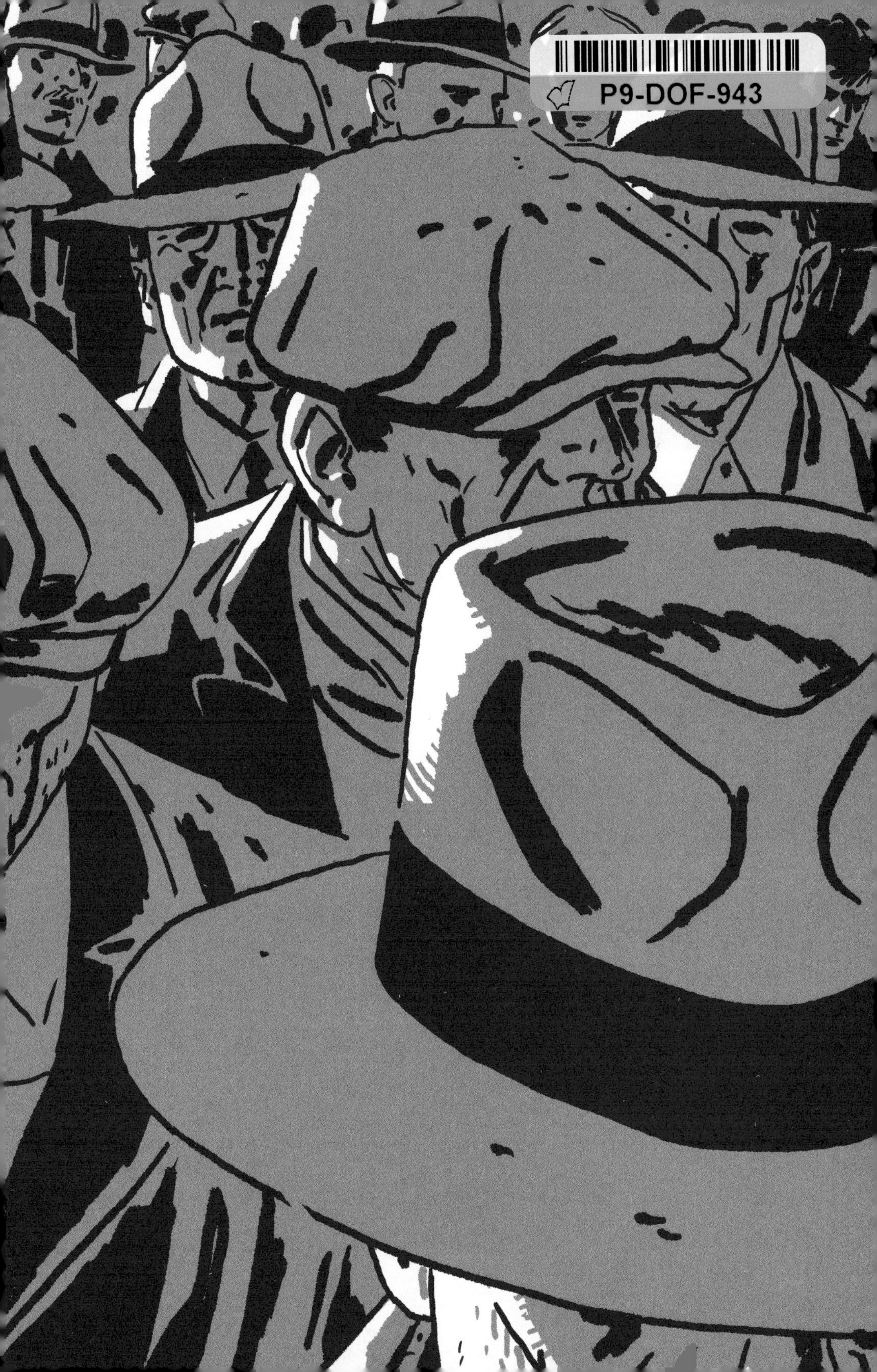

ALSO BY AMITY SHLAES

COOLIDGE

THE FORGOTTEN MAN

THE GREEDY HAND

GERMANY

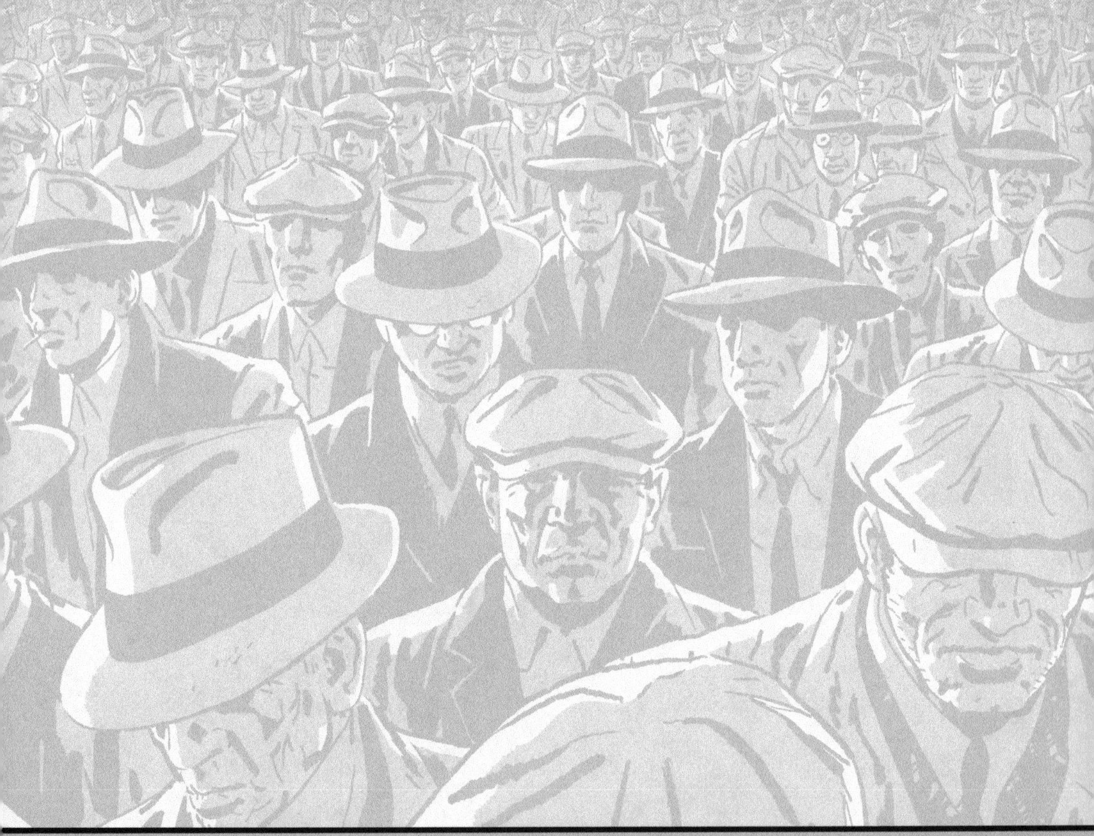

HARPER PERENNIAL

NEW YORK • LONDON • TORONTO • SYDNEY • NEW DELHI • AUCKLAND

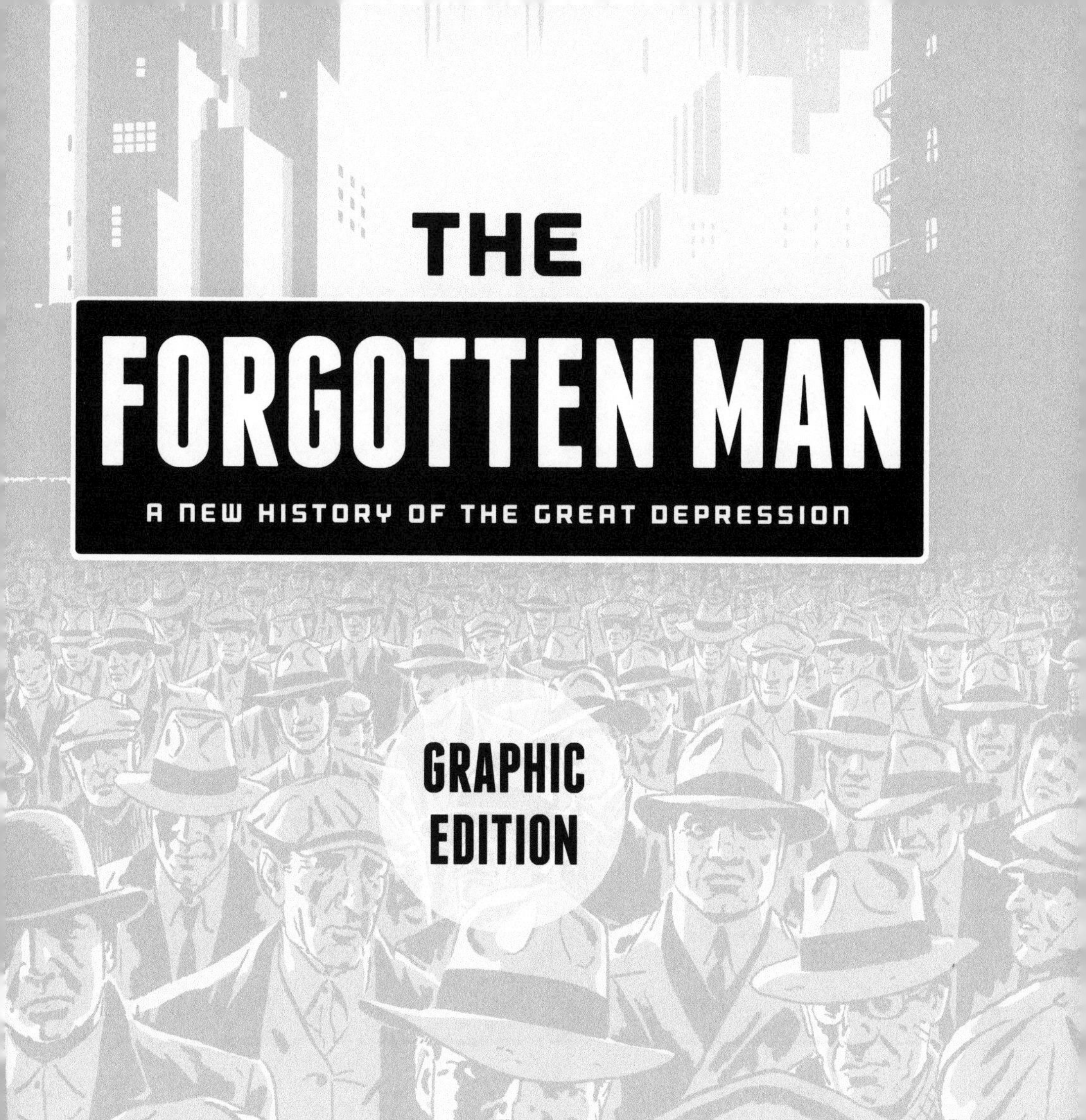

THE FORGOTTEN MAN

A NEW HISTORY OF THE GREAT DEPRESSION

GRAPHIC EDITION

AMITY SHLAES

ILLUSTRATED BY PAUL RIVOCHE

ADAPTED BY CHUCK DIXON

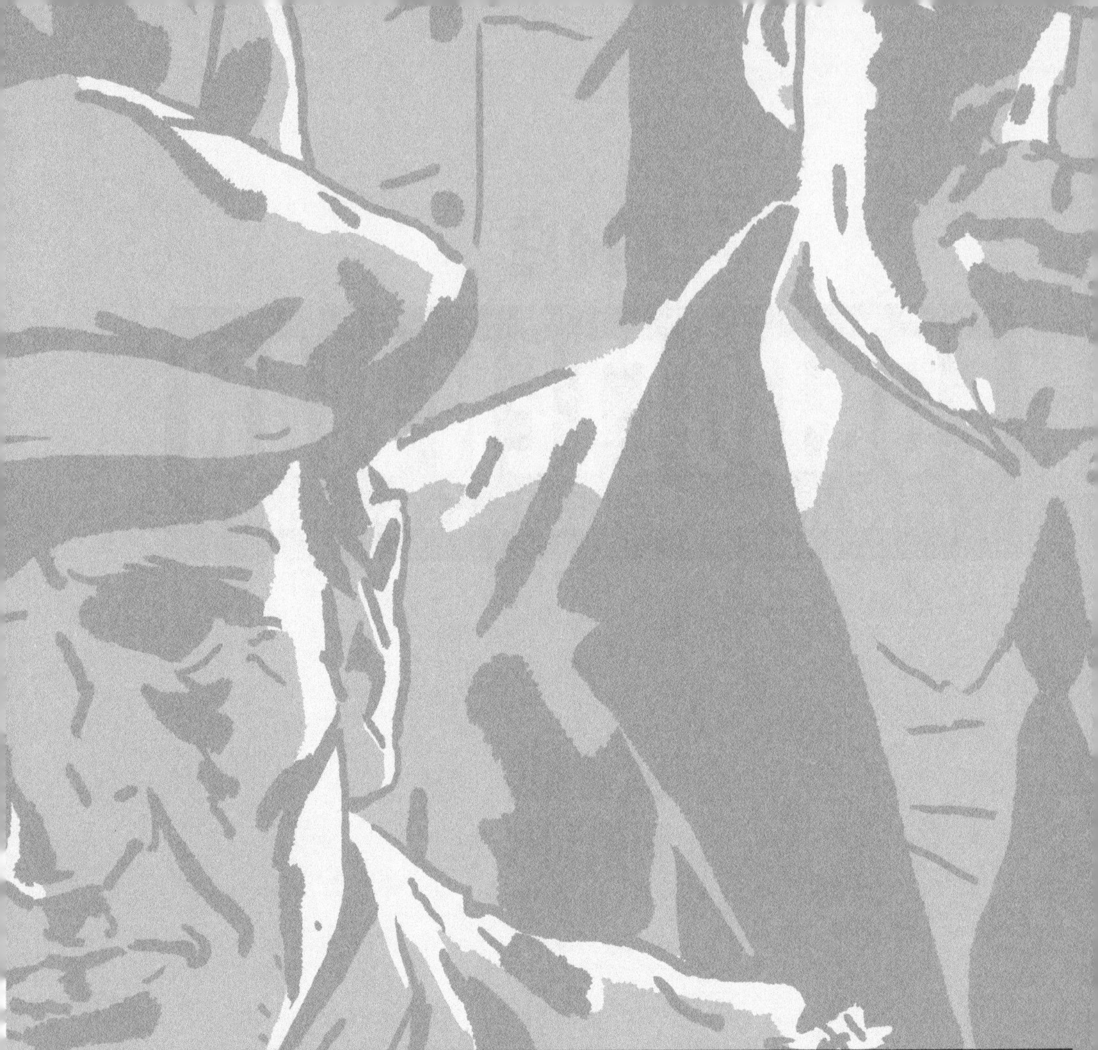

HARPER  PERENNIAL

HarperCollins books may be purchased for educational, business, or sales promotional use. For information, please email the Special Markets Department at SPsales@harpercollins.com.

FIRST EDITION

Designed by William Ruoto
Timeline designed by Nick Springer for Springer Cartographics.

Library of Congress Cataloging-in-Publication Data is available upon request.

ISBN: 978-0-06-196764-1

14 15 16 17 18 /RRD 10 9 8 7 6 5 4 3 2

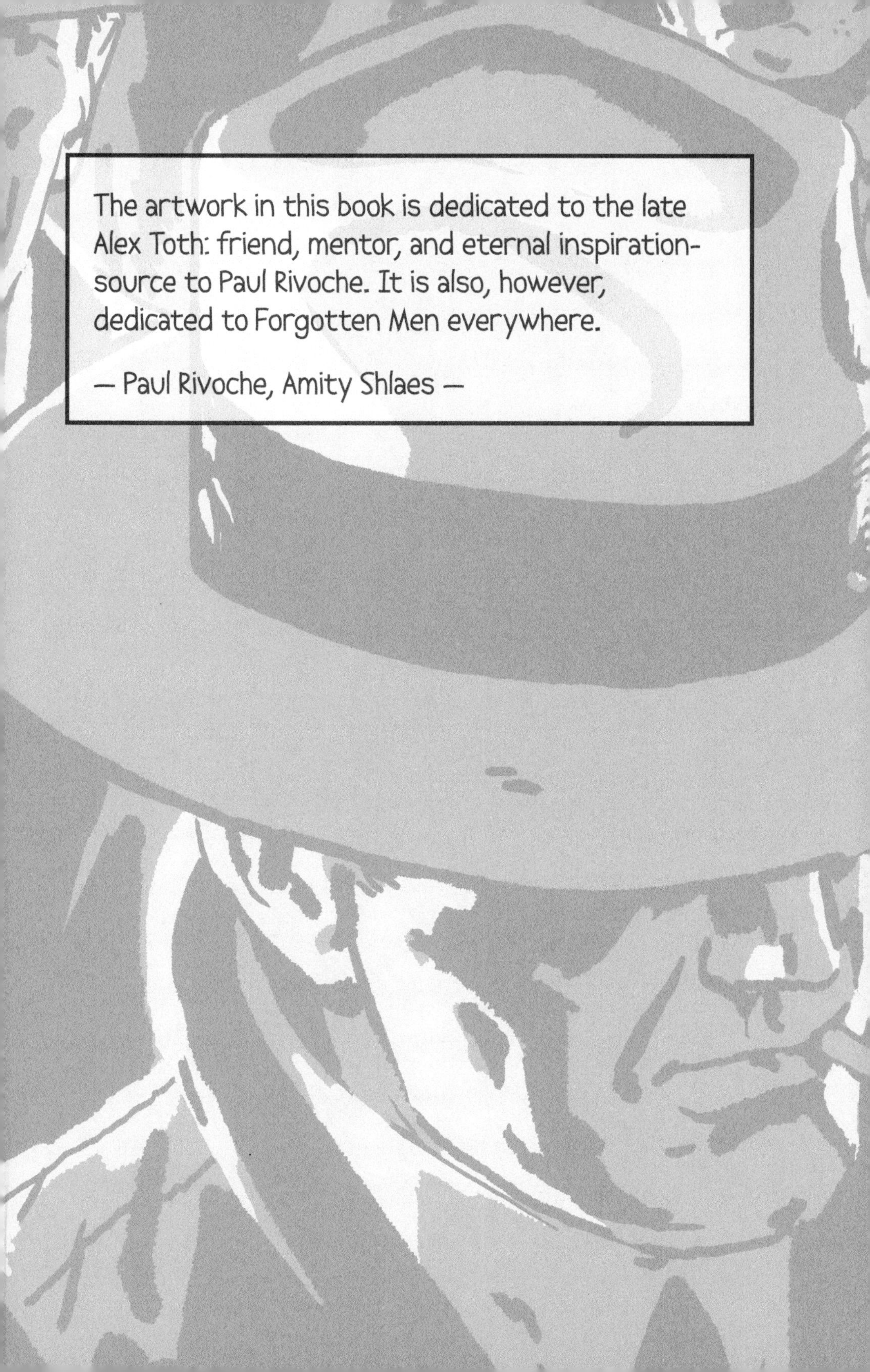

The artwork in this book is dedicated to the late Alex Toth: friend, mentor, and eternal inspiration-source to Paul Rivoche. It is also, however, dedicated to Forgotten Men everywhere.

— Paul Rivoche, Amity Shlaes —

THE FORGOTTEN MAN

GRAPHIC EDITION

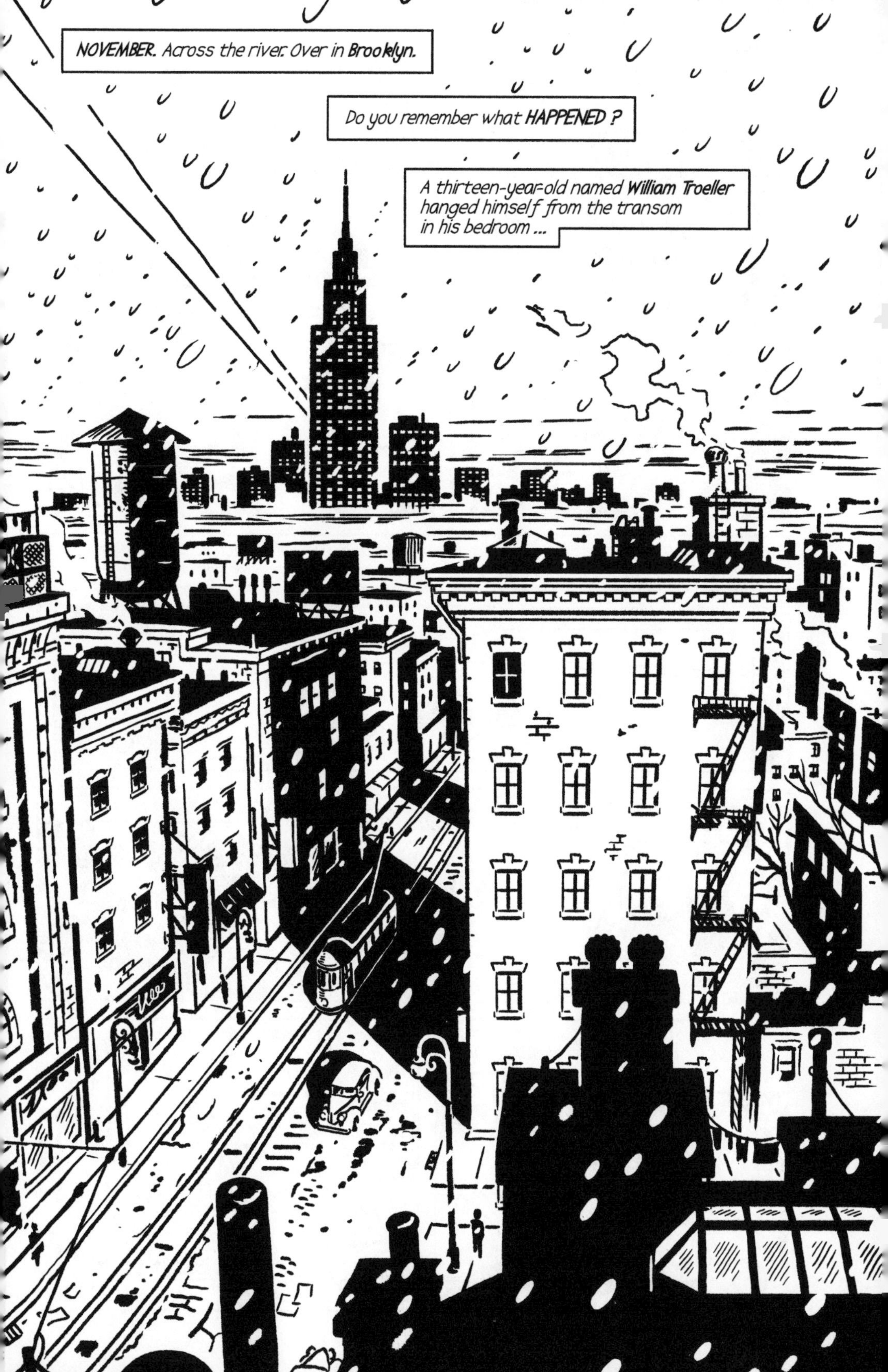
NOVEMBER. Across the river. Over in Brooklyn.
Do you remember what HAPPENED ?
A thirteen-year-old named William Troeller hanged himself from the transom in his bedroom ...

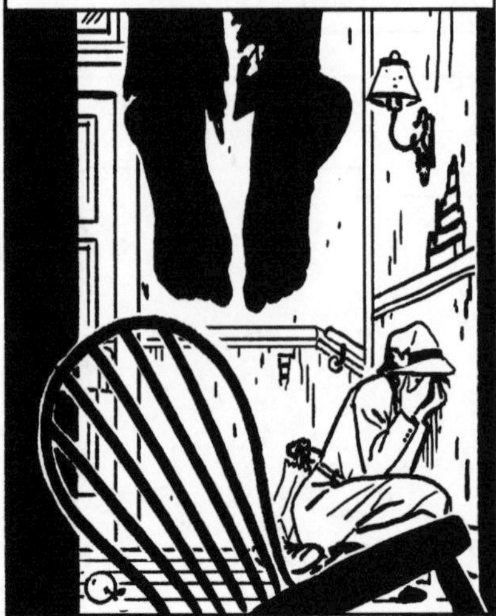
That boy had watched his family slide into an increasingly **desperate** situation.

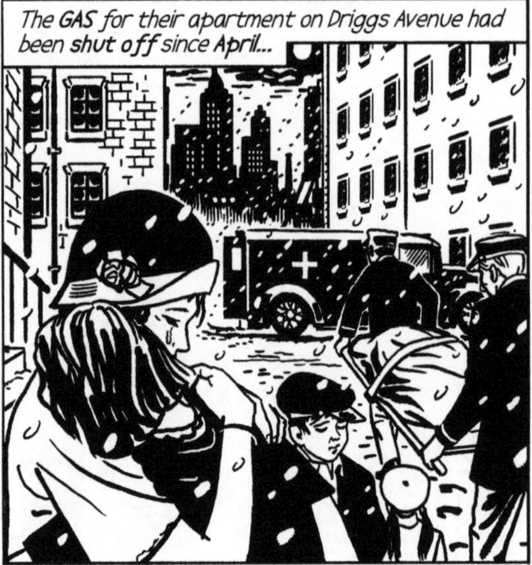
The **GAS** for their apartment on Driggs Avenue had been **shut off** since **April...**

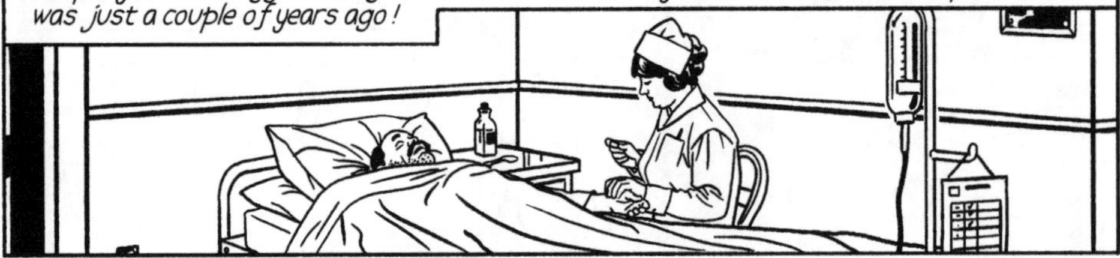
His father, Harold, had lost his job at **Brooklyn Edison** and was waiting for surgery for a hernia. The Brooklyn Edison, **LAYING PEOPLE OFF!** I can't **believe** it. Do you remember when that company was the biggest thing in the world -- when they **added on** 430,000 horsepower? That was just a couple of years ago!

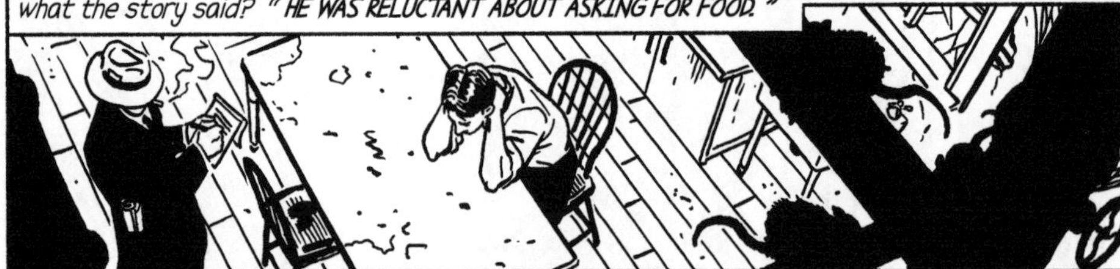
His older brother, **Harold Jr.**, told a reporter what happened. It was **unbelievable.** Do you remember what the story said? "**HE WAS RELUCTANT ABOUT ASKING FOR FOOD.**"

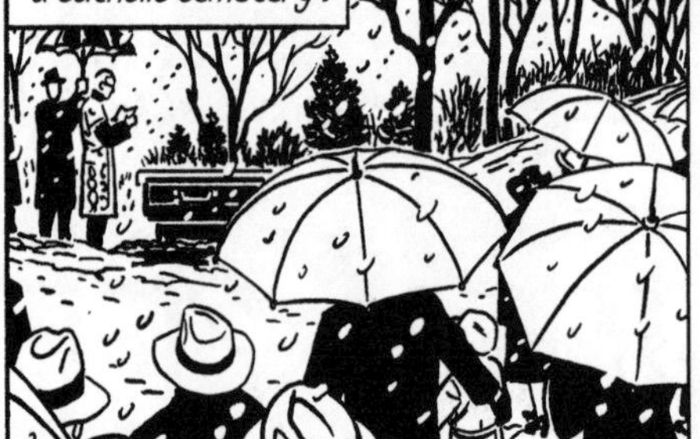
The Herbert Street police station helped to arrange for the boy's funeral and burial at a Catholic cemetery.

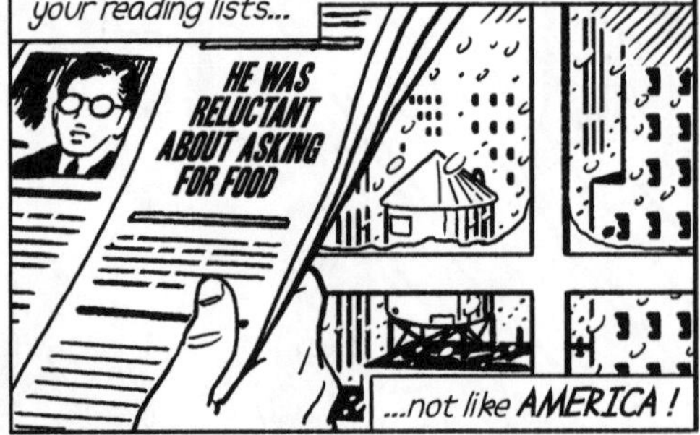
You know, **NEW YORK** felt to me like a city in one of those **Charles Dickens novels** you put on your reading lists...
HE WAS RELUCTANT ABOUT ASKING FOR FOOD
...not like **AMERICA!**

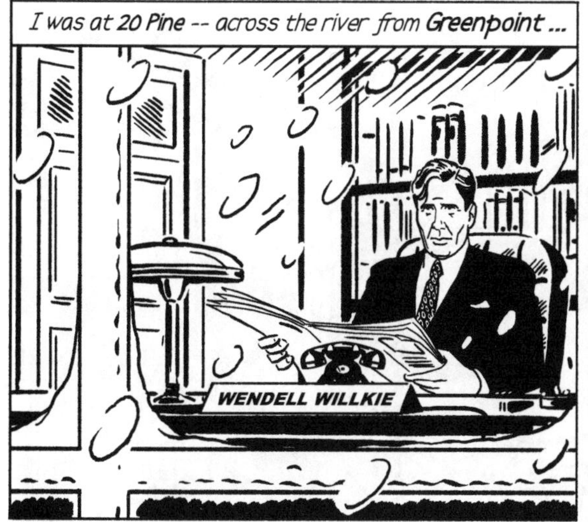
I was at 20 Pine -- across the river from Greenpoint ...
WENDELL WILLKIE

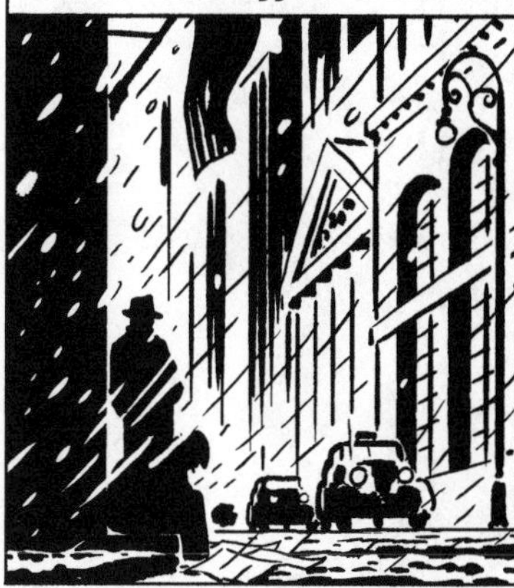
New York was in DESPAIR. We -- the businessmen, the companies-- ALL knew what the boy had only sensed: NOBODY could afford to HIRE!

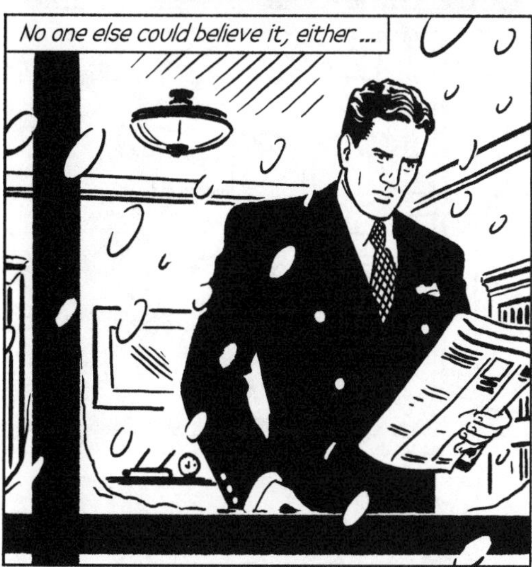
No one else could believe it, either ...

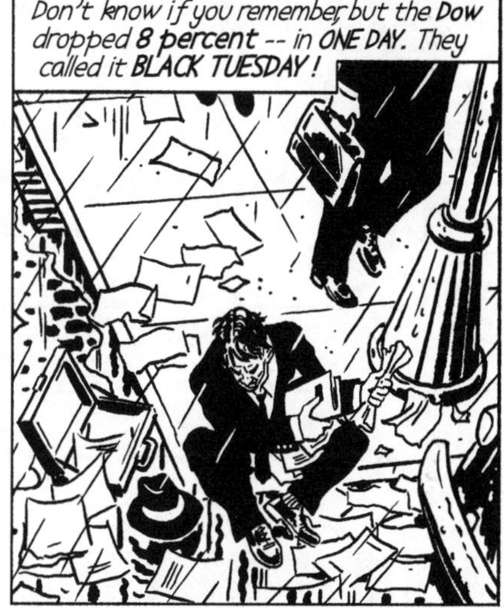
Don't know if you remember, but the Dow dropped 8 percent -- in ONE DAY. They called it BLACK TUESDAY!

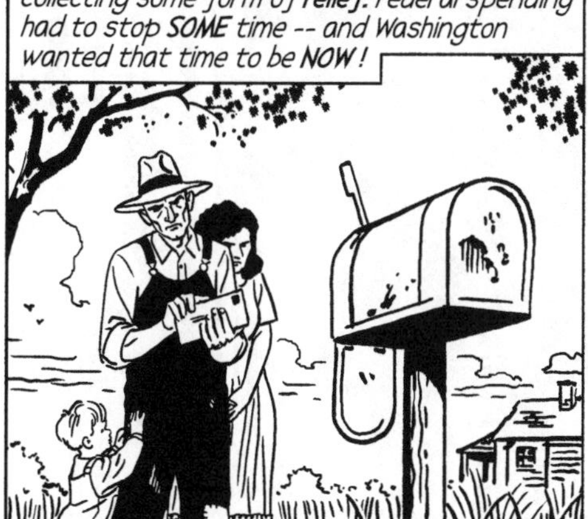
TWO in TEN farm families were in trouble and collecting some form of relief. Federal spending had to stop SOME time -- and Washington wanted that time to be NOW!

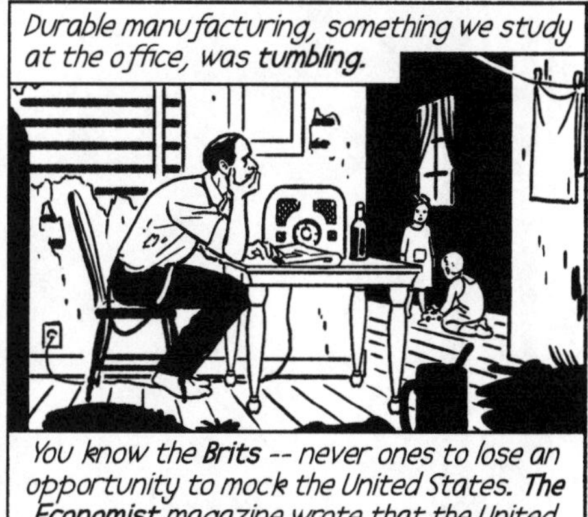
Durable manufacturing, something we study at the office, was tumbling.
You know the Brits -- never ones to lose an opportunity to mock the United States. The Economist magazine wrote that the United States ... "SEEMED TO HAVE FORGOTTEN, FOR THE MOMENT, HOW TO GROW."

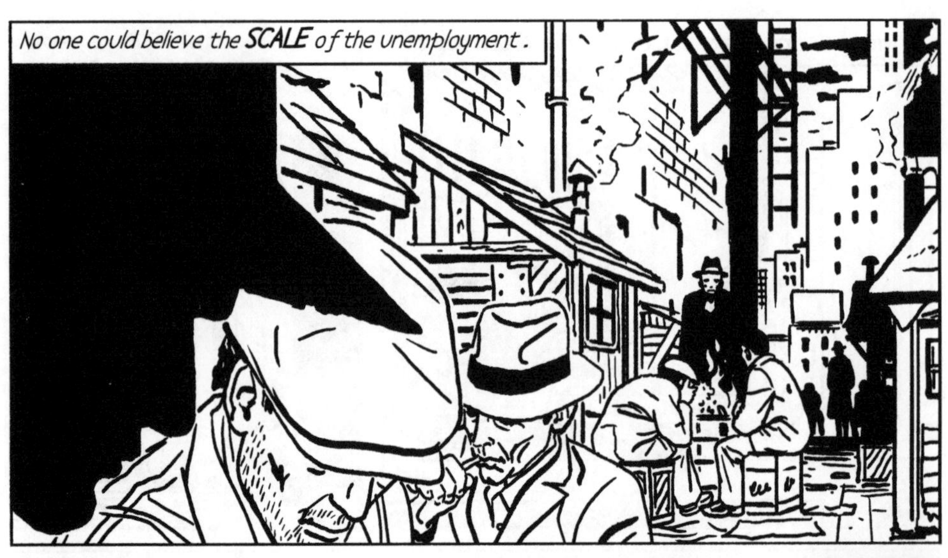
No one could believe the SCALE of the unemployment.

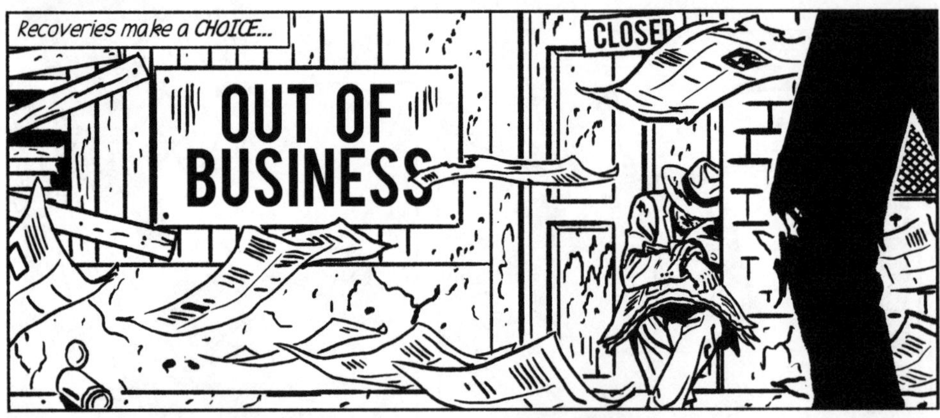
Recoveries make a CHOICE...
OUT OF BUSINESS
CLOSED

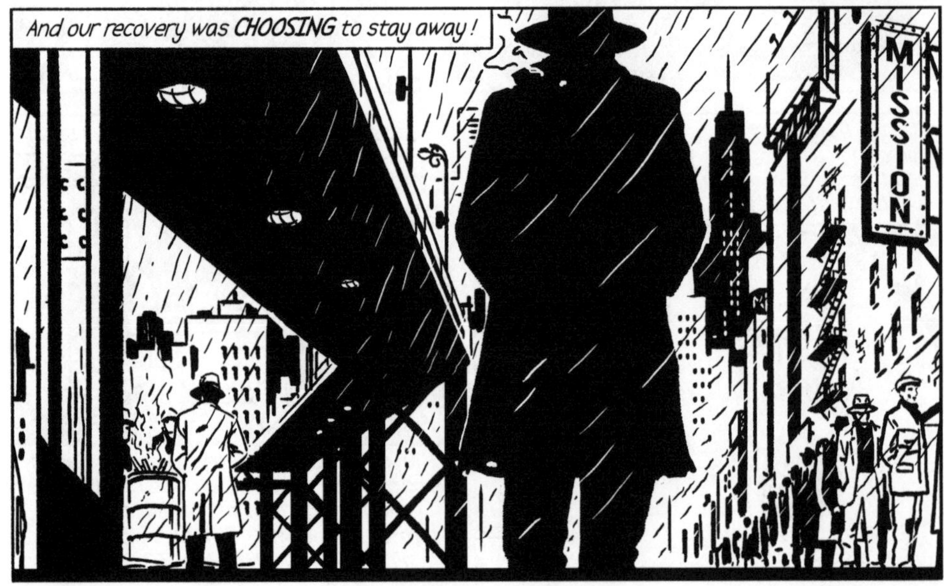
And our recovery was CHOOSING to stay away!
MISSION

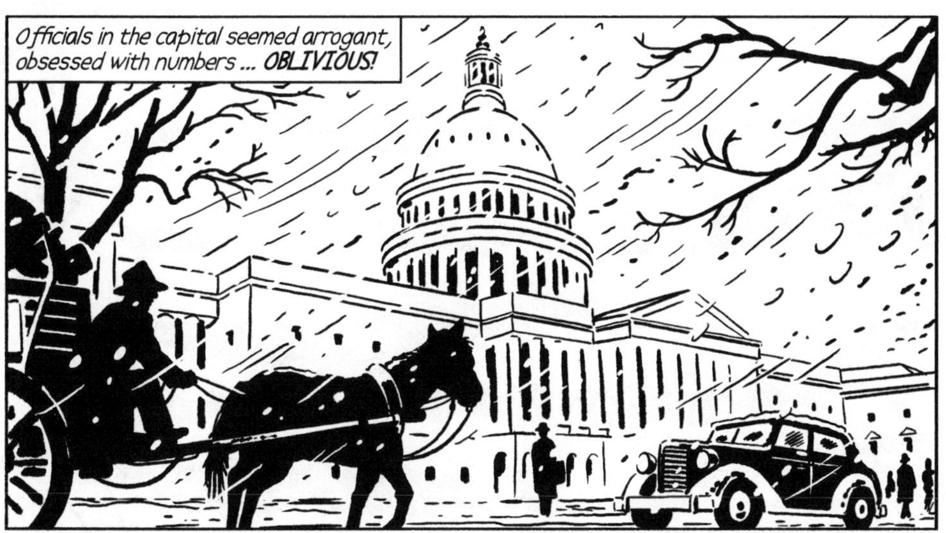
Officials in the capital seemed arrogant, obsessed with numbers ... OBLIVIOUS!

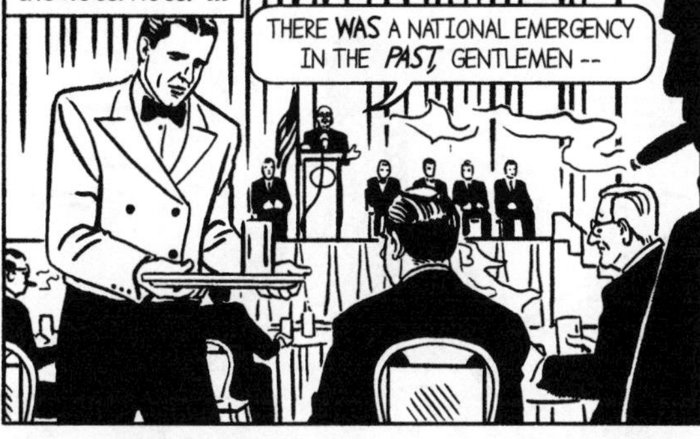
The Treasury Secretary was up in New York to address it all. Gave a talk to the Academy of Political Science at the Hotel Astor ...
THERE WAS A NATIONAL EMERGENCY IN THE PAST, GENTLEMEN --

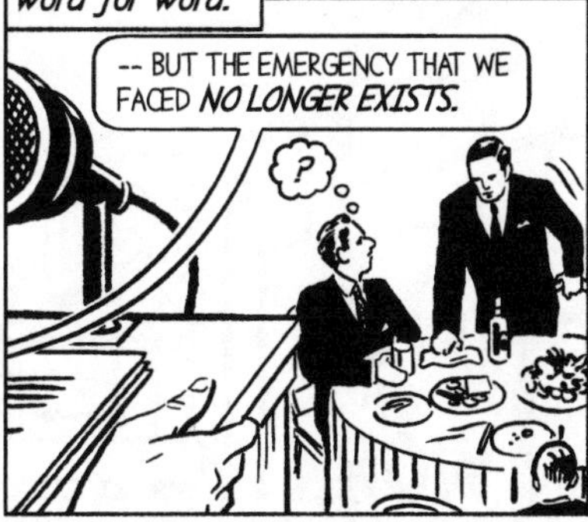
Treasury was so anxious, they insisted the president approve that speech word for word.
-- BUT THE EMERGENCY THAT WE FACED NO LONGER EXISTS.
?

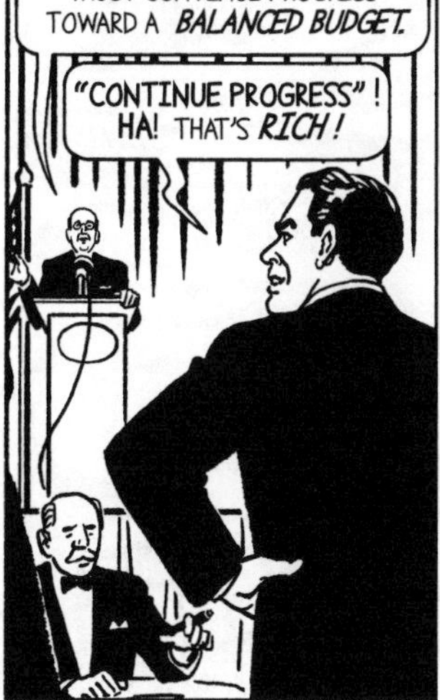
WE BELIEVE THAT MUCH OF THE REMAINING UNEMPLOYMENT WILL DISAPPEAR. THE COUNTRY MUST CONTINUE PROGRESS TOWARD A BALANCED BUDGET.
"CONTINUE PROGRESS"! HA! THAT'S RICH!

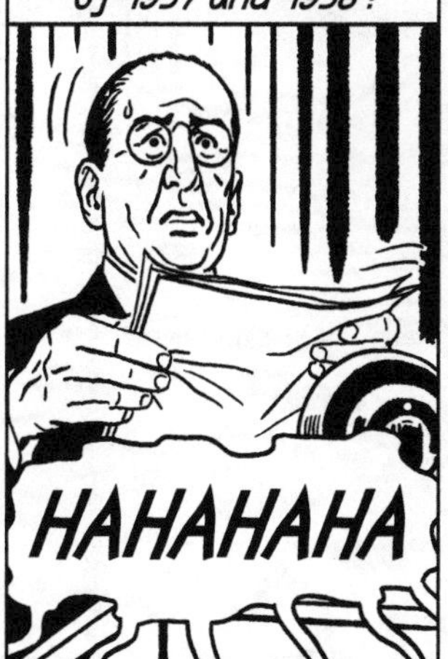
Sounds like 1929, right? But these events were taking place recently. The fall and winter of 1937 and 1938!
HAHAHAHA

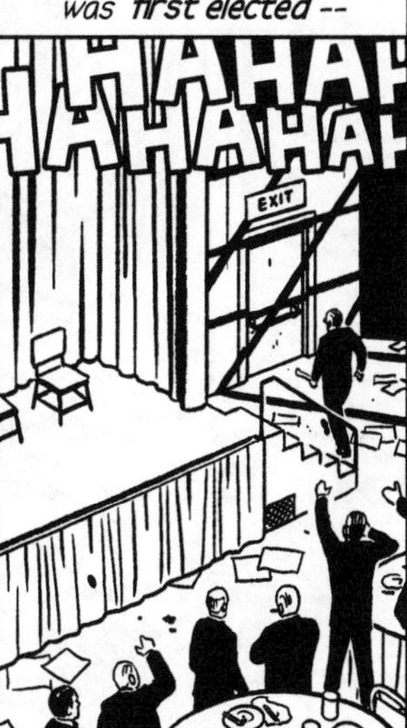
And this was all occurring FIVE YEARS after Roosevelt was first elected --
HAHAHA
HAHAHAH
EXIT

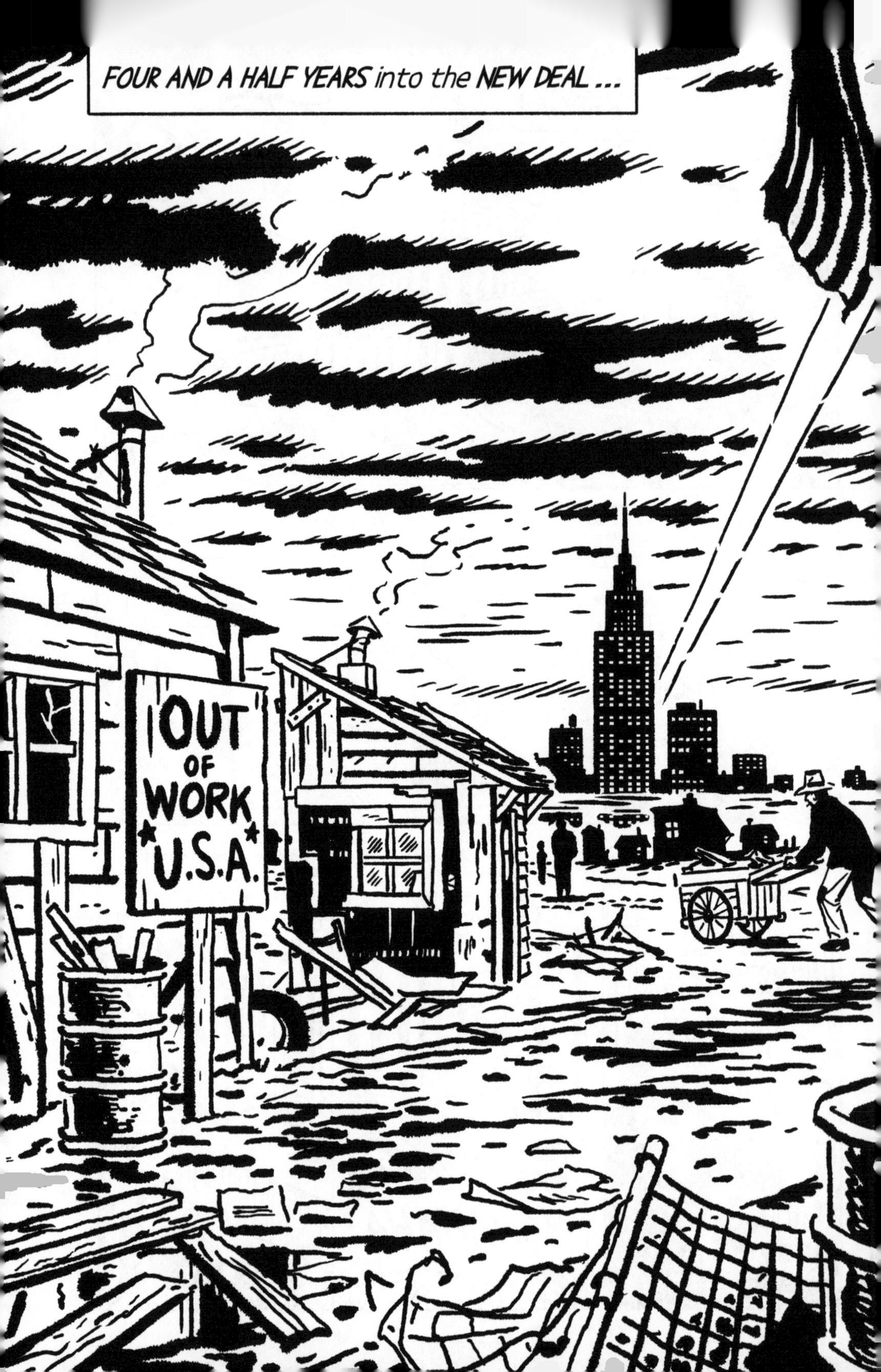
FOUR AND A HALF YEARS into the NEW DEAL ...
OUT OF WORK U.S.A.

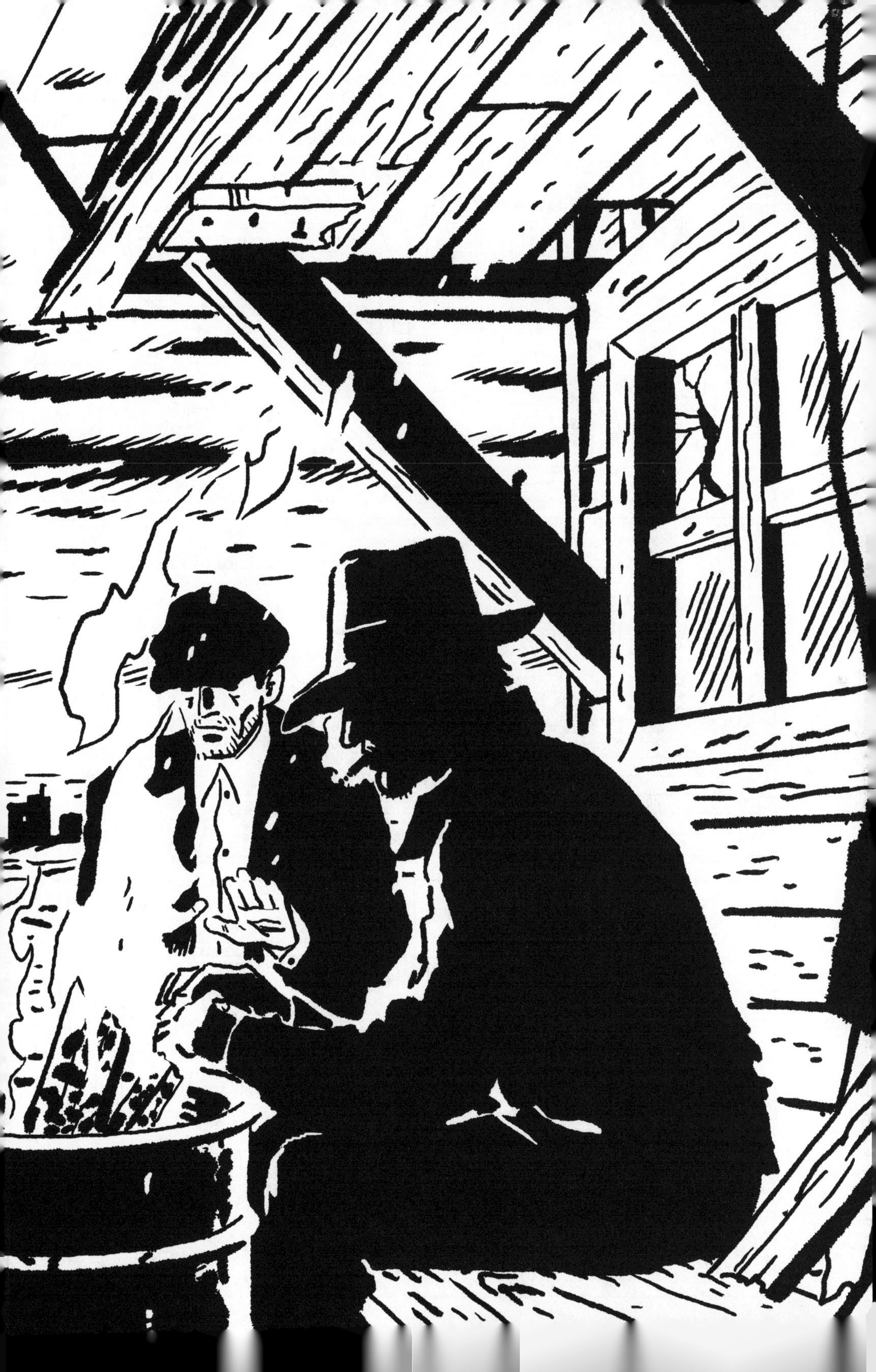

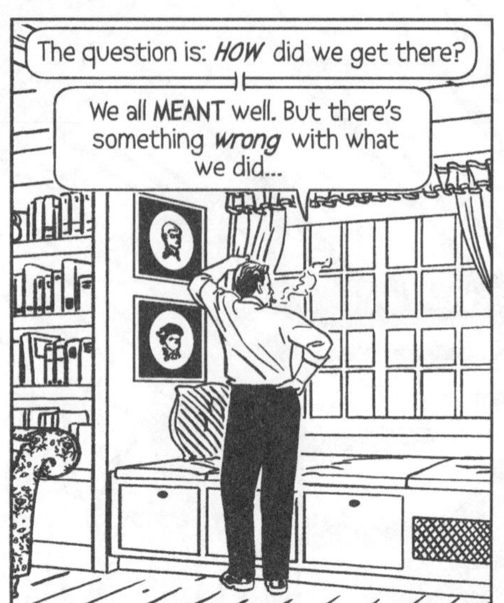
The question is: HOW did we get there?
We all MEANT well. But there's something wrong with what we did...

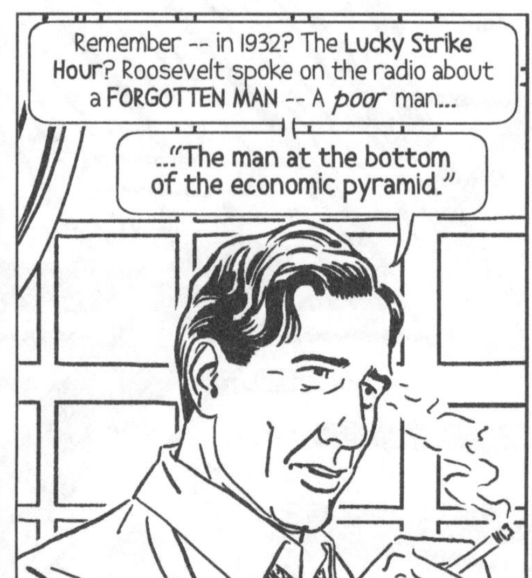
Remember -- in 1932? The Lucky Strike Hour? Roosevelt spoke on the radio about a FORGOTTEN MAN -- A poor man...
..."The man at the bottom of the economic pyramid."

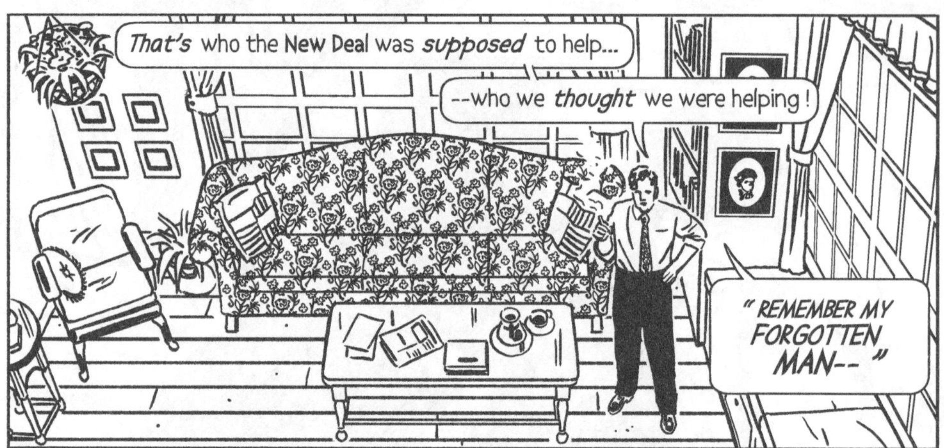
That's who the New Deal was supposed to help...
--who we thought we were helping!
" REMEMBER MY FORGOTTEN MAN-- "

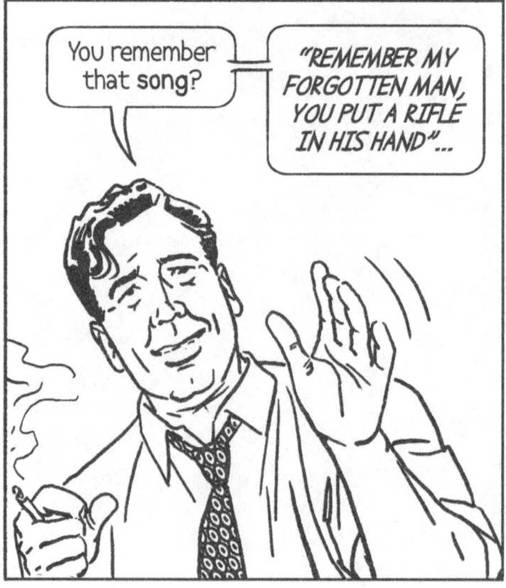
You remember that song?
"REMEMBER MY FORGOTTEN MAN, YOU PUT A RIFLE IN HIS HAND"...

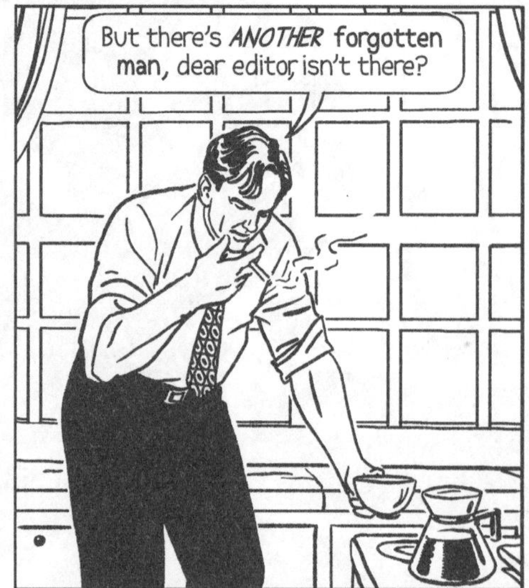
But there's ANOTHER forgotten man, dear editor, isn't there?

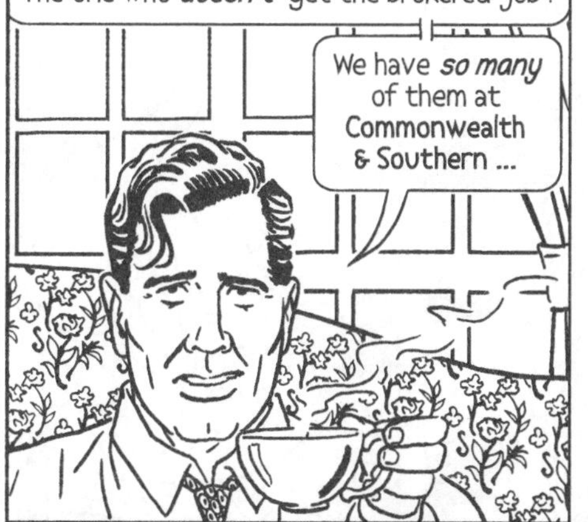
The FORGOTTEN MAN who's waiting for the recovery. The one who pays the tax on the beer...the one who pays the income tax. The one who doesn't get the brokered job!
We have so many of them at Commonwealth & Southern ...

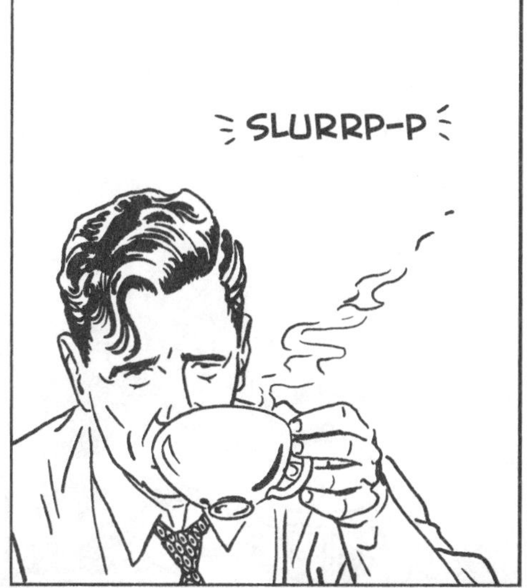
SLURRP-P

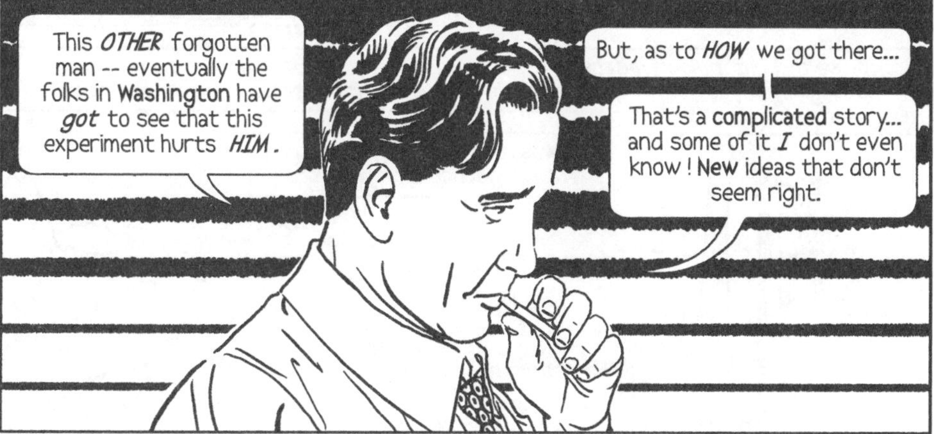
This OTHER forgotten man -- eventually the folks in Washington have got to see that this experiment hurts HIM.
But, as to HOW we got there...
That's a complicated story... and some of it I don't even know! New ideas that don't seem right.

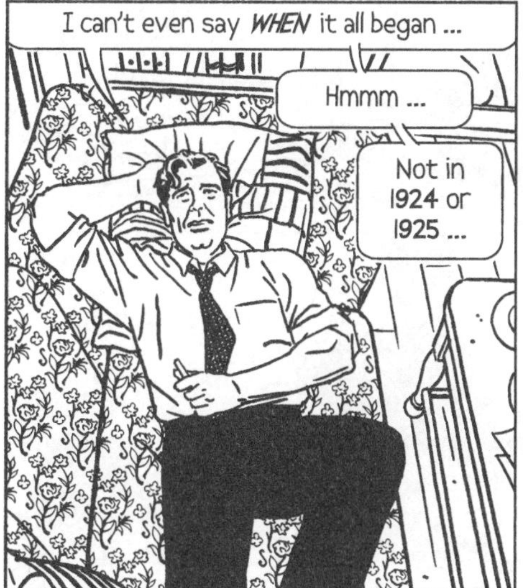
I can't even say WHEN it all began ...
Hmmm ...
Not in 1924 or 1925 ...

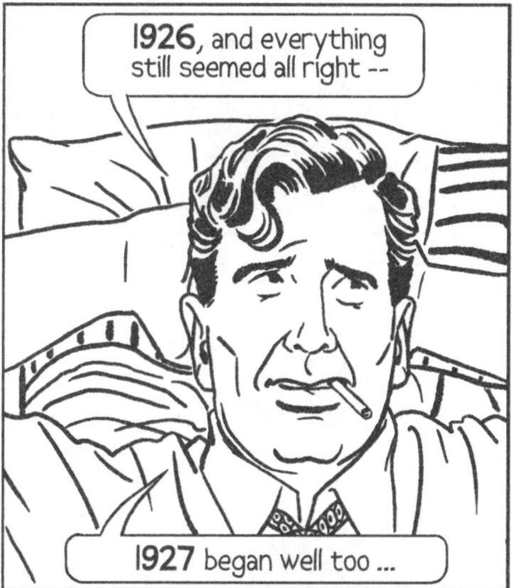
1926, and everything still seemed all right --
1927 began well too ...

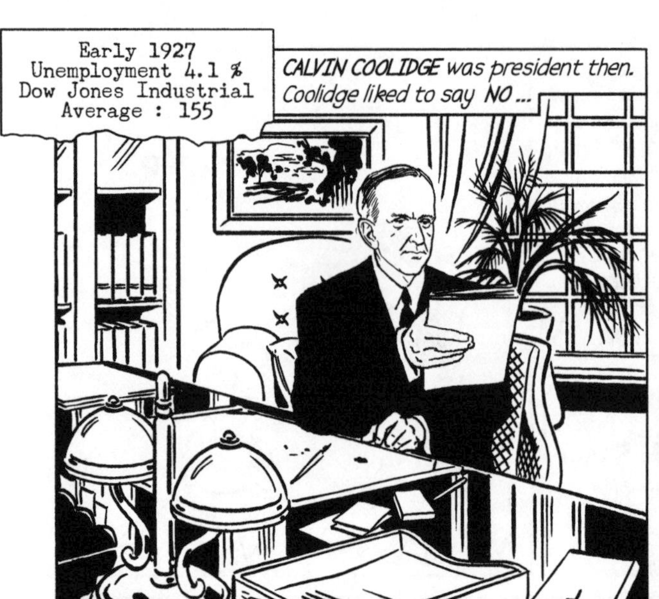
Early 1927
Unemployment 4.1 %
Dow Jones Industrial
Average : 155
CALVIN COOLIDGE was president then. Coolidge liked to say NO...

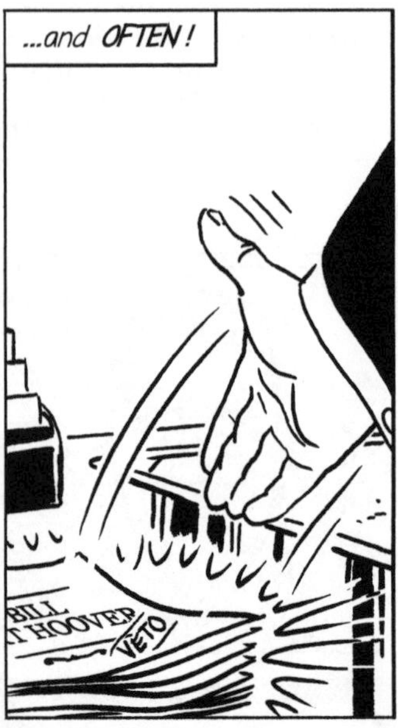
...and OFTEN!
BILL
HOOVER
VETO

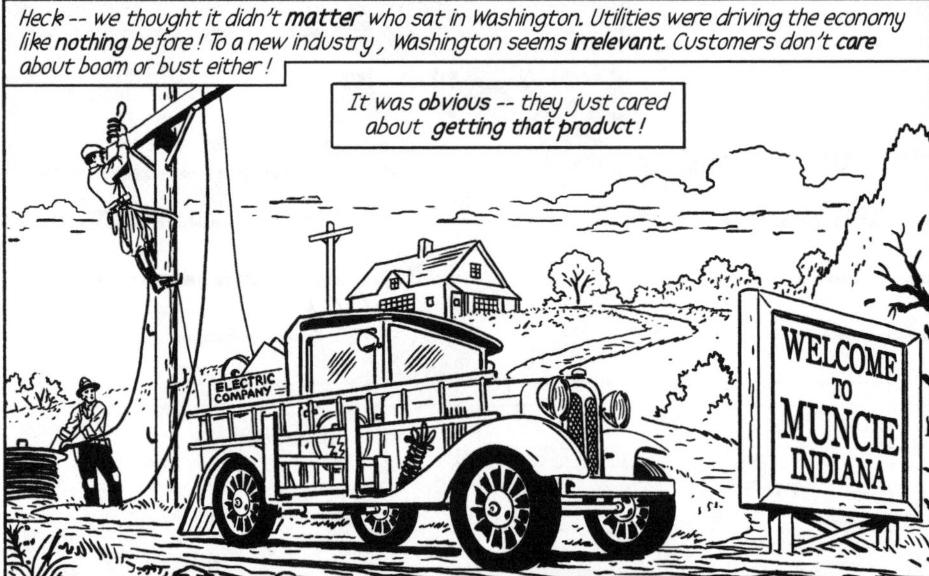
Heck -- we thought it didn't matter who sat in Washington. Utilities were driving the economy like nothing before! To a new industry, Washington seems irrelevant. Customers don't care about boom or bust either!
It was obvious -- they just cared about getting that product!
ELECTRIC COMPANY
WELCOME TO MUNCIE INDIANA

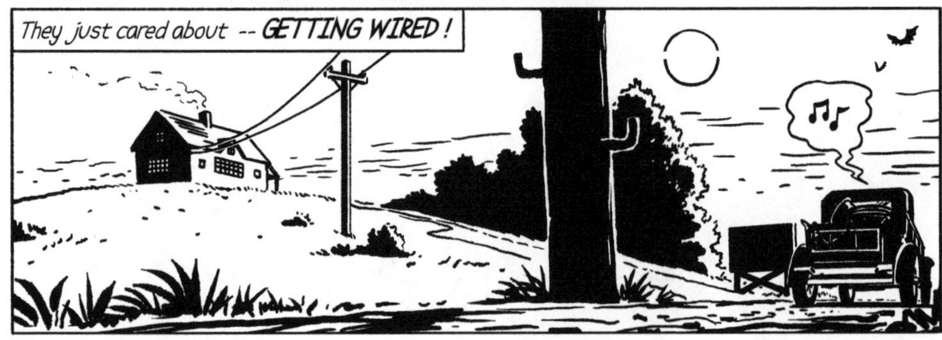
They just cared about -- GETTING WIRED!

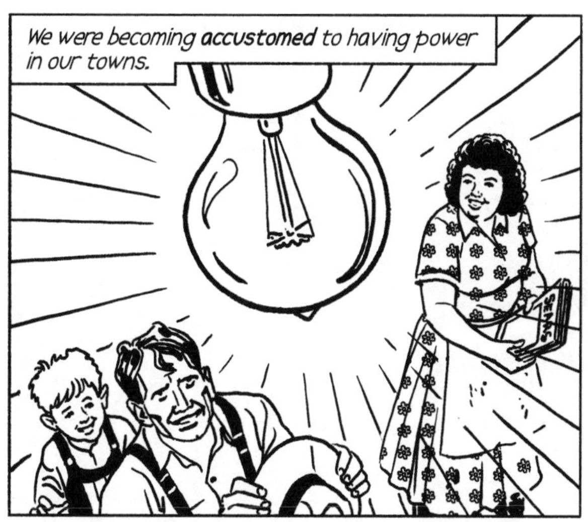
We were becoming **accustomed** to having power in our towns.

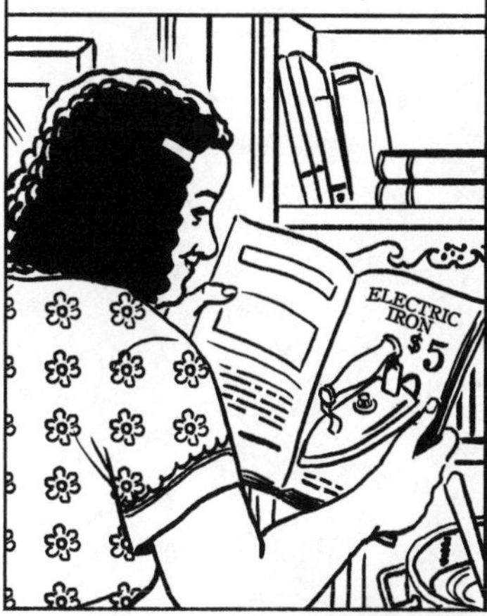
Though people weren't really sure yet what to **DO** with that power...
ELECTRIC IRON
$5

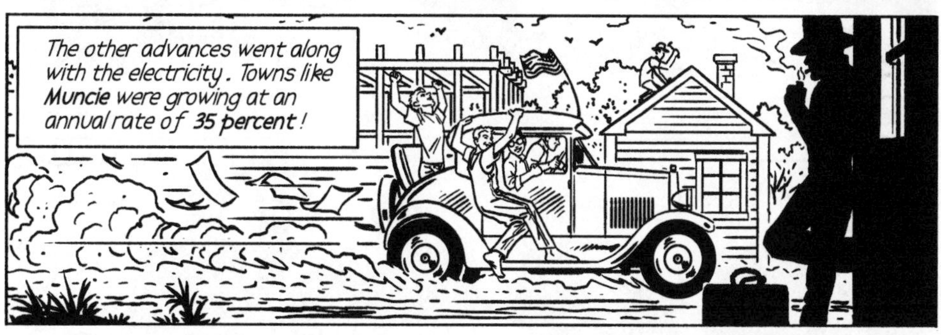
The other advances went along with the electricity. Towns like **Muncie** were growing at an annual rate of **35 percent**!

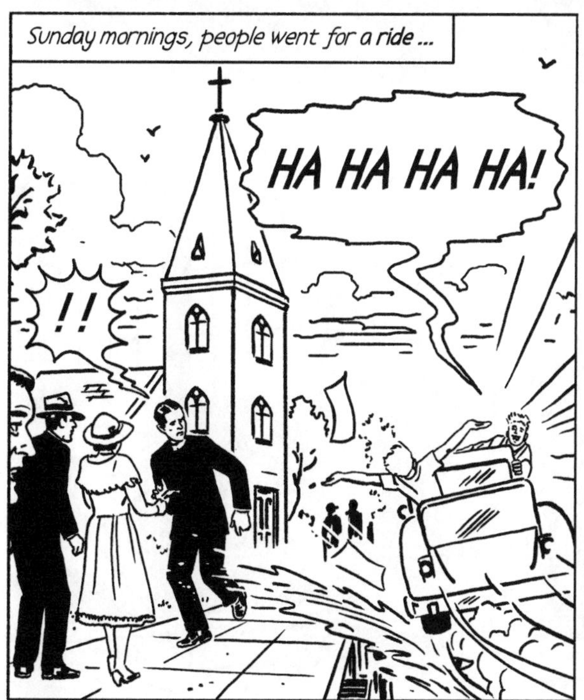
Sunday mornings, people went for a **ride** ...
HA HA HA HA!
!!

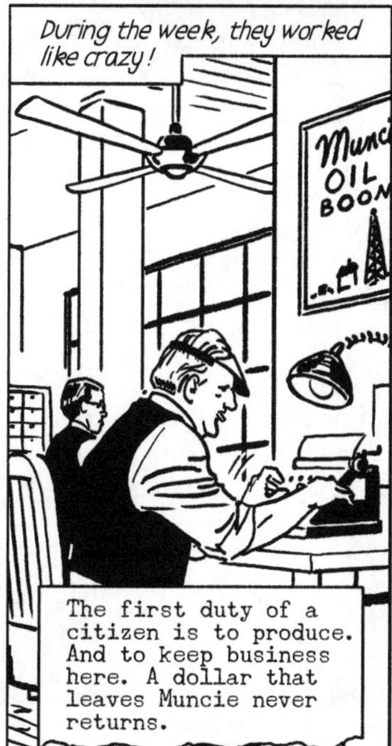
During the week, they worked like crazy!
Munci
OIL
BOOM
The first duty of a citizen is to produce. And to keep business here. A dollar that leaves Muncie never returns.

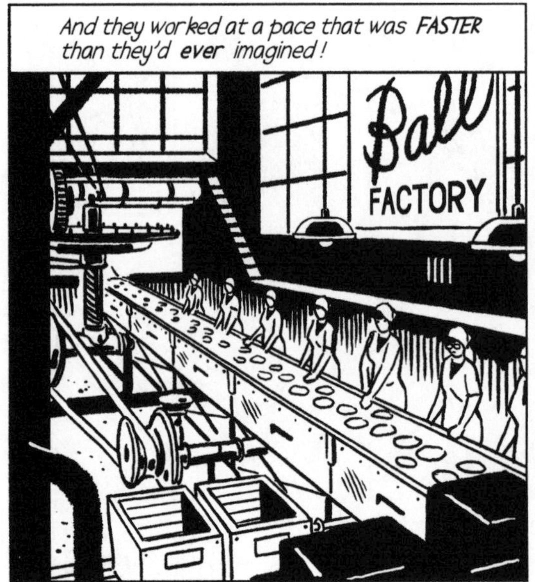
And they worked at a pace that was FASTER than they'd ever imagined!
Ball FACTORY

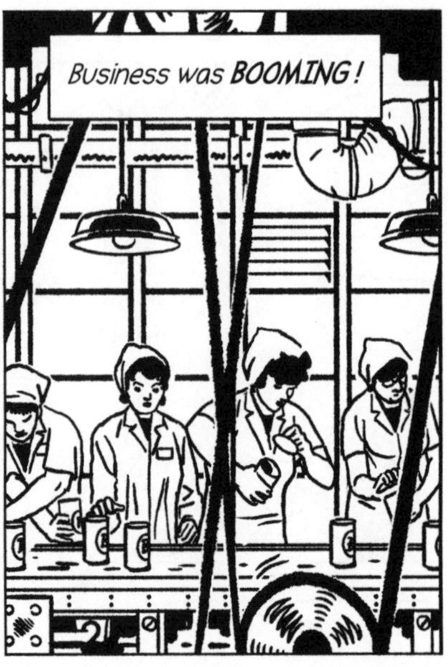
Business was BOOMING!

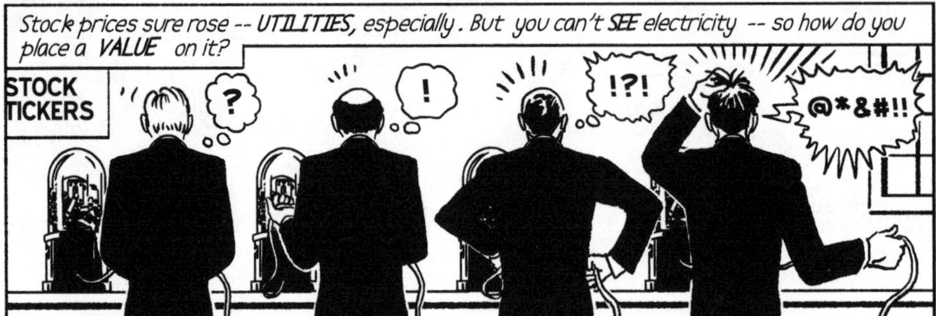
Stock prices sure rose -- UTILITIES, especially. But you can't SEE electricity -- so how do you place a VALUE on it?
STOCK TICKERS
?
!
!?!
@*&#!!

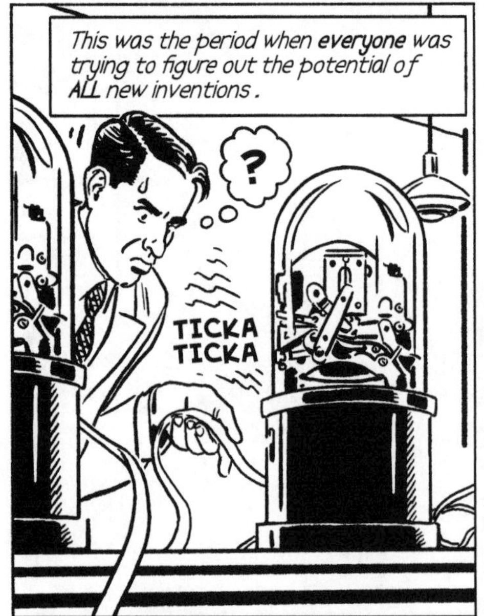
This was the period when everyone was trying to figure out the potential of ALL new inventions.
?
TICKA TICKA

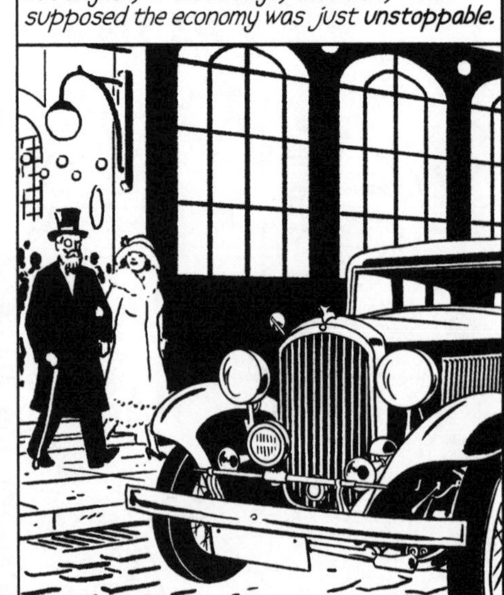
But anyhow, in those days, the 1920s, we all supposed the economy was just unstoppable.

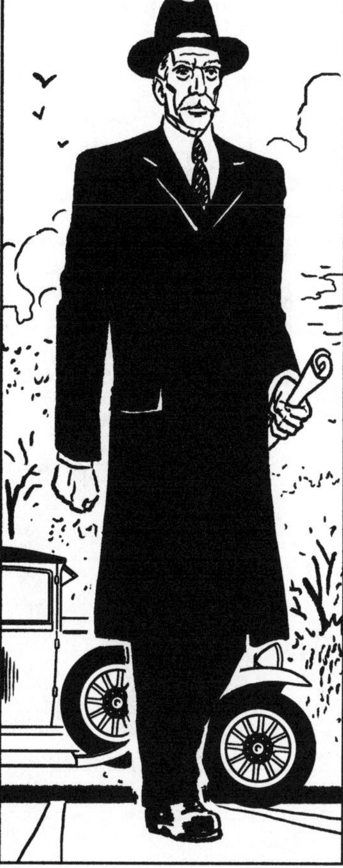
In the 1920s, the government knew how to make things stable for business. **Andrew Mellon** was **Treasury secretary** the whole time.
He was a **FIXTURE**. You know what they said about Mellon: "**Three presidents** served under him."

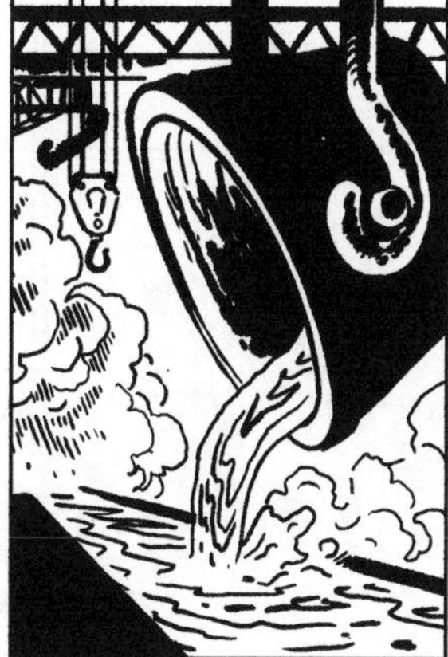
People **respected** the Mellons because they had holdings in **steel** and **aluminum.**

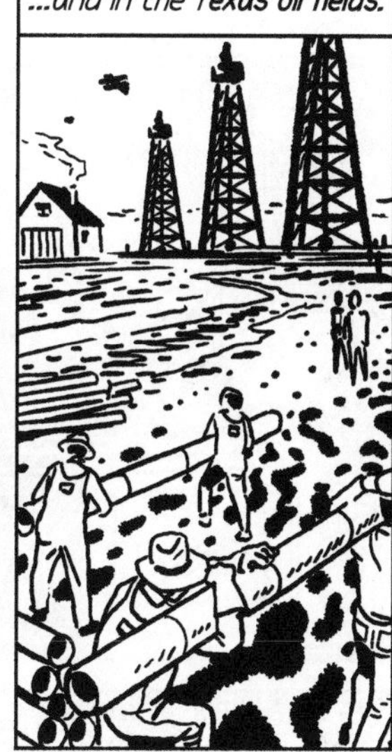
...and in the Texas **oil fields.**

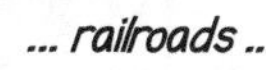
... **railroads** ...

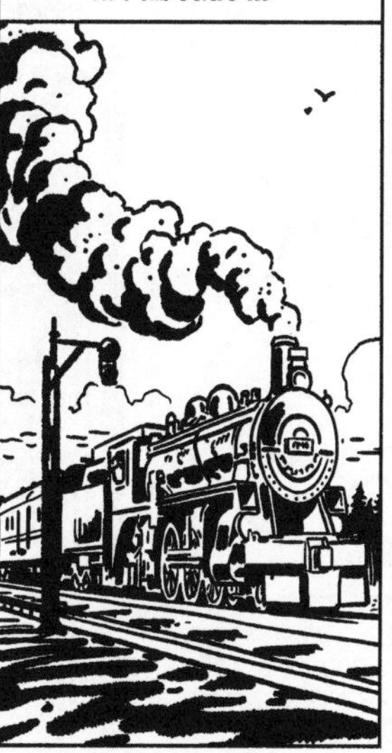

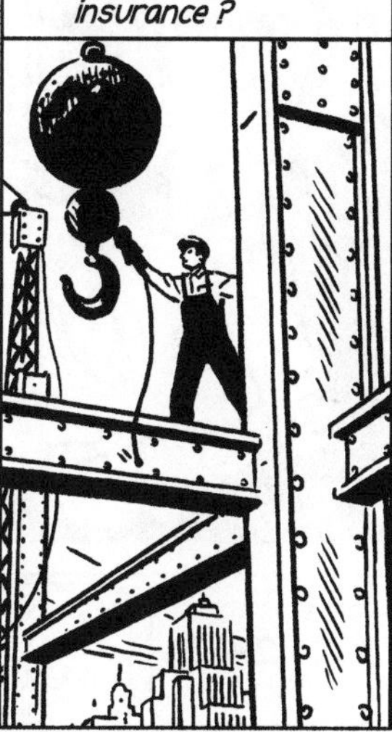
...and did I mention **construction** and **insurance** ?

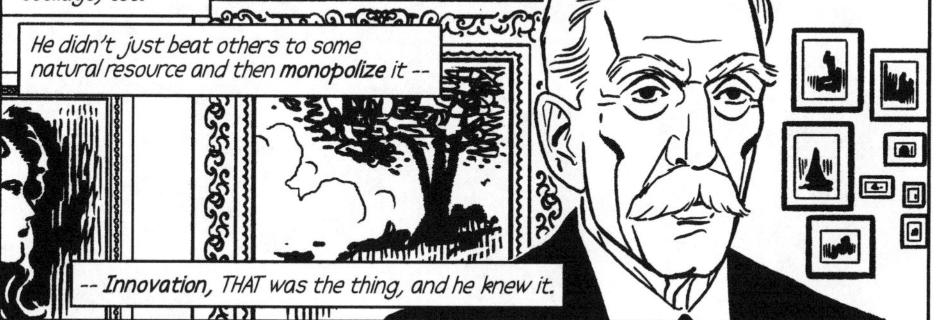
Nowadays, people remember Mellon like a **relic. Victorian.** But he was an **innovator.** Silent like Coolidge, too.
He didn't just beat others to some natural resource and then **monopolize** it --
-- **Innovation,** THAT was the thing, and he knew it.

Mellon preached and practiced a few **basic principles.** His son Paul always got a ***LESSON*...**

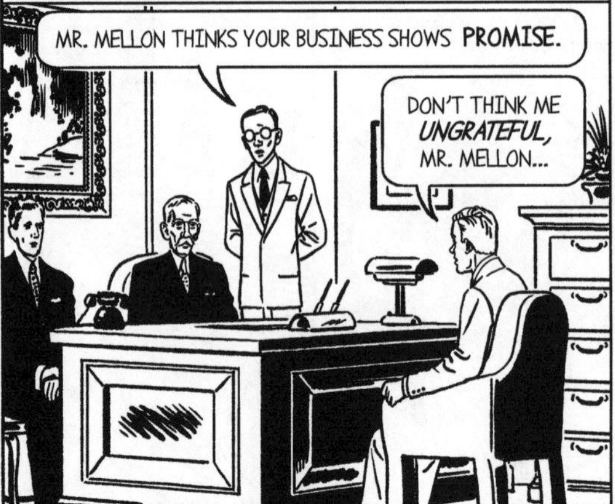

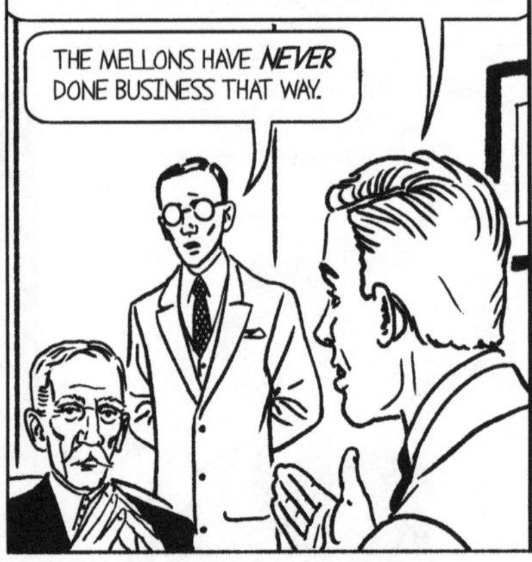

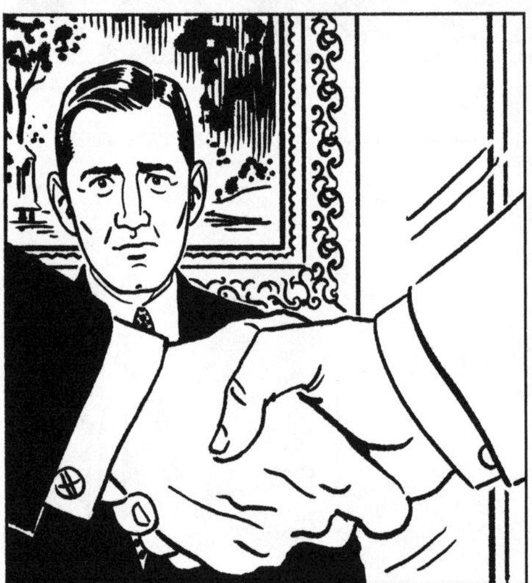

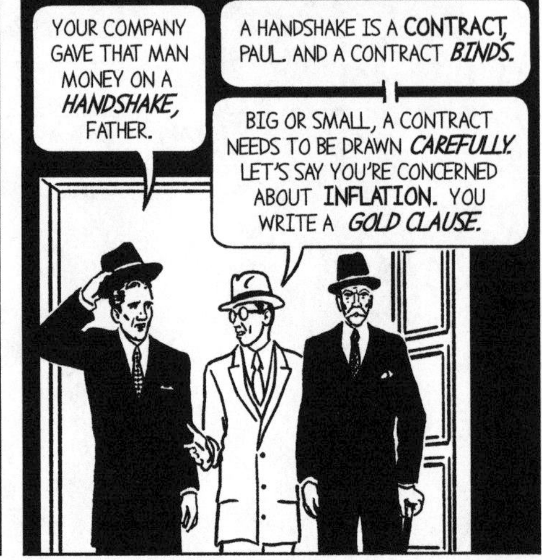

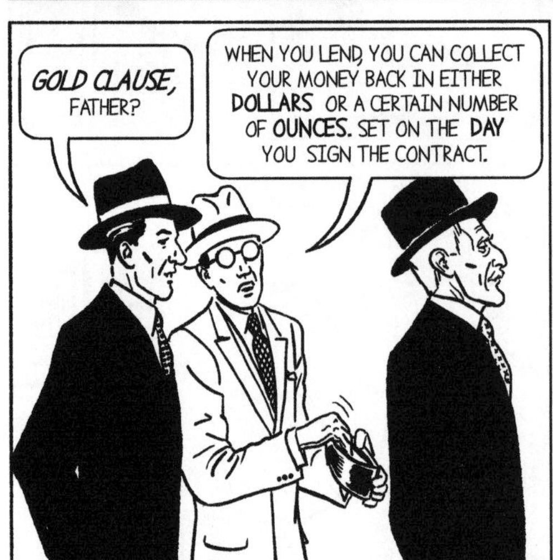

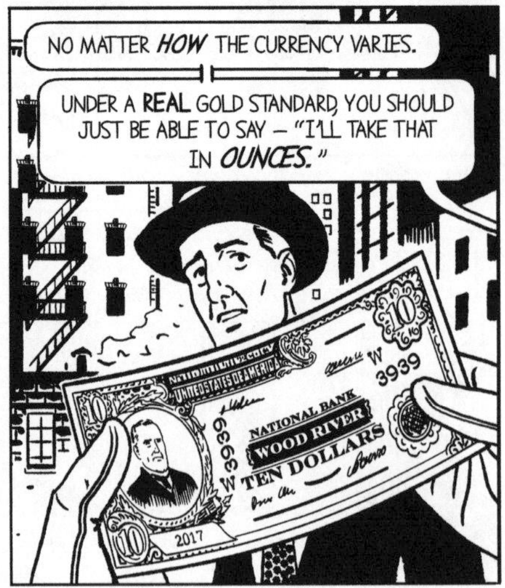

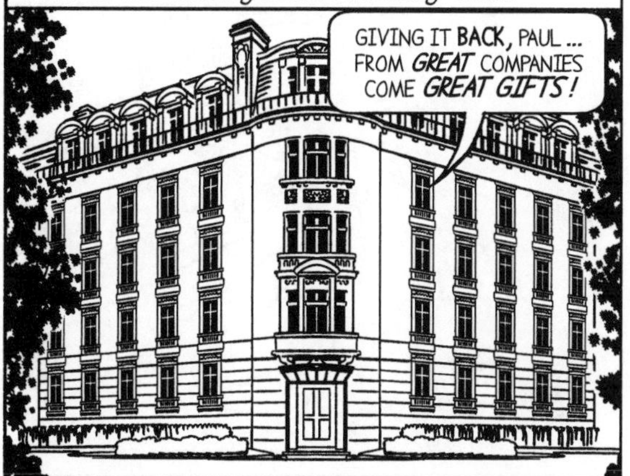

Of course by the late 1920s, Mellon's mind wasn't just on his old holding, or his job as treasury secretary, even. He was thinking about something *else*...
GIVING IT **BACK**, PAUL ... FROM *GREAT* COMPANIES COME *GREAT GIFTS*!

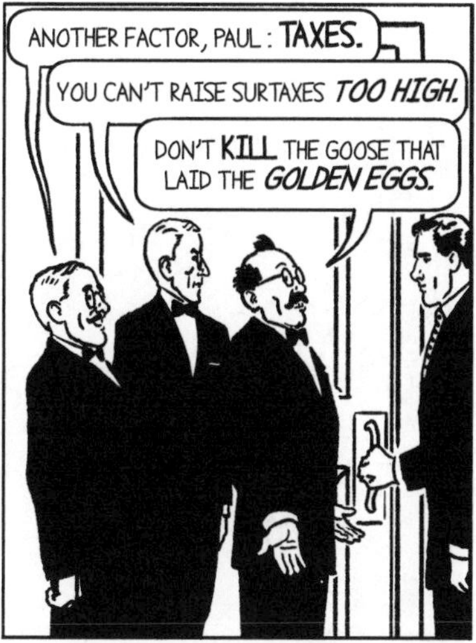

ANOTHER FACTOR, PAUL: **TAXES.**
YOU CAN'T RAISE SURTAXES *TOO HIGH.*
DON'T **KILL** THE GOOSE THAT LAID THE *GOLDEN EGGS.*

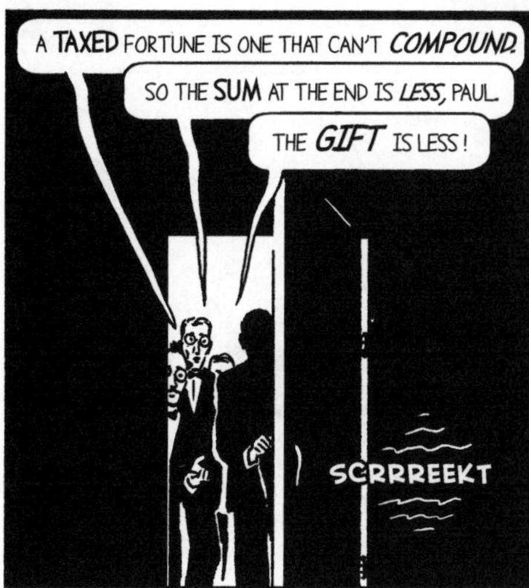

A **TAXED** FORTUNE IS ONE THAT CAN'T *COMPOUND.*
SO THE **SUM** AT THE END IS *LESS*, PAUL.
THE *GIFT* IS LESS!
SCRRREEKT

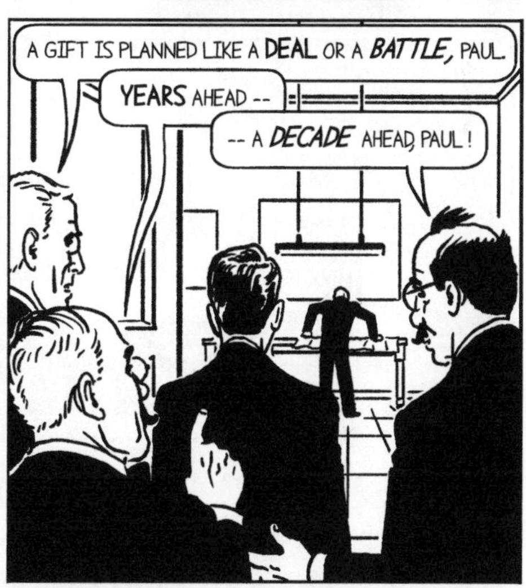

A GIFT IS PLANNED LIKE A **DEAL** OR A *BATTLE*, PAUL.
YEARS AHEAD --
-- A *DECADE* AHEAD, PAUL!

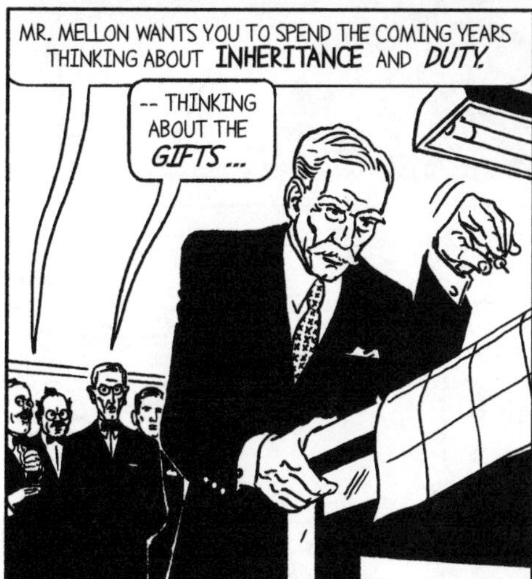

MR. MELLON WANTS YOU TO SPEND THE COMING YEARS THINKING ABOUT **INHERITANCE** AND *DUTY.*
-- THINKING ABOUT THE *GIFTS* ...

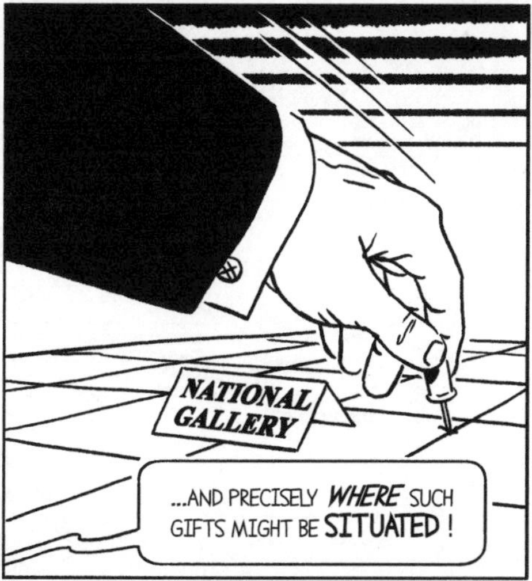

NATIONAL GALLERY
...AND PRECISELY *WHERE* SUCH GIFTS MIGHT BE **SITUATED**!

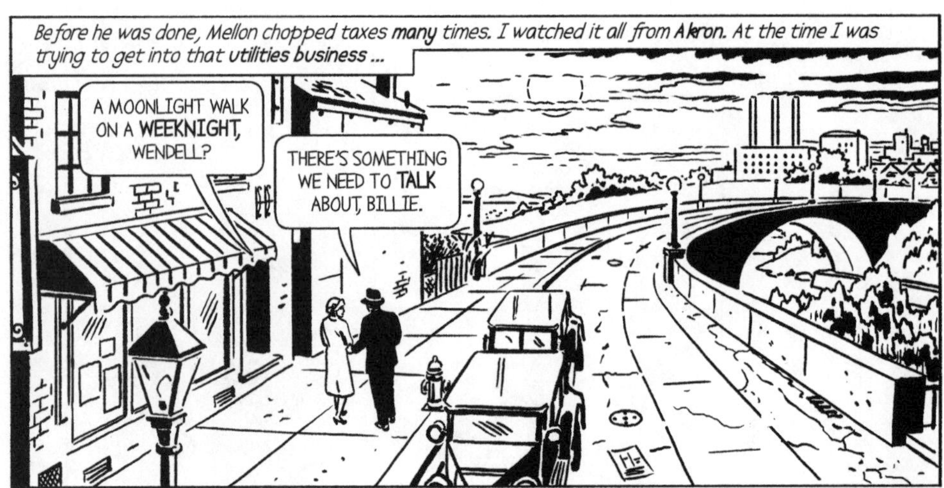
Before he was done, Mellon chopped taxes many times. I watched it all from Akron. At the time I was trying to get into that utilities business ...
A MOONLIGHT WALK ON A WEEKNIGHT, WENDELL?
THERE'S SOMETHING WE NEED TO TALK ABOUT, BILLIE.

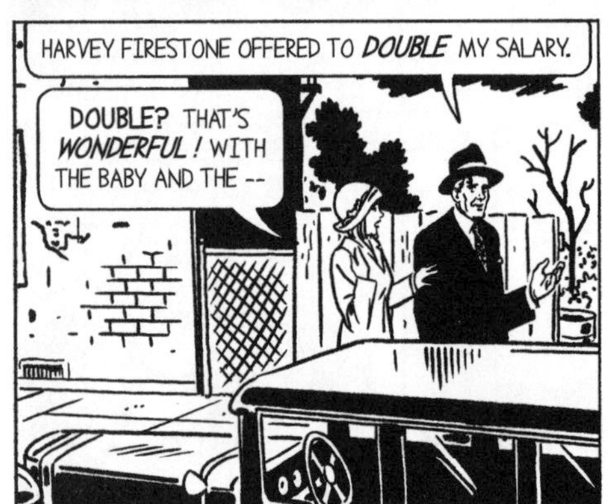
HARVEY FIRESTONE OFFERED TO DOUBLE MY SALARY.
DOUBLE? THAT'S WONDERFUL! WITH THE BABY AND THE --

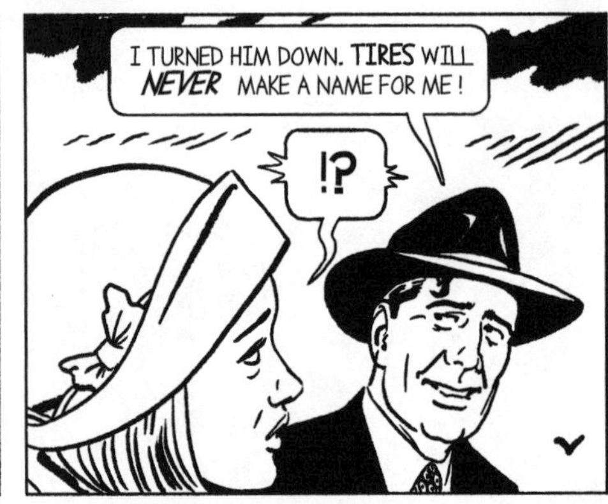
I TURNED HIM DOWN. TIRES WILL NEVER MAKE A NAME FOR ME!
!?

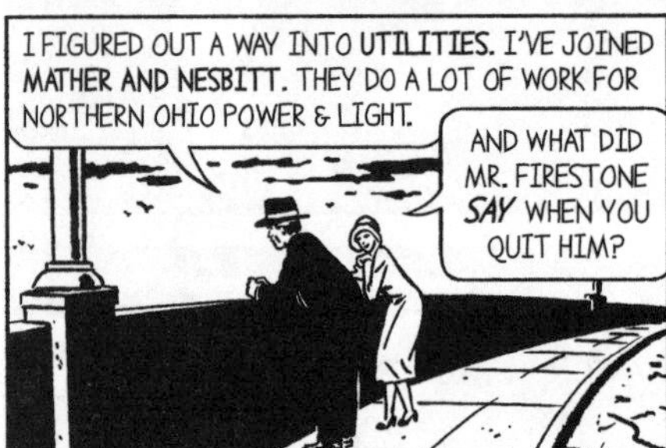
I FIGURED OUT A WAY INTO UTILITIES. I'VE JOINED MATHER AND NESBITT. THEY DO A LOT OF WORK FOR NORTHERN OHIO POWER & LIGHT.
AND WHAT DID MR. FIRESTONE SAY WHEN YOU QUIT HIM?

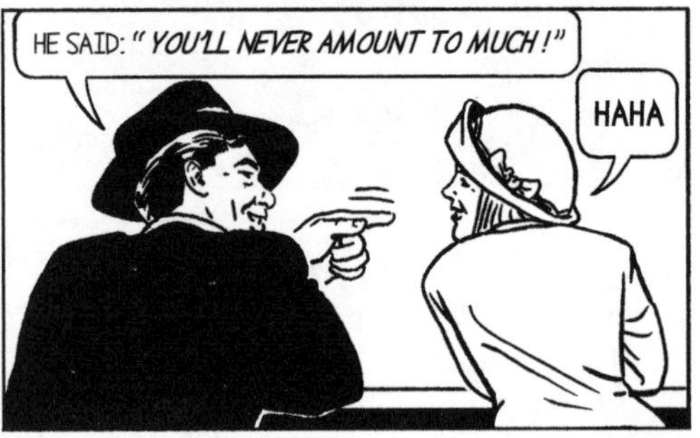
HE SAID: "YOU'LL NEVER AMOUNT TO MUCH!"
HAHA

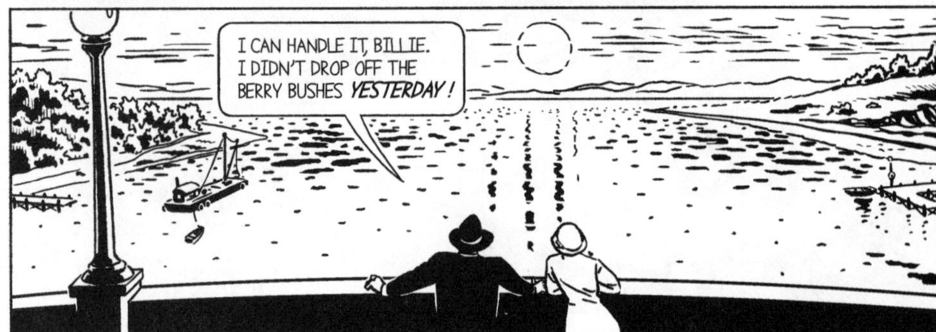
I CAN HANDLE IT, BILLIE. I DIDN'T DROP OFF THE BERRY BUSHES YESTERDAY!

We were going to make utilities **all over** the country. Some had already shown the way, like **Samuel Insull.**

You remember the name -- he'd come from the **UK,** worked with **Edison.** He began operating in **Chicago,** with the **World's Columbian Exposition.**

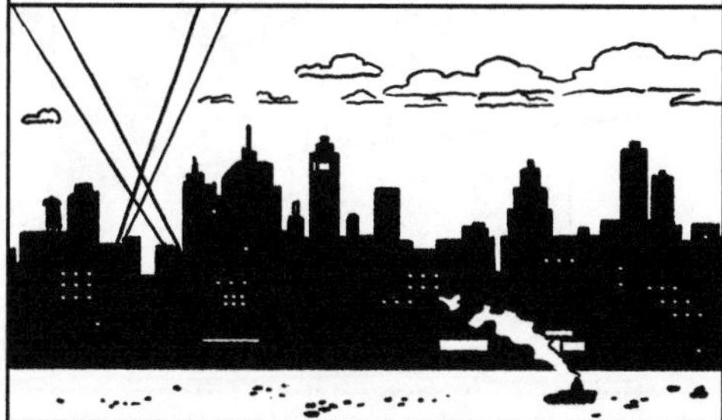

Chicagoans **LOVED** Insull. They turned out for the man, rain or shine. When he sold **war bonds,** they **bought** them -- I **learned** from that.

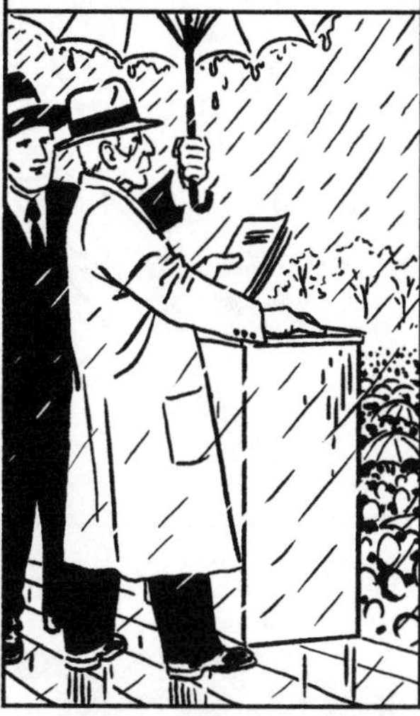

All the while I was growing up, I was aware of Insull. He **formatted** the modern grid in **Chicago,** and did it despite what Edison said in **New York.**

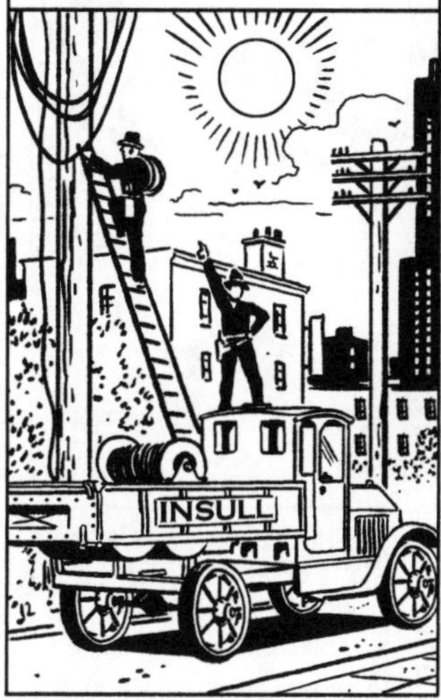

Insull knew it wasn't enough to just **lay wires** -- you had to **SHOW** people how to **USE** power -- sell the housewives the irons!

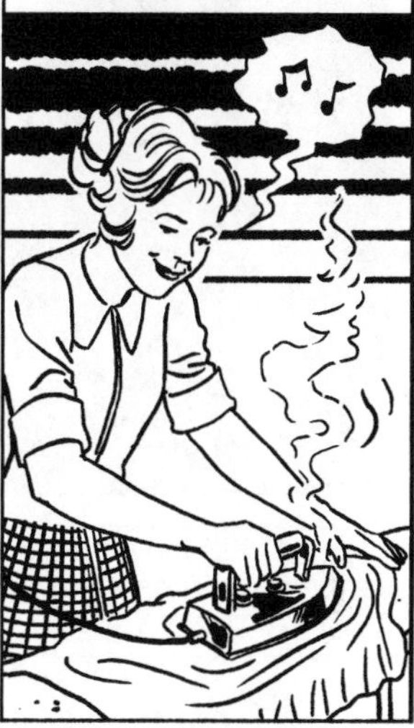

He installed electric elevators to **every box** in his opera house. Like Mellon, he was an **INNOVATOR.** I **learned** from that, too.

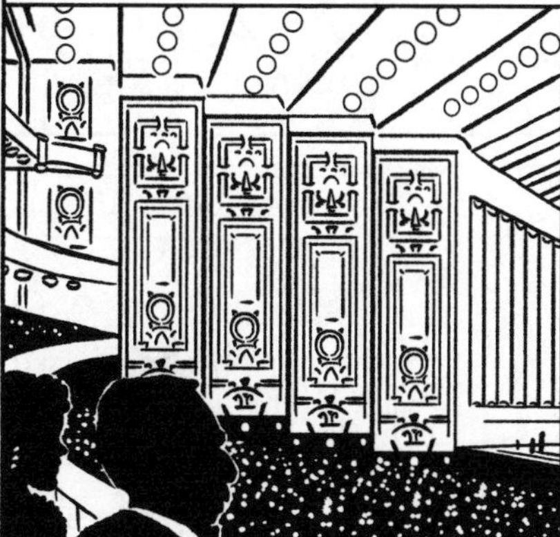

Insull even made his opera house look like an **armchair** facing west. That was his joke - **Chicago's** joke. **LaSalle Street** turns its back on **Wall Street...**

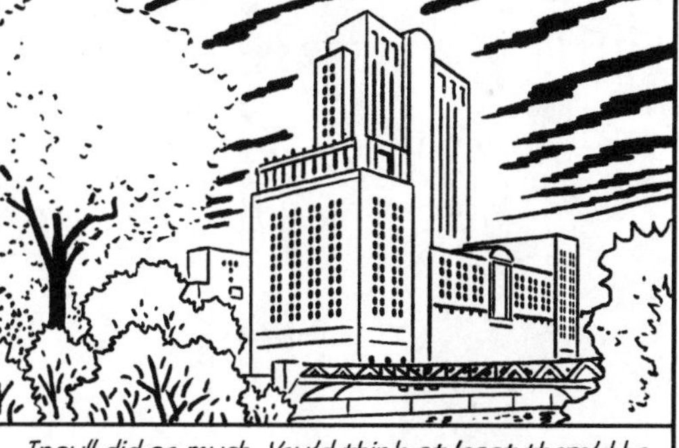

Insull did **so** much. You'd think **at least** there'd be a **big street** named after him...

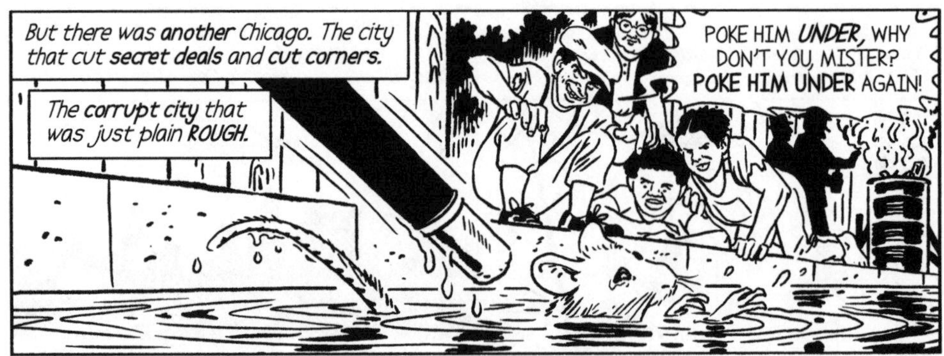
But there was another Chicago. The city that cut secret deals and cut corners.
The corrupt city that was just plain ROUGH.
POKE HIM UNDER, WHY DON'T YOU, MISTER? POKE HIM UNDER AGAIN!

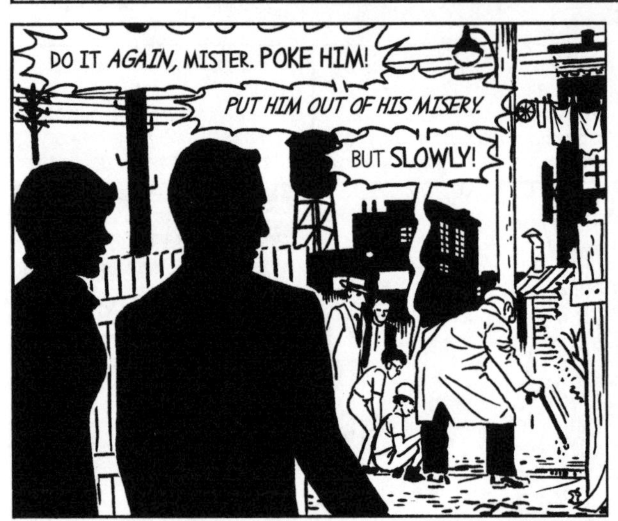
DO IT AGAIN, MISTER. POKE HIM!
PUT HIM OUT OF HIS MISERY.
BUT SLOWLY!

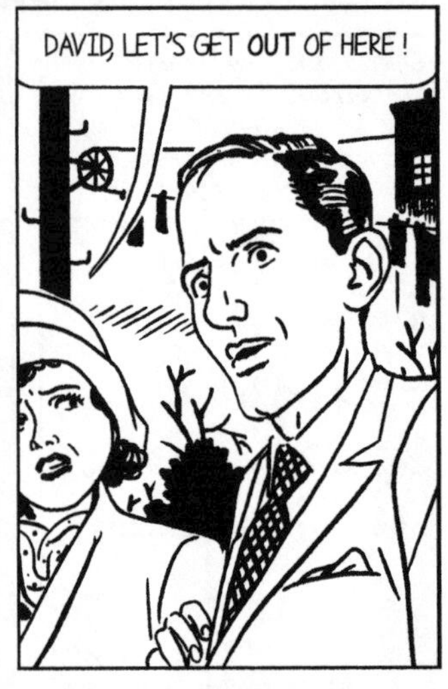
DAVID, LET'S GET OUT OF HERE!

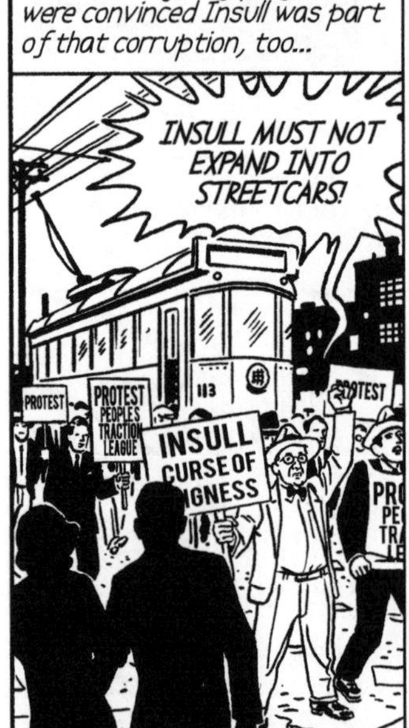
And a lot of young progressives were convinced Insull was part of that corruption, too...
INSULL MUST NOT EXPAND INTO STREETCARS!
PROTEST
PROTEST PEOPLES TRACTION LEAGUE
INSULL CURSE OF BIGNESS
PROTEST

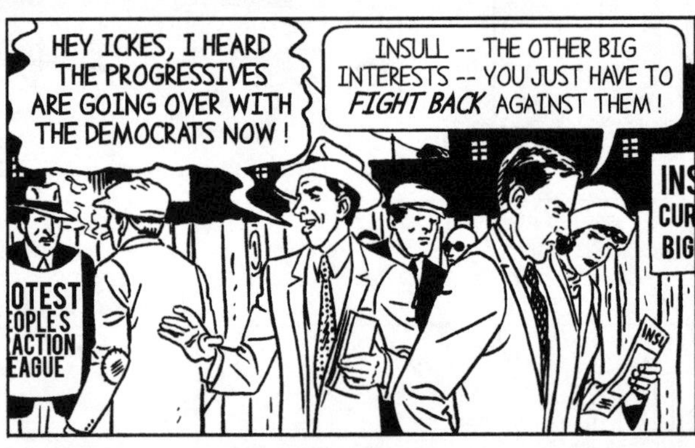
HEY ICKES, I HEARD THE PROGRESSIVES ARE GOING OVER WITH THE DEMOCRATS NOW!
INSULL -- THE OTHER BIG INTERESTS -- YOU JUST HAVE TO FIGHT BACK AGAINST THEM!
PROTEST PEOPLES TRACTION LEAGUE

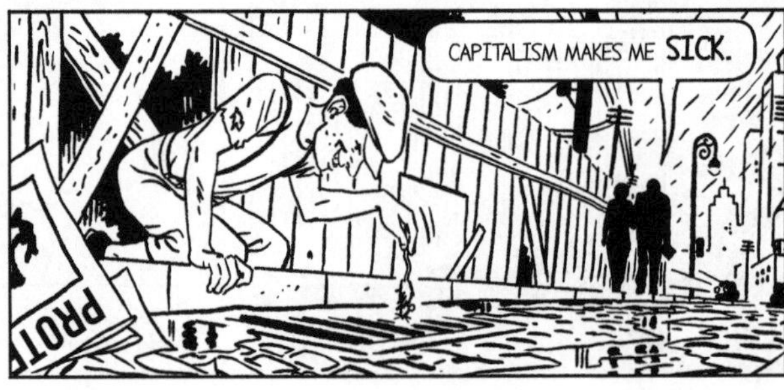
CAPITALISM MAKES ME SICK.

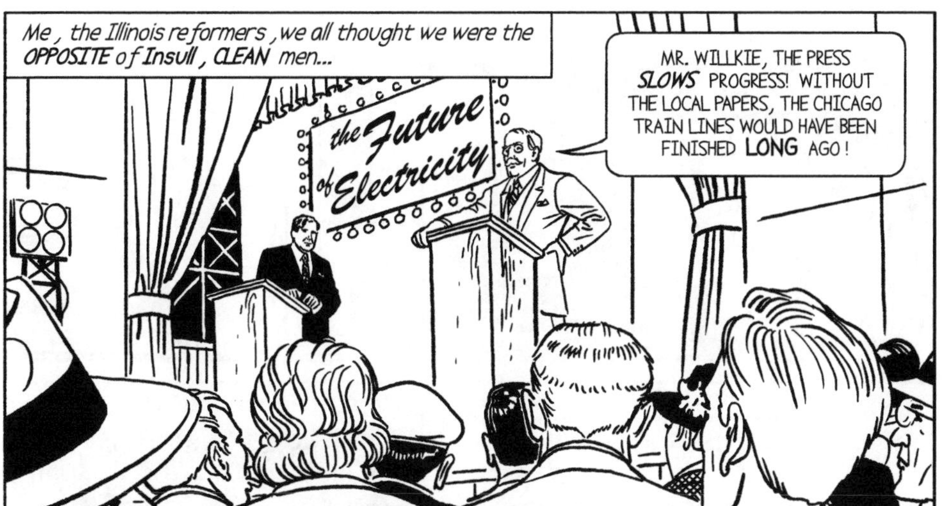
Me, the Illinois reformers, we all thought we were the OPPOSITE of Insull, CLEAN men...
MR. WILLKIE, THE PRESS SLOWS PROGRESS! WITHOUT THE LOCAL PAPERS, THE CHICAGO TRAIN LINES WOULD HAVE BEEN FINISHED LONG AGO!
the Future of Electricity

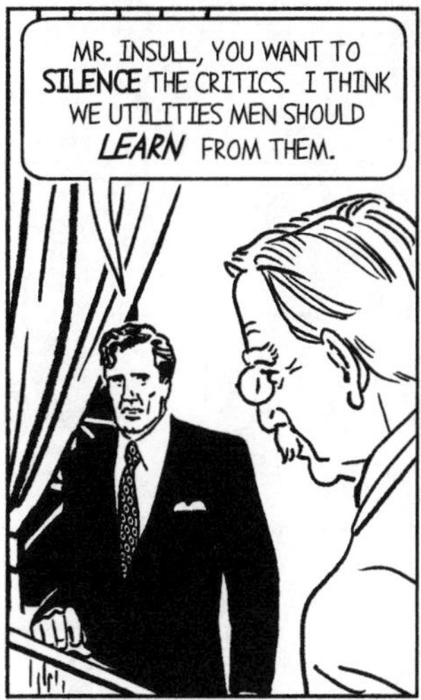
MR. INSULL, YOU WANT TO SILENCE THE CRITICS. I THINK WE UTILITIES MEN SHOULD LEARN FROM THEM.

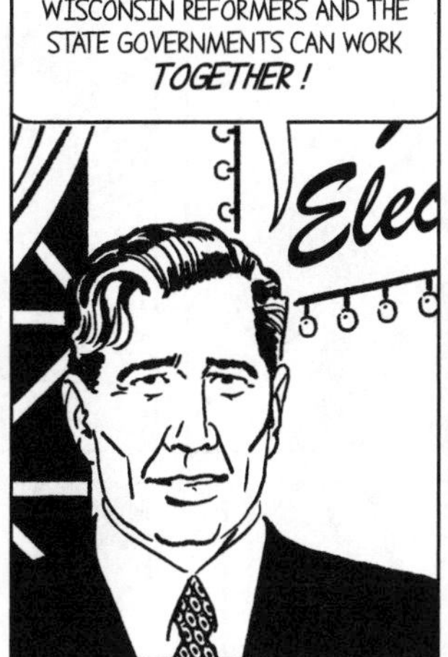
MY OWN SENSE IS THAT THE WISCONSIN REFORMERS AND THE STATE GOVERNMENTS CAN WORK TOGETHER!

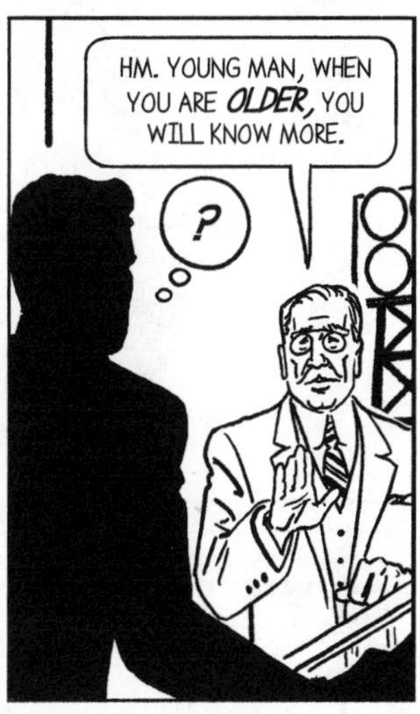
HM. YOUNG MAN, WHEN YOU ARE OLDER, YOU WILL KNOW MORE.
?

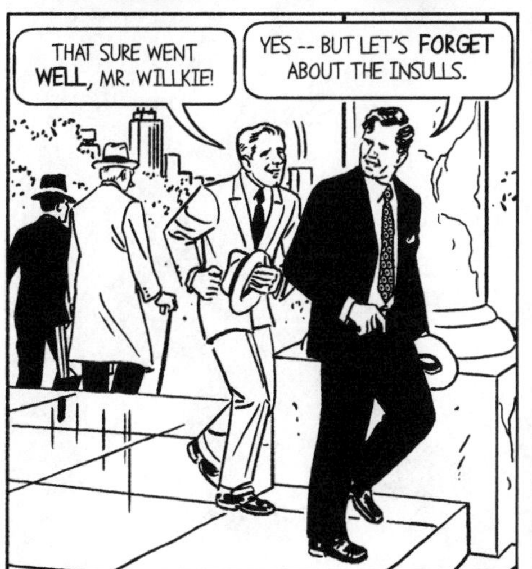
THAT SURE WENT WELL, MR. WILLKIE!
YES -- BUT LET'S FORGET ABOUT THE INSULLS.

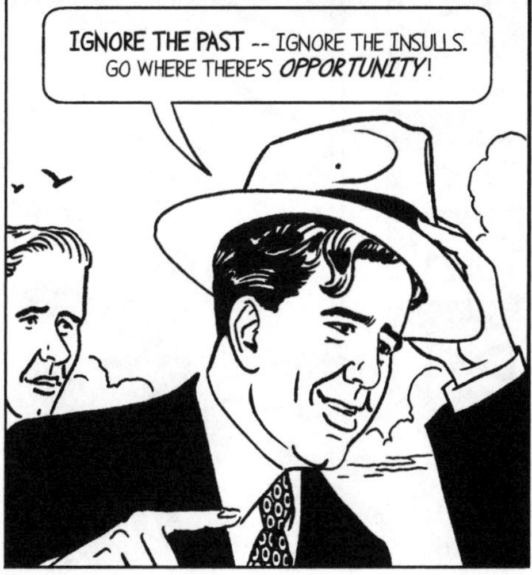
IGNORE THE PAST -- IGNORE THE INSULLS. GO WHERE THERE'S OPPORTUNITY!

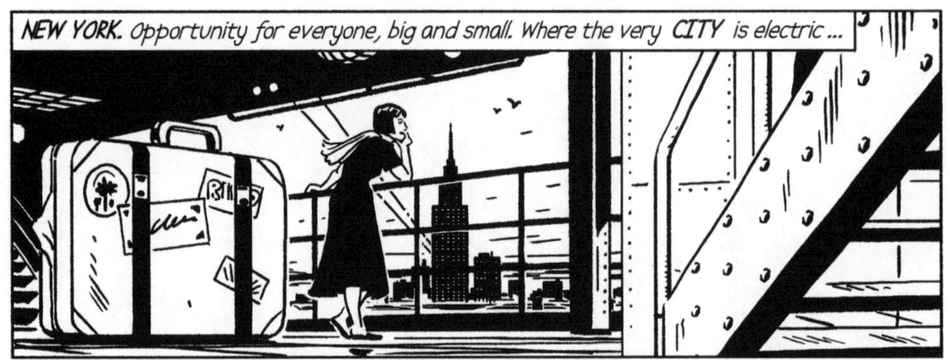
NEW YORK. Opportunity for everyone, big and small. Where the very CITY is electric ...

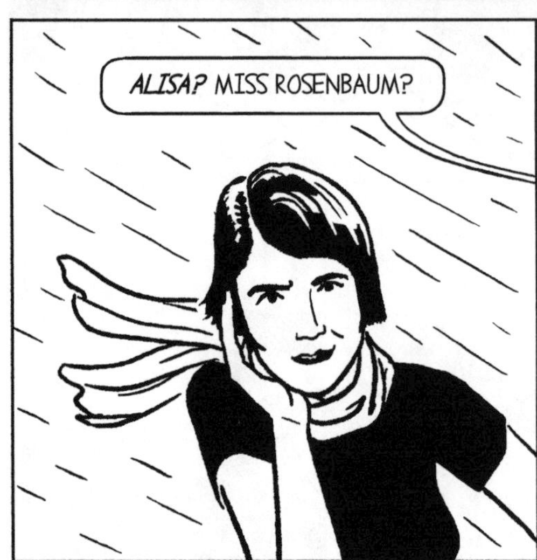
ALISA? MISS ROSENBAUM?

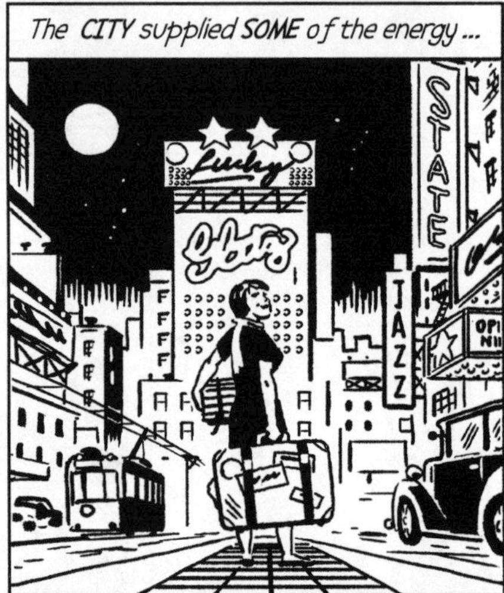
The CITY supplied SOME of the energy ...
STATE
JAZZ

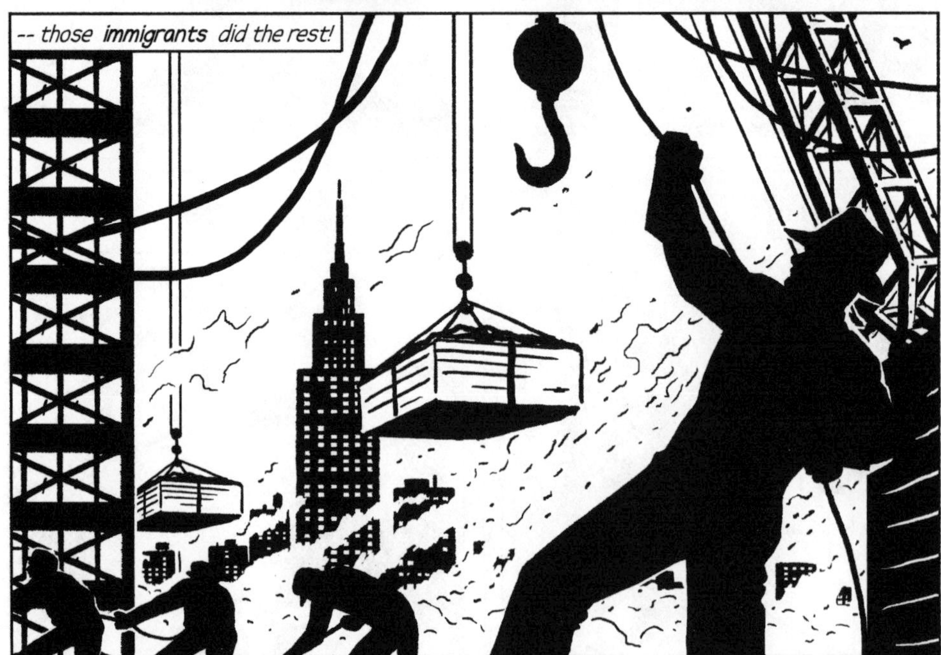
-- those immigrants did the rest!

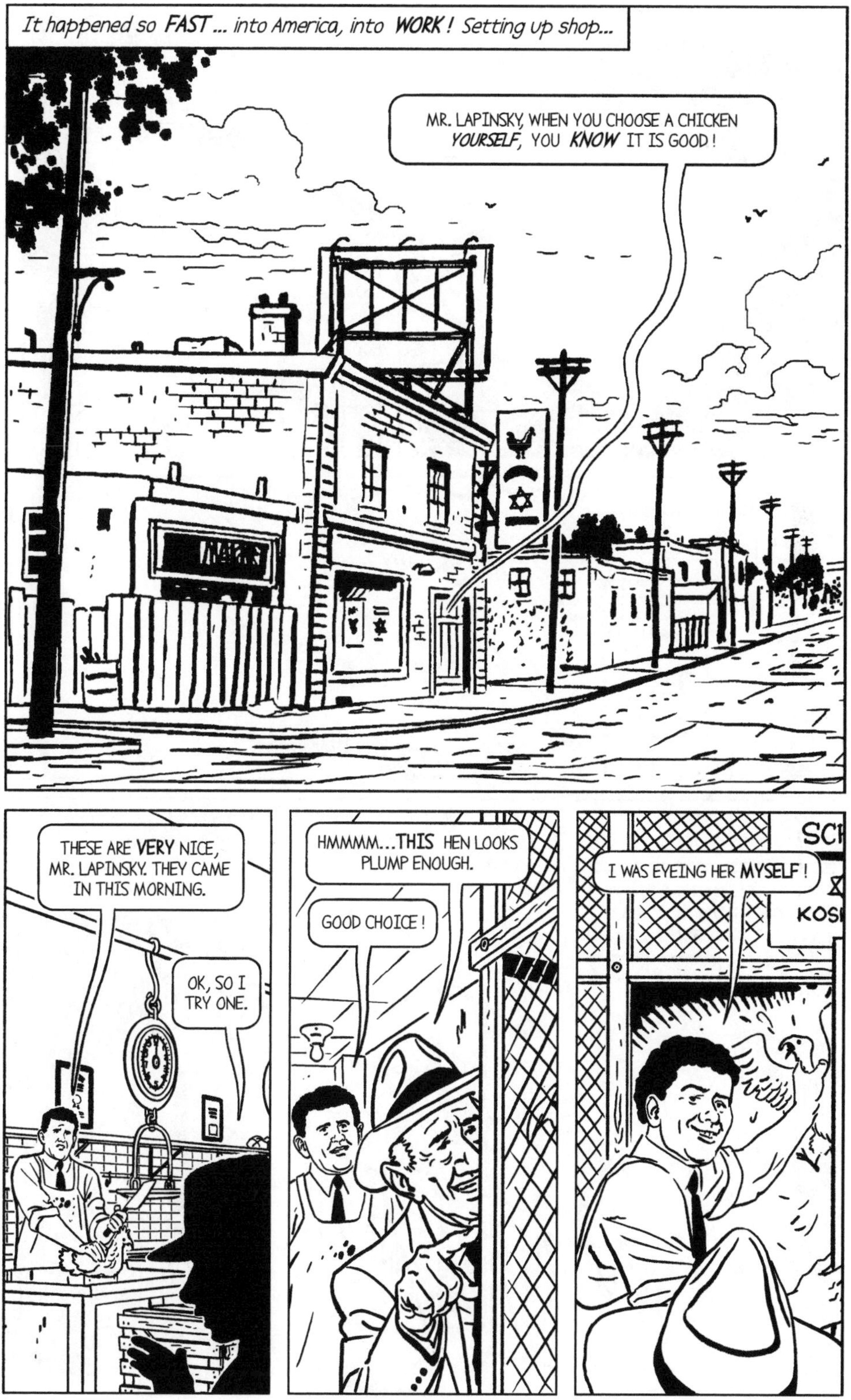

*It happened so **FAST** ... into America, into **WORK**! Setting up shop...*

MR. LAPINSKY, WHEN YOU CHOOSE A CHICKEN ***YOURSELF***, YOU ***KNOW*** IT IS GOOD!

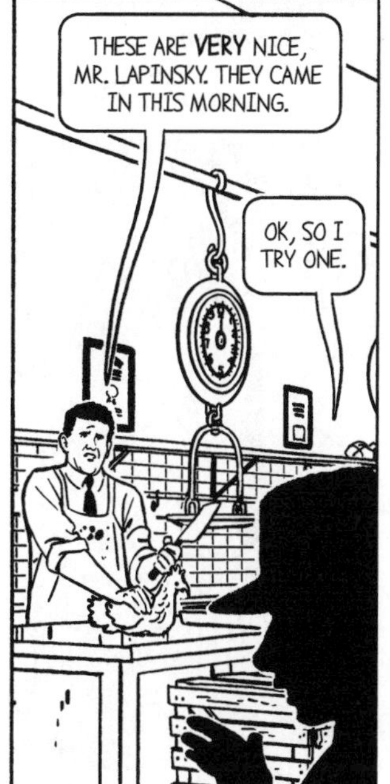

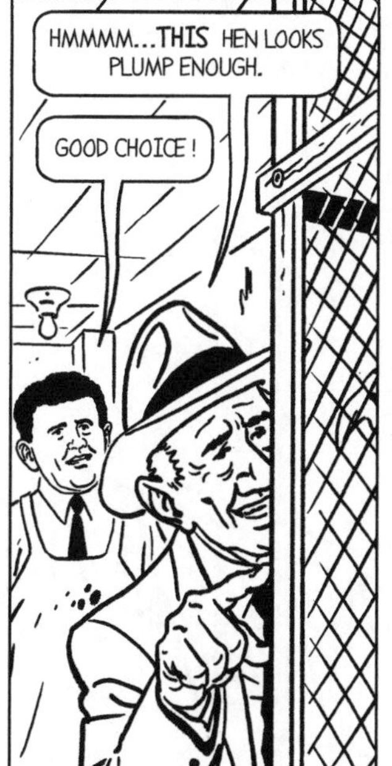

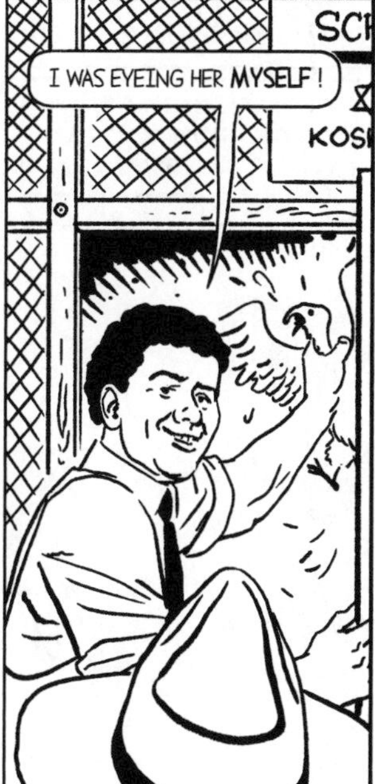

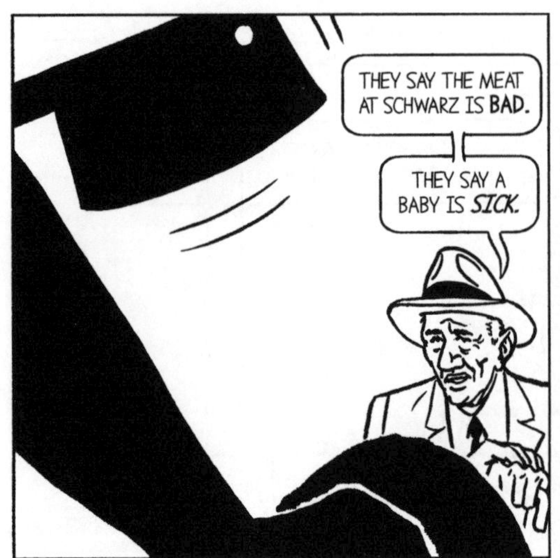

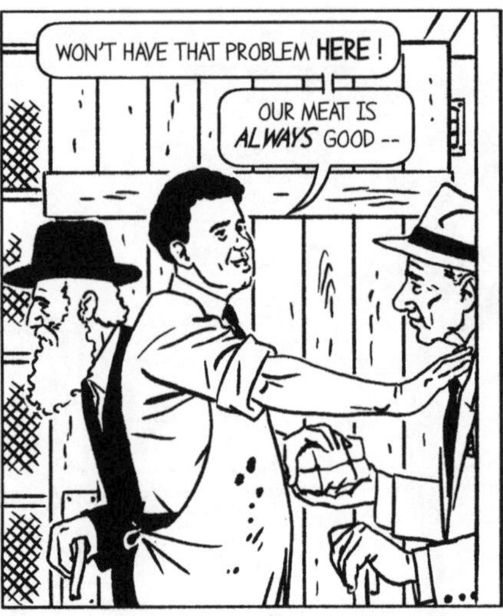

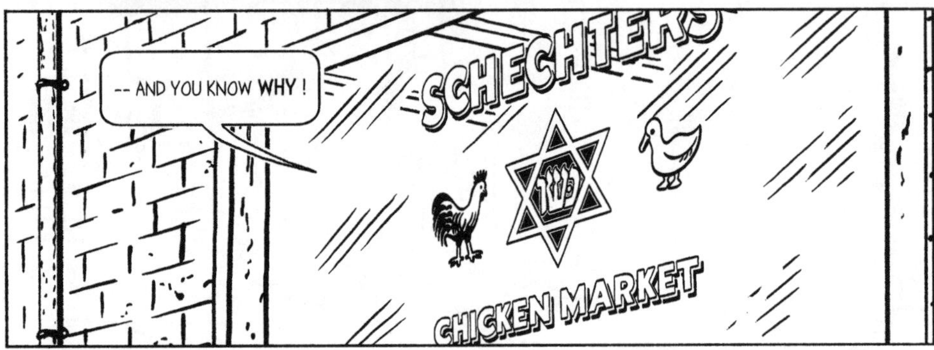

*It wasn't just **immigrants** who grew New York.*

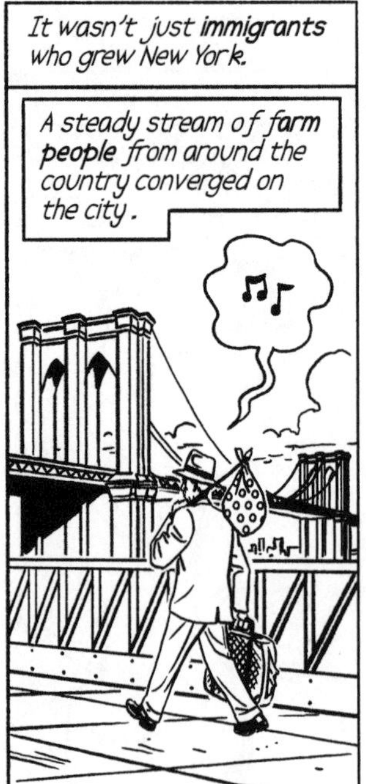

*Maybe they wanted to try their hands in **business** or on **Wall Street**.*

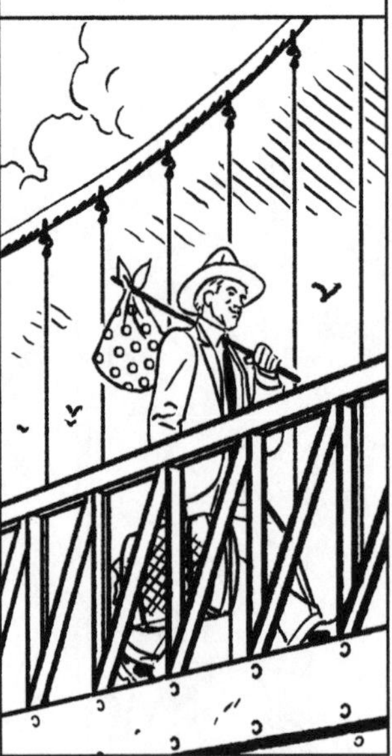

*Maybe they wanted to leave their pasts **behind...***

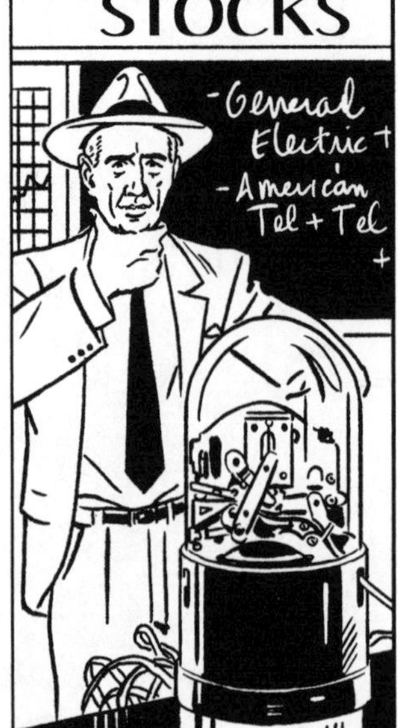

*The Negroes were part of the New York story, **too.** Some were coming up in a **great migration.** Some were **already** established ... **Strivers' Row** was **HOPPING**!*

*Even in **Akron** they spoke of **FATHER DIVINE**, the Negro preacher in New York spreading the **GOSPEL OF PLENTY.** His followers said he was **GOD** ...*

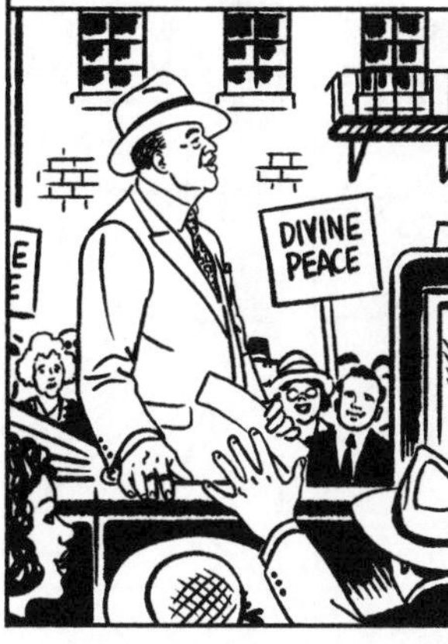

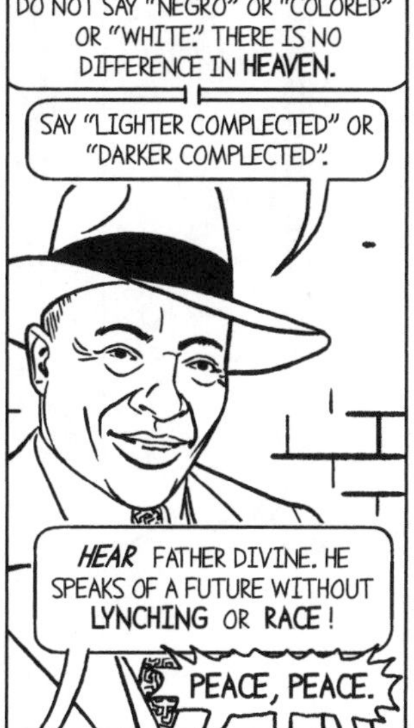

WHEN MEN *LIVE* THE CONSTITUTION OF THIS COUNTRY, **ONLY** THEN WILL WE NOT BE REPRESENTED NARROWLY AND AMERICANISM WILL BE CONVERTED INTO **TRUE EVANGELISM.**

WE SHALL **NOT** BE DISCOURAGED. WE SHALL BE MORE PRACTICAL AND PROFITABLE. WE *CAN* BUILD OUR OWN HEAVEN! **PEACE.**

PEACE. PEACE.

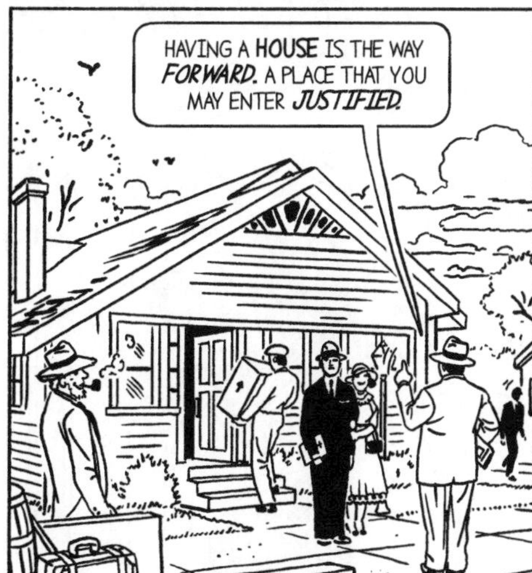

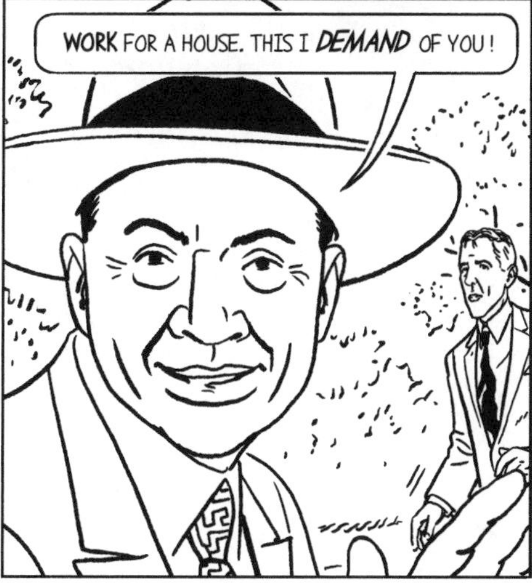

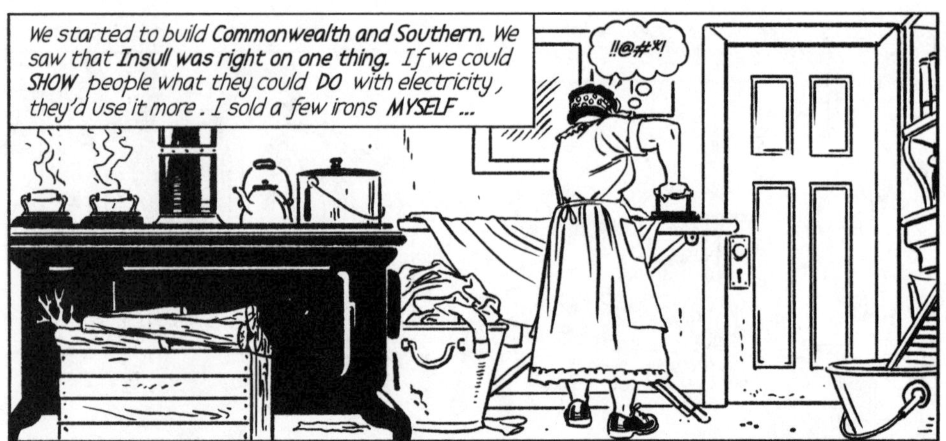
We started to build **Commonwealth and Southern.** We saw that **Insull was right on one thing.** If we could **SHOW** people what they could **DO** with electricity, they'd use it more. I sold a few irons **MYSELF ...**
!!@#*!

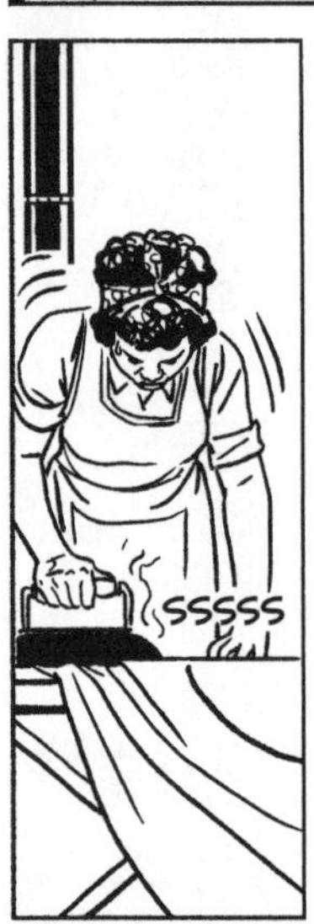
SSSSS

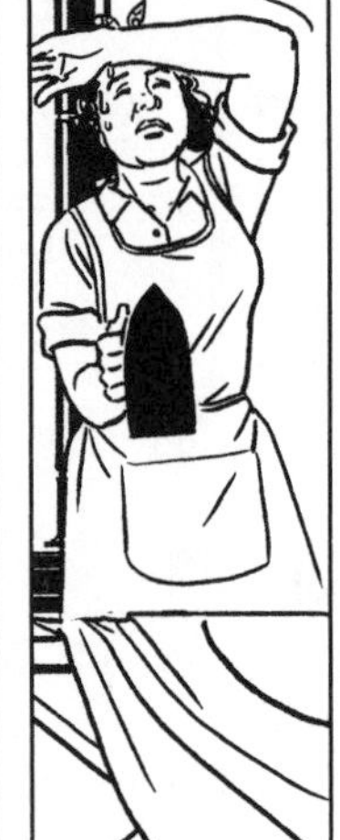

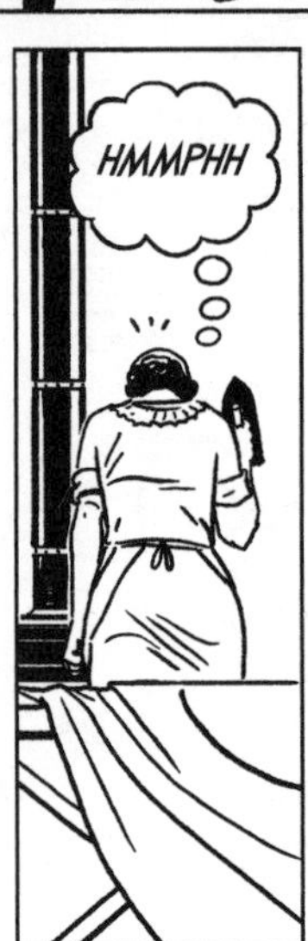
HMMPHH

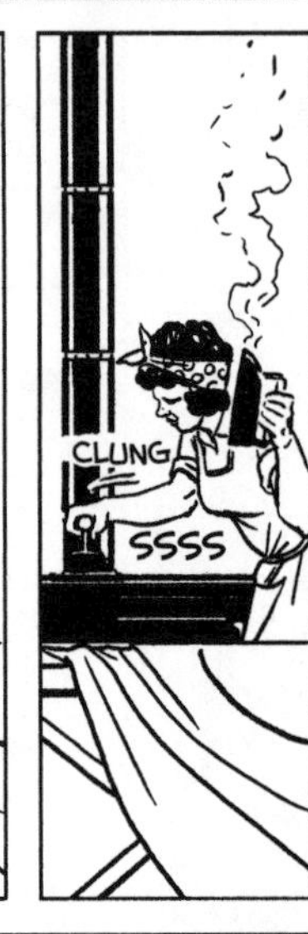
CLUNG
SSSS

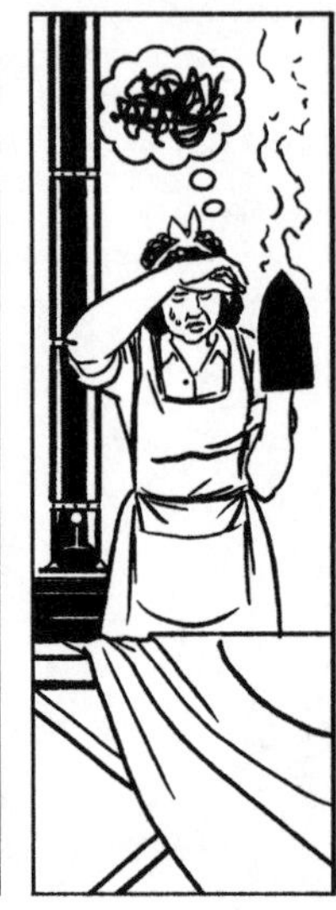

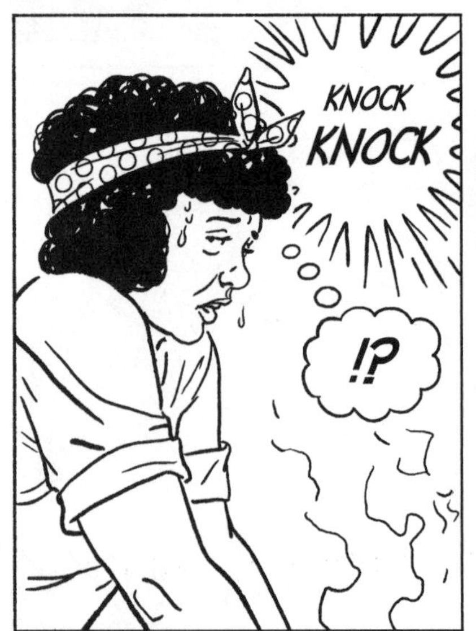
KNOCK
KNOCK
!?

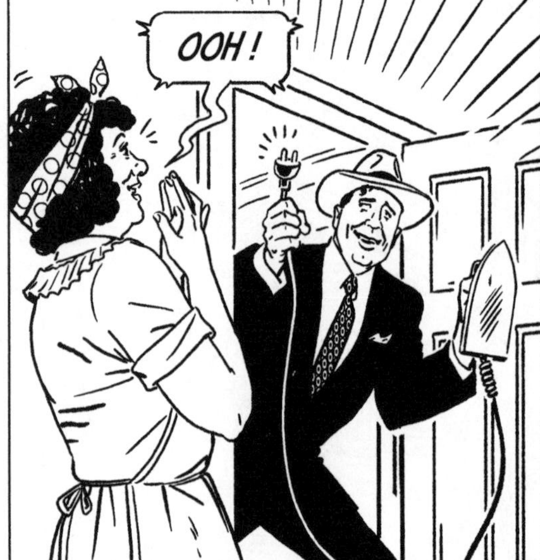
OOH!

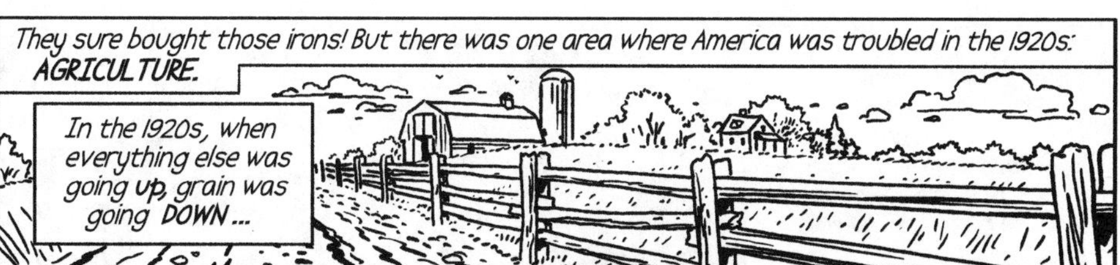
They sure bought those irons! But there was one area where America was troubled in the 1920s: AGRICULTURE.
In the 1920s, when everything else was going up, grain was going DOWN...

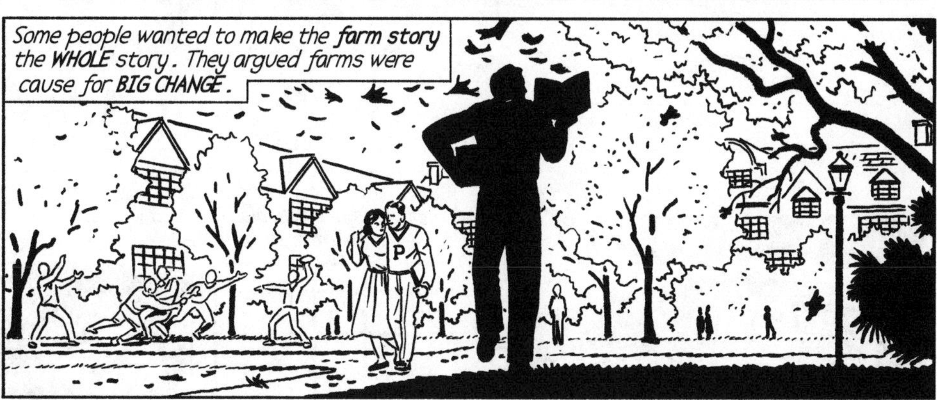
Some people wanted to make the farm story the WHOLE story. They argued farms were cause for BIG CHANGE.

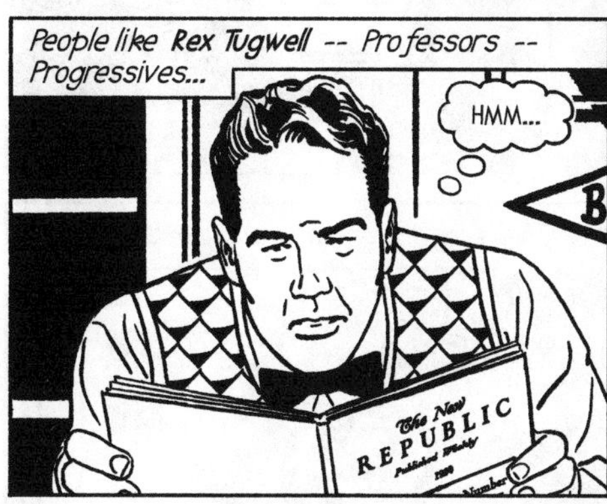
People like Rex Tugwell -- Professors -- Progressives...
HMM...
The New REPUBLIC

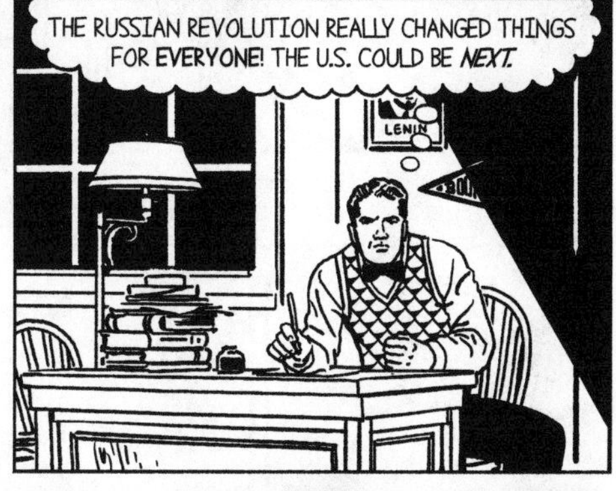
THE RUSSIAN REVOLUTION REALLY CHANGED THINGS FOR EVERYONE! THE U.S. COULD BE NEXT.
LENIN

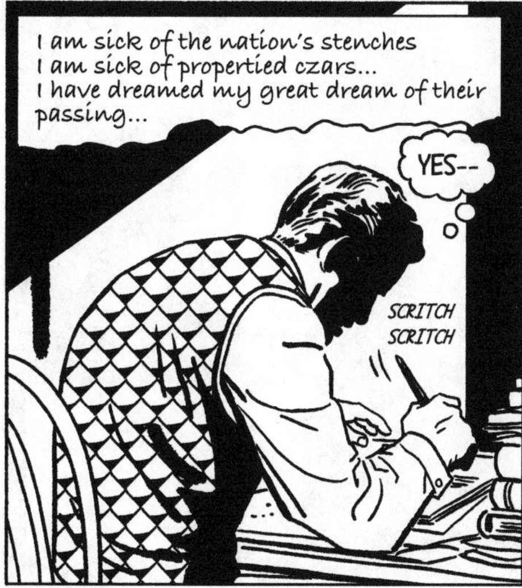
I am sick of the nation's stenches
I am sick of propertied czars...
I have dreamed my great dream of their passing...
YES--
SCRITCH
SCRITCH

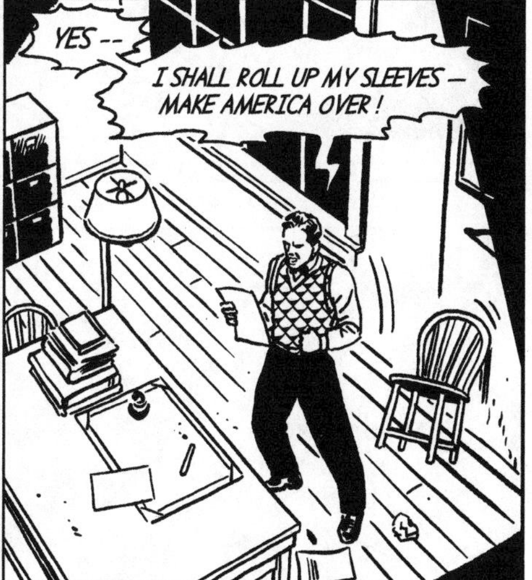
YES --
I SHALL ROLL UP MY SLEEVES — MAKE AMERICA OVER!

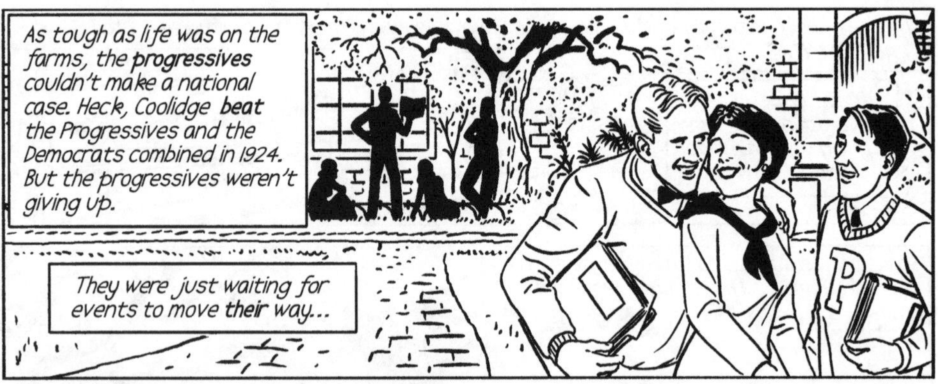
As tough as life was on the farms, the **progressives** couldn't make a national case. Heck, Coolidge **beat** the Progressives and the Democrats combined in 1924. But the progressives weren't giving up.
They were just waiting for events to move **their** way...
P

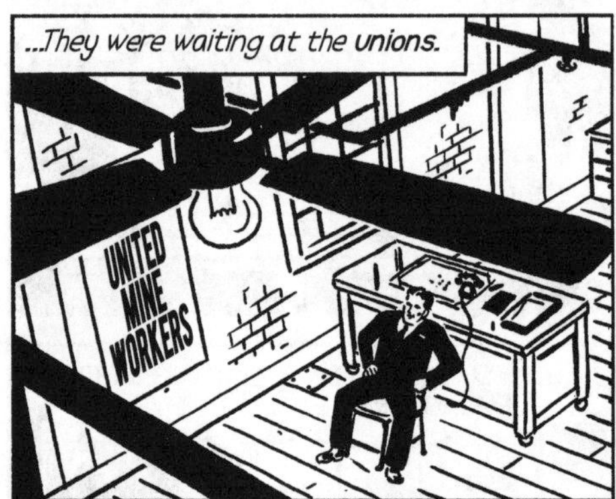
...They were waiting at the **unions.**
UNITED MINE WORKERS

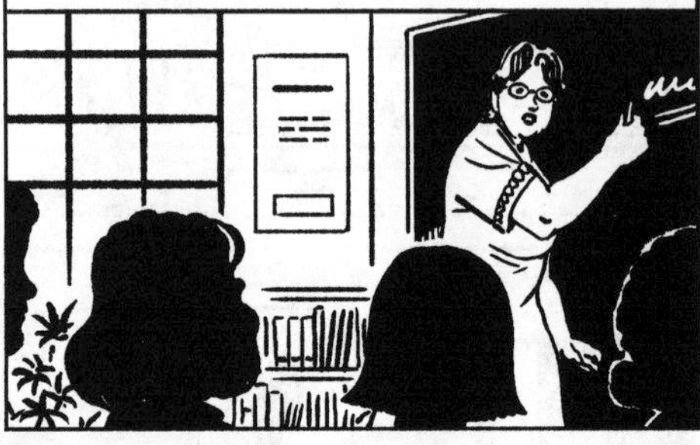
...They were waiting at those **John Dewey progressive schools.** The kind we **never** heard about in **Indiana.**

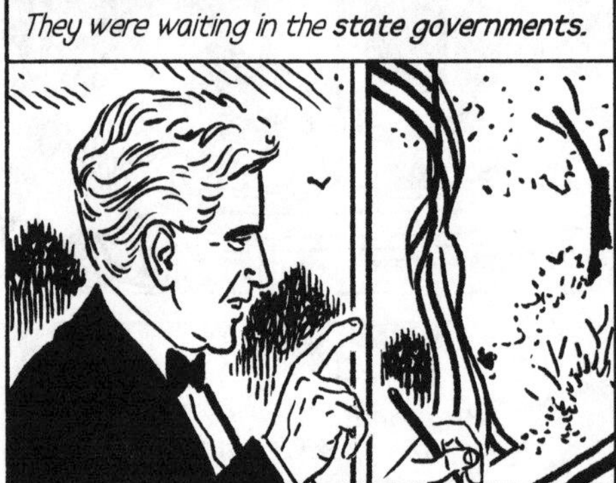
They were waiting in the **state governments.**

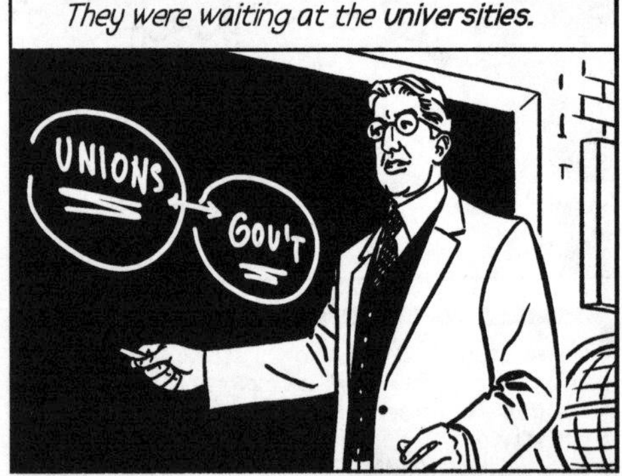
They were waiting at the **universities.**
UNIONS
GOV'T

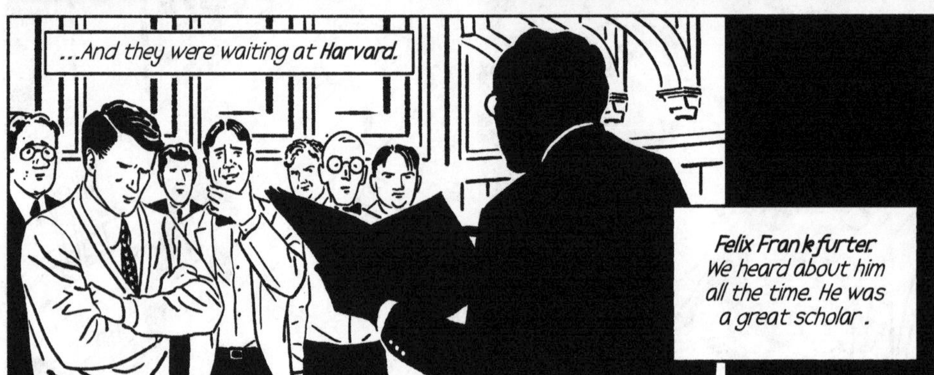
...And they were waiting at **Harvard.**
Felix Frankfurter. We heard about him all the time. He was a great scholar.

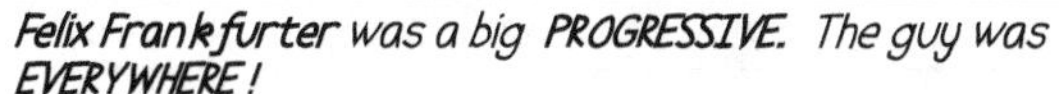
Felix Frankfurter was a big **PROGRESSIVE.** The guy was **EVERYWHERE!**

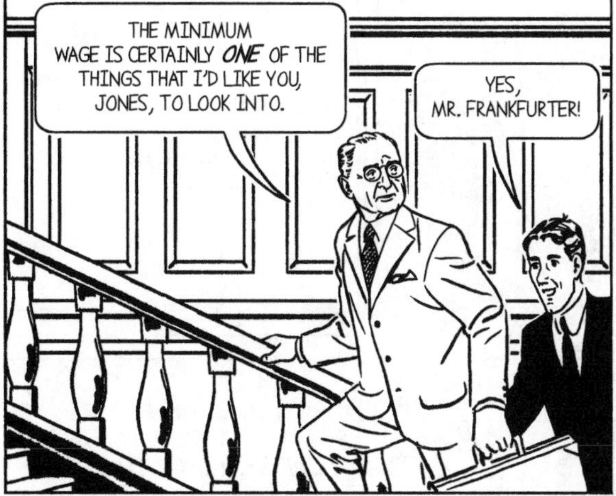
THE MINIMUM WAGE IS CERTAINLY ***ONE*** OF THE THINGS THAT I'D LIKE YOU, JONES, TO LOOK INTO.
YES, MR. FRANKFURTER!

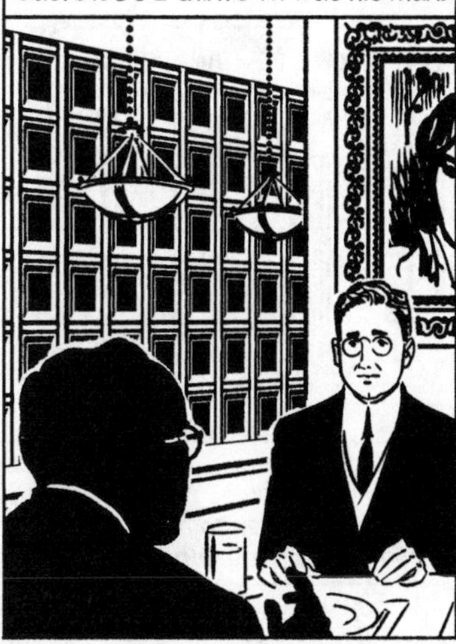
He knew the Roosevelt Family **way** back. 1906 I think. TR was his man.

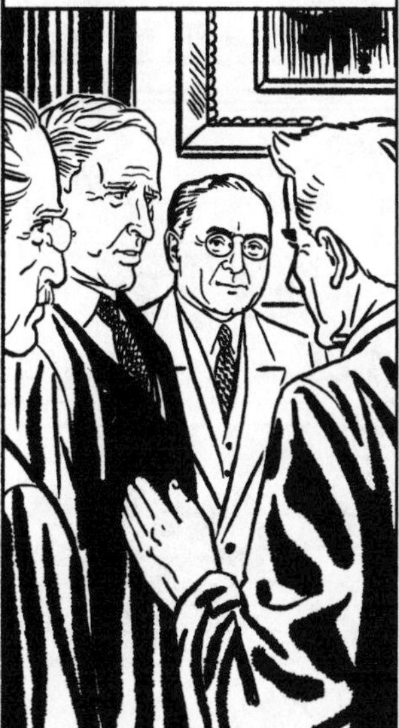
He knew **all** the justices. And to **Justice Brandeis,** Frankfurter was like a **SON.**

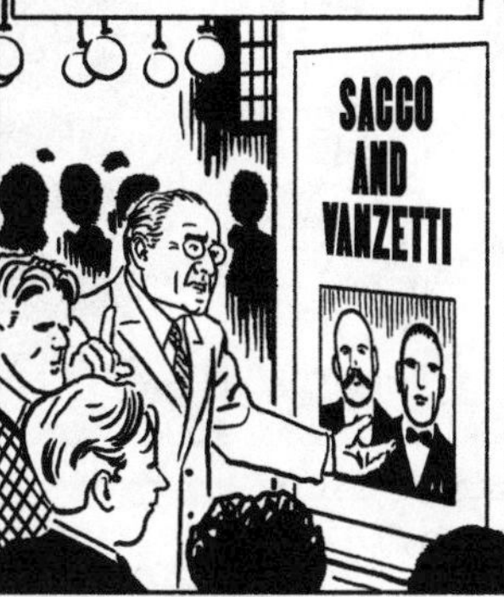
In the 1920s Frankfurter argued **Adkins.** That's the case where the Court ruled **against** the minimum wage -- said it **intruded** on the **individual contract** between man and man.
Frankfurter also jumped in to defend **Sacco** and **Vanzetti.**
SACCO AND VANZETTI

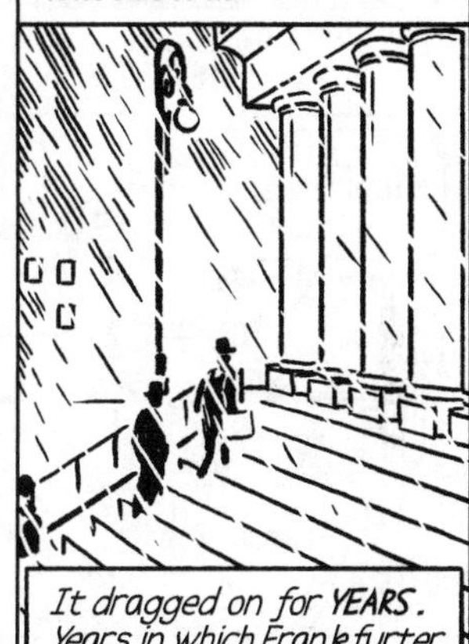
This was the kind of case that I would jump at too. Sacco and Vanzetti **murdered.** But they probably didn't get a fair trial because they were **anarchists ...**
It dragged on for **YEARS.** Years in which Frankfurter was also picking **Supreme Court** clerks.

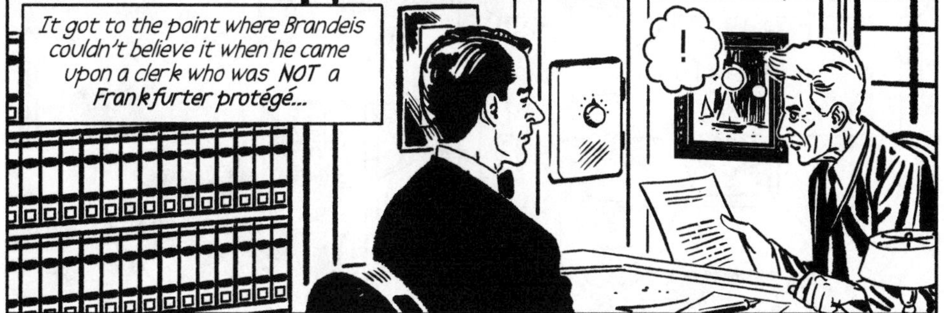
It got to the point where Brandeis couldn't believe it when he came upon a clerk who was **NOT** a **Frankfurter protégé...**
!

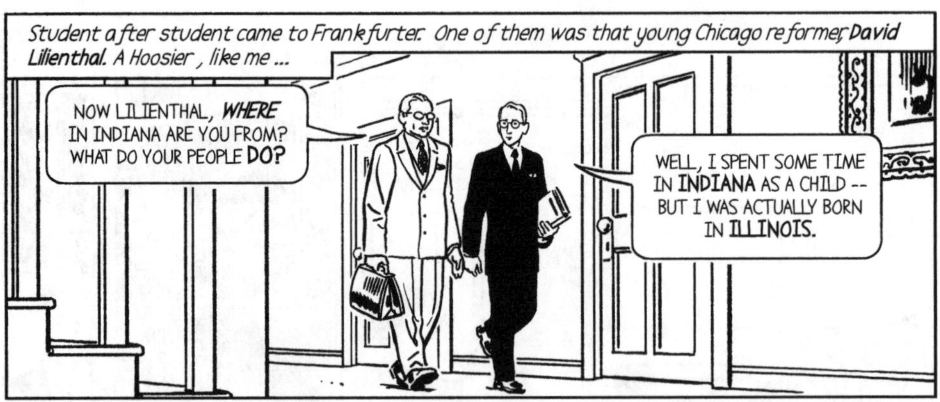
Student after student came to Frankfurter. One of them was that young Chicago reformer, David Lilienthal. A Hoosier, like me ...
NOW LILIENTHAL, WHERE IN INDIANA ARE YOU FROM? WHAT DO YOUR PEOPLE DO?
WELL, I SPENT SOME TIME IN INDIANA AS A CHILD -- BUT I WAS ACTUALLY BORN IN ILLINOIS.

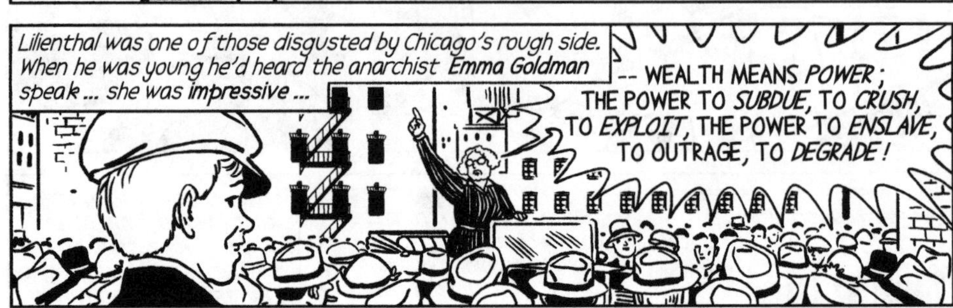
Lilienthal was one of those disgusted by Chicago's rough side. When he was young he'd heard the anarchist Emma Goldman speak ... she was impressive ...
-- WEALTH MEANS POWER; THE POWER TO SUBDUE, TO CRUSH, TO EXPLOIT, THE POWER TO ENSLAVE, TO OUTRAGE, TO DEGRADE!

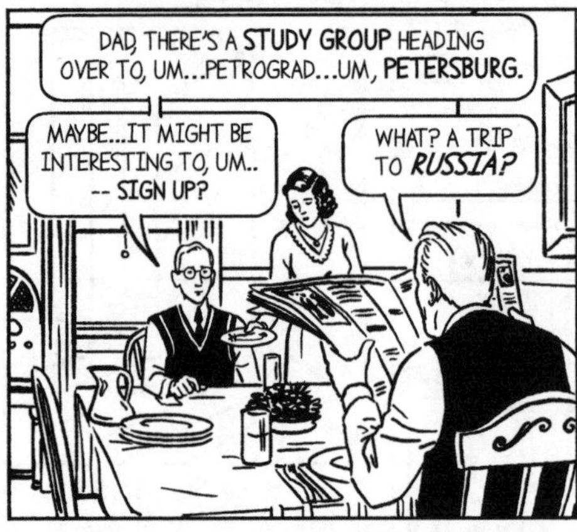
DAD, THERE'S A STUDY GROUP HEADING OVER TO, UM...PETROGRAD...UM, PETERSBURG.
MAYBE...IT MIGHT BE INTERESTING TO, UM.. -- SIGN UP?
WHAT? A TRIP TO RUSSIA?

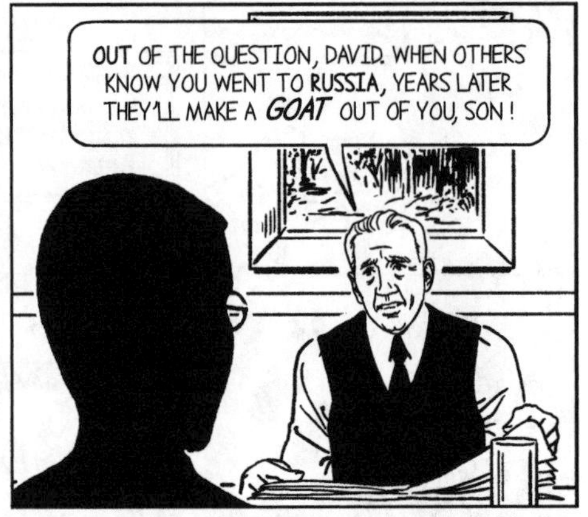
OUT OF THE QUESTION, DAVID. WHEN OTHERS KNOW YOU WENT TO RUSSIA, YEARS LATER THEY'LL MAKE A GOAT OUT OF YOU, SON!

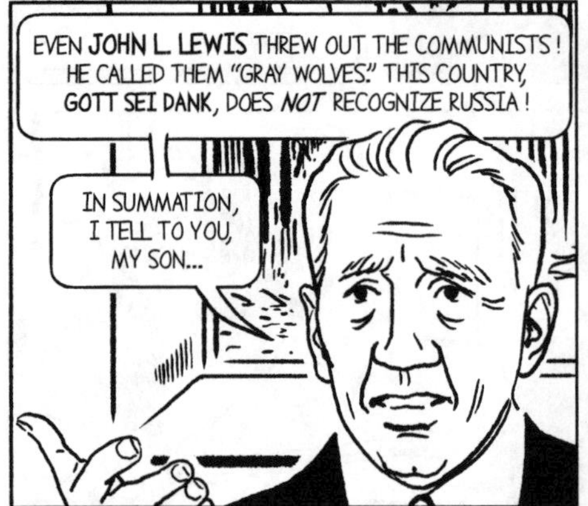
EVEN JOHN L. LEWIS THREW OUT THE COMMUNISTS! HE CALLED THEM "GRAY WOLVES." THIS COUNTRY, GOTT SEI DANK, DOES NOT RECOGNIZE RUSSIA!
IN SUMMATION, I TELL TO YOU, MY SON...

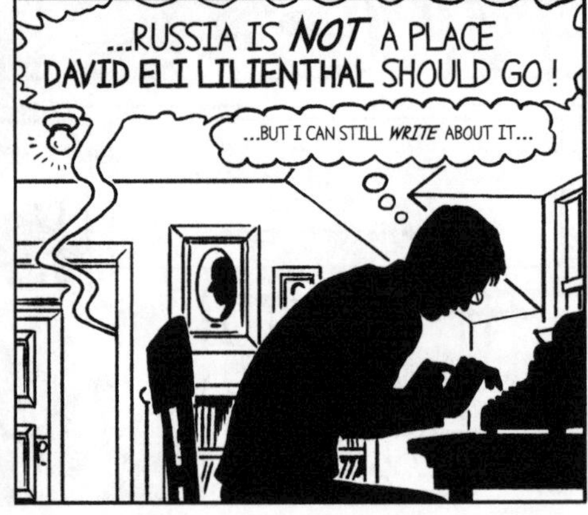
...RUSSIA IS NOT A PLACE DAVID ELI LILIENTHAL SHOULD GO!
...BUT I CAN STILL WRITE ABOUT IT...

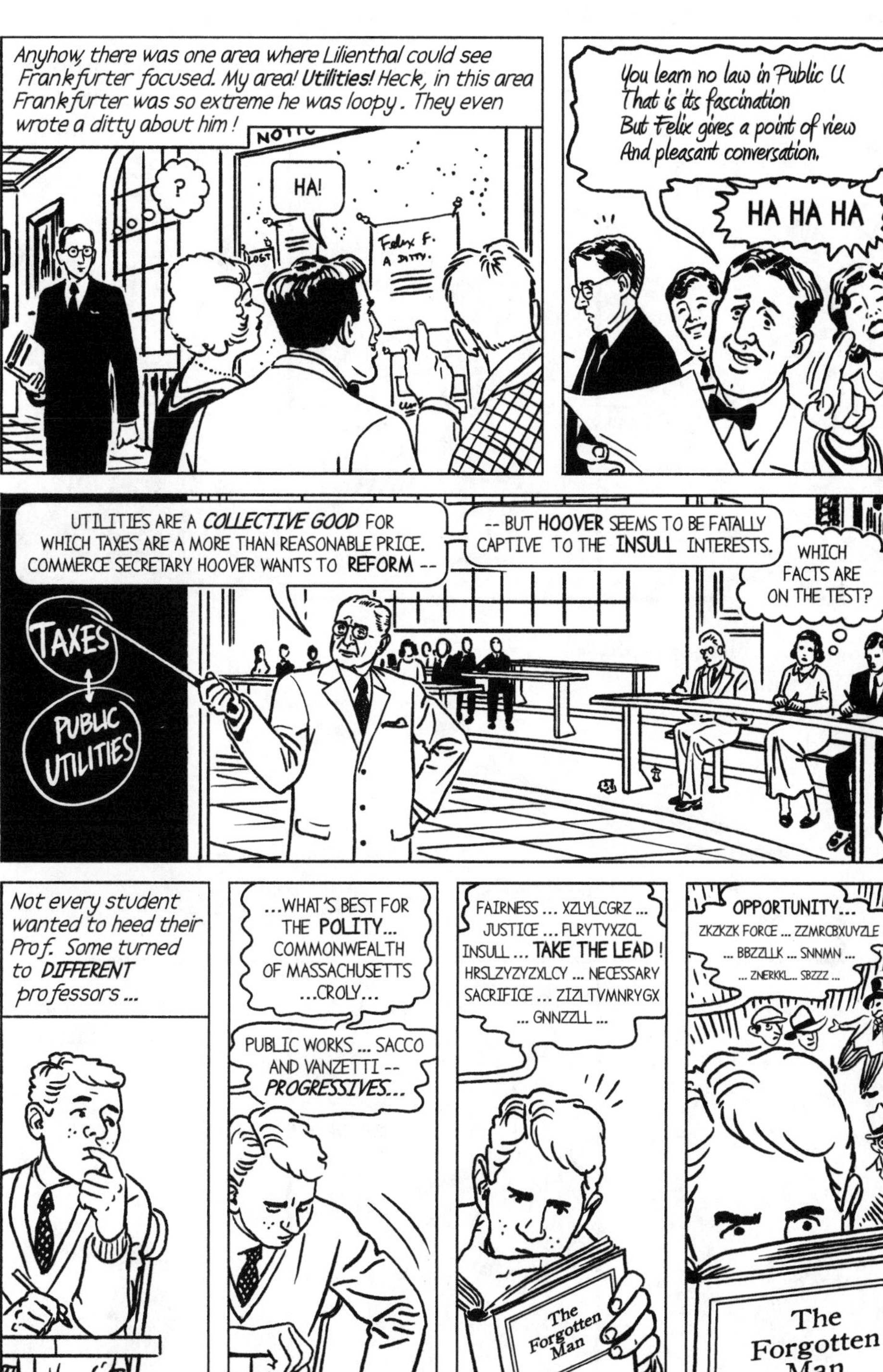
Anyhow, there was one area where Lilienthal could see Frankfurter focused. My area! Utilities! Heck, in this area Frankfurter was so extreme he was loopy. They even wrote a ditty about him!
?
HA!
Felix F. A DITTY.
You learn no law in Public U
That is its fascination
But Felix gives a point of view
And pleasant conversation.
HA HA HA
UTILITIES ARE A COLLECTIVE GOOD FOR WHICH TAXES ARE A MORE THAN REASONABLE PRICE. COMMERCE SECRETARY HOOVER WANTS TO REFORM --
-- BUT HOOVER SEEMS TO BE FATALLY CAPTIVE TO THE INSULL INTERESTS.
WHICH FACTS ARE ON THE TEST?
TAXES
PUBLIC UTILITIES
Not every student wanted to heed their Prof. Some turned to DIFFERENT professors ...
...WHAT'S BEST FOR THE POLITY... COMMONWEALTH OF MASSACHUSETTS ...CROLY...
PUBLIC WORKS ... SACCO AND VANZETTI -- PROGRESSIVES...
FAIRNESS ... XZLYLCGRZ ... JUSTICE ... FLRYTYXZCL INSULL ... TAKE THE LEAD! HRSLZYZYZXLCY ... NECESSARY SACRIFICE ... ZIZLTVMNRYGX ... GNNZZLL ...
The Forgotten Man William Graham Sumner
OPPORTUNITY... ZKZKZK FORCE ... ZZMRCBXUYZLE ... BBZZLLK ... SNNMN ... ... ZNERKKL... SBZZZ ...
The Forgotten Man William Graham Sumner

*That Sumner sketched his "**forgotten man**" so clear you could **VISUALIZE** it, like a movie.*

A observes something which seems to him to be wrong, from which X is suffering.

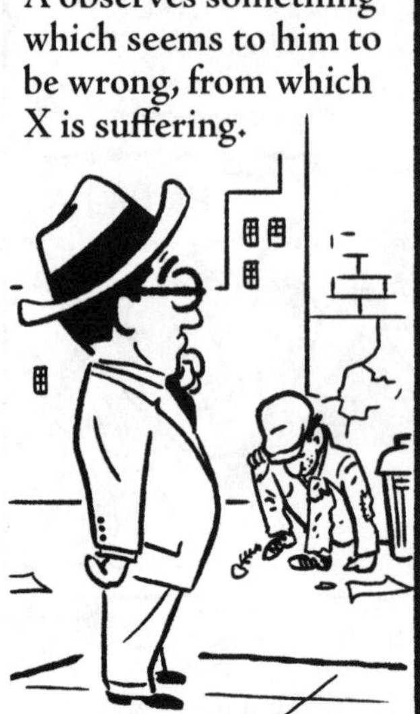

A talks it over with B.

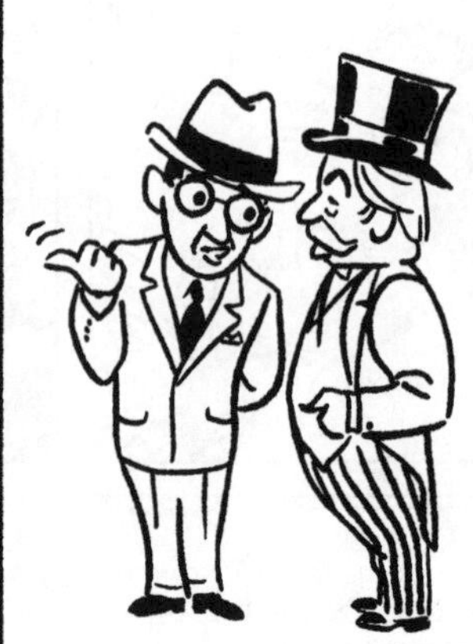

A and B then propose to get a law passed to remedy the evil and help X.

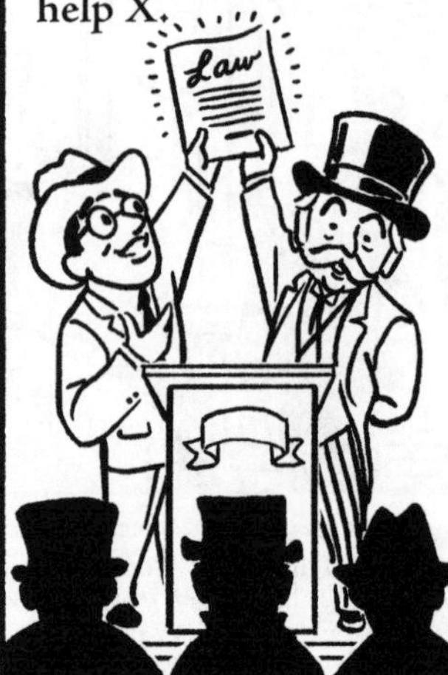

Their law always proposes to determine... what A, B, and C shall do for X.

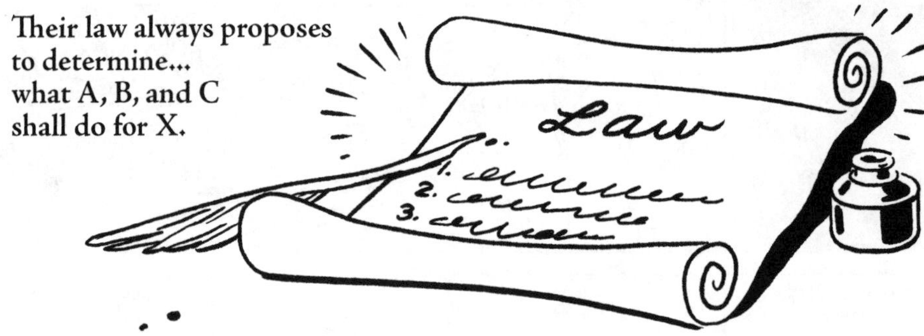

This can benefit X.

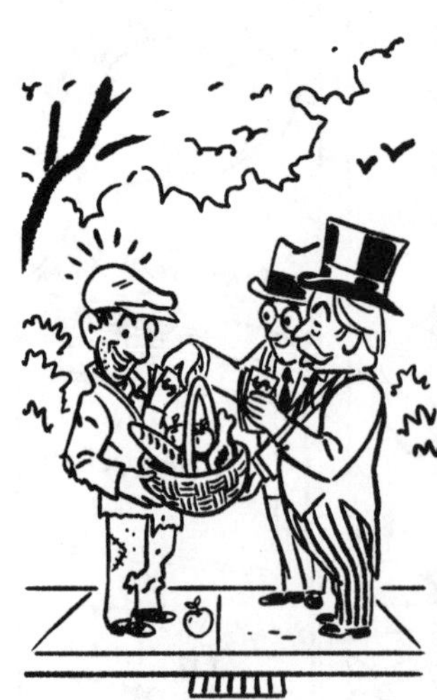

But what about C ?

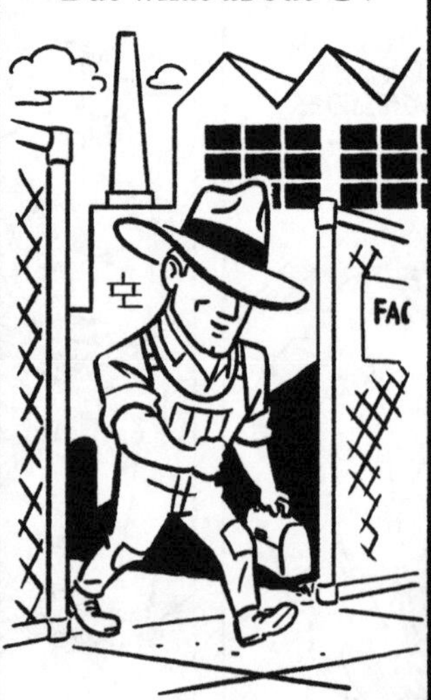

C is not allowed a voice in the matter.

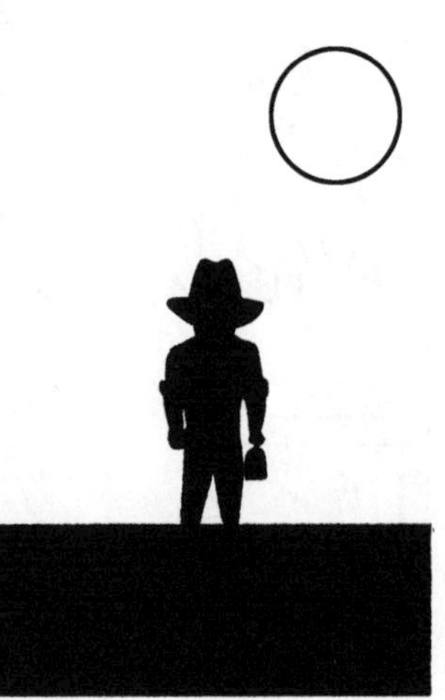

… is the forgotten man.
The man who pays.
The man who prays.
The man who is
never thought of.

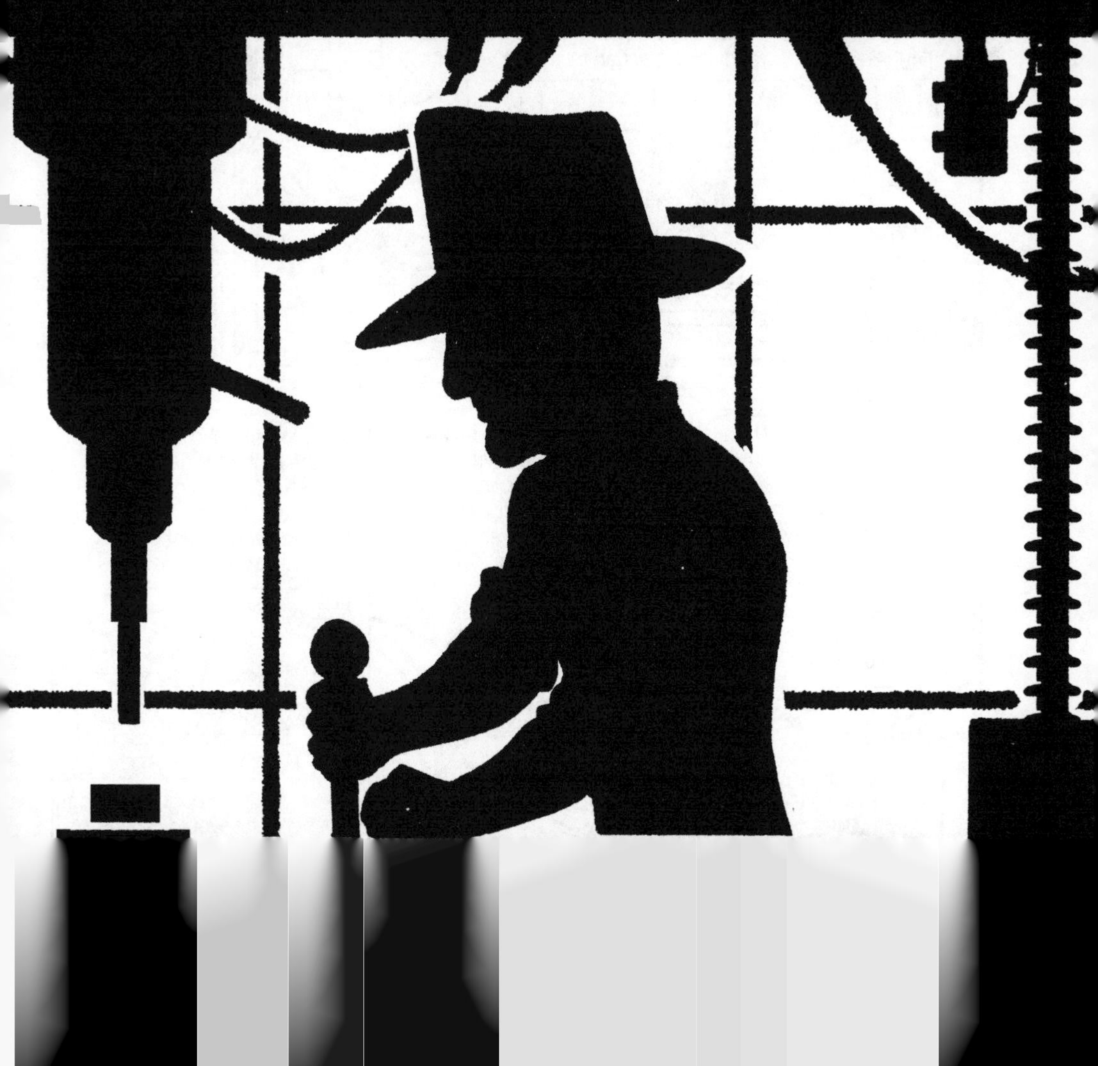

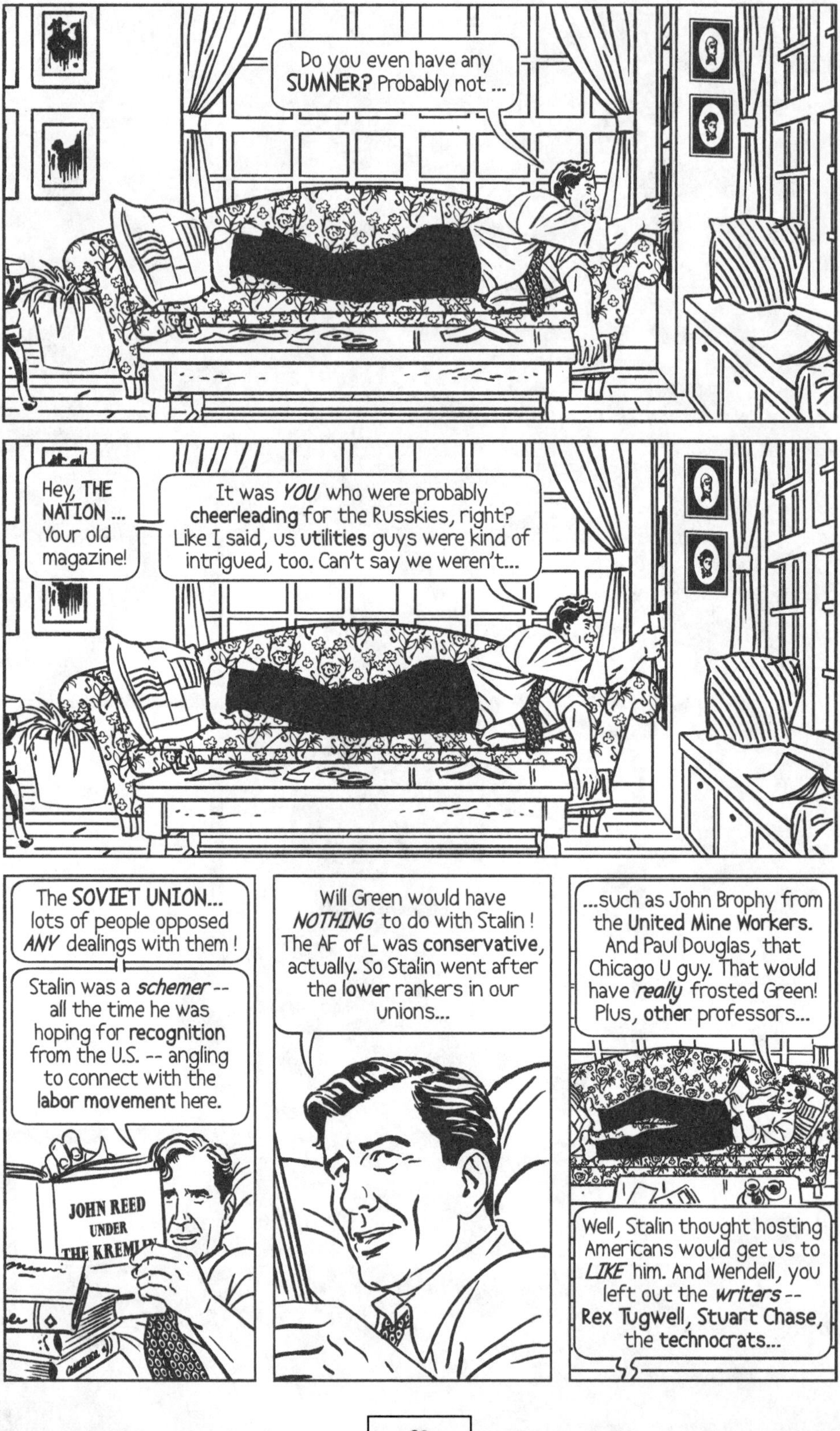

Do you even have any **SUMNER?** Probably not ...

Hey, **THE NATION** ... Your old magazine!

It was *YOU* who were probably **cheerleading** for the Russkies, right? Like I said, us **utilities** guys were kind of intrigued, too. Can't say we weren't...

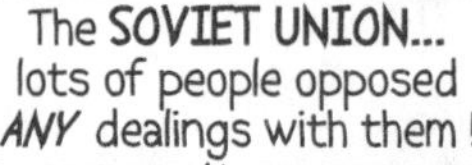

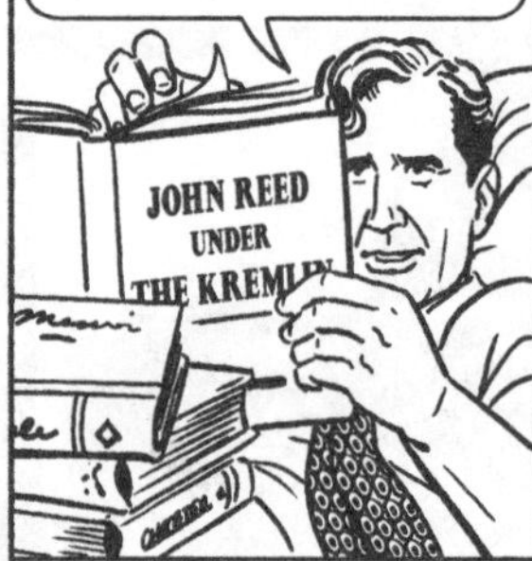

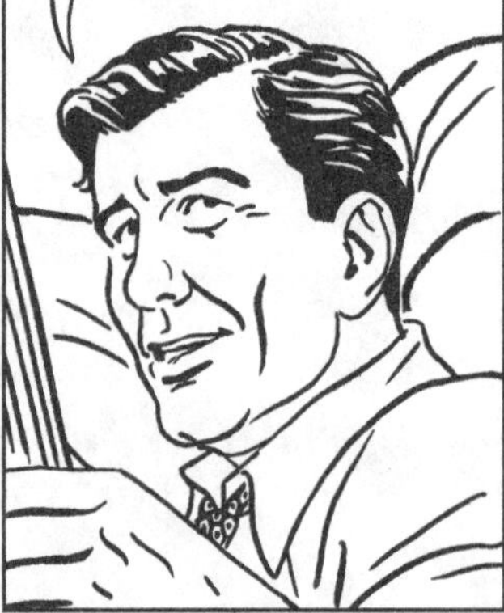

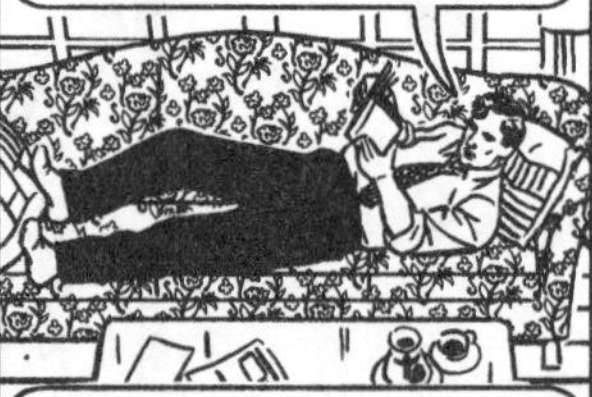

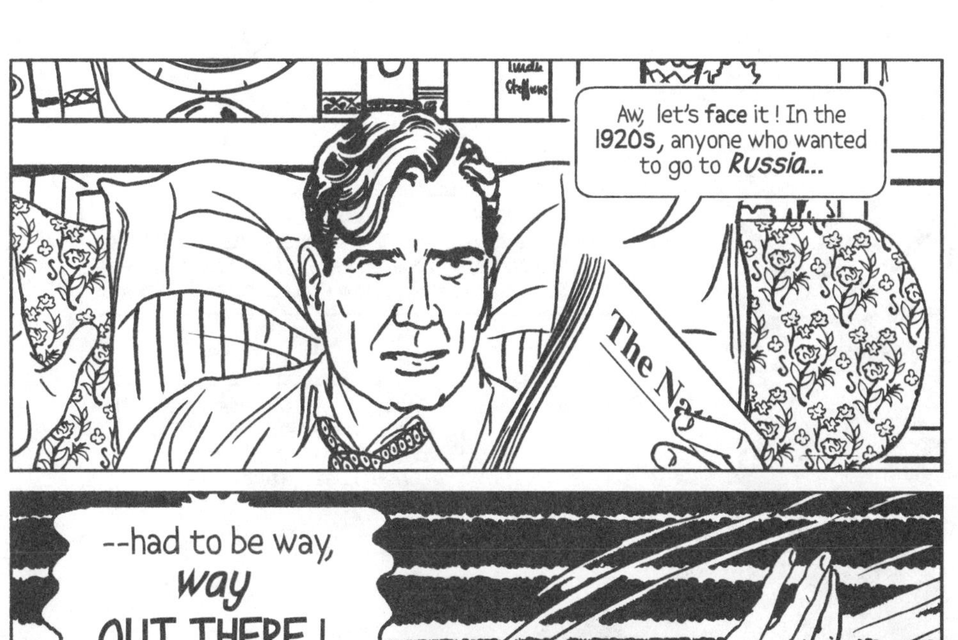
Aw, let's face it! In the 1920s, anyone who wanted to go to *Russia...*
The Na

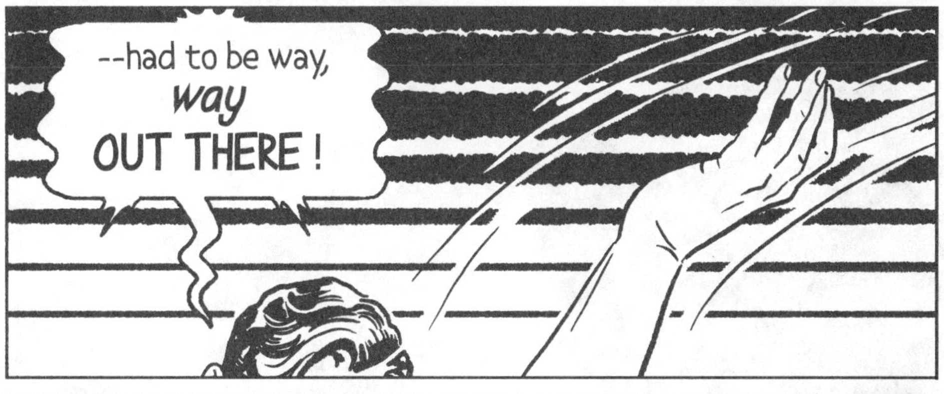
--had to be way, *way* OUT THERE!

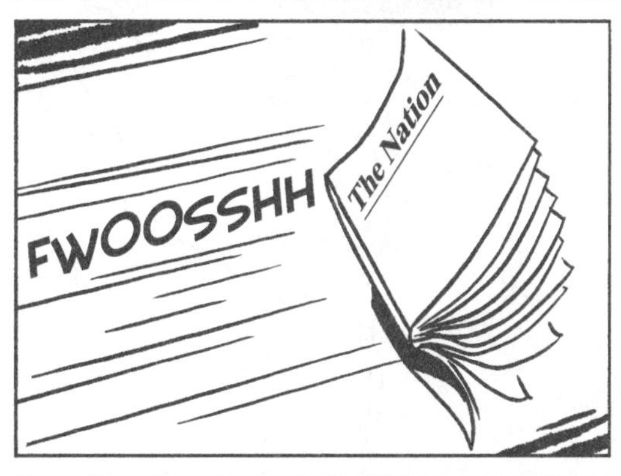
FWOOSSHH
The Nation

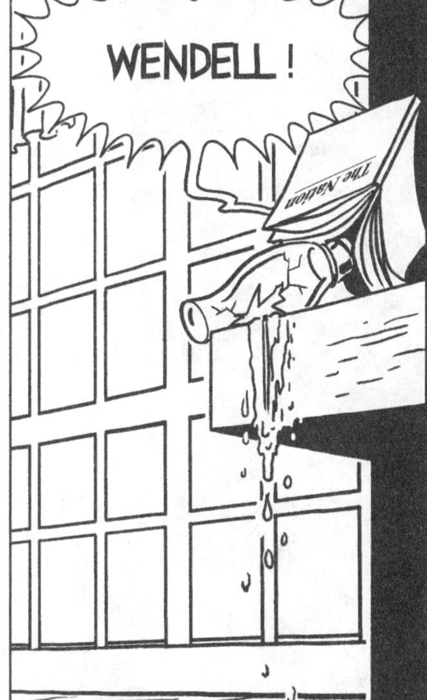
WENDELL!
The Nation

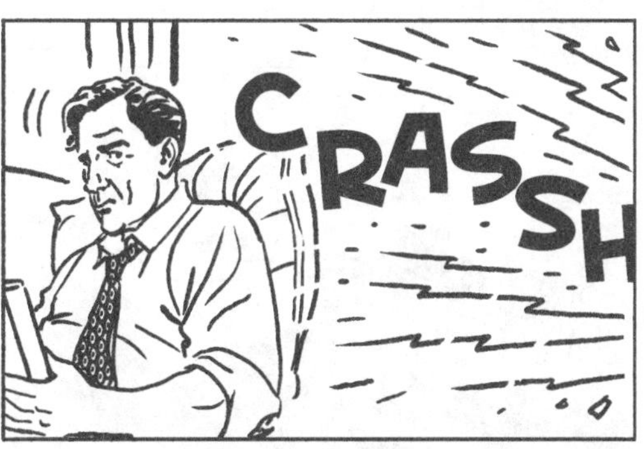
CRASSH

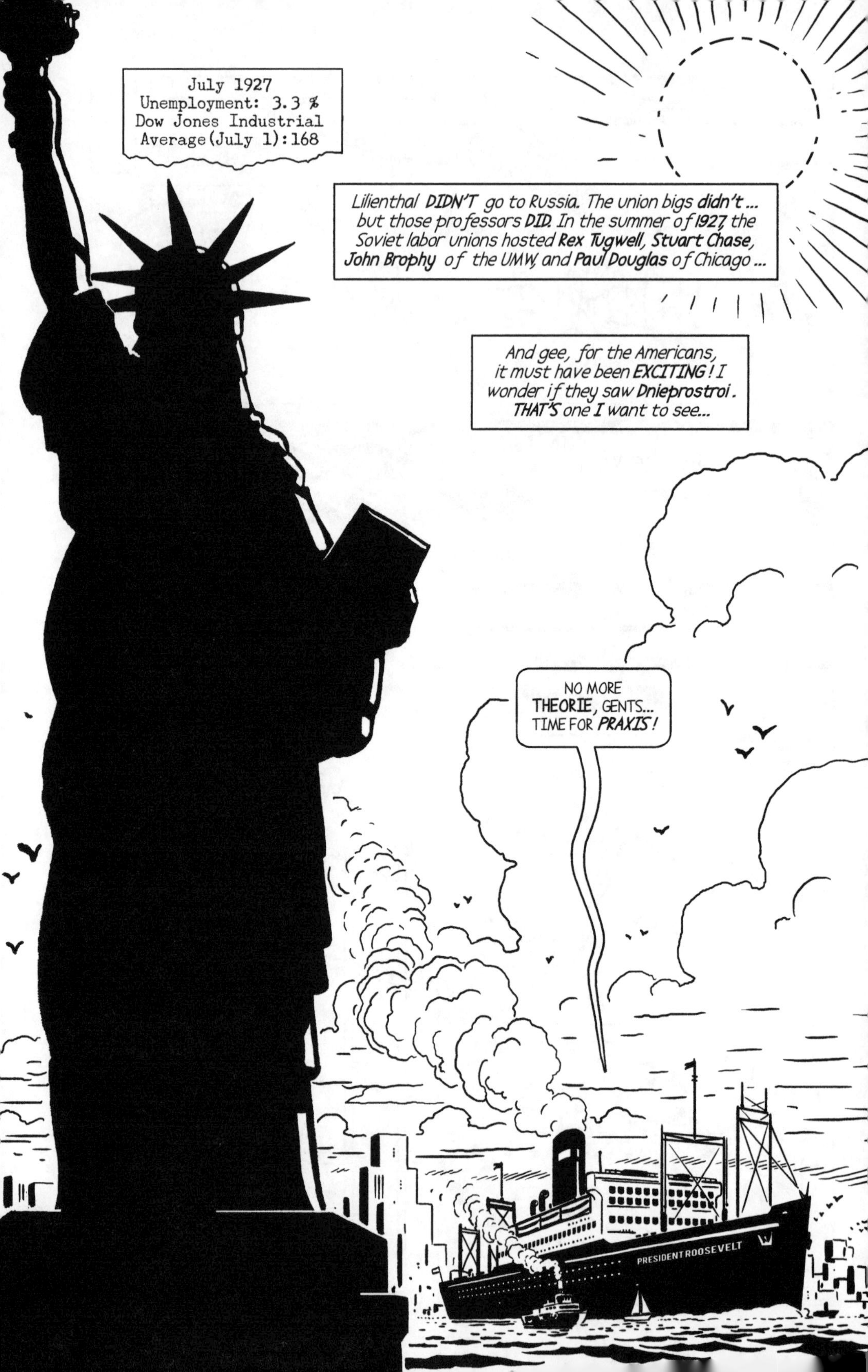
July 1927
Unemployment: 3.3 %
Dow Jones Industrial
Average (July 1): 168
Lilienthal DIDN'T go to Russia. The union bigs didn't ... but those professors DID. In the summer of 1927, the Soviet labor unions hosted Rex Tugwell, Stuart Chase, John Brophy of the UMW, and Paul Douglas of Chicago ...
And gee, for the Americans, it must have been EXCITING! I wonder if they saw Dnieprostroi. THAT'S one I want to see...
NO MORE THEORIE, GENTS... TIME FOR PRAXIS!
PRESIDENT ROOSEVELT

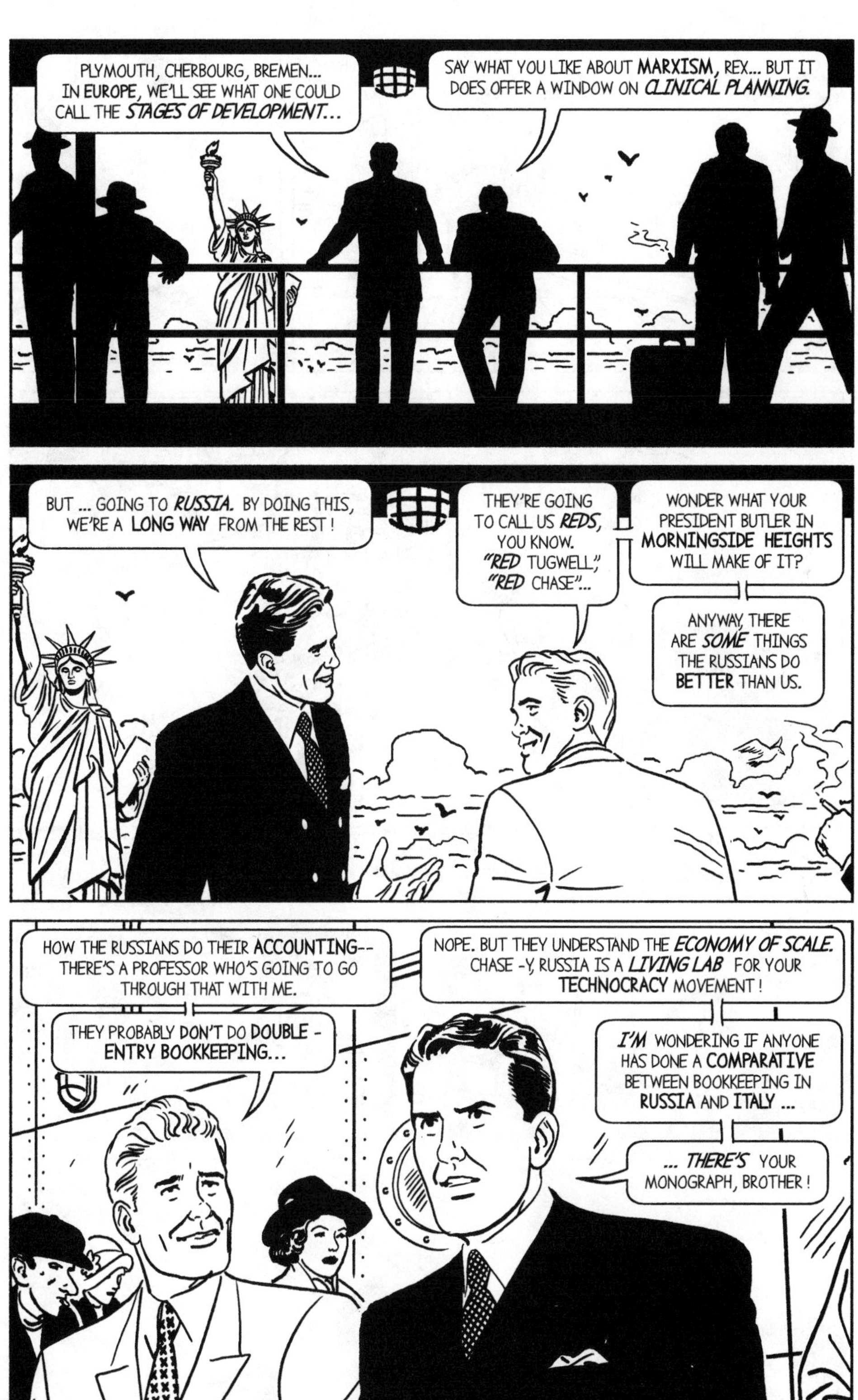
PLYMOUTH, CHERBOURG, BREMEN... IN EUROPE, WE'LL SEE WHAT ONE COULD CALL THE STAGES OF DEVELOPMENT...
SAY WHAT YOU LIKE ABOUT MARXISM, REX... BUT IT DOES OFFER A WINDOW ON CLINICAL PLANNING.
BUT ... GOING TO RUSSIA. BY DOING THIS, WE'RE A LONG WAY FROM THE REST!
THEY'RE GOING TO CALL US REDS, YOU KNOW. "RED TUGWELL," "RED CHASE"...
WONDER WHAT YOUR PRESIDENT BUTLER IN MORNINGSIDE HEIGHTS WILL MAKE OF IT?
ANYWAY, THERE ARE SOME THINGS THE RUSSIANS DO BETTER THAN US.
HOW THE RUSSIANS DO THEIR ACCOUNTING-- THERE'S A PROFESSOR WHO'S GOING TO GO THROUGH THAT WITH ME.
THEY PROBABLY DON'T DO DOUBLE - ENTRY BOOKKEEPING...
NOPE. BUT THEY UNDERSTAND THE ECONOMY OF SCALE. CHASE -Y, RUSSIA IS A LIVING LAB FOR YOUR TECHNOCRACY MOVEMENT!
I'M WONDERING IF ANYONE HAS DONE A COMPARATIVE BETWEEN BOOKKEEPING IN RUSSIA AND ITALY ...
... THERE'S YOUR MONOGRAPH, BROTHER!

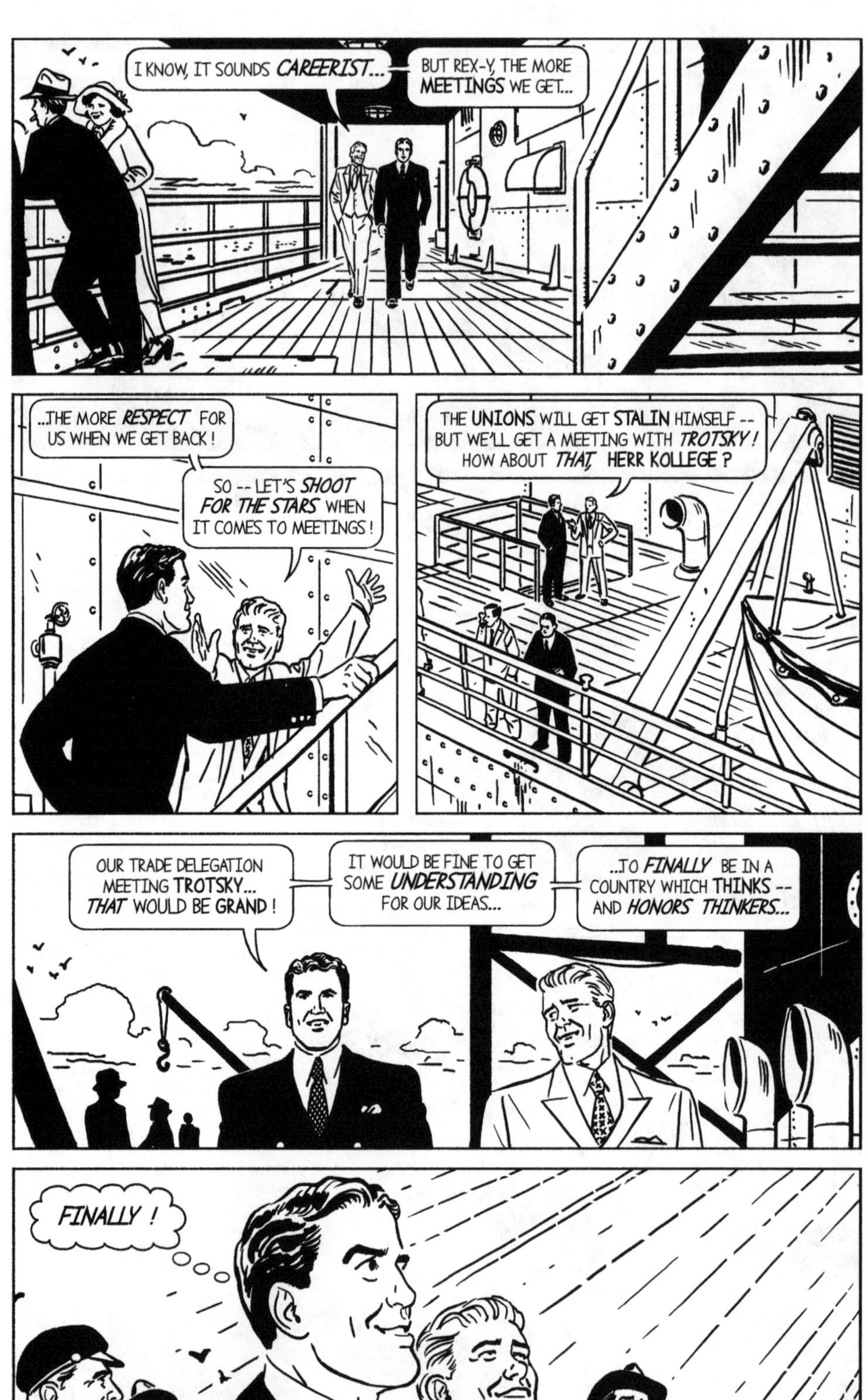
I KNOW, IT SOUNDS CAREERIST...
BUT REX-Y, THE MORE MEETINGS WE GET...
...THE MORE RESPECT FOR US WHEN WE GET BACK!
SO -- LET'S SHOOT FOR THE STARS WHEN IT COMES TO MEETINGS!
THE UNIONS WILL GET STALIN HIMSELF -- BUT WE'LL GET A MEETING WITH TROTSKY! HOW ABOUT THAT, HERR KOLLEGE?
OUR TRADE DELEGATION MEETING TROTSKY... THAT WOULD BE GRAND!
IT WOULD BE FINE TO GET SOME UNDERSTANDING FOR OUR IDEAS...
...TO FINALLY BE IN A COUNTRY WHICH THINKS -- AND HONORS THINKERS...
FINALLY!

The Russians made the trip **easy** for the Americans, labelling everything for them, prettying things up. It was another **Potemkin Village ...**

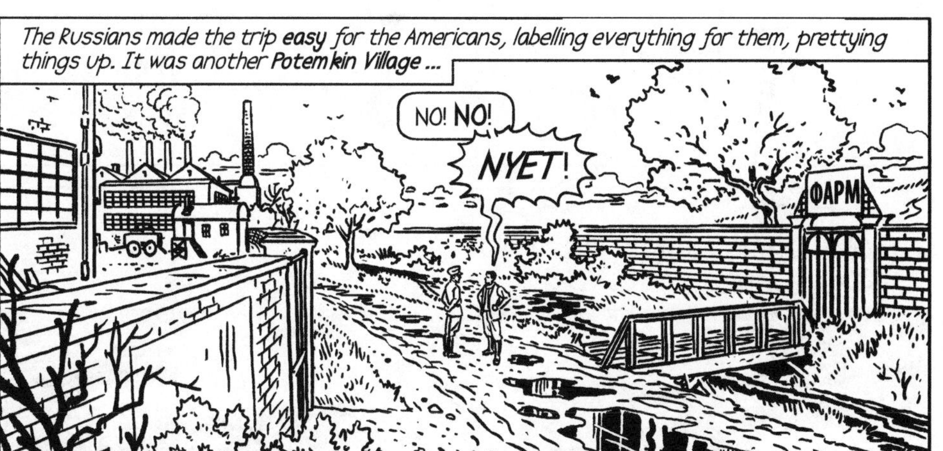

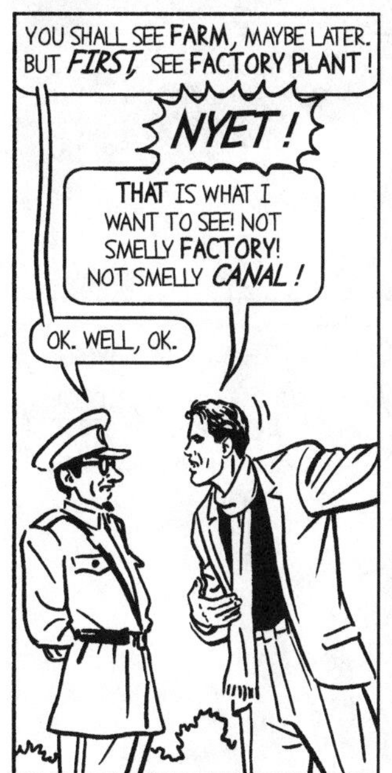

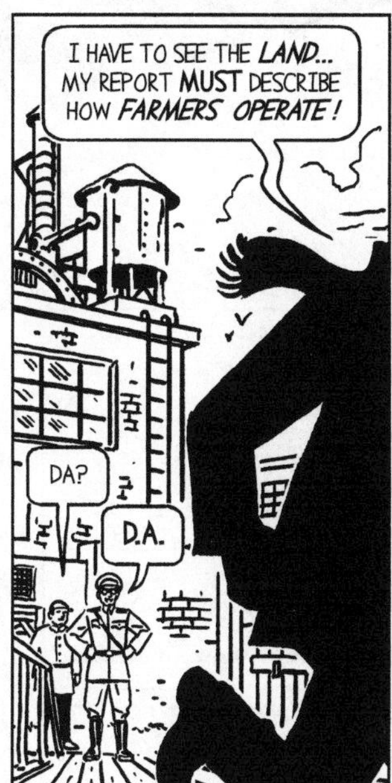

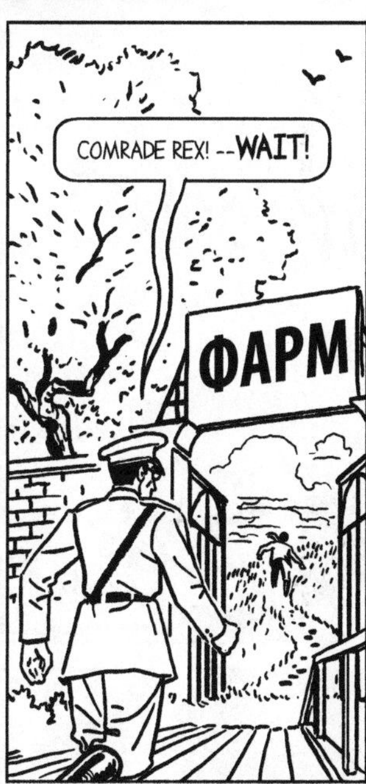

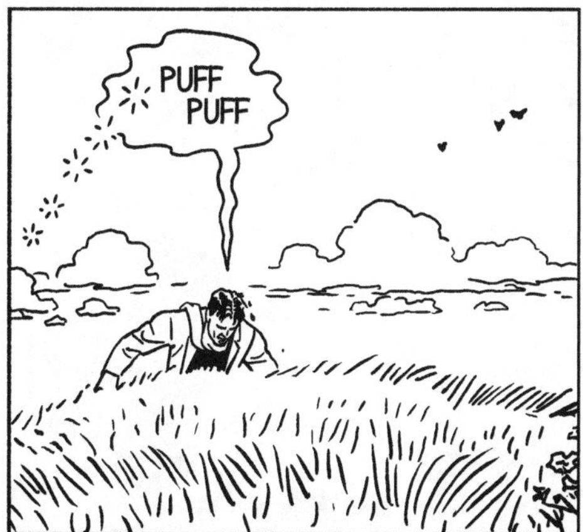

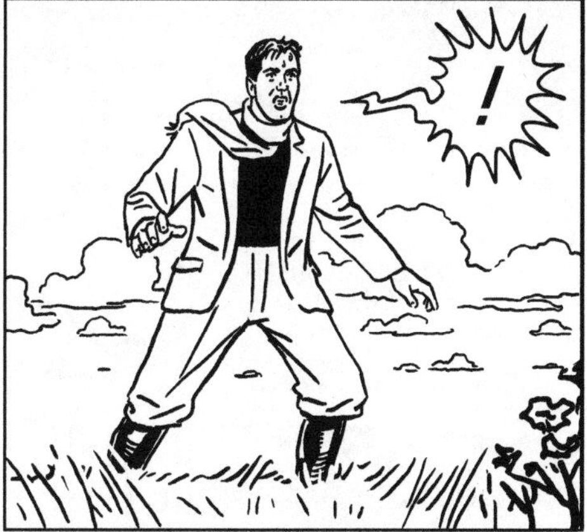

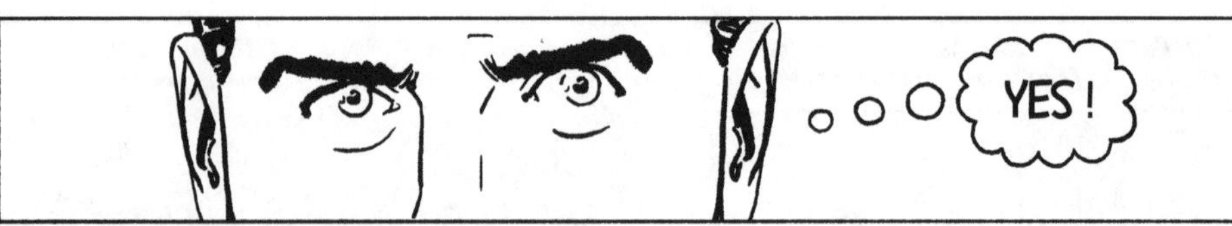
YES!

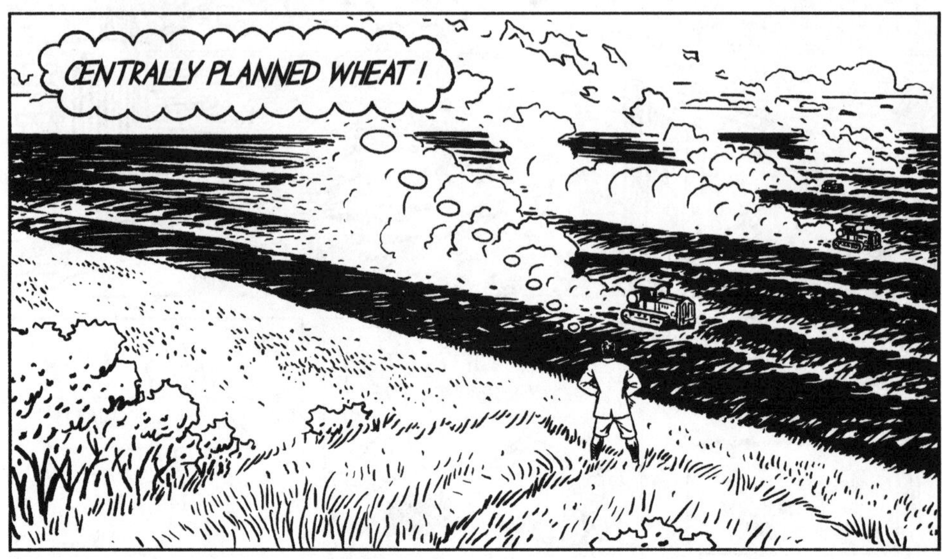
CENTRALLY PLANNED WHEAT!

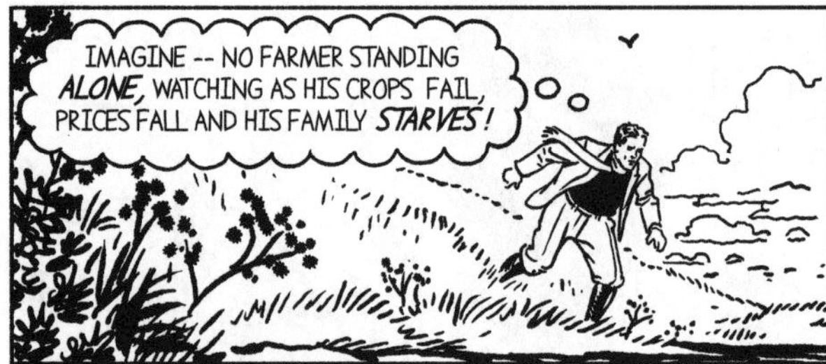
IMAGINE -- NO FARMER STANDING ALONE, WATCHING AS HIS CROPS FAIL, PRICES FALL AND HIS FAMILY STARVES!

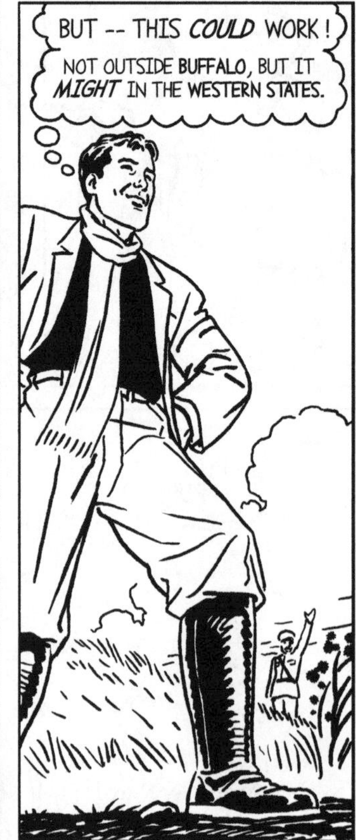
BUT -- THIS COULD WORK!
NOT OUTSIDE BUFFALO, BUT IT MIGHT IN THE WESTERN STATES.

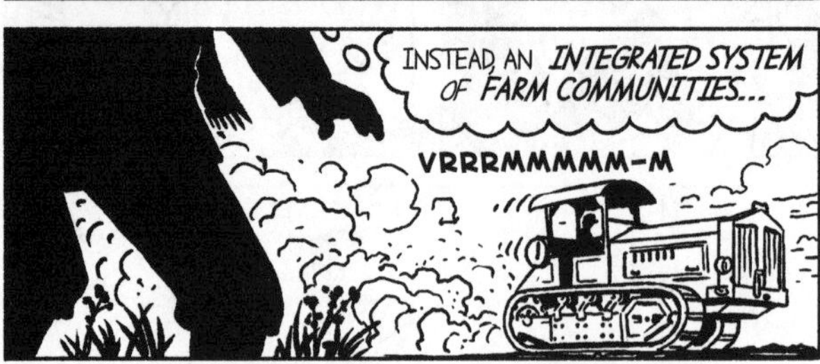
INSTEAD, AN INTEGRATED SYSTEM OF FARM COMMUNITIES...
VRRRMMMMM-M

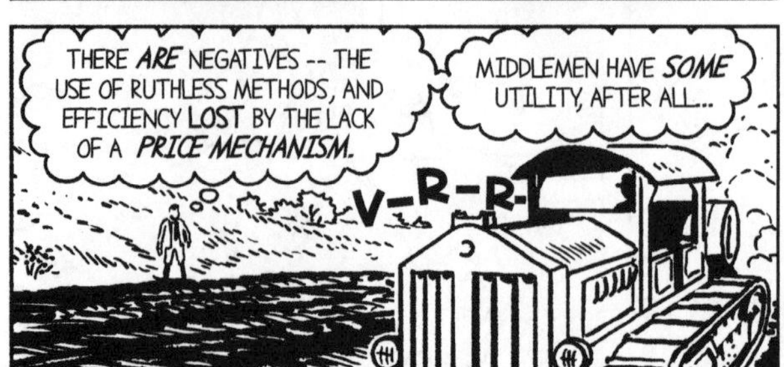
THERE ARE NEGATIVES -- THE USE OF RUTHLESS METHODS, AND EFFICIENCY LOST BY THE LACK OF A PRICE MECHANISM.
MIDDLEMEN HAVE SOME UTILITY, AFTER ALL...
V-R-R-

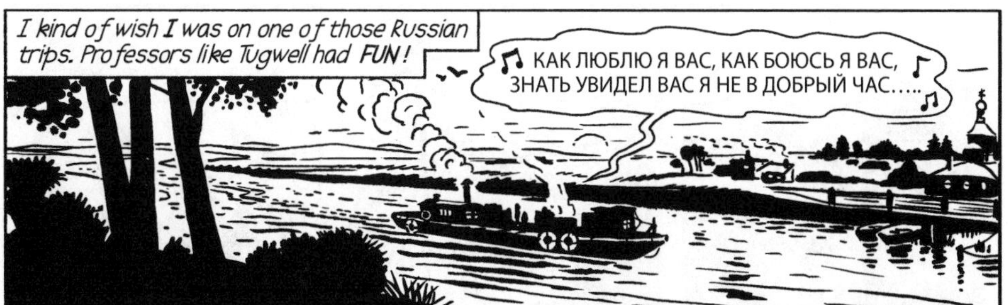
I kind of wish I was on one of those Russian trips. Professors like Tugwell had FUN!
КАК ЛЮБЛЮ Я ВАС, КАК БОЮСЬ Я ВАС, ЗНАТЬ УВИДЕЛ ВАС Я НЕ В ДОБРЫЙ ЧАС.....

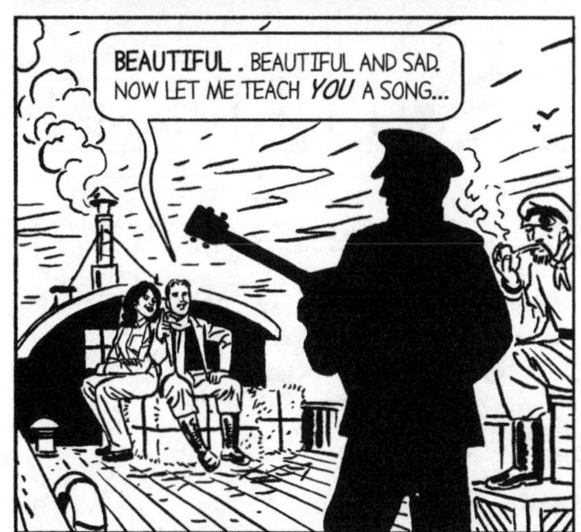
BEAUTIFUL. BEAUTIFUL AND SAD. NOW LET ME TEACH YOU A SONG...

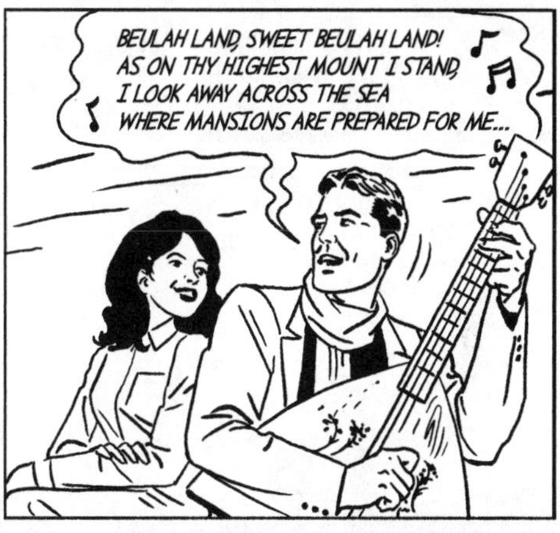
BEULAH LAND, SWEET BEULAH LAND! AS ON THY HIGHEST MOUNT I STAND, I LOOK AWAY ACROSS THE SEA WHERE MANSIONS ARE PREPARED FOR ME...

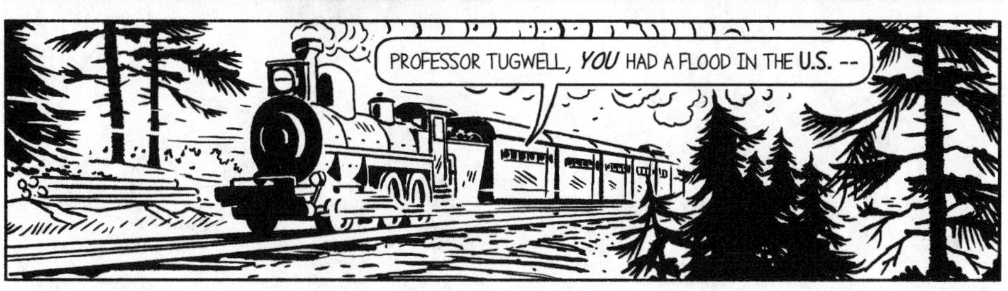
PROFESSOR TUGWELL, YOU HAD A FLOOD IN THE U.S. --

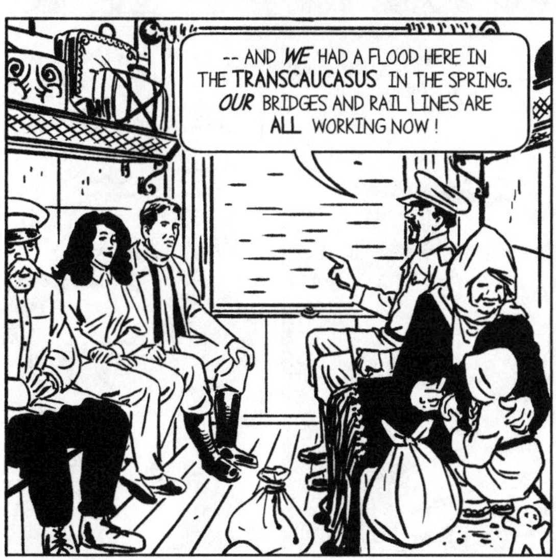
-- AND WE HAD A FLOOD HERE IN THE TRANSCAUCASUS IN THE SPRING. OUR BRIDGES AND RAIL LINES ARE ALL WORKING NOW!

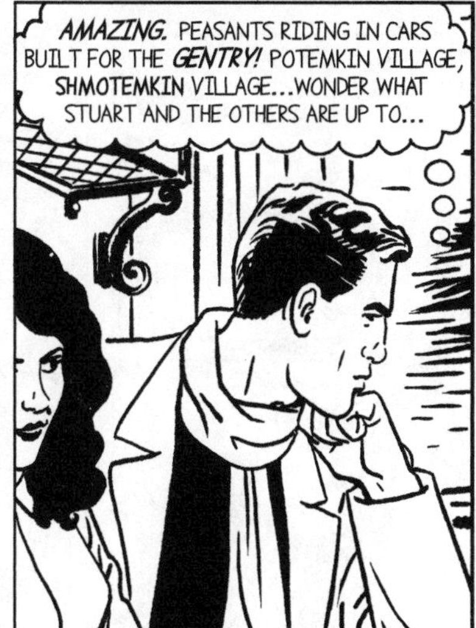
AMAZING. PEASANTS RIDING IN CARS BUILT FOR THE GENTRY! POTEMKIN VILLAGE, SHMOTEMKIN VILLAGE...WONDER WHAT STUART AND THE OTHERS ARE UP TO...

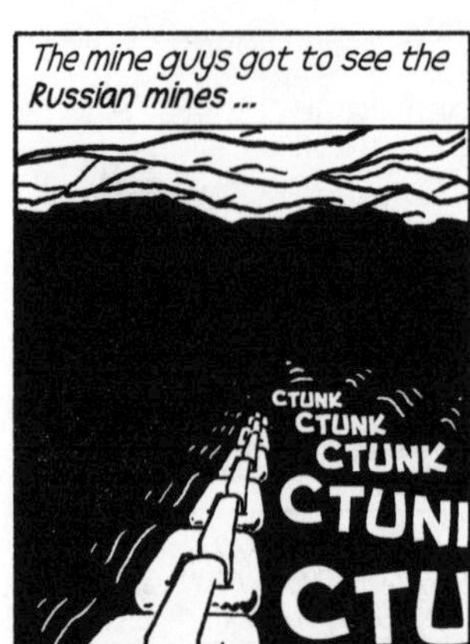
The mine guys got to see the **Russian mines ...**
CTUNK
CTUNK
CTUNK
CTUNI
CTU

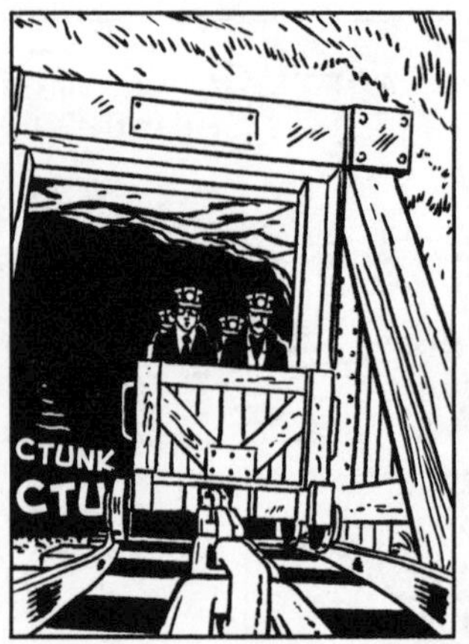
CTUNK
CTU

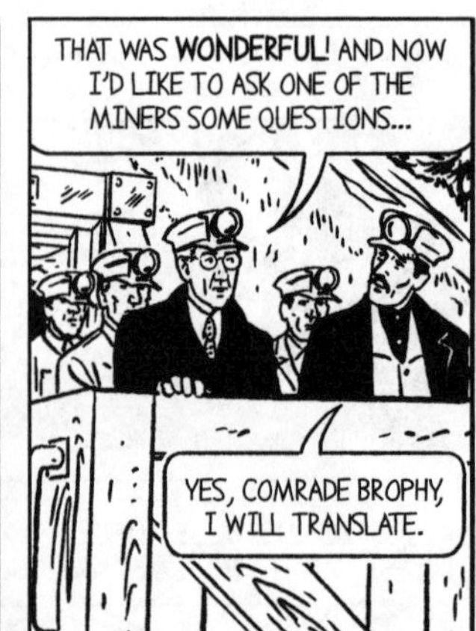
THAT WAS **WONDERFUL**! AND NOW I'D LIKE TO ASK ONE OF THE MINERS SOME QUESTIONS...
YES, COMRADE BROPHY, I WILL TRANSLATE.

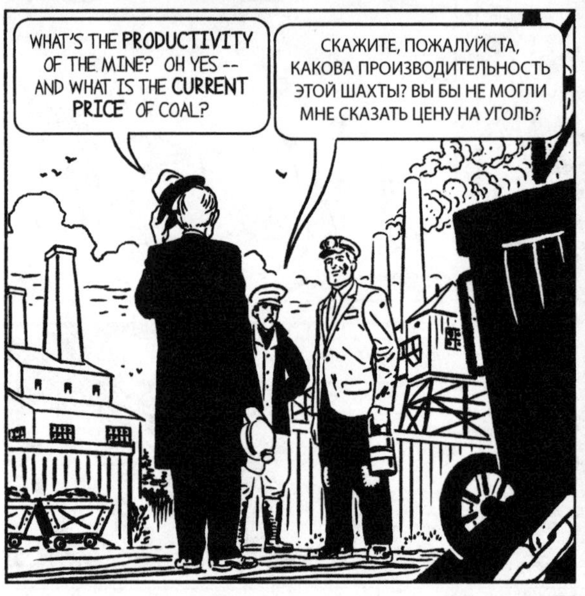
WHAT'S THE **PRODUCTIVITY** OF THE MINE? OH YES -- AND WHAT IS THE **CURRENT PRICE** OF COAL?
СКАЖИТЕ, ПОЖАЛУЙСТА, КАКОВА ПРОИЗВОДИТЕЛЬНОСТЬ ЭТОЙ ШАХТЫ? ВЫ БЫ НЕ МОГЛИ МНЕ СКАЗАТЬ ЦЕНУ НА УГОЛЬ?

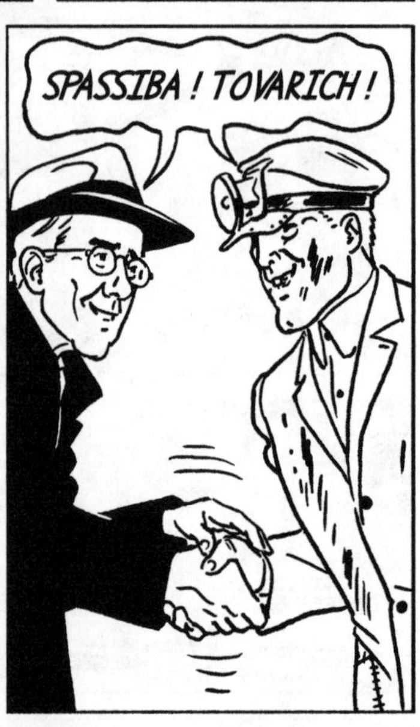
SPASSIBA ! TOVARICH !

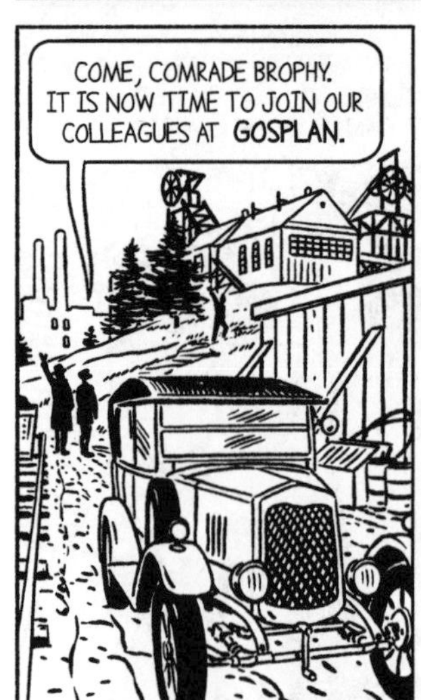
COME, COMRADE BROPHY. IT IS NOW TIME TO JOIN OUR COLLEAGUES AT **GOSPLAN.**

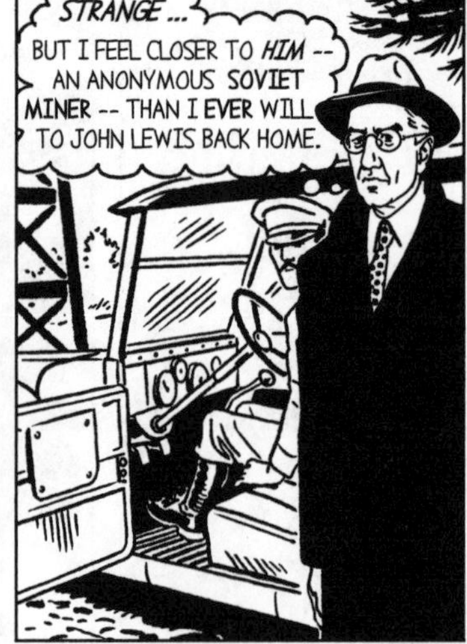
STRANGE ...
BUT I FEEL CLOSER TO *HIM* -- AN ANONYMOUS **SOVIET MINER** -- THAN I **EVER** WILL TO JOHN LEWIS BACK HOME.

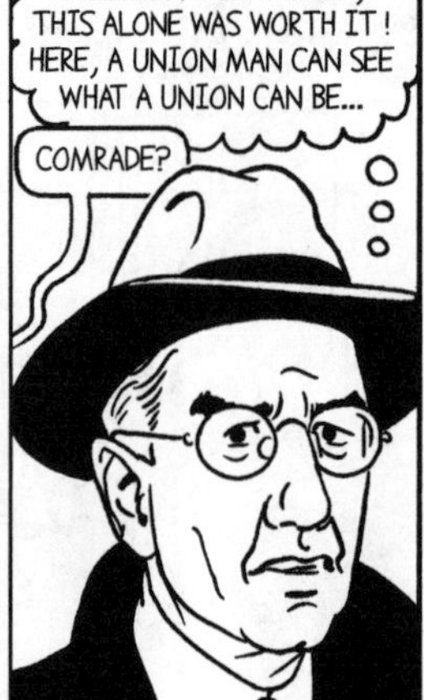
NO MATTER HOW **LEWIS** OR **HILLMAN** SHUT ME OUT, THIS ALONE WAS WORTH IT ! HERE, A UNION MAN CAN SEE WHAT A UNION CAN BE...
COMRADE?

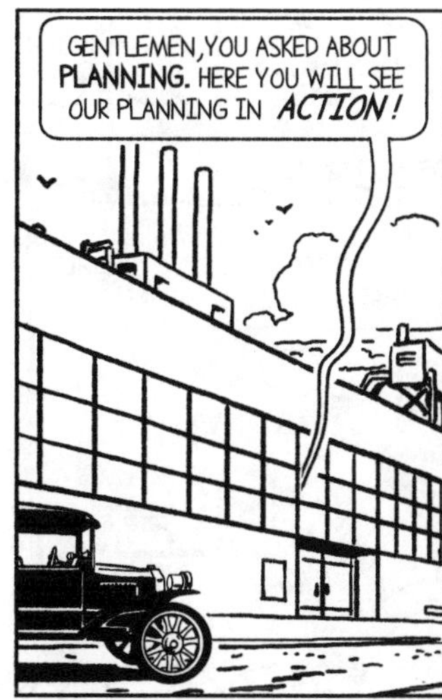
GENTLEMEN, YOU ASKED ABOUT PLANNING. HERE YOU WILL SEE OUR PLANNING IN ACTION!

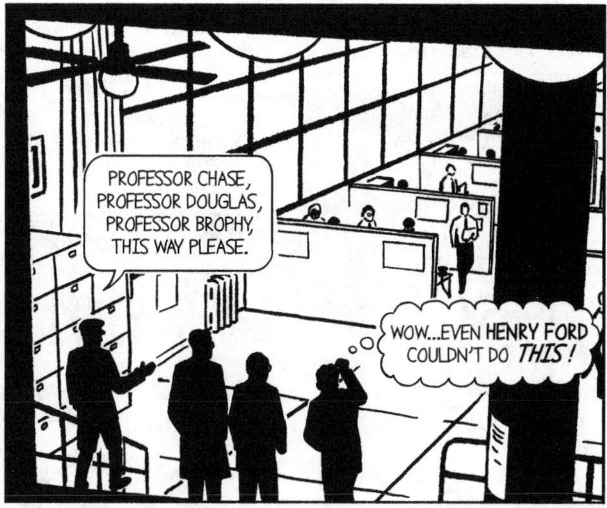
PROFESSOR CHASE, PROFESSOR DOUGLAS, PROFESSOR BROPHY, THIS WAY PLEASE.
WOW...EVEN HENRY FORD COULDN'T DO THIS!

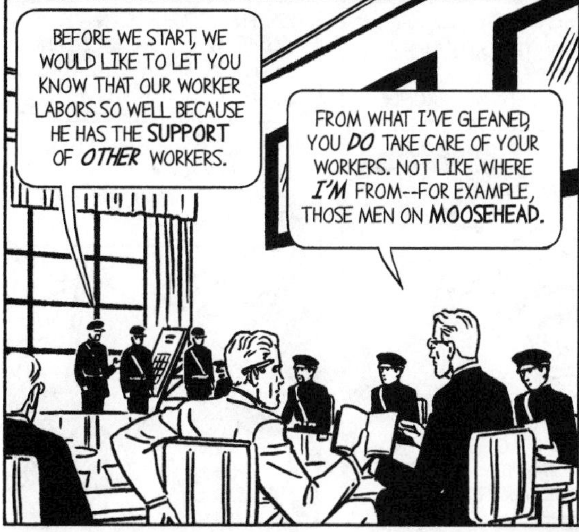
BEFORE WE START, WE WOULD LIKE TO LET YOU KNOW THAT OUR WORKER LABORS SO WELL BECAUSE HE HAS THE SUPPORT OF OTHER WORKERS.
FROM WHAT I'VE GLEANED, YOU DO TAKE CARE OF YOUR WORKERS. NOT LIKE WHERE I'M FROM--FOR EXAMPLE, THOSE MEN ON MOOSEHEAD.

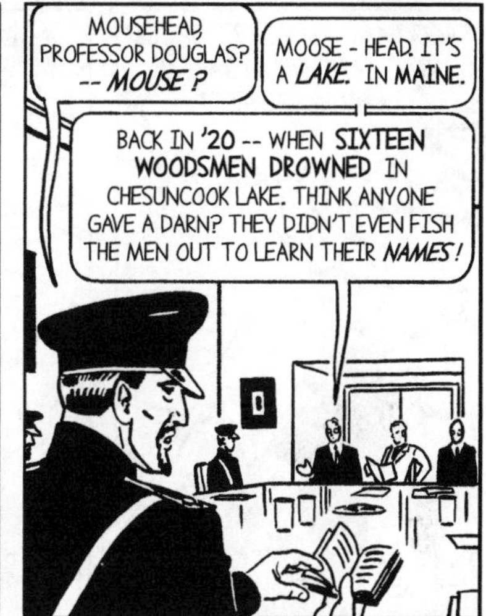
MOUSEHEAD, PROFESSOR DOUGLAS? -- MOUSE?
MOOSE - HEAD. IT'S A LAKE. IN MAINE.
BACK IN '20 -- WHEN SIXTEEN WOODSMEN DROWNED IN CHESUNCOOK LAKE. THINK ANYONE GAVE A DARN? THEY DIDN'T EVEN FISH THE MEN OUT TO LEARN THEIR NAMES!

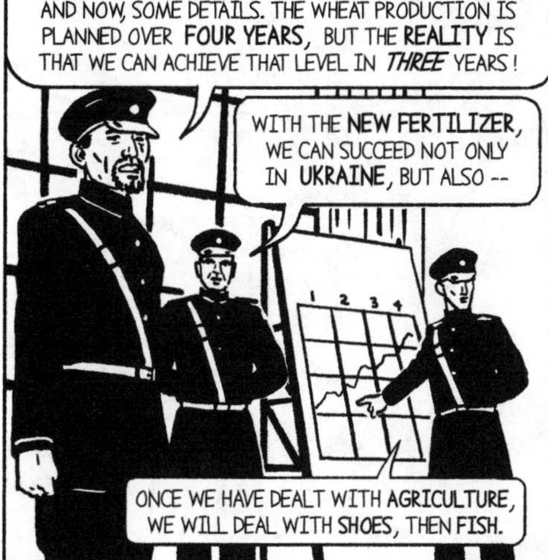
AND NOW, SOME DETAILS. THE WHEAT PRODUCTION IS PLANNED OVER FOUR YEARS, BUT THE REALITY IS THAT WE CAN ACHIEVE THAT LEVEL IN THREE YEARS!
WITH THE NEW FERTILIZER, WE CAN SUCCEED NOT ONLY IN UKRAINE, BUT ALSO --
1 2 3 4
ONCE WE HAVE DEALT WITH AGRICULTURE, WE WILL DEAL WITH SHOES, THEN FISH.

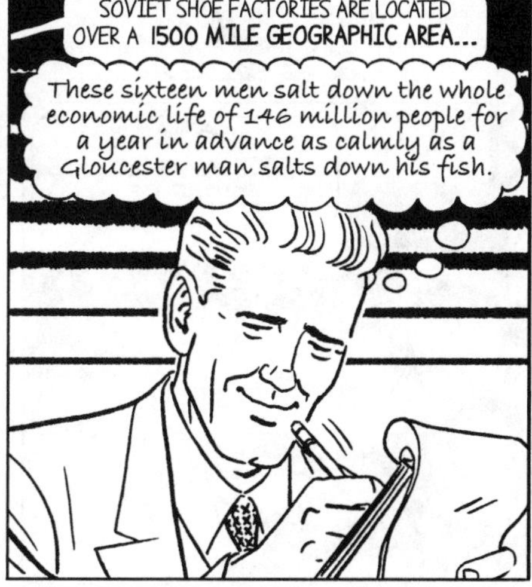
SOVIET SHOE FACTORIES ARE LOCATED OVER A 1500 MILE GEOGRAPHIC AREA...
These sixteen men salt down the whole economic life of 146 million people for a year in advance as calmly as a Gloucester man salts down his fish.

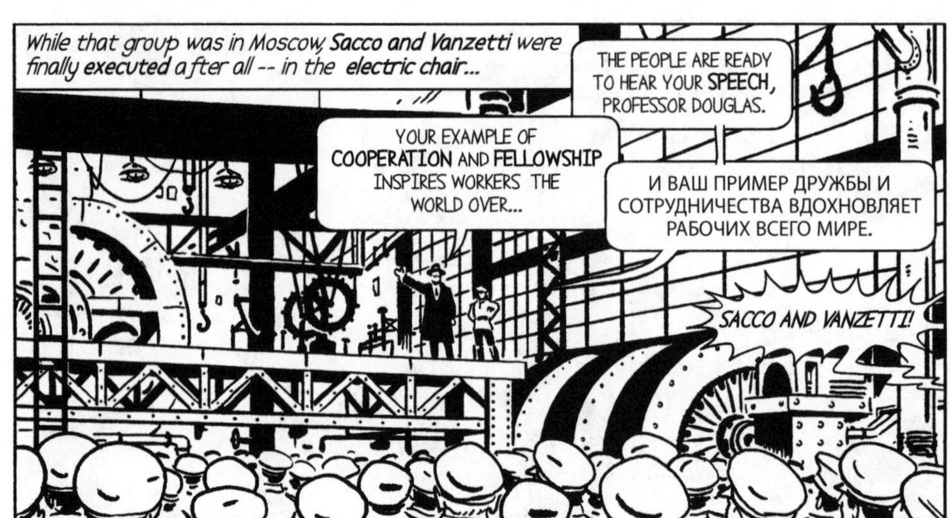

While that group was in Moscow, Sacco and Vanzetti were finally executed after all -- in the electric chair...
THE PEOPLE ARE READY TO HEAR YOUR SPEECH, PROFESSOR DOUGLAS.
YOUR EXAMPLE OF COOPERATION AND FELLOWSHIP INSPIRES WORKERS THE WORLD OVER...
И ВАШ ПРИМЕР ДРУЖБЫ И СОТРУДНИЧЕСТВА ВДОХНОВЛЯЕТ РАБОЧИХ ВСЕГО МИРЕ.
SACCO AND VANZETTI!

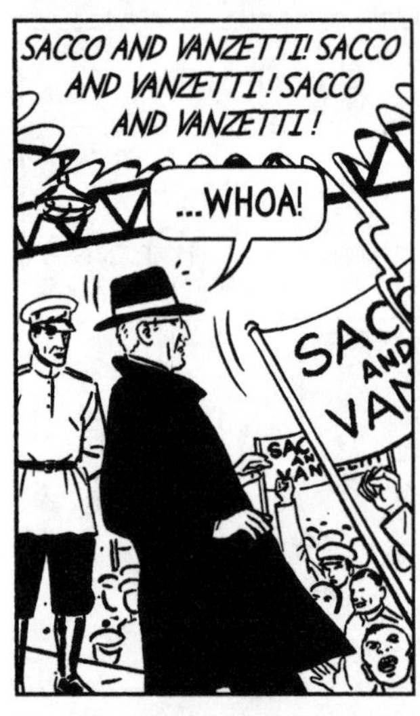

SACCO AND VANZETTI! SACCO AND VANZETTI! SACCO AND VANZETTI!
...WHOA!

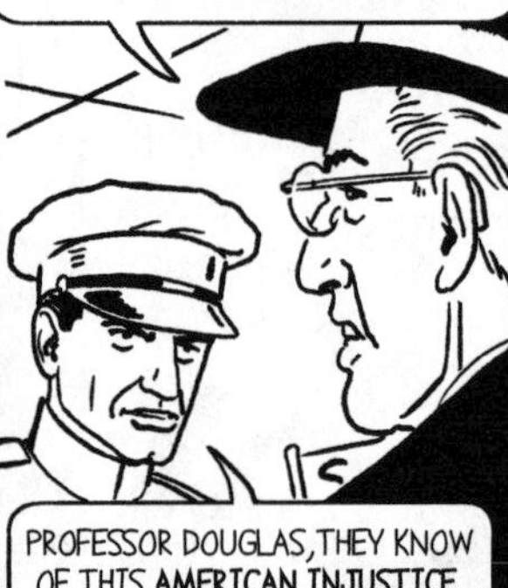

IS THIS FOR MY BENEFIT? BUT WE ARE ON THE SAME SIDE ON THIS, THEY AND I! WE BOTH BELIEVE THE PAIR WAS WRONGED.
PROFESSOR DOUGLAS, THEY KNOW OF THIS AMERICAN INJUSTICE. WE ARE TAUGHT OF THIS.

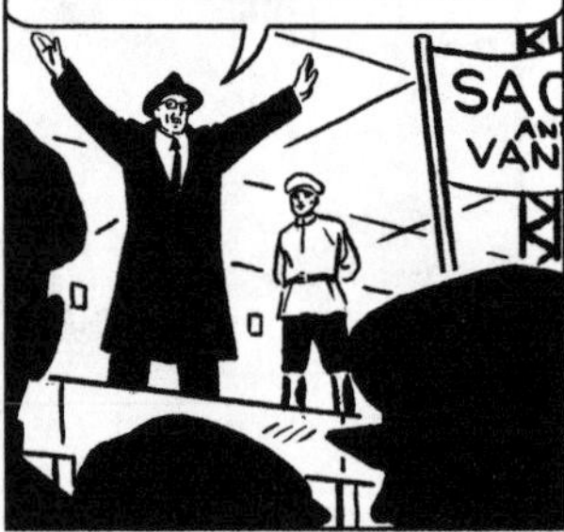

LISTEN...LISTEN... IT'S NOT AS CLEAR AS ALL THAT. SACCO AND VANZETTI ENJOYED THE FULL DEFENSE OF THE LAW!
WHY, PROFESSOR FRANKFURTER FROM HARVARD ACTUALLY WROTE AN ARTICLE ABOUT THIS -- IN THE ATLANTIC MAGAZINE...

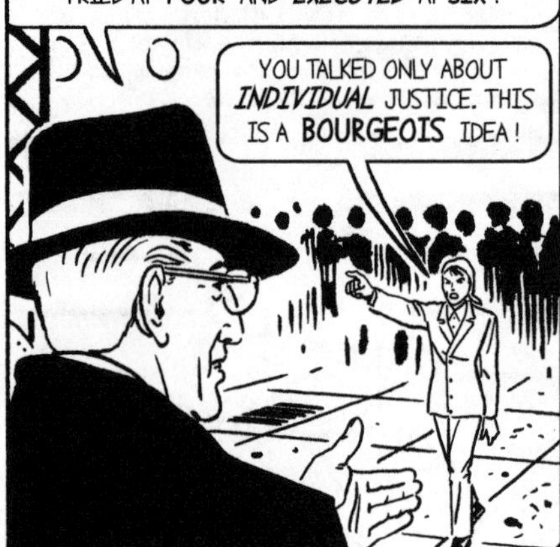

WHAT ABOUT YOURSELVES? TWO MONTHS AGO A GROUP OF BANK CLERKS WERE ARRESTED AT TWO, TRIED AT FOUR AND EXECUTED AT SIX!
YOU TALKED ONLY ABOUT INDIVIDUAL JUSTICE. THIS IS A BOURGEOIS IDEA!

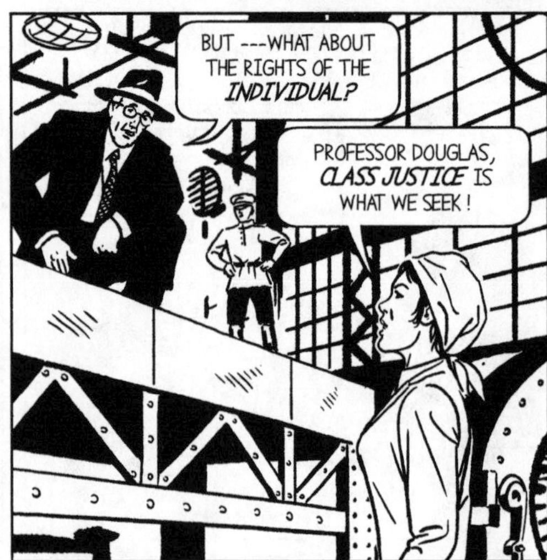

BUT ---WHAT ABOUT THE RIGHTS OF THE INDIVIDUAL?
PROFESSOR DOUGLAS, CLASS JUSTICE IS WHAT WE SEEK!

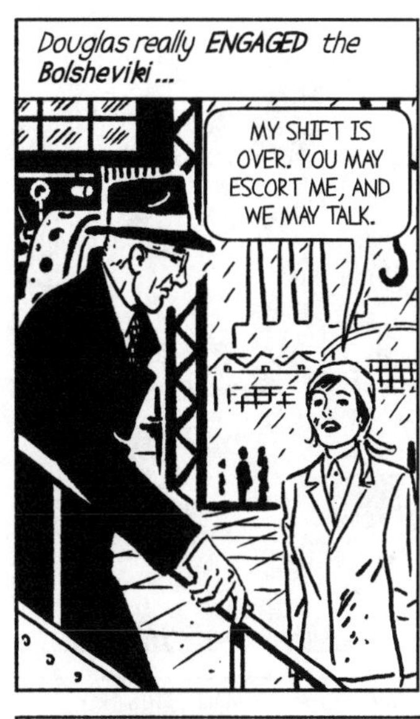
Douglas really ENGAGED the Bolsheviki...
MY SHIFT IS OVER. YOU MAY ESCORT ME, AND WE MAY TALK.

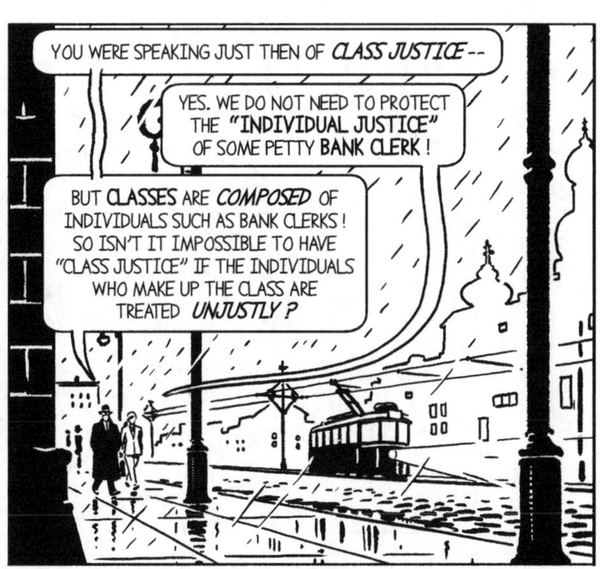
YOU WERE SPEAKING JUST THEN OF CLASS JUSTICE--
YES. WE DO NOT NEED TO PROTECT THE "INDIVIDUAL JUSTICE" OF SOME PETTY BANK CLERK!
BUT CLASSES ARE COMPOSED OF INDIVIDUALS SUCH AS BANK CLERKS! SO ISN'T IT IMPOSSIBLE TO HAVE "CLASS JUSTICE" IF THE INDIVIDUALS WHO MAKE UP THE CLASS ARE TREATED UNJUSTLY?

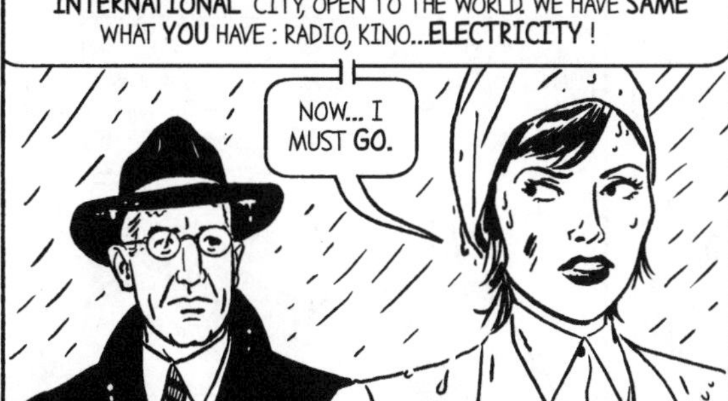
WE DO NOT NEED SUCH THING. YOU CAN SEE THAT MOSCOW IS AN INTERNATIONAL CITY, OPEN TO THE WORLD. WE HAVE SAME WHAT YOU HAVE: RADIO, KINO...ELECTRICITY!
NOW... I MUST GO.

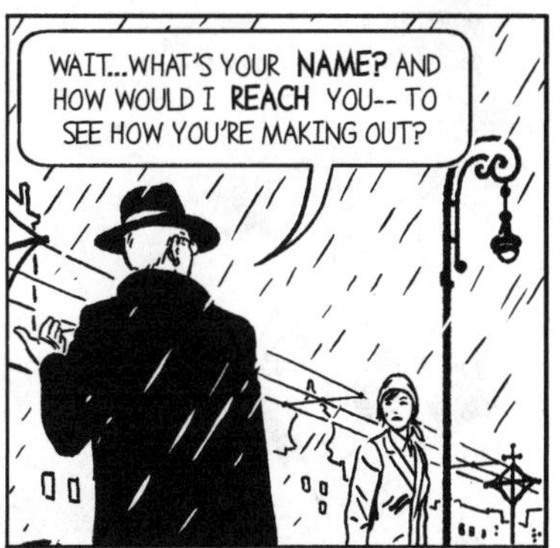
WAIT...WHAT'S YOUR NAME? AND HOW WOULD I REACH YOU-- TO SEE HOW YOU'RE MAKING OUT?

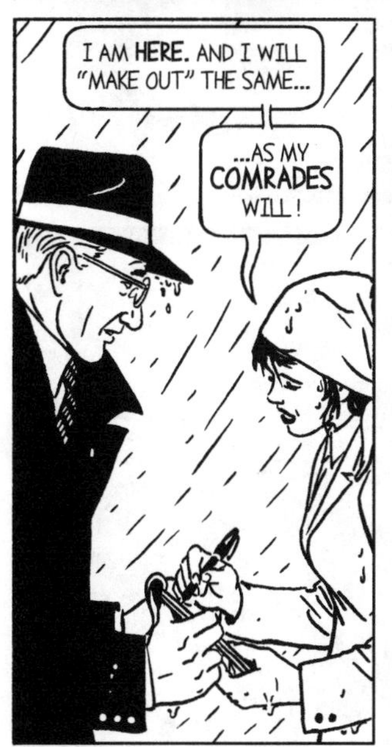
I AM HERE. AND I WILL "MAKE OUT" THE SAME...
...AS MY COMRADES WILL!

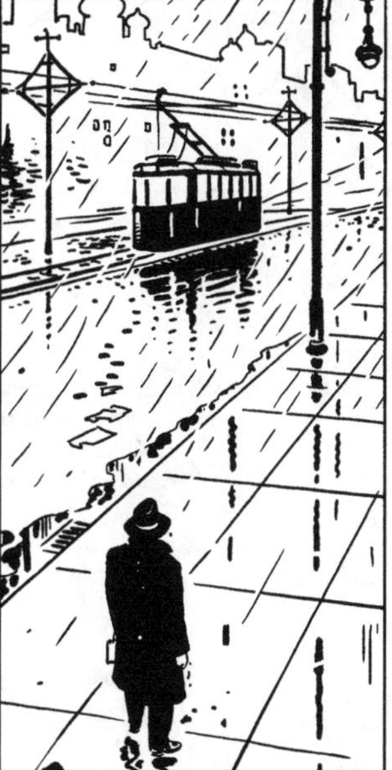

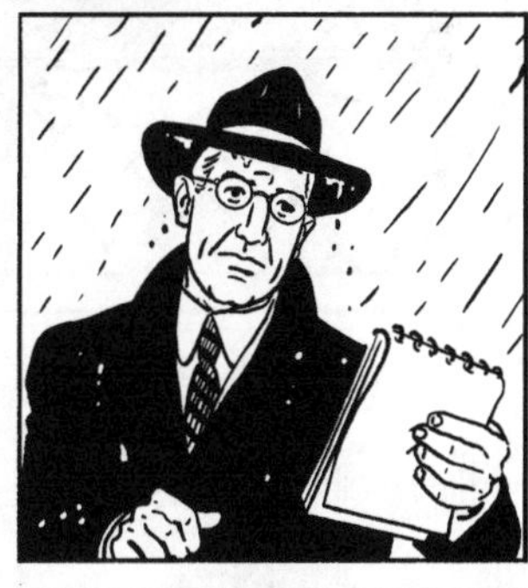

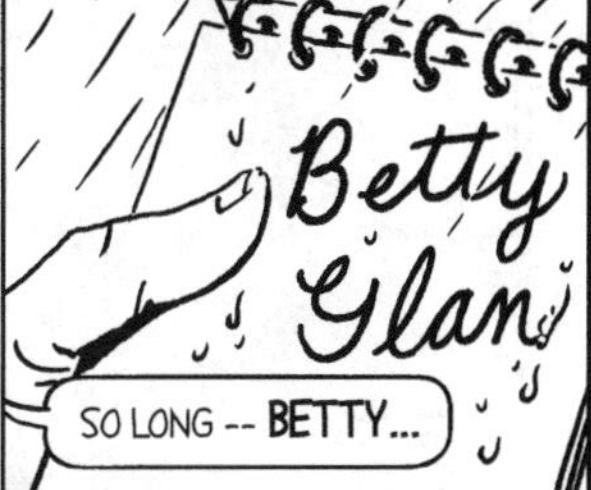
Betty Glan
SO LONG -- BETTY...

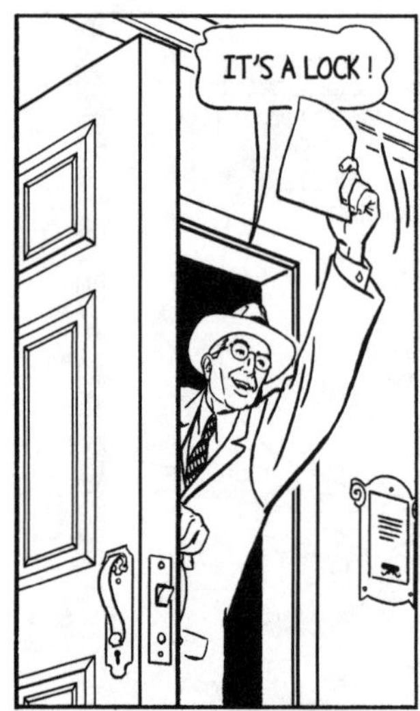
IT'S A LOCK!

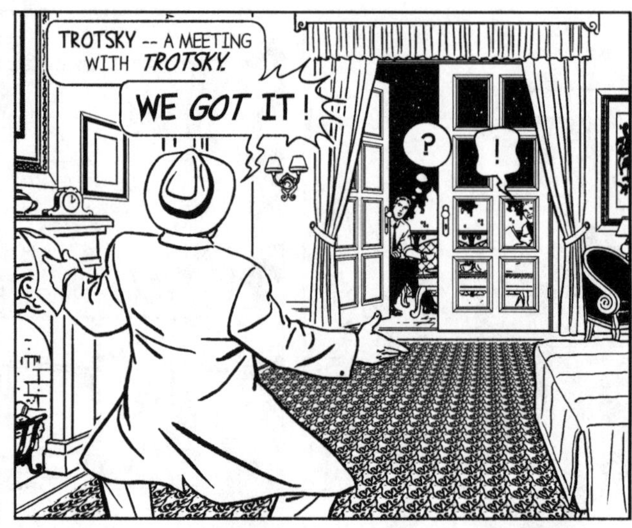
TROTSKY -- A MEETING WITH TROTSKY.
WE GOT IT!
?
!

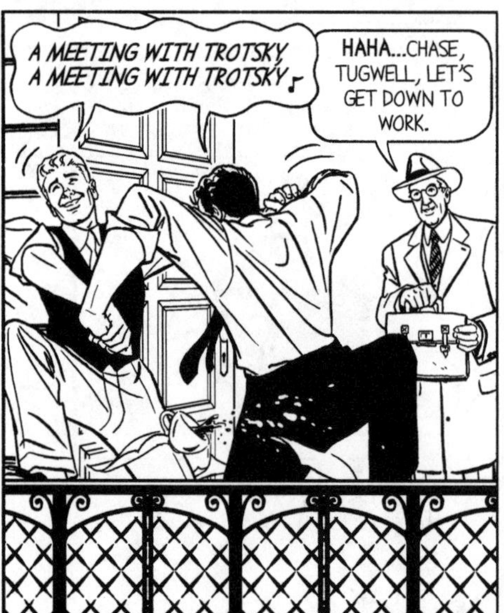
A MEETING WITH TROTSKY, A MEETING WITH TROTSKY
HAHA...CHASE, TUGWELL, LET'S GET DOWN TO WORK.

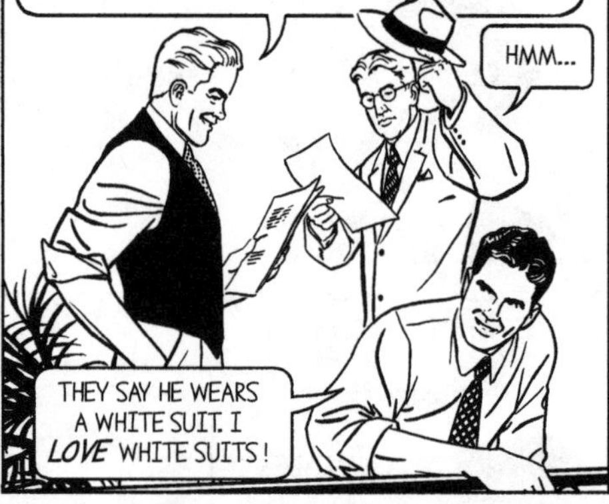
SURE, PAUL. TROTSKY ALONE MAKES THIS TRIP WORTHWHILE! OUR LIST OF QUESTIONS: ELECTRIC POWER, WORKPLACE INJURY COMPENSATION...
THIS IS ONE MEETING WHERE WE MAY ACTUALLY GET TO TALK IN DETAIL ABOUT OUR OWN WORK! LET'S SEE WHAT HE SUGGESTS -- MAYBE WE CAN GET DOWN TO THE DETAIL LEVEL WITH HIM.
HMM...
THEY SAY HE WEARS A WHITE SUIT. I LOVE WHITE SUITS!

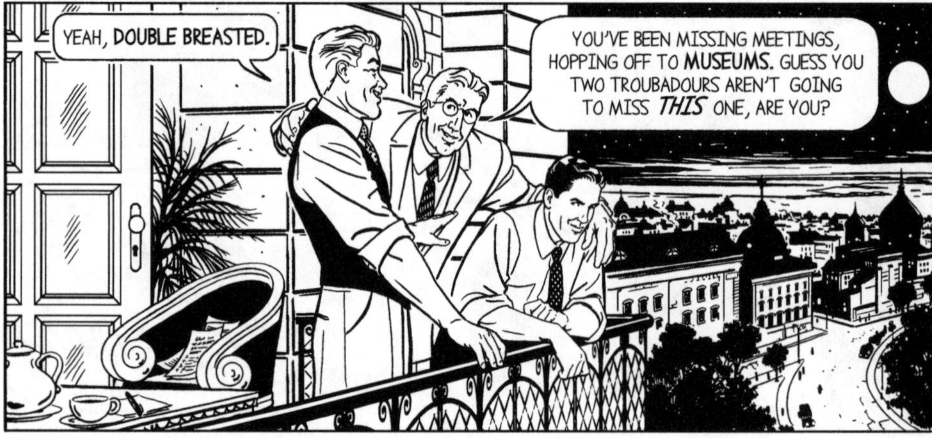
YEAH, DOUBLE BREASTED.
YOU'VE BEEN MISSING MEETINGS, HOPPING OFF TO MUSEUMS. GUESS YOU TWO TROUBADOURS AREN'T GOING TO MISS THIS ONE, ARE YOU?

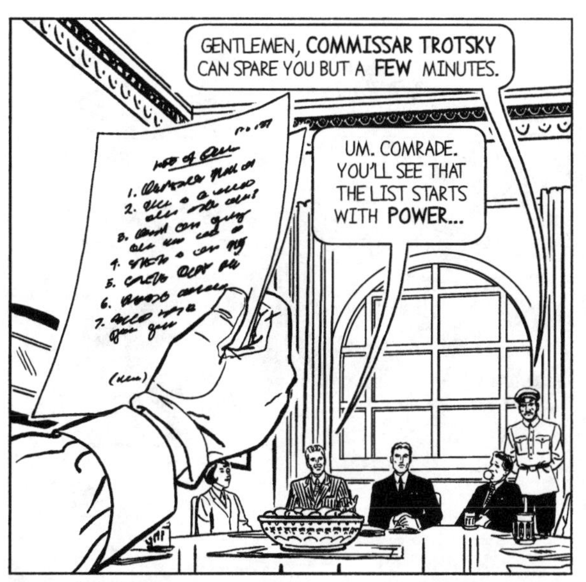

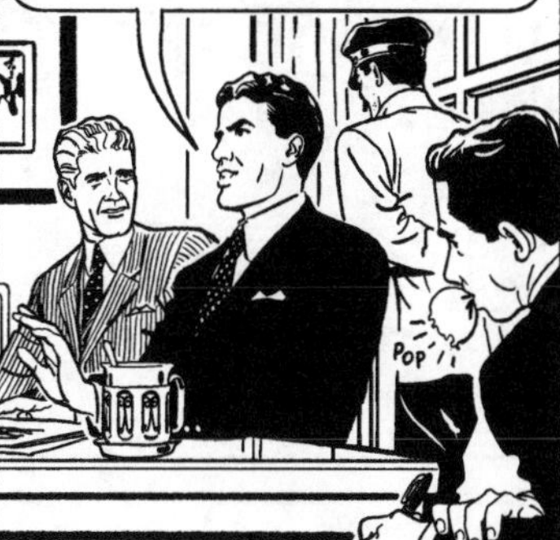

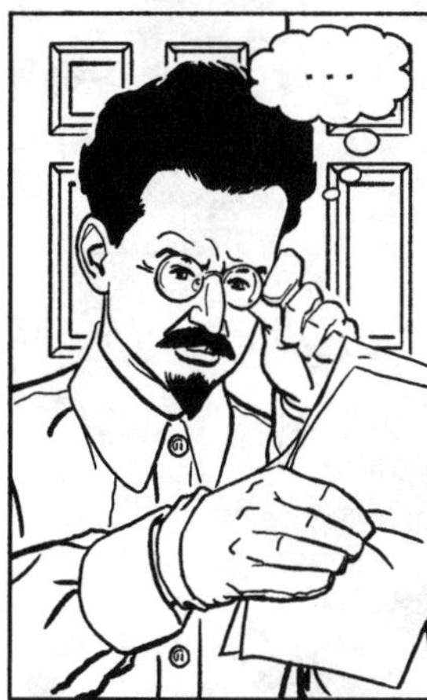

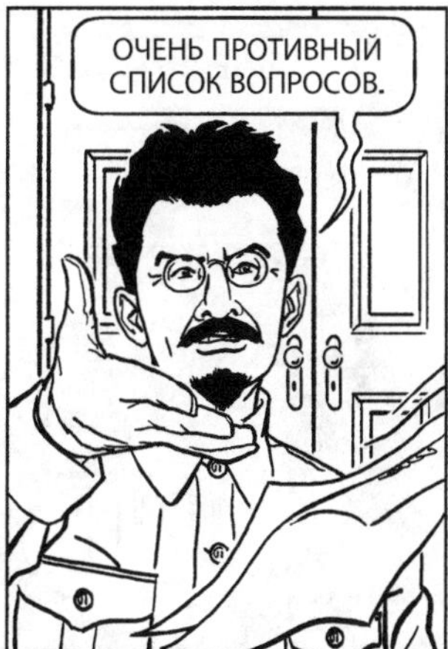

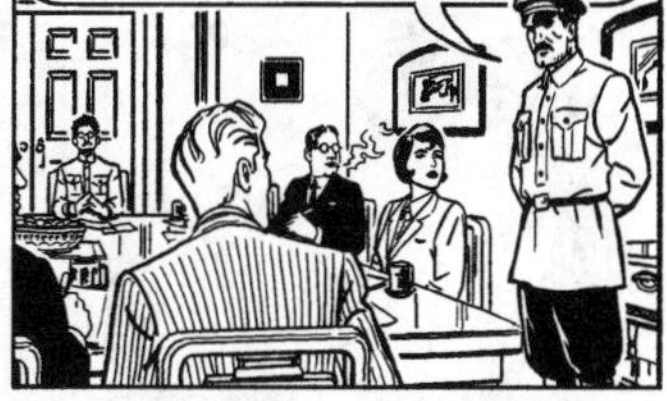

SIR, THE HOUR IS PASSING. THE AGRICULTURE SCHOLARS HERE, ESPECIALLY, HAVE WONDERED ABOUT YOUR VIEWS ON PRODUCTIVITY IN AGRICULTURE...

THE COMMISSAR PREFERS TO MOVE TO THE TOPIC OF YOUR PRESS FREEDOM. HE SAYS THAT IT IS NO FREEDOM TO PAY TWO CENTS FOR A NEWSPAPER PRODUCED BY BOURGEOIS JOURNALISTS!

WELL, WE THINK...

THANK YOU COMRADES, THE MEETING IS NOW CONCLUDED.

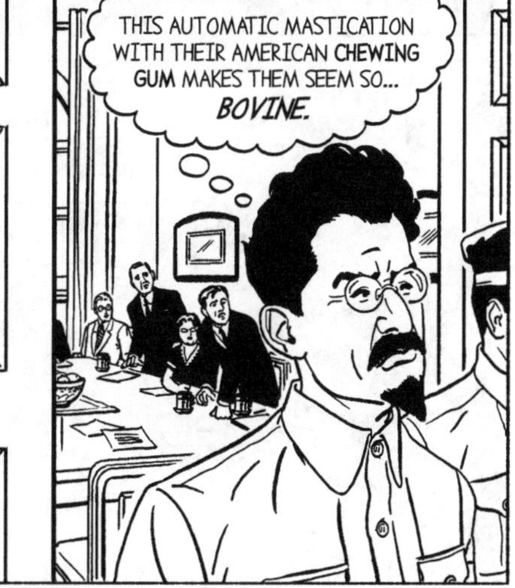

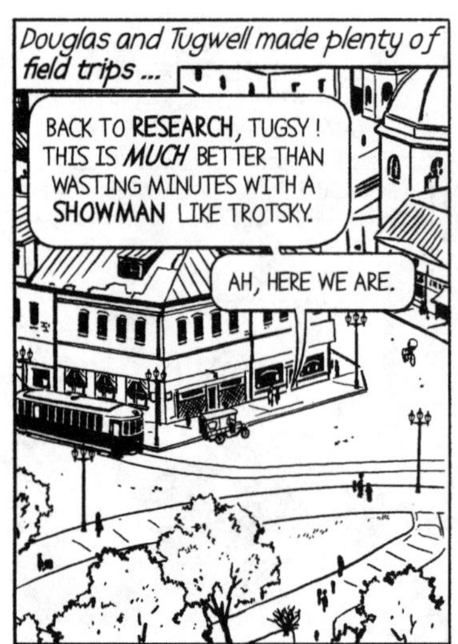
Douglas and Tugwell made plenty of field trips ...
BACK TO **RESEARCH**, TUGSY! THIS IS ***MUCH*** BETTER THAN WASTING MINUTES WITH A **SHOWMAN** LIKE TROTSKY.
AH, HERE WE ARE.

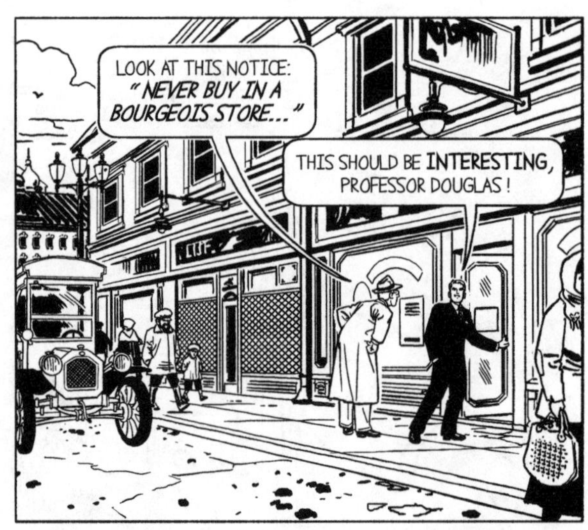
LOOK AT THIS NOTICE: ***"NEVER BUY IN A BOURGEOIS STORE..."***
THIS SHOULD BE **INTERESTING**, PROFESSOR DOUGLAS!

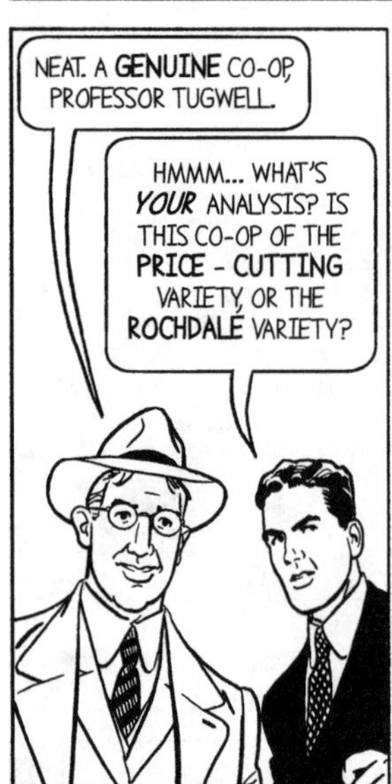
NEAT. A **GENUINE** CO-OP, PROFESSOR TUGWELL.
HMMM... WHAT'S ***YOUR*** ANALYSIS? IS THIS CO-OP OF THE **PRICE - CUTTING** VARIETY, OR THE **ROCHDALE** VARIETY?

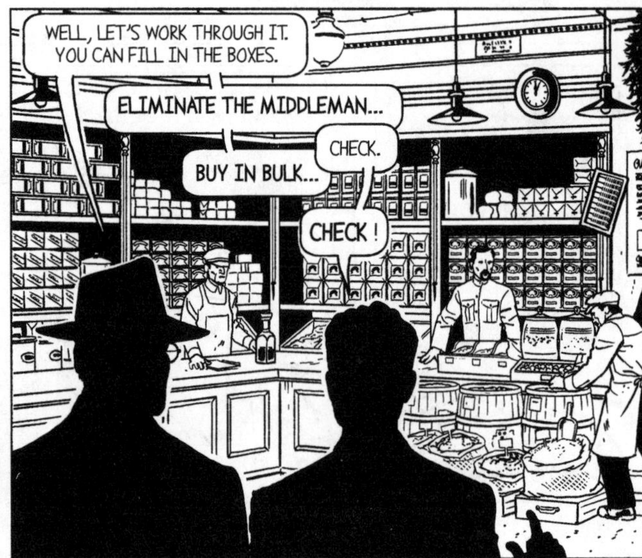
WELL, LET'S WORK THROUGH IT. YOU CAN FILL IN THE BOXES.
ELIMINATE THE MIDDLEMAN...
CHECK.
BUY IN BULK...
CHECK!

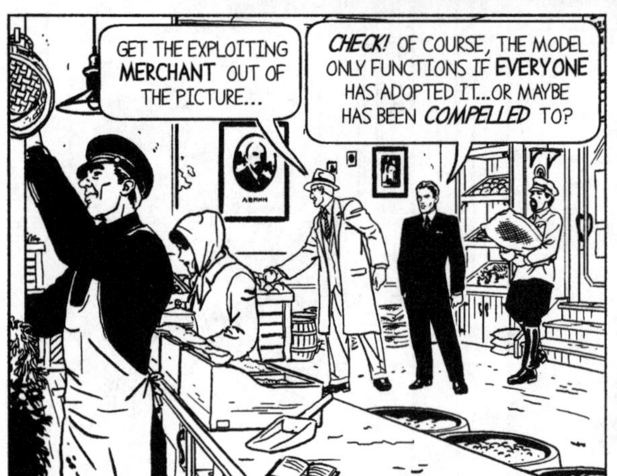
GET THE EXPLOITING **MERCHANT** OUT OF THE PICTURE...
CHECK! OF COURSE, THE MODEL ONLY FUNCTIONS IF **EVERYONE** HAS ADOPTED IT...OR MAYBE HAS BEEN ***COMPELLED*** TO?

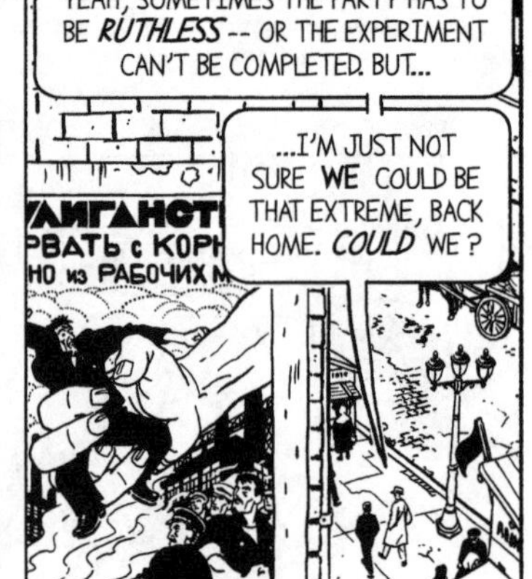
YEAH, SOMETIMES THE PARTY HAS TO BE ***RUTHLESS*** -- OR THE EXPERIMENT CAN'T BE COMPLETED. BUT...
...I'M JUST NOT SURE **WE** COULD BE THAT EXTREME, BACK HOME. ***COULD*** WE?
УЛИГАНСТ
РВАТЬ с КОРН
НО из РАБОЧИХ М

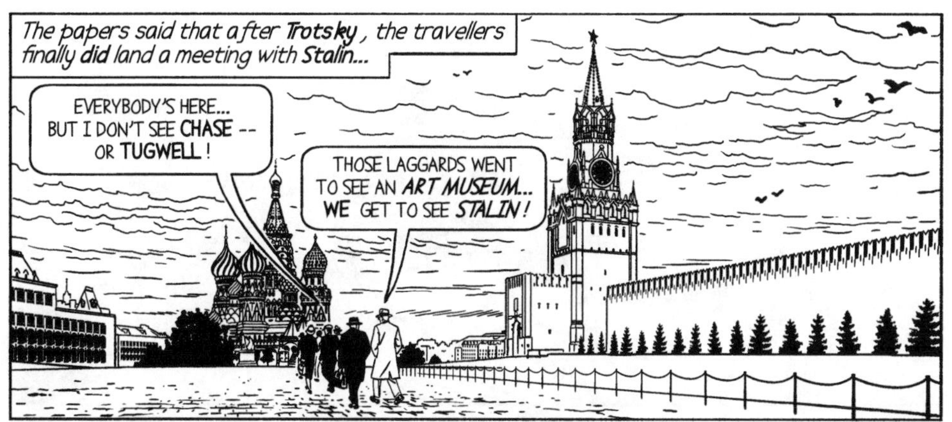
The papers said that after Trotsky, the travellers finally did land a meeting with Stalin...
EVERYBODY'S HERE... BUT I DON'T SEE CHASE -- OR TUGWELL!
THOSE LAGGARDS WENT TO SEE AN ART MUSEUM... WE GET TO SEE STALIN!

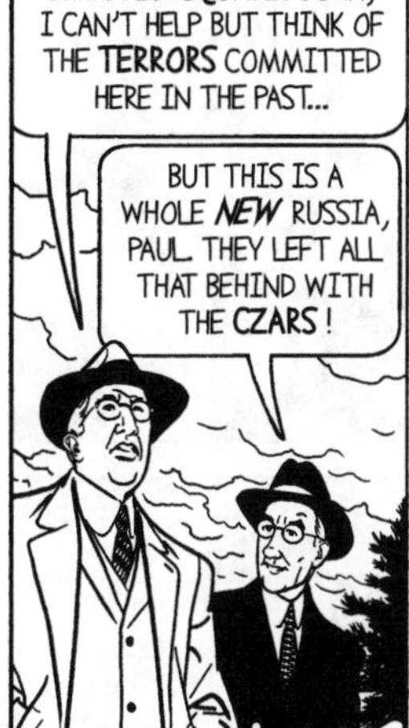
BRRR. RED SQUARE. JOHN, I CAN'T HELP BUT THINK OF THE TERRORS COMMITTED HERE IN THE PAST...
BUT THIS IS A WHOLE NEW RUSSIA, PAUL. THEY LEFT ALL THAT BEHIND WITH THE CZARS!

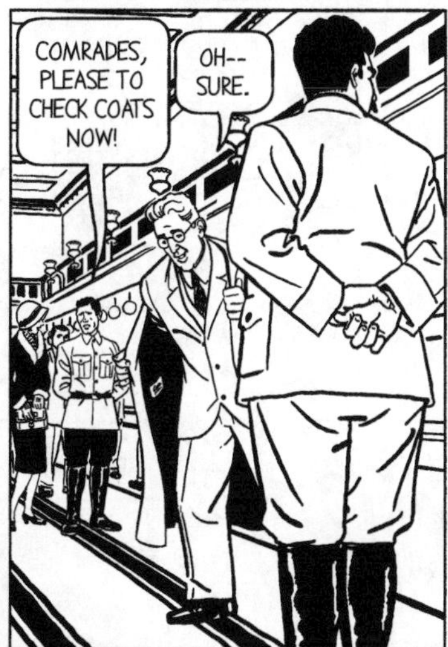
COMRADES, PLEASE TO CHECK COATS NOW!
OH-- SURE.

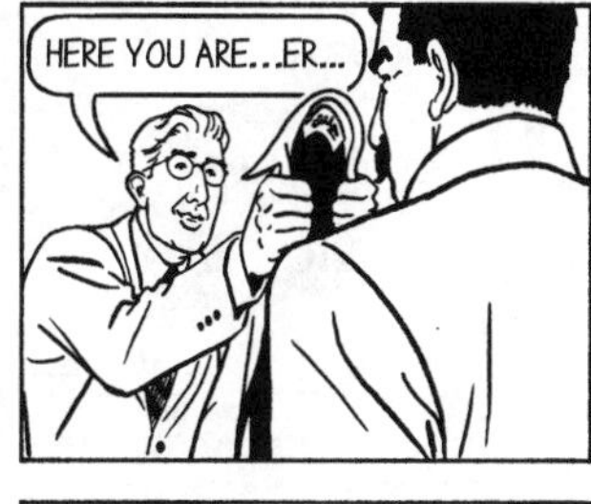
HERE YOU ARE...ER...

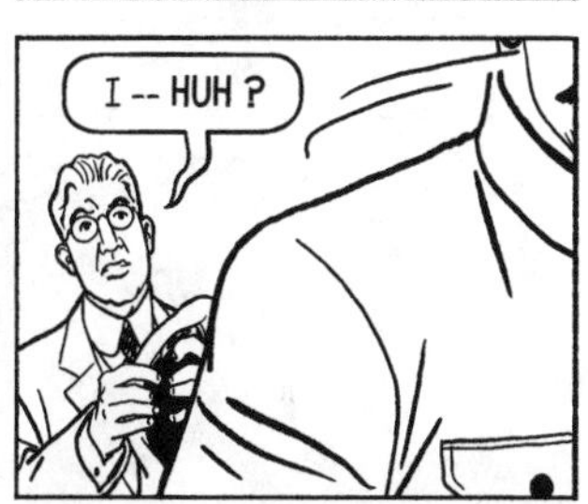
I -- HUH?

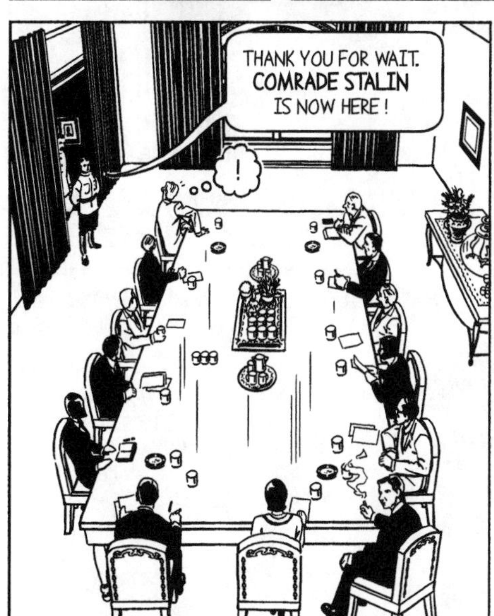
THANK YOU FOR WAIT. COMRADE STALIN IS NOW HERE!
!

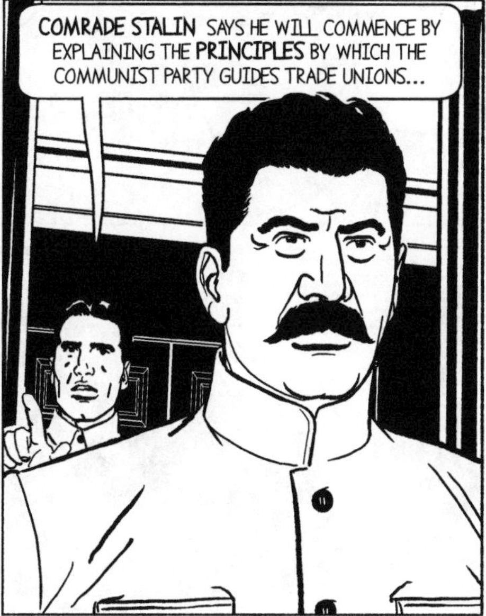
COMRADE STALIN SAYS HE WILL COMMENCE BY EXPLAINING THE PRINCIPLES BY WHICH THE COMMUNIST PARTY GUIDES TRADE UNIONS...

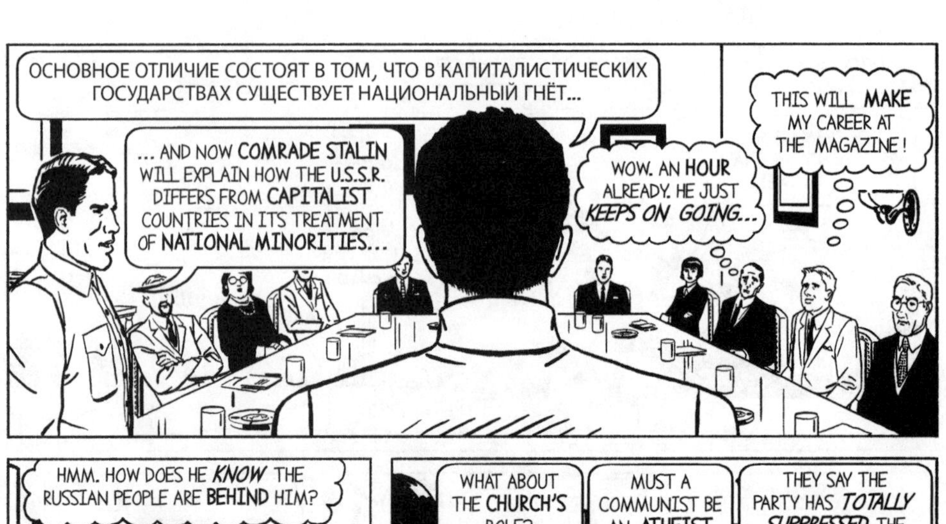
ОСНОВНОЕ ОТЛИЧИЕ СОСТОЯТ В ТОМ, ЧТО В КАПИТАЛИСТИЧЕСКИХ ГОСУДАРСТВАХ СУЩЕСТВУЕТ НАЦИОНАЛЬНЫЙ ГНЁТ...
... AND NOW COMRADE STALIN WILL EXPLAIN HOW THE U.S.S.R. DIFFERS FROM CAPITALIST COUNTRIES IN ITS TREATMENT OF NATIONAL MINORITIES...
WOW. AN HOUR ALREADY. HE JUST KEEPS ON GOING...
THIS WILL MAKE MY CAREER AT THE MAGAZINE!

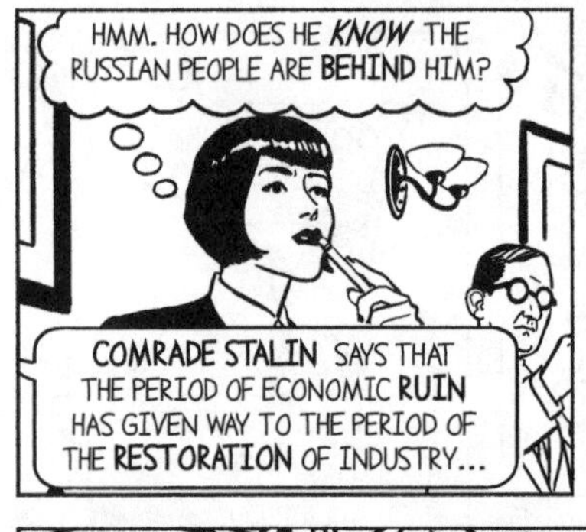
HMM. HOW DOES HE KNOW THE RUSSIAN PEOPLE ARE BEHIND HIM?
COMRADE STALIN SAYS THAT THE PERIOD OF ECONOMIC RUIN HAS GIVEN WAY TO THE PERIOD OF THE RESTORATION OF INDUSTRY...

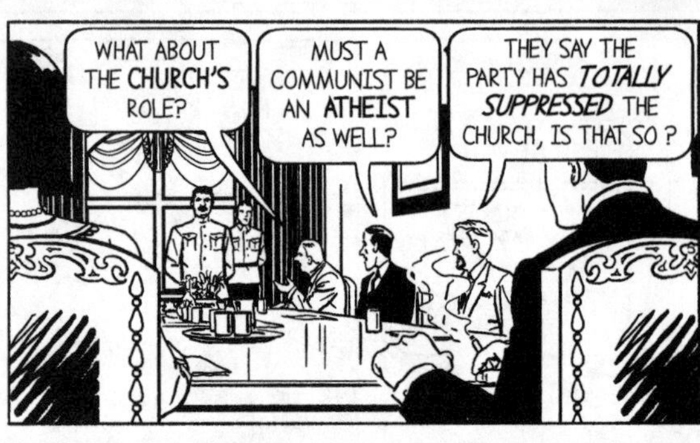
WHAT ABOUT THE CHURCH'S ROLE?
MUST A COMMUNIST BE AN ATHEIST AS WELL?
THEY SAY THE PARTY HAS TOTALLY SUPPRESSED THE CHURCH, IS THAT SO?

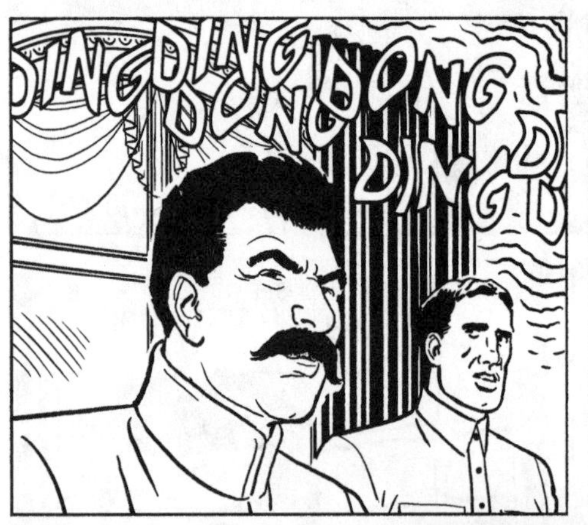
DING DING DONG DONG DING

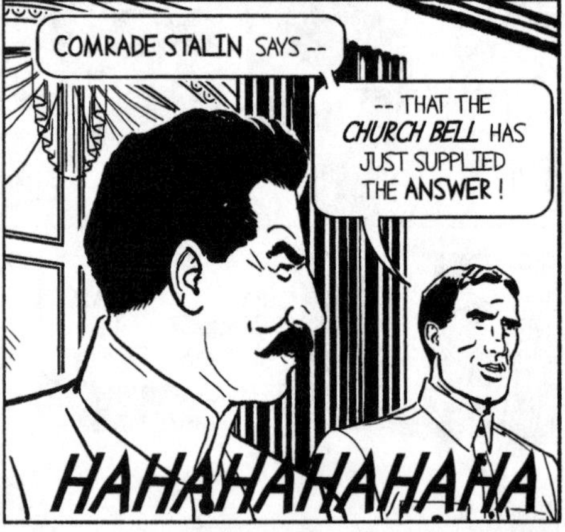
COMRADE STALIN SAYS --
-- THAT THE CHURCH BELL HAS JUST SUPPLIED THE ANSWER!
HAHAHAHAHAHAHA

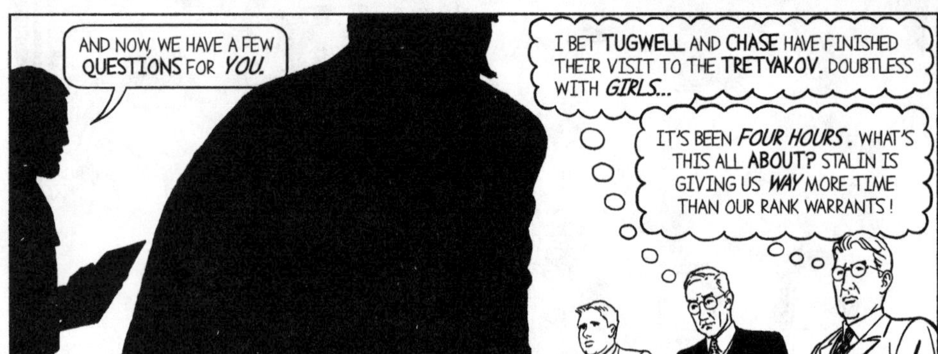
AND NOW, WE HAVE A FEW QUESTIONS FOR YOU.
I BET TUGWELL AND CHASE HAVE FINISHED THEIR VISIT TO THE TRETYAKOV. DOUBTLESS WITH GIRLS...
IT'S BEEN FOUR HOURS. WHAT'S THIS ALL ABOUT? STALIN IS GIVING US WAY MORE TIME THAN OUR RANK WARRANTS!

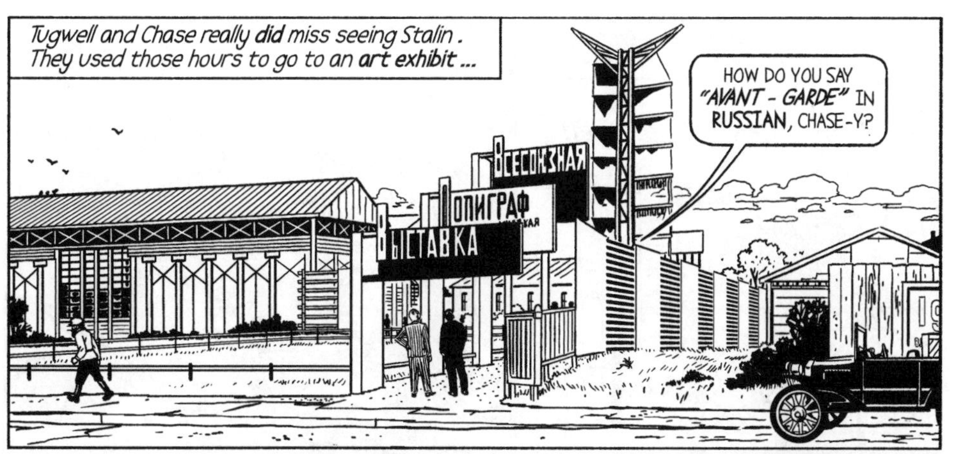
Tugwell and Chase really did miss seeing Stalin. They used those hours to go to an art exhibit...
HOW DO YOU SAY "AVANT - GARDE" IN RUSSIAN, CHASE-Y?
ВСЕСОЮЗНАЯ
ПОЛИГРАФ
ВЫСТАВКА

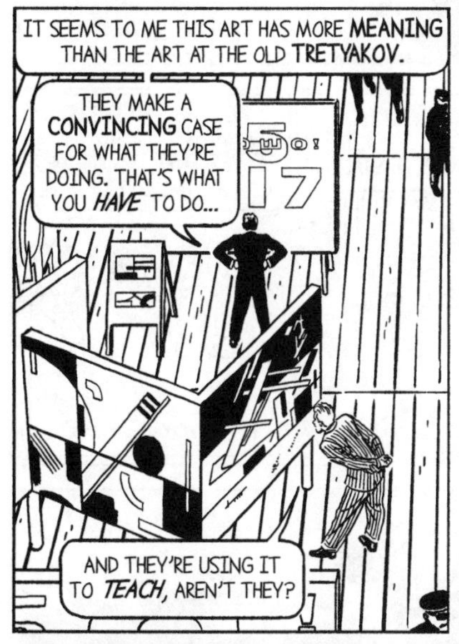
IT SEEMS TO ME THIS ART HAS MORE MEANING THAN THE ART AT THE OLD TRETYAKOV.
THEY MAKE A CONVINCING CASE FOR WHAT THEY'RE DOING. THAT'S WHAT YOU HAVE TO DO...
AND THEY'RE USING IT TO TEACH, AREN'T THEY?

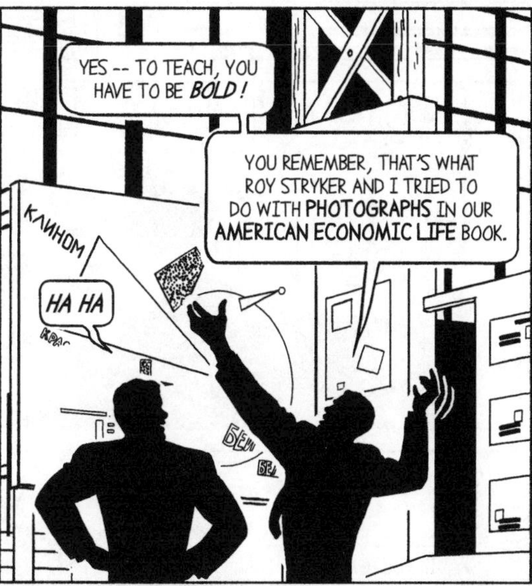
YES -- TO TEACH, YOU HAVE TO BE BOLD!
YOU REMEMBER, THAT'S WHAT ROY STRYKER AND I TRIED TO DO WITH PHOTOGRAPHS IN OUR AMERICAN ECONOMIC LIFE BOOK.
КЛИНОМ
НА НА

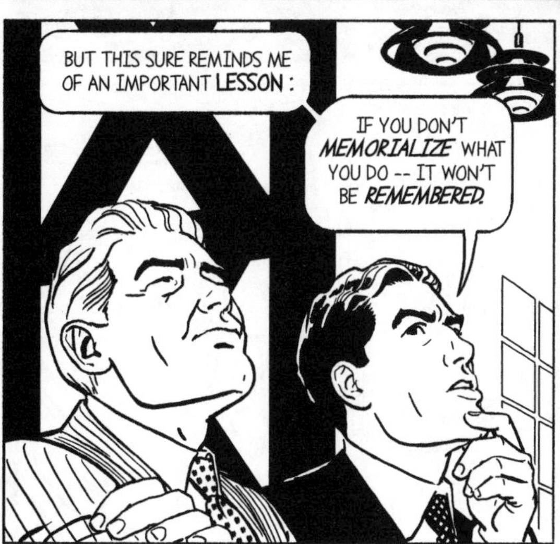
BUT THIS SURE REMINDS ME OF AN IMPORTANT LESSON:
IF YOU DON'T MEMORIALIZE WHAT YOU DO -- IT WON'T BE REMEMBERED.

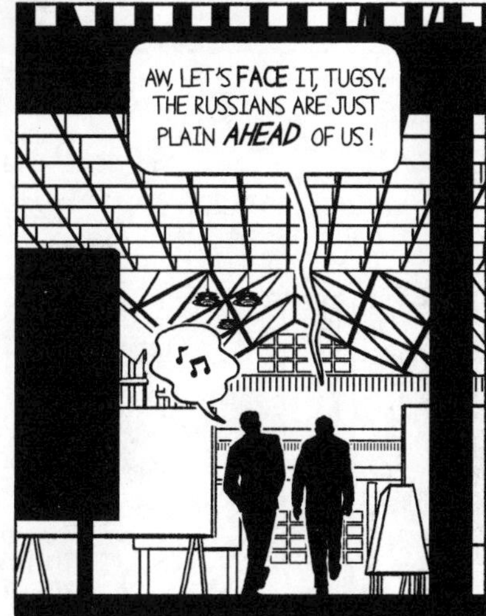
AW, LET'S FACE IT, TUGSY. THE RUSSIANS ARE JUST PLAIN AHEAD OF US!

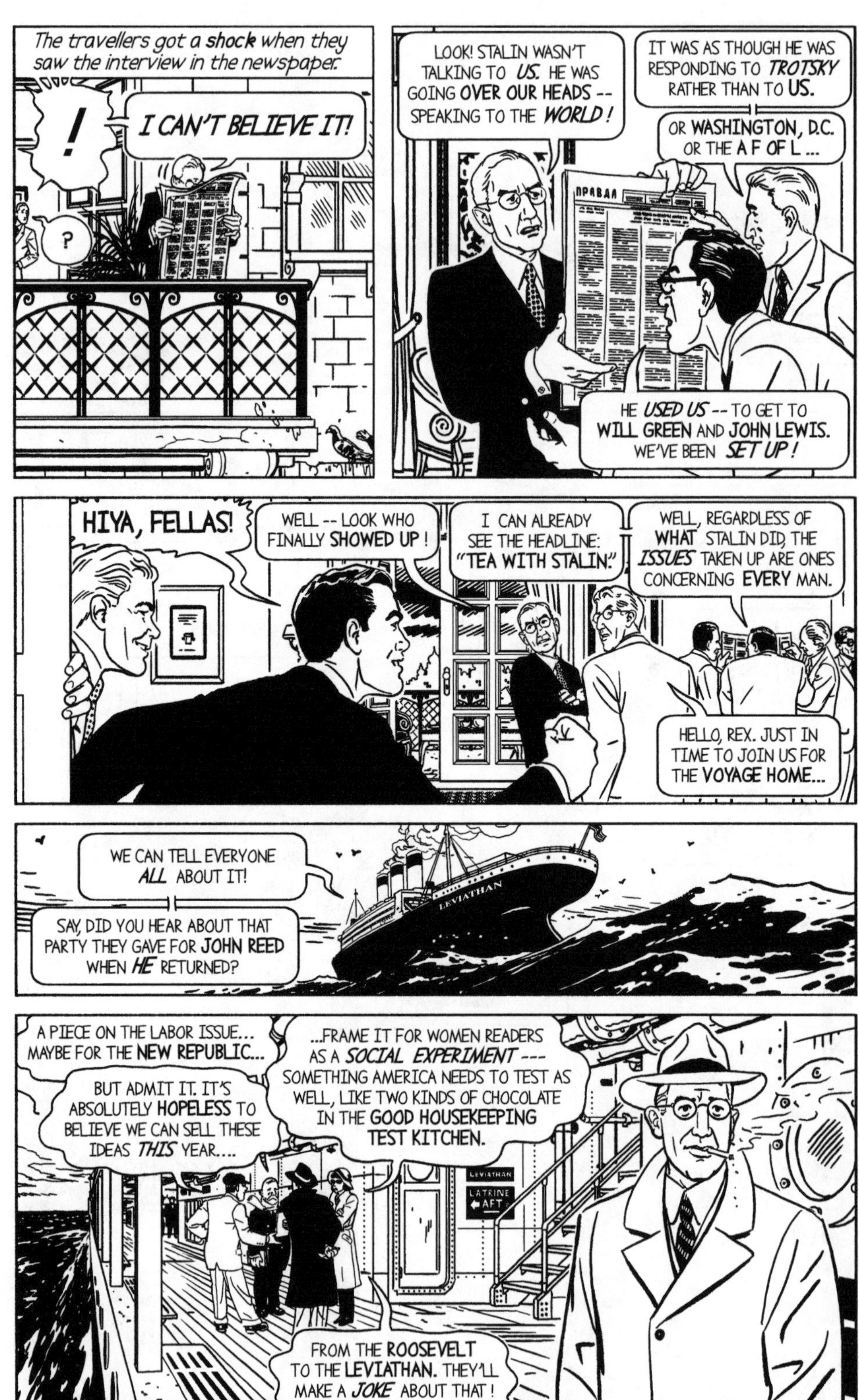
The travellers got a shock when they saw the interview in the newspaper.
!
I CAN'T BELIEVE IT!
?
LOOK! STALIN WASN'T TALKING TO US. HE WAS GOING OVER OUR HEADS -- SPEAKING TO THE WORLD!
IT WAS AS THOUGH HE WAS RESPONDING TO TROTSKY RATHER THAN TO US.
OR WASHINGTON, D.C. OR THE A F OF L...
ПРАВДА
HE USED US -- TO GET TO WILL GREEN AND JOHN LEWIS. WE'VE BEEN SET UP!
HIYA, FELLAS!
WELL -- LOOK WHO FINALLY SHOWED UP!
I CAN ALREADY SEE THE HEADLINE: "TEA WITH STALIN."
WELL, REGARDLESS OF WHAT STALIN DID, THE ISSUES TAKEN UP ARE ONES CONCERNING EVERY MAN.
HELLO, REX. JUST IN TIME TO JOIN US FOR THE VOYAGE HOME...
WE CAN TELL EVERYONE ALL ABOUT IT!
SAY, DID YOU HEAR ABOUT THAT PARTY THEY GAVE FOR JOHN REED WHEN HE RETURNED?
LEVIATHAN
A PIECE ON THE LABOR ISSUE... MAYBE FOR THE NEW REPUBLIC...
BUT ADMIT IT. IT'S ABSOLUTELY HOPELESS TO BELIEVE WE CAN SELL THESE IDEAS THIS YEAR....
...FRAME IT FOR WOMEN READERS AS A SOCIAL EXPERIMENT --- SOMETHING AMERICA NEEDS TO TEST AS WELL, LIKE TWO KINDS OF CHOCOLATE IN THE GOOD HOUSEKEEPING TEST KITCHEN.
LEVIATHAN
LATRINE AFT
FROM THE ROOSEVELT TO THE LEVIATHAN. THEY'LL MAKE A JOKE ABOUT THAT!

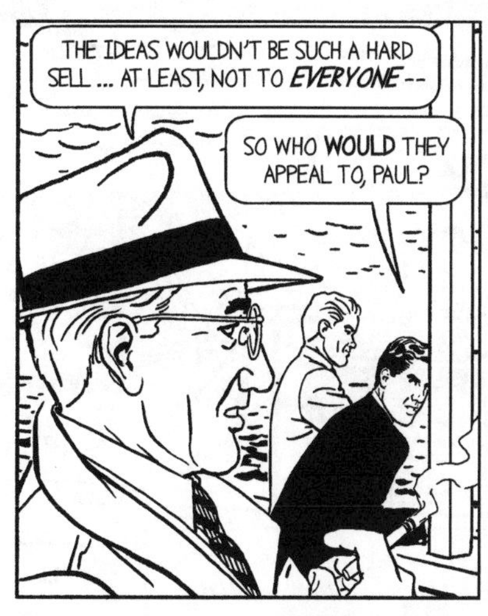
THE IDEAS WOULDN'T BE SUCH A HARD SELL ... AT LEAST, NOT TO *EVERYONE* --
SO WHO **WOULD** THEY APPEAL TO, PAUL?

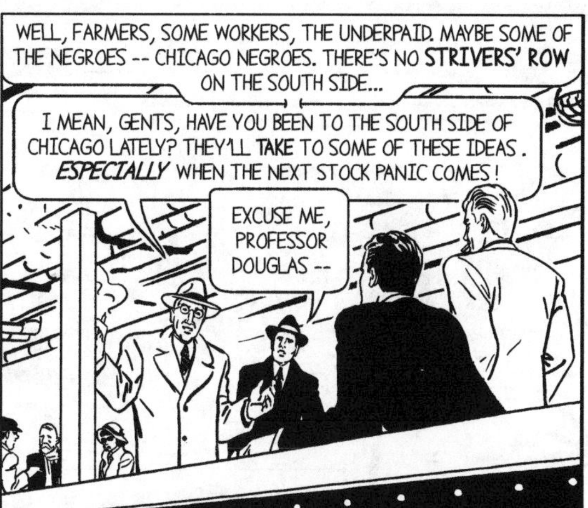
WELL, FARMERS, SOME WORKERS, THE UNDERPAID. MAYBE SOME OF THE NEGROES -- CHICAGO NEGROES. THERE'S NO **STRIVERS' ROW** ON THE SOUTH SIDE...
I MEAN, GENTS, HAVE YOU BEEN TO THE SOUTH SIDE OF CHICAGO LATELY? THEY'LL **TAKE** TO SOME OF THESE IDEAS . ***ESPECIALLY*** WHEN THE NEXT STOCK PANIC COMES !
EXCUSE ME, PROFESSOR DOUGLAS --

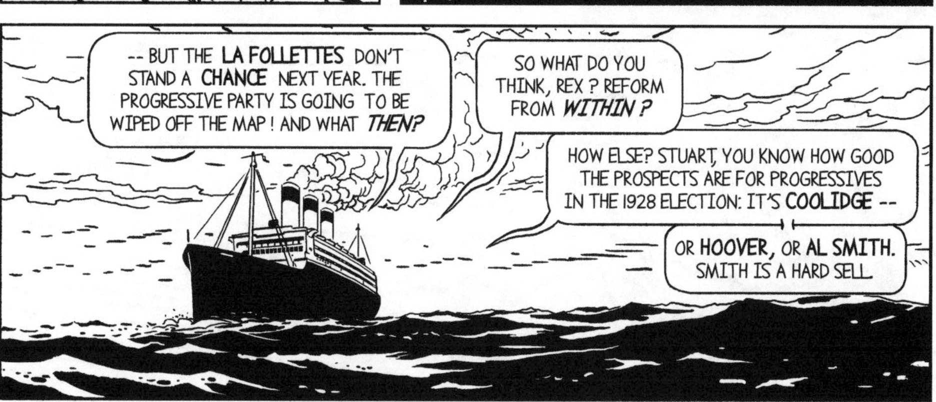
-- BUT THE **LA FOLLETTES** DON'T STAND A **CHANCE** NEXT YEAR. THE PROGRESSIVE PARTY IS GOING TO BE WIPED OFF THE MAP ! AND WHAT *THEN?*
SO WHAT DO YOU THINK, REX ? REFORM FROM *WITHIN ?*
HOW ELSE? STUART, YOU KNOW HOW GOOD THE PROSPECTS ARE FOR PROGRESSIVES IN THE 1928 ELECTION: IT'S **COOLIDGE** --
OR **HOOVER**, OR **AL SMITH.** SMITH IS A HARD SELL.

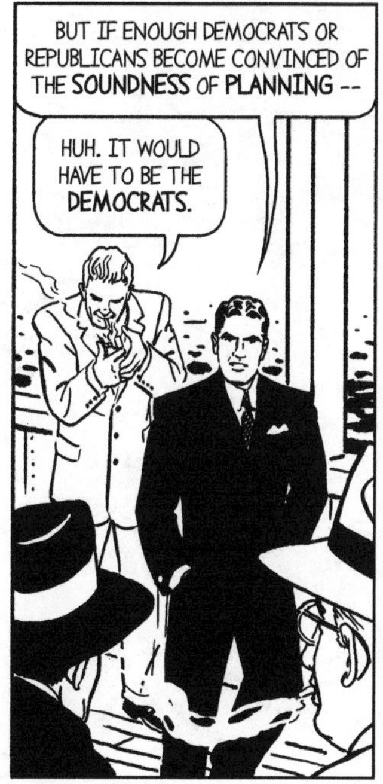
BUT IF ENOUGH DEMOCRATS OR REPUBLICANS BECOME CONVINCED OF THE **SOUNDNESS** OF **PLANNING** --
HUH. IT WOULD HAVE TO BE THE **DEMOCRATS.**

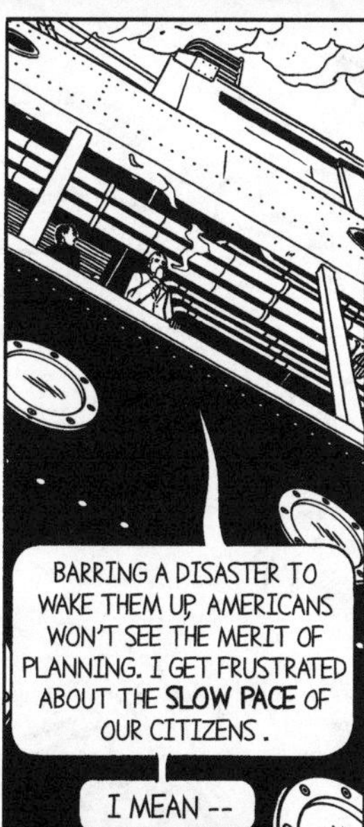
BARRING A DISASTER TO WAKE THEM UP, AMERICANS WON'T SEE THE MERIT OF PLANNING. I GET FRUSTRATED ABOUT THE **SLOW PACE** OF OUR CITIZENS .
I MEAN --

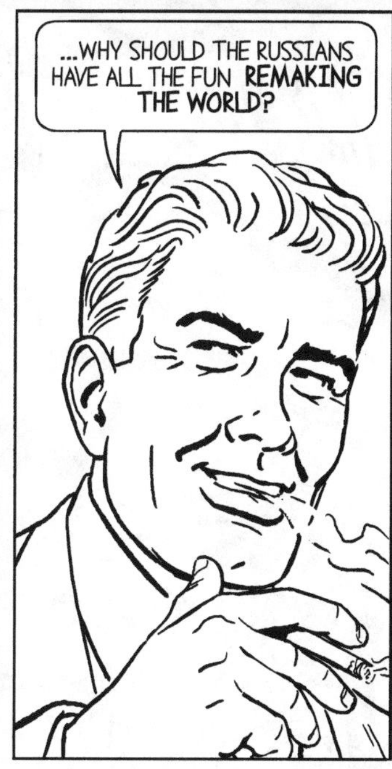
...WHY SHOULD THE RUSSIANS HAVE ALL THE FUN **REMAKING THE WORLD?**

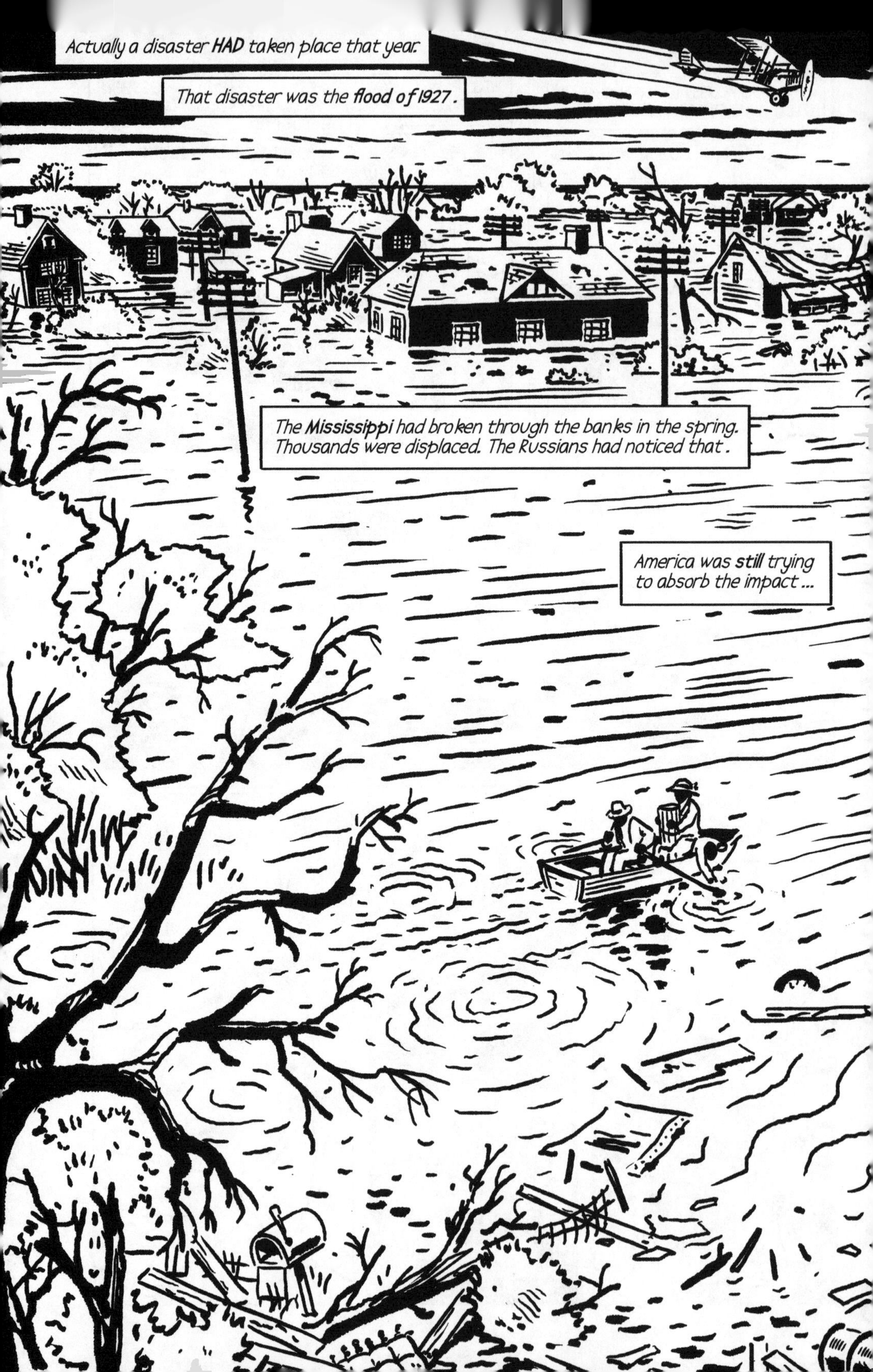
Actually a disaster HAD taken place that year.
That disaster was the flood of 1927.
The Mississippi had broken through the banks in the spring. Thousands were displaced. The Russians had noticed that.
America was still trying to absorb the impact...

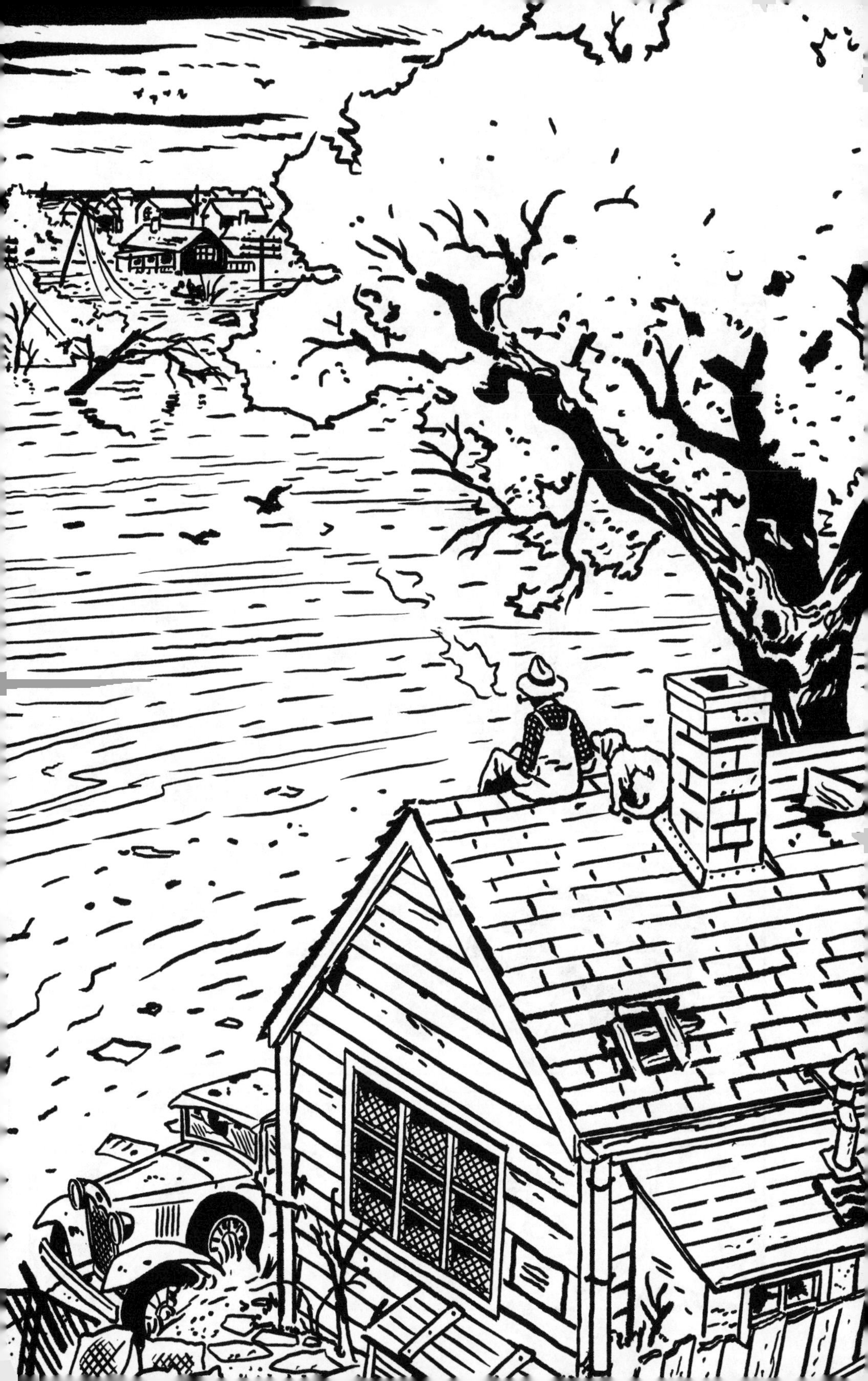

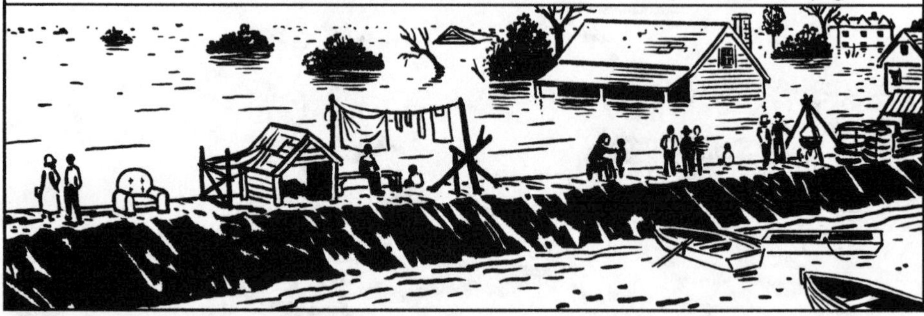
That flood reminded me of the **war** -- **A MILLION PEOPLE** displaced! There was a **WALL OF WATER** -- in Nashville it even rose as high as **56 feet!** The flood **changed** our geography ...

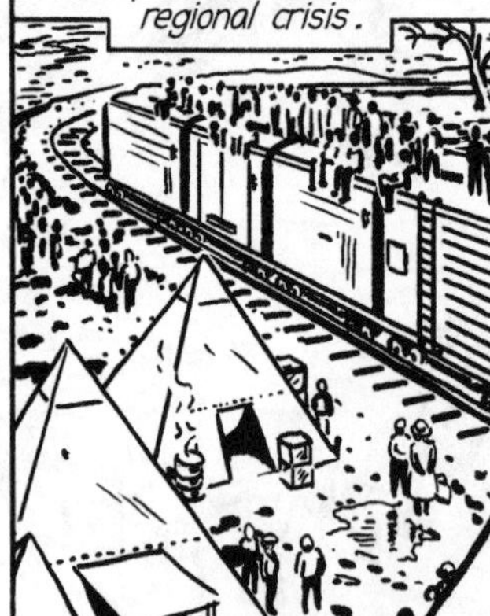
How does a president deal with a disaster? **Calvin Coolidge** didn't go down South -- he believed the executive should keep his **distance** from regional crisis.

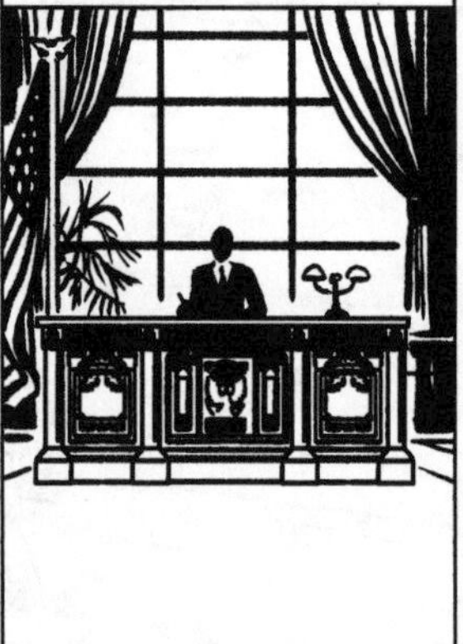
Coolidge thought **states** and the **Red Cross** ought to take the lead, with maybe a federal official to coordinate -- to direct.

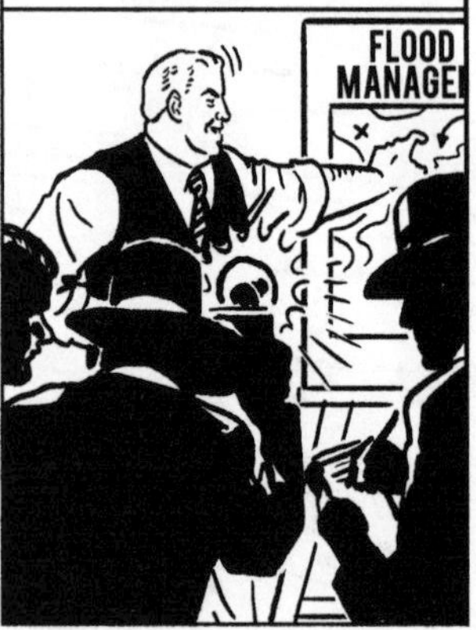
Herbert Hoover, the Commerce Secretary, was **another** story, though! He liked to **JUMP IN** -- and Coolidge **LET** him!
FLOOD
MANAGE

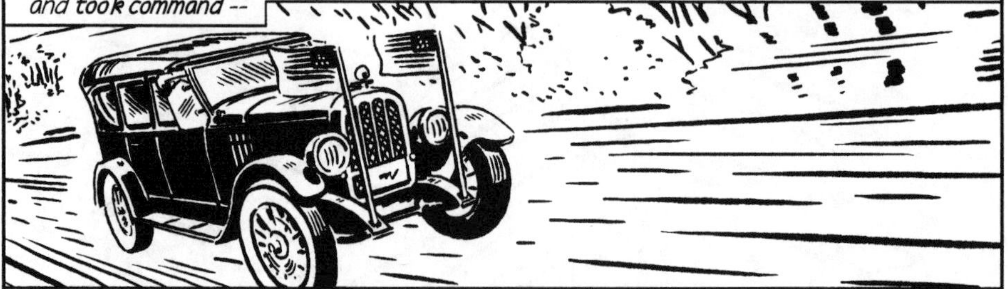
Hoover took that job and **ROLLED** with it! The commerce secretary **raced** down to Memphis and **took command** --

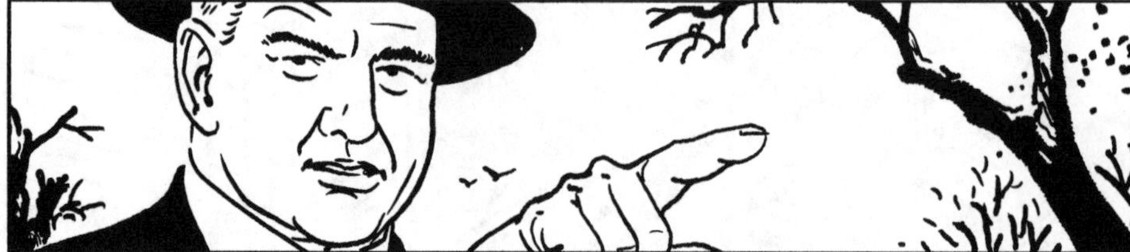
-- and everybody reported to **HIM.** Herbert talked the railroads into transporting the displaced, for **FREE.** He commandeered private outboard motors -- and built motorboats of plywood!

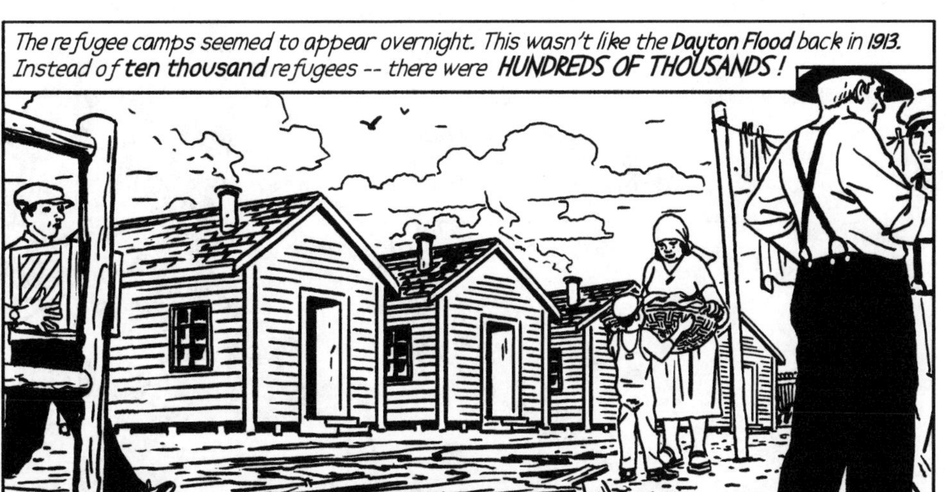
The refugee camps seemed to appear overnight. This wasn't like the Dayton Flood back in 1913. Instead of ten thousand refugees -- there were HUNDREDS OF THOUSANDS!

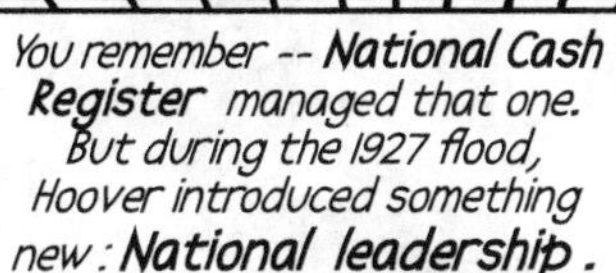
You remember -- National Cash Register managed that one. But during the 1927 flood, Hoover introduced something new: National leadership.

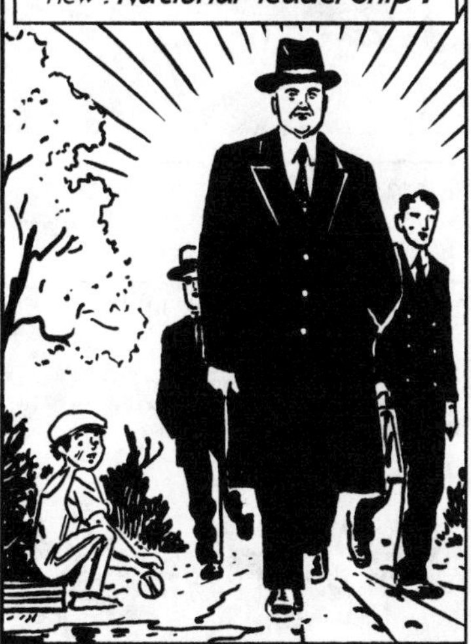

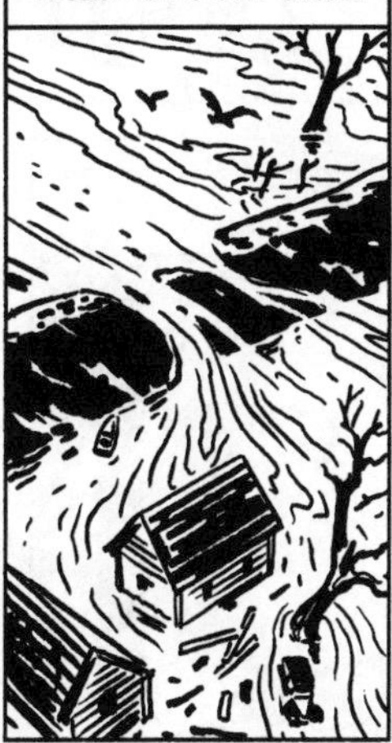
And it was necessary, because EVERYONE was scrambling! A whole 65-acre LAKE opened up at Mounds Landing, near a levee break! It's still there.

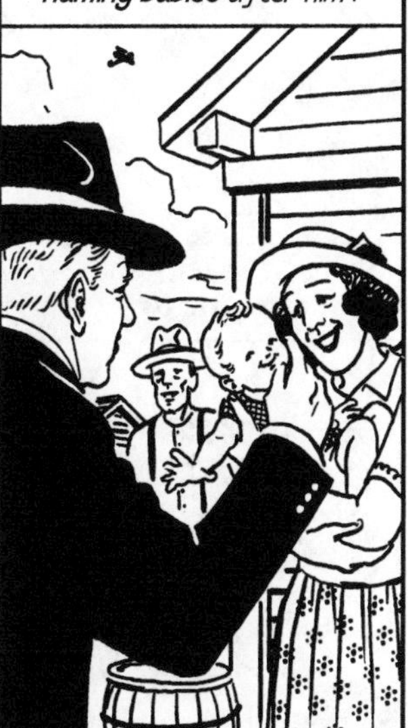
And Herbert got so popular that people actually started naming babies after him!

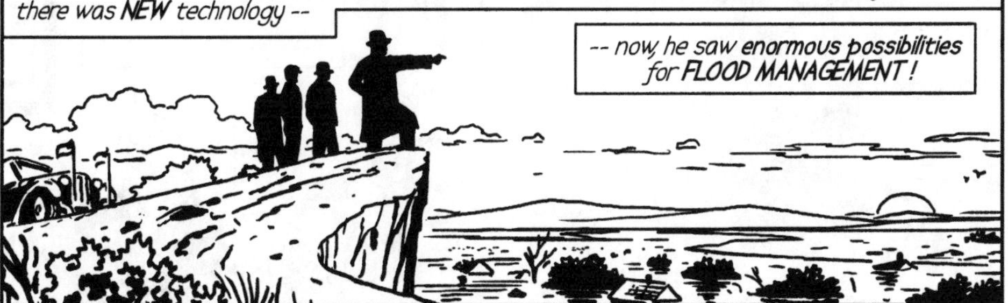
Sheesh, BEFORE Herbert, the Commerce Department was kind of a joke. You know -- the secretary's job was "put the fish to bed at night and turn out the lights in the lighthouses." Hoover had restructured dozens of mines. Now he wanted to restructure the country. And now, there was NEW technology --
-- now, he saw enormous possibilities for FLOOD MANAGEMENT!

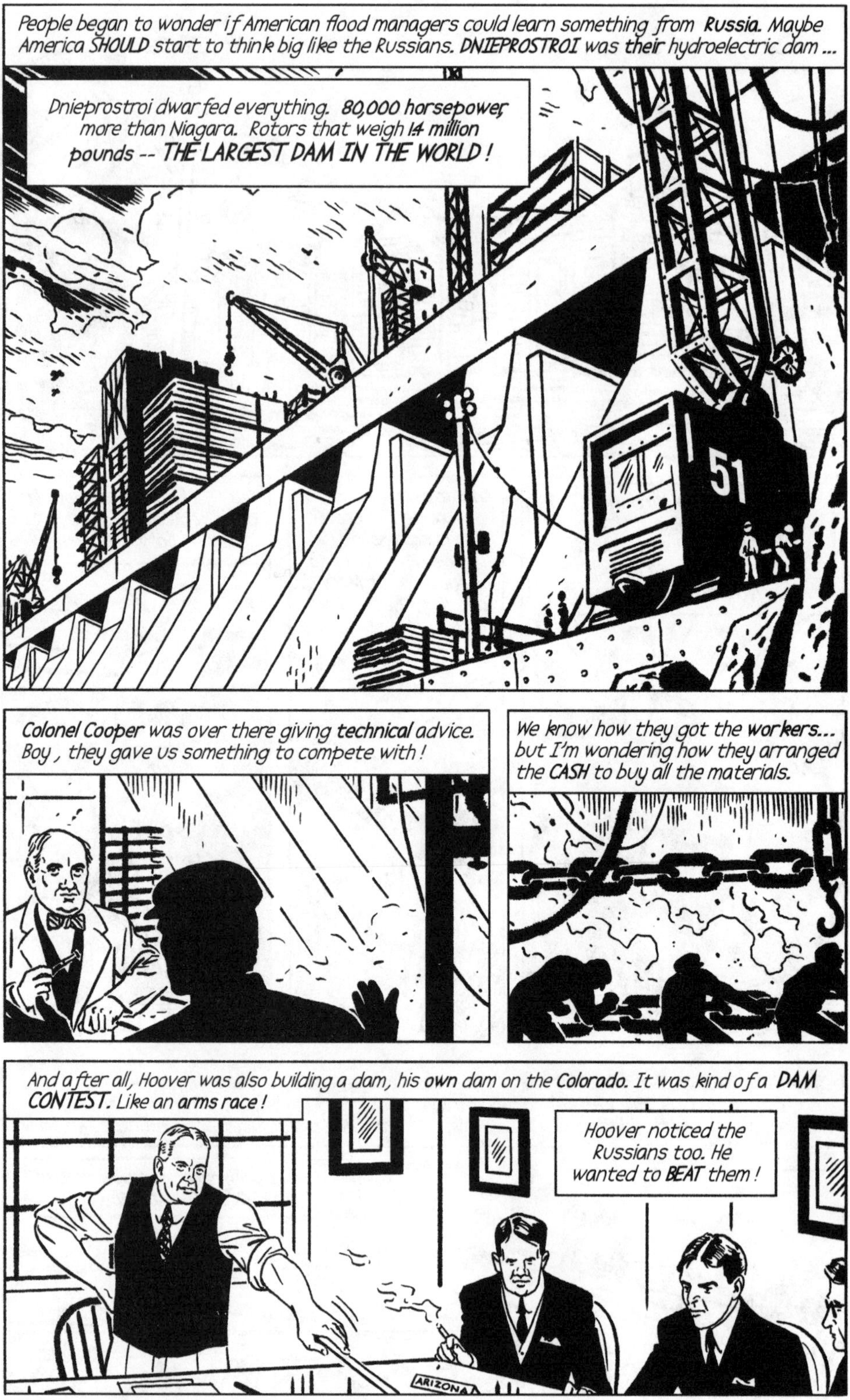

People began to wonder if American flood managers could learn something from **Russia.** Maybe America **SHOULD** start to think big like the Russians. **DNIEPROSTROI** was **their** hydroelectric dam ...

Dnieprostroi dwarfed everything. **80,000 horsepower,** more than Niagara. Rotors that weigh **1.4 million** pounds -- **THE LARGEST DAM IN THE WORLD !**

51

Colonel Cooper was over there giving **technical** advice. Boy, they gave us something to compete with !

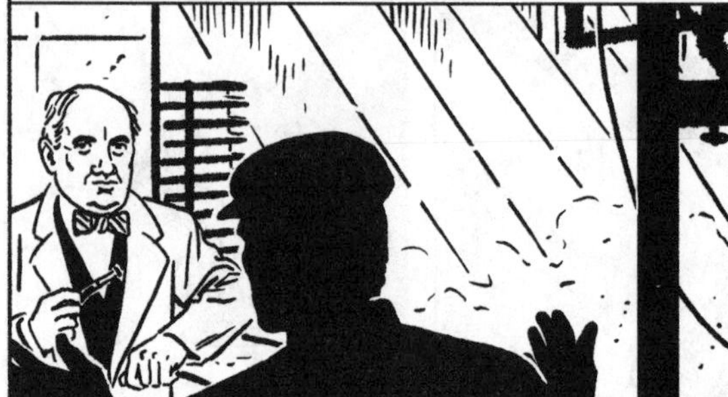

We know how they got the **workers...** but I'm wondering how they arranged the **CASH** to buy all the materials.

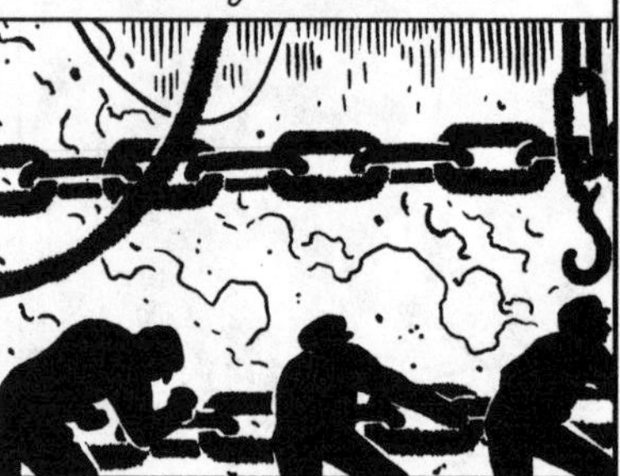

And after all, Hoover was also building a dam, his **own** dam on the **Colorado.** It was kind of a **DAM CONTEST.** Like an **arms race !**

Hoover noticed the Russians too. He wanted to **BEAT** them !

ARIZONA

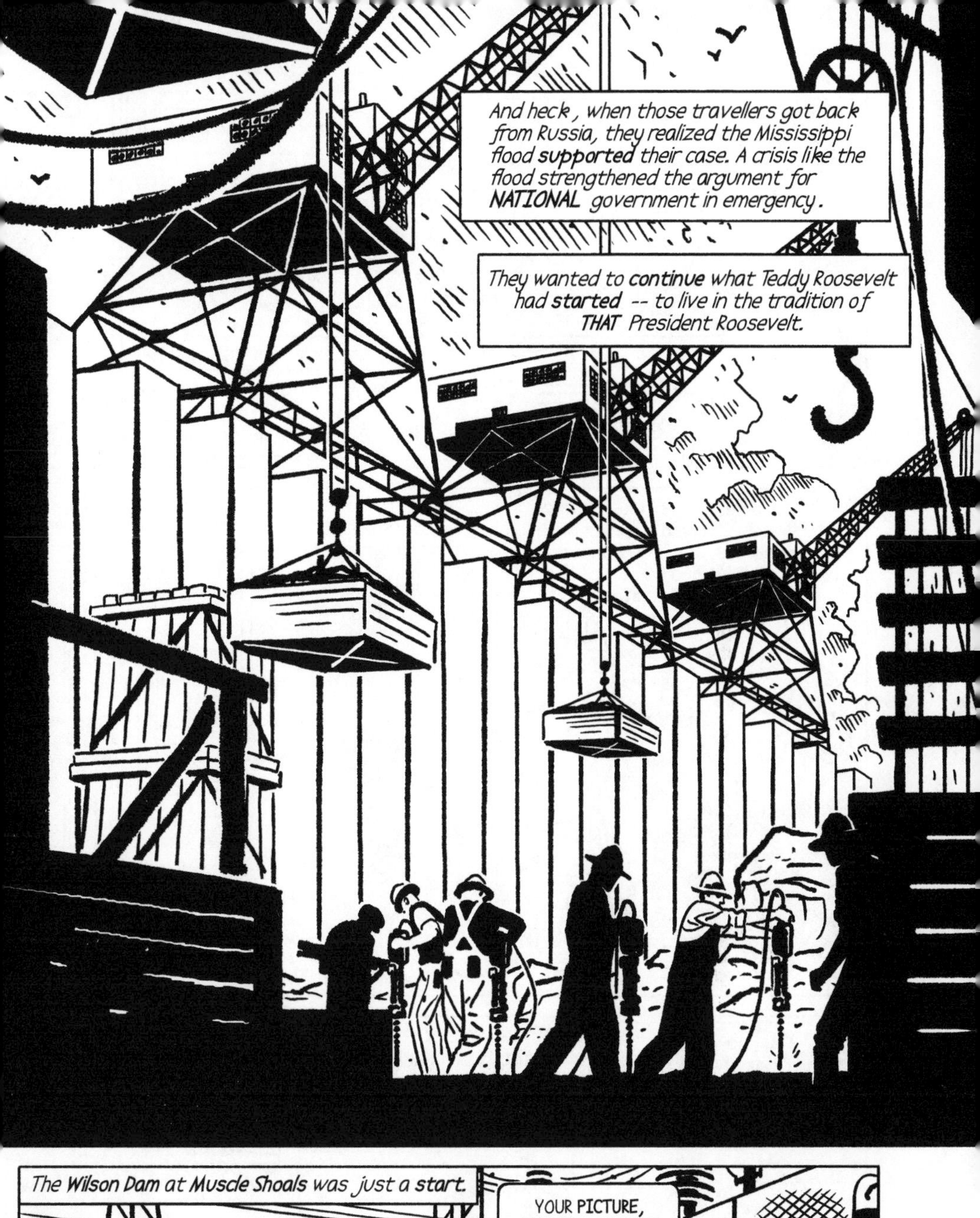

And heck, when those travellers got back from Russia, they realized the Mississippi flood **supported** their case. A crisis like the flood strengthened the argument for **NATIONAL** government in emergency.

They wanted to **continue** what Teddy Roosevelt had **started** -- to live in the tradition of **THAT** President Roosevelt.

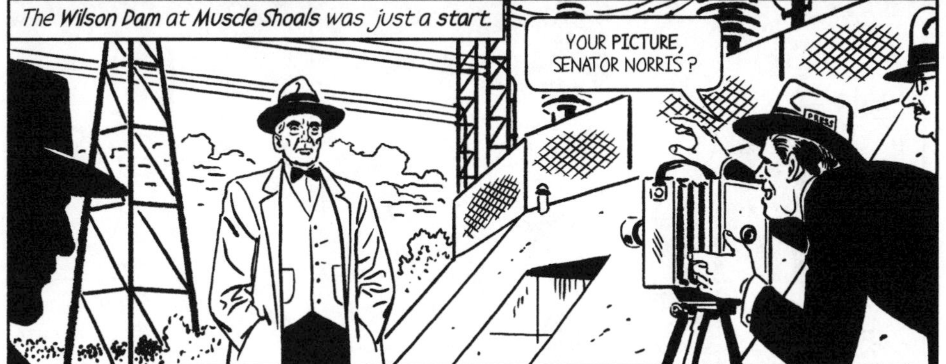

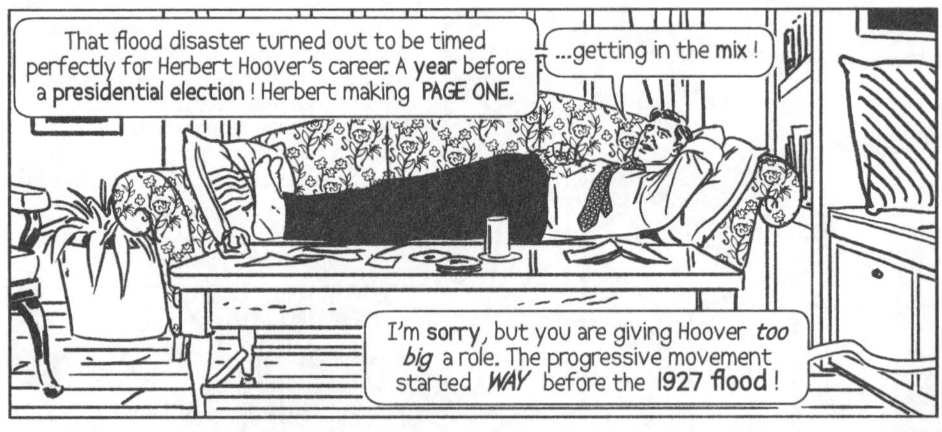

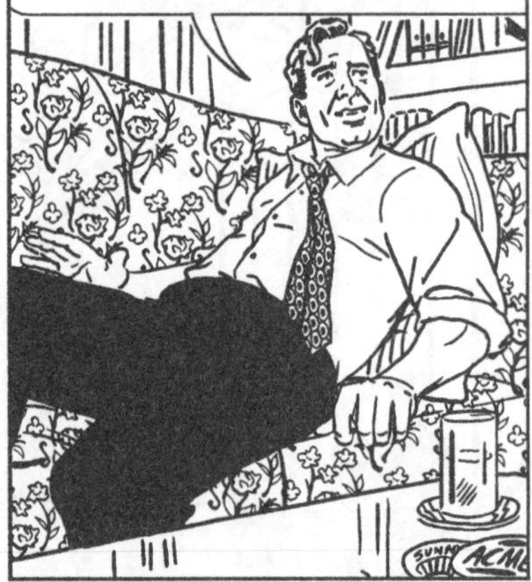

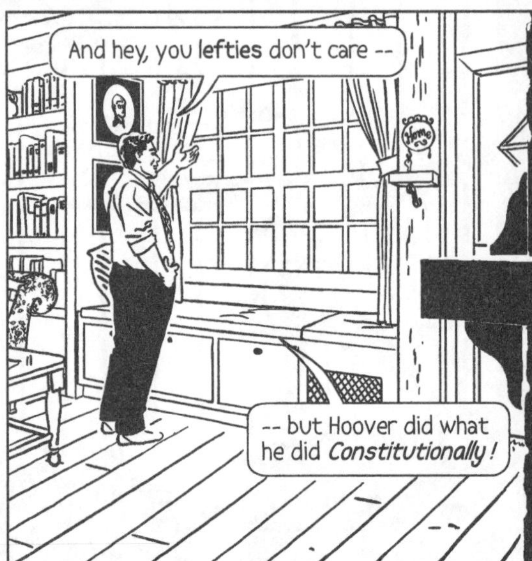

You know, we in utilities shared this sense of ***possibility***.

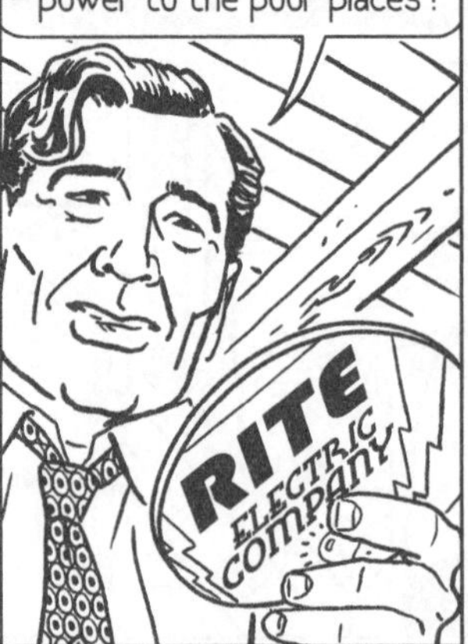

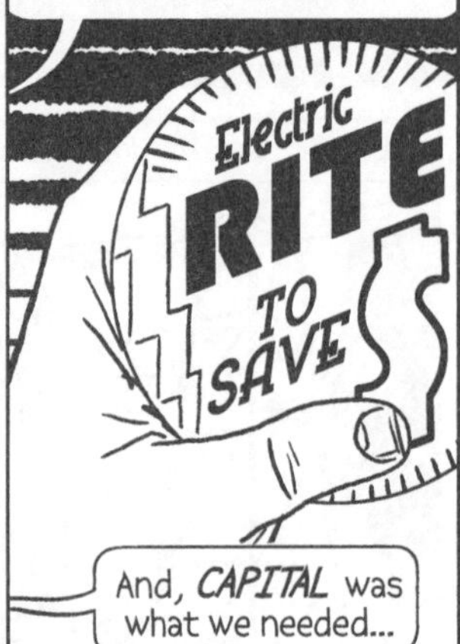

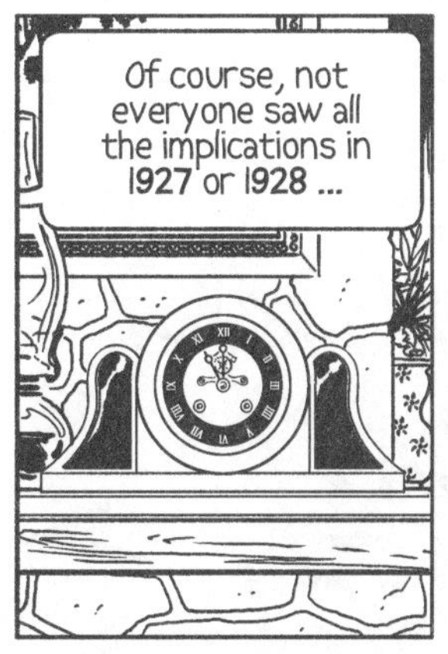
Of course, not everyone saw all the implications in 1927 or 1928 ...

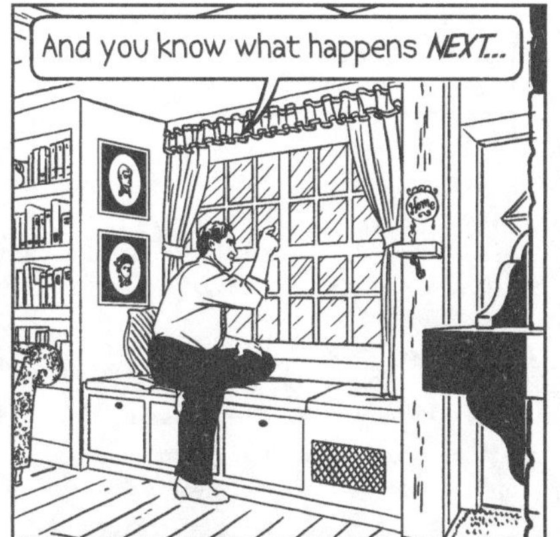
And you know what happens *NEXT...*

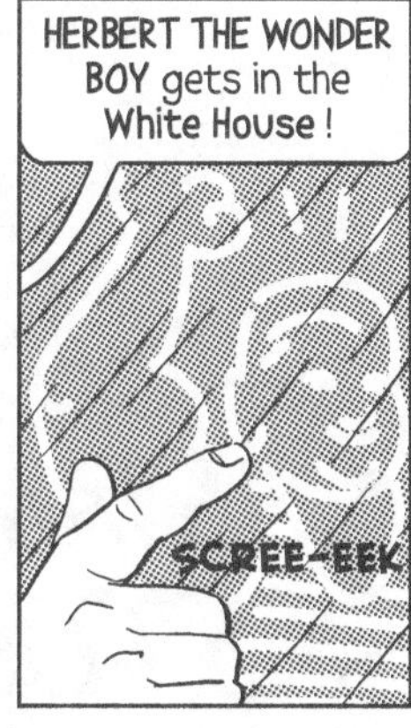
HERBERT THE WONDER BOY gets in the **White House** !
SCREE-EEK

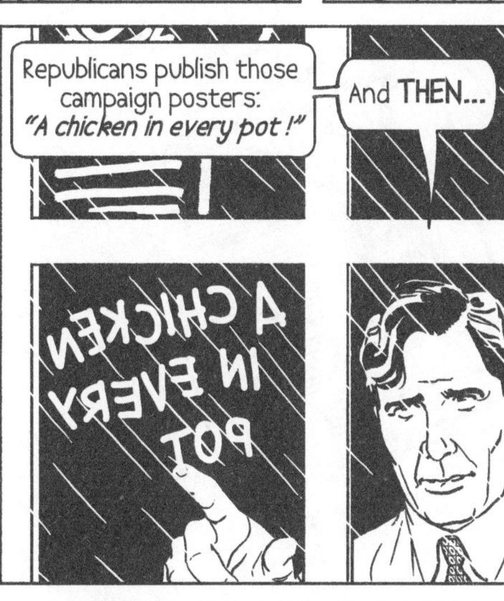
Republicans publish those campaign posters: *"A chicken in every pot !"*
And **THEN...**
A CHICKEN IN EVERY POT

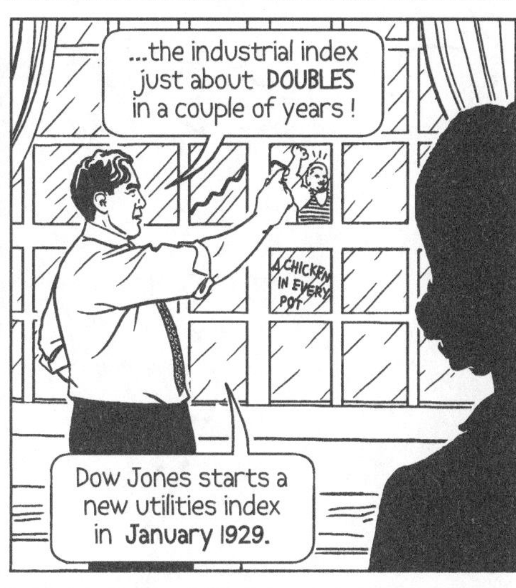
...the industrial index just about **DOUBLES** in a couple of years !
A CHICKEN IN EVERY POT
Dow Jones starts a new utilities index in **January** 1929.

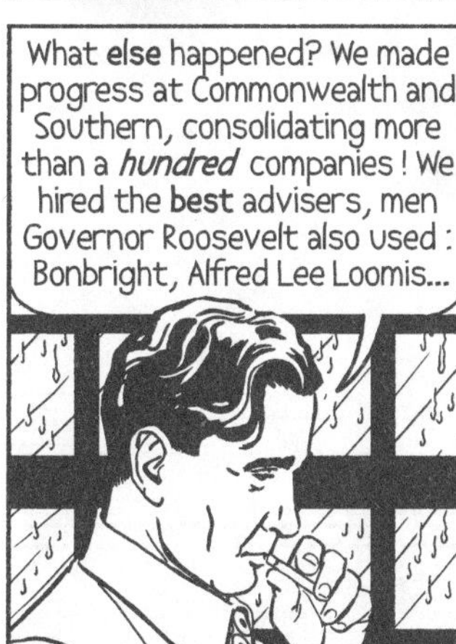
What **else** happened? We made progress at Commonwealth and Southern, consolidating more than a *hundred* companies ! We hired the **best** advisers, men Governor Roosevelt also used : Bonbright, Alfred Lee Loomis...

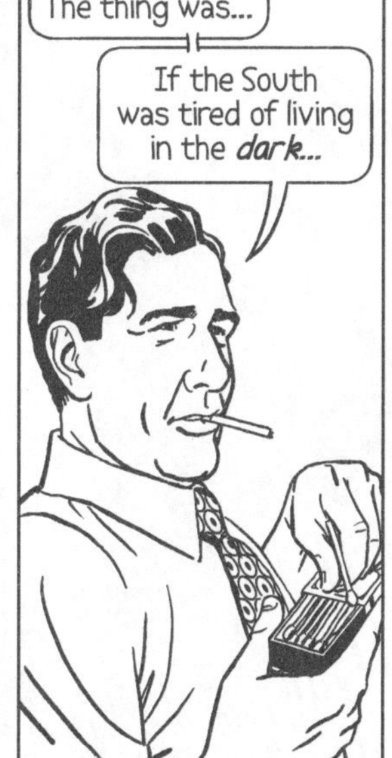
The thing was...
If the South was tired of living in the *dark...*

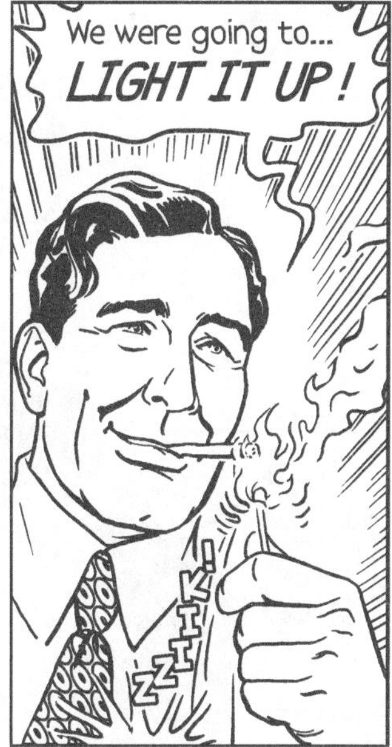
We were going to... *LIGHT IT UP !*
ZZZIIIK!

October 1929
Unemployment: 5.0%
Dow Jones Industrial Average (Oct.1): 343

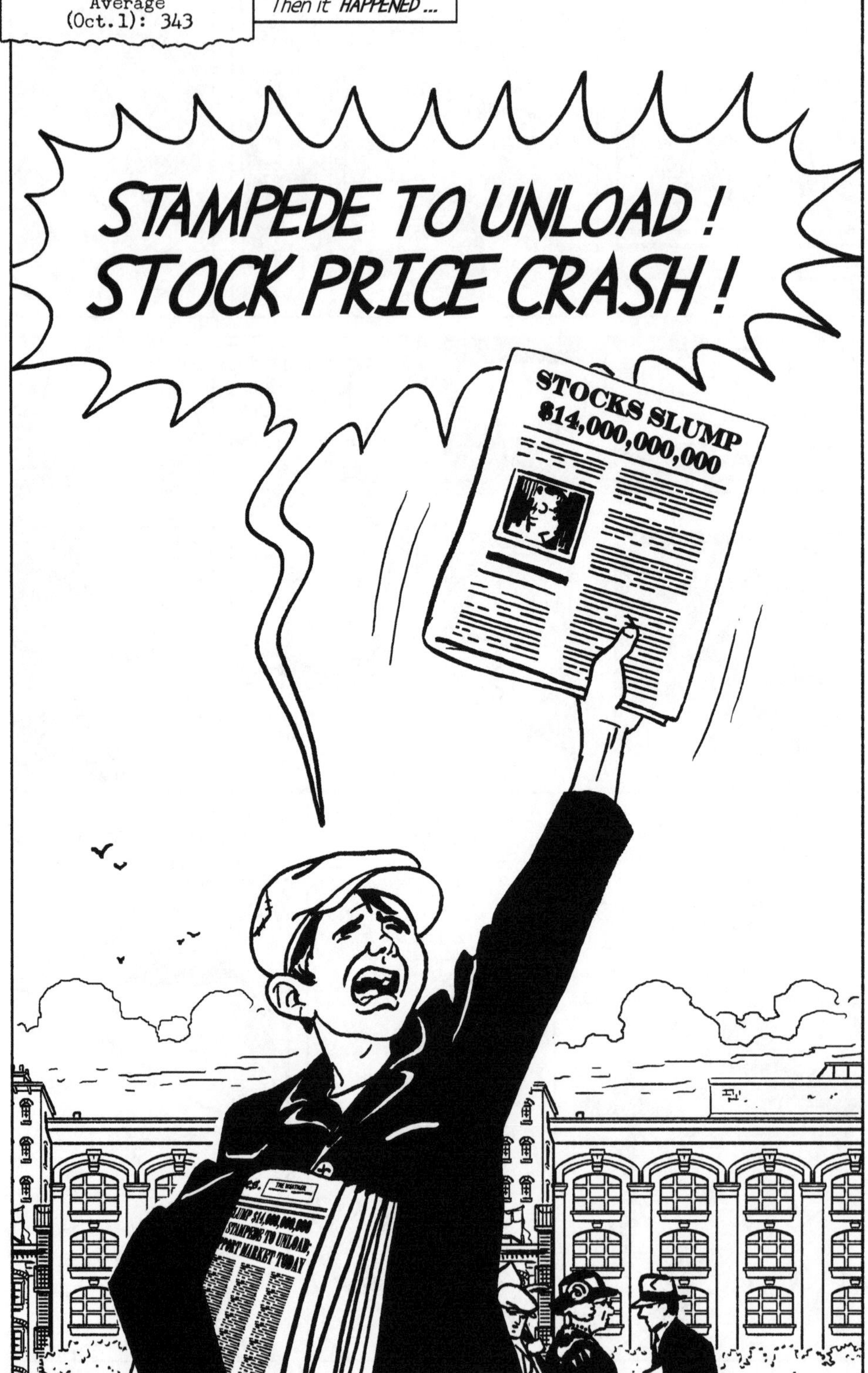

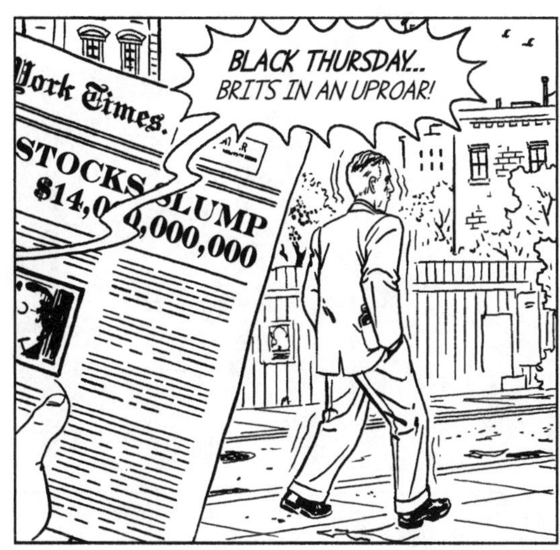
York Times.
STOCKS SLUMP
$14,0 ,000,000
BLACK THURSDAY...
BRITS IN AN UPROAR!

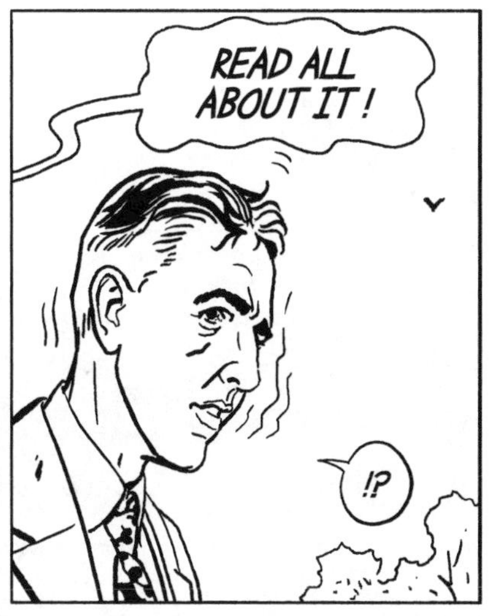
READ ALL
ABOUT IT!
!?

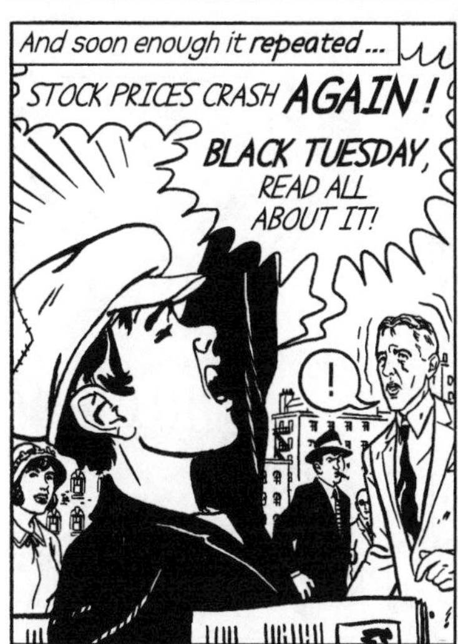
And soon enough it repeated ...
STOCK PRICES CRASH AGAIN!
BLACK TUESDAY,
READ ALL
ABOUT IT!
!

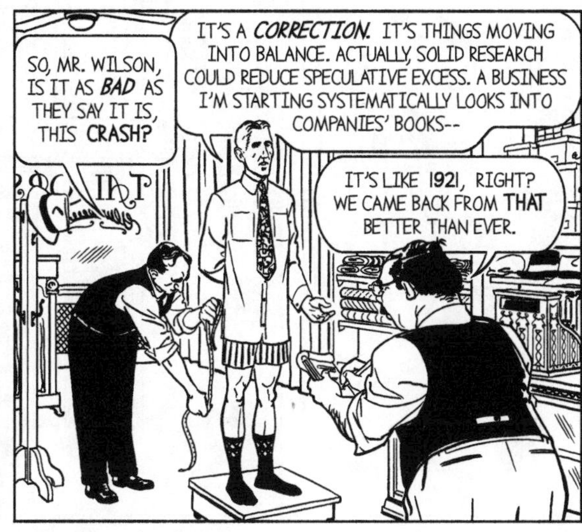
SO, MR. WILSON, IS IT AS BAD AS THEY SAY IT IS, THIS CRASH?
IT'S A CORRECTION. IT'S THINGS MOVING INTO BALANCE. ACTUALLY, SOLID RESEARCH COULD REDUCE SPECULATIVE EXCESS. A BUSINESS I'M STARTING SYSTEMATICALLY LOOKS INTO COMPANIES' BOOKS--
IT'S LIKE 1921, RIGHT? WE CAME BACK FROM THAT BETTER THAN EVER.

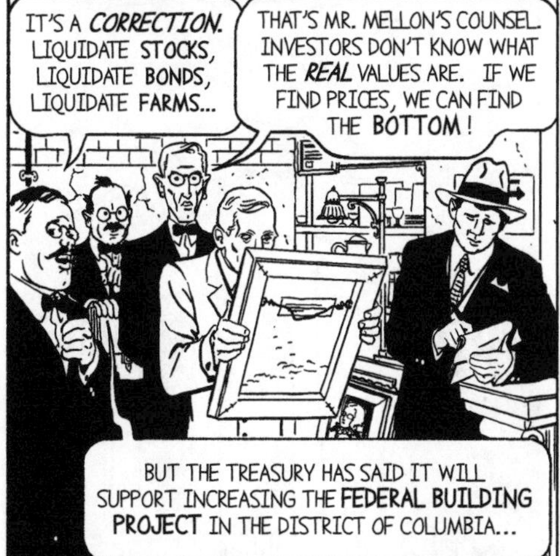
IT'S A CORRECTION. LIQUIDATE STOCKS, LIQUIDATE BONDS, LIQUIDATE FARMS...
THAT'S MR. MELLON'S COUNSEL. INVESTORS DON'T KNOW WHAT THE REAL VALUES ARE. IF WE FIND PRICES, WE CAN FIND THE BOTTOM!
BUT THE TREASURY HAS SAID IT WILL SUPPORT INCREASING THE FEDERAL BUILDING PROJECT IN THE DISTRICT OF COLUMBIA...

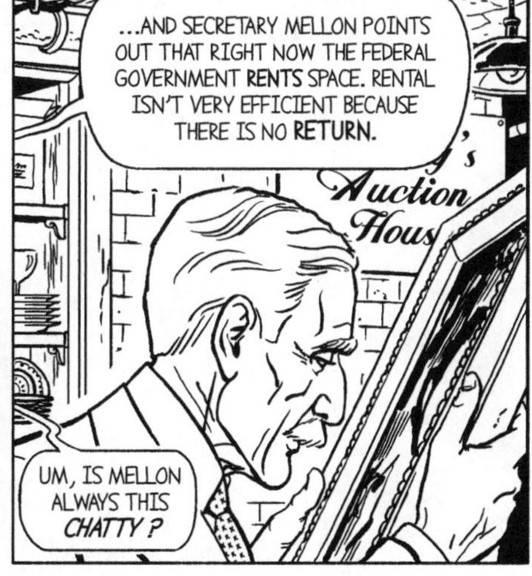
...AND SECRETARY MELLON POINTS OUT THAT RIGHT NOW THE FEDERAL GOVERNMENT RENTS SPACE. RENTAL ISN'T VERY EFFICIENT BECAUSE THERE IS NO RETURN.
Auction
Hous
UM, IS MELLON ALWAYS THIS CHATTY?

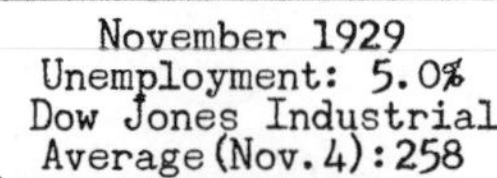
November 1929
Unemployment: 5.0%
Dow Jones Industrial
Average (Nov. 4): 258

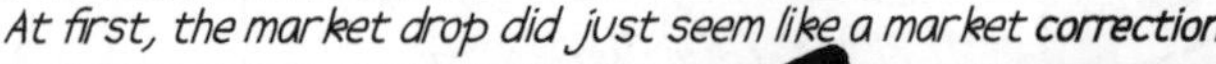
At first, the market drop did just seem like a market correction.

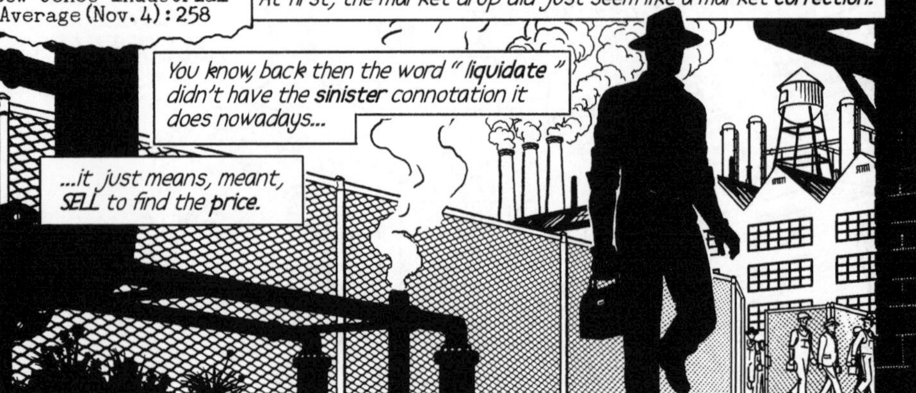
You know, back then the word "liquidate" didn't have the sinister connotation it does nowadays...
...it just means, meant, SELL to find the price.

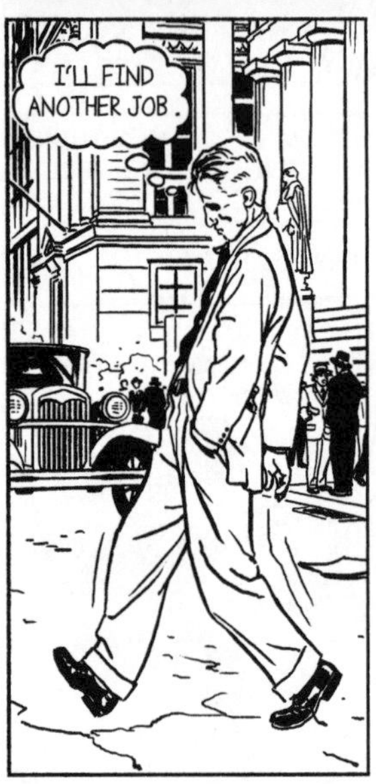
I'LL FIND ANOTHER JOB.

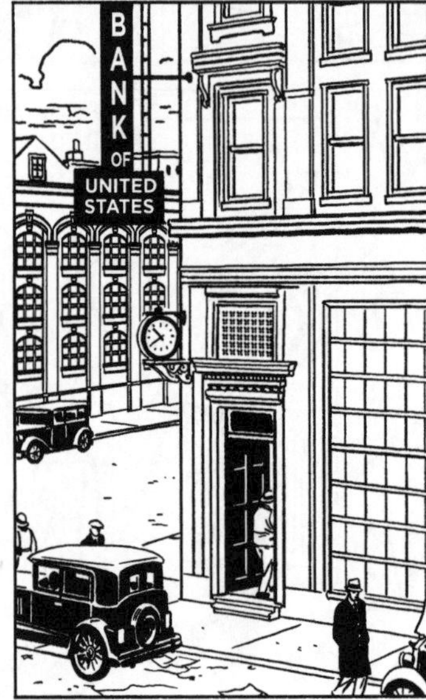
BANK OF UNITED STATES

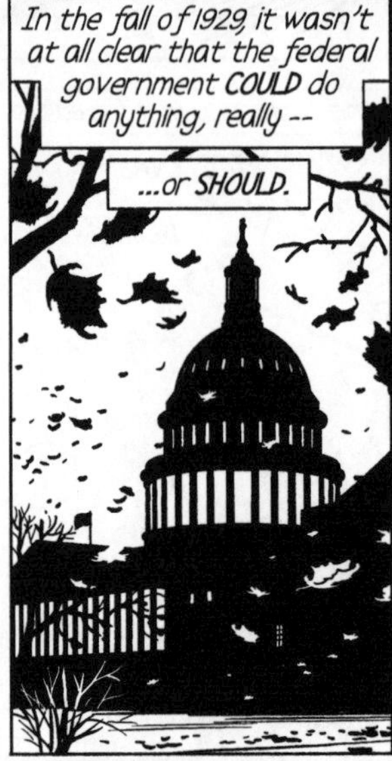
In the fall of 1929, it wasn't at all clear that the federal government COULD do anything, really --
...or SHOULD.

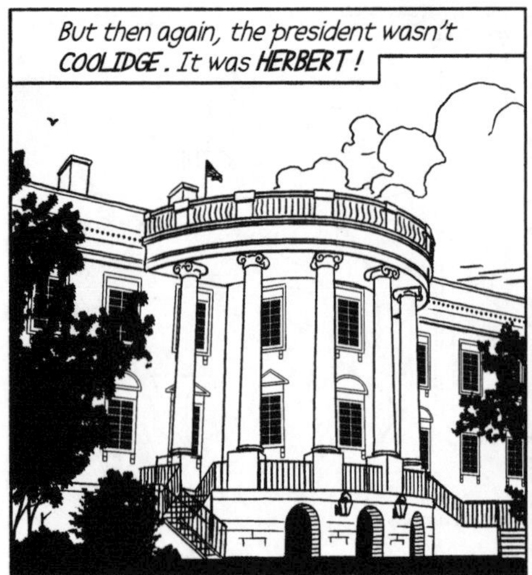
But then again, the president wasn't COOLIDGE. It was HERBERT!

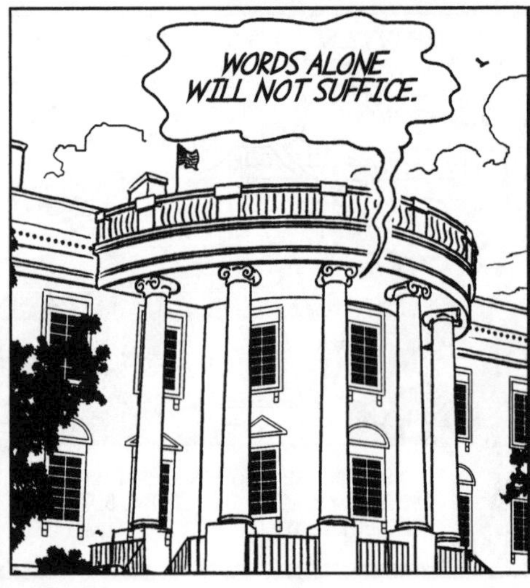
WORDS ALONE WILL NOT SUFFICE.

Less than a month after **Black Tuesday**, Hoover did act. He got ready to sign a temporary tax stimulus. He called in **railroad presidents ...**

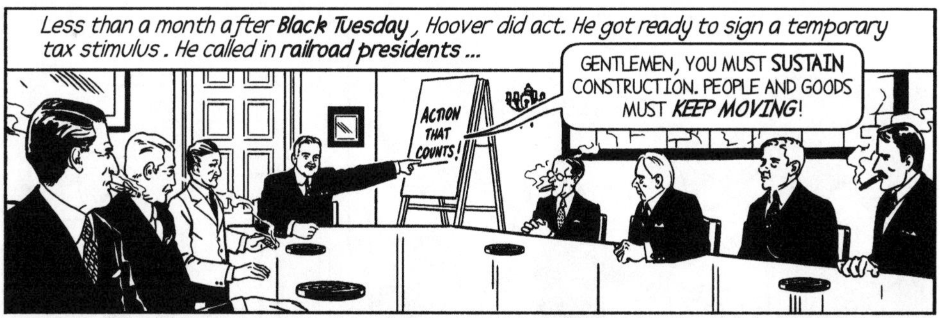

Next it was **heads of industry ...**

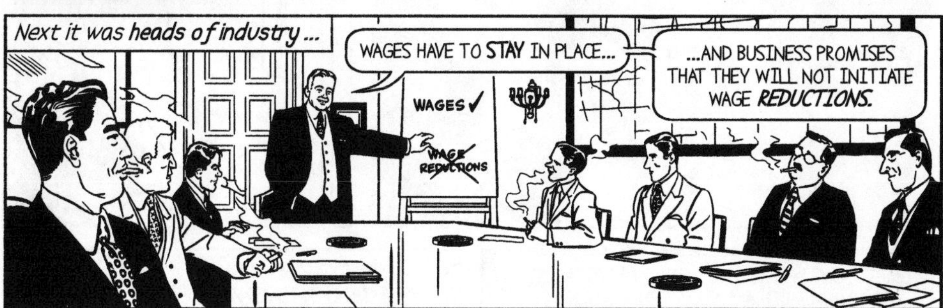

Then -- the **unions.**

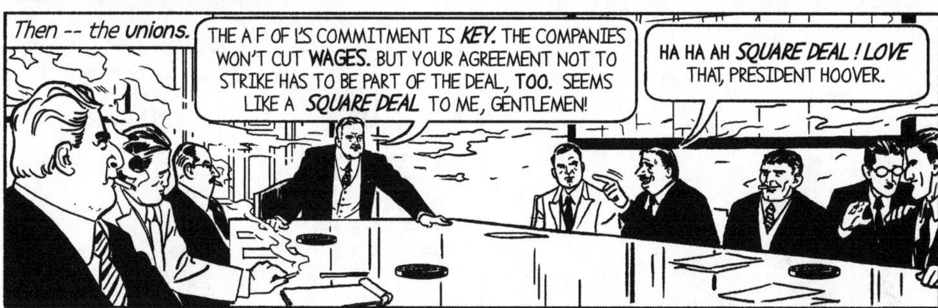

At the firms' offices, they saw matters **differently ...**

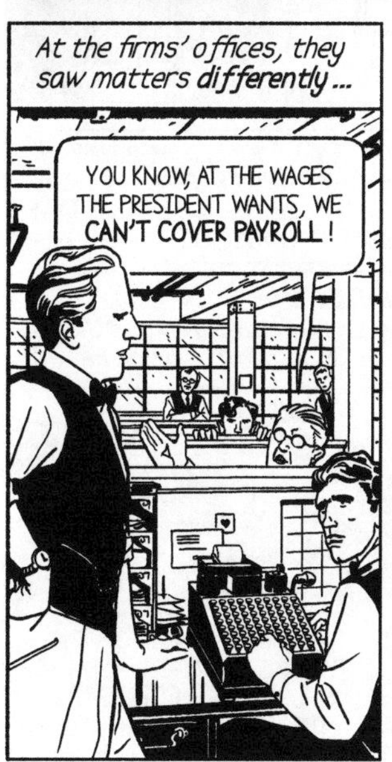

That winter, Hoover pushed Congress to endorse large **public spending projects.**

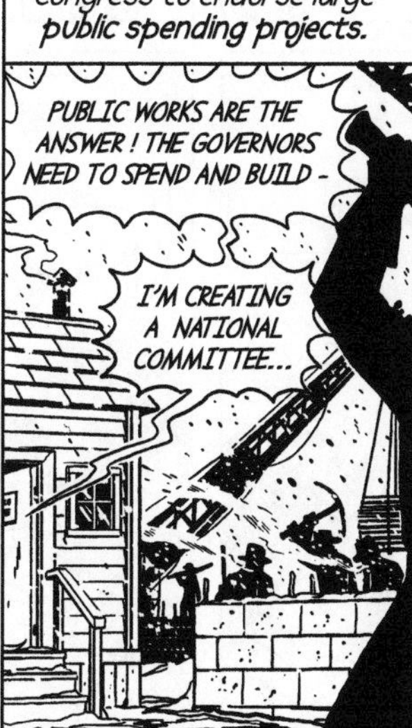

Along with all that, Hoover went to work on **farm prices**, trying to keep them high.

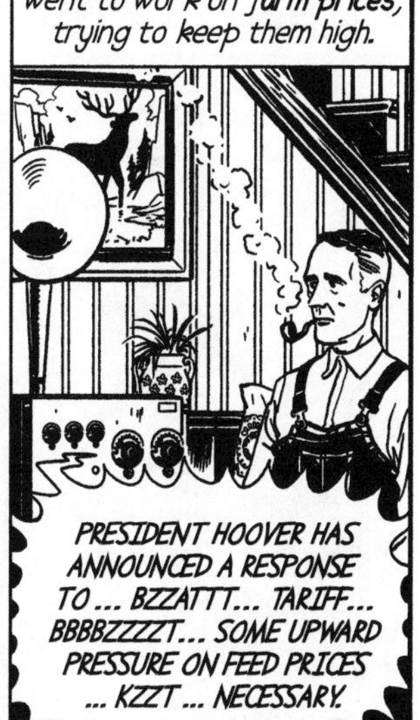

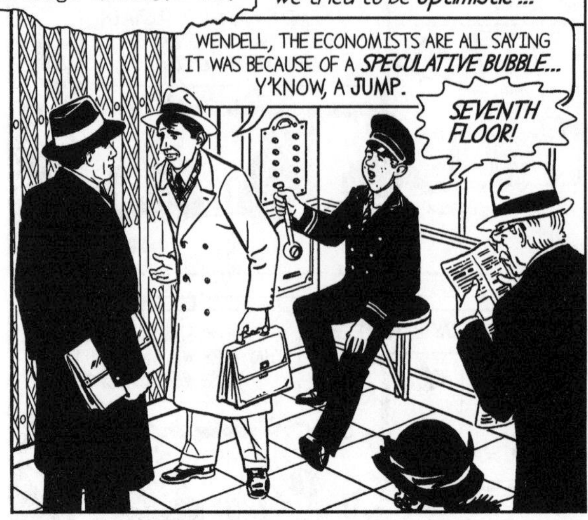

LOOK, WE'RE GETTING PAST THE *CREEPY* PART NOW!

THE FARMS HAVE YET TO BE **ELECTRIFIED**, AND *FIVE* CONCERNS VOTED TO MAKE COMMONWEALTH AND SOUTHERN THEIR *LEAD COMPANY*!

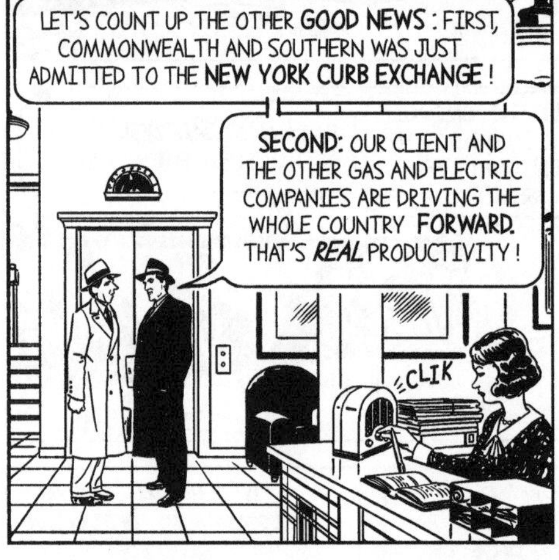

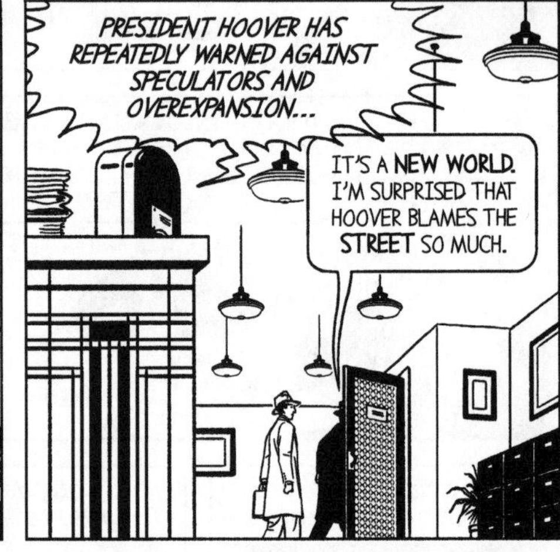

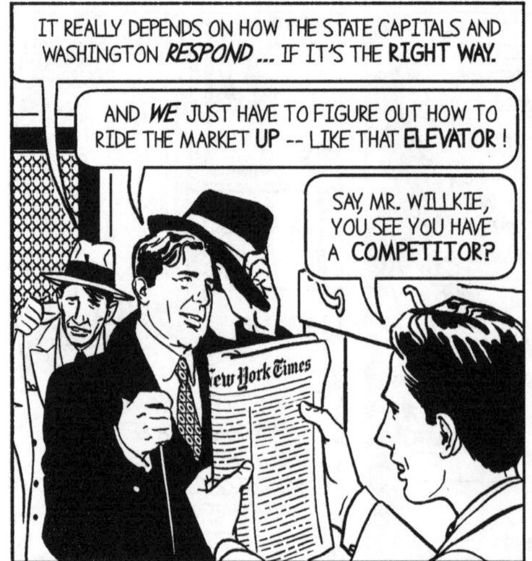

GOVERNOR ROOSEVELT SIGNED THE POWER LEGISLATION -- STATE OWNERSHIP OF WATER POWER. NOW HE WANTS TO CUT A DEAL WITH THE **CANADIANS** ON THE **ST. LAWRENCE**.

AND *ANOTHER* COMPETITOR: INSULL'S EXPANDING A PLANT NEAR HAMMOND, INDIANA. THAT'S WILLKIE TERRITORY! *HA HA HA*

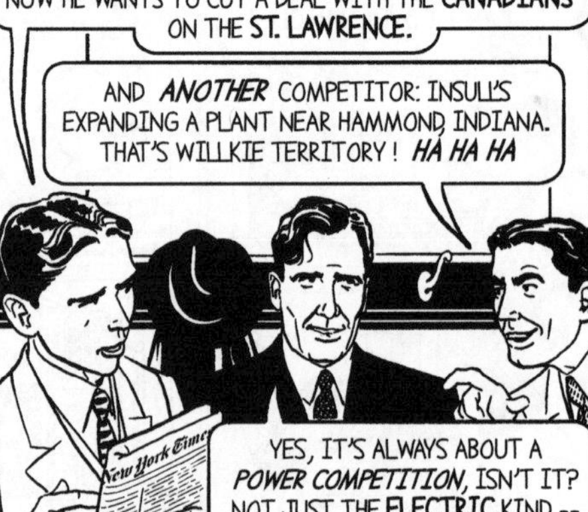

May 1930
Unemployment: 6.8%
Dow Jones (May 1): 275

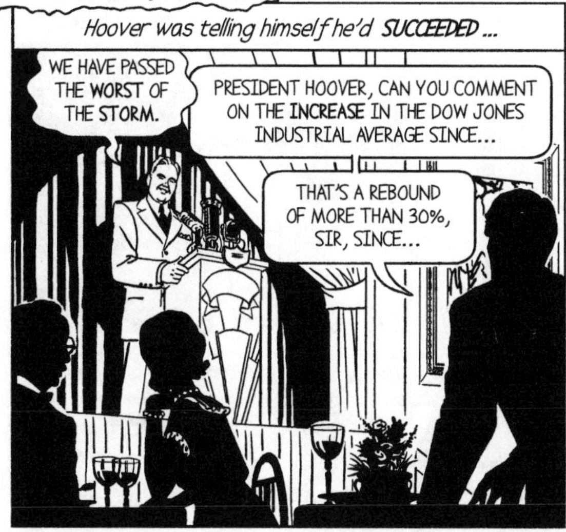

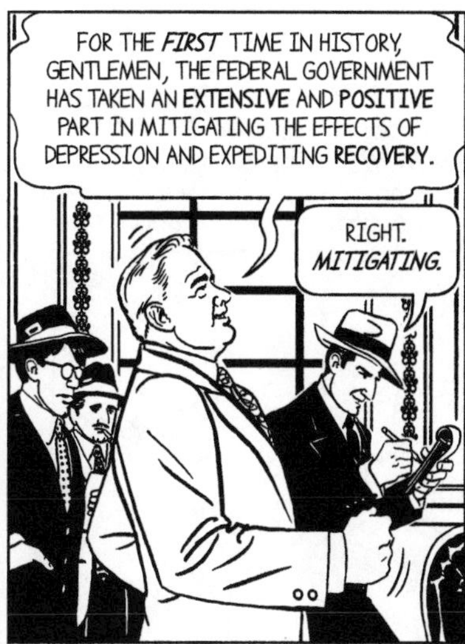

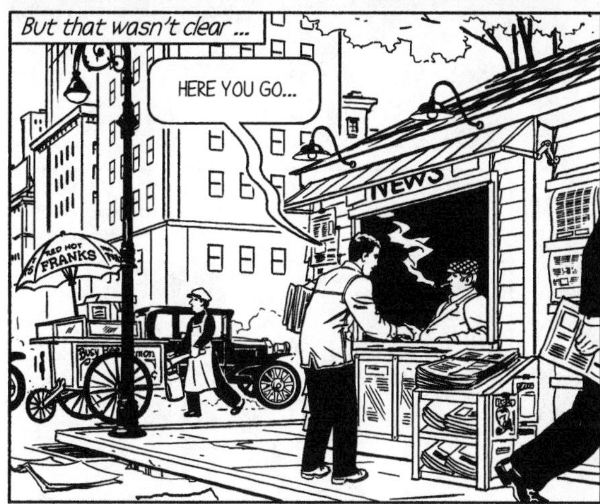

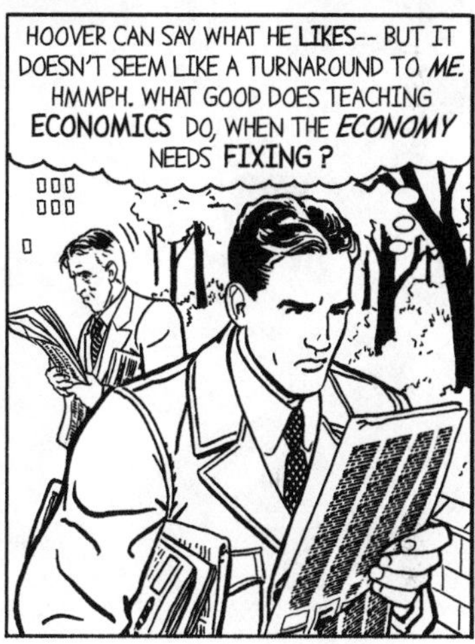

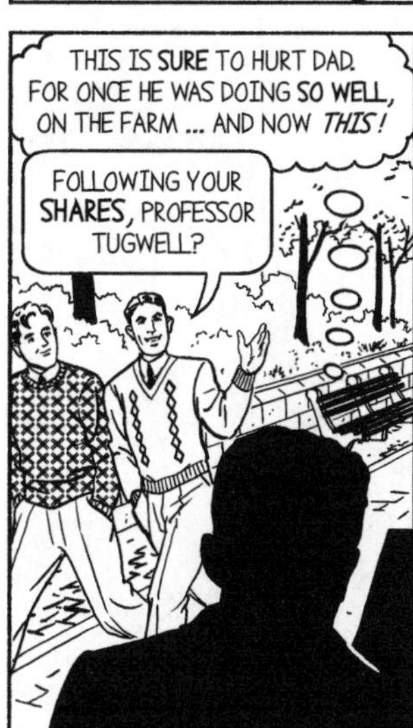

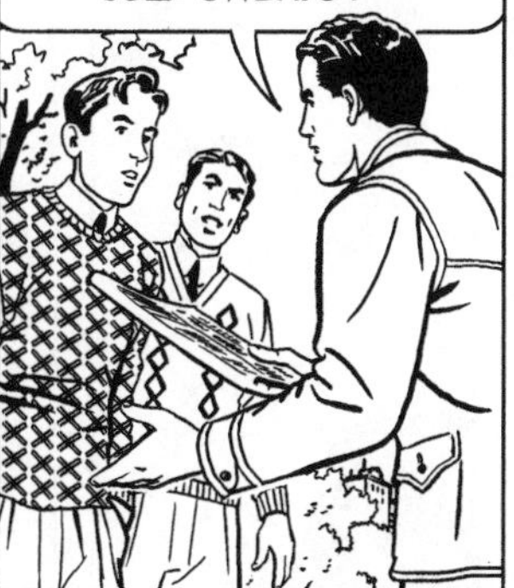

WEATHER, INSECTS, PRICE OF SEED... ...PRICE AT MARKET, ACTS OF GOD AND MAN...

UNPRODUCTIVE FARMS -- AND MAYBE THE MARKET DOESN'T STAY UP ...

GENTLEMEN, MARK MY WORDS: YOU'LL SEE TROUBLE REFLECTED IN THE MIDTERMS, COME NOVEMBER !

And Hoover made some **BAD** errors. The stock market was indeed trying to come back, like they said. But Congress was proposing the **BIGGEST TARIFF INCREASE IN HISTORY**! Ol' Herbert just couldn't **stop** himself -- he went and helped the **Republicans push through** that tariff!

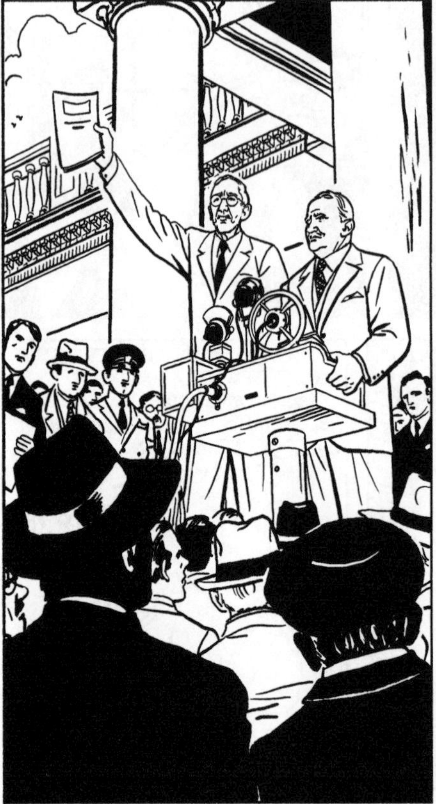

Everyone **else** seemed to know that the tariff was **wrong**...

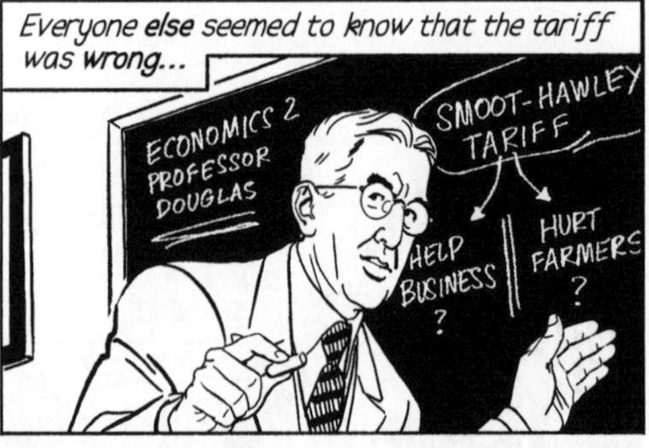

We even heard that the profs were wondering **overseas**.

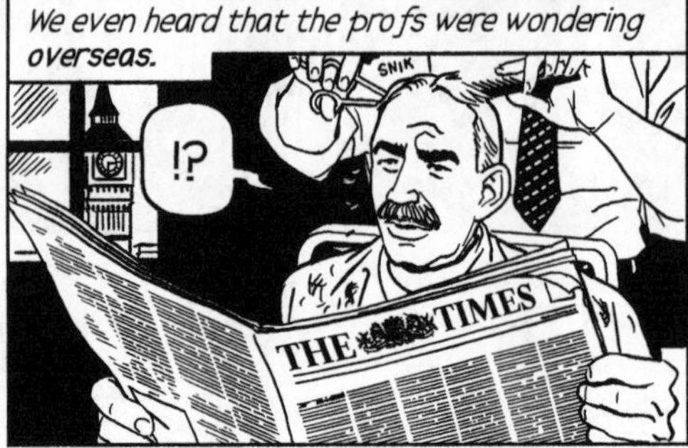

In the U.S., the **academics** were so **angry** that a **thousand professors** signed a **petition** against the tariff--even some from Hoover's old school!

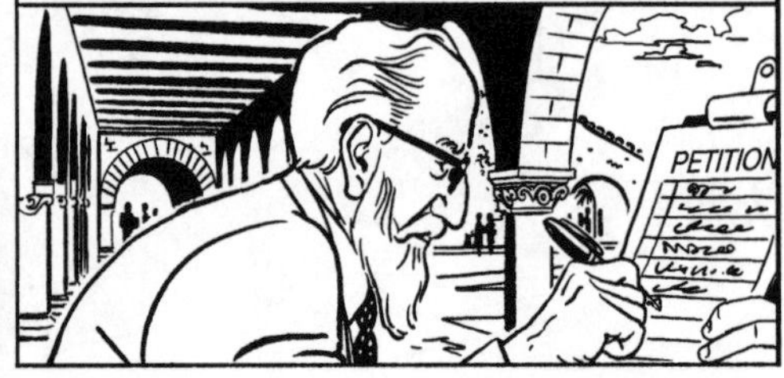

Hoover saw that he was doing **damage** ...

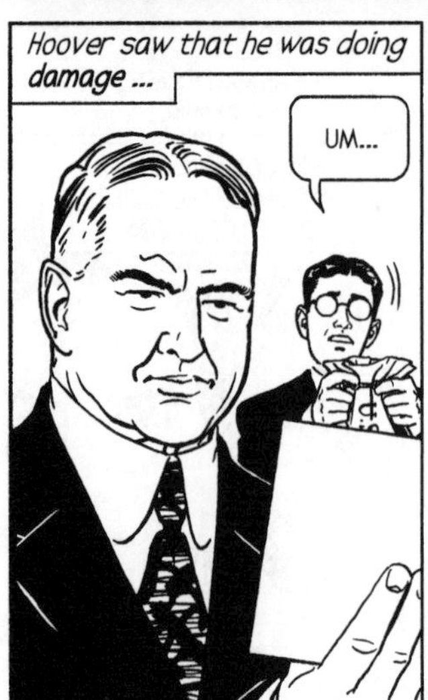

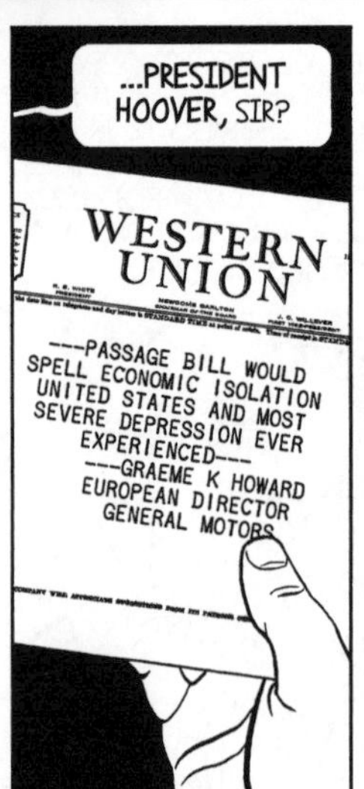

...But still, he flattered himself that he had it all under **control**!

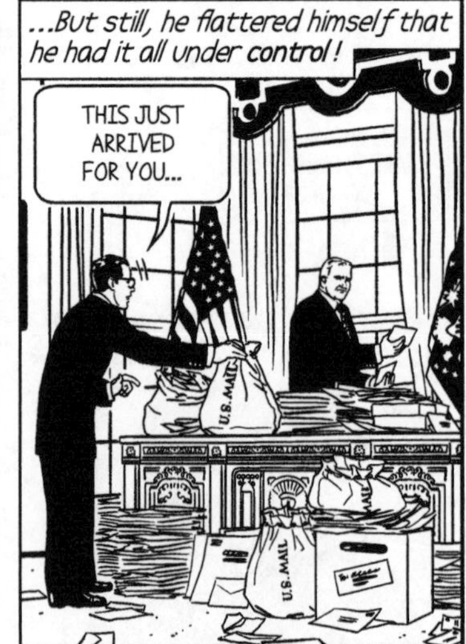

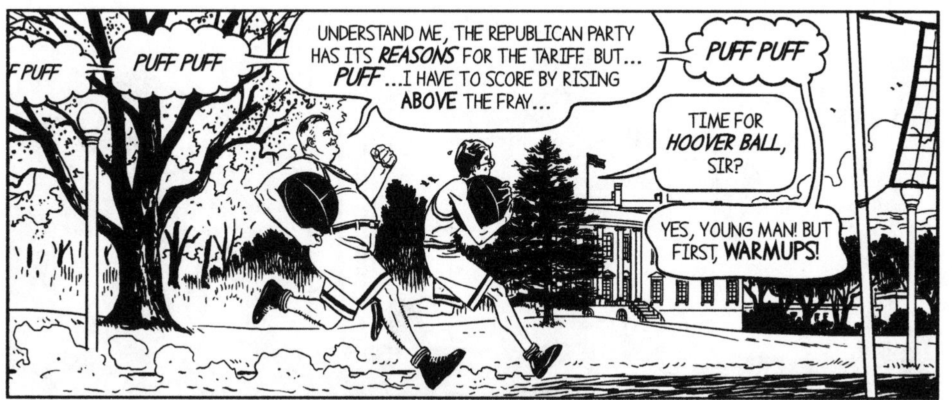
PUFF
PUFF PUFF
UNDERSTAND ME, THE REPUBLICAN PARTY HAS ITS REASONS FOR THE TARIFF. BUT... PUFF...I HAVE TO SCORE BY RISING ABOVE THE FRAY...
PUFF PUFF
TIME FOR HOOVER BALL, SIR?
YES, YOUNG MAN! BUT FIRST, WARMUPS!

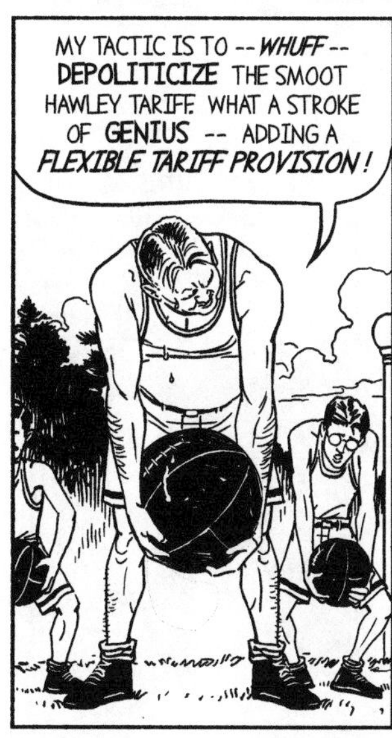
MY TACTIC IS TO --WHUFF-- DEPOLITICIZE THE SMOOT HAWLEY TARIFF. WHAT A STROKE OF GENIUS -- ADDING A FLEXIBLE TARIFF PROVISION!

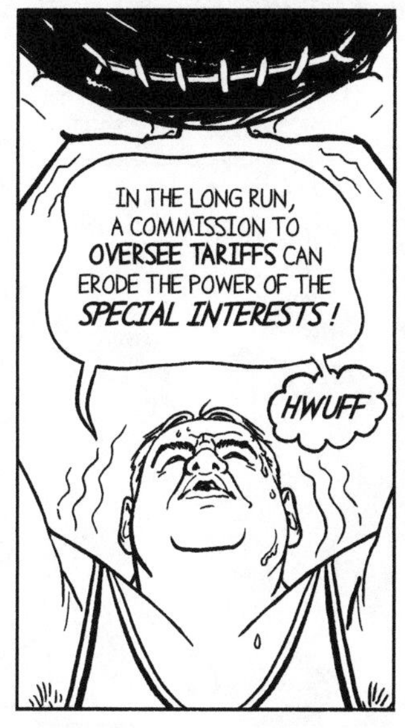
IN THE LONG RUN, A COMMISSION TO OVERSEE TARIFFS CAN ERODE THE POWER OF THE SPECIAL INTERESTS!
HWUFF

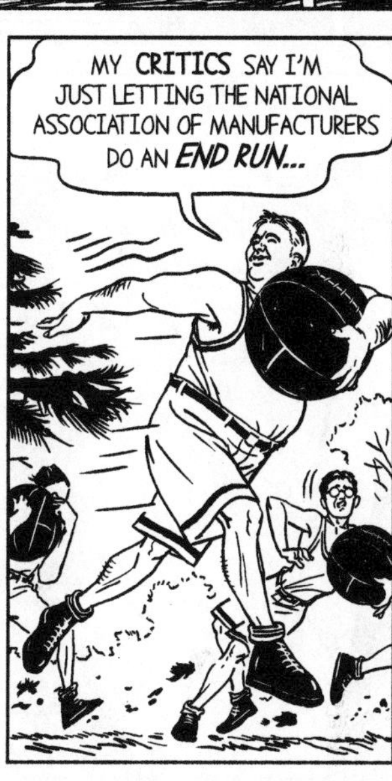
MY CRITICS SAY I'M JUST LETTING THE NATIONAL ASSOCIATION OF MANUFACTURERS DO AN END RUN...

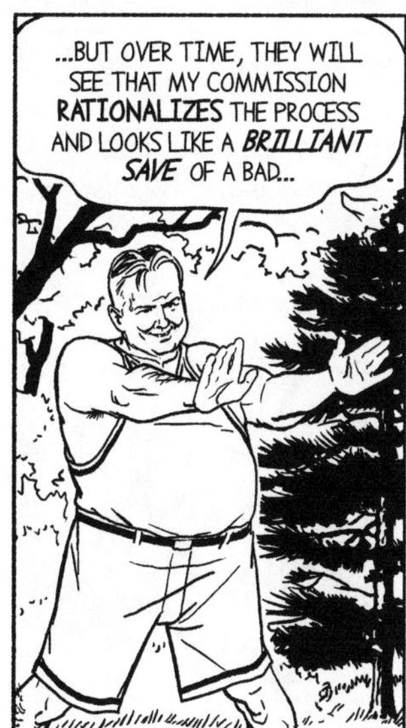
...BUT OVER TIME, THEY WILL SEE THAT MY COMMISSION RATIONALIZES THE PROCESS AND LOOKS LIKE A BRILLIANT SAVE OF A BAD...

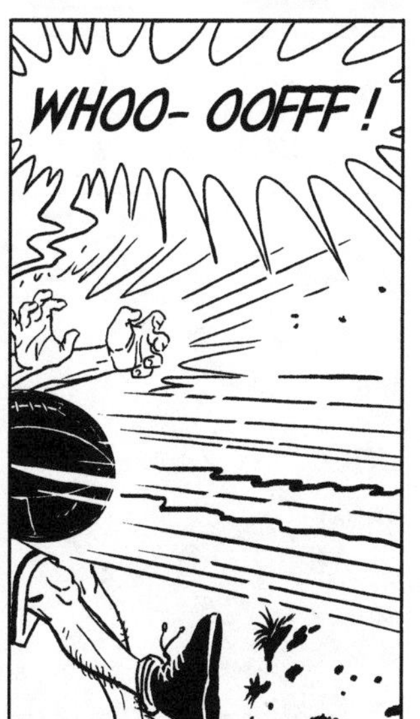
WHOO- OOFFF!

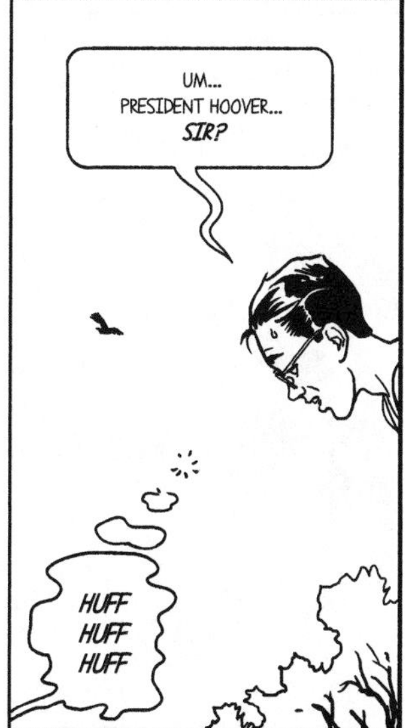
UM... PRESIDENT HOOVER... SIR?
HUFF HUFF HUFF

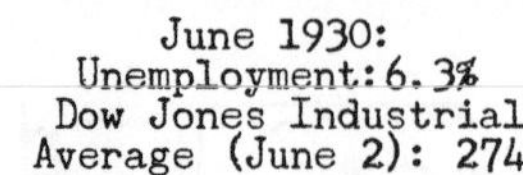
June 1930:
Unemployment: 6.3%
Dow Jones Industrial Average (June 2): 274

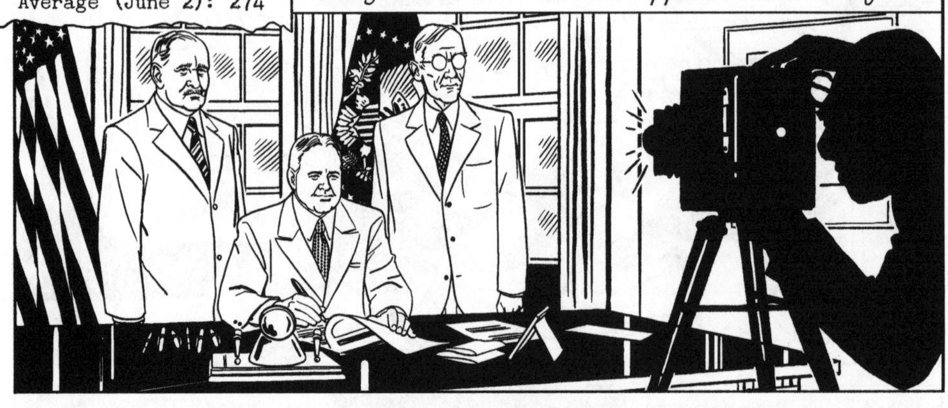
Washington knew that Hoover had slipped on Smoot - Hawley.

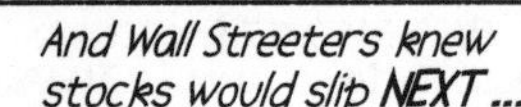
And Wall Streeters knew stocks would slip NEXT ...

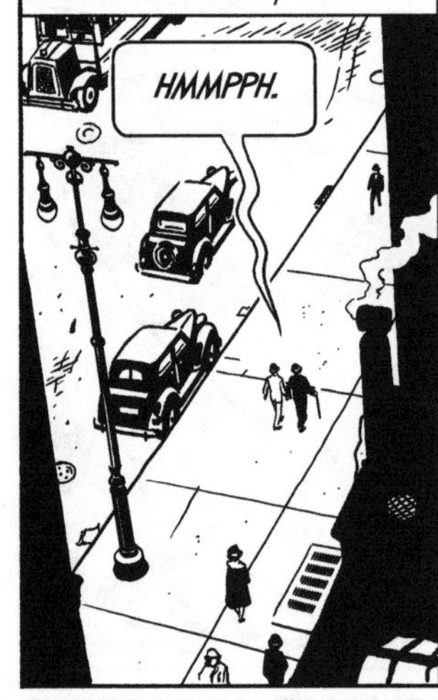
HMMPPH.

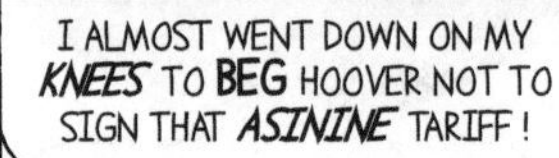
I ALMOST WENT DOWN ON MY KNEES TO BEG HOOVER NOT TO SIGN THAT ASININE TARIFF !

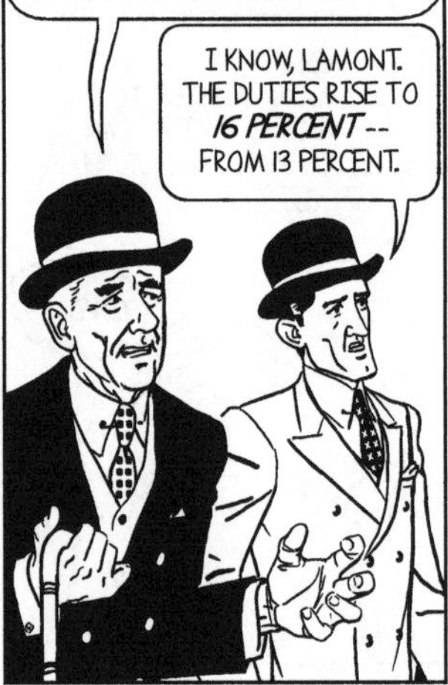
I KNOW, LAMONT. THE DUTIES RISE TO 16 PERCENT -- FROM 13 PERCENT.

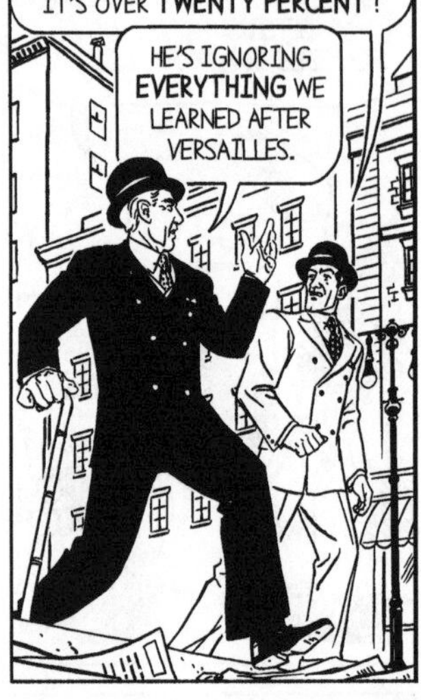
DOESN'T SOUND LIKE A LOT, BUT IT'S OVER TWENTY PERCENT !
HE'S IGNORING EVERYTHING WE LEARNED AFTER VERSAILLES.

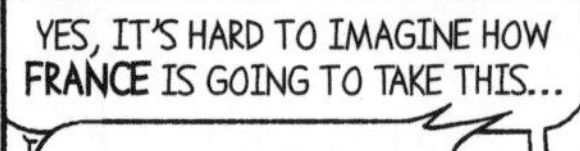
YES, IT'S HARD TO IMAGINE HOW FRANCE IS GOING TO TAKE THIS...

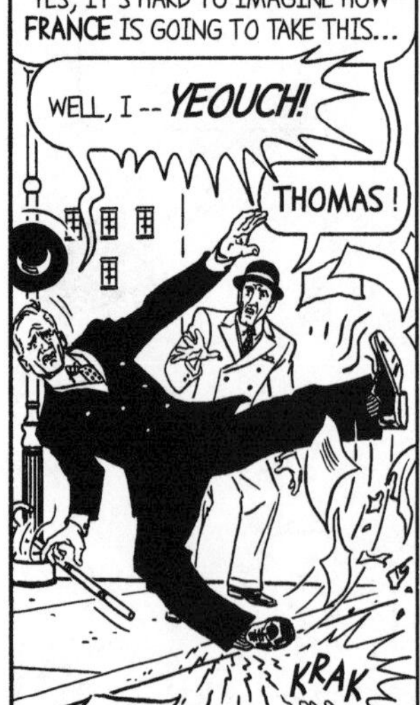
WELL, I -- YEOUCH!
THOMAS !
KRAK

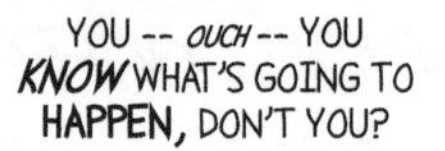
YOU -- OUCH -- YOU KNOW WHAT'S GOING TO HAPPEN, DON'T YOU?

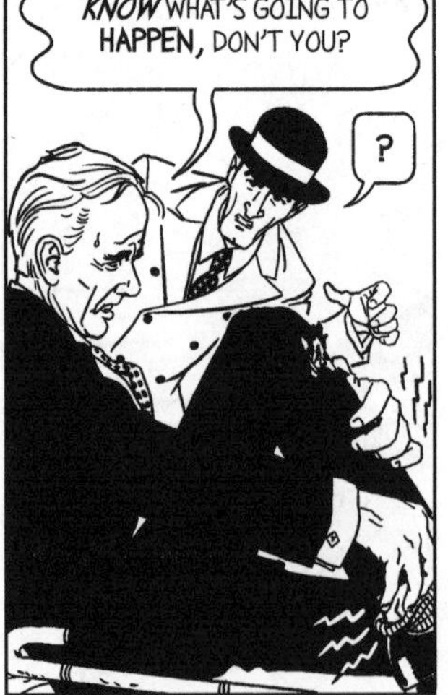
?

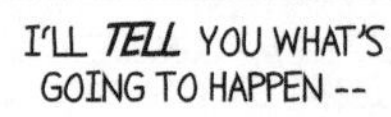
I'LL TELL YOU WHAT'S GOING TO HAPPEN --
-- THE MARKET IS GOING TO DROP OFF A CLIFF !
OUCH

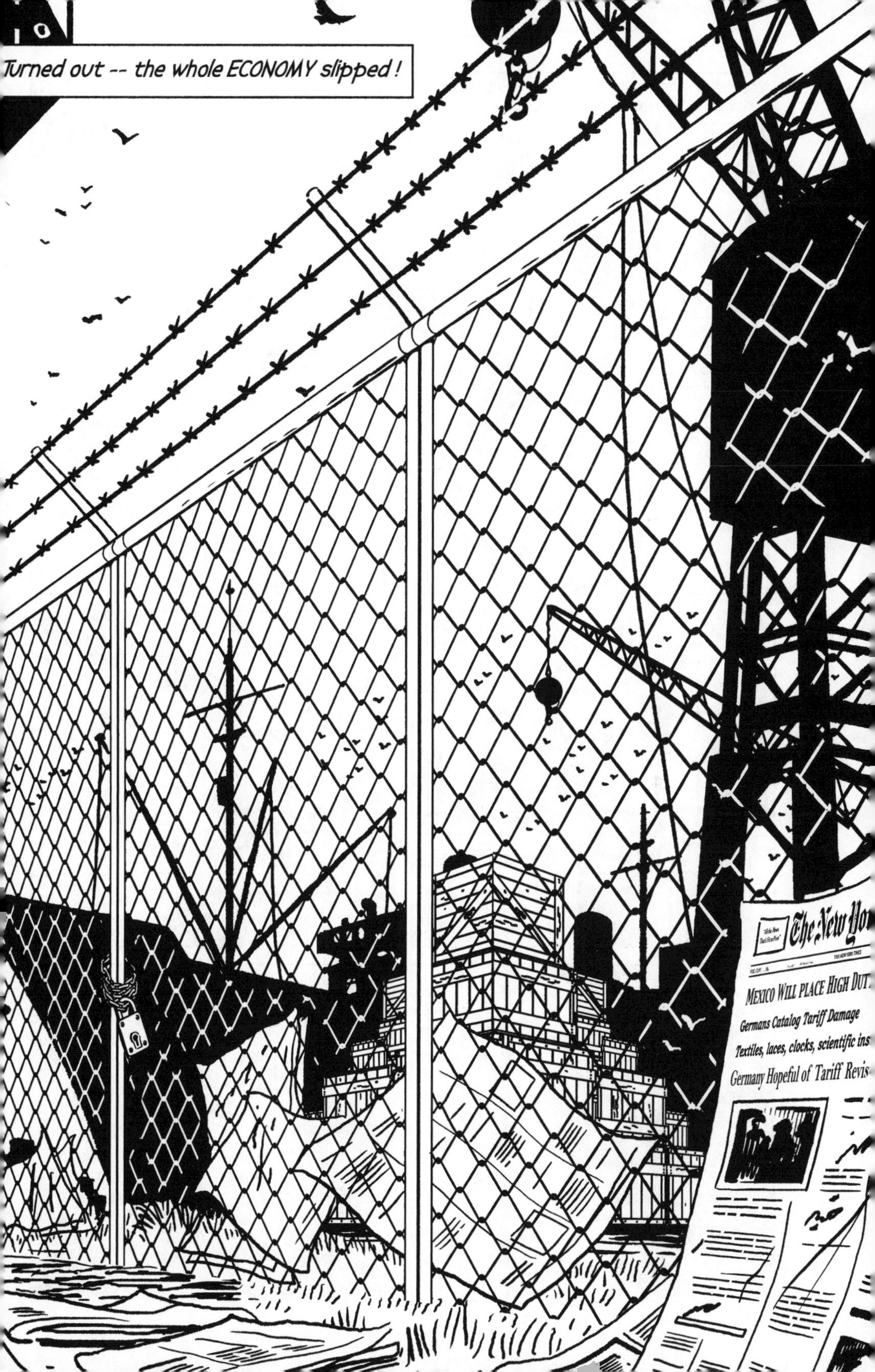
10
Turned out -- the whole ECONOMY slipped!
MEXICO WILL PLACE HIGH DUT
Germans Catalog Tariff Damage
Textiles, laces, clocks, scientific ins
Germany Hopeful of Tariff Revis

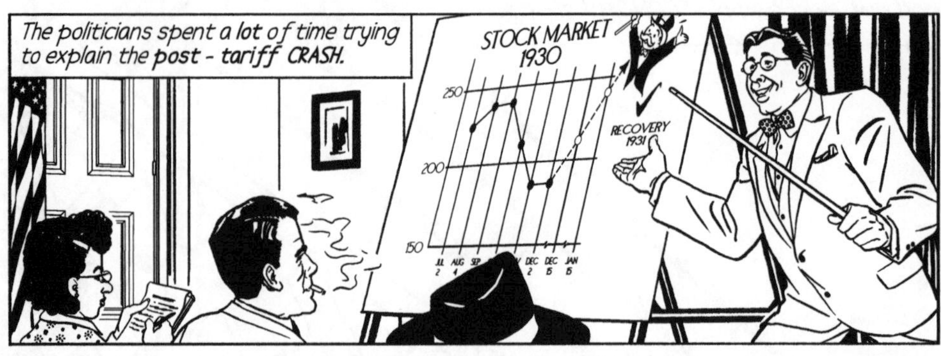

The politicians spent a lot of time trying to explain the post - tariff CRASH.
STOCK MARKET 1930
250
200
150
RECOVERY 1931

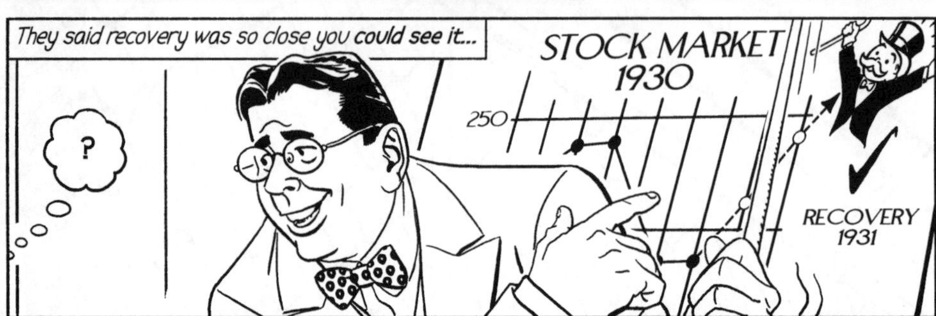

They said recovery was so close you could see it...
?
STOCK MARKET 1930
250
RECOVERY 1931

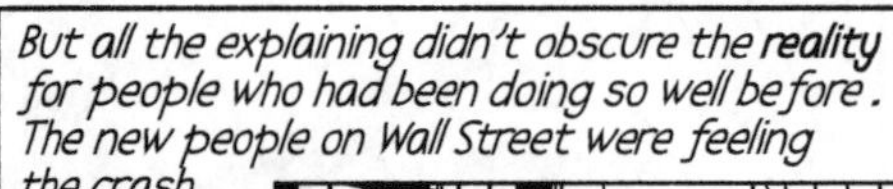

But all the explaining didn't obscure the reality for people who had been doing so well before. The new people on Wall Street were feeling the crash...

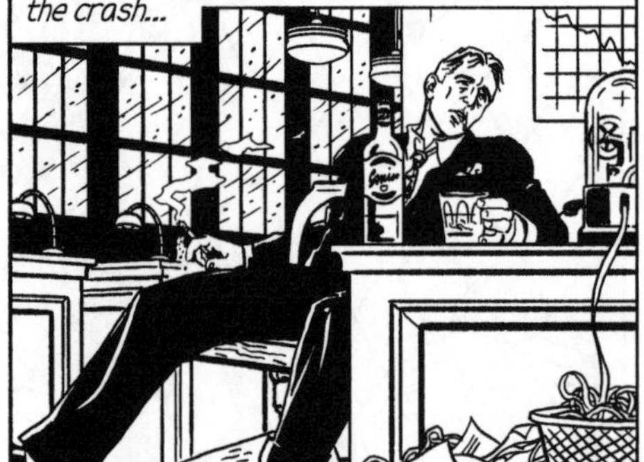

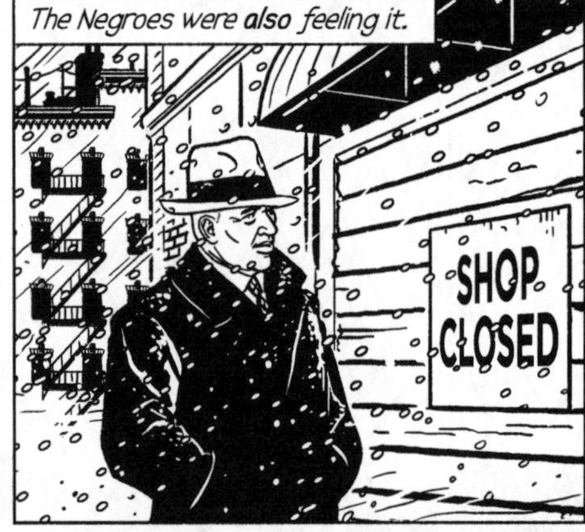

The Negroes were also feeling it.
SHOP CLOSED

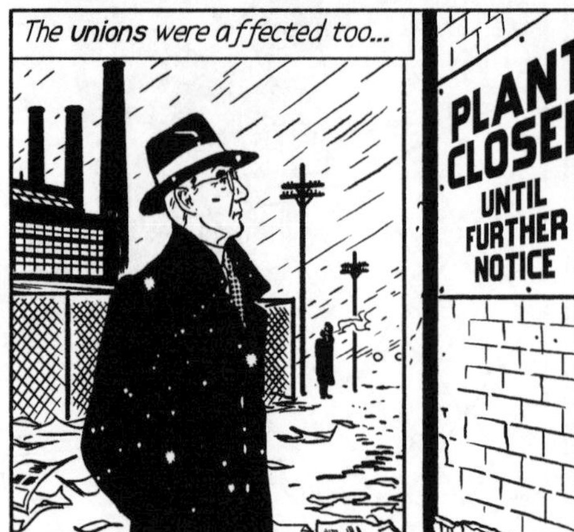

The unions were affected too...
PLANT
CLOSE
UNTIL FURTHER NOTICE

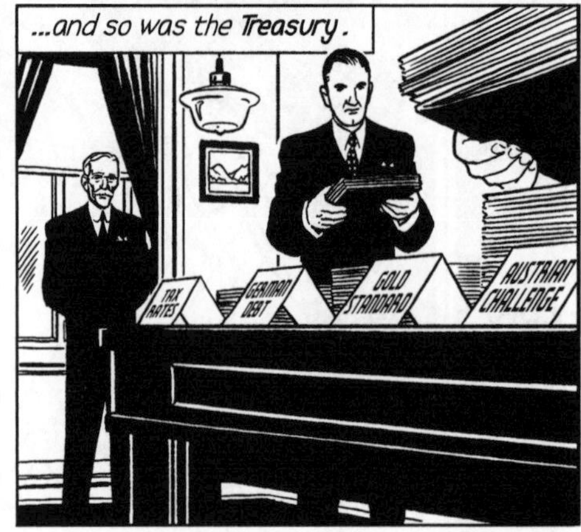

...and so was the Treasury.
TAX RATES
GERMAN DEBT
GOLD STANDARD
AUSTRIAN CHALLENGE

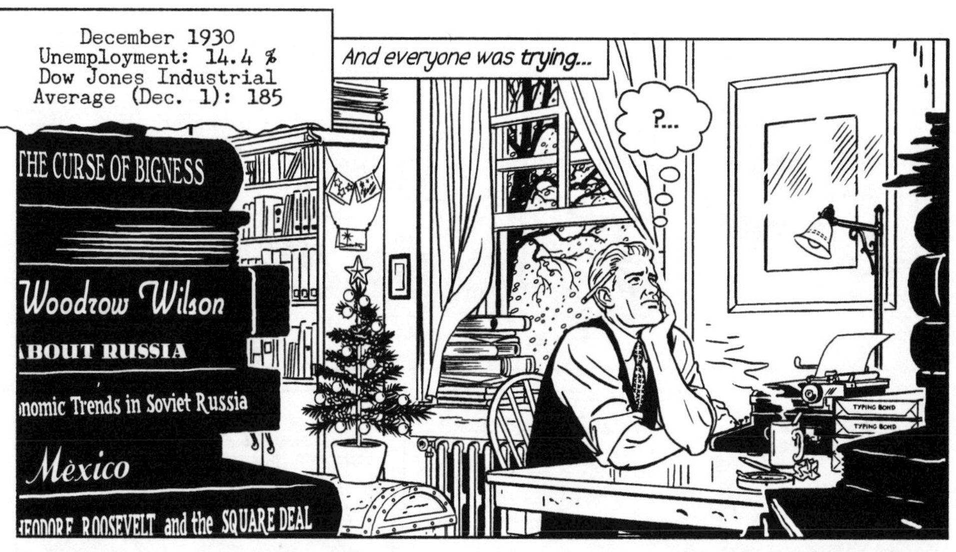
December 1930
Unemployment: 14.4 %
Dow Jones Industrial
Average (Dec. 1): 185
And everyone was trying...
?...
THE CURSE OF BIGNESS
Woodrow Wilson
ABOUT RUSSIA
nomic Trends in Soviet Russia
Mèxico
HEODORE ROOSEVELT and the SQUARE DEAL
TYPING BOND
TYPING BOND

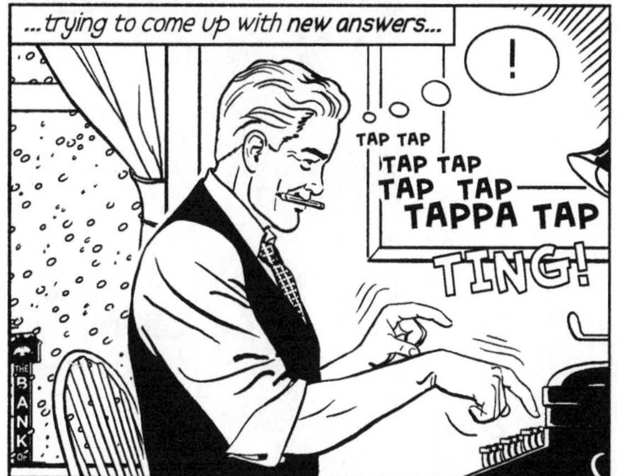
...trying to come up with new answers...
!
TAP TAP
TAP TAP
TAP TAP
TAPPA TAP
TING!

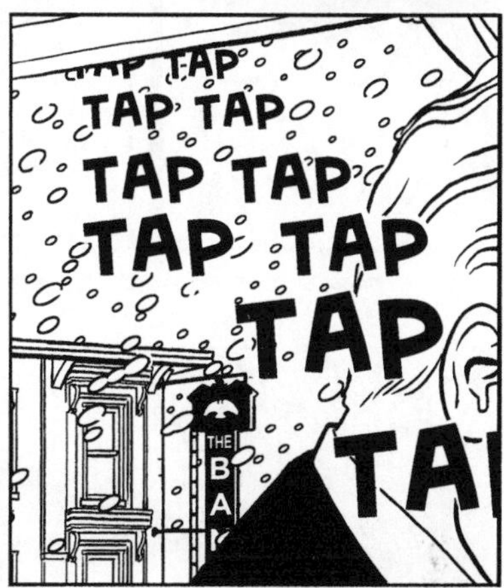
TAP TAP
TAP TAP
TAP TAP
TAP TAP
TAP

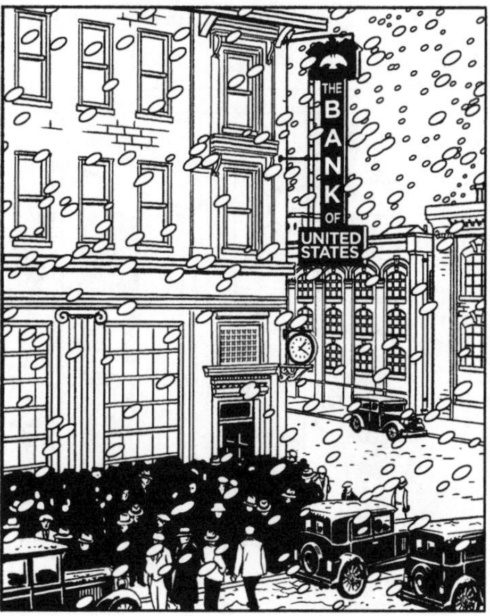
THE BANK OF UNITED STATES

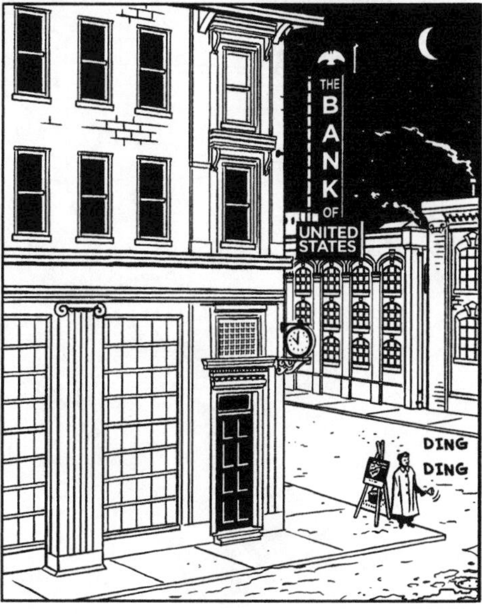
THE BANK OF UNITED STATES
DING
DING

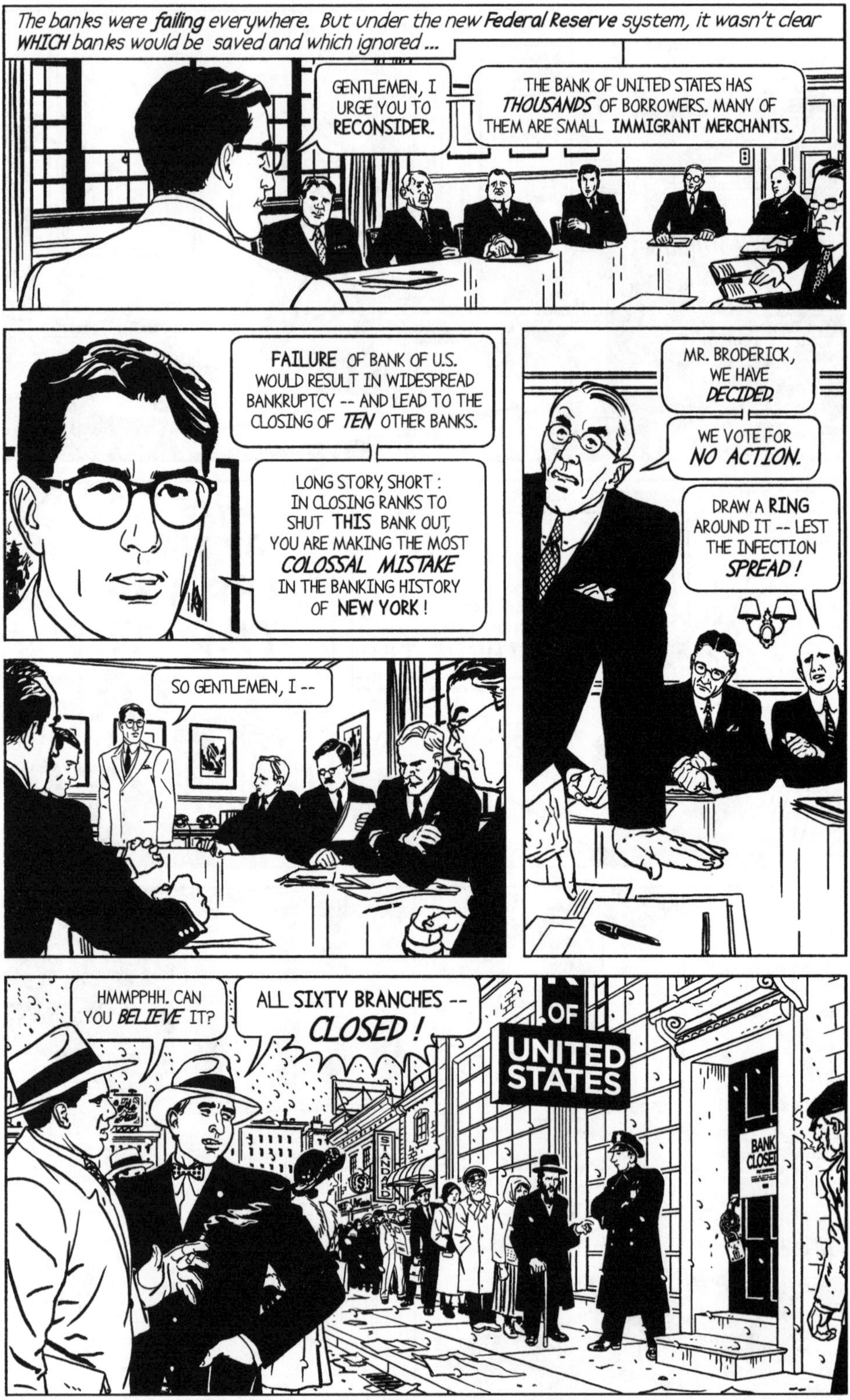

*The banks were **failing** everywhere. But under the new **Federal Reserve** system, it wasn't clear **WHICH** banks would be saved and which ignored ...*

GENTLEMEN, I URGE YOU TO **RECONSIDER.**

THE BANK OF UNITED STATES HAS ***THOUSANDS*** OF BORROWERS. MANY OF THEM ARE SMALL **IMMIGRANT MERCHANTS.**

FAILURE OF BANK OF U.S. WOULD RESULT IN WIDESPREAD BANKRUPTCY -- AND LEAD TO THE CLOSING OF ***TEN*** OTHER BANKS.

LONG STORY, SHORT : IN CLOSING RANKS TO SHUT **THIS** BANK OUT, YOU ARE MAKING THE MOST ***COLOSSAL MISTAKE*** IN THE BANKING HISTORY OF **NEW YORK** !

MR. BRODERICK, WE HAVE ***DECIDED.***

WE VOTE FOR ***NO ACTION.***

DRAW A **RING** AROUND IT -- LEST THE INFECTION ***SPREAD !***

SO GENTLEMEN, I --

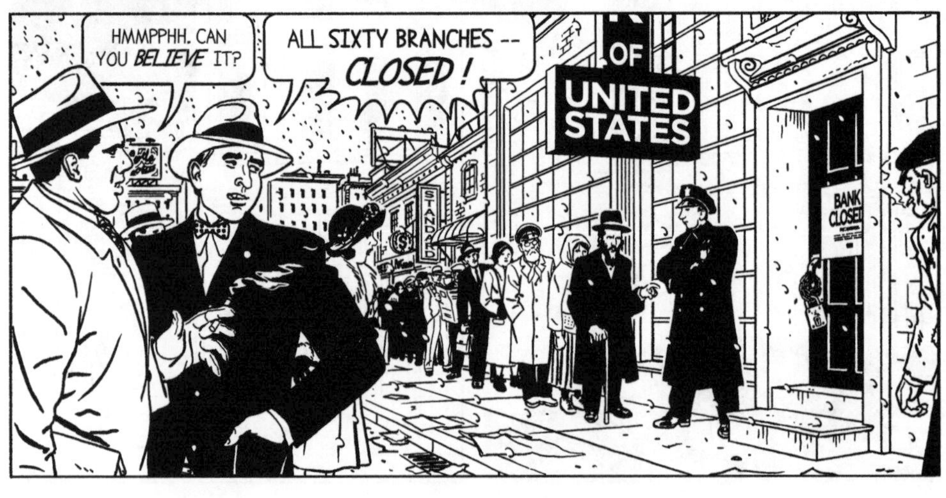

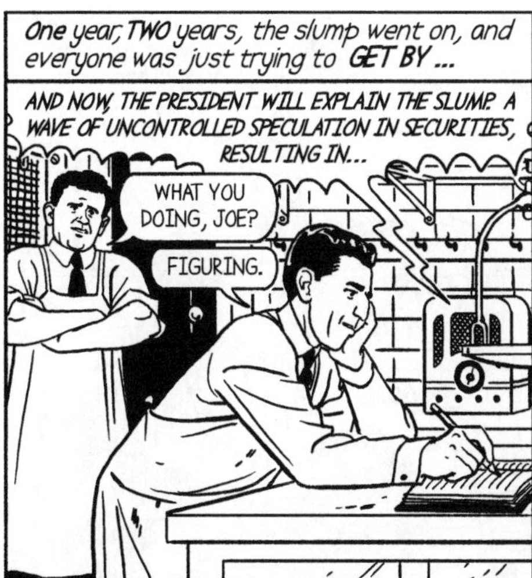
One year, TWO years, the slump went on, and everyone was just trying to GET BY ...
AND NOW, THE PRESIDENT WILL EXPLAIN THE SLUMP. A WAVE OF UNCONTROLLED SPECULATION IN SECURITIES, RESULTING IN...
WHAT YOU DOING, JOE?
FIGURING.

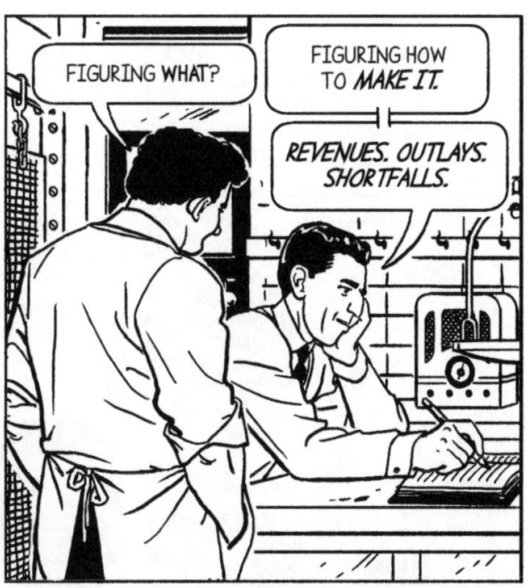
FIGURING WHAT?
FIGURING HOW TO MAKE IT.
REVENUES. OUTLAYS. SHORTFALLS.

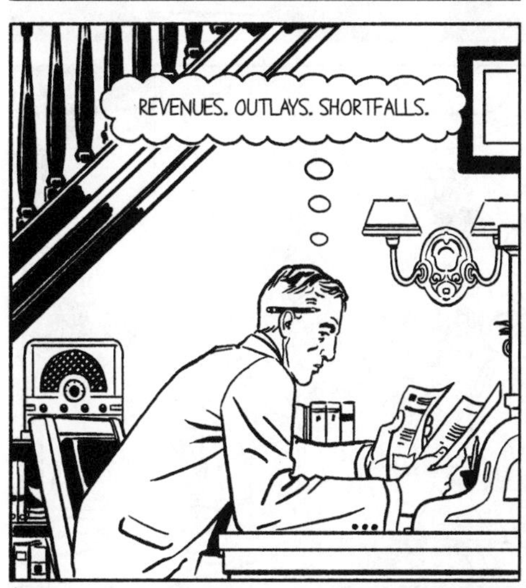
REVENUES. OUTLAYS. SHORTFALLS.

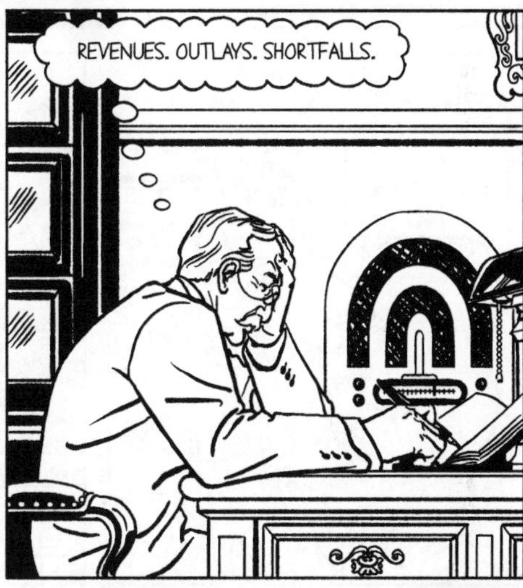
REVENUES. OUTLAYS. SHORTFALLS.

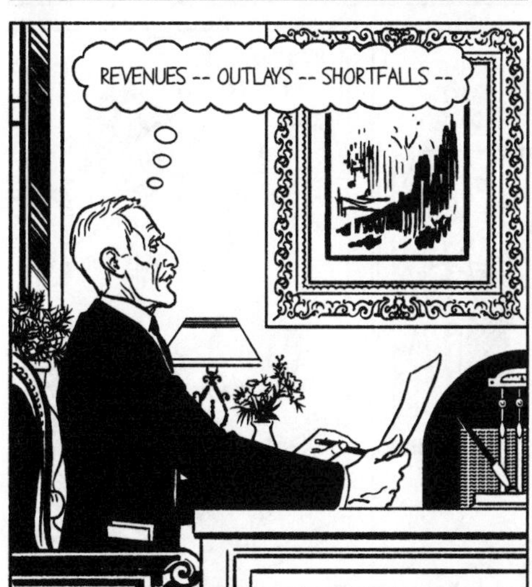
REVENUES -- OUTLAYS -- SHORTFALLS --

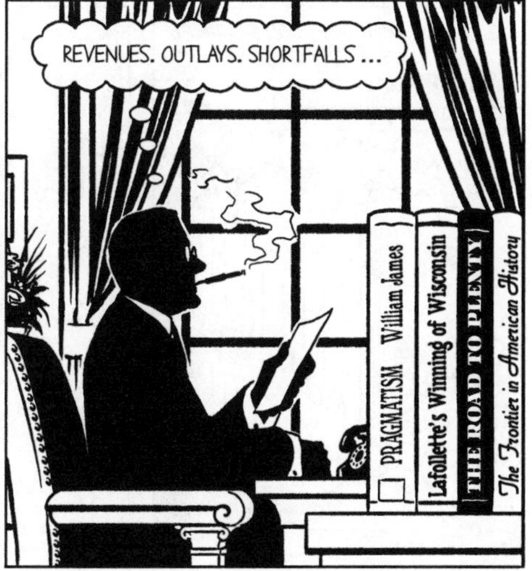
REVENUES. OUTLAYS. SHORTFALLS ...
PRAGMATISM William James
Lafollette's Winning of Wisconsin
THE ROAD TO PLENTY
The Frontier in American History

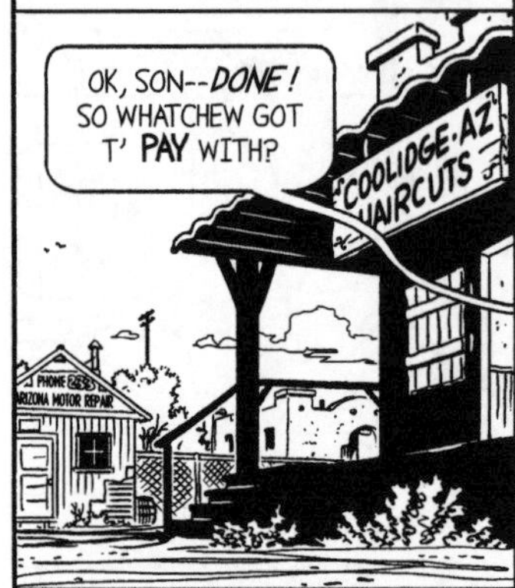
As 1931 passed, men all over were out of work. The radio gave us news about foreign banks, but all we knew was that money was running out -- LITERALLY.
OK, SON--DONE! SO WHATCHEW GOT T' PAY WITH?
COOLIDGE, AZ HAIRCUTS
PHONE
ARIZONA MOTOR REPAIR

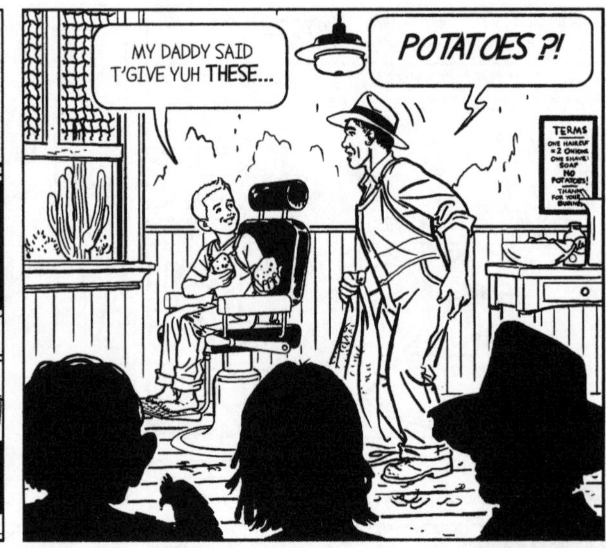
MY DADDY SAID T'GIVE YUH THESE...
POTATOES ?!
TERMS

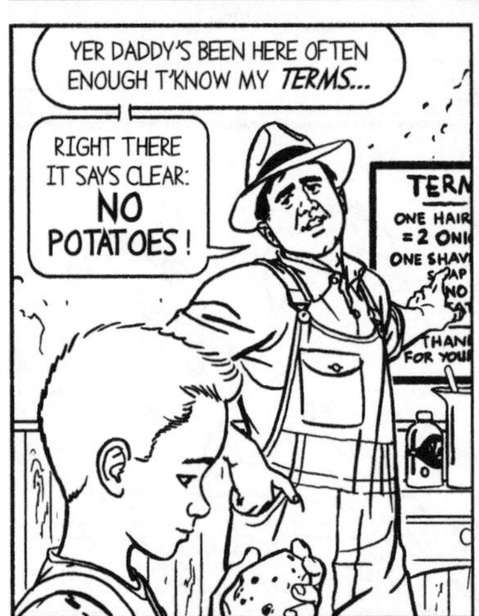
YER DADDY'S BEEN HERE OFTEN ENOUGH T'KNOW MY TERMS...
RIGHT THERE IT SAYS CLEAR: NO POTATOES!

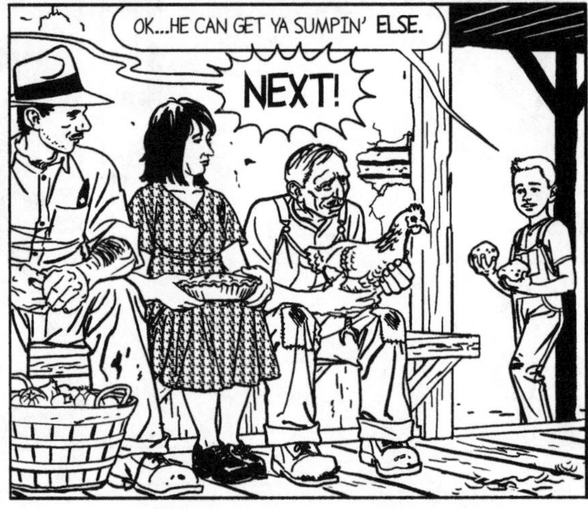
OK...HE CAN GET YA SUMPIN' ELSE.
NEXT!

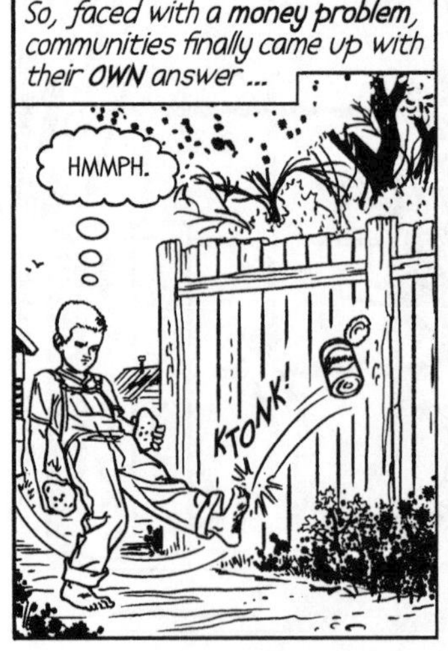
So, faced with a money problem, communities finally came up with their OWN answer ...
HMMPH.
KTONK!

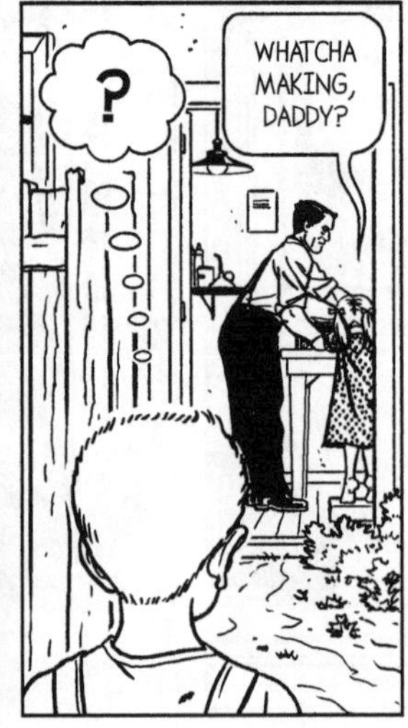
?
WHATCHA MAKING, DADDY?

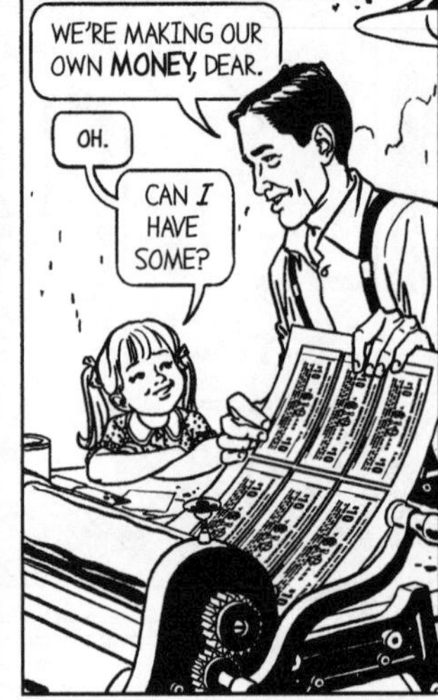
WE'RE MAKING OUR OWN MONEY, DEAR.
OH.
CAN I HAVE SOME?

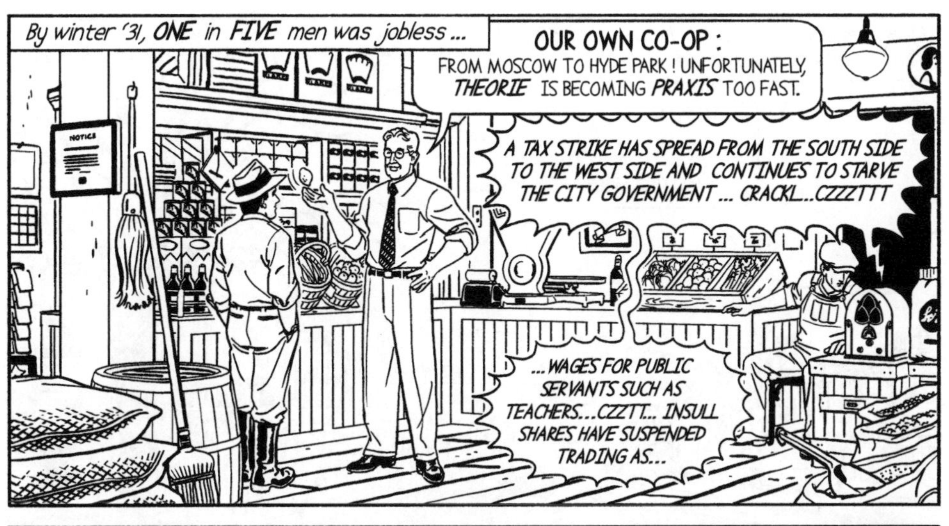
By winter '31, ONE in FIVE men was jobless ...
OUR OWN CO-OP : FROM MOSCOW TO HYDE PARK ! UNFORTUNATELY, THEORIE IS BECOMING PRAXIS TOO FAST.
A TAX STRIKE HAS SPREAD FROM THE SOUTH SIDE TO THE WEST SIDE AND CONTINUES TO STARVE THE CITY GOVERNMENT ... CRACKL...CZZZTTT
...WAGES FOR PUBLIC SERVANTS SUCH AS TEACHERS...CZZTT... INSULL SHARES HAVE SUSPENDED TRADING AS...

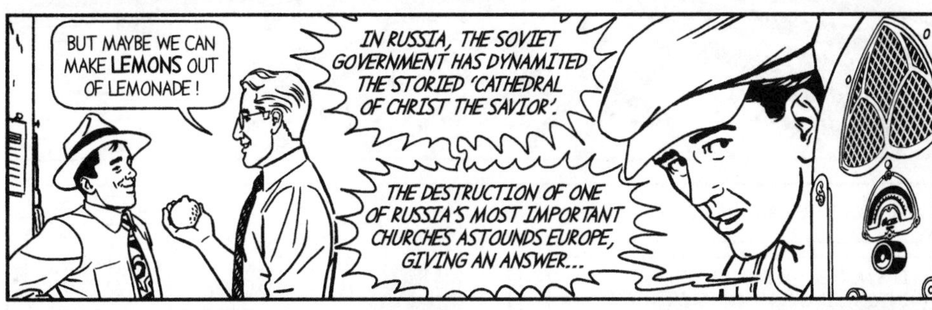
BUT MAYBE WE CAN MAKE LEMONS OUT OF LEMONADE !
IN RUSSIA, THE SOVIET GOVERNMENT HAS DYNAMITED THE STORIED 'CATHEDRAL OF CHRIST THE SAVIOR'.
THE DESTRUCTION OF ONE OF RUSSIA'S MOST IMPORTANT CHURCHES ASTOUNDS EUROPE, GIVING AN ANSWER...

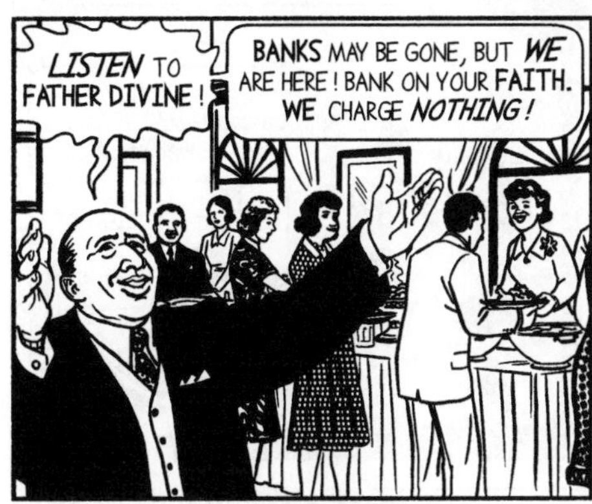
LISTEN TO FATHER DIVINE !
BANKS MAY BE GONE, BUT WE ARE HERE ! BANK ON YOUR FAITH. WE CHARGE NOTHING !

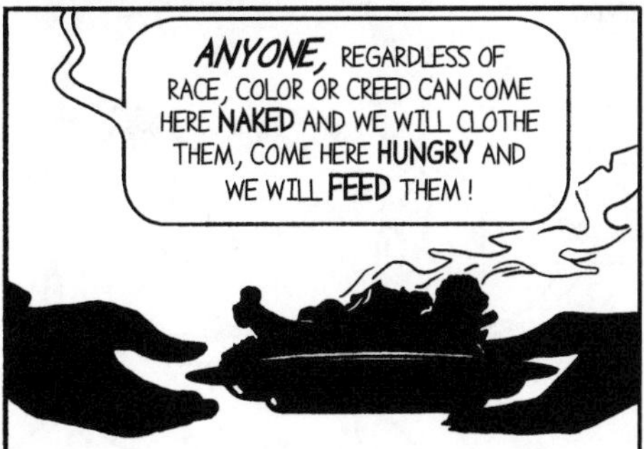
ANYONE, REGARDLESS OF RACE, COLOR OR CREED CAN COME HERE NAKED AND WE WILL CLOTHE THEM, COME HERE HUNGRY AND WE WILL FEED THEM !

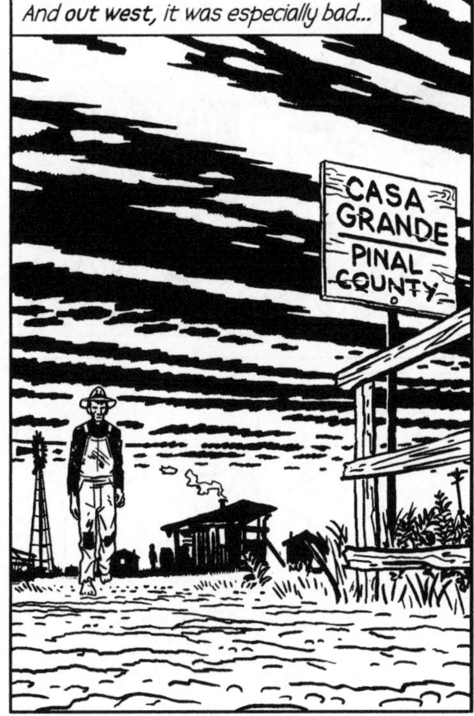
And out west, it was especially bad...
CASA GRANDE
PINAL COUNTY

Everyone knew someone who was **losing his shirt**. Rex Tugwell's father struggled especially hard. That made Rex **determined ...**

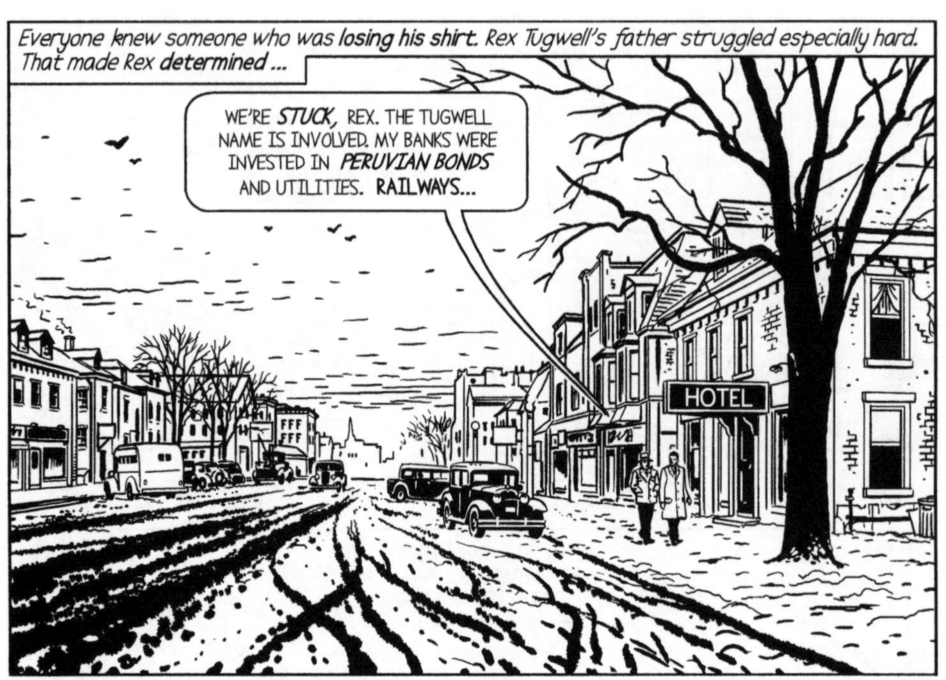

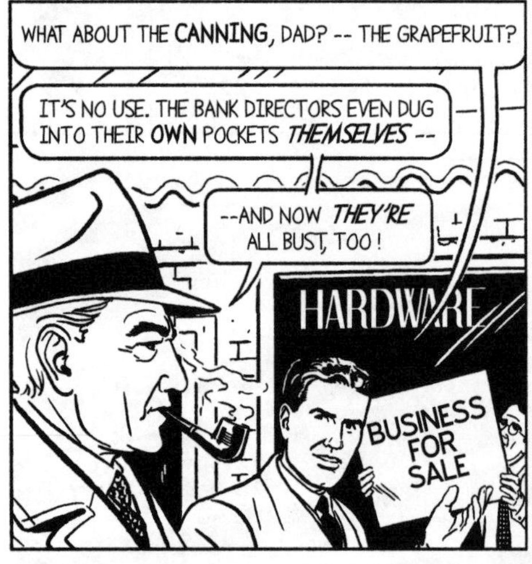

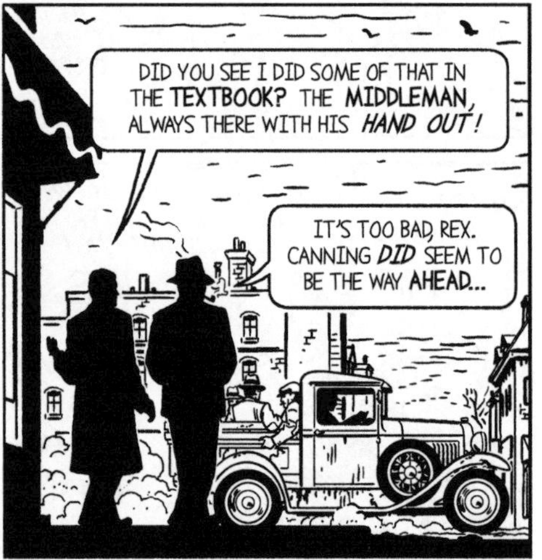

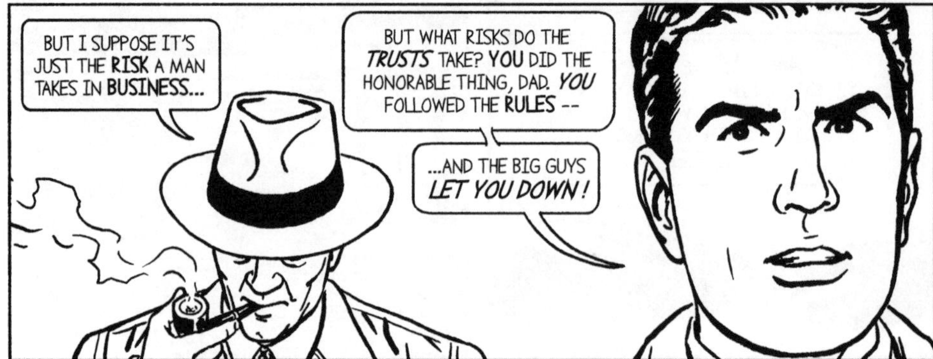

January 1932
Unemployment: 19.7%
Dow Jones Industrial
Average: (Jan. 4): 72

The professors couldn't agree on solutions. Inflation? Credit? Deflation? No one really knew what was going on.

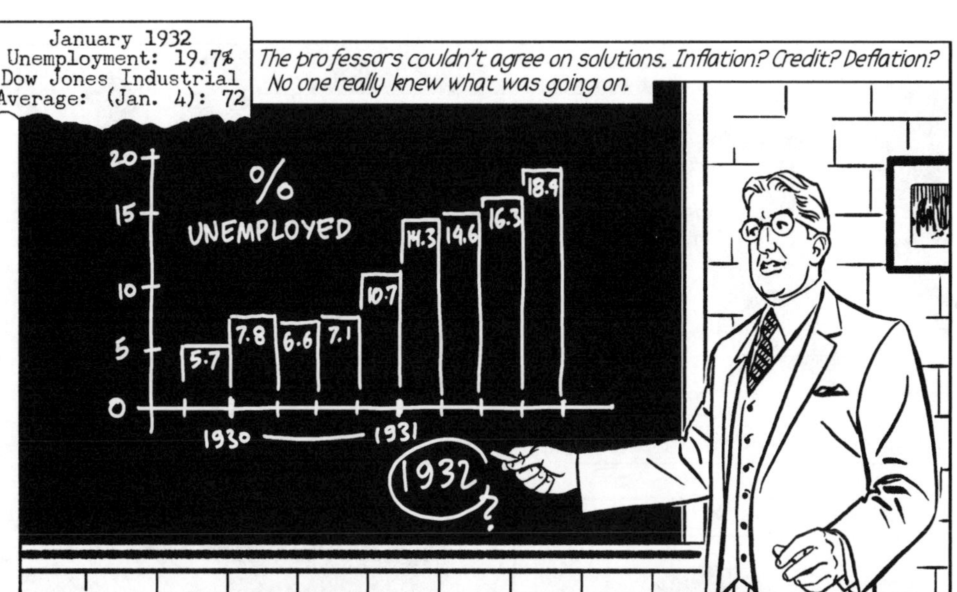

*People started to believe recovery **wouldn't come** ...*

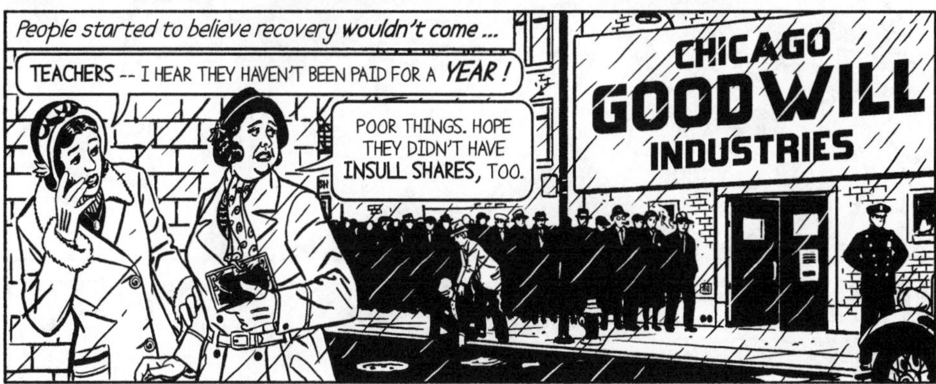

*Do you recall that **article** about the downturn? It spoke of "men who have never before had this sort of experience, for whom it is a personal tragedy too deep for words"...*

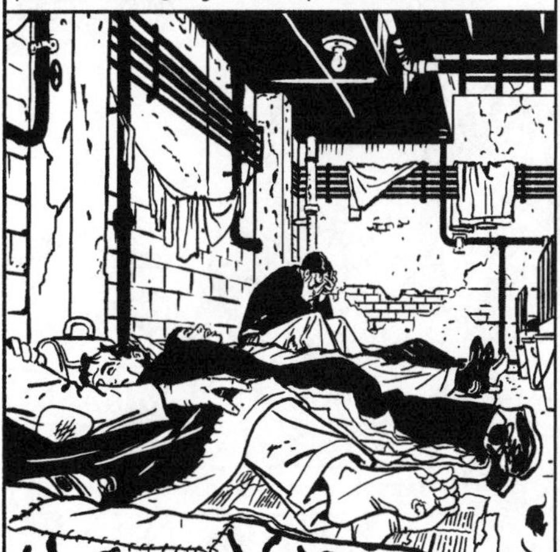

***Shanty towns** of homeless people sprang up all over. They called them **HOOVERVILLES** ...*

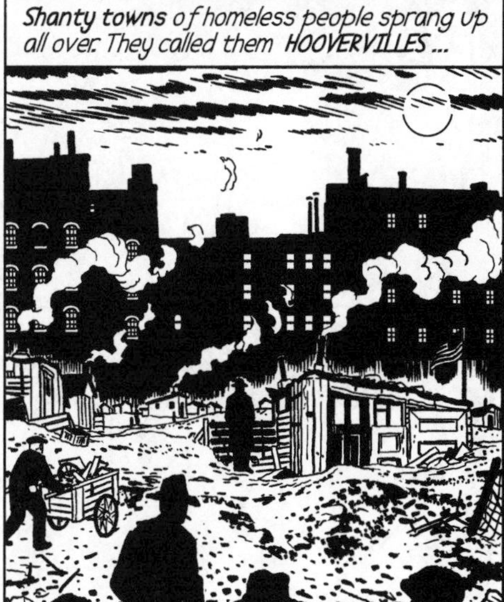

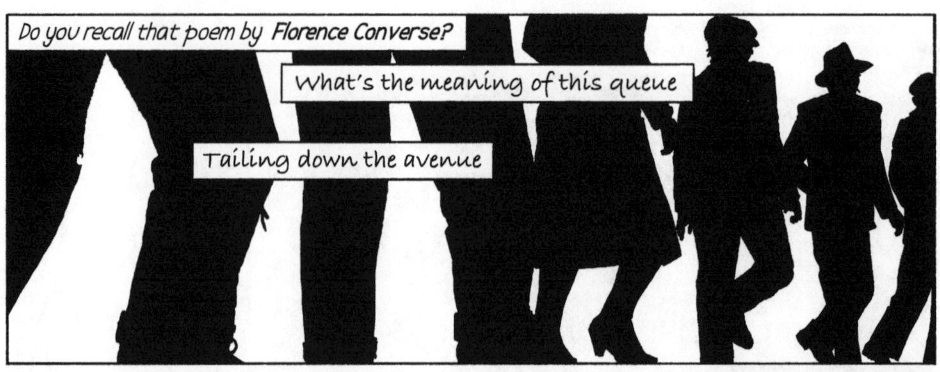

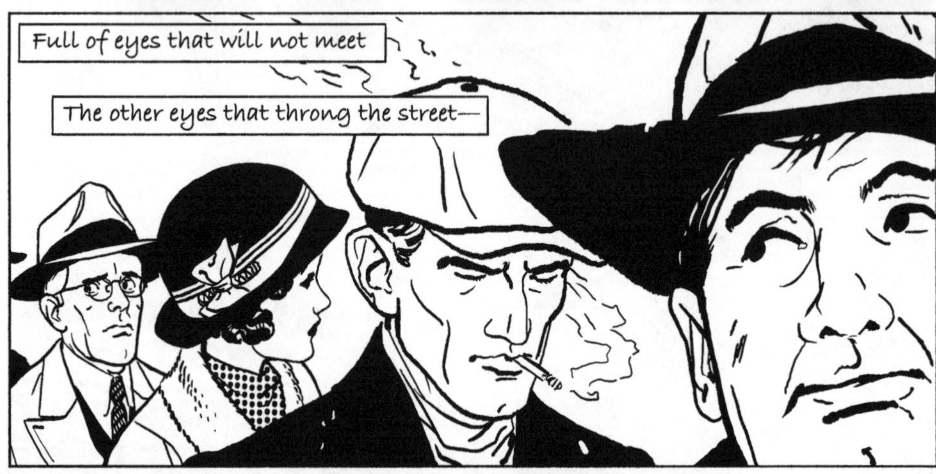

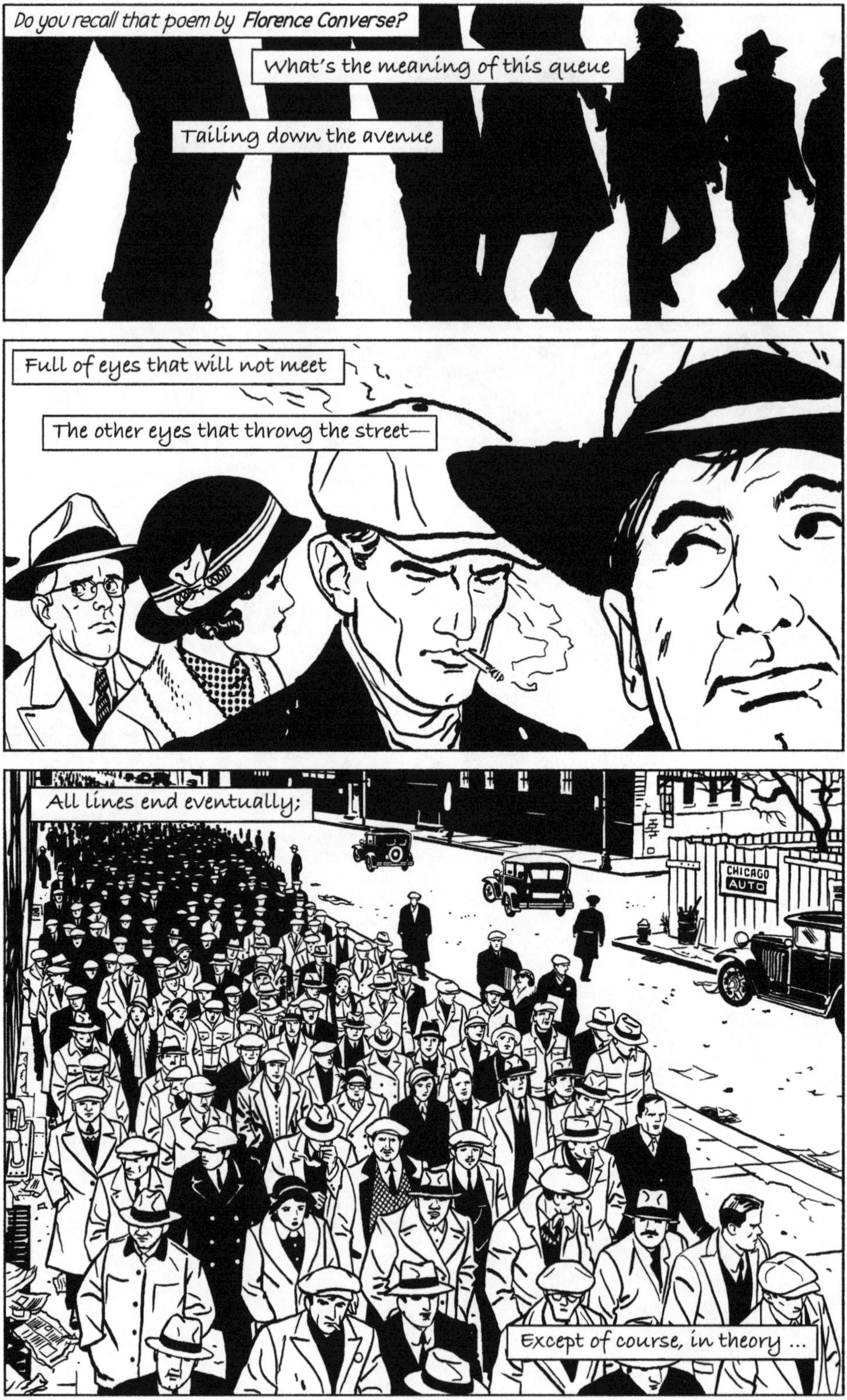

All lines end eventually;

CHICAGO AUTO

Except of course, in theory ...

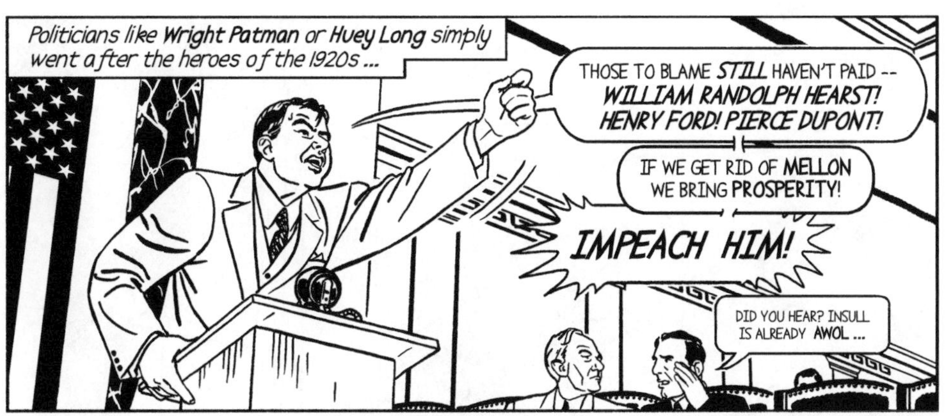
Politicians like **Wright Patman** or **Huey Long** simply went after the heroes of the 1920s ...
THOSE TO BLAME ***STILL*** HAVEN'T PAID -- ***WILLIAM RANDOLPH HEARST! HENRY FORD! PIERCE DUPONT!***
IF WE GET RID OF **MELLON** WE BRING **PROSPERITY**!
IMPEACH HIM!
DID YOU HEAR? INSULL IS ALREADY **AWOL ...**

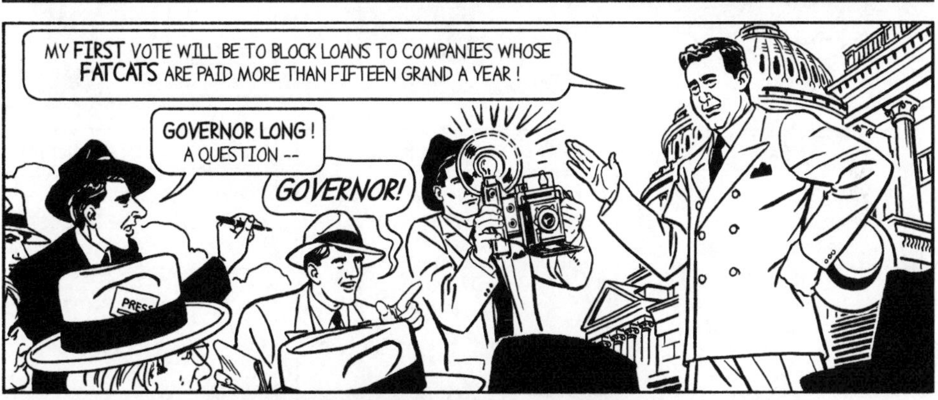
MY **FIRST** VOTE WILL BE TO BLOCK LOANS TO COMPANIES WHOSE **FATCATS** ARE PAID MORE THAN FIFTEEN GRAND A YEAR !
GOVERNOR LONG ! A QUESTION --
GOVERNOR!
PRESS

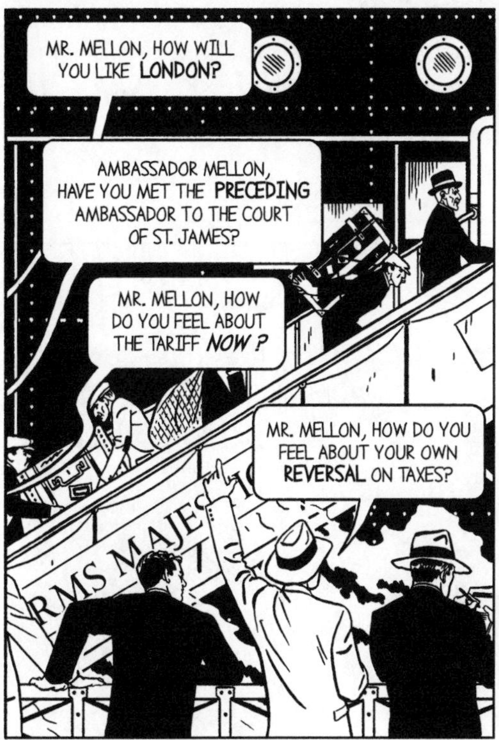
MR. MELLON, HOW WILL YOU LIKE **LONDON?**
AMBASSADOR MELLON, HAVE YOU MET THE **PRECEDING** AMBASSADOR TO THE COURT OF ST. JAMES?
MR. MELLON, HOW DO YOU FEEL ABOUT THE TARIFF ***NOW ?***
MR. MELLON, HOW DO YOU FEEL ABOUT YOUR OWN **REVERSAL** ON TAXES?
RMS MAJES

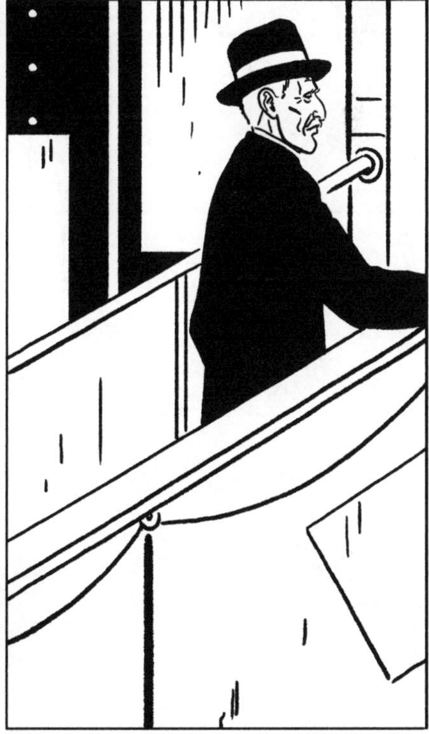

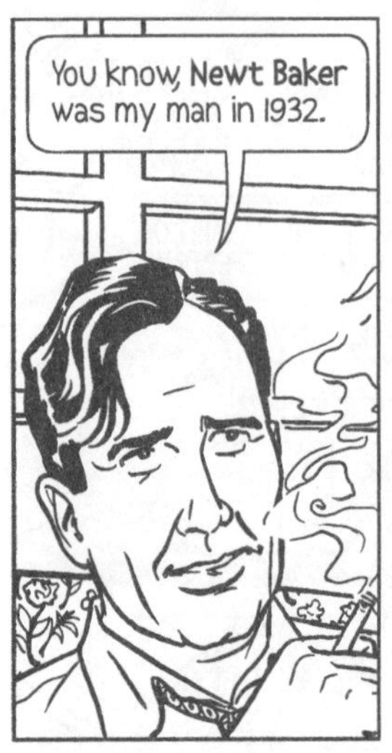
You know, Newt Baker was my man in 1932.

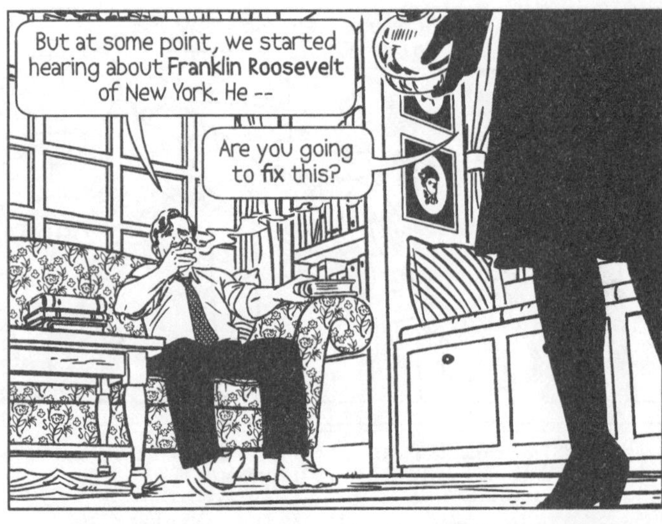
But at some point, we started hearing about Franklin Roosevelt of New York. He --
Are you going to fix this?

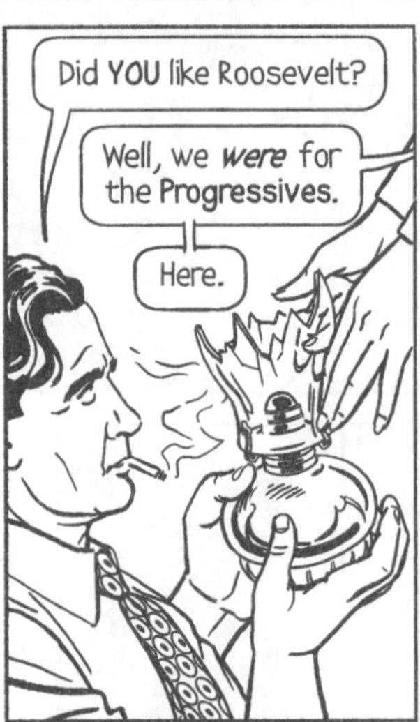
Did YOU like Roosevelt?
Well, we *were* for the Progressives.
Here.

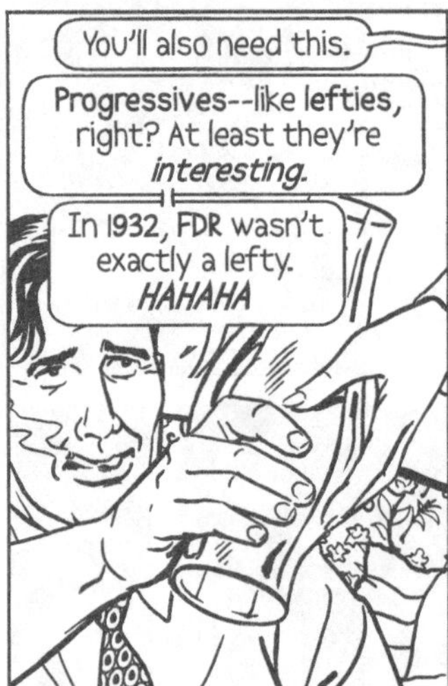
You'll also need this.
Progressives--like lefties, right? At least they're *interesting.*
In 1932, FDR wasn't exactly a lefty. *HAHAHA*

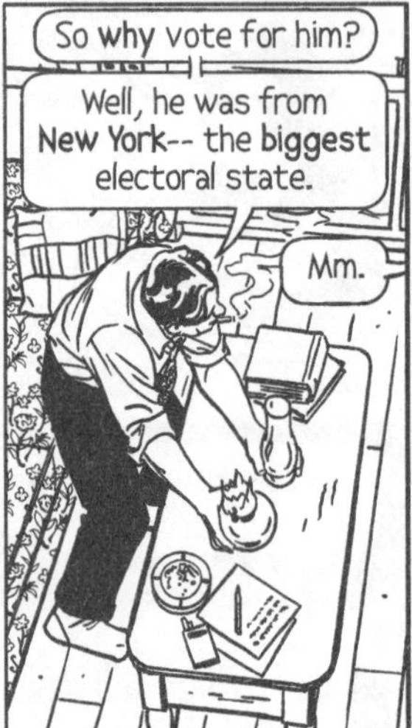
So why vote for him?
Well, he was from New York-- the biggest electoral state.
Mm.

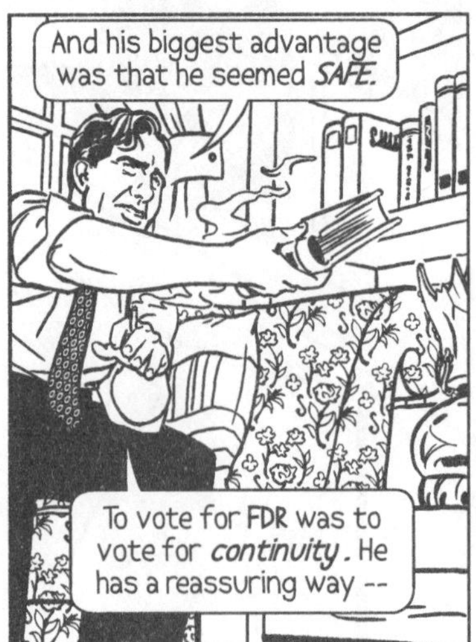
And his biggest advantage was that he seemed *SAFE.*
To vote for FDR was to vote for *continuity*. He has a reassuring way --

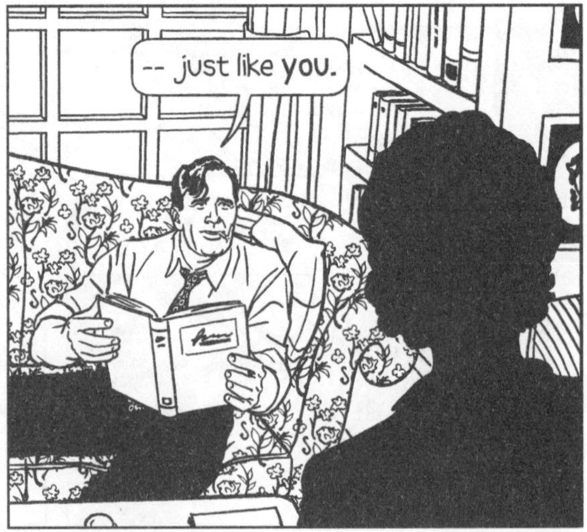
-- just like you.

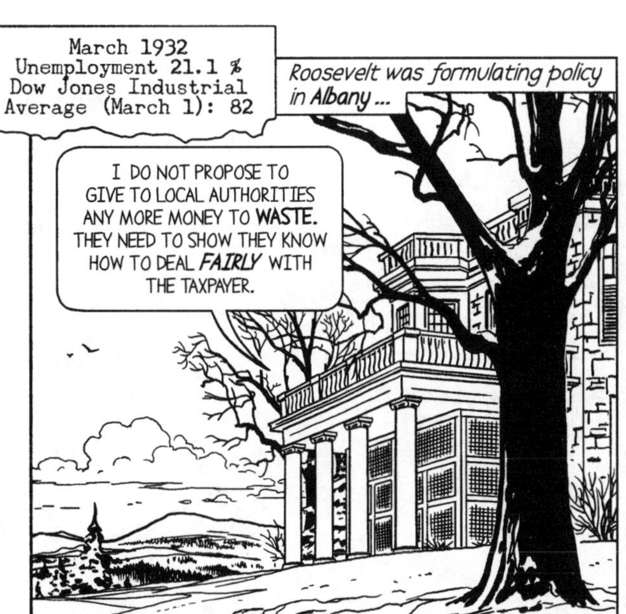
March 1932
Unemployment 21.1 %
Dow Jones Industrial
Average (March 1): 82
Roosevelt was formulating policy in Albany ...
I DO NOT PROPOSE TO GIVE TO LOCAL AUTHORITIES ANY MORE MONEY TO WASTE. THEY NEED TO SHOW THEY KNOW HOW TO DEAL FAIRLY WITH THE TAXPAYER.

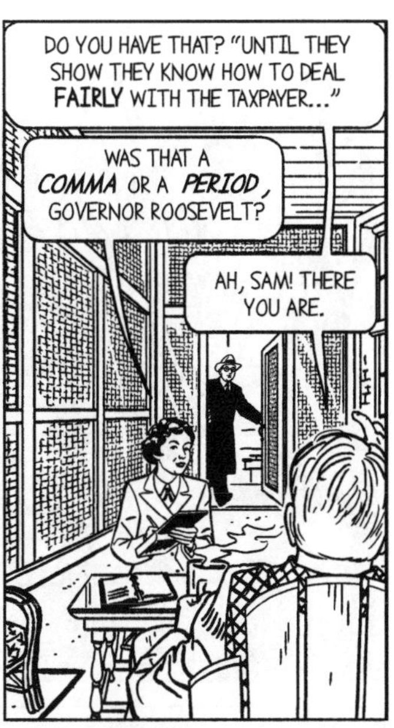
DO YOU HAVE THAT? "UNTIL THEY SHOW THEY KNOW HOW TO DEAL FAIRLY WITH THE TAXPAYER..."
WAS THAT A COMMA OR A PERIOD, GOVERNOR ROOSEVELT?
AH, SAM! THERE YOU ARE.

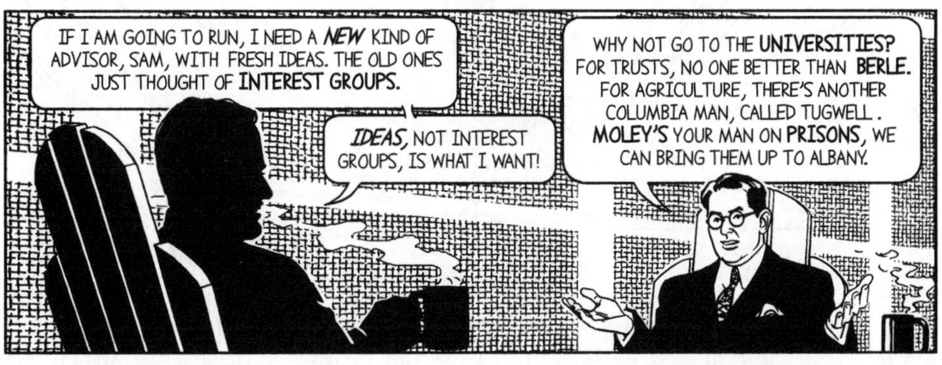
IF I AM GOING TO RUN, I NEED A NEW KIND OF ADVISOR, SAM, WITH FRESH IDEAS. THE OLD ONES JUST THOUGHT OF INTEREST GROUPS.
IDEAS, NOT INTEREST GROUPS, IS WHAT I WANT!
WHY NOT GO TO THE UNIVERSITIES? FOR TRUSTS, NO ONE BETTER THAN BERLE. FOR AGRICULTURE, THERE'S ANOTHER COLUMBIA MAN, CALLED TUGWELL. MOLEY'S YOUR MAN ON PRISONS, WE CAN BRING THEM UP TO ALBANY.

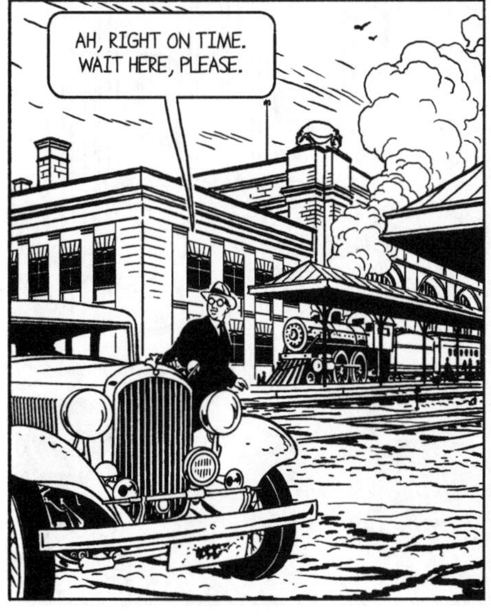
AH, RIGHT ON TIME. WAIT HERE, PLEASE.

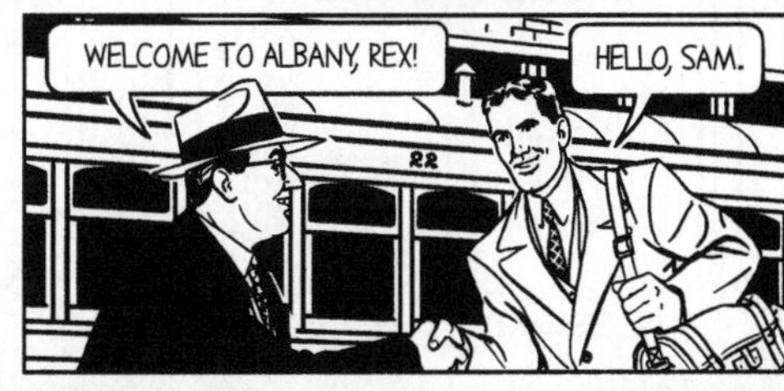
WELCOME TO ALBANY, REX!
HELLO, SAM.

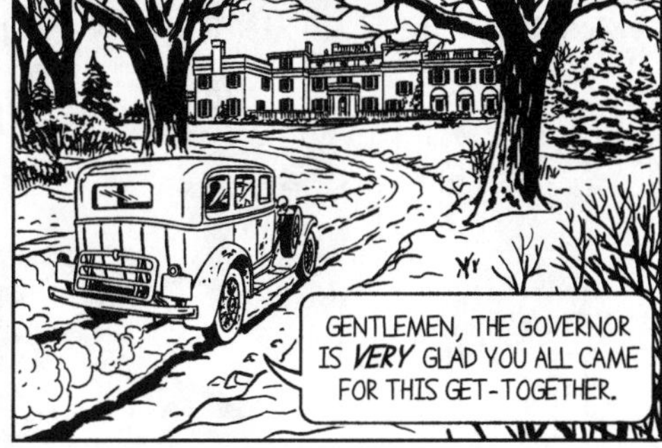
GENTLEMEN, THE GOVERNOR IS VERY GLAD YOU ALL CAME FOR THIS GET-TOGETHER.

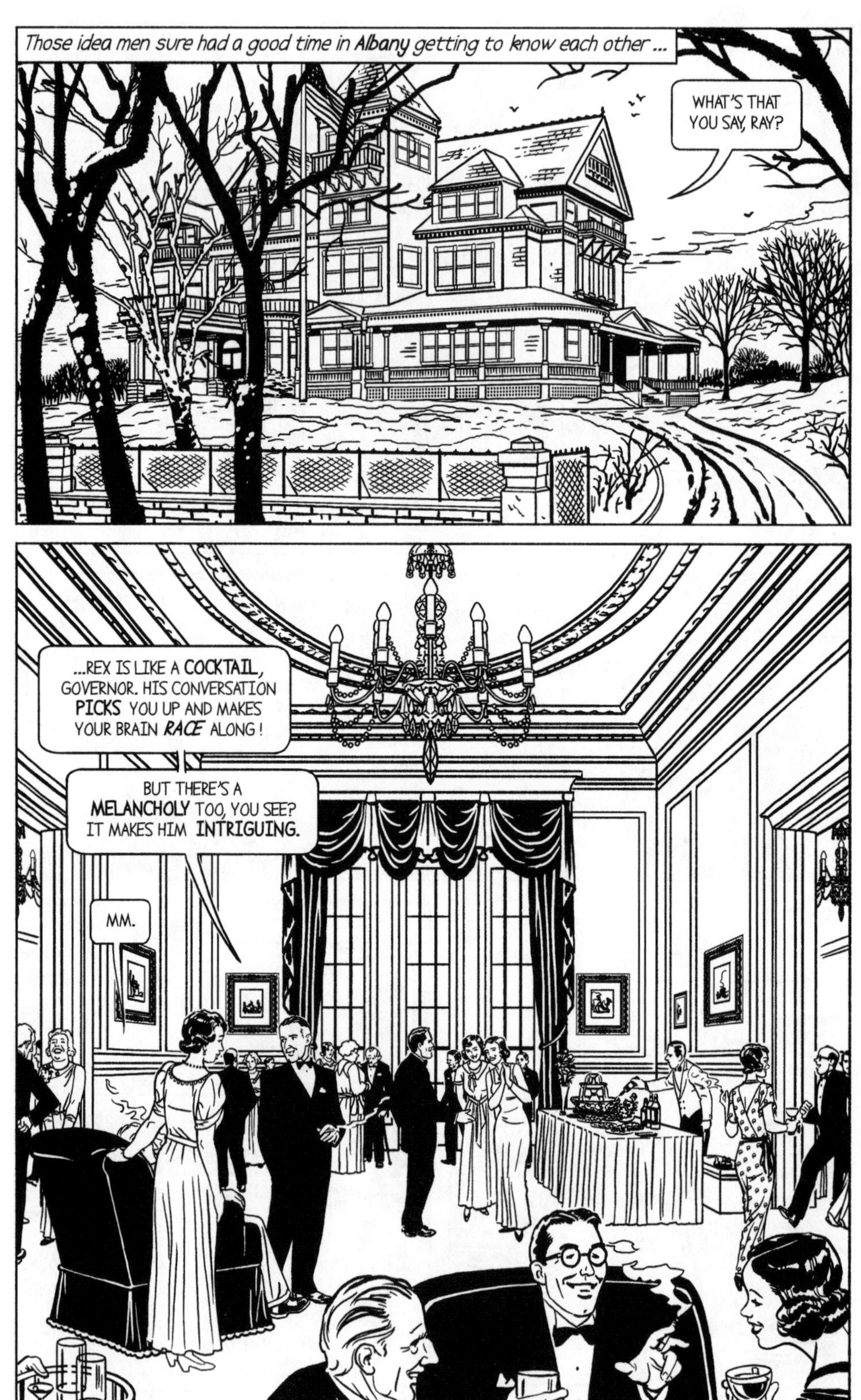
Those idea men sure had a good time in Albany getting to know each other ...
WHAT'S THAT YOU SAY, RAY?
...REX IS LIKE A COCKTAIL, GOVERNOR. HIS CONVERSATION PICKS YOU UP AND MAKES YOUR BRAIN RACE ALONG!
BUT THERE'S A MELANCHOLY TOO, YOU SEE? IT MAKES HIM INTRIGUING.
MM.

It's got to have been **swell.** Suddenly those marginal professors were in the ***MIDDLE*** of it!

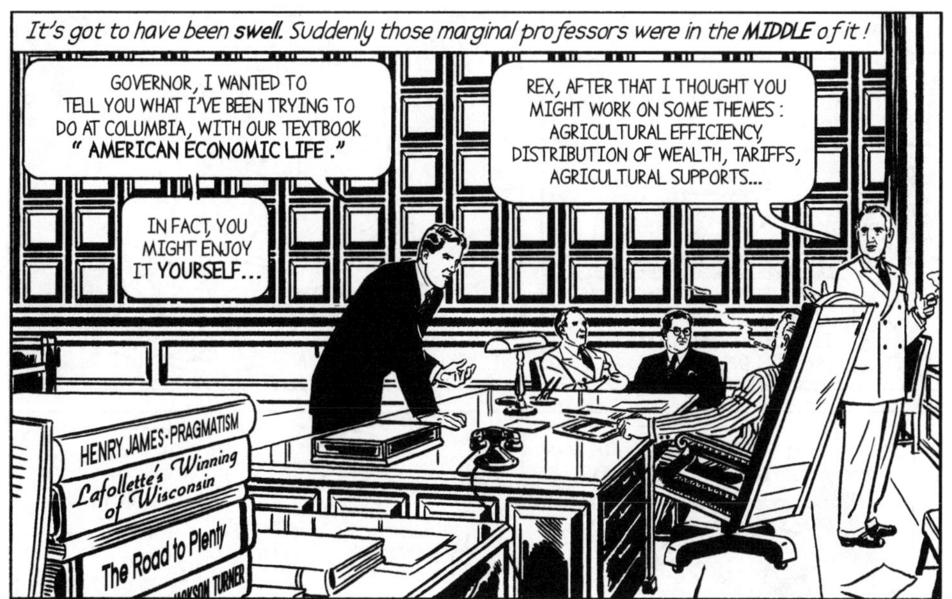

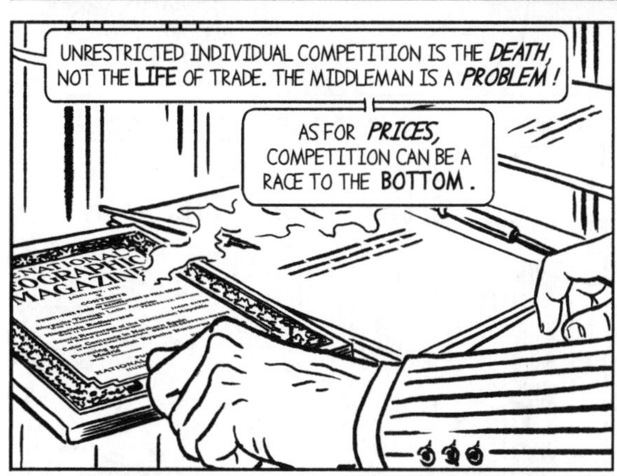

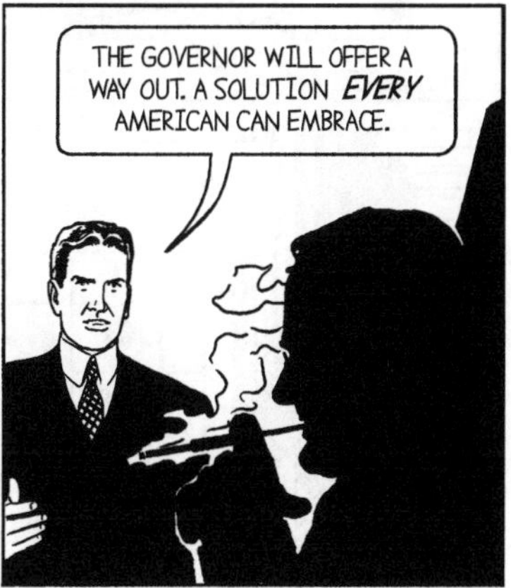

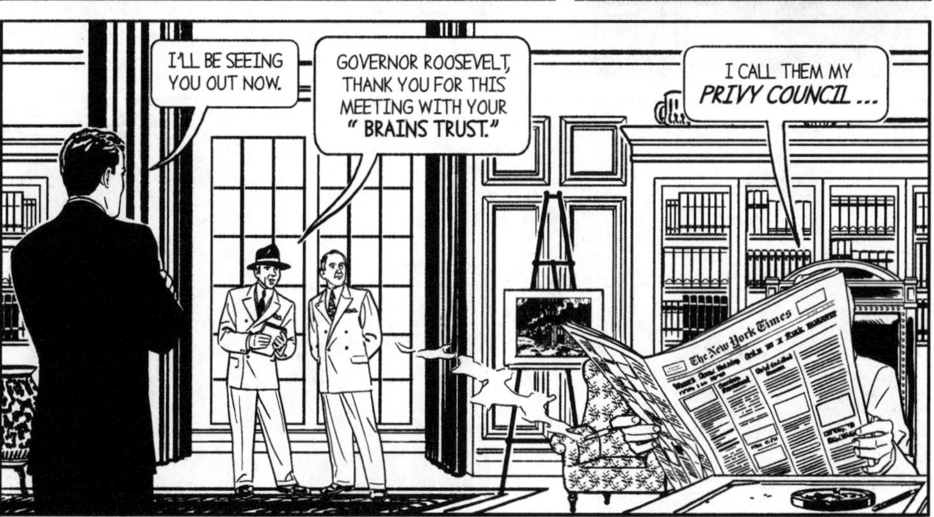

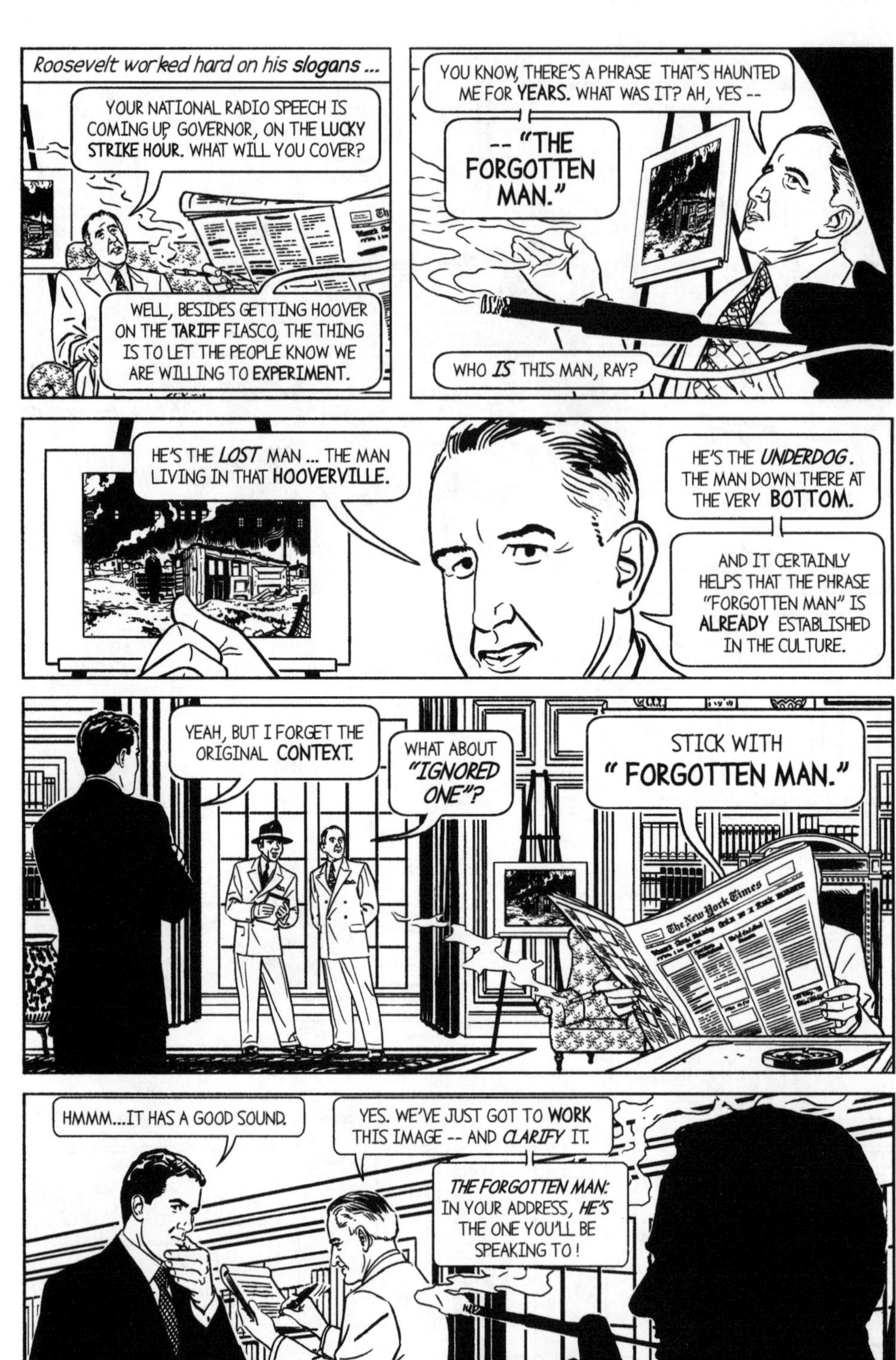
Roosevelt worked hard on his slogans ...
YOUR NATIONAL RADIO SPEECH IS COMING UP, GOVERNOR, ON THE LUCKY STRIKE HOUR. WHAT WILL YOU COVER?
WELL, BESIDES GETTING HOOVER ON THE TARIFF FIASCO, THE THING IS TO LET THE PEOPLE KNOW WE ARE WILLING TO EXPERIMENT.
YOU KNOW, THERE'S A PHRASE THAT'S HAUNTED ME FOR YEARS. WHAT WAS IT? AH, YES --
-- "THE FORGOTTEN MAN."
WHO IS THIS MAN, RAY?
HE'S THE LOST MAN ... THE MAN LIVING IN THAT HOOVERVILLE.
HE'S THE UNDERDOG. THE MAN DOWN THERE AT THE VERY BOTTOM.
AND IT CERTAINLY HELPS THAT THE PHRASE "FORGOTTEN MAN" IS ALREADY ESTABLISHED IN THE CULTURE.
YEAH, BUT I FORGET THE ORIGINAL CONTEXT.
WHAT ABOUT "IGNORED ONE"?
STICK WITH " FORGOTTEN MAN."
The New York Times
HMMM...IT HAS A GOOD SOUND.
YES. WE'VE JUST GOT TO WORK THIS IMAGE -- AND CLARIFY IT.
THE FORGOTTEN MAN: IN YOUR ADDRESS, HE'S THE ONE YOU'LL BE SPEAKING TO !

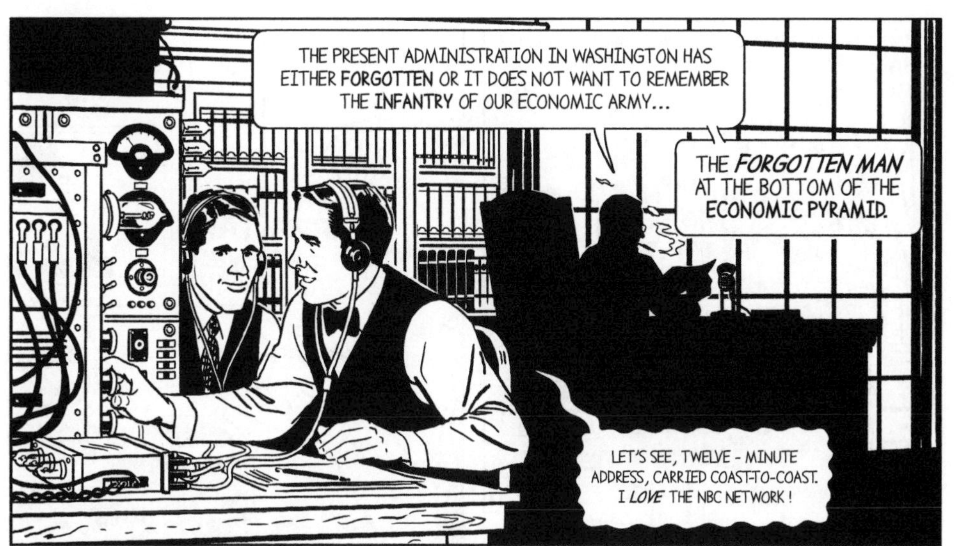
THE PRESENT ADMINISTRATION IN WASHINGTON HAS EITHER FORGOTTEN OR IT DOES NOT WANT TO REMEMBER THE INFANTRY OF OUR ECONOMIC ARMY...
THE *FORGOTTEN MAN* AT THE BOTTOM OF THE ECONOMIC PYRAMID.
LET'S SEE, TWELVE - MINUTE ADDRESS, CARRIED COAST-TO-COAST. I *LOVE* THE NBC NETWORK !

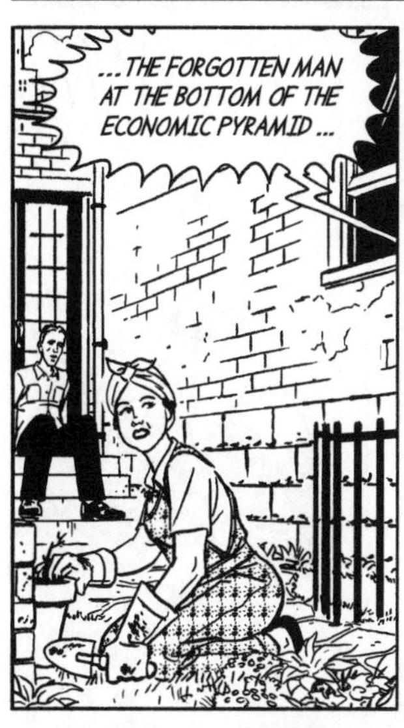
...THE FORGOTTEN MAN AT THE BOTTOM OF THE ECONOMIC PYRAMID ...

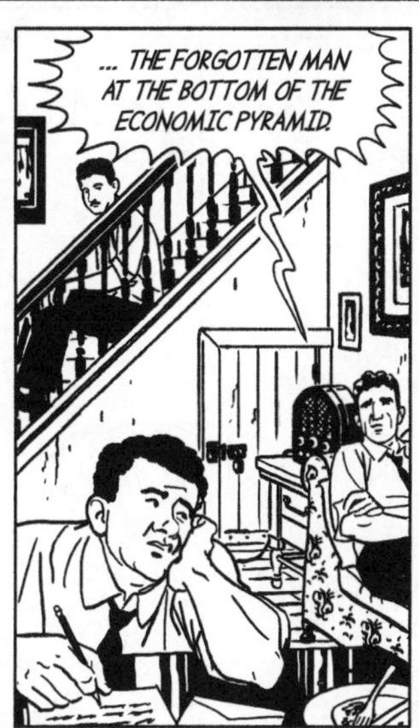
... THE FORGOTTEN MAN AT THE BOTTOM OF THE ECONOMIC PYRAMID.

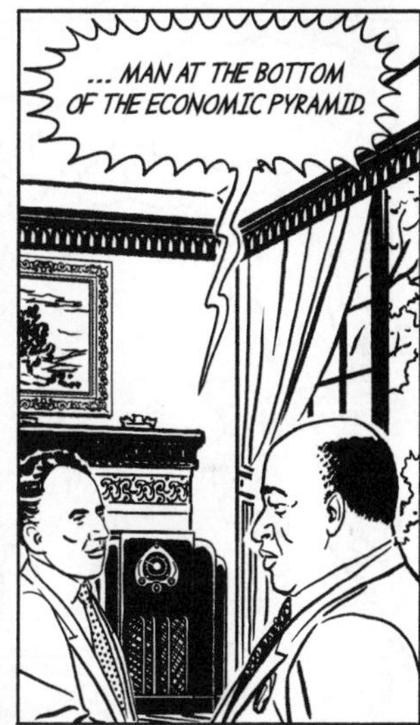
... MAN AT THE BOTTOM OF THE ECONOMIC PYRAMID.

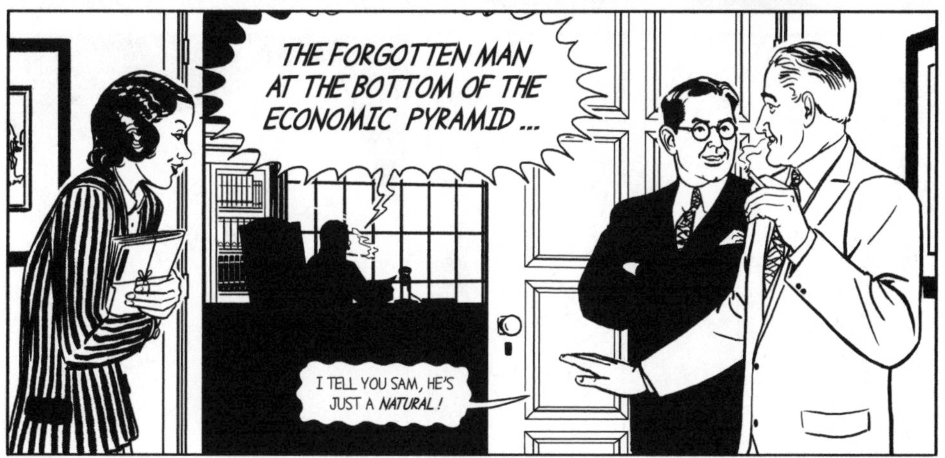
THE FORGOTTEN MAN AT THE BOTTOM OF THE ECONOMIC PYRAMID ...
I TELL YOU SAM, HE'S JUST A *NATURAL* !

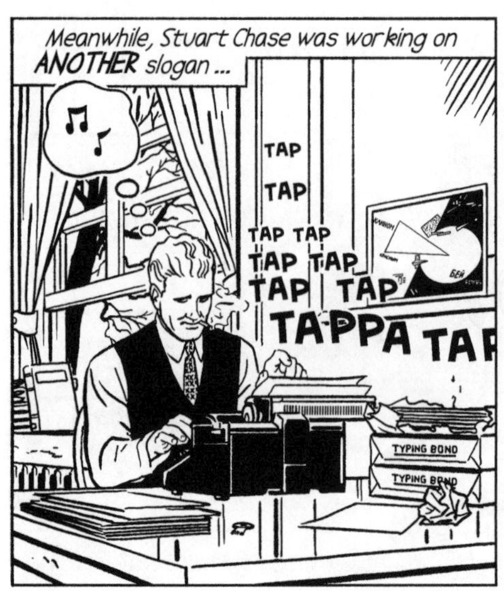
Meanwhile, Stuart Chase was working on ANOTHER slogan ...
TAP
TAP
TAP TAP
TAP TAP
TAP TAP
TAPPA TAP
TYPING BOND
TYPING BOND

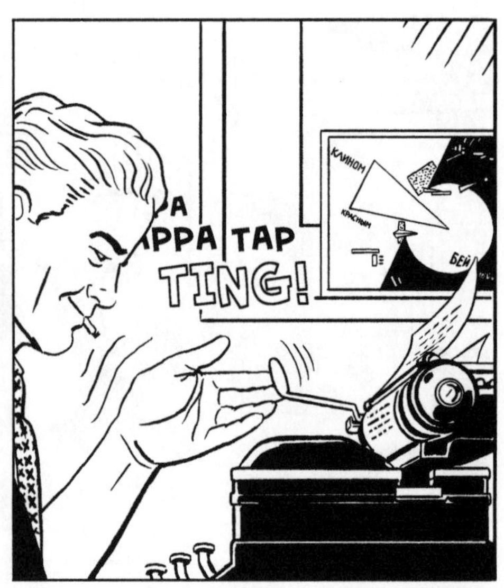
APPA TAP
TING!

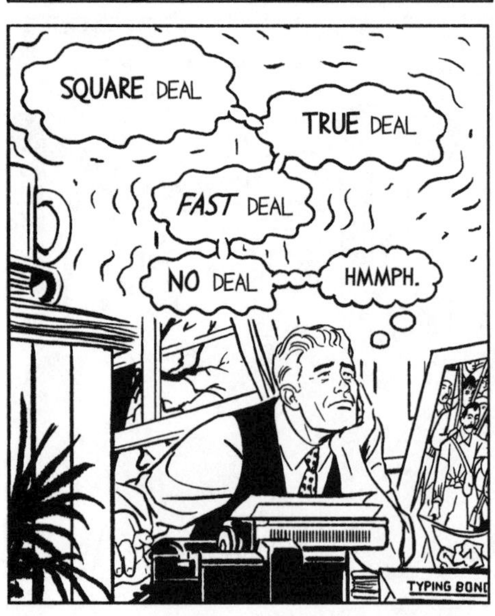
SQUARE DEAL
TRUE DEAL
FAST DEAL
NO DEAL
HMMPH.
TYPING BOND

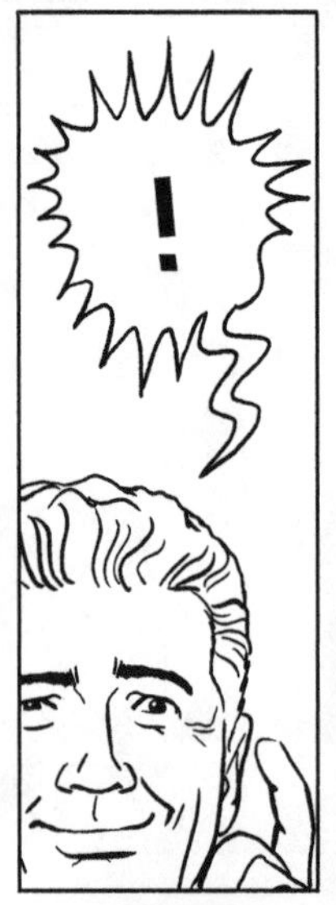
!

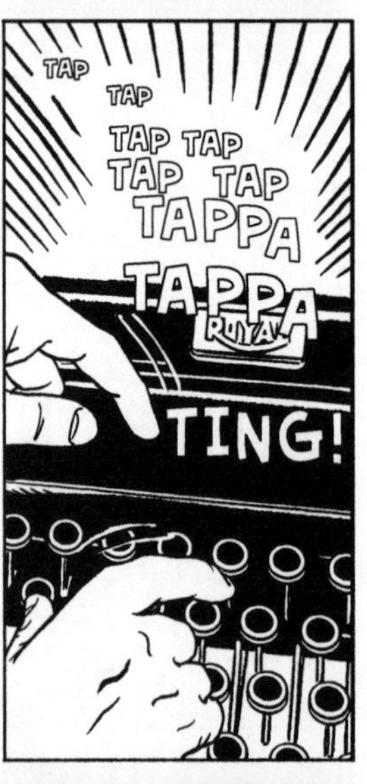
TAP
TAP
TAP TAP
TAP TAP
TAPPA
TAPPA
TING!

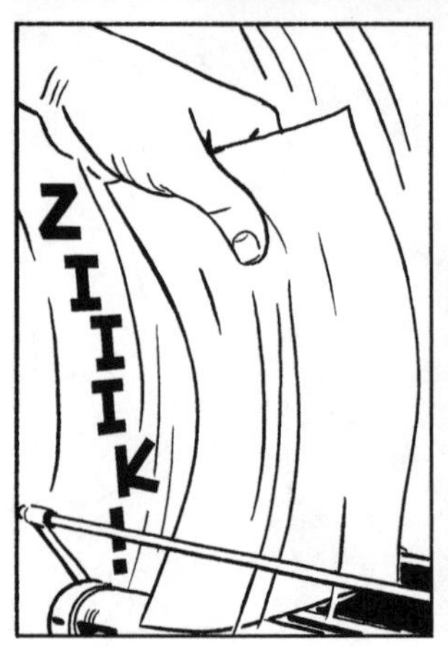
ZIIIK!!

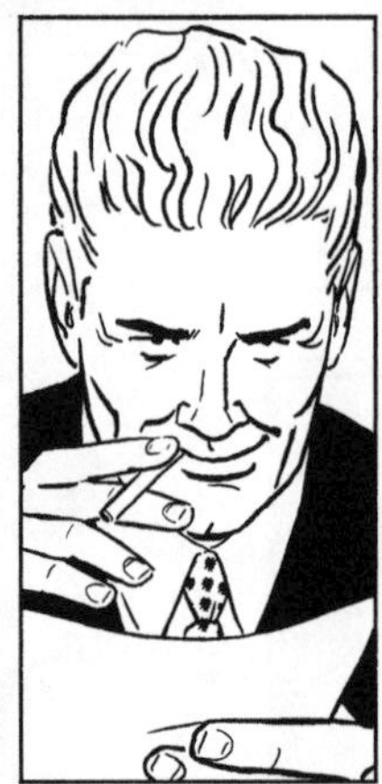

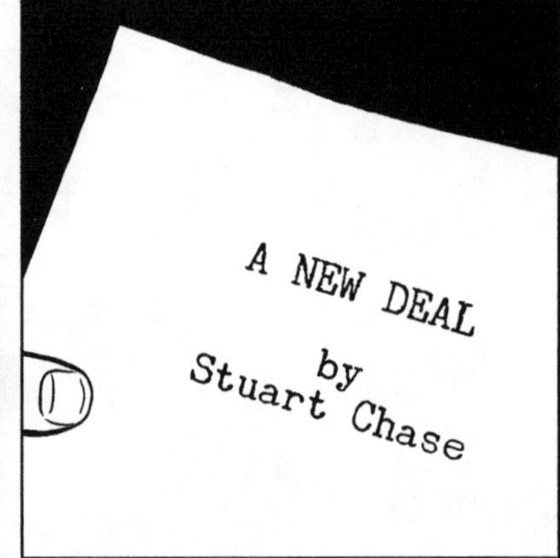
A NEW DEAL
by
Stuart Chase

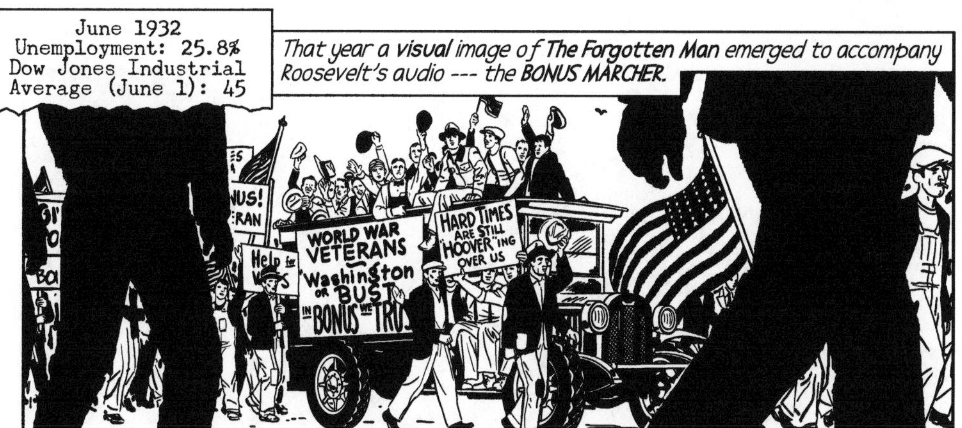
June 1932
Unemployment: 25.8%
Dow Jones Industrial
Average (June 1): 45
That year a **visual** image of **The Forgotten Man** emerged to accompany Roosevelt's audio --- the **BONUS MARCHER.**
WORLD WAR VETERANS
Washington or BUST
HARD TIMES ARE STILL HOOVER'ING OVER US

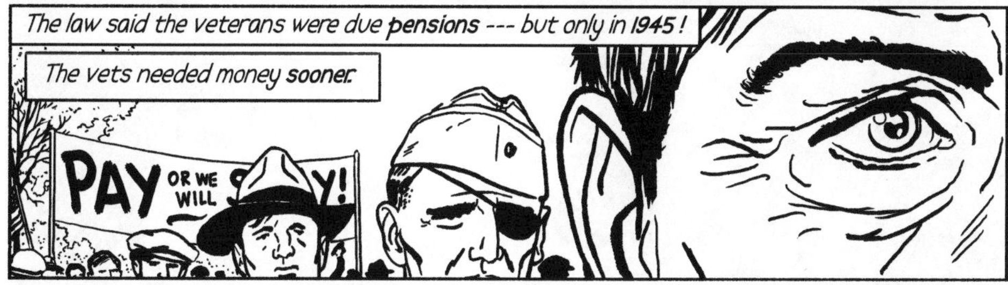
The law said the veterans were due **pensions** --- but only in **1945**!
The vets needed money **sooner.**

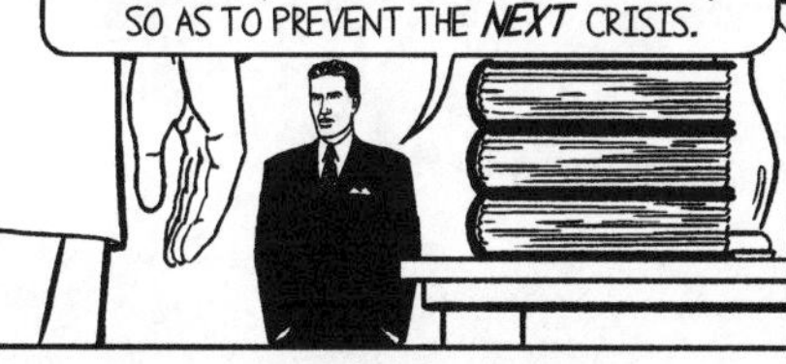
SURE, WE CAN REGULATE, JUST AS TR PLANNED. BUT THIS ROOSEVELT WANTS SOMETHING *MORE* -- THE DEVELOPMENT OF **CONTROLS** TO STIMULATE AND STABILIZE ECONOMIC ACTIVITY.
RAY, BETWEEN THE FLOOD AND THE CRASH, PEOPLE EXPECT GOVERNMENT BE READY TO HELP THEM **NOW.** WE NEED MORE FARM PLANNING, A MORE POWERFUL TREASURY, SO AS TO PREVENT THE *NEXT* CRISIS.

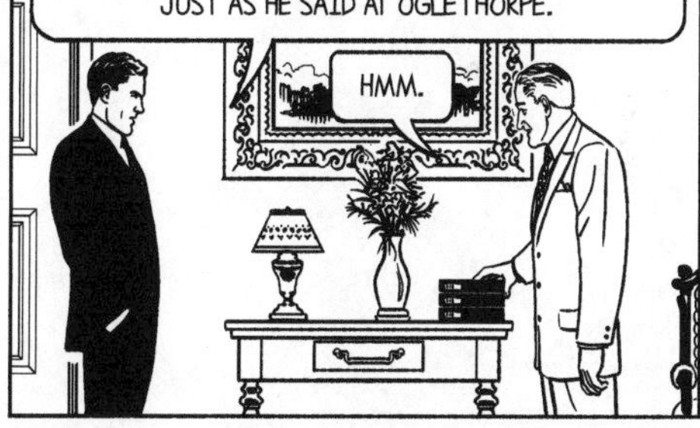
THE TRICK IS FOR THE GOVERNOR TO PRESENT HIMSELF AS **SCIENTIFIC** -- *FLEXIBLE*. WE DON'T **PIN** OURSELVES TO DOCTRINE LIKE BUGS. INSTEAD, WE SHOW THAT WE'RE READY TO **EXPERIMENT,** JUST AS HE SAID AT OGLETHORPE.
HMM.

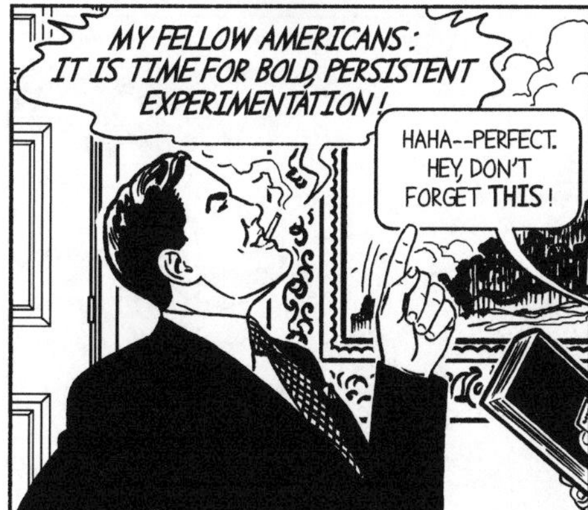
MY FELLOW AMERICANS: IT IS TIME FOR BOLD, PERSISTENT EXPERIMENTATION!
HAHA--PERFECT. HEY, DON'T FORGET **THIS**!

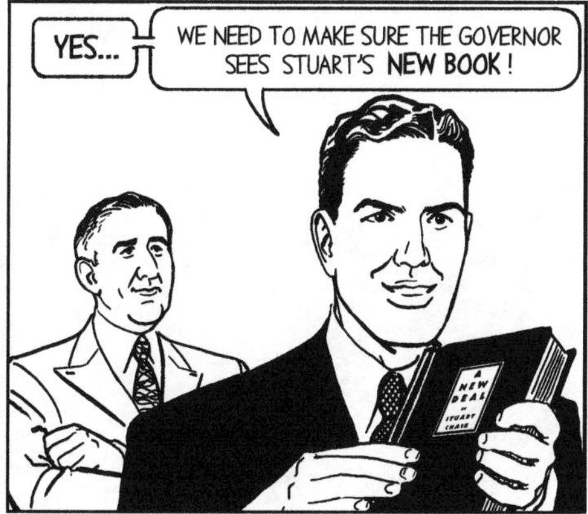
YES...
WE NEED TO MAKE SURE THE GOVERNOR SEES STUART'S **NEW BOOK**!

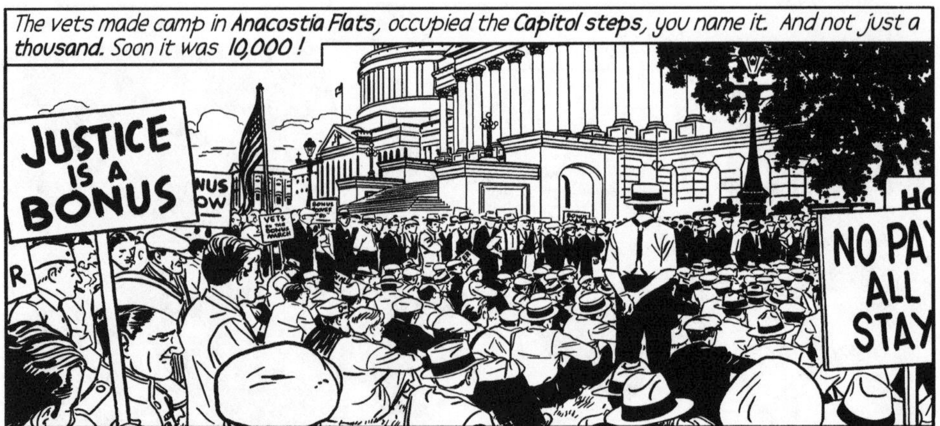
The vets made camp in **Anacostia Flats**, occupied the **Capitol steps**, you name it. And not just a **thousand**. Soon it was **10,000**!
JUSTICE IS A BONUS
NUS
OW
NO PA
ALL
STAY

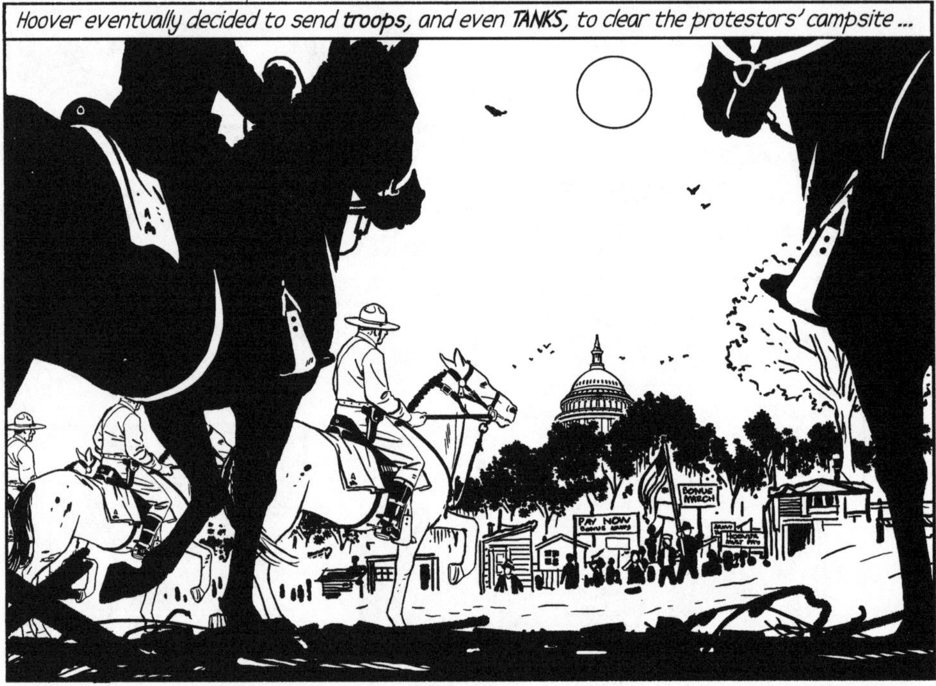
Hoover eventually decided to send **troops**, and even **TANKS**, to clear the protestors' campsite ...
PAY NOW
BONUS MARCH

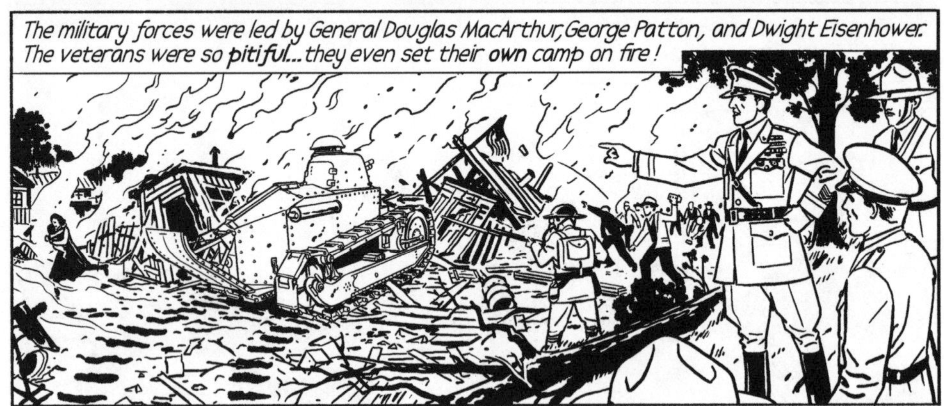
The military forces were led by General Douglas MacArthur, George Patton, and Dwight Eisenhower. The veterans were so **pitiful**... they even set their **own** camp on fire!

Suddenly, the election was Roosevelt's to win! Tugwell was ***one step ahead*** *of politicians ...*

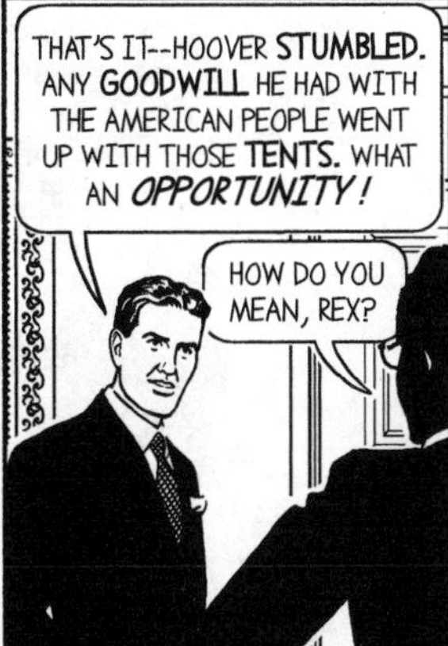

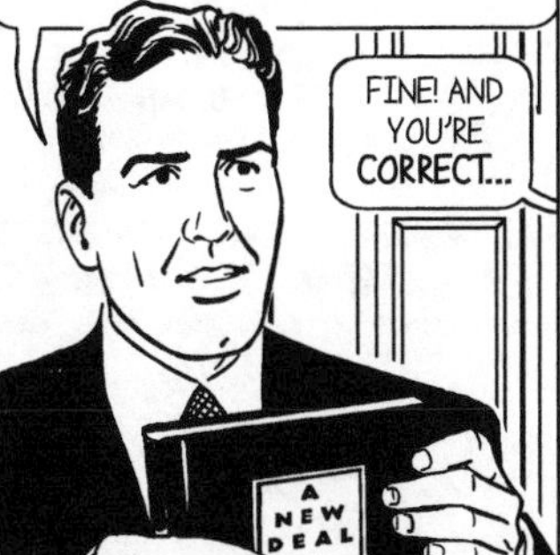

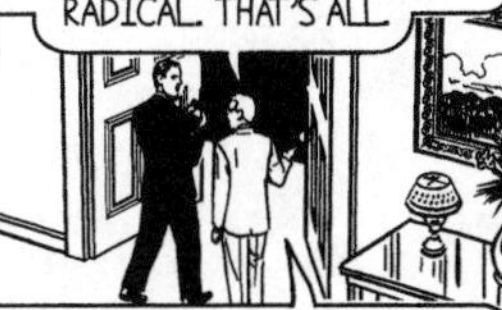

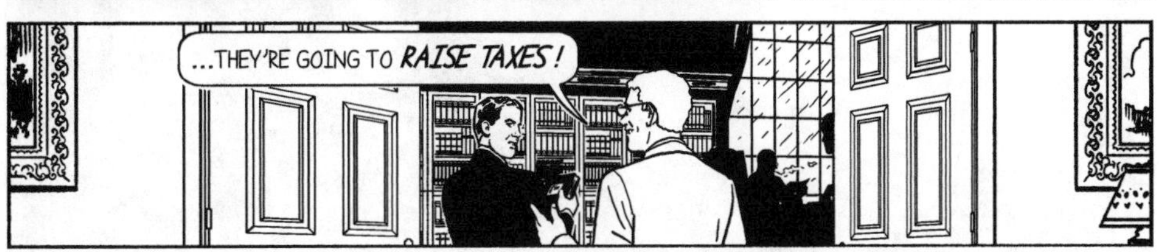

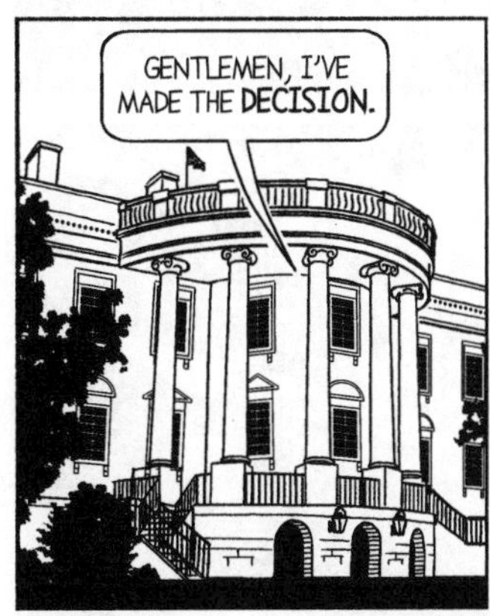

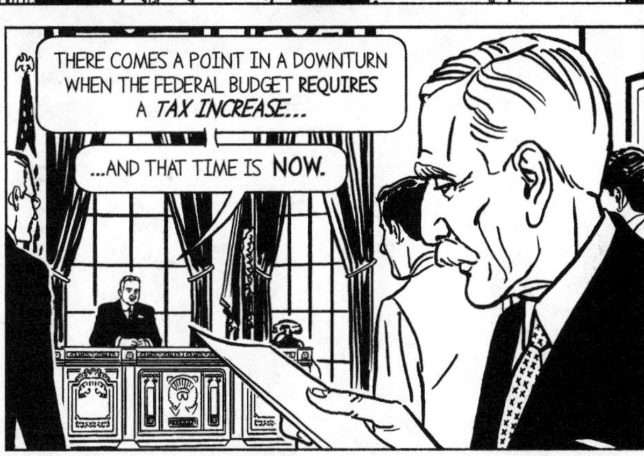

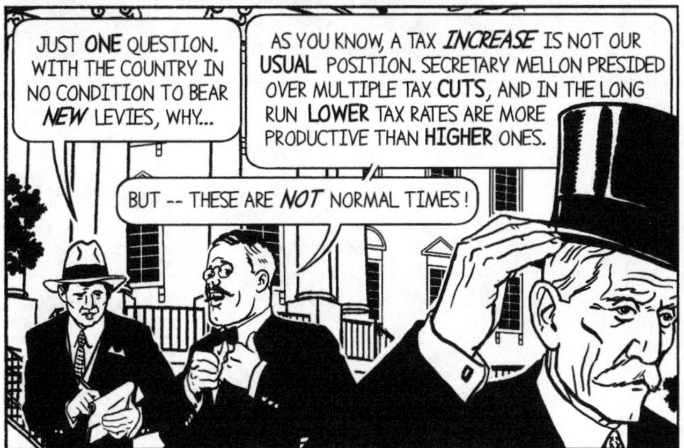

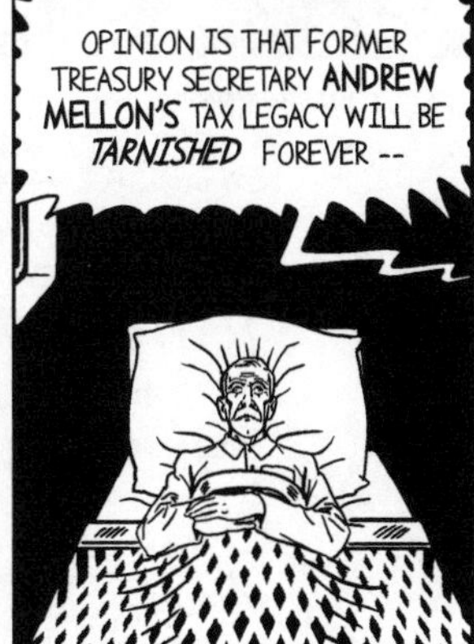

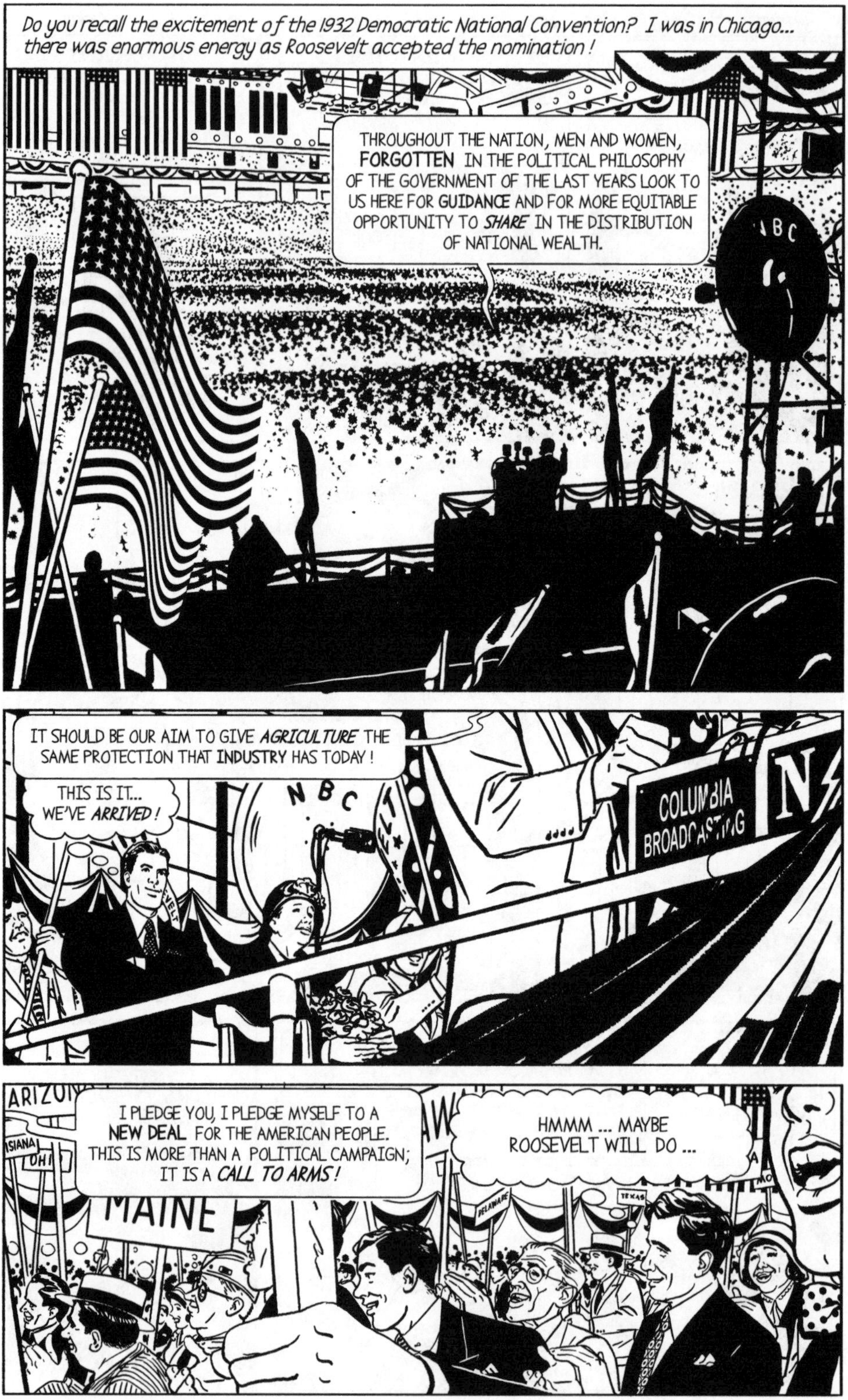

Do you recall the excitement of the 1932 Democratic National Convention? I was in Chicago... there was enormous energy as Roosevelt accepted the nomination!

THROUGHOUT THE NATION, MEN AND WOMEN, **FORGOTTEN** IN THE POLITICAL PHILOSOPHY OF THE GOVERNMENT OF THE LAST YEARS LOOK TO US HERE FOR **GUIDANCE** AND FOR MORE EQUITABLE OPPORTUNITY TO *SHARE* IN THE DISTRIBUTION OF NATIONAL WEALTH.

NBC

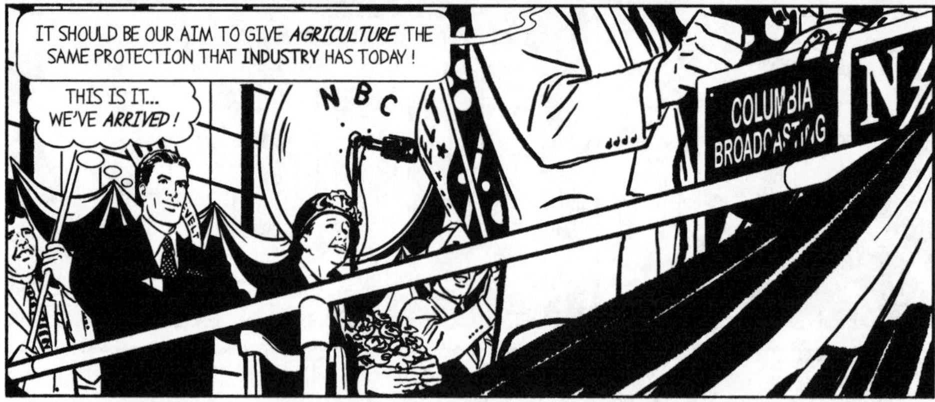

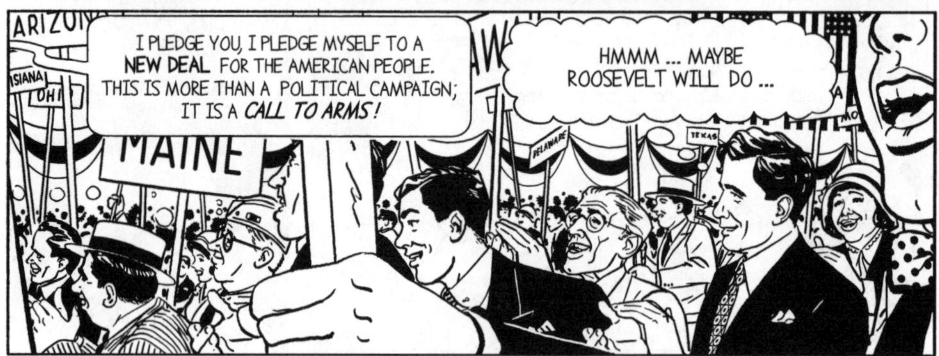

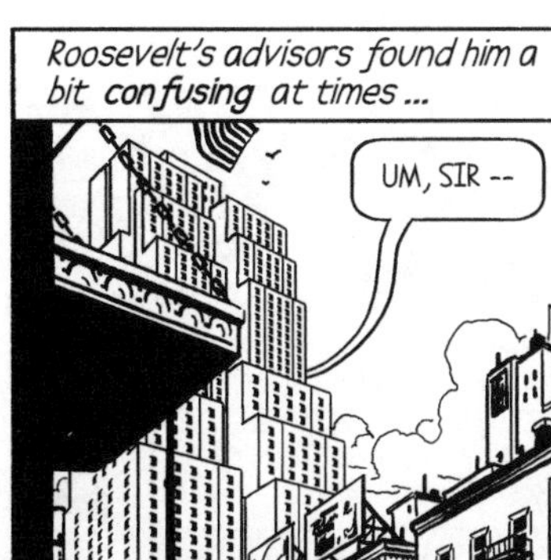
Roosevelt's advisors found him a bit confusing at times ...
UM, SIR --

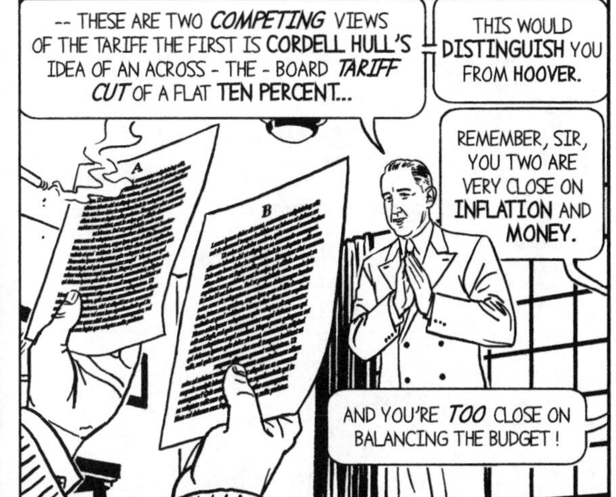
-- THESE ARE TWO COMPETING VIEWS OF THE TARIFF. THE FIRST IS CORDELL HULL'S IDEA OF AN ACROSS - THE - BOARD TARIFF CUT OF A FLAT TEN PERCENT...
THIS WOULD DISTINGUISH YOU FROM HOOVER.
REMEMBER, SIR, YOU TWO ARE VERY CLOSE ON INFLATION AND MONEY.
AND YOU'RE TOO CLOSE ON BALANCING THE BUDGET !

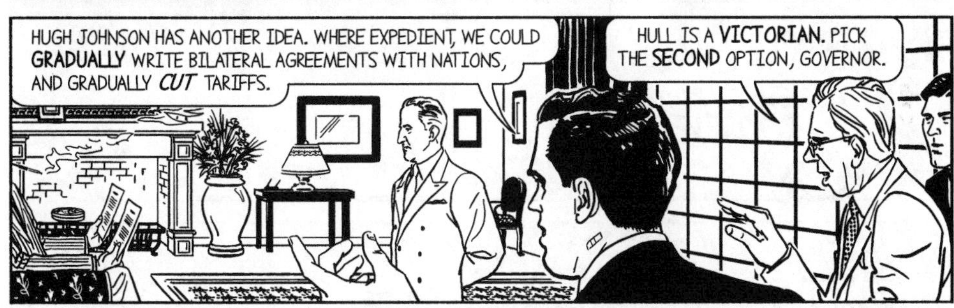
HUGH JOHNSON HAS ANOTHER IDEA. WHERE EXPEDIENT, WE COULD GRADUALLY WRITE BILATERAL AGREEMENTS WITH NATIONS, AND GRADUALLY CUT TARIFFS.
HULL IS A VICTORIAN. PICK THE SECOND OPTION, GOVERNOR.

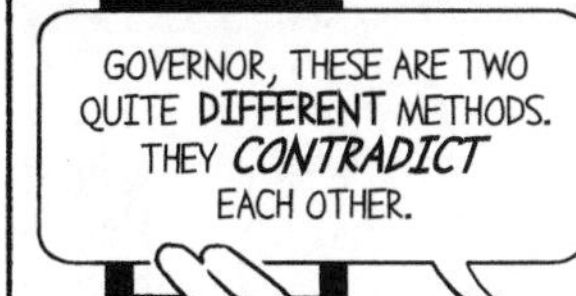
GOVERNOR, THESE ARE TWO QUITE DIFFERENT METHODS. THEY CONTRADICT EACH OTHER.

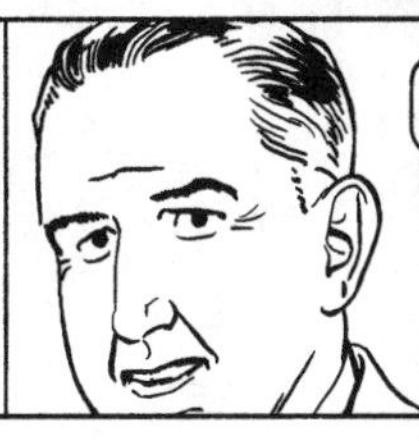

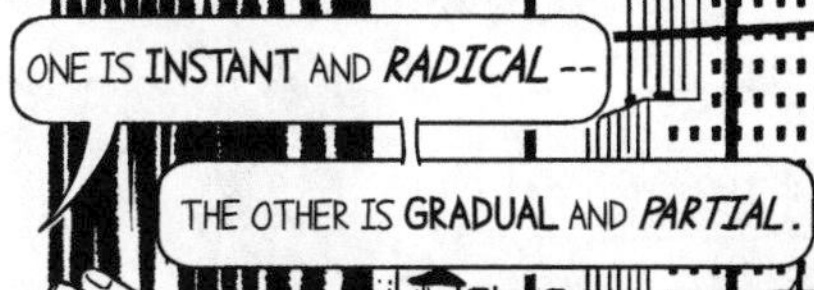
ONE IS INSTANT AND RADICAL --
THE OTHER IS GRADUAL AND PARTIAL.

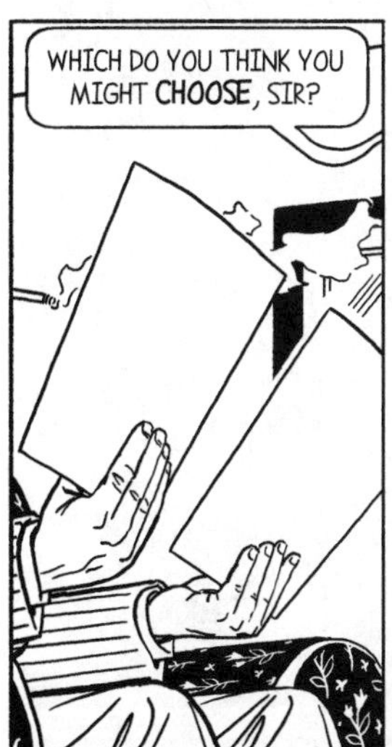
WHICH DO YOU THINK YOU MIGHT CHOOSE, SIR?

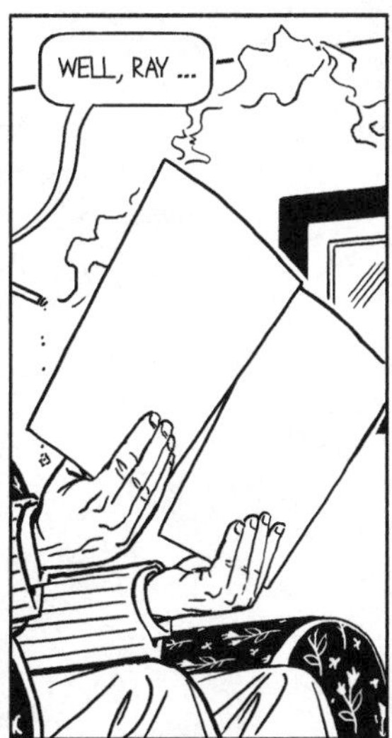
WELL, RAY ...

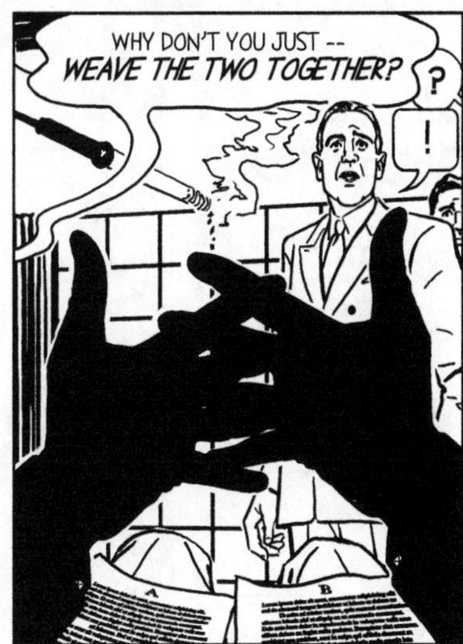
WHY DON'T YOU JUST -- WEAVE THE TWO TOGETHER?
?
!

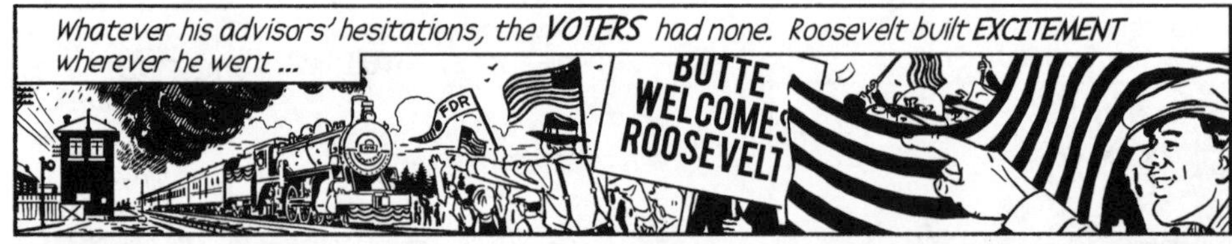
Whatever his advisors' hesitations, the **VOTERS** had none. Roosevelt built **EXCITEMENT** wherever he went ...
FDR
BUTTE WELCOMES ROOSEVELT

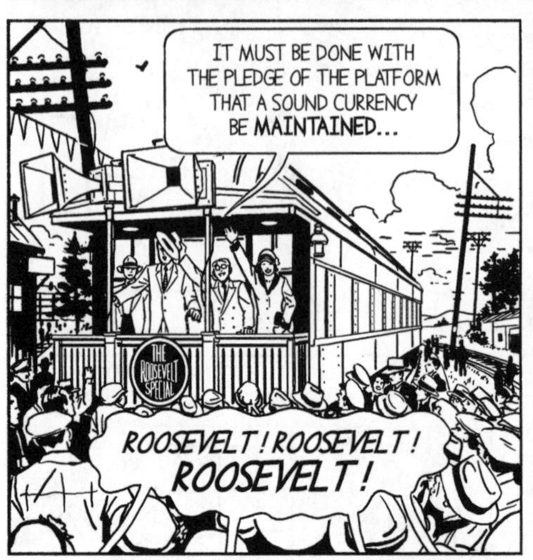
IT MUST BE DONE WITH THE PLEDGE OF THE PLATFORM THAT A SOUND CURRENCY BE MAINTAINED...
THE ROOSEVELT SPECIAL
ROOSEVELT! ROOSEVELT! ROOSEVELT!

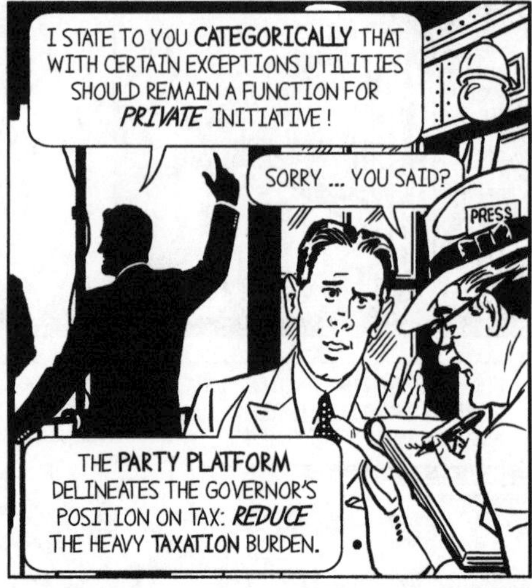
I STATE TO YOU CATEGORICALLY THAT WITH CERTAIN EXCEPTIONS UTILITIES SHOULD REMAIN A FUNCTION FOR PRIVATE INITIATIVE!
SORRY ... YOU SAID?
PRESS
THE PARTY PLATFORM DELINEATES THE GOVERNOR'S POSITION ON TAX: REDUCE THE HEAVY TAXATION BURDEN.

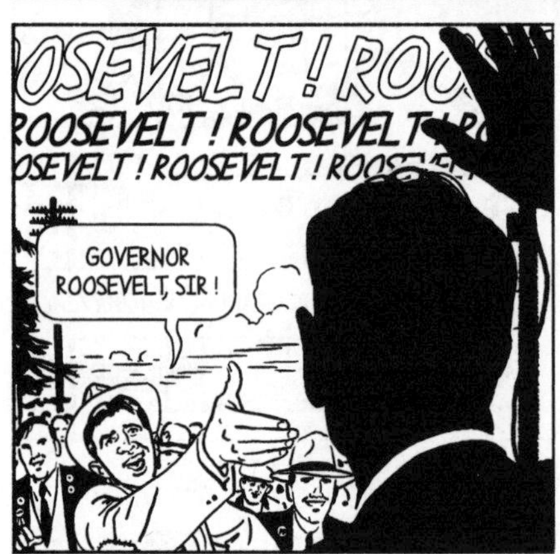
OSEVELT! ROO
ROOSEVELT! ROOSEVELT!
OSEVELT! ROOSEVELT!
GOVERNOR ROOSEVELT, SIR!

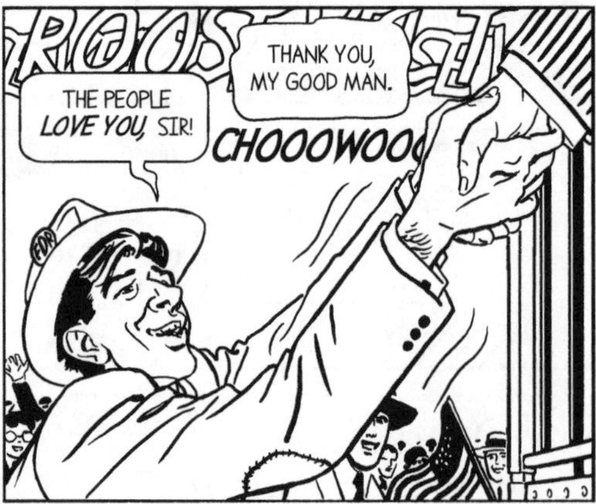
THE PEOPLE LOVE YOU, SIR!
THANK YOU, MY GOOD MAN.
CHOOOWOO

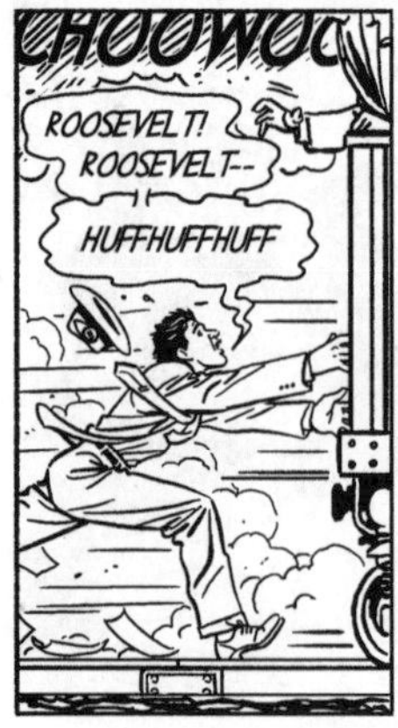
CHOOWOO
ROOSEVELT! ROOSEVELT--
HUFFHUFFHUFF

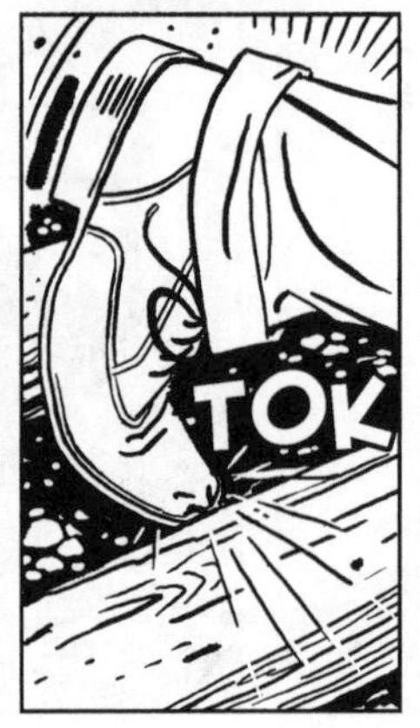
TOK

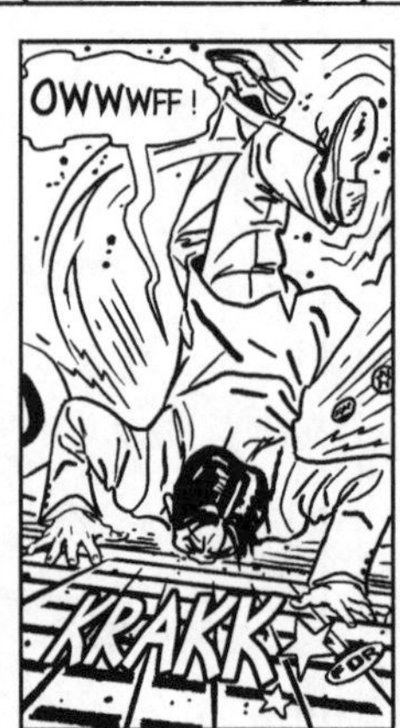
OWWWFF!
KRAKK

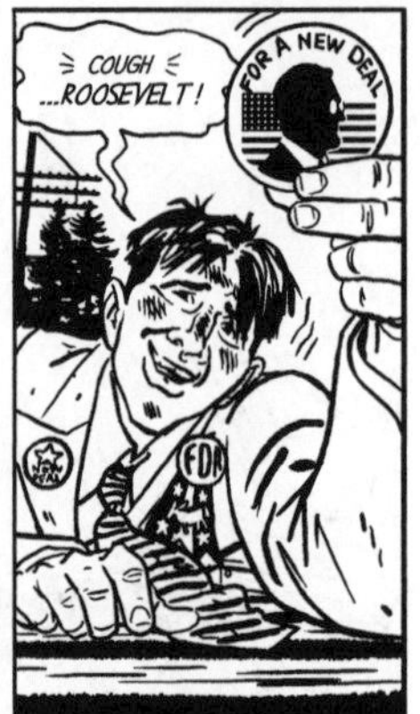
COUGH ...ROOSEVELT!
FOR A NEW DEAL
FDR

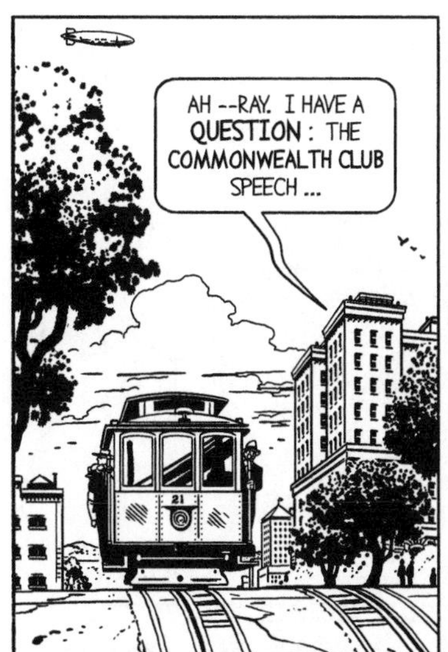
AH --RAY. I HAVE A QUESTION : THE COMMONWEALTH CLUB SPEECH ...
21

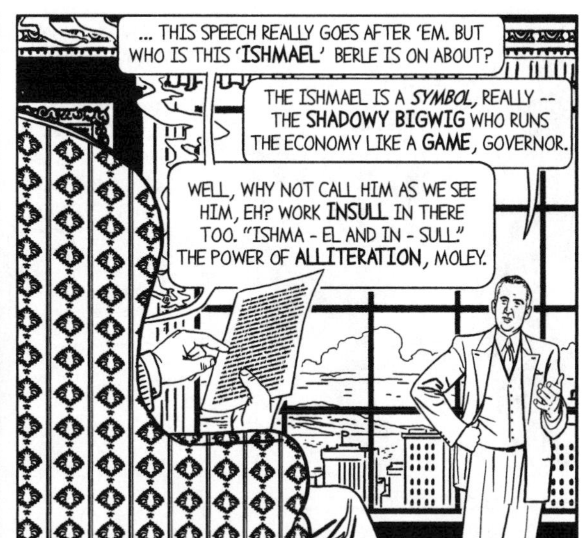
... THIS SPEECH REALLY GOES AFTER 'EM. BUT WHO IS THIS 'ISHMAEL' BERLE IS ON ABOUT?
THE ISHMAEL IS A SYMBOL, REALLY -- THE SHADOWY BIGWIG WHO RUNS THE ECONOMY LIKE A GAME, GOVERNOR.
WELL, WHY NOT CALL HIM AS WE SEE HIM, EH? WORK INSULL IN THERE TOO. "ISHMA - EL AND IN - SULL." THE POWER OF ALLITERATION, MOLEY.

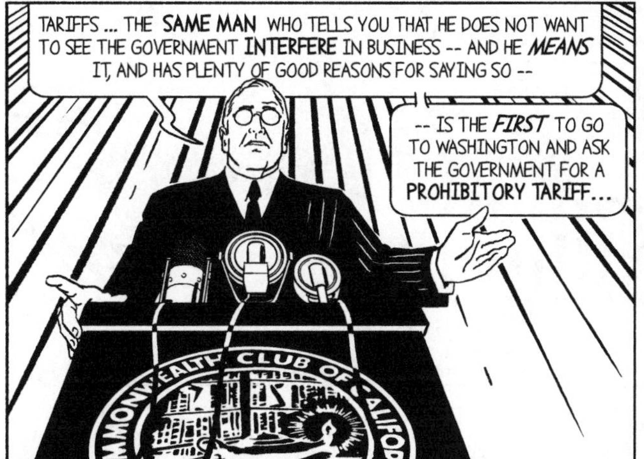
TARIFFS ... THE SAME MAN WHO TELLS YOU THAT HE DOES NOT WANT TO SEE THE GOVERNMENT INTERFERE IN BUSINESS -- AND HE MEANS IT, AND HAS PLENTY OF GOOD REASONS FOR SAYING SO --
-- IS THE FIRST TO GO TO WASHINGTON AND ASK THE GOVERNMENT FOR A PROHIBITORY TARIFF...

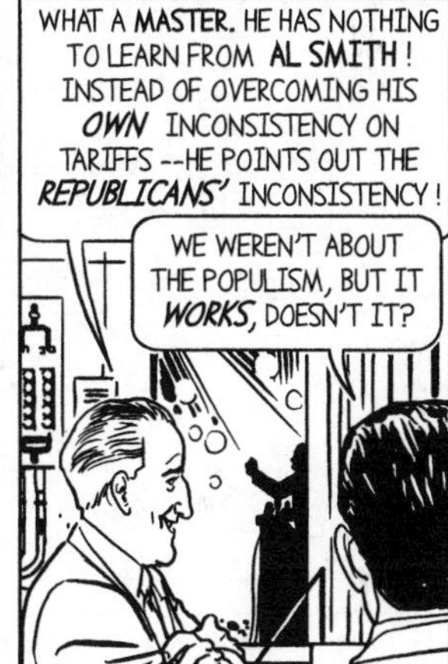
WHAT A MASTER. HE HAS NOTHING TO LEARN FROM AL SMITH ! INSTEAD OF OVERCOMING HIS OWN INCONSISTENCY ON TARIFFS --HE POINTS OUT THE REPUBLICANS' INCONSISTENCY !
WE WEREN'T ABOUT THE POPULISM, BUT IT WORKS, DOESN'T IT?

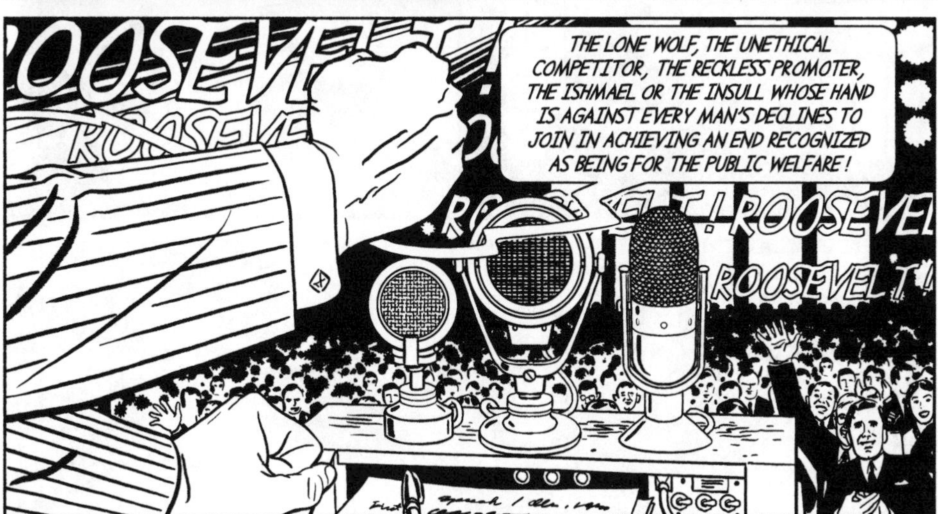
THE LONE WOLF, THE UNETHICAL COMPETITOR, THE RECKLESS PROMOTER, THE ISHMAEL OR THE INSULL WHOSE HAND IS AGAINST EVERY MAN'S DECLINES TO JOIN IN ACHIEVING AN END RECOGNIZED AS BEING FOR THE PUBLIC WELFARE !
ROOSEVELT!
ROOSEVELT! ROOSEVEL
ROOSEVELT!

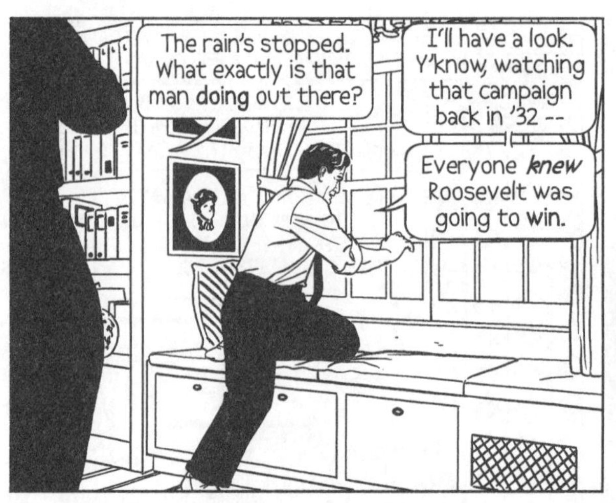
The rain's stopped. What exactly is that man **doing** out there?
I'll have a look. Y'know, watching that campaign back in '32 --
Everyone *knew* Roosevelt was going to **win**.

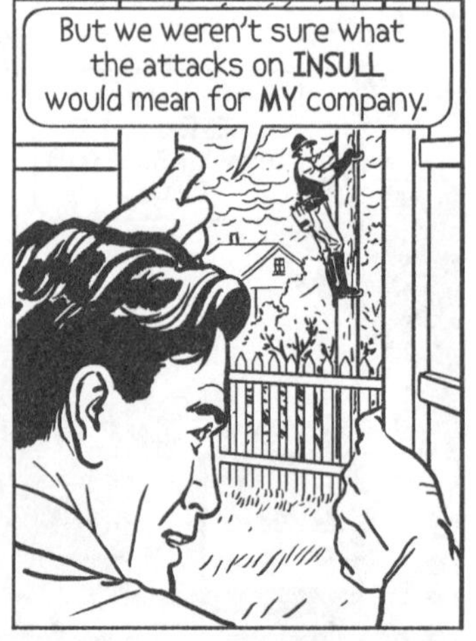
But we weren't sure what the attacks on **INSULL** would mean for **MY** company.

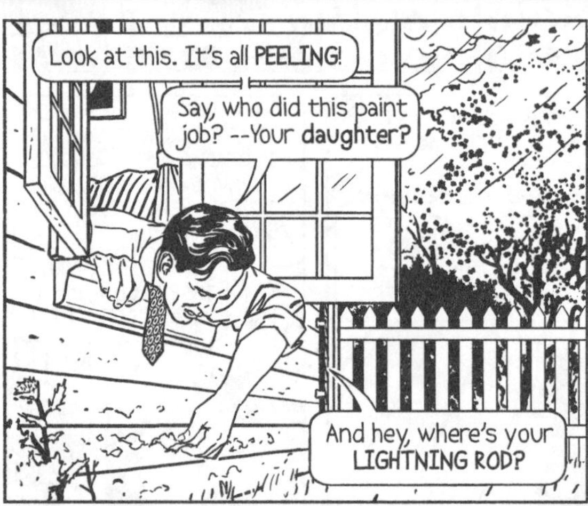
Look at this. It's all **PEELING**!
Say, who did this paint job? --Your **daughter?**
And hey, where's your **LIGHTNING ROD?**

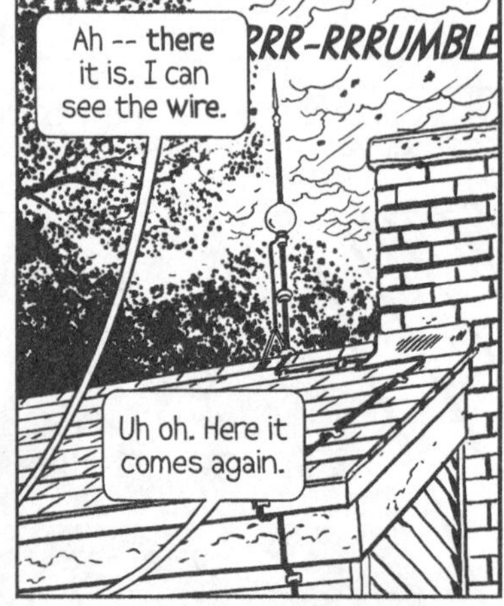
Ah -- **there** it is. I can see the **wire**.
RRR-RRRUMBLE
Uh oh. Here it comes again.

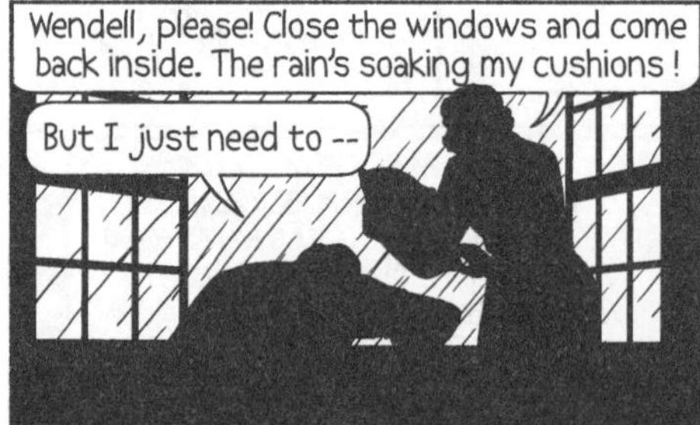
Wendell, please! Close the windows and come back inside. The rain's soaking my cushions !
But I just need to --

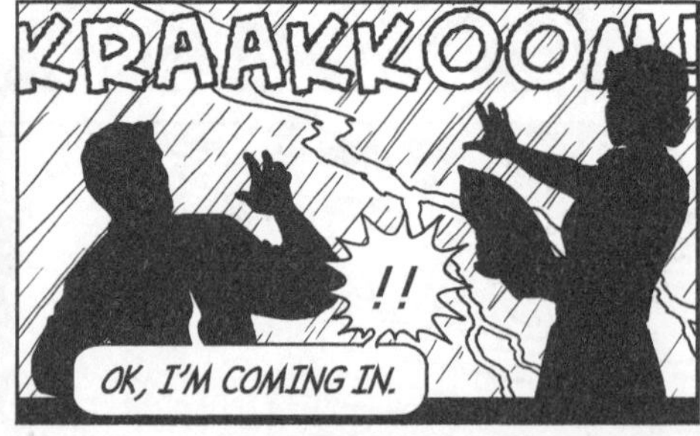
KRAAKKOOM
!!
OK, I'M COMING IN.

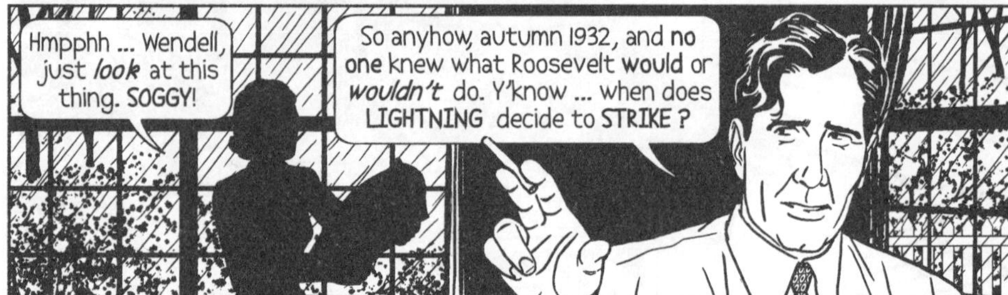
Hmpphh ... Wendell, just *look* at this thing. **SOGGY!**
So anyhow, autumn 1932, and **no one** knew what Roosevelt **would** or ***wouldn't*** do. Y'know ... when does **LIGHTNING** decide to **STRIKE ?**

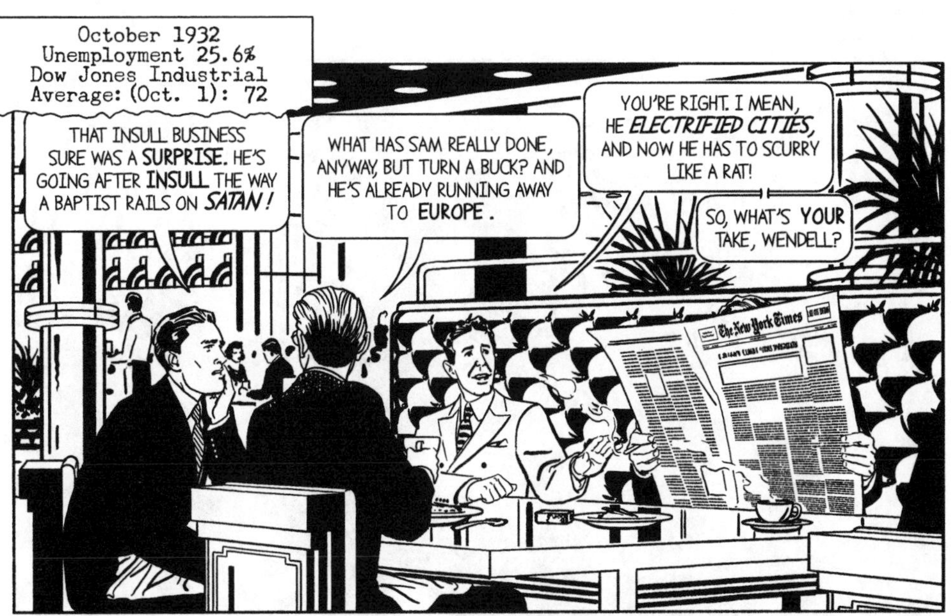
October 1932
Unemployment 25.6%
Dow Jones Industrial
Average: (Oct. 1): 72
THAT INSULL BUSINESS SURE WAS A SURPRISE. HE'S GOING AFTER INSULL THE WAY A BAPTIST RAILS ON SATAN!
WHAT HAS SAM REALLY DONE, ANYWAY, BUT TURN A BUCK? AND HE'S ALREADY RUNNING AWAY TO EUROPE.
YOU'RE RIGHT. I MEAN, HE ELECTRIFIED CITIES, AND NOW HE HAS TO SCURRY LIKE A RAT!
SO, WHAT'S YOUR TAKE, WENDELL?
The New York Times

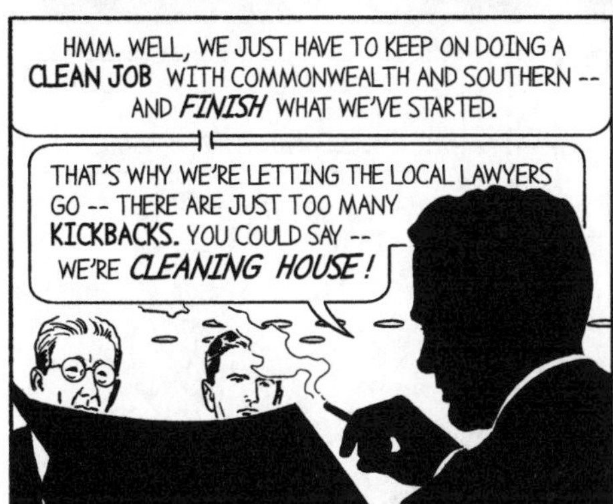
HMM. WELL, WE JUST HAVE TO KEEP ON DOING A CLEAN JOB WITH COMMONWEALTH AND SOUTHERN -- AND FINISH WHAT WE'VE STARTED.
THAT'S WHY WE'RE LETTING THE LOCAL LAWYERS GO -- THERE ARE JUST TOO MANY KICKBACKS. YOU COULD SAY -- WE'RE CLEANING HOUSE!

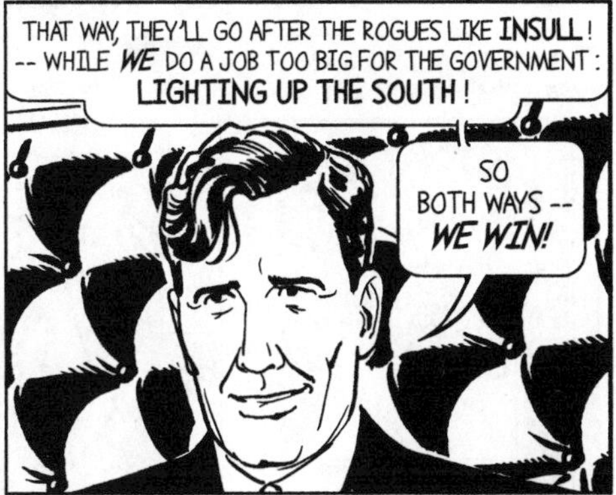
THAT WAY, THEY'LL GO AFTER THE ROGUES LIKE INSULL! -- WHILE WE DO A JOB TOO BIG FOR THE GOVERNMENT: LIGHTING UP THE SOUTH!
SO BOTH WAYS -- WE WIN!

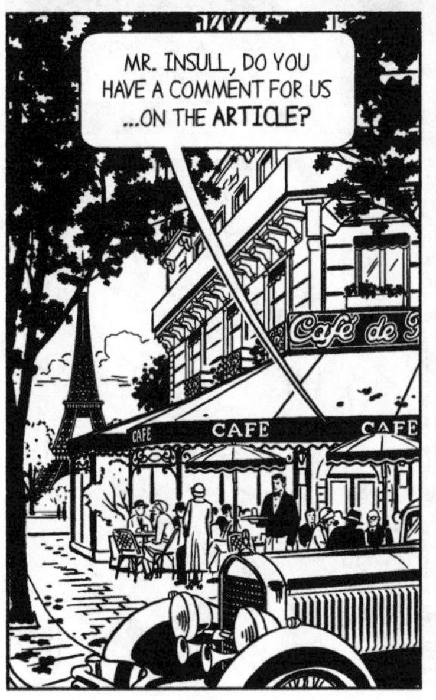
MR. INSULL, DO YOU HAVE A COMMENT FOR US ...ON THE ARTICLE?
CAFE
CAFE
CAFE

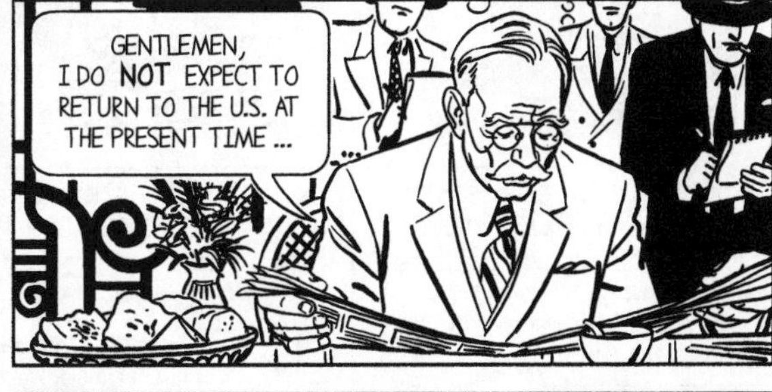
GENTLEMEN, I DO NOT EXPECT TO RETURN TO THE U.S. AT THE PRESENT TIME ...

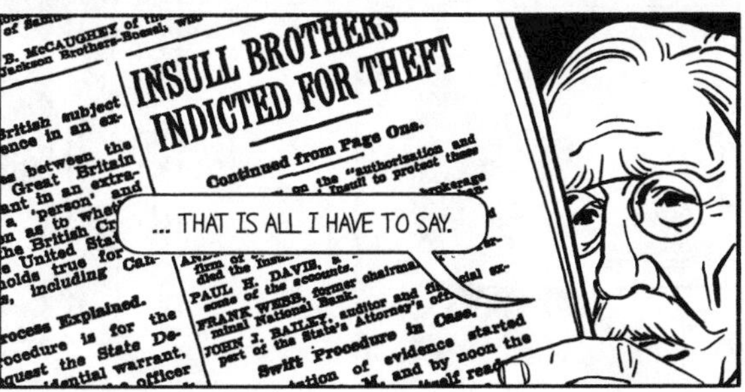
INSULL BROTHERS INDICTED FOR THEFT
Continued from Page One.
... THAT IS ALL I HAVE TO SAY.

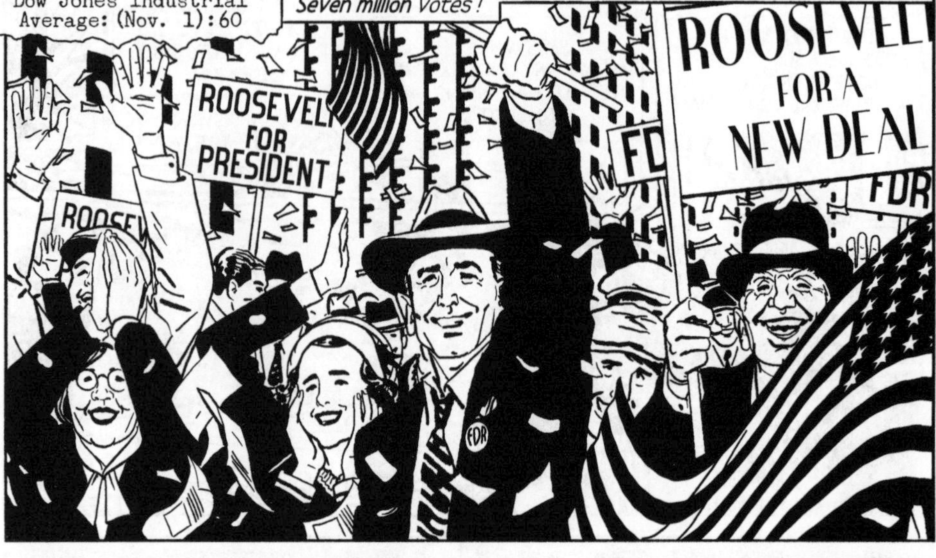
November 1932
Unemployment 23.2%
Dow Jones Industrial
Average: (Nov. 1): 60
The SIZE of the Roosevelt victory was something we didn't expect. Seven million votes!
ROOSEVELT FOR PRESIDENT
ROOSEV
FDR
ROOSEVEL FOR A NEW DEAL
FDR
FDR

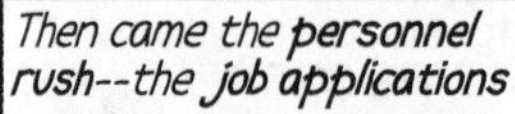
Then came the personnel rush--the job applications!

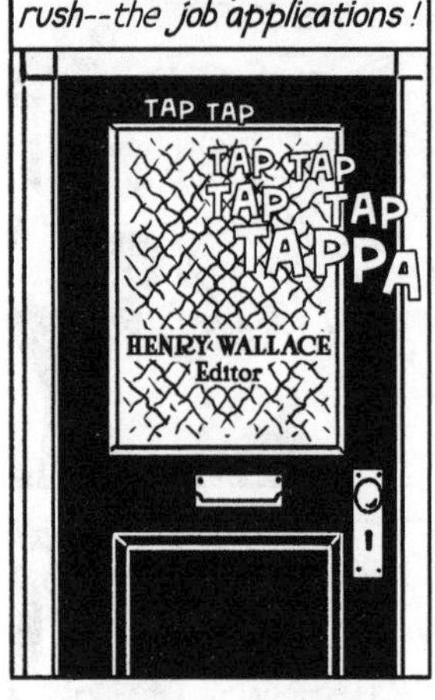
TAP TAP
TAP TAP TAP TAP TAPPA
HENRY WALLACE
Editor

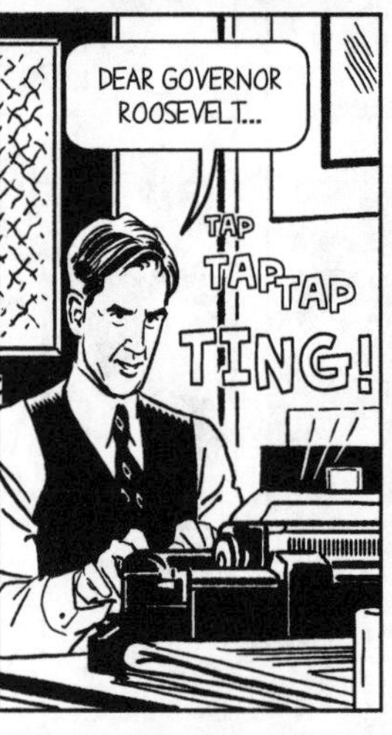
DEAR GOVERNOR ROOSEVELT...
TAP TAP TAP TING!

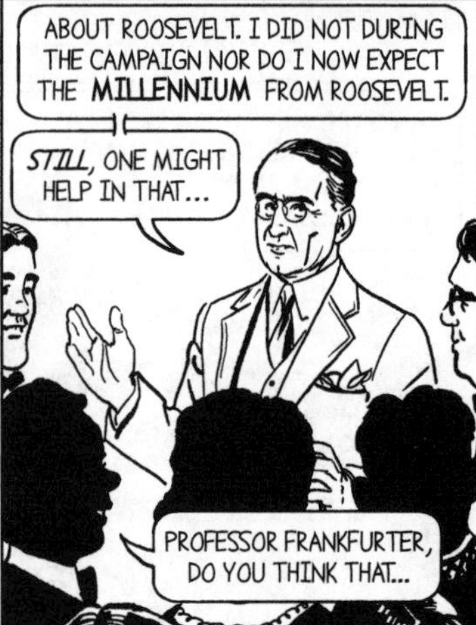
ABOUT ROOSEVELT. I DID NOT DURING THE CAMPAIGN NOR DO I NOW EXPECT THE MILLENNIUM FROM ROOSEVELT.
STILL, ONE MIGHT HELP IN THAT...
PROFESSOR FRANKFURTER, DO YOU THINK THAT...

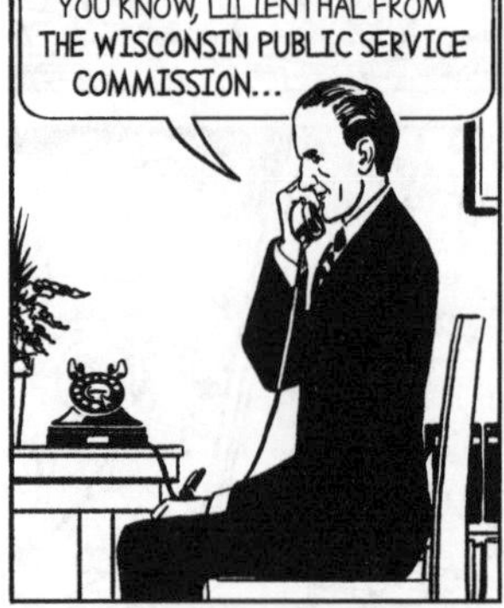
~ CRACKLE ~~ PROFESSOR BERLE? -- IT'S DAVID LILIENTHAL.
YOU KNOW, LILIENTHAL FROM THE WISCONSIN PUBLIC SERVICE COMMISSION...

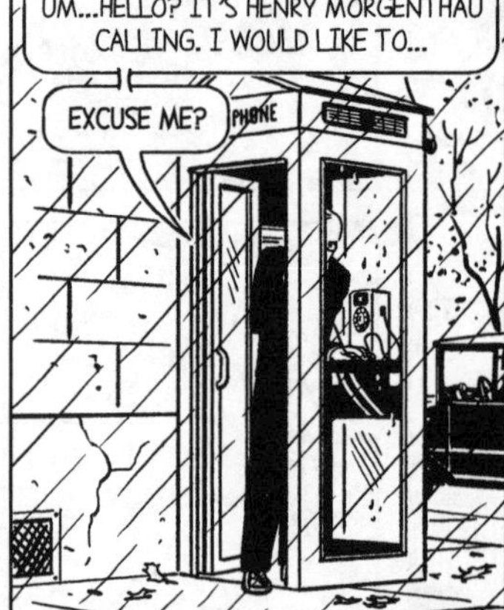
UM...HELLO? IT'S HENRY MORGENTHAU CALLING. I WOULD LIKE TO...
EXCUSE ME?
PHONE

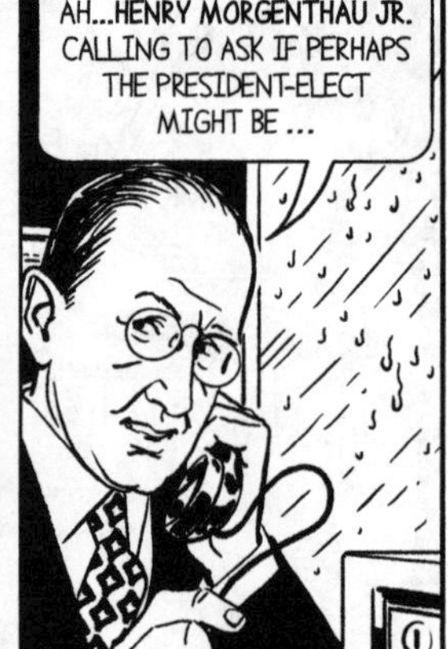
AH...HENRY MORGENTHAU JR. CALLING TO ASK IF PERHAPS THE PRESIDENT-ELECT MIGHT BE ...

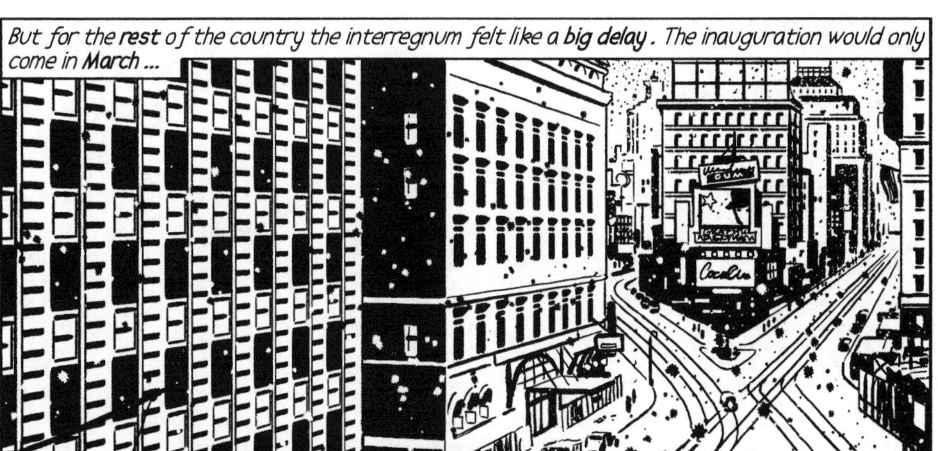
But for the **rest** of the country the interregnum felt like a **big delay**. The inauguration would only come in **March** ...

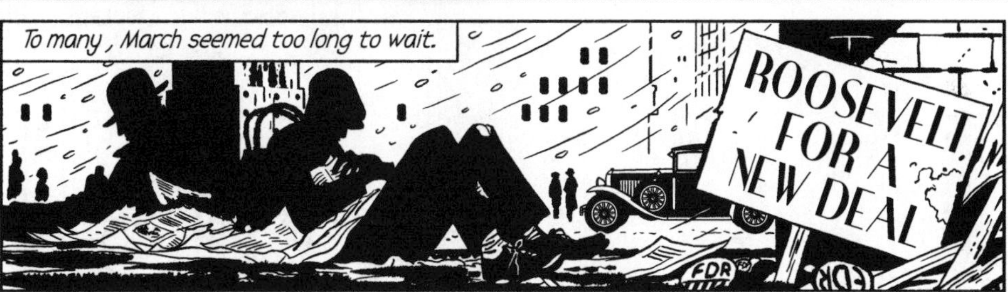
To many, March seemed too long to wait.
ROOSEVELT FOR A NEW DEAL
FDR

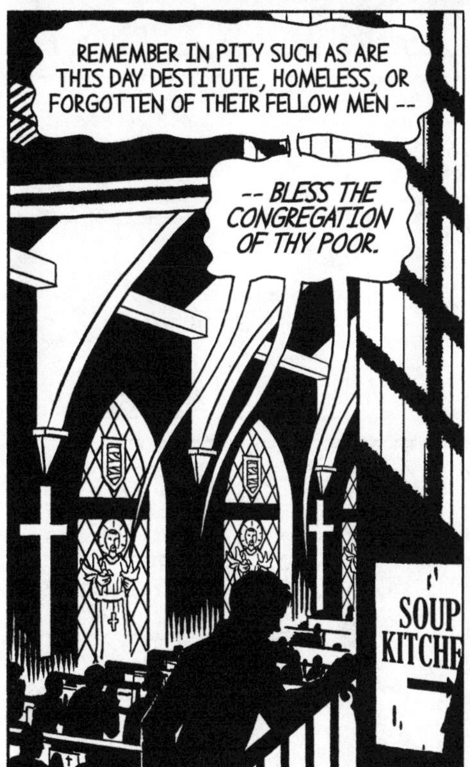
REMEMBER IN PITY SUCH AS ARE THIS DAY DESTITUTE, HOMELESS, OR FORGOTTEN OF THEIR FELLOW MEN --
-- BLESS THE CONGREGATION OF THY POOR.
SOUP KITCHE

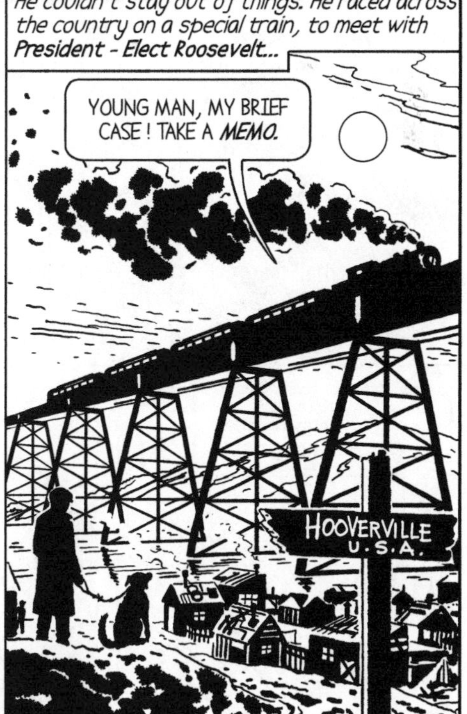
The wait seemed too long to **Herbert**, as well! He couldn't stay out of things. He raced across the country on a special train, to meet with **President - Elect Roosevelt**...
YOUNG MAN, MY BRIEF CASE! TAKE A *MEMO*.
HOOVERVILLE U.S.A.

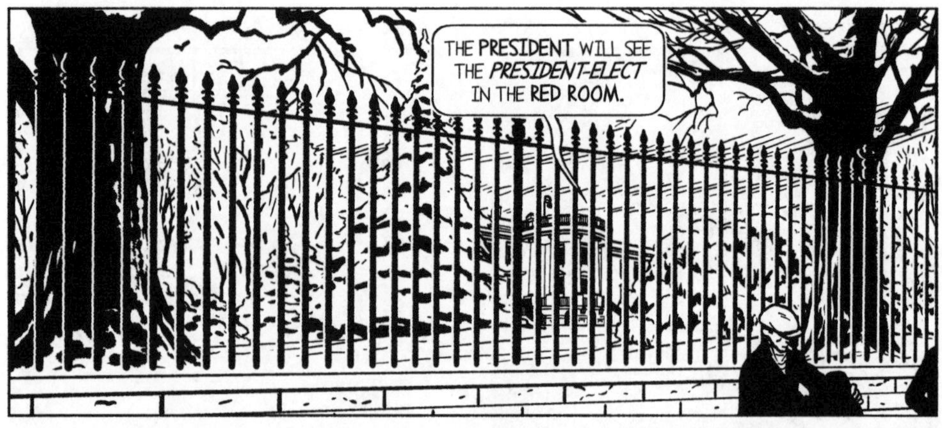
THE PRESIDENT WILL SEE
THE PRESIDENT-ELECT
IN THE RED ROOM.

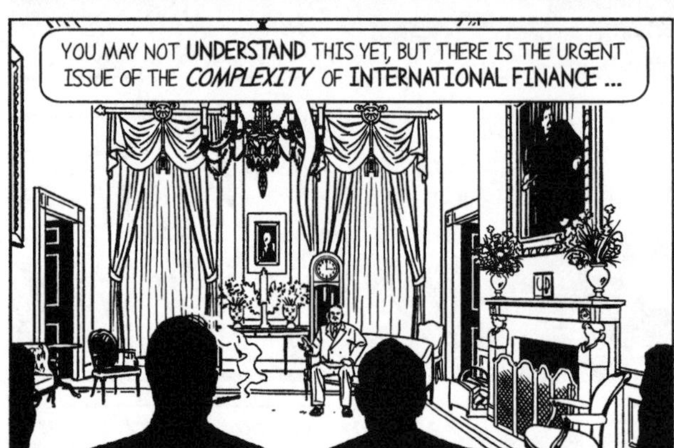
YOU MAY NOT UNDERSTAND THIS YET, BUT THERE IS THE URGENT ISSUE OF THE COMPLEXITY OF INTERNATIONAL FINANCE ...

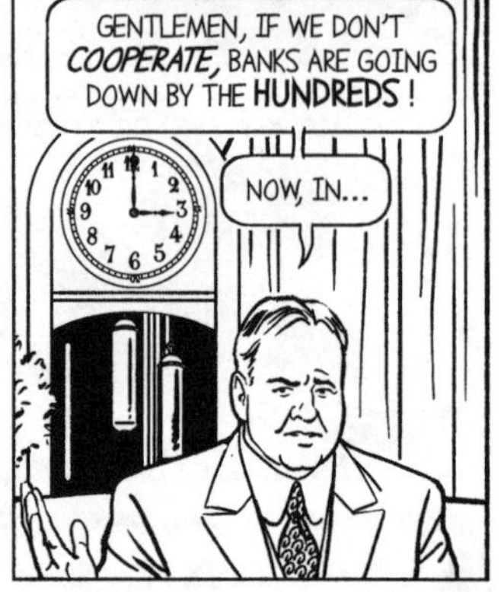
GENTLEMEN, IF WE DON'T COOPERATE, BANKS ARE GOING DOWN BY THE HUNDREDS !
NOW, IN...

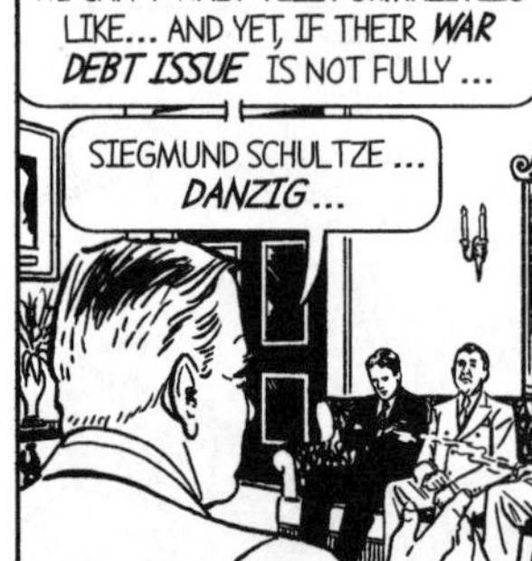
WE CAN'T WAIT TILL FORMALITIES LIKE... AND YET, IF THEIR WAR DEBT ISSUE IS NOT FULLY ...
SIEGMUND SCHULTZE ... DANZIG ...

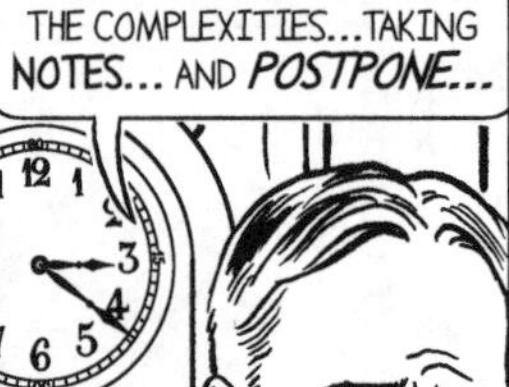
WE CAN HELP YOU DELVE INTO THE COMPLEXITIES...TAKING NOTES... AND POSTPONE...

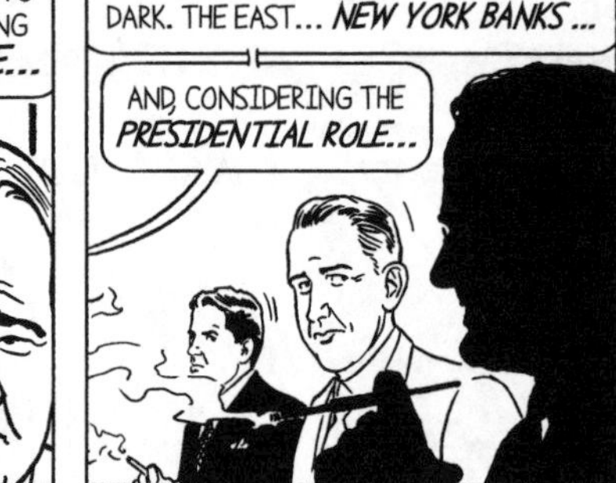
... MY MORATORIUM ... GERMAN OUTLOOK DARK. THE EAST... NEW YORK BANKS ...
AND, CONSIDERING THE PRESIDENTIAL ROLE...

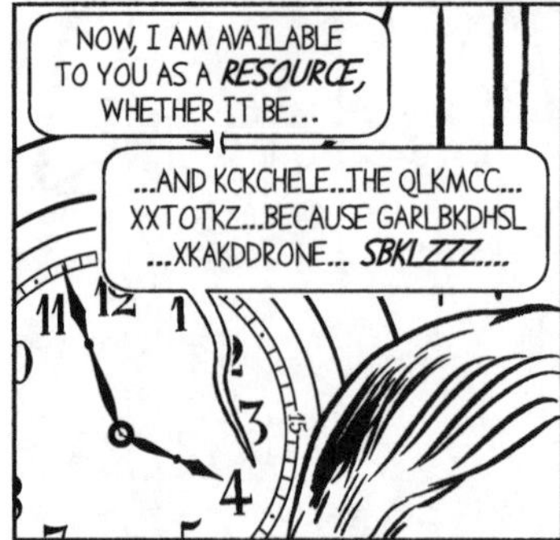
NOW, I AM AVAILABLE TO YOU AS A RESOURCE, WHETHER IT BE...
...AND KCKCHELE...THE QLKMCC... XXTOTKZ...BECAUSE GARLBKDHSL ...XKAKDDRONE... SBKLZZZ....

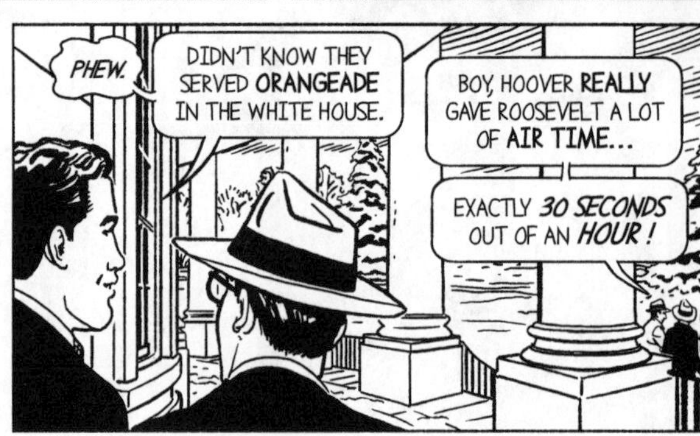
PHEW.
DIDN'T KNOW THEY SERVED ORANGEADE IN THE WHITE HOUSE.
BOY, HOOVER REALLY GAVE ROOSEVELT A LOT OF AIR TIME...
EXACTLY 30 SECONDS OUT OF AN HOUR !

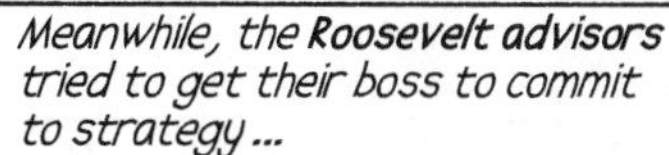

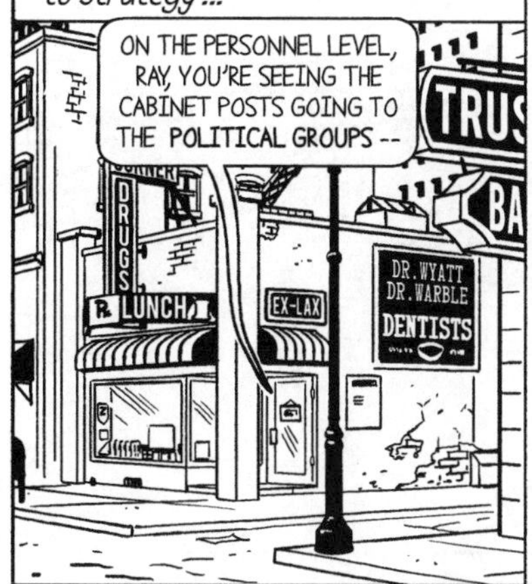

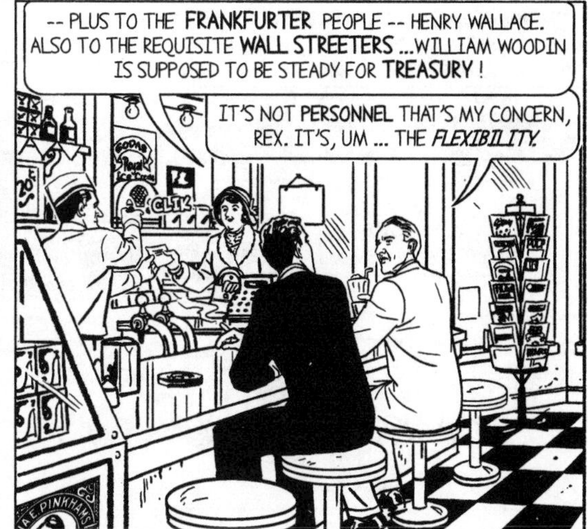

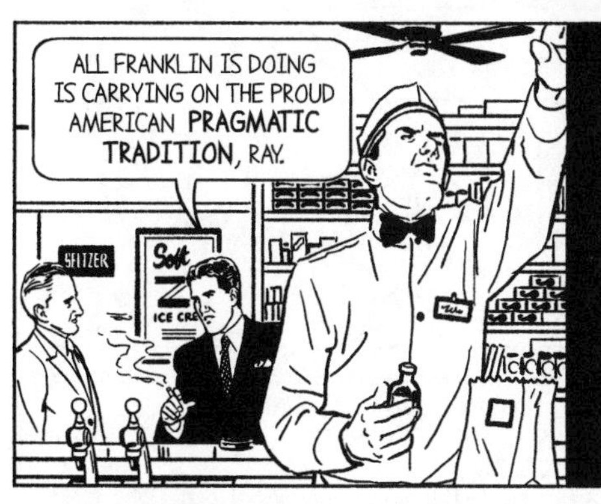

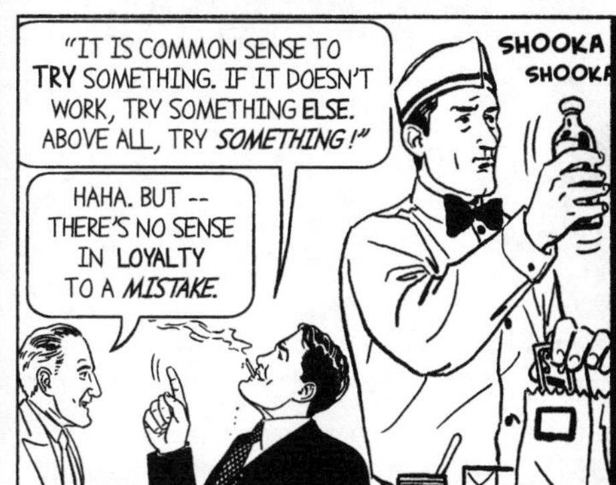

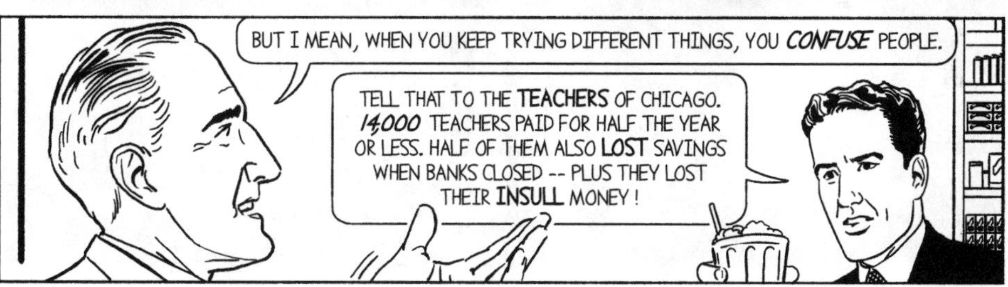

SEEMS LIKE IT'S A **DISEASE**. BANKS FAIL. THEN, EIGHTEEN MONTHS LATER, **MUNICIPALITIES** ARE THE CRISIS. WONDER WHAT THE RIGHT MEDICINE IS FOR ***THAT ?***

THE RIGHT **MEDICINE?**

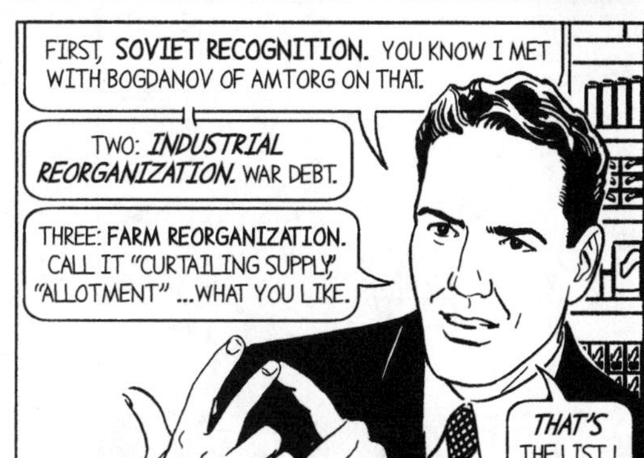

By January, 1933 it became clear that FDR wanted his administration to do something **dramatic** on utilities. Roosevelt was going to reverse the Coolidge policy and get into the hydropower business at Muscle Shoals, and quick ...

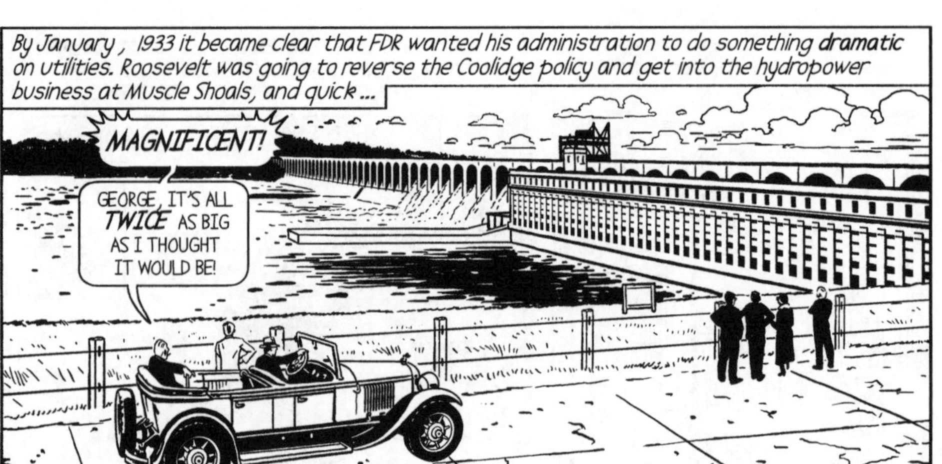

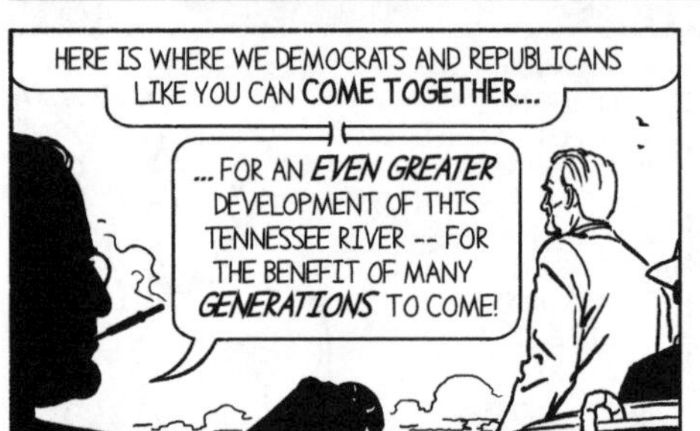

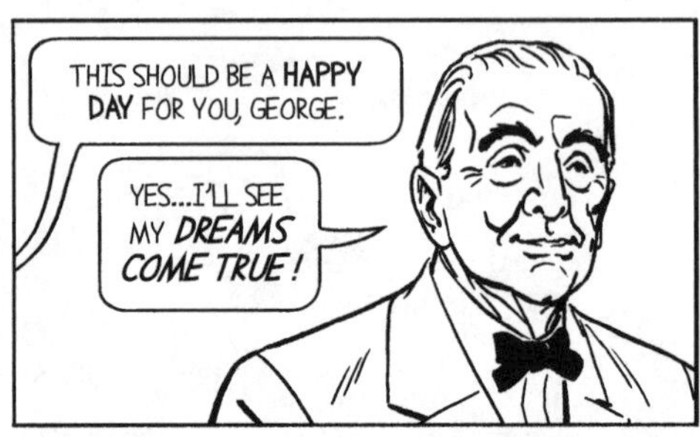

Sam Insull was a true *fugitive* by then, heading to *Greece.*

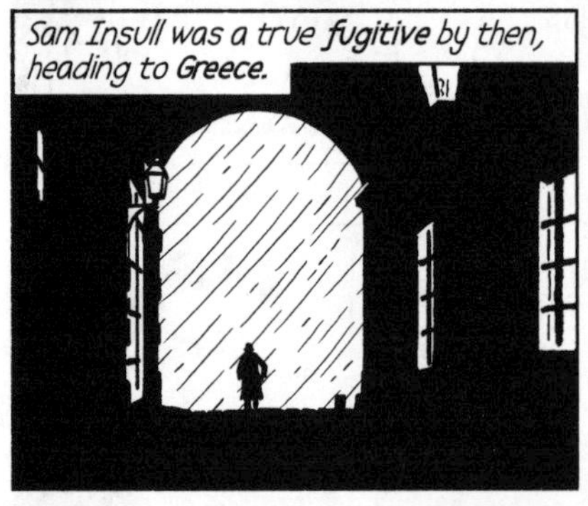

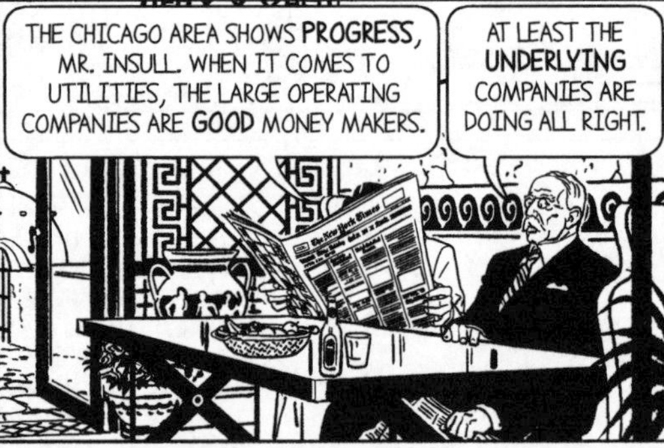

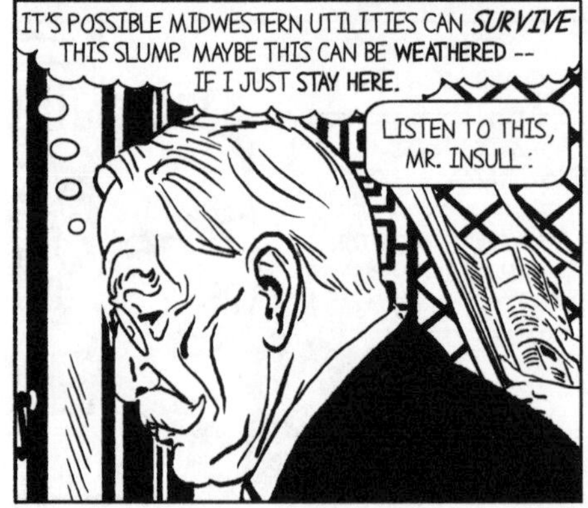

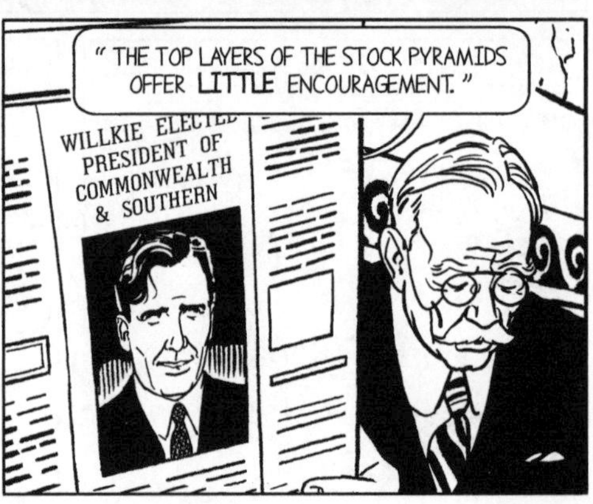

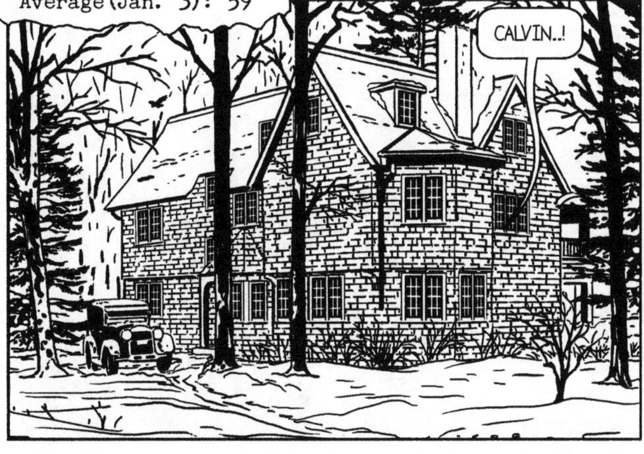
January 1933
Unemployment 25.9%
Dow Jones Industrial
Average(Jan. 3): 59
Those who might have **protested** didn't -- or **couldn't** ...
CALVIN..!

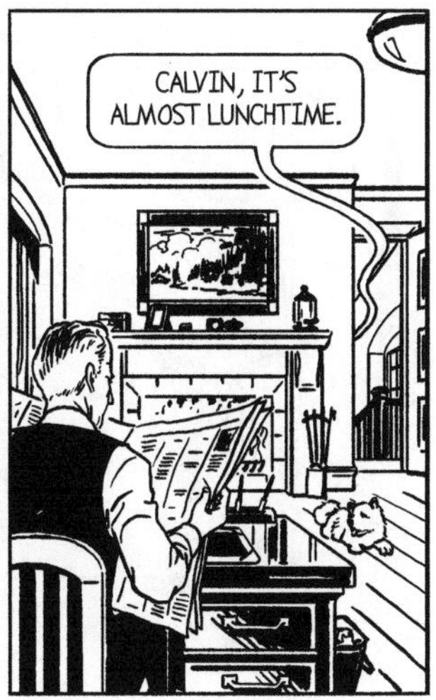
CALVIN, IT'S ALMOST LUNCHTIME.

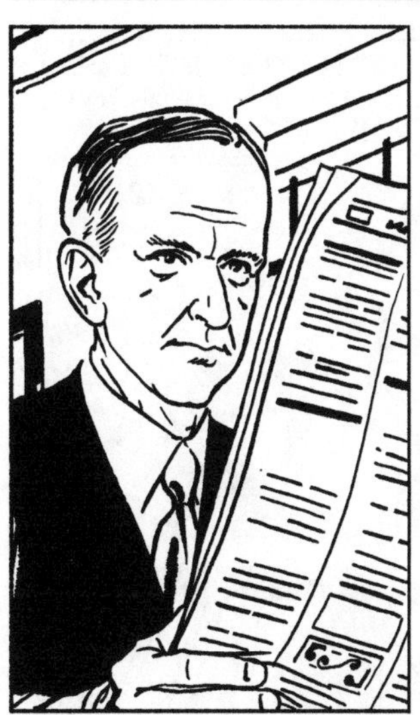

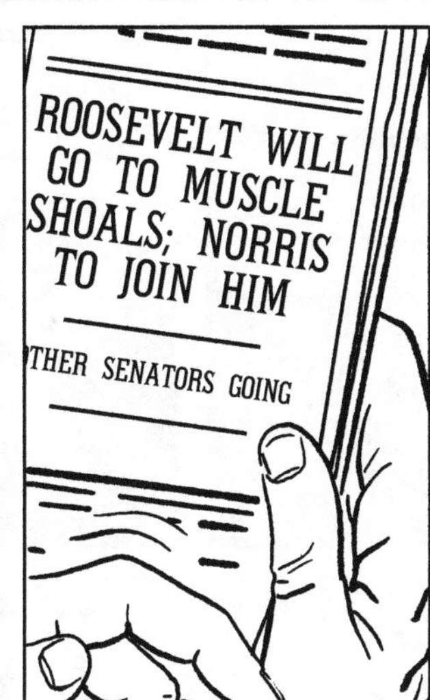
ROOSEVELT WILL GO TO MUSCLE SHOALS; NORRIS TO JOIN HIM
THER SENATORS GOING

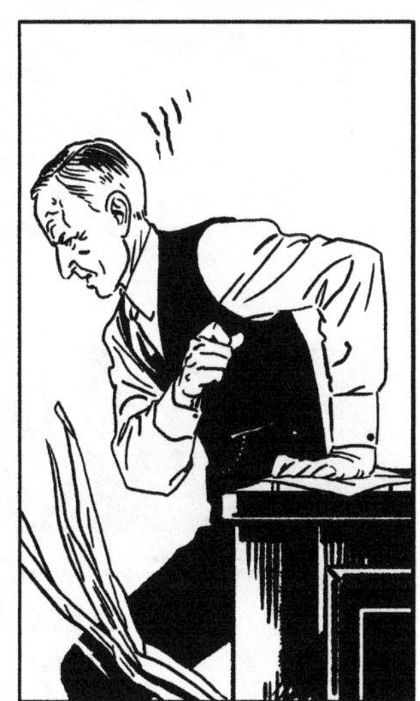

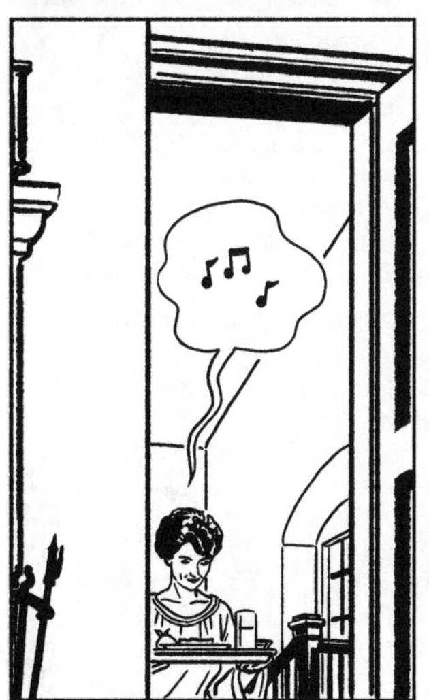

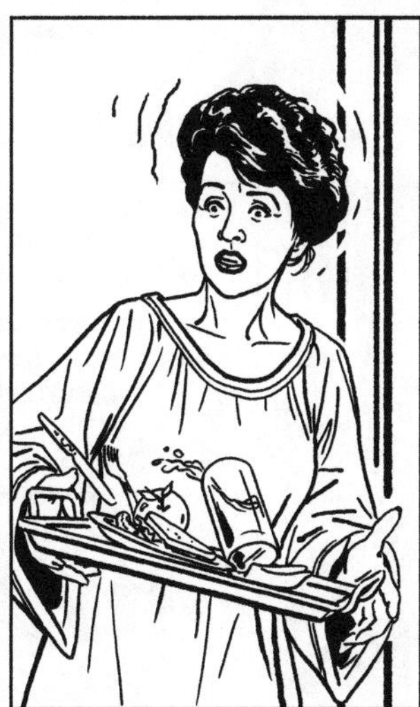

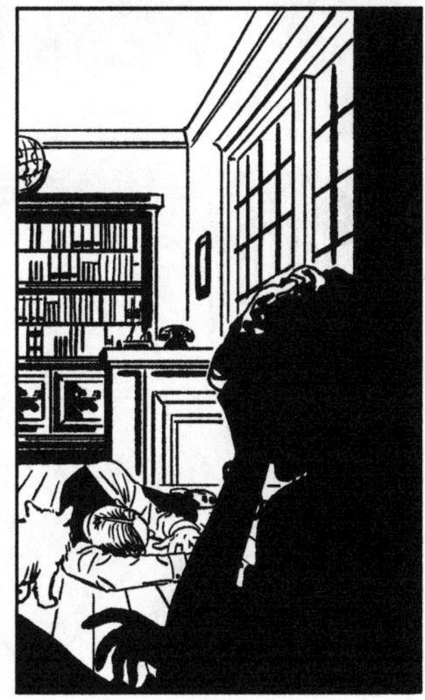

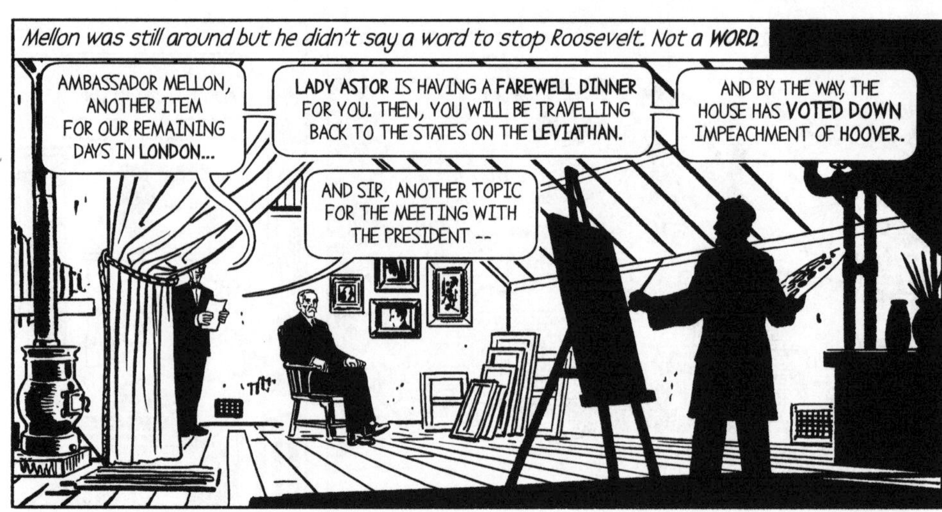

-- DEPOSIT INSURANCE. MAKE THE POINT "REFORMS PERHAPS YES, BUT DEPOSIT INSURANCE IS THE WRONG ONE TO BACK"...

RECALL THAT YOUR ATTORNEY SAID ROOSEVELT COULD BE REASONABLE. OUR SOURCES SAY HE MAY NOT ENDORSE DEPOSIT INSURANCE, WHICH FAILED IN NEW YORK STATE WHEN THEY TRIED IT...

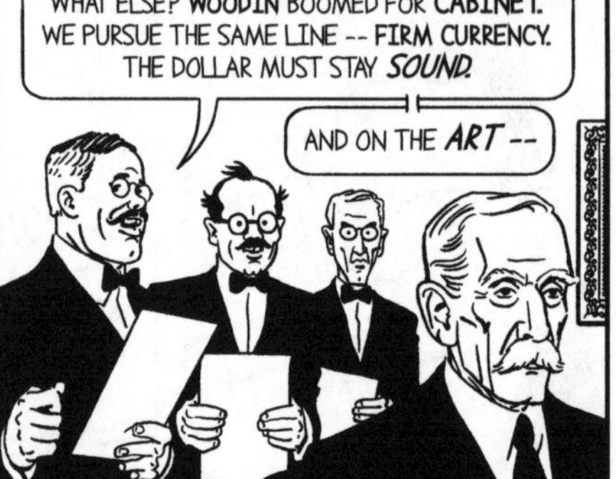

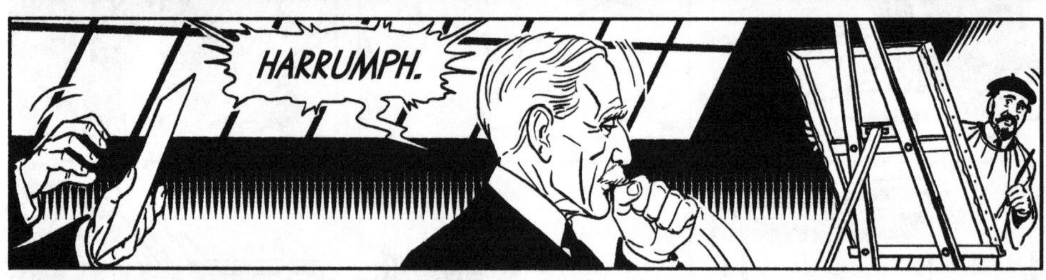

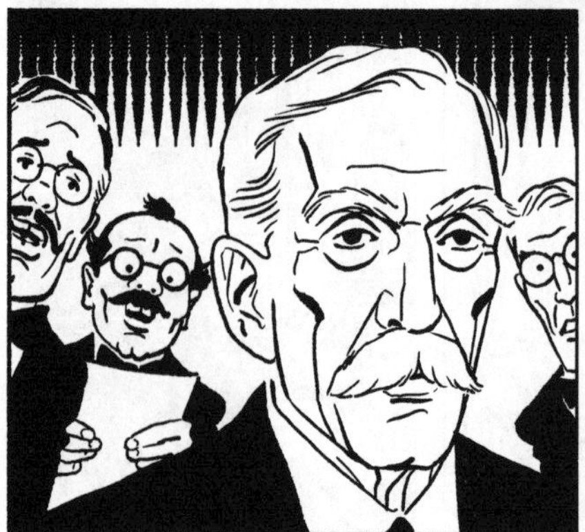

ANYHOW, SIR, YOU KNOW THE TALKING POINTS TO OUTLINE AT THE WHITE HOUSE. MONEY -- SOUND. NO TINKERING. NEW YORK FAILURE PROVED DEPOSIT INSURANCE'S FLAWS.

IF, WHILE TRAVELLING, YOU ARE TRAPPED IN AN INTERVIEW, MAKE THE OLD ARGUMENT : IF THE GOVERNMENT INSURES A BANK, THE BANK KNOWS IT CAN DO WRONG WITH NO CONSEQUENCE. CLASSIC MORAL HAZARD ...

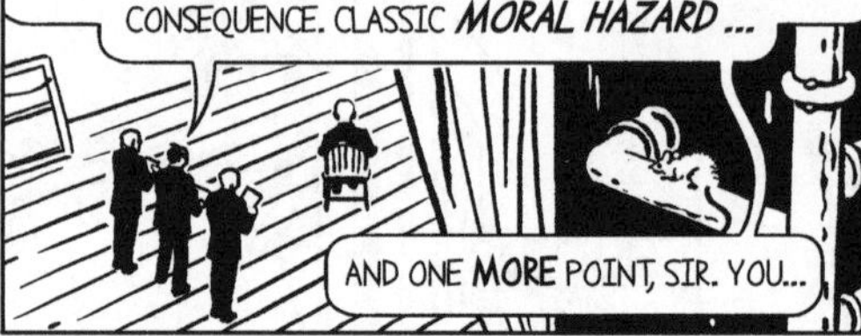

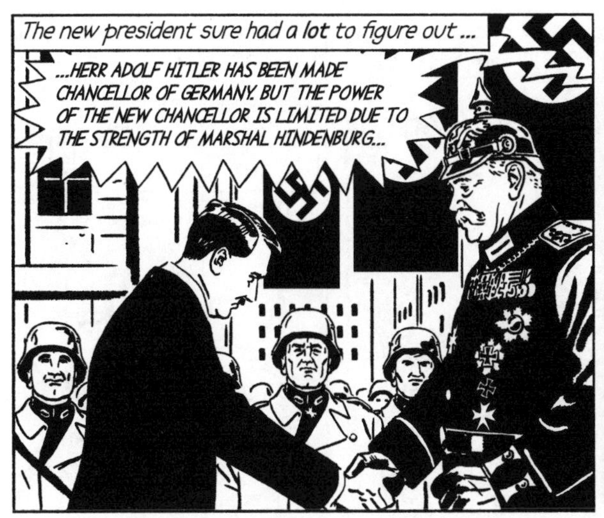
The new president sure had a lot to figure out ...
...HERR ADOLF HITLER HAS BEEN MADE CHANCELLOR OF GERMANY. BUT THE POWER OF THE NEW CHANCELLOR IS LIMITED DUE TO THE STRENGTH OF MARSHAL HINDENBURG...

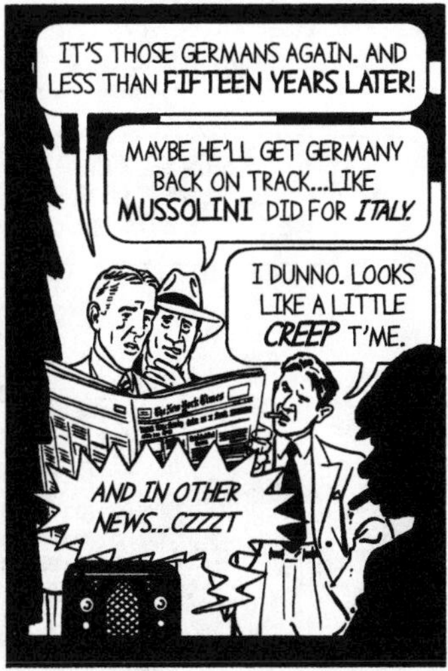
IT'S THOSE GERMANS AGAIN. AND LESS THAN FIFTEEN YEARS LATER!
MAYBE HE'LL GET GERMANY BACK ON TRACK...LIKE MUSSOLINI DID FOR ITALY.
I DUNNO. LOOKS LIKE A LITTLE CREEP T'ME.
AND IN OTHER NEWS...CZZZT

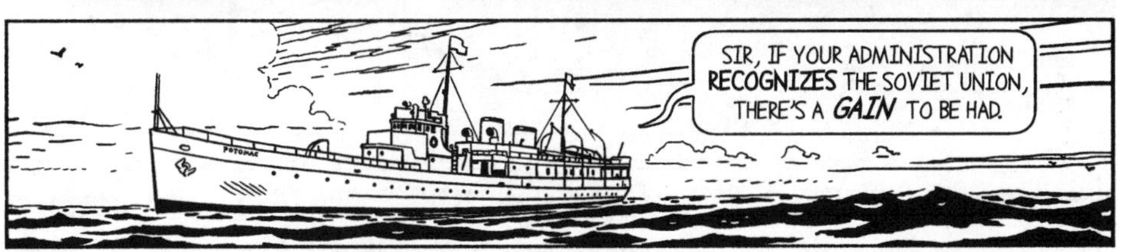
SIR, IF YOUR ADMINISTRATION RECOGNIZES THE SOVIET UNION, THERE'S A GAIN TO BE HAD.
POTOMAC

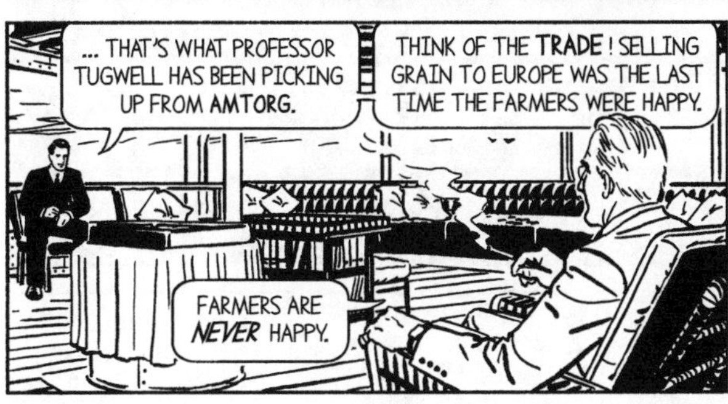
... THAT'S WHAT PROFESSOR TUGWELL HAS BEEN PICKING UP FROM AMTORG.
THINK OF THE TRADE! SELLING GRAIN TO EUROPE WAS THE LAST TIME THE FARMERS WERE HAPPY.
FARMERS ARE NEVER HAPPY.

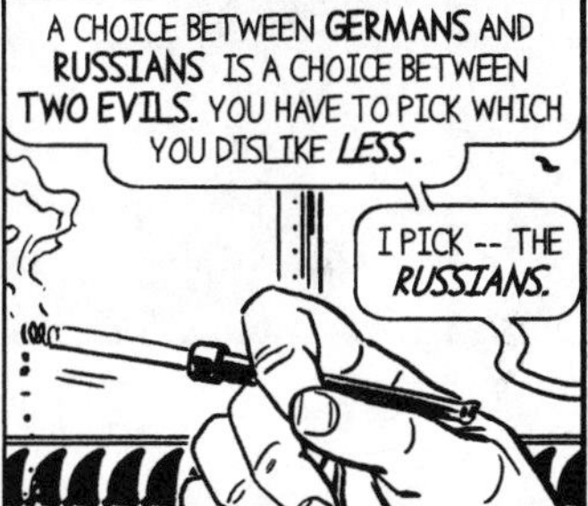
A CHOICE BETWEEN GERMANS AND RUSSIANS IS A CHOICE BETWEEN TWO EVILS. YOU HAVE TO PICK WHICH YOU DISLIKE LESS.
I PICK -- THE RUSSIANS.

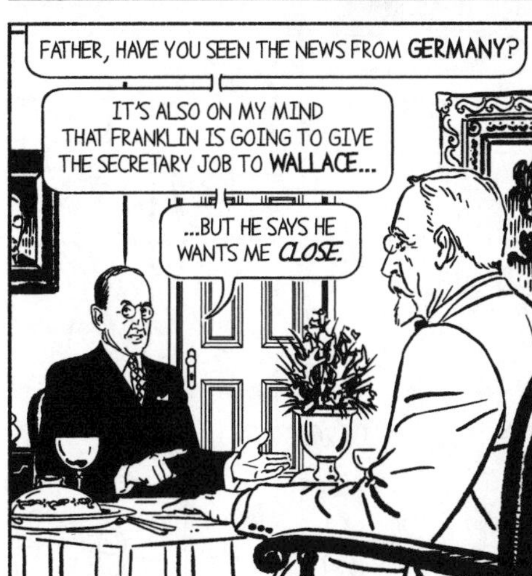
FATHER, HAVE YOU SEEN THE NEWS FROM GERMANY?
IT'S ALSO ON MY MIND THAT FRANKLIN IS GOING TO GIVE THE SECRETARY JOB TO WALLACE...
...BUT HE SAYS HE WANTS ME CLOSE.

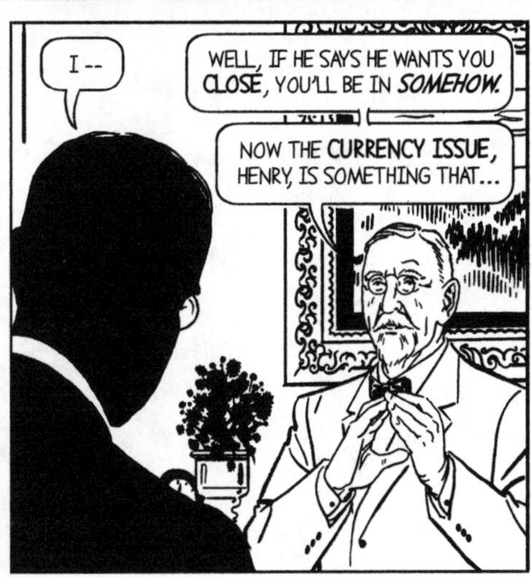
I --
WELL, IF HE SAYS HE WANTS YOU CLOSE, YOU'LL BE IN SOMEHOW.
NOW THE CURRENCY ISSUE, HENRY, IS SOMETHING THAT...

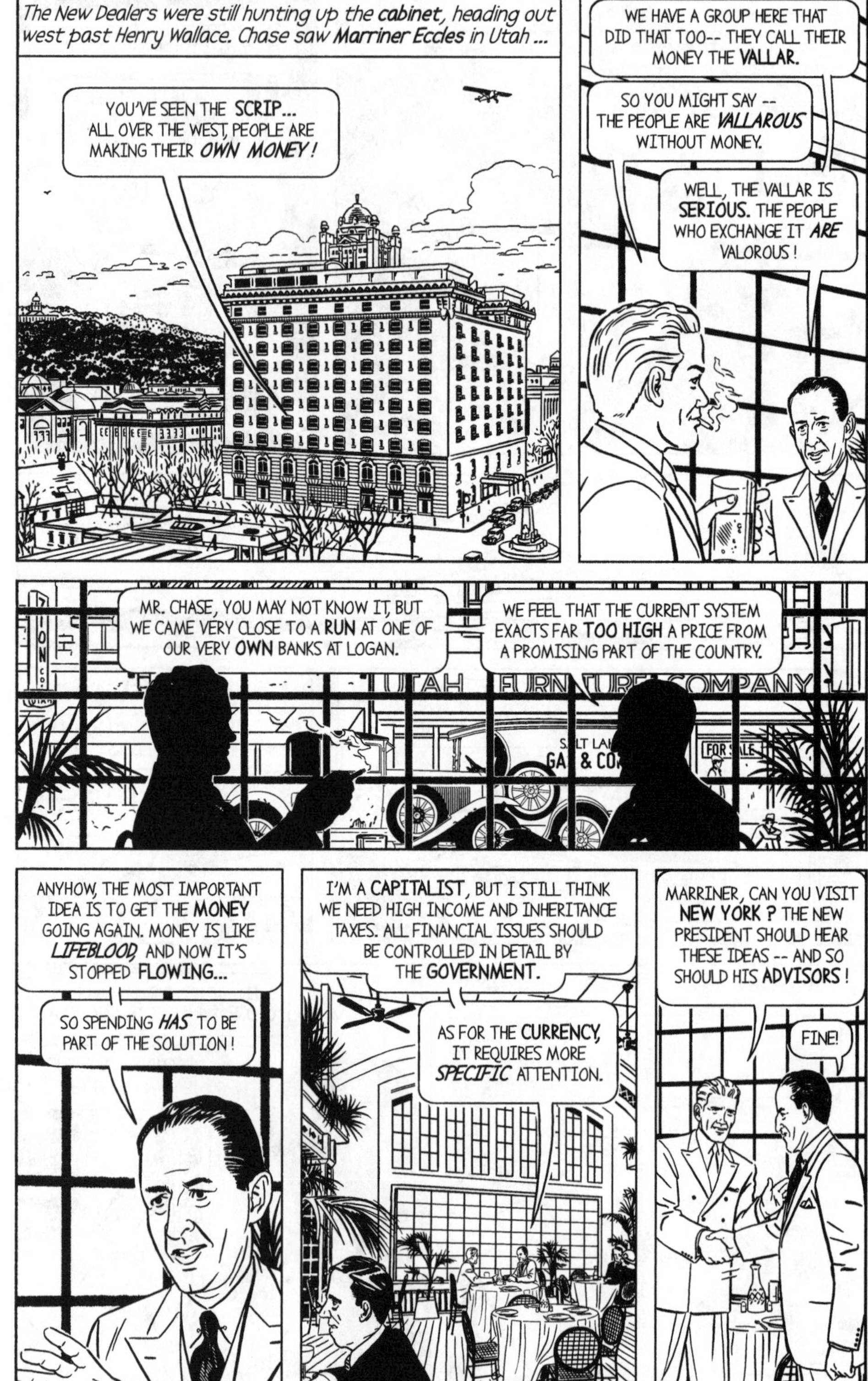
The New Dealers were still hunting up the **cabinet**, heading out west past Henry Wallace. Chase saw **Marriner Eccles** in Utah ...
YOU'VE SEEN THE SCRIP... ALL OVER THE WEST, PEOPLE ARE MAKING THEIR OWN MONEY!
WE HAVE A GROUP HERE THAT DID THAT TOO-- THEY CALL THEIR MONEY THE VALLAR.
SO YOU MIGHT SAY -- THE PEOPLE ARE VALLAROUS WITHOUT MONEY.
WELL, THE VALLAR IS SERIOUS. THE PEOPLE WHO EXCHANGE IT ARE VALOROUS!
MR. CHASE, YOU MAY NOT KNOW IT, BUT WE CAME VERY CLOSE TO A RUN AT ONE OF OUR VERY OWN BANKS AT LOGAN.
WE FEEL THAT THE CURRENT SYSTEM EXACTS FAR TOO HIGH A PRICE FROM A PROMISING PART OF THE COUNTRY.
UTAH FURNITURE COMPANY
FOR SALE
ANYHOW, THE MOST IMPORTANT IDEA IS TO GET THE MONEY GOING AGAIN. MONEY IS LIKE LIFEBLOOD, AND NOW IT'S STOPPED FLOWING...
SO SPENDING HAS TO BE PART OF THE SOLUTION!
I'M A CAPITALIST, BUT I STILL THINK WE NEED HIGH INCOME AND INHERITANCE TAXES. ALL FINANCIAL ISSUES SHOULD BE CONTROLLED IN DETAIL BY THE GOVERNMENT.
AS FOR THE CURRENCY, IT REQUIRES MORE SPECIFIC ATTENTION.
MARRINER, CAN YOU VISIT NEW YORK? THE NEW PRESIDENT SHOULD HEAR THESE IDEAS -- AND SO SHOULD HIS ADVISORS!
FINE!

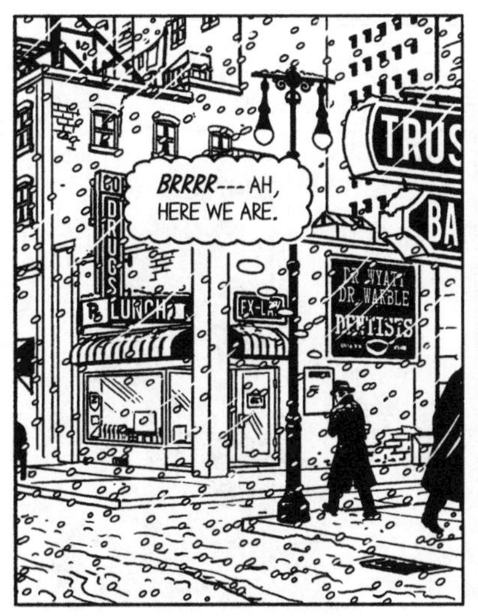
BRRRR--- AH, HERE WE ARE.
TRUS
BA
DRUGS
LURCH
EX-LA
DR. WYATT
DR. WARBLE
DENTISTS

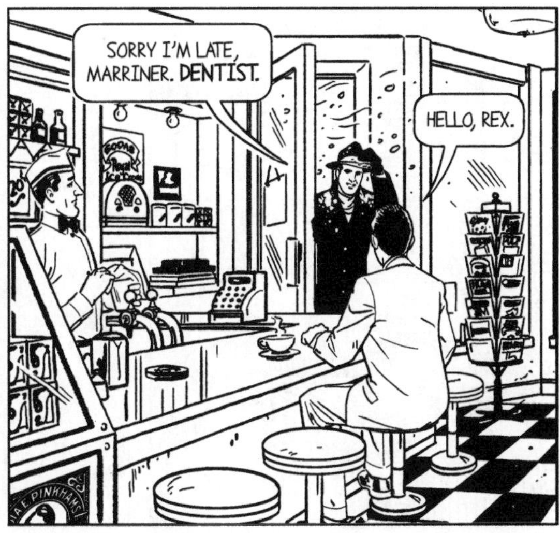
SORRY I'M LATE, MARRINER. DENTIST.
HELLO, REX.

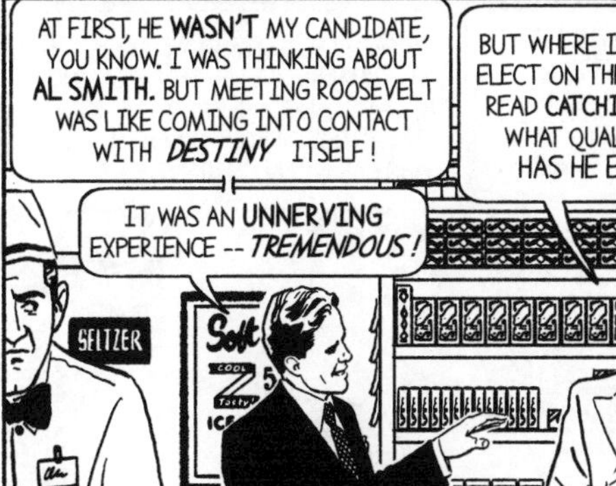
AT FIRST, HE WASN'T MY CANDIDATE, YOU KNOW. I WAS THINKING ABOUT AL SMITH. BUT MEETING ROOSEVELT WAS LIKE COMING INTO CONTACT WITH DESTINY ITSELF!
IT WAS AN UNNERVING EXPERIENCE -- TREMENDOUS!
BUT WHERE IS THE PRESIDENT - ELECT ON THE ISSUES? HAS HE READ CATCHINGS AND FOSTER? WHAT QUALITY OF BANKER HAS HE EXPERIENCED?
SELTZER
Choc-O Hearts

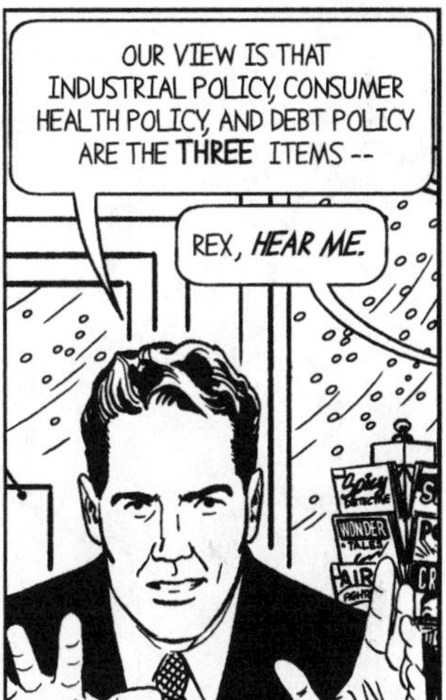
OUR VIEW IS THAT INDUSTRIAL POLICY, CONSUMER HEALTH POLICY, AND DEBT POLICY ARE THE THREE ITEMS --
REX, HEAR ME.

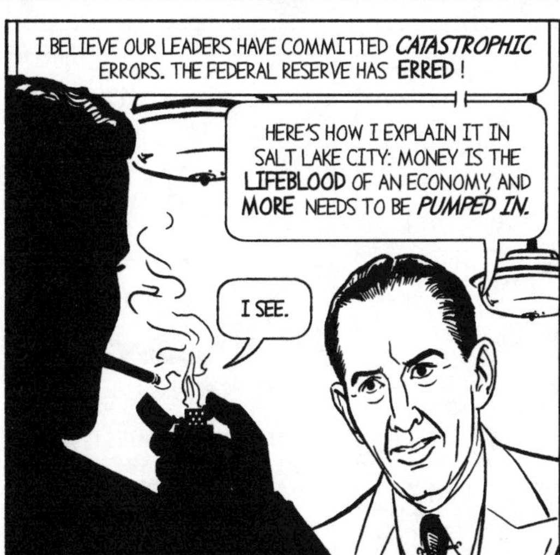
I BELIEVE OUR LEADERS HAVE COMMITTED CATASTROPHIC ERRORS. THE FEDERAL RESERVE HAS ERRED!
HERE'S HOW I EXPLAIN IT IN SALT LAKE CITY: MONEY IS THE LIFEBLOOD OF AN ECONOMY, AND MORE NEEDS TO BE PUMPED IN.
I SEE.

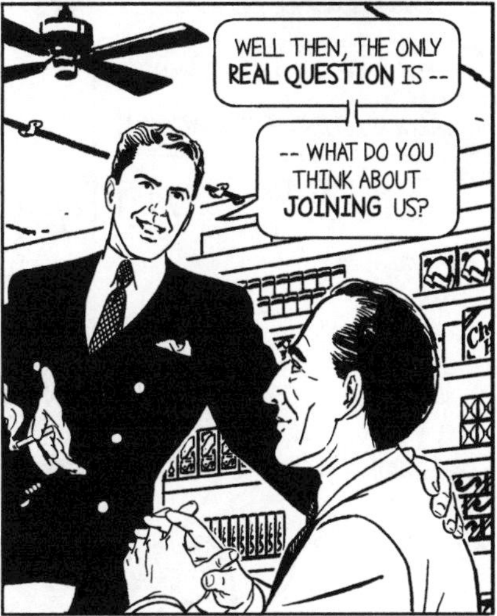
WELL THEN, THE ONLY REAL QUESTION IS --
-- WHAT DO YOU THINK ABOUT JOINING US?

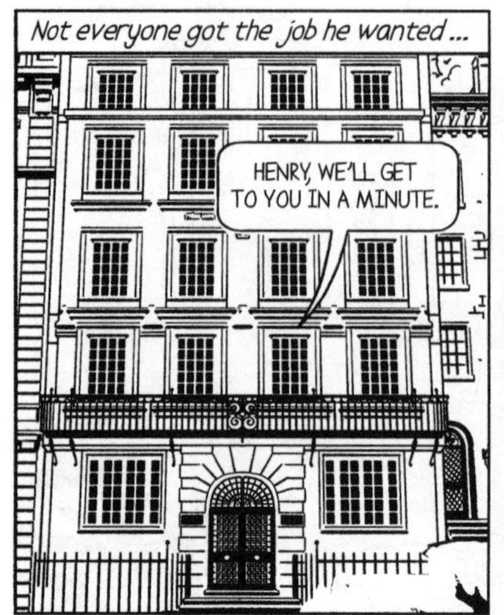
Not everyone got the job he wanted...
HENRY, WE'LL GET TO YOU IN A MINUTE.

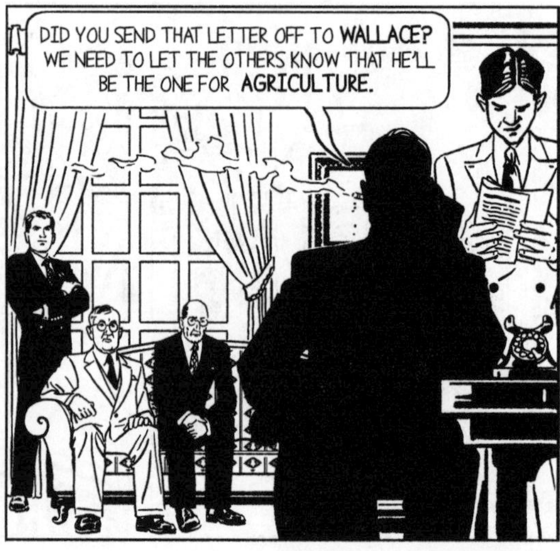
DID YOU SEND THAT LETTER OFF TO WALLACE? WE NEED TO LET THE OTHERS KNOW THAT HE'LL BE THE ONE FOR AGRICULTURE.

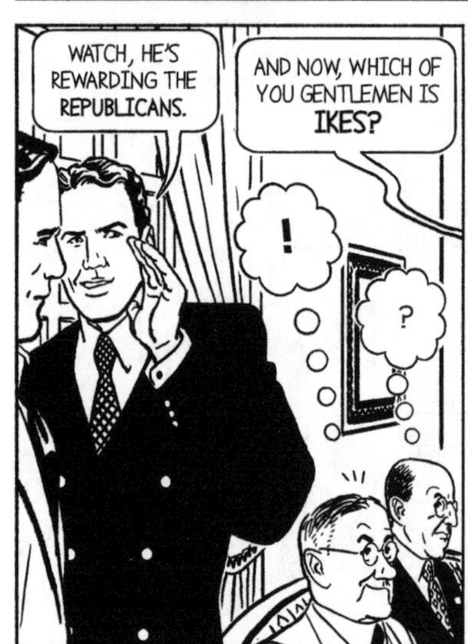
WATCH, HE'S REWARDING THE REPUBLICANS.
AND NOW, WHICH OF YOU GENTLEMEN IS IKES?
!
?

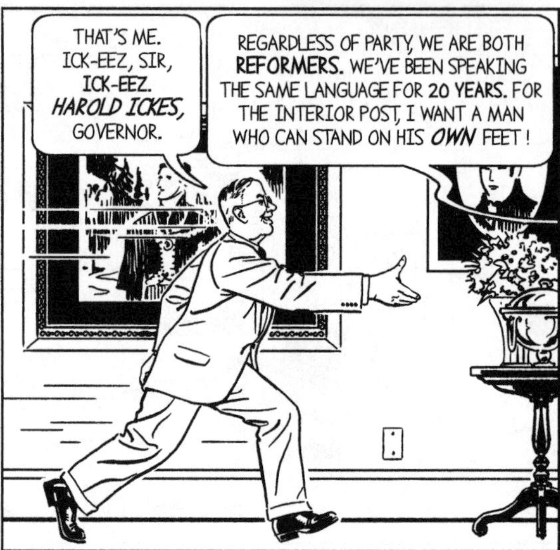
THAT'S ME. ICK-EEZ, SIR, ICK-EEZ. HAROLD ICKES, GOVERNOR.
REGARDLESS OF PARTY, WE ARE BOTH REFORMERS. WE'VE BEEN SPEAKING THE SAME LANGUAGE FOR 20 YEARS. FOR THE INTERIOR POST, I WANT A MAN WHO CAN STAND ON HIS OWN FEET!

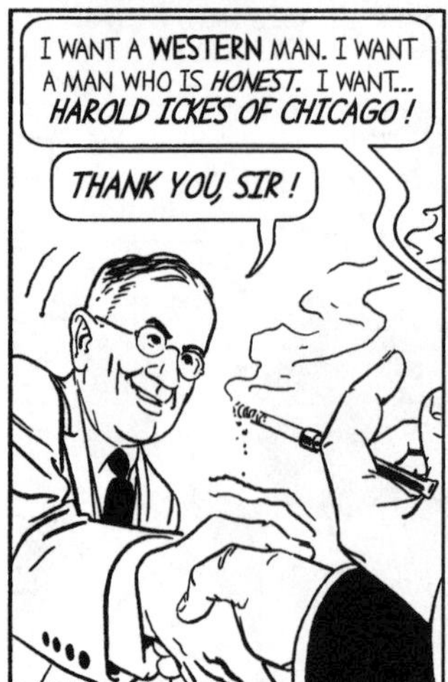
I WANT A WESTERN MAN. I WANT A MAN WHO IS HONEST. I WANT... HAROLD ICKES OF CHICAGO!
THANK YOU, SIR!

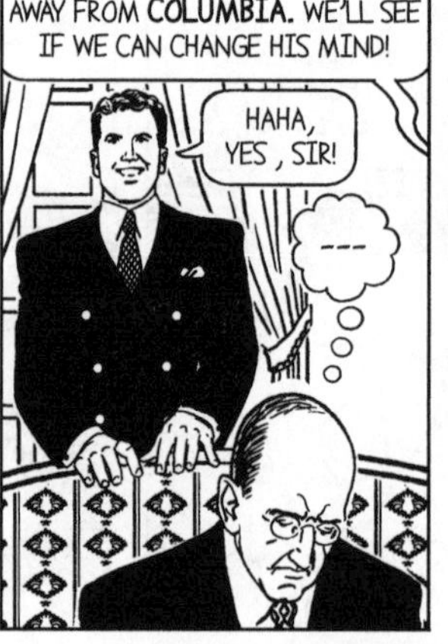
AND REX -- THEY SAY PRESIDENT BUTLER WON'T LET US PRY YOU AWAY FROM COLUMBIA. WE'LL SEE IF WE CAN CHANGE HIS MIND!
HAHA, YES, SIR!

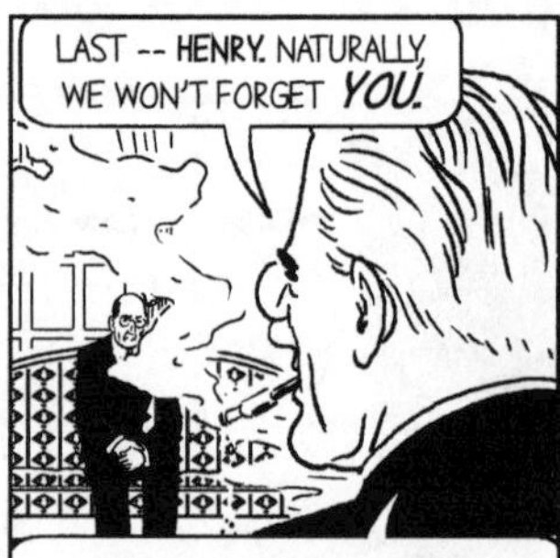
LAST -- HENRY. NATURALLY, WE WON'T FORGET YOU.
BUT THAT REMINDS ME...HMM. THE TENNESSEE VALLEY. GOT SOME NAMES HERE... AND MISS PERKINS WILL BE AT LABOR. SHE'S ALREADY PROVEN HERSELF HERE IN NEW YORK. SHE HAS A BETTER HANDLE ON UNEMPLOYMENT THAN HOOVER...

*We could see Roosevelt was a **master** coalition builder. He didn't need Hoover's help. And right before inauguration something happened that made FDR seem **dearer** to Americans ...*

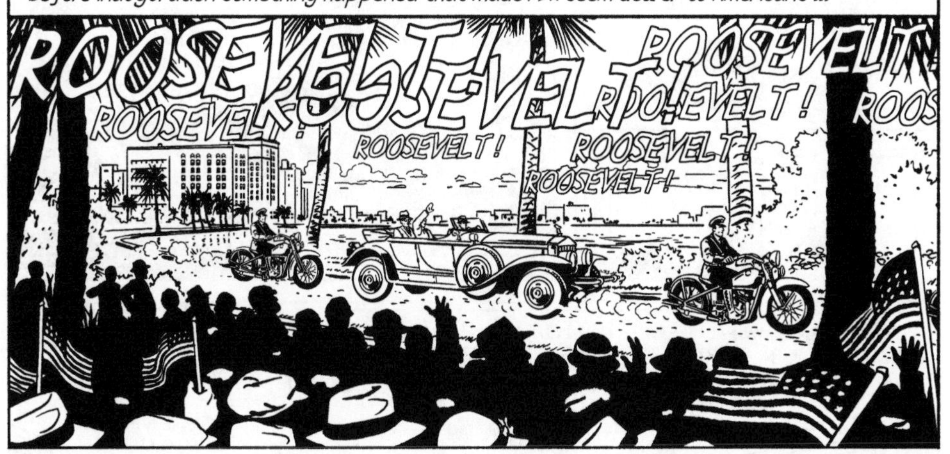

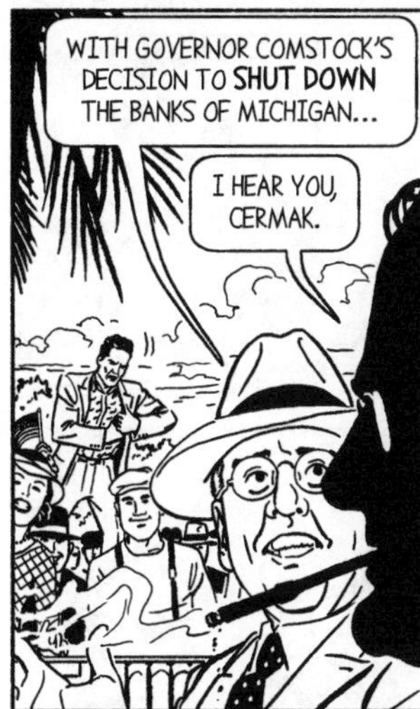

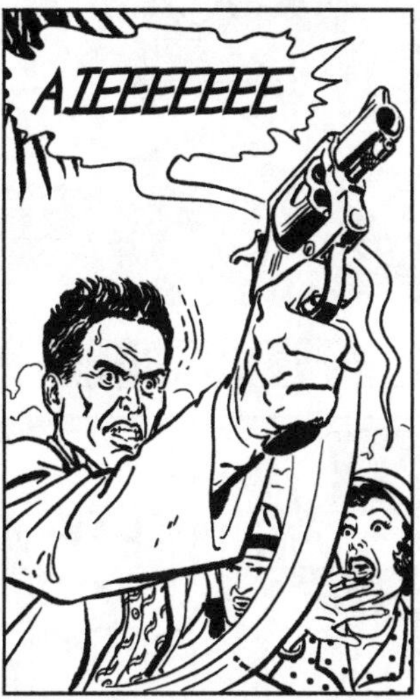

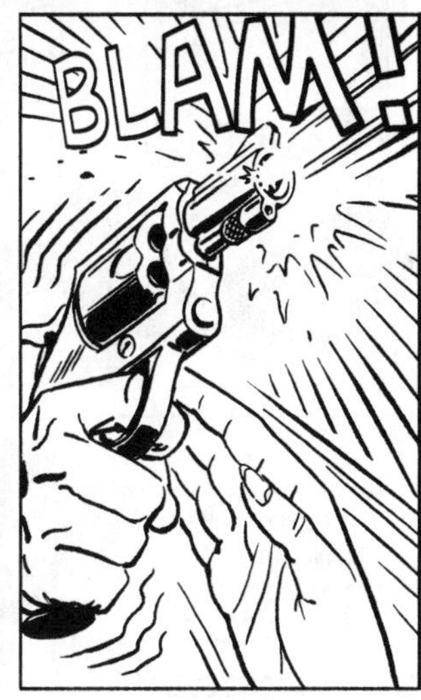

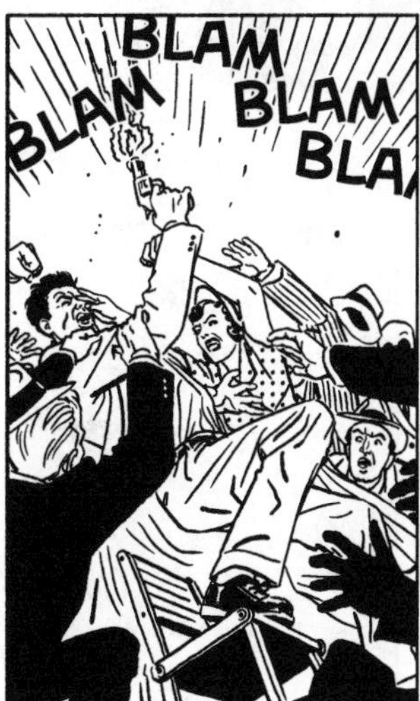

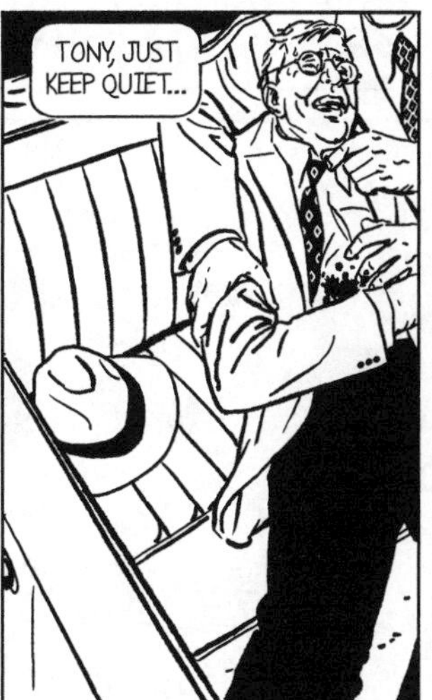

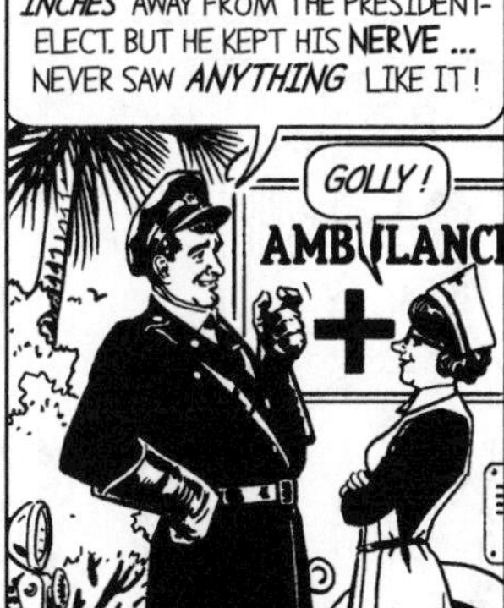

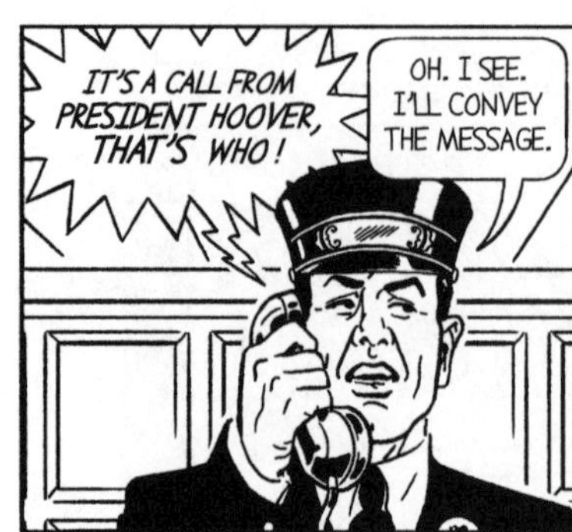
IT'S A CALL FROM PRESIDENT HOOVER, THAT'S WHO!
OH. I SEE. I'LL CONVEY THE MESSAGE.

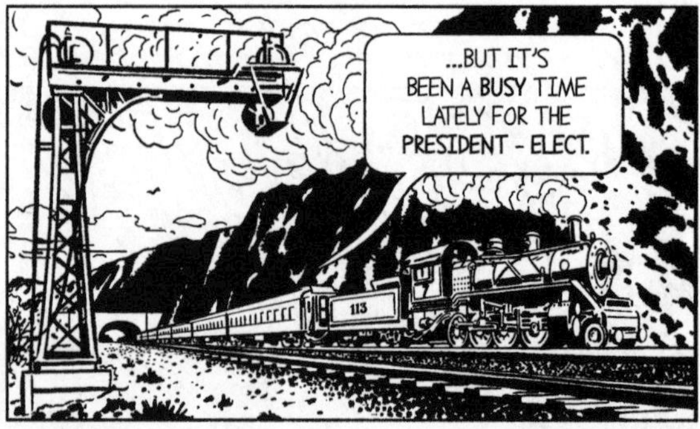
...BUT IT'S BEEN A BUSY TIME LATELY FOR THE PRESIDENT - ELECT.
113

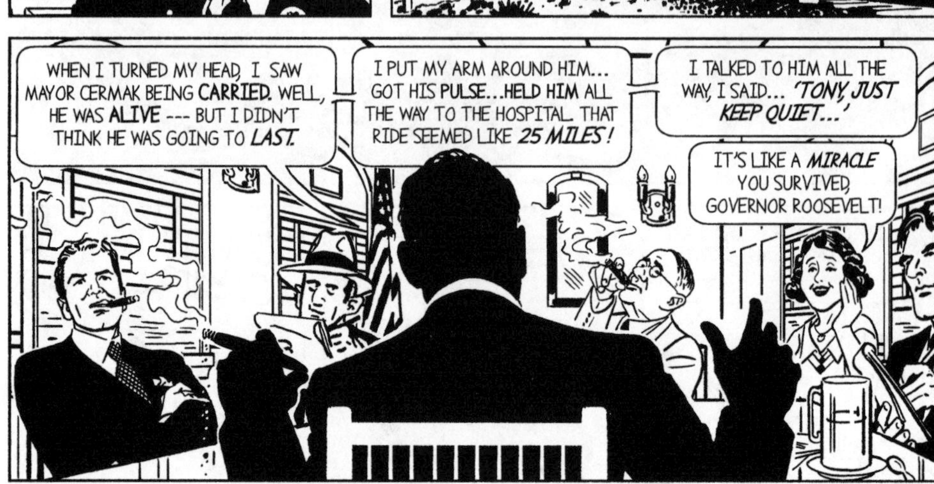
WHEN I TURNED MY HEAD, I SAW MAYOR CERMAK BEING CARRIED. WELL, HE WAS ALIVE --- BUT I DIDN'T THINK HE WAS GOING TO LAST.
I PUT MY ARM AROUND HIM... GOT HIS PULSE...HELD HIM ALL THE WAY TO THE HOSPITAL. THAT RIDE SEEMED LIKE 25 MILES!
I TALKED TO HIM ALL THE WAY, I SAID... 'TONY, JUST KEEP QUIET...'
IT'S LIKE A MIRACLE YOU SURVIVED, GOVERNOR ROOSEVELT!

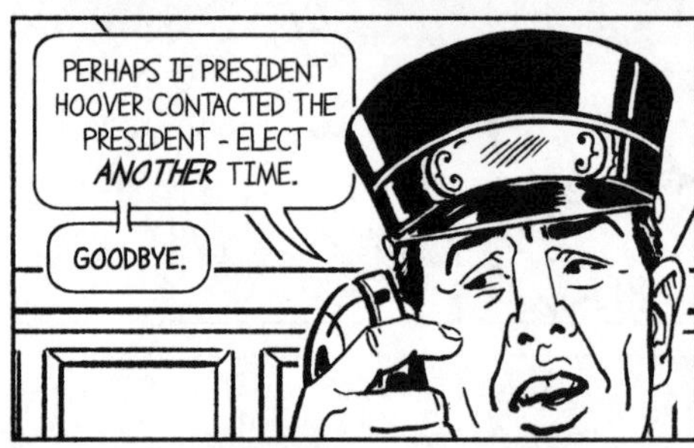
PERHAPS IF PRESIDENT HOOVER CONTACTED THE PRESIDENT - ELECT ANOTHER TIME.
GOODBYE.

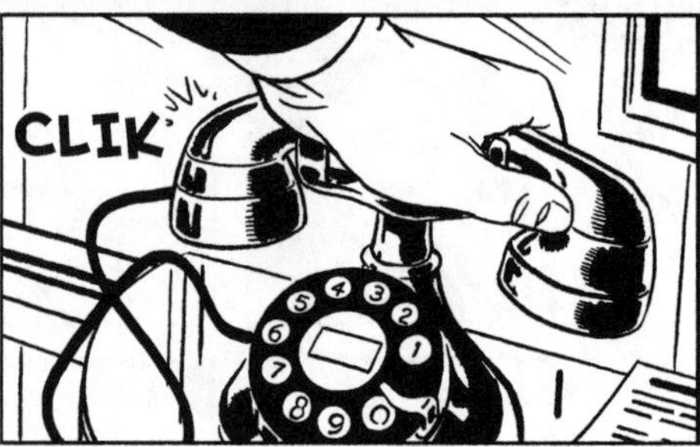
CLIK

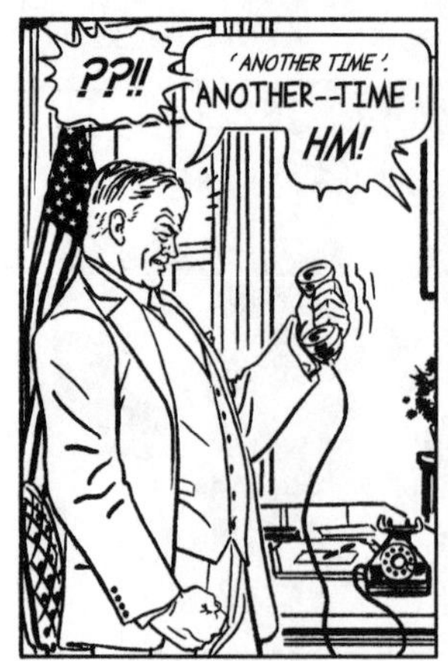
??!!
'ANOTHER TIME'. ANOTHER--TIME! HM!

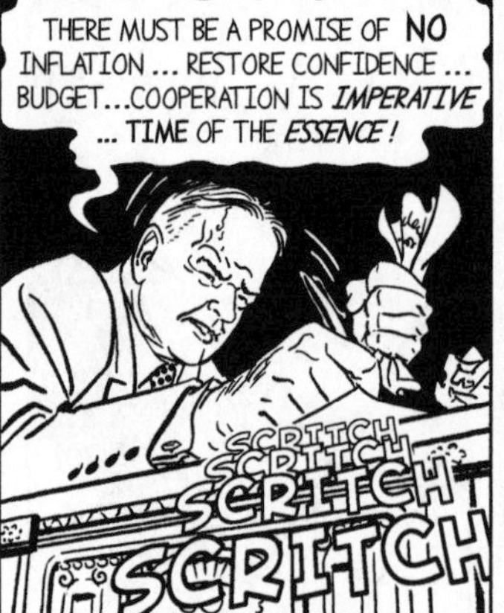
THERE MUST BE A PROMISE OF NO INFLATION ... RESTORE CONFIDENCE ... BUDGET...COOPERATION IS IMPERATIVE ... TIME OF THE ESSENCE!
SCRITCH SCRITCH SCRITCH SCRITCH

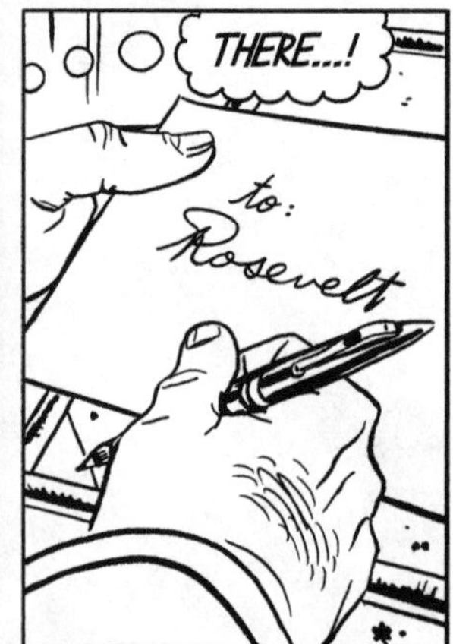
THERE...!
to: Roosevelt

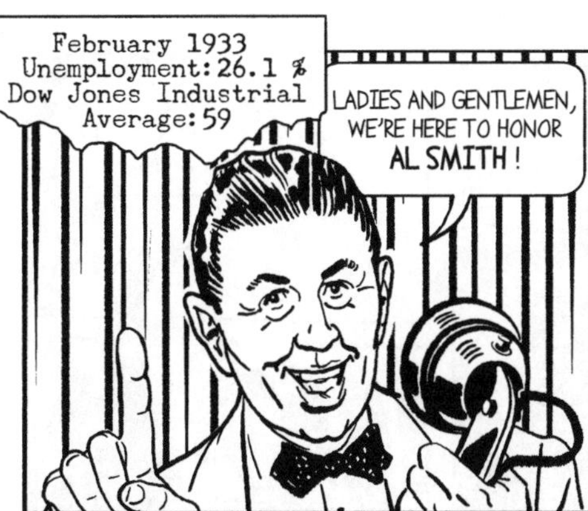
February 1933
Unemployment: 26.1 %
Dow Jones Industrial Average: 59
LADIES AND GENTLEMEN, WE'RE HERE TO HONOR AL SMITH !

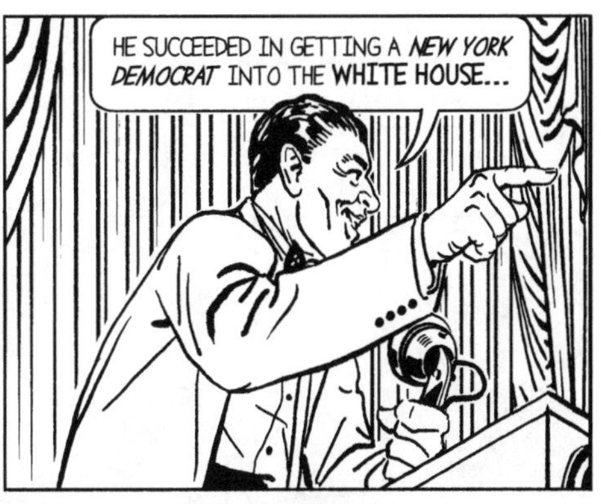
HE SUCCEEDED IN GETTING A NEW YORK DEMOCRAT INTO THE WHITE HOUSE...

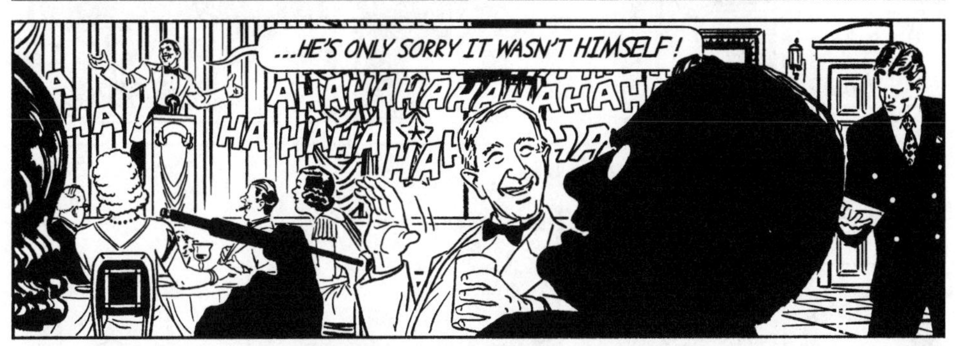
...HE'S ONLY SORRY IT WASN'T HIMSELF !
AHAHAHAHAHAHAHAHAH
HA HA HAHA HA

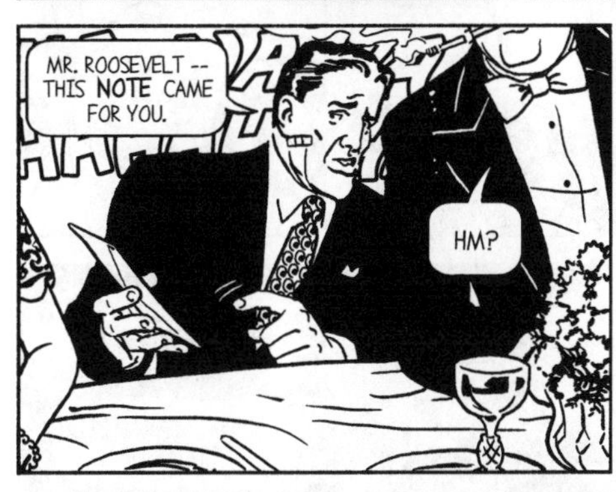
MR. ROOSEVELT -- THIS NOTE CAME FOR YOU.
HM?

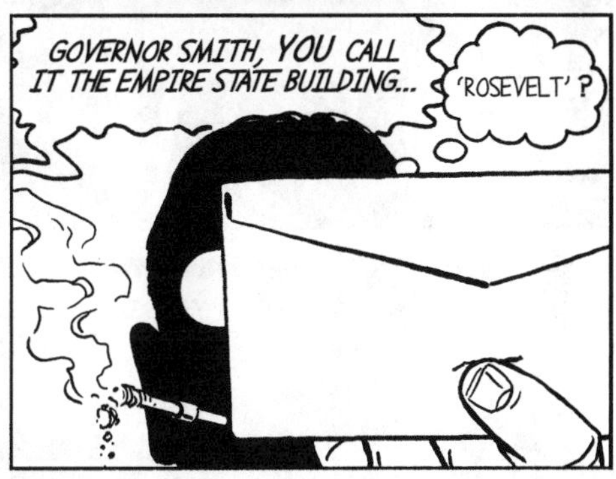
GOVERNOR SMITH, YOU CALL IT THE EMPIRE STATE BUILDING...
'ROSEVELT' ?

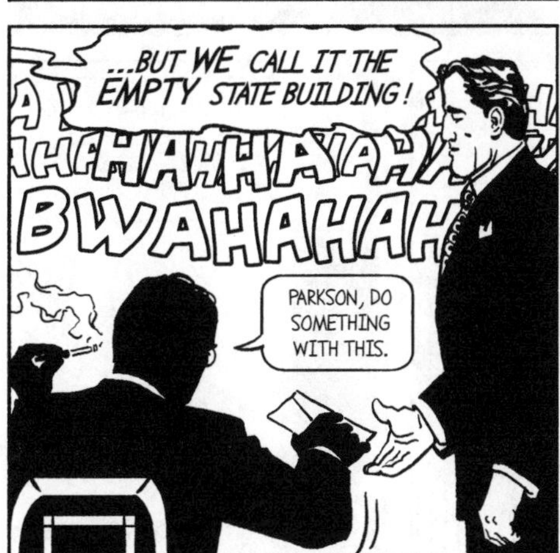
...BUT WE CALL IT THE EMPTY STATE BUILDING !
BWAHAHAHAH
PARKSON, DO SOMETHING WITH THIS.

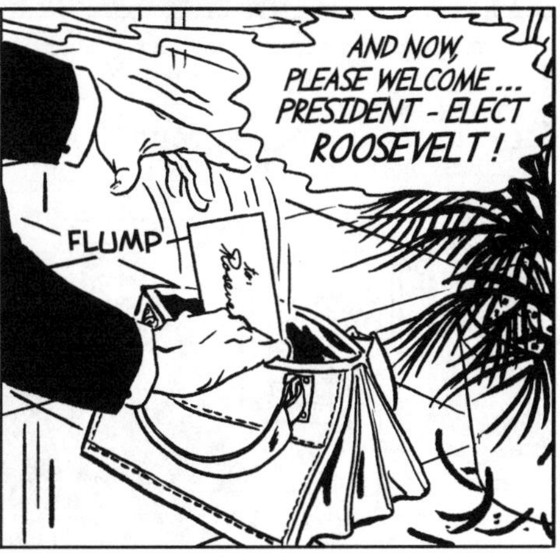
AND NOW, PLEASE WELCOME ... PRESIDENT - ELECT ROOSEVELT !
FLUMP

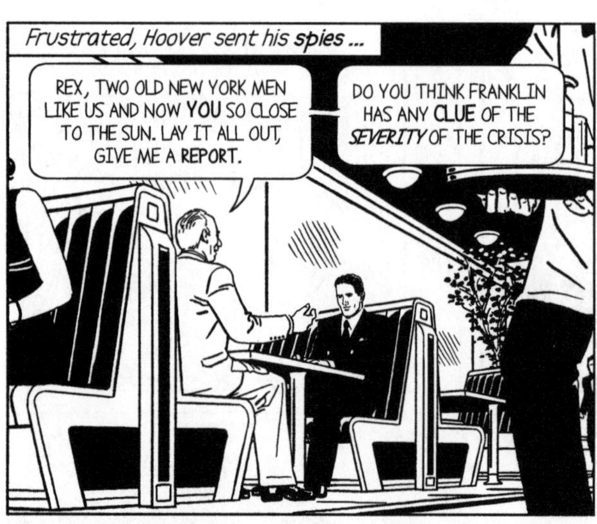

Frustrated, Hoover sent his spies ...
REX, TWO OLD NEW YORK MEN LIKE US AND NOW YOU SO CLOSE TO THE SUN. LAY IT ALL OUT, GIVE ME A REPORT.
DO YOU THINK FRANKLIN HAS ANY CLUE OF THE SEVERITY OF THE CRISIS?

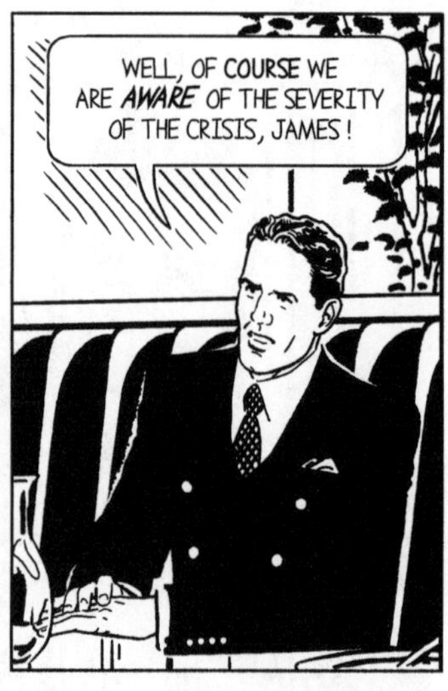

WELL, OF COURSE WE ARE AWARE OF THE SEVERITY OF THE CRISIS, JAMES!

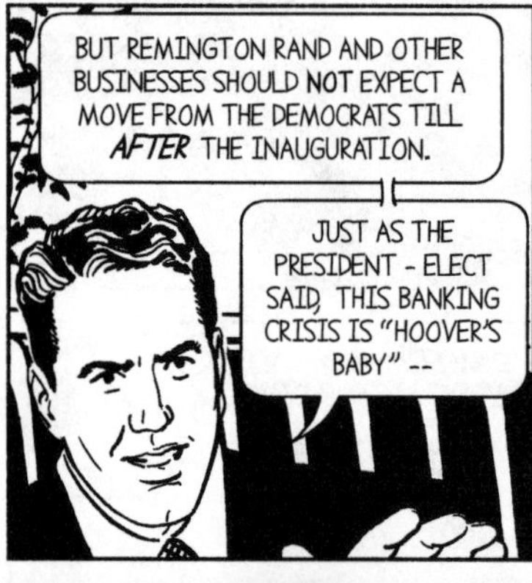

BUT REMINGTON RAND AND OTHER BUSINESSES SHOULD NOT EXPECT A MOVE FROM THE DEMOCRATS TILL AFTER THE INAUGURATION.
JUST AS THE PRESIDENT - ELECT SAID, THIS BANKING CRISIS IS "HOOVER'S BABY" --

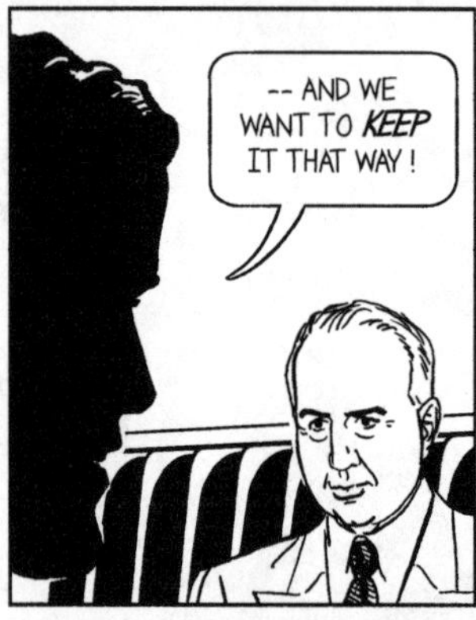

-- AND WE WANT TO KEEP IT THAT WAY!

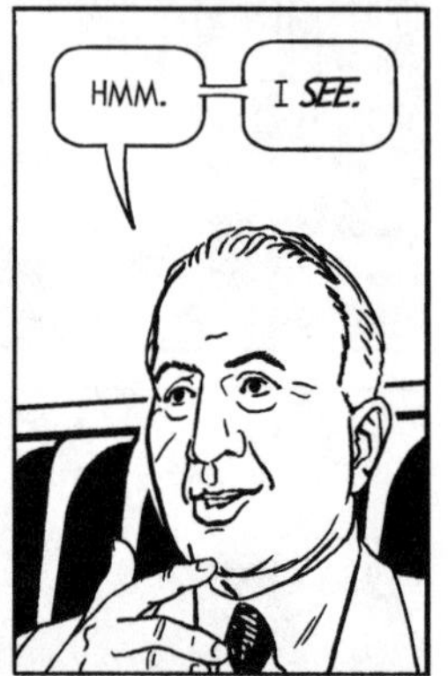

HMM.
I SEE.

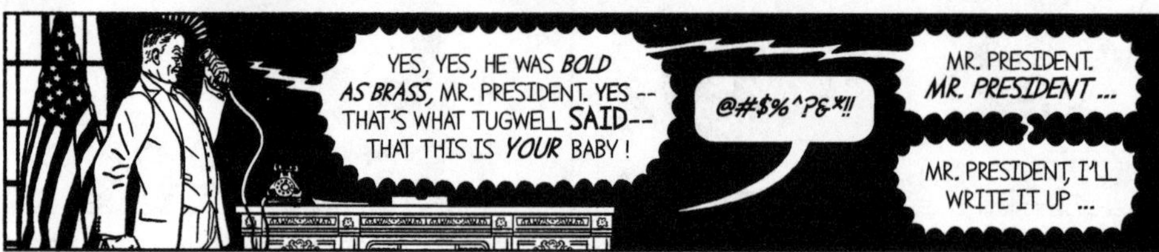

YES, YES, HE WAS BOLD AS BRASS, MR. PRESIDENT. YES -- THAT'S WHAT TUGWELL SAID-- THAT THIS IS YOUR BABY!
@#$%^?&*!!
MR. PRESIDENT. MR. PRESIDENT ...
MR. PRESIDENT, I'LL WRITE IT UP ...

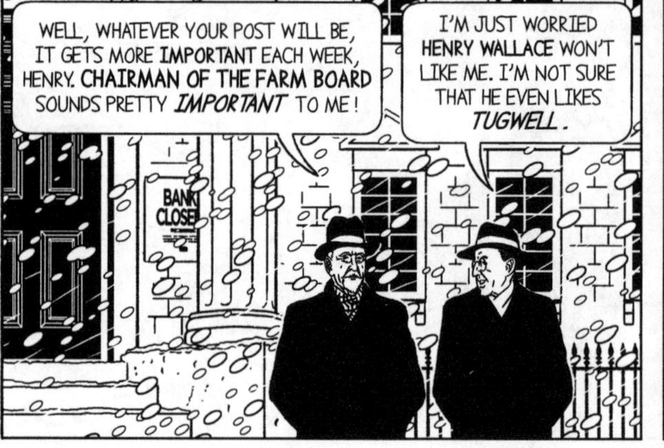

WELL, WHATEVER YOUR POST WILL BE, IT GETS MORE IMPORTANT EACH WEEK, HENRY. CHAIRMAN OF THE FARM BOARD SOUNDS PRETTY IMPORTANT TO ME!
I'M JUST WORRIED HENRY WALLACE WON'T LIKE ME. I'M NOT SURE THAT HE EVEN LIKES TUGWELL.

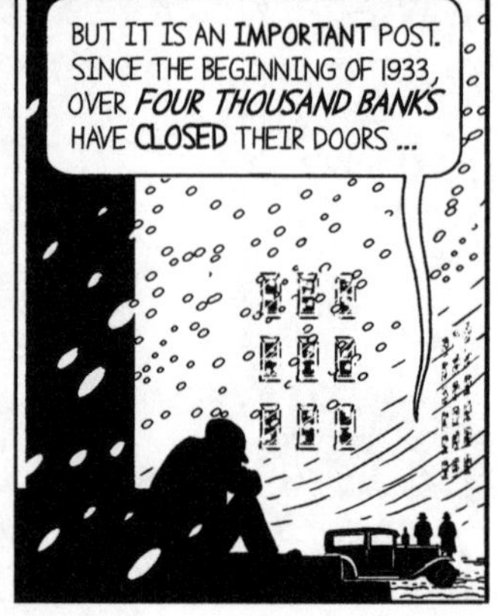

BUT IT IS AN IMPORTANT POST. SINCE THE BEGINNING OF 1933, OVER FOUR THOUSAND BANKS HAVE CLOSED THEIR DOORS ...

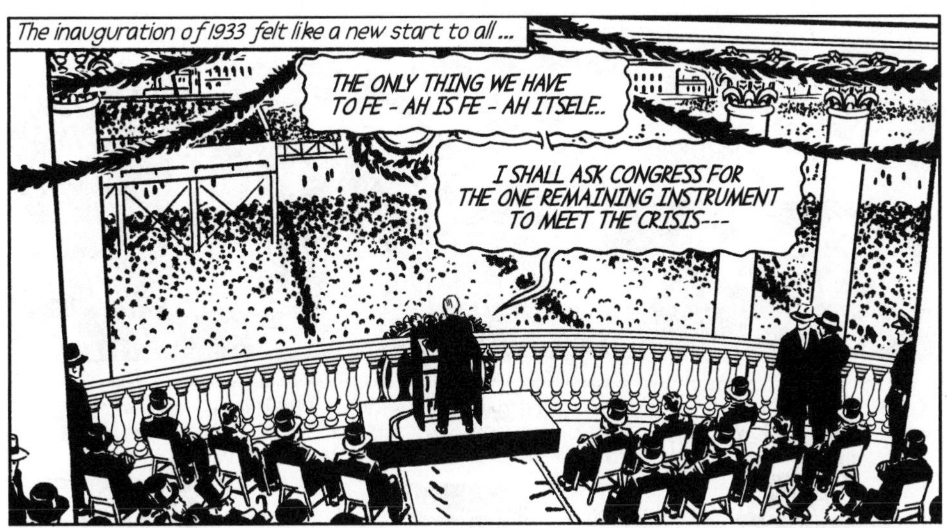
The inauguration of 1933 felt like a new start to all ...
THE ONLY THING WE HAVE TO FE - AH IS FE - AH ITSELF...
I SHALL ASK CONGRESS FOR THE ONE REMAINING INSTRUMENT TO MEET THE CRISIS---

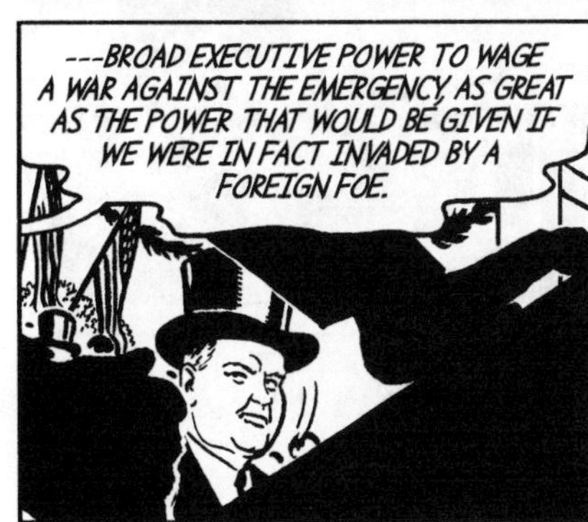
---BROAD EXECUTIVE POWER TO WAGE A WAR AGAINST THE EMERGENCY, AS GREAT AS THE POWER THAT WOULD BE GIVEN IF WE WERE IN FACT INVADED BY A FOREIGN FOE.

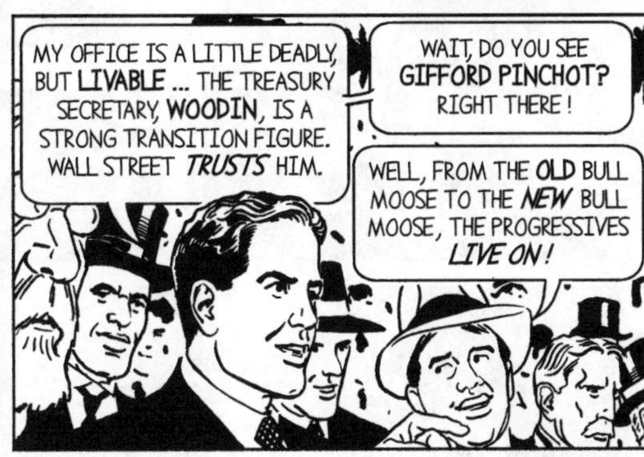
MY OFFICE IS A LITTLE DEADLY, BUT LIVABLE ... THE TREASURY SECRETARY, WOODIN, IS A STRONG TRANSITION FIGURE. WALL STREET TRUSTS HIM.
WAIT, DO YOU SEE GIFFORD PINCHOT? RIGHT THERE!
WELL, FROM THE OLD BULL MOOSE TO THE NEW BULL MOOSE, THE PROGRESSIVES LIVE ON!

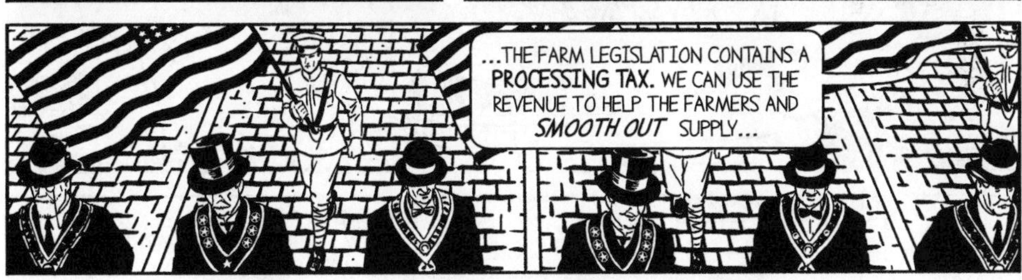
...THE FARM LEGISLATION CONTAINS A PROCESSING TAX. WE CAN USE THE REVENUE TO HELP THE FARMERS AND SMOOTH OUT SUPPLY...

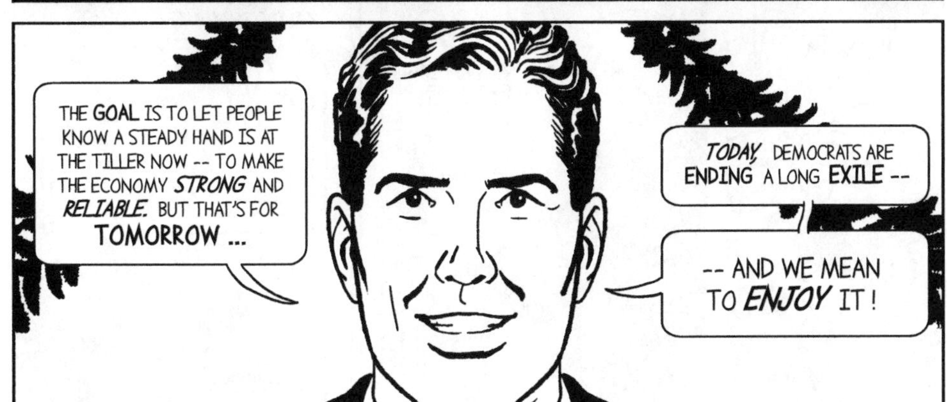
THE GOAL IS TO LET PEOPLE KNOW A STEADY HAND IS AT THE TILLER NOW -- TO MAKE THE ECONOMY STRONG AND RELIABLE. BUT THAT'S FOR TOMORROW ...
TODAY, DEMOCRATS ARE ENDING A LONG EXILE --
-- AND WE MEAN TO ENJOY IT!

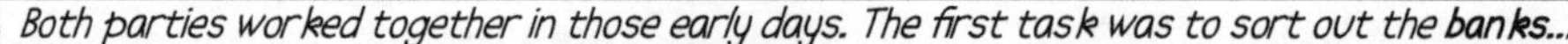
Both parties worked together in those early days. The first task was to sort out the banks...

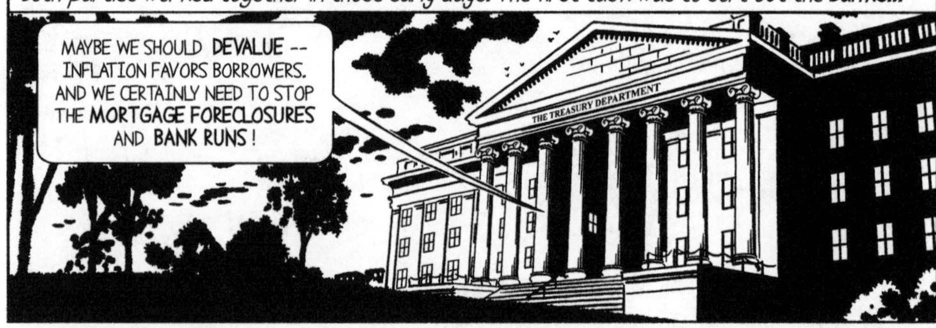
THE TREASURY DEPARTMENT
MAYBE WE SHOULD DEVALUE -- INFLATION FAVORS BORROWERS. AND WE CERTAINLY NEED TO STOP THE MORTGAGE FORECLOSURES AND BANK RUNS !

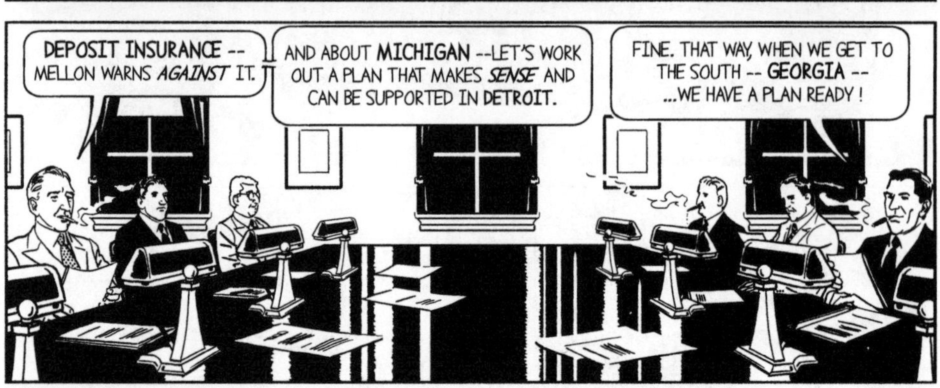
DEPOSIT INSURANCE -- MELLON WARNS AGAINST IT.
AND ABOUT MICHIGAN --LET'S WORK OUT A PLAN THAT MAKES SENSE AND CAN BE SUPPORTED IN DETROIT.
FINE. THAT WAY, WHEN WE GET TO THE SOUTH -- GEORGIA -- ...WE HAVE A PLAN READY !

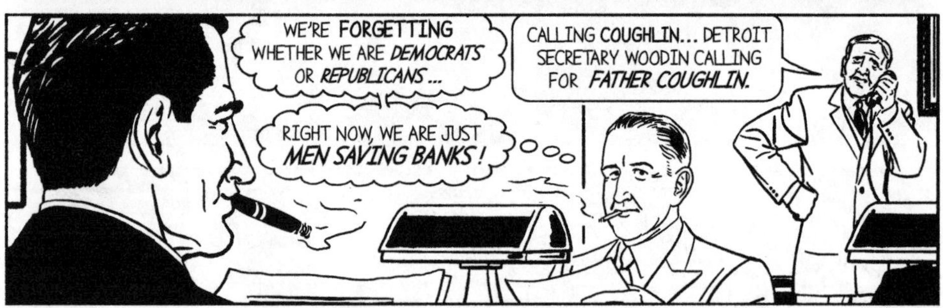
WE'RE FORGETTING WHETHER WE ARE DEMOCRATS OR REPUBLICANS ...
RIGHT NOW, WE ARE JUST MEN SAVING BANKS !
CALLING COUGHLIN... DETROIT SECRETARY WOODIN CALLING FOR FATHER COUGHLIN.

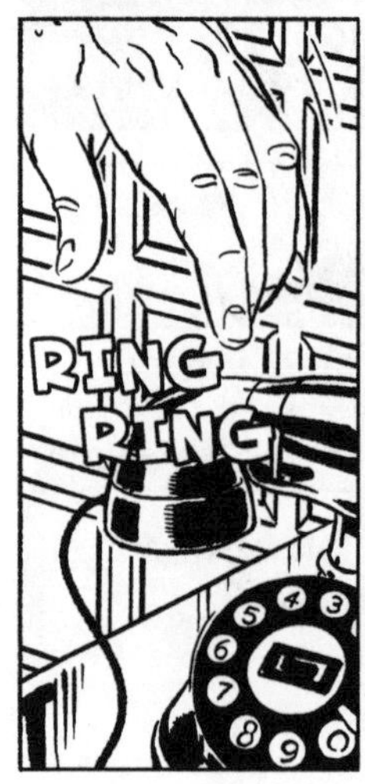
RING
RING

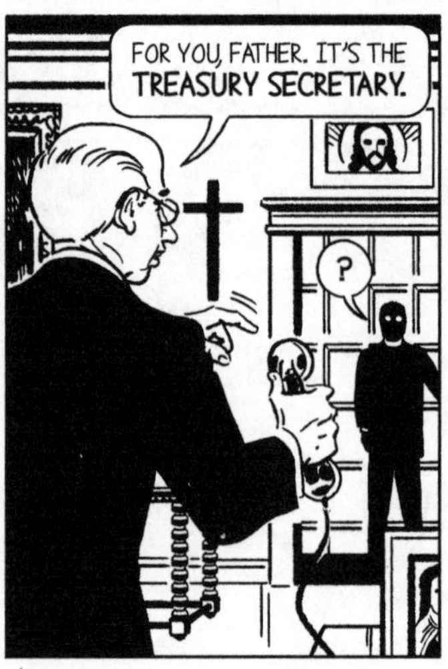
FOR YOU, FATHER. IT'S THE TREASURY SECRETARY.
?

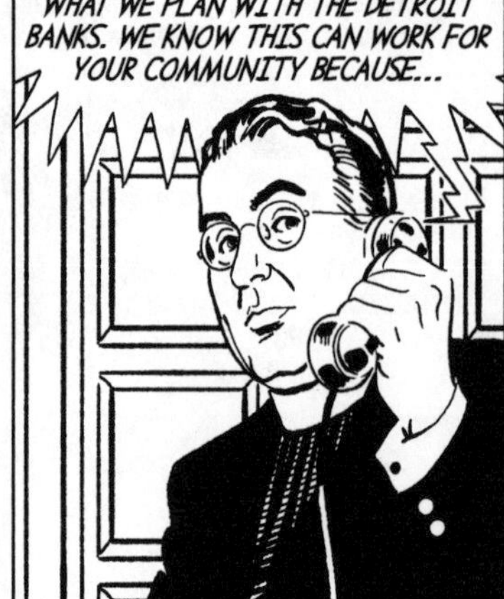
FATHER? WILLIAM WOODIN. HERE IS WHAT WE PLAN WITH THE DETROIT BANKS. WE KNOW THIS CAN WORK FOR YOUR COMMUNITY BECAUSE...

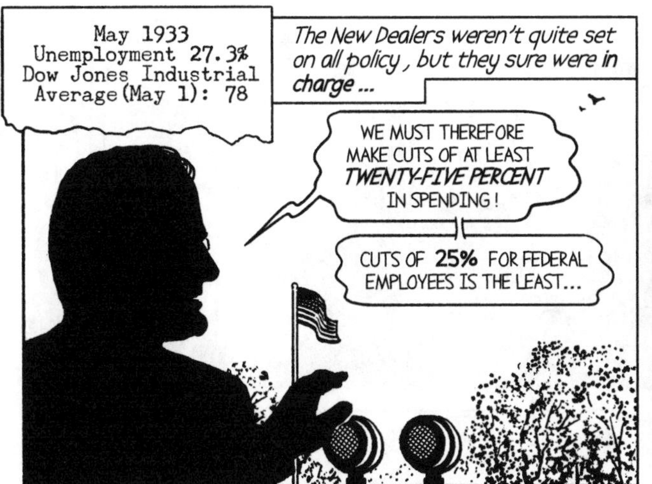
May 1933
Unemployment 27.3%
Dow Jones Industrial
Average(May 1): 78
The New Dealers weren't quite set on all policy, but they sure were in charge...
WE MUST THEREFORE MAKE CUTS OF AT LEAST TWENTY-FIVE PERCENT IN SPENDING!
CUTS OF 25% FOR FEDERAL EMPLOYEES IS THE LEAST...

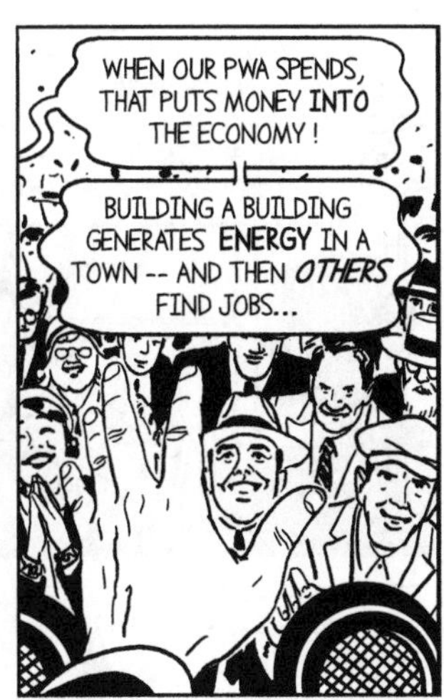
WHEN OUR PWA SPENDS, THAT PUTS MONEY INTO THE ECONOMY!
BUILDING A BUILDING GENERATES ENERGY IN A TOWN -- AND THEN OTHERS FIND JOBS...

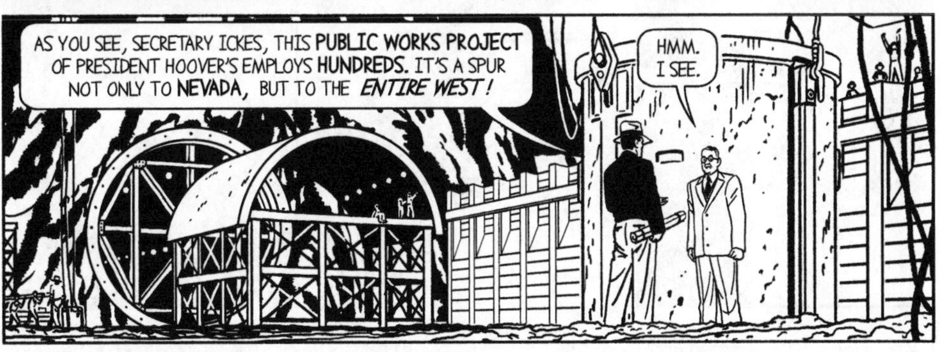
AS YOU SEE, SECRETARY ICKES, THIS PUBLIC WORKS PROJECT OF PRESIDENT HOOVER'S EMPLOYS HUNDREDS. IT'S A SPUR NOT ONLY TO NEVADA, BUT TO THE ENTIRE WEST!
HMM. I SEE.

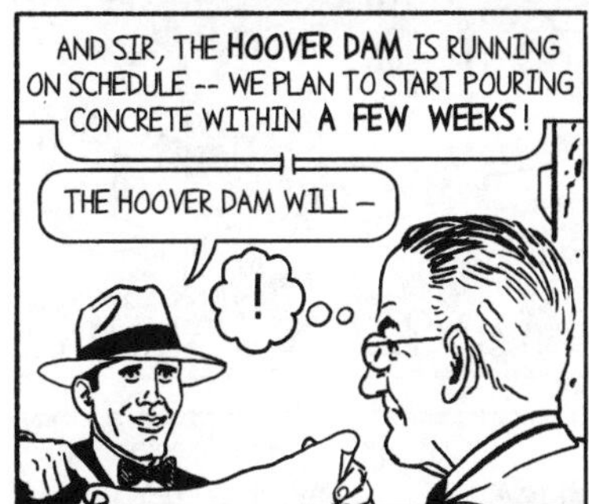
AND SIR, THE HOOVER DAM IS RUNNING ON SCHEDULE -- WE PLAN TO START POURING CONCRETE WITHIN A FEW WEEKS!
THE HOOVER DAM WILL –
!

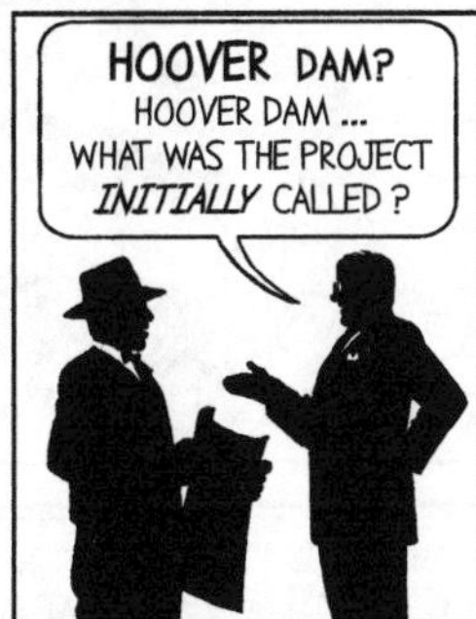
HOOVER DAM? HOOVER DAM ... WHAT WAS THE PROJECT INITIALLY CALLED?

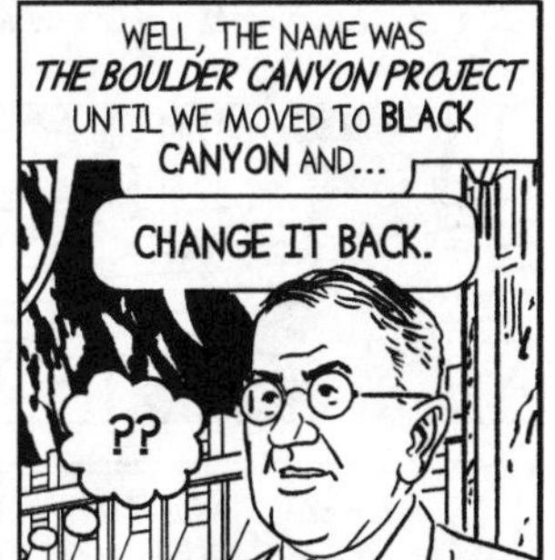
WELL, THE NAME WAS THE BOULDER CANYON PROJECT UNTIL WE MOVED TO BLACK CANYON AND...
CHANGE IT BACK.
??

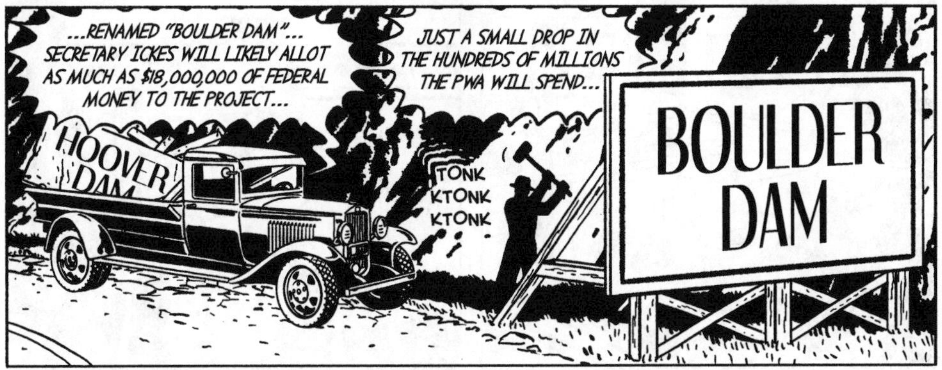
...RENAMED "BOULDER DAM"... SECRETARY ICKES WILL LIKELY ALLOT AS MUCH AS $18,000,000 OF FEDERAL MONEY TO THE PROJECT...
JUST A SMALL DROP IN THE HUNDREDS OF MILLIONS THE PWA WILL SPEND...
HOOVER DAM
TONK
KTONK
KTONK
BOULDER DAM

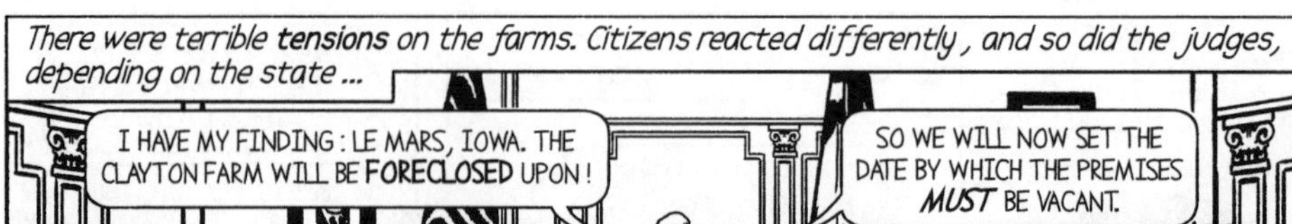
There were terrible **tensions** on the farms. Citizens reacted differently, and so did the judges, depending on the state ...

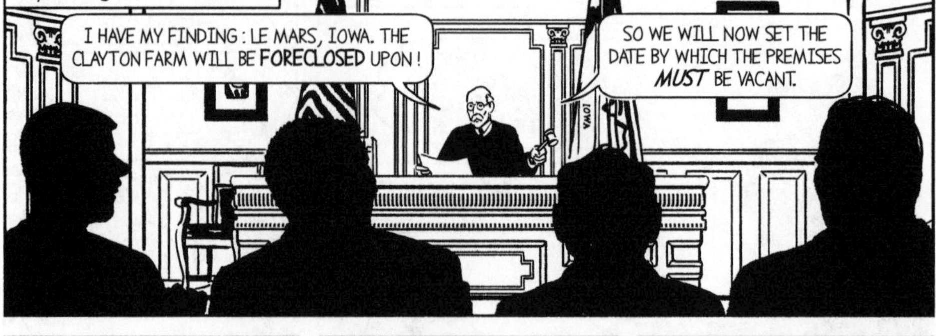
I HAVE MY FINDING : LE MARS, IOWA. THE CLAYTON FARM WILL BE **FORECLOSED** UPON !
SO WE WILL NOW SET THE DATE BY WHICH THE PREMISES *MUST* BE VACANT.

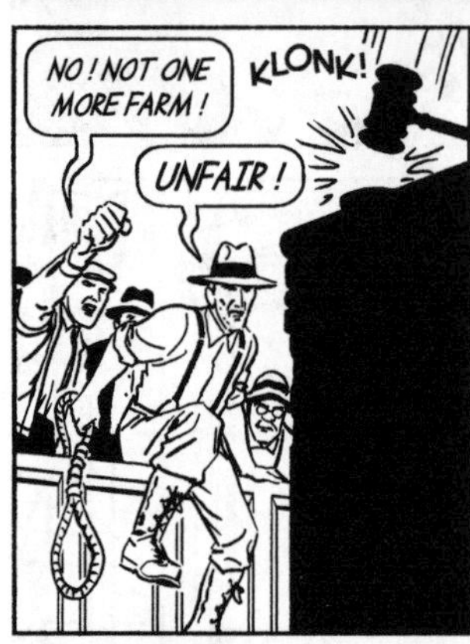
NO ! NOT ONE MORE FARM !
KLONK!
UNFAIR !

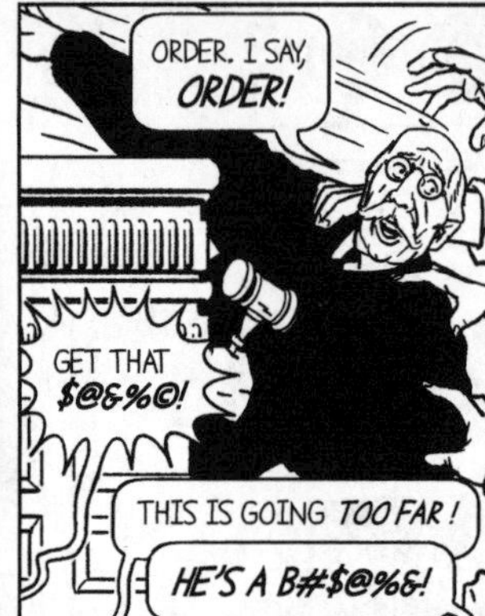
ORDER. I SAY, *ORDER!*
GET THAT $@&%©!
THIS IS GOING *TOO FAR !*
HE'S A B#$@%&!

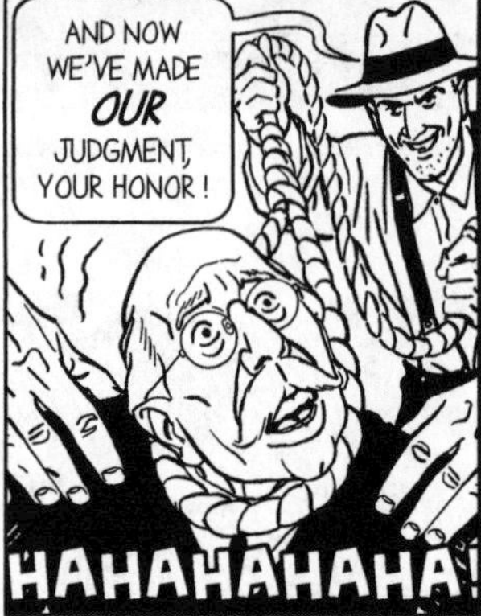
AND NOW WE'VE MADE *OUR* JUDGMENT, YOUR HONOR !
HAHAHAHAHAHA!

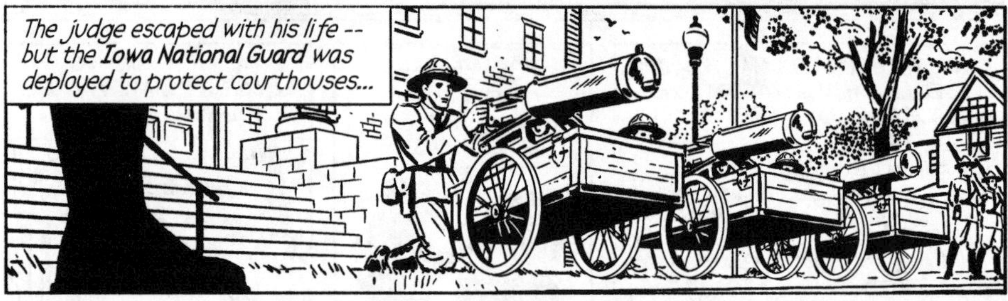
The judge escaped with his life -- but the **Iowa National Guard** was deployed to protect courthouses...

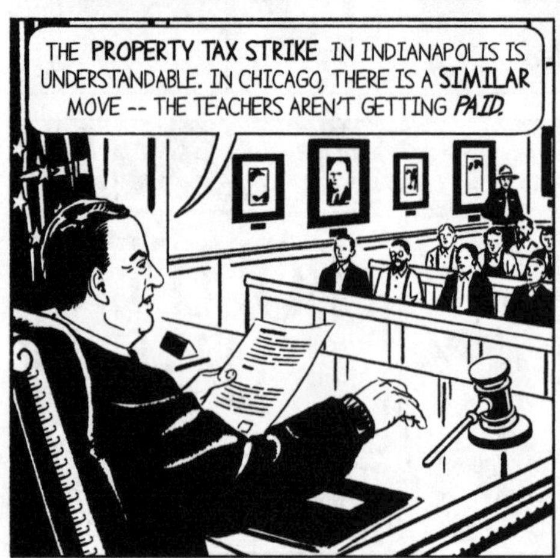
THE **PROPERTY TAX STRIKE** IN INDIANAPOLIS IS UNDERSTANDABLE. IN CHICAGO, THERE IS A **SIMILAR** MOVE -- THE TEACHERS AREN'T GETTING *PAID.*

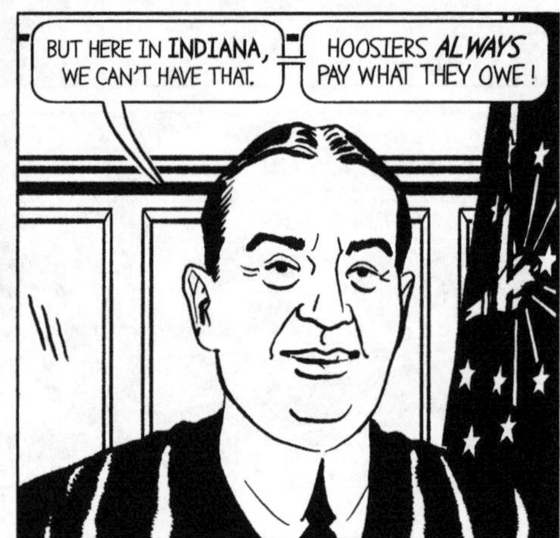
BUT HERE IN **INDIANA**, WE CAN'T HAVE THAT.
HOOSIERS *ALWAYS* PAY WHAT THEY OWE !

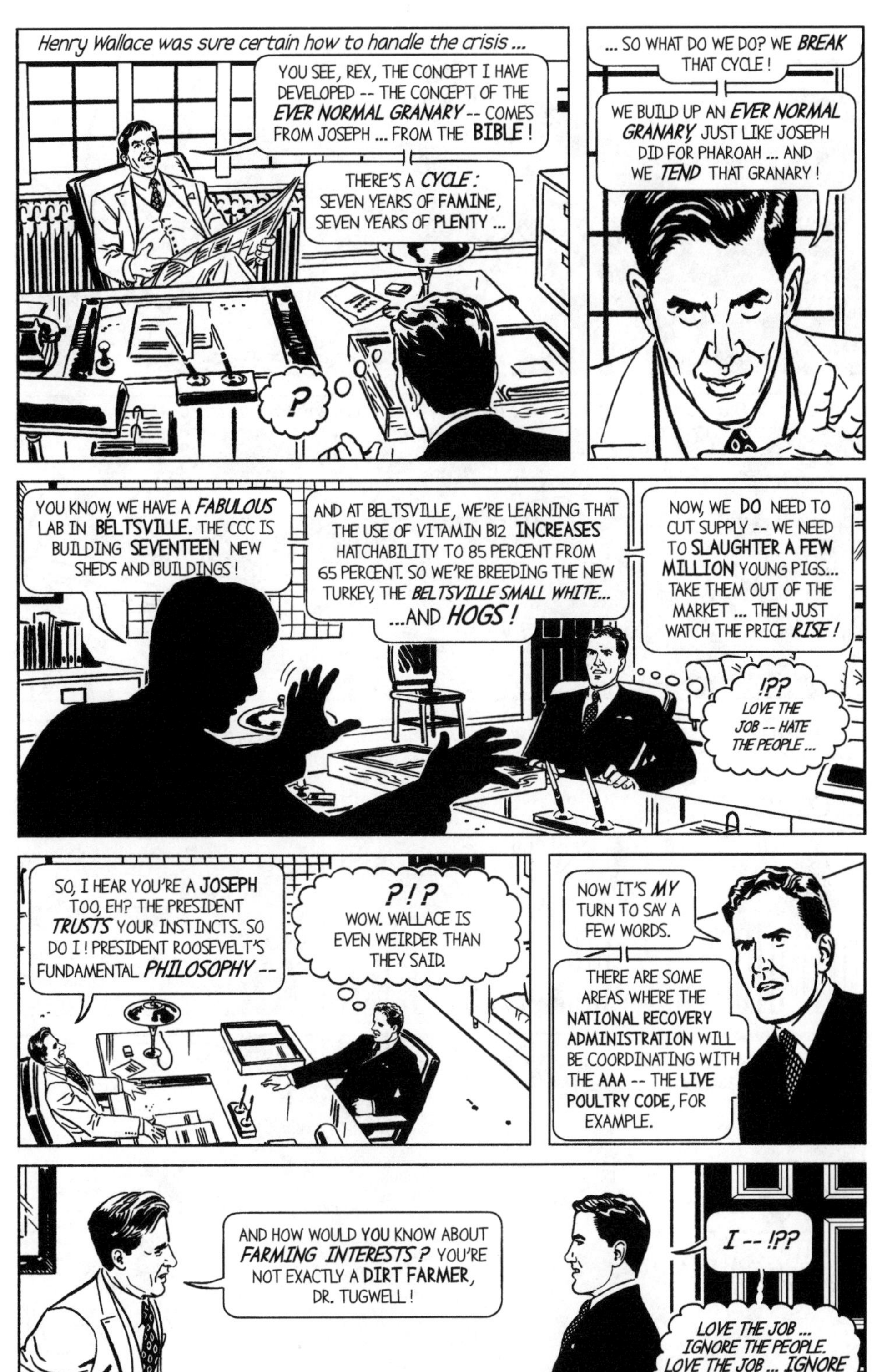

Henry Wallace was sure certain how to handle the crisis ...
YOU SEE, REX, THE CONCEPT I HAVE DEVELOPED -- THE CONCEPT OF THE EVER NORMAL GRANARY -- COMES FROM JOSEPH ... FROM THE BIBLE!
THERE'S A CYCLE: SEVEN YEARS OF FAMINE, SEVEN YEARS OF PLENTY ...
?
... SO WHAT DO WE DO? WE BREAK THAT CYCLE!
WE BUILD UP AN EVER NORMAL GRANARY, JUST LIKE JOSEPH DID FOR PHAROAH ... AND WE TEND THAT GRANARY!
YOU KNOW, WE HAVE A FABULOUS LAB IN BELTSVILLE. THE CCC IS BUILDING SEVENTEEN NEW SHEDS AND BUILDINGS!
AND AT BELTSVILLE, WE'RE LEARNING THAT THE USE OF VITAMIN B12 INCREASES HATCHABILITY TO 85 PERCENT FROM 65 PERCENT. SO WE'RE BREEDING THE NEW TURKEY, THE BELTSVILLE SMALL WHITE...
...AND HOGS!
NOW, WE DO NEED TO CUT SUPPLY -- WE NEED TO SLAUGHTER A FEW MILLION YOUNG PIGS... TAKE THEM OUT OF THE MARKET ... THEN JUST WATCH THE PRICE RISE!
!?? LOVE THE JOB -- HATE THE PEOPLE ...
SO, I HEAR YOU'RE A JOSEPH TOO, EH? THE PRESIDENT TRUSTS YOUR INSTINCTS. SO DO I! PRESIDENT ROOSEVELT'S FUNDAMENTAL PHILOSOPHY --
?!? WOW. WALLACE IS EVEN WEIRDER THAN THEY SAID.
NOW IT'S MY TURN TO SAY A FEW WORDS.
THERE ARE SOME AREAS WHERE THE NATIONAL RECOVERY ADMINISTRATION WILL BE COORDINATING WITH THE AAA -- THE LIVE POULTRY CODE, FOR EXAMPLE.
AND HOW WOULD YOU KNOW ABOUT FARMING INTERESTS? YOU'RE NOT EXACTLY A DIRT FARMER, DR. TUGWELL!
I -- !??
LOVE THE JOB ... IGNORE THE PEOPLE. LOVE THE JOB ... IGNORE THE PEOPLE. LOVE THE...

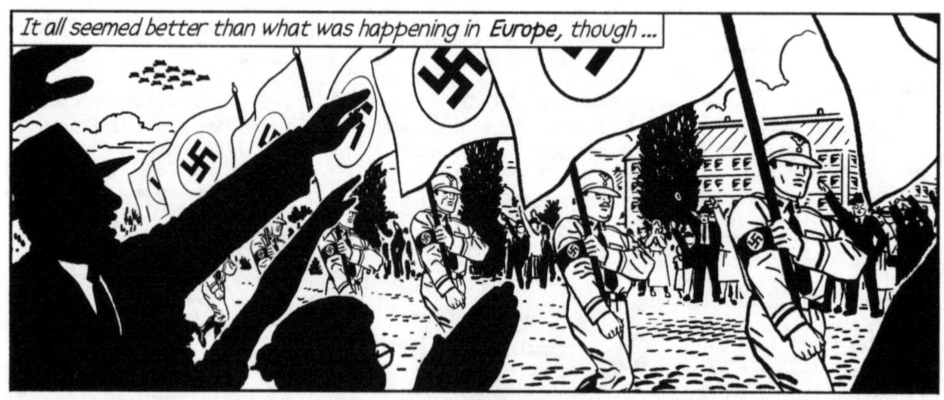
It all seemed better than what was happening in Europe, though ...

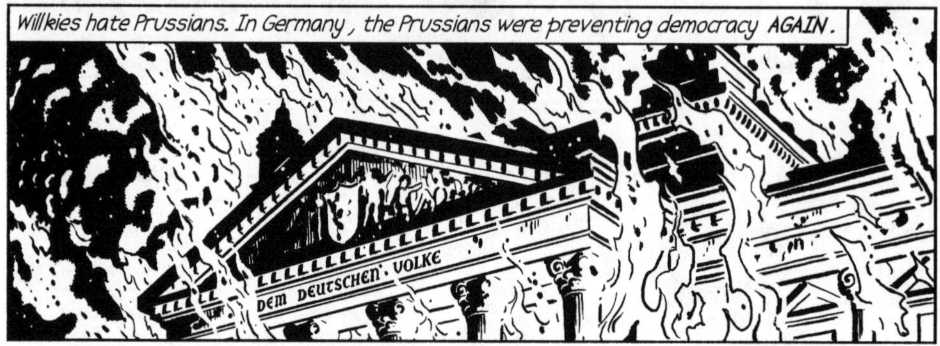
Willkies hate Prussians. In Germany, the Prussians were preventing democracy AGAIN.
DEM DEUTSCHEN VOLKE

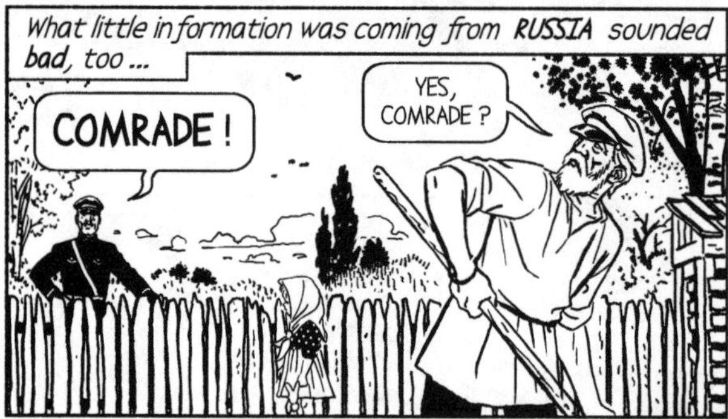
What little information was coming from RUSSIA sounded bad, too ...
COMRADE!
YES, COMRADE?

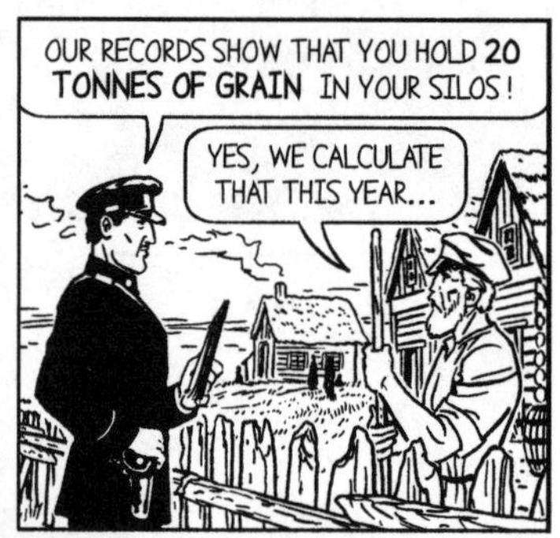
OUR RECORDS SHOW THAT YOU HOLD 20 TONNES OF GRAIN IN YOUR SILOS!
YES, WE CALCULATE THAT THIS YEAR...

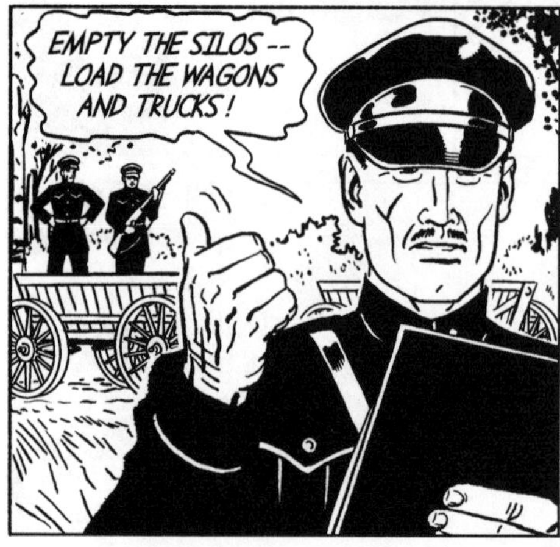
EMPTY THE SILOS -- LOAD THE WAGONS AND TRUCKS!

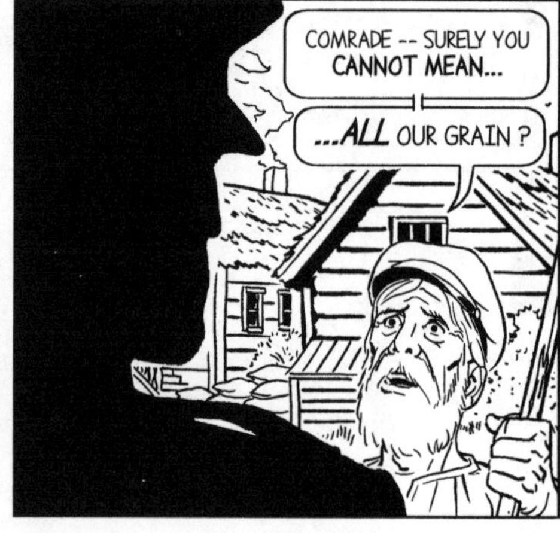
COMRADE -- SURELY YOU CANNOT MEAN...
...ALL OUR GRAIN?

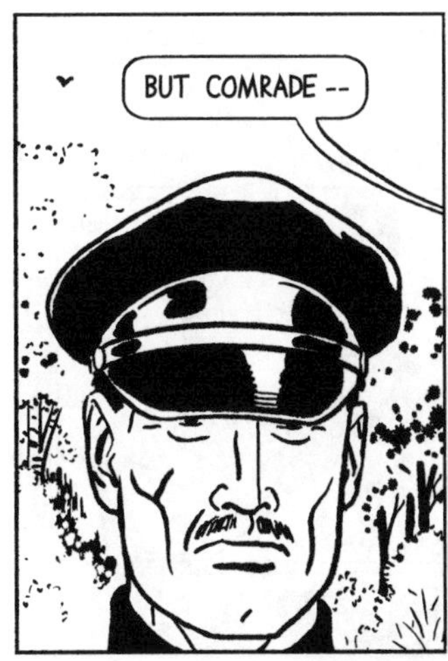
BUT COMRADE --

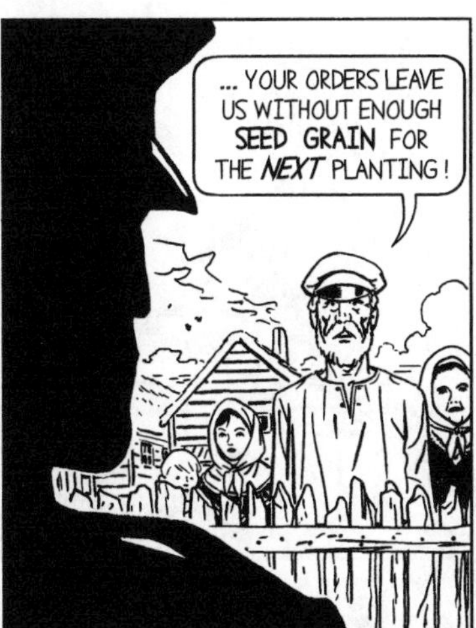
... YOUR ORDERS LEAVE US WITHOUT ENOUGH **SEED GRAIN** FOR THE ***NEXT*** PLANTING!

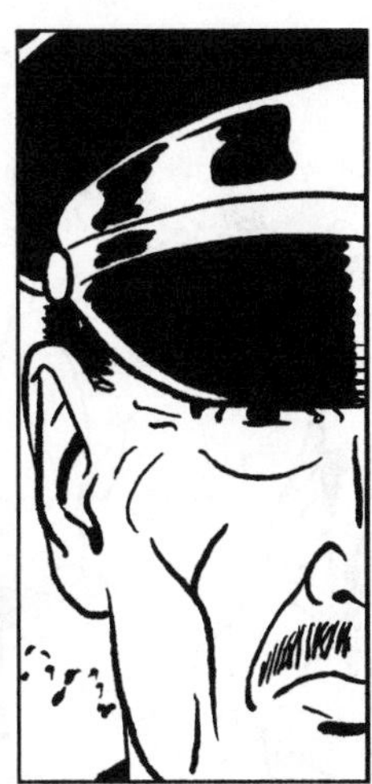

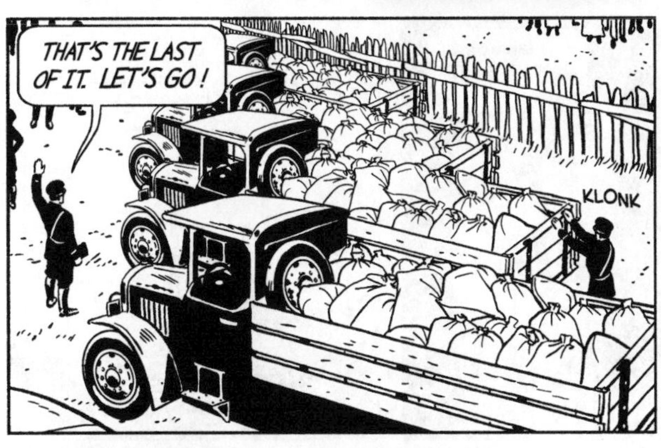
THAT'S THE LAST OF IT. LET'S GO!
KLONK

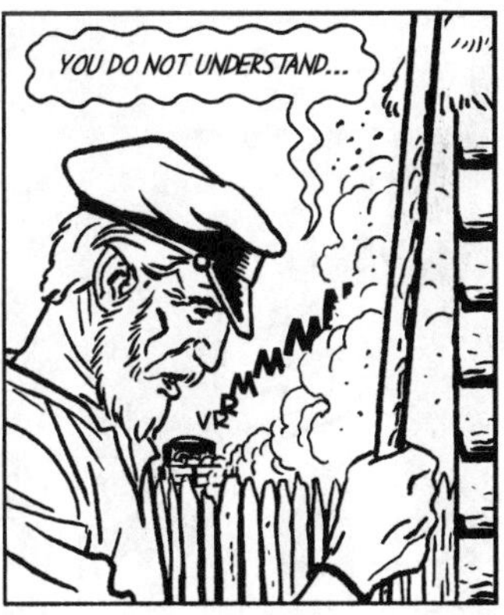
YOU DO NOT UNDERSTAND...
VRMMMM

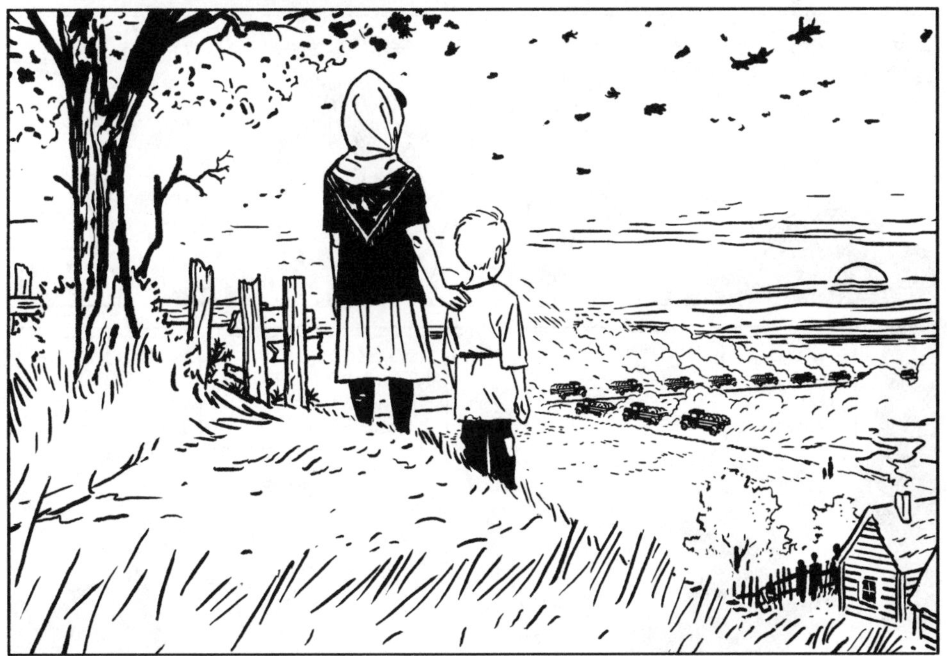

Finance was the international issue Roosevelt was dealing with. Not always predictably ...

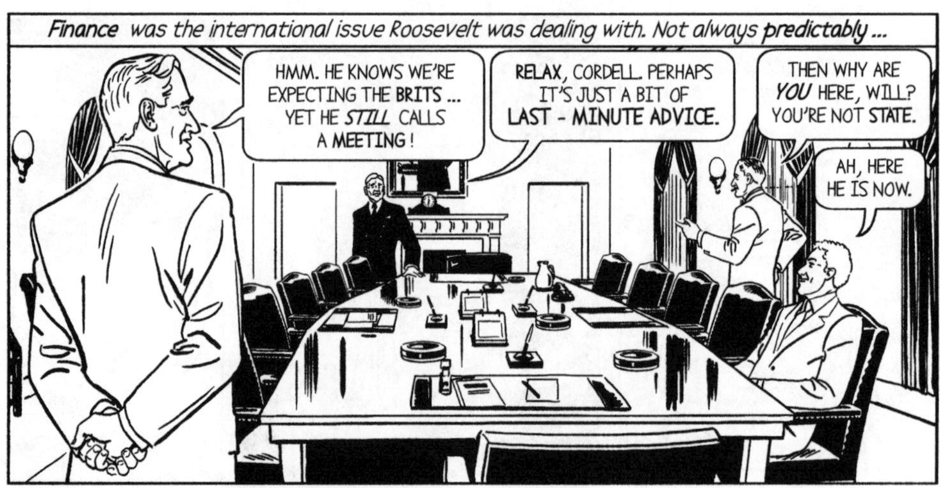

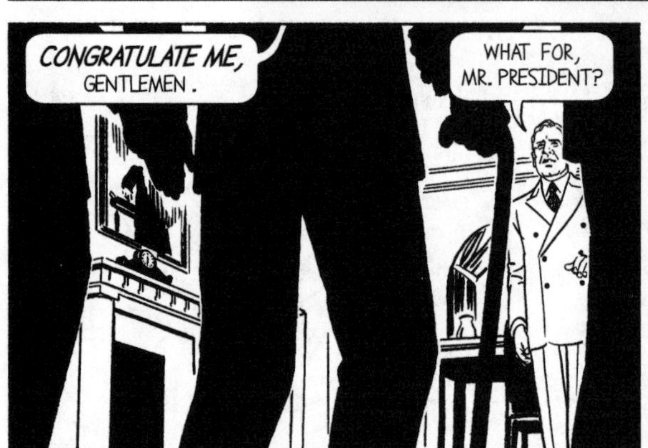

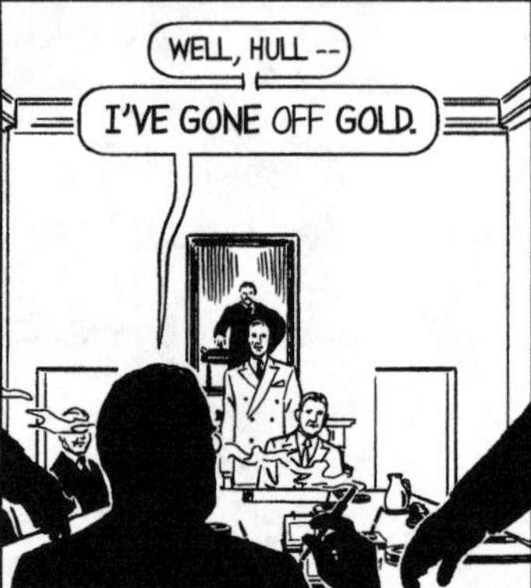

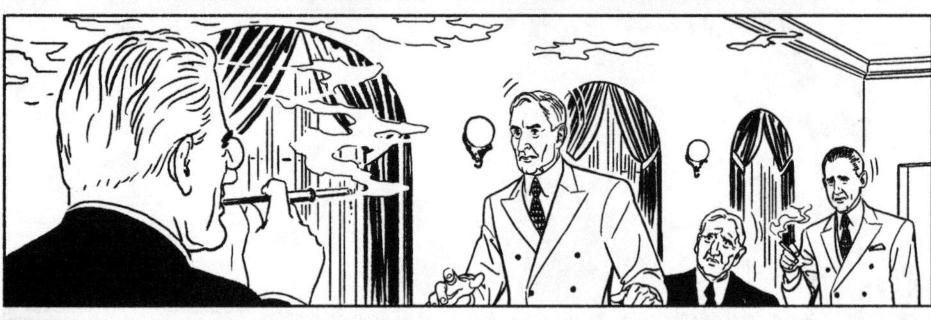

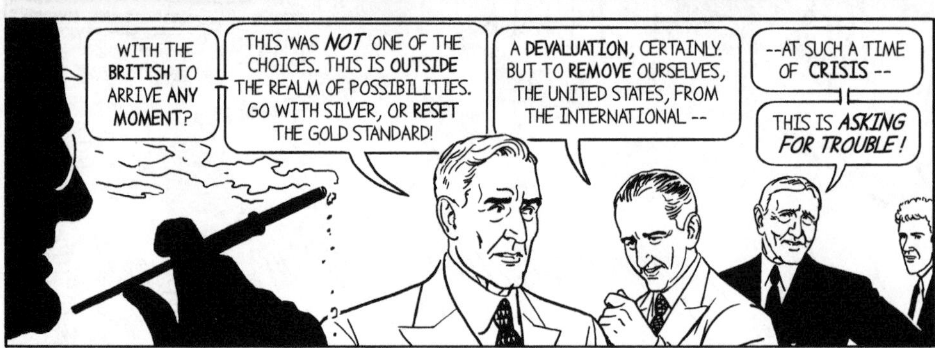

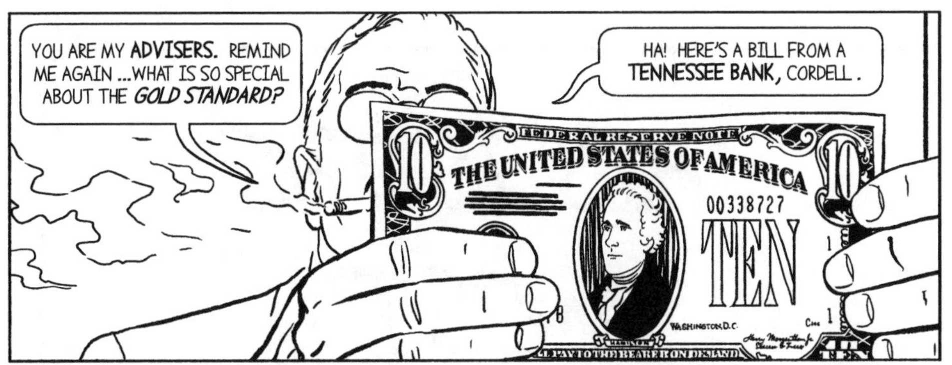
YOU ARE MY ADVISERS. REMIND ME AGAIN ...WHAT IS SO SPECIAL ABOUT THE GOLD STANDARD?
HA! HERE'S A BILL FROM A TENNESSEE BANK, CORDELL.
FEDERAL RESERVE NOTE
THE UNITED STATES OF AMERICA
00338727
TEN
WASHINGTON D.C.

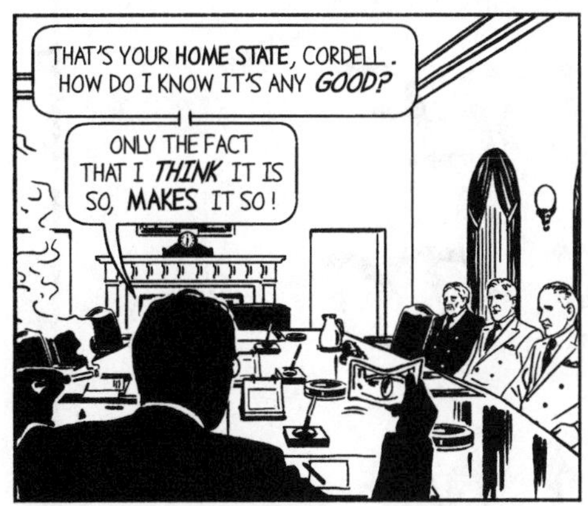
THAT'S YOUR HOME STATE, CORDELL. HOW DO I KNOW IT'S ANY GOOD?
ONLY THE FACT THAT I THINK IT IS SO, MAKES IT SO!

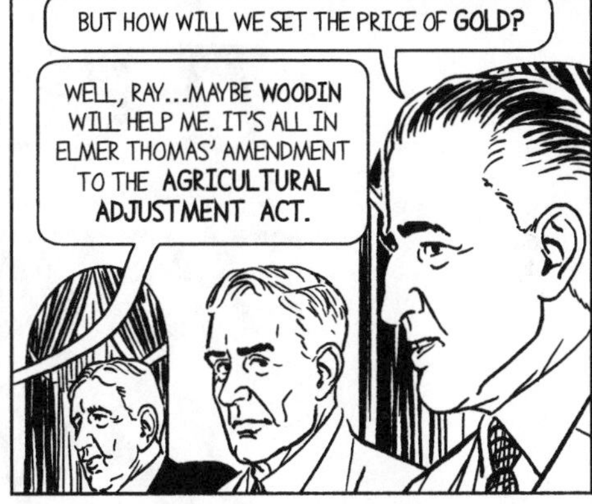
BUT HOW WILL WE SET THE PRICE OF GOLD?
WELL, RAY...MAYBE WOODIN WILL HELP ME. IT'S ALL IN ELMER THOMAS' AMENDMENT TO THE AGRICULTURAL ADJUSTMENT ACT.

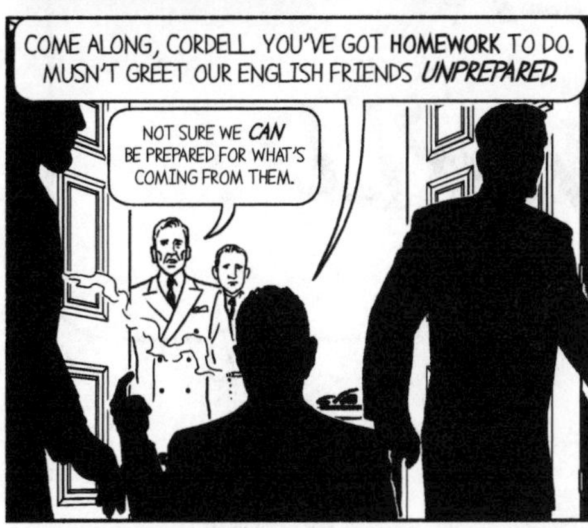
COME ALONG, CORDELL. YOU'VE GOT HOMEWORK TO DO. MUSN'T GREET OUR ENGLISH FRIENDS UNPREPARED.
NOT SURE WE CAN BE PREPARED FOR WHAT'S COMING FROM THEM.

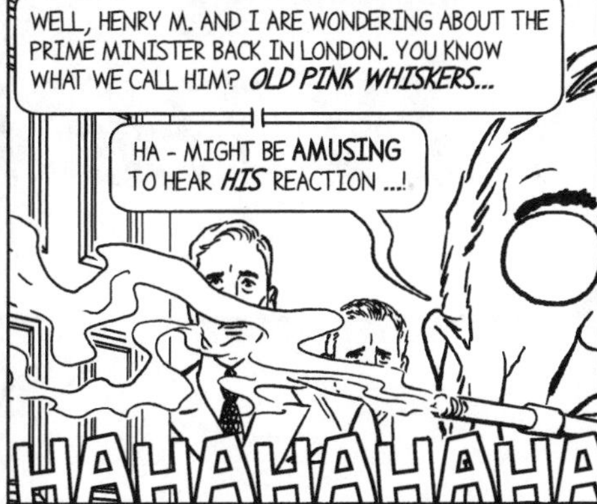
WELL, HENRY M. AND I ARE WONDERING ABOUT THE PRIME MINISTER BACK IN LONDON. YOU KNOW WHAT WE CALL HIM? OLD PINK WHISKERS...
HA - MIGHT BE AMUSING TO HEAR HIS REACTION ...!
HAHAHAHAHAHA

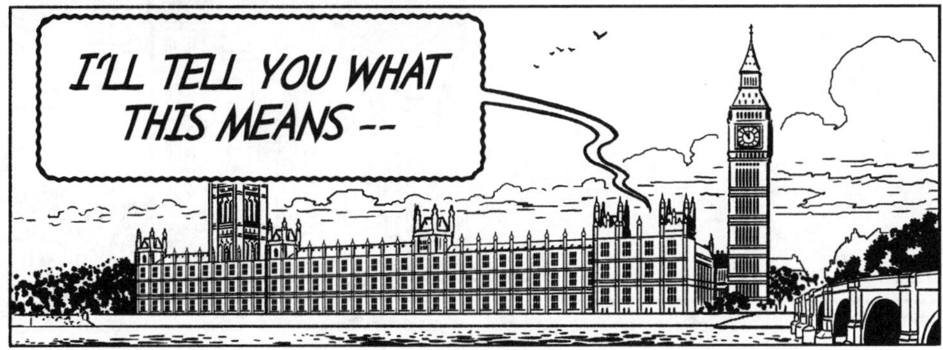
I'LL TELL YOU WHAT THIS MEANS --

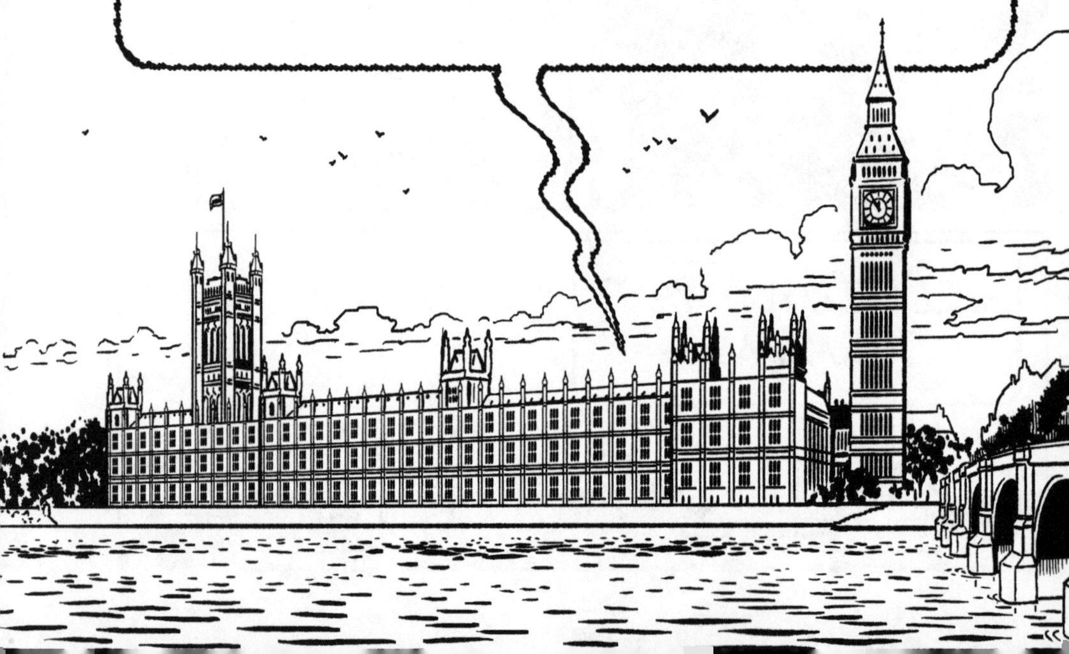
THIS IS THE MOST TERRIBLE THING TO HAPPEN IN THE WORLD!

August 1933
Unemployment 23.4%
Dow Jones Industrial
Average (Aug. 1): 93

Out in the country, though, they weren't second guessing Roosevelt on the money -- the President was trying to put people back ***TO WORK!*** *The* ***Public Works Administration*** *was starting to* ***BUILD...***

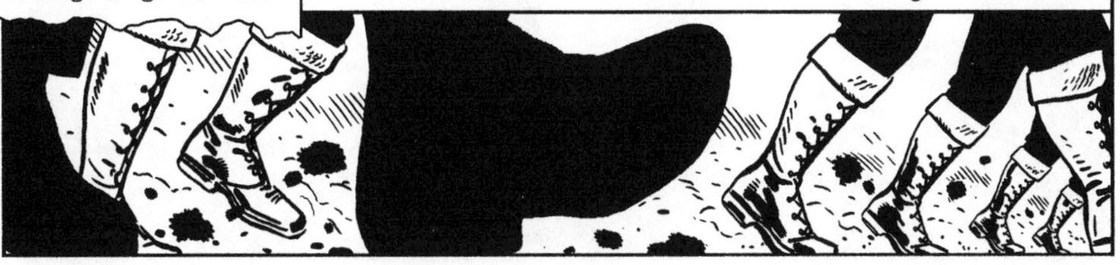

The ***Civilian Conservation Corps****, for example, sure seemed like another good idea. It was* ***smaller*** *than the Public Works Administration, Ickes's project. But the CCC still had* ***HALF A MILLION*** *men enlisted, with almost 3000 camps going up -- from* ***Hawaii*** *to* ***Puerto Rico.***

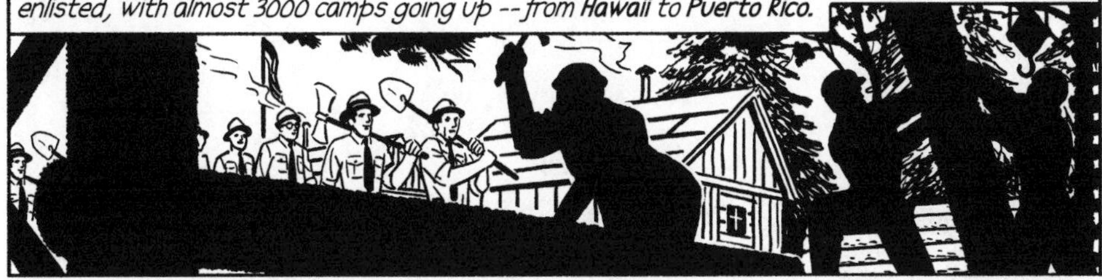

Roosevelt *visited camps when he could, with the press, to show the* ***progress*** *he was making....*

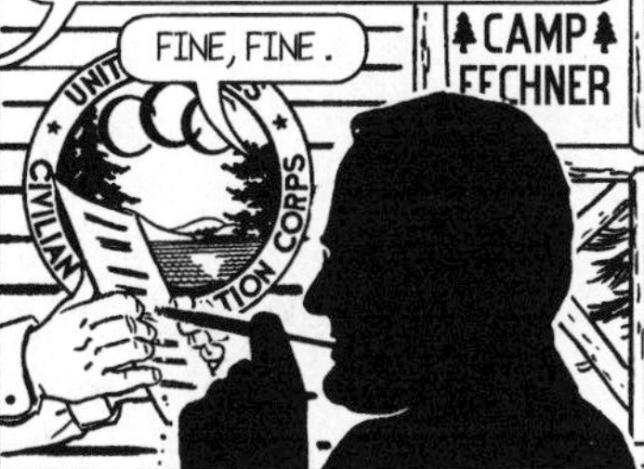

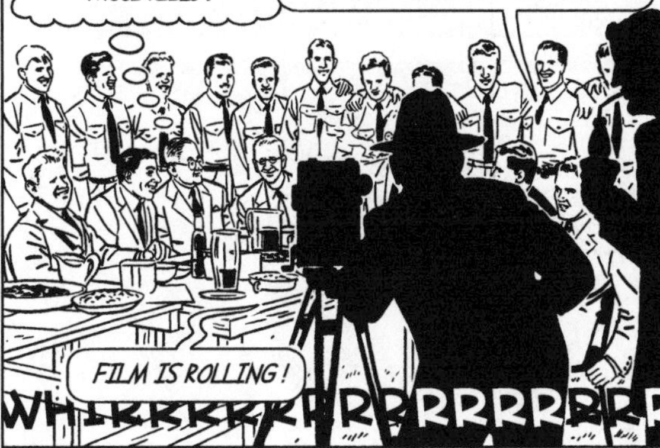

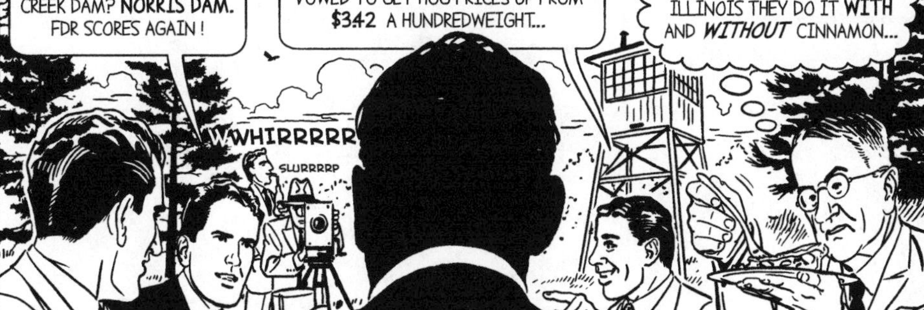

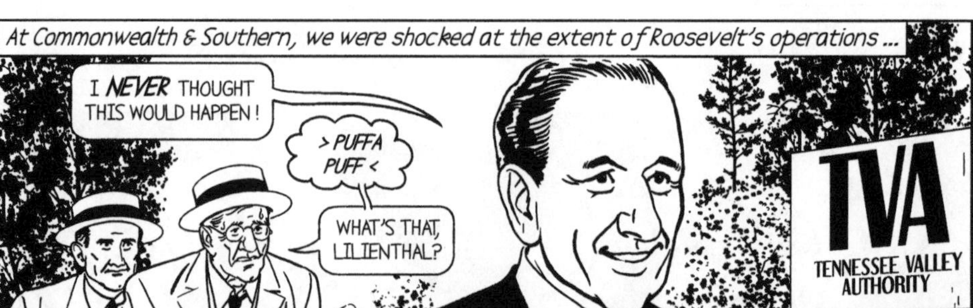
At Commonwealth & Southern, we were shocked at the extent of Roosevelt's operations ...
I NEVER THOUGHT THIS WOULD HAPPEN!
>PUFFA PUFF<
WHAT'S THAT, LILIENTHAL?
TVA
TENNESSEE VALLEY AUTHORITY

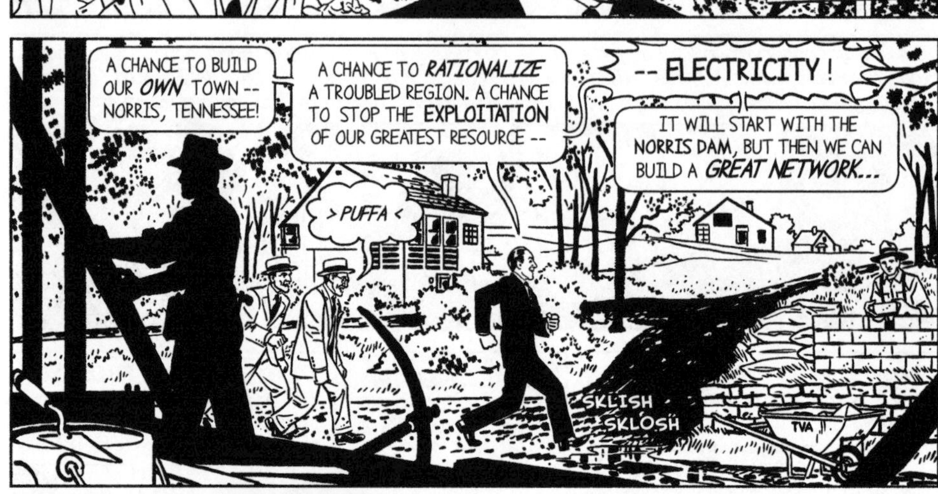
A CHANCE TO BUILD OUR OWN TOWN -- NORRIS, TENNESSEE!
A CHANCE TO RATIONALIZE A TROUBLED REGION. A CHANCE TO STOP THE EXPLOITATION OF OUR GREATEST RESOURCE --
-- ELECTRICITY!
IT WILL START WITH THE NORRIS DAM, BUT THEN WE CAN BUILD A GREAT NETWORK...
>PUFFA<
SKLISH
SKLOSH
TVA

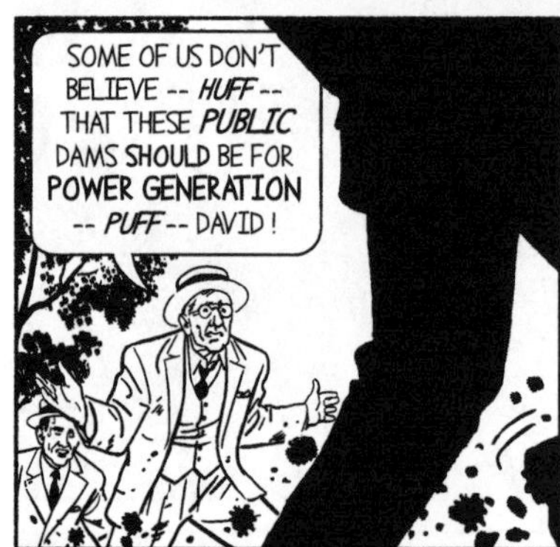
SOME OF US DON'T BELIEVE -- HUFF -- THAT THESE PUBLIC DAMS SHOULD BE FOR POWER GENERATION -- PUFF -- DAVID!

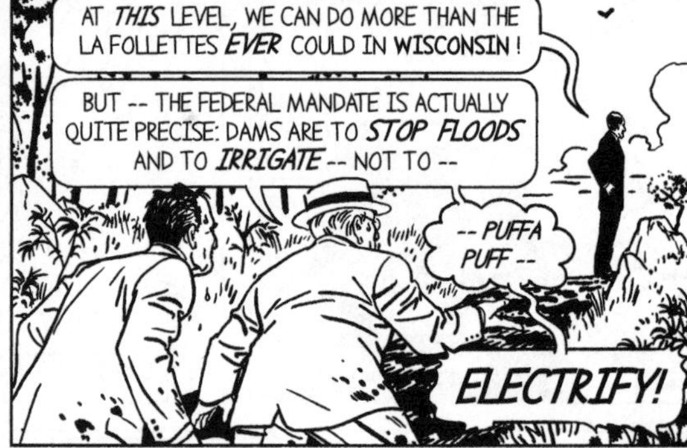
AT THIS LEVEL, WE CAN DO MORE THAN THE LA FOLLETTES EVER COULD IN WISCONSIN!
BUT -- THE FEDERAL MANDATE IS ACTUALLY QUITE PRECISE: DAMS ARE TO STOP FLOODS AND TO IRRIGATE -- NOT TO --
-- PUFFA PUFF --
ELECTRIFY!

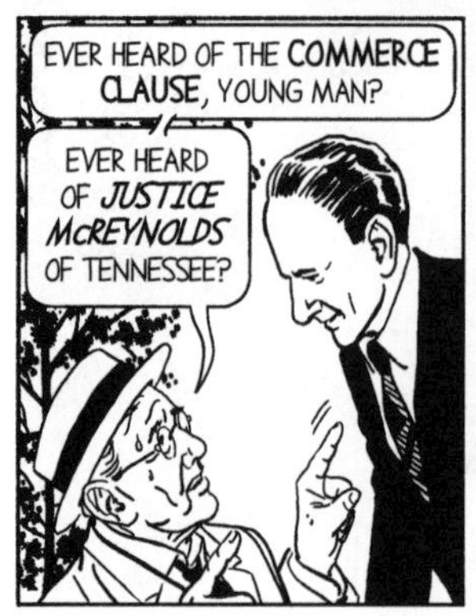
EVER HEARD OF THE COMMERCE CLAUSE, YOUNG MAN?
EVER HEARD OF JUSTICE McREYNOLDS OF TENNESSEE?

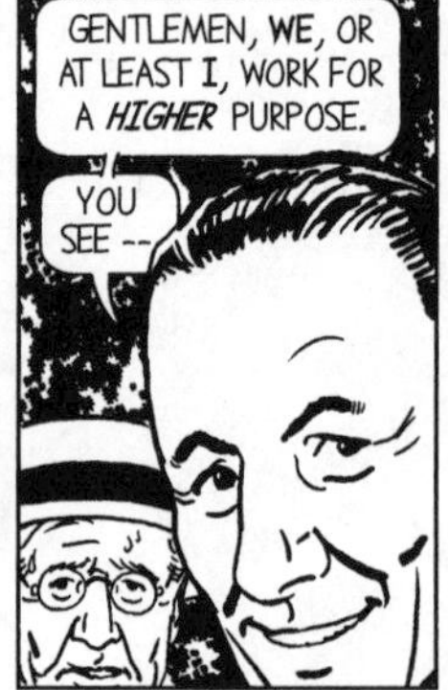
GENTLEMEN, WE, OR AT LEAST I, WORK FOR A HIGHER PURPOSE.
YOU SEE --

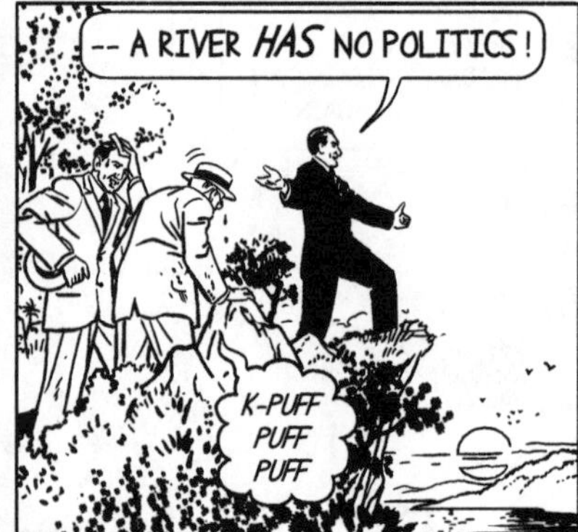
-- A RIVER HAS NO POLITICS!
K-PUFF PUFF PUFF

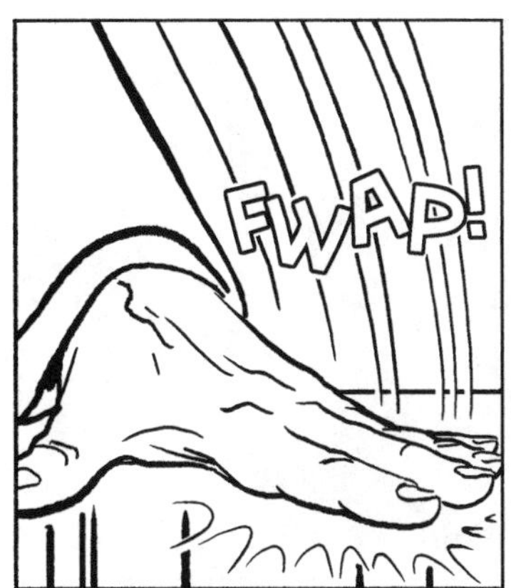
FWAP!

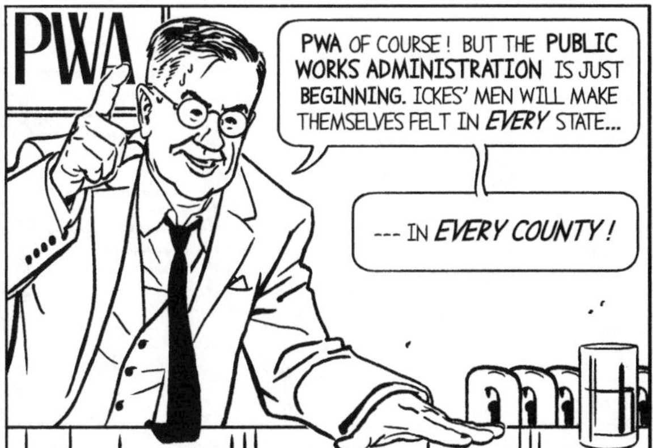
PWA
PWA OF COURSE! BUT THE PUBLIC WORKS ADMINISTRATION IS JUST BEGINNING. ICKES' MEN WILL MAKE THEMSELVES FELT IN EVERY STATE...
--- IN EVERY COUNTY!

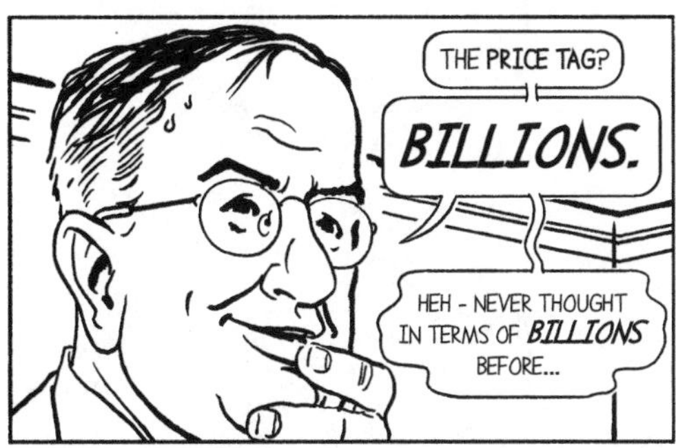
THE PRICE TAG?
BILLIONS.
HEH - NEVER THOUGHT IN TERMS OF BILLIONS BEFORE...

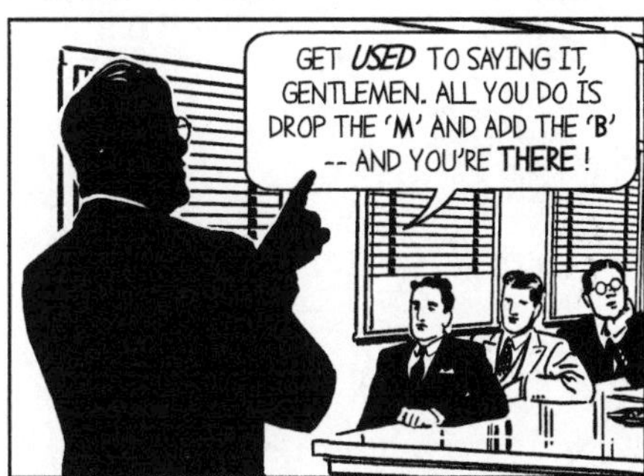
GET USED TO SAYING IT, GENTLEMEN. ALL YOU DO IS DROP THE 'M' AND ADD THE 'B' -- AND YOU'RE THERE!

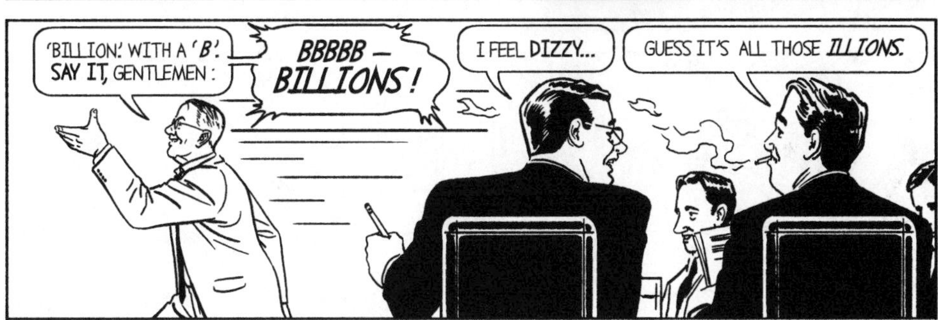
'BILLION.' WITH A 'B'. SAY IT, GENTLEMEN:
BBBBB — BILLIONS!
I FEEL DIZZY...
GUESS IT'S ALL THOSE ILLIONS.

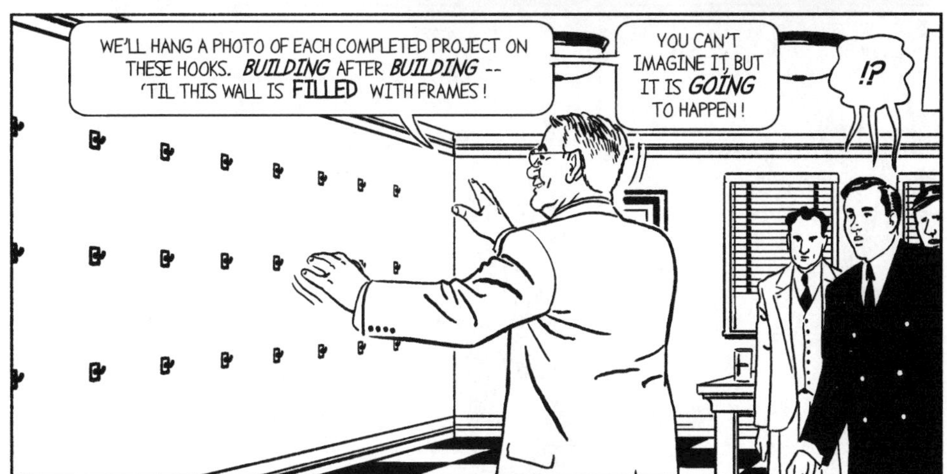
WE'LL HANG A PHOTO OF EACH COMPLETED PROJECT ON THESE HOOKS. BUILDING AFTER BUILDING -- 'TIL THIS WALL IS FILLED WITH FRAMES!
YOU CAN'T IMAGINE IT, BUT IT IS GOING TO HAPPEN!
!?

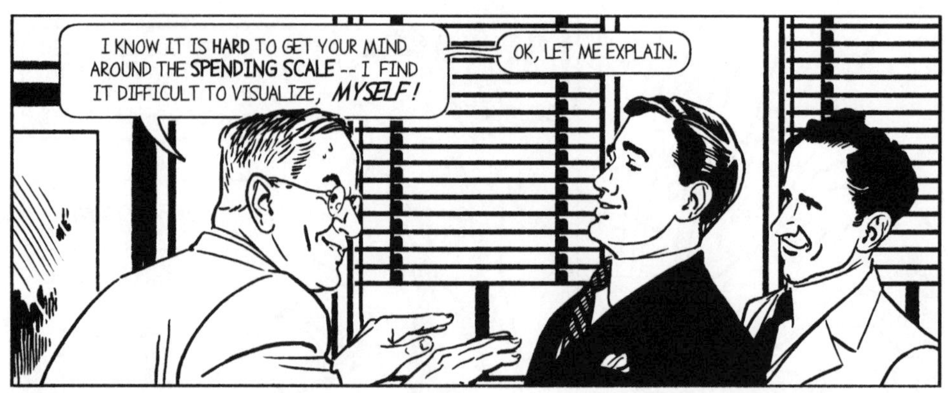
I KNOW IT IS HARD TO GET YOUR MIND AROUND THE SPENDING SCALE -- I FIND IT DIFFICULT TO VISUALIZE, MYSELF!
OK, LET ME EXPLAIN.

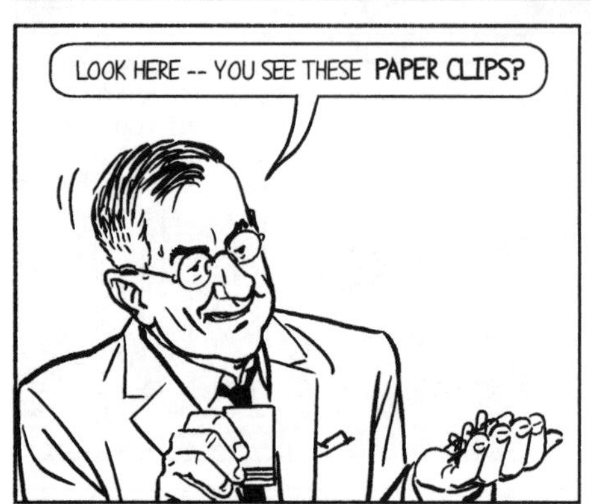
LOOK HERE -- YOU SEE THESE PAPER CLIPS?

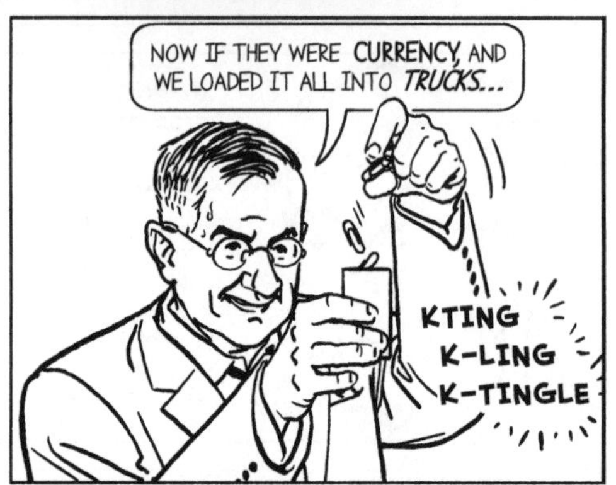
NOW IF THEY WERE CURRENCY, AND WE LOADED IT ALL INTO TRUCKS...
KTING
K-LING
K-TINGLE

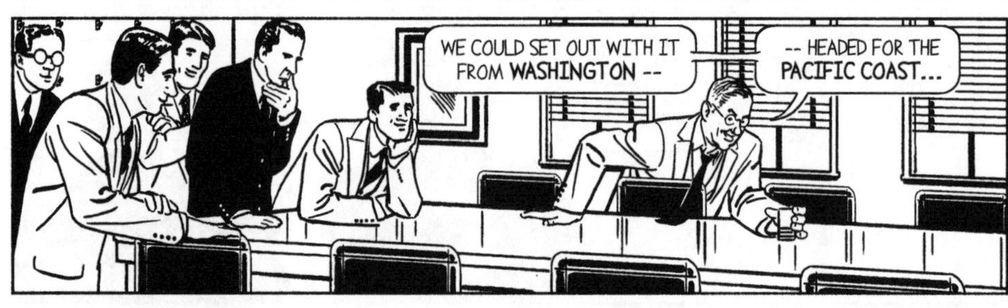
WE COULD SET OUT WITH IT FROM WASHINGTON --
-- HEADED FOR THE PACIFIC COAST...

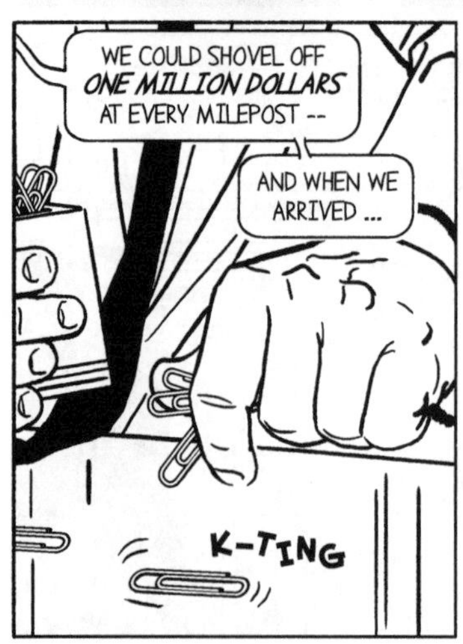
WE COULD SHOVEL OFF ONE MILLION DOLLARS AT EVERY MILEPOST --
AND WHEN WE ARRIVED ...
K-TING

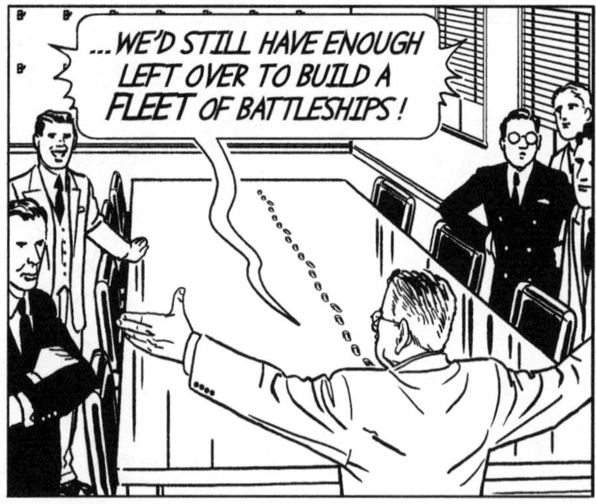
...WE'D STILL HAVE ENOUGH LEFT OVER TO BUILD A FLEET OF BATTLESHIPS!

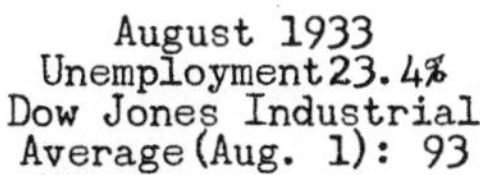
August 1933
Unemployment 23.4%
Dow Jones Industrial
Average (Aug. 1): 93

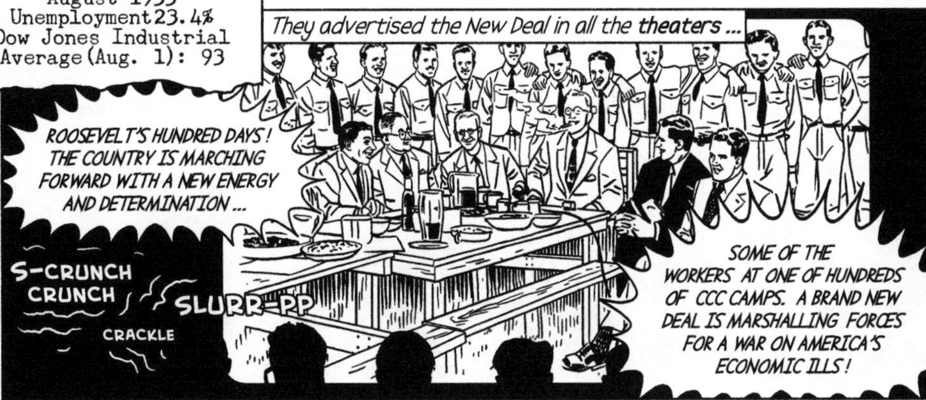
They advertised the New Deal in all the theaters ...
ROOSEVELT'S HUNDRED DAYS! THE COUNTRY IS MARCHING FORWARD WITH A NEW ENERGY AND DETERMINATION ...
S-CRUNCH CRUNCH
SLURR-PP
CRACKLE
SOME OF THE WORKERS AT ONE OF HUNDREDS OF CCC CAMPS. A BRAND NEW DEAL IS MARSHALLING FORCES FOR A WAR ON AMERICA'S ECONOMIC ILLS!

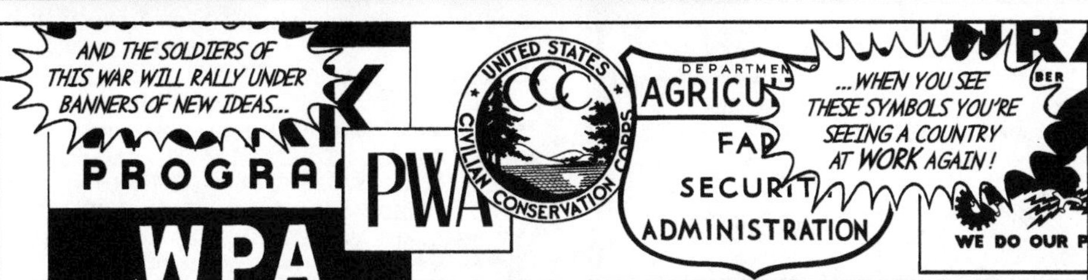
AND THE SOLDIERS OF THIS WAR WILL RALLY UNDER BANNERS OF NEW IDEAS...
PROGRA
WPA
PWA
UNITED STATES
CCC
CIVILIAN CONSERVATION CORPS
DEPARTMEN
AGRICU
FA
SECURIT
ADMINISTRATION
...WHEN YOU SEE THESE SYMBOLS YOU'RE SEEING A COUNTRY AT WORK AGAIN!
WE DO OUR P

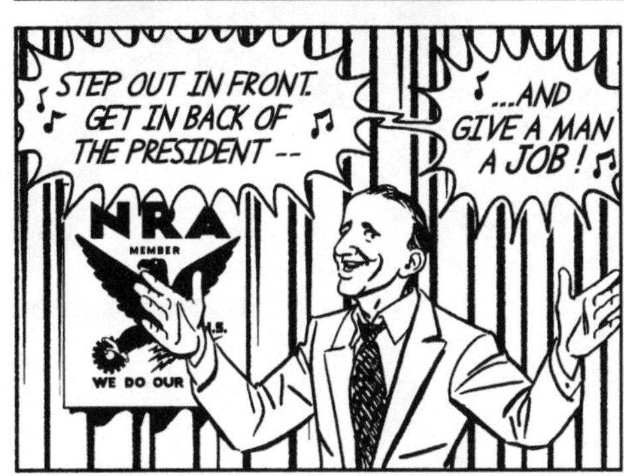
STEP OUT IN FRONT. GET IN BACK OF THE PRESIDENT --
...AND GIVE A MAN A JOB!
NRA
MEMBER
WE DO OUR

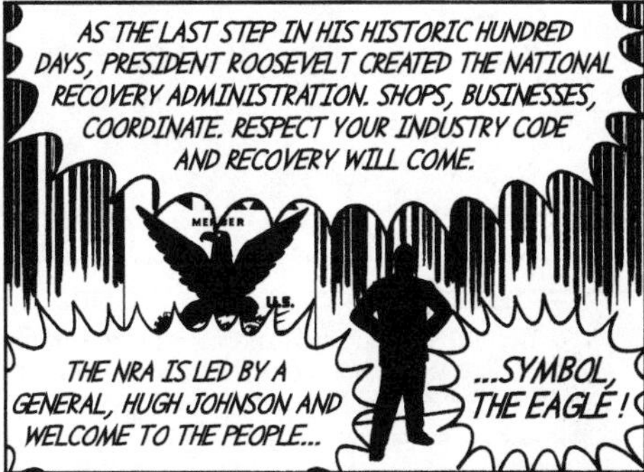
AS THE LAST STEP IN HIS HISTORIC HUNDRED DAYS, PRESIDENT ROOSEVELT CREATED THE NATIONAL RECOVERY ADMINISTRATION. SHOPS, BUSINESSES, COORDINATE. RESPECT YOUR INDUSTRY CODE AND RECOVERY WILL COME.
MEMBER
U.S.
THE NRA IS LED BY A GENERAL, HUGH JOHNSON AND WELCOME TO THE PEOPLE...
...SYMBOL, THE EAGLE!

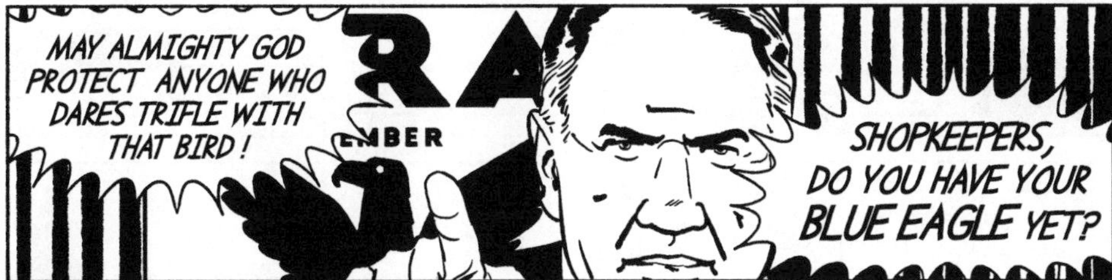
MAY ALMIGHTY GOD PROTECT ANYONE WHO DARES TRIFLE WITH THAT BIRD!
RA
EMBER
SHOPKEEPERS, DO YOU HAVE YOUR BLUE EAGLE YET?

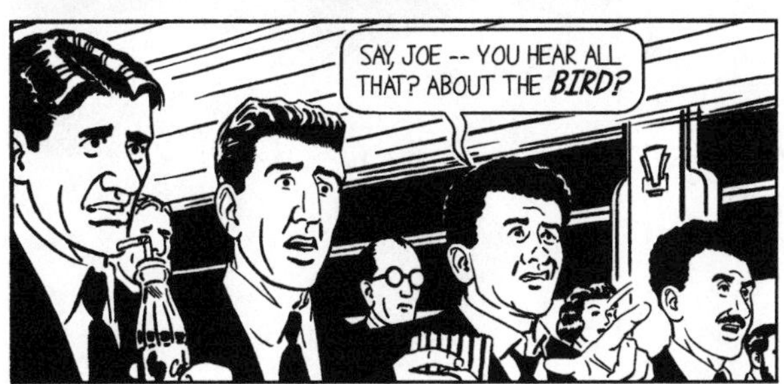
SAY, JOE -- YOU HEAR ALL THAT? ABOUT THE BIRD?

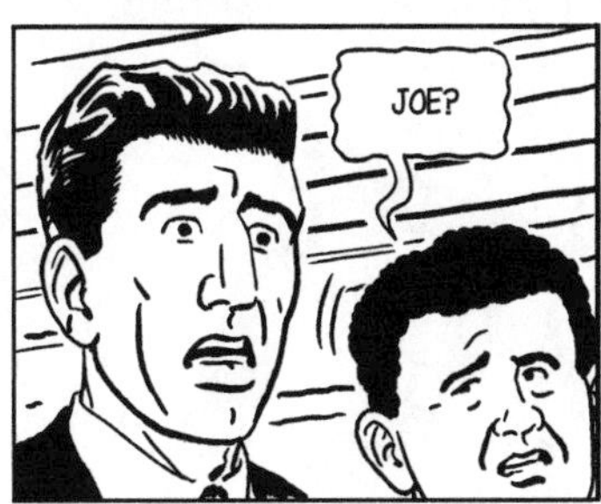
JOE?

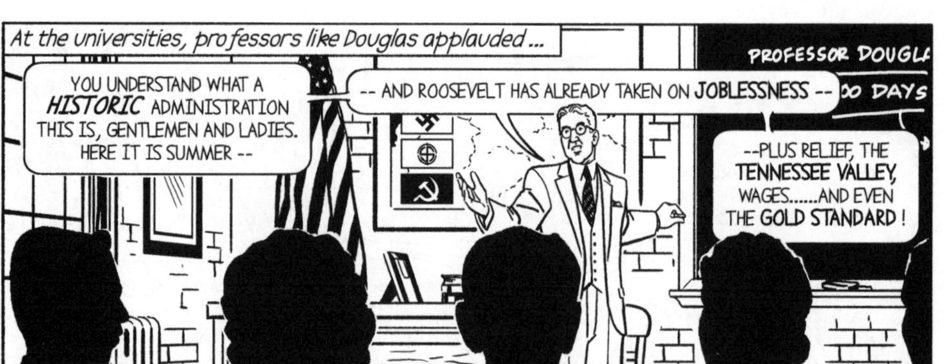
At the universities, professors like Douglas applauded...
PROFESSOR DOUGL
00 DAYS
YOU UNDERSTAND WHAT A HISTORIC ADMINISTRATION THIS IS, GENTLEMEN AND LADIES. HERE IT IS SUMMER --
-- AND ROOSEVELT HAS ALREADY TAKEN ON JOBLESSNESS --
--PLUS RELIEF, THE TENNESSEE VALLEY, WAGES......AND EVEN THE GOLD STANDARD !

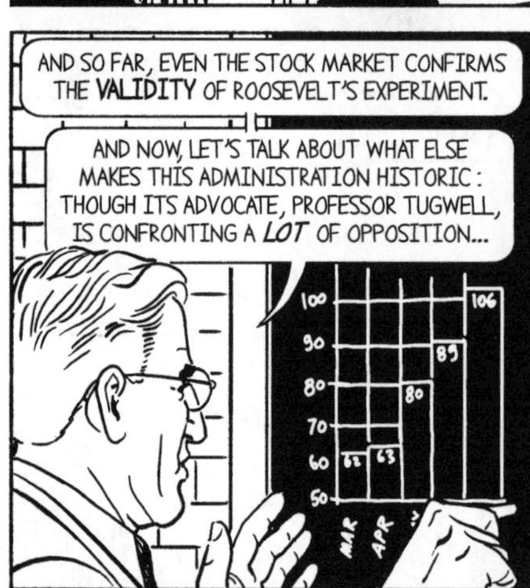
AND SO FAR, EVEN THE STOCK MARKET CONFIRMS THE VALIDITY OF ROOSEVELT'S EXPERIMENT.
AND NOW, LET'S TALK ABOUT WHAT ELSE MAKES THIS ADMINISTRATION HISTORIC : THOUGH ITS ADVOCATE, PROFESSOR TUGWELL, IS CONFRONTING A LOT OF OPPOSITION...
100
90
80
70
60
50
62
63
80
89
106
MAR
APR

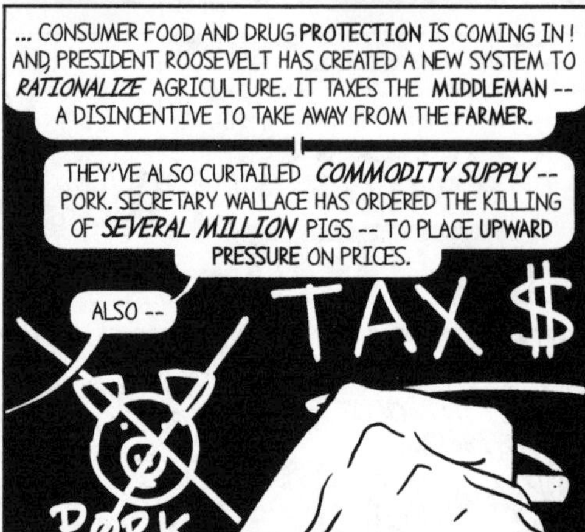
... CONSUMER FOOD AND DRUG PROTECTION IS COMING IN ! AND, PRESIDENT ROOSEVELT HAS CREATED A NEW SYSTEM TO RATIONALIZE AGRICULTURE. IT TAXES THE MIDDLEMAN -- A DISINCENTIVE TO TAKE AWAY FROM THE FARMER.
THEY'VE ALSO CURTAILED COMMODITY SUPPLY -- PORK. SECRETARY WALLACE HAS ORDERED THE KILLING OF SEVERAL MILLION PIGS -- TO PLACE UPWARD PRESSURE ON PRICES.
ALSO --
TAX $
PØRK

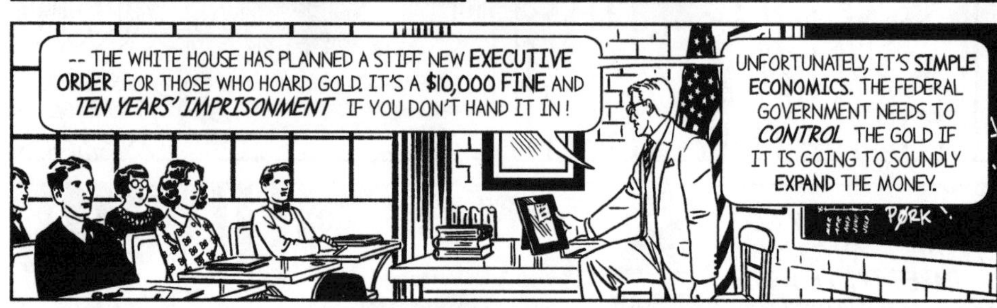
-- THE WHITE HOUSE HAS PLANNED A STIFF NEW EXECUTIVE ORDER FOR THOSE WHO HOARD GOLD. IT'S A $10,000 FINE AND TEN YEARS' IMPRISONMENT IF YOU DON'T HAND IT IN !
UNFORTUNATELY, IT'S SIMPLE ECONOMICS. THE FEDERAL GOVERNMENT NEEDS TO CONTROL THE GOLD IF IT IS GOING TO SOUNDLY EXPAND THE MONEY.
PØRK

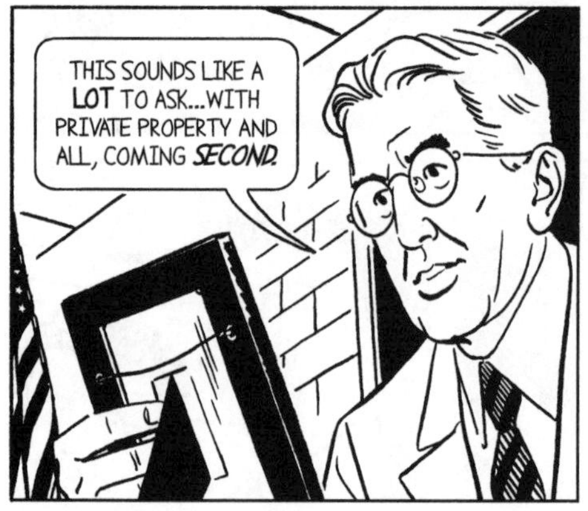
THIS SOUNDS LIKE A LOT TO ASK...WITH PRIVATE PROPERTY AND ALL, COMING SECOND.

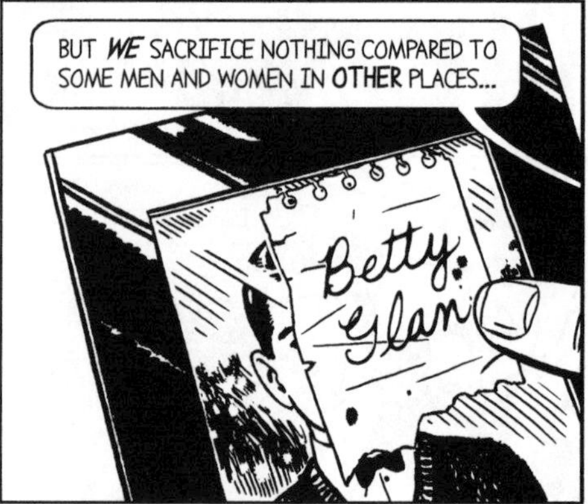
BUT WE SACRIFICE NOTHING COMPARED TO SOME MEN AND WOMEN IN OTHER PLACES...
Betty Glan

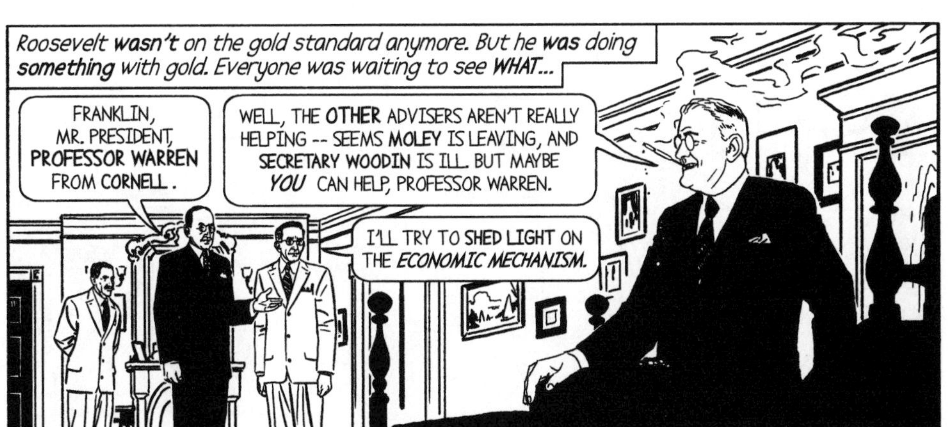
Roosevelt **wasn't** on the gold standard anymore. But he **was** doing **something** with gold. Everyone was waiting to see **WHAT...**
FRANKLIN, MR. PRESIDENT, **PROFESSOR WARREN** FROM **CORNELL**.
WELL, THE **OTHER** ADVISERS AREN'T REALLY HELPING -- SEEMS **MOLEY** IS LEAVING, AND **SECRETARY WOODIN** IS ILL. BUT MAYBE ***YOU*** CAN HELP, PROFESSOR WARREN.
I'LL TRY TO **SHED LIGHT** ON THE *ECONOMIC MECHANISM.*

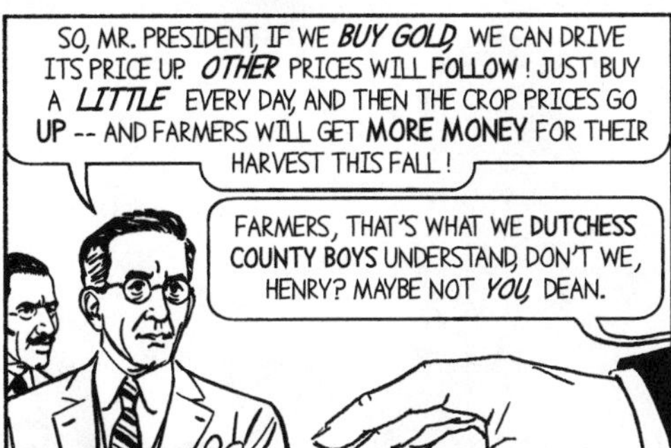
SO, MR. PRESIDENT, IF WE ***BUY GOLD,*** WE CAN DRIVE ITS PRICE UP. ***OTHER*** PRICES WILL **FOLLOW**! JUST BUY A ***LITTLE*** EVERY DAY, AND THEN THE CROP PRICES GO **UP** -- AND FARMERS WILL GET **MORE MONEY** FOR THEIR HARVEST THIS FALL!
FARMERS, THAT'S WHAT WE **DUTCHESS COUNTY BOYS** UNDERSTAND, DON'T WE, HENRY? MAYBE NOT *YOU,* DEAN.

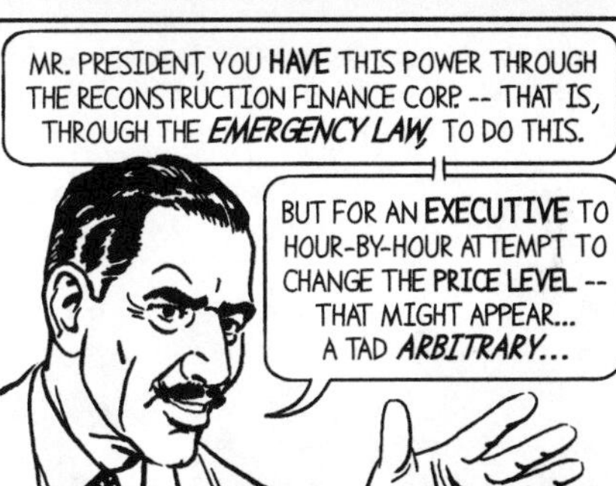
MR. PRESIDENT, YOU **HAVE** THIS POWER THROUGH THE RECONSTRUCTION FINANCE CORP. -- THAT IS, THROUGH THE ***EMERGENCY LAW,*** TO DO THIS.
BUT FOR AN **EXECUTIVE** TO HOUR-BY-HOUR ATTEMPT TO CHANGE THE **PRICE LEVEL** -- THAT MIGHT APPEAR... A TAD ***ARBITRARY...***

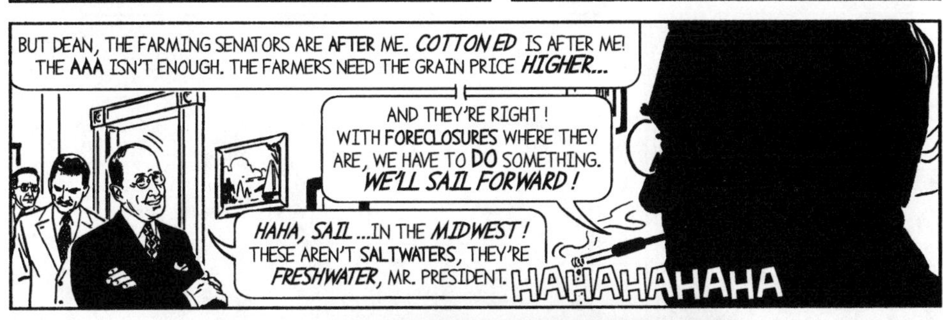
BUT DEAN, THE FARMING SENATORS ARE **AFTER** ME. ***COTTON ED*** IS AFTER ME! THE **AAA** ISN'T ENOUGH. THE FARMERS NEED THE GRAIN PRICE ***HIGHER...***
AND THEY'RE RIGHT! WITH **FORECLOSURES** WHERE THEY ARE, WE HAVE TO **DO** SOMETHING. ***WE'LL SAIL FORWARD!***
HAHA, SAIL...IN THE ***MIDWEST!*** THESE AREN'T **SALTWATERS**, THEY'RE ***FRESHWATER***, MR. PRESIDENT.
HAHAHAHAHA

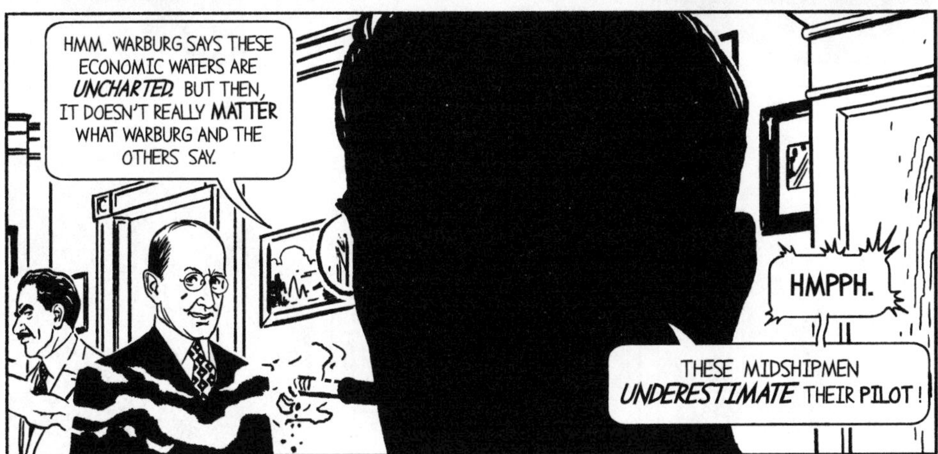
HMM. WARBURG SAYS THESE ECONOMIC WATERS ARE ***UNCHARTED.*** BUT THEN, IT DOESN'T REALLY **MATTER** WHAT WARBURG AND THE OTHERS SAY.
HMPPH.
THESE MIDSHIPMEN ***UNDERESTIMATE*** THEIR **PILOT**!

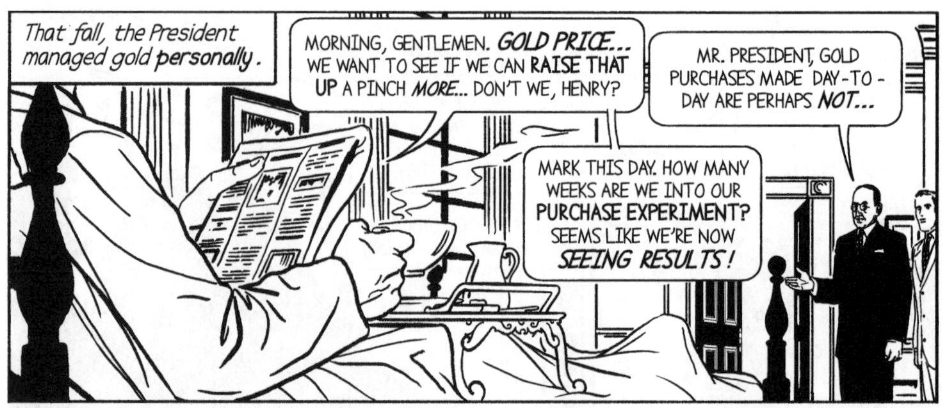
That fall, the President managed gold personally.
MORNING, GENTLEMEN. GOLD PRICE... WE WANT TO SEE IF WE CAN RAISE THAT UP A PINCH MORE... DON'T WE, HENRY?
MARK THIS DAY. HOW MANY WEEKS ARE WE INTO OUR PURCHASE EXPERIMENT? SEEMS LIKE WE'RE NOW SEEING RESULTS!
MR. PRESIDENT, GOLD PURCHASES MADE DAY-TO-DAY ARE PERHAPS NOT...

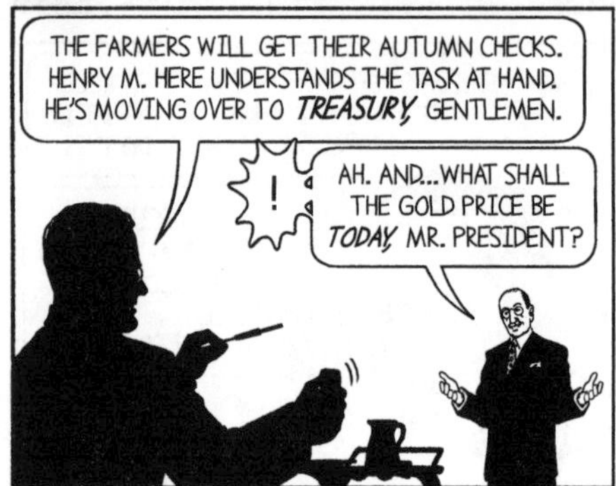
THE FARMERS WILL GET THEIR AUTUMN CHECKS. HENRY M. HERE UNDERSTANDS THE TASK AT HAND. HE'S MOVING OVER TO TREASURY, GENTLEMEN.
!
AH. AND...WHAT SHALL THE GOLD PRICE BE TODAY, MR. PRESIDENT?

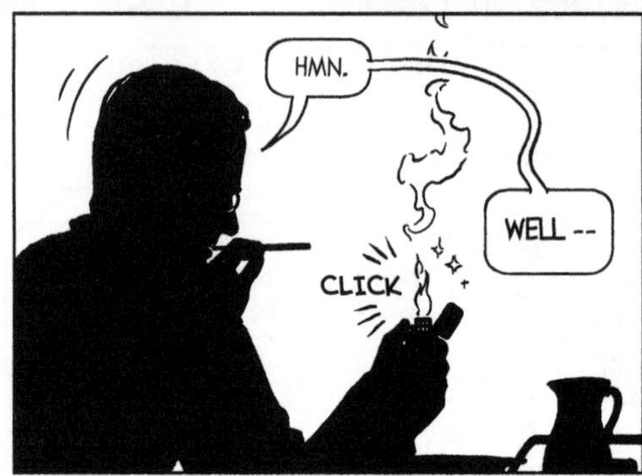
HMN.
CLICK
WELL --

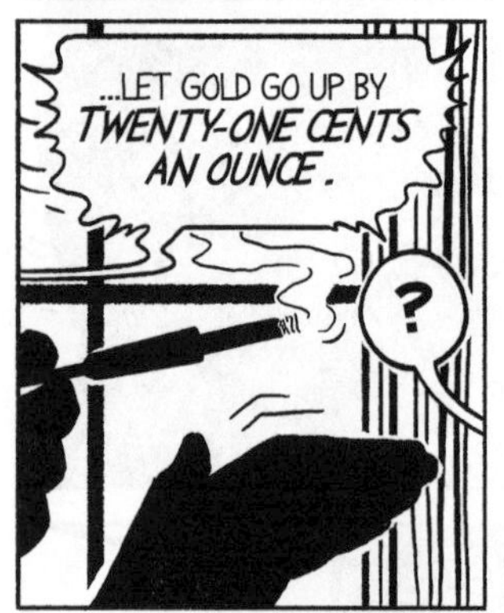
...LET GOLD GO UP BY TWENTY-ONE CENTS AN OUNCE.
?

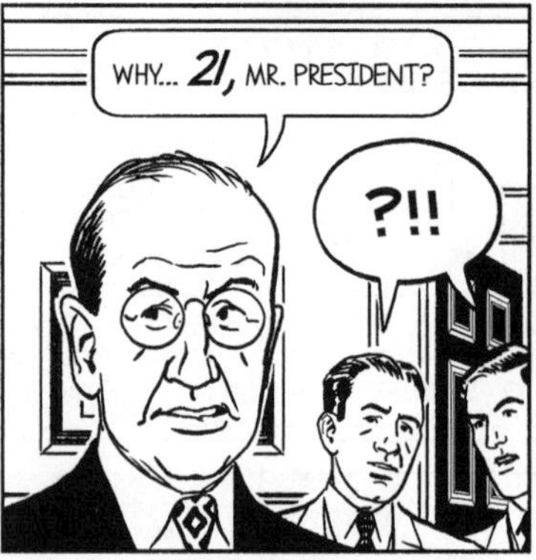
WHY... 21, MR. PRESIDENT?
?!!

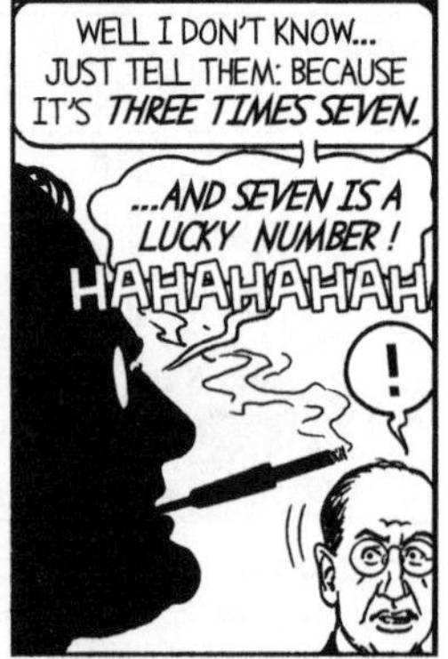
WELL I DON'T KNOW... JUST TELL THEM: BECAUSE IT'S THREE TIMES SEVEN.
...AND SEVEN IS A LUCKY NUMBER!
HAHAHAHAHAH
!

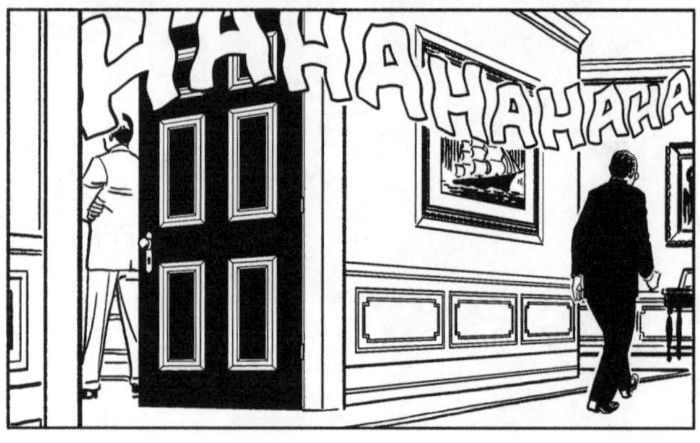
HAHAHAHAHAHAHA

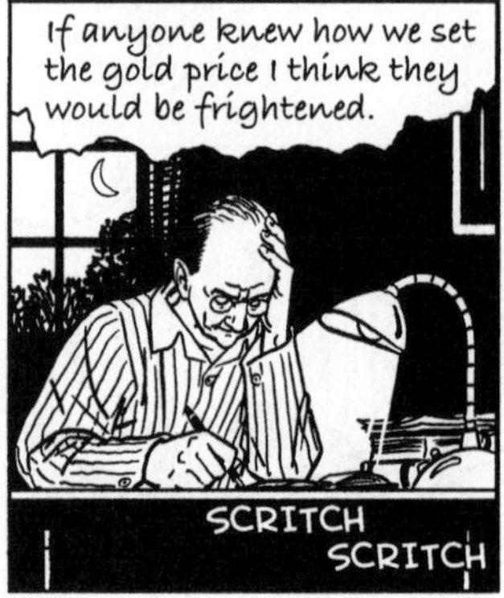
If anyone knew how we set the gold price I think they would be frightened.
SCRITCH
SCRITCH

As *head* of Commonwealth & Southern, I was confronting the business challenge of a **CAREER** ...

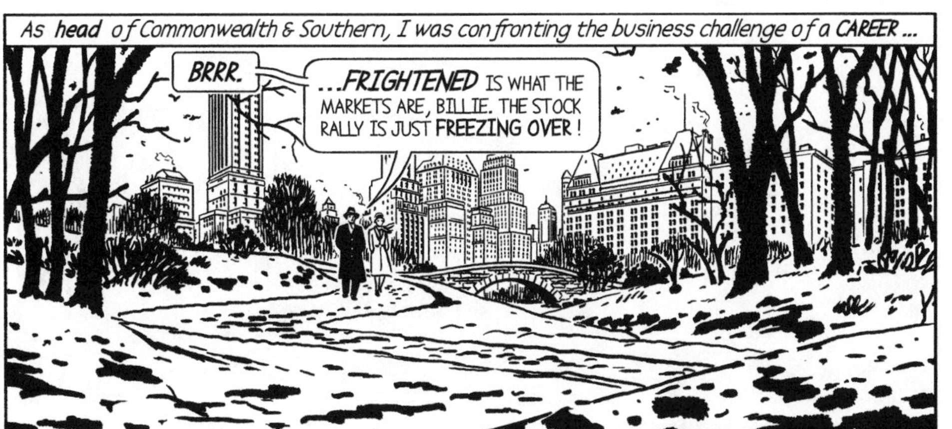

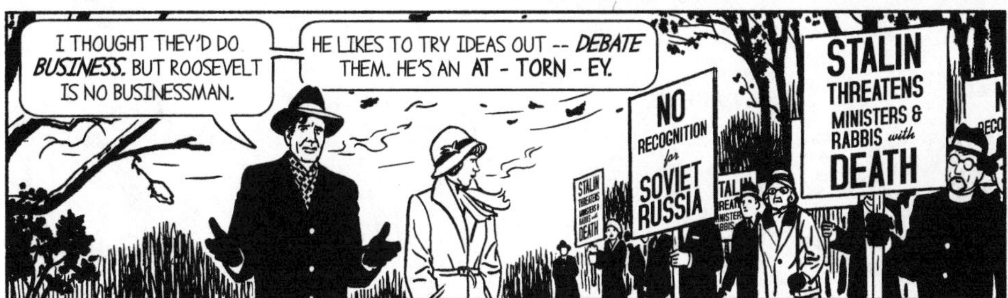

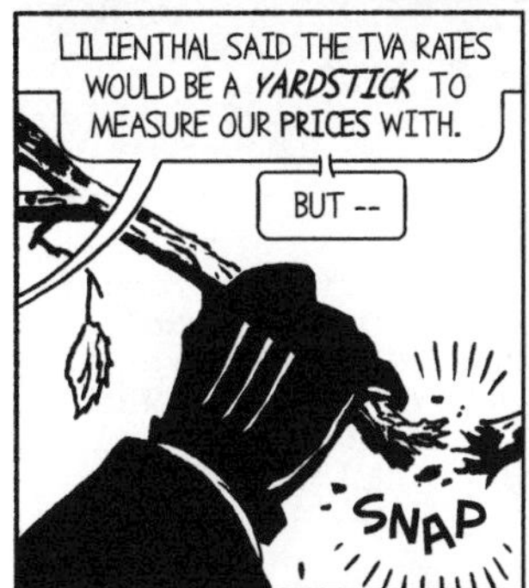

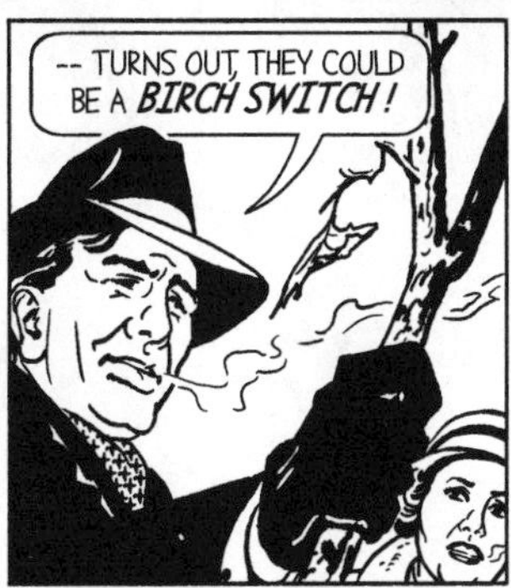

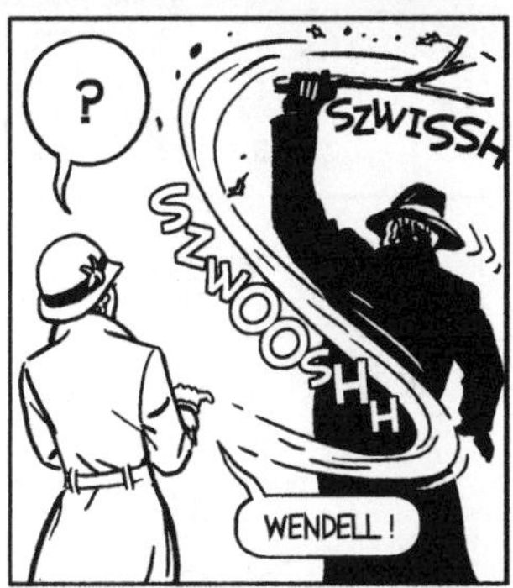

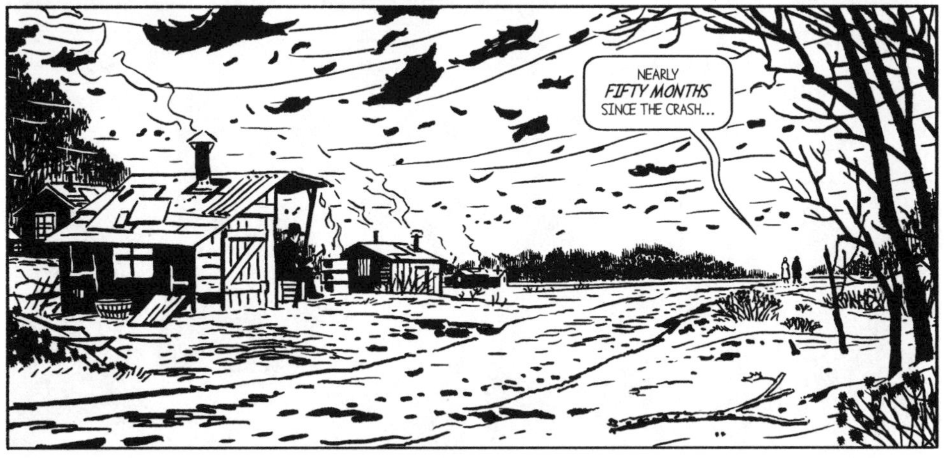

October 1933
Unemployment: 22.9 %
Dow Jones Industrial
Average (Oct. 2): 93

*That fall, I met with **Lilienthal** for the first time. He was still the junior member of the TVA management, behind the two Morgans. We settled on the **Cosmos Club** as neutral ground...*

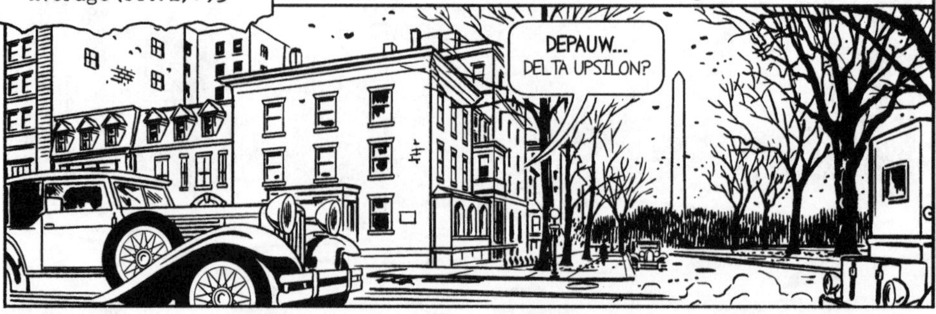

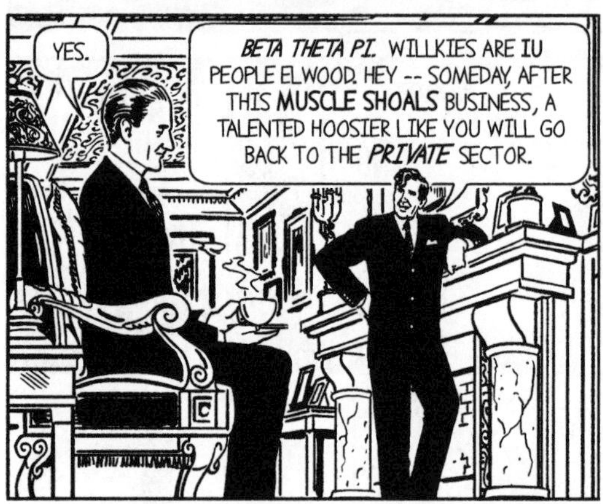

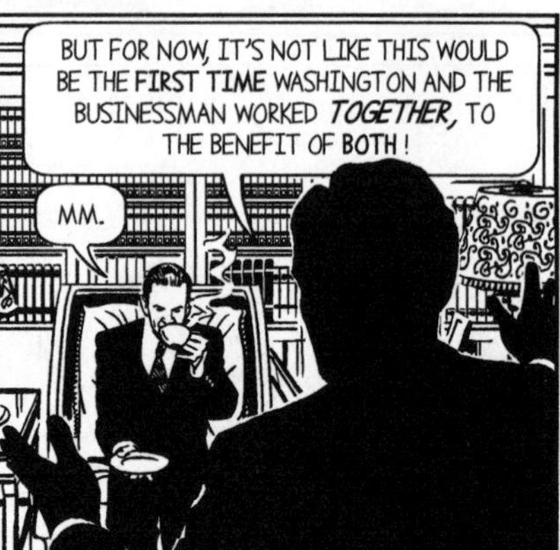

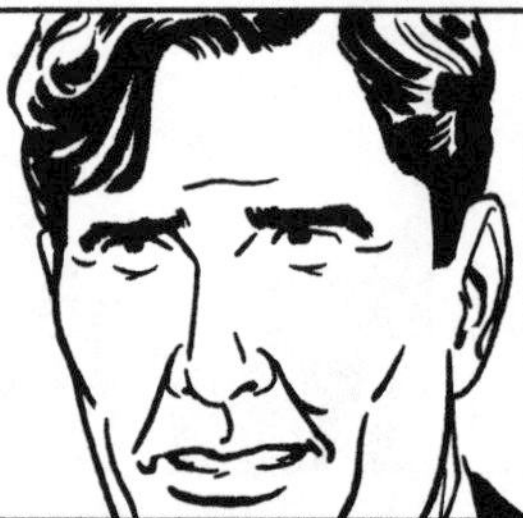

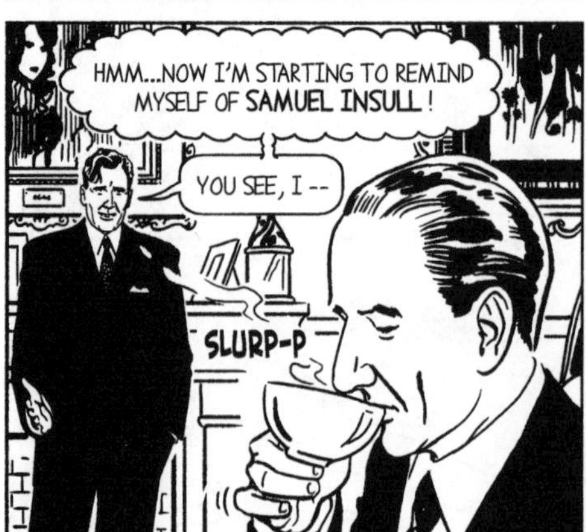

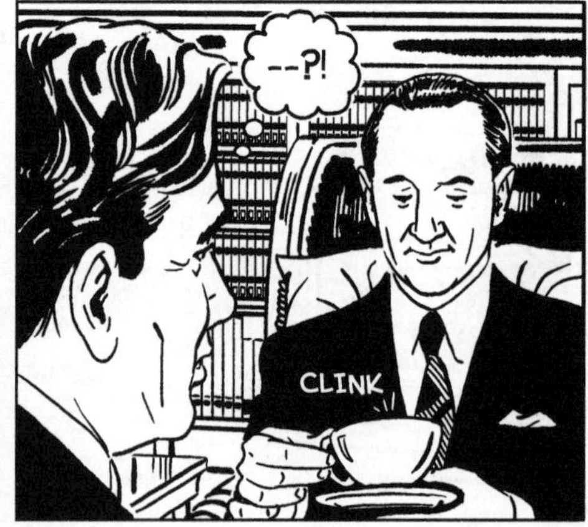

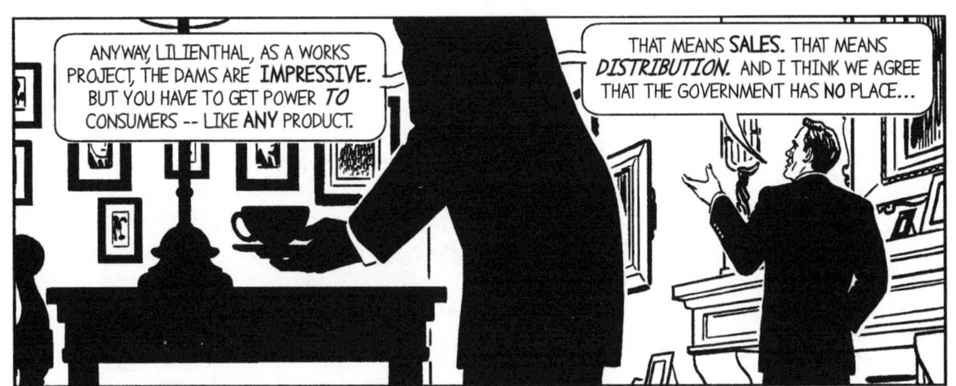
ANYWAY, LILIENTHAL, AS A WORKS PROJECT, THE DAMS ARE IMPRESSIVE. BUT YOU HAVE TO GET POWER TO CONSUMERS -- LIKE ANY PRODUCT.
THAT MEANS SALES. THAT MEANS DISTRIBUTION. AND I THINK WE AGREE THAT THE GOVERNMENT HAS NO PLACE...

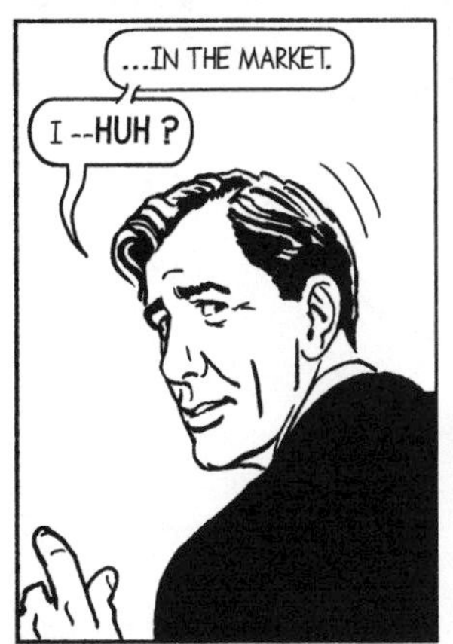
...IN THE MARKET.
I --HUH ?

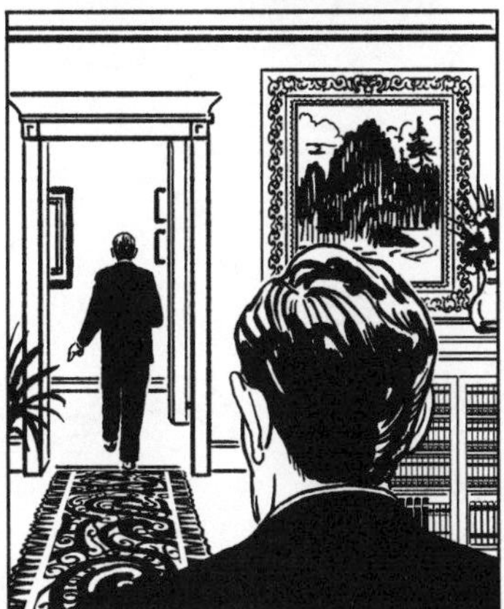

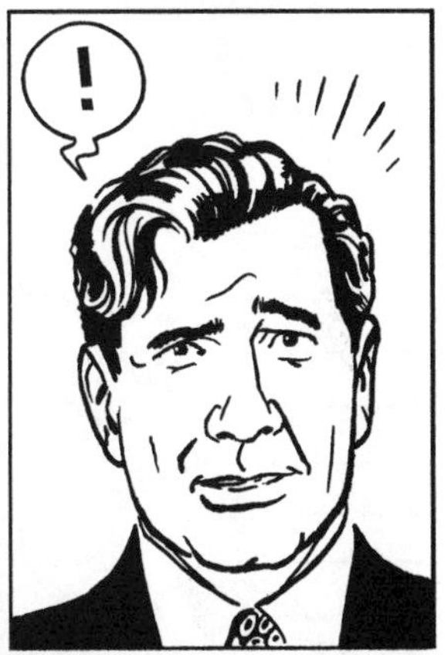
!

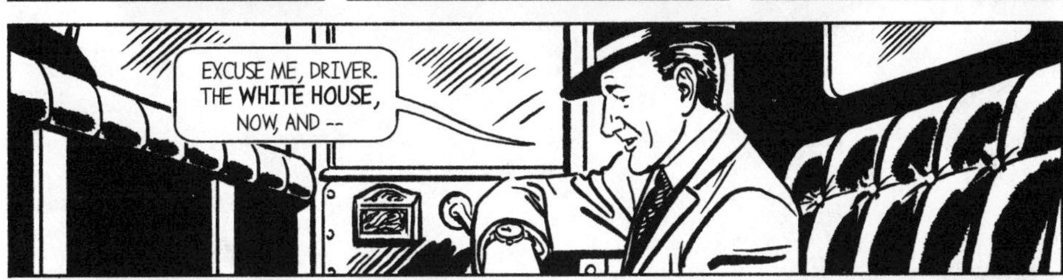
EXCUSE ME, DRIVER. THE WHITE HOUSE, NOW, AND --

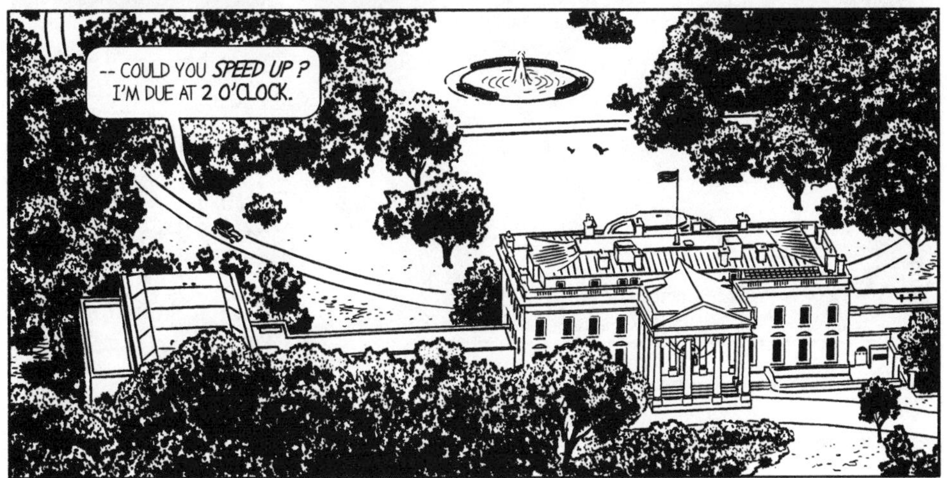
-- COULD YOU SPEED UP ? I'M DUE AT 2 O'CLOCK.

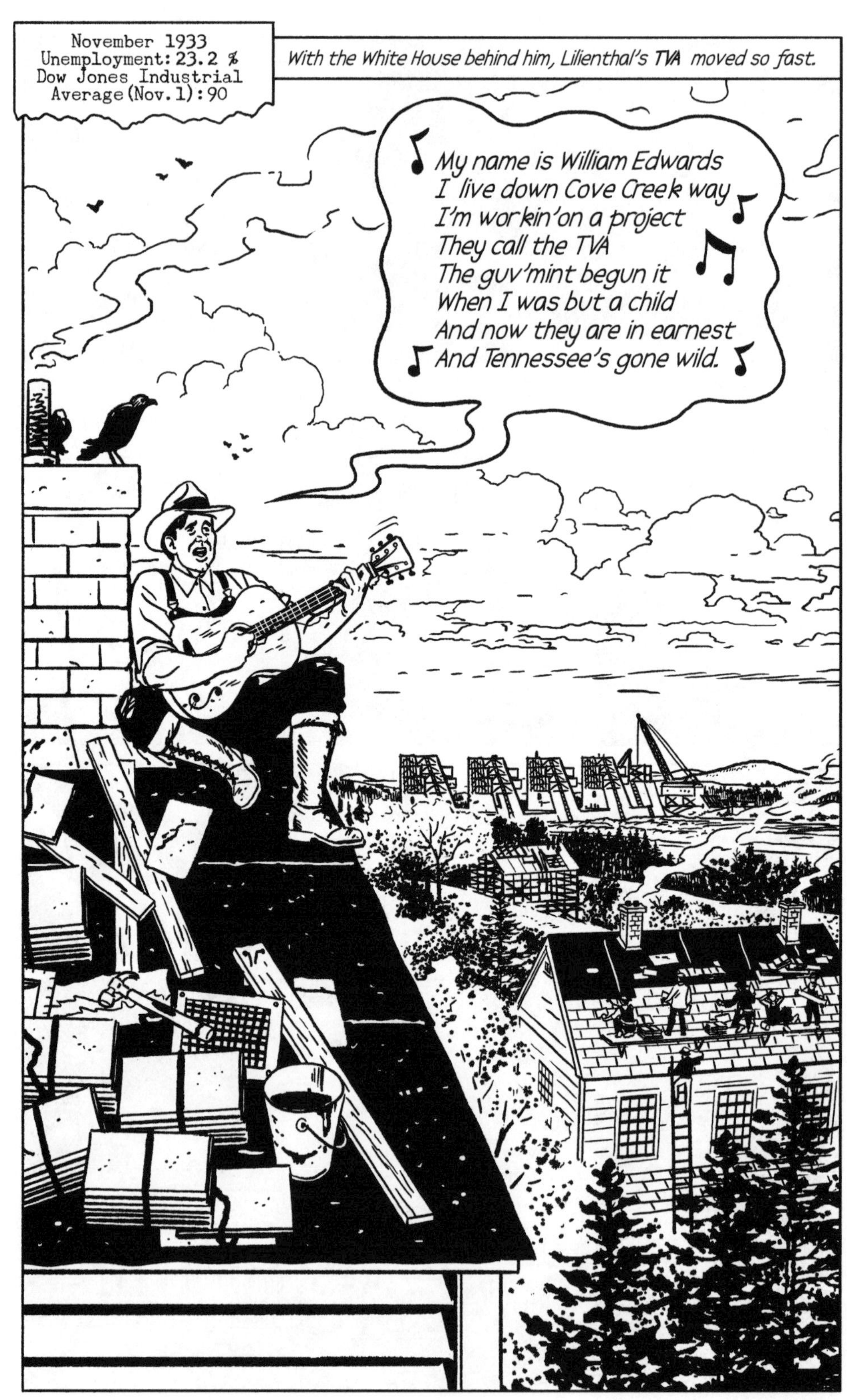
November 1933
Unemployment: 23.2 %
Dow Jones Industrial
Average (Nov. 1): 90
With the White House behind him, Lilienthal's TVA moved so fast.
My name is William Edwards
I live down Cove Creek way
I'm workin' on a project
They call the TVA
The guv'mint begun it
When I was but a child
And now they are in earnest
And Tennessee's gone wild.

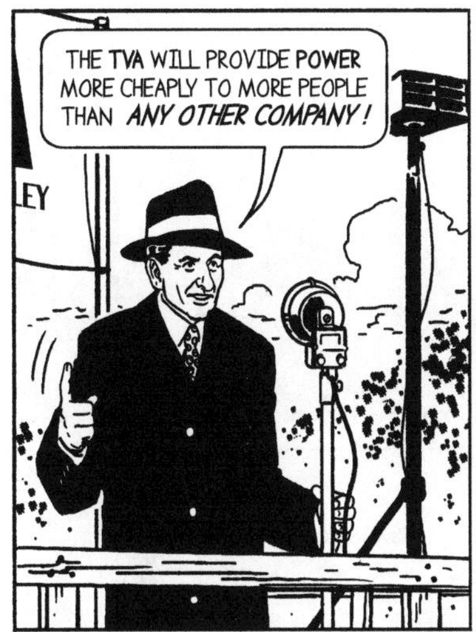
THE TVA WILL PROVIDE POWER MORE CHEAPLY TO MORE PEOPLE THAN ANY OTHER COMPANY!
LEY

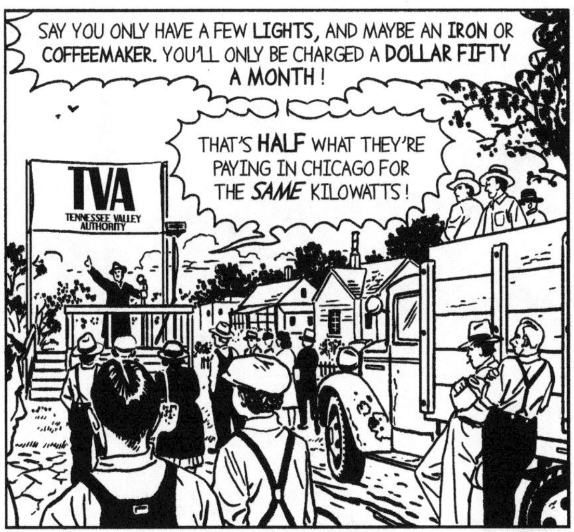
SAY YOU ONLY HAVE A FEW LIGHTS, AND MAYBE AN IRON OR COFFEEMAKER. YOU'LL ONLY BE CHARGED A DOLLAR FIFTY A MONTH!
THAT'S HALF WHAT THEY'RE PAYING IN CHICAGO FOR THE SAME KILOWATTS!
TVA
TENNESSEE VALLEY AUTHORITY

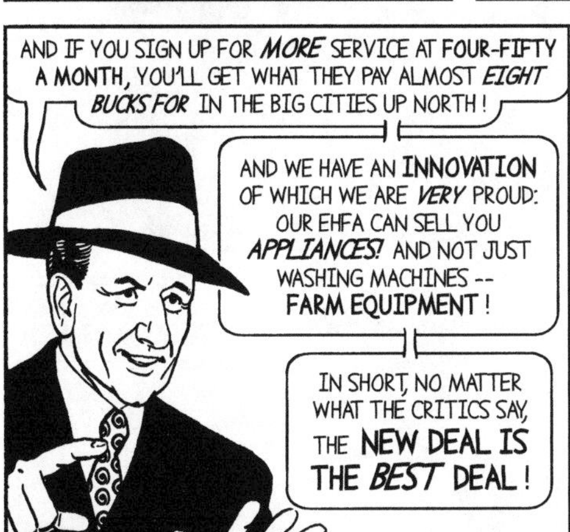
AND IF YOU SIGN UP FOR MORE SERVICE AT FOUR-FIFTY A MONTH, YOU'LL GET WHAT THEY PAY ALMOST EIGHT BUCKS FOR IN THE BIG CITIES UP NORTH!
AND WE HAVE AN INNOVATION OF WHICH WE ARE VERY PROUD: OUR EHFA CAN SELL YOU APPLIANCES! AND NOT JUST WASHING MACHINES -- FARM EQUIPMENT!
IN SHORT, NO MATTER WHAT THE CRITICS SAY, THE NEW DEAL IS THE BEST DEAL!

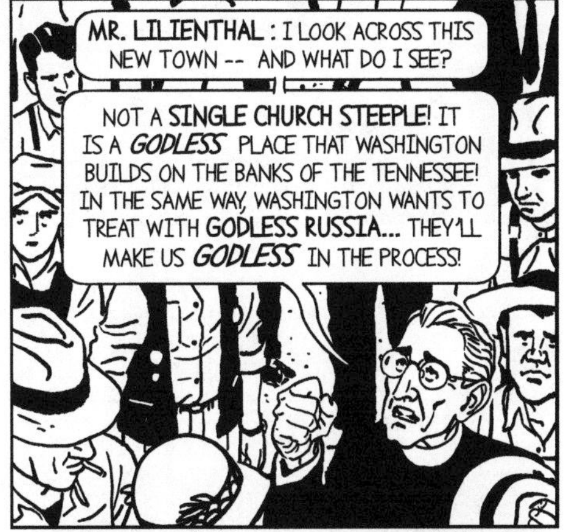
MR. LILIENTHAL: I LOOK ACROSS THIS NEW TOWN -- AND WHAT DO I SEE?
NOT A SINGLE CHURCH STEEPLE! IT IS A GODLESS PLACE THAT WASHINGTON BUILDS ON THE BANKS OF THE TENNESSEE! IN THE SAME WAY, WASHINGTON WANTS TO TREAT WITH GODLESS RUSSIA... THEY'LL MAKE US GODLESS IN THE PROCESS!

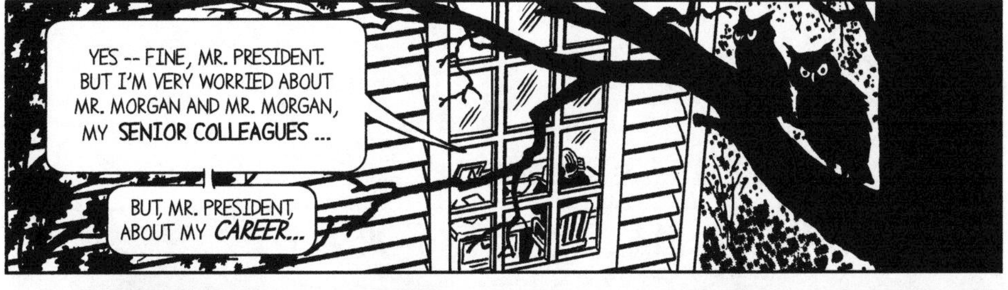
YES -- FINE, MR. PRESIDENT. BUT I'M VERY WORRIED ABOUT MR. MORGAN AND MR. MORGAN, MY SENIOR COLLEAGUES ...
BUT, MR. PRESIDENT, ABOUT MY CAREER...

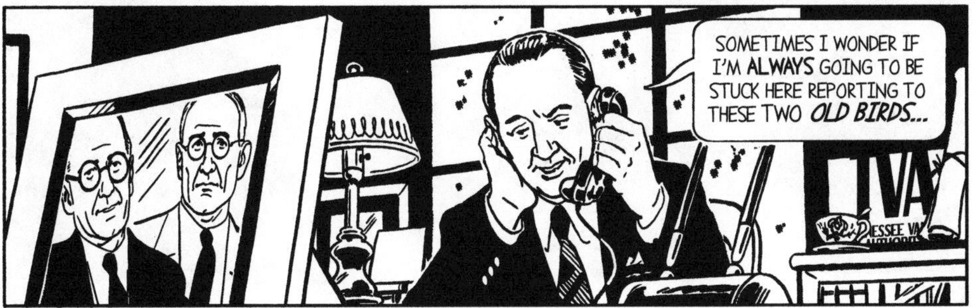
SOMETIMES I WONDER IF I'M ALWAYS GOING TO BE STUCK HERE REPORTING TO THESE TWO OLD BIRDS...
TVA

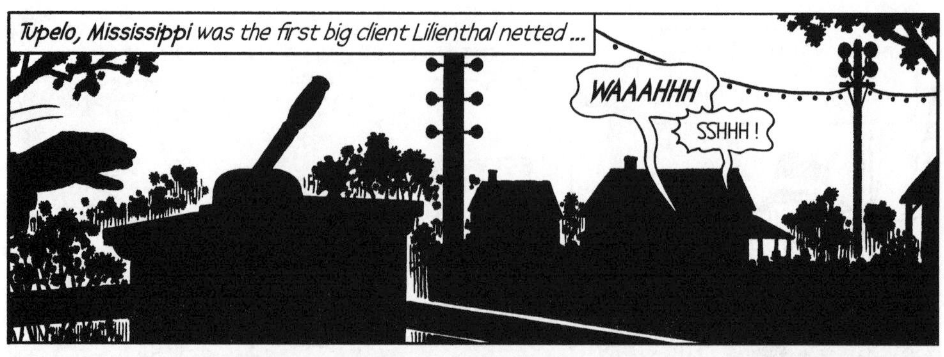
Tupelo, Mississippi was the first big client Lilienthal netted ...
WAAAHHH
SSHHH !

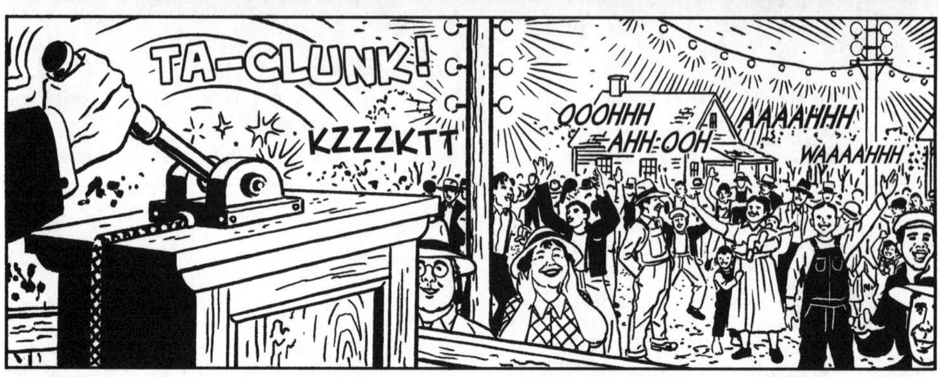
TA-CLUNK!
KZZZKTT
OOOHHH
AHH-OOH
AAAAHHH
WAAAAHHH

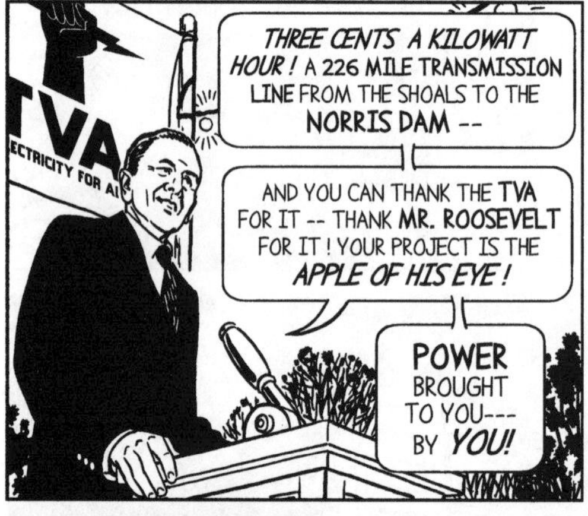
THREE CENTS A KILOWATT HOUR ! A 226 MILE TRANSMISSION LINE FROM THE SHOALS TO THE NORRIS DAM --
AND YOU CAN THANK THE TVA FOR IT -- THANK MR. ROOSEVELT FOR IT ! YOUR PROJECT IS THE APPLE OF HIS EYE !
POWER BROUGHT TO YOU--- BY YOU!
TVA
ECTRICITY FOR AL

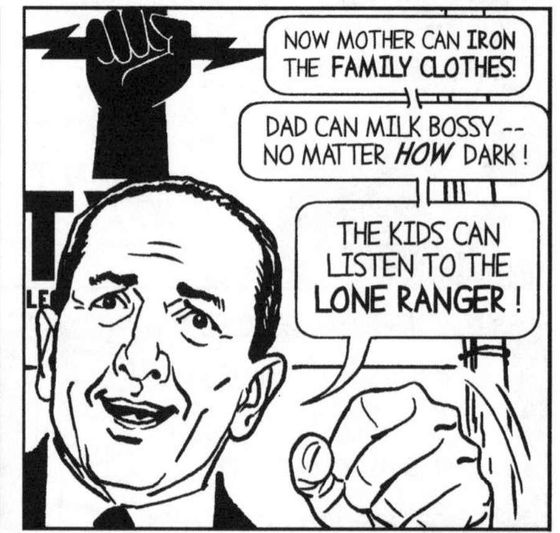
NOW MOTHER CAN IRON THE FAMILY CLOTHES!
DAD CAN MILK BOSSY -- NO MATTER HOW DARK !
THE KIDS CAN LISTEN TO THE LONE RANGER !

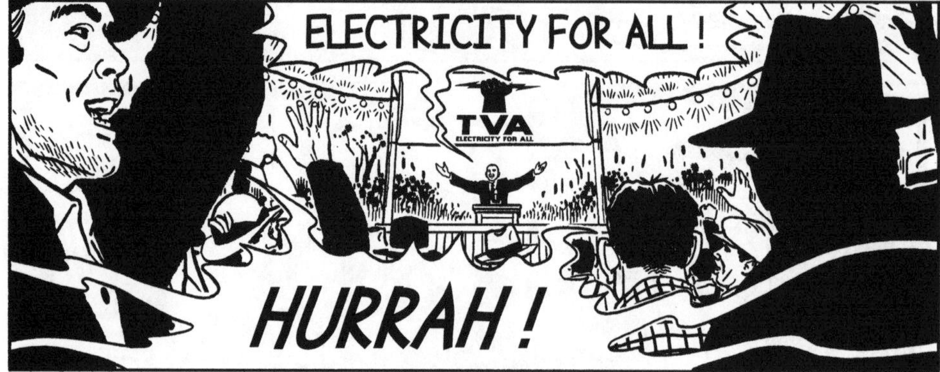
ELECTRICITY FOR ALL !
TVA
ELECTRICITY FOR ALL
HURRAH !

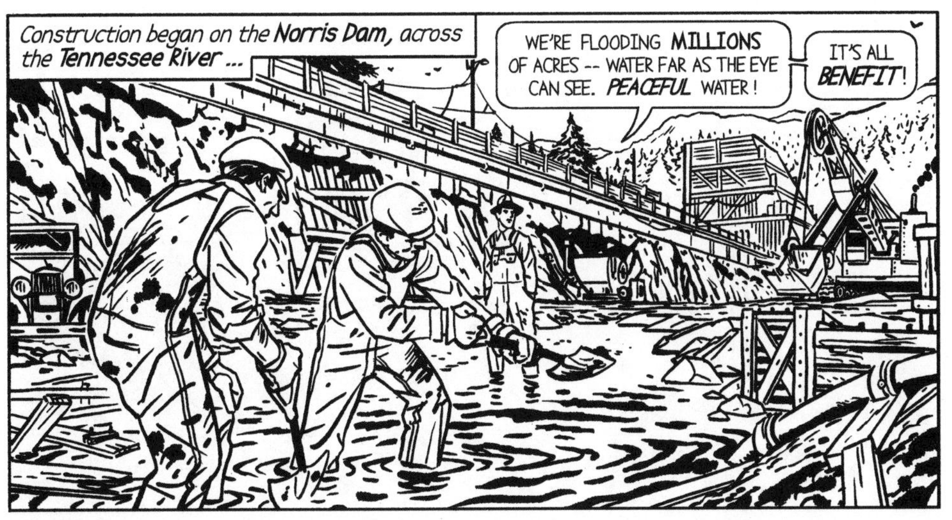

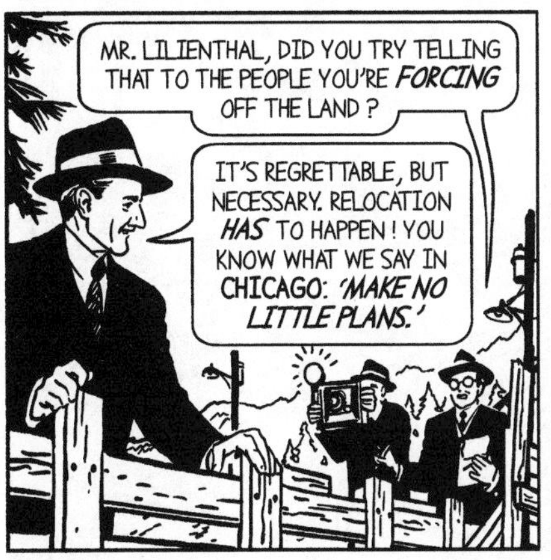

AS I'VE SAID BEFORE, THE PRICE OF ELECTRICITY GENERATED BY THIS DAM WILL PROVIDE A YARDSTICK FOR MEASURING THE RATES OF PRIVATE SECTOR UTILITIES -- COMPANIES LIKE INSULL'S -- YOU KNOW, THE FUGITIVE.

BUT HAVE YOU SPOKEN WITH MR. WILLKIE OF COMMONWEALTH AND SOUTHERN? AREN'T YOU TREADING ON THEIR TERRITORY?

SOME UNEXPECTED PARTNERSHIPS ARE COMING TOGETHER IN THE NEW DEAL. WILL YOU AND WILLKIE TEAM UP?

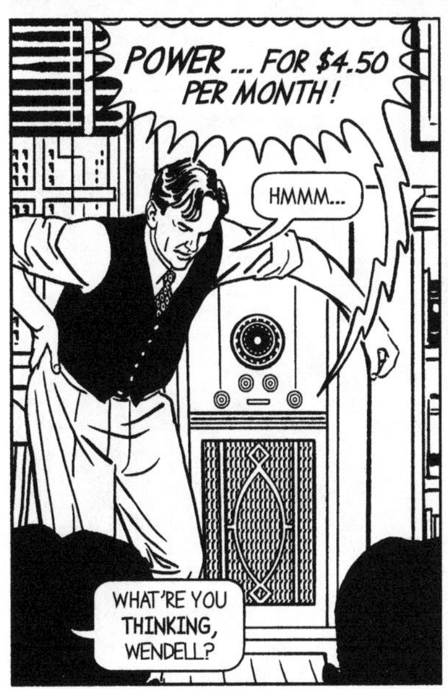

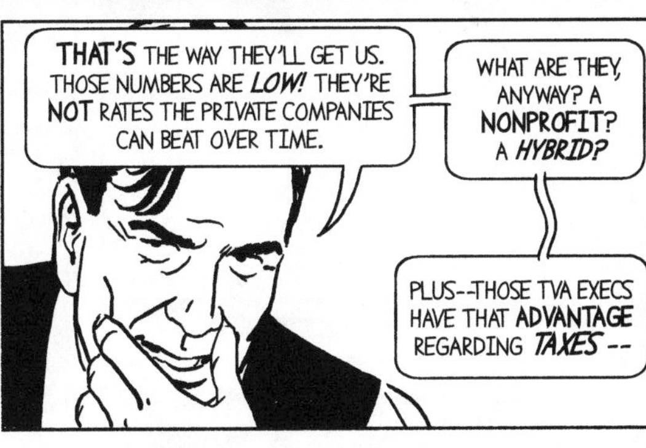

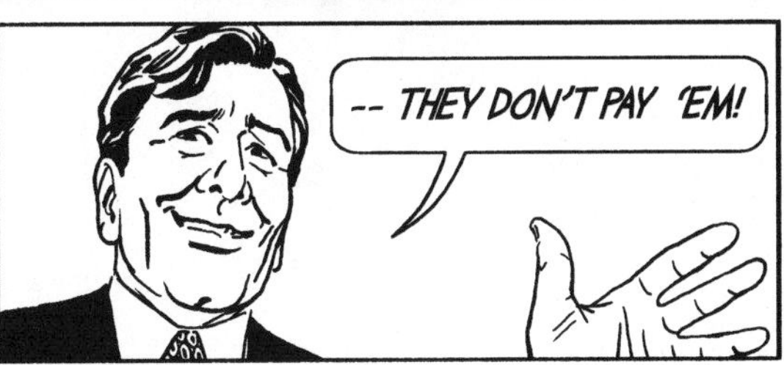

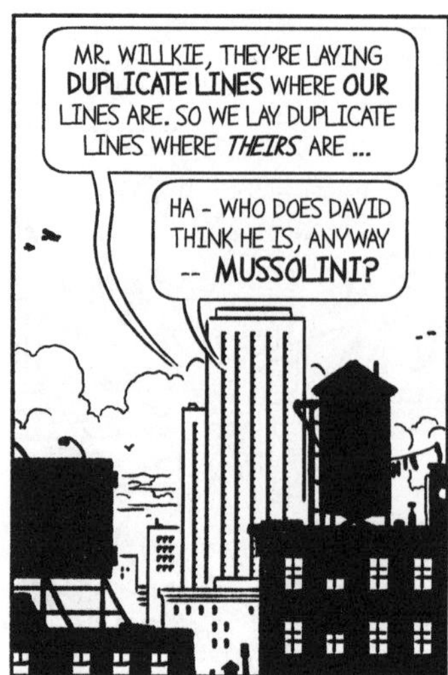
MR. WILLKIE, THEY'RE LAYING DUPLICATE LINES WHERE OUR LINES ARE. SO WE LAY DUPLICATE LINES WHERE *THEIRS* ARE ...
HA - WHO DOES DAVID THINK HE IS, ANYWAY -- MUSSOLINI?

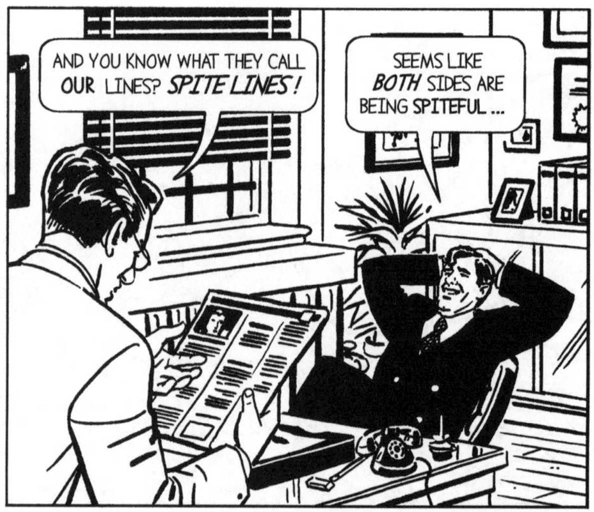
AND YOU KNOW WHAT THEY CALL OUR LINES? *SPITE LINES!*
SEEMS LIKE *BOTH* SIDES ARE BEING SPITEFUL ...

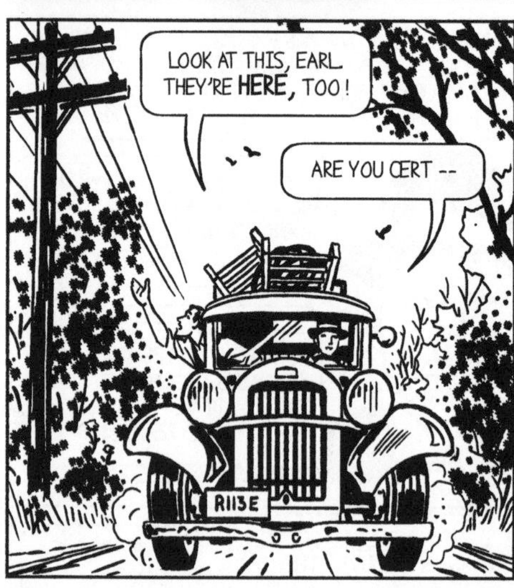
LOOK AT THIS, EARL. THEY'RE HERE, TOO!
ARE YOU CERT --
R113E

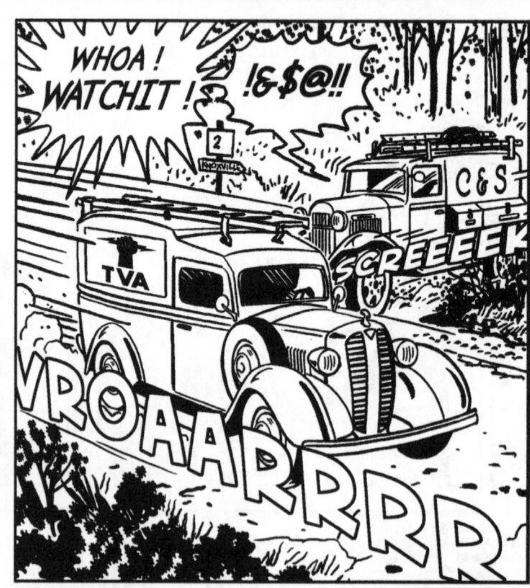
WHOA! WATCHIT!
!&$@!!
C & S
TVA
SCREEEEK
VROAARRRR

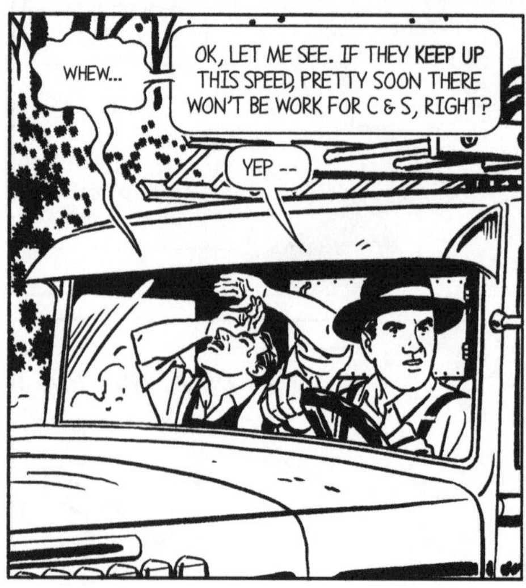
WHEW...
OK, LET ME SEE. IF THEY KEEP UP THIS SPEED, PRETTY SOON THERE WON'T BE WORK FOR C & S, RIGHT?
YEP --

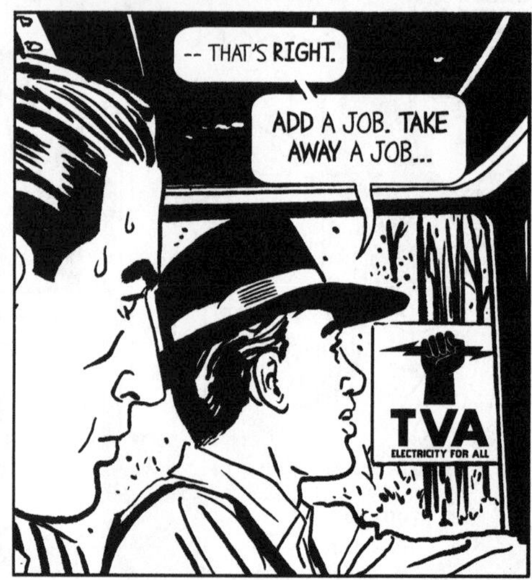
-- THAT'S RIGHT.
ADD A JOB. TAKE AWAY A JOB...
TVA
ELECTRICITY FOR ALL

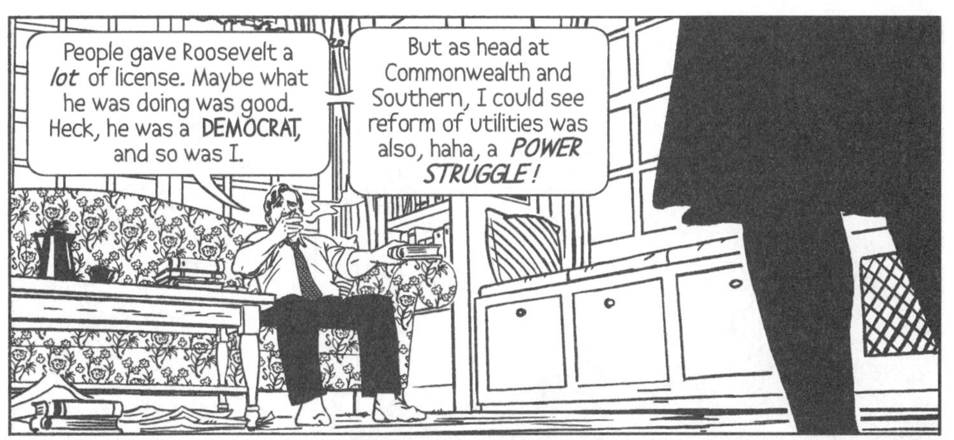

Lilienthal and I, we were like *wrestlers*...the PRIVATE utility versus the PUBLIC utility!

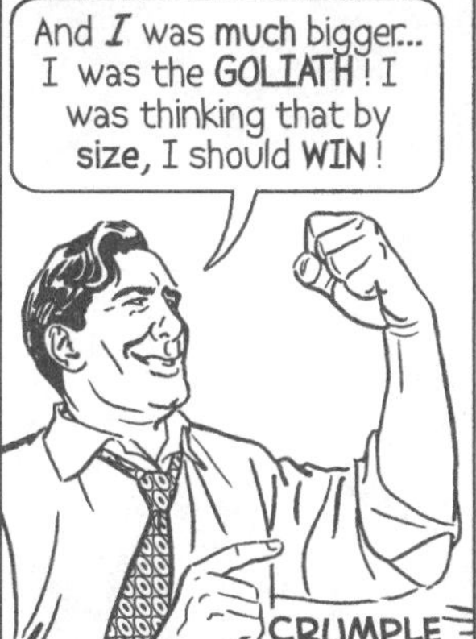

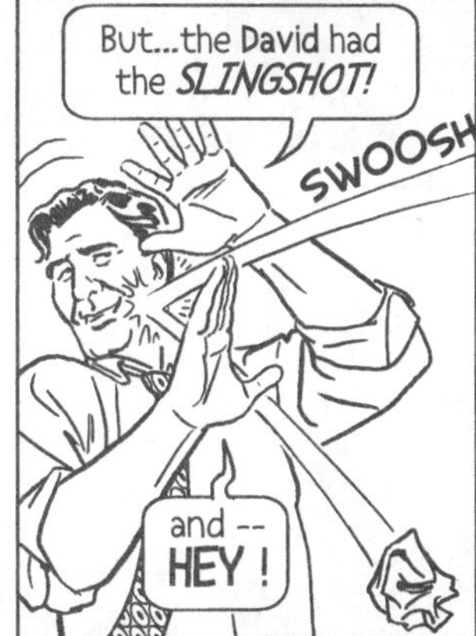

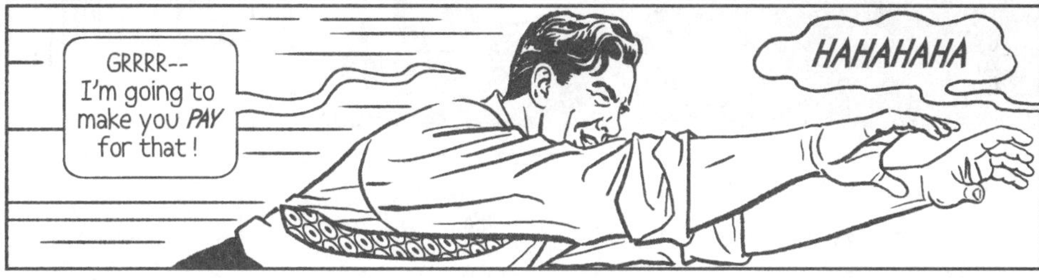

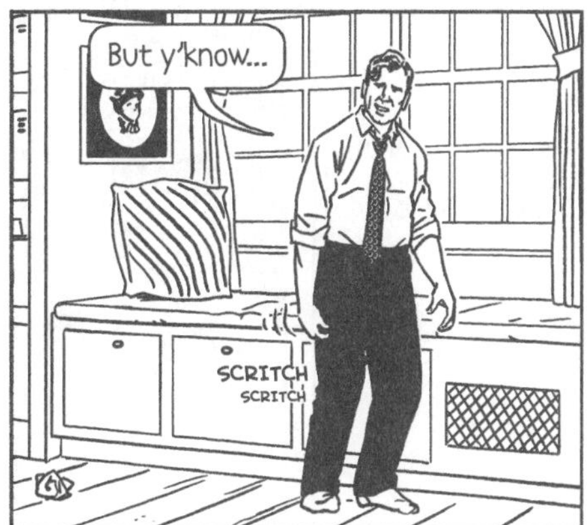

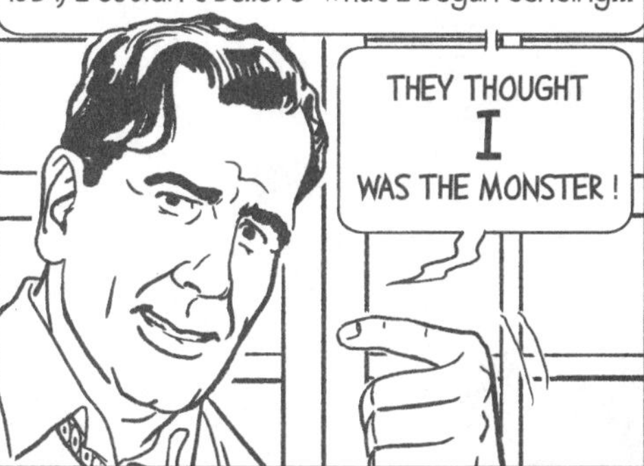

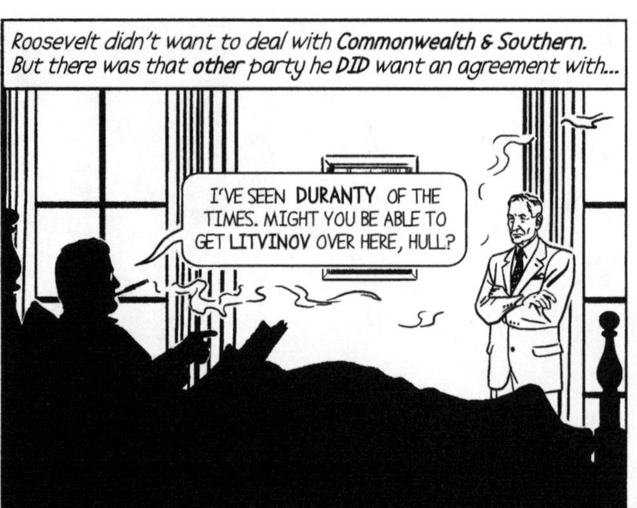

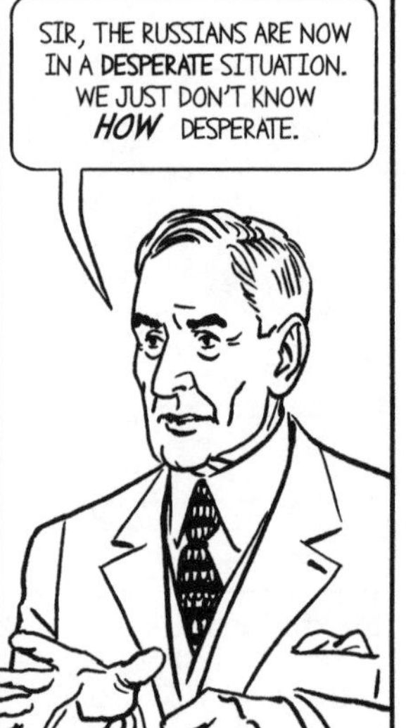

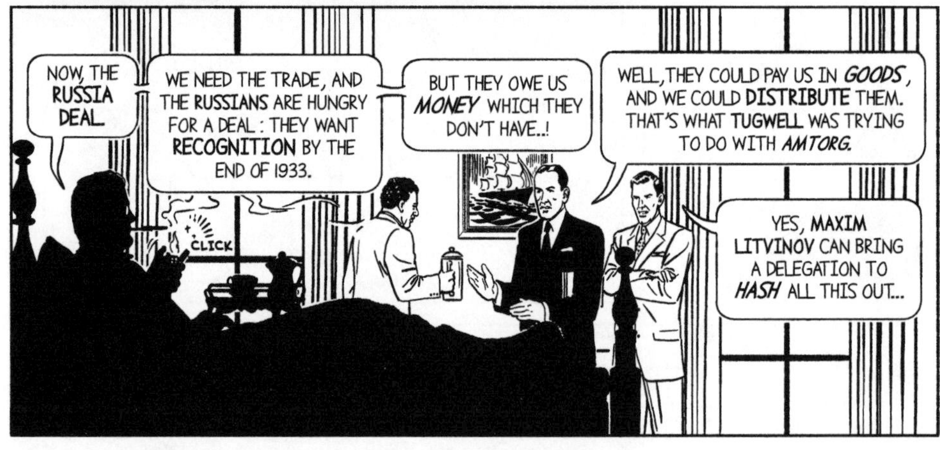

BUT THE ***FREEDOM OF WORSHIP*** ISSUE IS STILL THERE. DO YOU RECALL WHEN THEY ***BLEW UP*** THE **CATHEDRAL OF CHRIST THE SAVIOUR?** WE CAN'T BE SEEN TO CONDONE THAT -- THE PUBLIC WON'T TAKE IT !

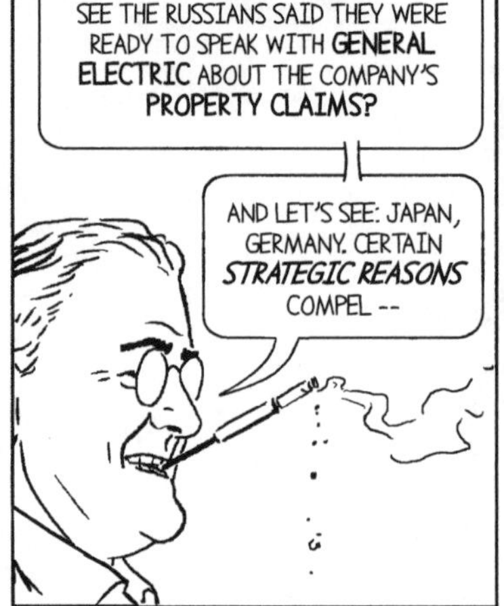

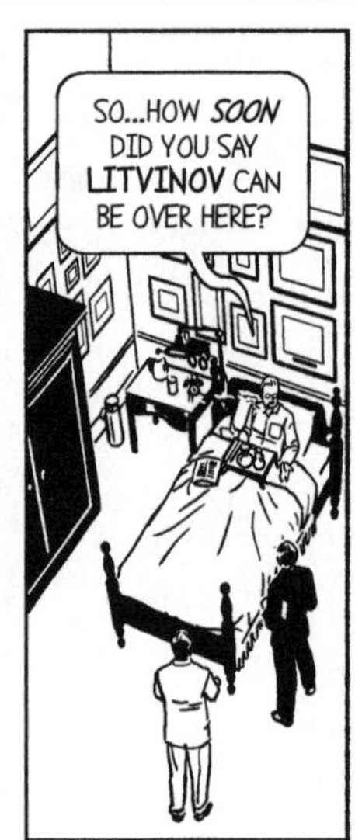

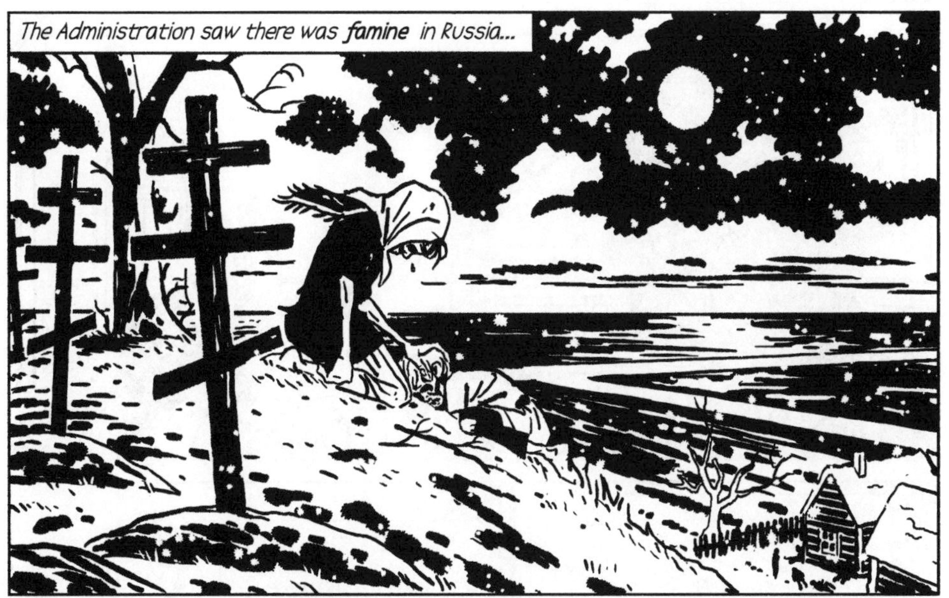
The Administration saw there was **famine** in Russia...

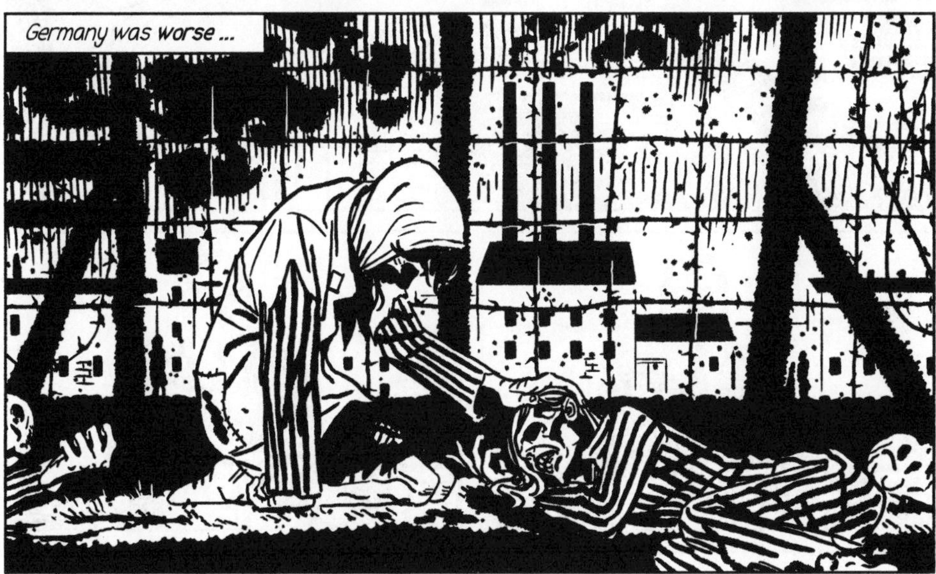
Germany was **worse** ...

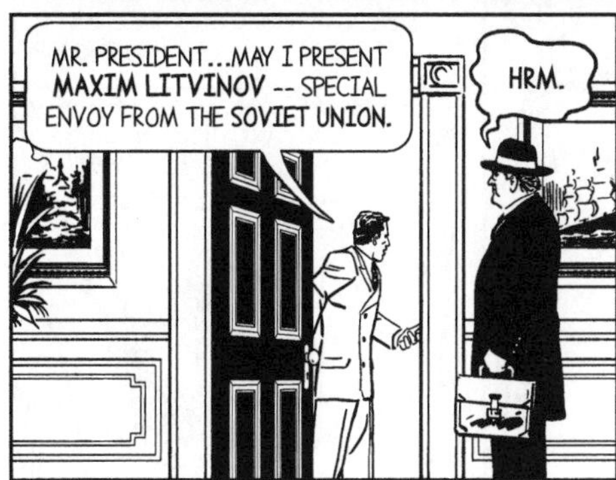
MR. PRESIDENT...MAY I PRESENT **MAXIM LITVINOV** -- SPECIAL ENVOY FROM THE **SOVIET UNION.**
HRM.

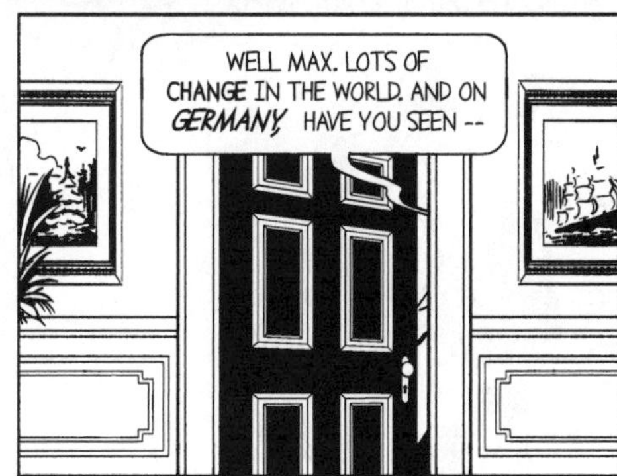
WELL MAX. LOTS OF **CHANGE** IN THE WORLD. AND ON ***GERMANY,*** HAVE YOU SEEN --

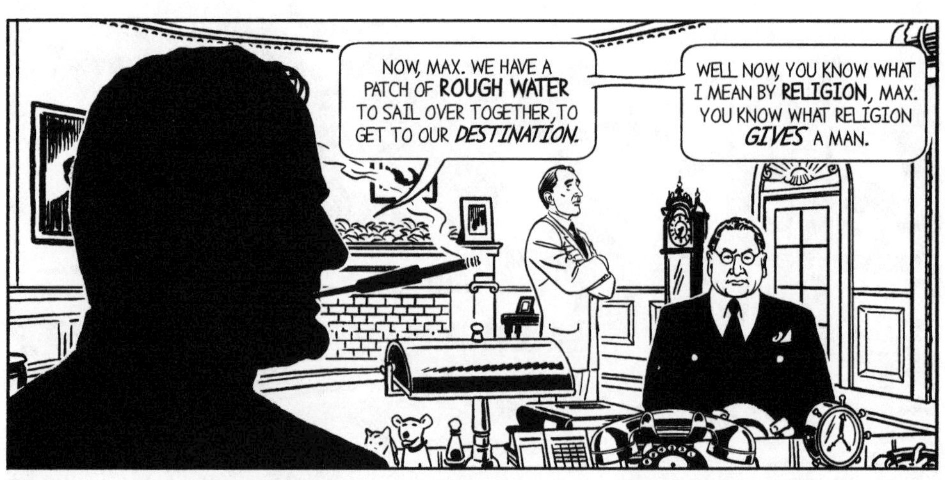
NOW, MAX. WE HAVE A PATCH OF ROUGH WATER TO SAIL OVER TOGETHER, TO GET TO OUR DESTINATION.
WELL NOW, YOU KNOW WHAT I MEAN BY RELIGION, MAX. YOU KNOW WHAT RELIGION GIVES A MAN.

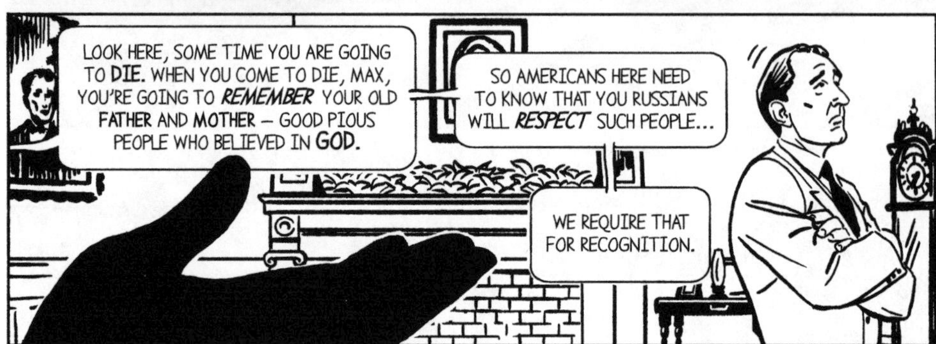
LOOK HERE, SOME TIME YOU ARE GOING TO DIE. WHEN YOU COME TO DIE, MAX, YOU'RE GOING TO REMEMBER YOUR OLD FATHER AND MOTHER – GOOD PIOUS PEOPLE WHO BELIEVED IN GOD.
SO AMERICANS HERE NEED TO KNOW THAT YOU RUSSIANS WILL RESPECT SUCH PEOPLE...
WE REQUIRE THAT FOR RECOGNITION.

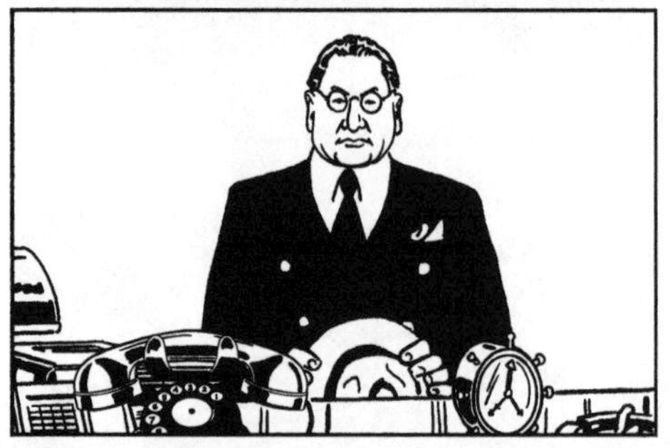

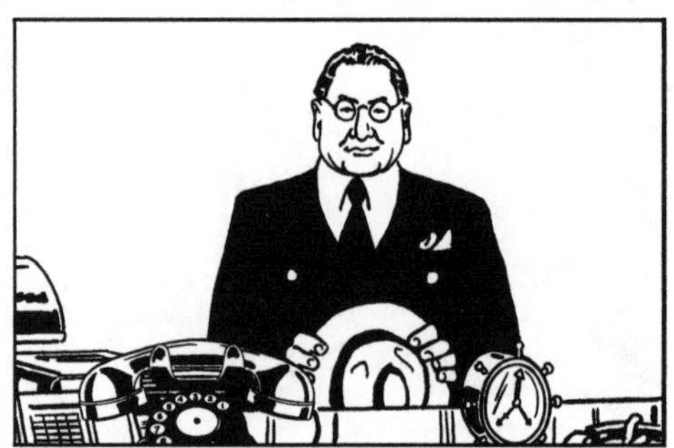

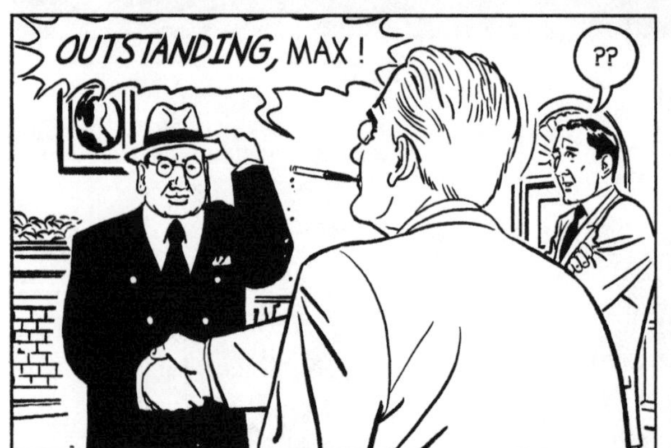
OUTSTANDING, MAX !
??

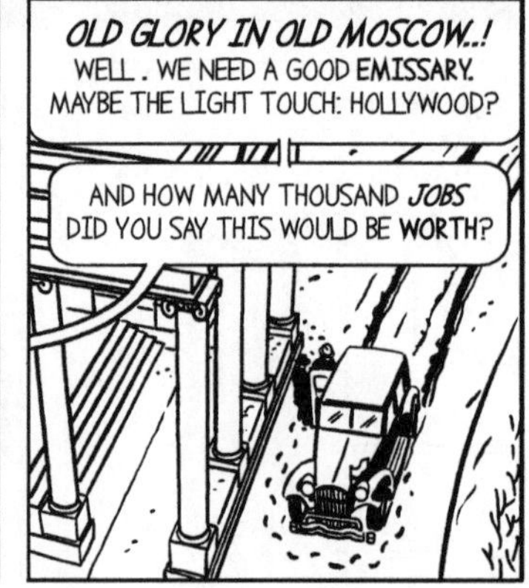
OLD GLORY IN OLD MOSCOW..! WELL . WE NEED A GOOD EMISSARY. MAYBE THE LIGHT TOUCH: HOLLYWOOD?
AND HOW MANY THOUSAND JOBS DID YOU SAY THIS WOULD BE WORTH?

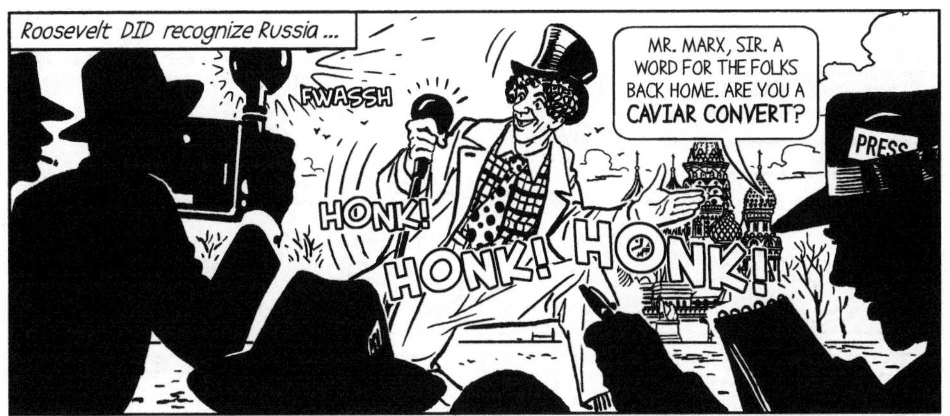
Roosevelt DID recognize Russia ...
FWASSH
MR. MARX, SIR. A WORD FOR THE FOLKS BACK HOME. ARE YOU A **CAVIAR CONVERT?**
HONK!
HONK! HONK!
PRESS

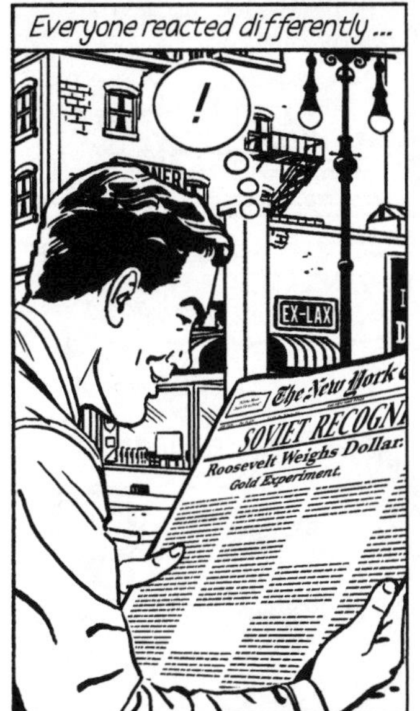
Everyone reacted differently ...
!
EX-LAX
The New York
SOVIET RECOGNI
Roosevelt Weighs Dollar.
Gold Experiment.

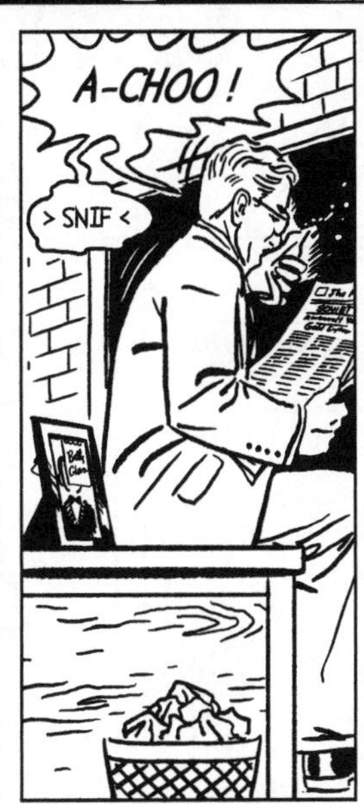
A-CHOO!
> SNIF <

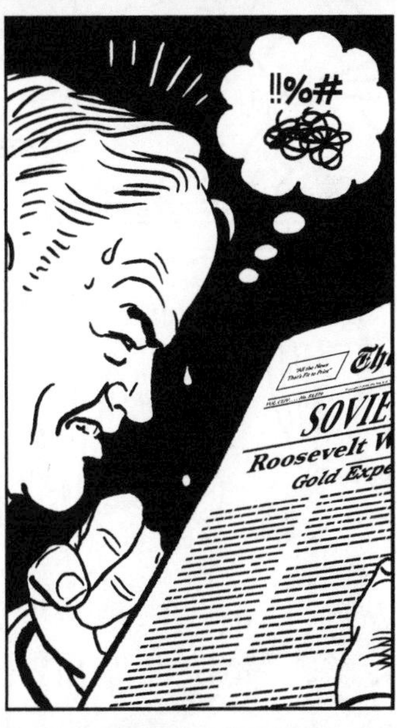
!!%#
SOVIET
Roosevelt W
Gold Expe

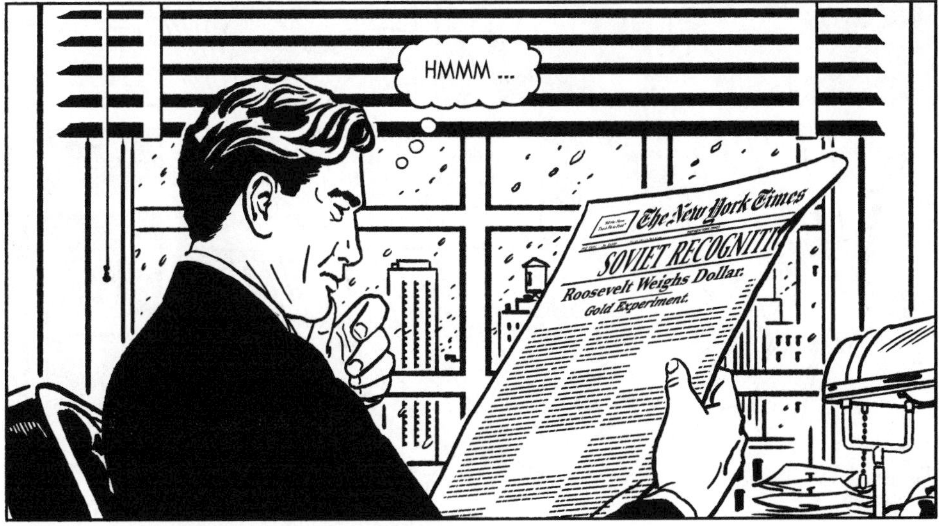
HMMM ...
The New York Times
SOVIET RECOGNITI
Roosevelt Weighs Dollar.
Gold Experiment.

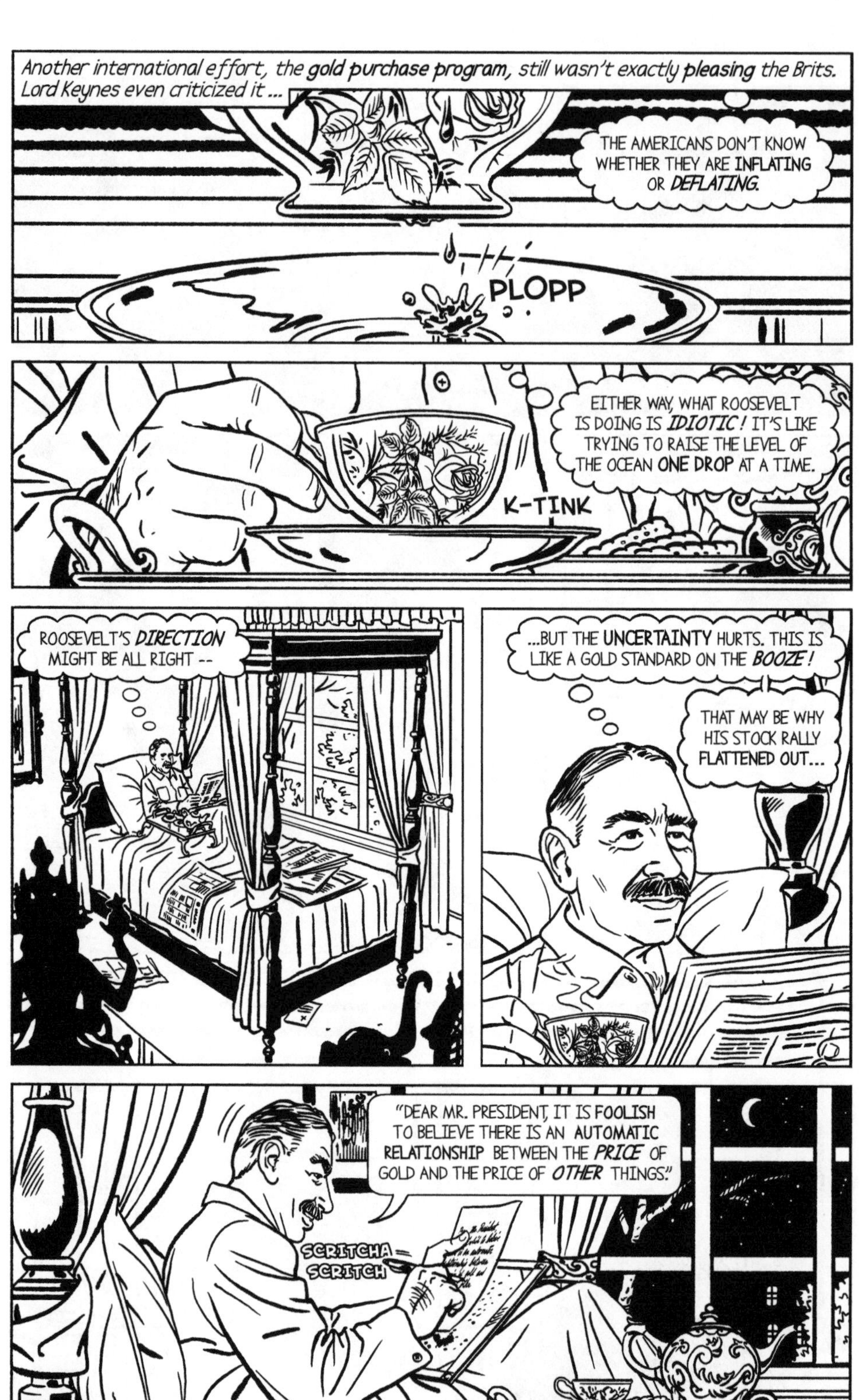
Another international effort, the **gold purchase program**, still wasn't exactly **pleasing** the Brits. Lord Keynes even criticized it ...
THE AMERICANS DON'T KNOW WHETHER THEY ARE INFLATING OR DEFLATING.
PLOPP
EITHER WAY, WHAT ROOSEVELT IS DOING IS IDIOTIC! IT'S LIKE TRYING TO RAISE THE LEVEL OF THE OCEAN ONE DROP AT A TIME.
K-TINK
ROOSEVELT'S DIRECTION MIGHT BE ALL RIGHT --
...BUT THE UNCERTAINTY HURTS. THIS IS LIKE A GOLD STANDARD ON THE BOOZE!
THAT MAY BE WHY HIS STOCK RALLY FLATTENED OUT...
"DEAR MR. PRESIDENT, IT IS FOOLISH TO BELIEVE THERE IS AN AUTOMATIC RELATIONSHIP BETWEEN THE PRICE OF GOLD AND THE PRICE OF OTHER THINGS."
SCRITCHA SCRITCH

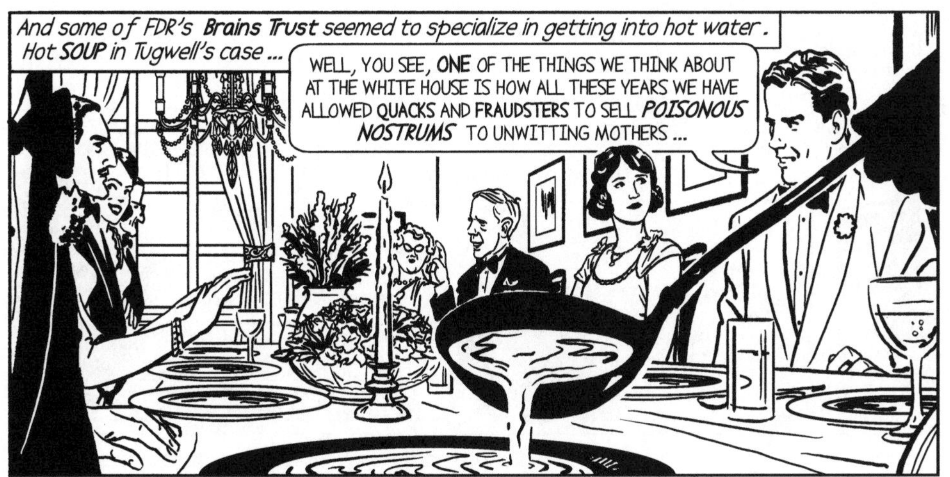
And some of FDR's Brains Trust seemed to specialize in getting into hot water. Hot SOUP in Tugwell's case ...
WELL, YOU SEE, ONE OF THE THINGS WE THINK ABOUT AT THE WHITE HOUSE IS HOW ALL THESE YEARS WE HAVE ALLOWED QUACKS AND FRAUDSTERS TO SELL POISONOUS NOSTRUMS TO UNWITTING MOTHERS ...

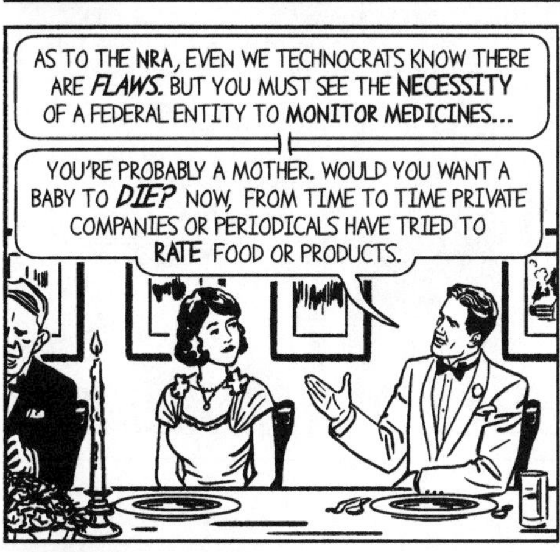
AS TO THE NRA, EVEN WE TECHNOCRATS KNOW THERE ARE FLAWS. BUT YOU MUST SEE THE NECESSITY OF A FEDERAL ENTITY TO MONITOR MEDICINES...
YOU'RE PROBABLY A MOTHER. WOULD YOU WANT A BABY TO DIE? NOW, FROM TIME TO TIME PRIVATE COMPANIES OR PERIODICALS HAVE TRIED TO RATE FOOD OR PRODUCTS.

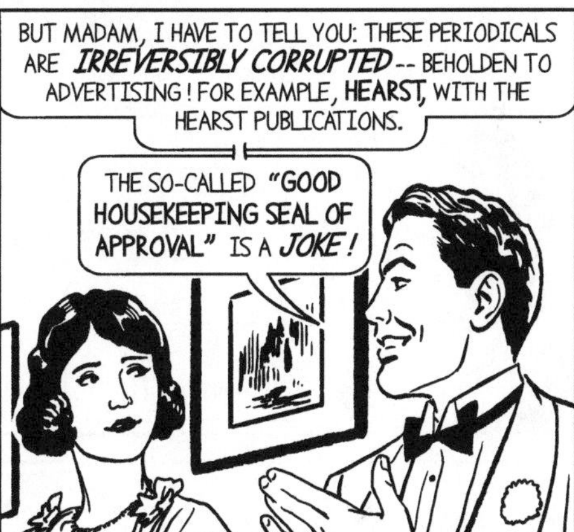
BUT MADAM, I HAVE TO TELL YOU: THESE PERIODICALS ARE IRREVERSIBLY CORRUPTED -- BEHOLDEN TO ADVERTISING! FOR EXAMPLE, HEARST, WITH THE HEARST PUBLICATIONS.
THE SO-CALLED "GOOD HOUSEKEEPING SEAL OF APPROVAL" IS A JOKE!

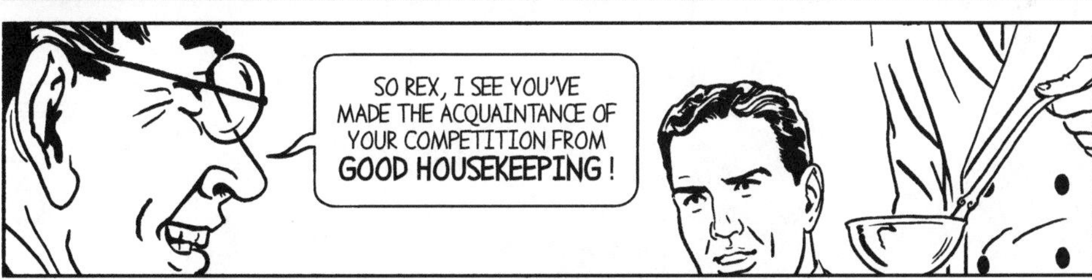
SO REX, I SEE YOU'VE MADE THE ACQUAINTANCE OF YOUR COMPETITION FROM GOOD HOUSEKEEPING!

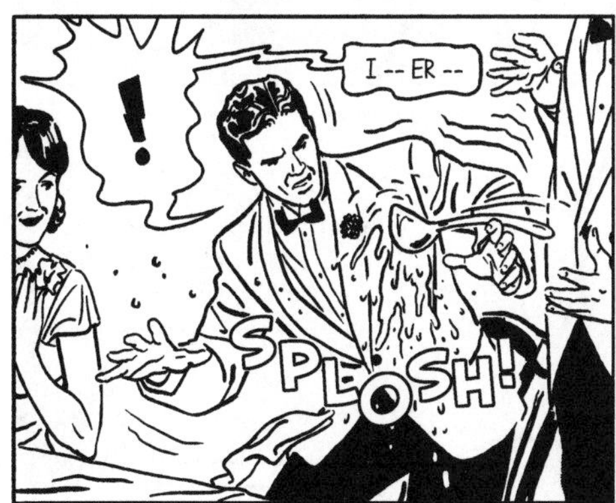
I -- ER --
!
SPLOSH!

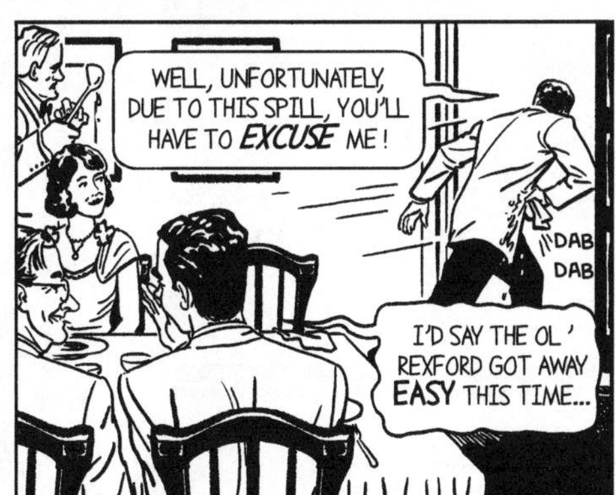
WELL, UNFORTUNATELY, DUE TO THIS SPILL, YOU'LL HAVE TO EXCUSE ME!
DAB
DAB
I'D SAY THE OL' REXFORD GOT AWAY EASY THIS TIME...

December 1933
Unemployment: 22.4 &
Dow Jones Industrial
Average: (Dec. 1): 99

But when one plan didn't work, Roosevelt's men tried another ...

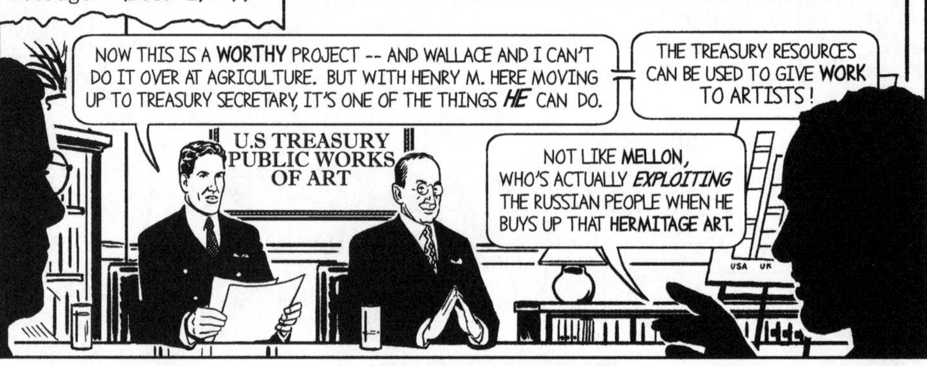

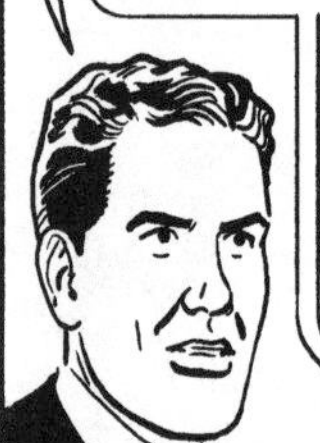

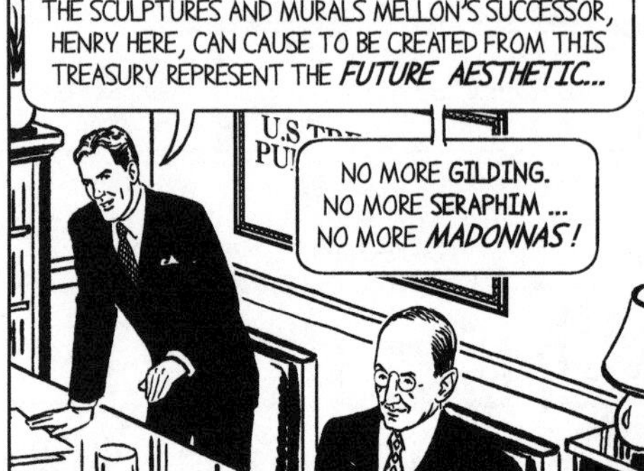

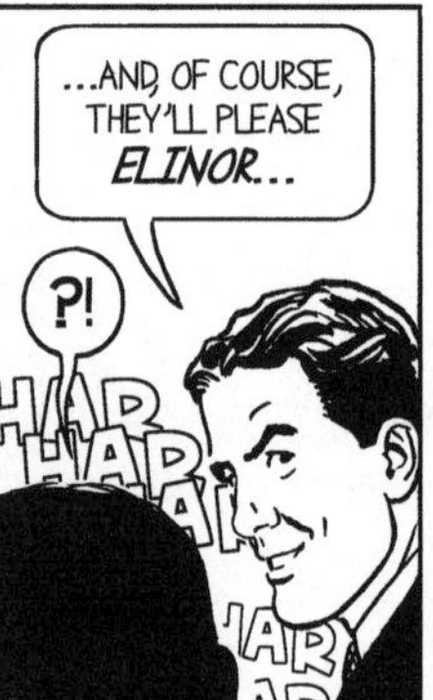

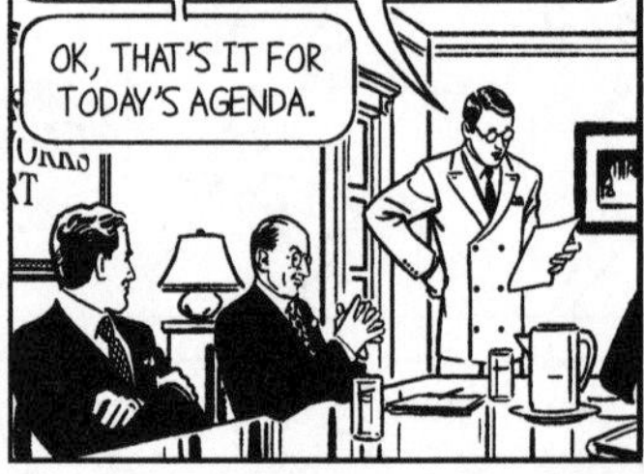

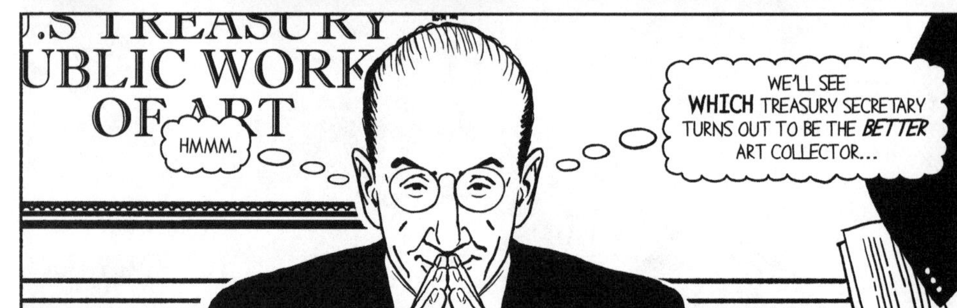

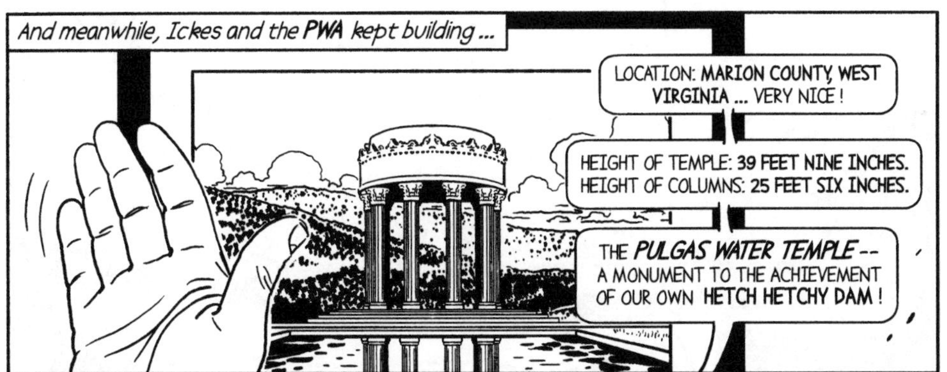
And meanwhile, Ickes and the PWA kept building ...
LOCATION: MARION COUNTY, WEST VIRGINIA ... VERY NICE!
HEIGHT OF TEMPLE: 39 FEET NINE INCHES. HEIGHT OF COLUMNS: 25 FEET SIX INCHES.
THE PULGAS WATER TEMPLE -- A MONUMENT TO THE ACHIEVEMENT OF OUR OWN HETCH HETCHY DAM!

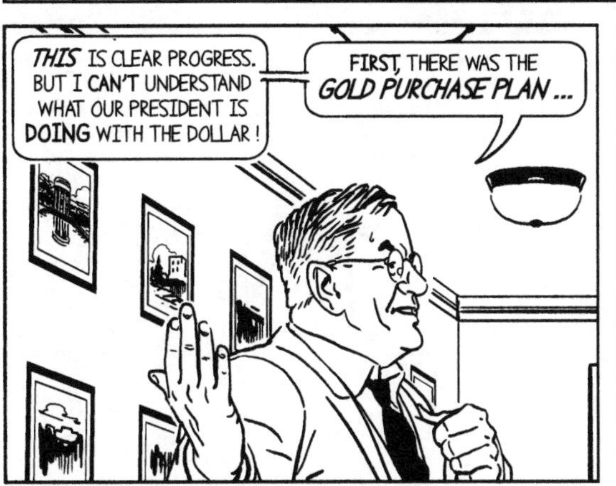
THIS IS CLEAR PROGRESS. BUT I CAN'T UNDERSTAND WHAT OUR PRESIDENT IS DOING WITH THE DOLLAR!
FIRST, THERE WAS THE GOLD PURCHASE PLAN ...

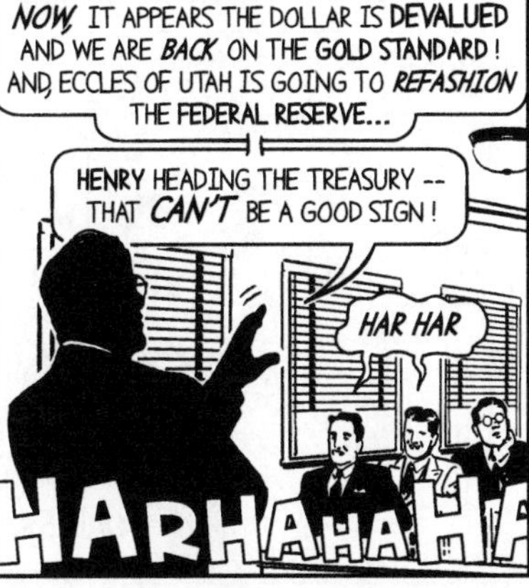
NOW, IT APPEARS THE DOLLAR IS DEVALUED AND WE ARE BACK ON THE GOLD STANDARD! AND, ECCLES OF UTAH IS GOING TO REFASHION THE FEDERAL RESERVE...
HENRY HEADING THE TREASURY -- THAT CAN'T BE A GOOD SIGN!
HAR HAR
HARHAHAHAHA

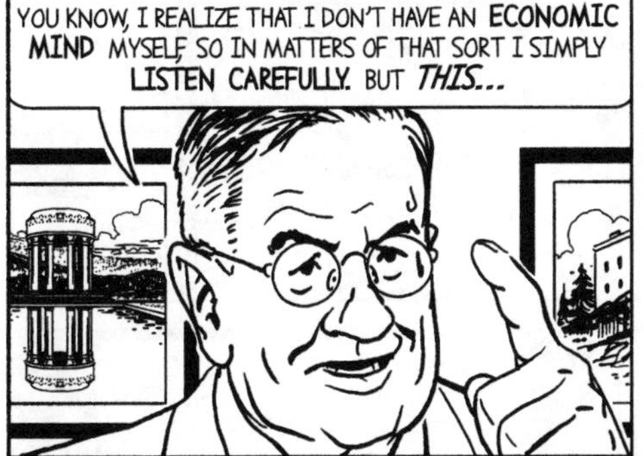
YOU KNOW, I REALIZE THAT I DON'T HAVE AN ECONOMIC MIND MYSELF, SO IN MATTERS OF THAT SORT I SIMPLY LISTEN CAREFULLY. BUT THIS...

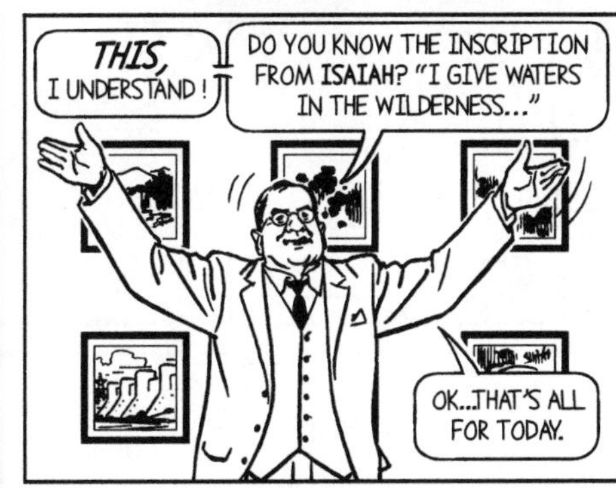
THIS, I UNDERSTAND!
DO YOU KNOW THE INSCRIPTION FROM ISAIAH? "I GIVE WATERS IN THE WILDERNESS..."
OK...THAT'S ALL FOR TODAY.

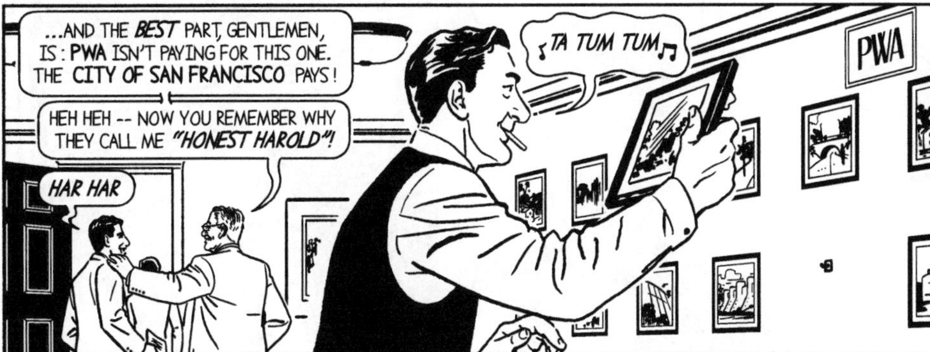
...AND THE BEST PART, GENTLEMEN, IS: PWA ISN'T PAYING FOR THIS ONE. THE CITY OF SAN FRANCISCO PAYS!
HEH HEH -- NOW YOU REMEMBER WHY THEY CALL ME "HONEST HAROLD"!
TA TUM TUM
PWA
HAR HAR

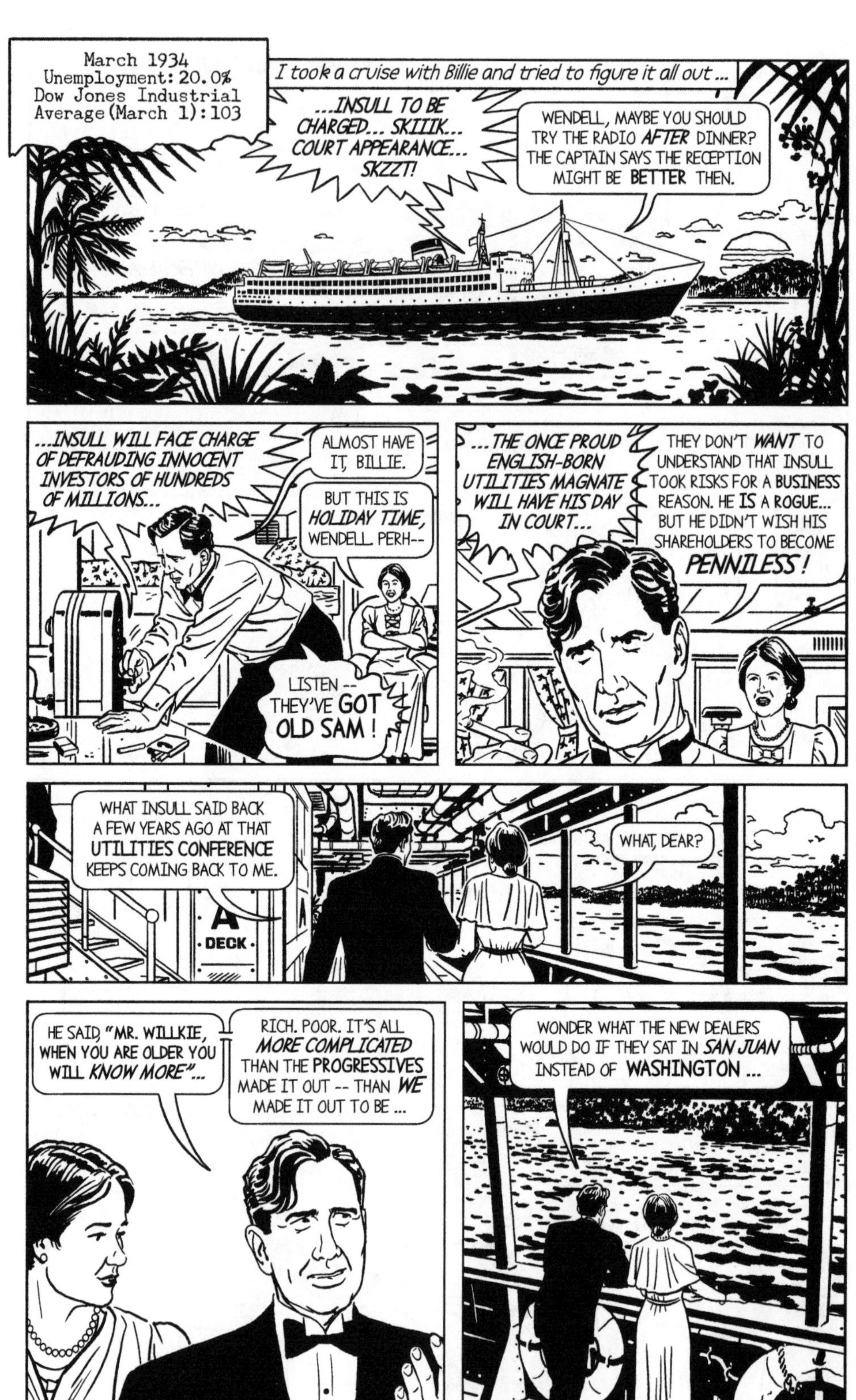
March 1934
Unemployment: 20.0%
Dow Jones Industrial
Average (March 1): 103
I took a cruise with Billie and tried to figure it all out ...
...INSULL TO BE CHARGED... SKIIIK... COURT APPEARANCE... SKZZT!
WENDELL, MAYBE YOU SHOULD TRY THE RADIO AFTER DINNER? THE CAPTAIN SAYS THE RECEPTION MIGHT BE BETTER THEN.
...INSULL WILL FACE CHARGE OF DEFRAUDING INNOCENT INVESTORS OF HUNDREDS OF MILLIONS...
ALMOST HAVE IT, BILLIE.
BUT THIS IS HOLIDAY TIME, WENDELL. PERH--
LISTEN -- THEY'VE GOT OLD SAM!
...THE ONCE PROUD ENGLISH-BORN UTILITIES MAGNATE WILL HAVE HIS DAY IN COURT...
THEY DON'T WANT TO UNDERSTAND THAT INSULL TOOK RISKS FOR A BUSINESS REASON. HE IS A ROGUE... BUT HE DIDN'T WISH HIS SHAREHOLDERS TO BECOME PENNILESS!
WHAT INSULL SAID BACK A FEW YEARS AGO AT THAT UTILITIES CONFERENCE KEEPS COMING BACK TO ME.
A DECK
WHAT, DEAR?
HE SAID, "MR. WILLKIE, WHEN YOU ARE OLDER YOU WILL KNOW MORE"...
RICH. POOR. IT'S ALL MORE COMPLICATED THAN THE PROGRESSIVES MADE IT OUT -- THAN WE MADE IT OUT TO BE ...
WONDER WHAT THE NEW DEALERS WOULD DO IF THEY SAT IN SAN JUAN INSTEAD OF WASHINGTON ...

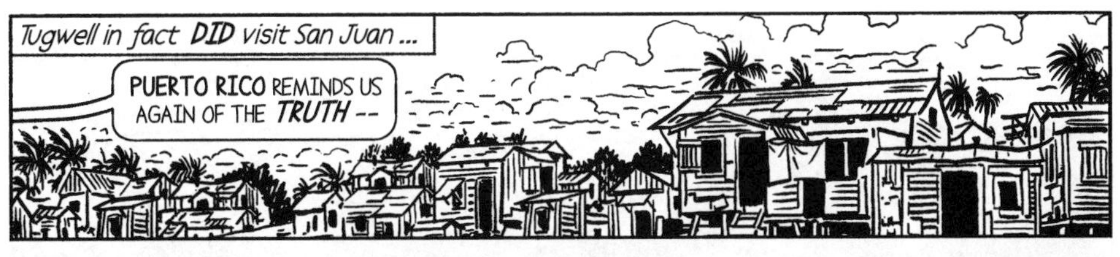
Tugwell in fact DID visit San Juan ...
PUERTO RICO REMINDS US AGAIN OF THE TRUTH --

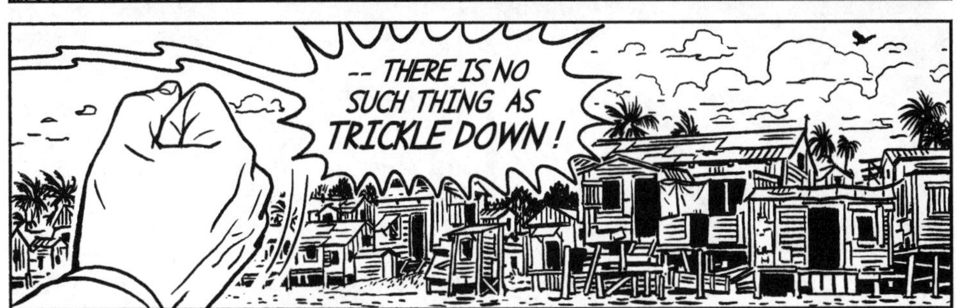
-- THERE IS NO SUCH THING AS TRICKLE DOWN!

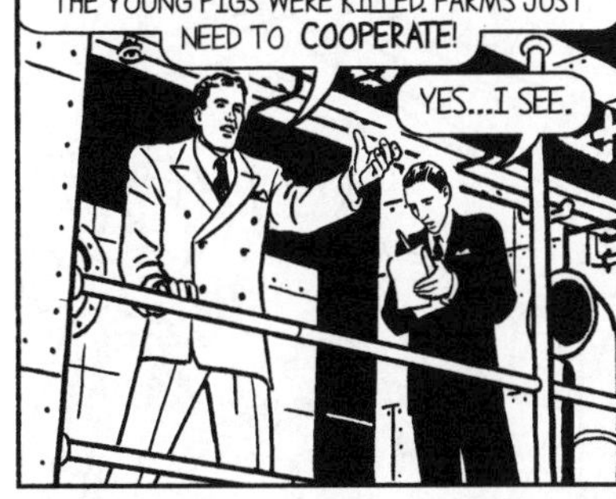
GOVERNMENT JUST HAS TO DO ITS PART, HEWES. FOR EXAMPLE, IN AGRICULTURE. FOR ALL OUR ERRORS, WE GOT THE PRICE OF HOGS UP TO $3.60 A HUNDREDWEIGHT AFTER THE YOUNG PIGS WERE KILLED. FARMS JUST NEED TO COOPERATE!
YES...I SEE.

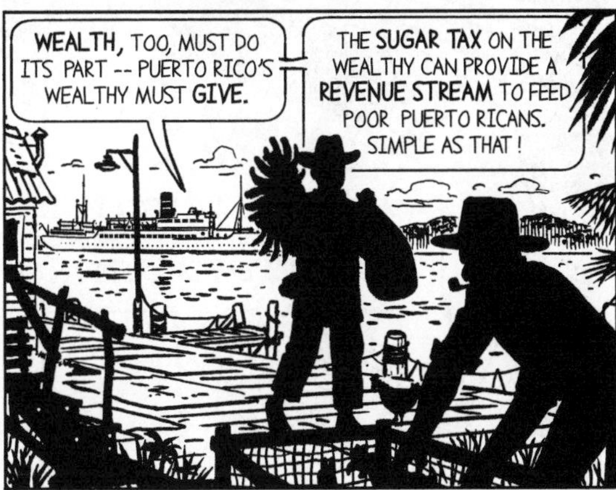
WEALTH, TOO, MUST DO ITS PART -- PUERTO RICO'S WEALTHY MUST GIVE.
THE SUGAR TAX ON THE WEALTHY CAN PROVIDE A REVENUE STREAM TO FEED POOR PUERTO RICANS. SIMPLE AS THAT!

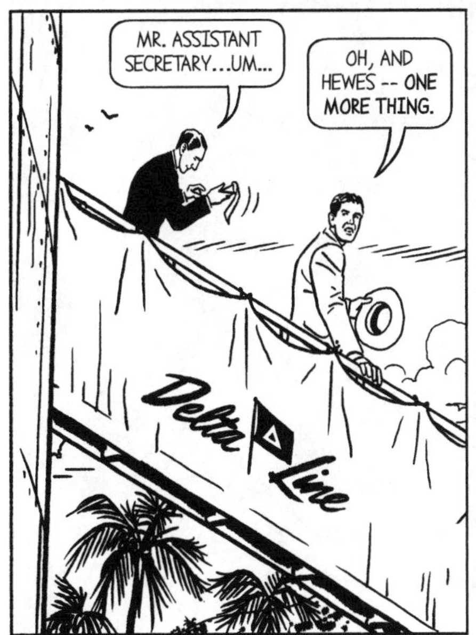
MR. ASSISTANT SECRETARY...UM...
OH, AND HEWES -- ONE MORE THING.
Delta Line

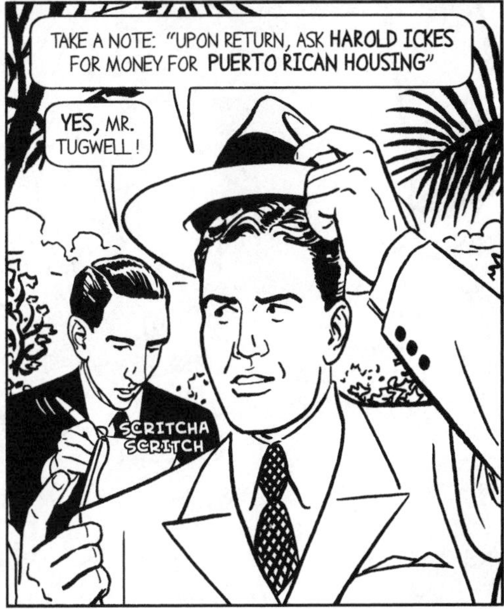
TAKE A NOTE: "UPON RETURN, ASK HAROLD ICKES FOR MONEY FOR PUERTO RICAN HOUSING"
YES, MR. TUGWELL!
SCRITCHA SCRITCH

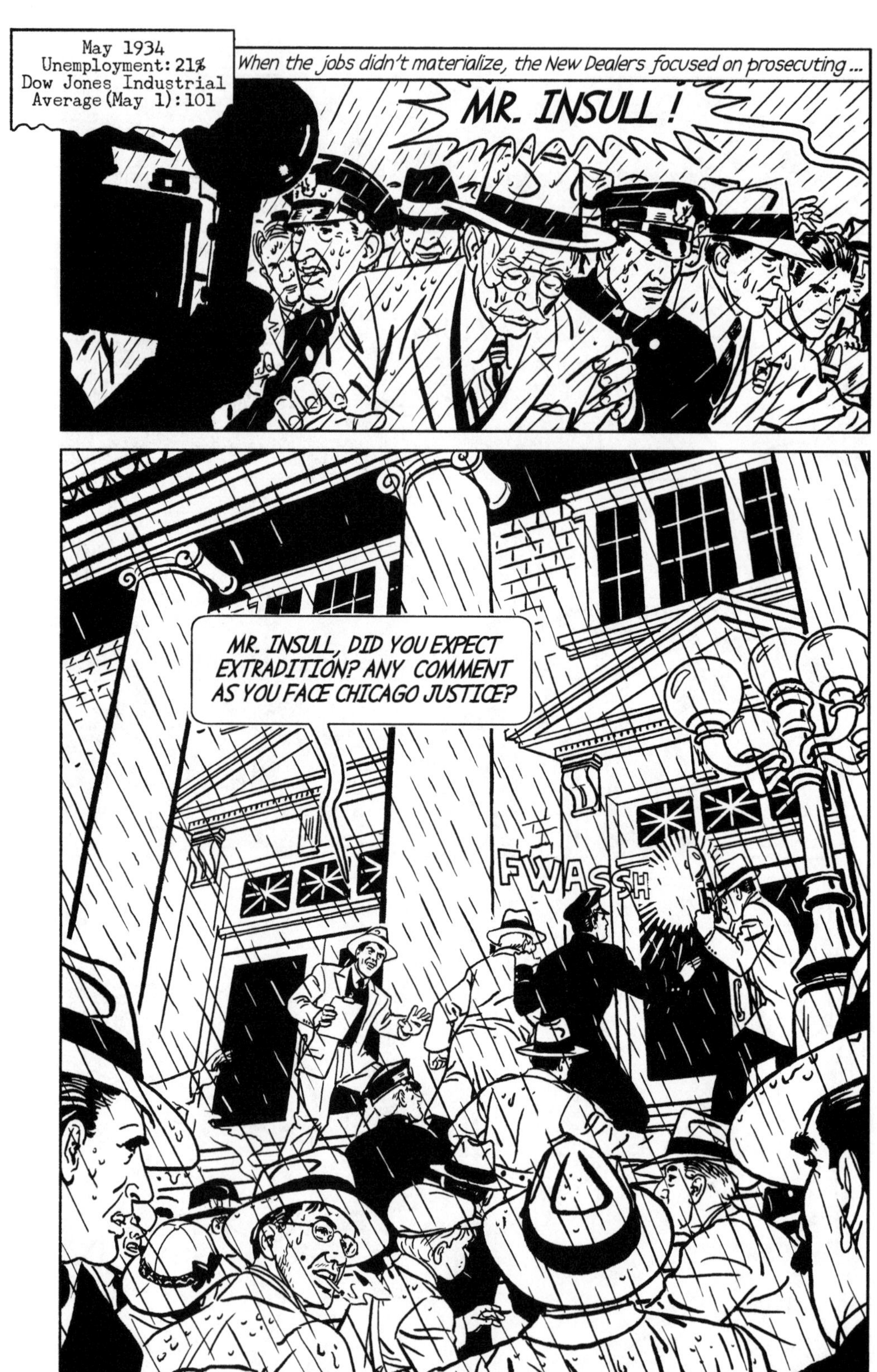
May 1934
Unemployment: 21%
Dow Jones Industrial
Average (May 1): 101
When the jobs didn't materialize, the New Dealers focused on prosecuting ...
MR. INSULL !
MR. INSULL, DID YOU EXPECT
EXTRADITION? ANY COMMENT
AS YOU FACE CHICAGO JUSTICE?
FWASSH

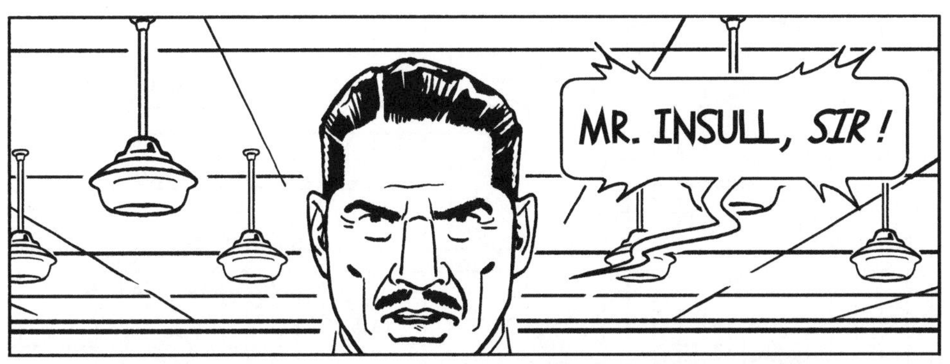
MR. INSULL, SIR!

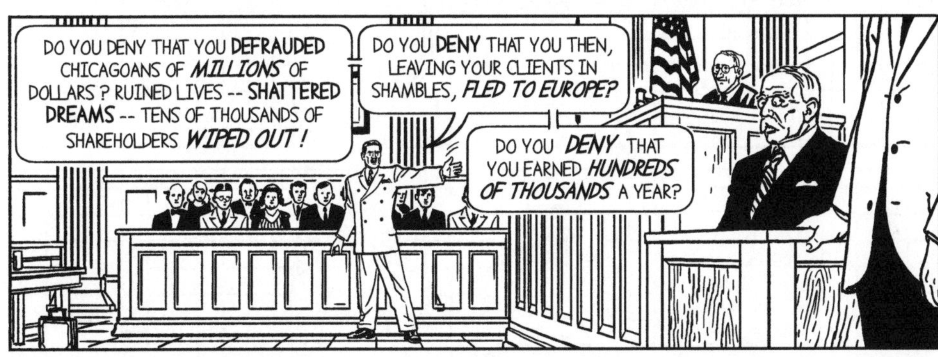
DO YOU DENY THAT YOU DEFRAUDED CHICAGOANS OF MILLIONS OF DOLLARS? RUINED LIVES -- SHATTERED DREAMS -- TENS OF THOUSANDS OF SHAREHOLDERS WIPED OUT!
DO YOU DENY THAT YOU THEN, LEAVING YOUR CLIENTS IN SHAMBLES, FLED TO EUROPE?
DO YOU DENY THAT YOU EARNED HUNDREDS OF THOUSANDS A YEAR?

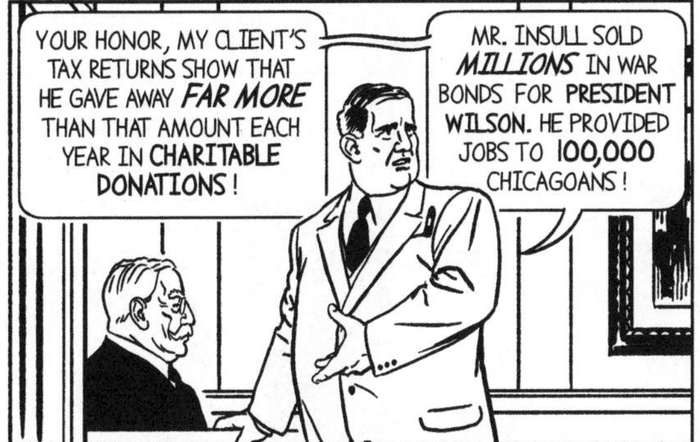
YOUR HONOR, MY CLIENT'S TAX RETURNS SHOW THAT HE GAVE AWAY FAR MORE THAN THAT AMOUNT EACH YEAR IN CHARITABLE DONATIONS!
MR. INSULL SOLD MILLIONS IN WAR BONDS FOR PRESIDENT WILSON. HE PROVIDED JOBS TO 100,000 CHICAGOANS!

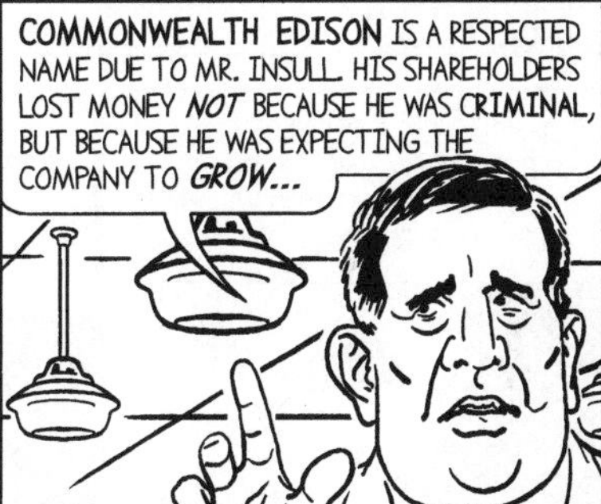
COMMONWEALTH EDISON IS A RESPECTED NAME DUE TO MR. INSULL. HIS SHAREHOLDERS LOST MONEY NOT BECAUSE HE WAS CRIMINAL, BUT BECAUSE HE WAS EXPECTING THE COMPANY TO GROW...

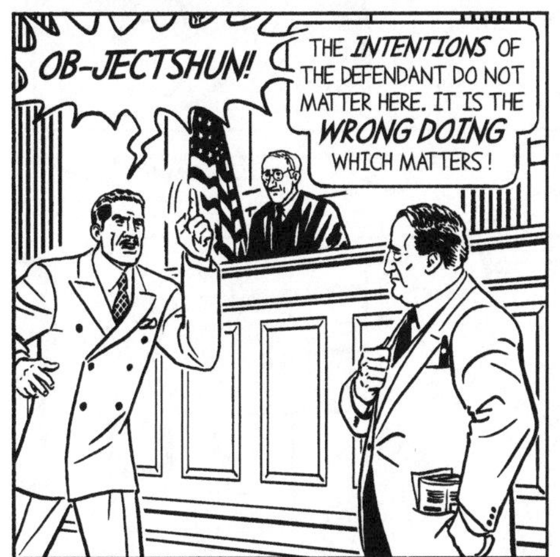
OB-JECTSHUN!
THE INTENTIONS OF THE DEFENDANT DO NOT MATTER HERE. IT IS THE WRONG DOING WHICH MATTERS!

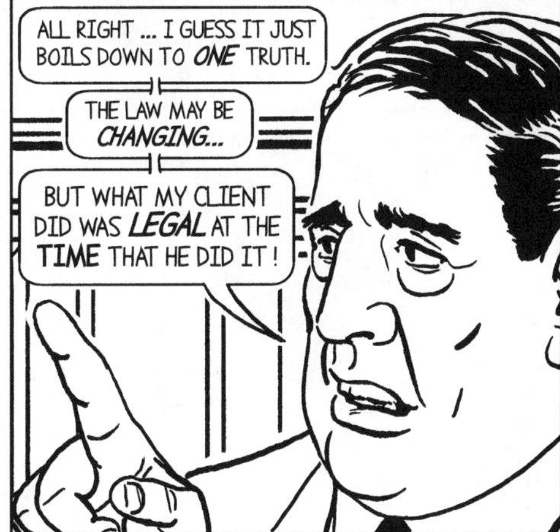
ALL RIGHT ... I GUESS IT JUST BOILS DOWN TO ONE TRUTH.
THE LAW MAY BE CHANGING...
BUT WHAT MY CLIENT DID WAS LEGAL AT THE TIME THAT HE DID IT!

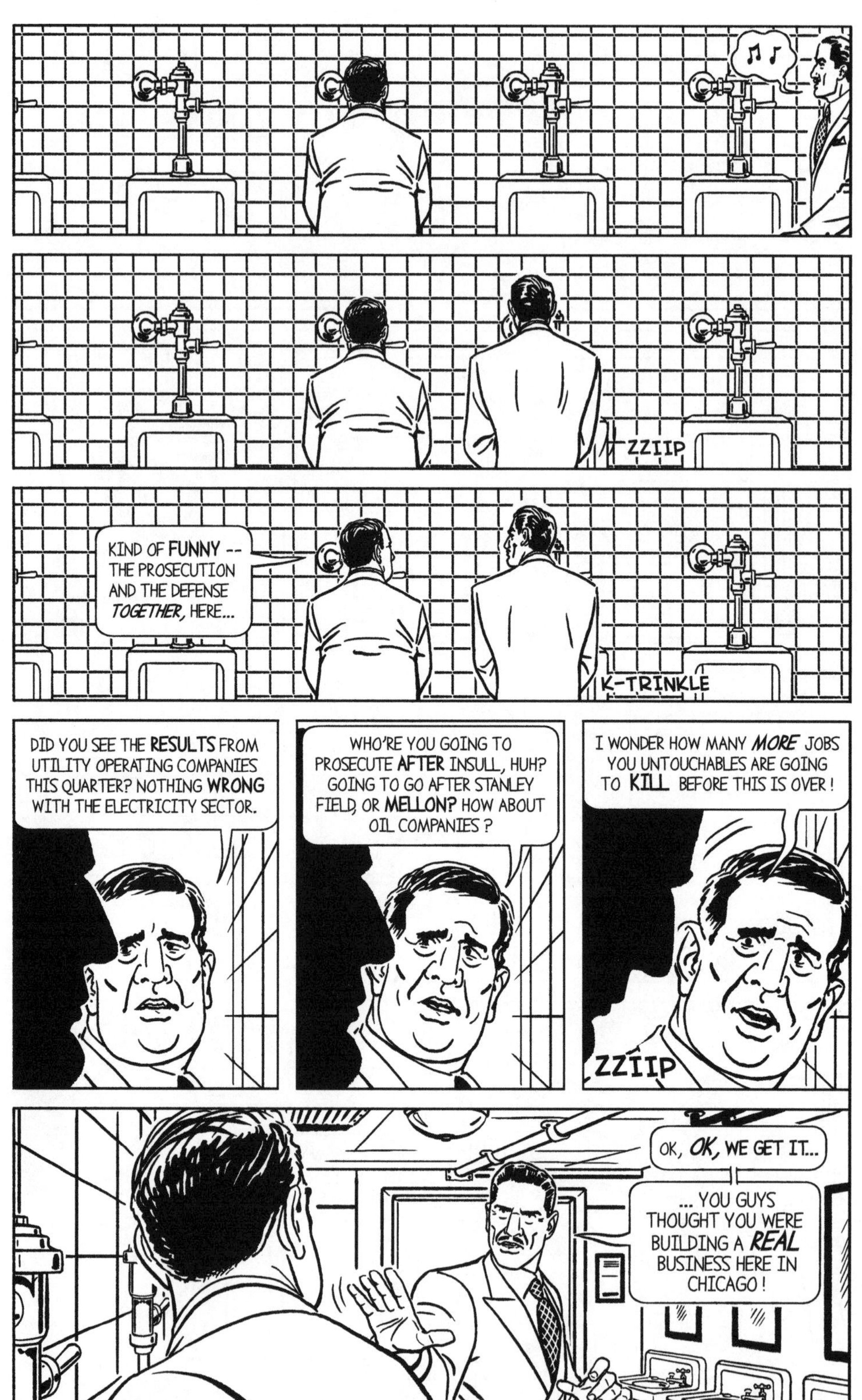
ZZIIP
KIND OF FUNNY -- THE PROSECUTION AND THE DEFENSE TOGETHER, HERE...
K-TRINKLE
DID YOU SEE THE RESULTS FROM UTILITY OPERATING COMPANIES THIS QUARTER? NOTHING WRONG WITH THE ELECTRICITY SECTOR.
WHO'RE YOU GOING TO PROSECUTE AFTER INSULL, HUH? GOING TO GO AFTER STANLEY FIELD, OR MELLON? HOW ABOUT OIL COMPANIES ?
I WONDER HOW MANY MORE JOBS YOU UNTOUCHABLES ARE GOING TO KILL BEFORE THIS IS OVER !
ZZIIP
OK, OK, WE GET IT...
... YOU GUYS THOUGHT YOU WERE BUILDING A REAL BUSINESS HERE IN CHICAGO !

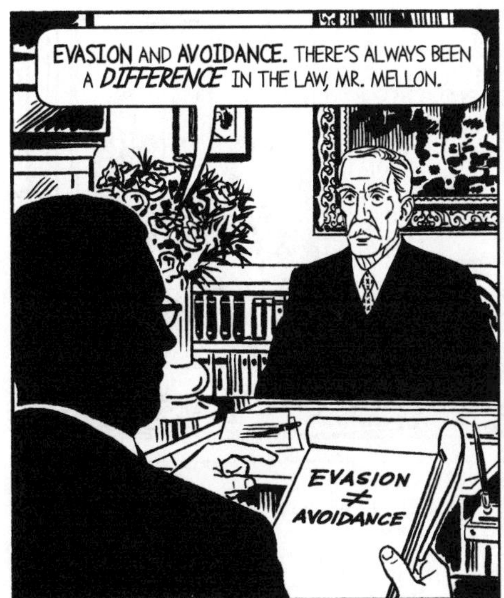
EVASION AND AVOIDANCE. THERE'S ALWAYS BEEN A DIFFERENCE IN THE LAW, MR. MELLON.
EVASION ≠ AVOIDANCE

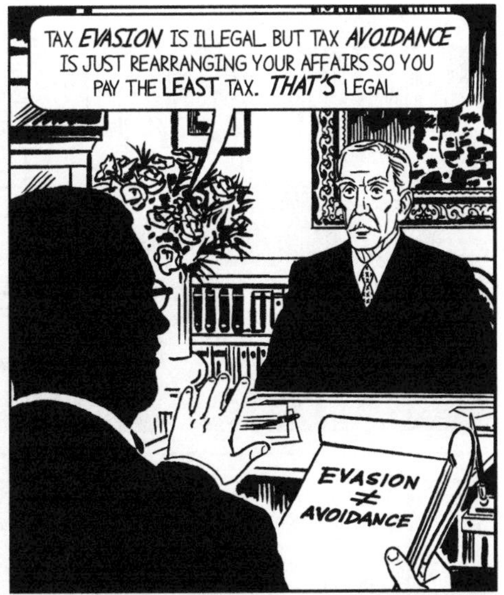
TAX EVASION IS ILLEGAL. BUT TAX AVOIDANCE IS JUST REARRANGING YOUR AFFAIRS SO YOU PAY THE LEAST TAX. THAT'S LEGAL.
EVASION ≠ AVOIDANCE

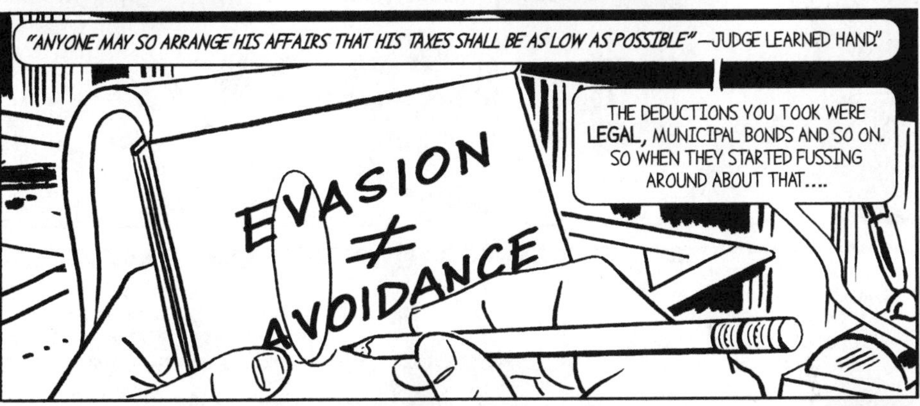
"ANYONE MAY SO ARRANGE HIS AFFAIRS THAT HIS TAXES SHALL BE AS LOW AS POSSIBLE" —JUDGE LEARNED HAND."
THE DEDUCTIONS YOU TOOK WERE LEGAL, MUNICIPAL BONDS AND SO ON. SO WHEN THEY STARTED FUSSING AROUND ABOUT THAT....
EVASION ≠ AVOIDANCE

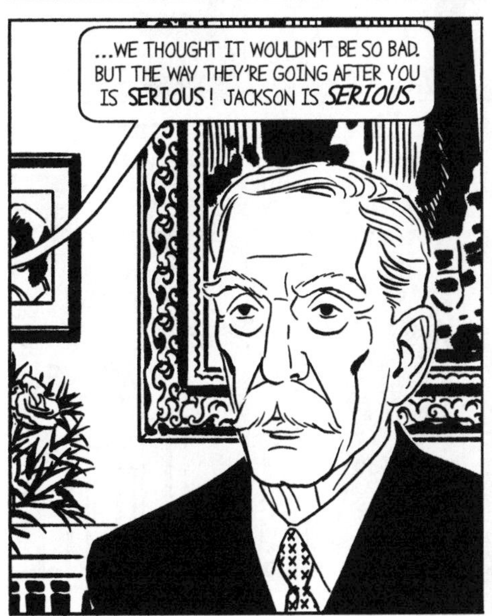
...WE THOUGHT IT WOULDN'T BE SO BAD. BUT THE WAY THEY'RE GOING AFTER YOU IS SERIOUS! JACKSON IS SERIOUS.

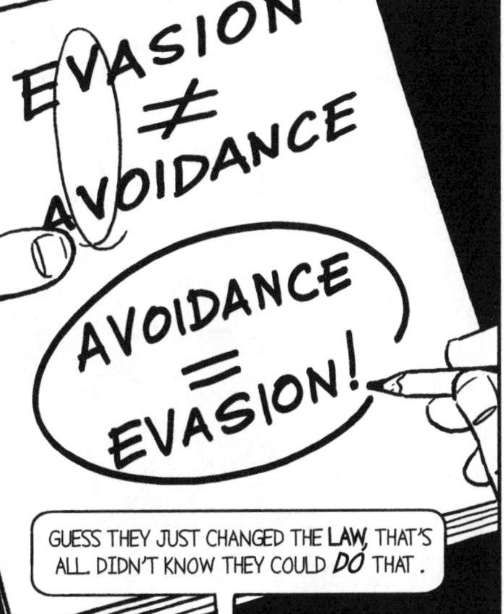
EVASION ≠ AVOIDANCE
AVOIDANCE = EVASION!
GUESS THEY JUST CHANGED THE LAW, THAT'S ALL. DIDN'T KNOW THEY COULD DO THAT.

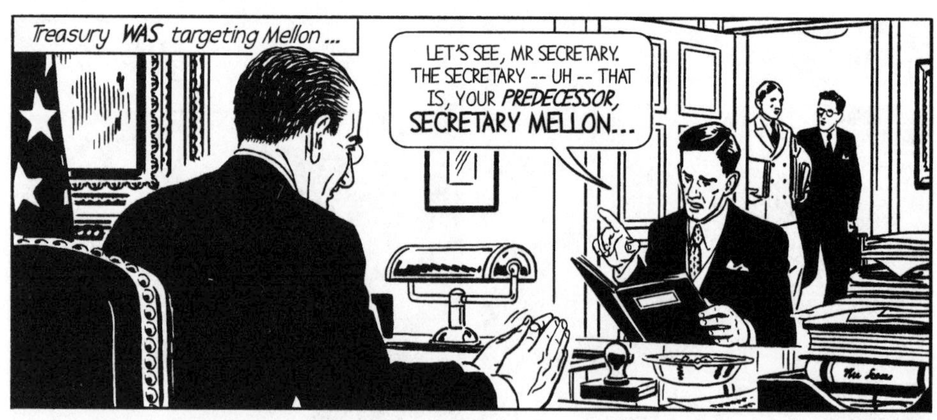
Treasury WAS targeting Mellon ...
LET'S SEE, MR SECRETARY. THE SECRETARY -- UH -- THAT IS, YOUR PREDECESSOR, SECRETARY MELLON...

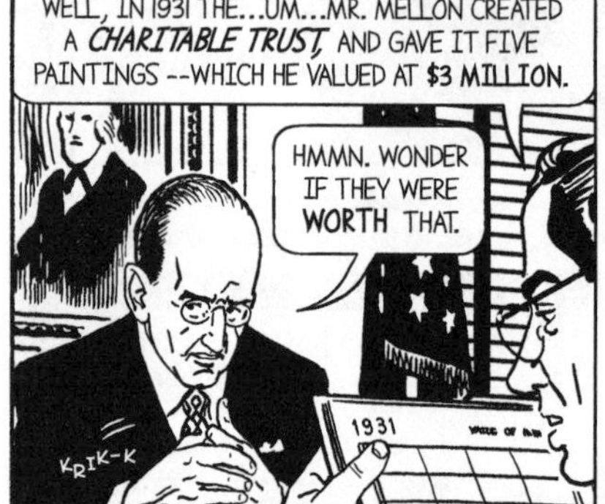
WELL, IN 1931 THE...UM...MR. MELLON CREATED A CHARITABLE TRUST, AND GAVE IT FIVE PAINTINGS --WHICH HE VALUED AT $3 MILLION.
HMMN. WONDER IF THEY WERE WORTH THAT.
KRIK-K
1931

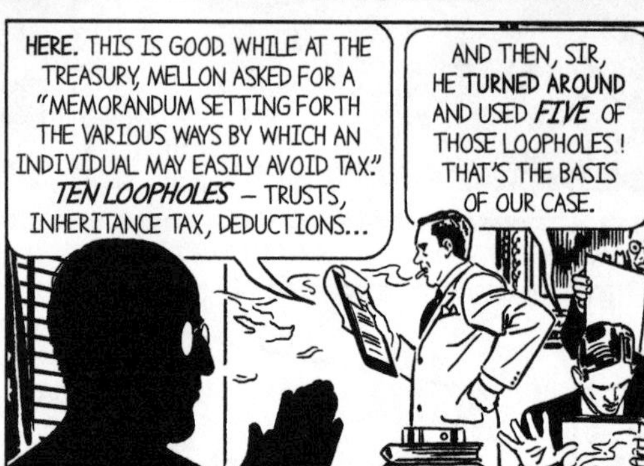
HERE. THIS IS GOOD. WHILE AT THE TREASURY, MELLON ASKED FOR A "MEMORANDUM SETTING FORTH THE VARIOUS WAYS BY WHICH AN INDIVIDUAL MAY EASILY AVOID TAX." TEN LOOPHOLES – TRUSTS, INHERITANCE TAX, DEDUCTIONS...
AND THEN, SIR, HE TURNED AROUND AND USED FIVE OF THOSE LOOPHOLES! THAT'S THE BASIS OF OUR CASE.

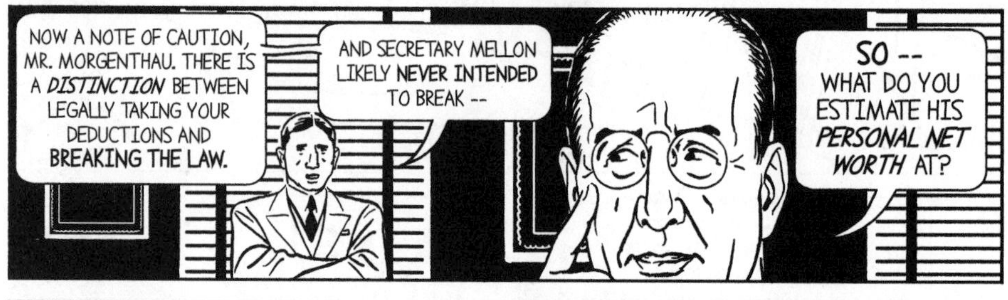
NOW A NOTE OF CAUTION, MR. MORGENTHAU. THERE IS A DISTINCTION BETWEEN LEGALLY TAKING YOUR DEDUCTIONS AND BREAKING THE LAW.
AND SECRETARY MELLON LIKELY NEVER INTENDED TO BREAK --
SO -- WHAT DO YOU ESTIMATE HIS PERSONAL NET WORTH AT?

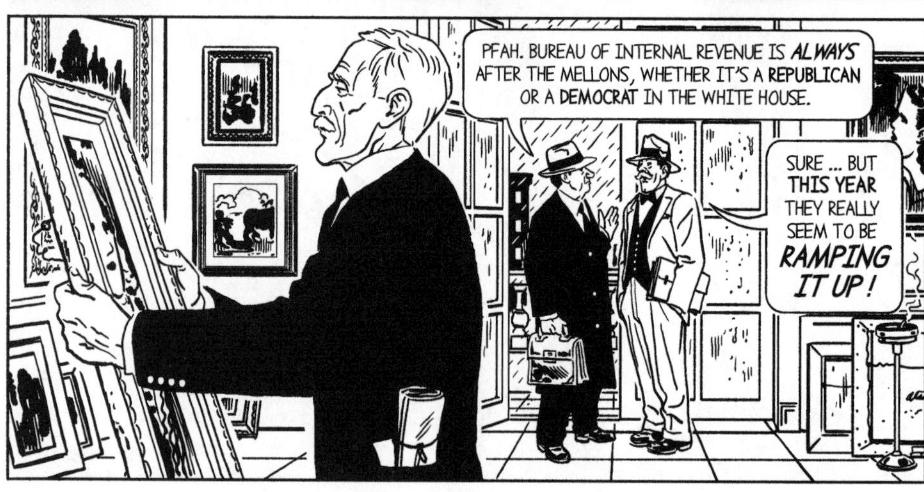
PFAH. BUREAU OF INTERNAL REVENUE IS ALWAYS AFTER THE MELLONS, WHETHER IT'S A REPUBLICAN OR A DEMOCRAT IN THE WHITE HOUSE.
SURE ... BUT THIS YEAR THEY REALLY SEEM TO BE RAMPING IT UP!

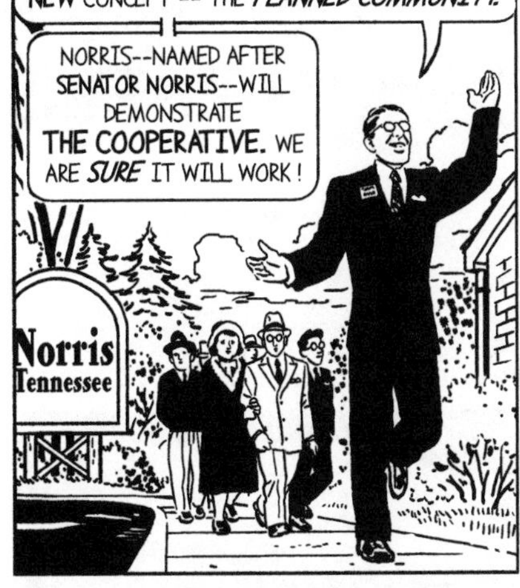
Even as they were taking Insull and Mellon DOWN, the New Dealers kept building UP!
IT'S NOT JUST THE MATERIALS WE HAVE USED. THE GOVERNANCE OF NORRIS REFLECTS A WHOLE NEW CONCEPT -- THE PLANNED COMMUNITY.
NORRIS--NAMED AFTER SENATOR NORRIS--WILL DEMONSTRATE THE COOPERATIVE. WE ARE SURE IT WILL WORK!
Norris Tennessee

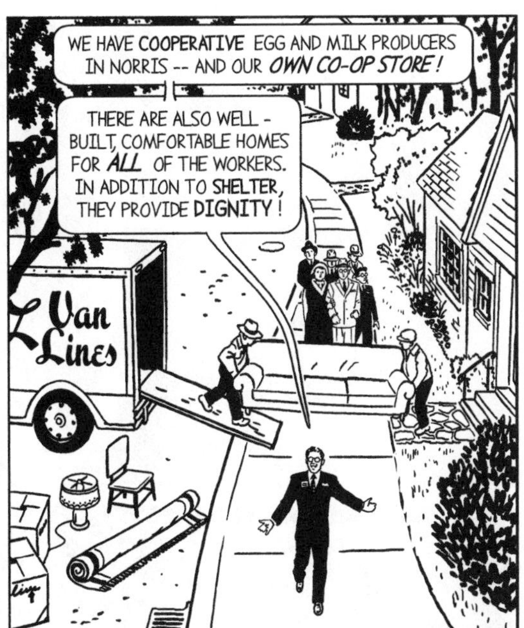
WE HAVE COOPERATIVE EGG AND MILK PRODUCERS IN NORRIS -- AND OUR OWN CO-OP STORE!
THERE ARE ALSO WELL - BUILT, COMFORTABLE HOMES FOR ALL OF THE WORKERS. IN ADDITION TO SHELTER, THEY PROVIDE DIGNITY!
Van Lines

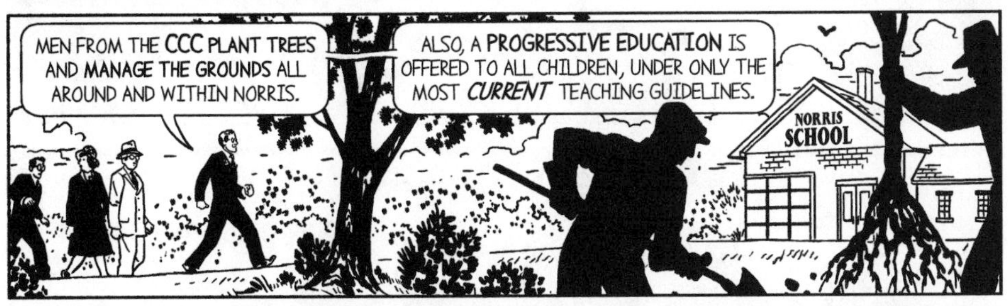
MEN FROM THE CCC PLANT TREES AND MANAGE THE GROUNDS ALL AROUND AND WITHIN NORRIS.
ALSO, A PROGRESSIVE EDUCATION IS OFFERED TO ALL CHILDREN, UNDER ONLY THE MOST CURRENT TEACHING GUIDELINES.
NORRIS SCHOOL

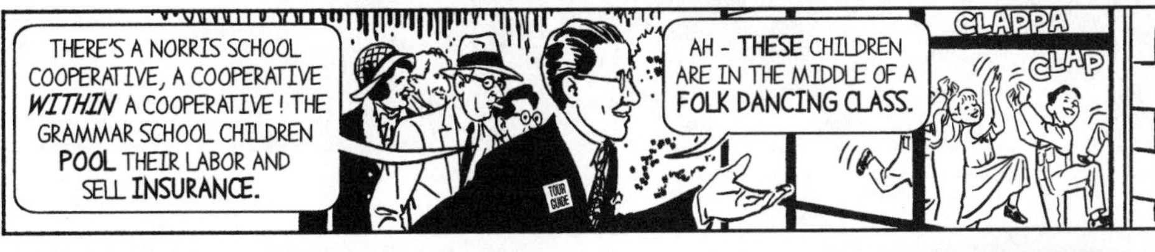
THERE'S A NORRIS SCHOOL COOPERATIVE, A COOPERATIVE WITHIN A COOPERATIVE! THE GRAMMAR SCHOOL CHILDREN POOL THEIR LABOR AND SELL INSURANCE.
AH - THESE CHILDREN ARE IN THE MIDDLE OF A FOLK DANCING CLASS.
CLAPPA
CLAP
TOUR GUIDE

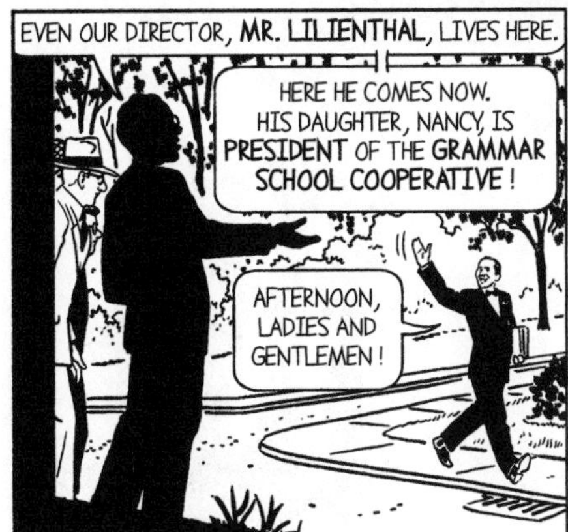
EVEN OUR DIRECTOR, MR. LILIENTHAL, LIVES HERE.
HERE HE COMES NOW. HIS DAUGHTER, NANCY, IS PRESIDENT OF THE GRAMMAR SCHOOL COOPERATIVE!
AFTERNOON, LADIES AND GENTLEMEN!

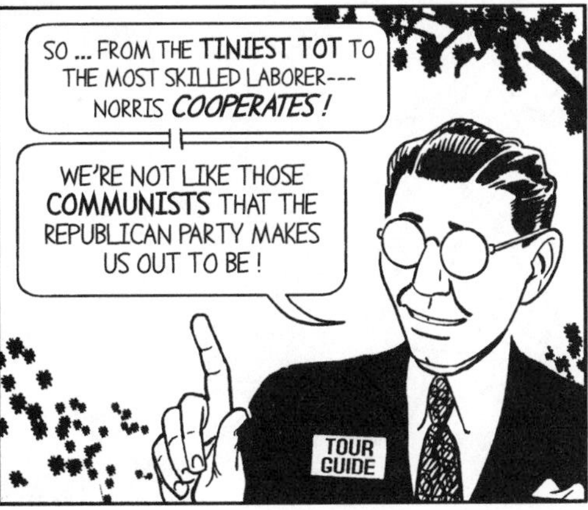
SO ... FROM THE TINIEST TOT TO THE MOST SKILLED LABORER--- NORRIS COOPERATES!
WE'RE NOT LIKE THOSE COMMUNISTS THAT THE REPUBLICAN PARTY MAKES US OUT TO BE!
TOUR GUIDE

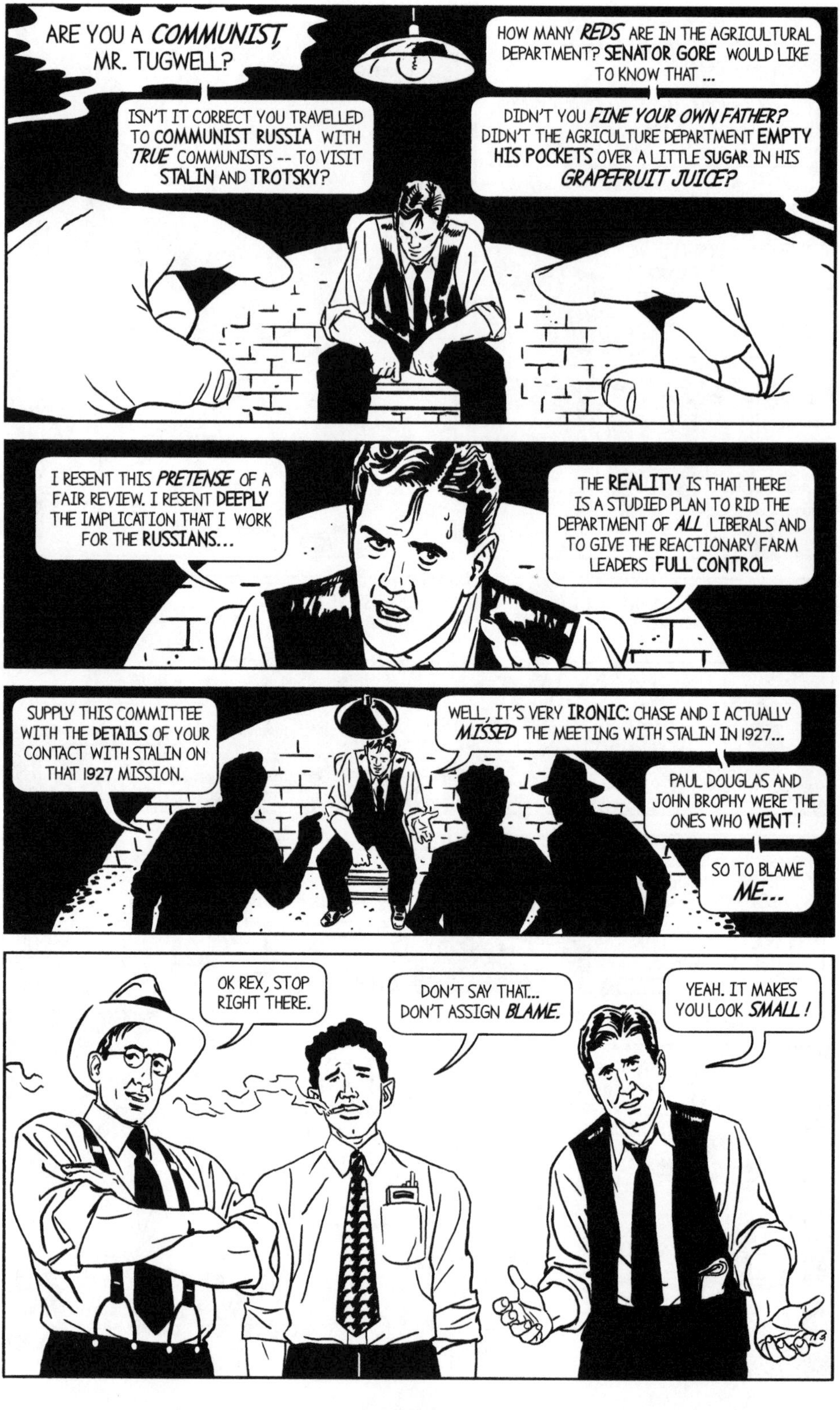

ARE YOU A COMMUNIST, MR. TUGWELL?
ISN'T IT CORRECT YOU TRAVELLED TO COMMUNIST RUSSIA WITH TRUE COMMUNISTS -- TO VISIT STALIN AND TROTSKY?
HOW MANY REDS ARE IN THE AGRICULTURAL DEPARTMENT? SENATOR GORE WOULD LIKE TO KNOW THAT ...
DIDN'T YOU FINE YOUR OWN FATHER? DIDN'T THE AGRICULTURE DEPARTMENT EMPTY HIS POCKETS OVER A LITTLE SUGAR IN HIS GRAPEFRUIT JUICE?

I RESENT THIS PRETENSE OF A FAIR REVIEW. I RESENT DEEPLY THE IMPLICATION THAT I WORK FOR THE RUSSIANS...
THE REALITY IS THAT THERE IS A STUDIED PLAN TO RID THE DEPARTMENT OF ALL LIBERALS AND TO GIVE THE REACTIONARY FARM LEADERS FULL CONTROL.

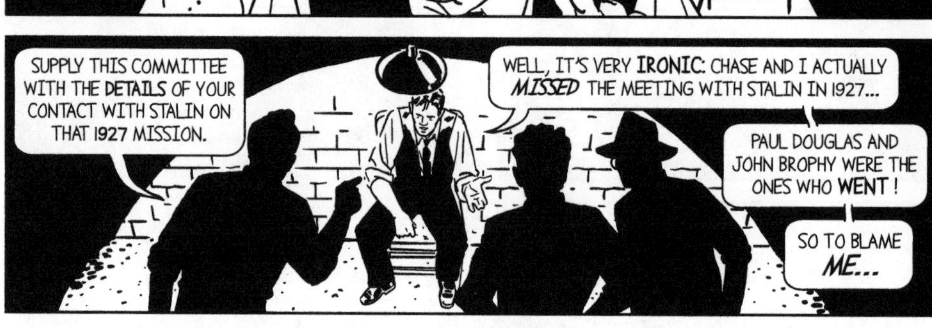

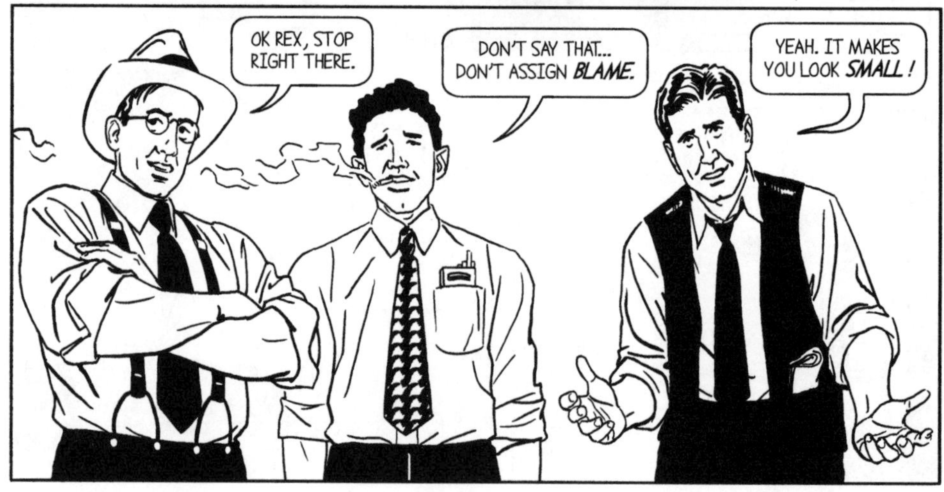

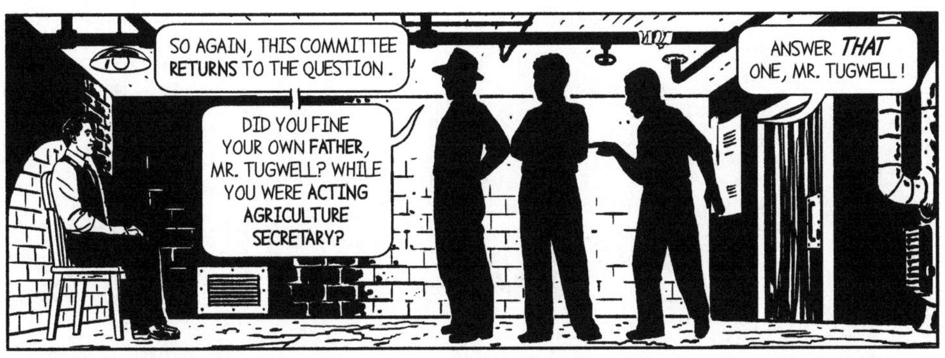
SO AGAIN, THIS COMMITTEE **RETURNS** TO THE QUESTION.
DID YOU FINE YOUR OWN **FATHER**, MR. TUGWELL? WHILE YOU WERE **ACTING AGRICULTURE SECRETARY?**
ANSWER ***THAT*** ONE, MR. TUGWELL!

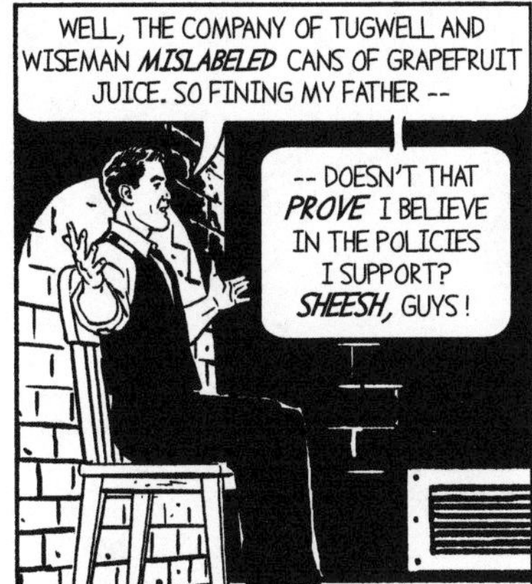
WELL, THE COMPANY OF TUGWELL AND WISEMAN ***MISLABELED*** CANS OF GRAPEFRUIT JUICE. SO FINING MY FATHER --
-- DOESN'T THAT ***PROVE*** I BELIEVE IN THE POLICIES I SUPPORT? ***SHEESH,*** GUYS!

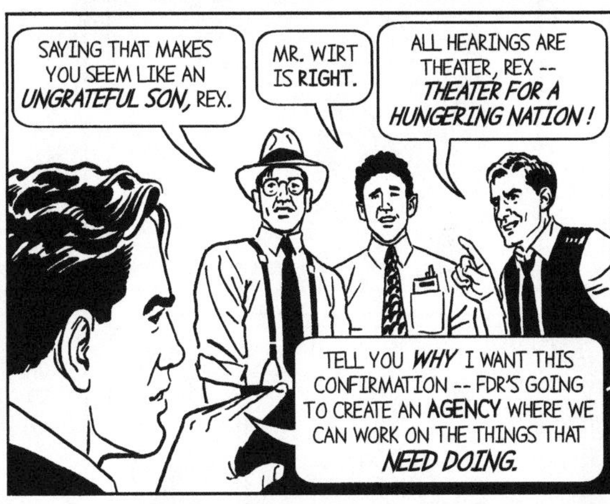
SAYING THAT MAKES YOU SEEM LIKE AN ***UNGRATEFUL SON,*** REX.
MR. WIRT IS **RIGHT**.
ALL HEARINGS ARE THEATER, REX -- ***THEATER FOR A HUNGERING NATION!***
TELL YOU ***WHY*** I WANT THIS CONFIRMATION -- FDR'S GOING TO CREATE AN **AGENCY** WHERE WE CAN WORK ON THE THINGS THAT ***NEED DOING.***

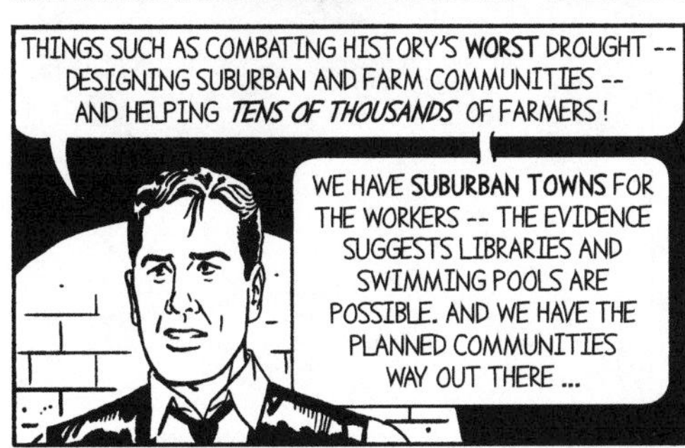
THINGS SUCH AS COMBATING HISTORY'S **WORST** DROUGHT -- DESIGNING SUBURBAN AND FARM COMMUNITIES -- AND HELPING ***TENS OF THOUSANDS*** OF FARMERS!
WE HAVE **SUBURBAN TOWNS** FOR THE WORKERS -- THE EVIDENCE SUGGESTS LIBRARIES AND SWIMMING POOLS ARE POSSIBLE. AND WE HAVE THE PLANNED COMMUNITIES WAY OUT THERE ...

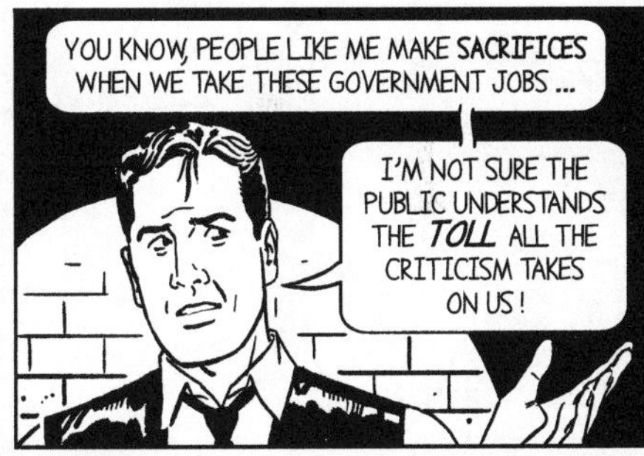
YOU KNOW, PEOPLE LIKE ME MAKE **SACRIFICES** WHEN WE TAKE THESE GOVERNMENT JOBS ...
I'M NOT SURE THE PUBLIC UNDERSTANDS THE ***TOLL*** ALL THE CRITICISM TAKES ON US!

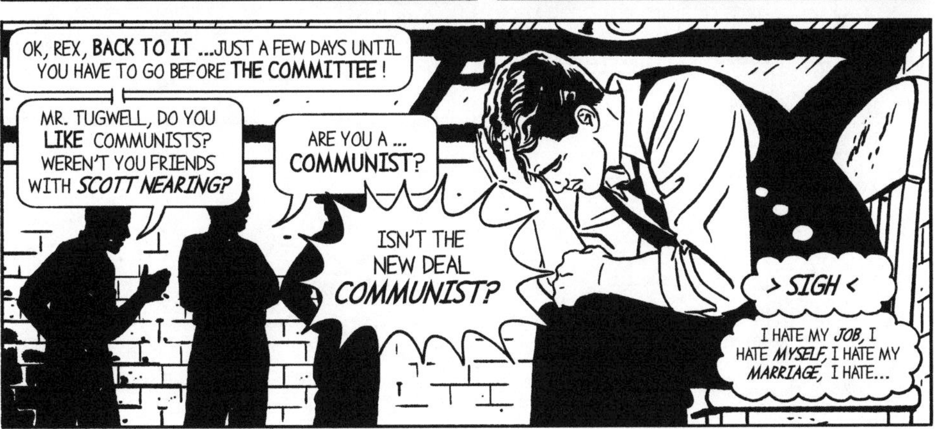
OK, REX, **BACK TO IT** ...JUST A FEW DAYS UNTIL YOU HAVE TO GO BEFORE **THE COMMITTEE**!
MR. TUGWELL, DO YOU **LIKE** COMMUNISTS? WEREN'T YOU FRIENDS WITH ***SCOTT NEARING?***
ARE YOU A ... **COMMUNIST**?
ISN'T THE NEW DEAL ***COMMUNIST?***
> ***SIGH*** <
I HATE MY ***JOB,*** I HATE ***MYSELF,*** I HATE MY ***MARRIAGE,*** I HATE...

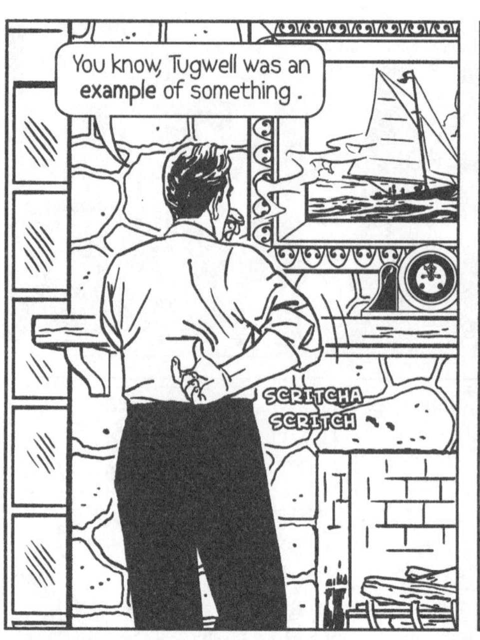
You know, Tugwell was an example of something.
SCRITCHA
SCRITCH

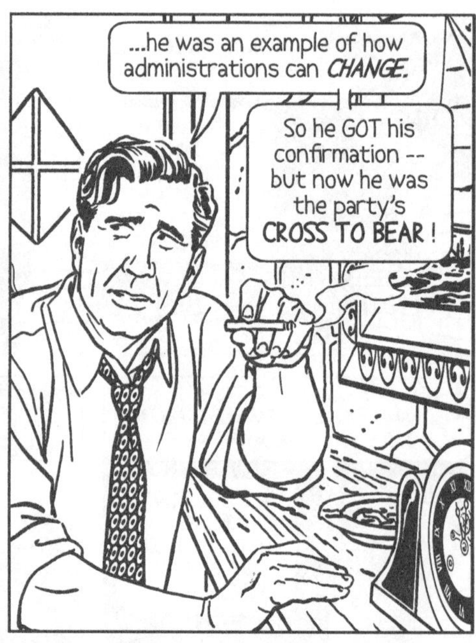
...he was an example of how administrations can CHANGE.
So he GOT his confirmation -- but now he was the party's CROSS TO BEAR!

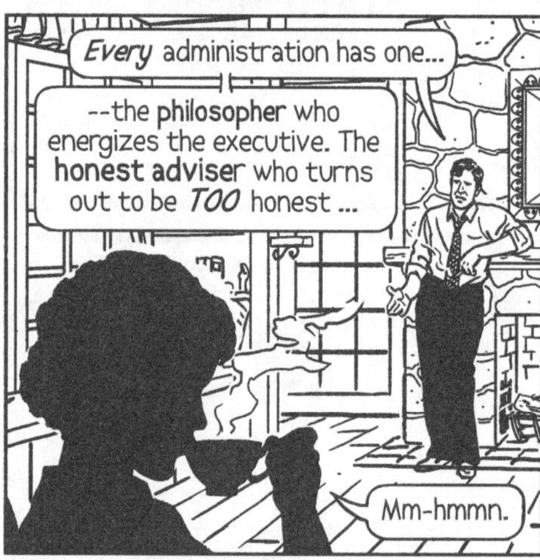
Every administration has one...
--the philosopher who energizes the executive. The honest adviser who turns out to be TOO honest ...
Mm-hmmn.

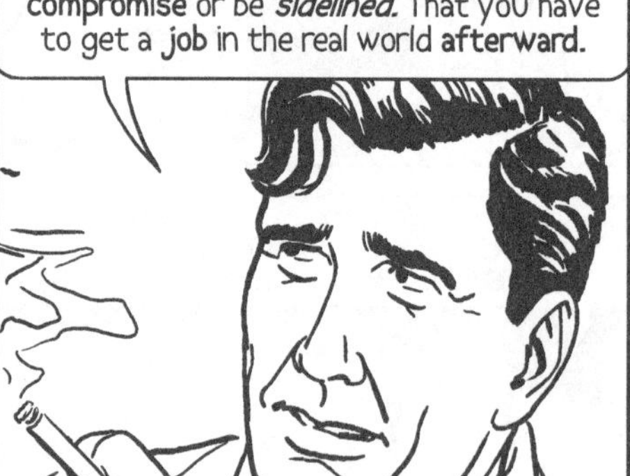
...who doesn't understand that you have to compromise or be sidelined. That you have to get a job in the real world afterward.

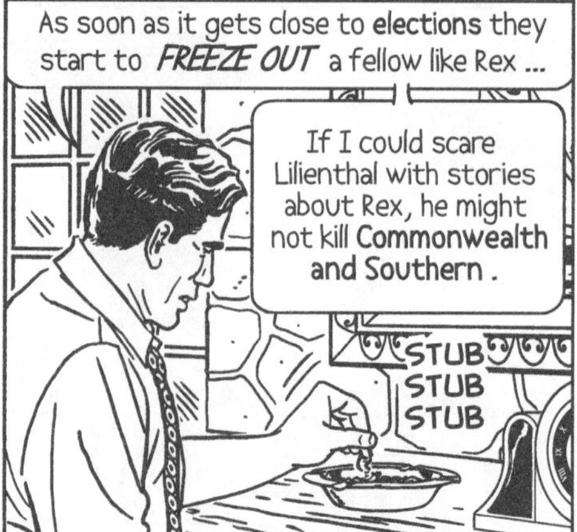
As soon as it gets close to elections they start to FREEZE OUT a fellow like Rex ...
If I could scare Lilienthal with stories about Rex, he might not kill Commonwealth and Southern.
STUB
STUB
STUB

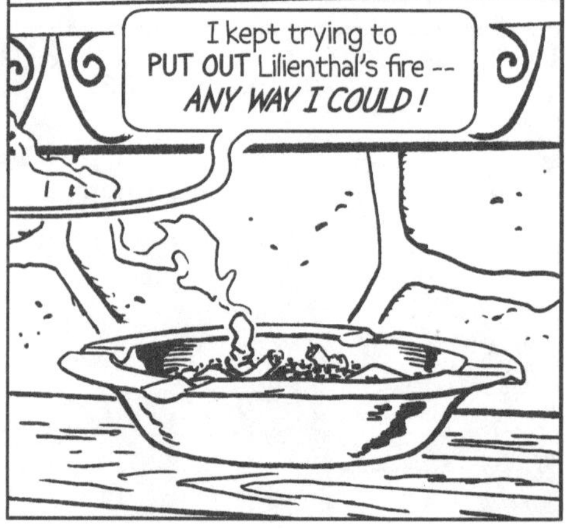
I kept trying to PUT OUT Lilienthal's fire -- ANY WAY I COULD!

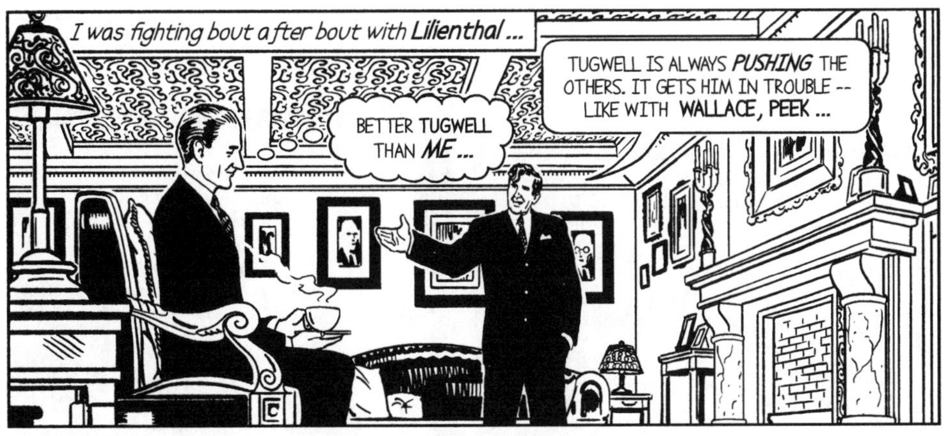
I was fighting bout after bout with Lilienthal ...
BETTER TUGWELL THAN ME ...
TUGWELL IS ALWAYS PUSHING THE OTHERS. IT GETS HIM IN TROUBLE -- LIKE WITH WALLACE, PEEK ...

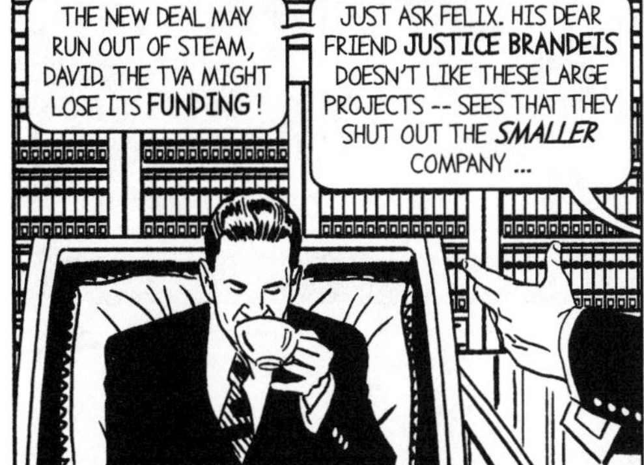
THE NEW DEAL MAY RUN OUT OF STEAM, DAVID. THE TVA MIGHT LOSE ITS FUNDING!
JUST ASK FELIX. HIS DEAR FRIEND JUSTICE BRANDEIS DOESN'T LIKE THESE LARGE PROJECTS -- SEES THAT THEY SHUT OUT THE SMALLER COMPANY ...

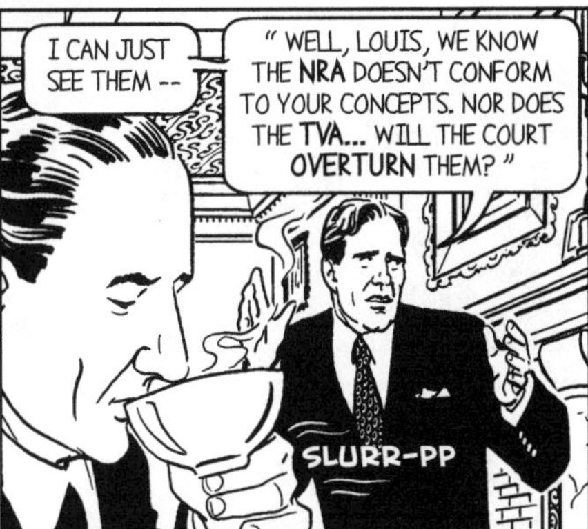
I CAN JUST SEE THEM --
" WELL, LOUIS, WE KNOW THE NRA DOESN'T CONFORM TO YOUR CONCEPTS. NOR DOES THE TVA... WILL THE COURT OVERTURN THEM? "
SLURR-PP

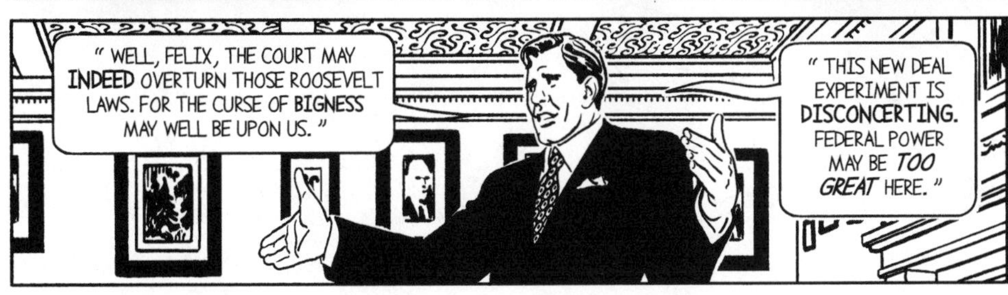
" WELL, FELIX, THE COURT MAY INDEED OVERTURN THOSE ROOSEVELT LAWS. FOR THE CURSE OF BIGNESS MAY WELL BE UPON US. "
" THIS NEW DEAL EXPERIMENT IS DISCONCERTING. FEDERAL POWER MAY BE TOO GREAT HERE. "

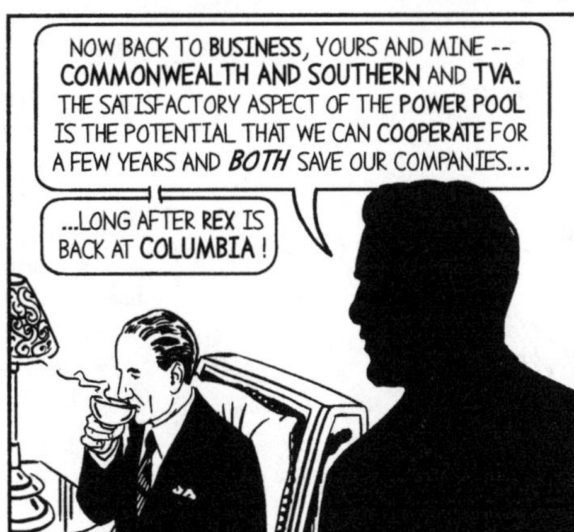
NOW BACK TO BUSINESS, YOURS AND MINE -- COMMONWEALTH AND SOUTHERN AND TVA. THE SATISFACTORY ASPECT OF THE POWER POOL IS THE POTENTIAL THAT WE CAN COOPERATE FOR A FEW YEARS AND BOTH SAVE OUR COMPANIES...
...LONG AFTER REX IS BACK AT COLUMBIA!

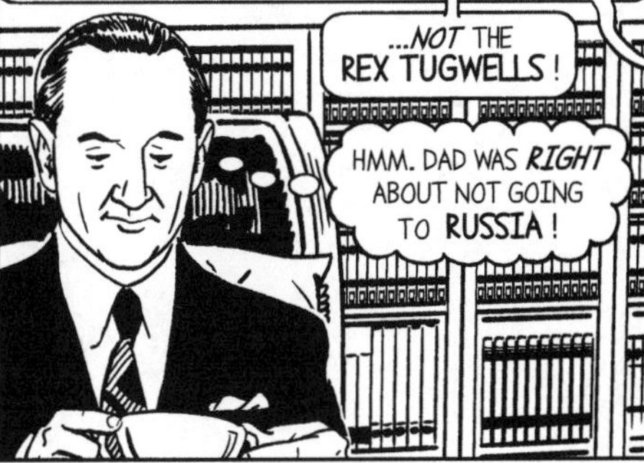
I KNOW I'VE TOLD YOU THIS BEFORE, DAVID, BUT HIRING COMPANIES LOOK AT CANDIDATES' COMPORTMENT WHILE THEY WERE IN GOVERNMENT. COMPANIES WANT TO HIRE FORMER OFFICIALS, BUT ONLY THE REASONABLE ONES.
...NOT THE REX TUGWELLS!
HMM. DAD WAS RIGHT ABOUT NOT GOING TO RUSSIA!

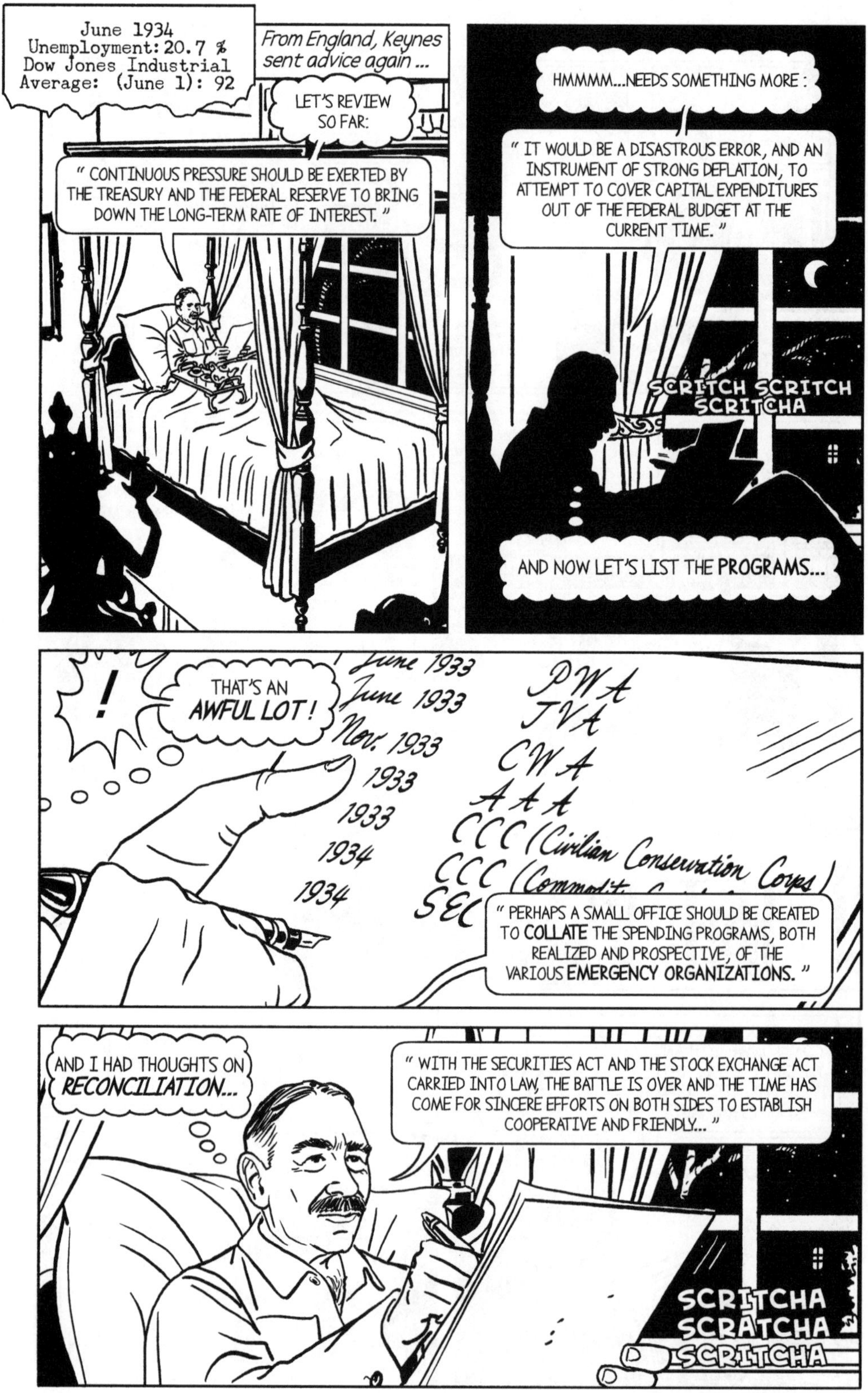

June 1934
Unemployment: 20.7 %
Dow Jones Industrial
Average: (June 1): 92

From England, Keynes sent advice again ...

LET'S REVIEW SO FAR:

" CONTINUOUS PRESSURE SHOULD BE EXERTED BY THE TREASURY AND THE FEDERAL RESERVE TO BRING DOWN THE LONG-TERM RATE OF INTEREST. "

HMMMM...NEEDS SOMETHING MORE :

" IT WOULD BE A DISASTROUS ERROR, AND AN INSTRUMENT OF STRONG DEFLATION, TO ATTEMPT TO COVER CAPITAL EXPENDITURES OUT OF THE FEDERAL BUDGET AT THE CURRENT TIME. "

SCRITCH SCRITCH SCRITCHA

AND NOW LET'S LIST THE **PROGRAMS...**

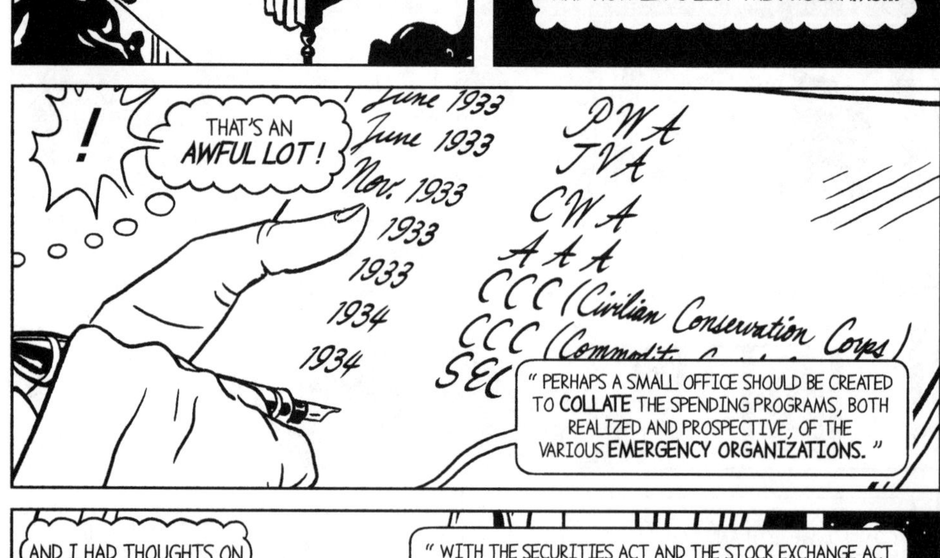

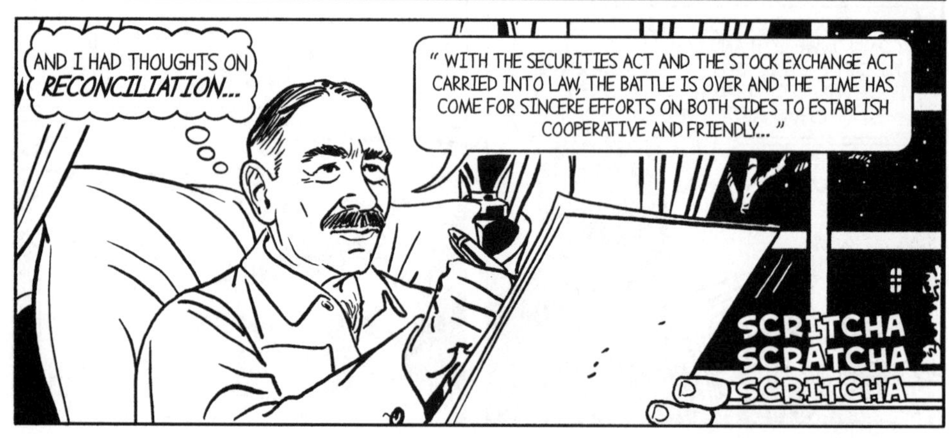

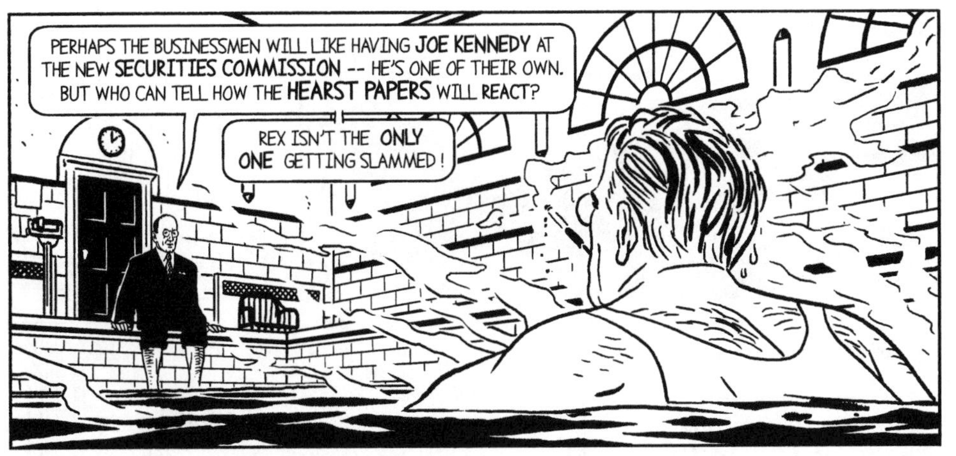
PERHAPS THE BUSINESSMEN WILL LIKE HAVING JOE KENNEDY AT THE NEW SECURITIES COMMISSION -- HE'S ONE OF THEIR OWN. BUT WHO CAN TELL HOW THE HEARST PAPERS WILL REACT?
REX ISN'T THE ONLY ONE GETTING SLAMMED!

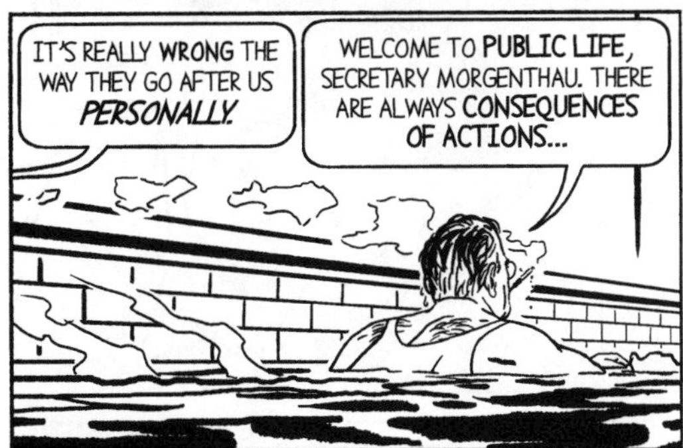
IT'S REALLY WRONG THE WAY THEY GO AFTER US PERSONALLY.
WELCOME TO PUBLIC LIFE, SECRETARY MORGENTHAU. THERE ARE ALWAYS CONSEQUENCES OF ACTIONS...

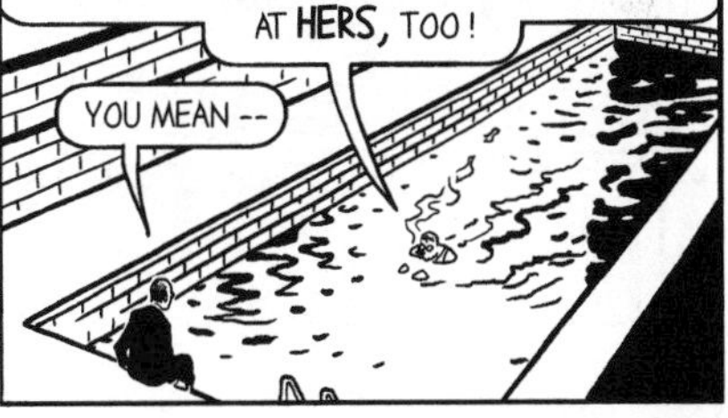
BUT WE CAN ALSO REACT! LET'S SEE -- HEARST AND THE HOSTILE PAPERS. MOE ANNENBERG IS HOSTILE. WHY DON'T YOU HAVE YOUR MEN LOOK AT HIS PERSONAL RETURNS? HAVE A LOOK AT HERS, TOO!
YOU MEAN --

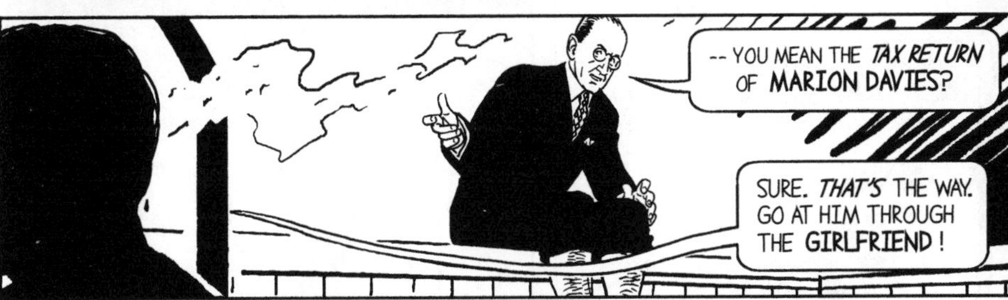
-- YOU MEAN THE TAX RETURN OF MARION DAVIES?
SURE. THAT'S THE WAY. GO AT HIM THROUGH THE GIRLFRIEND!

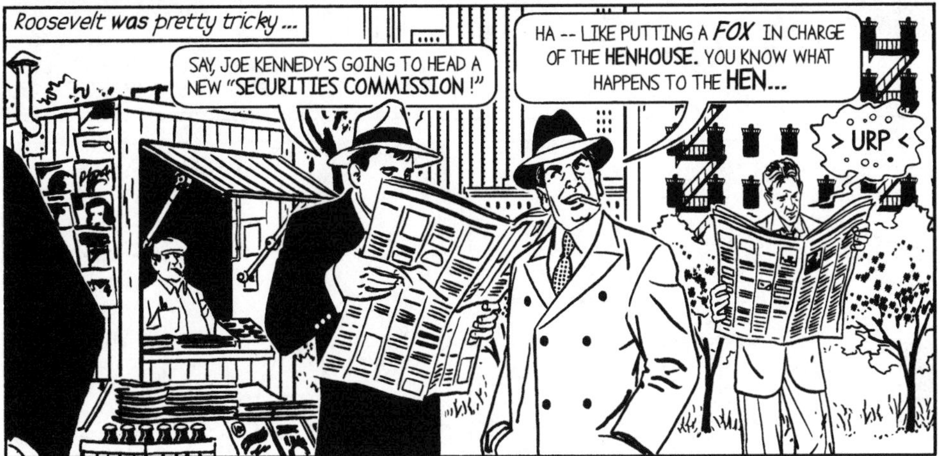
Roosevelt was pretty tricky...
SAY, JOE KENNEDY'S GOING TO HEAD A NEW "SECURITIES COMMISSION!"
HA -- LIKE PUTTING A FOX IN CHARGE OF THE HENHOUSE. YOU KNOW WHAT HAPPENS TO THE HEN...
> URP <

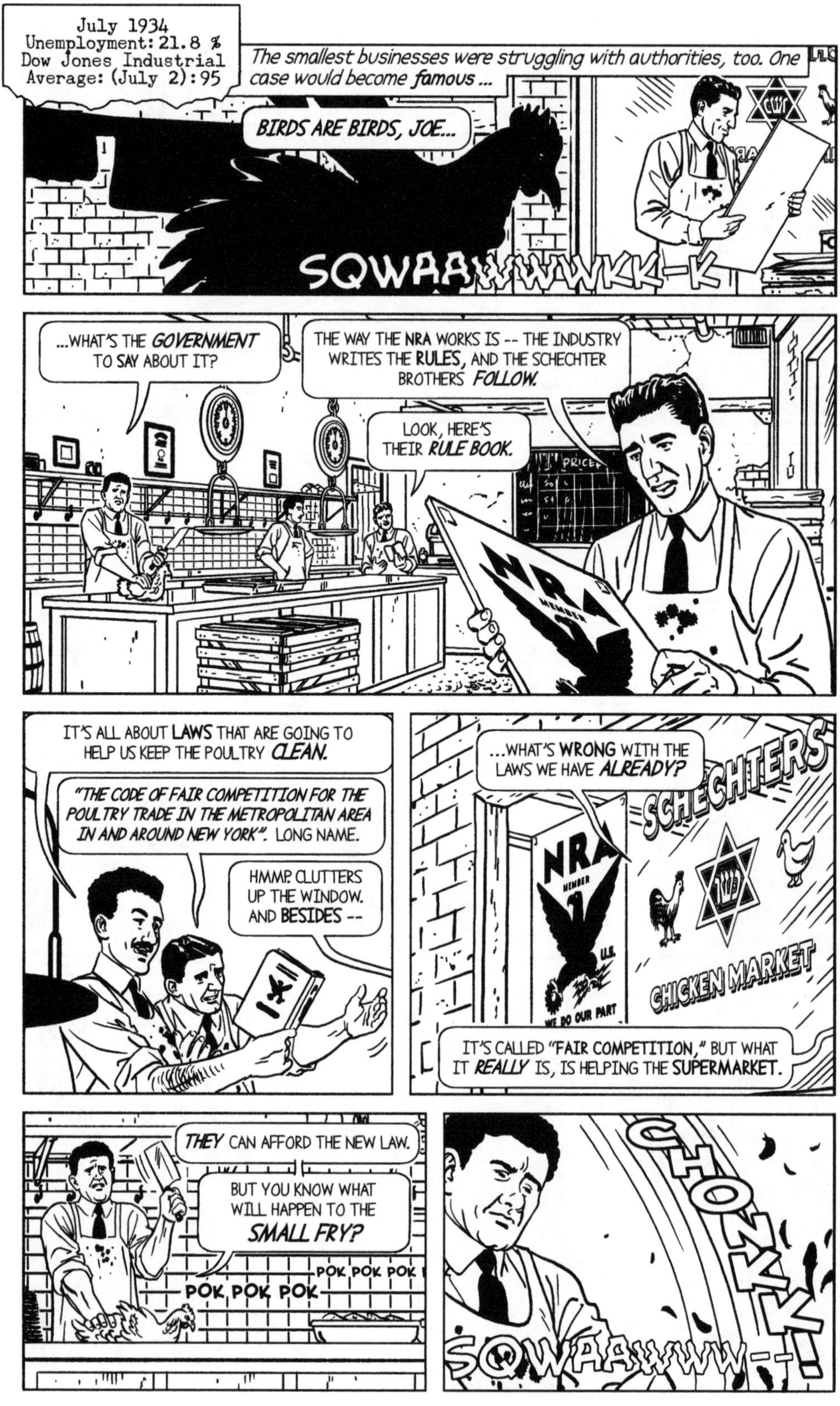

July 1934
Unemployment: 21.8 %
Dow Jones Industrial
Average: (July 2): 95

*The smallest businesses were struggling with authorities, too. One case would become **famous** ...*

BIRDS ARE BIRDS, JOE...

SQWAAWWWKK-K

...WHAT'S THE ***GOVERNMENT*** TO **SAY** ABOUT IT?

THE WAY THE **NRA** WORKS IS -- THE INDUSTRY WRITES THE **RULES,** AND THE SCHECHTER BROTHERS ***FOLLOW.***

LOOK, HERE'S THEIR ***RULE BOOK.***

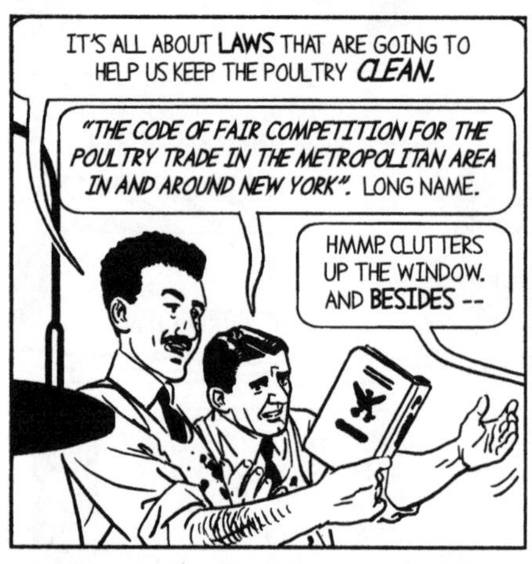

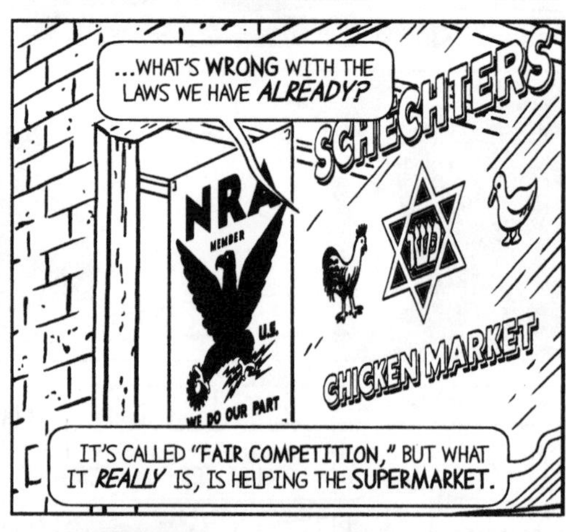

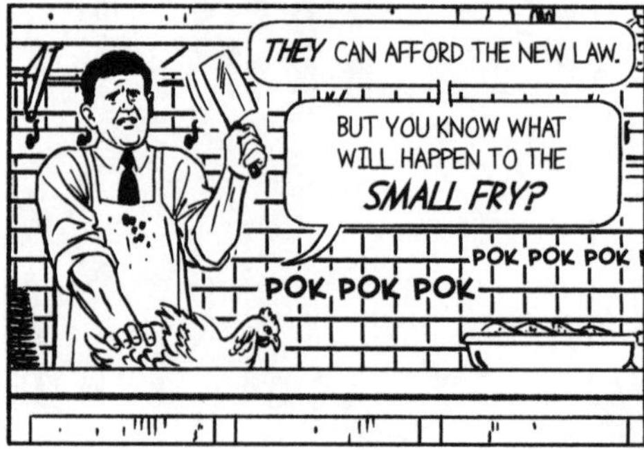

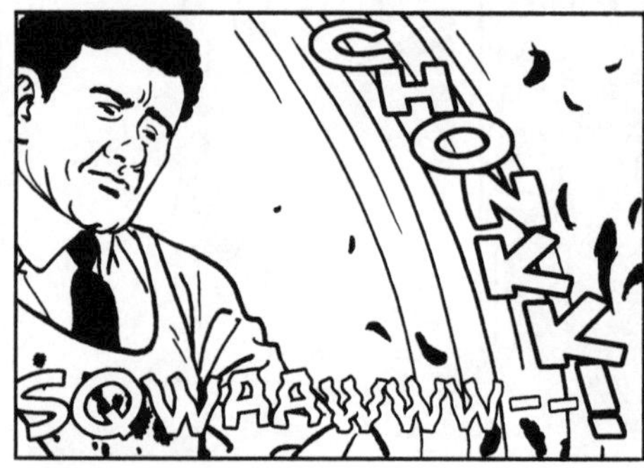

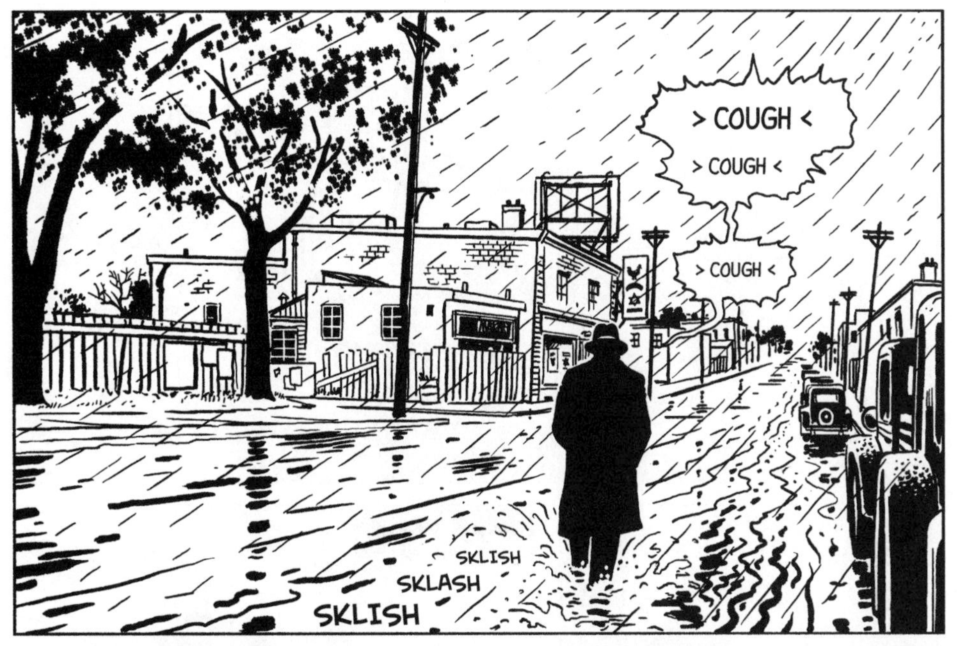
> COUGH <
> COUGH <
> COUGH <
SKLISH
SKLASH
SKLISH

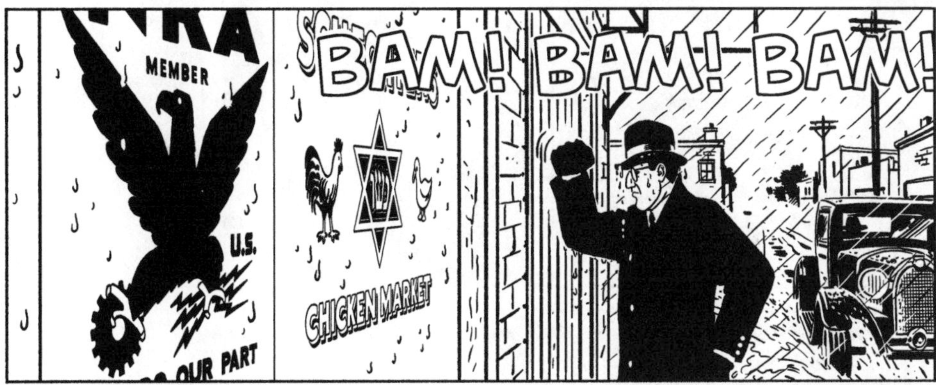
NRA
MEMBER
U.S.
OUR PART
CHICKEN MARKET
BAM! BAM! BAM!

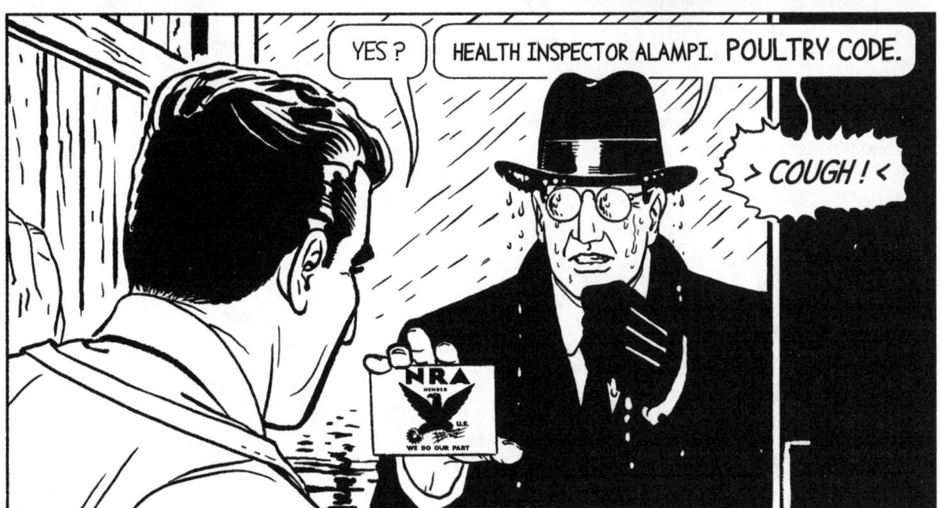
YES ?
HEALTH INSPECTOR ALAMPI. POULTRY CODE.
> COUGH ! <
NRA
MEMBER
U.S.
WE DO OUR PART

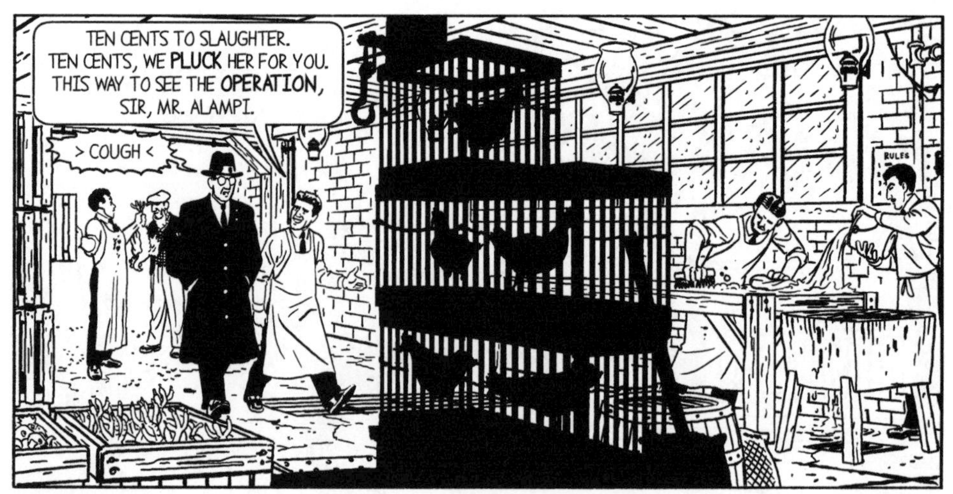
TEN CENTS TO SLAUGHTER. TEN CENTS, WE PLUCK HER FOR YOU. THIS WAY TO SEE THE OPERATION, SIR, MR. ALAMPI.
> COUGH <
RULES

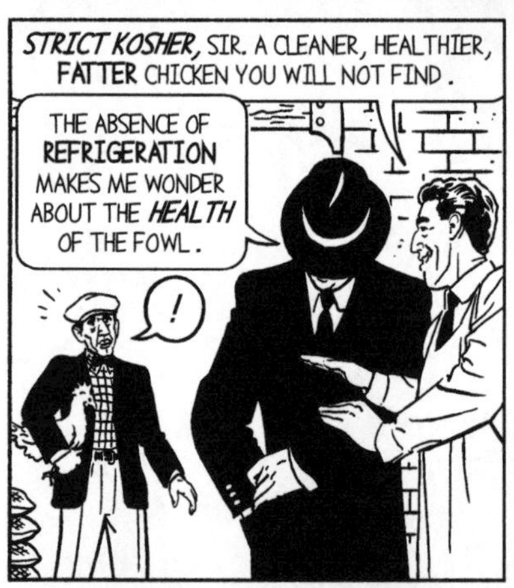
STRICT KOSHER, SIR. A CLEANER, HEALTHIER, FATTER CHICKEN YOU WILL NOT FIND.
THE ABSENCE OF REFRIGERATION MAKES ME WONDER ABOUT THE HEALTH OF THE FOWL.
!

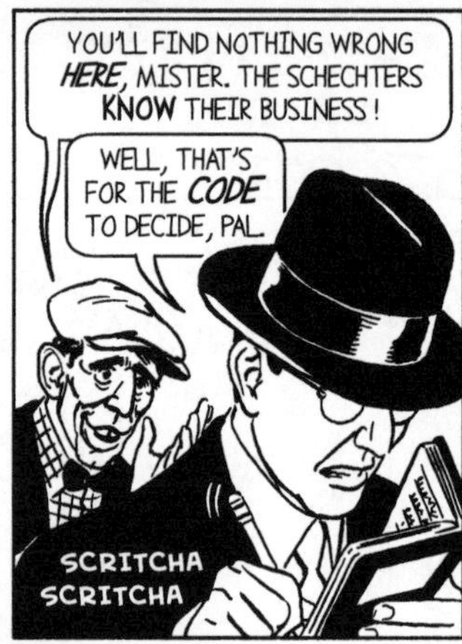
YOU'LL FIND NOTHING WRONG HERE, MISTER. THE SCHECHTERS KNOW THEIR BUSINESS!
WELL, THAT'S FOR THE CODE TO DECIDE, PAL.
SCRITCHA SCRITCHA

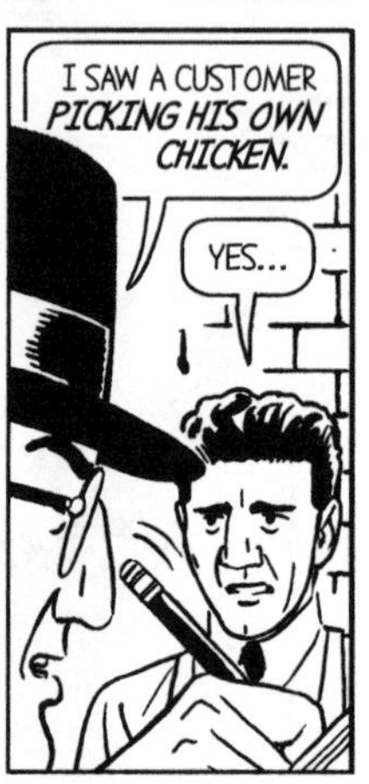
I SAW A CUSTOMER PICKING HIS OWN CHICKEN.
YES...

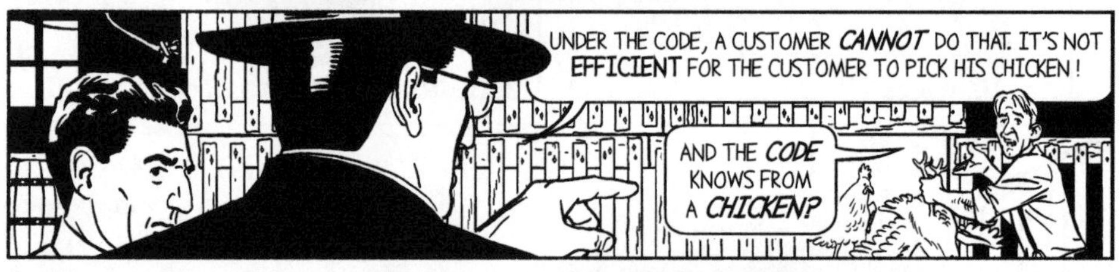
UNDER THE CODE, A CUSTOMER CANNOT DO THAT. IT'S NOT EFFICIENT FOR THE CUSTOMER TO PICK HIS CHICKEN!
AND THE CODE KNOWS FROM A CHICKEN?

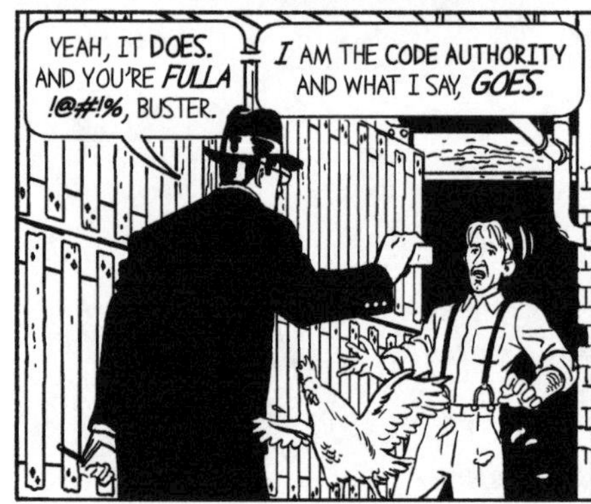
YEAH, IT DOES. AND YOU'RE FULLA !@#!%, BUSTER.
I AM THE CODE AUTHORITY AND WHAT I SAY, GOES.

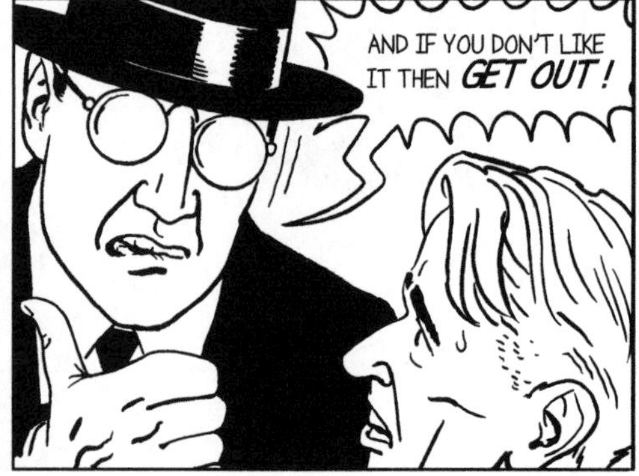
AND IF YOU DON'T LIKE IT THEN GET OUT!

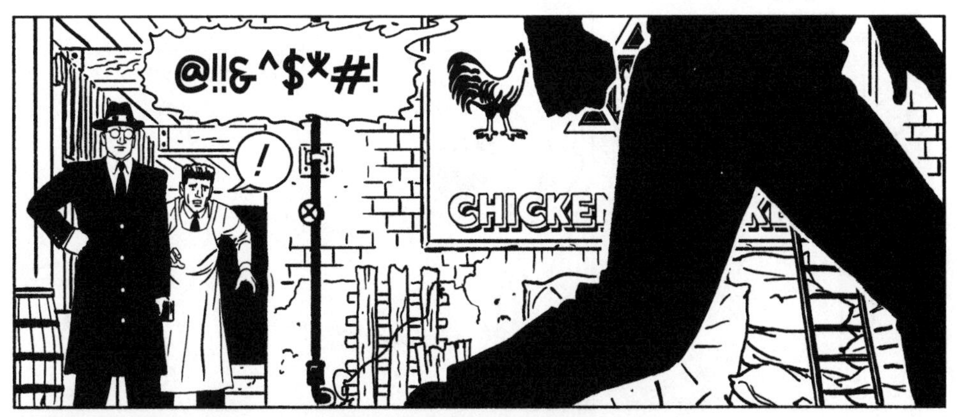
@!!&^$*#!
!
CHICKEN

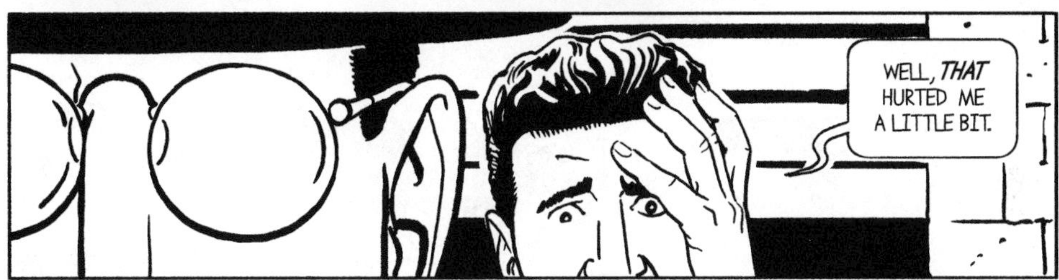
WELL, *THAT* HURTED ME A LITTLE BIT.

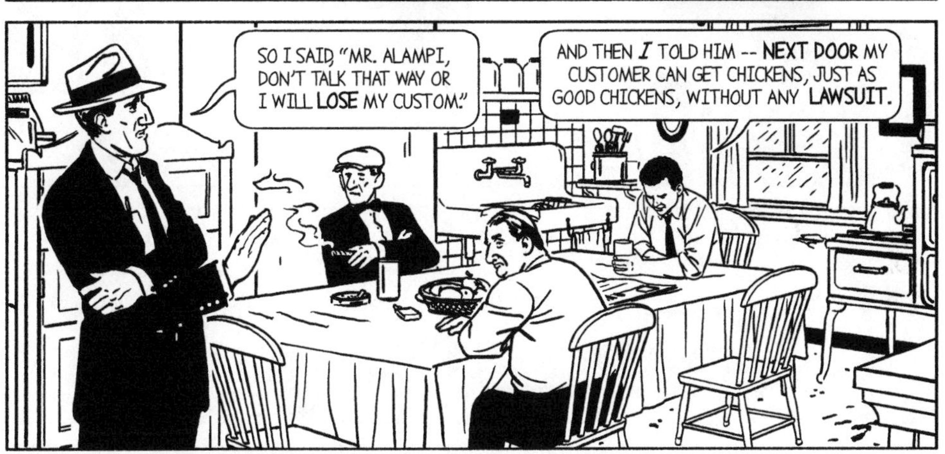
SO I SAID, "MR. ALAMPI, DON'T TALK THAT WAY OR I WILL **LOSE** MY CUSTOM."
AND THEN *I* TOLD HIM -- **NEXT DOOR** MY CUSTOMER CAN GET CHICKENS, JUST AS GOOD CHICKENS, WITHOUT ANY **LAWSUIT**.

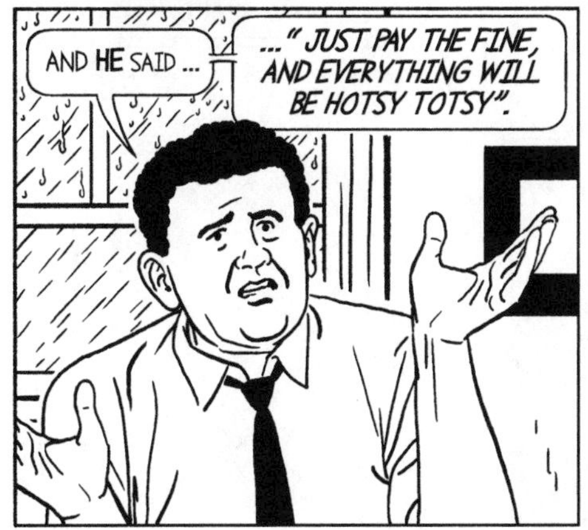
AND **HE** SAID ...
..." JUST PAY THE FINE, AND EVERYTHING WILL BE HOTSY TOTSY".

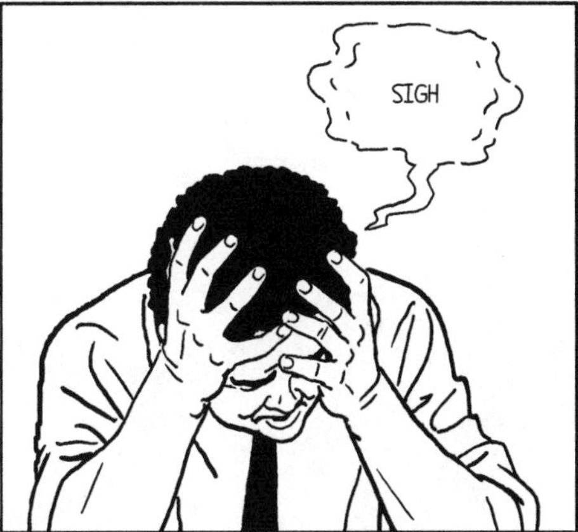
SIGH

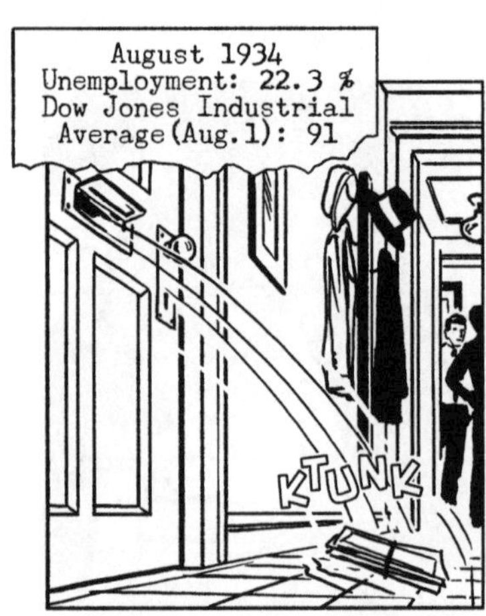
August 1934
Unemployment: 22.3 %
Dow Jones Industrial
Average(Aug.1): 91
KTUNK

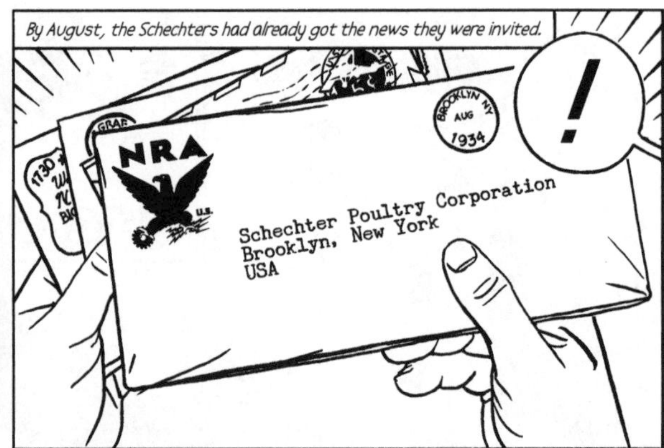
By August, the Schechters had already got the news they were invited.
NRA
BROOKLYN NY AUG 1934
Schechter Poultry Corporation
Brooklyn, New York
USA
!

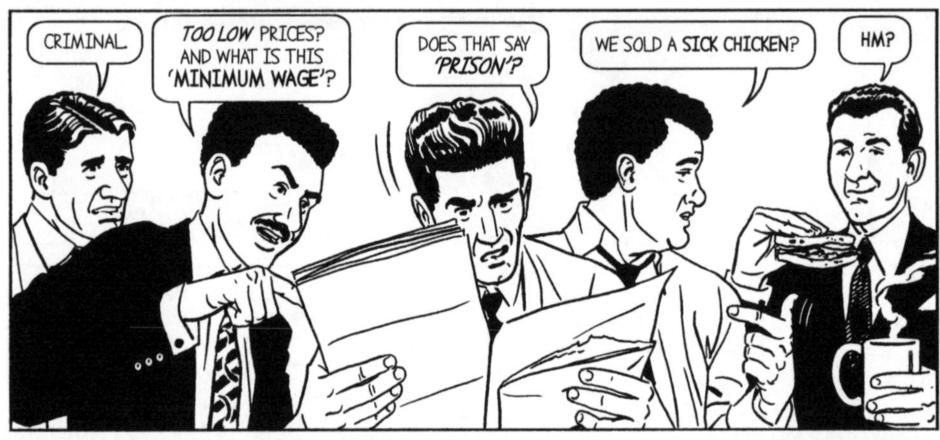
CRIMINAL.
TOO LOW PRICES? AND WHAT IS THIS 'MINIMUM WAGE'?
DOES THAT SAY 'PRISON'?
WE SOLD A SICK CHICKEN?
HM?

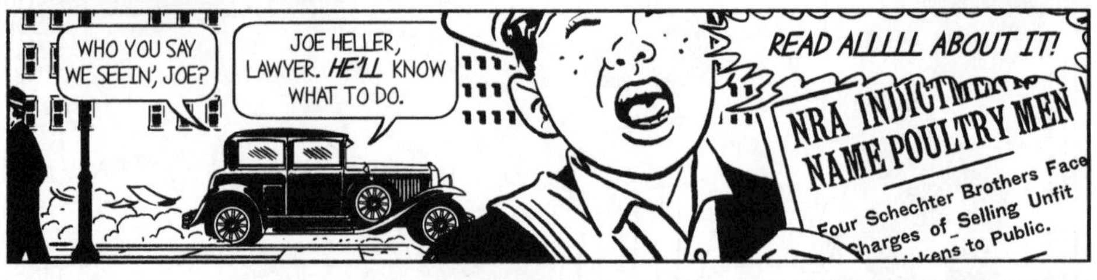
WHO YOU SAY WE SEEIN', JOE?
JOE HELLER, LAWYER. HE'LL KNOW WHAT TO DO.
READ ALLLLL ABOUT IT!
NRA INDICTMENTS NAME POULTRY MEN
Four Schechter Brothers Face Charges of Selling Unfit Chickens to Public.

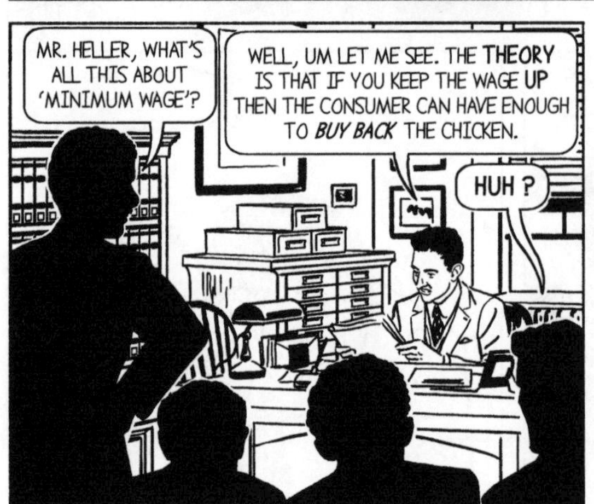
MR. HELLER, WHAT'S ALL THIS ABOUT 'MINIMUM WAGE'?
WELL, UM LET ME SEE. THE THEORY IS THAT IF YOU KEEP THE WAGE UP THEN THE CONSUMER CAN HAVE ENOUGH TO BUY BACK THE CHICKEN.
HUH ?

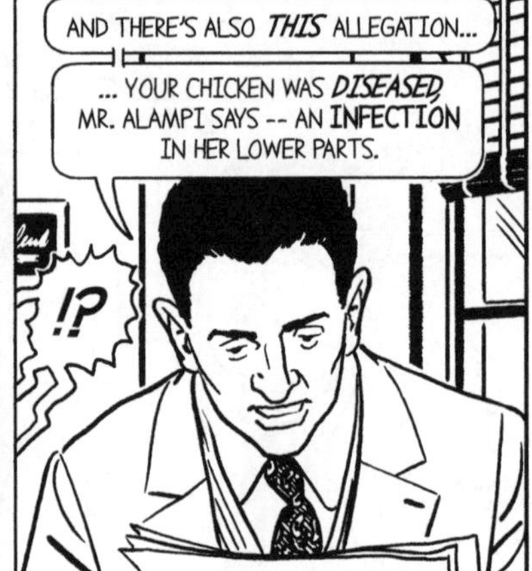
AND THERE'S ALSO THIS ALLEGATION...
... YOUR CHICKEN WAS DISEASED, MR. ALAMPI SAYS -- AN INFECTION IN HER LOWER PARTS.
!?

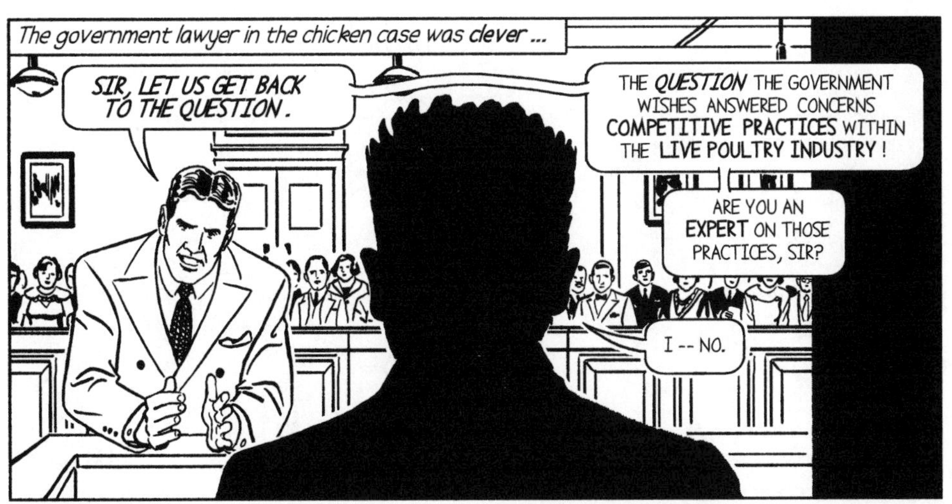

The government lawyer in the chicken case was **clever** ...
SIR, LET US GET BACK TO THE QUESTION.
THE *QUESTION* THE GOVERNMENT WISHES ANSWERED CONCERNS **COMPETITIVE PRACTICES** WITHIN THE **LIVE POULTRY INDUSTRY**!
ARE YOU AN **EXPERT** ON THOSE PRACTICES, SIR?
I -- NO.

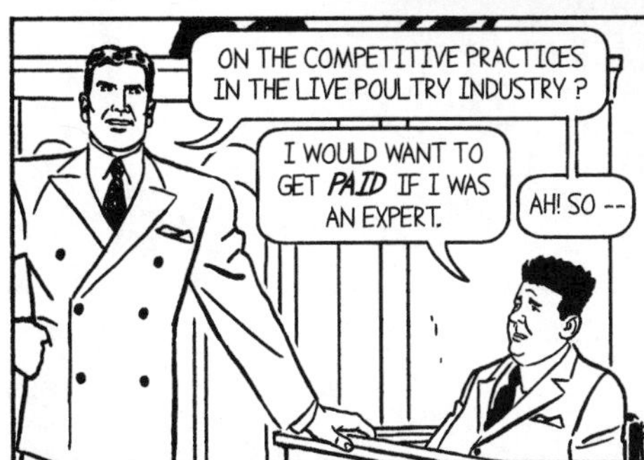

ON THE COMPETITIVE PRACTICES IN THE LIVE POULTRY INDUSTRY?
I WOULD WANT TO GET *PAID* IF I WAS AN EXPERT.
AH! SO --

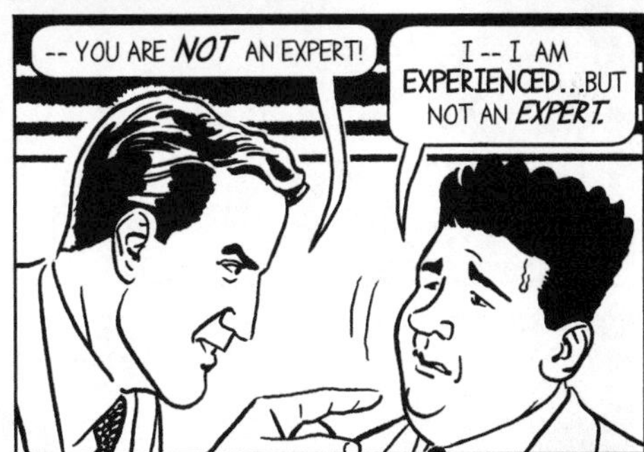

-- YOU ARE *NOT* AN EXPERT!
I -- I AM **EXPERIENCED**...BUT NOT AN *EXPERT.*

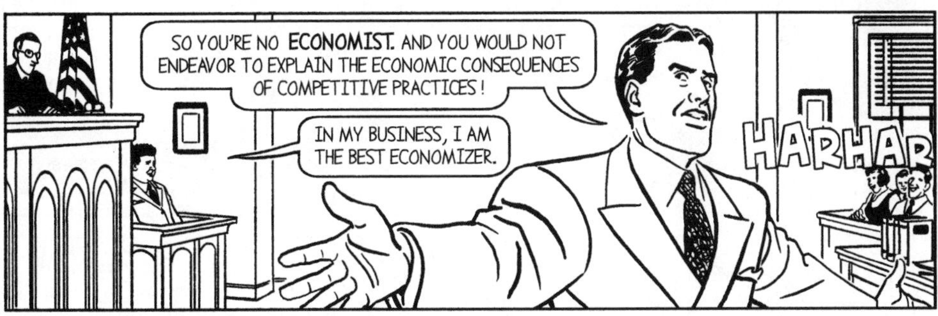

SO YOU'RE NO **ECONOMIST.** AND YOU WOULD NOT ENDEAVOR TO EXPLAIN THE ECONOMIC CONSEQUENCES OF COMPETITIVE PRACTICES!
IN MY BUSINESS, I AM THE BEST ECONOMIZER.
HARHAR

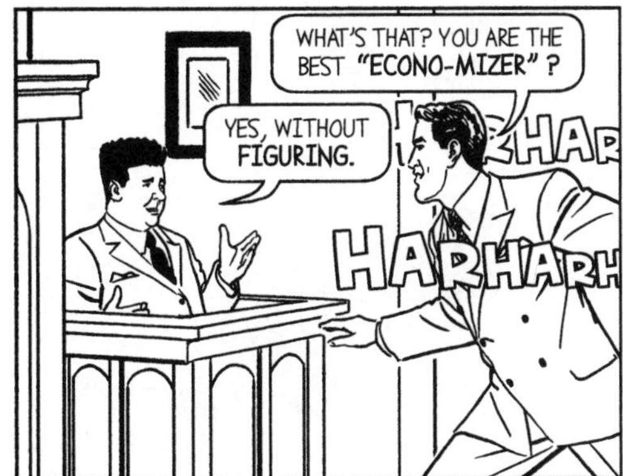

WHAT'S THAT? YOU ARE THE BEST **"ECONO-MIZER"**?
YES, WITHOUT **FIGURING.**
HARHARH

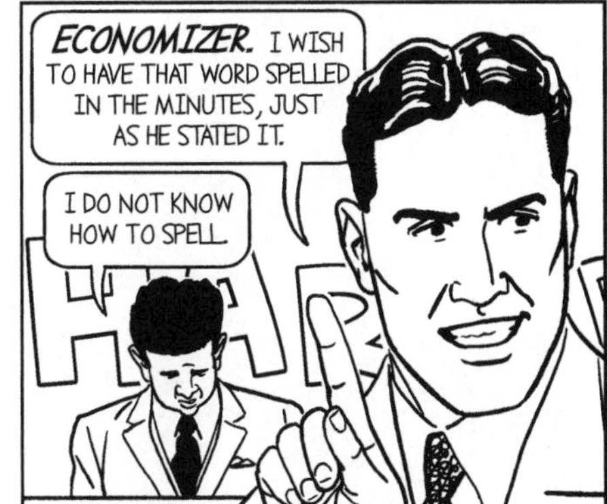

ECONOMIZER. I WISH TO HAVE THAT WORD SPELLED IN THE MINUTES, JUST AS HE STATED IT.
I DO NOT KNOW HOW TO SPELL.

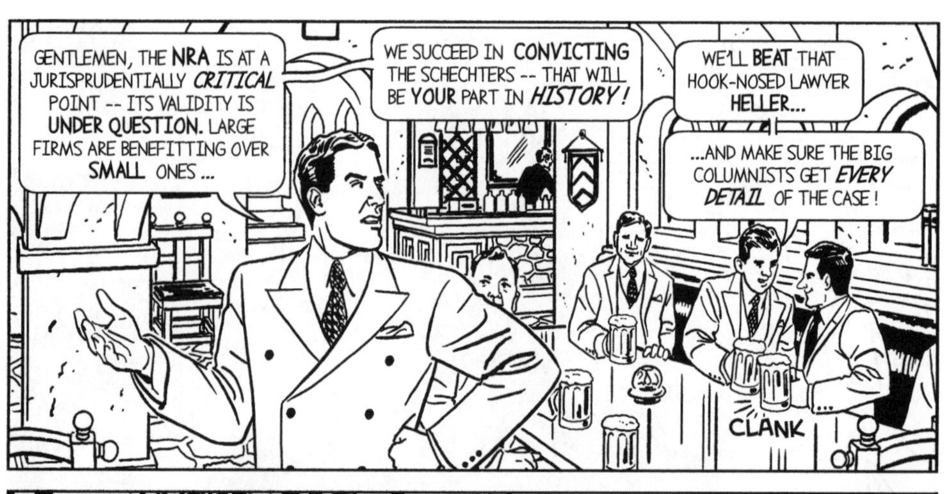
GENTLEMEN, THE NRA IS AT A JURISPRUDENTIALLY CRITICAL POINT -- ITS VALIDITY IS UNDER QUESTION. LARGE FIRMS ARE BENEFITTING OVER SMALL ONES ...
WE SUCCEED IN CONVICTING THE SCHECHTERS -- THAT WILL BE YOUR PART IN HISTORY!
WE'LL BEAT THAT HOOK-NOSED LAWYER HELLER...
...AND MAKE SURE THE BIG COLUMNISTS GET EVERY DETAIL OF THE CASE!
CLANK

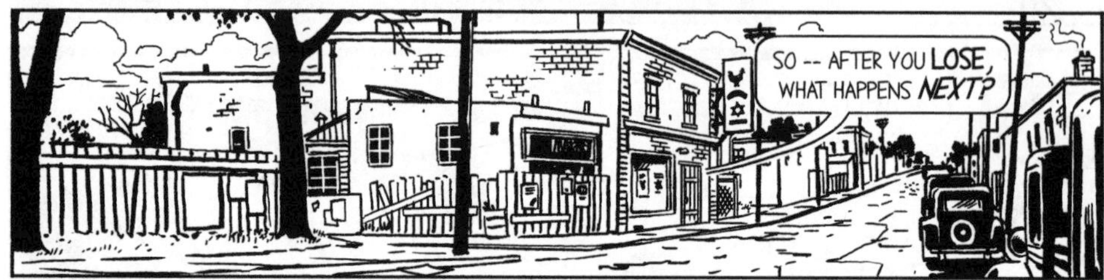
SO -- AFTER YOU LOSE, WHAT HAPPENS NEXT?

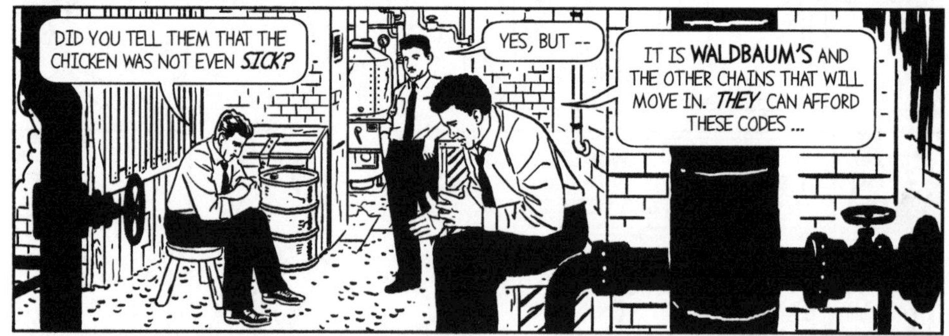
DID YOU TELL THEM THAT THE CHICKEN WAS NOT EVEN SICK?
YES, BUT --
IT IS WALDBAUM'S AND THE OTHER CHAINS THAT WILL MOVE IN. THEY CAN AFFORD THESE CODES ...

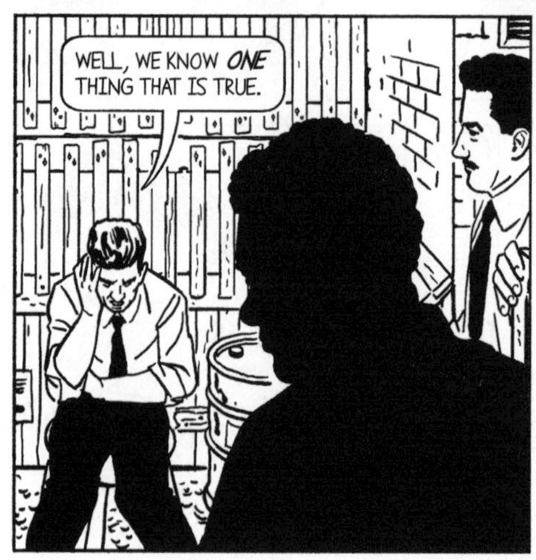
WELL, WE KNOW ONE THING THAT IS TRUE.

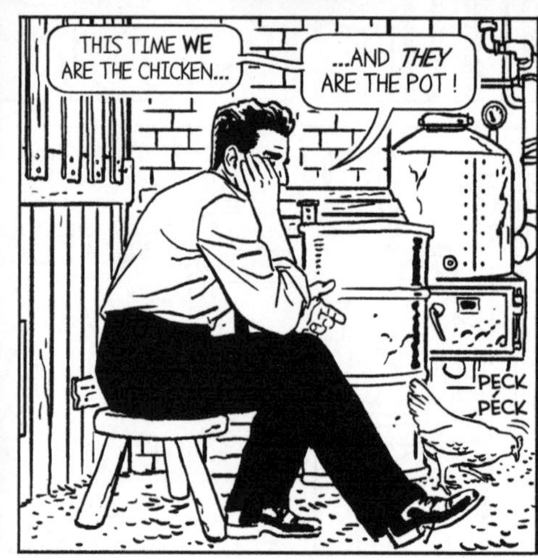
THIS TIME WE ARE THE CHICKEN...
...AND THEY ARE THE POT!
PECK
PECK

Heck, the New Dealers seemed to know how to play **any** game to their advantage ...

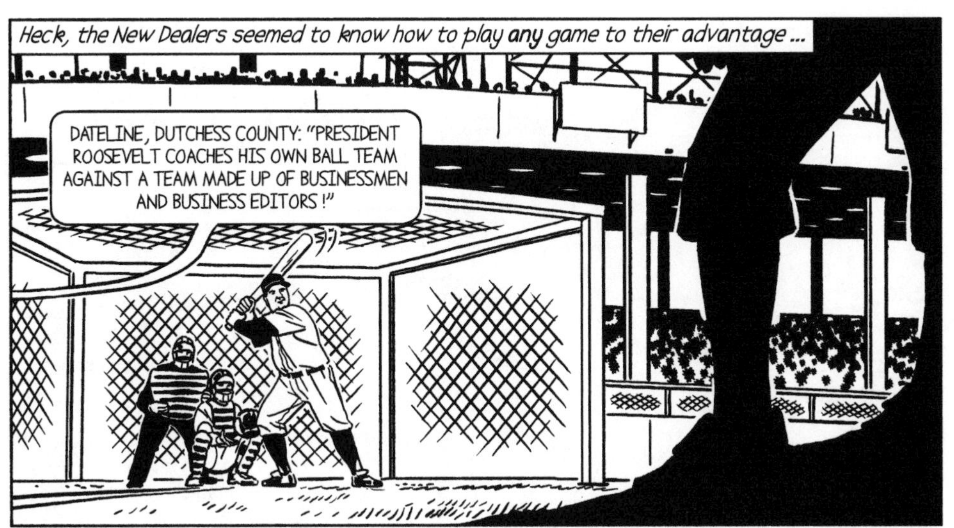

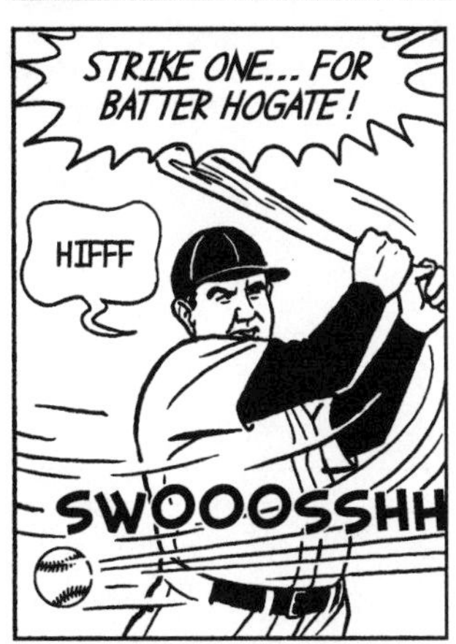

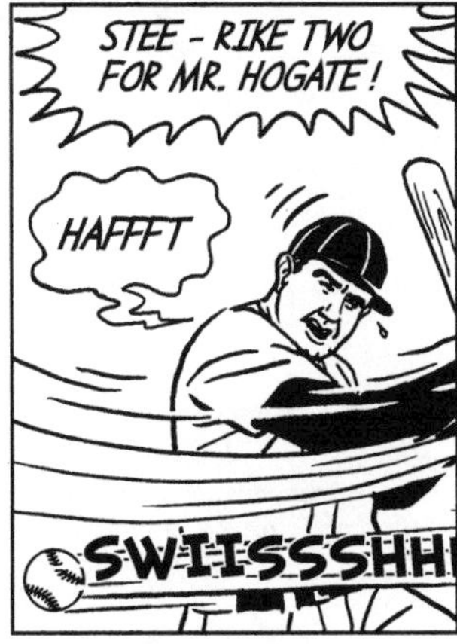

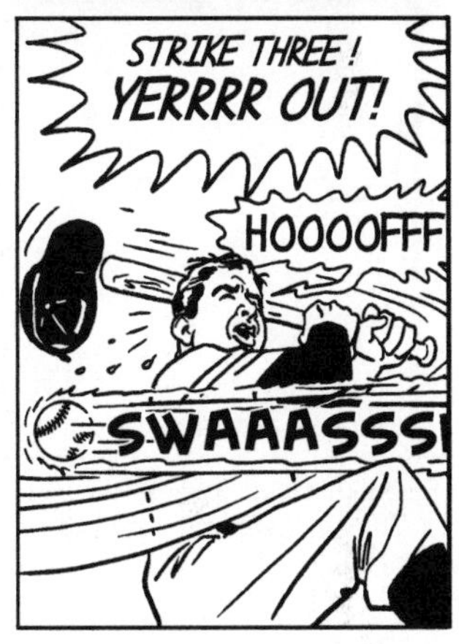

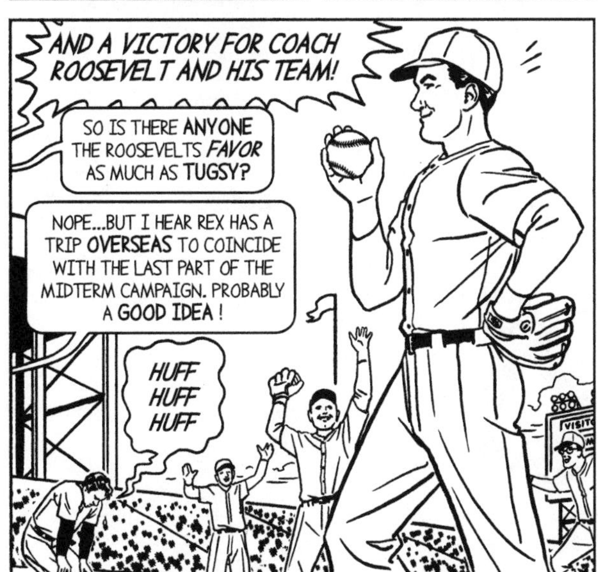

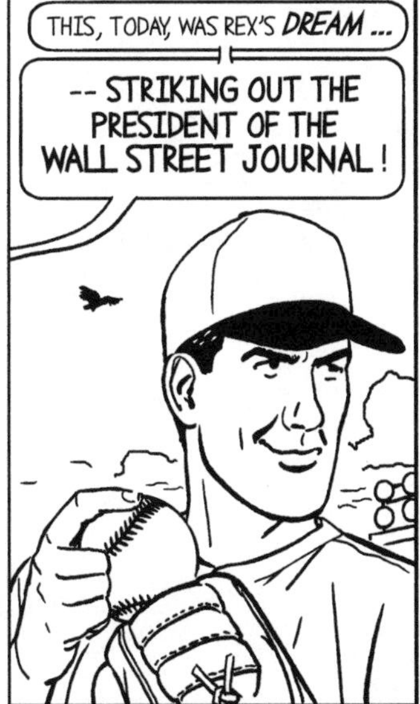

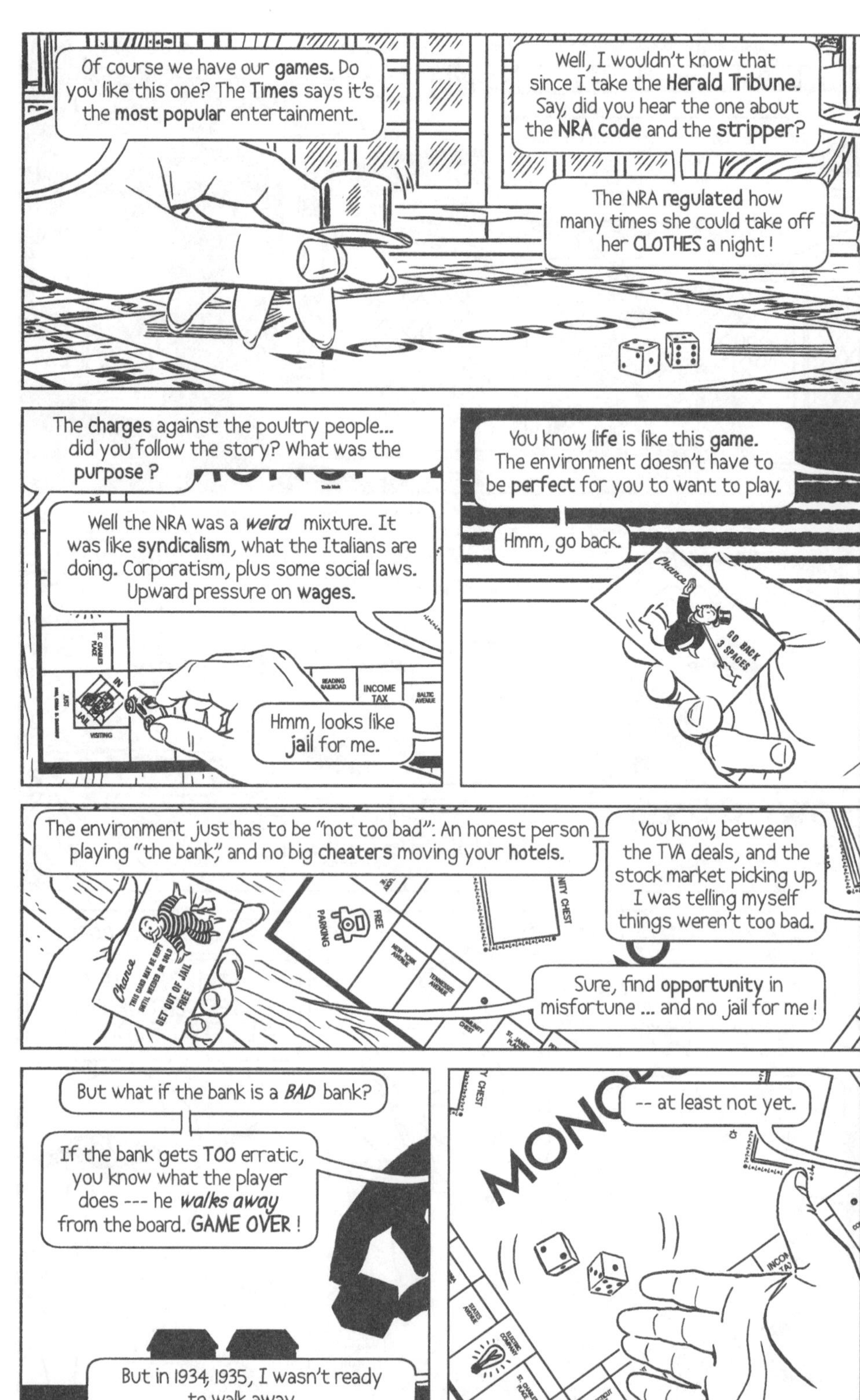
Of course we have our games. Do you like this one? The Times says it's the most popular entertainment.
Well, I wouldn't know that since I take the Herald Tribune. Say, did you hear the one about the NRA code and the stripper?
The NRA regulated how many times she could take off her CLOTHES a night!
MONOPOLY
The charges against the poultry people... did you follow the story? What was the purpose ?
Well the NRA was a weird mixture. It was like syndicalism, what the Italians are doing. Corporatism, plus some social laws. Upward pressure on wages.
Hmm, looks like jail for me.
You know, life is like this game. The environment doesn't have to be perfect for you to want to play.
Hmm, go back.
Chance
GO BACK 3 SPACES
The environment just has to be "not too bad": An honest person playing "the bank," and no big cheaters moving your hotels.
You know, between the TVA deals, and the stock market picking up, I was telling myself things weren't too bad.
Chance
GET OUT OF JAIL FREE
Sure, find opportunity in misfortune ... and no jail for me!
But what if the bank is a BAD bank?
If the bank gets TOO erratic, you know what the player does --- he walks away from the board. GAME OVER!
But in 1934, 1935, I wasn't ready to walk away ...
-- at least not yet.

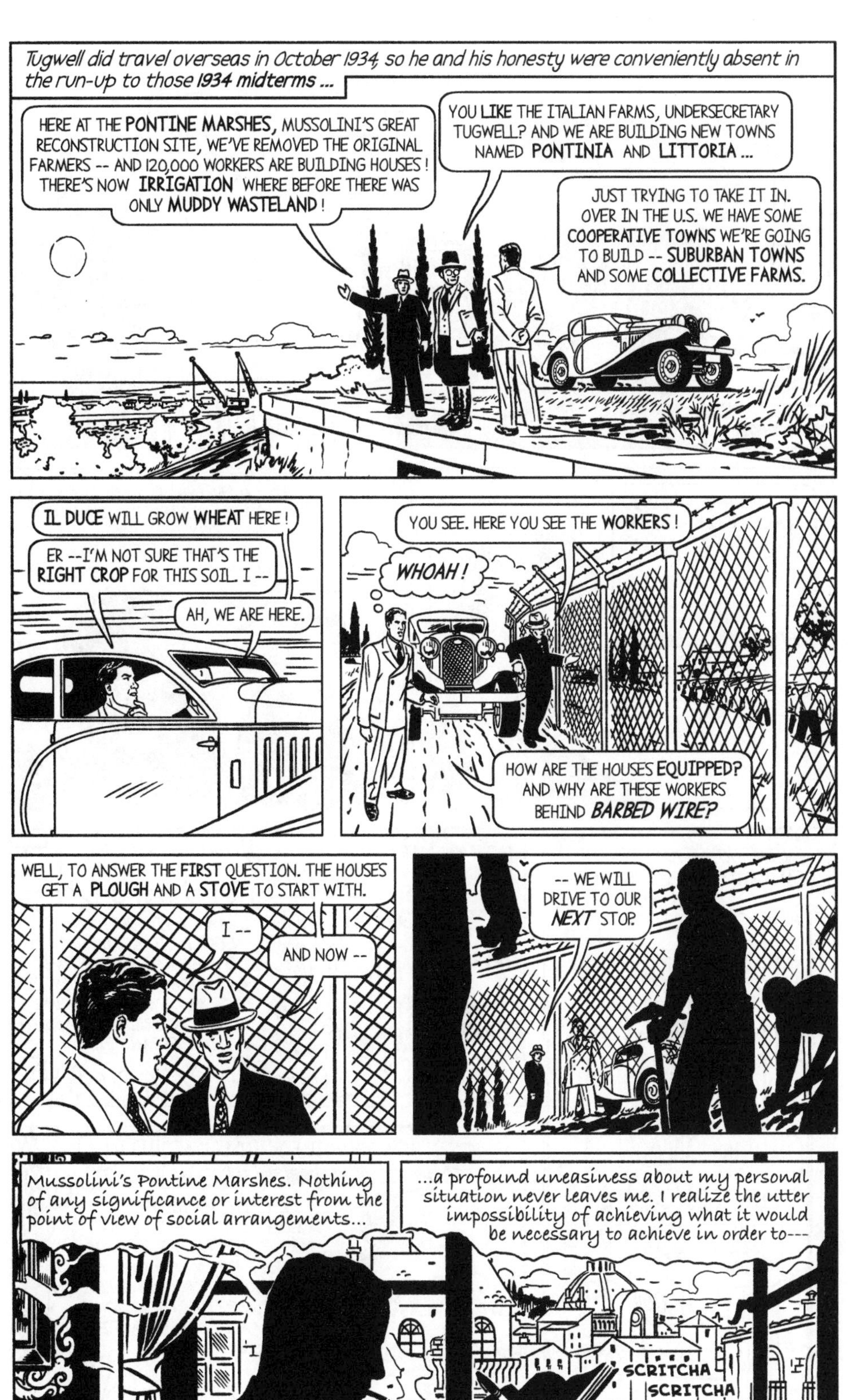
Tugwell did travel overseas in October 1934, so he and his honesty were conveniently absent in the run-up to those 1934 midterms ...
HERE AT THE PONTINE MARSHES, MUSSOLINI'S GREAT RECONSTRUCTION SITE, WE'VE REMOVED THE ORIGINAL FARMERS -- AND 120,000 WORKERS ARE BUILDING HOUSES! THERE'S NOW IRRIGATION WHERE BEFORE THERE WAS ONLY MUDDY WASTELAND!
YOU LIKE THE ITALIAN FARMS, UNDERSECRETARY TUGWELL? AND WE ARE BUILDING NEW TOWNS NAMED PONTINIA AND LITTORIA ...
JUST TRYING TO TAKE IT IN. OVER IN THE U.S. WE HAVE SOME COOPERATIVE TOWNS WE'RE GOING TO BUILD -- SUBURBAN TOWNS AND SOME COLLECTIVE FARMS.
IL DUCE WILL GROW WHEAT HERE!
ER --I'M NOT SURE THAT'S THE RIGHT CROP FOR THIS SOIL. I --
AH, WE ARE HERE.
WHOAH!
YOU SEE. HERE YOU SEE THE WORKERS!
HOW ARE THE HOUSES EQUIPPED? AND WHY ARE THESE WORKERS BEHIND BARBED WIRE?
WELL, TO ANSWER THE FIRST QUESTION. THE HOUSES GET A PLOUGH AND A STOVE TO START WITH.
I --
AND NOW --
-- WE WILL DRIVE TO OUR NEXT STOP.
Mussolini's Pontine Marshes. Nothing of any significance or interest from the point of view of social arrangements...
...a profound uneasiness about my personal situation never leaves me. I realize the utter impossibility of achieving what it would be necessary to achieve in order to---
SCRITCHA
SCRITCHA

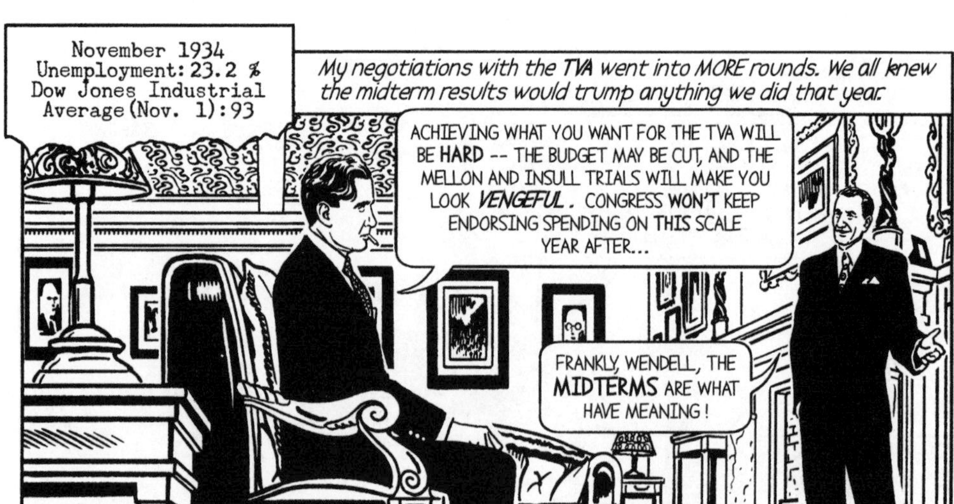
November 1934
Unemployment: 23.2 %
Dow Jones Industrial Average (Nov. 1): 93
My negotiations with the TVA went into MORE rounds. We all knew the midterm results would trump anything we did that year.
ACHIEVING WHAT YOU WANT FOR THE TVA WILL BE HARD -- THE BUDGET MAY BE CUT, AND THE MELLON AND INSULL TRIALS WILL MAKE YOU LOOK VENGEFUL. CONGRESS WON'T KEEP ENDORSING SPENDING ON THIS SCALE YEAR AFTER...
FRANKLY, WENDELL, THE MIDTERMS ARE WHAT HAVE MEANING!

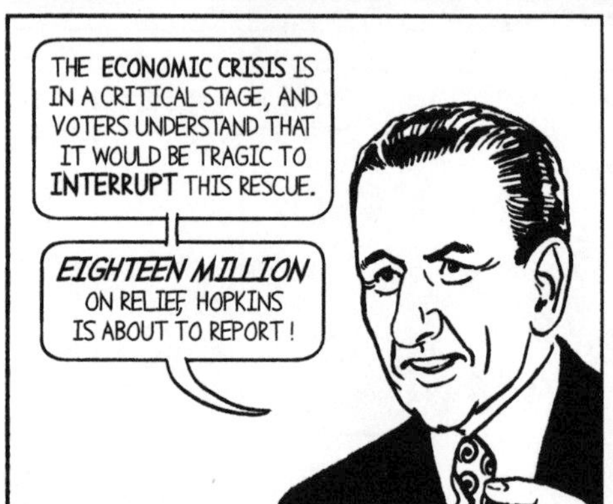
THE ECONOMIC CRISIS IS IN A CRITICAL STAGE, AND VOTERS UNDERSTAND THAT IT WOULD BE TRAGIC TO INTERRUPT THIS RESCUE.
EIGHTEEN MILLION ON RELIEF, HOPKINS IS ABOUT TO REPORT!

I KNOW YOU'RE WONDERING IF THOSE AT THE ADMINISTRATION HAVE ALREADY DISCOUNTED FOR THEM. WE KNOW HOW THE COURTS WILL DECIDE. MELLON? OF COURSE PITTSBURGH WILL BE LOYAL. INSULL? DITTO FOR CHICAGO ...

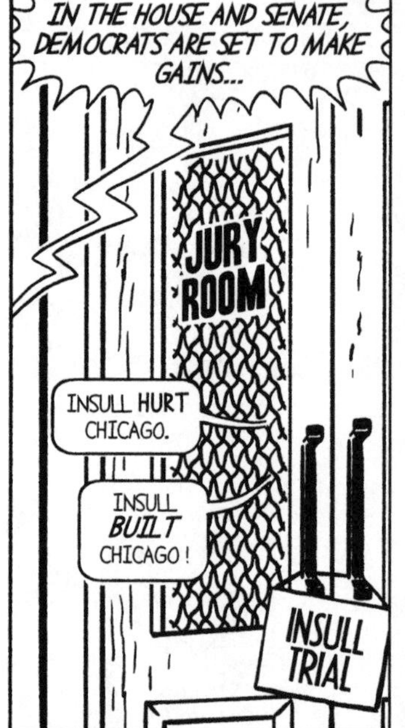
IN THE HOUSE AND SENATE, DEMOCRATS ARE SET TO MAKE GAINS...
JURY ROOM
INSULL HURT CHICAGO.
INSULL BUILT CHICAGO!
INSULL TRIAL

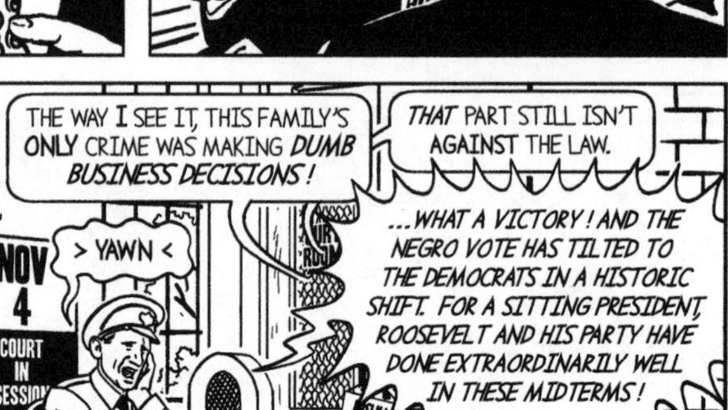
THE WAY I SEE IT, THIS FAMILY'S ONLY CRIME WAS MAKING DUMB BUSINESS DECISIONS!
THAT PART STILL ISN'T AGAINST THE LAW.
NOV 4
COURT IN SESSION
> YAWN <
...WHAT A VICTORY! AND THE NEGRO VOTE HAS TILTED TO THE DEMOCRATS IN A HISTORIC SHIFT. FOR A SITTING PRESIDENT, ROOSEVELT AND HIS PARTY HAVE DONE EXTRAORDINARILY WELL IN THESE MIDTERMS!
INSULL TRIAL

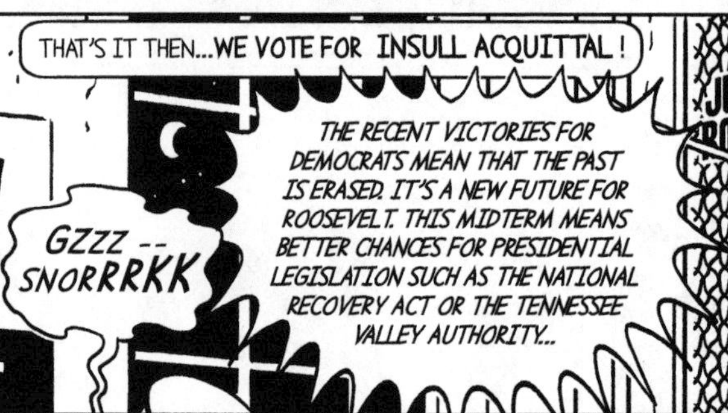
THAT'S IT THEN...WE VOTE FOR INSULL ACQUITTAL!
THE RECENT VICTORIES FOR DEMOCRATS MEAN THAT THE PAST IS ERASED. IT'S A NEW FUTURE FOR ROOSEVELT. THIS MIDTERM MEANS BETTER CHANCES FOR PRESIDENTIAL LEGISLATION SUCH AS THE NATIONAL RECOVERY ACT OR THE TENNESSEE VALLEY AUTHORITY...
GZZZ -- SNORRRKK

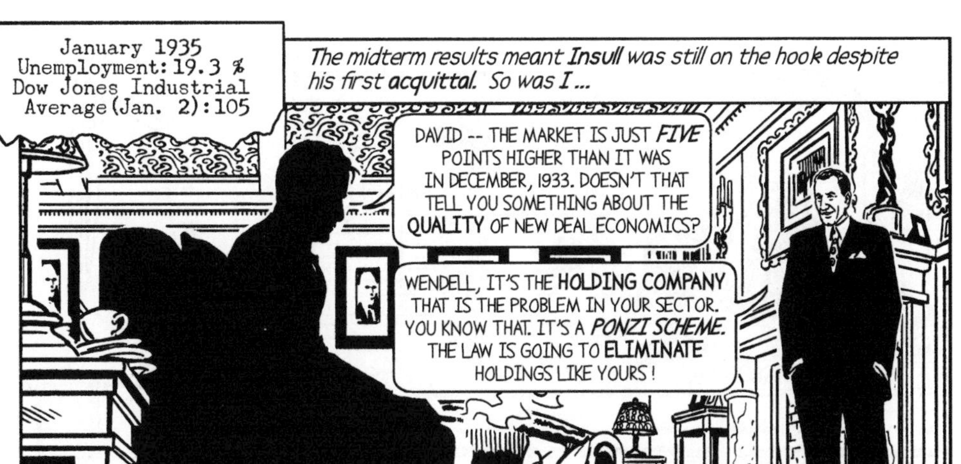
January 1935
Unemployment: 19.3 %
Dow Jones Industrial Average (Jan. 2): 105
The midterm results meant **Insull** was still on the hook despite his first **acquittal**. So was **I**...
DAVID -- THE MARKET IS JUST ***FIVE*** POINTS HIGHER THAN IT WAS IN DECEMBER, 1933. DOESN'T THAT TELL YOU SOMETHING ABOUT THE **QUALITY** OF NEW DEAL ECONOMICS?
WENDELL, IT'S THE **HOLDING COMPANY** THAT IS THE PROBLEM IN YOUR SECTOR. YOU KNOW THAT. IT'S A ***PONZI SCHEME.*** THE LAW IS GOING TO **ELIMINATE** HOLDINGS LIKE YOURS!

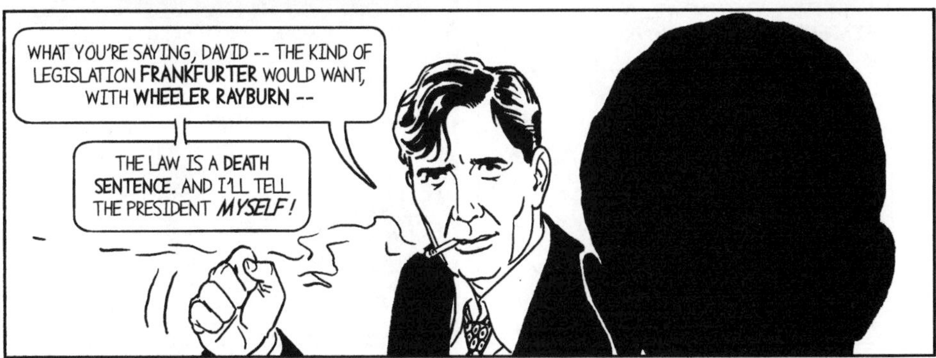
WHAT YOU'RE SAYING, DAVID -- THE KIND OF LEGISLATION **FRANKFURTER** WOULD WANT, WITH **WHEELER RAYBURN** --
THE LAW IS A **DEATH SENTENCE**. AND I'LL TELL THE PRESIDENT ***MYSELF!***

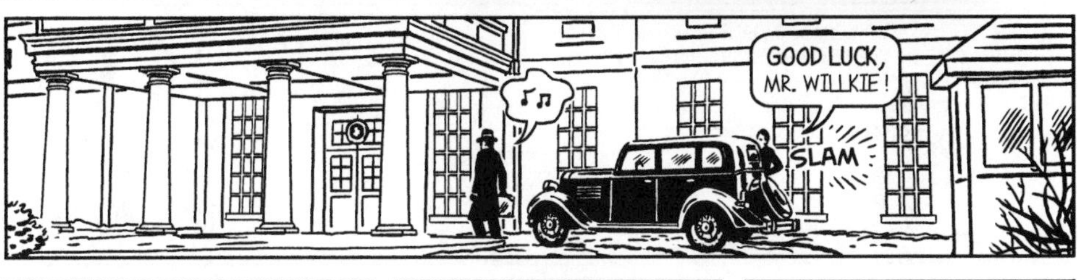
GOOD LUCK, MR. WILLKIE!
SLAM

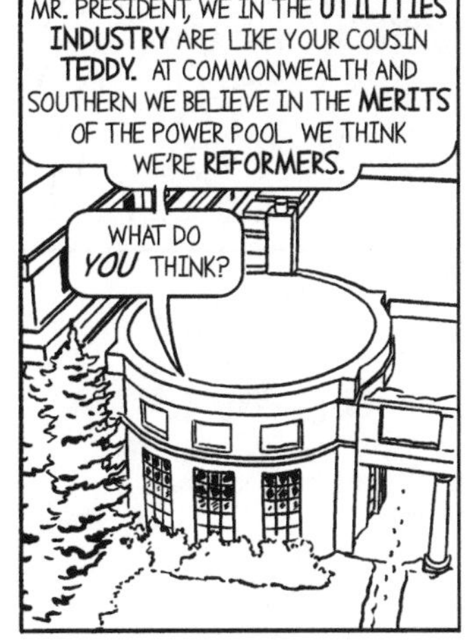
MR. PRESIDENT, WE IN THE **UTILITIES INDUSTRY** ARE LIKE YOUR COUSIN **TEDDY.** AT COMMONWEALTH AND SOUTHERN WE BELIEVE IN THE **MERITS** OF THE POWER POOL. WE THINK WE'RE **REFORMERS.**
WHAT DO ***YOU*** THINK?

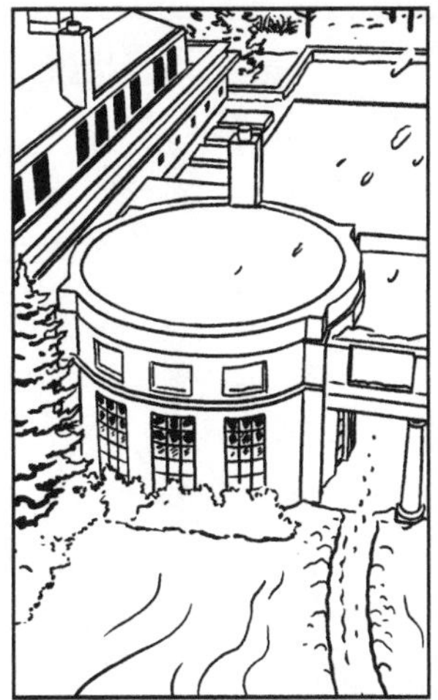

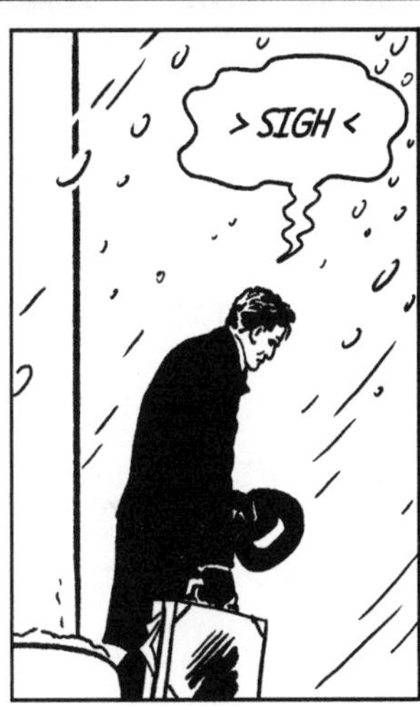
> SIGH <

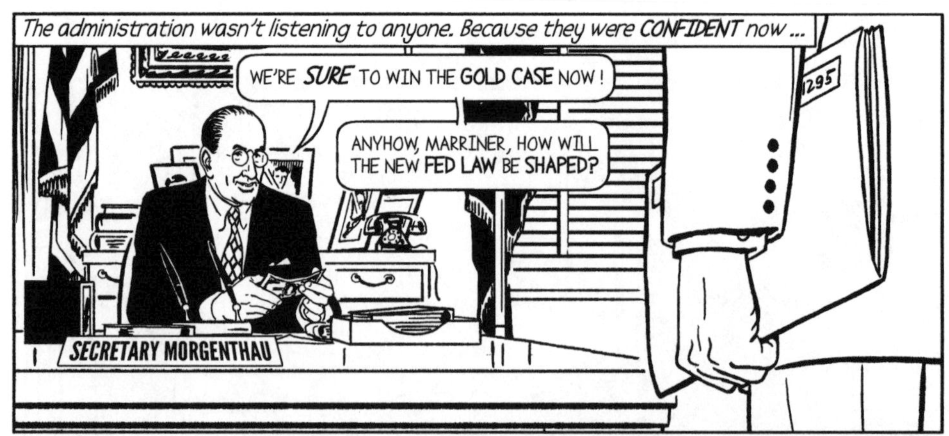
The administration wasn't listening to anyone. Because they were CONFIDENT now ...
WE'RE SURE TO WIN THE GOLD CASE NOW!
ANYHOW, MARRINER, HOW WILL THE NEW FED LAW BE SHAPED?
1295
SECRETARY MORGENTHAU

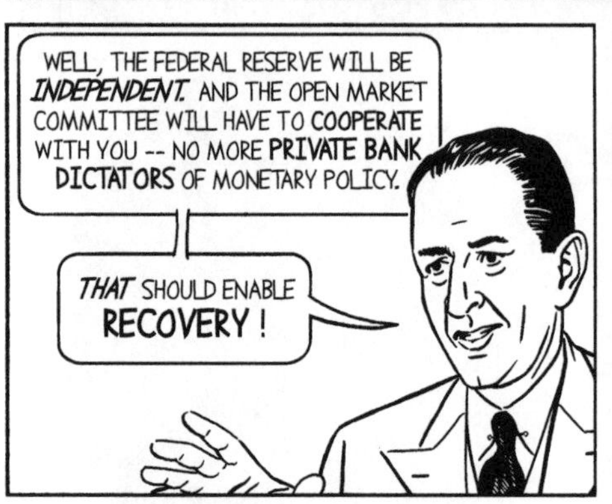
WELL, THE FEDERAL RESERVE WILL BE INDEPENDENT. AND THE OPEN MARKET COMMITTEE WILL HAVE TO COOPERATE WITH YOU -- NO MORE PRIVATE BANK DICTATORS OF MONETARY POLICY.
THAT SHOULD ENABLE RECOVERY!

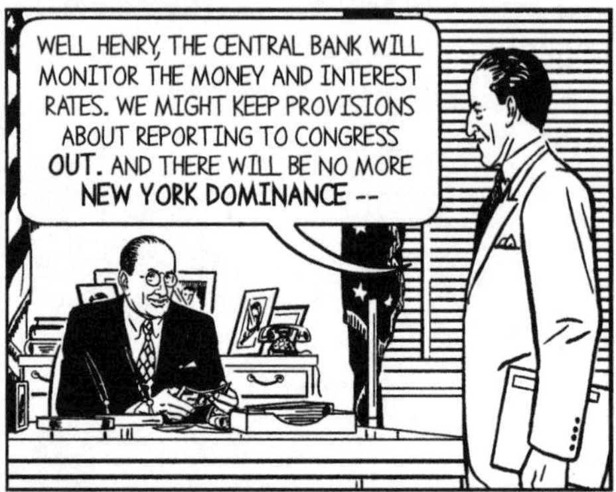
WELL HENRY, THE CENTRAL BANK WILL MONITOR THE MONEY AND INTEREST RATES. WE MIGHT KEEP PROVISIONS ABOUT REPORTING TO CONGRESS OUT. AND THERE WILL BE NO MORE NEW YORK DOMINANCE --

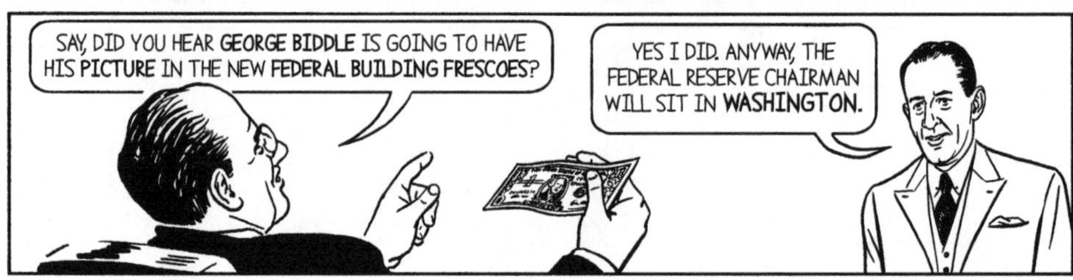
SAY, DID YOU HEAR GEORGE BIDDLE IS GOING TO HAVE HIS PICTURE IN THE NEW FEDERAL BUILDING FRESCOES?
YES I DID. ANYWAY, THE FEDERAL RESERVE CHAIRMAN WILL SIT IN WASHINGTON.

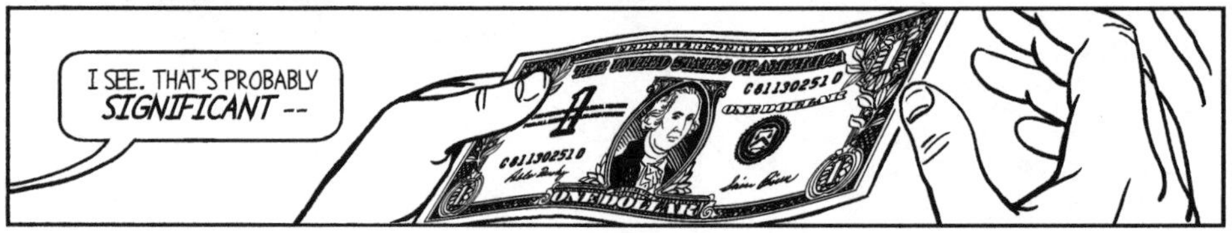
I SEE. THAT'S PROBABLY SIGNIFICANT --
THE UNITED STATES OF AMERICA
C 61130251 D
ONE DOLLAR

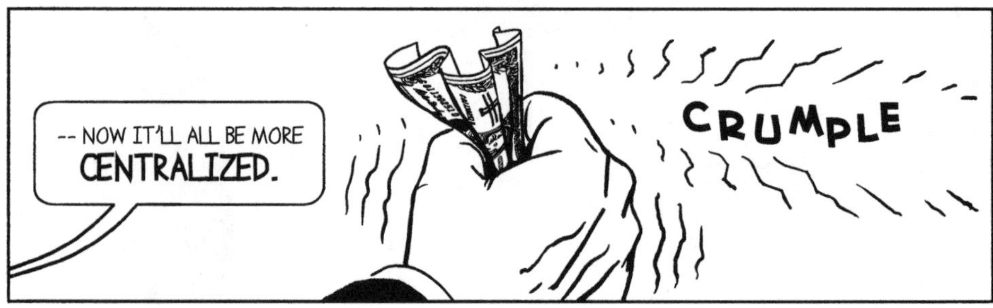
-- NOW IT'LL ALL BE MORE CENTRALIZED.
CRUMPLE

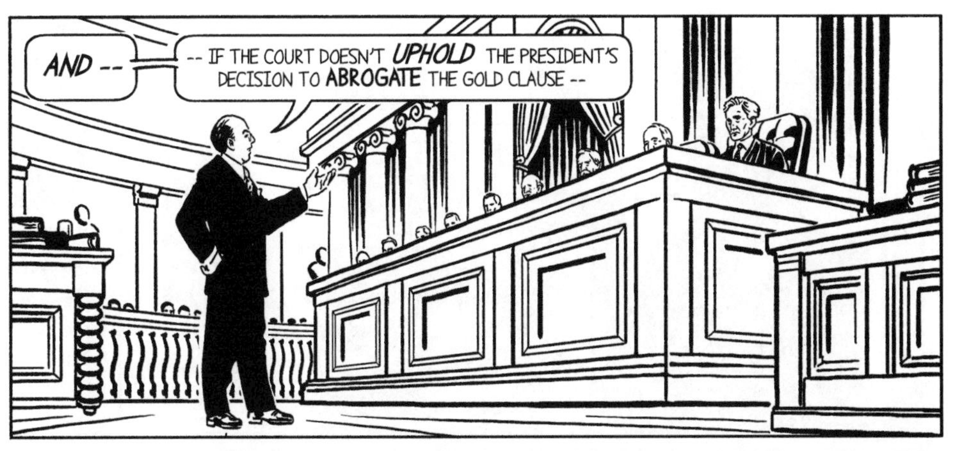
AND --
-- IF THE COURT DOESN'T UPHOLD THE PRESIDENT'S DECISION TO ABROGATE THE GOLD CLAUSE --

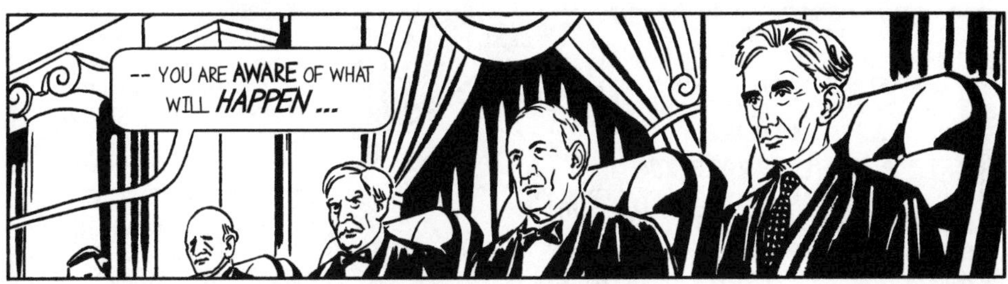
-- YOU ARE AWARE OF WHAT WILL HAPPEN ...

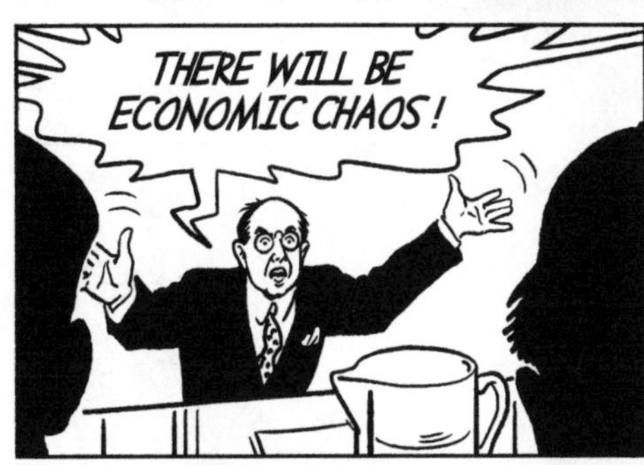
THERE WILL BE ECONOMIC CHAOS !

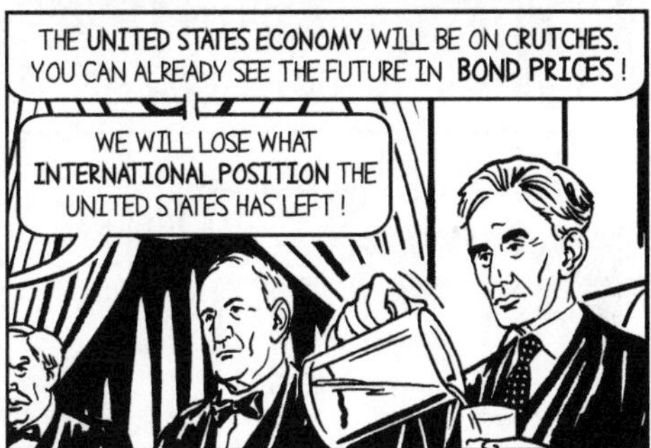
THE UNITED STATES ECONOMY WILL BE ON CRUTCHES. YOU CAN ALREADY SEE THE FUTURE IN BOND PRICES !
WE WILL LOSE WHAT INTERNATIONAL POSITION THE UNITED STATES HAS LEFT !

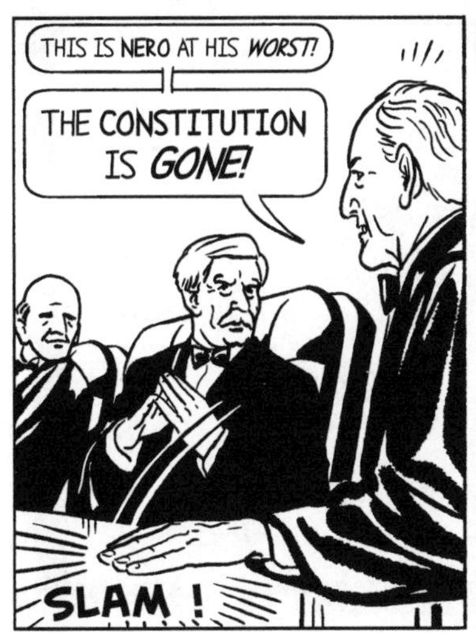
THIS IS NERO AT HIS WORST!
THE CONSTITUTION IS GONE!
SLAM !

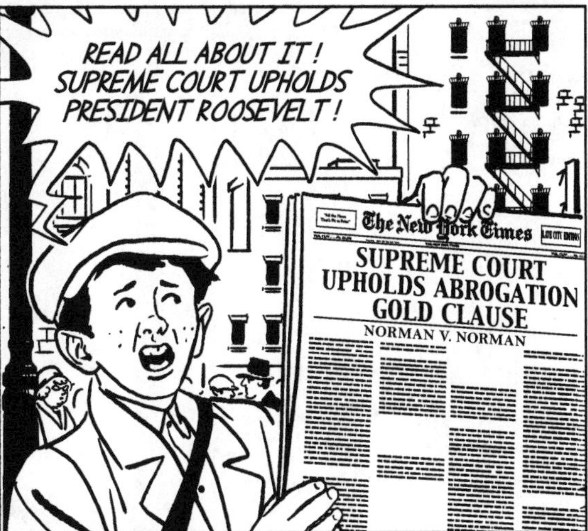
READ ALL ABOUT IT ! SUPREME COURT UPHOLDS PRESIDENT ROOSEVELT !
The New York Times
SUPREME COURT UPHOLDS ABROGATION GOLD CLAUSE
NORMAN V. NORMAN

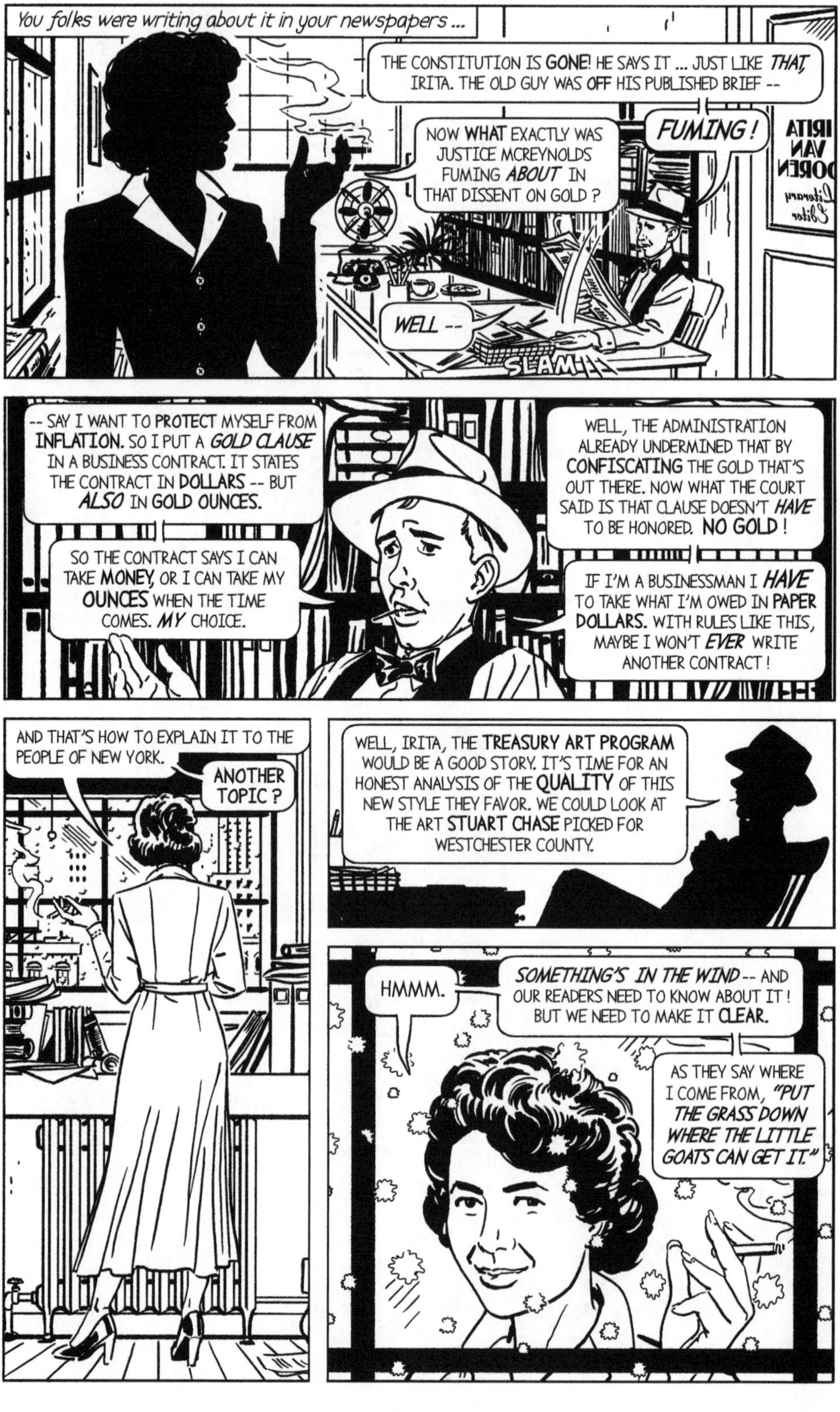

You folks were writing about it in your newspapers ...

THE CONSTITUTION IS **GONE**! HE SAYS IT ... JUST LIKE *THAT*, IRITA. THE OLD GUY WAS **OFF** HIS PUBLISHED BRIEF --

FUMING!

NOW **WHAT** EXACTLY WAS JUSTICE MCREYNOLDS FUMING ***ABOUT*** IN THAT DISSENT ON GOLD ?

WELL --

SLAM!!

-- SAY I WANT TO **PROTECT** MYSELF FROM **INFLATION.** SO I PUT A ***GOLD CLAUSE*** IN A BUSINESS CONTRACT. IT STATES THE CONTRACT IN **DOLLARS** -- BUT ***ALSO*** IN **GOLD OUNCES.**

SO THE CONTRACT SAYS I CAN TAKE **MONEY,** OR I CAN TAKE MY **OUNCES** WHEN THE TIME COMES. ***MY*** CHOICE.

WELL, THE ADMINISTRATION ALREADY UNDERMINED THAT BY **CONFISCATING** THE GOLD THAT'S OUT THERE. NOW WHAT THE COURT SAID IS THAT CLAUSE DOESN'T ***HAVE*** TO BE HONORED. **NO GOLD** !

IF I'M A BUSINESSMAN I ***HAVE*** TO TAKE WHAT I'M OWED IN **PAPER DOLLARS.** WITH RULES LIKE THIS, MAYBE I WON'T ***EVER*** WRITE ANOTHER CONTRACT !

AND THAT'S HOW TO EXPLAIN IT TO THE PEOPLE OF NEW YORK.

ANOTHER TOPIC ?

WELL, IRITA, THE **TREASURY ART PROGRAM** WOULD BE A GOOD STORY. IT'S TIME FOR AN HONEST ANALYSIS OF THE **QUALITY** OF THIS NEW STYLE THEY FAVOR. WE COULD LOOK AT THE ART **STUART CHASE** PICKED FOR WESTCHESTER COUNTY.

HMMM.

SOMETHING'S IN THE WIND -- AND OUR READERS NEED TO KNOW ABOUT IT ! BUT WE NEED TO MAKE IT **CLEAR.**

AS THEY SAY WHERE I COME FROM, ***"PUT THE GRASS DOWN WHERE THE LITTLE GOATS CAN GET IT."***

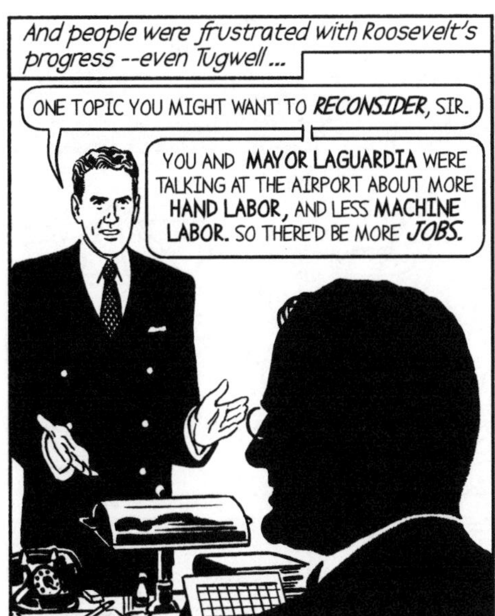
And people were frustrated with Roosevelt's progress --even Tugwell ...
ONE TOPIC YOU MIGHT WANT TO RECONSIDER, SIR.
YOU AND MAYOR LAGUARDIA WERE TALKING AT THE AIRPORT ABOUT MORE HAND LABOR, AND LESS MACHINE LABOR. SO THERE'D BE MORE JOBS.

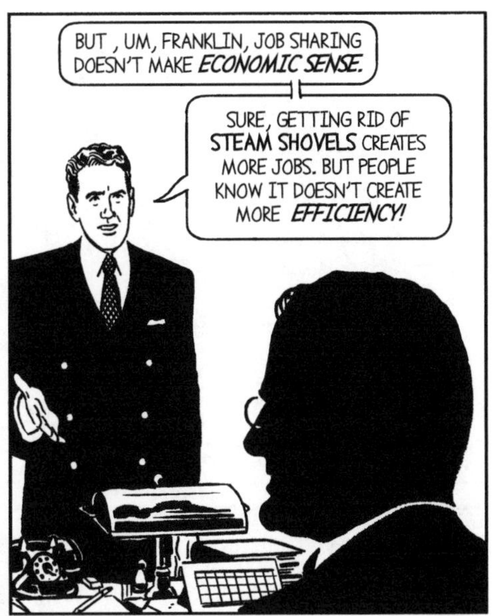
BUT , UM, FRANKLIN, JOB SHARING DOESN'T MAKE ECONOMIC SENSE.
SURE, GETTING RID OF STEAM SHOVELS CREATES MORE JOBS. BUT PEOPLE KNOW IT DOESN'T CREATE MORE EFFICIENCY!

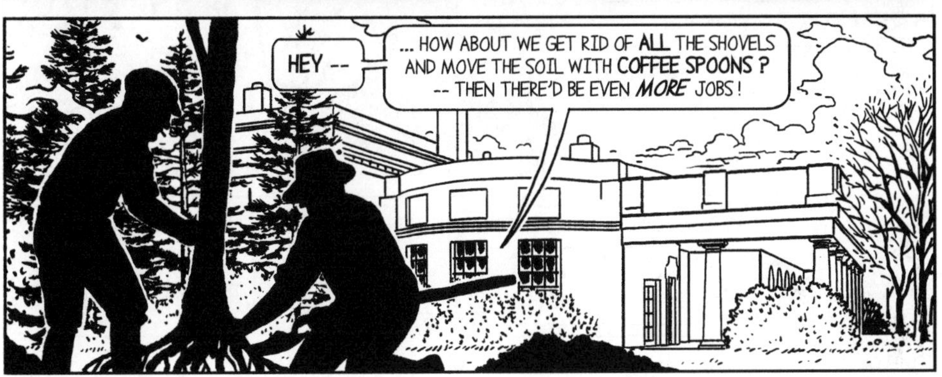
HEY --
... HOW ABOUT WE GET RID OF ALL THE SHOVELS AND MOVE THE SOIL WITH COFFEE SPOONS ? -- THEN THERE'D BE EVEN MORE JOBS !

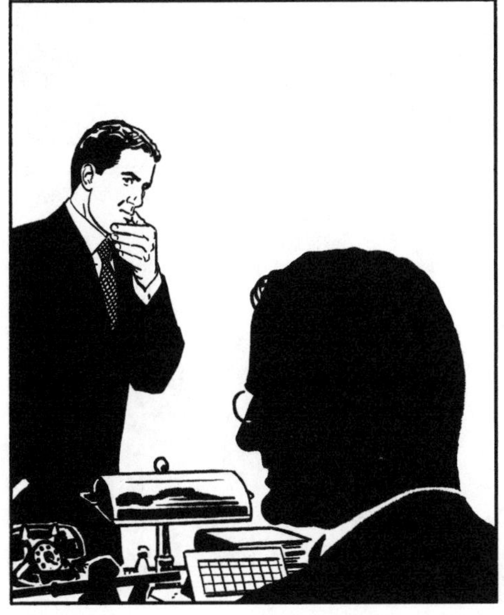

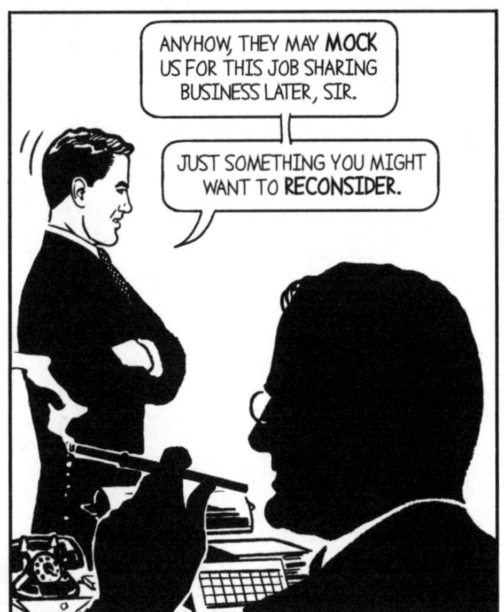
ANYHOW, THEY MAY MOCK US FOR THIS JOB SHARING BUSINESS LATER, SIR.
JUST SOMETHING YOU MIGHT WANT TO RECONSIDER.

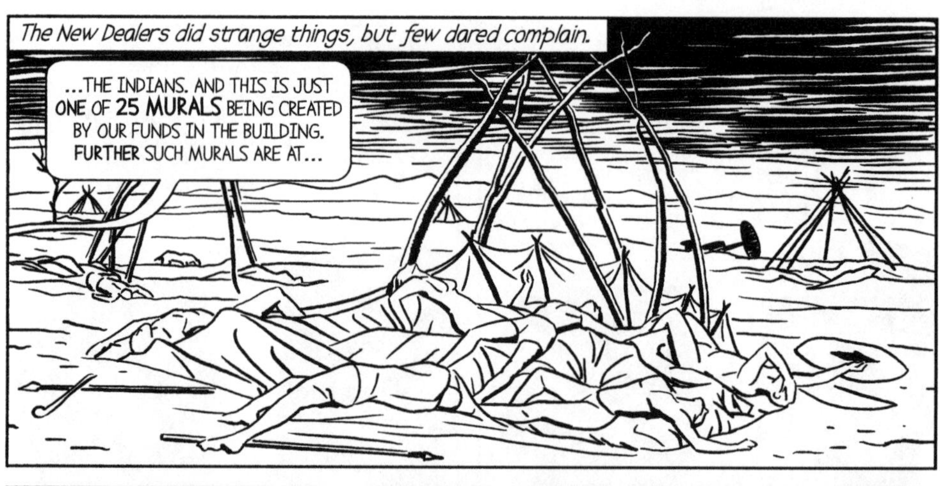
The New Dealers did strange things, but few dared complain.
...THE INDIANS. AND THIS IS JUST ONE OF 25 MURALS BEING CREATED BY OUR FUNDS IN THE BUILDING. FURTHER SUCH MURALS ARE AT...

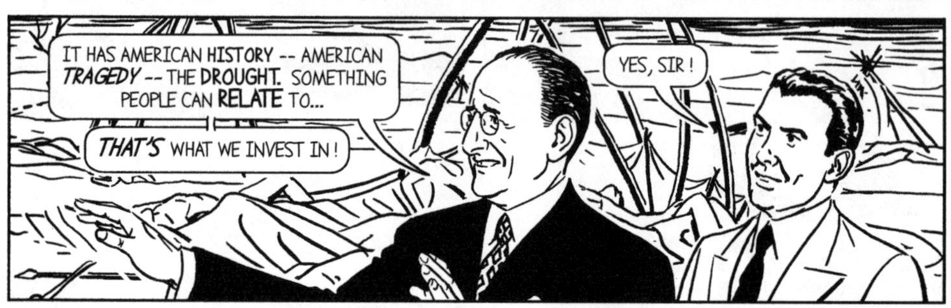
IT HAS AMERICAN HISTORY -- AMERICAN TRAGEDY -- THE DROUGHT. SOMETHING PEOPLE CAN RELATE TO...
THAT'S WHAT WE INVEST IN!
YES, SIR!

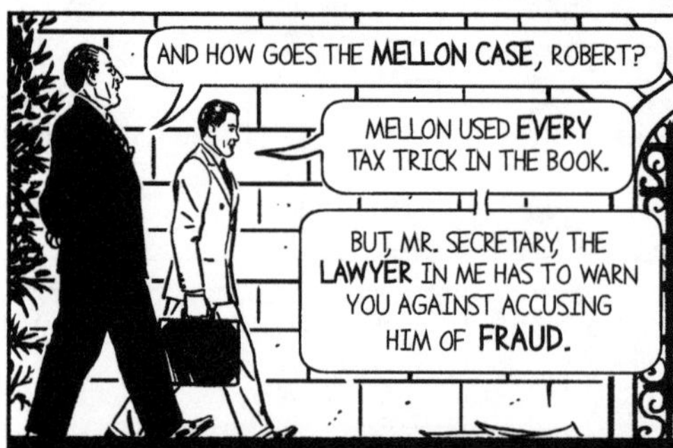
AND HOW GOES THE MELLON CASE, ROBERT?
MELLON USED EVERY TAX TRICK IN THE BOOK.
BUT, MR. SECRETARY, THE LAWYER IN ME HAS TO WARN YOU AGAINST ACCUSING HIM OF FRAUD.

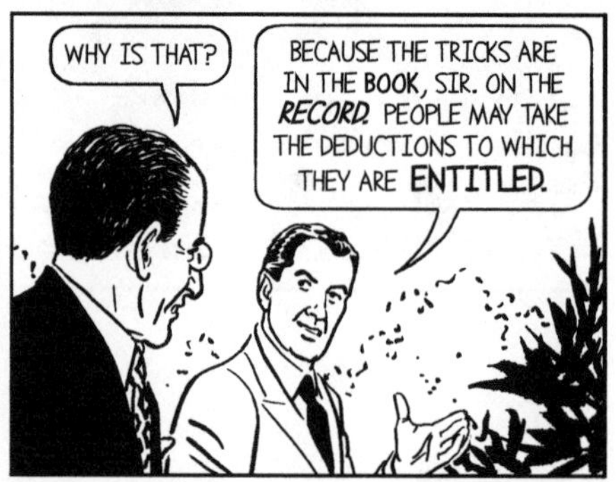
WHY IS THAT?
BECAUSE THE TRICKS ARE IN THE BOOK, SIR. ON THE RECORD. PEOPLE MAY TAKE THE DEDUCTIONS TO WHICH THEY ARE ENTITLED.

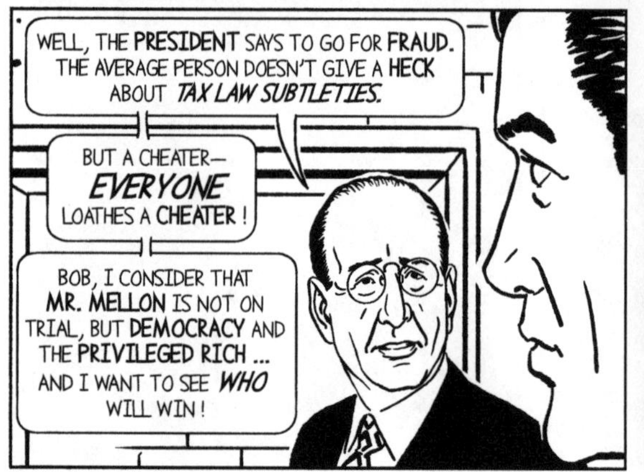
WELL, THE PRESIDENT SAYS TO GO FOR FRAUD. THE AVERAGE PERSON DOESN'T GIVE A HECK ABOUT TAX LAW SUBTLETIES.
BUT A CHEATER— EVERYONE LOATHES A CHEATER!
BOB, I CONSIDER THAT MR. MELLON IS NOT ON TRIAL, BUT DEMOCRACY AND THE PRIVILEGED RICH ... AND I WANT TO SEE WHO WILL WIN!

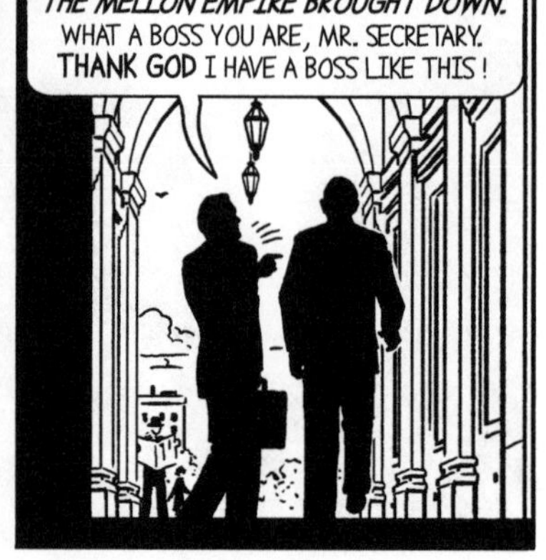
THE MELLON EMPIRE BROUGHT DOWN. WHAT A BOSS YOU ARE, MR. SECRETARY. THANK GOD I HAVE A BOSS LIKE THIS!

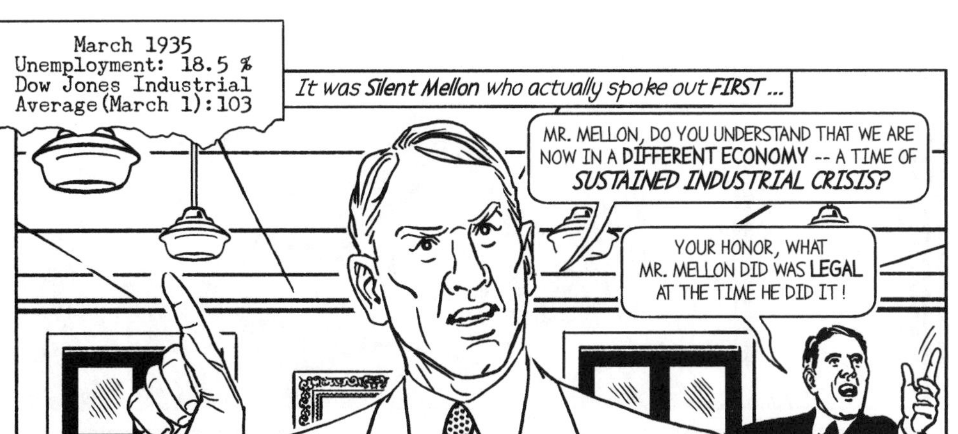
March 1935
Unemployment: 18.5 %
Dow Jones Industrial
Average (March 1): 103
It was Silent Mellon who actually spoke out FIRST ...
MR. MELLON, DO YOU UNDERSTAND THAT WE ARE NOW IN A DIFFERENT ECONOMY -- A TIME OF SUSTAINED INDUSTRIAL CRISIS?
YOUR HONOR, WHAT MR. MELLON DID WAS LEGAL AT THE TIME HE DID IT !

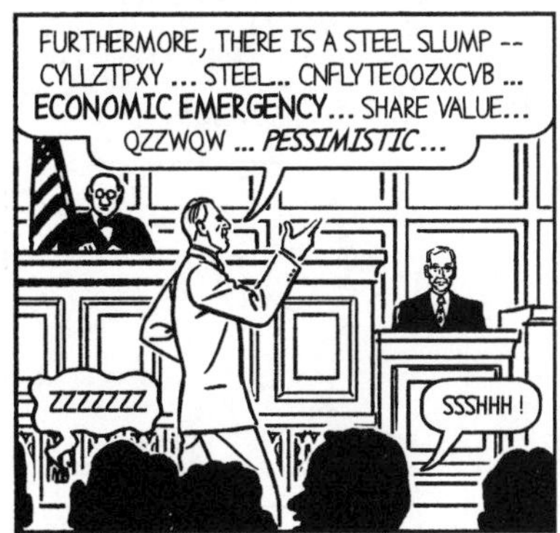
FURTHERMORE, THERE IS A STEEL SLUMP -- CYLLZTPXY ... STEEL... CNFLYTEOOZXCVB ... ECONOMIC EMERGENCY... SHARE VALUE... QZZWQW ... PESSIMISTIC ...
ZZZZZZZ
SSSHHH !

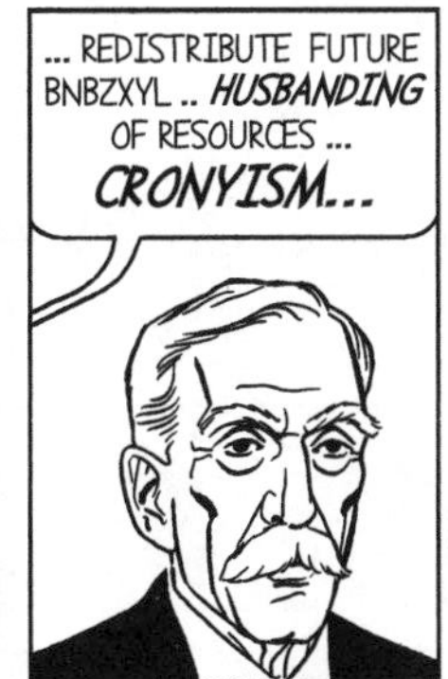
... REDISTRIBUTE FUTURE BNBZXYL .. HUSBANDING OF RESOURCES ... CRONYISM...

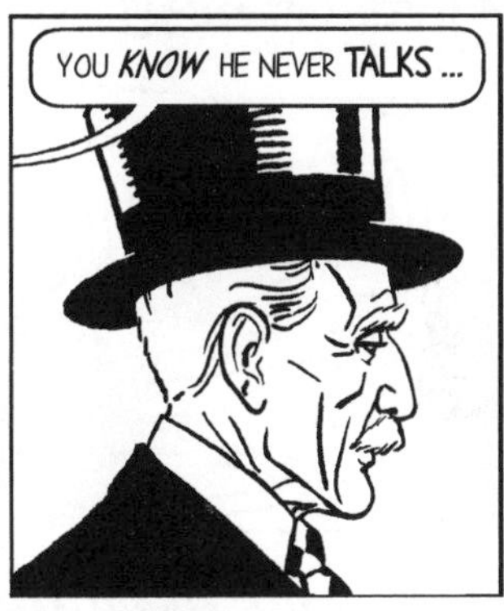
YOU KNOW HE NEVER TALKS ...

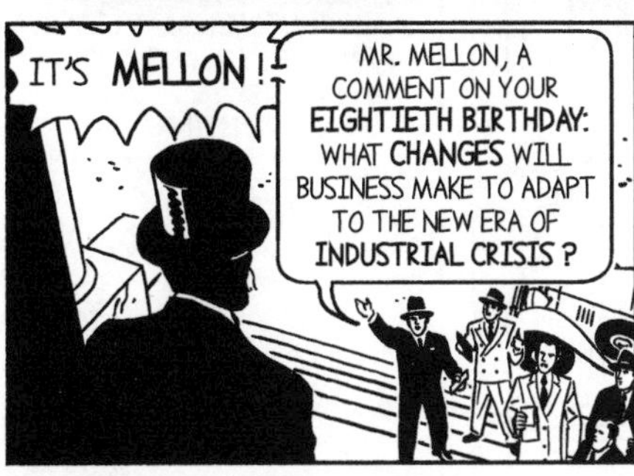
IT'S MELLON !
MR. MELLON, A COMMENT ON YOUR EIGHTIETH BIRTHDAY: WHAT CHANGES WILL BUSINESS MAKE TO ADAPT TO THE NEW ERA OF INDUSTRIAL CRISIS ?

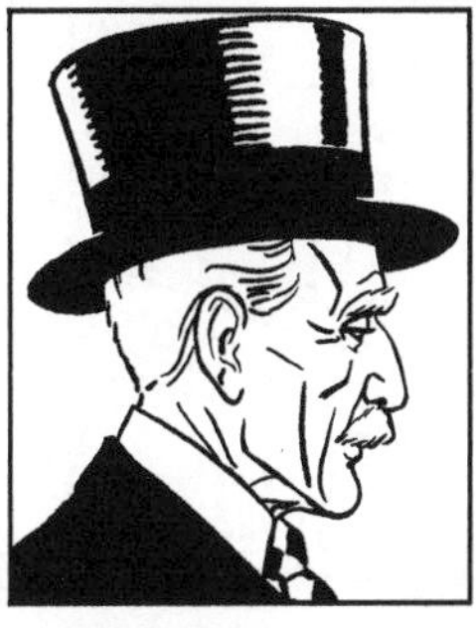

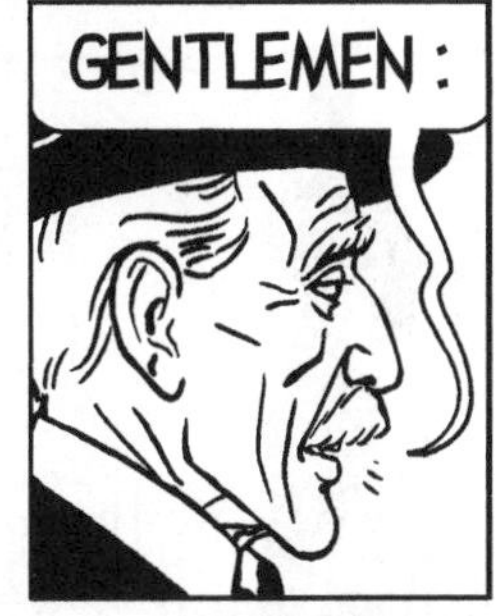
GENTLEMEN :

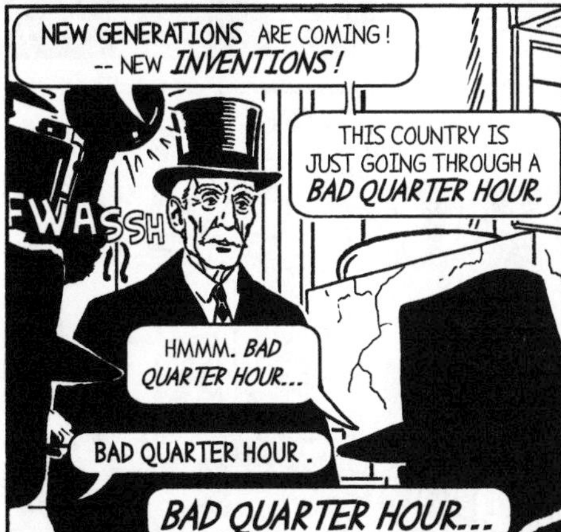
NEW GENERATIONS ARE COMING ! -- NEW INVENTIONS !
THIS COUNTRY IS JUST GOING THROUGH A BAD QUARTER HOUR.
FWASSH
HMMM. BAD QUARTER HOUR...
BAD QUARTER HOUR .
BAD QUARTER HOUR...

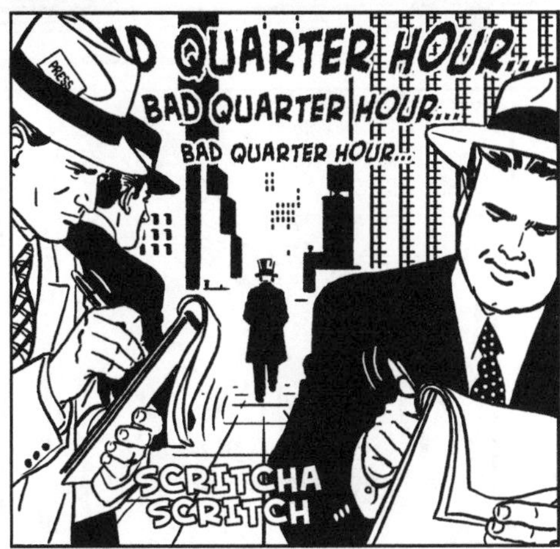
PRESS
D QUARTER HOUR...
BAD QUARTER HOUR...
BAD QUARTER HOUR...
SCRITCHA
SCRITCH ...

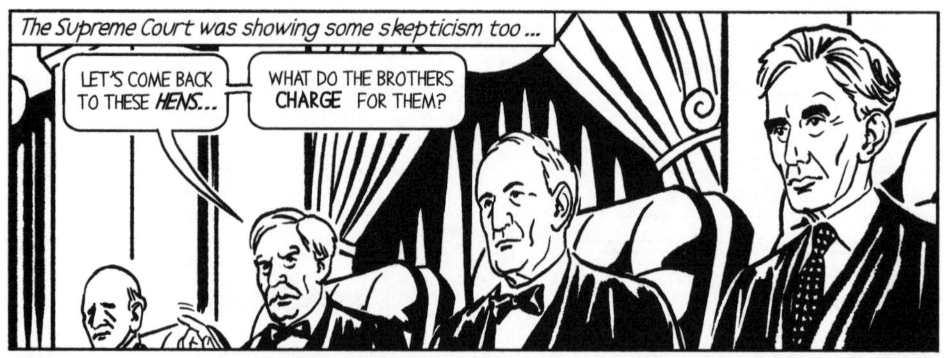
The Supreme Court was showing some skepticism too ...
LET'S COME BACK TO THESE HENS...
WHAT DO THE BROTHERS CHARGE FOR THEM?

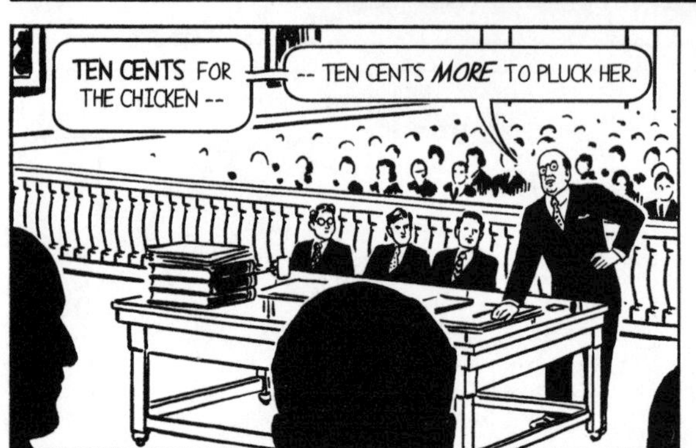
TEN CENTS FOR THE CHICKEN --
-- TEN CENTS MORE TO PLUCK HER.

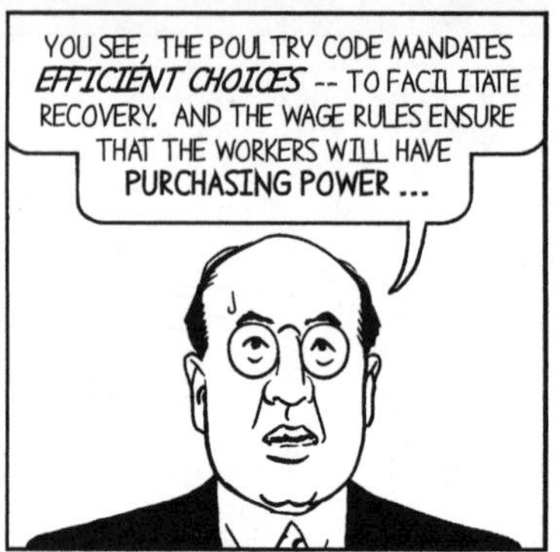
YOU SEE, THE POULTRY CODE MANDATES EFFICIENT CHOICES -- TO FACILITATE RECOVERY. AND THE WAGE RULES ENSURE THAT THE WORKERS WILL HAVE PURCHASING POWER ...

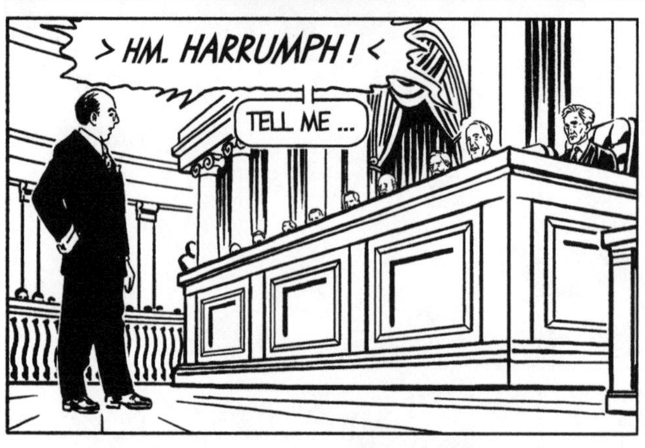
> HM. HARRUMPH! <
TELL ME ...

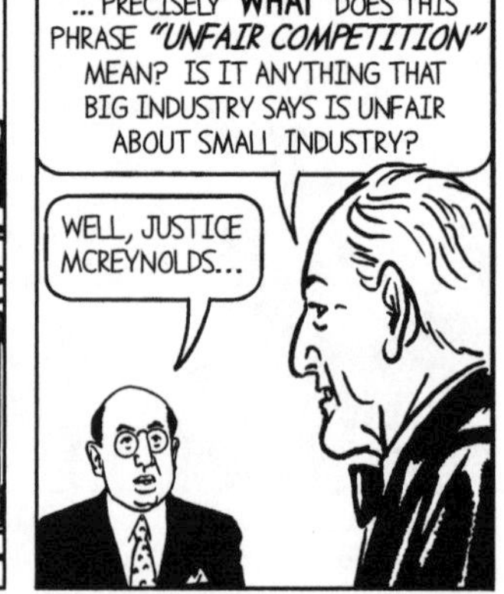
... PRECISELY WHAT DOES THIS PHRASE "UNFAIR COMPETITION" MEAN? IS IT ANYTHING THAT BIG INDUSTRY SAYS IS UNFAIR ABOUT SMALL INDUSTRY?
WELL, JUSTICE MCREYNOLDS...

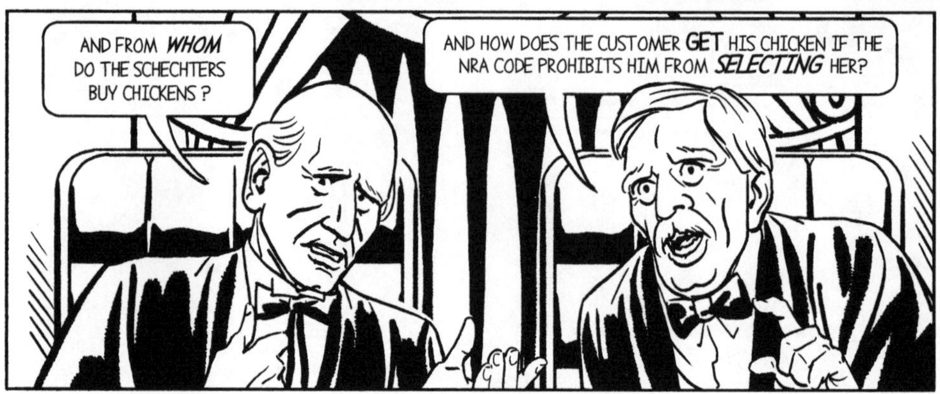
AND FROM WHOM DO THE SCHECHTERS BUY CHICKENS ?
AND HOW DOES THE CUSTOMER GET HIS CHICKEN IF THE NRA CODE PROHIBITS HIM FROM SELECTING HER?

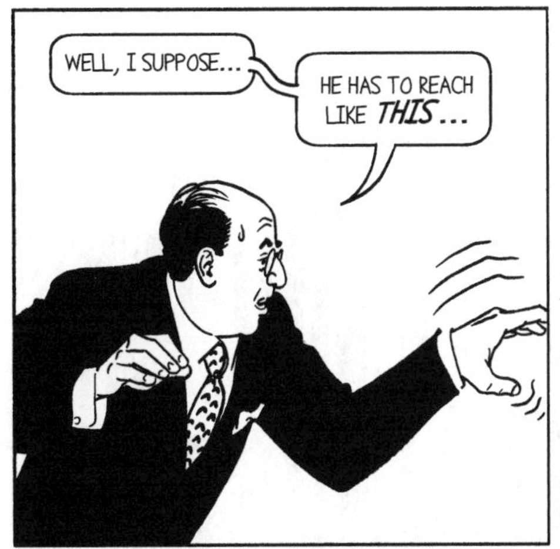
WELL, I SUPPOSE...
HE HAS TO REACH LIKE *THIS*...

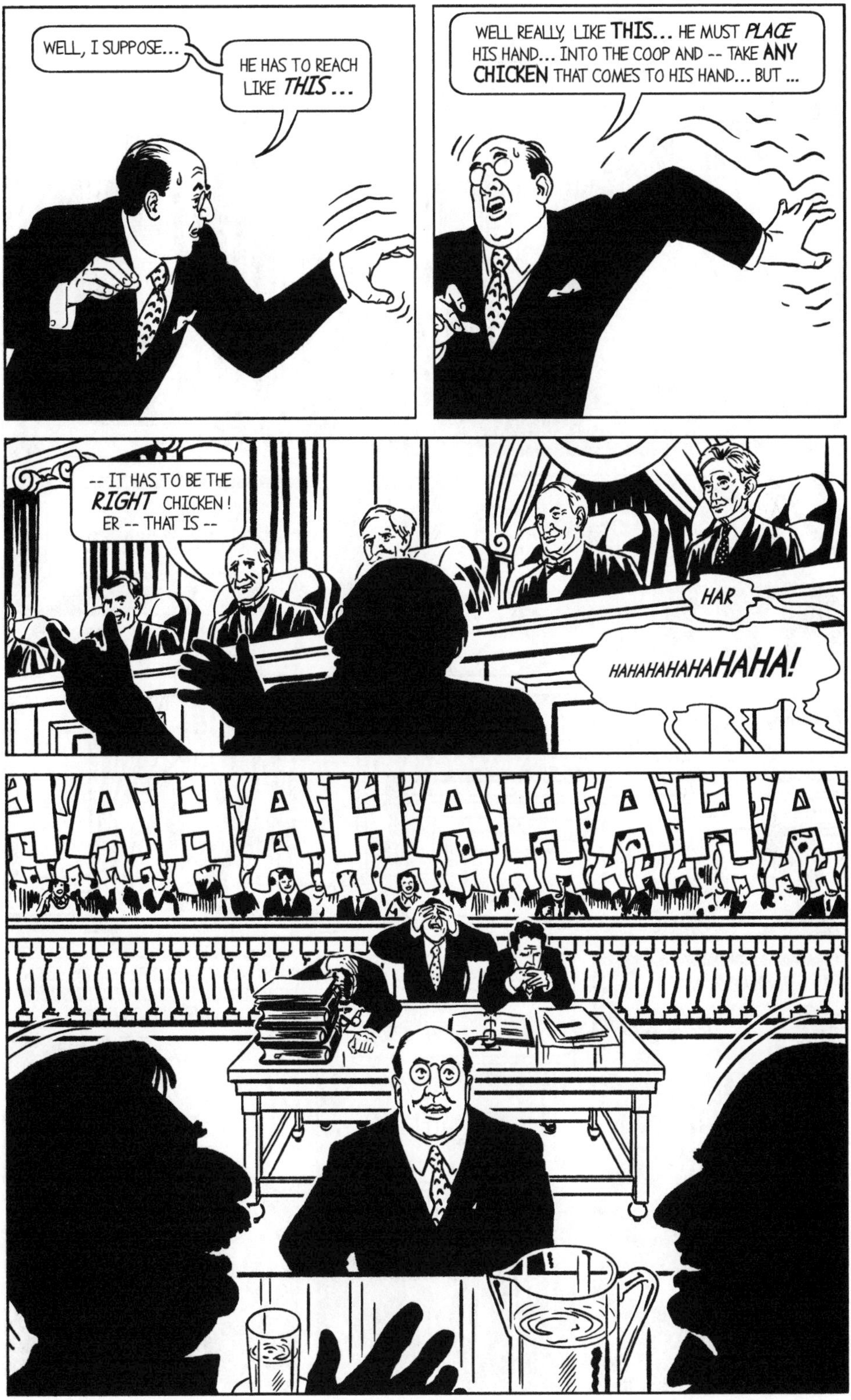

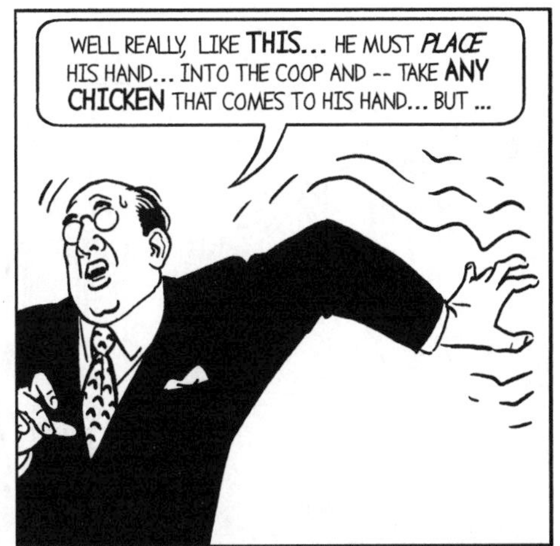
WELL REALLY, LIKE **THIS**... HE MUST *PLACE* HIS HAND... INTO THE COOP AND -- TAKE **ANY CHICKEN** THAT COMES TO HIS HAND... BUT ...

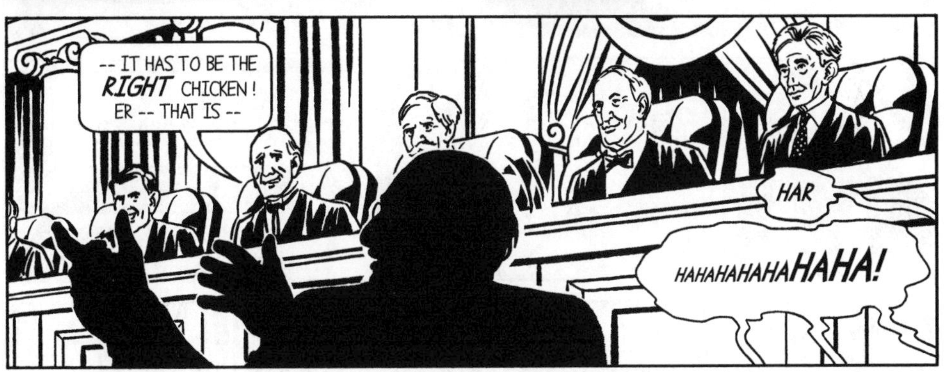
-- IT HAS TO BE THE *RIGHT* CHICKEN! ER -- THAT IS --
HAR
HAHAHAHAHAHAHA!

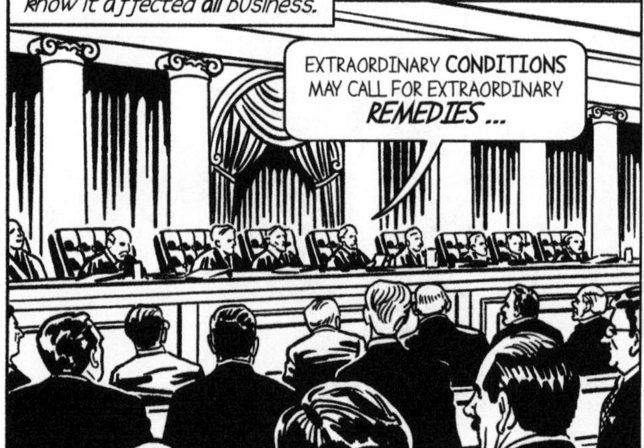
Eventually the justices did get to their opinion on Schechter. We really weren't sure how it would come out -- but we did know it affected all business.
EXTRAORDINARY CONDITIONS MAY CALL FOR EXTRAORDINARY REMEDIES ...

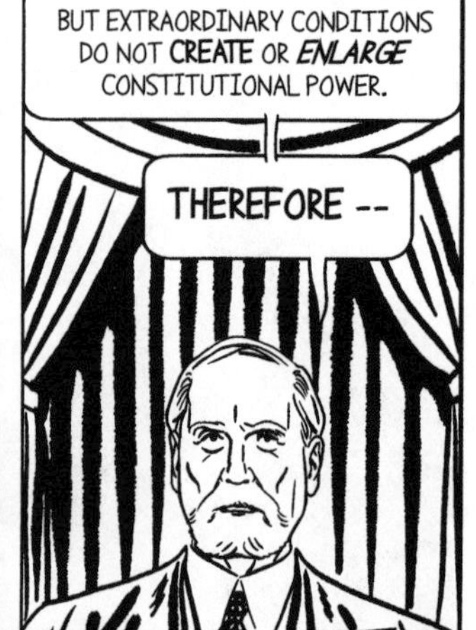
BUT EXTRAORDINARY CONDITIONS DO NOT CREATE OR ENLARGE CONSTITUTIONAL POWER.
THEREFORE --

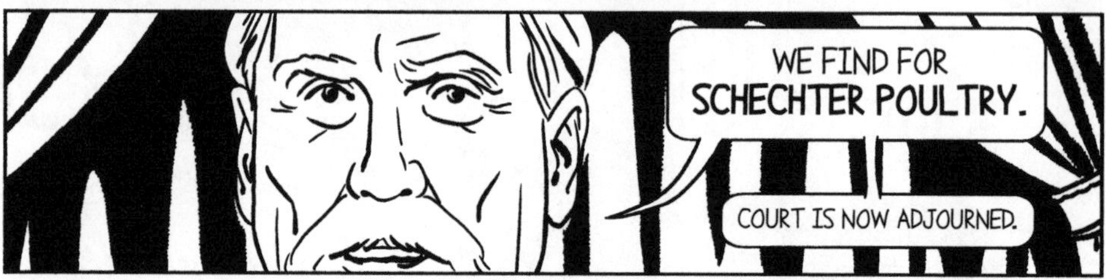
WE FIND FOR SCHECHTER POULTRY.
COURT IS NOW ADJOURNED.

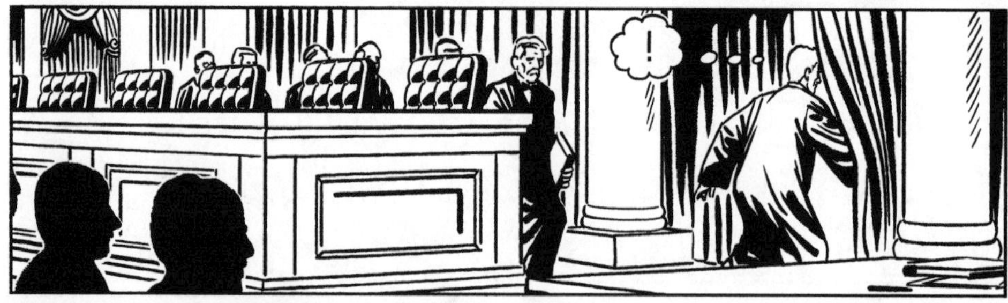
!

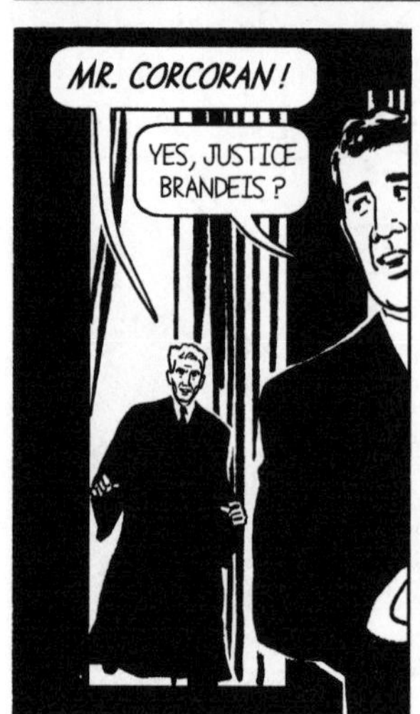
MR. CORCORAN!
YES, JUSTICE BRANDEIS?

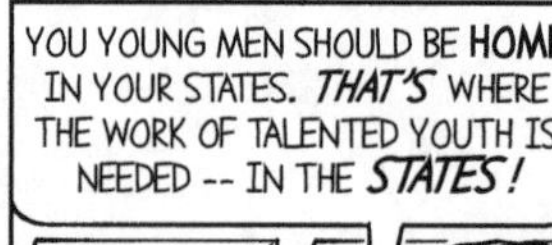
YOU YOUNG MEN SHOULD BE HOME IN YOUR STATES. THAT'S WHERE THE WORK OF TALENTED YOUTH IS NEEDED -- IN THE STATES!

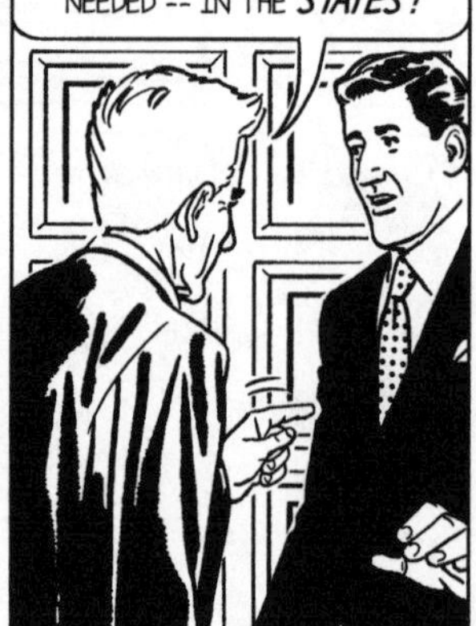

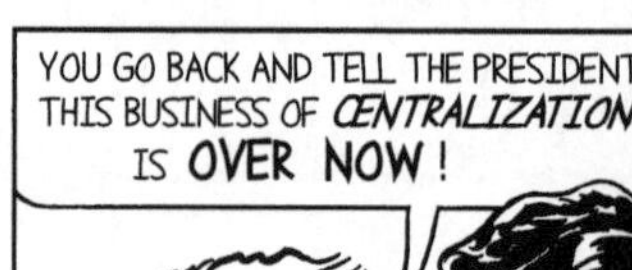
YOU GO BACK AND TELL THE PRESIDENT THIS BUSINESS OF CENTRALIZATION IS OVER NOW!

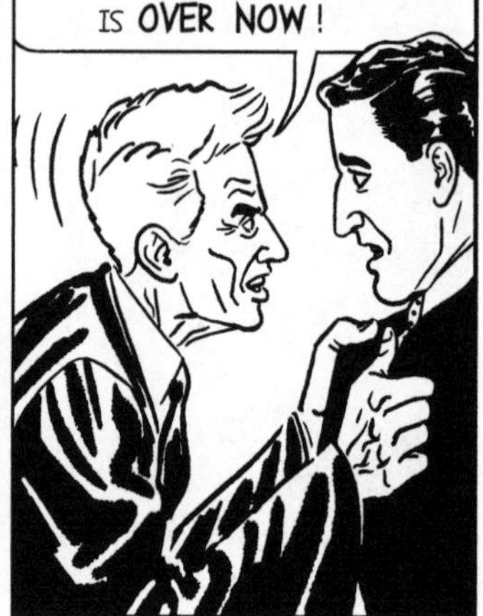

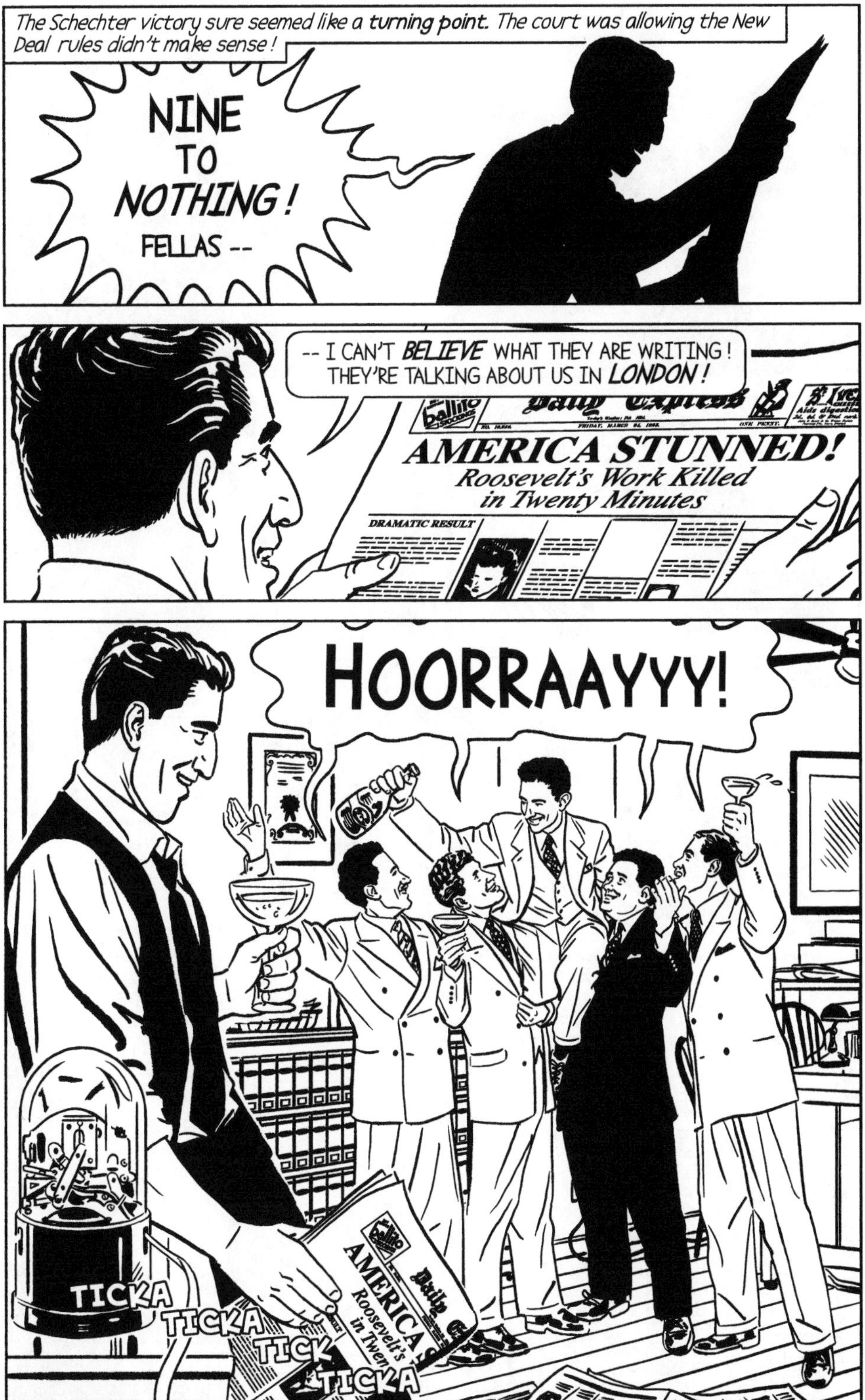

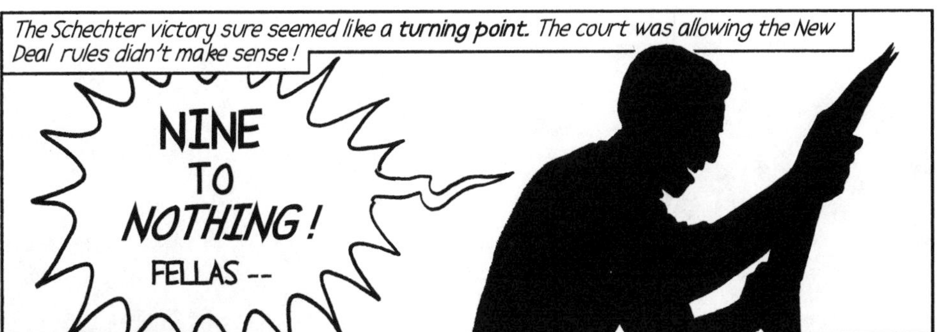

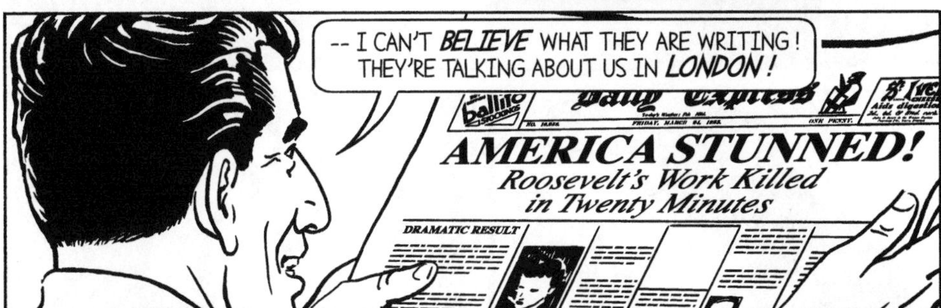

HOORRAAYYY!

TICKA TICKA TICK TICKA

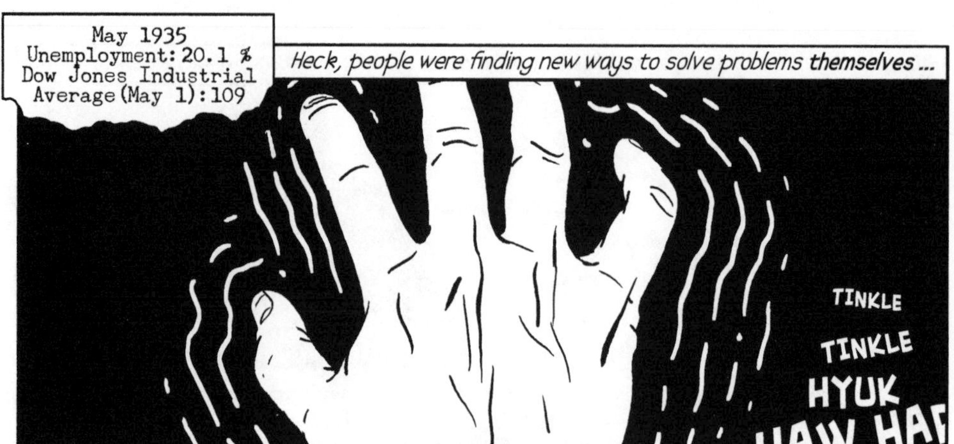
May 1935
Unemployment: 20.1 %
Dow Jones Industrial
Average (May 1): 109
Heck, people were finding new ways to solve problems **themselves** ...
TINKLE
TINKLE
HYUK

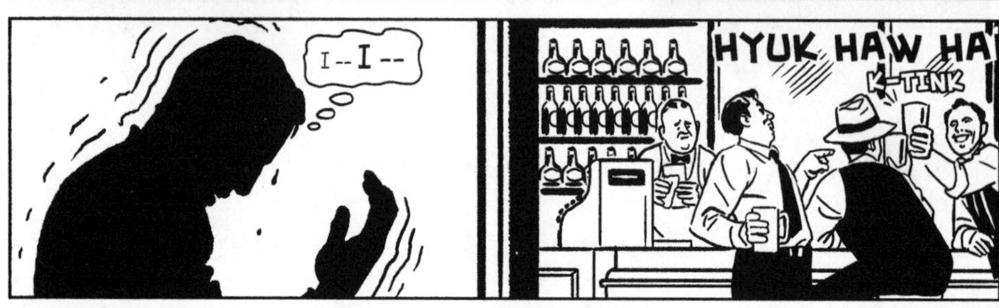
I -- I --
HYUK HAW HA
K-TINK

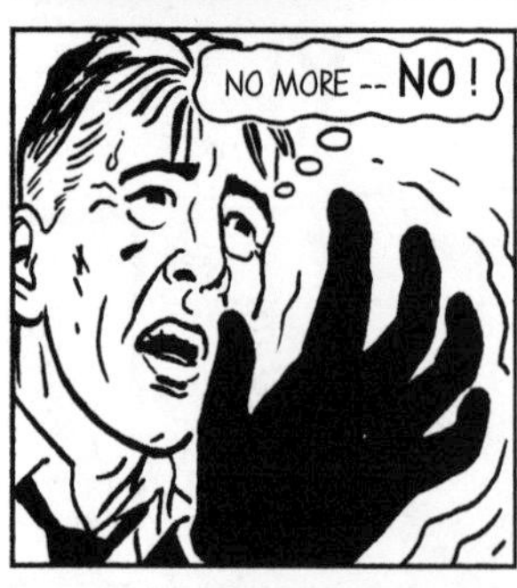
NO MORE -- **NO** !

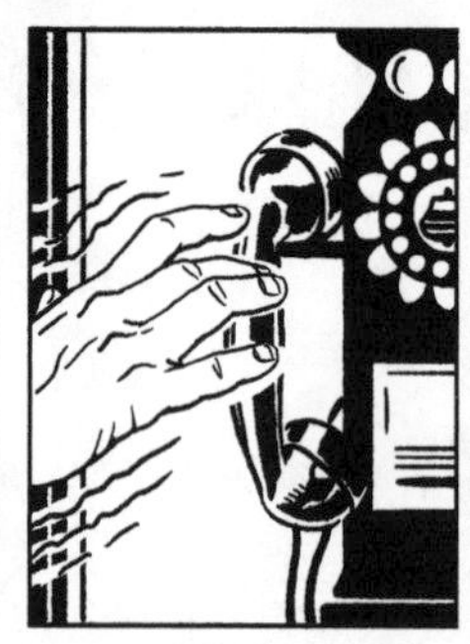

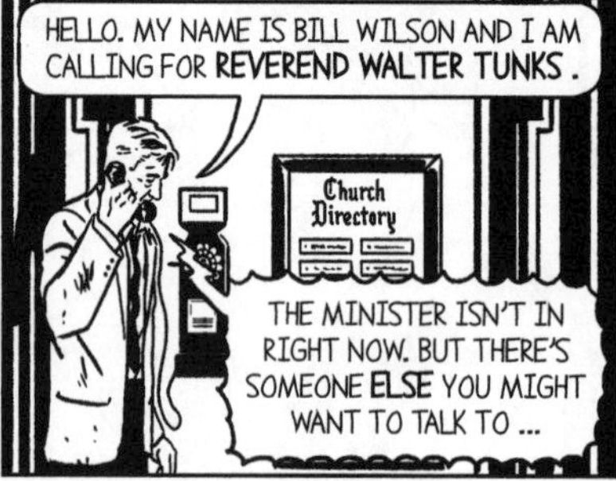
HELLO. MY NAME IS BILL WILSON AND I AM CALLING FOR **REVEREND WALTER TUNKS** .
Church Directory
THE MINISTER ISN'T IN RIGHT NOW. BUT THERE'S SOMEONE **ELSE** YOU MIGHT WANT TO TALK TO ...

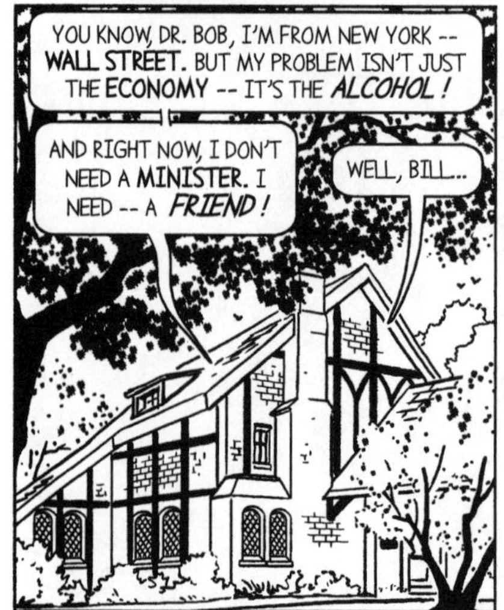
YOU KNOW, DR. BOB, I'M FROM NEW YORK -- **WALL STREET.** BUT MY PROBLEM ISN'T JUST THE **ECONOMY** -- IT'S THE ***ALCOHOL*** !
AND RIGHT NOW, I DON'T NEED A **MINISTER.** I NEED -- A ***FRIEND*** !
WELL, BILL...

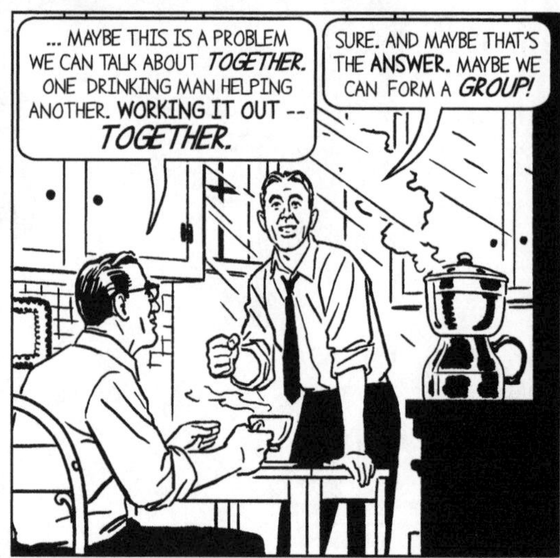
... MAYBE THIS IS A PROBLEM WE CAN TALK ABOUT *TOGETHER.* ONE DRINKING MAN HELPING ANOTHER. **WORKING IT OUT** -- *TOGETHER.*
SURE. AND MAYBE THAT'S THE **ANSWER.** MAYBE WE CAN FORM A ***GROUP!***

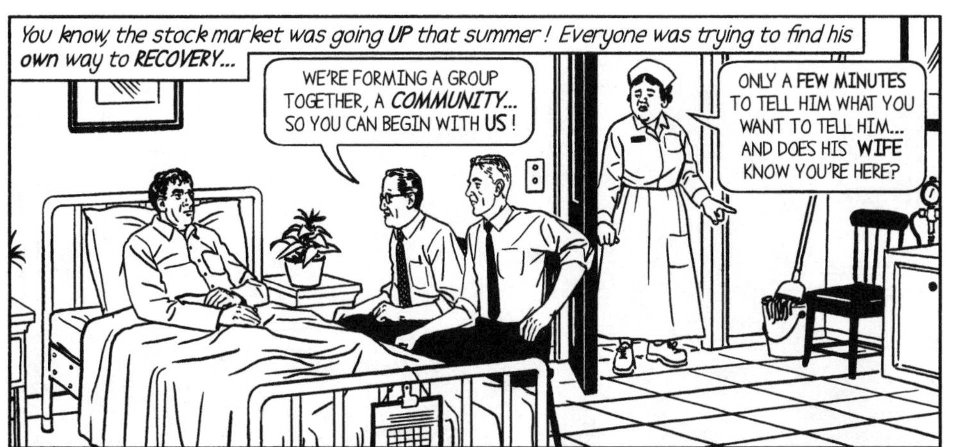
You know, the stock market was going UP that summer! Everyone was trying to find his own way to RECOVERY...
WE'RE FORMING A GROUP TOGETHER, A COMMUNITY... SO YOU CAN BEGIN WITH US!
ONLY A FEW MINUTES TO TELL HIM WHAT YOU WANT TO TELL HIM... AND DOES HIS WIFE KNOW YOU'RE HERE?

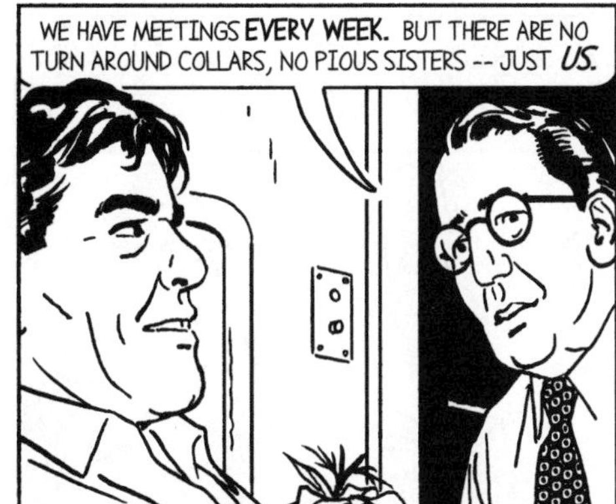
WE HAVE MEETINGS EVERY WEEK. BUT THERE ARE NO TURN AROUND COLLARS, NO PIOUS SISTERS -- JUST US.

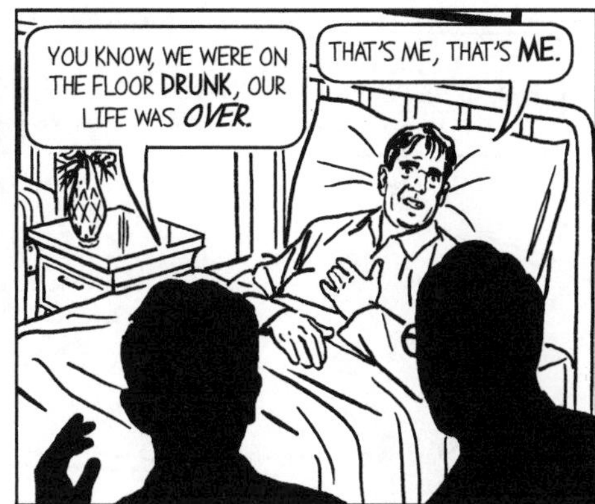
YOU KNOW, WE WERE ON THE FLOOR DRUNK, OUR LIFE WAS OVER.
THAT'S ME, THAT'S ME.

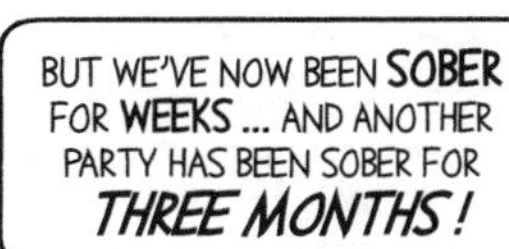
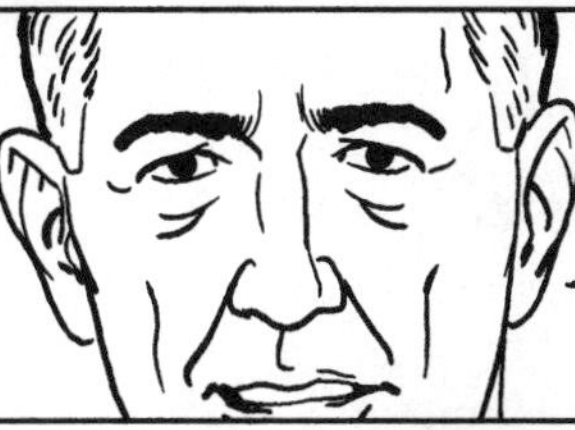
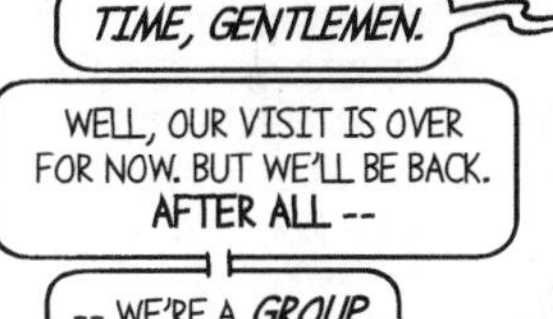
BUT WE'VE NOW BEEN SOBER FOR WEEKS ... AND ANOTHER PARTY HAS BEEN SOBER FOR THREE MONTHS!
TIME, GENTLEMEN.
WELL, OUR VISIT IS OVER FOR NOW. BUT WE'LL BE BACK. AFTER ALL --
-- WE'RE A GROUP.

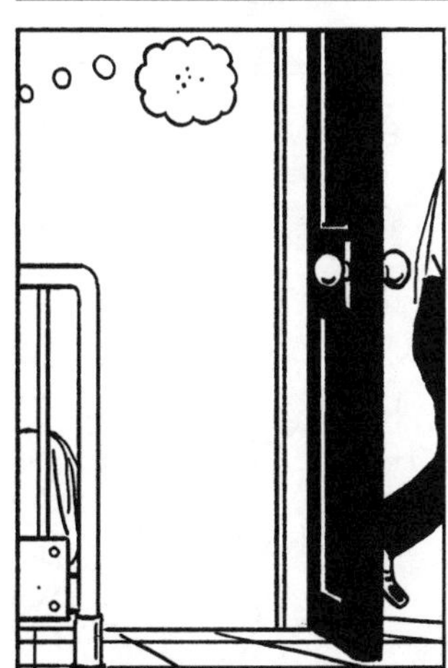
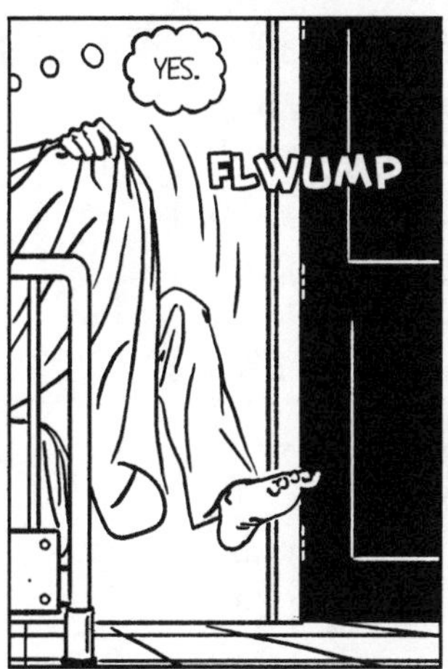
YES.
FLWUMP

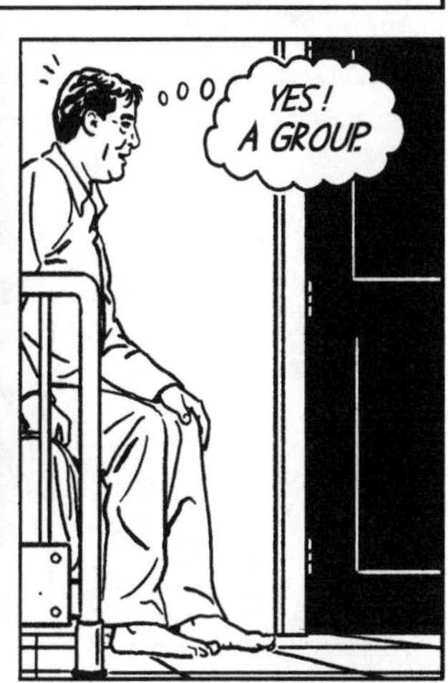
YES! A GROUP.

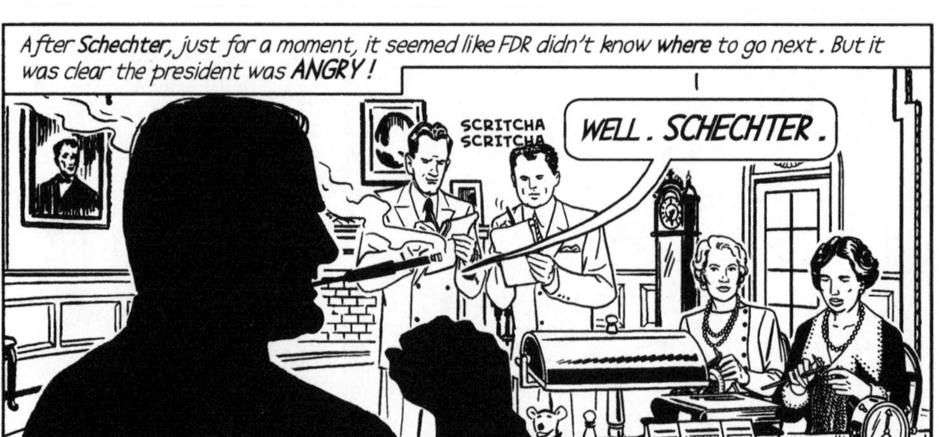
After Schechter, just for a moment, it seemed like FDR didn't know where to go next. But it was clear the president was ANGRY!
SCRITCHA
SCRITCHA
WELL. SCHECHTER.

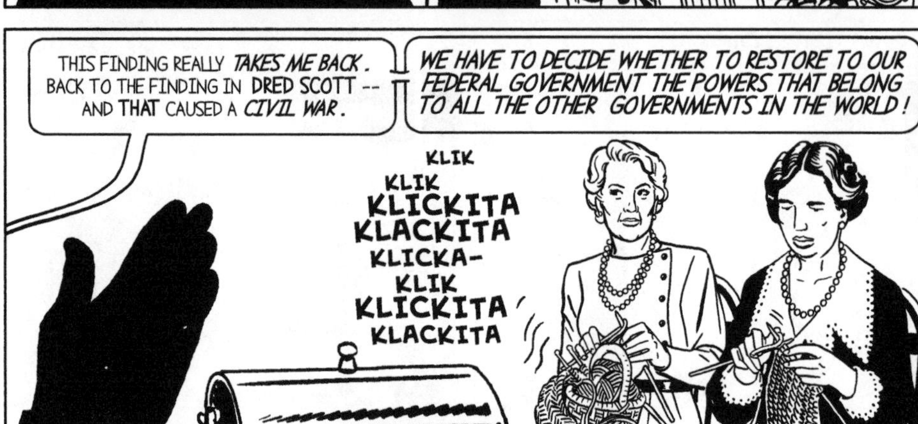
THIS FINDING REALLY TAKES ME BACK. BACK TO THE FINDING IN DRED SCOTT -- AND THAT CAUSED A CIVIL WAR.
WE HAVE TO DECIDE WHETHER TO RESTORE TO OUR FEDERAL GOVERNMENT THE POWERS THAT BELONG TO ALL THE OTHER GOVERNMENTS IN THE WORLD!
KLIK
KLIK
KLICKITA
KLACKITA
KLICKA-
KLIK
KLICKITA
KLACKITA

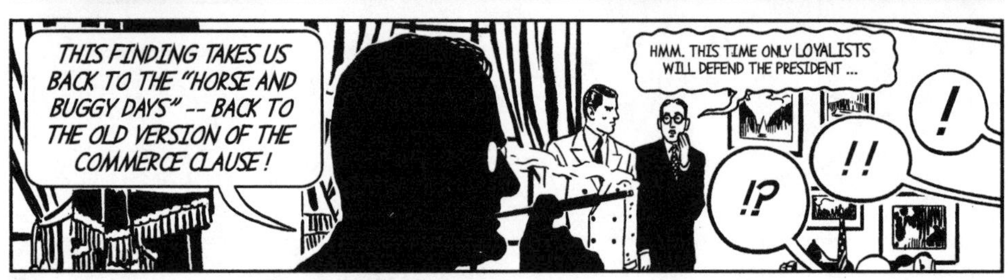
THIS FINDING TAKES US BACK TO THE "HORSE AND BUGGY DAYS" -- BACK TO THE OLD VERSION OF THE COMMERCE CLAUSE!
HMM. THIS TIME ONLY LOYALISTS WILL DEFEND THE PRESIDENT ...
!
!!
!?

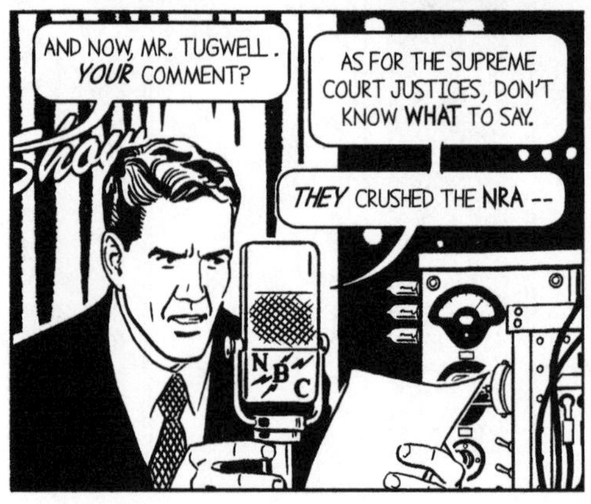
AND NOW, MR. TUGWELL. YOUR COMMENT?
AS FOR THE SUPREME COURT JUSTICES, DON'T KNOW WHAT TO SAY.
THEY CRUSHED THE NRA --
NBC

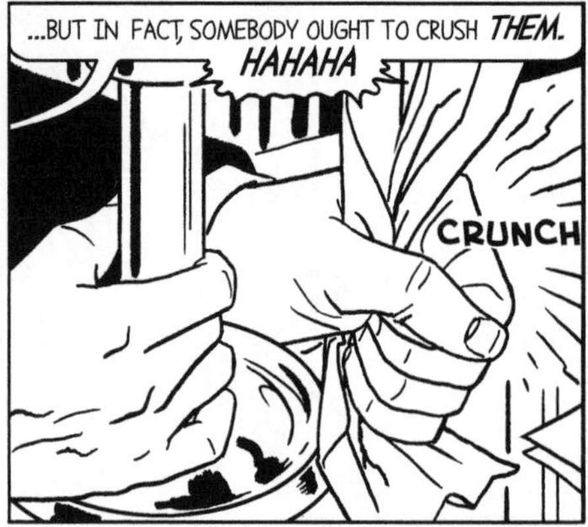
...BUT IN FACT, SOMEBODY OUGHT TO CRUSH THEM.
HAHAHA
CRUNCH

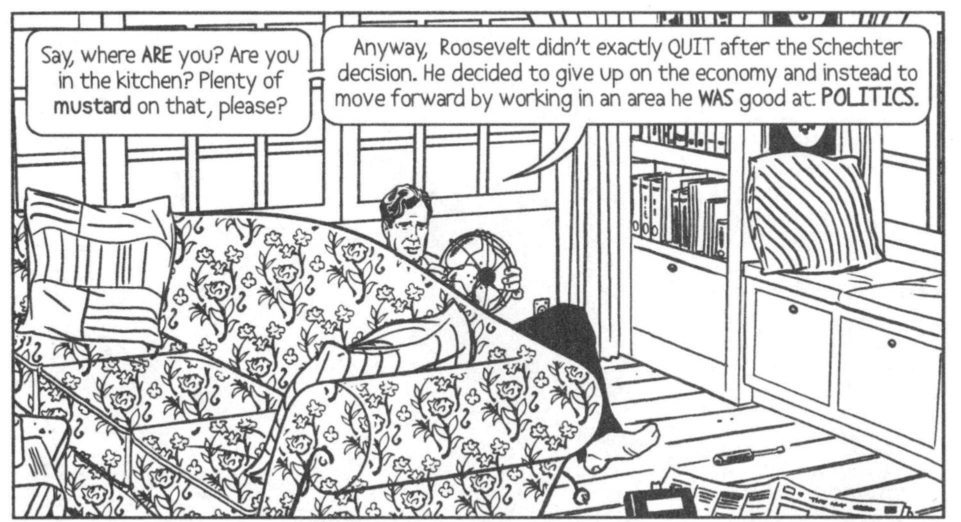
Say, where ARE you? Are you in the kitchen? Plenty of mustard on that, please?
Anyway, Roosevelt didn't exactly QUIT after the Schechter decision. He decided to give up on the economy and instead to move forward by working in an area he WAS good at: POLITICS.

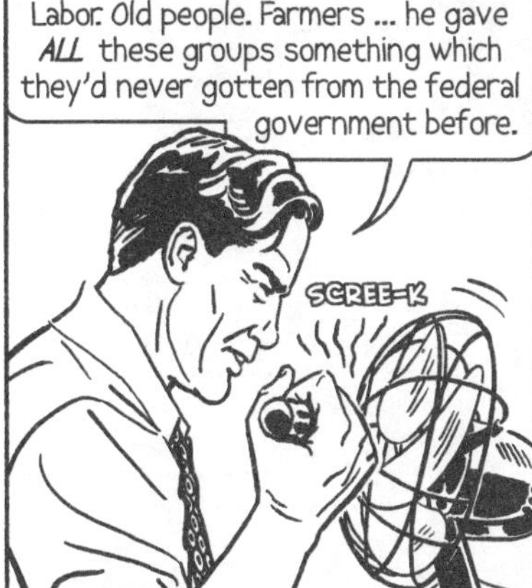
Labor. Old people. Farmers ... he gave ALL these groups something which they'd never gotten from the federal government before.
SCREE-K

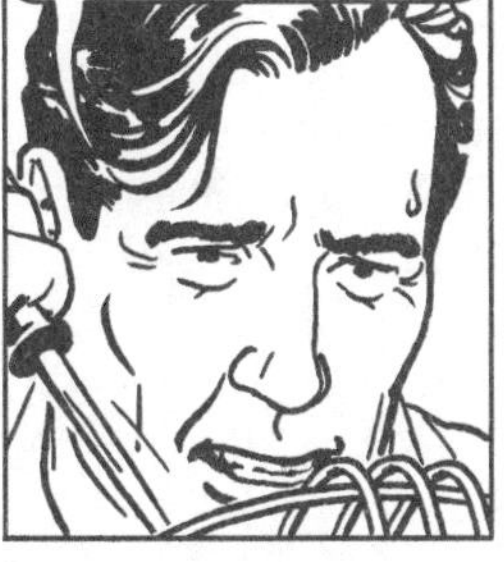
All those buildings that Ickes built were GIFTS for towns in Georgia, Mississippi, New England, everywhere. Washington was going to --

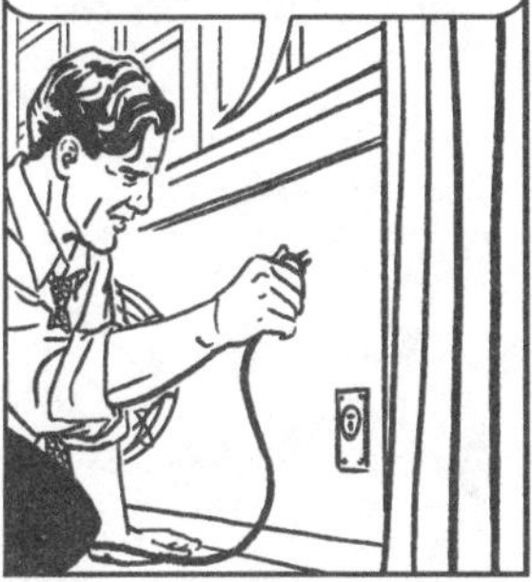
-- CONNECT with them. That's how he was going to remember his FORGOTTEN MAN -- by connecting to GROUPS, not individuals!

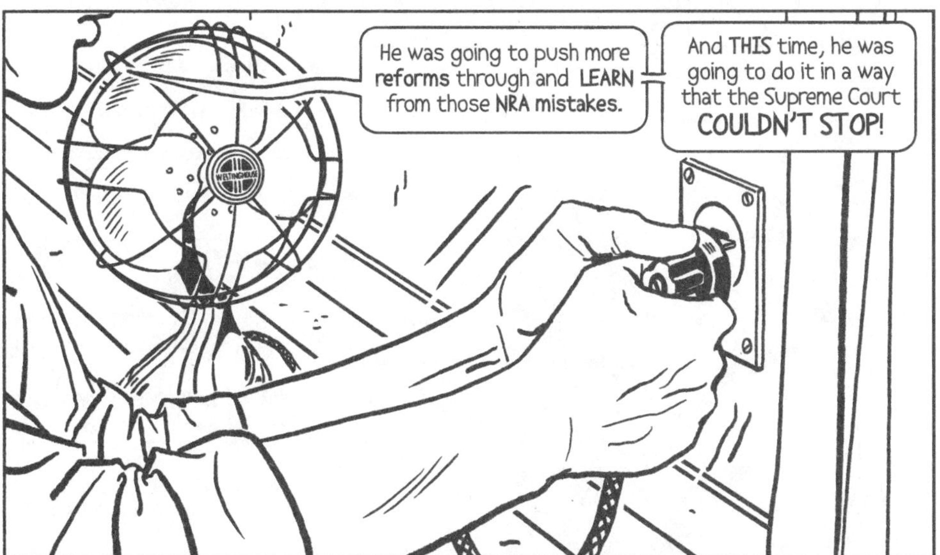
He was going to push more reforms through and LEARN from those NRA mistakes.
And THIS time, he was going to do it in a way that the Supreme Court COULDN'T STOP!

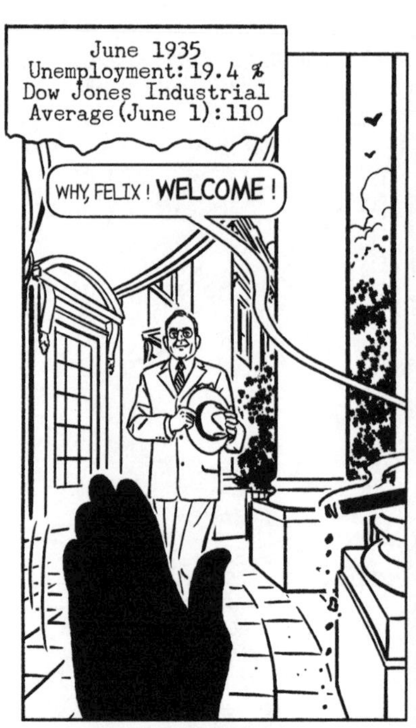
June 1935
Unemployment: 19.4 %
Dow Jones Industrial
Average (June 1): 110
WHY, FELIX! **WELCOME**!

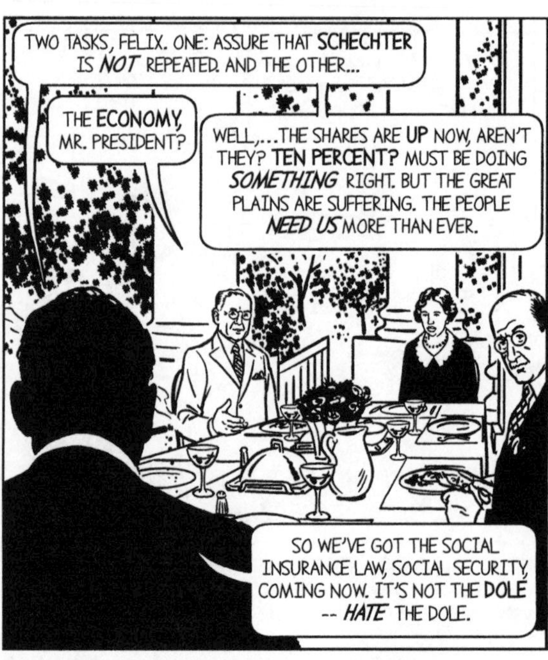
TWO TASKS, FELIX. ONE: ASSURE THAT **SCHECHTER** IS ***NOT*** REPEATED. AND THE OTHER...
THE **ECONOMY**, MR. PRESIDENT?
WELL,...THE SHARES ARE **UP** NOW, AREN'T THEY? **TEN PERCENT?** MUST BE DOING ***SOMETHING*** RIGHT. BUT THE GREAT PLAINS ARE SUFFERING. THE PEOPLE ***NEED US*** MORE THAN EVER.
SO WE'VE GOT THE SOCIAL INSURANCE LAW, SOCIAL SECURITY, COMING NOW. IT'S NOT THE **DOLE** -- ***HATE*** THE DOLE.

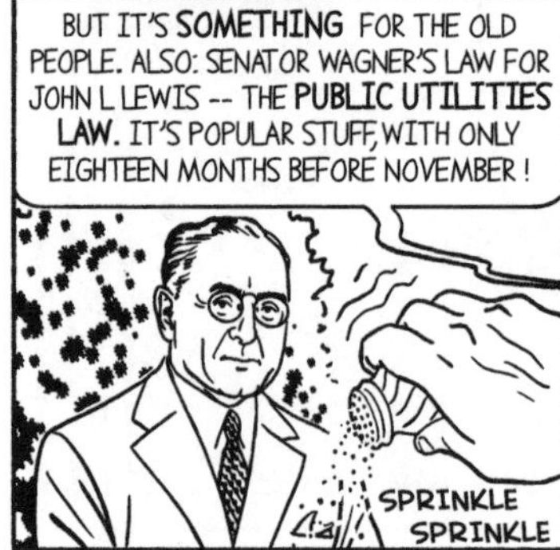
BUT IT'S **SOMETHING** FOR THE OLD PEOPLE. ALSO: SENATOR WAGNER'S LAW FOR JOHN L LEWIS -- THE **PUBLIC UTILITIES LAW**. IT'S POPULAR STUFF, WITH ONLY EIGHTEEN MONTHS BEFORE NOVEMBER!
SPRINKLE
SPRINKLE

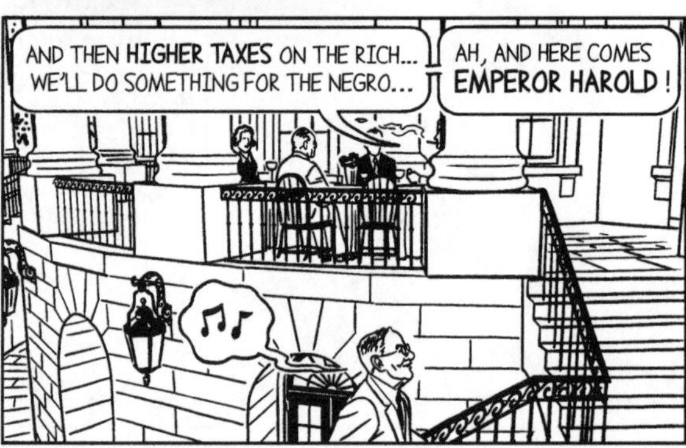
AND THEN **HIGHER TAXES** ON THE RICH... WE'LL DO SOMETHING FOR THE NEGRO...
AH, AND HERE COMES **EMPEROR HAROLD**!
♫ ♪

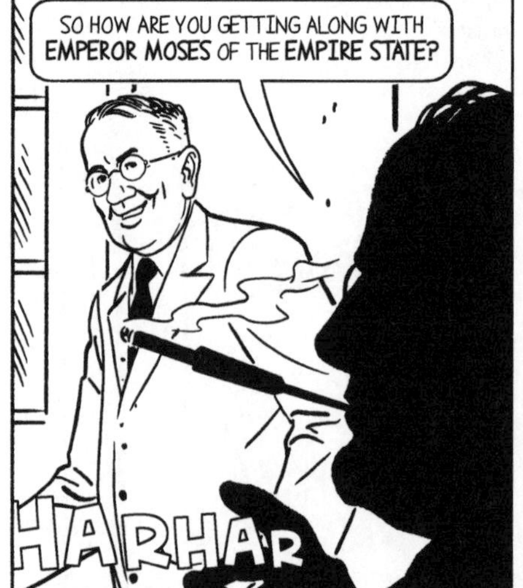
SO HOW ARE YOU GETTING ALONG WITH **EMPEROR MOSES** OF THE **EMPIRE STATE?**
HARHAR

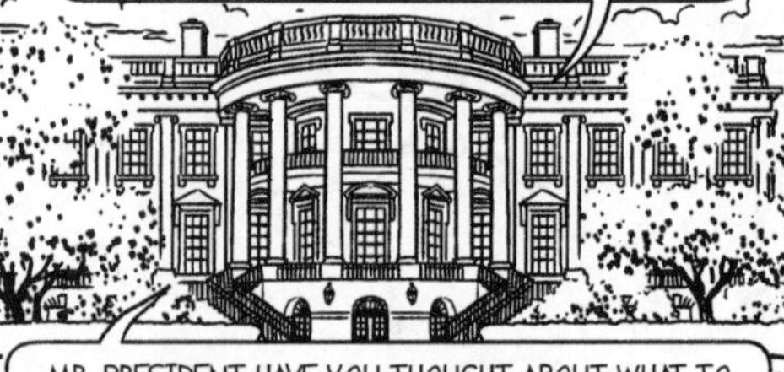
GOOD TO HAVE THE **TEAM** HERE! OUR PWA BUILDINGS THAT HAROLD IS CREATING ARE DESIGNED TO **PLEASE.** NO SKYSCRAPERS ... A PARK AROUND EVERY PROJECT! IT IS IMPORTANT THAT THE ARCHITECTURE BE ***REGIONAL***.
I HOPE **REX** IS HAPPY WITH HIS NEW POSITION. NOW HE'S GOT HIS VERY OWN **PLAYPEN** TO BUILD IN. QUITE A ***BUDGET***, TOO.
MR. PRESIDENT, HAVE YOU THOUGHT ABOUT WHAT TO SAY ON THE **CATASTROPHE** IN THE GREAT PLAINS? REX SAYS WE SHOULD POUR RESOURCES INTO ***THAT***, TOO. AND HE'S ***RIGHT.***

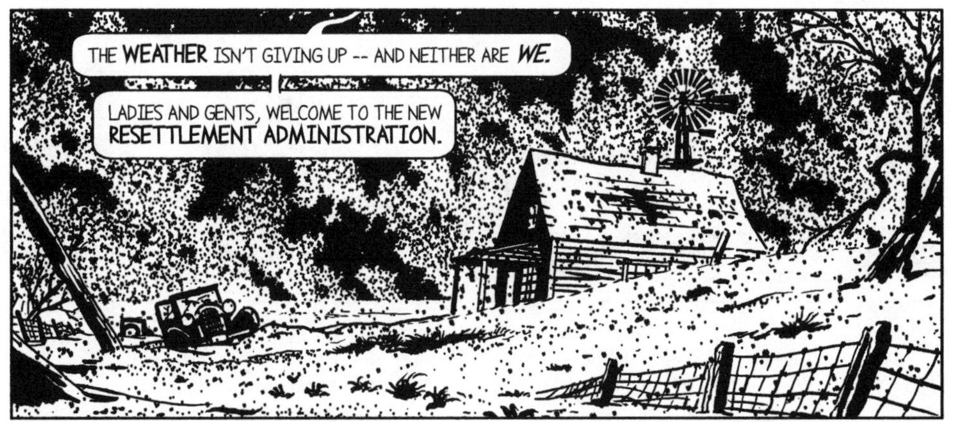
THE WEATHER ISN'T GIVING UP -- AND NEITHER ARE WE.
LADIES AND GENTS, WELCOME TO THE NEW RESETTLEMENT ADMINISTRATION.

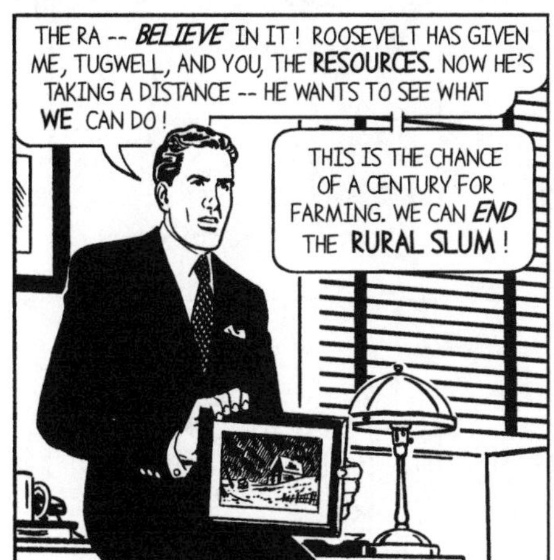
THE RA -- BELIEVE IN IT! ROOSEVELT HAS GIVEN ME, TUGWELL, AND YOU, THE RESOURCES. NOW HE'S TAKING A DISTANCE -- HE WANTS TO SEE WHAT WE CAN DO!
THIS IS THE CHANCE OF A CENTURY FOR FARMING. WE CAN END THE RURAL SLUM!

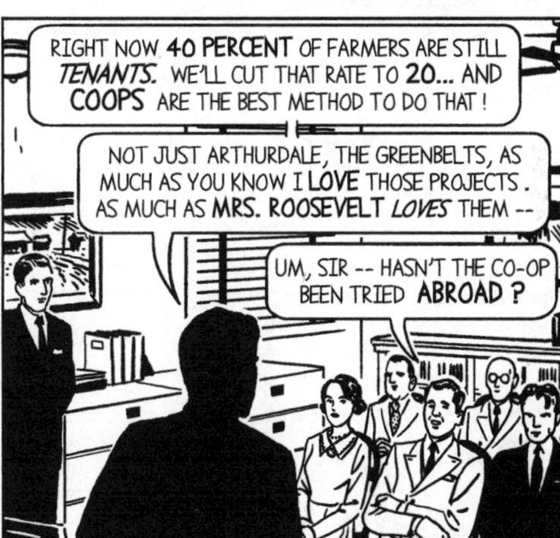
RIGHT NOW 40 PERCENT OF FARMERS ARE STILL TENANTS. WE'LL CUT THAT RATE TO 20... AND COOPS ARE THE BEST METHOD TO DO THAT!
NOT JUST ARTHURDALE, THE GREENBELTS, AS MUCH AS YOU KNOW I LOVE THOSE PROJECTS. AS MUCH AS MRS. ROOSEVELT LOVES THEM --
UM, SIR -- HASN'T THE CO-OP BEEN TRIED ABROAD?

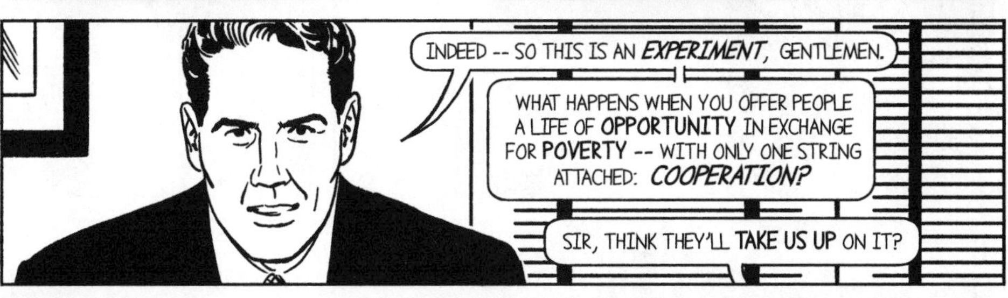
INDEED -- SO THIS IS AN EXPERIMENT, GENTLEMEN.
WHAT HAPPENS WHEN YOU OFFER PEOPLE A LIFE OF OPPORTUNITY IN EXCHANGE FOR POVERTY -- WITH ONLY ONE STRING ATTACHED: COOPERATION?
SIR, THINK THEY'LL TAKE US UP ON IT?

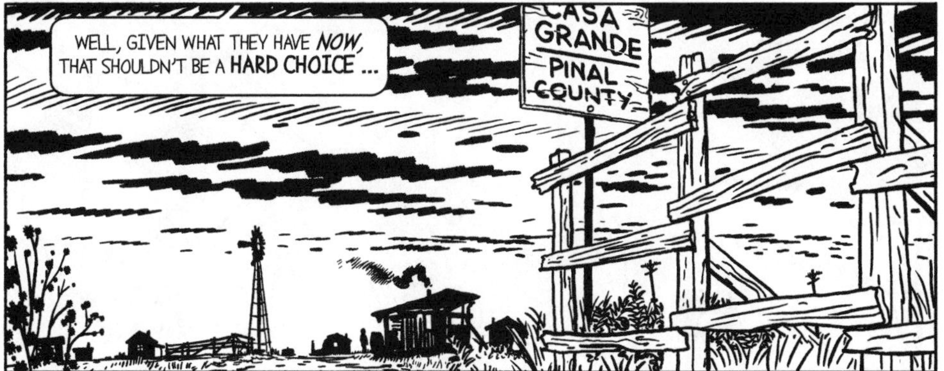
WELL, GIVEN WHAT THEY HAVE NOW, THAT SHOULDN'T BE A HARD CHOICE...
CASA GRANDE
PINAL COUNTY

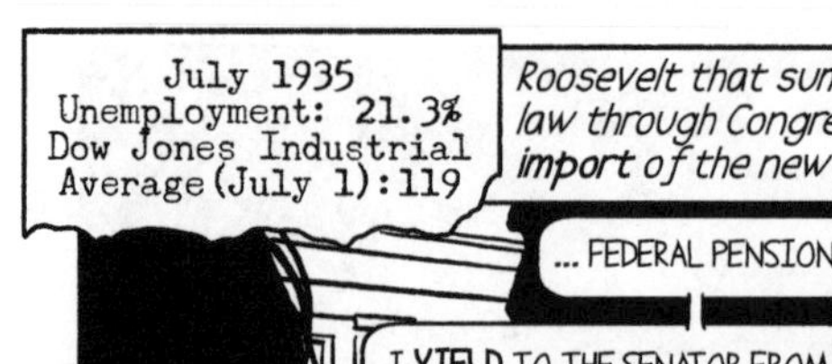
July 1935
Unemployment: 21.3%
Dow Jones Industrial
Average(July 1):119

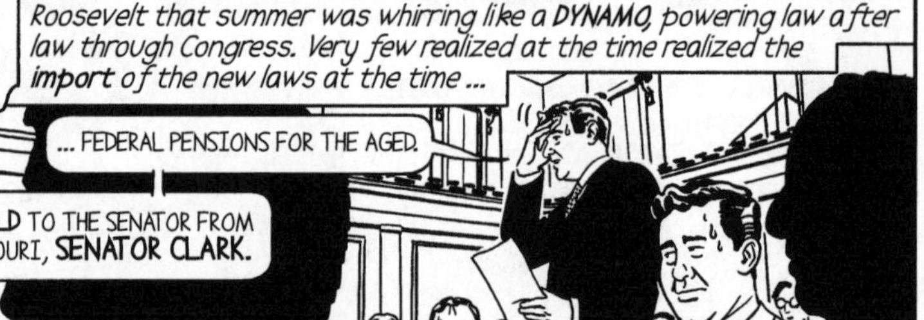
Roosevelt that summer was whirring like a DYNAMO, powering law after law through Congress. Very few realized at the time realized the import of the new laws at the time ...
... FEDERAL PENSIONS FOR THE AGED.
I YIELD TO THE SENATOR FROM MISSOURI, SENATOR CLARK.
> WHEW <

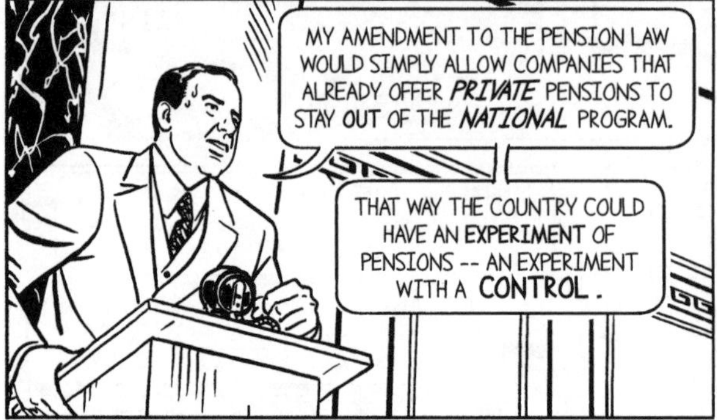
MY AMENDMENT TO THE PENSION LAW WOULD SIMPLY ALLOW COMPANIES THAT ALREADY OFFER PRIVATE PENSIONS TO STAY OUT OF THE NATIONAL PROGRAM.
THAT WAY THE COUNTRY COULD HAVE AN EXPERIMENT OF PENSIONS -- AN EXPERIMENT WITH A CONTROL.

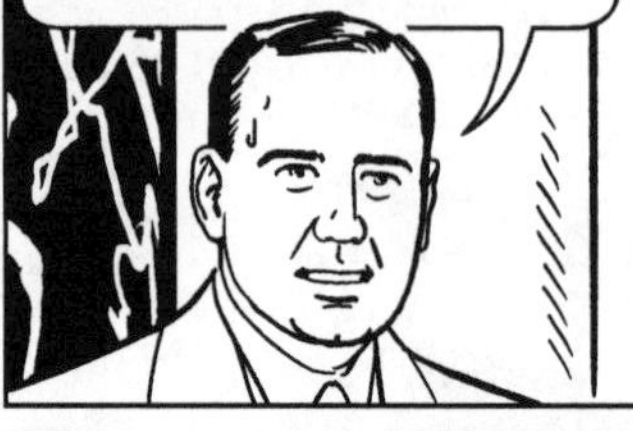
WITH MY AMENDMENT, THEN WE CAN SEE OVER TIME WHICH PENSION PLAN FARES BETTER!
SENATOR HUEY LONG MIGHT BE INTERESTED IN THE OUTCOME ...

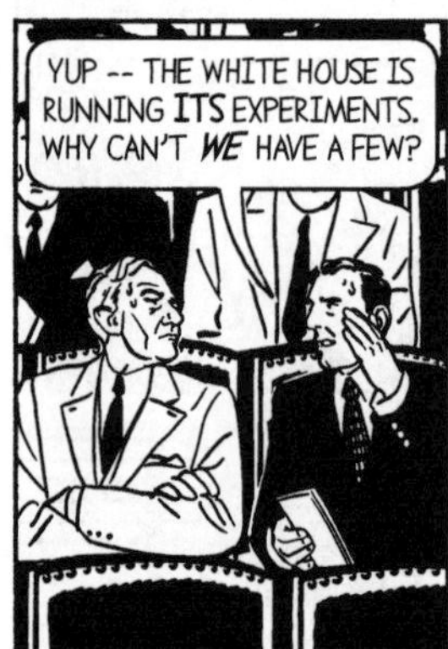
YUP -- THE WHITE HOUSE IS RUNNING ITS EXPERIMENTS. WHY CAN'T WE HAVE A FEW?

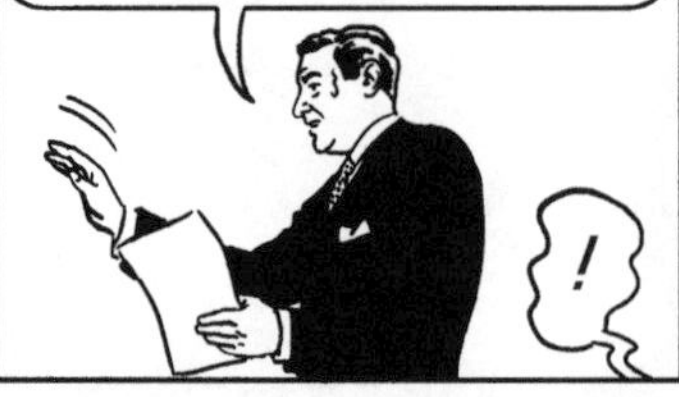
TAXES. IF YOU'LL ALLOW, I'LL CONTINUE TO READ THE PRESIDENTIAL MESSAGE. WE HAVE ESTABLISHED THE PRINCIPLE OF GRADUATED TAXES.
WE SHOULD APPLY THE SAME PRINCIPLE TO CORPORATIONS: A TAX ON DIVIDENDS BETWEEN CORPORATIONS. UM...RATES TO GO UP.
!

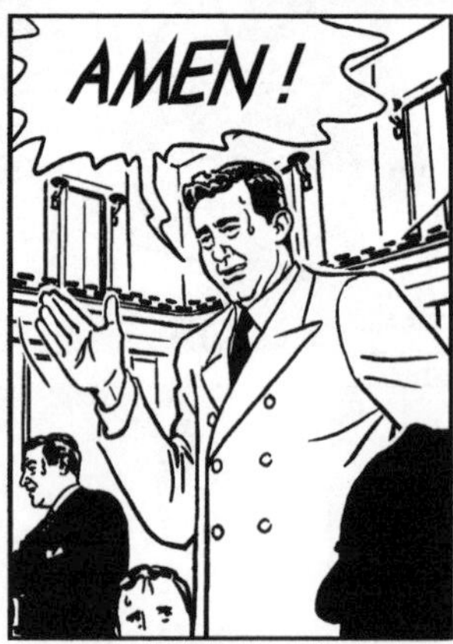
AMEN!

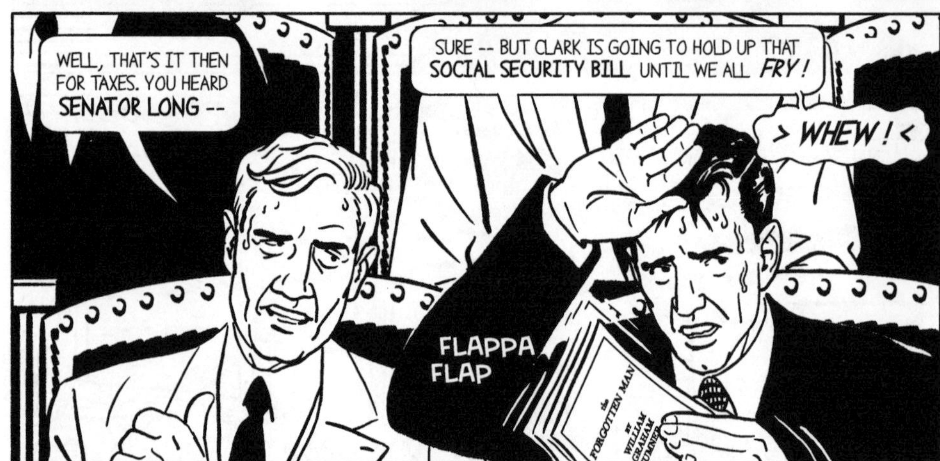
WELL, THAT'S IT THEN FOR TAXES. YOU HEARD SENATOR LONG --
SURE -- BUT CLARK IS GOING TO HOLD UP THAT SOCIAL SECURITY BILL UNTIL WE ALL FRY!
> WHEW! <
FLAPPA FLAP
the FORGOTTEN MAN
BY WILLIAM GRAHAM SUMNER

August 1935
Unemployment: 20.0 %
Dow Jones Industrial Average (Aug. 1): 126

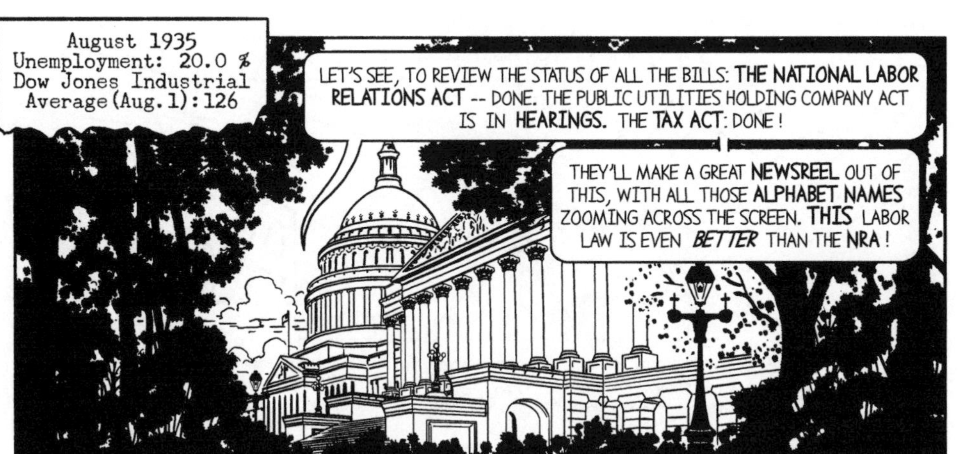

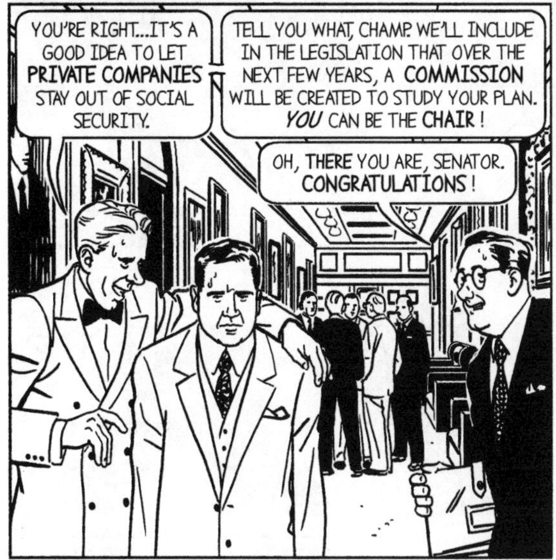

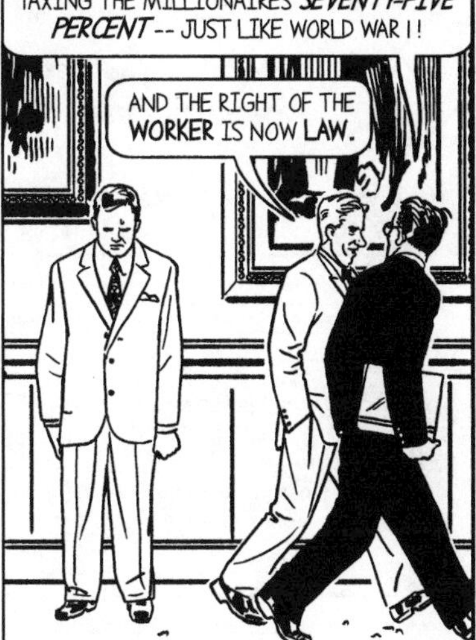

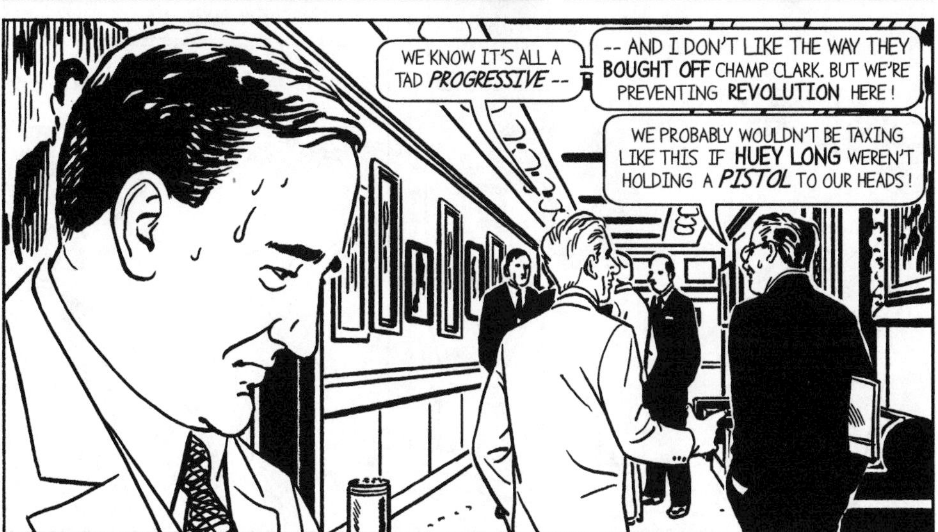

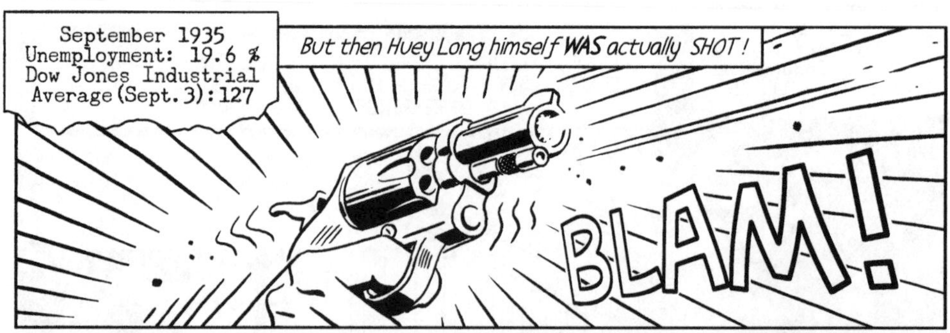
September 1935
Unemployment: 19.6 %
Dow Jones Industrial
Average (Sept. 3): 127
But then Huey Long himself WAS actually SHOT!
BLAM!

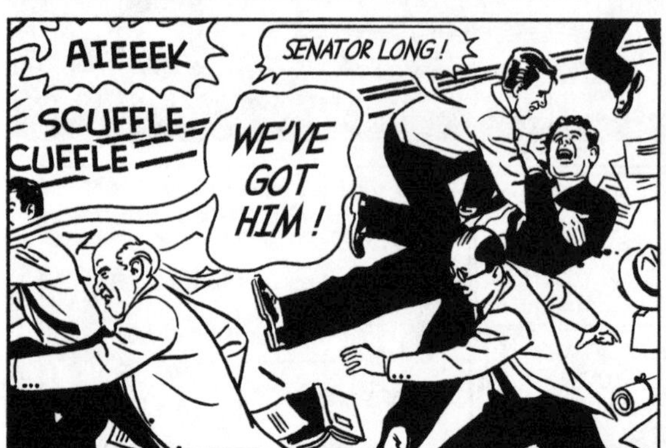
AIEEEK
SENATOR LONG!
SCUFFLE
CUFFLE
WE'VE GOT HIM!

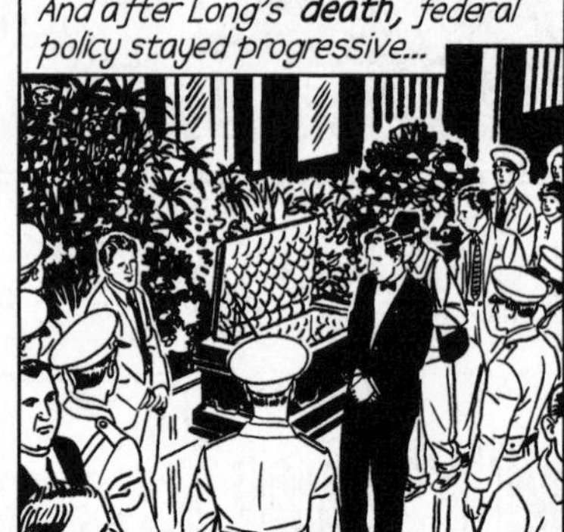
And after Long's death, federal policy stayed progressive...

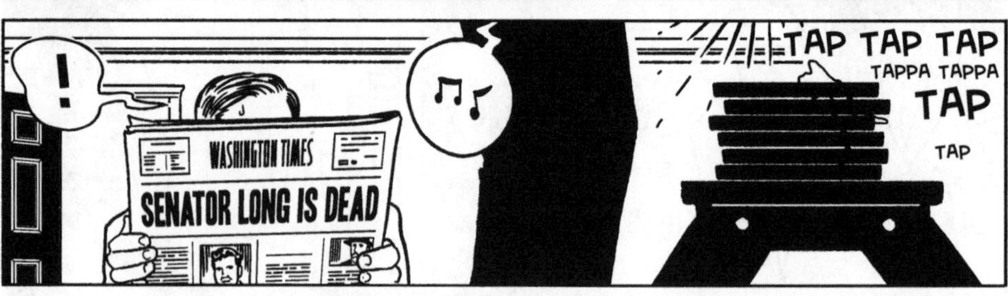
!
WASHINGTON TIMES
SENATOR LONG IS DEAD
TAP TAP TAP
TAPPA TAPPA
TAP
TAP

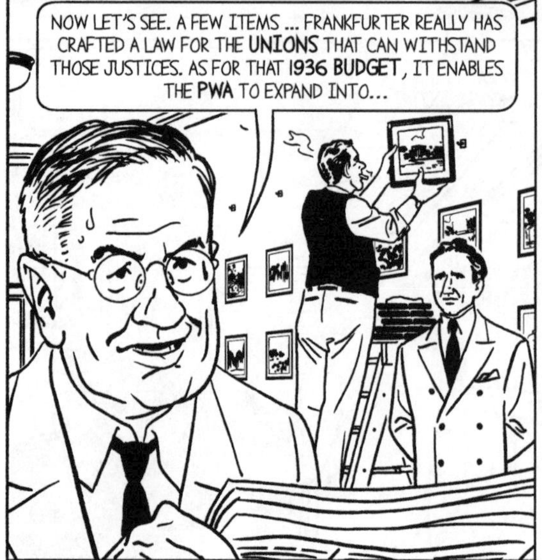
NOW LET'S SEE. A FEW ITEMS ... FRANKFURTER REALLY HAS CRAFTED A LAW FOR THE UNIONS THAT CAN WITHSTAND THOSE JUSTICES. AS FOR THAT 1936 BUDGET, IT ENABLES THE PWA TO EXPAND INTO...

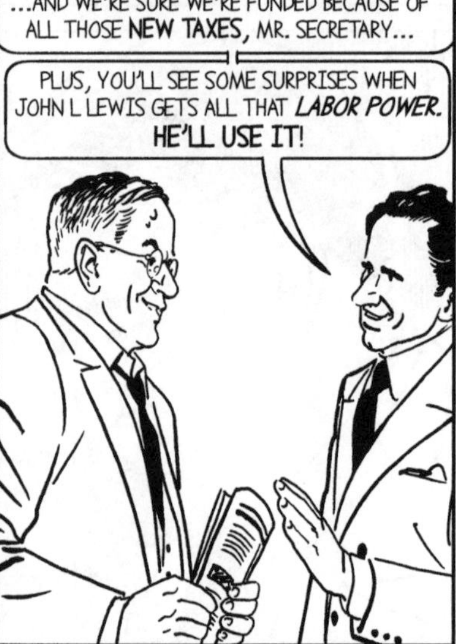
...AND WE'RE SURE WE'RE FUNDED BECAUSE OF ALL THOSE NEW TAXES, MR. SECRETARY...
PLUS, YOU'LL SEE SOME SURPRISES WHEN JOHN L LEWIS GETS ALL THAT LABOR POWER. HE'LL USE IT!

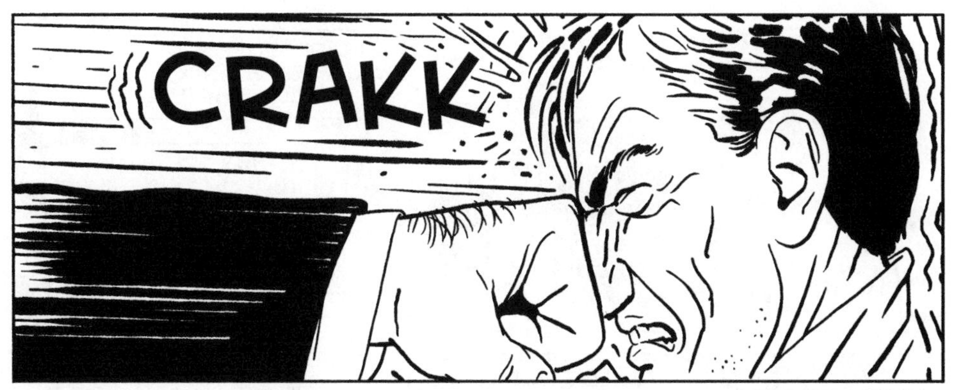
CRAKK

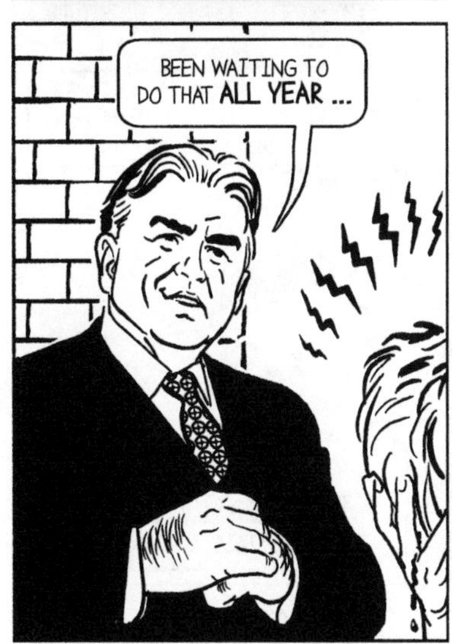
BEEN WAITING TO DO THAT ALL YEAR ...

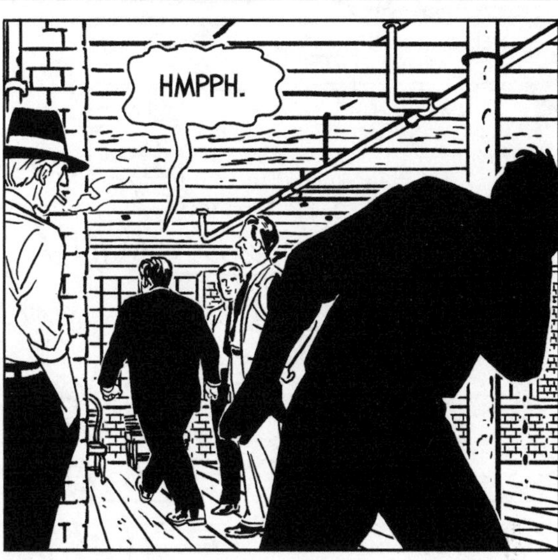
HMPPH.

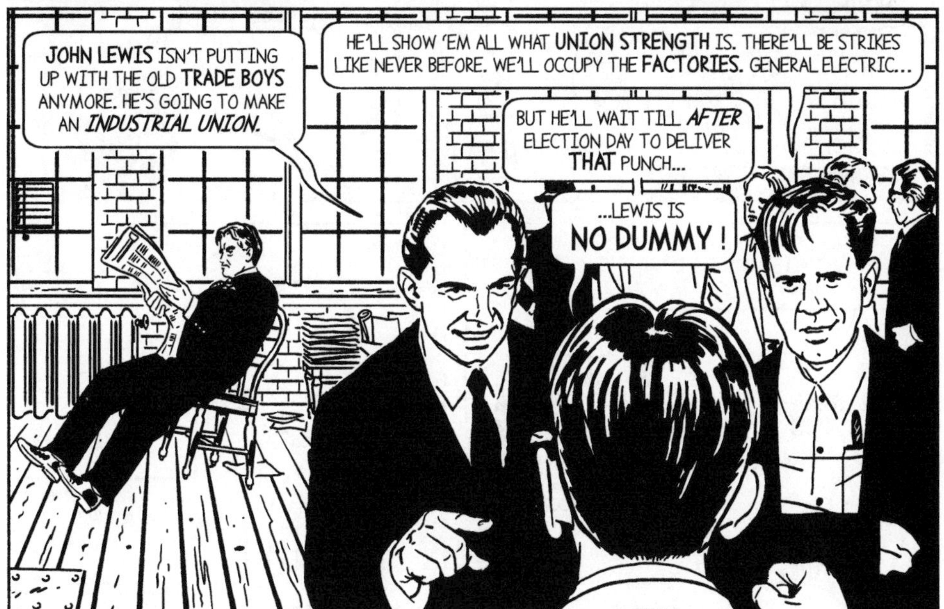
JOHN LEWIS ISN'T PUTTING UP WITH THE OLD TRADE BOYS ANYMORE. HE'S GOING TO MAKE AN *INDUSTRIAL UNION.*
HE'LL SHOW 'EM ALL WHAT UNION STRENGTH IS. THERE'LL BE STRIKES LIKE NEVER BEFORE. WE'LL OCCUPY THE FACTORIES. GENERAL ELECTRIC...
BUT HE'LL WAIT TILL *AFTER* ELECTION DAY TO DELIVER THAT PUNCH...
...LEWIS IS NO DUMMY !

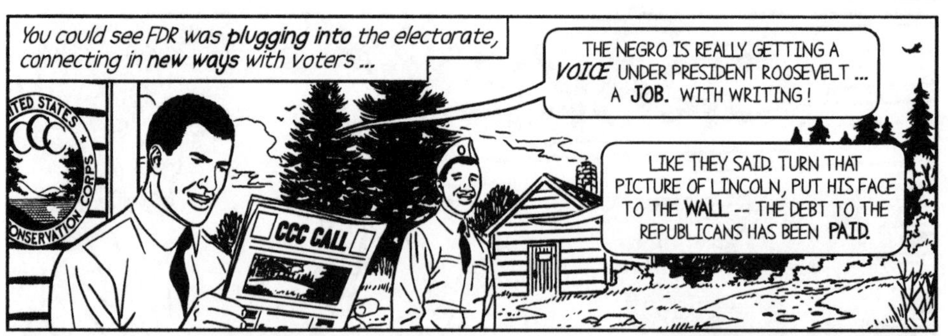
You could see FDR was **plugging into** the electorate, connecting in **new ways** with voters ...
THE NEGRO IS REALLY GETTING A *VOICE* UNDER PRESIDENT ROOSEVELT ... A **JOB.** WITH WRITING!
LIKE THEY SAID. TURN THAT PICTURE OF LINCOLN, PUT HIS FACE TO THE **WALL** -- THE DEBT TO THE REPUBLICANS HAS BEEN **PAID.**
UNITED STATES CCC CONSERVATION CORPS
CCC CALL

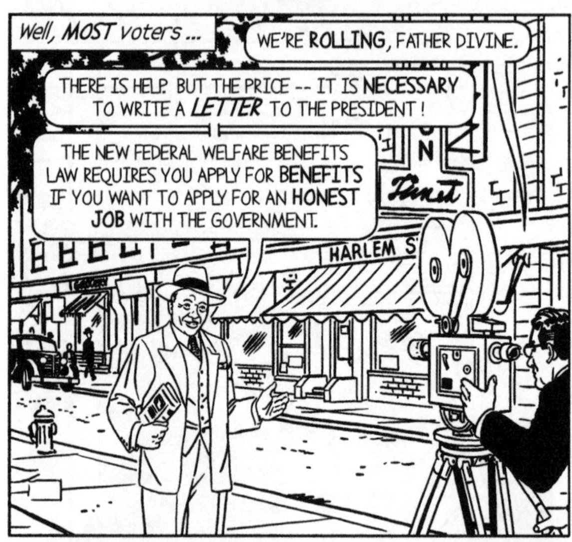
Well, *MOST* voters ...
WE'RE **ROLLING**, FATHER DIVINE.
THERE IS HELP. BUT THE PRICE -- IT IS **NECESSARY** TO WRITE A ***LETTER*** TO THE PRESIDENT!
THE NEW FEDERAL WELFARE BENEFITS LAW REQUIRES YOU APPLY FOR **BENEFITS** IF YOU WANT TO APPLY FOR AN **HONEST JOB** WITH THE GOVERNMENT.
HARLEM

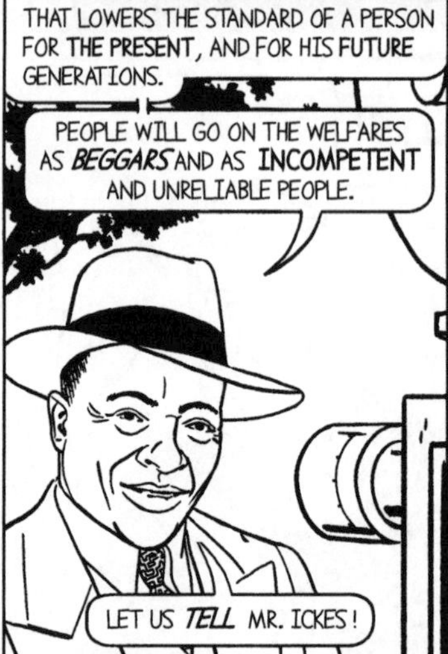
THAT LOWERS THE STANDARD OF A PERSON FOR **THE PRESENT**, AND FOR HIS **FUTURE** GENERATIONS.
PEOPLE WILL GO ON THE WELFARES AS ***BEGGARS*** AND AS **INCOMPETENT** AND UNRELIABLE PEOPLE.
LET US ***TELL*** MR. ICKES!

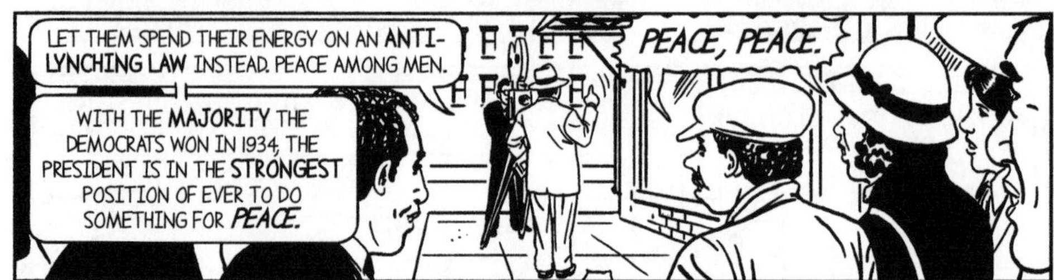
LET THEM SPEND THEIR ENERGY ON AN **ANTI-LYNCHING LAW** INSTEAD. PEACE AMONG MEN.
WITH THE **MAJORITY** THE DEMOCRATS WON IN 1934, THE PRESIDENT IS IN THE **STRONGEST** POSITION OF EVER TO DO SOMETHING FOR ***PEACE.***
PEACE, PEACE.

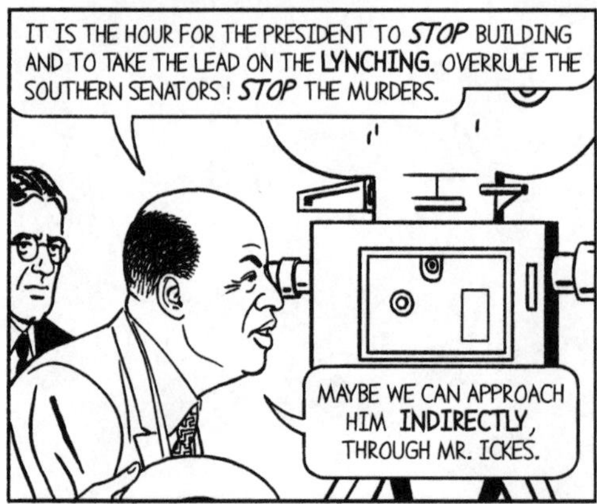
IT IS THE HOUR FOR THE PRESIDENT TO ***STOP*** BUILDING AND TO TAKE THE LEAD ON THE **LYNCHING.** OVERRULE THE SOUTHERN SENATORS! ***STOP*** THE MURDERS.
MAYBE WE CAN APPROACH HIM **INDIRECTLY**, THROUGH MR. ICKES.

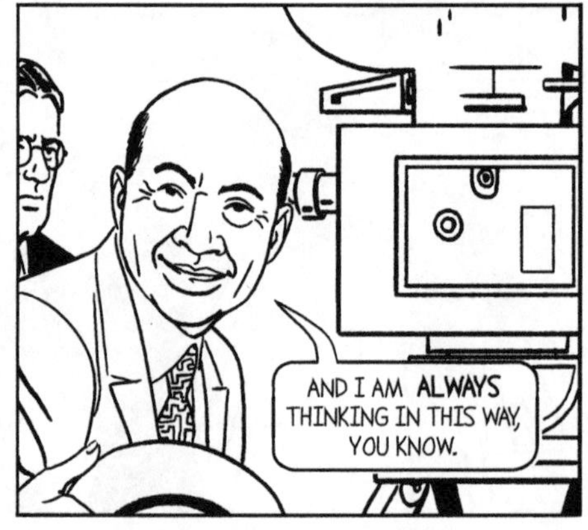
AND I AM **ALWAYS** THINKING IN THIS WAY, YOU KNOW.

The New Deal leaders' response to criticism was to **SCALE UP** the New Deal.

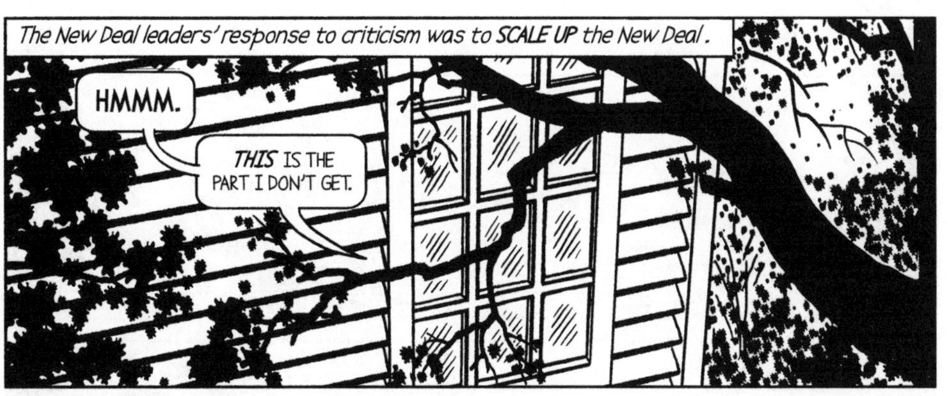

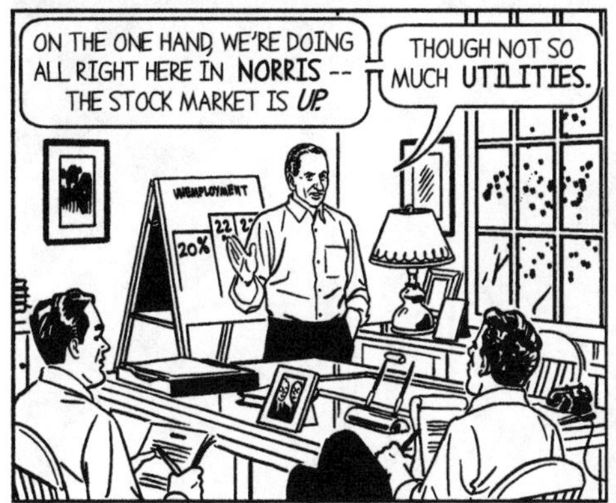

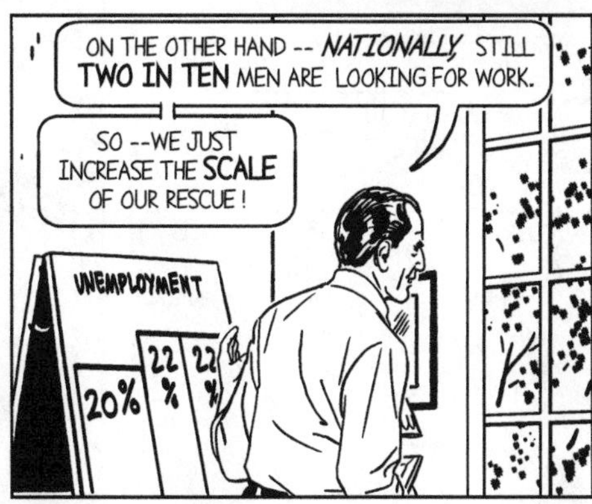

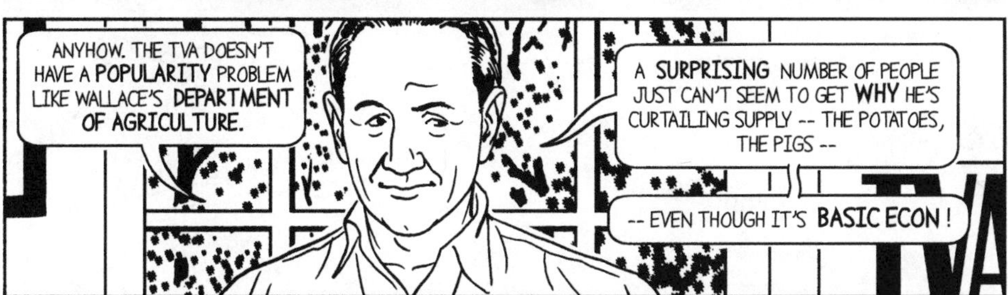

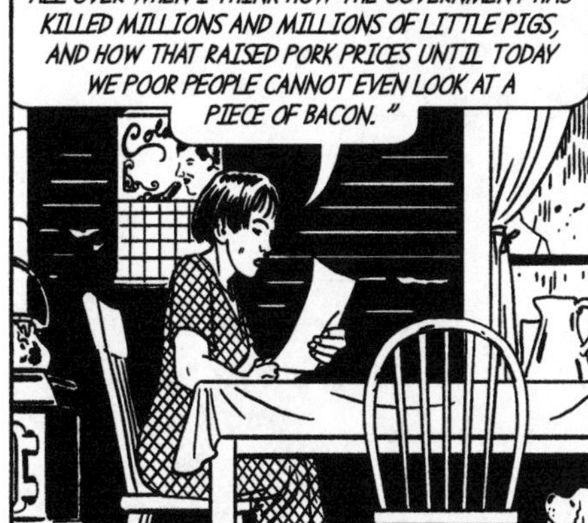

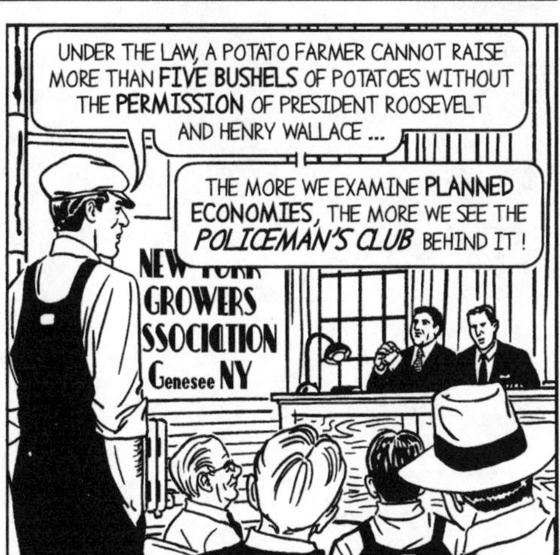

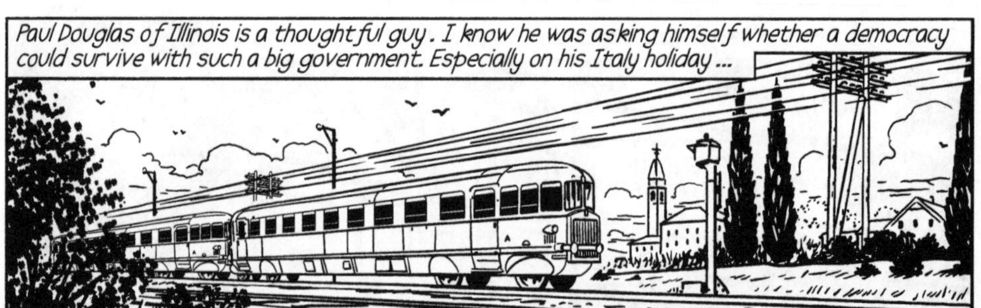
Paul Douglas of Illinois is a thoughtful guy. I know he was asking himself whether a democracy could survive with such a big government. Especially on his Italy holiday ...

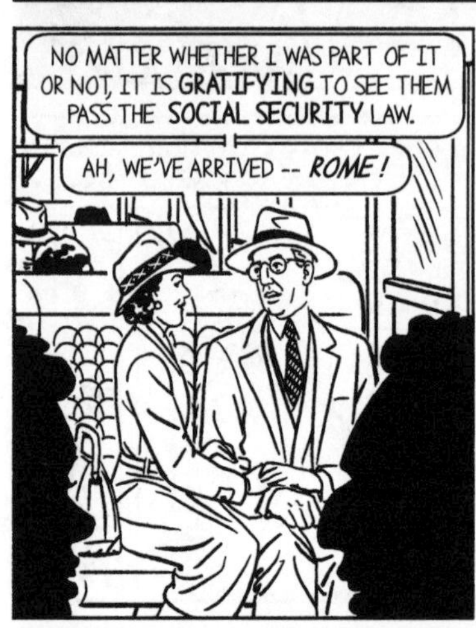
NO MATTER WHETHER I WAS PART OF IT OR NOT, IT IS GRATIFYING TO SEE THEM PASS THE SOCIAL SECURITY LAW.
AH, WE'VE ARRIVED -- ROME!

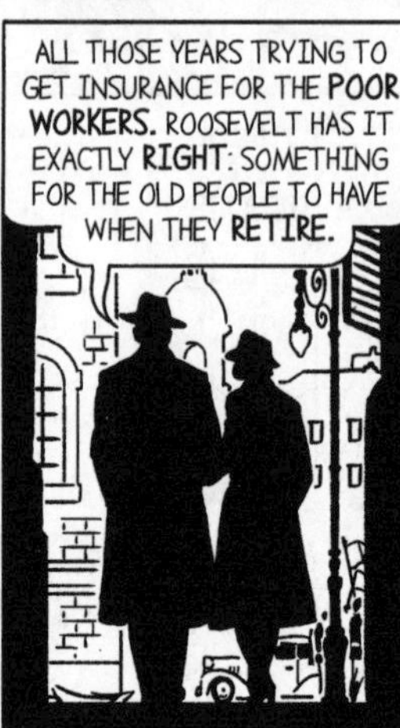
ALL THOSE YEARS TRYING TO GET INSURANCE FOR THE POOR WORKERS. ROOSEVELT HAS IT EXACTLY RIGHT: SOMETHING FOR THE OLD PEOPLE TO HAVE WHEN THEY RETIRE.

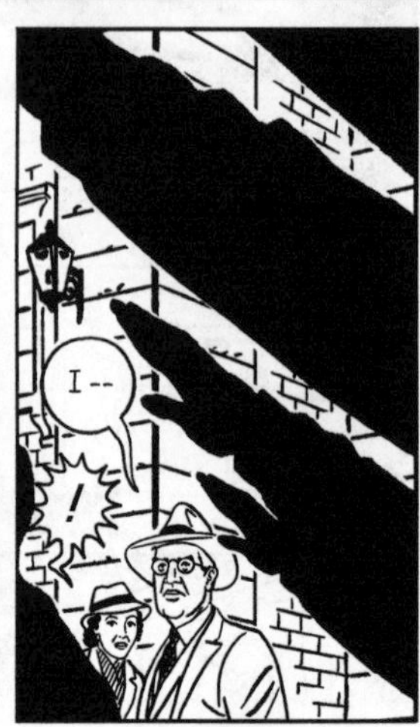
I --
!

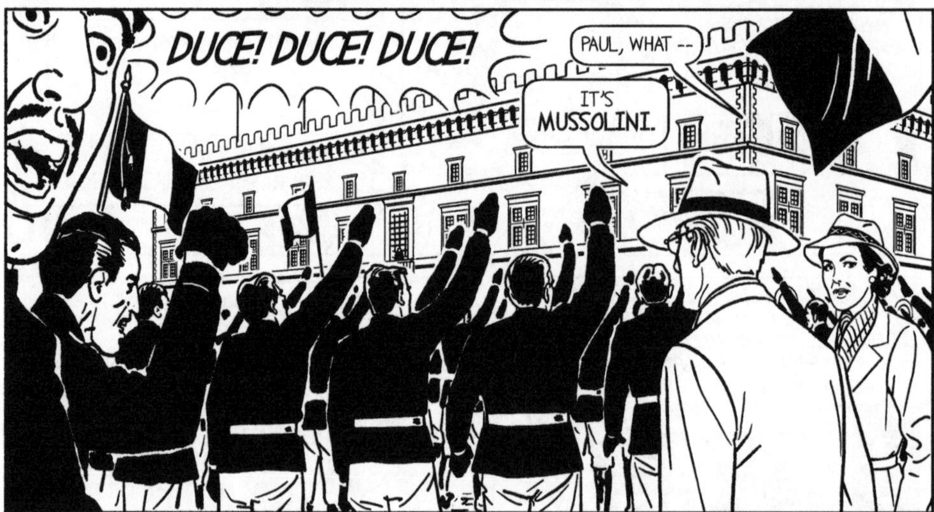
DUCE! DUCE! DUCE!
PAUL, WHAT --
IT'S MUSSOLINI.

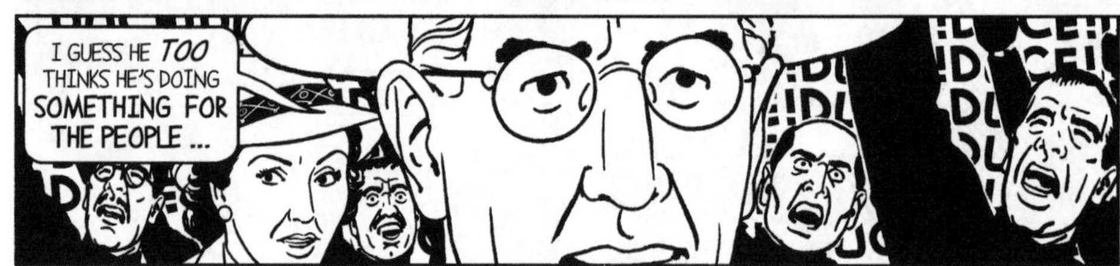
I GUESS HE TOO THINKS HE'S DOING SOMETHING FOR THE PEOPLE ...

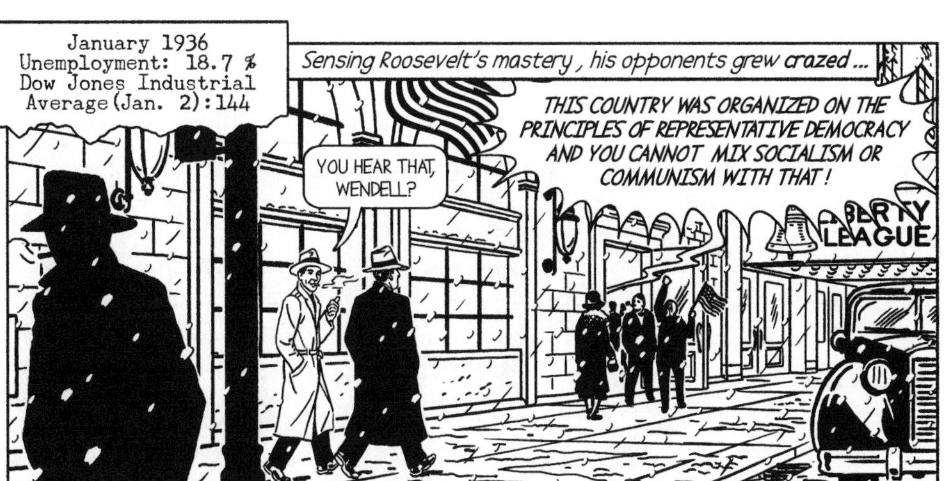
January 1936
Unemployment: 18.7 %
Dow Jones Industrial
Average (Jan. 2): 144
Sensing Roosevelt's mastery, his opponents grew crazed...
THIS COUNTRY WAS ORGANIZED ON THE PRINCIPLES OF REPRESENTATIVE DEMOCRACY AND YOU CANNOT MIX SOCIALISM OR COMMUNISM WITH THAT!
YOU HEAR THAT, WENDELL?
LEAGUE

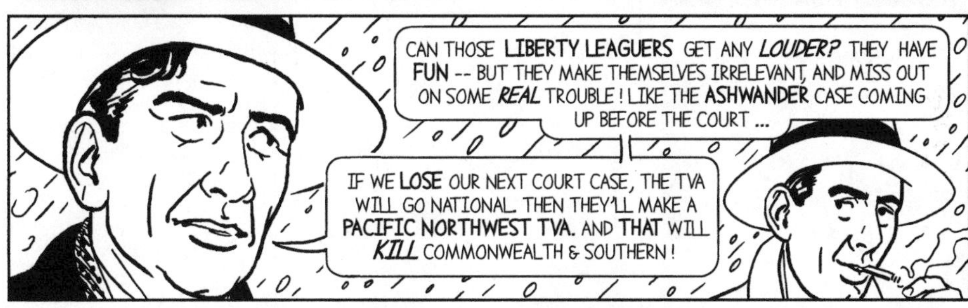
CAN THOSE LIBERTY LEAGUERS GET ANY LOUDER? THEY HAVE FUN -- BUT THEY MAKE THEMSELVES IRRELEVANT, AND MISS OUT ON SOME REAL TROUBLE! LIKE THE ASHWANDER CASE COMING UP BEFORE THE COURT ...
IF WE LOSE OUR NEXT COURT CASE, THE TVA WILL GO NATIONAL. THEN THEY'LL MAKE A PACIFIC NORTHWEST TVA. AND THAT WILL KILL COMMONWEALTH & SOUTHERN!

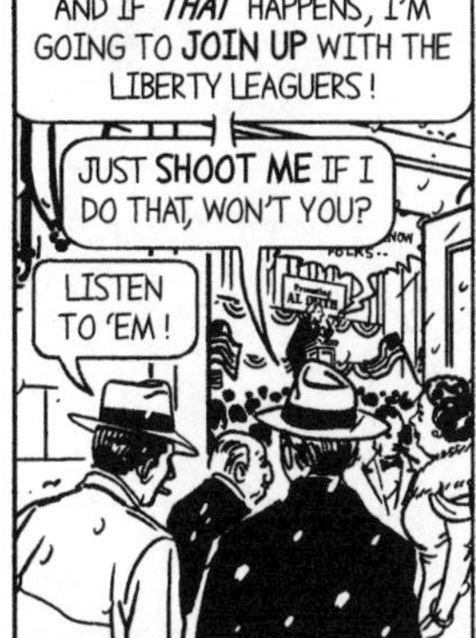
AND IF THAT HAPPENS, I'M GOING TO JOIN UP WITH THE LIBERTY LEAGUERS!
JUST SHOOT ME IF I DO THAT, WON'T YOU?
LISTEN TO 'EM!

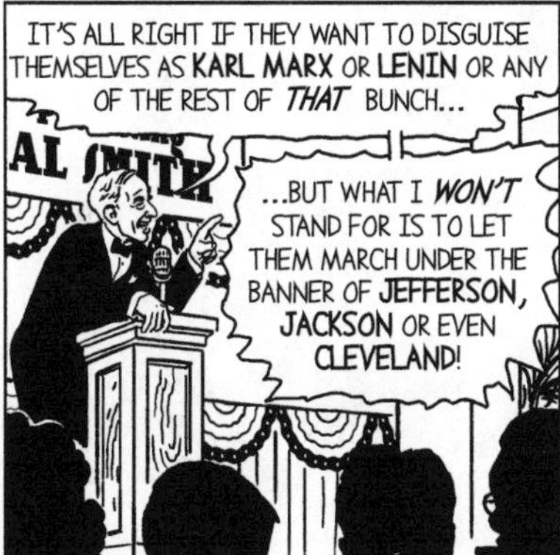
IT'S ALL RIGHT IF THEY WANT TO DISGUISE THEMSELVES AS KARL MARX OR LENIN OR ANY OF THE REST OF THAT BUNCH...
AL SMITH
...BUT WHAT I WON'T STAND FOR IS TO LET THEM MARCH UNDER THE BANNER OF JEFFERSON, JACKSON OR EVEN CLEVELAND!

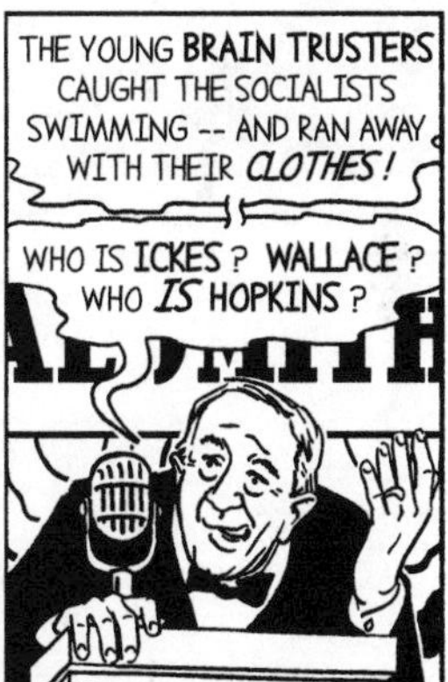
THE YOUNG BRAIN TRUSTERS CAUGHT THE SOCIALISTS SWIMMING -- AND RAN AWAY WITH THEIR CLOTHES!
WHO IS ICKES? WALLACE? WHO IS HOPKINS?

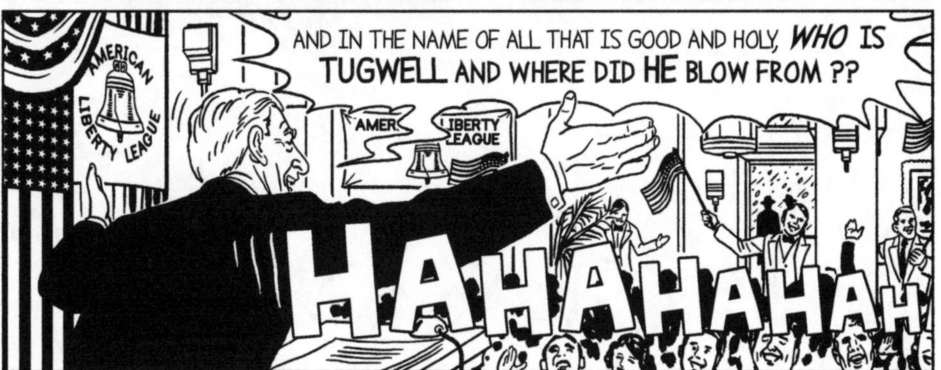
AND IN THE NAME OF ALL THAT IS GOOD AND HOLY, WHO IS TUGWELL AND WHERE DID HE BLOW FROM??
AMERICAN LIBERTY LEAGUE
AMER
LIBERTY LEAGUE
HAHAHAHAHAH

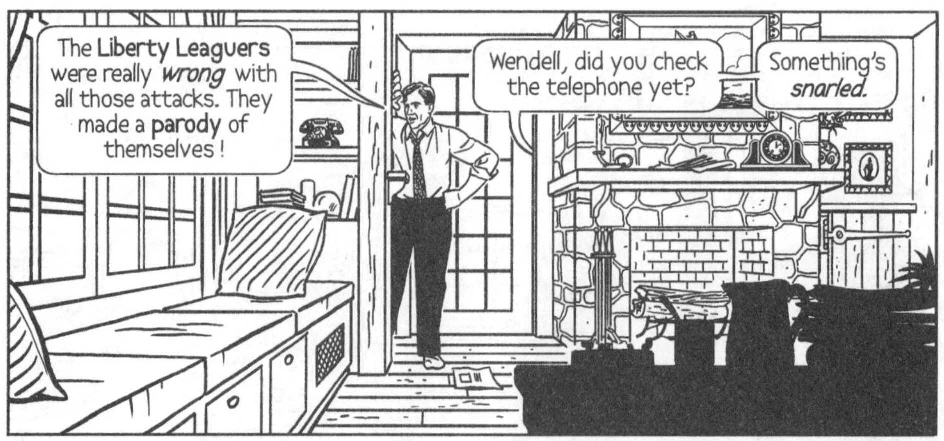
The Liberty Leaguers were really *wrong* with all those attacks. They made a **parody** of themselves !
Wendell, did you check the telephone yet?
Something's *snarled.*

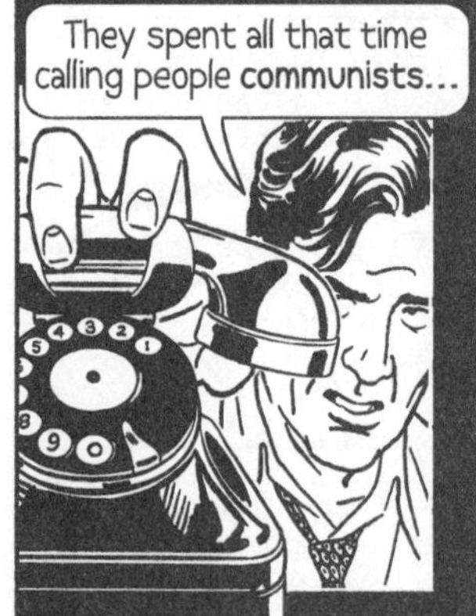
They spent all that time calling people **communists**...

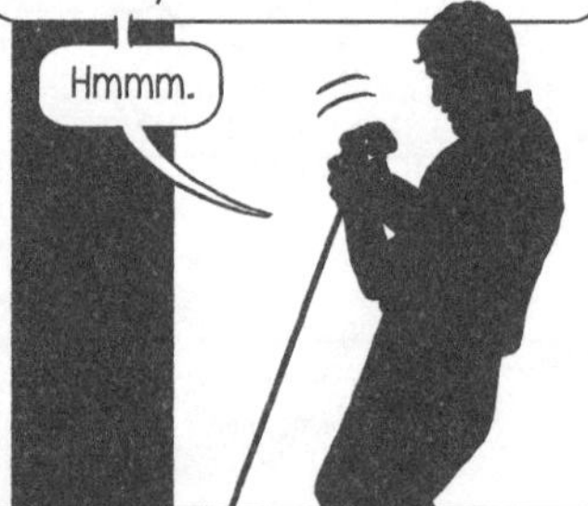
Sure, there *were* communists reporting to Moscow in the U.S. **Yes**, there were communists in **Knoxville** trying to **wire** their way into the TVA.
Hmmm.

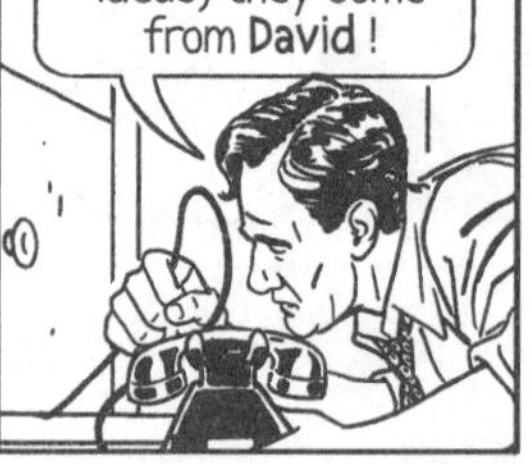
But those communists had almost *no* success influencing the TVA officials.
So if David has lefty ideas, they come from **David** !

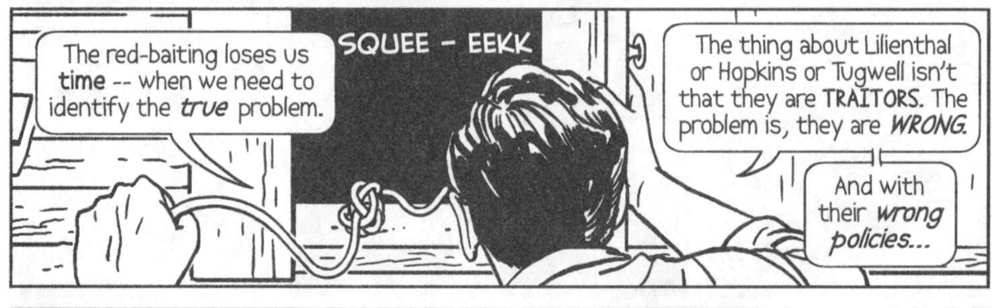
The red-baiting loses us **time** -- when we need to identify the *true* problem.
SQUEE - EEKK
The thing about Lilienthal or Hopkins or Tugwell isn't that they are **TRAITORS.** The problem is, they are *WRONG.*
And with their *wrong policies...*

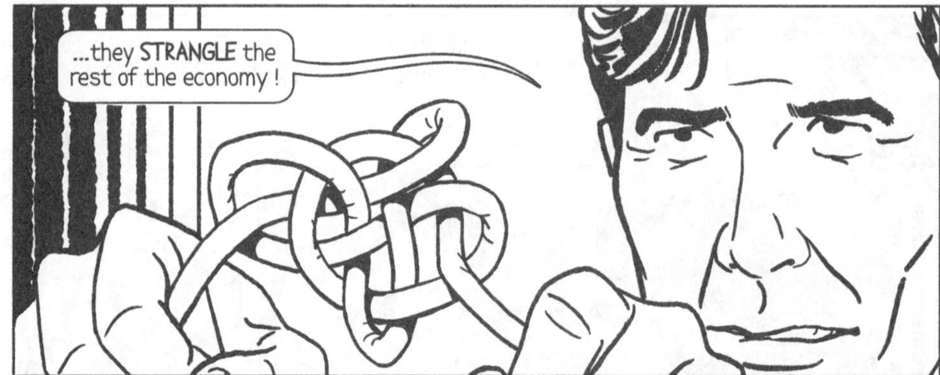
...they **STRANGLE** the rest of the economy !

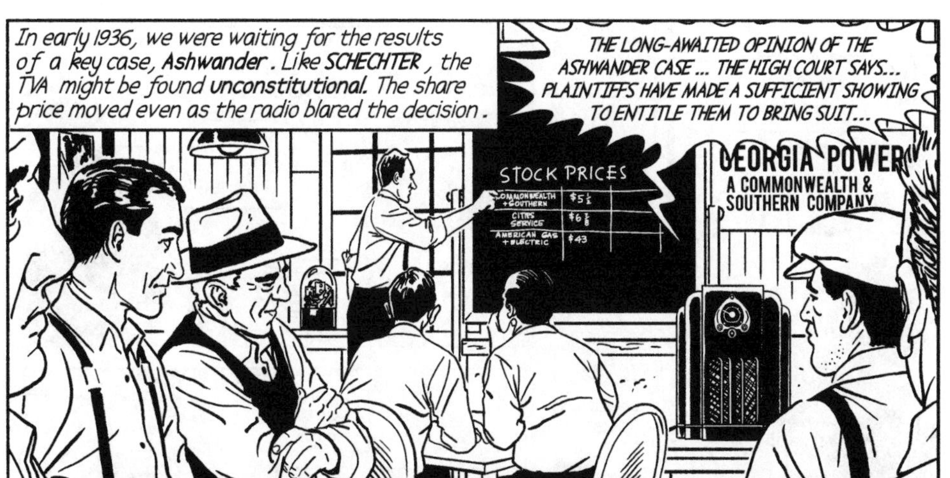
In early 1936, we were waiting for the results of a key case, Ashwander. Like SCHECHTER, the TVA might be found unconstitutional. The share price moved even as the radio blared the decision.
THE LONG-AWAITED OPINION OF THE ASHWANDER CASE... THE HIGH COURT SAYS... PLAINTIFFS HAVE MADE A SUFFICIENT SHOWING TO ENTITLE THEM TO BRING SUIT...
STOCK PRICES
COMMONWEALTH + SOUTHERN $5½
CITIES SERVICE $6⅞
AMERICAN GAS + ELECTRIC $43
GEORGIA POWER
A COMMONWEALTH & SOUTHERN COMPANY

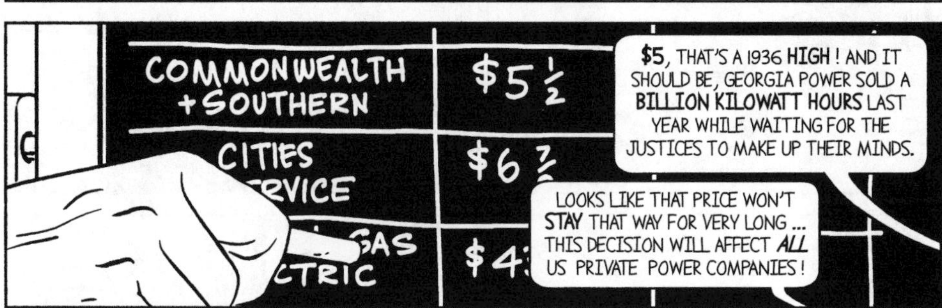
COMMONWEALTH + SOUTHERN $5½
CITIES SERVICE $6⅞
$5, THAT'S A 1936 HIGH! AND IT SHOULD BE, GEORGIA POWER SOLD A BILLION KILOWATT HOURS LAST YEAR WHILE WAITING FOR THE JUSTICES TO MAKE UP THEIR MINDS.
LOOKS LIKE THAT PRICE WON'T STAY THAT WAY FOR VERY LONG... THIS DECISION WILL AFFECT ALL US PRIVATE POWER COMPANIES!

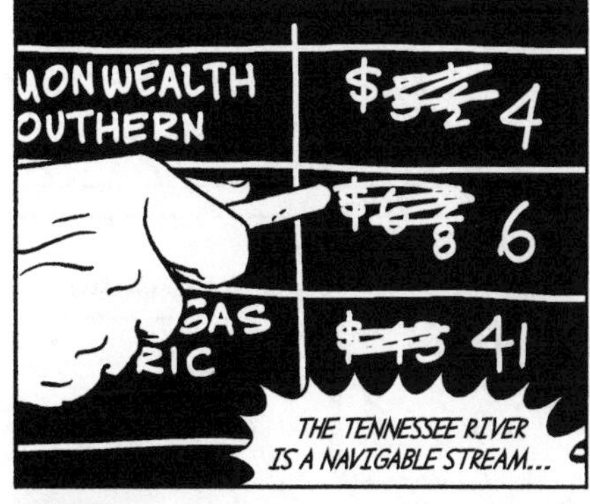
4
6
41
THE TENNESSEE RIVER IS A NAVIGABLE STREAM...

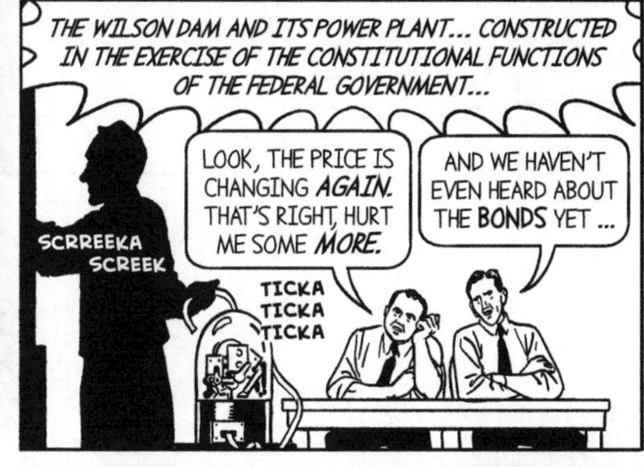
THE WILSON DAM AND ITS POWER PLANT... CONSTRUCTED IN THE EXERCISE OF THE CONSTITUTIONAL FUNCTIONS OF THE FEDERAL GOVERNMENT...
SCRREEKA SCREEK
TICKA TICKA TICKA
LOOK, THE PRICE IS CHANGING AGAIN. THAT'S RIGHT, HURT ME SOME MORE.
AND WE HAVEN'T EVEN HEARD ABOUT THE BONDS YET...

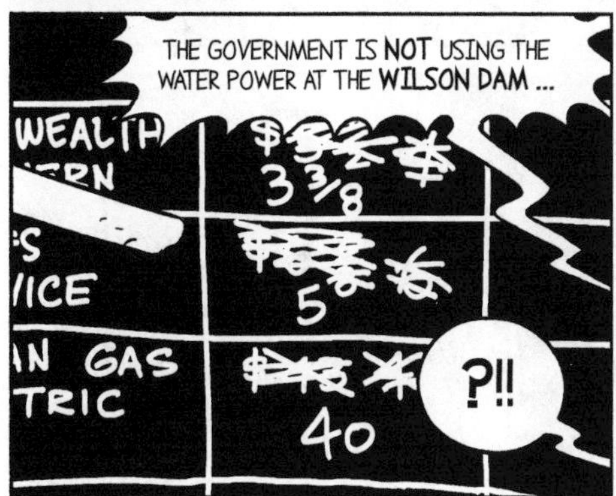
THE GOVERNMENT IS NOT USING THE WATER POWER AT THE WILSON DAM...
3⅜
5
40
?!!

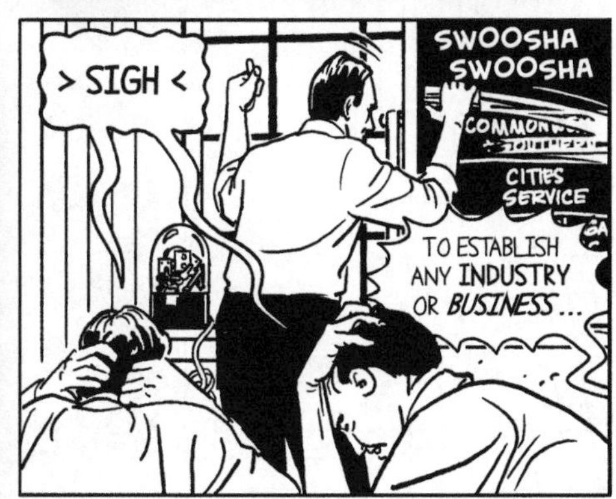
> SIGH <
SWOOSHA SWOOSHA
CITIES SERVICE
TO ESTABLISH ANY INDUSTRY OR BUSINESS...

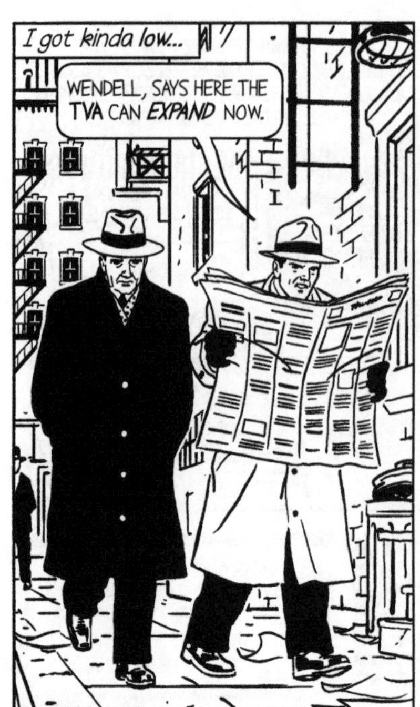
I got kinda low...
WENDELL, SAYS HERE THE TVA CAN EXPAND NOW.

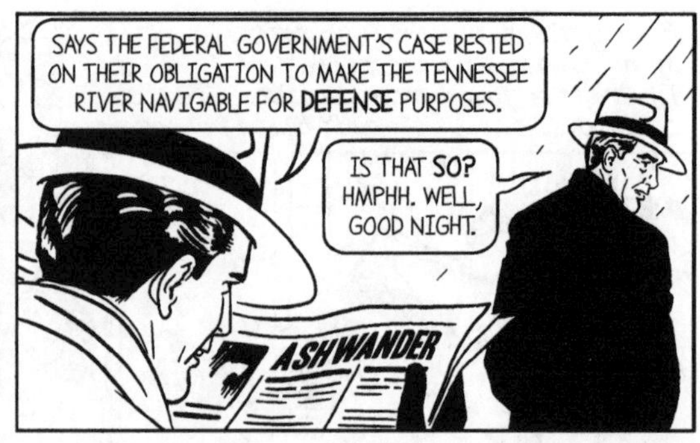
SAYS THE FEDERAL GOVERNMENT'S CASE RESTED ON THEIR OBLIGATION TO MAKE THE TENNESSEE RIVER NAVIGABLE FOR DEFENSE PURPOSES.
IS THAT SO? HMPHH. WELL, GOOD NIGHT.
ASHWANDER

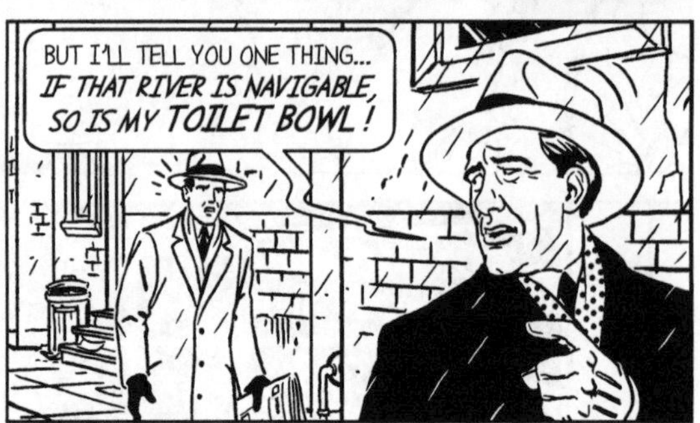
BUT I'LL TELL YOU ONE THING... IF THAT RIVER IS NAVIGABLE, SO IS MY TOILET BOWL !

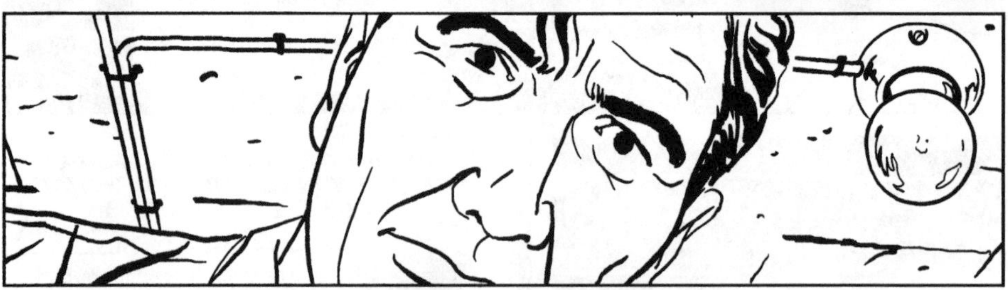

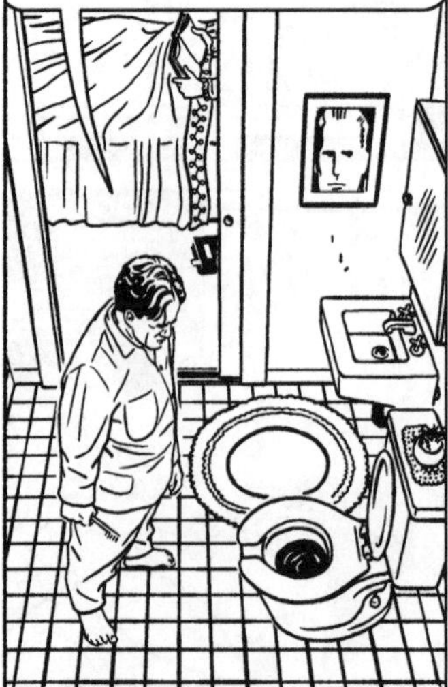
BILLIE, I DON'T KNOW WHAT'LL HAPPEN NEXT. THIS ACT IS THE BEGINNING OF SOMETHING I CAN'T STOP.

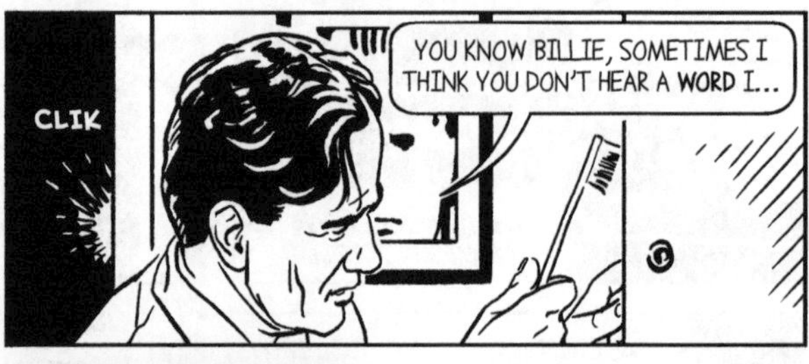
CLIK
YOU KNOW BILLIE, SOMETIMES I THINK YOU DON'T HEAR A WORD I...

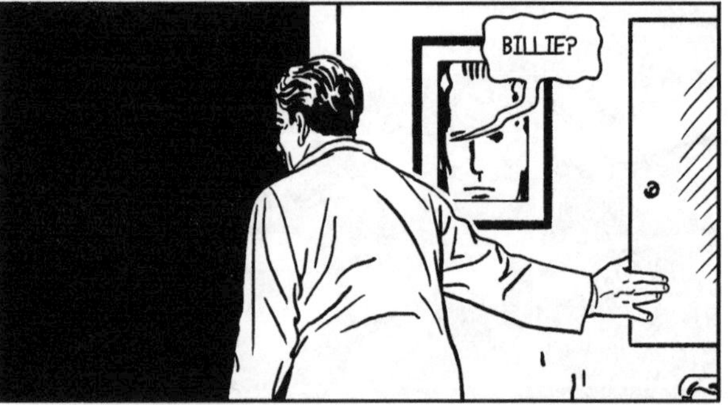
BILLIE?

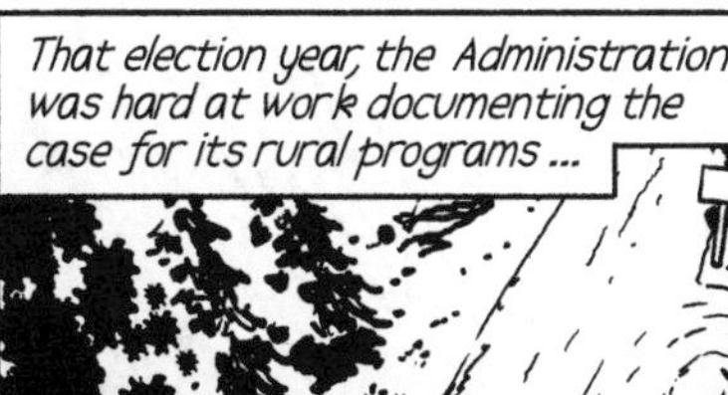
That election year, the Administration was hard at work documenting the case for its rural programs ...

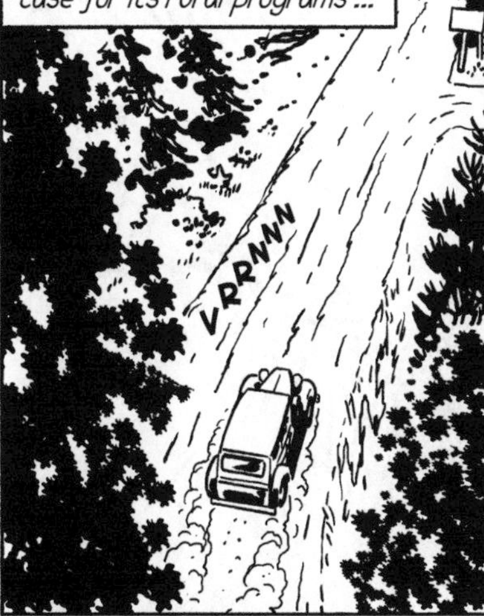
VRRNNN

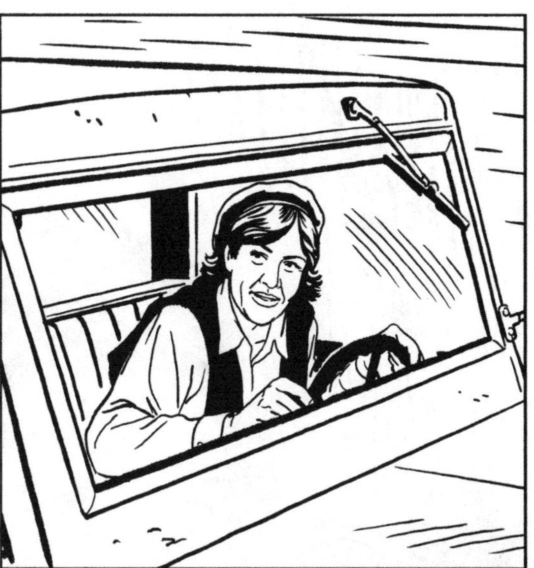

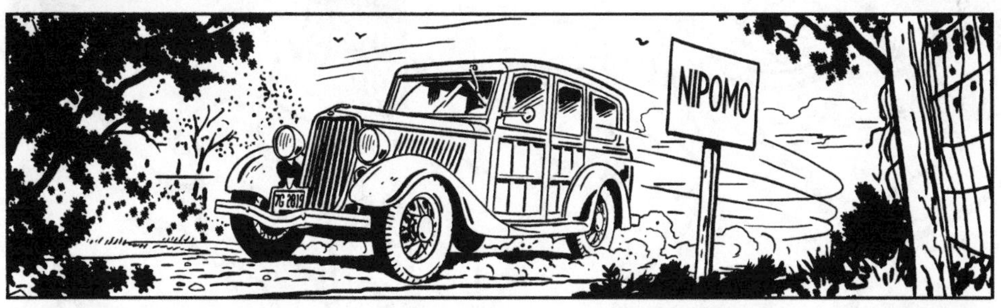
NIPOMO

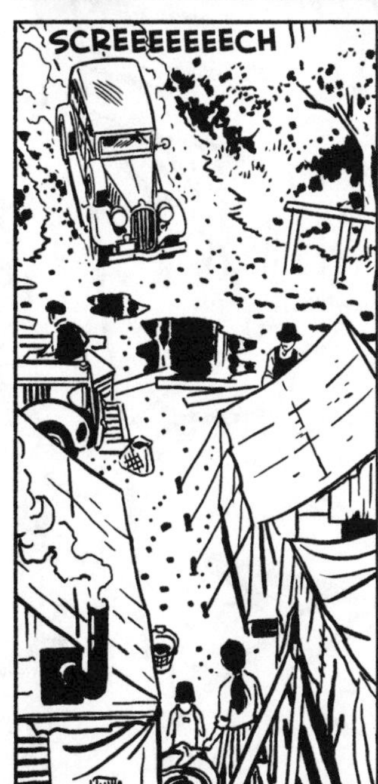
SCREEEEEEECH

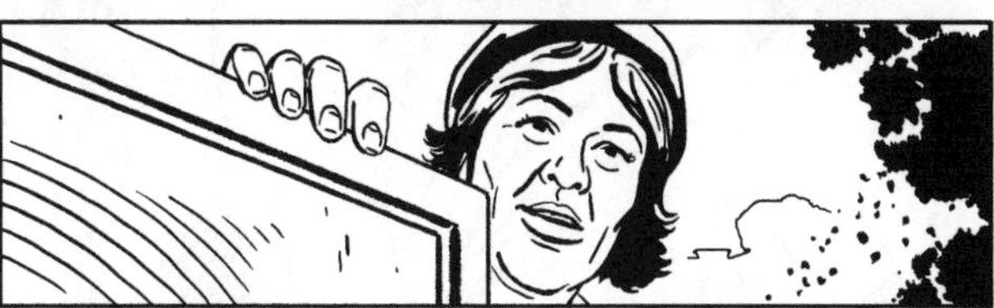

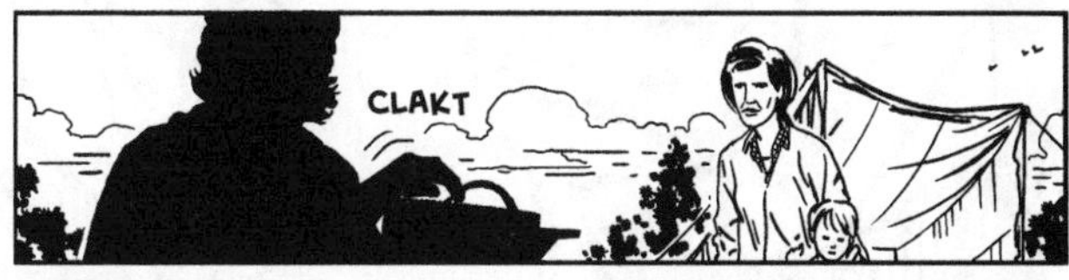
CLAKT

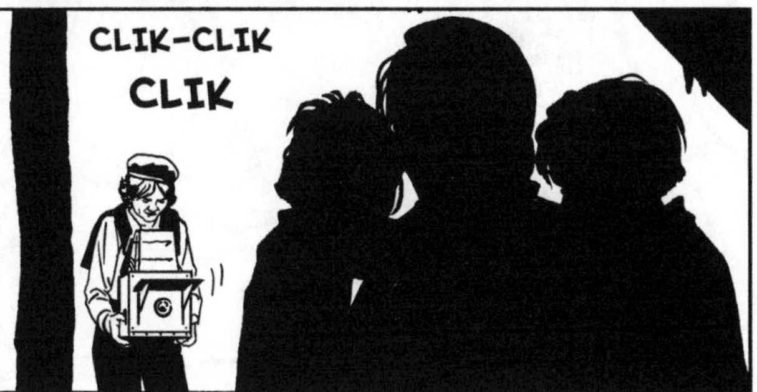
CLIK-CLIK
CLIK

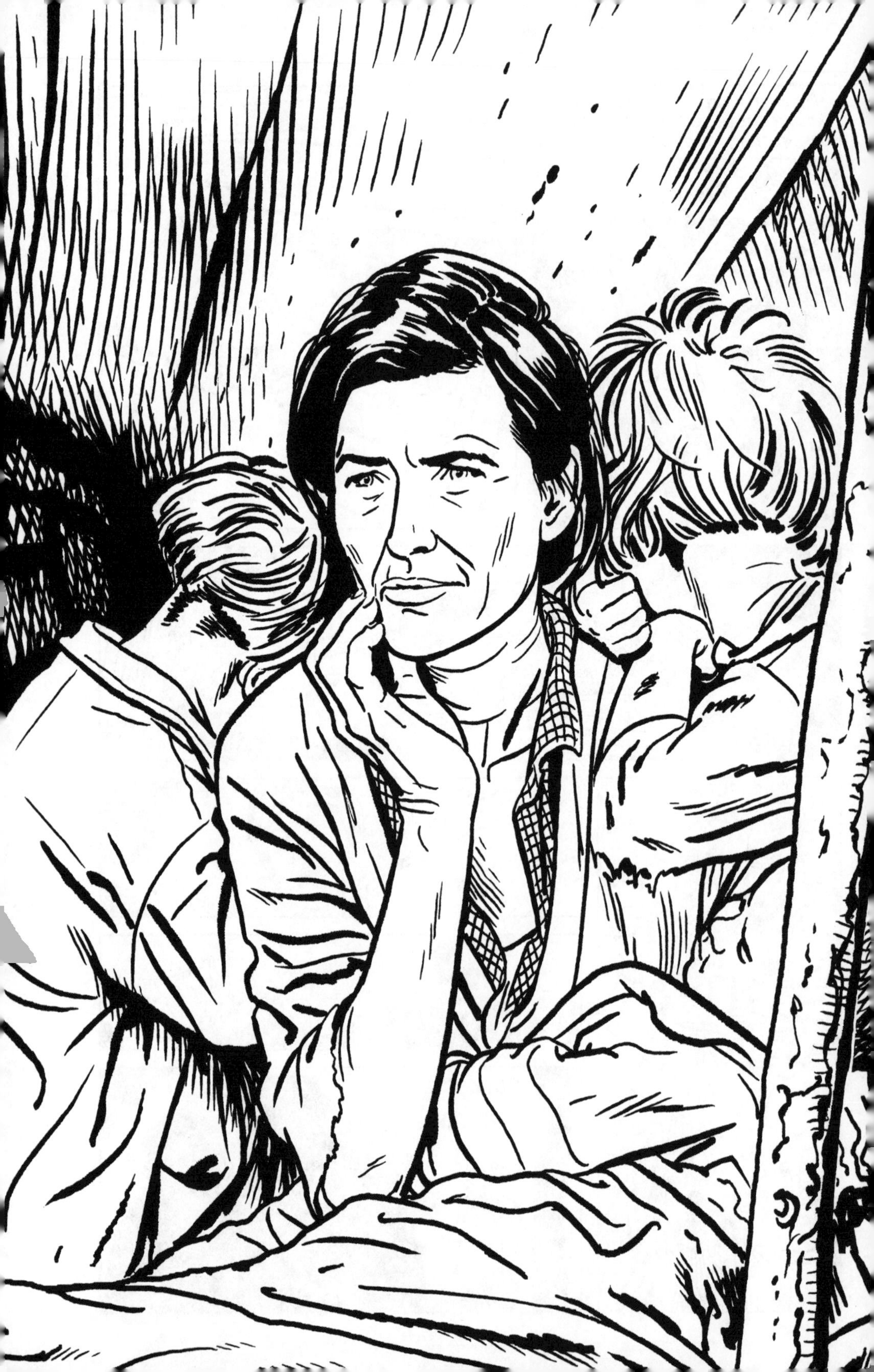

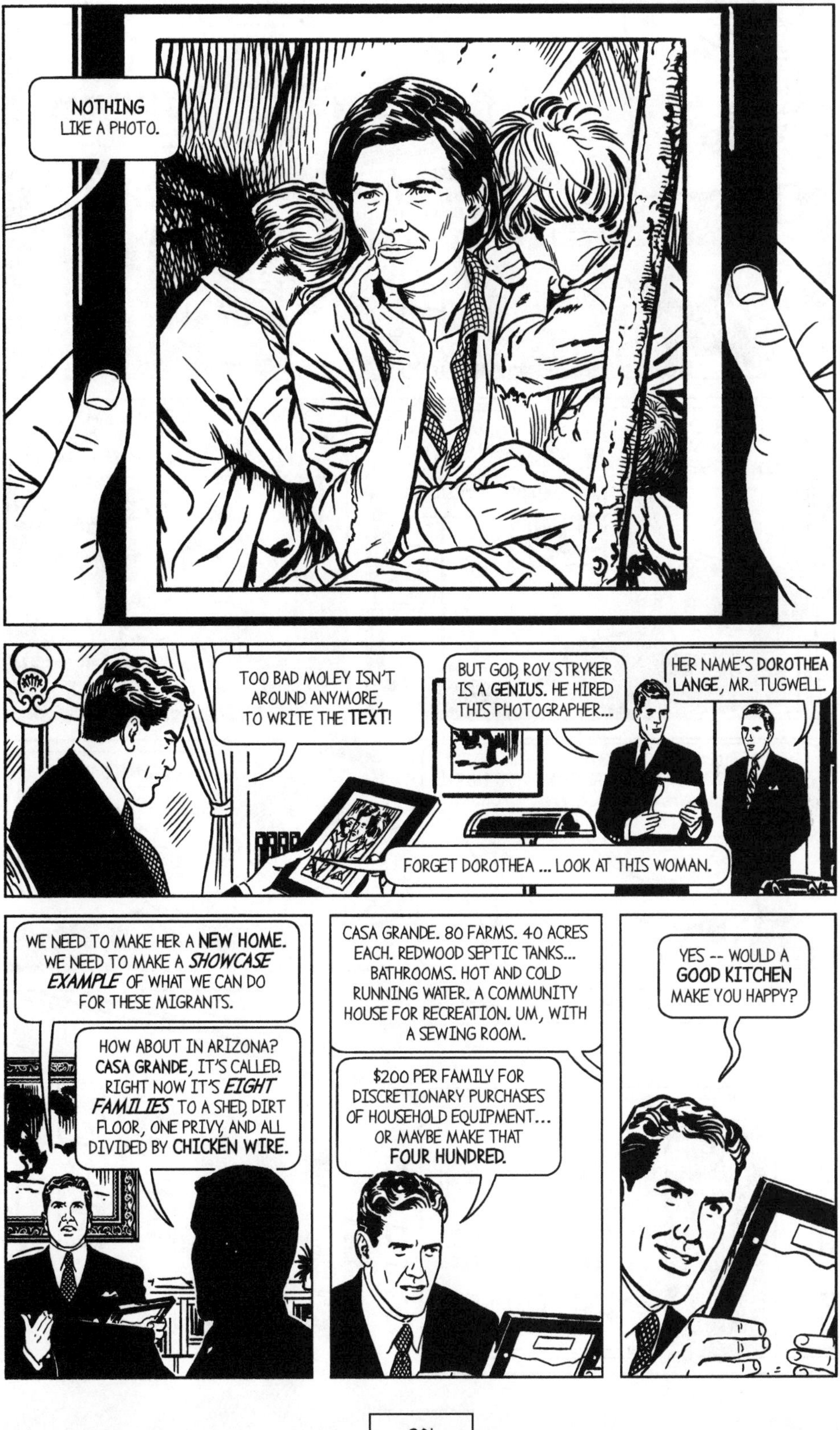

NOTHING
LIKE A PHOTO.

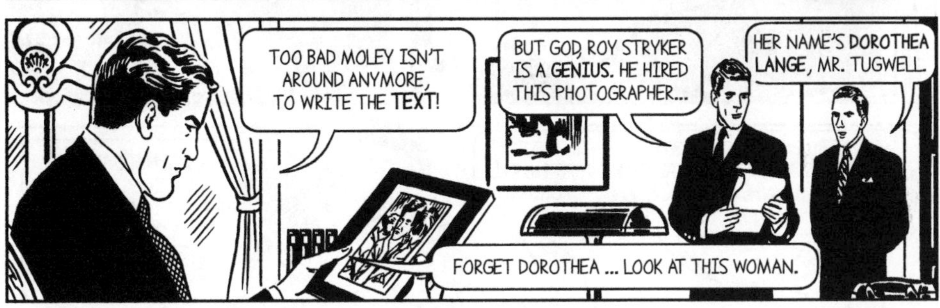

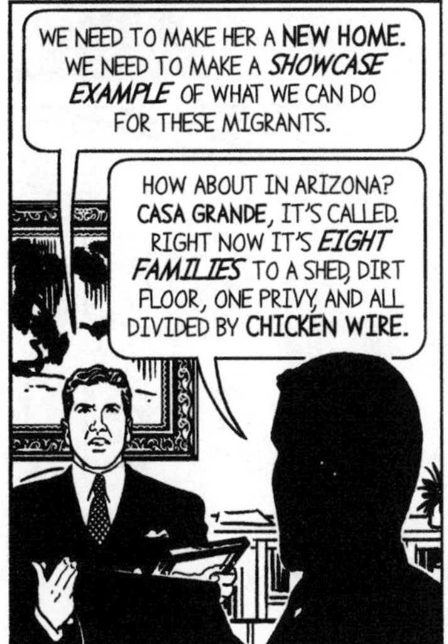

CASA GRANDE. 80 FARMS. 40 ACRES EACH. REDWOOD SEPTIC TANKS... BATHROOMS. HOT AND COLD RUNNING WATER. A COMMUNITY HOUSE FOR RECREATION. UM, WITH A SEWING ROOM.

$200 PER FAMILY FOR DISCRETIONARY PURCHASES OF HOUSEHOLD EQUIPMENT... OR MAYBE MAKE THAT **FOUR HUNDRED**.

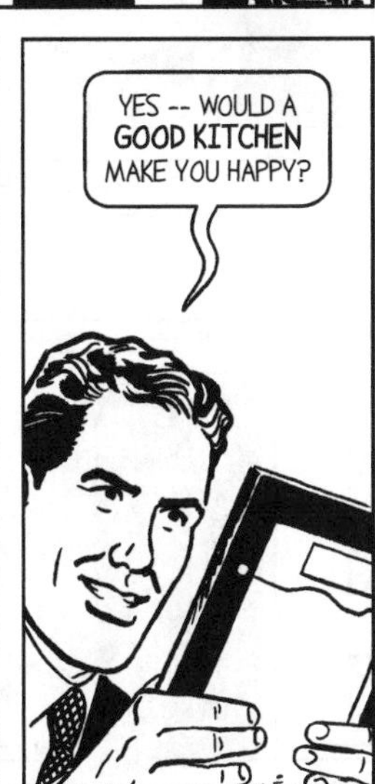

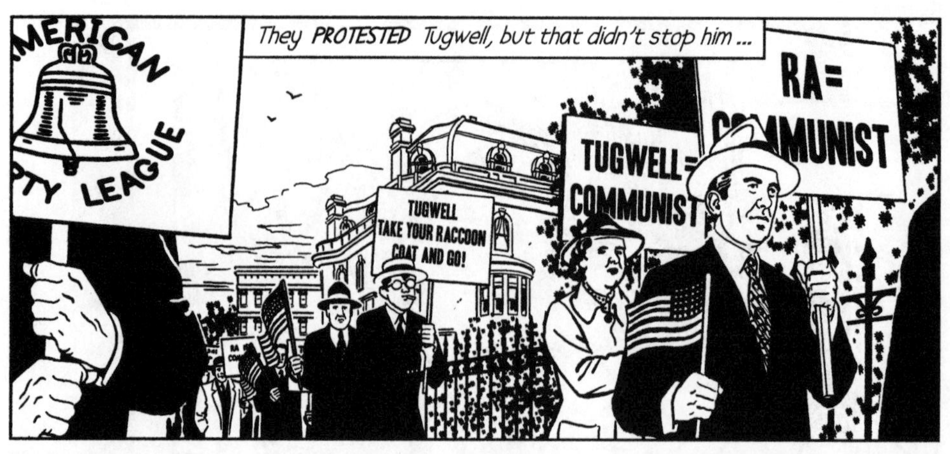
They PROTESTED Tugwell, but that didn't stop him ...
MERICAN
PTY LEAGUE
TUGWELL TAKE YOUR RACCOON COAT AND GO!
TUGWELL= COMMUNIST
RA= COMMUNIST

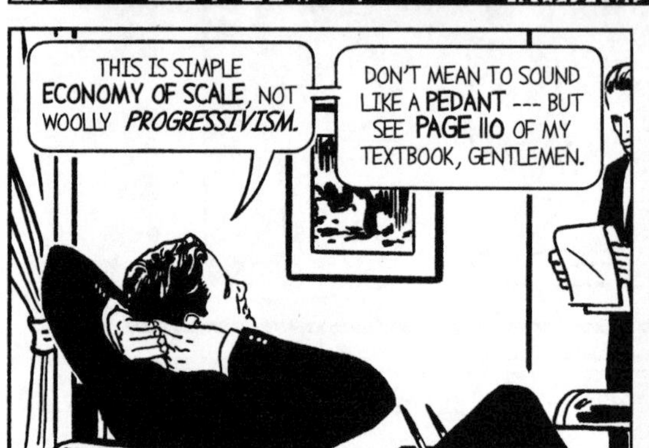
THIS IS SIMPLE ECONOMY OF SCALE, NOT WOOLLY PROGRESSIVISM.
DON'T MEAN TO SOUND LIKE A PEDANT --- BUT SEE PAGE 110 OF MY TEXTBOOK, GENTLEMEN.

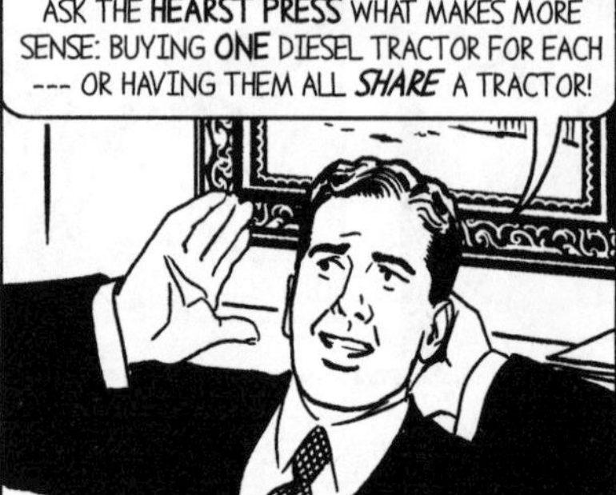
ASK THE HEARST PRESS WHAT MAKES MORE SENSE: BUYING ONE DIESEL TRACTOR FOR EACH --- OR HAVING THEM ALL SHARE A TRACTOR!

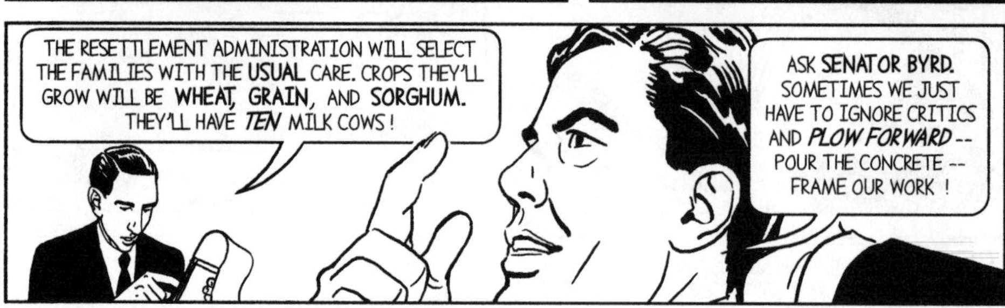
THE RESETTLEMENT ADMINISTRATION WILL SELECT THE FAMILIES WITH THE USUAL CARE. CROPS THEY'LL GROW WILL BE WHEAT, GRAIN, AND SORGHUM. THEY'LL HAVE TEN MILK COWS!
ASK SENATOR BYRD. SOMETIMES WE JUST HAVE TO IGNORE CRITICS AND PLOW FORWARD -- POUR THE CONCRETE -- FRAME OUR WORK !

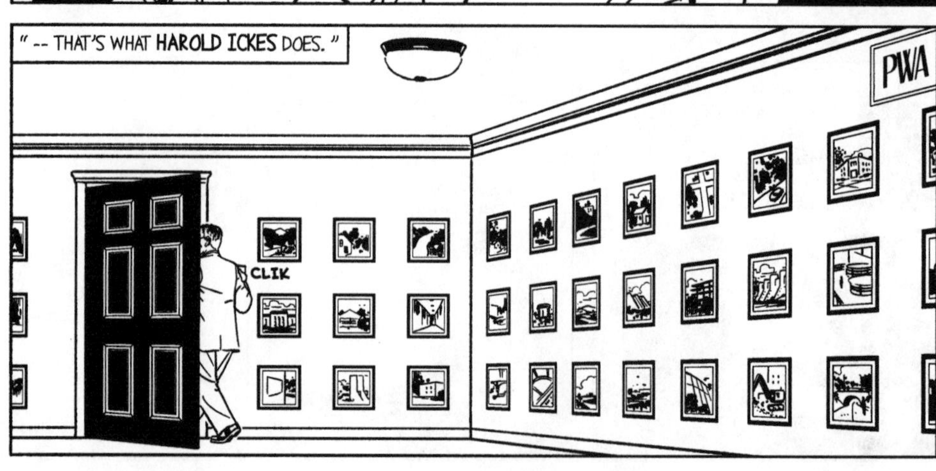
" -- THAT'S WHAT HAROLD ICKES DOES. "
PWA
CLIK

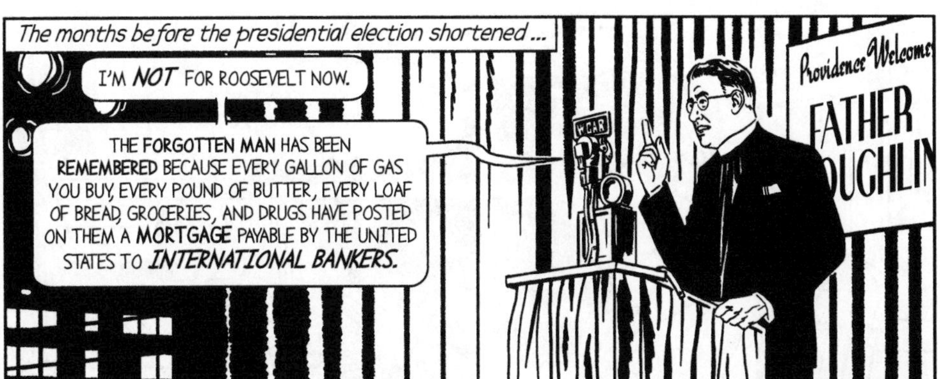
The months before the presidential election shortened ...
I'M NOT FOR ROOSEVELT NOW.
THE FORGOTTEN MAN HAS BEEN REMEMBERED BECAUSE EVERY GALLON OF GAS YOU BUY, EVERY POUND OF BUTTER, EVERY LOAF OF BREAD, GROCERIES, AND DRUGS HAVE POSTED ON THEM A MORTGAGE PAYABLE BY THE UNITED STATES TO INTERNATIONAL BANKERS.
Providence Welcomes
FATHER
OUGHLIN

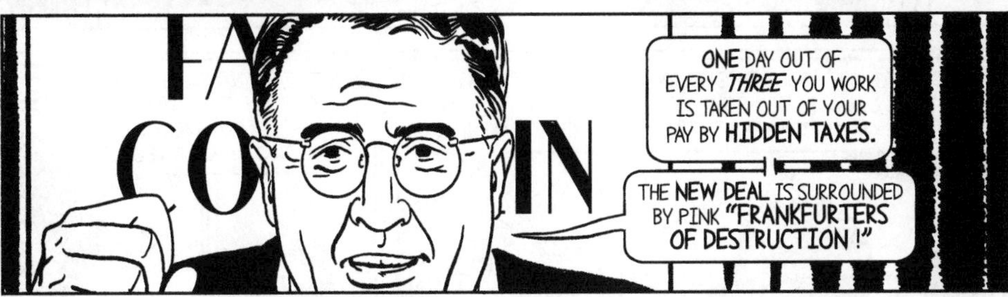
ONE DAY OUT OF EVERY THREE YOU WORK IS TAKEN OUT OF YOUR PAY BY HIDDEN TAXES.
THE NEW DEAL IS SURROUNDED BY PINK "FRANKFURTERS OF DESTRUCTION!"

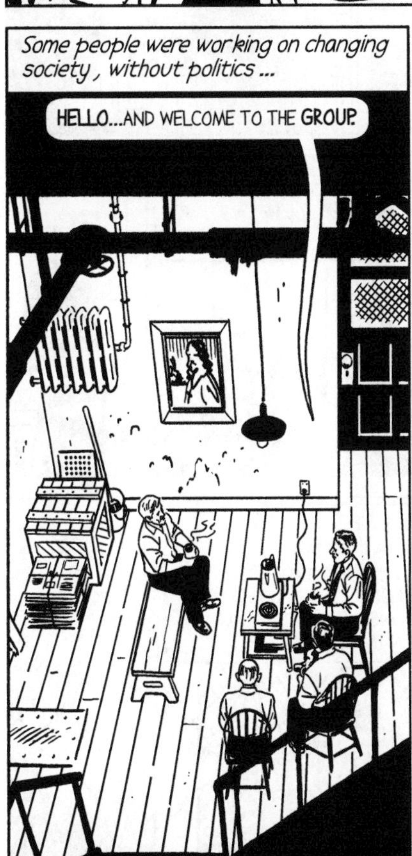
Some people were working on changing society, without politics ...
HELLO...AND WELCOME TO THE GROUP.

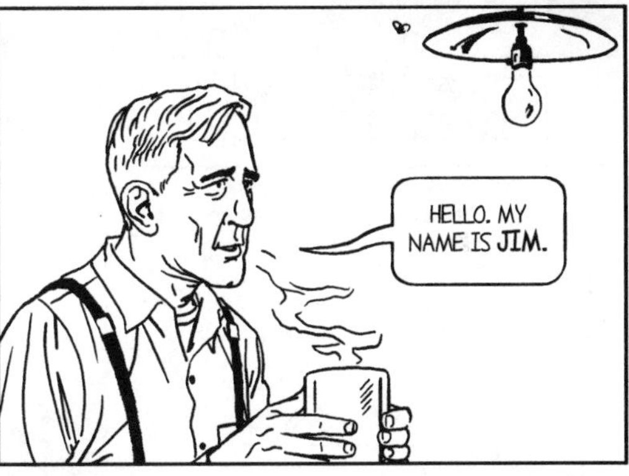
HELLO. MY NAME IS JIM.

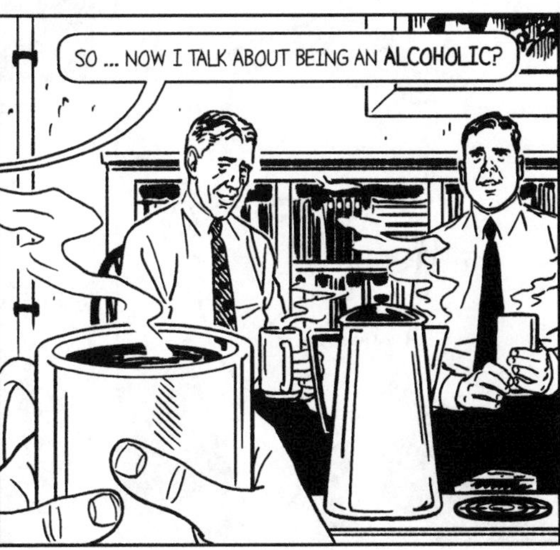
SO ... NOW I TALK ABOUT BEING AN ALCOHOLIC?

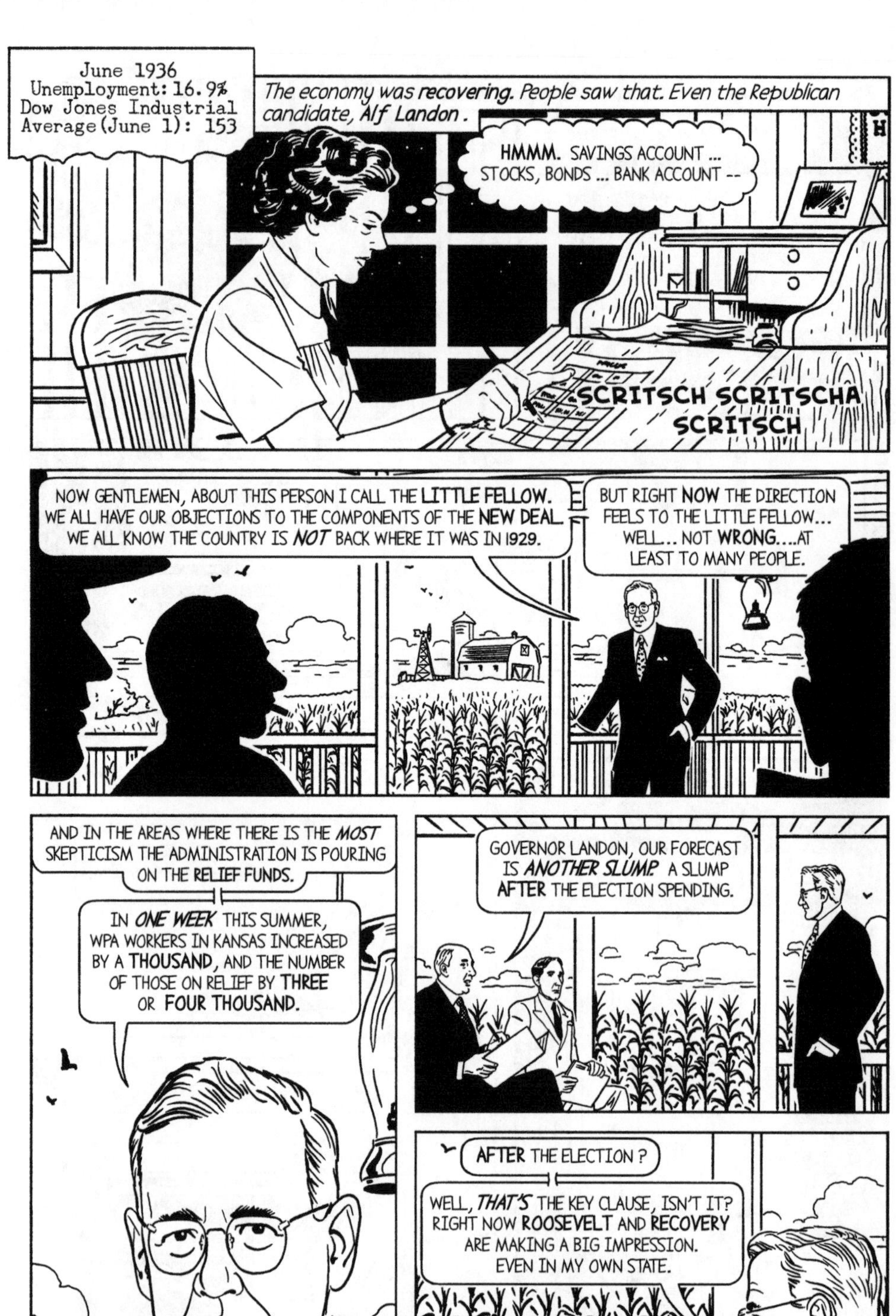
June 1936
Unemployment: 16.9%
Dow Jones Industrial
Average (June 1): 153
The economy was recovering. People saw that. Even the Republican candidate, Alf Landon.
HMMM. SAVINGS ACCOUNT ... STOCKS, BONDS ... BANK ACCOUNT --
SCRITSCH SCRITSCHA SCRITSCH
NOW GENTLEMEN, ABOUT THIS PERSON I CALL THE LITTLE FELLOW. WE ALL HAVE OUR OBJECTIONS TO THE COMPONENTS OF THE NEW DEAL. WE ALL KNOW THE COUNTRY IS NOT BACK WHERE IT WAS IN 1929.
BUT RIGHT NOW THE DIRECTION FEELS TO THE LITTLE FELLOW... WELL... NOT WRONG....AT LEAST TO MANY PEOPLE.
AND IN THE AREAS WHERE THERE IS THE MOST SKEPTICISM THE ADMINISTRATION IS POURING ON THE RELIEF FUNDS.
IN ONE WEEK THIS SUMMER, WPA WORKERS IN KANSAS INCREASED BY A THOUSAND, AND THE NUMBER OF THOSE ON RELIEF BY THREE OR FOUR THOUSAND.
GOVERNOR LANDON, OUR FORECAST IS ANOTHER SLUMP. A SLUMP AFTER THE ELECTION SPENDING.
AFTER THE ELECTION?
WELL, THAT'S THE KEY CLAUSE, ISN'T IT? RIGHT NOW ROOSEVELT AND RECOVERY ARE MAKING A BIG IMPRESSION. EVEN IN MY OWN STATE.

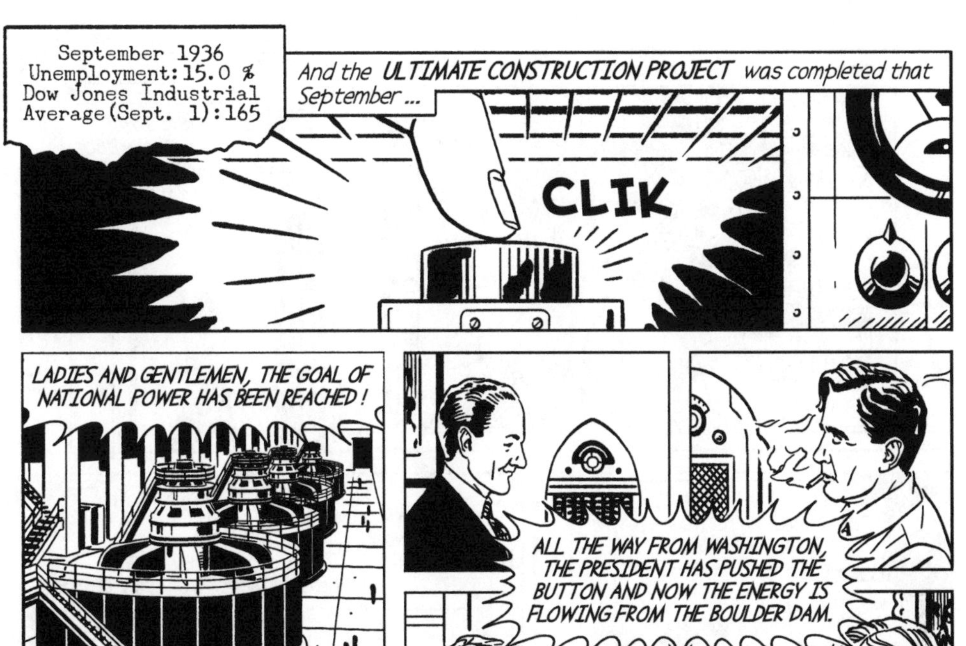
September 1936
Unemployment: 15.0 %
Dow Jones Industrial
Average (Sept. 1): 165
And the ULTIMATE CONSTRUCTION PROJECT was completed that September...
CLIK
LADIES AND GENTLEMEN, THE GOAL OF NATIONAL POWER HAS BEEN REACHED!
THRUMM-M-M
ALL THE WAY FROM WASHINGTON, THE PRESIDENT HAS PUSHED THE BUTTON AND NOW THE ENERGY IS FLOWING FROM THE BOULDER DAM.
THE CROWDS ARE STUNNED BY THE WATERFALL, 13 FEET HIGHER THAN NIAGARA!
MAN ACHIEVES MORE THAN NATURE...

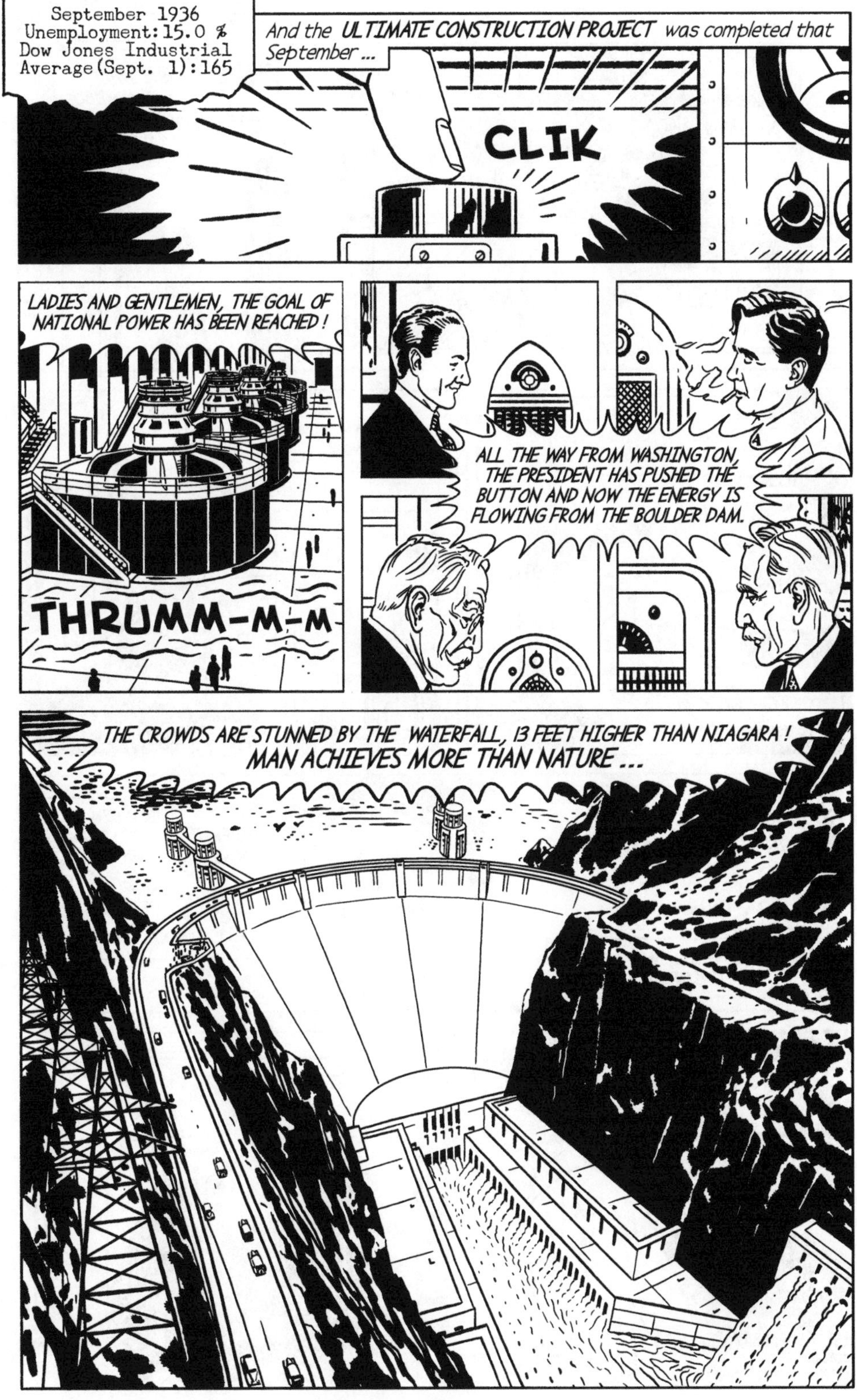

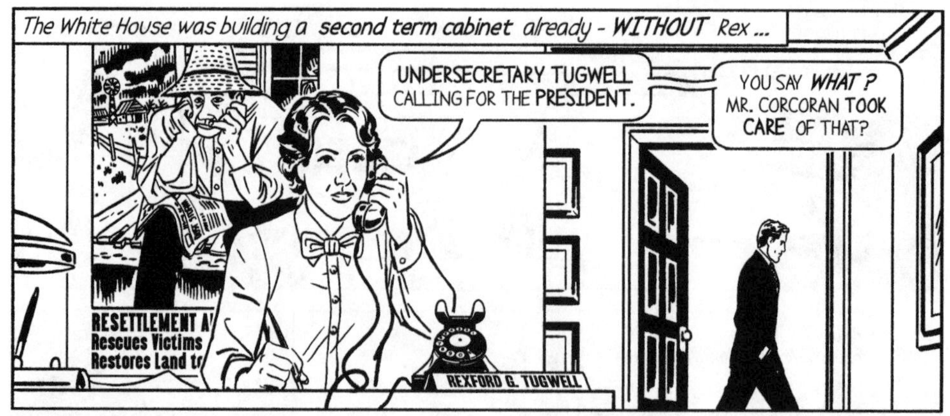
The White House was building a **second term cabinet** already - **WITHOUT** Rex ...
UNDERSECRETARY TUGWELL CALLING FOR THE PRESIDENT.
YOU SAY *WHAT?* MR. CORCORAN TOOK CARE OF THAT?
RESETTLEMENT A
Rescues Victims
Restores Land t
REXFORD G. TUGWELL

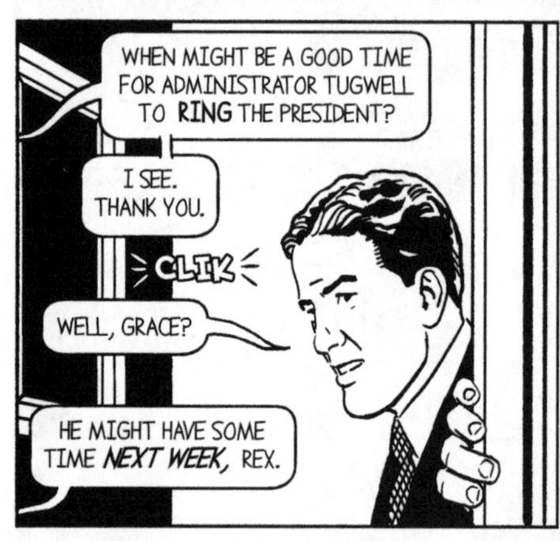
WHEN MIGHT BE A GOOD TIME FOR ADMINISTRATOR TUGWELL TO RING THE PRESIDENT?
I SEE. THANK YOU.
CLIK
WELL, GRACE?
HE MIGHT HAVE SOME TIME *NEXT WEEK,* REX.

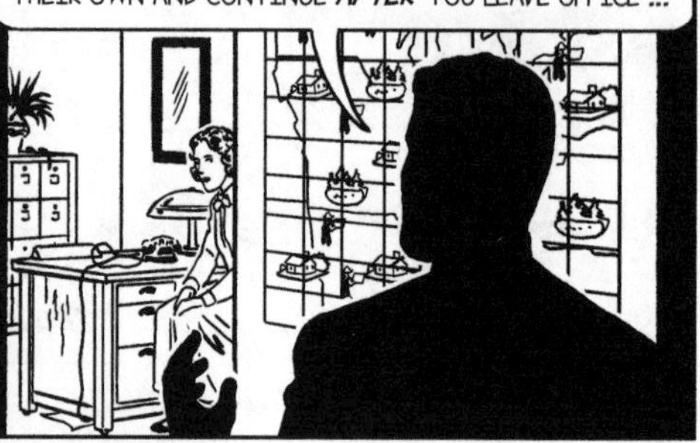
WELL -- THERE ARE *LOTS* OF THINGS TO DO AFTER GOVERNMENT. MOLEY IS HAVING THE TIME OF HIS LIFE WORKING AS AN EDITOR TODAY ! AND -- THE PROJECTS YOU START IN GOVERNMENT GET A LIFE OF THEIR OWN AND CONTINUE *AFTER* YOU LEAVE OFFICE ...

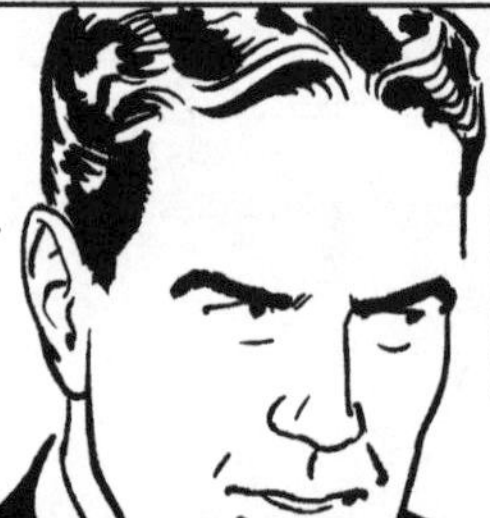
BUT IT'S ABSOLUTELY *IRONIC* THAT SYCOPHANTS LIKE MORGENTHAU GET CLOSER AND CLOSER TO THE PRESIDENT -- HE CAN'T BE TRUSTED TO DO ANYTHING ALONE --
-- BUT THE CAMPAIGN HASN'T ASKED *THIS* BRAIN TRUSTER FOR HELP !
AFTER ALL, BETWEEN THE GREENBELTS AND THE FARMS, OUR ACHIEVEMENTS *DO* STACK UP WELL AGAINST THE OTHERS. AND SOME OF THE BEST PROJECTS WON'T EVEN BE *FINISHED* UNTIL LATE NEXT YEAR --

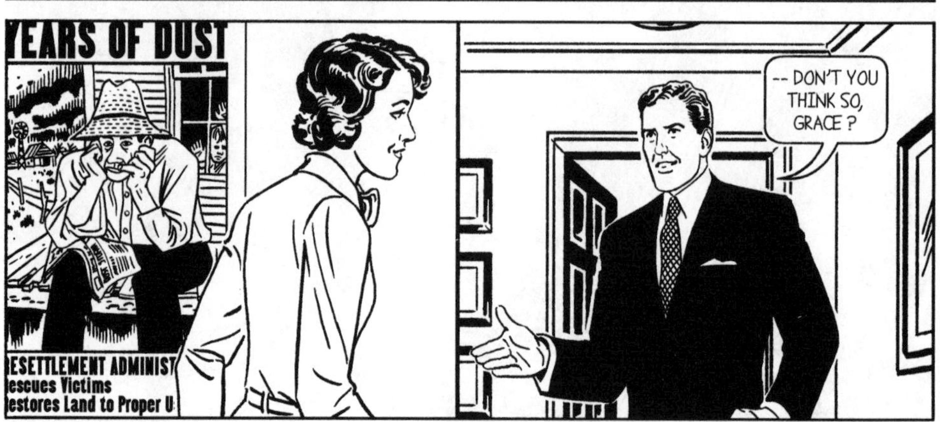
YEARS OF DUST
RESETTLEMENT ADMINIST
Rescues Victims
Restores Land to Proper U
-- DON'T YOU THINK SO, GRACE ?

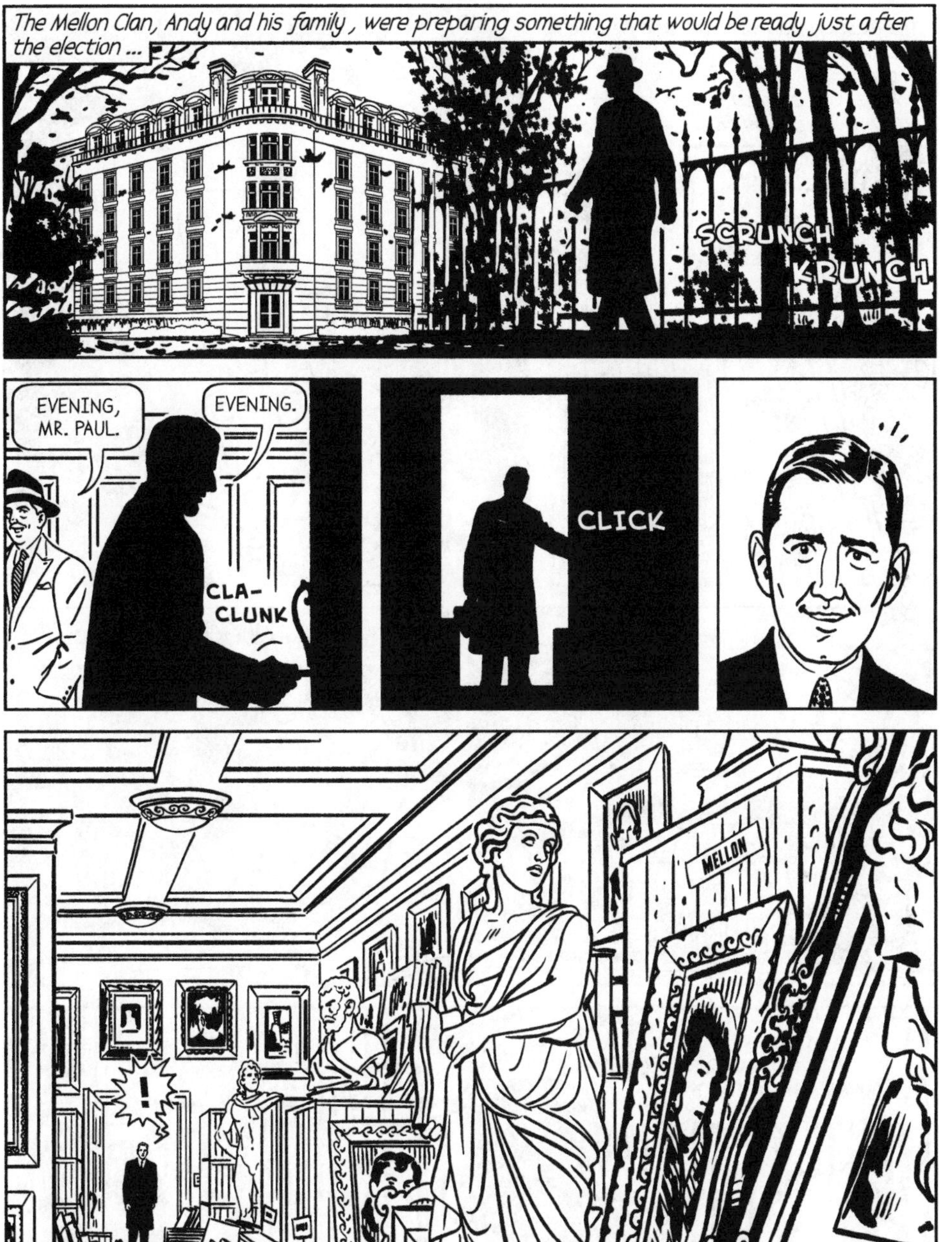

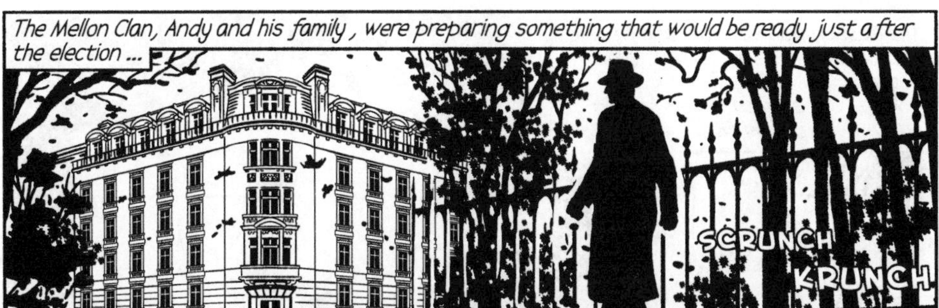
The Mellon Clan, Andy and his family, were preparing something that would be ready just after the election ...
SCRUNCH
KRUNCH

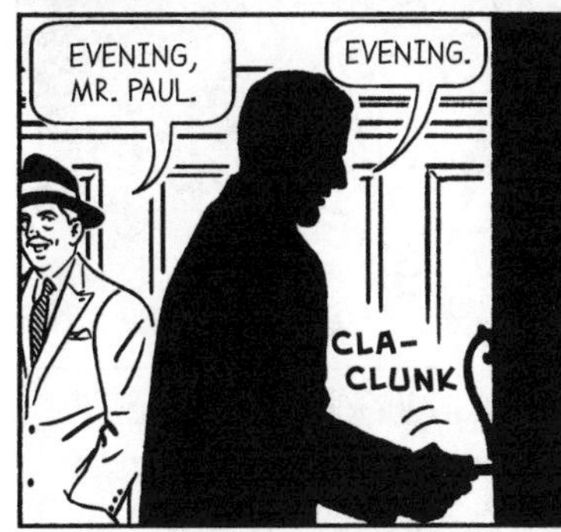
EVENING, MR. PAUL.
EVENING.
CLA-
CLUNK

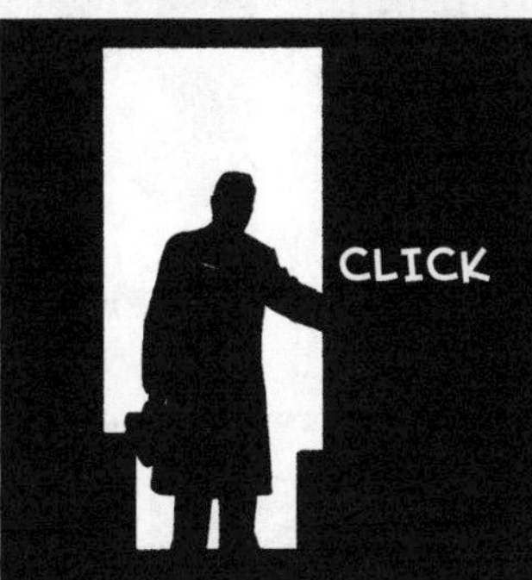
CLICK

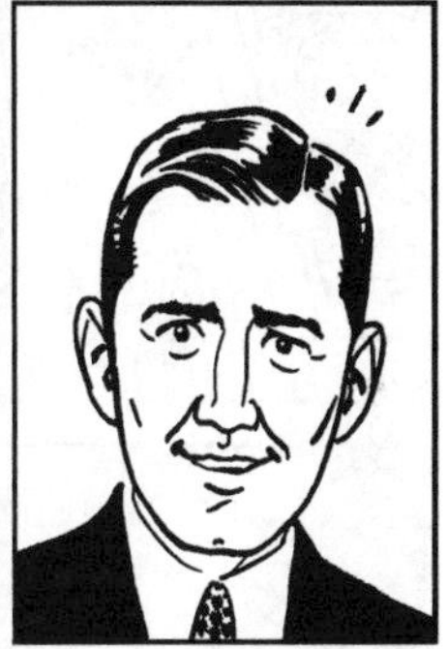

*The election was **so close**, and people were kind of hopeful. You get tired of being down about the economy. Roosevelt seemed to be offering **SO MUCH** ...*

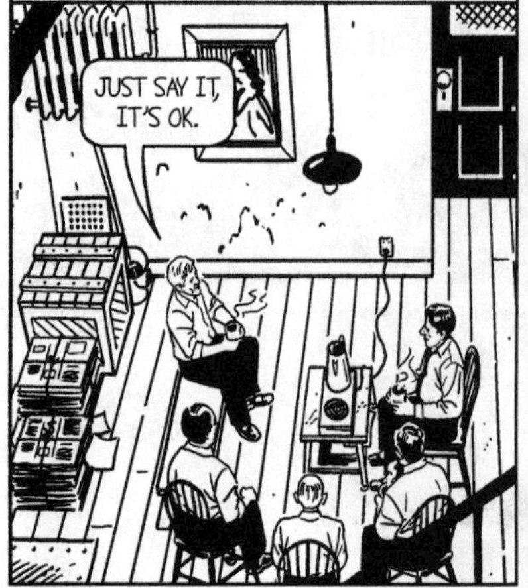

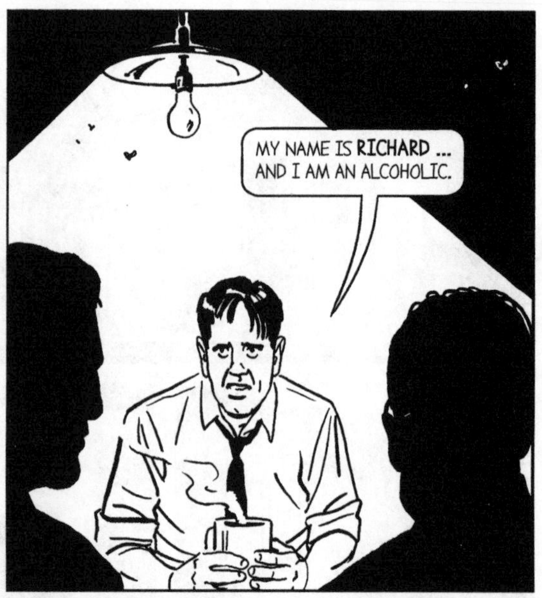

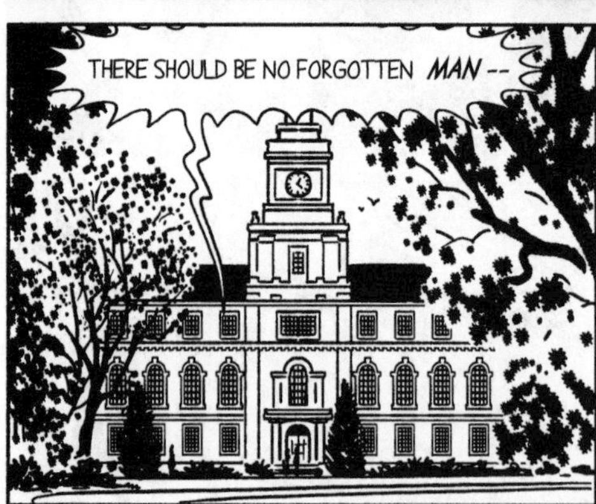

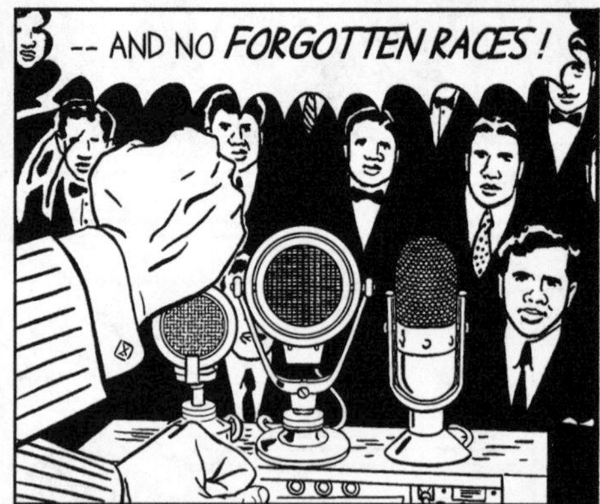

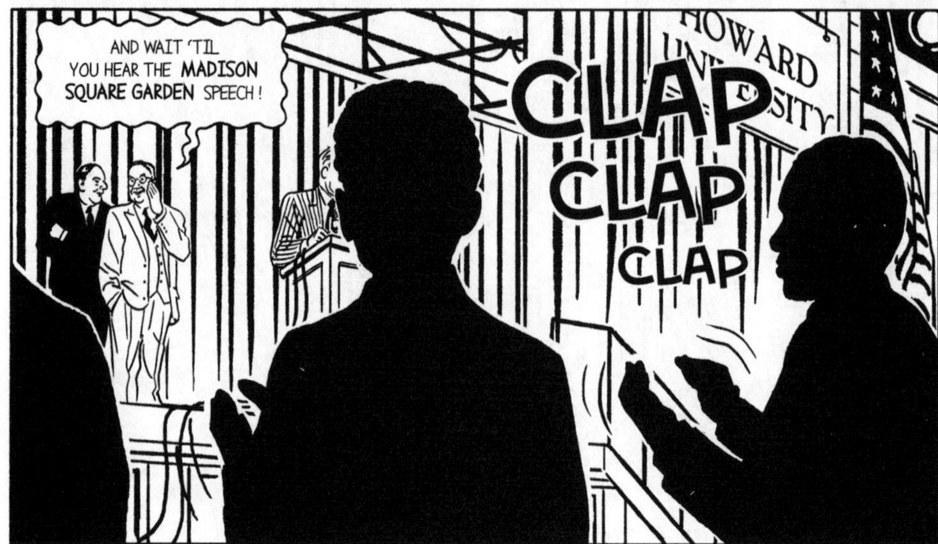

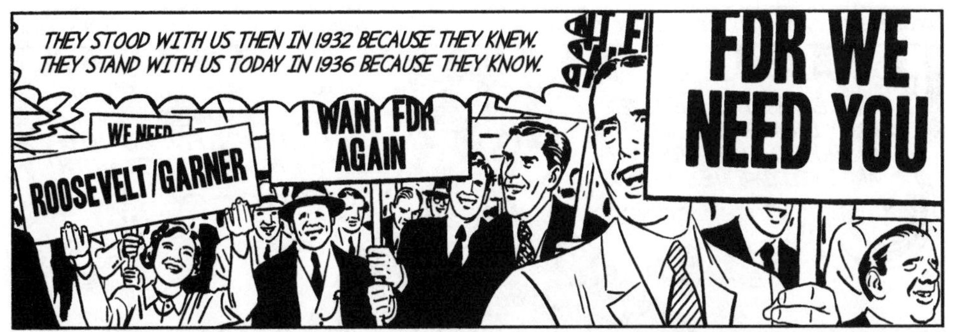
THEY STOOD WITH US THEN IN 1932 BECAUSE THEY KNEW.
THEY STAND WITH US TODAY IN 1936 BECAUSE THEY KNOW.
ROOSEVELT/GARNER
I WANT FDR AGAIN
FDR WE NEED YOU

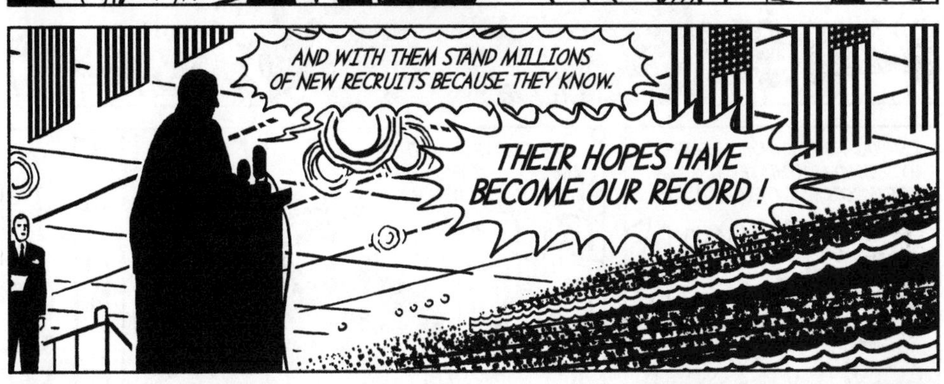
AND WITH THEM STAND MILLIONS OF NEW RECRUITS BECAUSE THEY KNOW.
THEIR HOPES HAVE BECOME OUR RECORD !

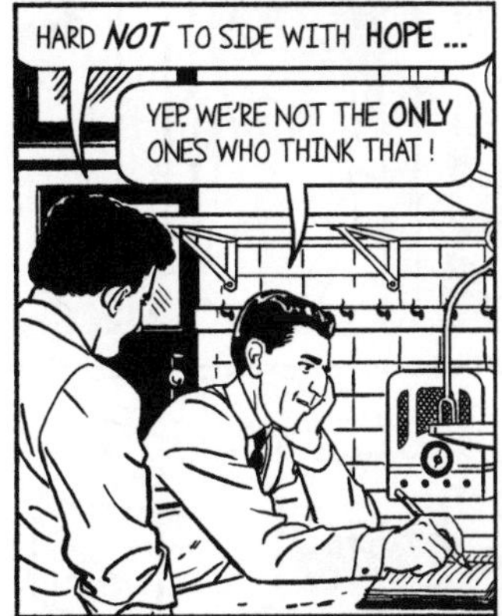
HARD NOT TO SIDE WITH HOPE ...
YEP. WE'RE NOT THE ONLY ONES WHO THINK THAT !

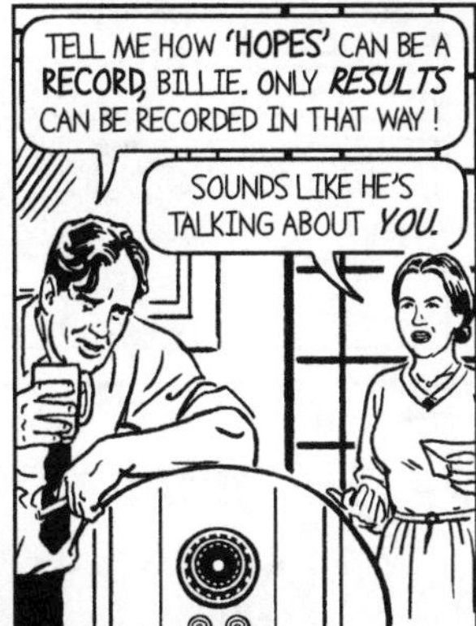
TELL ME HOW 'HOPES' CAN BE A RECORD, BILLIE. ONLY RESULTS CAN BE RECORDED IN THAT WAY !
SOUNDS LIKE HE'S TALKING ABOUT YOU.

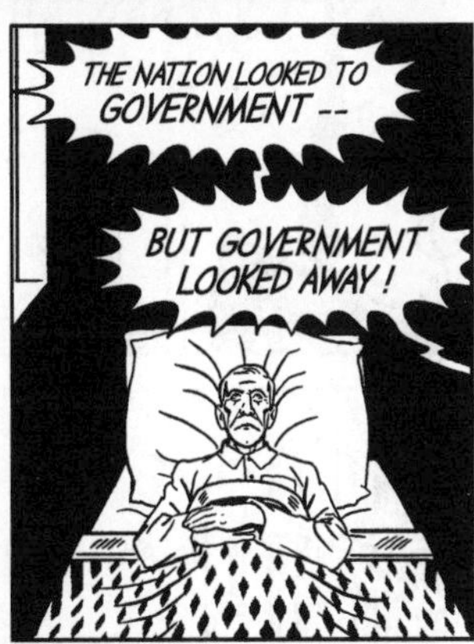
THE NATION LOOKED TO GOVERNMENT --
BUT GOVERNMENT LOOKED AWAY !

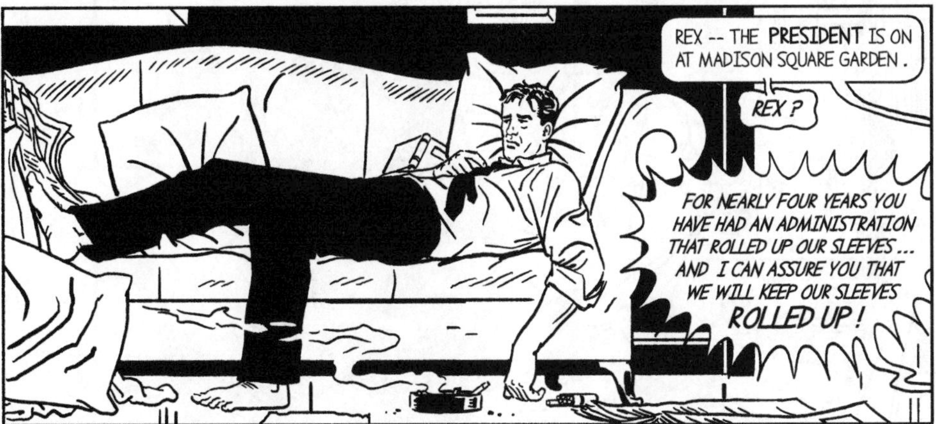
REX -- THE PRESIDENT IS ON AT MADISON SQUARE GARDEN .
REX ?
FOR NEARLY FOUR YEARS YOU HAVE HAD AN ADMINISTRATION THAT ROLLED UP OUR SLEEVES ... AND I CAN ASSURE YOU THAT WE WILL KEEP OUR SLEEVES ROLLED UP !

Roosevelt's campaign rhetoric got far harsher as the election moment neared. I tried to ignore it.

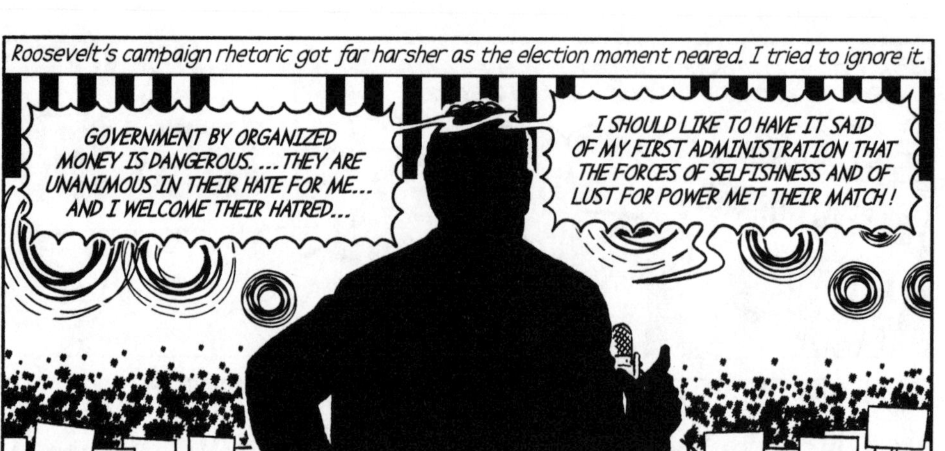

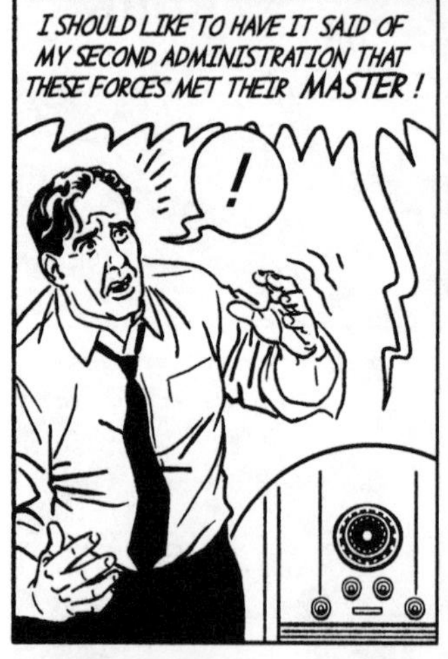

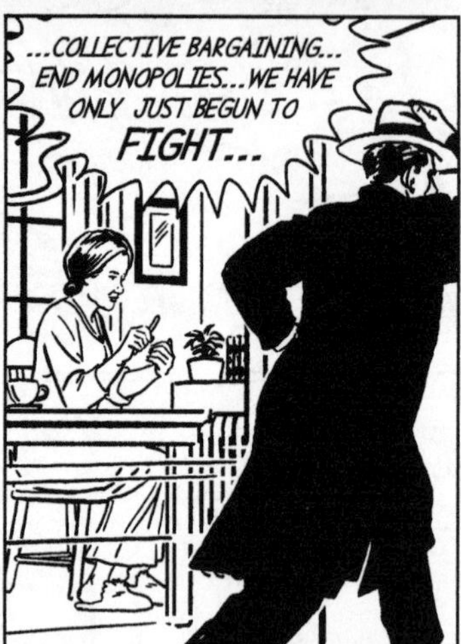

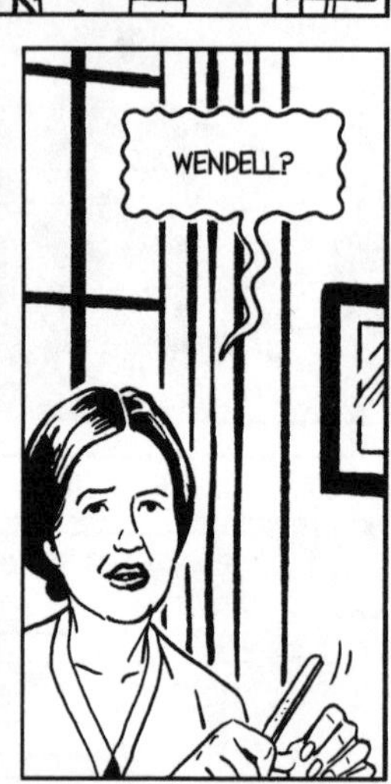

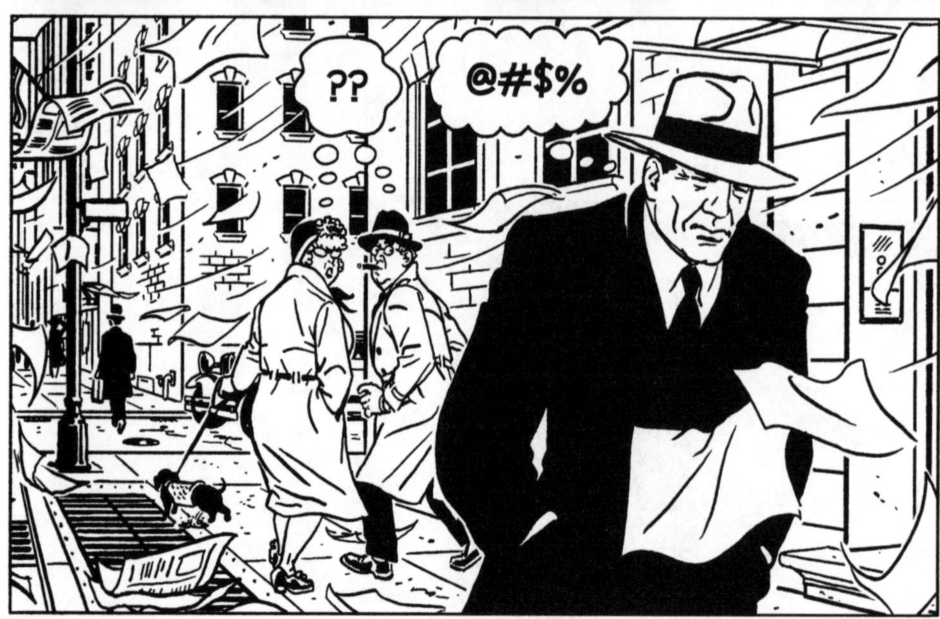

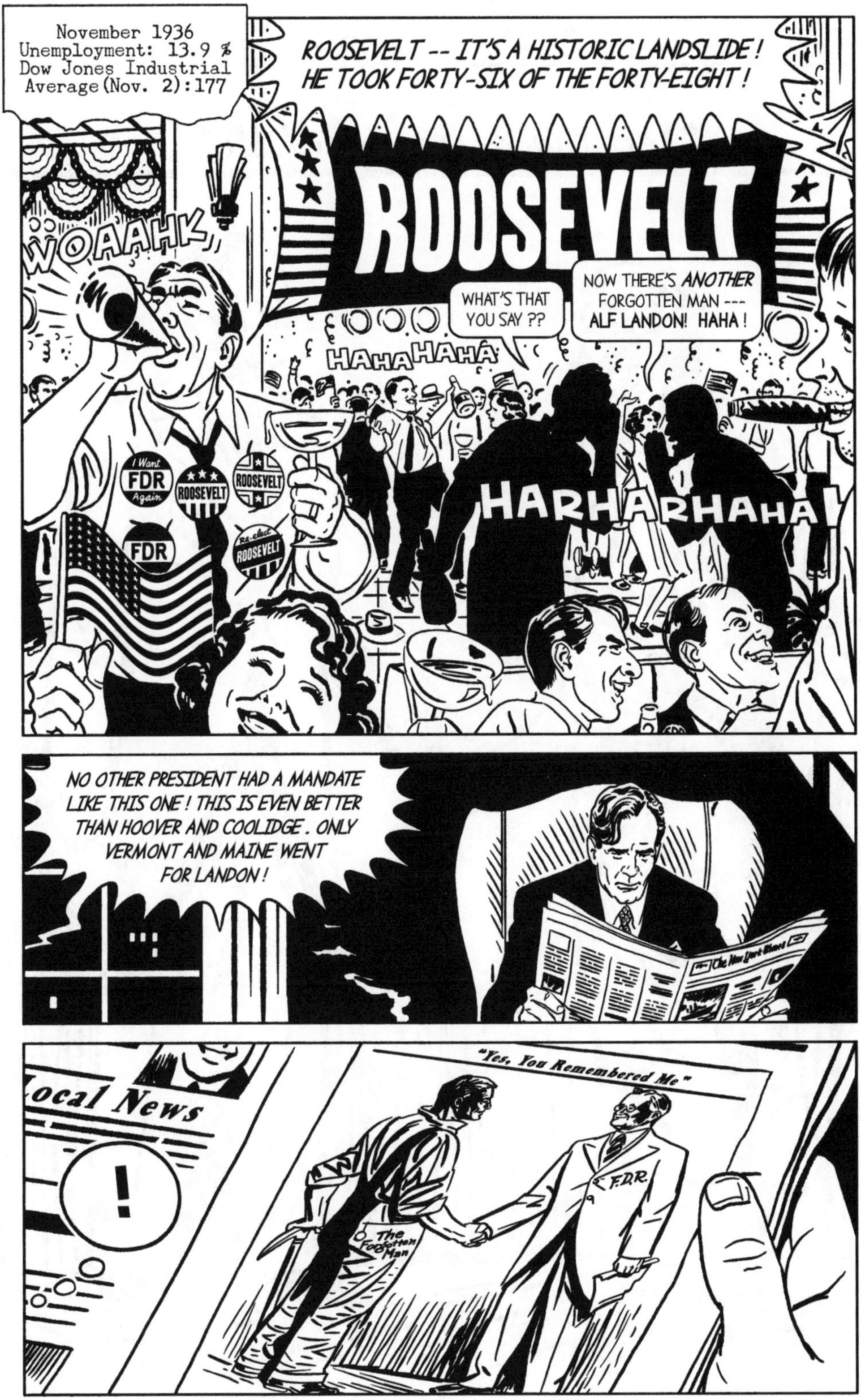

November 1936
Unemployment: 13.9 %
Dow Jones Industrial
Average (Nov. 2): 177

ROOSEVELT -- IT'S A HISTORIC LANDSLIDE!
HE TOOK FORTY-SIX OF THE FORTY-EIGHT!

WOAAHK!

ROOSEVELT

WHAT'S THAT YOU SAY??

NOW THERE'S *ANOTHER* FORGOTTEN MAN --- **ALF LANDON! HAHA!**

HAHAHAHAHA

HARHARHAHA!

I Want FDR Again

ROOSEVELT

ROOSEVELT

FDR

Re-elect ROOSEVELT

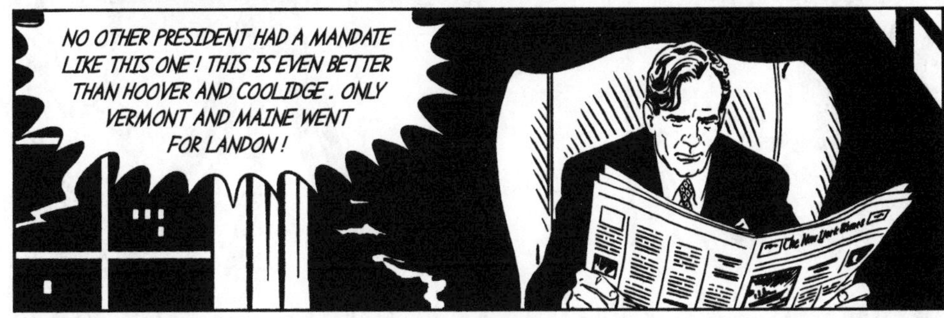

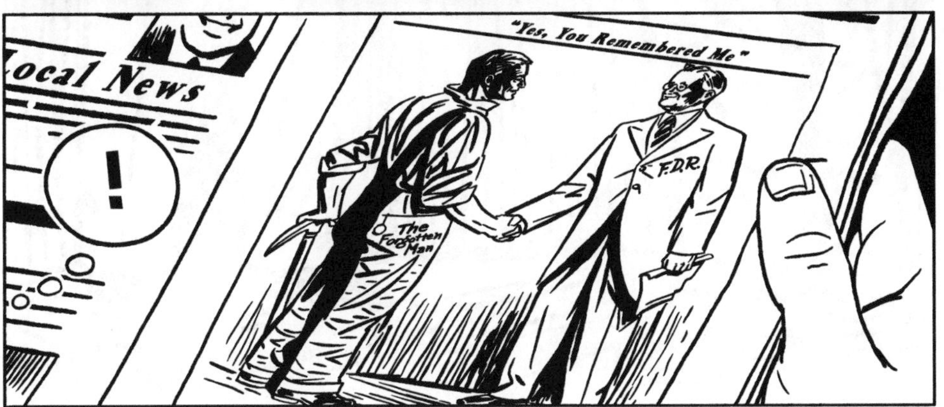

Roosevelt was a ***MASTER****, and he had served his* ***FORGOTTEN MAN ...***

"Yes, You Remembered Me"

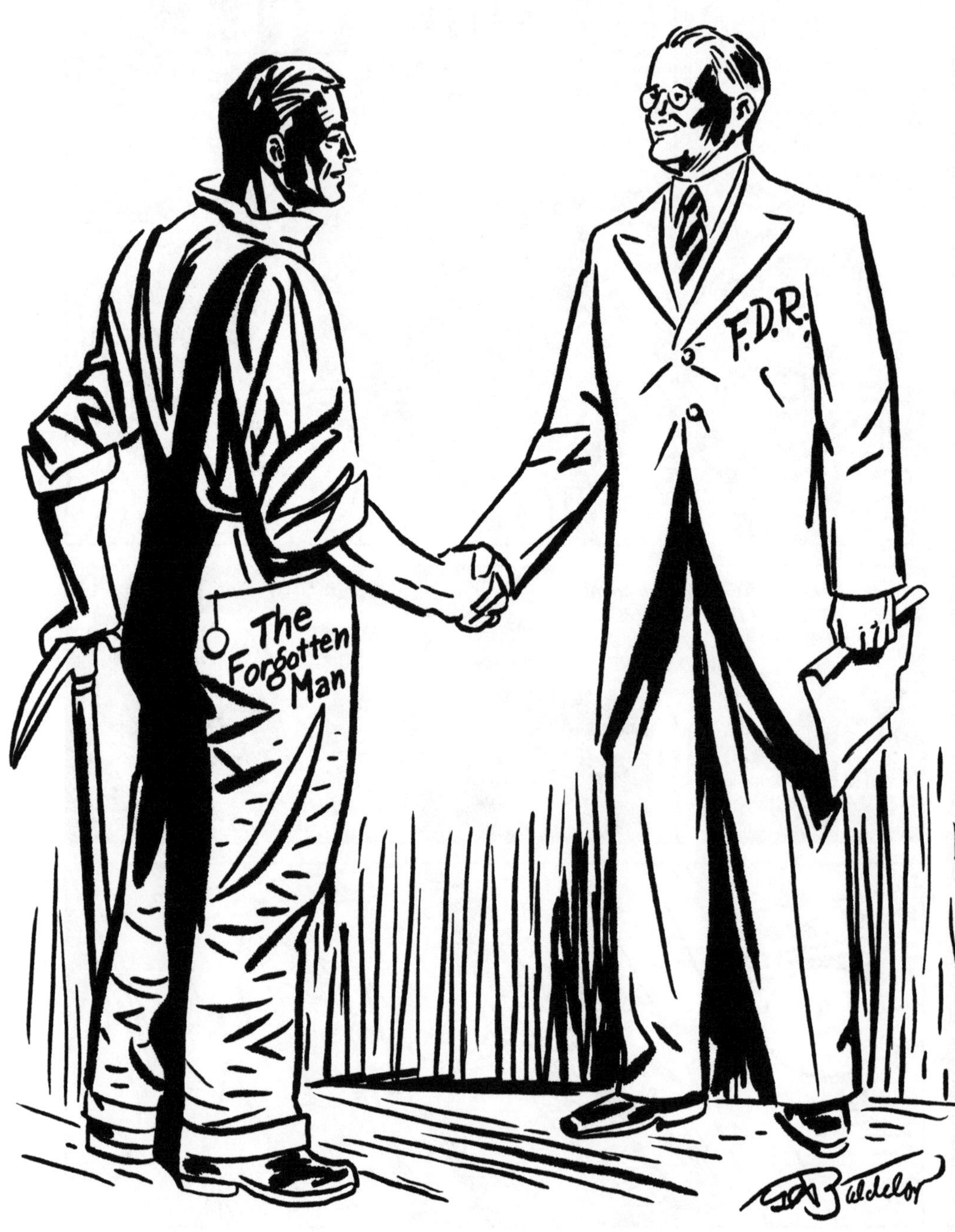

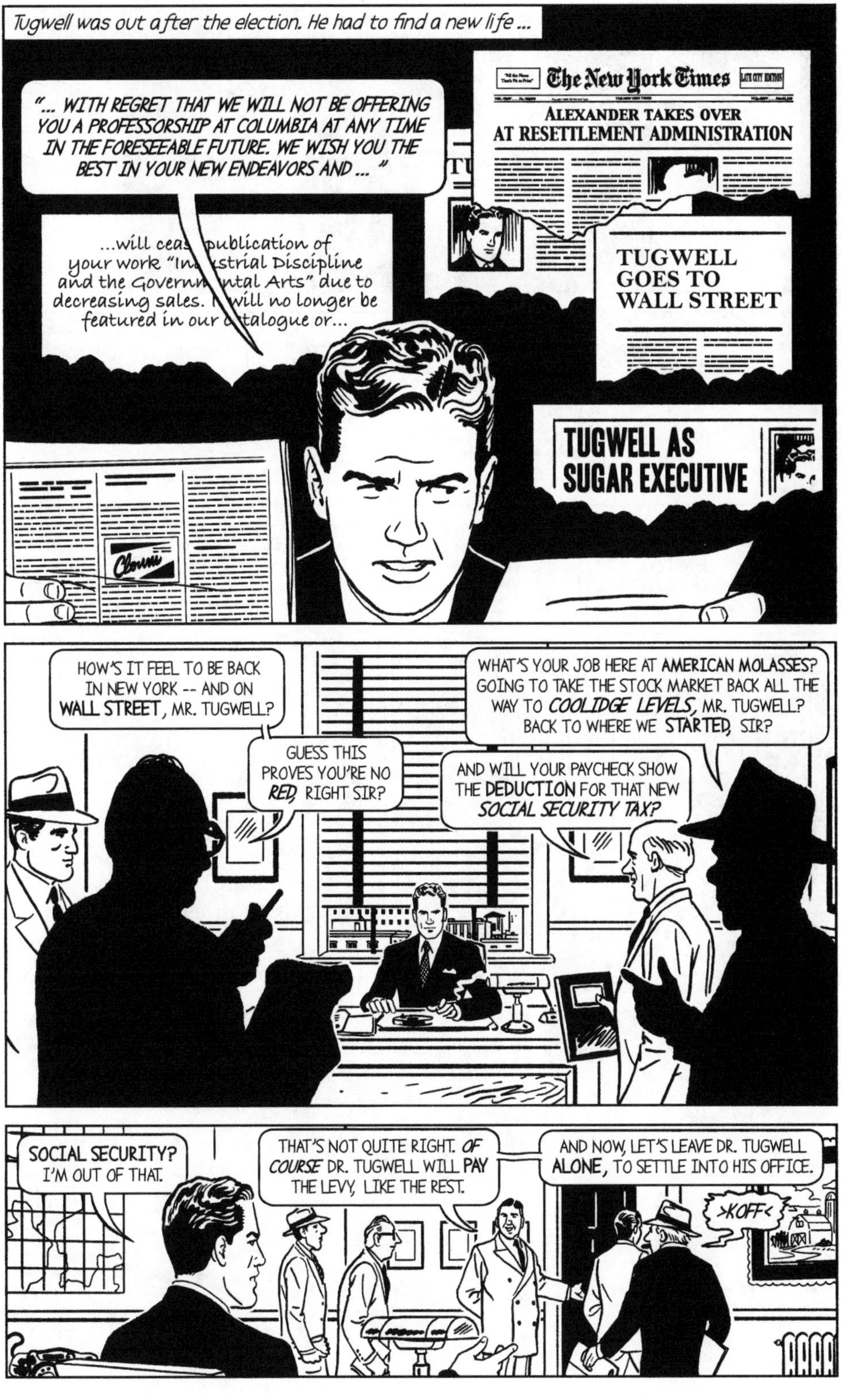

Tugwell was out after the election. He had to find a new life ...

"... WITH REGRET THAT WE WILL NOT BE OFFERING YOU A PROFESSORSHIP AT COLUMBIA AT ANY TIME IN THE FORESEEABLE FUTURE. WE WISH YOU THE BEST IN YOUR NEW ENDEAVORS AND ... "

The New York Times

ALEXANDER TAKES OVER AT RESETTLEMENT ADMINISTRATION

...will ceas publication of your work "In strial Discipline and the Governm ntal Arts" due to decreasing sales. will no longer be featured in our atalogue or...

TUGWELL GOES TO WALL STREET

TUGWELL AS SUGAR EXECUTIVE

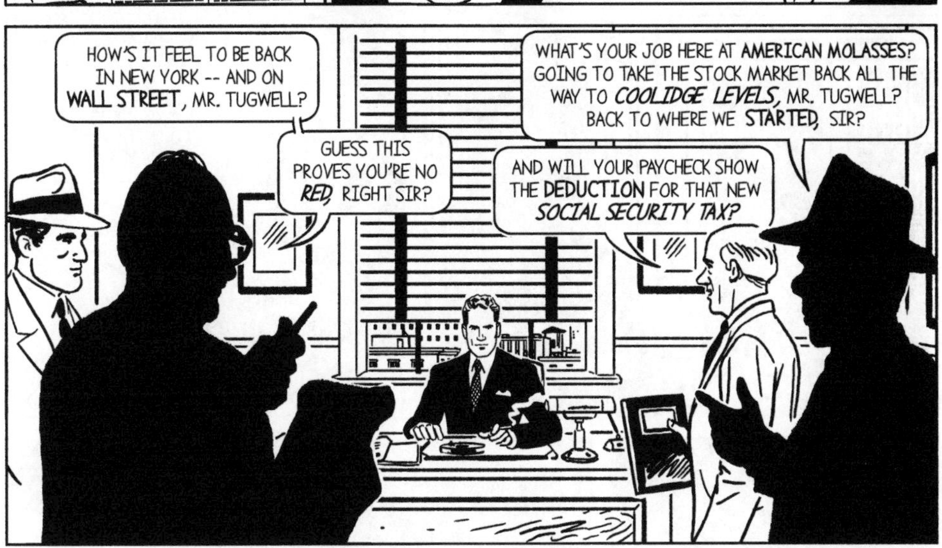

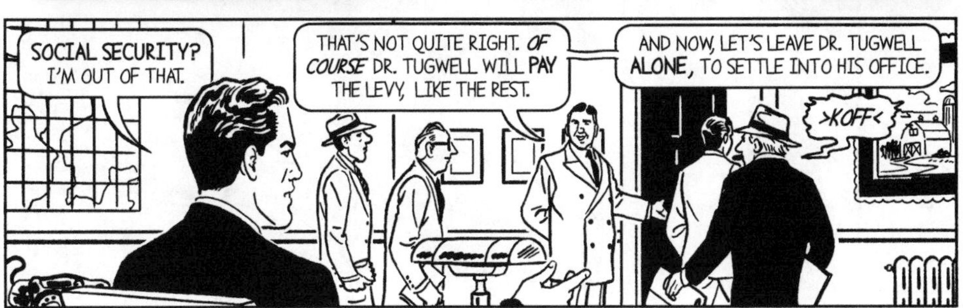

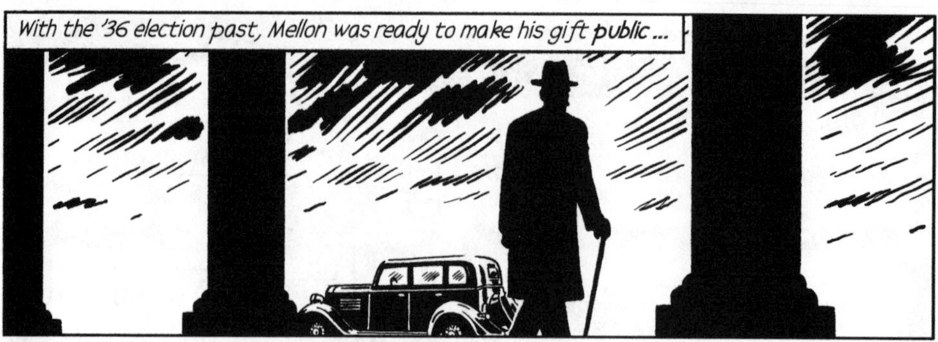
With the '36 election past, Mellon was ready to make his gift public ...

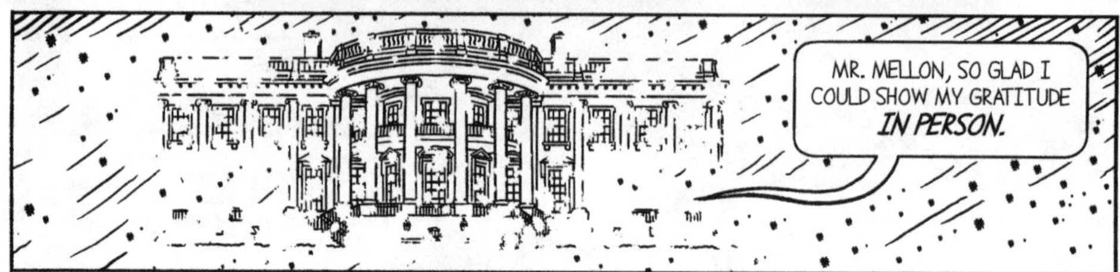
MR. MELLON, SO GLAD I COULD SHOW MY GRATITUDE IN PERSON.

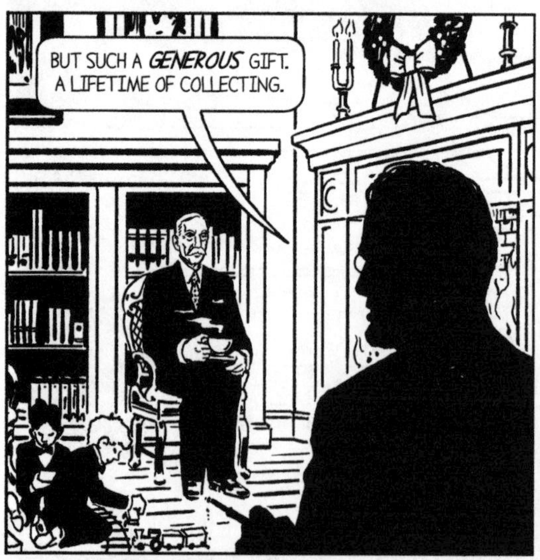
BUT SUCH A GENEROUS GIFT. A LIFETIME OF COLLECTING.

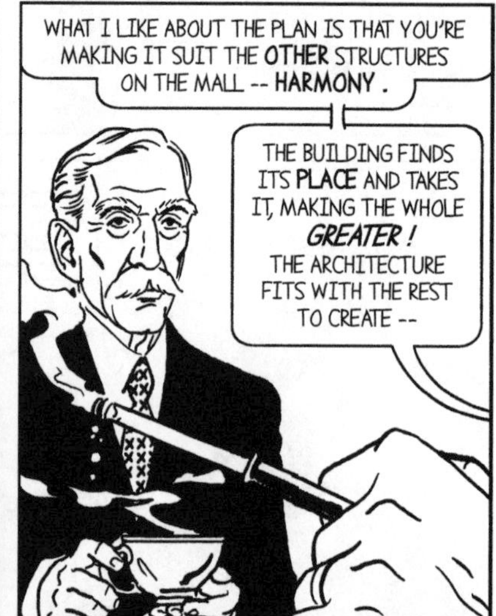
WHAT I LIKE ABOUT THE PLAN IS THAT YOU'RE MAKING IT SUIT THE OTHER STRUCTURES ON THE MALL -- HARMONY .
THE BUILDING FINDS ITS PLACE AND TAKES IT, MAKING THE WHOLE GREATER ! THE ARCHITECTURE FITS WITH THE REST TO CREATE --

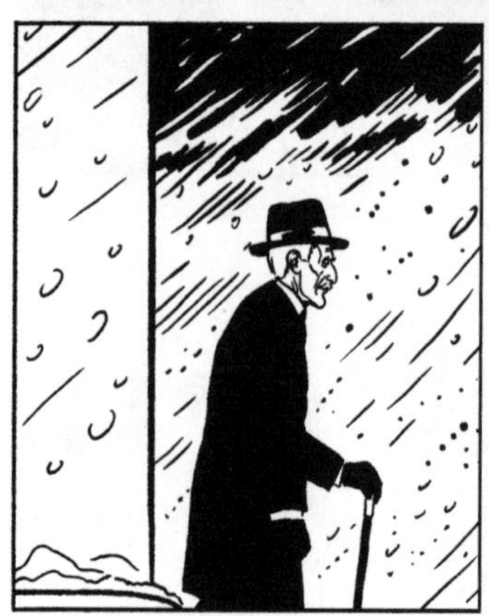

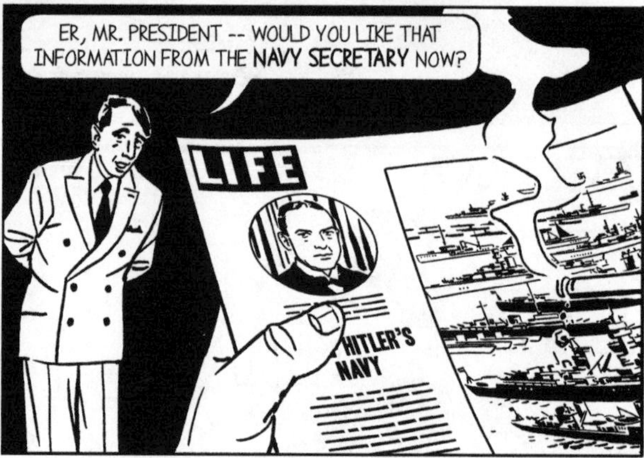
ER, MR. PRESIDENT -- WOULD YOU LIKE THAT INFORMATION FROM THE NAVY SECRETARY NOW?
LIFE
HITLER'S NAVY

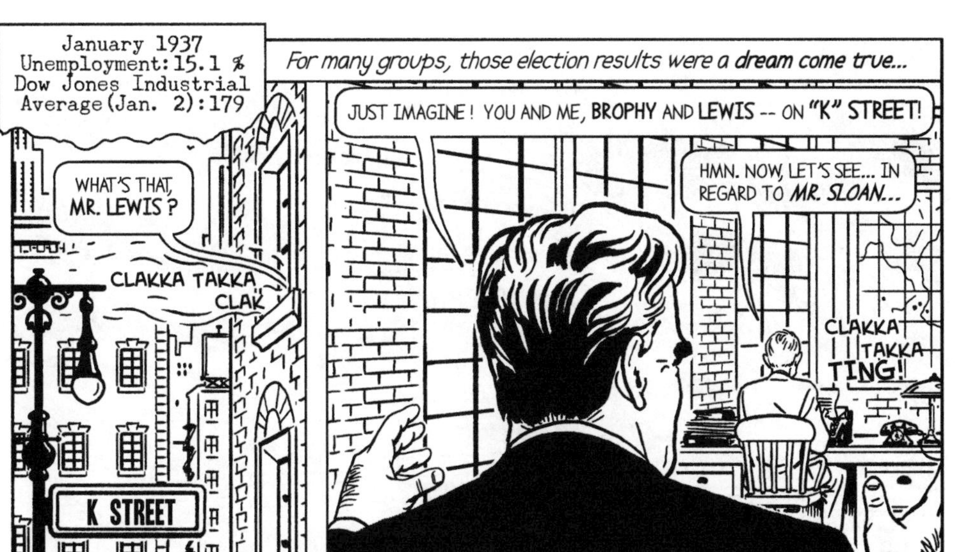
January 1937
Unemployment: 15.1 %
Dow Jones Industrial
Average (Jan. 2): 179
For many groups, those election results were a dream come true...
WHAT'S THAT, MR. LEWIS?
CLAKKA TAKKA CLAK
K STREET
JUST IMAGINE! YOU AND ME, BROPHY AND LEWIS -- ON "K" STREET!
HMN. NOW, LET'S SEE... IN REGARD TO MR. SLOAN...
CLAKKA TAKKA TING!

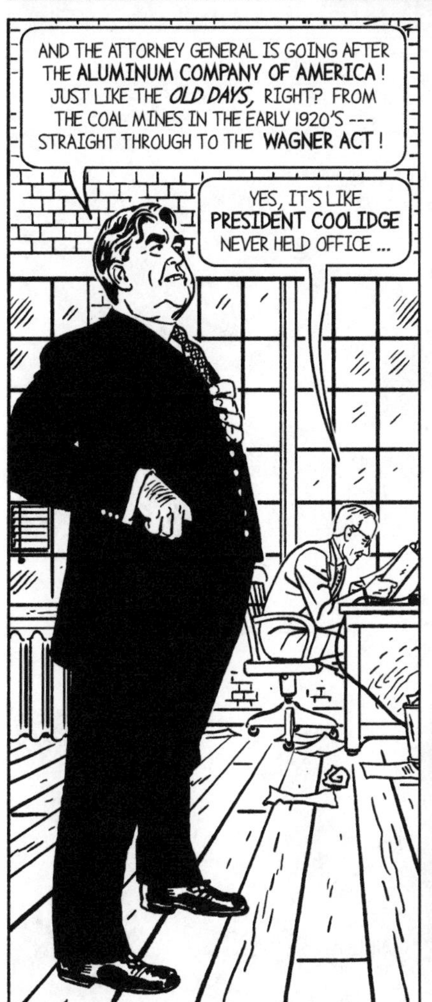
AND THE ATTORNEY GENERAL IS GOING AFTER THE ALUMINUM COMPANY OF AMERICA! JUST LIKE THE OLD DAYS, RIGHT? FROM THE COAL MINES IN THE EARLY 1920'S --- STRAIGHT THROUGH TO THE WAGNER ACT!
YES, IT'S LIKE PRESIDENT COOLIDGE NEVER HELD OFFICE ...

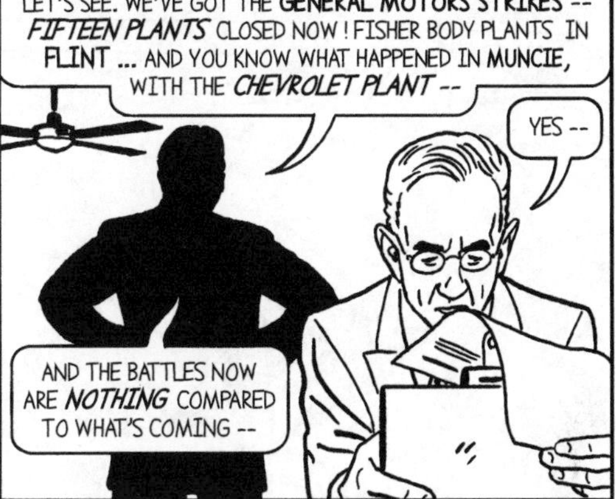
LET'S SEE. WE'VE GOT THE GENERAL MOTORS STRIKES -- FIFTEEN PLANTS CLOSED NOW! FISHER BODY PLANTS IN FLINT ... AND YOU KNOW WHAT HAPPENED IN MUNCIE, WITH THE CHEVROLET PLANT --
YES --
AND THE BATTLES NOW ARE NOTHING COMPARED TO WHAT'S COMING --

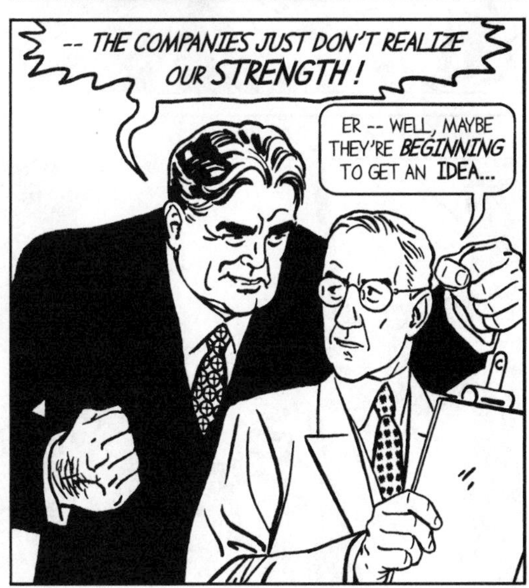
-- THE COMPANIES JUST DON'T REALIZE OUR STRENGTH!
ER -- WELL, MAYBE THEY'RE BEGINNING TO GET AN IDEA...

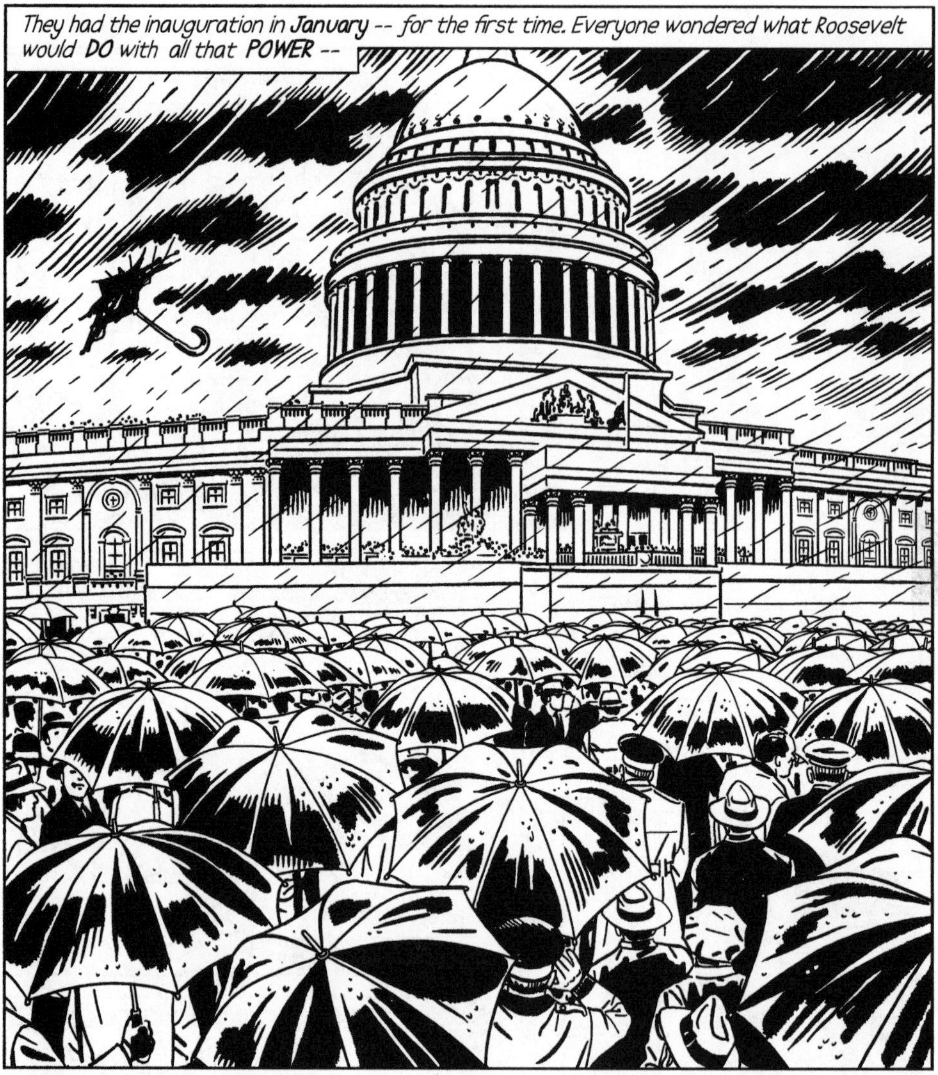

They had the inauguration in **January** -- for the first time. Everyone wondered what Roosevelt would **DO** with all that **POWER** --

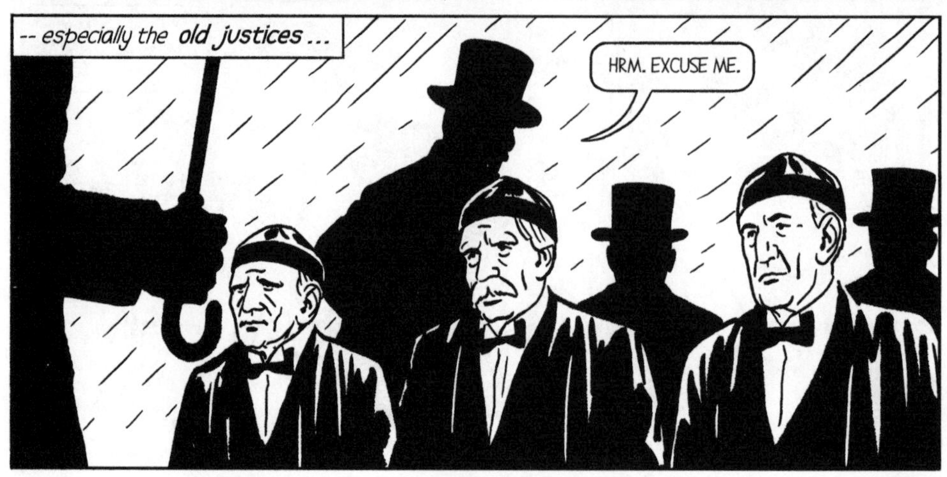

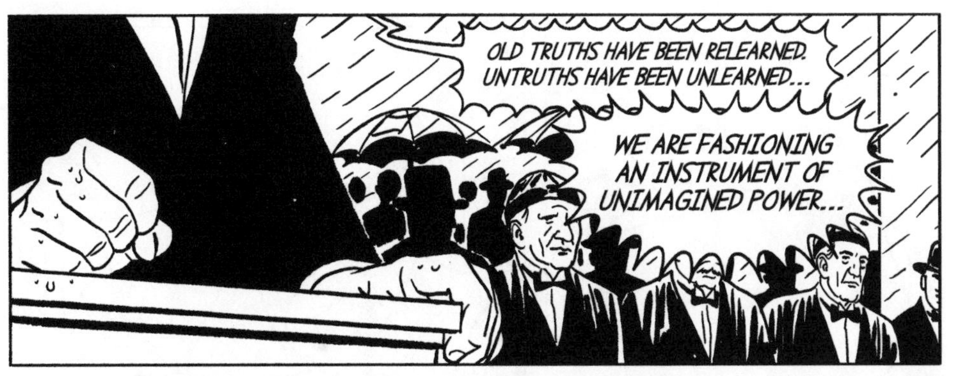
OLD TRUTHS HAVE BEEN RELEARNED. UNTRUTHS HAVE BEEN UNLEARNED...
WE ARE FASHIONING AN INSTRUMENT OF UNIMAGINED POWER...

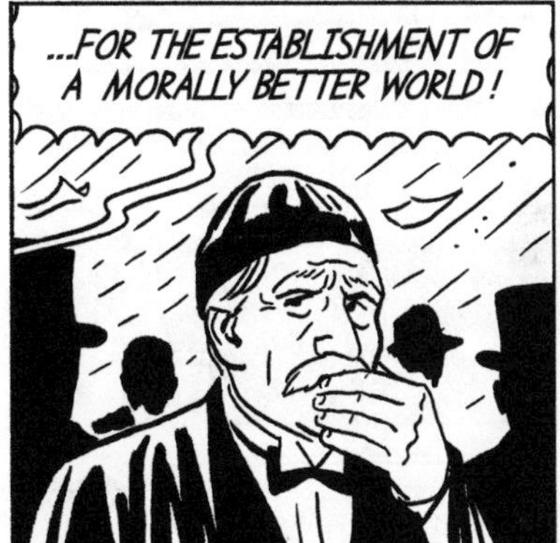
...FOR THE ESTABLISHMENT OF A MORALLY BETTER WORLD!

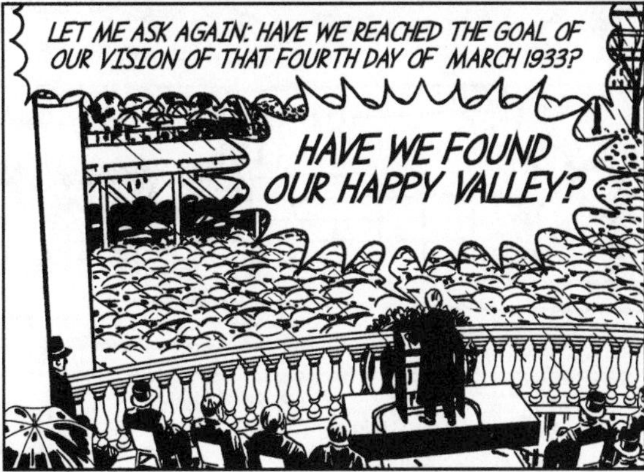
LET ME ASK AGAIN: HAVE WE REACHED THE GOAL OF OUR VISION OF THAT FOURTH DAY OF MARCH 1933?
HAVE WE FOUND OUR HAPPY VALLEY?

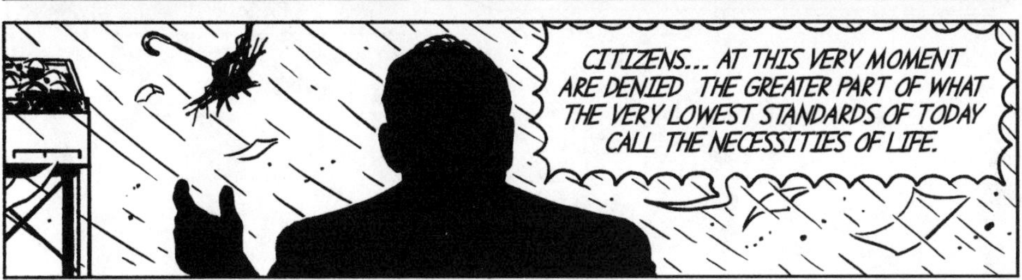
CITIZENS... AT THIS VERY MOMENT ARE DENIED THE GREATER PART OF WHAT THE VERY LOWEST STANDARDS OF TODAY CALL THE NECESSITIES OF LIFE.

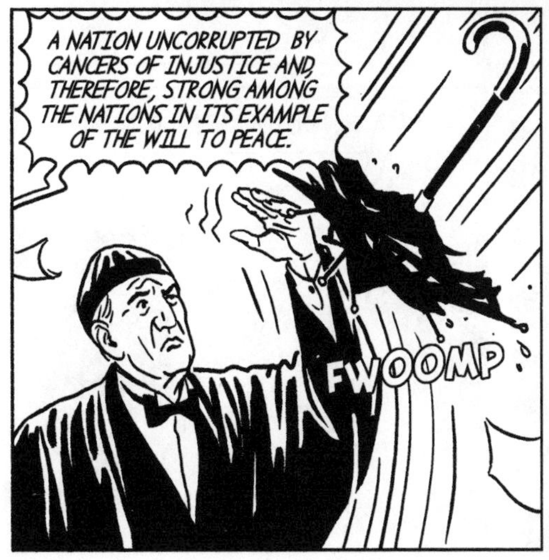
A NATION UNCORRUPTED BY CANCERS OF INJUSTICE AND, THEREFORE, STRONG AMONG THE NATIONS IN ITS EXAMPLE OF THE WILL TO PEACE.
FWOOMP

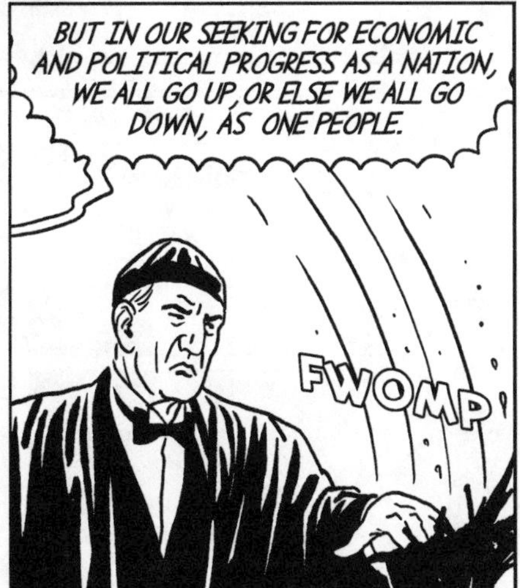
BUT IN OUR SEEKING FOR ECONOMIC AND POLITICAL PROGRESS AS A NATION, WE ALL GO UP, OR ELSE WE ALL GO DOWN, AS ONE PEOPLE.
FWOMP

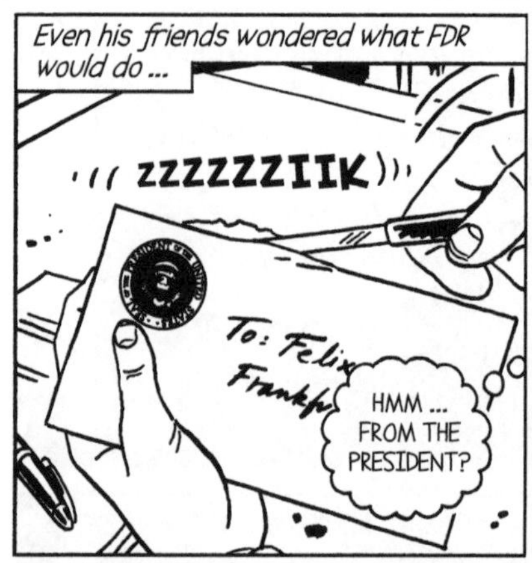
Even his friends wondered what FDR would do ...
ZZZZZZIIK
To: Felix Frankf
HMM ... FROM THE PRESIDENT?

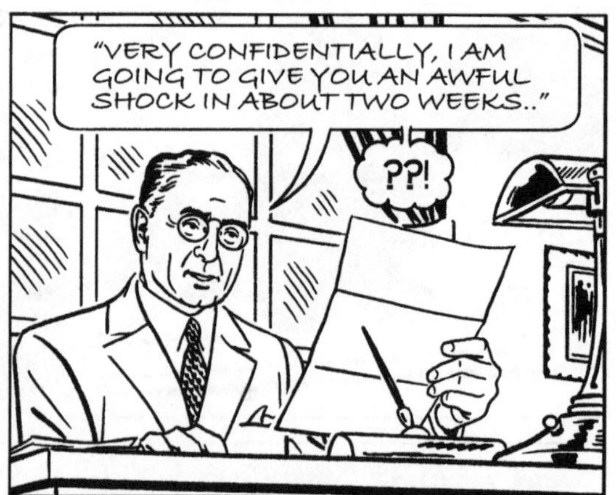
"VERY CONFIDENTIALLY, I AM GOING TO GIVE YOU AN AWFUL SHOCK IN ABOUT TWO WEEKS.."
??!

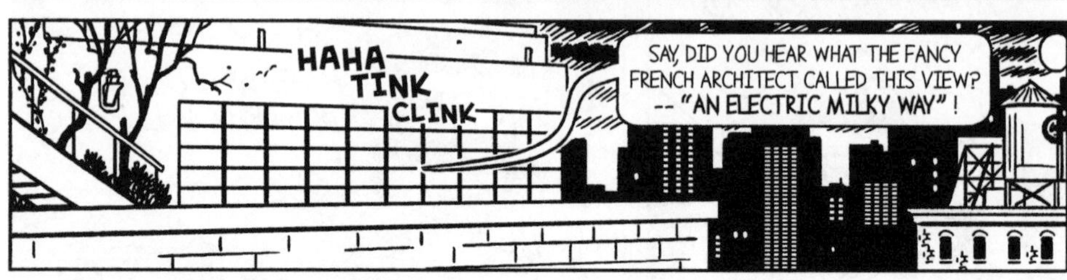
HAHA
TINK
CLINK
SAY, DID YOU HEAR WHAT THE FANCY FRENCH ARCHITECT CALLED THIS VIEW? -- "AN ELECTRIC MILKY WAY"!

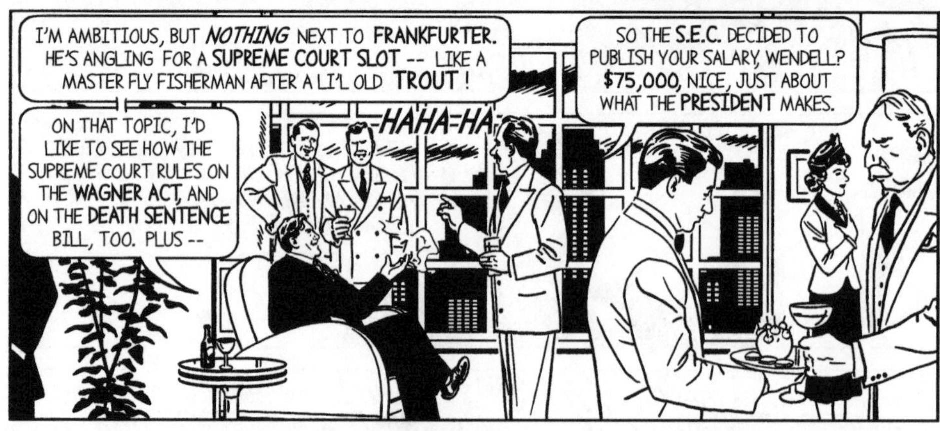
I'M AMBITIOUS, BUT NOTHING NEXT TO FRANKFURTER. HE'S ANGLING FOR A SUPREME COURT SLOT -- LIKE A MASTER FLY FISHERMAN AFTER A LI'L OLD TROUT!
ON THAT TOPIC, I'D LIKE TO SEE HOW THE SUPREME COURT RULES ON THE WAGNER ACT, AND ON THE DEATH SENTENCE BILL, TOO. PLUS --
HAHA-HA
SO THE S.E.C. DECIDED TO PUBLISH YOUR SALARY, WENDELL? $75,000, NICE, JUST ABOUT WHAT THE PRESIDENT MAKES.

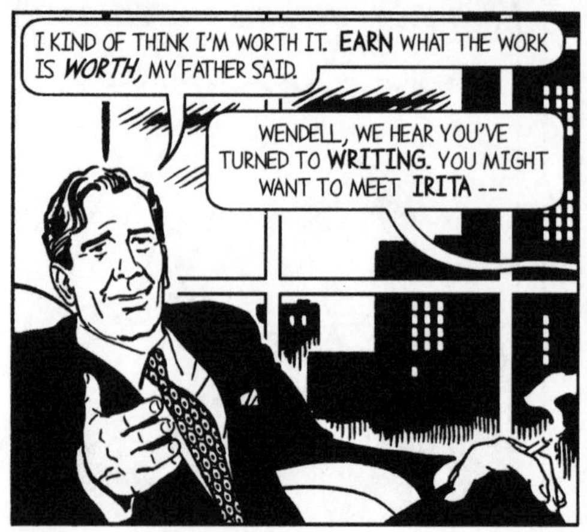
I KIND OF THINK I'M WORTH IT. EARN WHAT THE WORK IS WORTH, MY FATHER SAID.
WENDELL, WE HEAR YOU'VE TURNED TO WRITING. YOU MIGHT WANT TO MEET IRITA ---

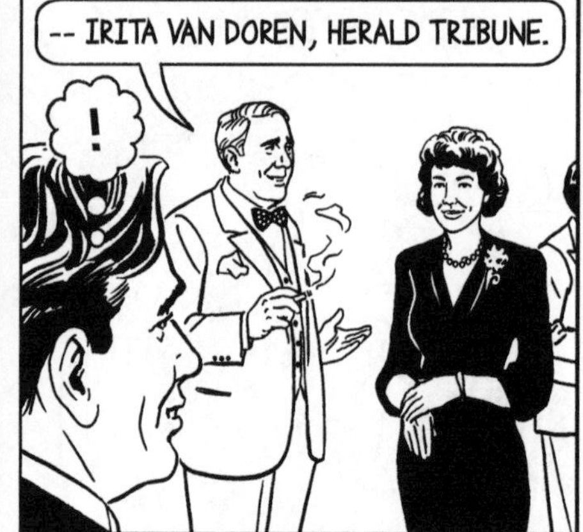
-- IRITA VAN DOREN, HERALD TRIBUNE.
!

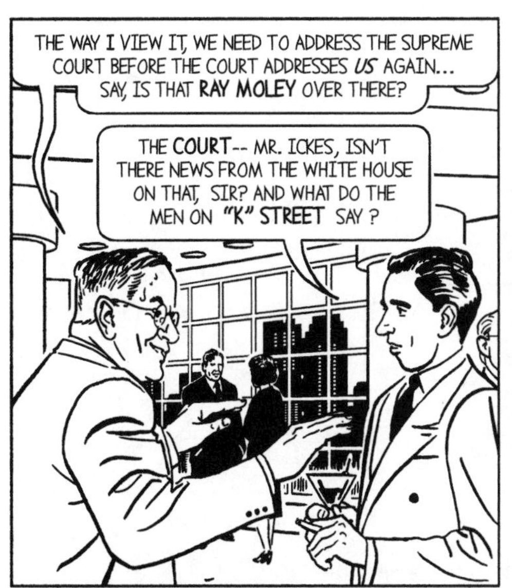
THE WAY I VIEW IT, WE NEED TO ADDRESS THE SUPREME COURT BEFORE THE COURT ADDRESSES US AGAIN... SAY, IS THAT RAY MOLEY OVER THERE?
THE COURT-- MR. ICKES, ISN'T THERE NEWS FROM THE WHITE HOUSE ON THAT, SIR? AND WHAT DO THE MEN ON "K" STREET SAY?

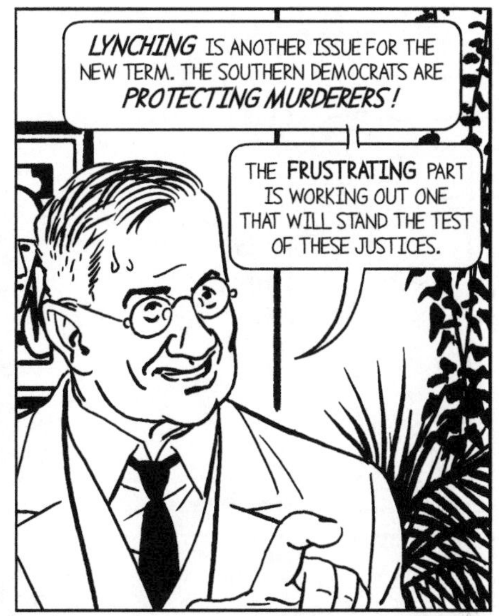
LYNCHING IS ANOTHER ISSUE FOR THE NEW TERM. THE SOUTHERN DEMOCRATS ARE PROTECTING MURDERERS!
THE FRUSTRATING PART IS WORKING OUT ONE THAT WILL STAND THE TEST OF THESE JUSTICES.

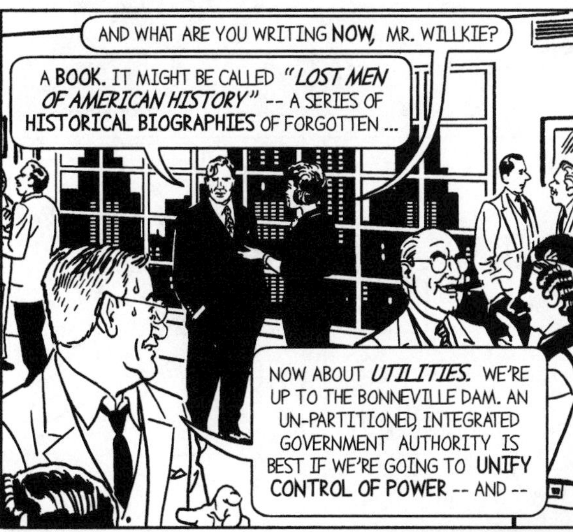
AND WHAT ARE YOU WRITING NOW, MR. WILLKIE?
A BOOK. IT MIGHT BE CALLED "LOST MEN OF AMERICAN HISTORY" -- A SERIES OF HISTORICAL BIOGRAPHIES OF FORGOTTEN ...
NOW ABOUT UTILITIES. WE'RE UP TO THE BONNEVILLE DAM. AN UN-PARTITIONED, INTEGRATED GOVERNMENT AUTHORITY IS BEST IF WE'RE GOING TO UNIFY CONTROL OF POWER -- AND --

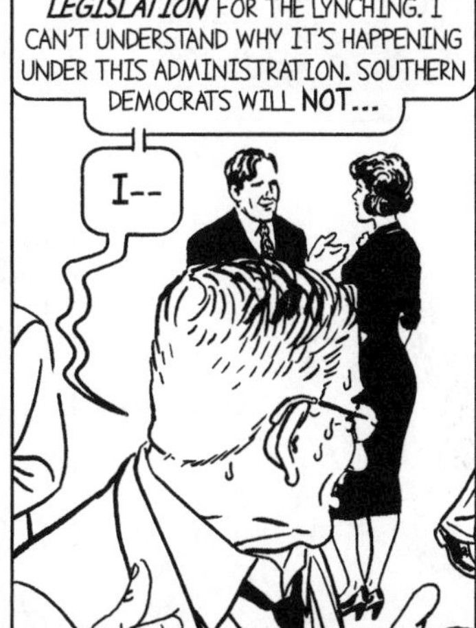
IN ANY CASE, SOMEDAY, WE ALSO NEED LEGISLATION FOR THE LYNCHING. I CAN'T UNDERSTAND WHY IT'S HAPPENING UNDER THIS ADMINISTRATION. SOUTHERN DEMOCRATS WILL NOT...
I--

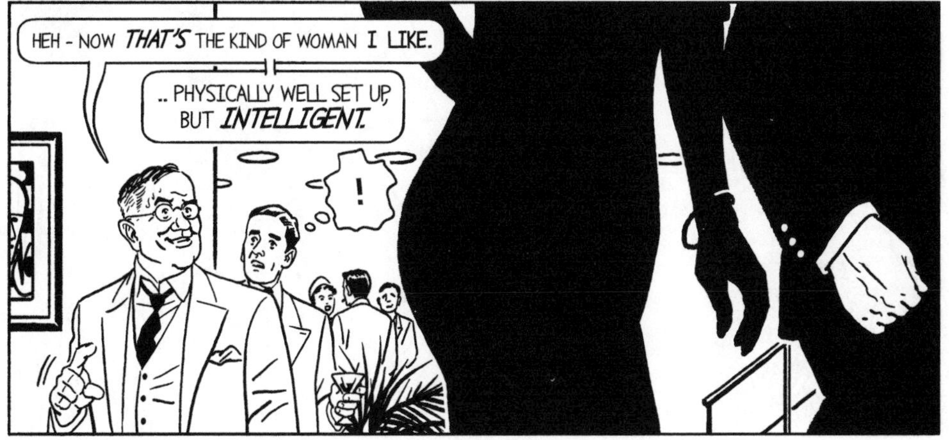
HEH - NOW THAT'S THE KIND OF WOMAN I LIKE.
.. PHYSICALLY WELL SET UP, BUT INTELLIGENT.
!

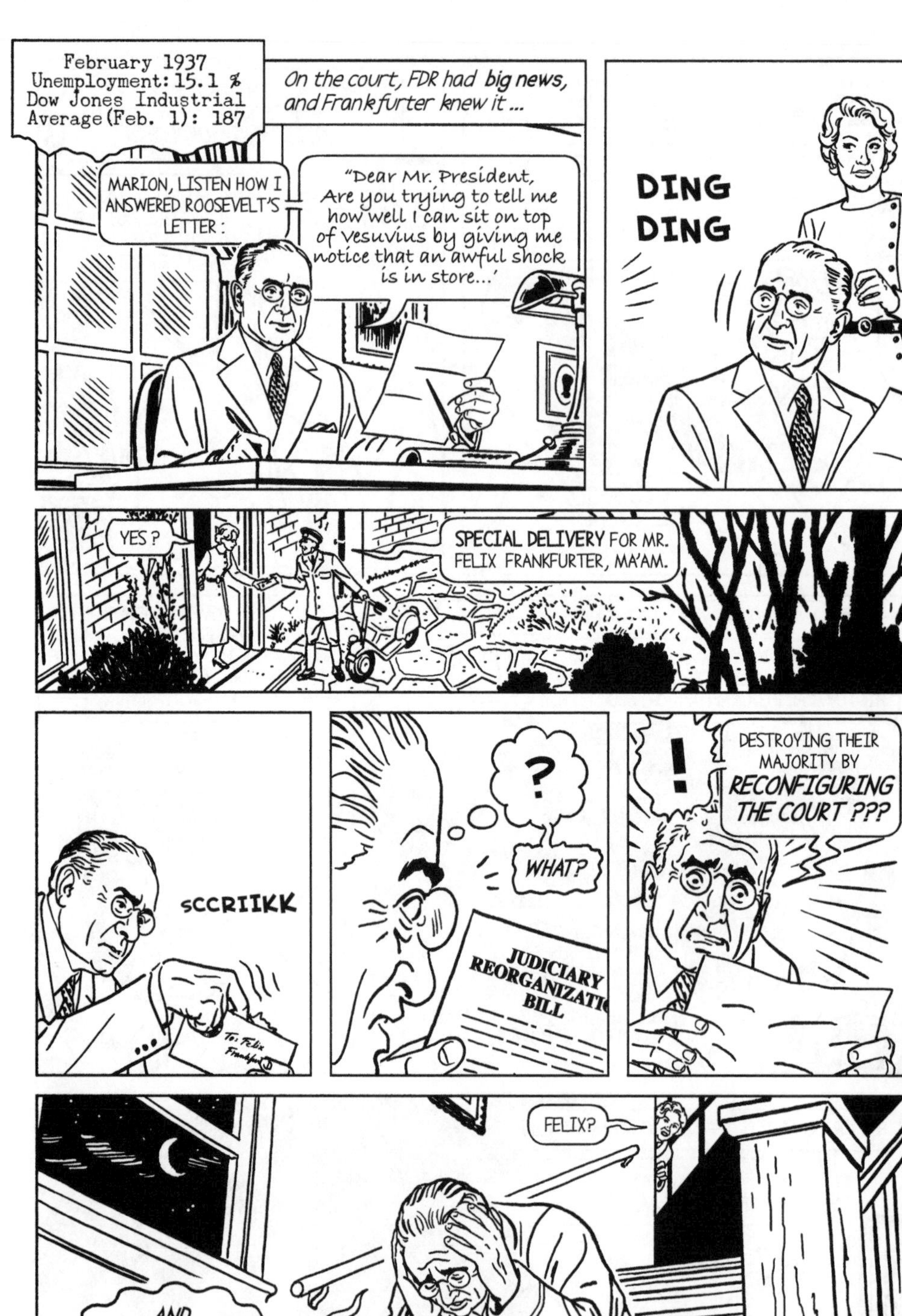
February 1937
Unemployment: 15.1 %
Dow Jones Industrial
Average (Feb. 1): 187
On the court, FDR had big news, and Frankfurter knew it ...
MARION, LISTEN HOW I ANSWERED ROOSEVELT'S LETTER:
"Dear Mr. President, Are you trying to tell me how well I can sit on top of vesuvius by giving me notice that an awful shock is in store...'
DING
DING
YES?
SPECIAL DELIVERY FOR MR. FELIX FRANKFURTER, MA'AM.
SCCRIIKK
To: Felix Frankfurter
?
WHAT?
JUDICIARY REORGANIZATI
BILL
!
DESTROYING THEIR MAJORITY BY RECONFIGURING THE COURT ???
FELIX?
AND EVERYONE WILL THINK THE PLAN IS MY IDEA ...
> CROAK <

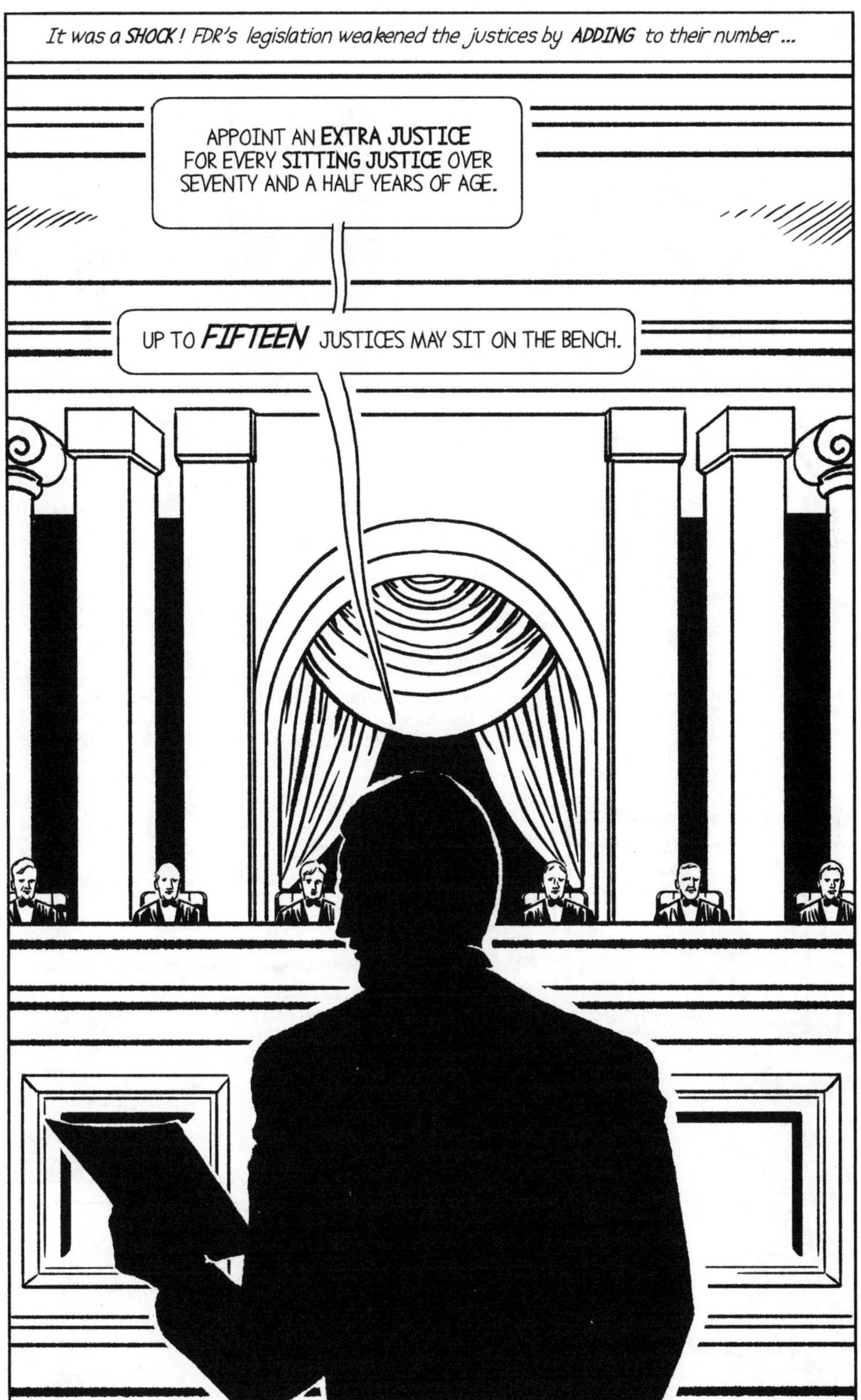
It was a SHOCK! FDR's legislation weakened the justices by ADDING to their number...
APPOINT AN EXTRA JUSTICE FOR EVERY SITTING JUSTICE OVER SEVENTY AND A HALF YEARS OF AGE.
UP TO FIFTEEN JUSTICES MAY SIT ON THE BENCH.

Right away, the justices started to switch their votes to favor Roosevelt in cases.

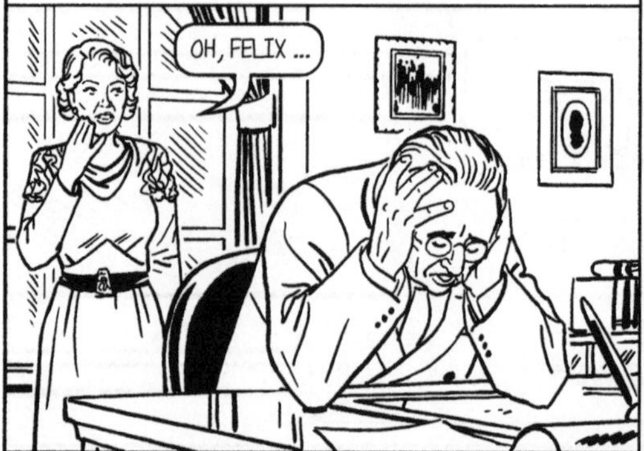

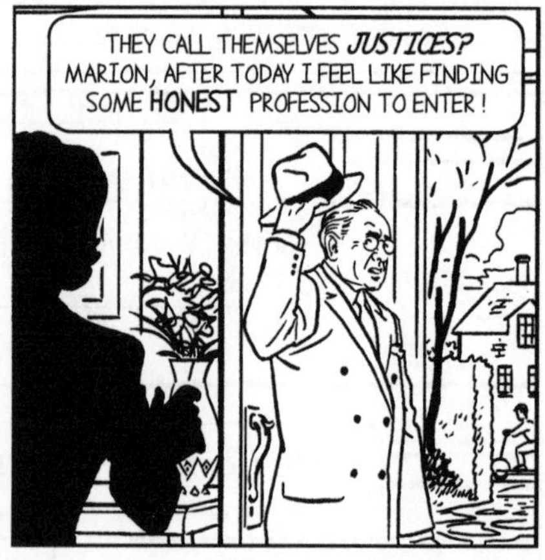

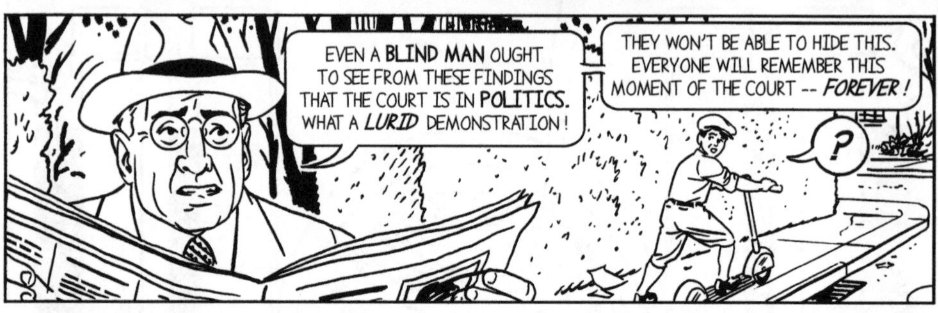

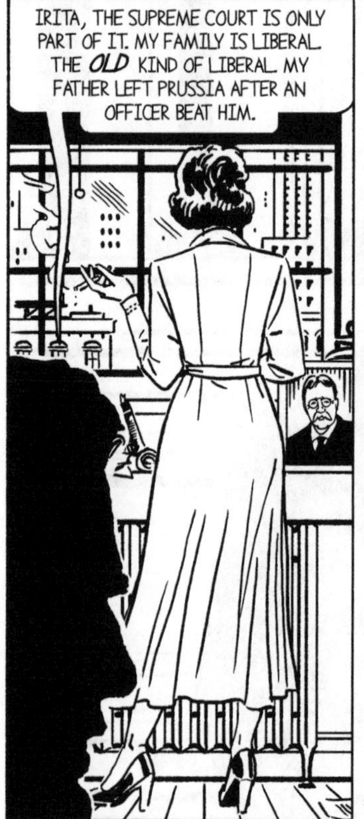

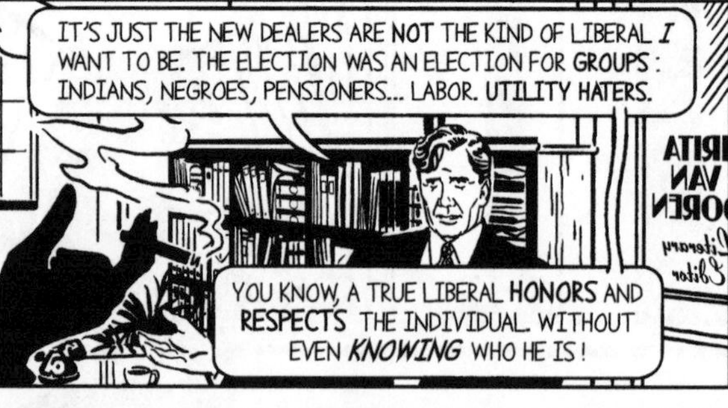

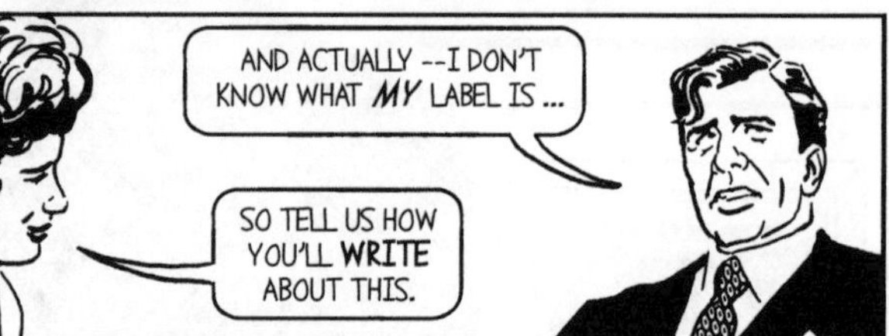

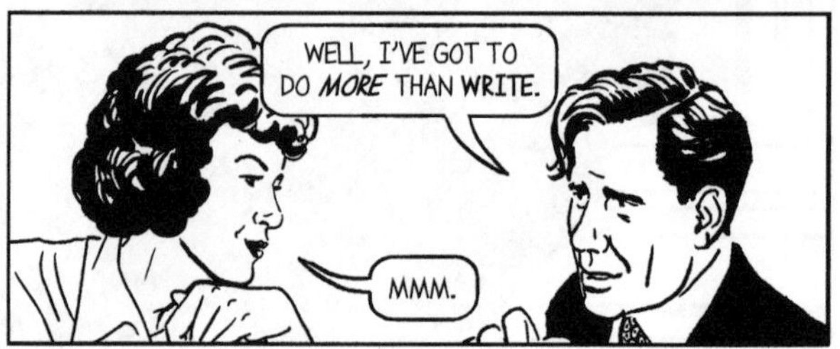

Our sector had **utilities propaganda** to counter, like the play *"POWER,"* You remember? That was our **first date**!

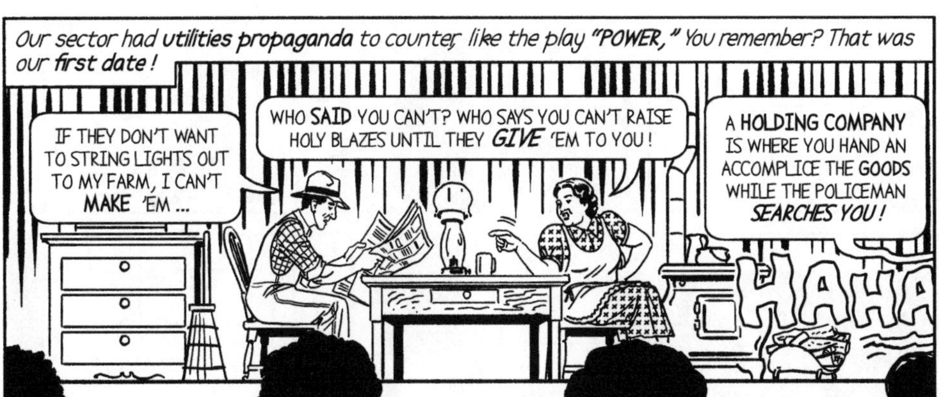

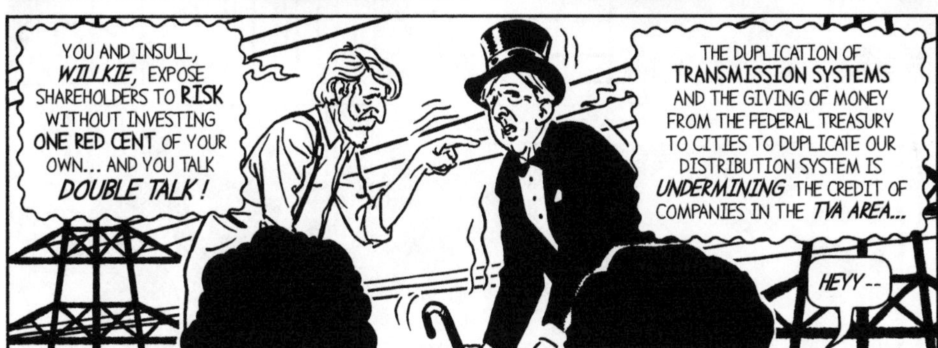

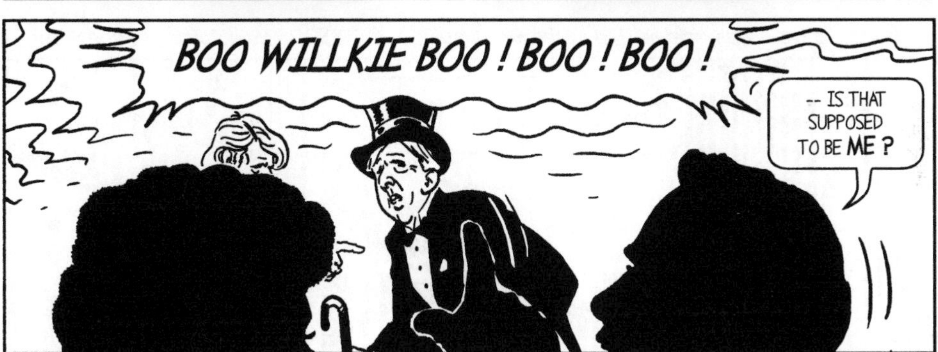

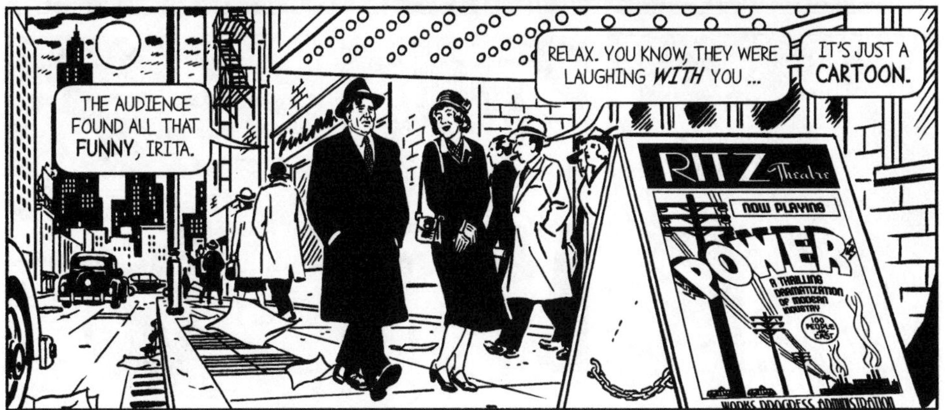

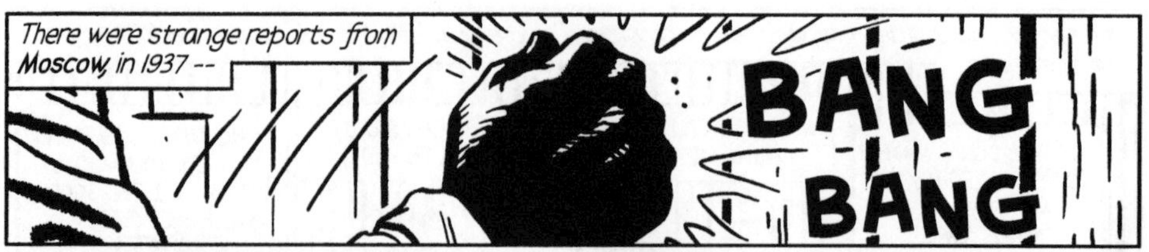
There were strange reports from **Moscow**, in 1937 --
BANG
BANG

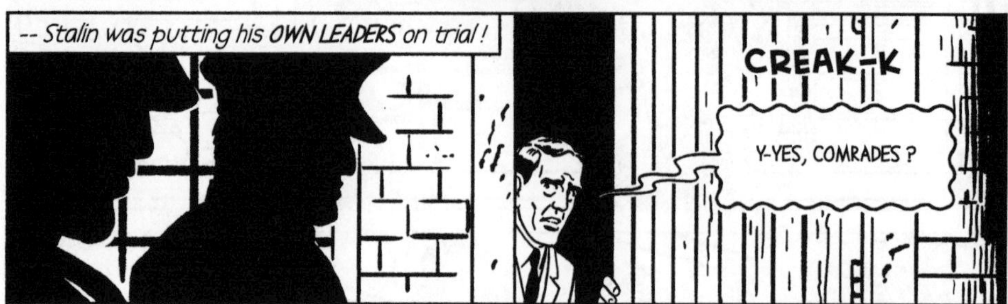
-- Stalin was putting his **OWN LEADERS** on trial!
CREAK-K
Y-YES, COMRADES ?

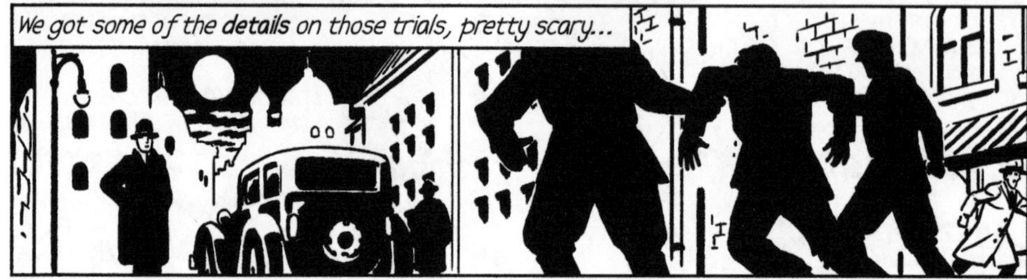
We got some of the **details** on those trials, pretty scary...

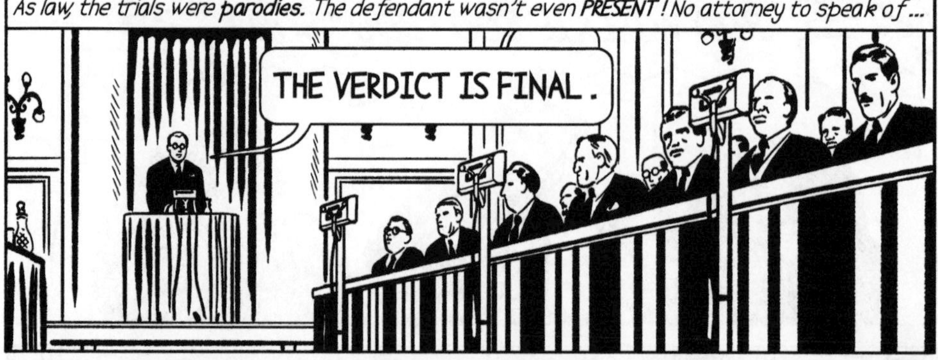
As law, the trials were **parodies.** The defendant wasn't even **PRESENT**! No attorney to speak of...
THE VERDICT IS FINAL .

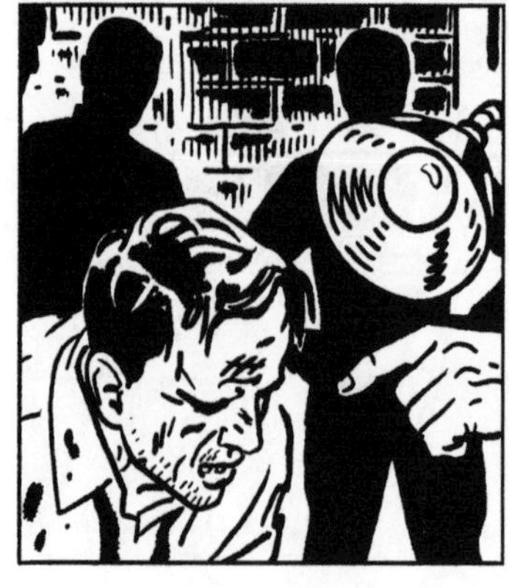

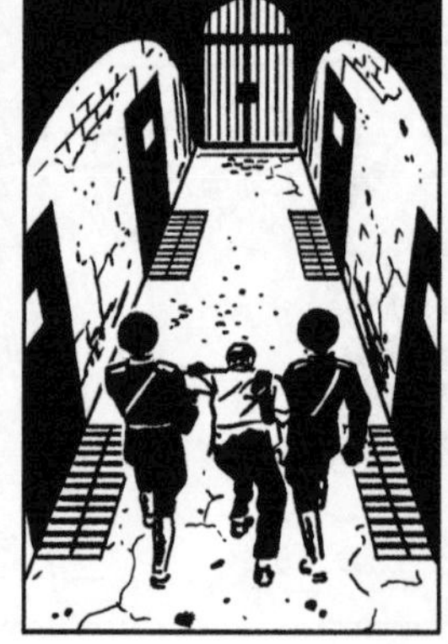

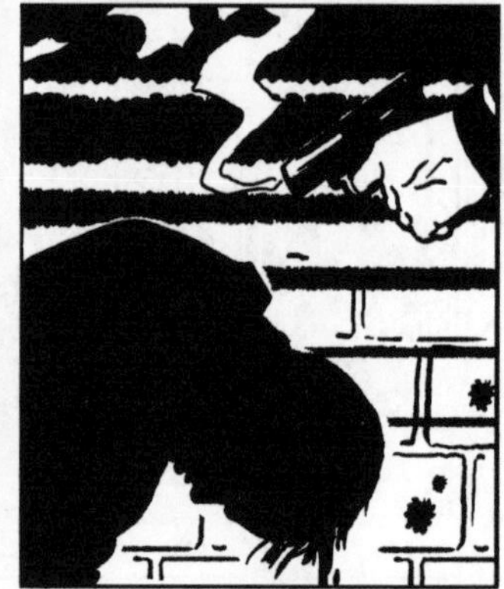

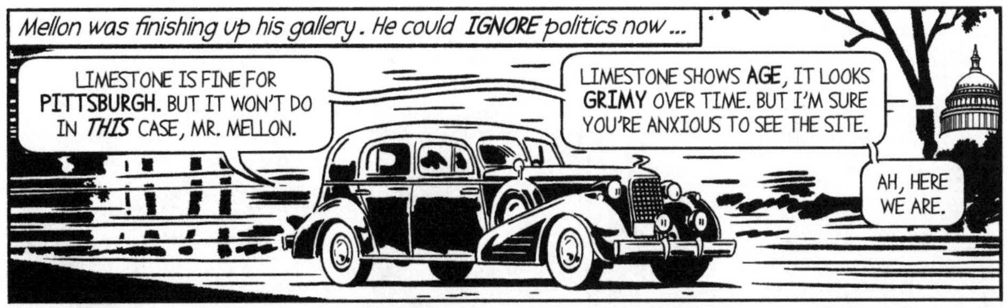
Mellon was finishing up his gallery. He could IGNORE politics now ...
LIMESTONE IS FINE FOR PITTSBURGH. BUT IT WON'T DO IN THIS CASE, MR. MELLON.
LIMESTONE SHOWS AGE, IT LOOKS GRIMY OVER TIME. BUT I'M SURE YOU'RE ANXIOUS TO SEE THE SITE.
AH, HERE WE ARE.

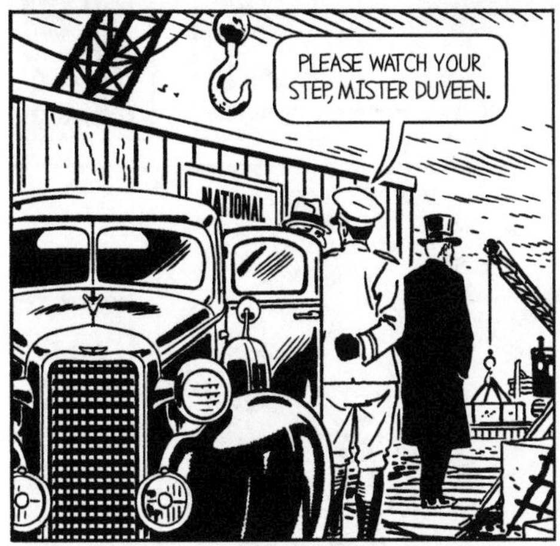
PLEASE WATCH YOUR STEP, MISTER DUVEEN.
NATIONAL

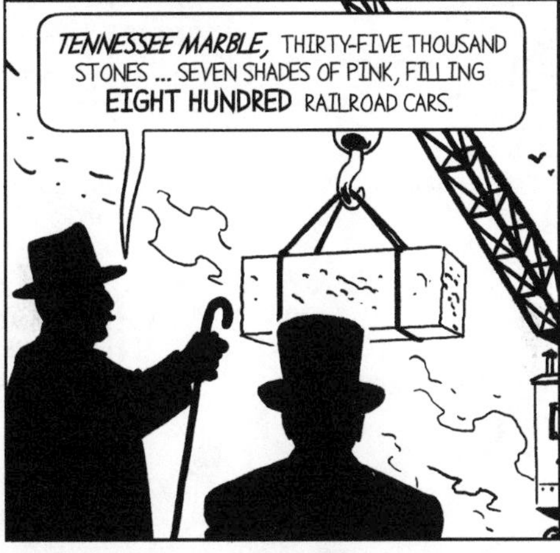
TENNESSEE MARBLE, THIRTY-FIVE THOUSAND STONES ... SEVEN SHADES OF PINK, FILLING EIGHT HUNDRED RAILROAD CARS.

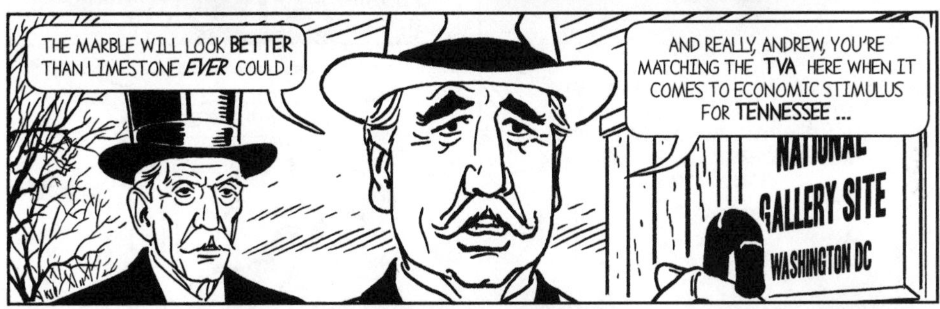
THE MARBLE WILL LOOK BETTER THAN LIMESTONE EVER COULD!
AND REALLY, ANDREW, YOU'RE MATCHING THE TVA HERE WHEN IT COMES TO ECONOMIC STIMULUS FOR TENNESSEE ...
GALLERY SITE
WASHINGTON DC

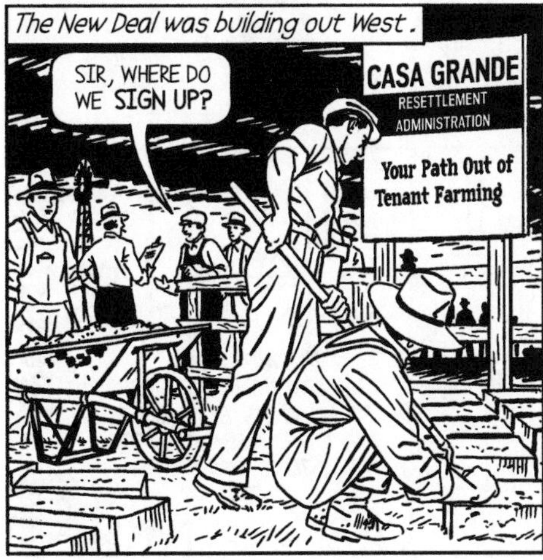
The New Deal was building out West.
SIR, WHERE DO WE SIGN UP?
CASA GRANDE
RESETTLEMENT ADMINISTRATION
Your Path Out of Tenant Farming

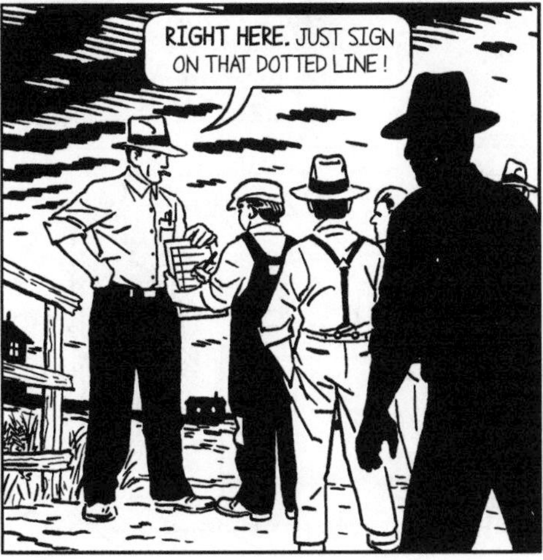
RIGHT HERE. JUST SIGN ON THAT DOTTED LINE!

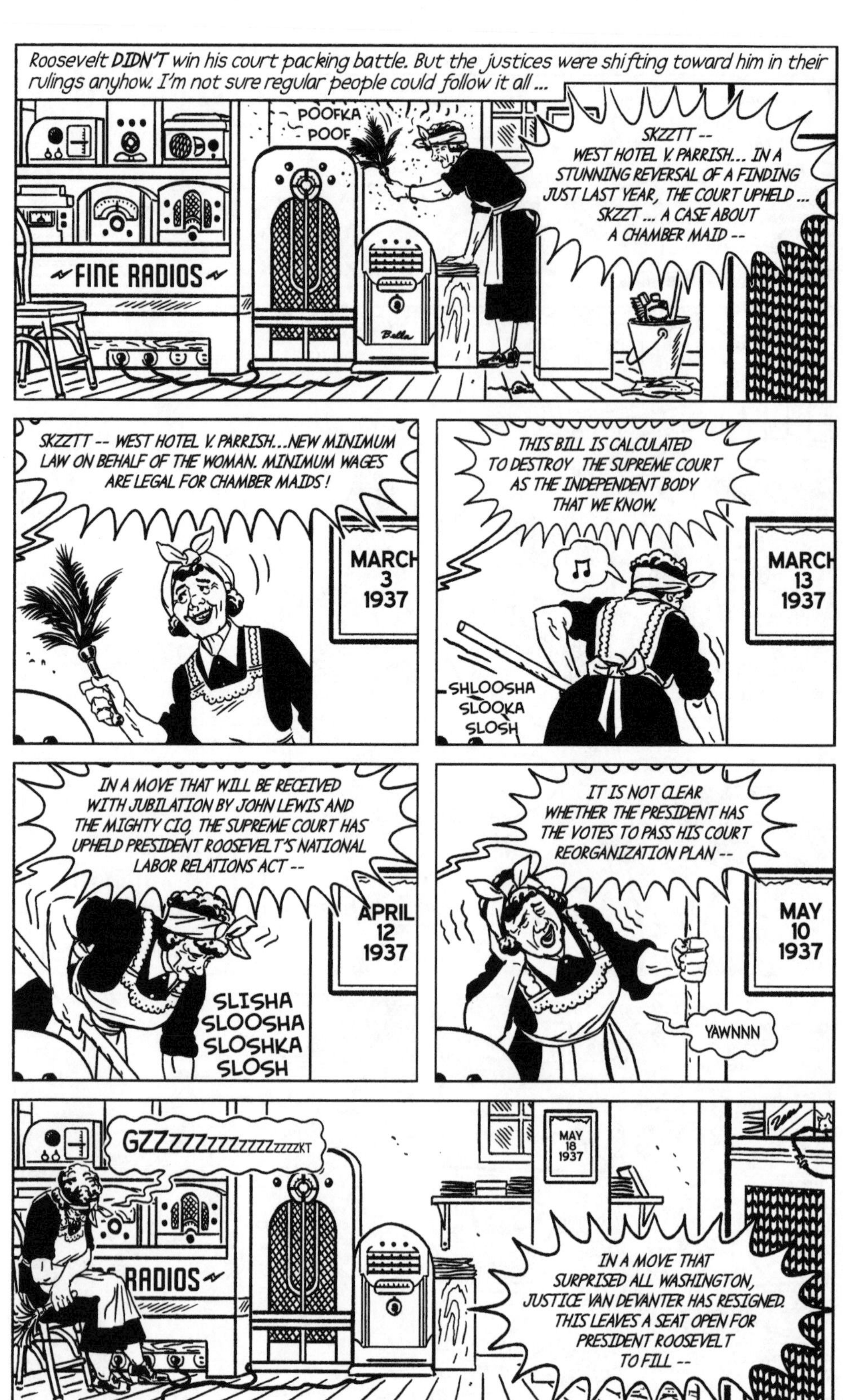
Roosevelt **DIDN'T** win his court packing battle. But the justices were shifting toward him in their rulings anyhow. I'm not sure regular people could follow it all ...
POOFKA POOF
SKZZTT -- WEST HOTEL V. PARRISH... IN A STUNNING REVERSAL OF A FINDING JUST LAST YEAR, THE COURT UPHELD ... SKZZT ... A CASE ABOUT A CHAMBER MAID --
FINE RADIOS
Bella
SKZZTT -- WEST HOTEL V. PARRISH...NEW MINIMUM LAW ON BEHALF OF THE WOMAN. MINIMUM WAGES ARE LEGAL FOR CHAMBER MAIDS!
MARCH 3 1937
THIS BILL IS CALCULATED TO DESTROY THE SUPREME COURT AS THE INDEPENDENT BODY THAT WE KNOW.
MARCH 13 1937
SHLOOSHA SLOOKA SLOSH
IN A MOVE THAT WILL BE RECEIVED WITH JUBILATION BY JOHN LEWIS AND THE MIGHTY CIO, THE SUPREME COURT HAS UPHELD PRESIDENT ROOSEVELT'S NATIONAL LABOR RELATIONS ACT --
APRIL 12 1937
SLISHA SLOOSHA SLOSHKA SLOSH
IT IS NOT CLEAR WHETHER THE PRESIDENT HAS THE VOTES TO PASS HIS COURT REORGANIZATION PLAN --
MAY 10 1937
YAWNNN
GZZzzzzzzzzzzzzzzKT
MAY 18 1937
RADIOS
IN A MOVE THAT SURPRISED ALL WASHINGTON, JUSTICE VAN DEVANTER HAS RESIGNED. THIS LEAVES A SEAT OPEN FOR PRESIDENT ROOSEVELT TO FILL --

In early 1937, Americans were wondering where it was all going. People were getting tired of **The Experiment.** The White House didn't seem to be picking that up...

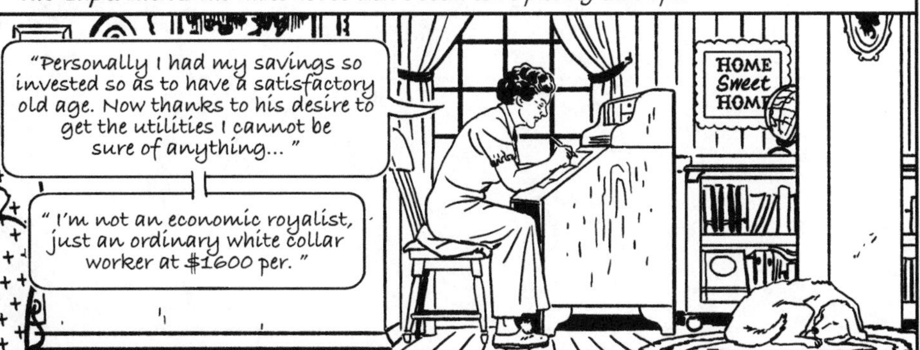

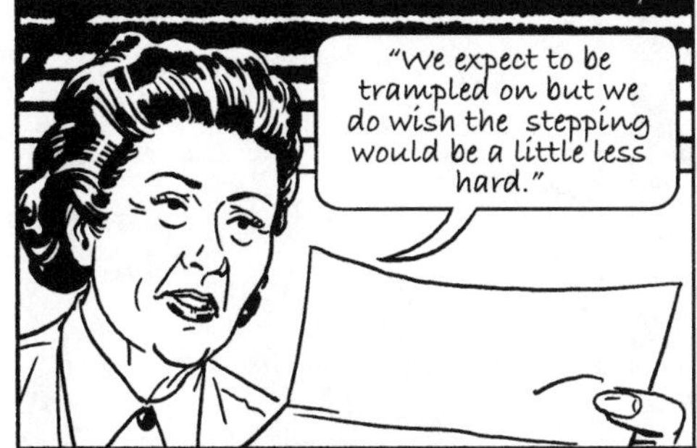

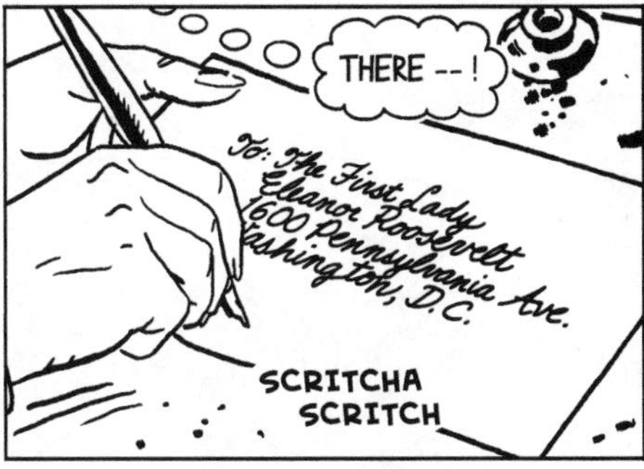

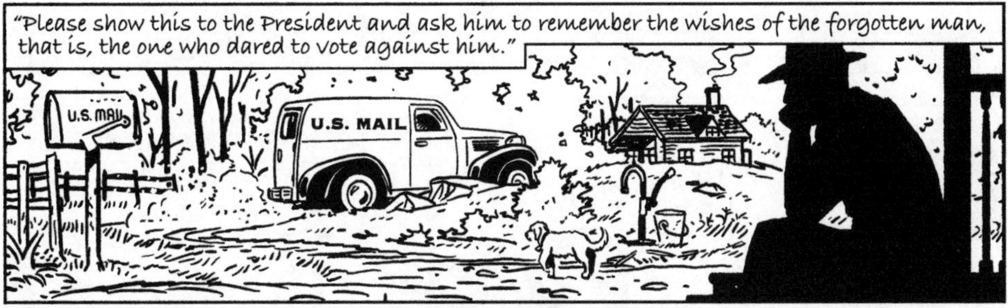

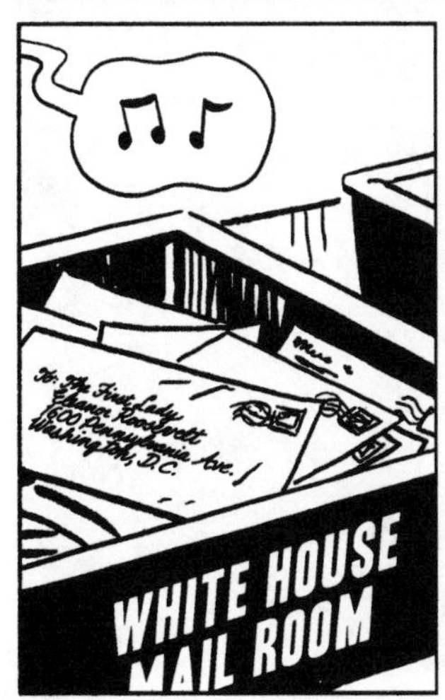

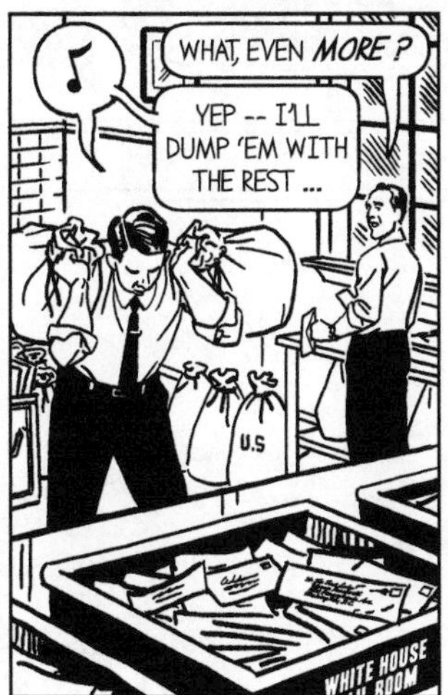

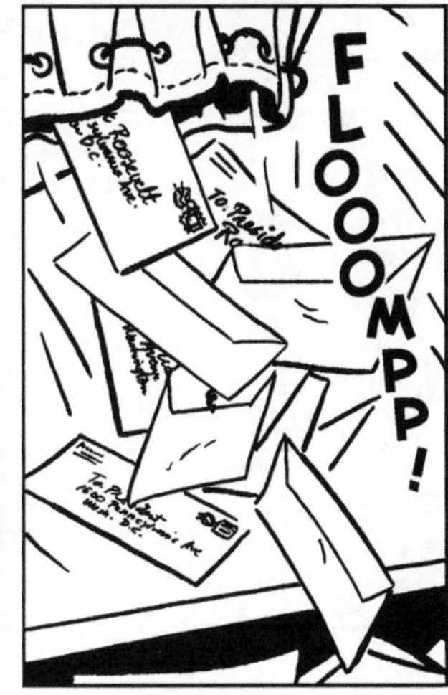

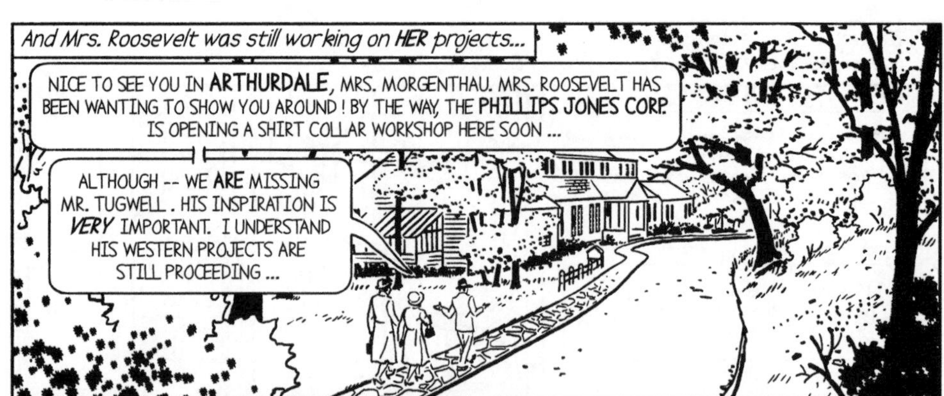

And Mrs. Roosevelt was still working on HER projects...
NICE TO SEE YOU IN ARTHURDALE, MRS. MORGENTHAU. MRS. ROOSEVELT HAS BEEN WANTING TO SHOW YOU AROUND! BY THE WAY, THE PHILLIPS JONES CORP. IS OPENING A SHIRT COLLAR WORKSHOP HERE SOON ...
ALTHOUGH -- WE ARE MISSING MR. TUGWELL. HIS INSPIRATION IS VERY IMPORTANT. I UNDERSTAND HIS WESTERN PROJECTS ARE STILL PROCEEDING ...

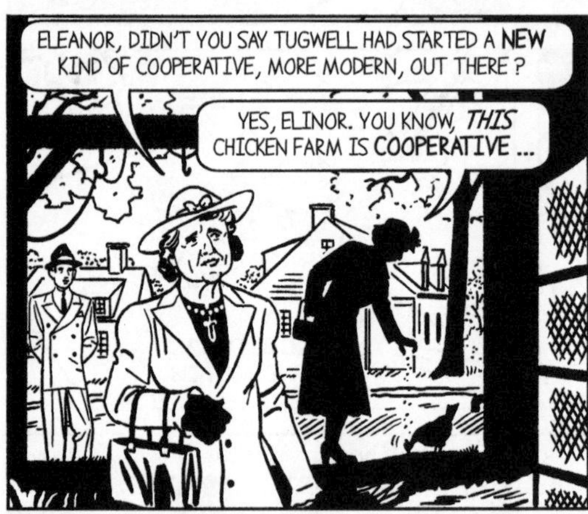

ELEANOR, DIDN'T YOU SAY TUGWELL HAD STARTED A NEW KIND OF COOPERATIVE, MORE MODERN, OUT THERE?
YES, ELINOR. YOU KNOW, THIS CHICKEN FARM IS COOPERATIVE ...

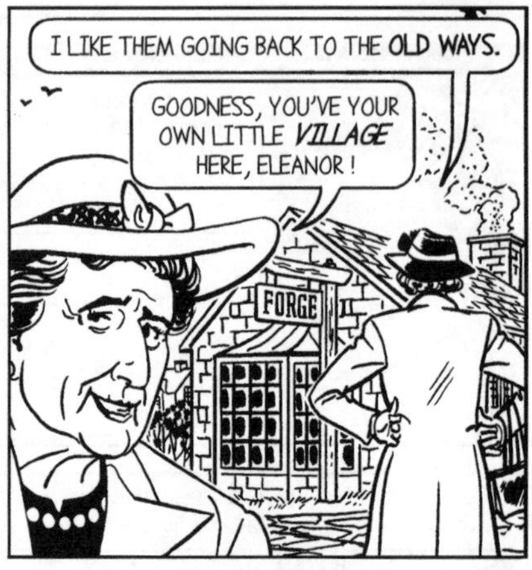

I LIKE THEM GOING BACK TO THE OLD WAYS.
GOODNESS, YOU'VE YOUR OWN LITTLE VILLAGE HERE, ELEANOR!
FORGE

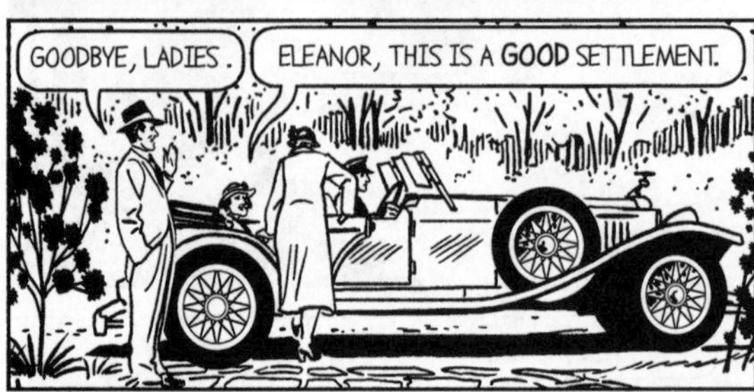

GOODBYE, LADIES.
ELEANOR, THIS IS A GOOD SETTLEMENT.

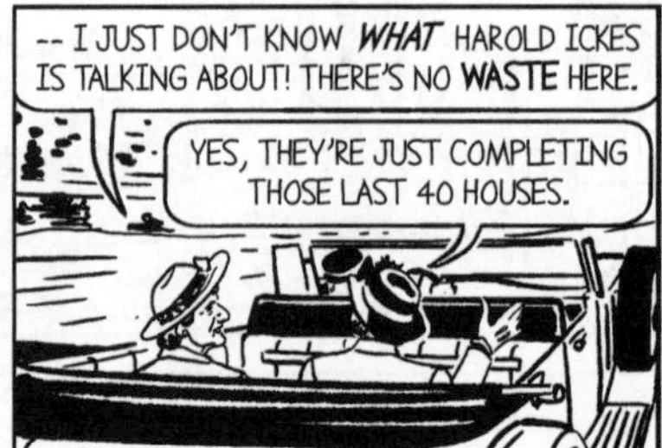

-- I JUST DON'T KNOW WHAT HAROLD ICKES IS TALKING ABOUT! THERE'S NO WASTE HERE.
YES, THEY'RE JUST COMPLETING THOSE LAST 40 HOUSES.

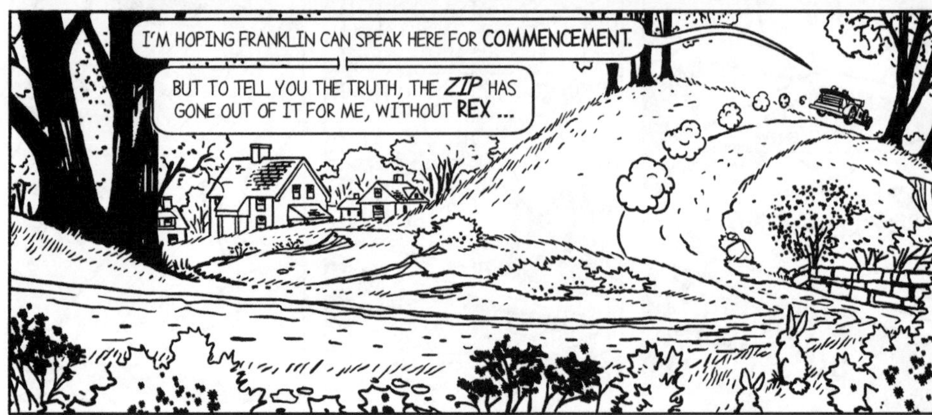

I'M HOPING FRANKLIN CAN SPEAK HERE FOR COMMENCEMENT.
BUT TO TELL YOU THE TRUTH, THE ZIP HAS GONE OUT OF IT FOR ME, WITHOUT REX ...

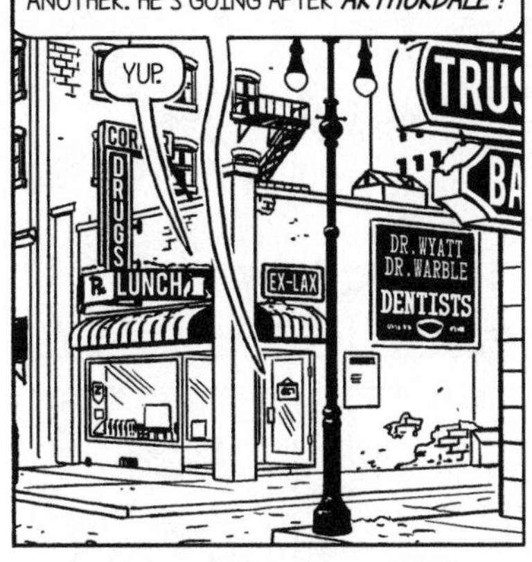
REX, DID YOU SEE WHERE HENRY WALLACE IS SHUTTING DOWN THE RESETTLEMENT ADMINISTRATION? SENATOR BYRD IS STILL GOING AFTER YOU. ONE APPLE GROWER AFTER ANOTHER. HE'S GOING AFTER ARTHURDALE!
YUP.
DRUGS
LUNCH
EX-LAX
DR. WYATT
DR. WARBLE
DENTISTS
TRUS

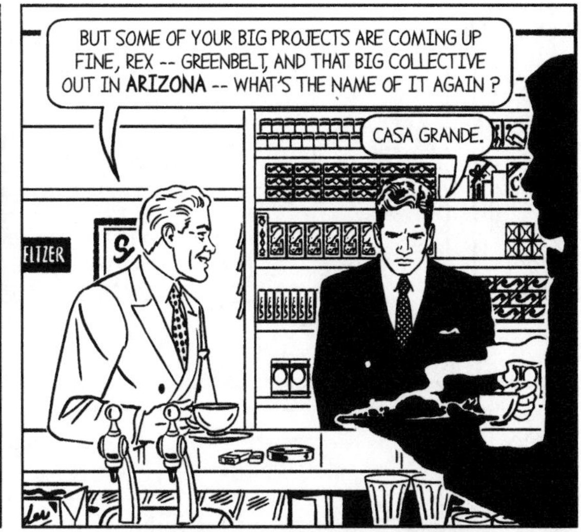
BUT SOME OF YOUR BIG PROJECTS ARE COMING UP FINE, REX -- GREENBELT, AND THAT BIG COLLECTIVE OUT IN ARIZONA -- WHAT'S THE NAME OF IT AGAIN?
CASA GRANDE.
ELTZER

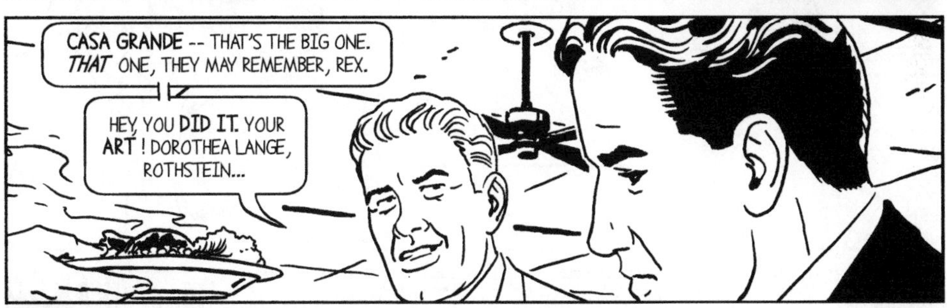
CASA GRANDE -- THAT'S THE BIG ONE. THAT ONE, THEY MAY REMEMBER, REX.
HEY, YOU DID IT. YOUR ART! DOROTHEA LANGE, ROTHSTEIN...

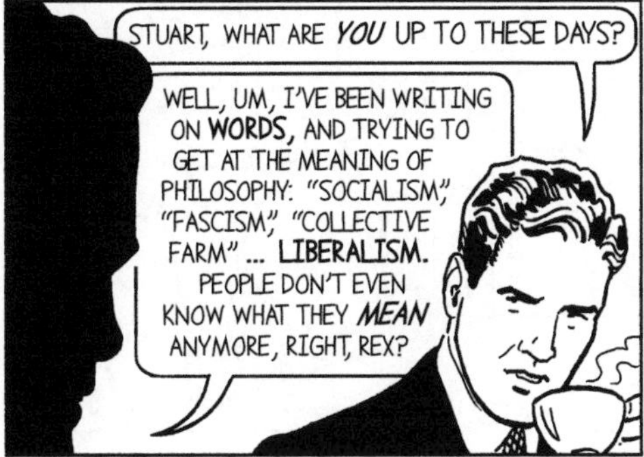
STUART, WHAT ARE YOU UP TO THESE DAYS?
WELL, UM, I'VE BEEN WRITING ON WORDS, AND TRYING TO GET AT THE MEANING OF PHILOSOPHY: "SOCIALISM," "FASCISM," "COLLECTIVE FARM" ... LIBERALISM. PEOPLE DON'T EVEN KNOW WHAT THEY MEAN ANYMORE, RIGHT, REX?

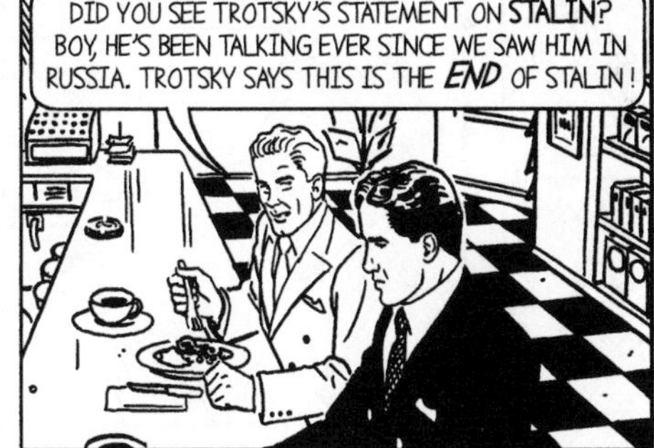
DID YOU SEE TROTSKY'S STATEMENT ON STALIN? BOY, HE'S BEEN TALKING EVER SINCE WE SAW HIM IN RUSSIA. TROTSKY SAYS THIS IS THE END OF STALIN!

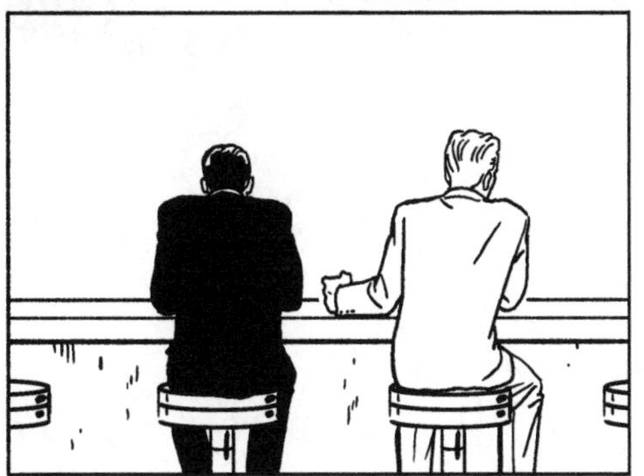

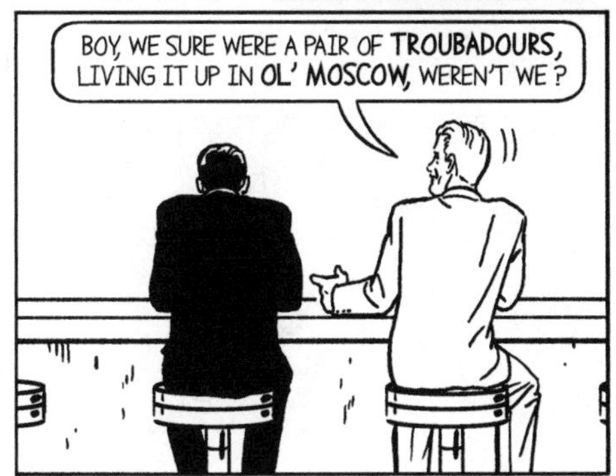
BOY, WE SURE WERE A PAIR OF TROUBADOURS, LIVING IT UP IN OL' MOSCOW, WEREN'T WE?

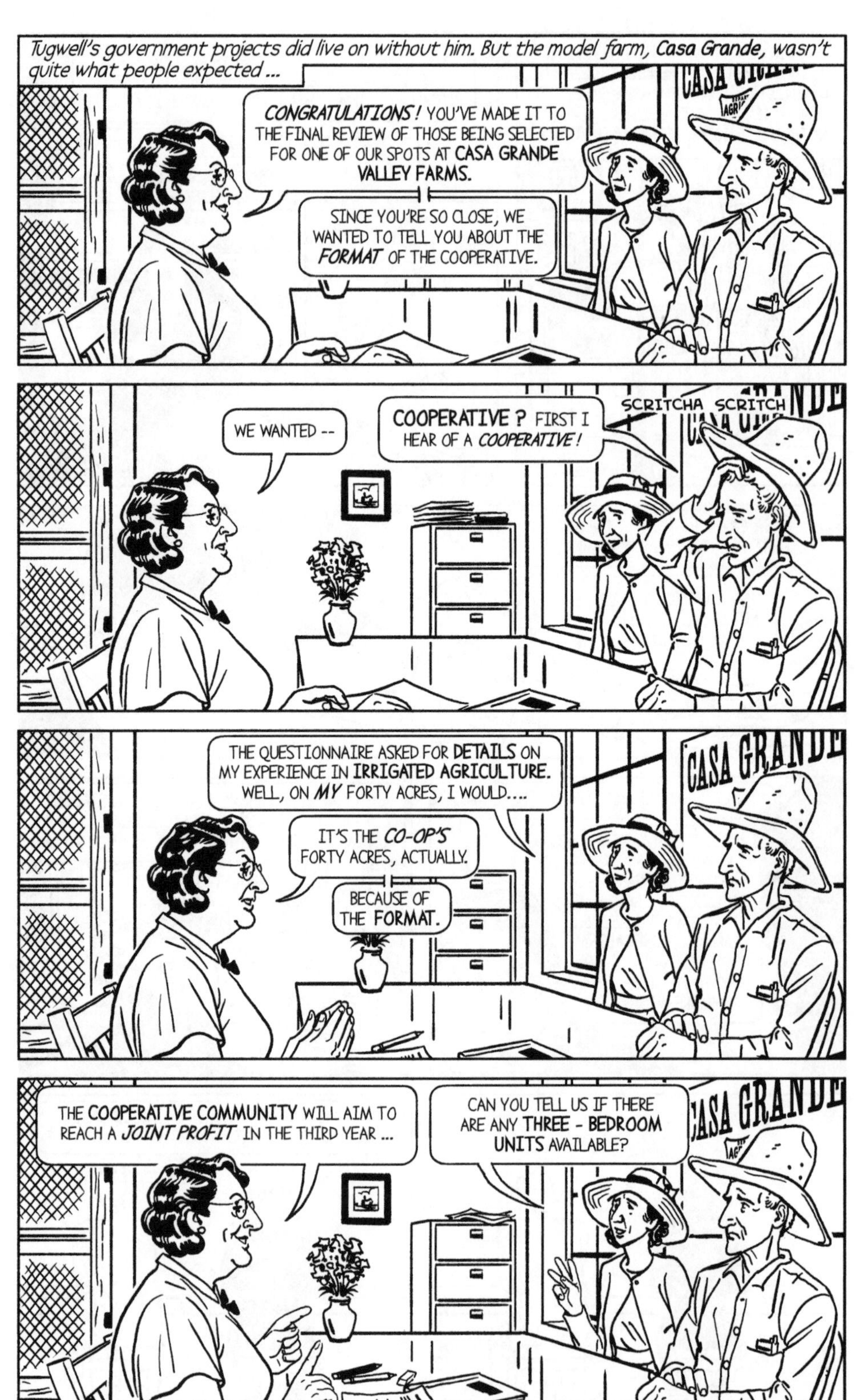

Tugwell's government projects did live on without him. But the model farm, Casa Grande, wasn't quite what people expected ...
CASA GRANDE
CONGRATULATIONS! YOU'VE MADE IT TO THE FINAL REVIEW OF THOSE BEING SELECTED FOR ONE OF OUR SPOTS AT CASA GRANDE VALLEY FARMS.
SINCE YOU'RE SO CLOSE, WE WANTED TO TELL YOU ABOUT THE FORMAT OF THE COOPERATIVE.
WE WANTED --
COOPERATIVE? FIRST I HEAR OF A COOPERATIVE!
SCRITCHA SCRITCH
THE QUESTIONNAIRE ASKED FOR DETAILS ON MY EXPERIENCE IN IRRIGATED AGRICULTURE. WELL, ON MY FORTY ACRES, I WOULD....
IT'S THE CO-OP'S FORTY ACRES, ACTUALLY.
BECAUSE OF THE FORMAT.
CASA GRANDE
THE COOPERATIVE COMMUNITY WILL AIM TO REACH A JOINT PROFIT IN THE THIRD YEAR ...
CAN YOU TELL US IF THERE ARE ANY THREE-BEDROOM UNITS AVAILABLE?
CASA GRANDE

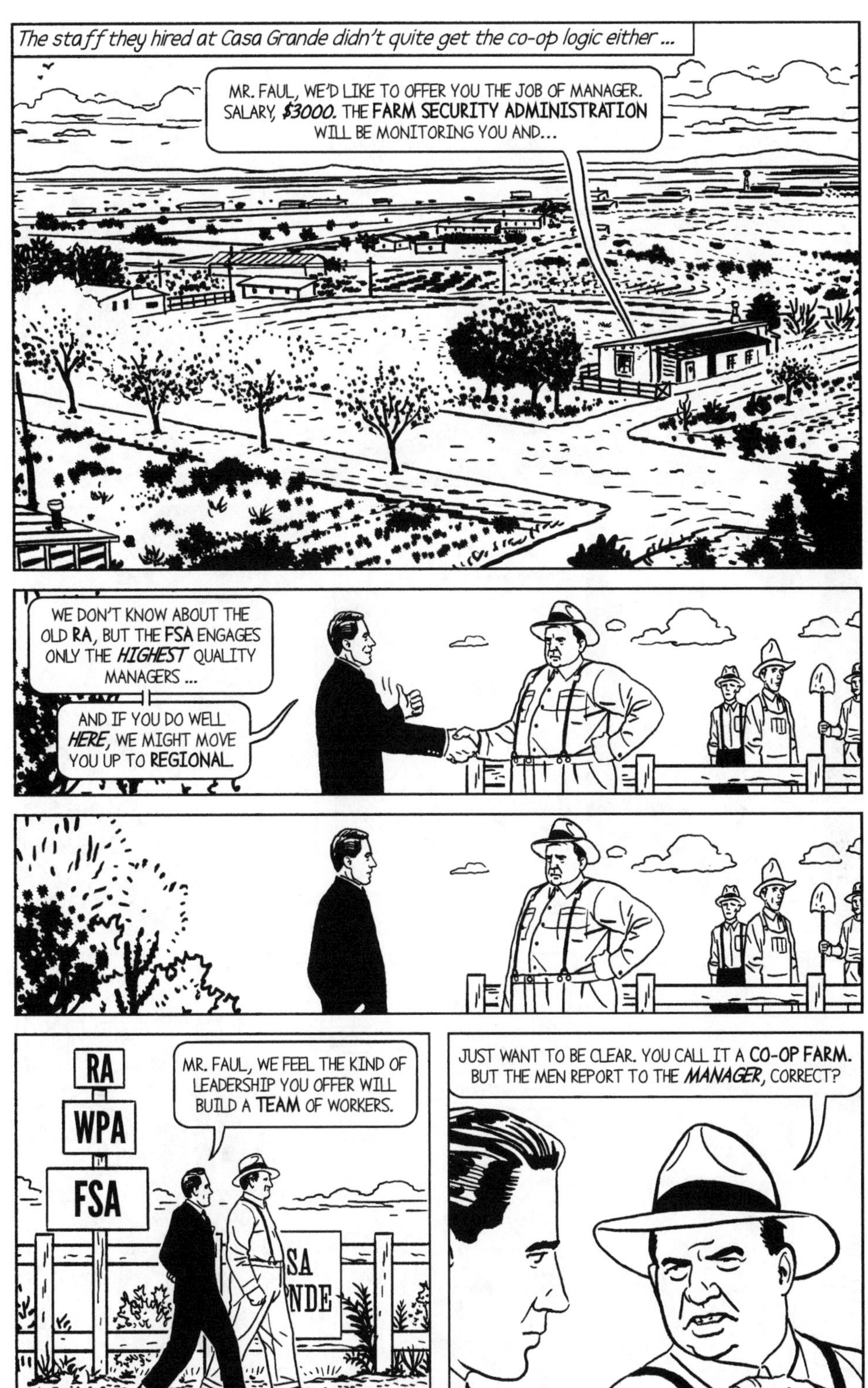
The staff they hired at Casa Grande didn't quite get the co-op logic either ...
MR. FAUL, WE'D LIKE TO OFFER YOU THE JOB OF MANAGER. SALARY, $3000. THE FARM SECURITY ADMINISTRATION WILL BE MONITORING YOU AND...
WE DON'T KNOW ABOUT THE OLD RA, BUT THE FSA ENGAGES ONLY THE HIGHEST QUALITY MANAGERS ...
AND IF YOU DO WELL HERE, WE MIGHT MOVE YOU UP TO REGIONAL.
RA
WPA
FSA
MR. FAUL, WE FEEL THE KIND OF LEADERSHIP YOU OFFER WILL BUILD A TEAM OF WORKERS.
JUST WANT TO BE CLEAR. YOU CALL IT A CO-OP FARM. BUT THE MEN REPORT TO THE MANAGER, CORRECT?

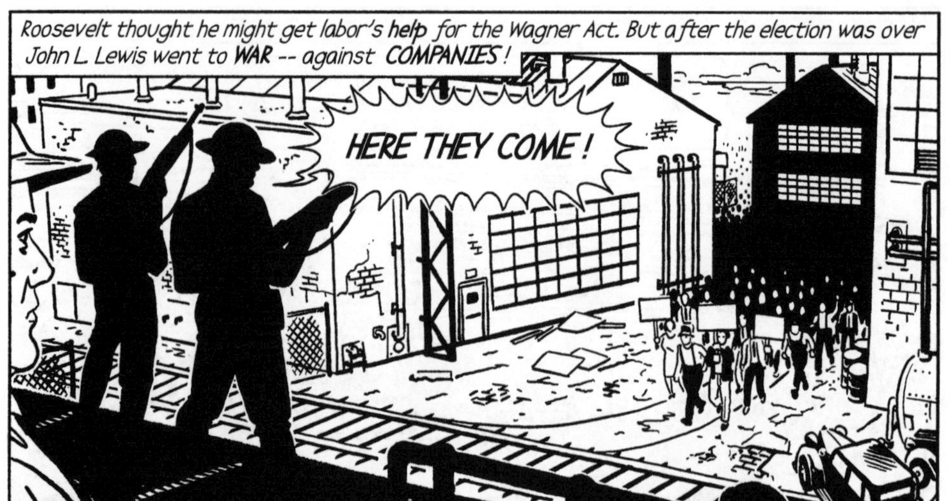
Roosevelt thought he might get labor's help for the Wagner Act. But after the election was over John L. Lewis went to WAR -- against COMPANIES!
HERE THEY COME!

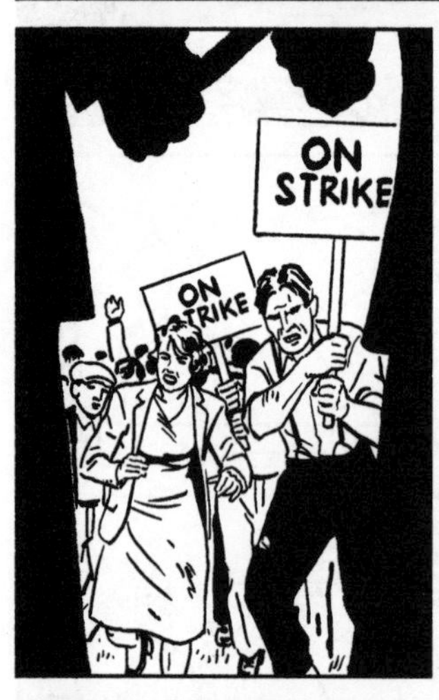
ON STRIKE
ON STRIKE

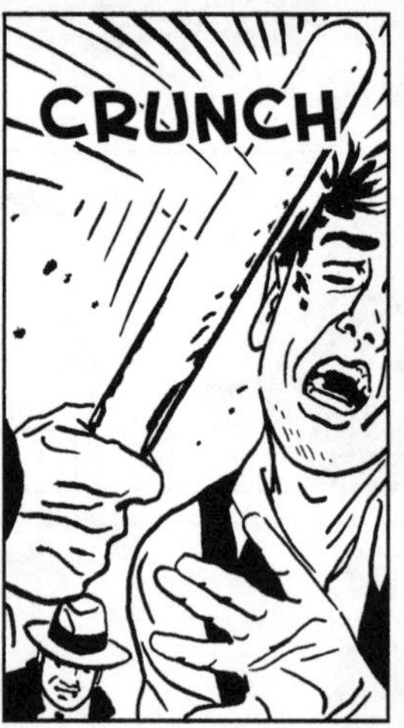
CRUNCH

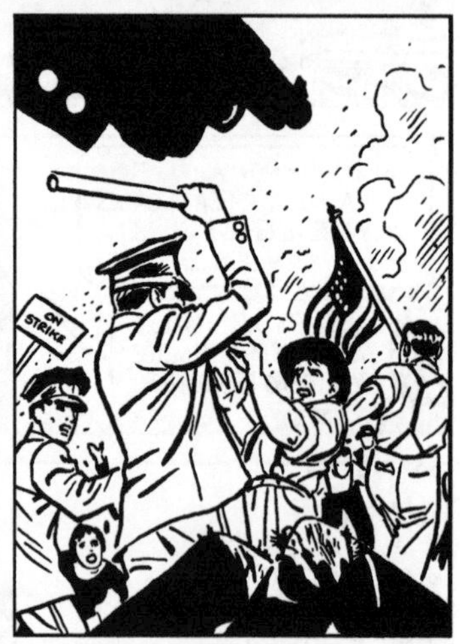
ON STRIKE

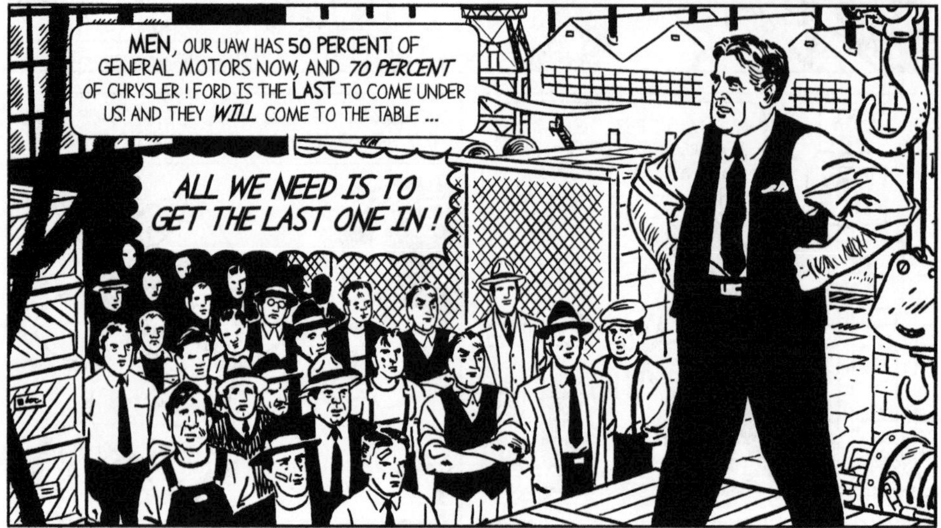
MEN, OUR UAW HAS 50 PERCENT OF GENERAL MOTORS NOW, AND 70 PERCENT OF CHRYSLER! FORD IS THE LAST TO COME UNDER US! AND THEY WILL COME TO THE TABLE ...
ALL WE NEED IS TO GET THE LAST ONE IN!

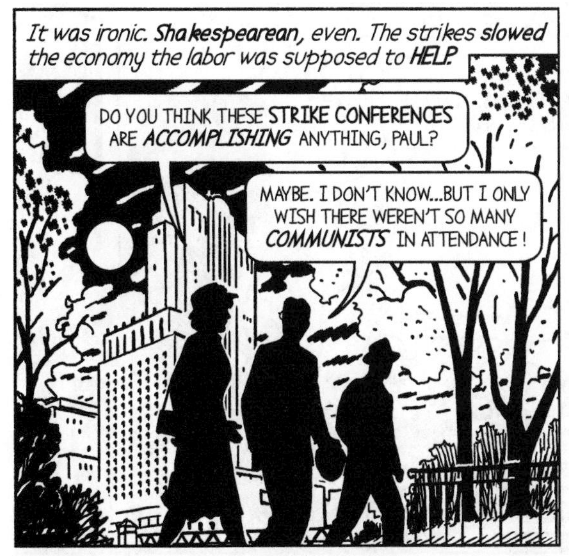
It was ironic. Shakespearean, even. The strikes slowed the economy the labor was supposed to HELP.
DO YOU THINK THESE STRIKE CONFERENCES ARE ACCOMPLISHING ANYTHING, PAUL?
MAYBE. I DON'T KNOW...BUT I ONLY WISH THERE WEREN'T SO MANY COMMUNISTS IN ATTENDANCE!

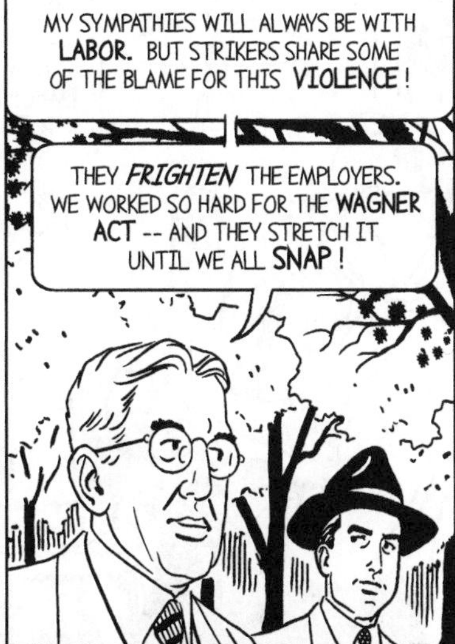
MY SYMPATHIES WILL ALWAYS BE WITH LABOR. BUT STRIKERS SHARE SOME OF THE BLAME FOR THIS VIOLENCE!
THEY FRIGHTEN THE EMPLOYERS. WE WORKED SO HARD FOR THE WAGNER ACT -- AND THEY STRETCH IT UNTIL WE ALL SNAP!

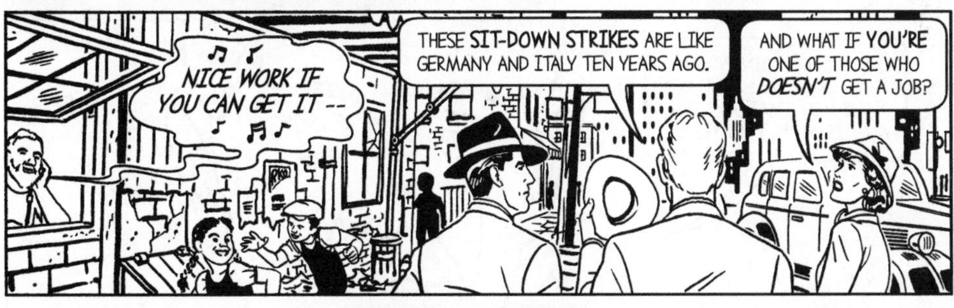
NICE WORK IF YOU CAN GET IT --
THESE SIT-DOWN STRIKES ARE LIKE GERMANY AND ITALY TEN YEARS AGO.
AND WHAT IF YOU'RE ONE OF THOSE WHO DOESN'T GET A JOB?

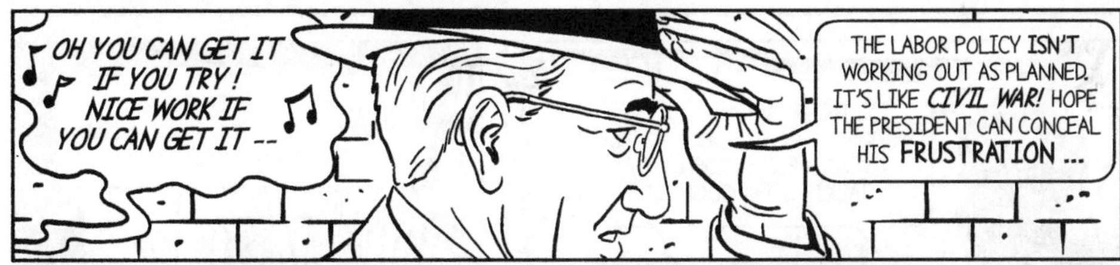
OH YOU CAN GET IT IF YOU TRY! NICE WORK IF YOU CAN GET IT --
THE LABOR POLICY ISN'T WORKING OUT AS PLANNED. IT'S LIKE CIVIL WAR! HOPE THE PRESIDENT CAN CONCEAL HIS FRUSTRATION ...

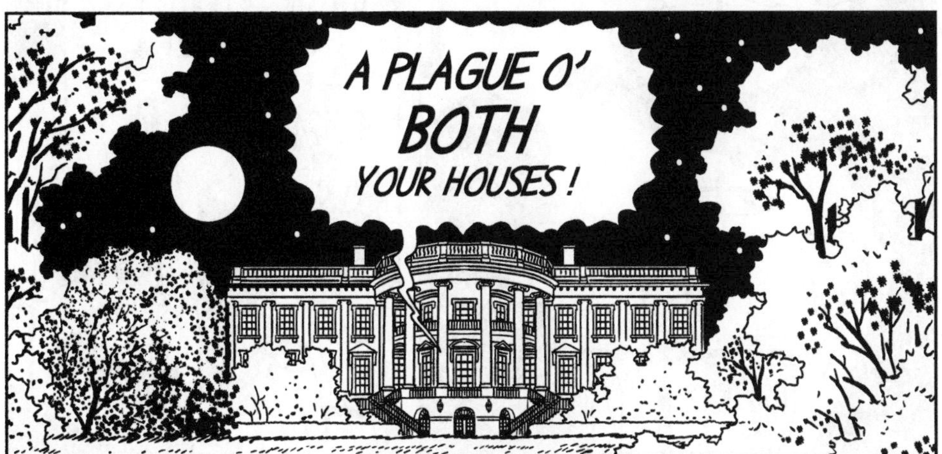
A PLAGUE O' BOTH YOUR HOUSES!

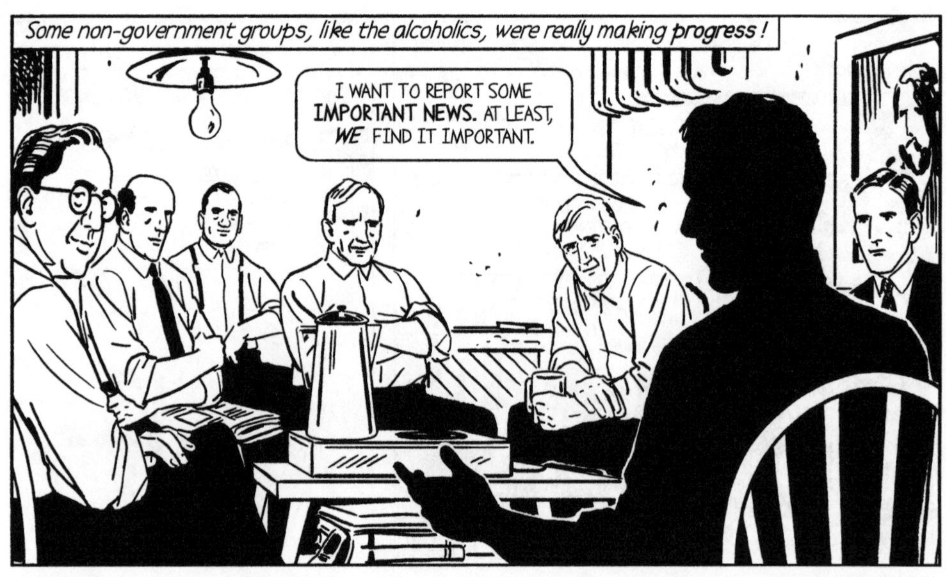
Some non-government groups, like the alcoholics, were really making progress!
I WANT TO REPORT SOME IMPORTANT NEWS. AT LEAST, WE FIND IT IMPORTANT.

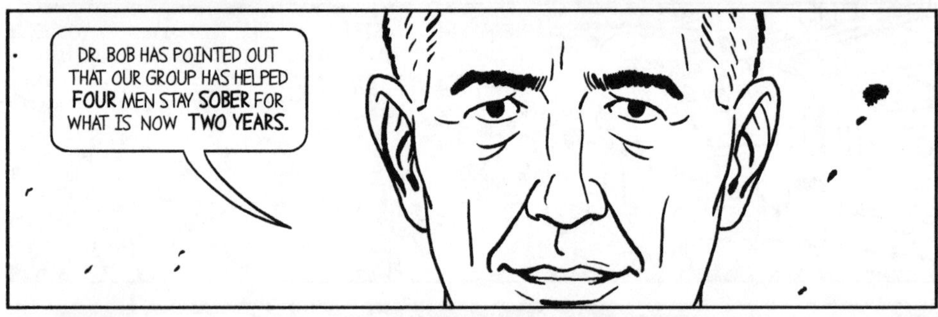
DR. BOB HAS POINTED OUT THAT OUR GROUP HAS HELPED FOUR MEN STAY SOBER FOR WHAT IS NOW TWO YEARS.

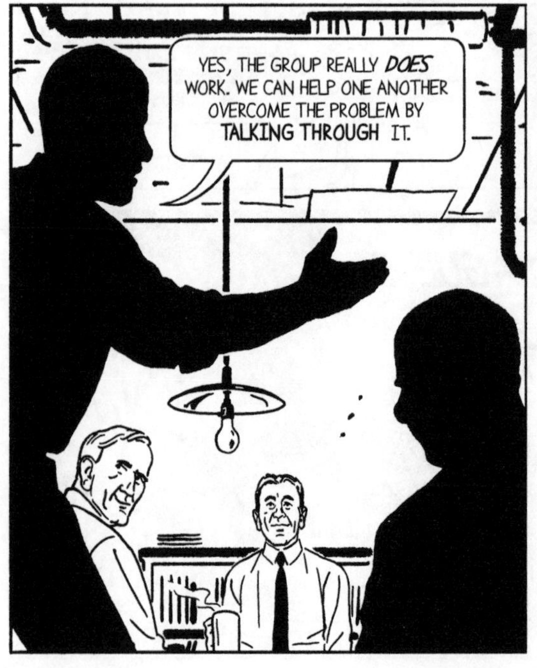
YES, THE GROUP REALLY DOES WORK. WE CAN HELP ONE ANOTHER OVERCOME THE PROBLEM BY TALKING THROUGH IT.

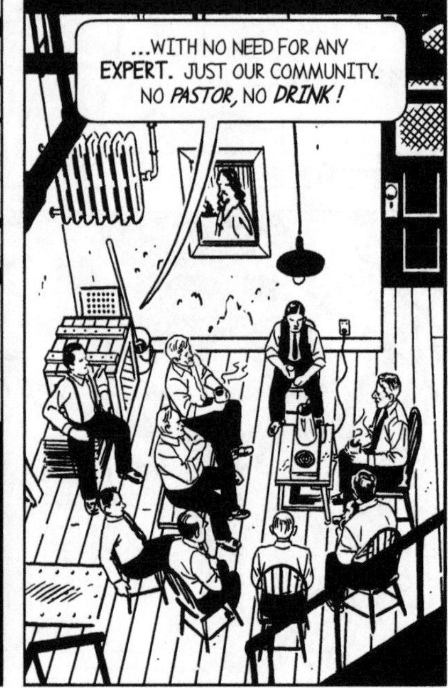
...WITH NO NEED FOR ANY EXPERT. JUST OUR COMMUNITY. NO PASTOR, NO DRINK!

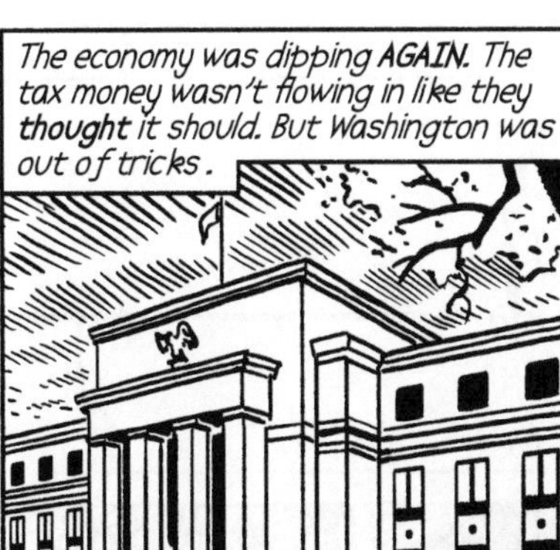
The economy was dipping **AGAIN.** The tax money wasn't flowing in like they **thought** it should. But Washington was out of tricks.

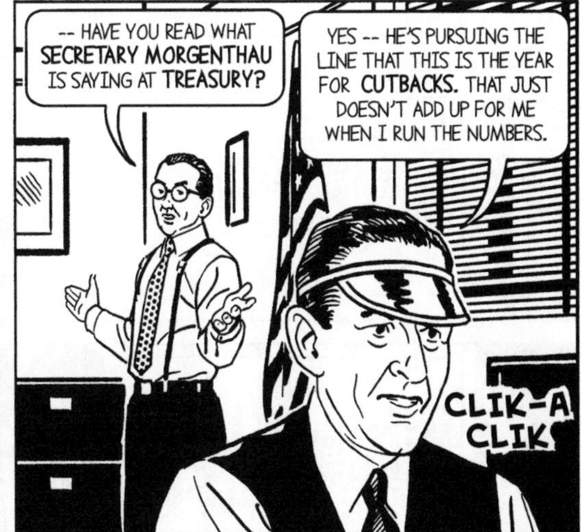
-- HAVE YOU READ WHAT **SECRETARY MORGENTHAU** IS SAYING AT **TREASURY?**
YES -- HE'S PURSUING THE LINE THAT THIS IS THE YEAR FOR **CUTBACKS.** THAT JUST DOESN'T ADD UP FOR ME WHEN I RUN THE NUMBERS.
CLIK-A CLIK

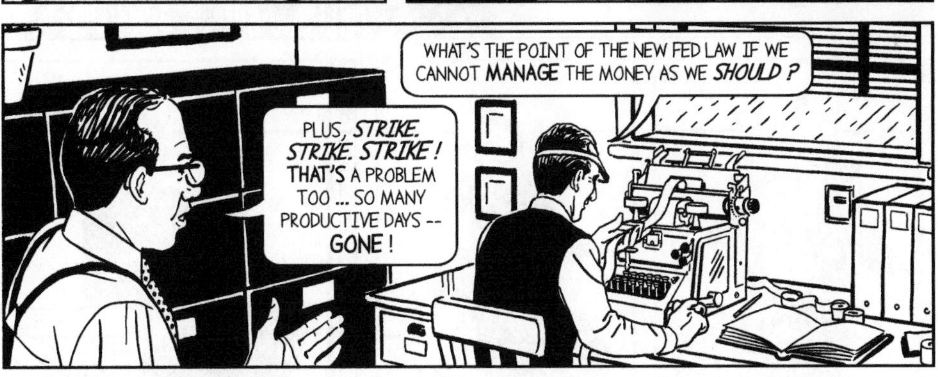
WHAT'S THE POINT OF THE NEW FED LAW IF WE CANNOT **MANAGE** THE MONEY AS WE ***SHOULD?***
PLUS, ***STRIKE. STRIKE. STRIKE!*** **THAT'S** A PROBLEM TOO ... SO MANY PRODUCTIVE DAYS -- **GONE!**

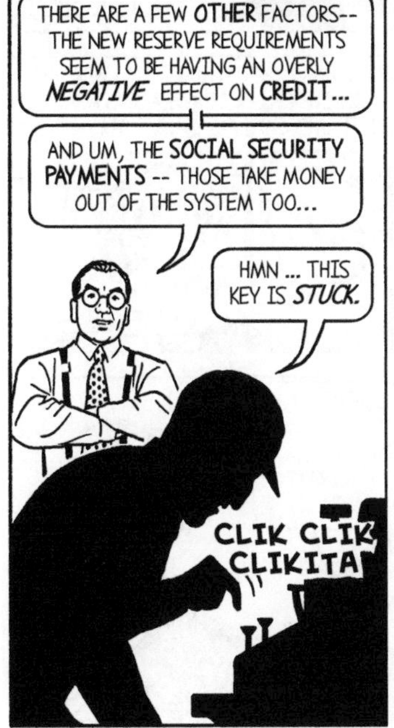
THERE ARE A FEW **OTHER** FACTORS-- THE NEW RESERVE REQUIREMENTS SEEM TO BE HAVING AN OVERLY ***NEGATIVE*** EFFECT ON **CREDIT...**
AND UM, THE **SOCIAL SECURITY PAYMENTS** -- THOSE TAKE MONEY OUT OF THE SYSTEM TOO...
HMN ... THIS KEY IS ***STUCK.***
CLIK CLIK CLIKITA

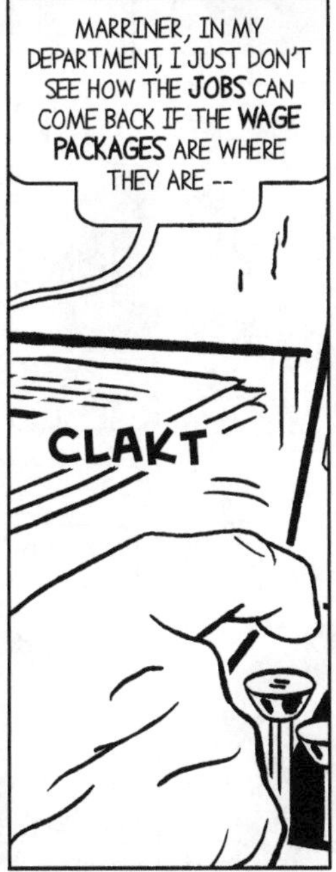
MARRINER, IN MY DEPARTMENT, I JUST DON'T SEE HOW THE **JOBS** CAN COME BACK IF THE **WAGE PACKAGES** ARE WHERE THEY ARE --
CLAKT

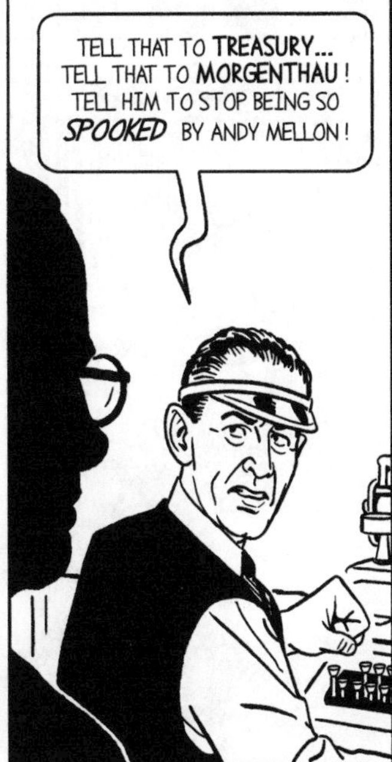
TELL THAT TO **TREASURY...** TELL THAT TO **MORGENTHAU!** TELL HIM TO STOP BEING SO ***SPOOKED*** BY ANDY MELLON!

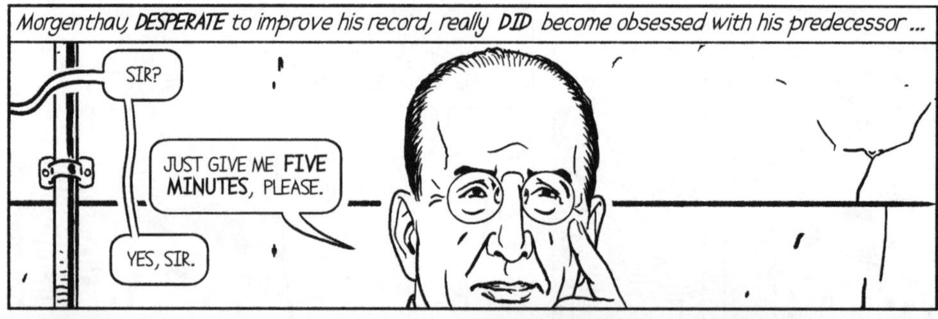
Morgenthau, **DESPERATE** to improve his record, really **DID** become obsessed with his predecessor ...
SIR?
JUST GIVE ME **FIVE MINUTES**, PLEASE.
YES, SIR.

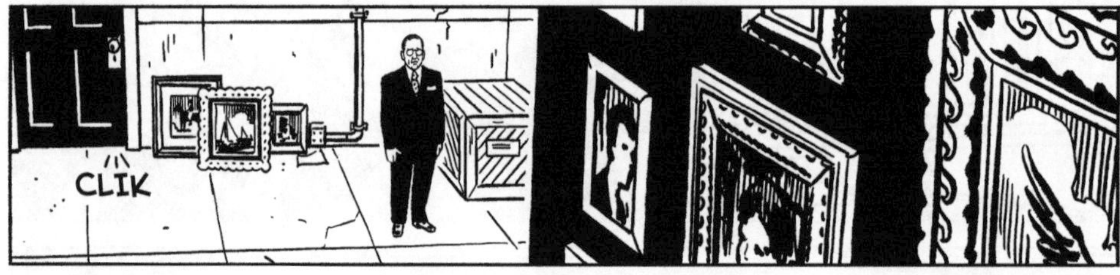
CLIK

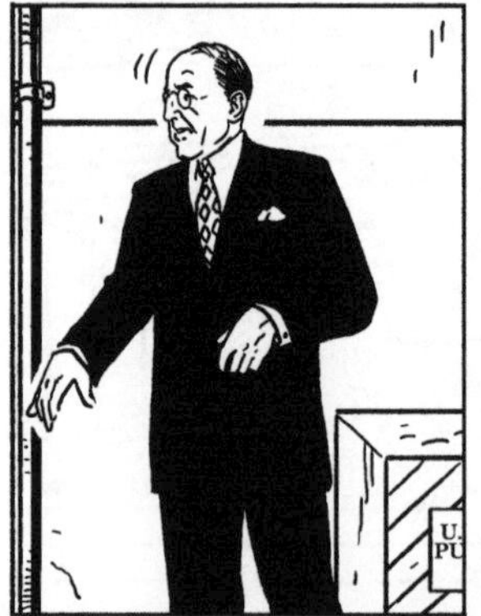

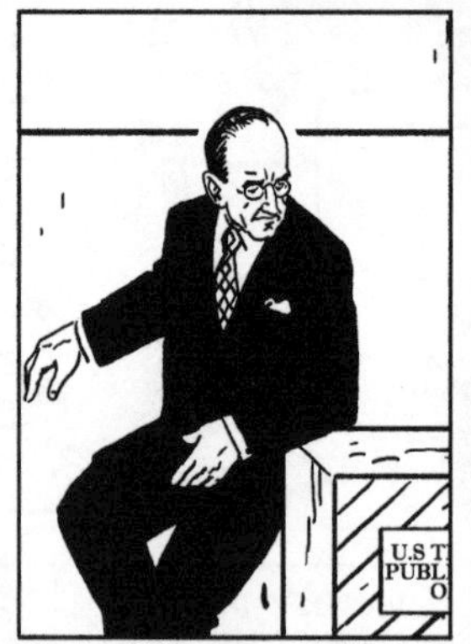

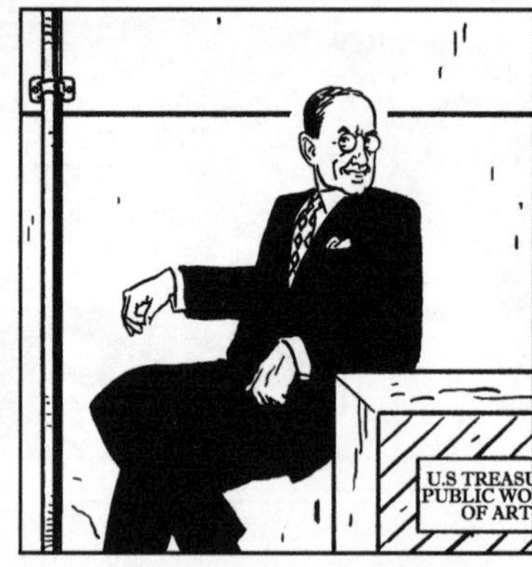

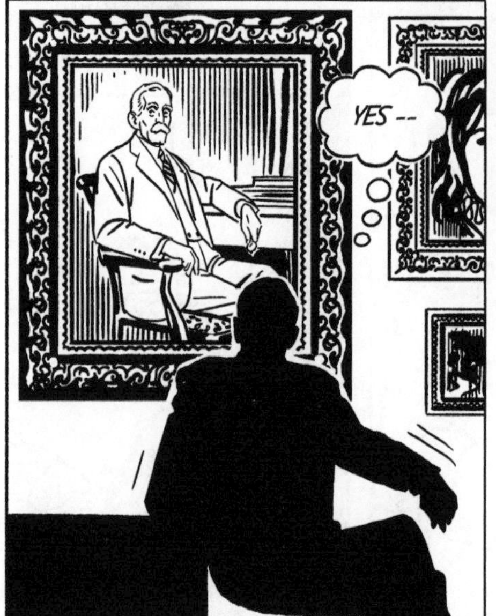
YES --

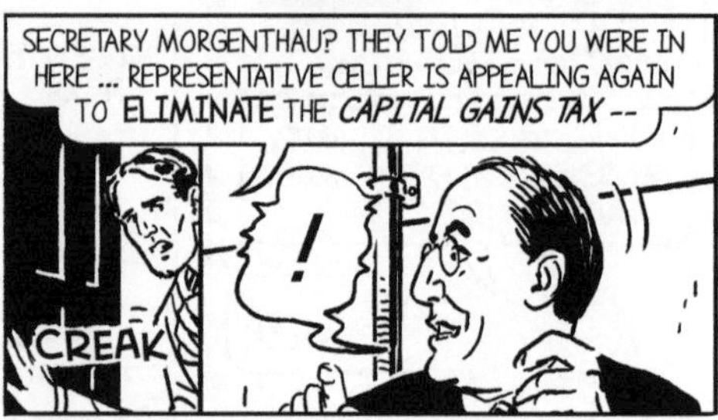
SECRETARY MORGENTHAU? THEY TOLD ME YOU WERE IN HERE ... REPRESENTATIVE CELLER IS APPEALING AGAIN TO **ELIMINATE** THE ***CAPITAL GAINS TAX*** --
!
CREAK

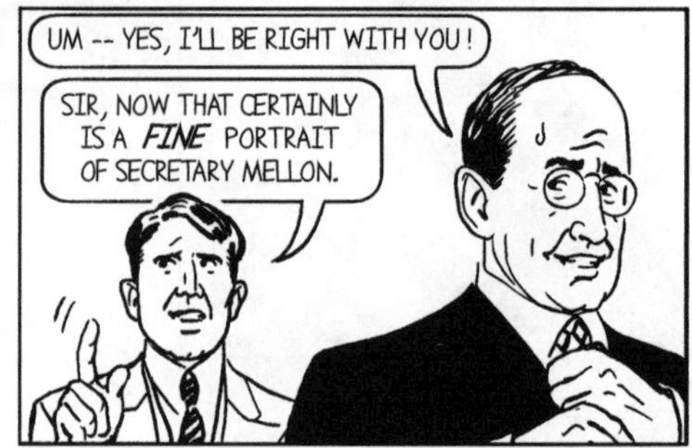
UM -- YES, I'LL BE RIGHT WITH YOU!
SIR, NOW THAT CERTAINLY IS A ***FINE*** PORTRAIT OF SECRETARY MELLON.

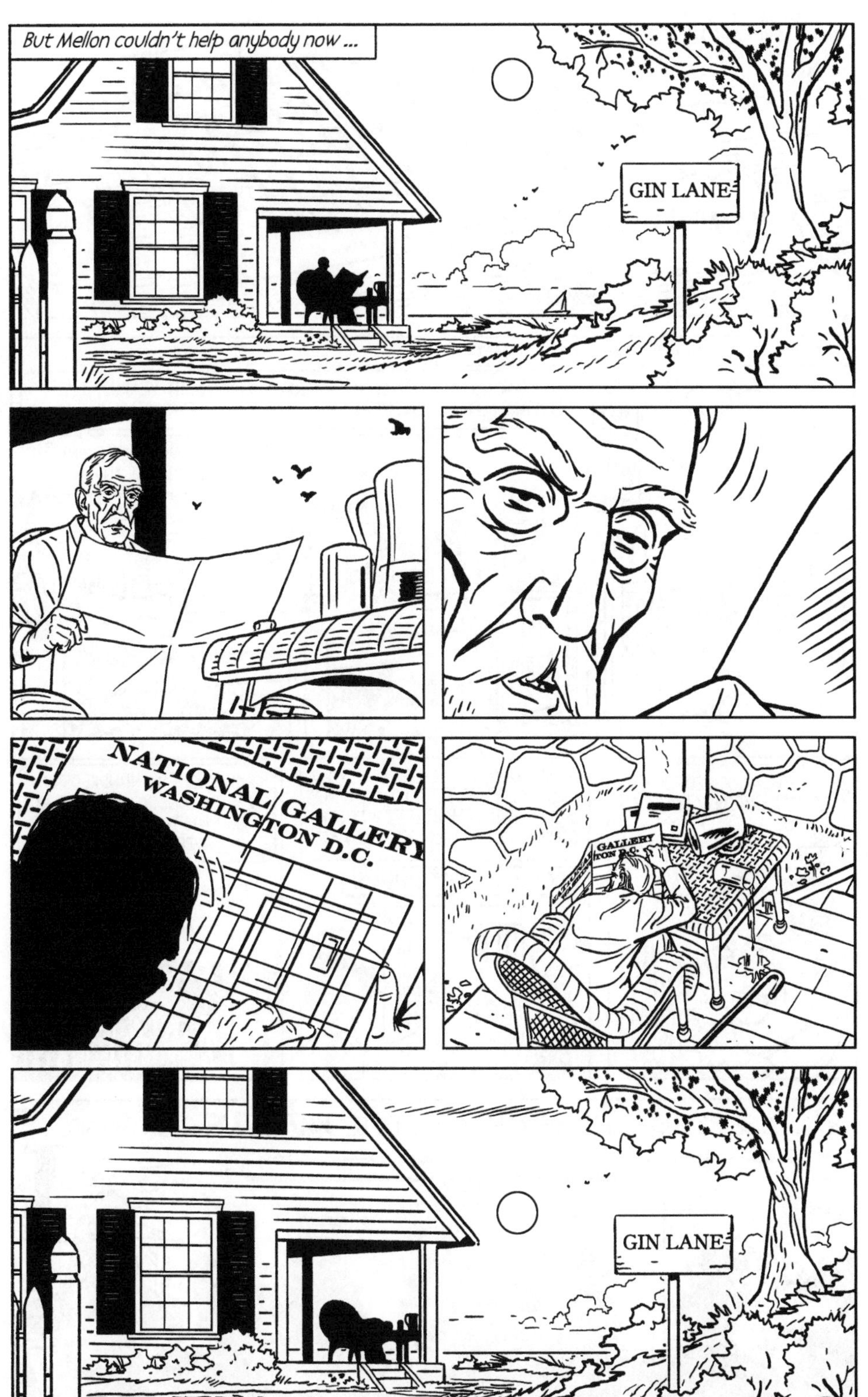
But Mellon couldn't help anybody now ...
GIN LANE
NATIONAL GALLERY
WASHINGTON D.C.
GALLERY
TON D.C.
GIN LANE

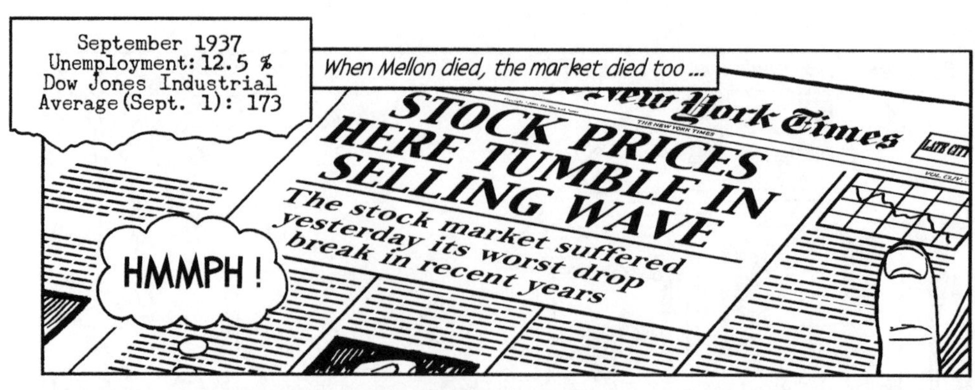
September 1937
Unemployment: 12.5 %
Dow Jones Industrial
Average (Sept. 1): 173
When Mellon died, the market died too ...
The New York Times
STOCK PRICES HERE TUMBLE IN SELLING WAVE
The stock market suffered yesterday its worst drop break in recent years
HMMPH!

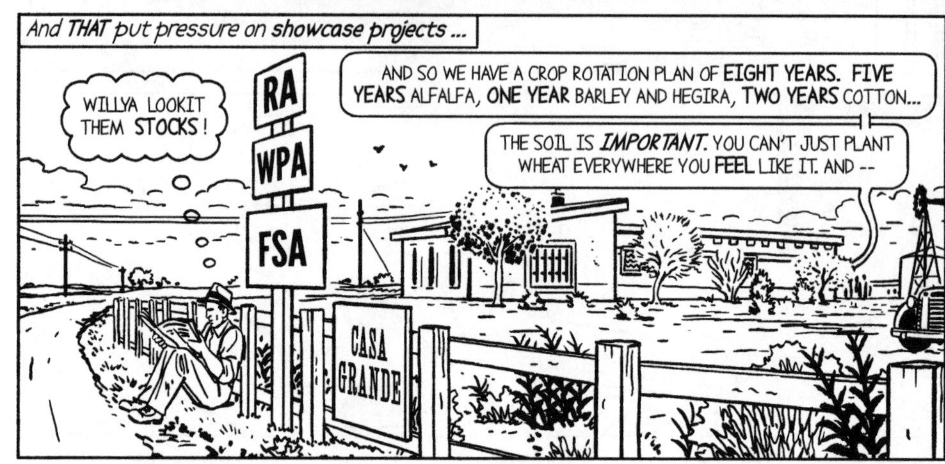
And THAT put pressure on showcase projects ...
WILLYA LOOKIT THEM STOCKS!
RA
WPA
FSA
CASA GRANDE
AND SO WE HAVE A CROP ROTATION PLAN OF EIGHT YEARS. FIVE YEARS ALFALFA, ONE YEAR BARLEY AND HEGIRA, TWO YEARS COTTON...
THE SOIL IS IMPORTANT. YOU CAN'T JUST PLANT WHEAT EVERYWHERE YOU FEEL LIKE IT. AND --

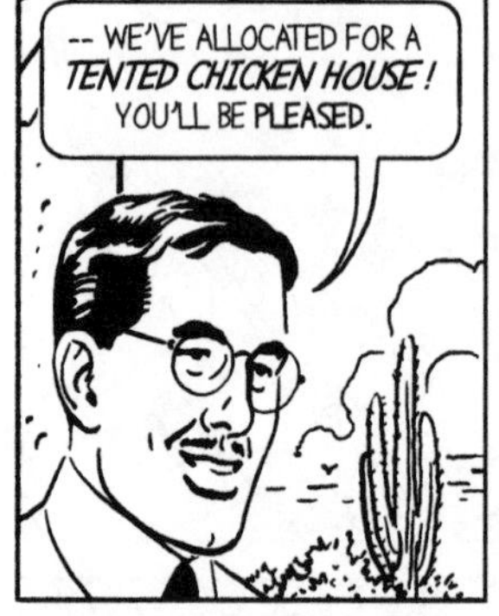
-- WE'VE ALLOCATED FOR A TENTED CHICKEN HOUSE! YOU'LL BE PLEASED.

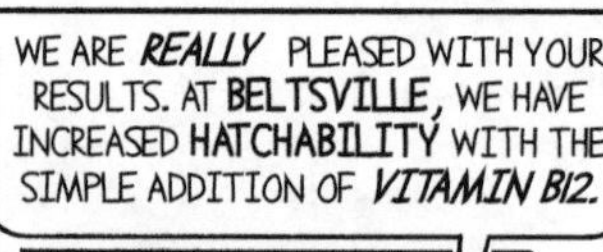
WE ARE REALLY PLEASED WITH YOUR RESULTS. AT BELTSVILLE, WE HAVE INCREASED HATCHABILITY WITH THE SIMPLE ADDITION OF VITAMIN B12.

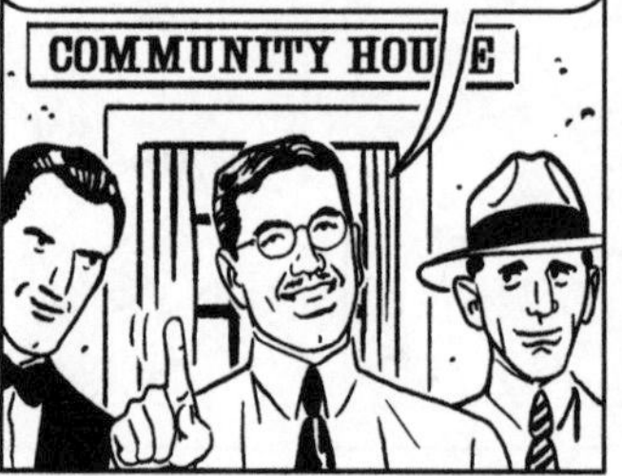
COMMUNITY HOU E

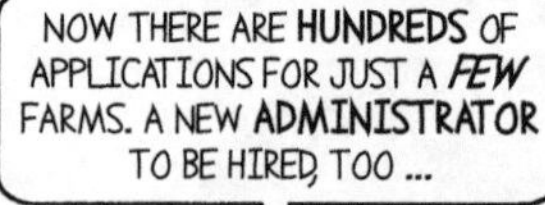
NOW THERE ARE HUNDREDS OF APPLICATIONS FOR JUST A FEW FARMS. A NEW ADMINISTRATOR TO BE HIRED, TOO ...

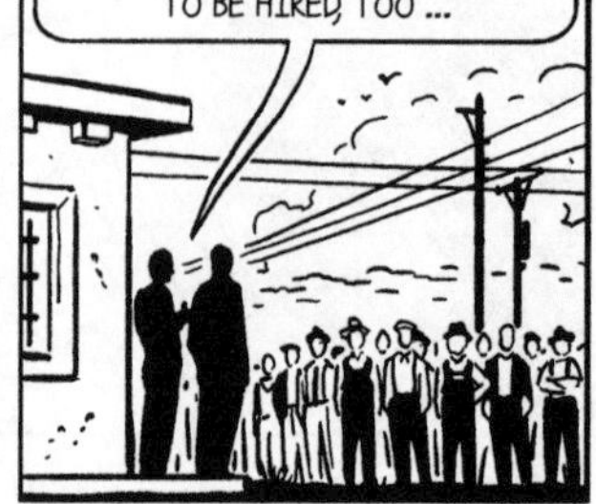

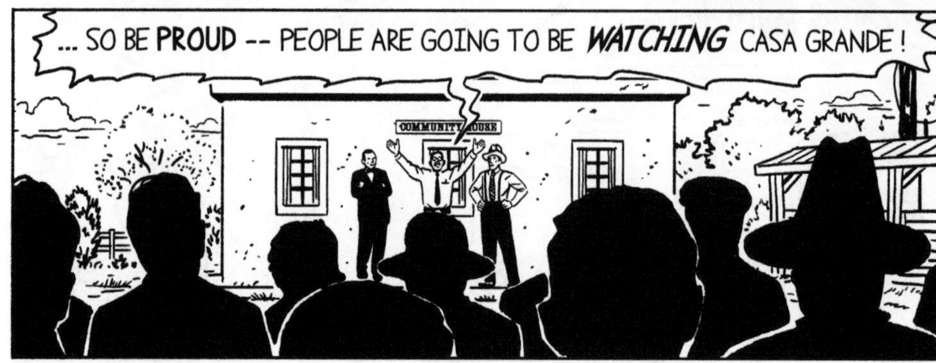
... SO BE PROUD -- PEOPLE ARE GOING TO BE WATCHING CASA GRANDE!
COMMUNITY HOUSE

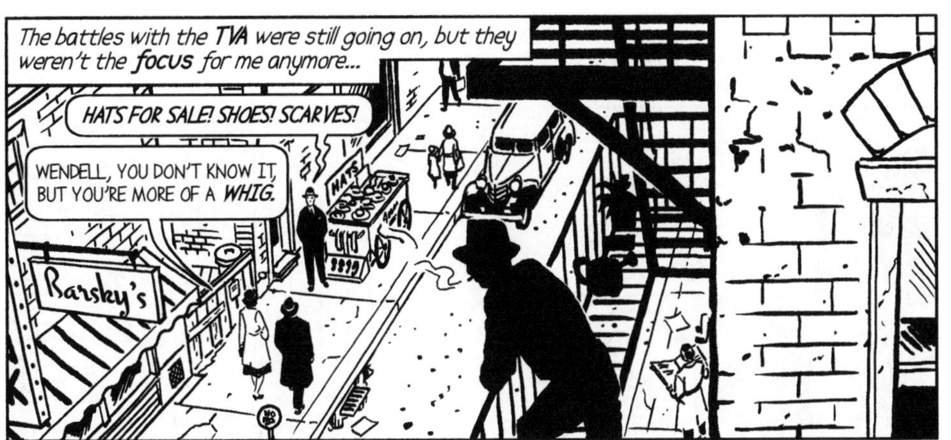

The battles with the TVA were still going on, but they weren't the focus for me anymore...
HATS FOR SALE! SHOES! SCARVES!
WENDELL, YOU DON'T KNOW IT, BUT YOU'RE MORE OF A WHIG.
Barsky's

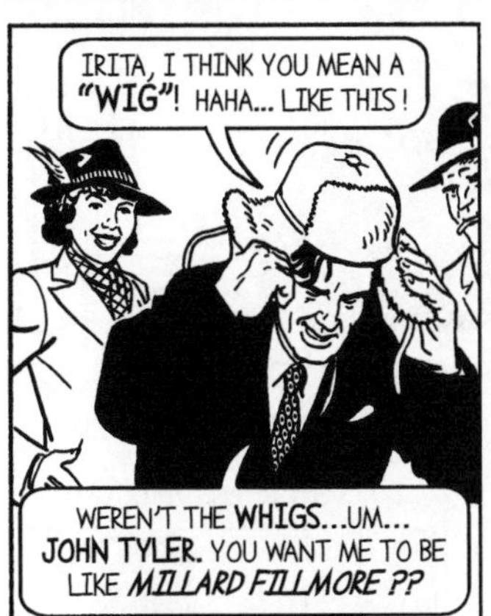

IRITA, I THINK YOU MEAN A "WIG"! HAHA... LIKE THIS!
WEREN'T THE WHIGS...UM... JOHN TYLER. YOU WANT ME TO BE LIKE MILLARD FILLMORE??

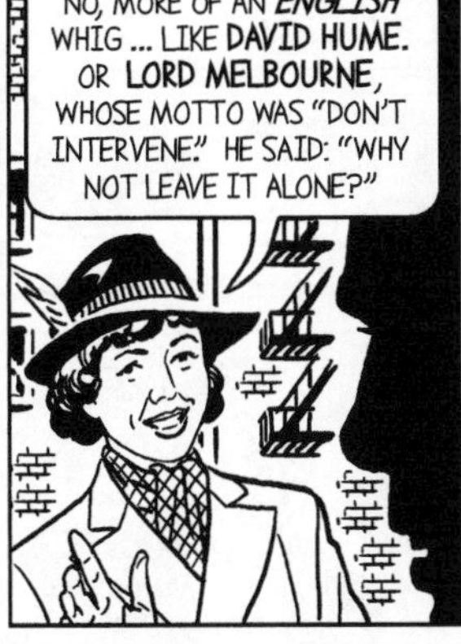

NO, MORE OF AN ENGLISH WHIG ... LIKE DAVID HUME. OR LORD MELBOURNE, WHOSE MOTTO WAS "DON'T INTERVENE." HE SAID: "WHY NOT LEAVE IT ALONE?"

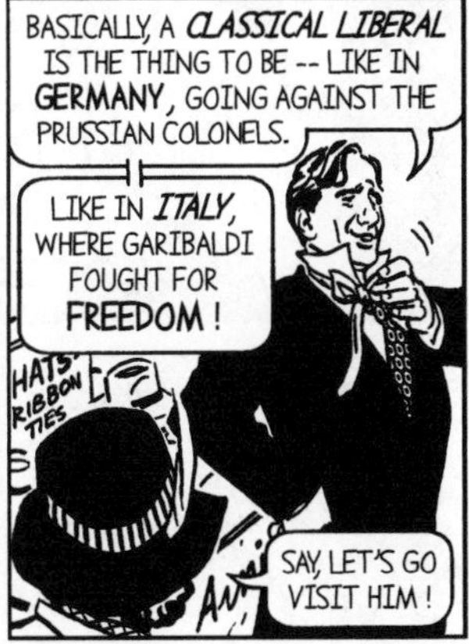

BASICALLY, A CLASSICAL LIBERAL IS THE THING TO BE -- LIKE IN GERMANY, GOING AGAINST THE PRUSSIAN COLONELS.
LIKE IN ITALY, WHERE GARIBALDI FOUGHT FOR FREEDOM!
HATS RIBBON TIES
SAY, LET'S GO VISIT HIM!

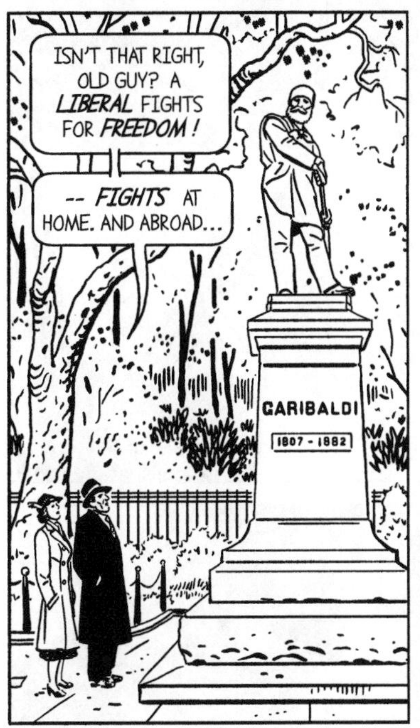

ISN'T THAT RIGHT, OLD GUY? A LIBERAL FIGHTS FOR FREEDOM!
-- FIGHTS AT HOME. AND ABROAD...
GARIBALDI
1807 - 1882

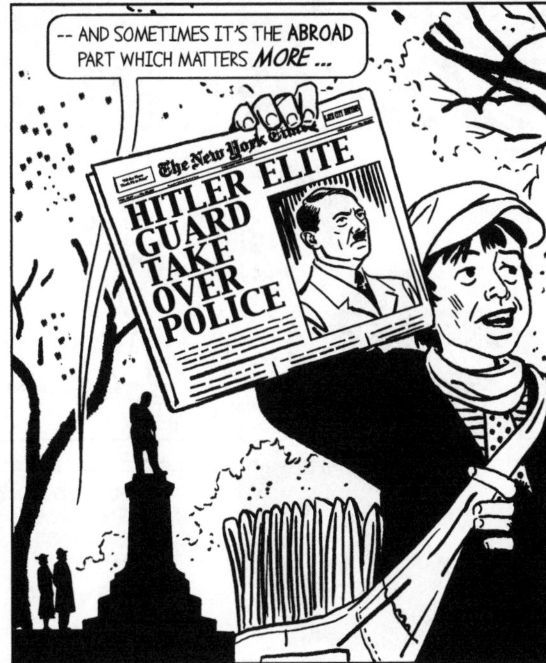

-- AND SOMETIMES IT'S THE ABROAD PART WHICH MATTERS MORE ...
The New York Times
HITLER ELITE GUARD TAKE OVER POLICE

It didn't help the economy that the squabble between Morgenthau and Eccles was ***ESCALATING.*** *Day in, day out, it was Morgenthau versus Eccles -- the Treasury vs. The Fed!* ***"Put more money into the economy!"*** *vs.* ***"STAY TIGHT!"***

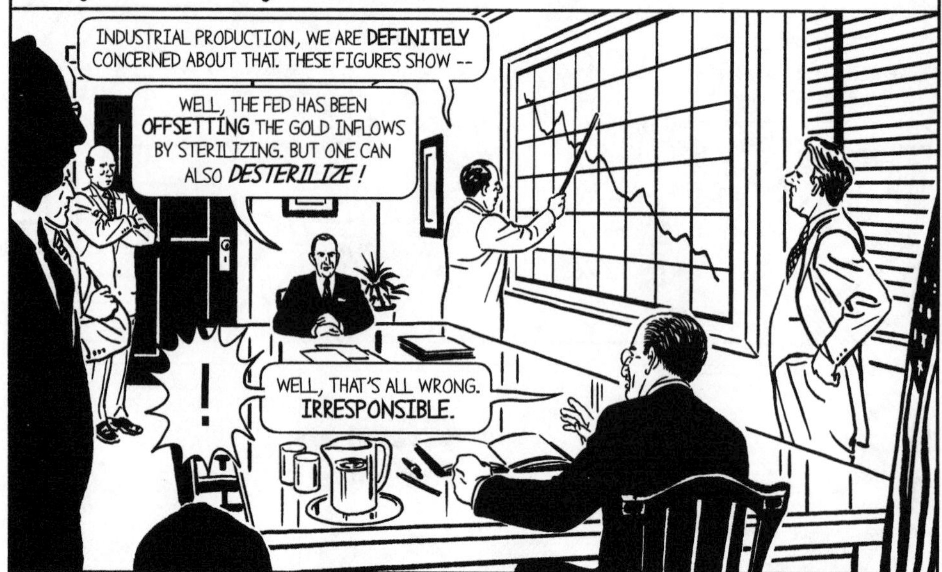

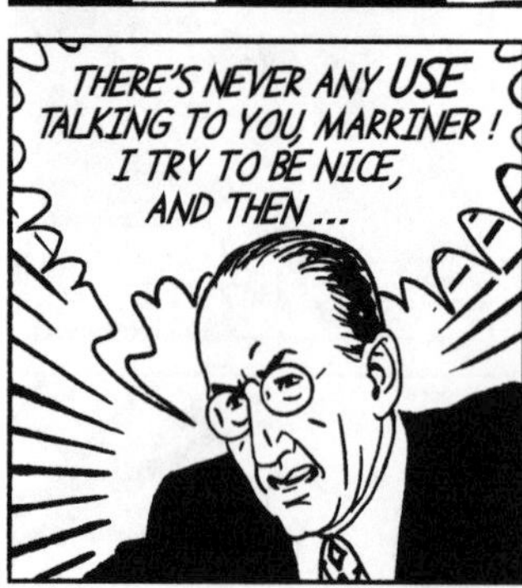

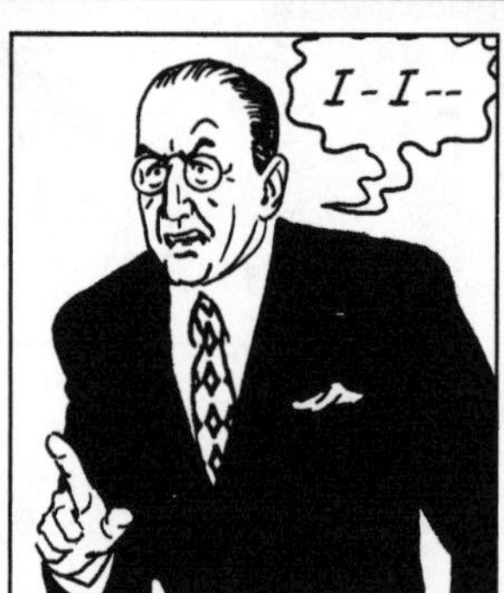

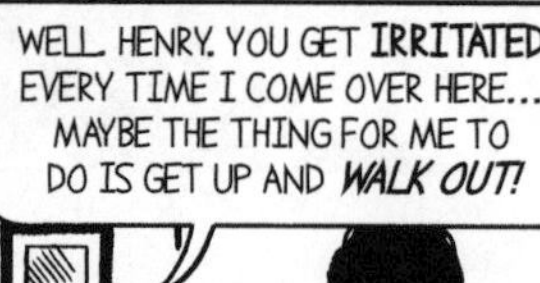

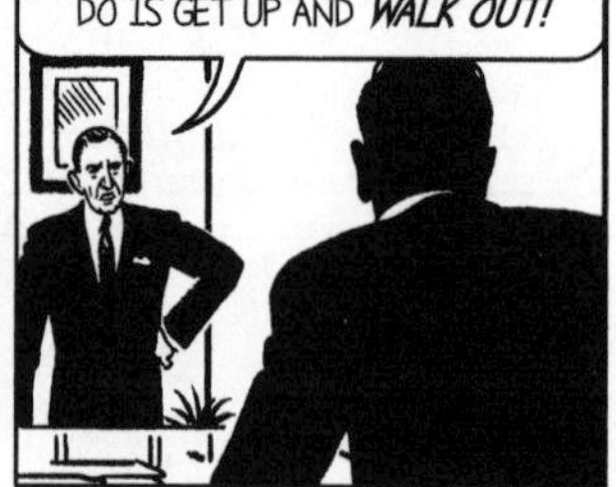

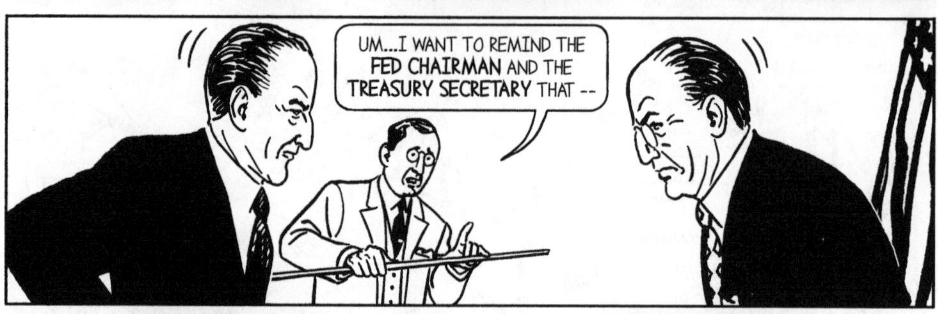

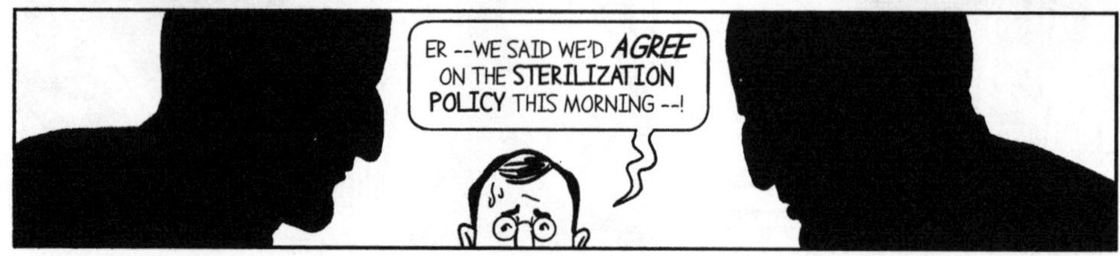

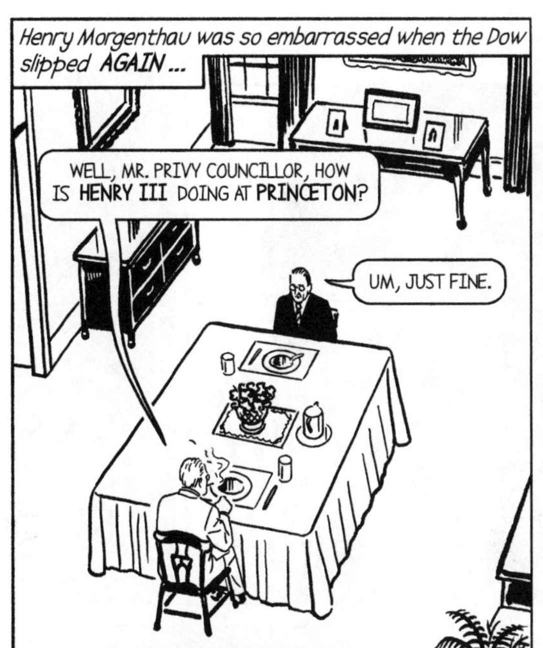
Henry Morgenthau was so embarrassed when the Dow slipped AGAIN...
WELL, MR. PRIVY COUNCILLOR, HOW IS HENRY III DOING AT PRINCETON?
UM, JUST FINE.

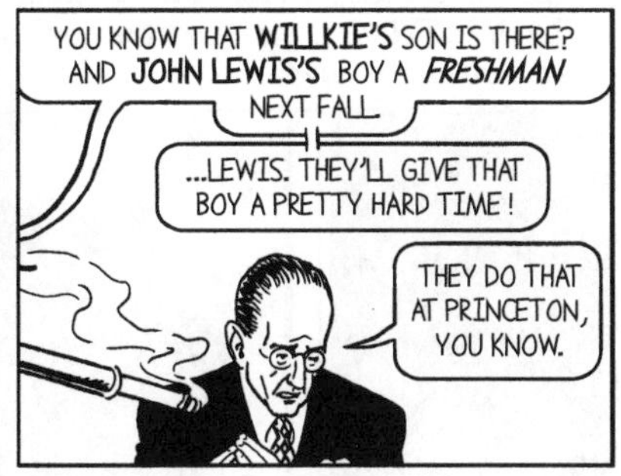
YOU KNOW THAT WILLKIE'S SON IS THERE? AND JOHN LEWIS'S BOY A FRESHMAN NEXT FALL.
...LEWIS. THEY'LL GIVE THAT BOY A PRETTY HARD TIME!
THEY DO THAT AT PRINCETON, YOU KNOW.

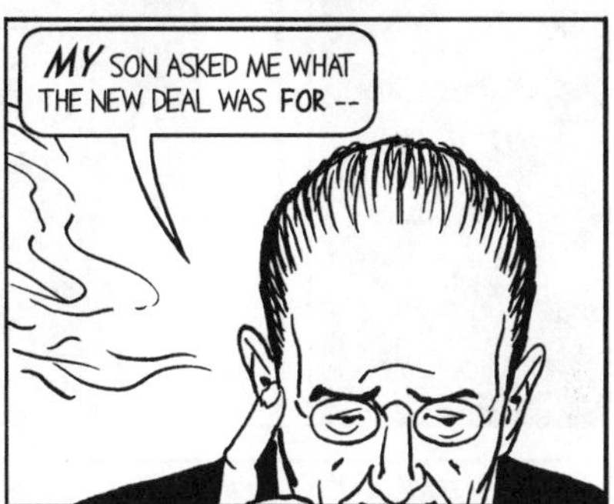
MY SON ASKED ME WHAT THE NEW DEAL WAS FOR --

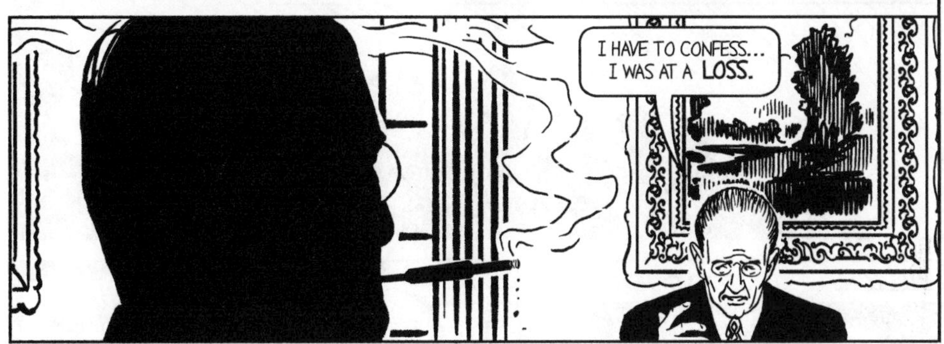
I HAVE TO CONFESS... I WAS AT A LOSS.

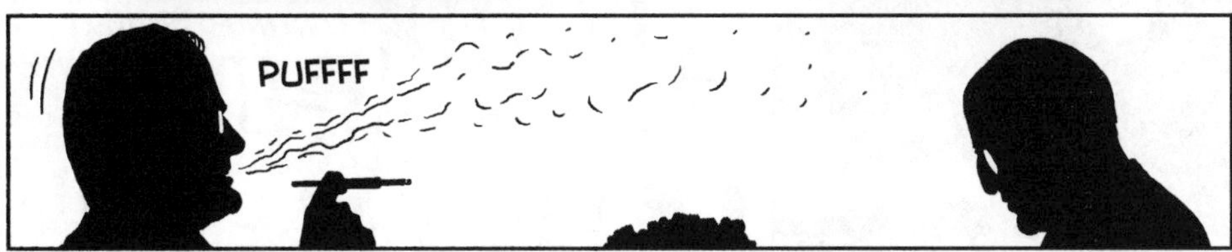
PUFFFF

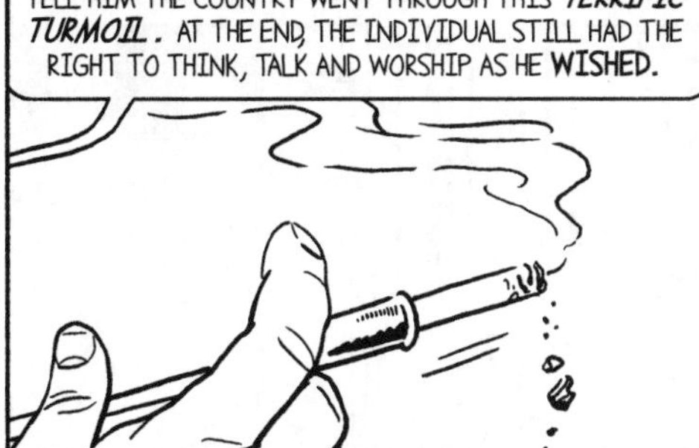
TELL HIM THE COUNTRY WENT THROUGH THIS TERRIFIC TURMOIL. AT THE END, THE INDIVIDUAL STILL HAD THE RIGHT TO THINK, TALK AND WORSHIP AS HE WISHED.

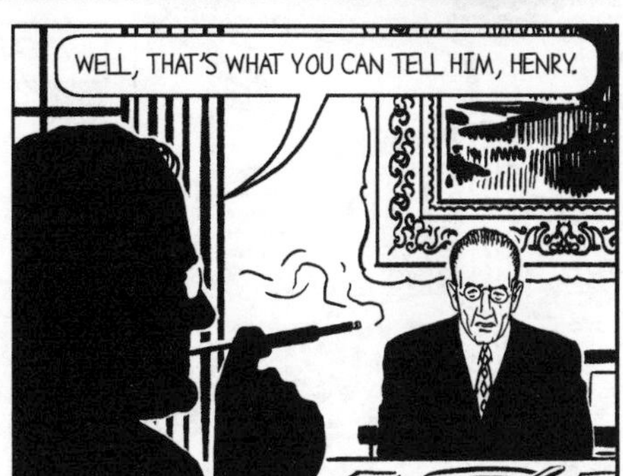
WELL, THAT'S WHAT YOU CAN TELL HIM, HENRY.

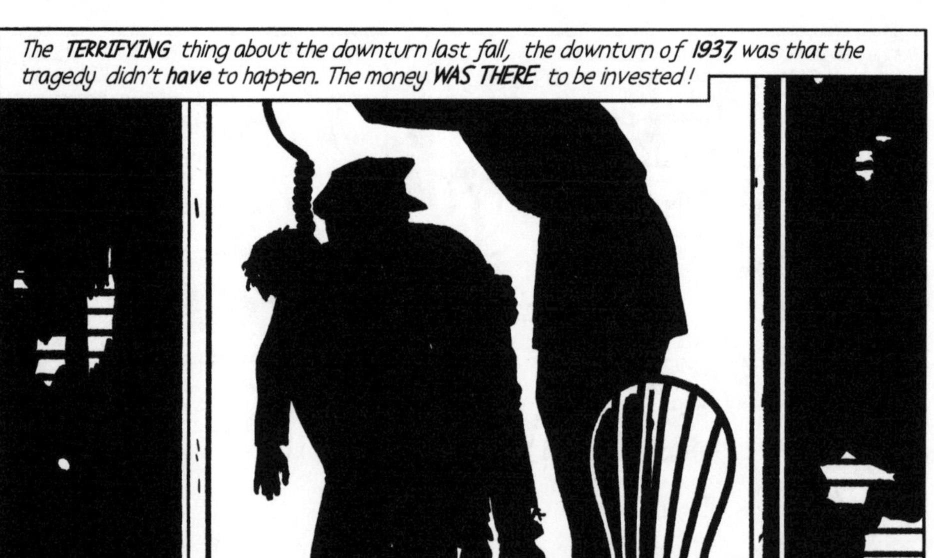
The TERRIFYING thing about the downturn last fall, the downturn of 1937, was that the tragedy didn't have to happen. The money WAS THERE to be invested!

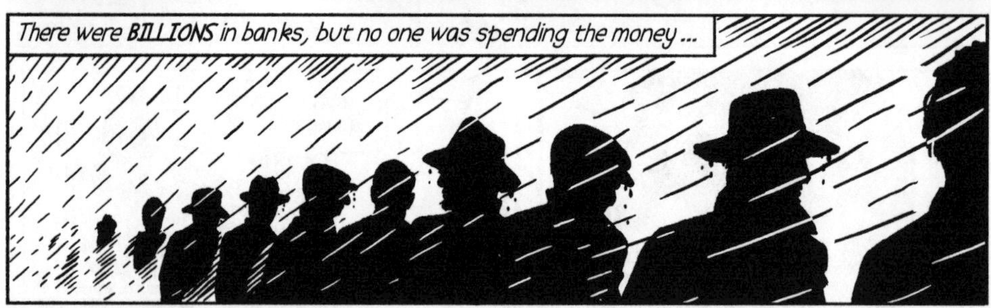
There were BILLIONS in banks, but no one was spending the money ...

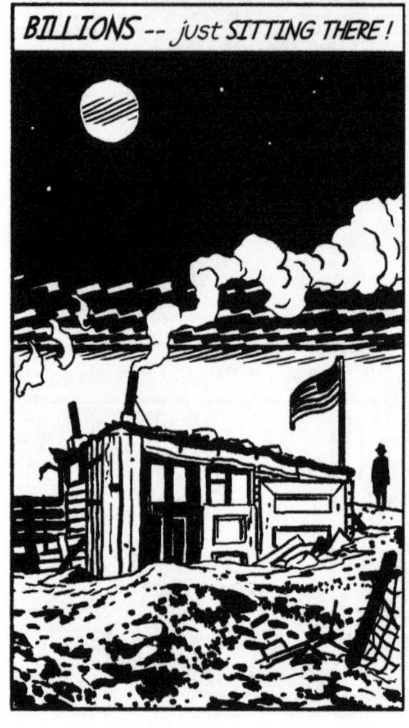
BILLIONS -- just SITTING THERE!

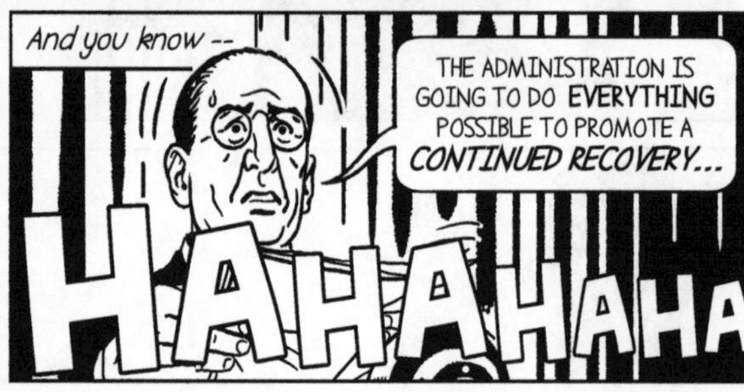
And you know --
THE ADMINISTRATION IS GOING TO DO EVERYTHING POSSIBLE TO PROMOTE A CONTINUED RECOVERY...
HAHAHAHAHA

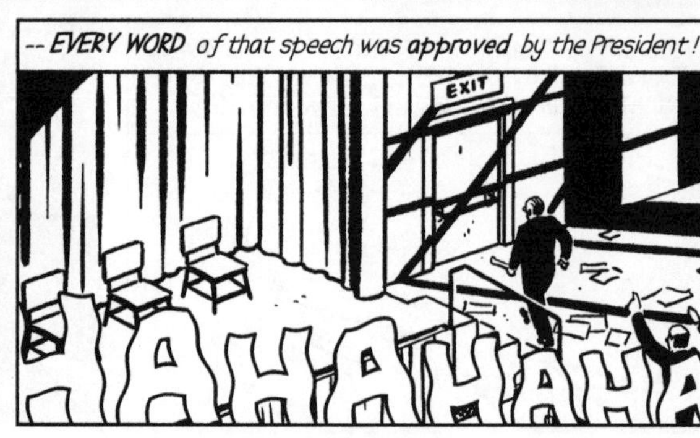
-- EVERY WORD of that speech was approved by the President!
EXIT
HAHAHAHAHA

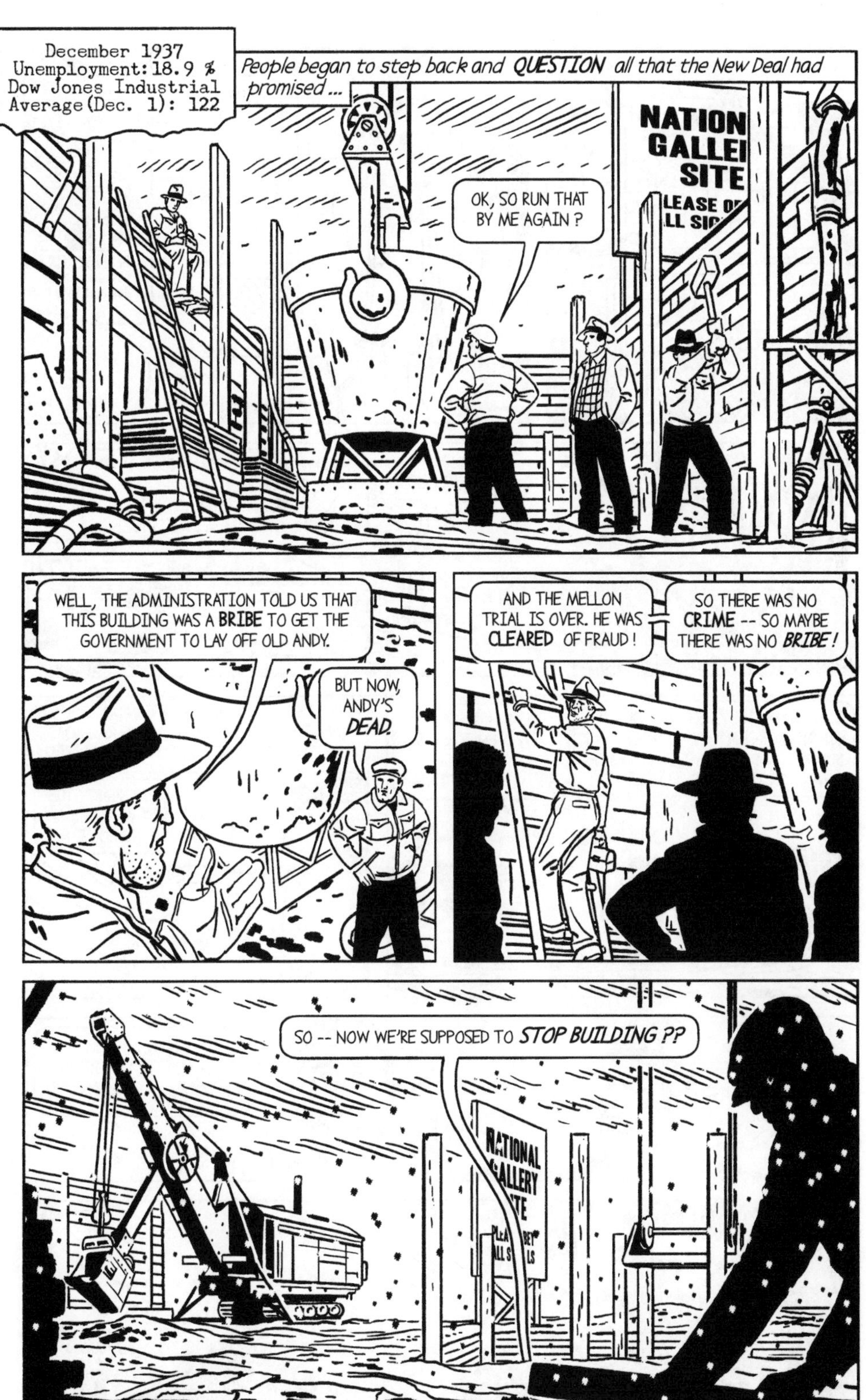
December 1937
Unemployment: 18.9 %
Dow Jones Industrial
Average (Dec. 1): 122
People began to step back and QUESTION all that the New Deal had promised ...
OK, SO RUN THAT BY ME AGAIN ?
WELL, THE ADMINISTRATION TOLD US THAT THIS BUILDING WAS A BRIBE TO GET THE GOVERNMENT TO LAY OFF OLD ANDY.
BUT NOW, ANDY'S DEAD.
AND THE MELLON TRIAL IS OVER. HE WAS CLEARED OF FRAUD !
SO THERE WAS NO CRIME -- SO MAYBE THERE WAS NO BRIBE !
SO -- NOW WE'RE SUPPOSED TO STOP BUILDING ??

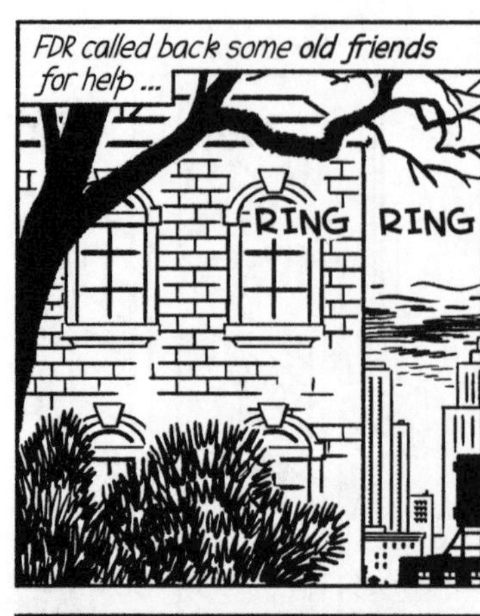

FDR called back some old friends for help ...
RING RING

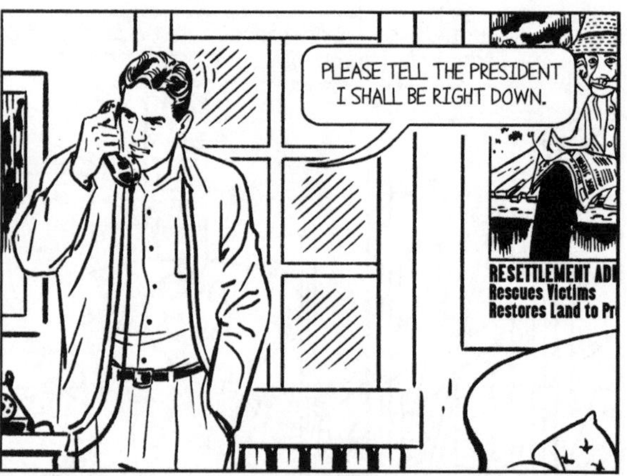

PLEASE TELL THE PRESIDENT I SHALL BE RIGHT DOWN.
RESETTLEMENT ADM
Rescues Victims
Restores Land to Pr

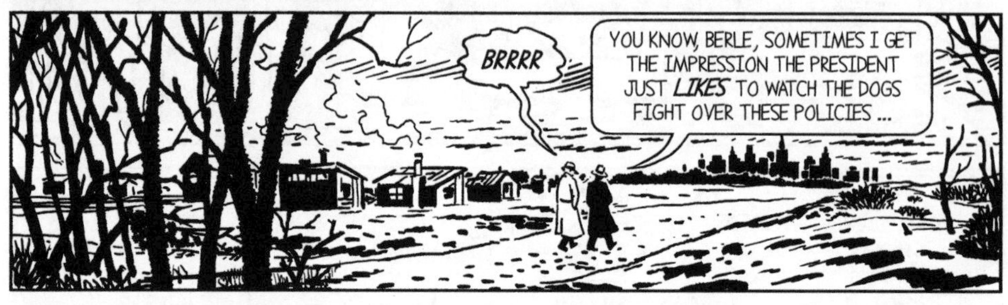

BRRRR
YOU KNOW, BERLE, SOMETIMES I GET THE IMPRESSION THE PRESIDENT JUST LIKES TO WATCH THE DOGS FIGHT OVER THESE POLICIES ...

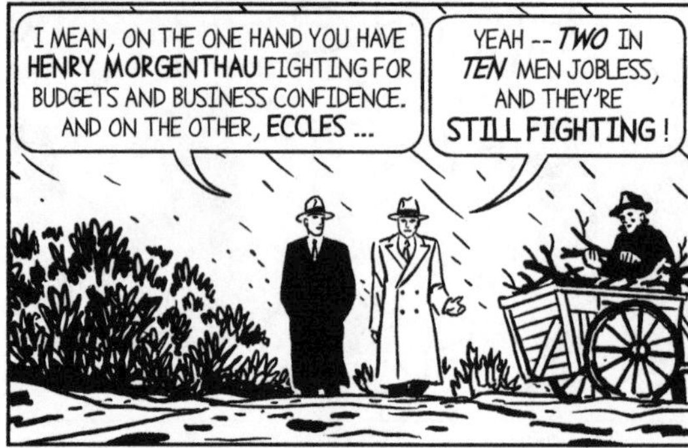

I MEAN, ON THE ONE HAND YOU HAVE HENRY MORGENTHAU FIGHTING FOR BUDGETS AND BUSINESS CONFIDENCE. AND ON THE OTHER, ECCLES ...
YEAH -- TWO IN TEN MEN JOBLESS, AND THEY'RE STILL FIGHTING!

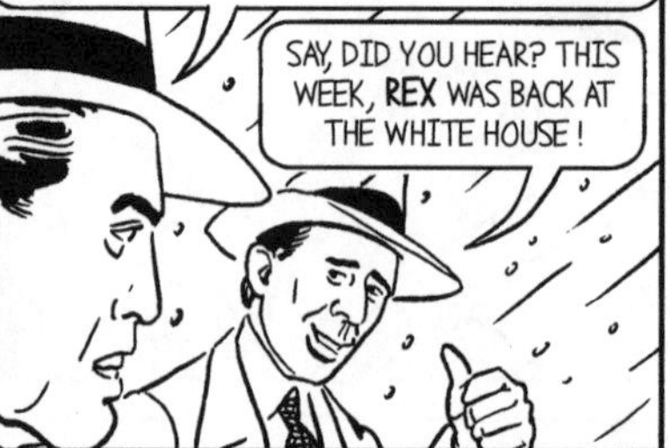

WELL, THERE'S NOT MUCH WE CAN DO ABOUT IT NOW, THE CRISIS IS SO DEEP. THE RAILROADS WILL PROBABLY HAVE TO BE NATIONALIZED!
SAY, DID YOU HEAR? THIS WEEK, REX WAS BACK AT THE WHITE HOUSE!

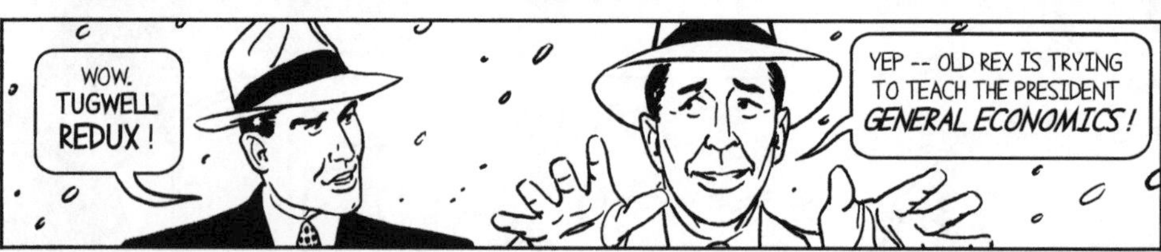

WOW. TUGWELL REDUX!
YEP -- OLD REX IS TRYING TO TEACH THE PRESIDENT GENERAL ECONOMICS!

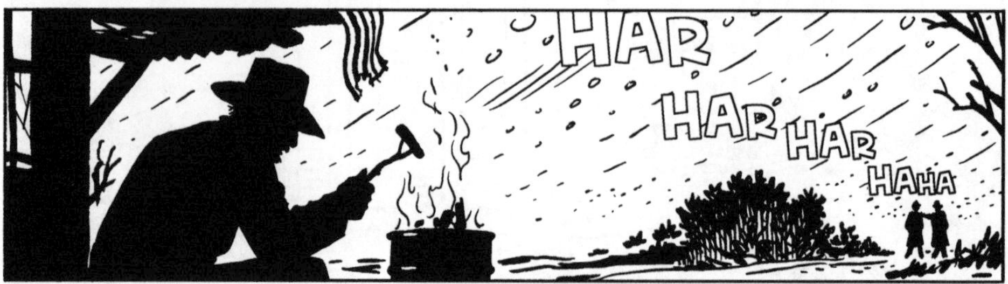

HAR
HAR HAR
HAHA

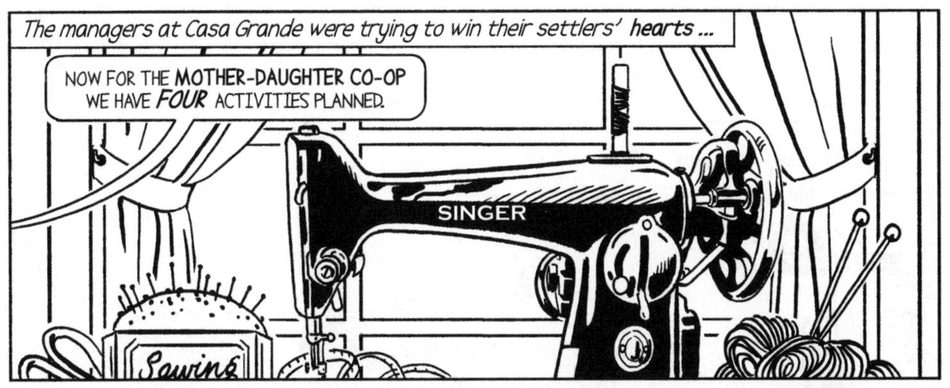
The managers at Casa Grande were trying to win their settlers' **hearts ...**
NOW FOR THE **MOTHER-DAUGHTER CO-OP** WE HAVE ***FOUR*** ACTIVITIES PLANNED.
SINGER
Sewing

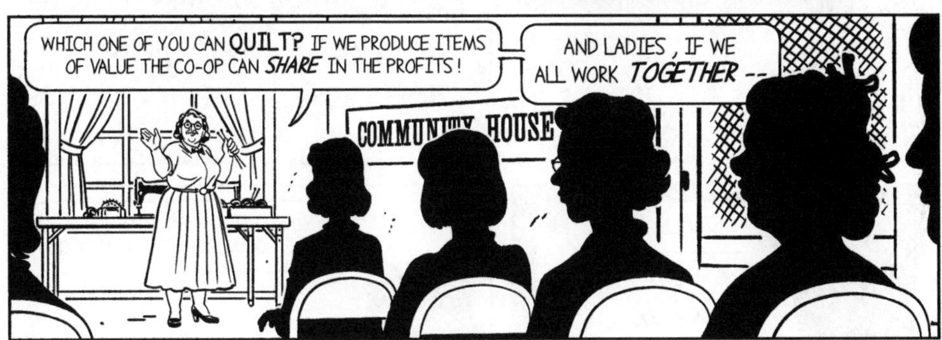
WHICH ONE OF YOU CAN **QUILT?** IF WE PRODUCE ITEMS OF VALUE THE CO-OP CAN ***SHARE*** IN THE PROFITS !
AND LADIES , IF WE ALL WORK ***TOGETHER*** --

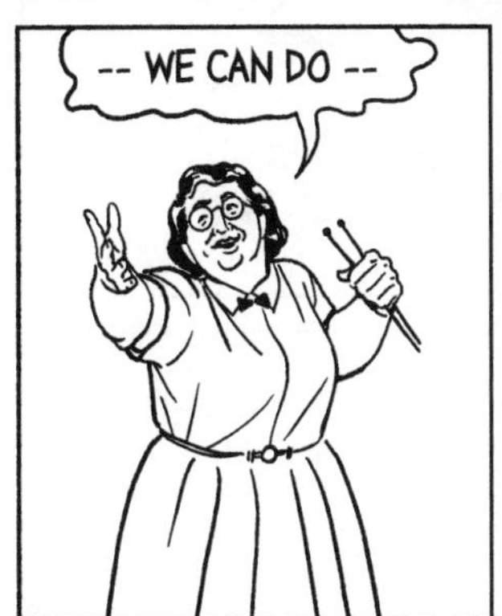
-- WE CAN DO --

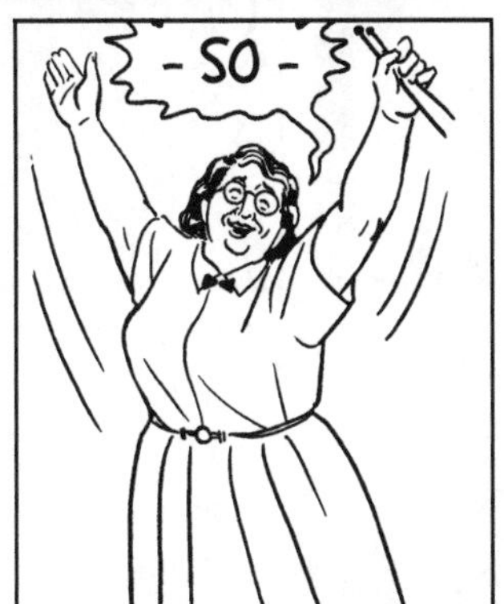
- SO -

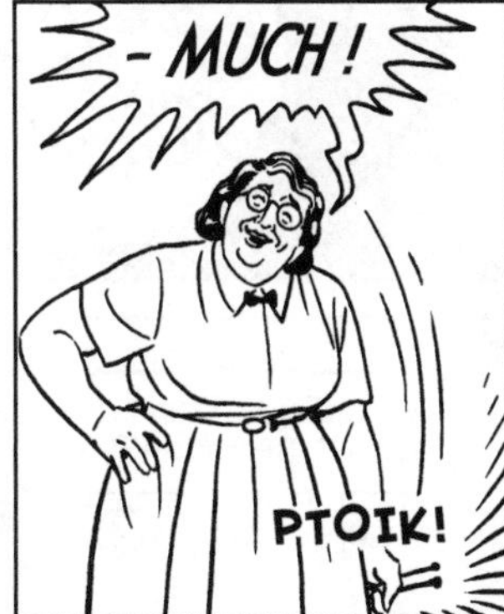
- MUCH !
PTOIK!

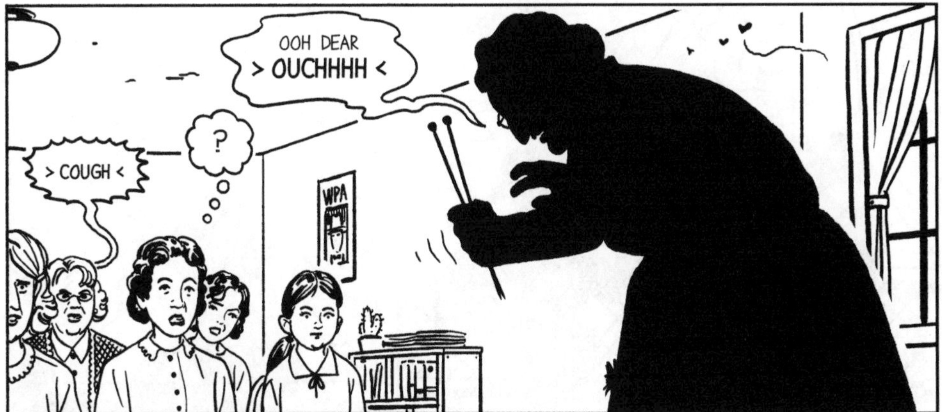
OOH DEAR
> OUCHHHH <
?
> COUGH <
WPA

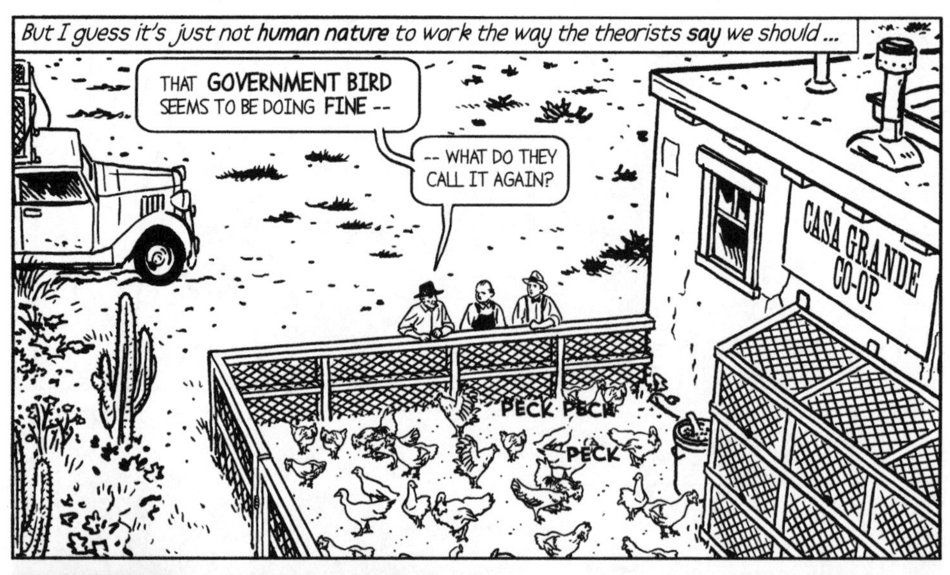
But I guess it's just not **human nature** to work the way the theorists **say** we should ...
THAT **GOVERNMENT BIRD** SEEMS TO BE DOING **FINE** --
-- WHAT DO THEY CALL IT AGAIN?
CASA GRANDE CO-OP
PECK PECK
PECK

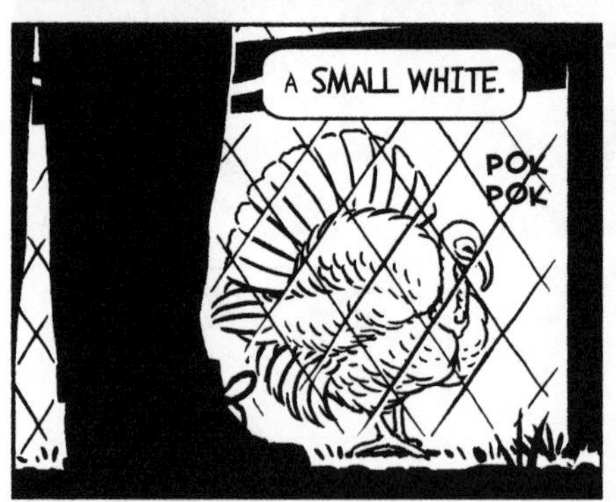
A **SMALL WHITE.**
POK POK

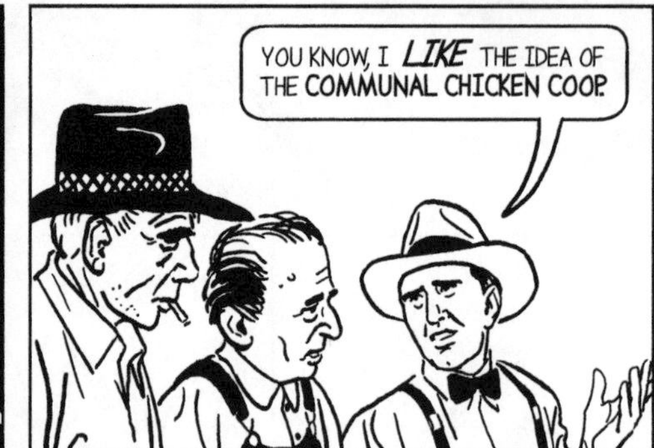
YOU KNOW, I ***LIKE*** THE IDEA OF THE **COMMUNAL CHICKEN COOP.**

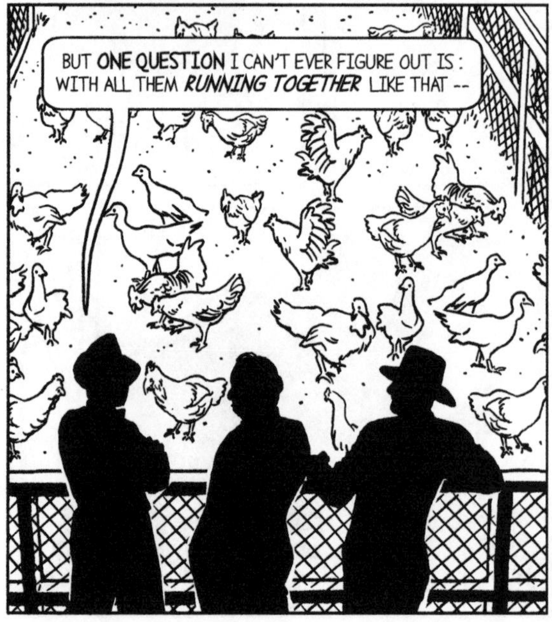
BUT **ONE QUESTION** I CAN'T EVER FIGURE OUT IS : WITH ALL THEM ***RUNNING TOGETHER*** LIKE THAT --

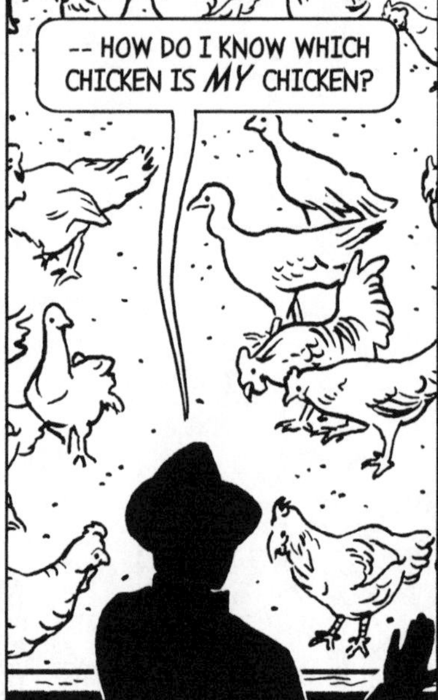
-- **HOW DO I KNOW WHICH CHICKEN IS *MY* CHICKEN?**

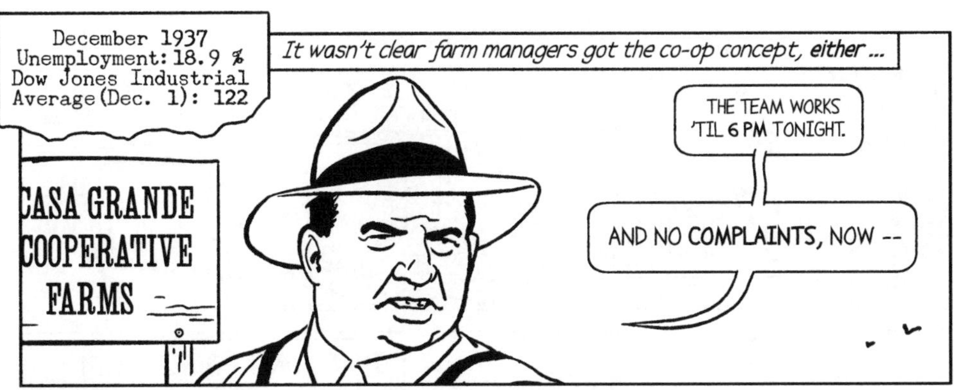
December 1937
Unemployment: 18.9 %
Dow Jones Industrial
Average (Dec. 1): 122
It wasn't clear farm managers got the co-op concept, either ...
CASA GRANDE
COOPERATIVE
FARMS
THE TEAM WORKS 'TIL 6 PM TONIGHT.
AND NO COMPLAINTS, NOW --

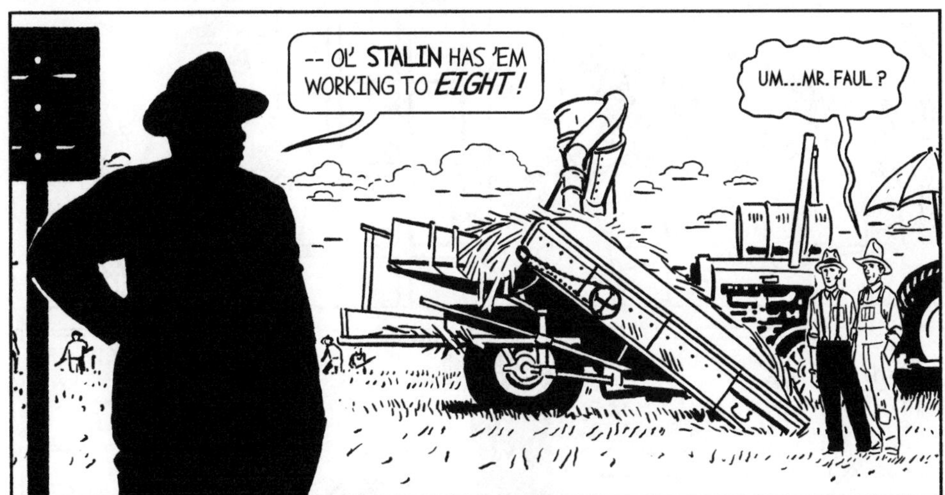
-- OL' STALIN HAS 'EM WORKING TO EIGHT!
UM...MR. FAUL ?

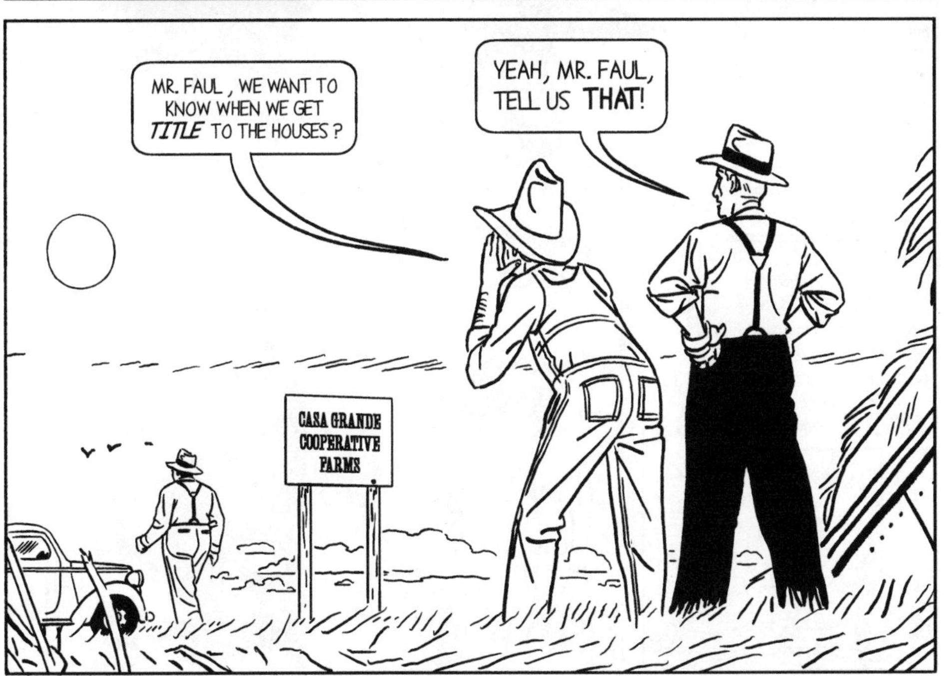
MR. FAUL, WE WANT TO KNOW WHEN WE GET TITLE TO THE HOUSES ?
YEAH, MR. FAUL, TELL US THAT!
CASA GRANDE
COOPERATIVE
FARMS

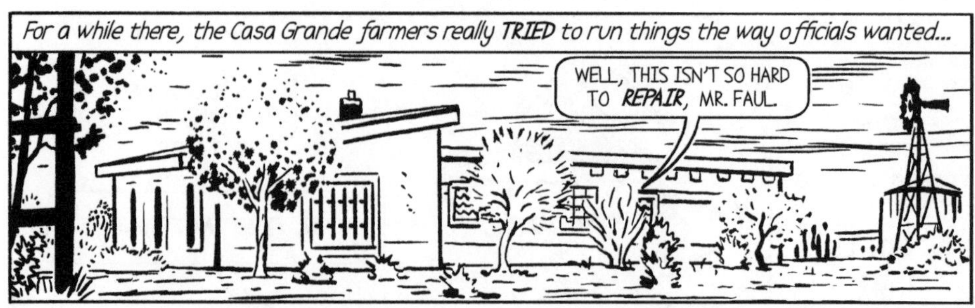
For a while there, the Casa Grande farmers really TRIED to run things the way officials wanted...
WELL, THIS ISN'T SO HARD TO REPAIR, MR. FAUL.

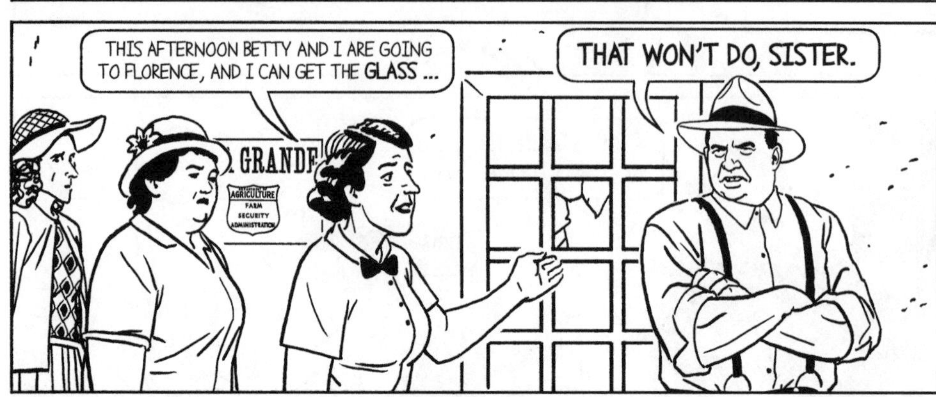
THIS AFTERNOON BETTY AND I ARE GOING TO FLORENCE, AND I CAN GET THE GLASS ...
THAT WON'T DO, SISTER.
GRANDE
AGRICULTURE
FARM
SECURITY
ADMINISTRATION

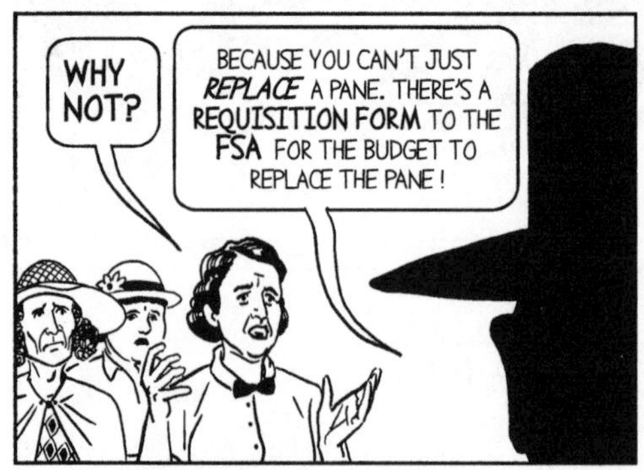
WHY NOT?
BECAUSE YOU CAN'T JUST REPLACE A PANE. THERE'S A REQUISITION FORM TO THE FSA FOR THE BUDGET TO REPLACE THE PANE!

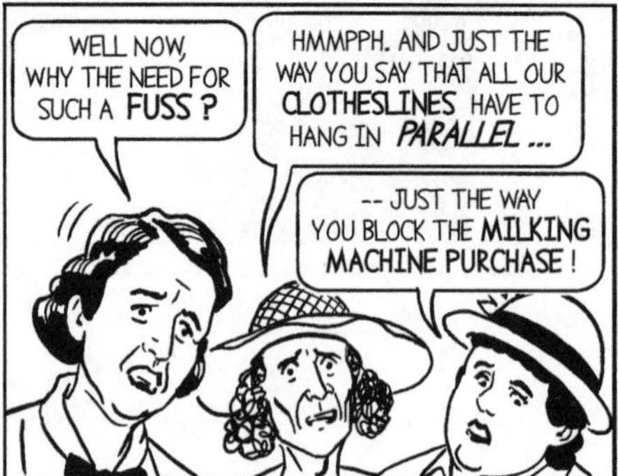
WELL NOW, WHY THE NEED FOR SUCH A FUSS?
HMMPPH. AND JUST THE WAY YOU SAY THAT ALL OUR CLOTHESLINES HAVE TO HANG IN PARALLEL ...
-- JUST THE WAY YOU BLOCK THE MILKING MACHINE PURCHASE!

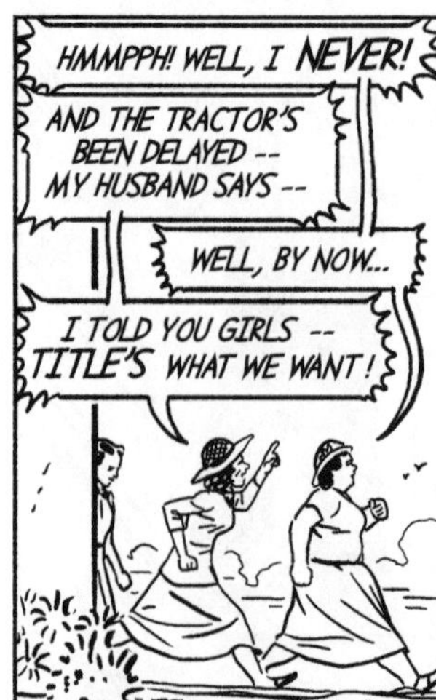
HMMPPH! WELL, I NEVER!
AND THE TRACTOR'S BEEN DELAYED -- MY HUSBAND SAYS --
WELL, BY NOW...
I TOLD YOU GIRLS -- TITLE'S WHAT WE WANT!

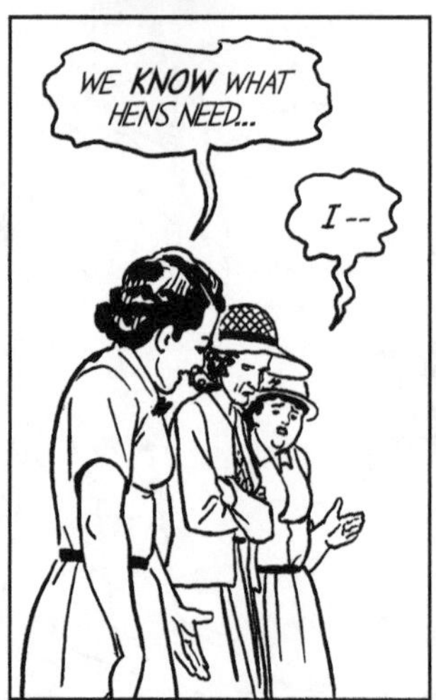
WE KNOW WHAT HENS NEED...
I --

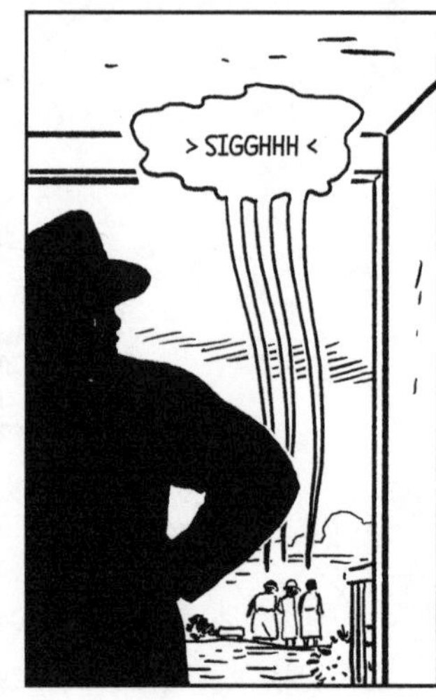
> SIGGHHH <

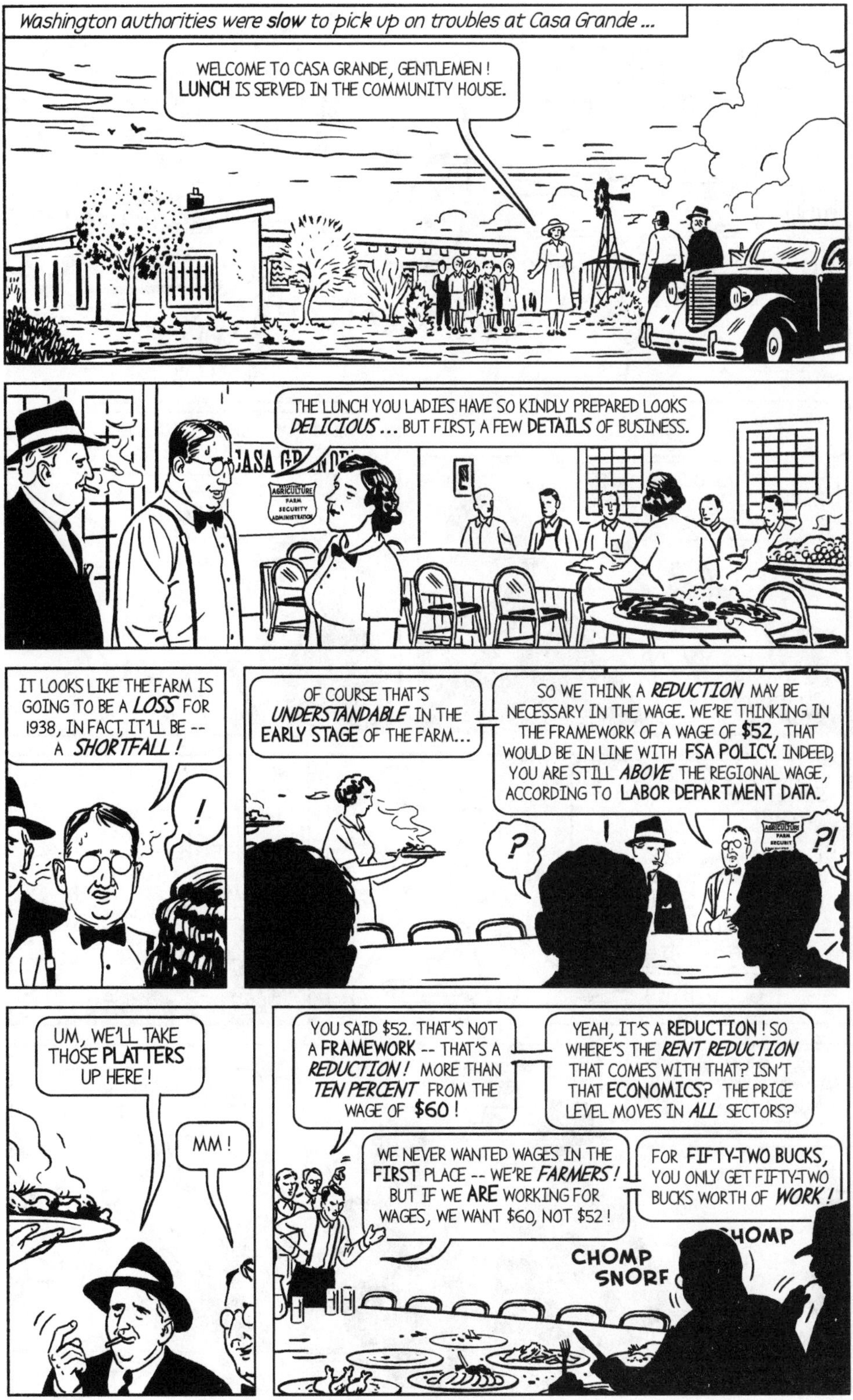

*Washington authorities were **slow** to pick up on troubles at Casa Grande ...*

WELCOME TO CASA GRANDE, GENTLEMEN! **LUNCH** IS SERVED IN THE COMMUNITY HOUSE.

THE LUNCH YOU LADIES HAVE SO KINDLY PREPARED LOOKS ***DELICIOUS...*** BUT FIRST, A FEW **DETAILS** OF BUSINESS.

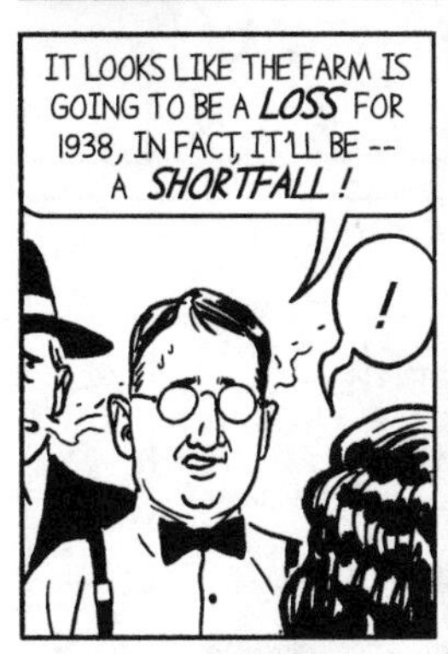

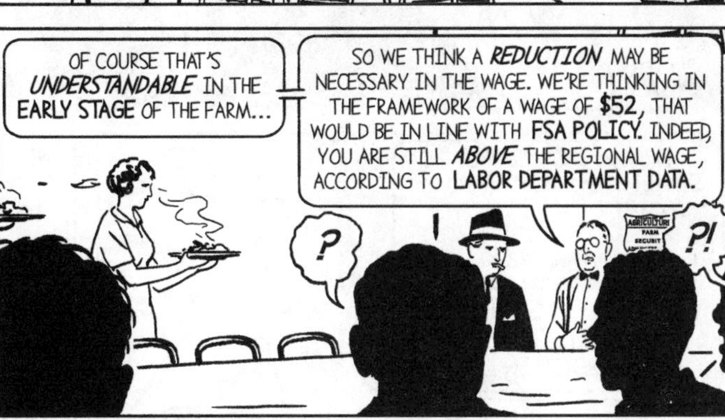

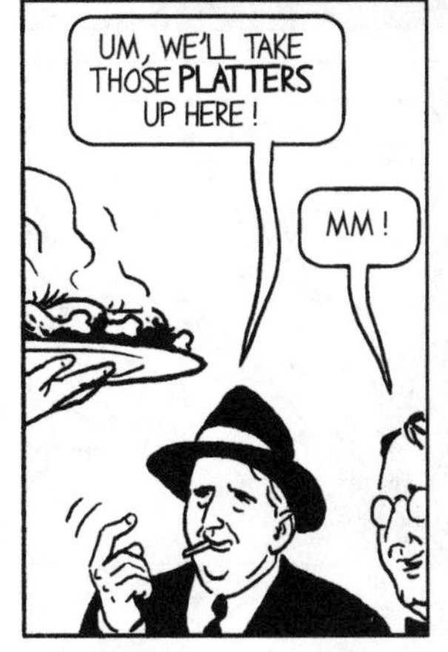

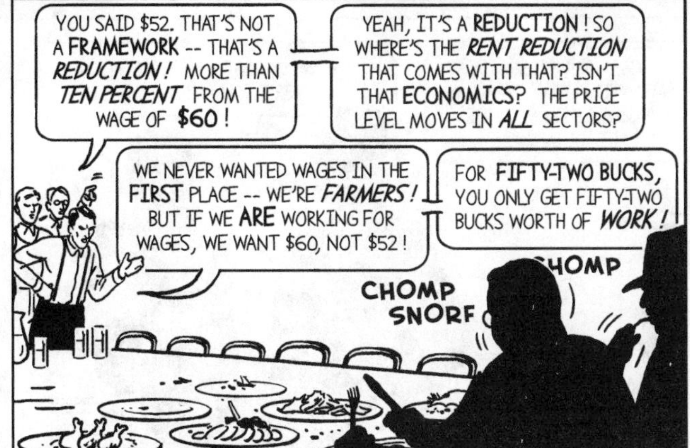

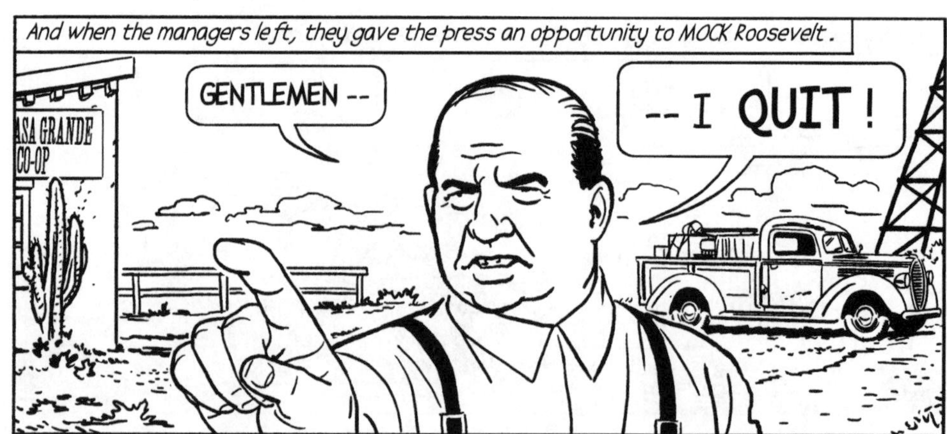
And when the managers left, they gave the press an opportunity to MOCK Roosevelt.
GENTLEMEN --
-- I QUIT!

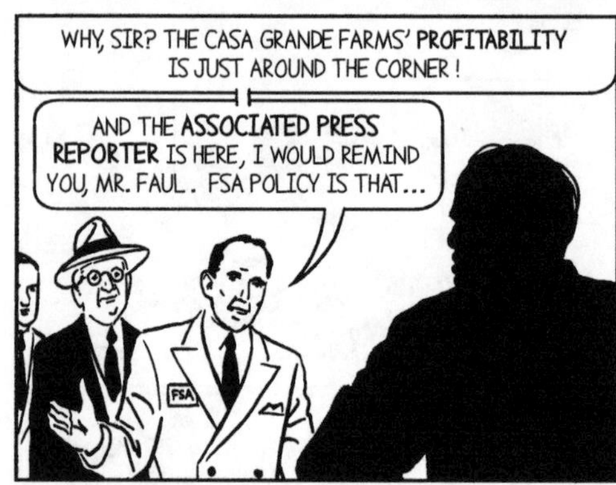
WHY, SIR? THE CASA GRANDE FARMS' PROFITABILITY IS JUST AROUND THE CORNER!
AND THE ASSOCIATED PRESS REPORTER IS HERE, I WOULD REMIND YOU, MR. FAUL. FSA POLICY IS THAT...
FSA

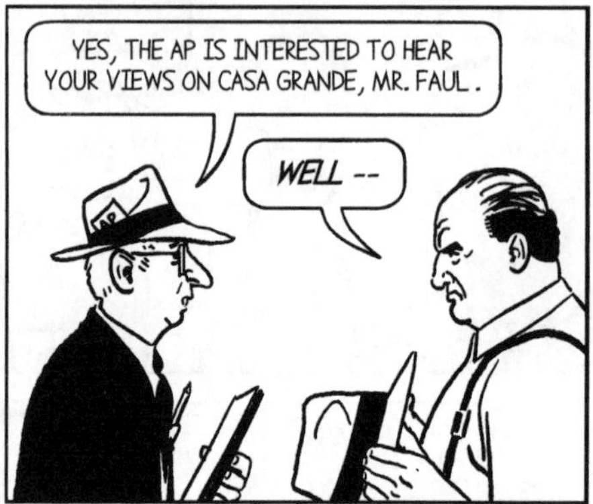
YES, THE AP IS INTERESTED TO HEAR YOUR VIEWS ON CASA GRANDE, MR. FAUL.
WELL --

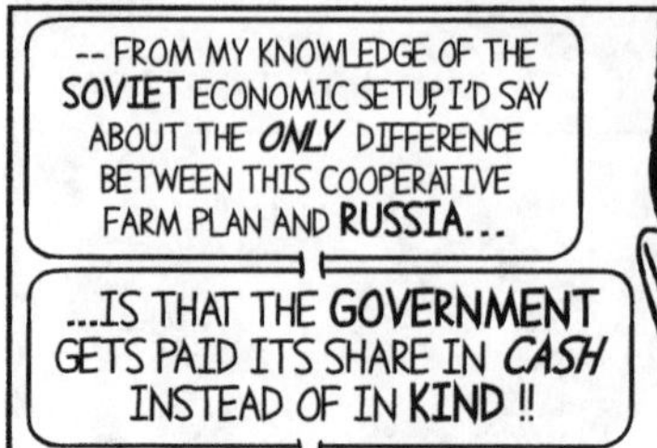
-- FROM MY KNOWLEDGE OF THE SOVIET ECONOMIC SETUP, I'D SAY ABOUT THE ONLY DIFFERENCE BETWEEN THIS COOPERATIVE FARM PLAN AND RUSSIA...
...IS THAT THE GOVERNMENT GETS PAID ITS SHARE IN CASH INSTEAD OF IN KIND!!
GOOD-BYE!

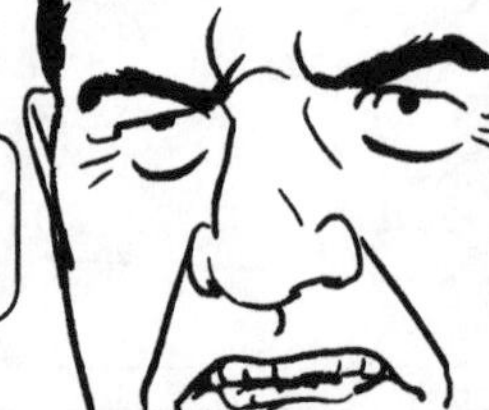

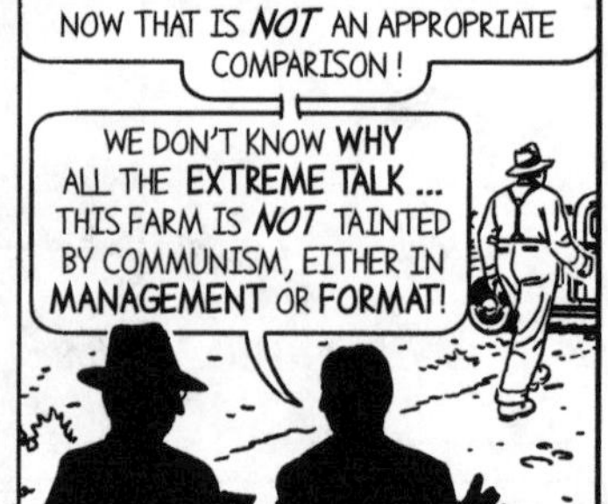
NOW THAT IS NOT AN APPROPRIATE COMPARISON!
WE DON'T KNOW WHY ALL THE EXTREME TALK ... THIS FARM IS NOT TAINTED BY COMMUNISM, EITHER IN MANAGEMENT OR FORMAT!

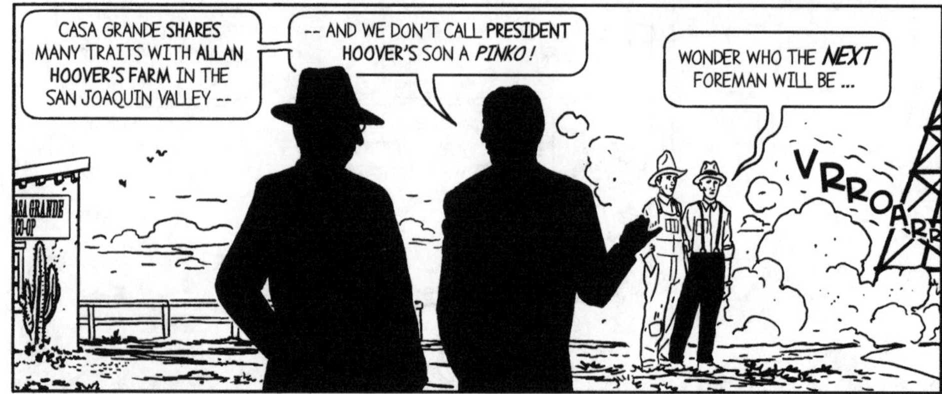
CASA GRANDE SHARES MANY TRAITS WITH ALLAN HOOVER'S FARM IN THE SAN JOAQUIN VALLEY --
-- AND WE DON'T CALL PRESIDENT HOOVER'S SON A PINKO!
WONDER WHO THE NEXT FOREMAN WILL BE ...
VRROARR

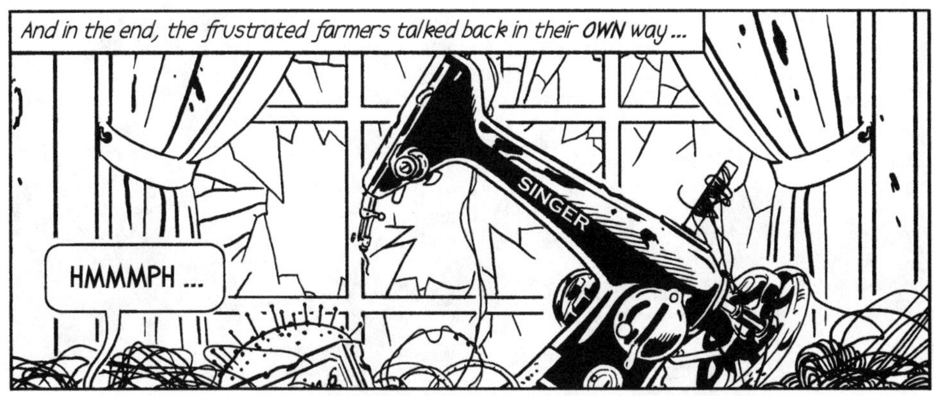

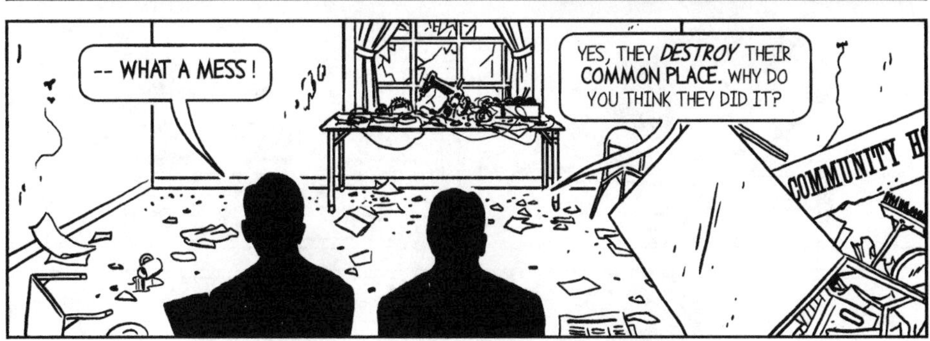

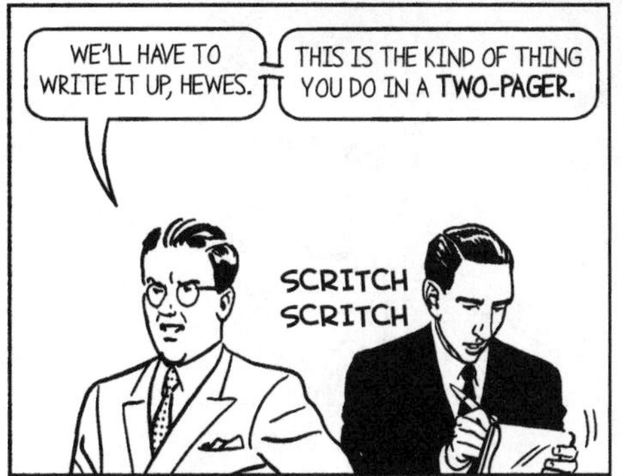

The present condition of the community house is more or less the symbol of community activities at Casa Grande. And there's a definite split in the membership here.

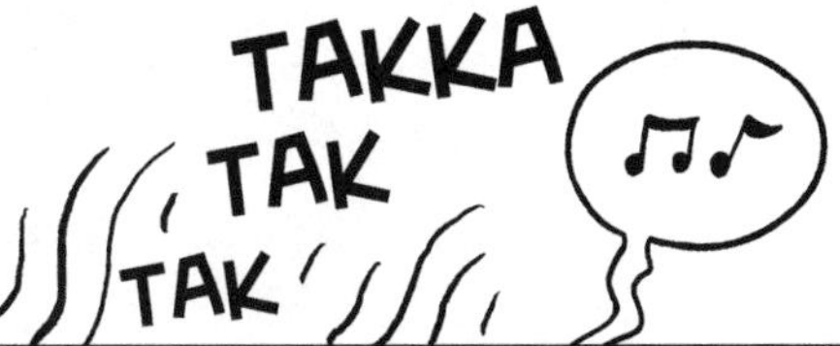

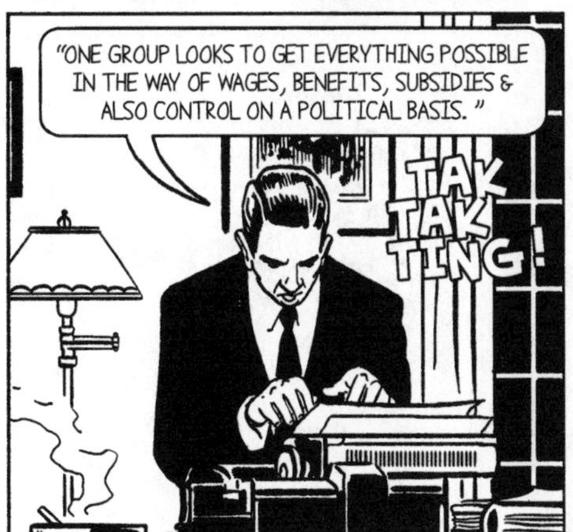

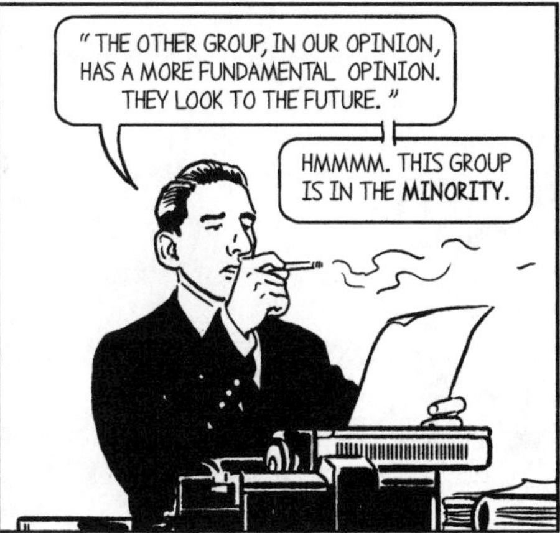

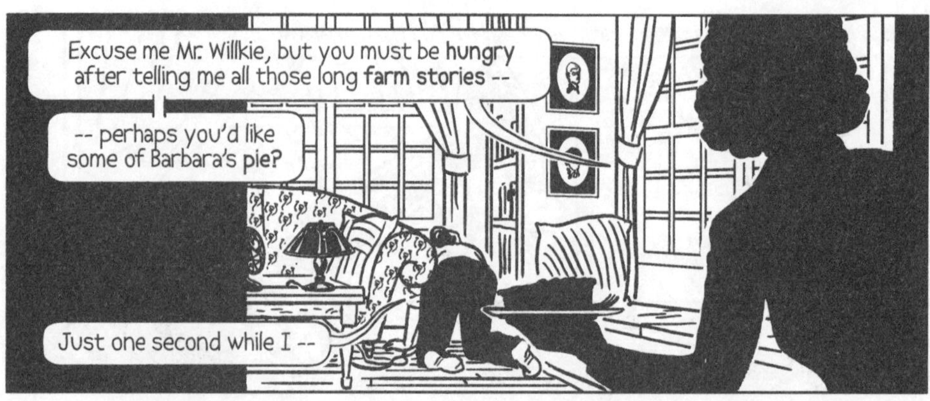
Excuse me Mr. Willkie, but you must be hungry after telling me all those long farm stories --
-- perhaps you'd like some of Barbara's pie?
Just one second while I --

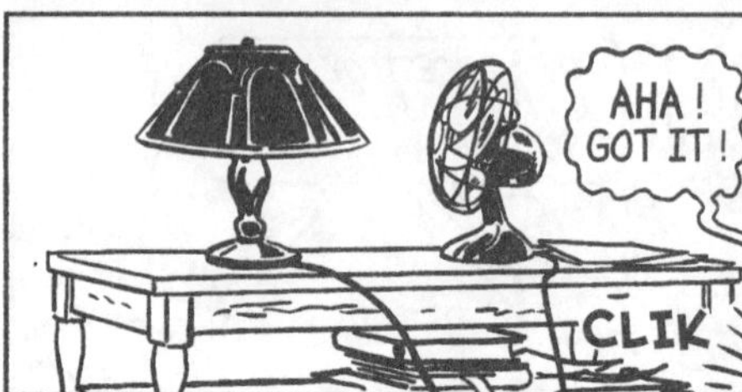
AHA! GOT IT!
CLIK

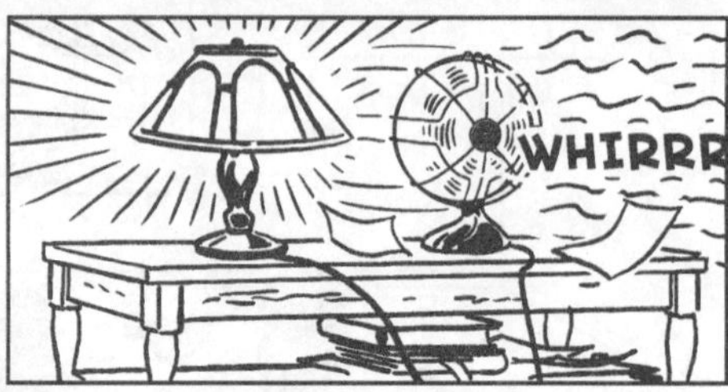
WHIRRR

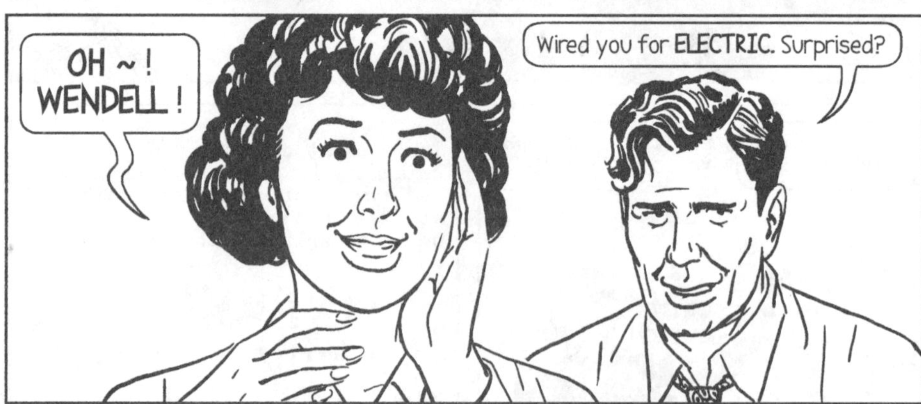
OH ~! WENDELL!
Wired you for ELECTRIC. Surprised?

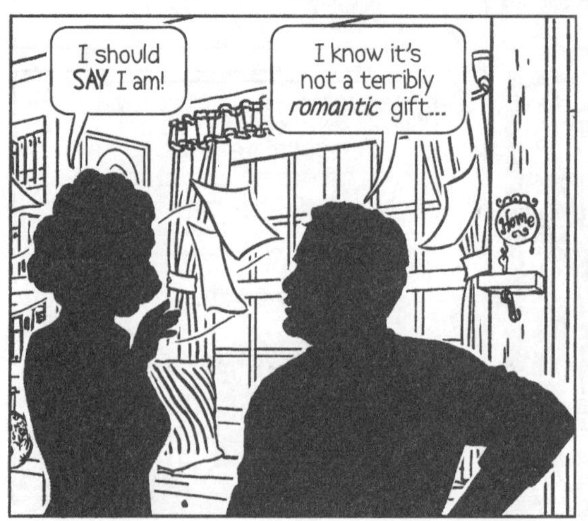
I should SAY I am!
I know it's not a terribly *romantic* gift...
Home

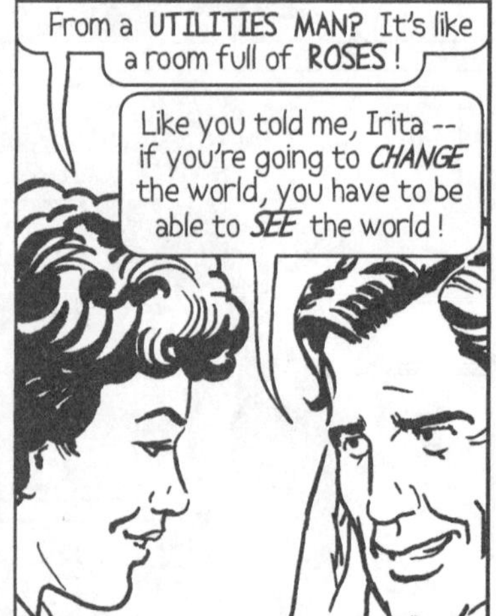
From a UTILITIES MAN? It's like a room full of ROSES!
Like you told me, Irita -- if you're going to *CHANGE* the world, you have to be able to *SEE* the world!

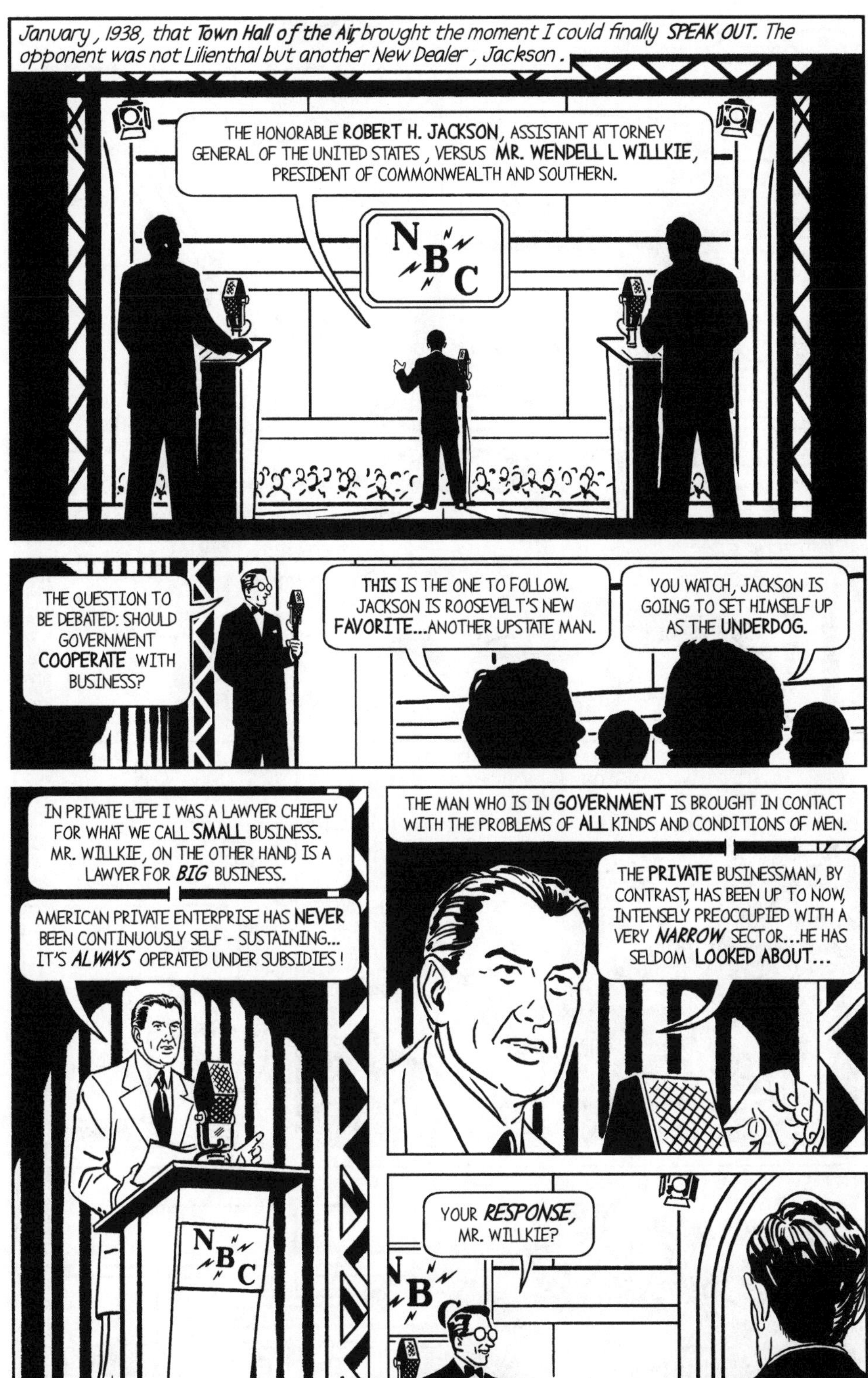
January, 1938, that Town Hall of the Air brought the moment I could finally SPEAK OUT. The opponent was not Lilienthal but another New Dealer, Jackson.
THE HONORABLE ROBERT H. JACKSON, ASSISTANT ATTORNEY GENERAL OF THE UNITED STATES, VERSUS MR. WENDELL L WILLKIE, PRESIDENT OF COMMONWEALTH AND SOUTHERN.
NBC
THE QUESTION TO BE DEBATED: SHOULD GOVERNMENT COOPERATE WITH BUSINESS?
THIS IS THE ONE TO FOLLOW. JACKSON IS ROOSEVELT'S NEW FAVORITE...ANOTHER UPSTATE MAN.
YOU WATCH, JACKSON IS GOING TO SET HIMSELF UP AS THE UNDERDOG.
IN PRIVATE LIFE I WAS A LAWYER CHIEFLY FOR WHAT WE CALL SMALL BUSINESS. MR. WILLKIE, ON THE OTHER HAND, IS A LAWYER FOR BIG BUSINESS.
AMERICAN PRIVATE ENTERPRISE HAS NEVER BEEN CONTINUOUSLY SELF - SUSTAINING... IT'S ALWAYS OPERATED UNDER SUBSIDIES!
NBC
THE MAN WHO IS IN GOVERNMENT IS BROUGHT IN CONTACT WITH THE PROBLEMS OF ALL KINDS AND CONDITIONS OF MEN.
THE PRIVATE BUSINESSMAN, BY CONTRAST, HAS BEEN UP TO NOW, INTENSELY PREOCCUPIED WITH A VERY NARROW SECTOR...HE HAS SELDOM LOOKED ABOUT...
YOUR RESPONSE, MR. WILLKIE?

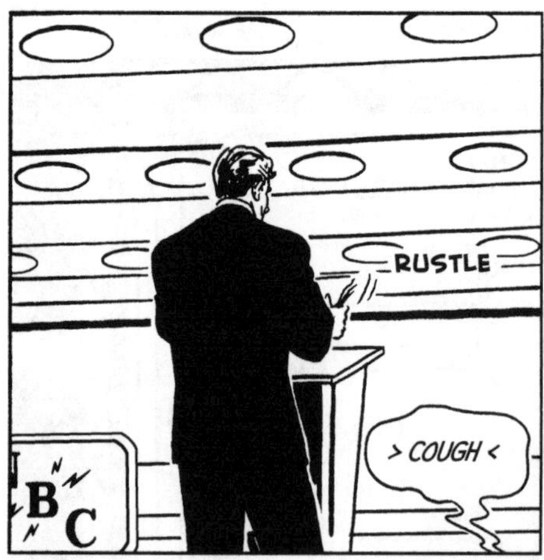

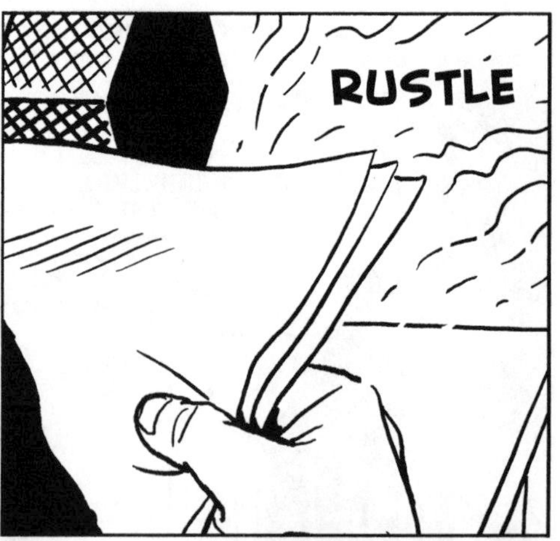

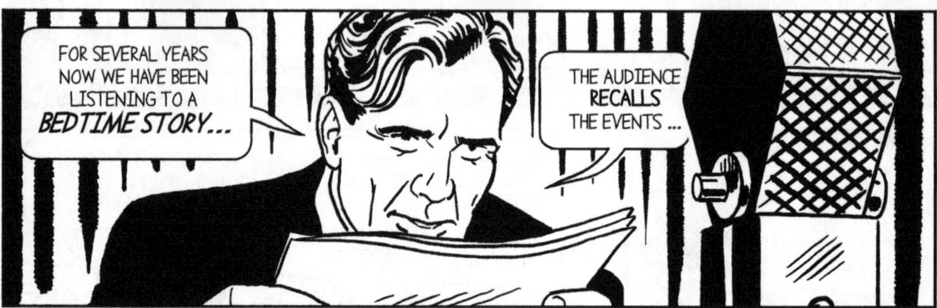

" THE BEDTIME STORY IS THAT MEN WHO HOLD OFFICE IN **WASHINGTON** ARE, BY THEIR VERY POSITIONS, ENDOWED WITH **SPECIAL VIRTUE.** "

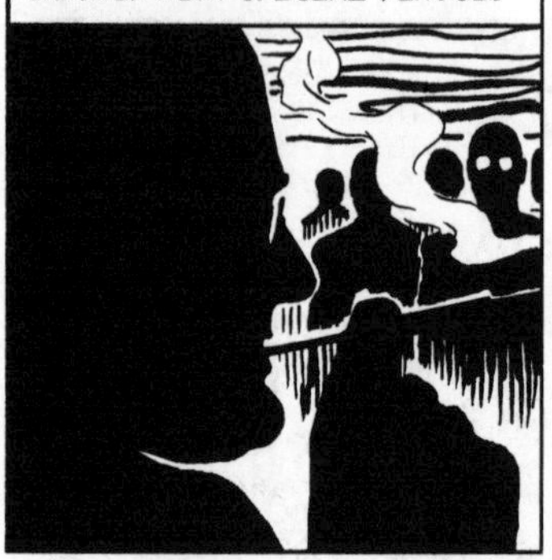

" IN AN **EPIDEMIC** IN A CITY, YOU CANNOT CONVINCE A MAN HE IS IN NO DANGER BECAUSE AT THE MOMENT ONLY **15 PERCENT** OF THE CITY IS AFFECTED. THE INVESTOR KNOWS IF THE GOVERNMENT CAN COMPETE IN **15 PERCENT** OF THE UNITED STATES, IT CAN COMPETE WITH ***ANY*** INDUSTRY ***ANYWHERE.*** "

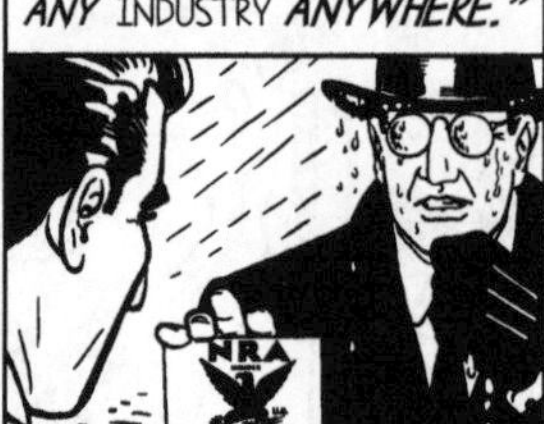

" MR. JACKSON SPOKE OF A '**STRIKE OF CAPITAL**' AGAINST THE GOVERNMENT. IF THERE IS ANY STRIKE OF CAPITAL, IT COMES FROM THOSE MILLIONS OF ***SMALL*** INVESTORS, NOT FROM THE **WEALTHY FEW** ! "

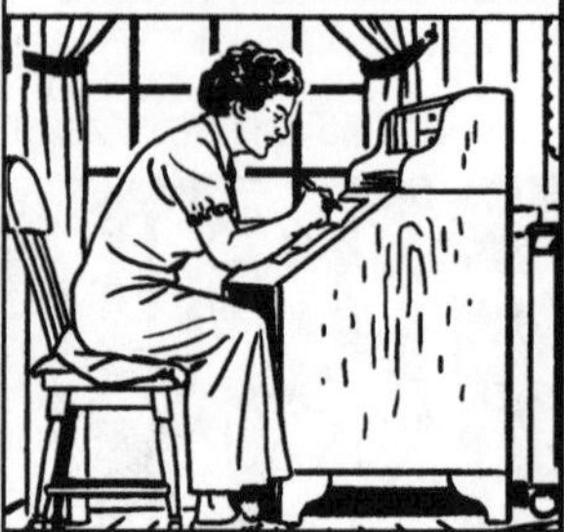

" FOR SEVERAL YEARS NOW, THE GOVERNMENT HAS TAKEN DEFINITE ACTION TO SHOW ITS ***HOSTILITY*** TOWARDS **BUSINESS.** "

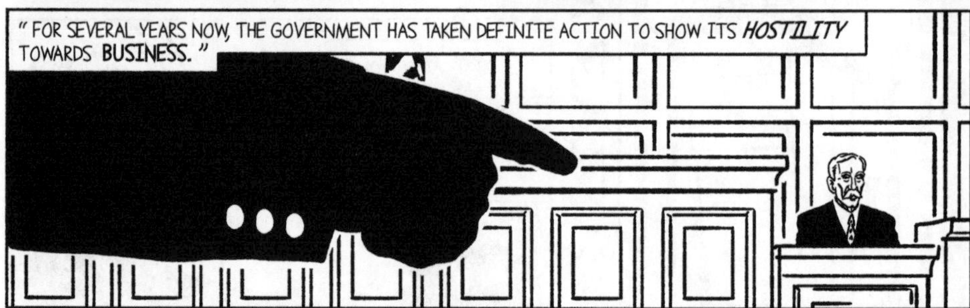

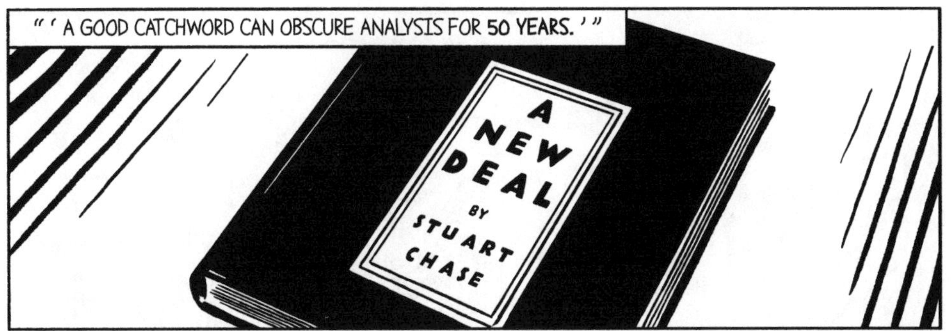
"'A GOOD CATCHWORD CAN OBSCURE ANALYSIS FOR 50 YEARS.'"
A NEW DEAL BY STUART CHASE

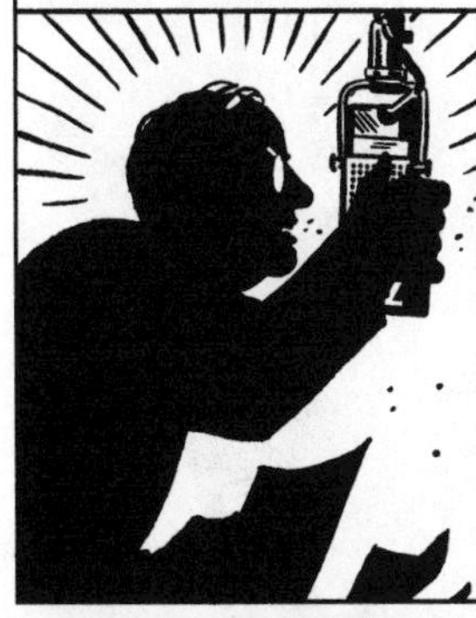
"THAT IS WHAT JUSTICE OLIVER WENDELL HOLMES SAID. TODAY GOVERNMENT OFFICIALS, WHO AT FIRST SOUGHT TO MINIMIZE OUR BUSINESS DECLINE, ARE NOW SEEKING FRANTICALLY TO MAKE BIG BUSINESS RESPONSIBLE!"

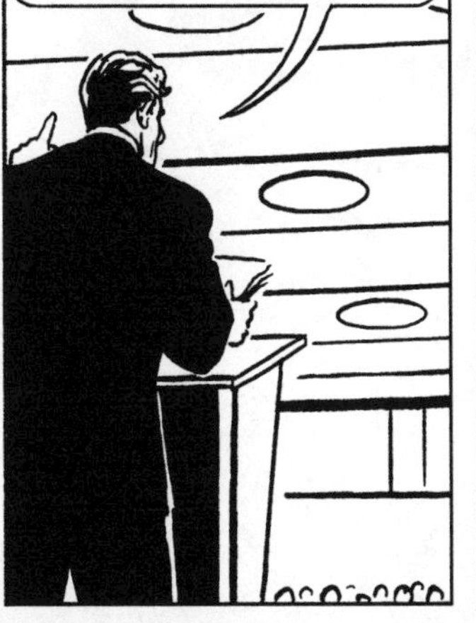
GOVERNMENT THINKS ECONOMIC FORCES CAN BE CONTROLLED BY POLITICS. BUT ECONOMIC FORCES ARE MORE POWERFUL THAN EITHER GOVERNMENT OR BUSINESS!

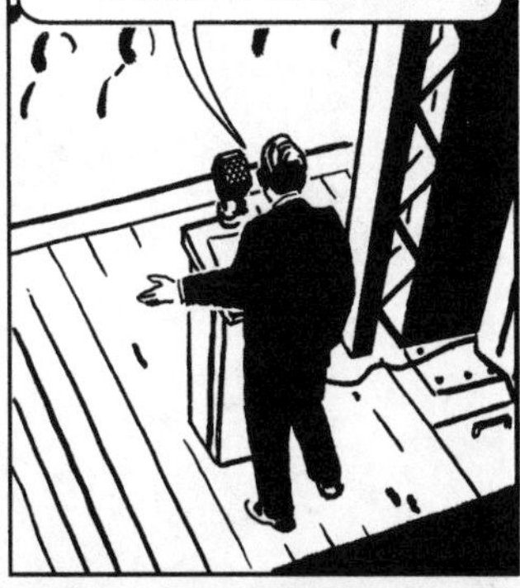
MY INDUSTRY IS SUPPOSED TO BE EXPENSIVE. BUT WHILE THE COST OF LIVING WENT UP SINCE THE PREWAR YEARS, THE COST OF ELECTRICITY HAS GONE DOWN. THE AMERICAN CONSUMER PAYS A SMALLER PART OF HIS INCOME FOR ELECTRICITY THAN CONSUMERS IN EUROPE!

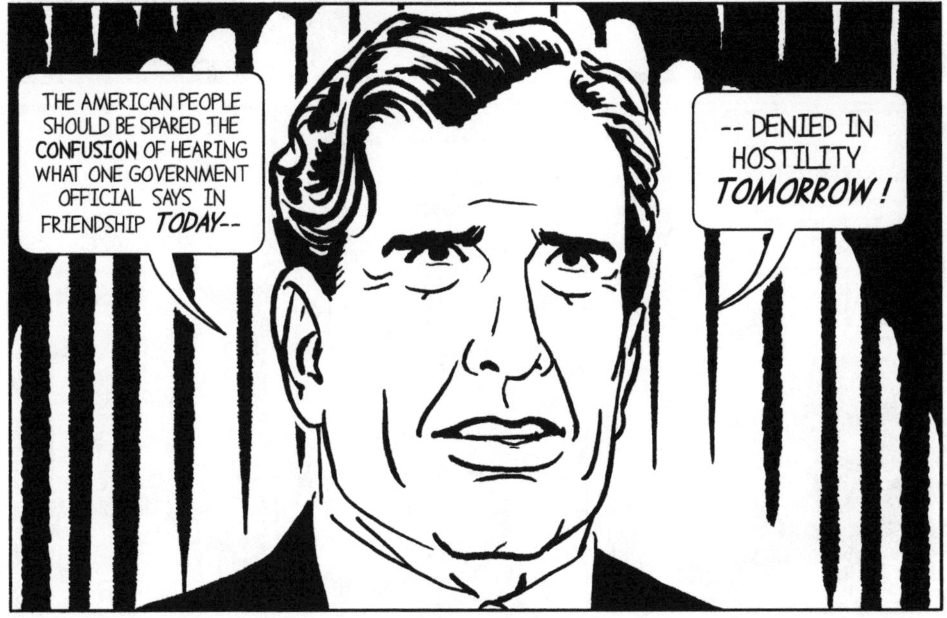
THE AMERICAN PEOPLE SHOULD BE SPARED THE CONFUSION OF HEARING WHAT ONE GOVERNMENT OFFICIAL SAYS IN FRIENDSHIP TODAY--
-- DENIED IN HOSTILITY TOMORROW!

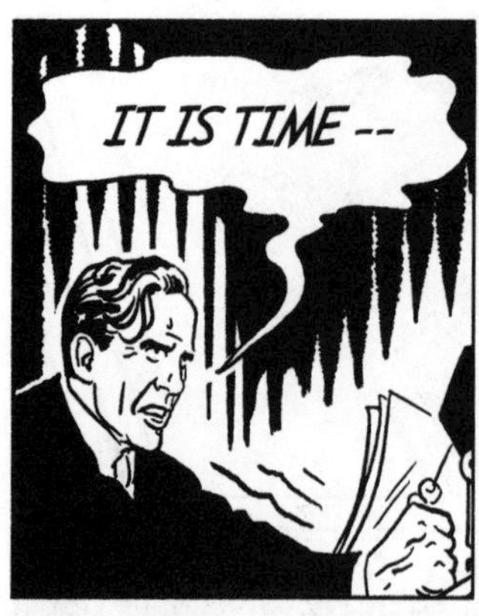
IT IS TIME --

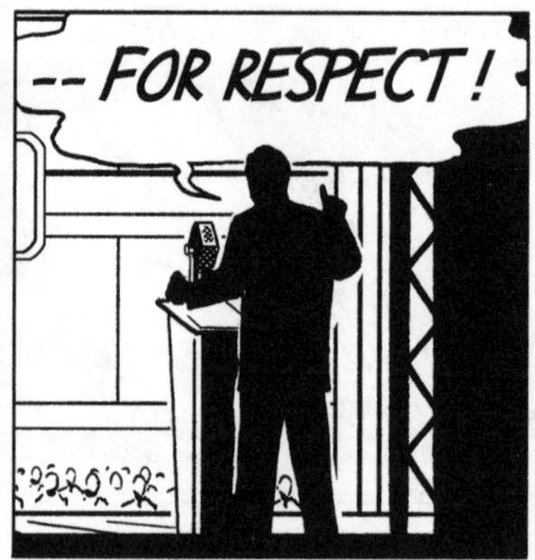
-- FOR RESPECT !

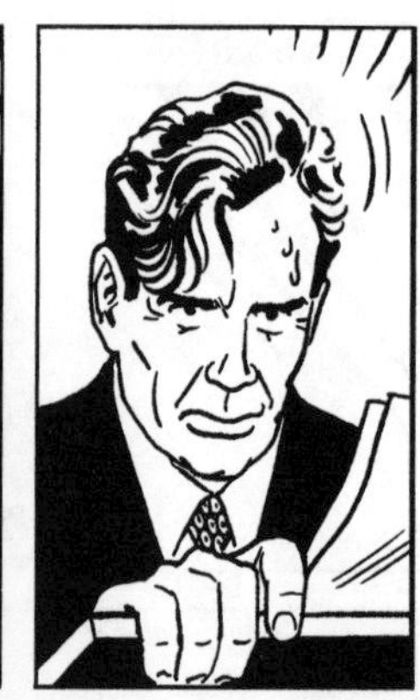

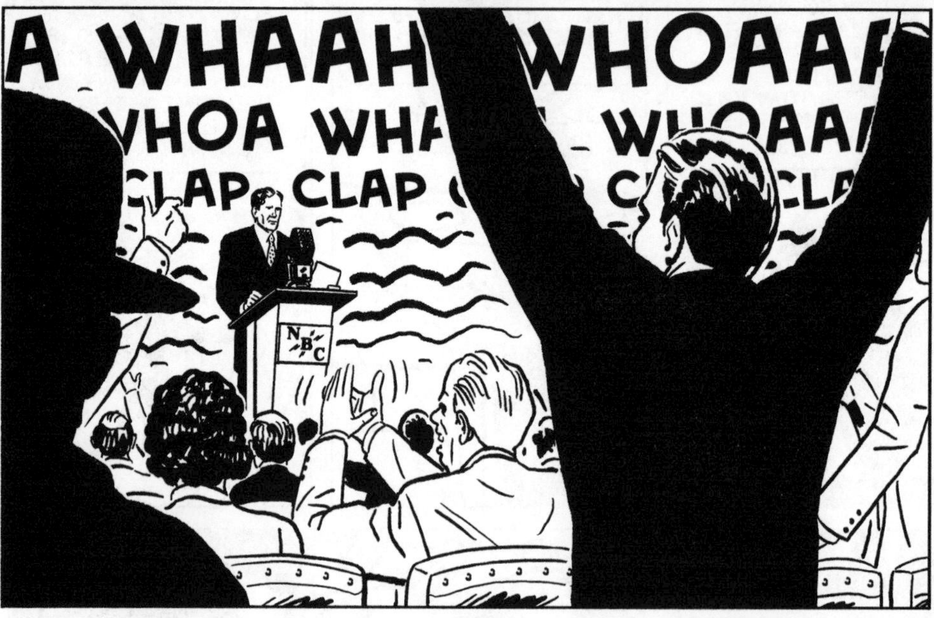
A WHAAH WHOAA
WHOA WHA WHOAA
CLAP CLAP CLA
NBC

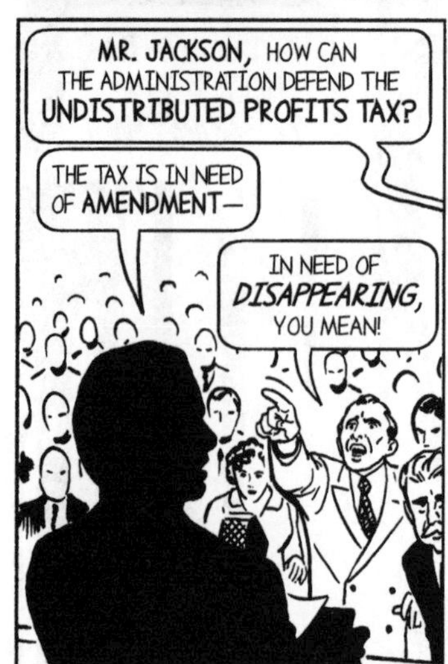
MR. JACKSON, HOW CAN THE ADMINISTRATION DEFEND THE UNDISTRIBUTED PROFITS TAX?
THE TAX IS IN NEED OF AMENDMENT—
IN NEED OF DISAPPEARING, YOU MEAN!

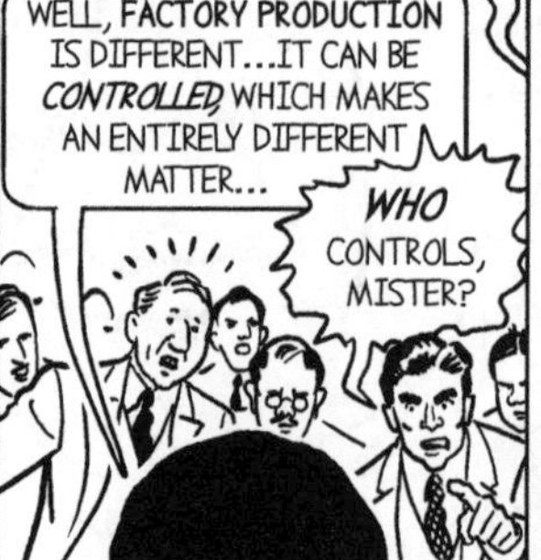
MR. JACKSON, RECONCILE THIS: THE NEW DEAL PROGRAM FOR FARMERS IS TO CUT PRODUCTION TO RAISE PRICES -- BUT THE NEW DEAL ALSO HAS A PLAN TO INCREASE INDUSTRIAL PRODUCTION TO LOWER PRICES !
WELL, FACTORY PRODUCTION IS DIFFERENT...IT CAN BE CONTROLLED, WHICH MAKES AN ENTIRELY DIFFERENT MATTER...
WHO CONTROLS, MISTER?

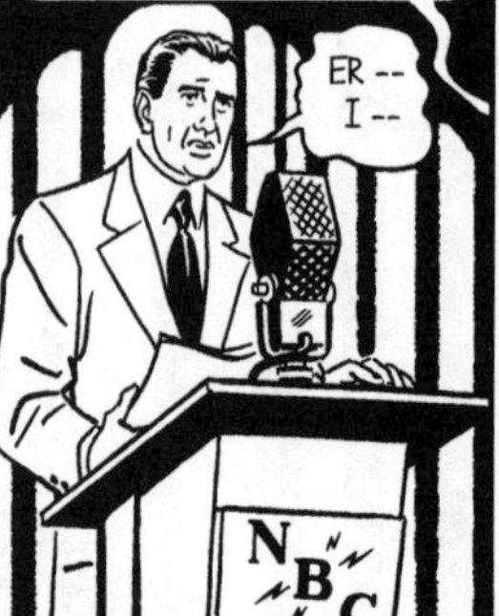
MR. JACKSON, DON'T WE THE PEOPLE FEAR AN UNDUE CONCENTRATION IN GOVERNMENT AS MUCH OR MORE THAN WE FEAR A CONCENTRATION IN BUSINESS ?
ER -- I --
NBC

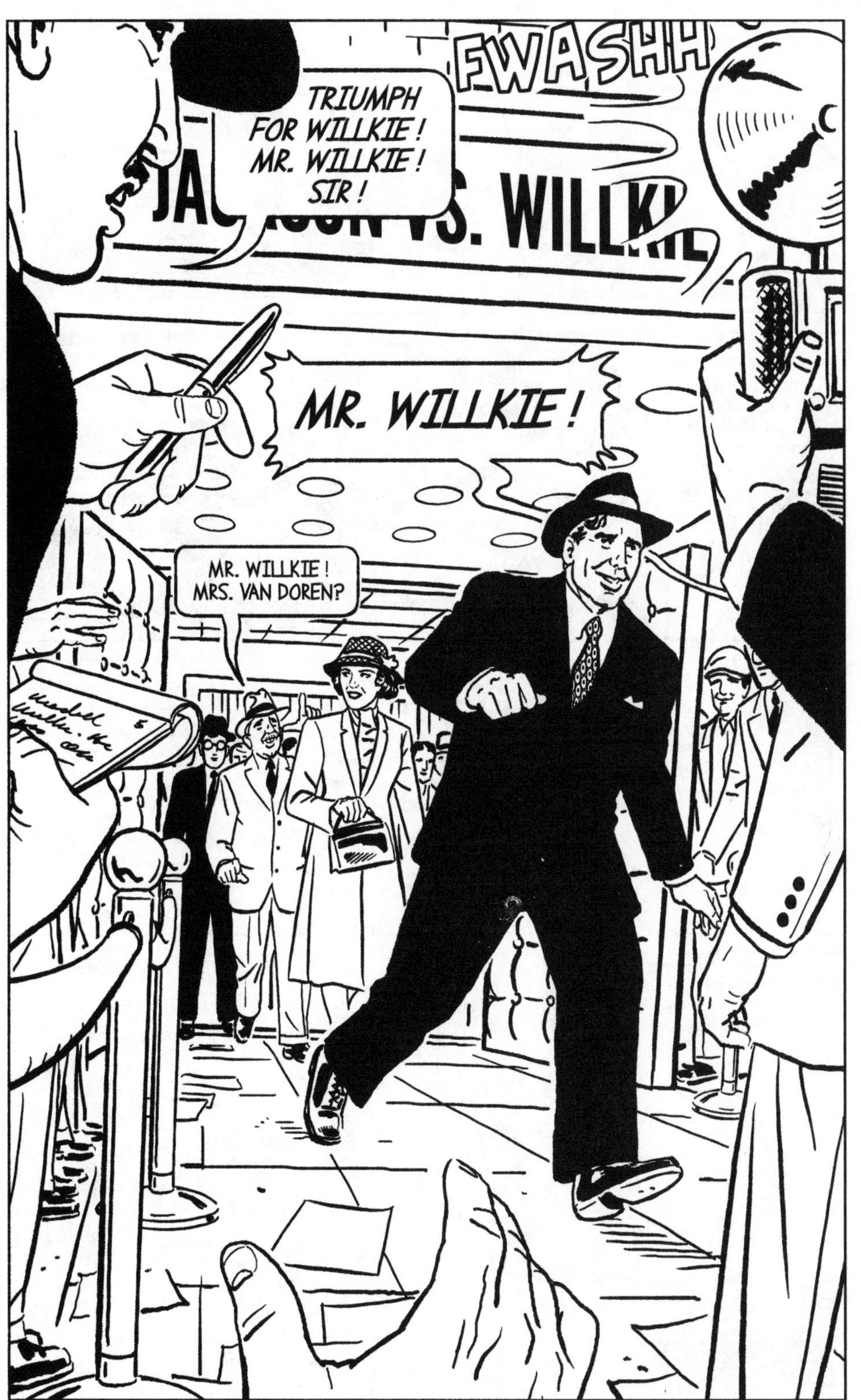
FWASHH
TRIUMPH FOR WILLKIE! MR. WILLKIE! SIR!
MR. WILLKIE!
MR. WILLKIE! MRS. VAN DOREN?

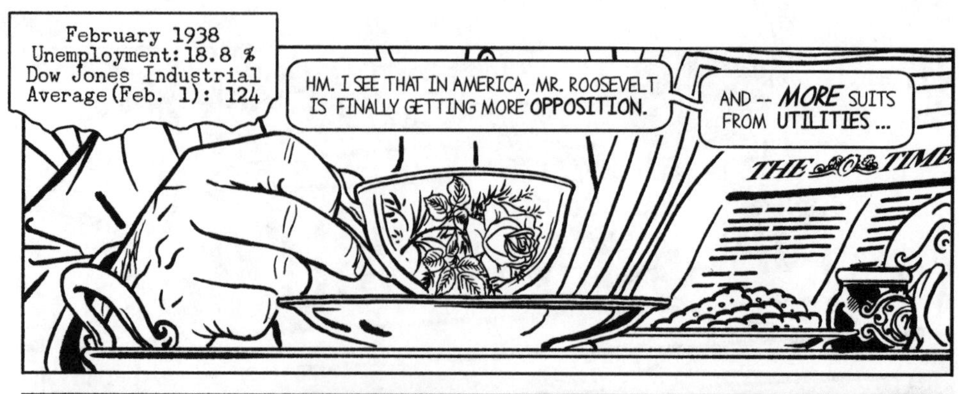
February 1938
Unemployment: 18.8 %
Dow Jones Industrial
Average (Feb. 1): 124
HM. I SEE THAT IN AMERICA, MR. ROOSEVELT IS FINALLY GETTING MORE OPPOSITION.
AND -- MORE SUITS FROM UTILITIES ...

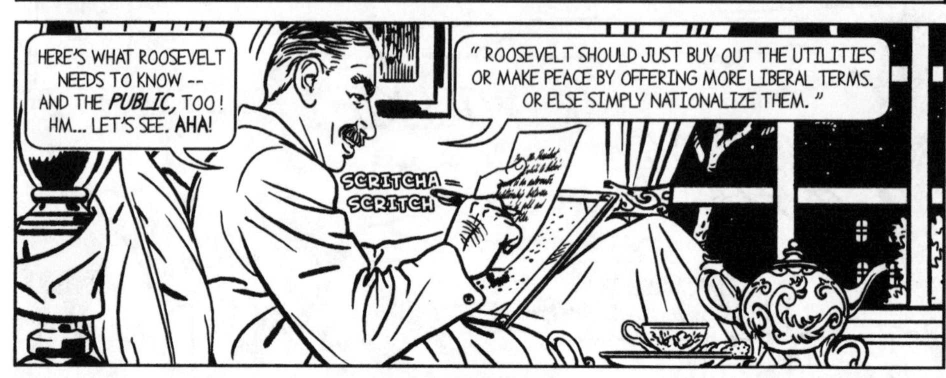
HERE'S WHAT ROOSEVELT NEEDS TO KNOW -- AND THE PUBLIC, TOO! HM... LET'S SEE. AHA!
" ROOSEVELT SHOULD JUST BUY OUT THE UTILITIES OR MAKE PEACE BY OFFERING MORE LIBERAL TERMS. OR ELSE SIMPLY NATIONALIZE THEM. "
SCRITCHA
SCRITCH

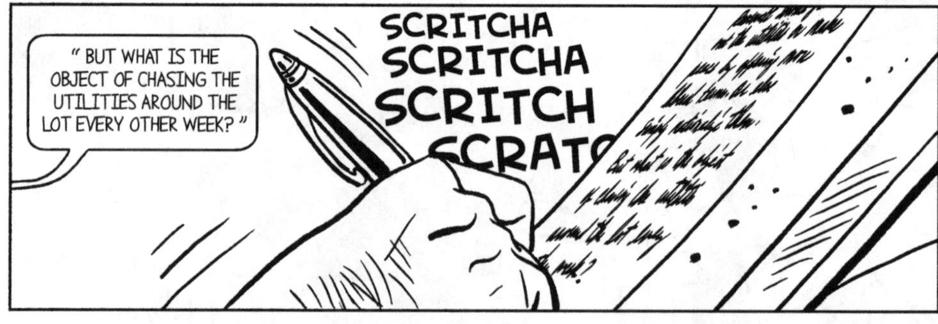
" BUT WHAT IS THE OBJECT OF CHASING THE UTILITIES AROUND THE LOT EVERY OTHER WEEK? "
SCRITCHA
SCRITCHA
SCRITCH

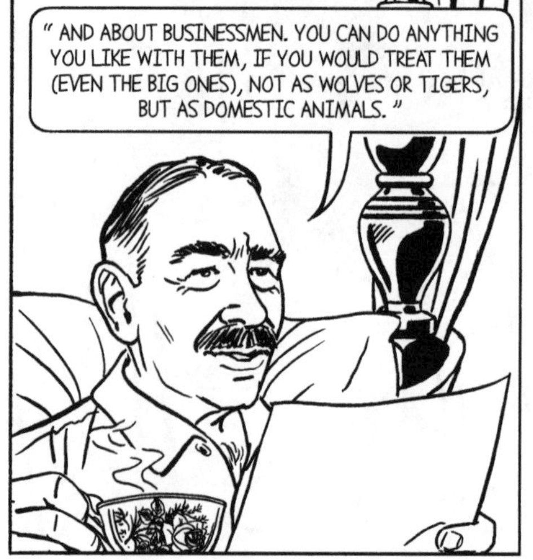
" AND ABOUT BUSINESSMEN. YOU CAN DO ANYTHING YOU LIKE WITH THEM, IF YOU WOULD TREAT THEM (EVEN THE BIG ONES), NOT AS WOLVES OR TIGERS, BUT AS DOMESTIC ANIMALS. "

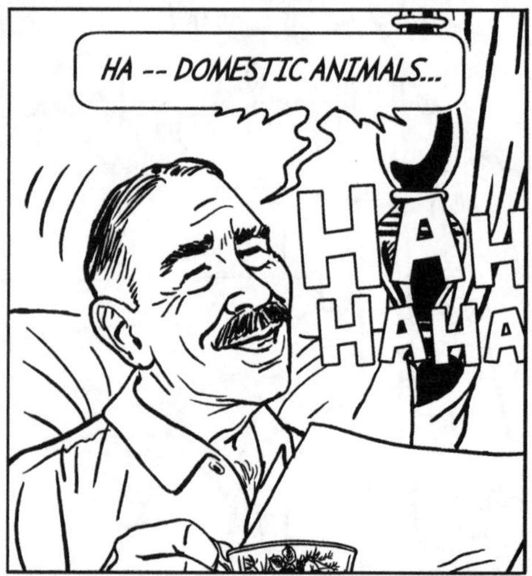
HA -- DOMESTIC ANIMALS...

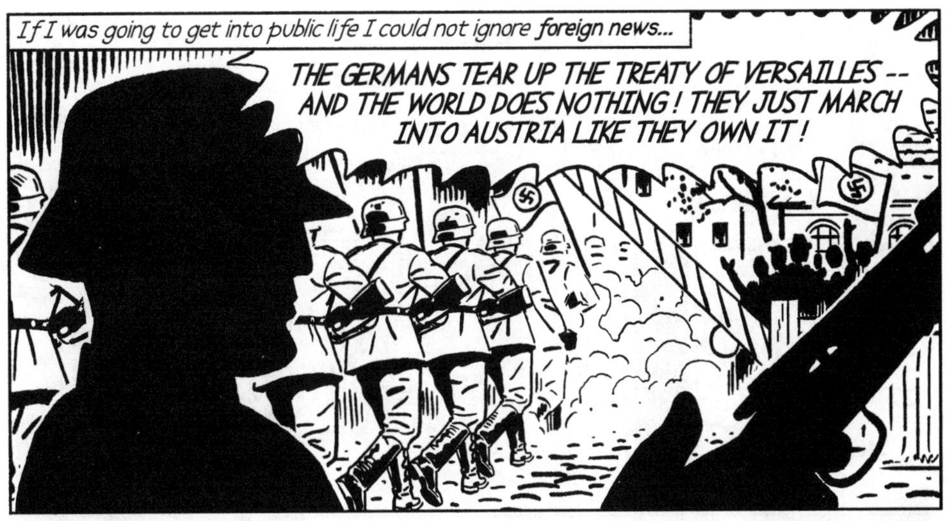
If I was going to get into public life I could not ignore foreign news...
THE GERMANS TEAR UP THE TREATY OF VERSAILLES -- AND THE WORLD DOES NOTHING! THEY JUST MARCH INTO AUSTRIA LIKE THEY OWN IT!

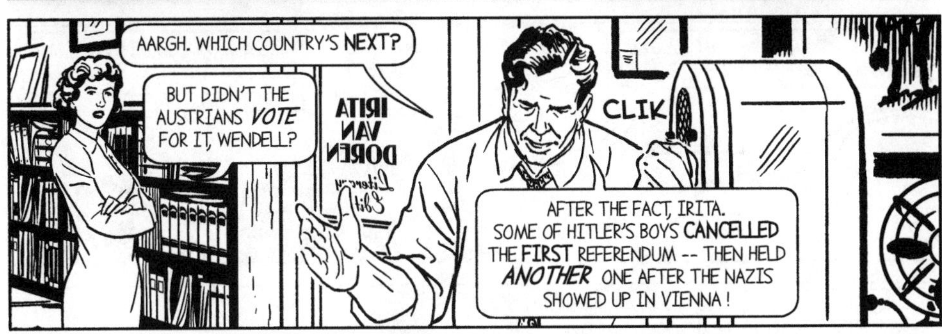
AARGH. WHICH COUNTRY'S NEXT?
BUT DIDN'T THE AUSTRIANS VOTE FOR IT, WENDELL?
IRITA VAN DOREN
CLIK
AFTER THE FACT, IRITA. SOME OF HITLER'S BOYS CANCELLED THE FIRST REFERENDUM -- THEN HELD ANOTHER ONE AFTER THE NAZIS SHOWED UP IN VIENNA!

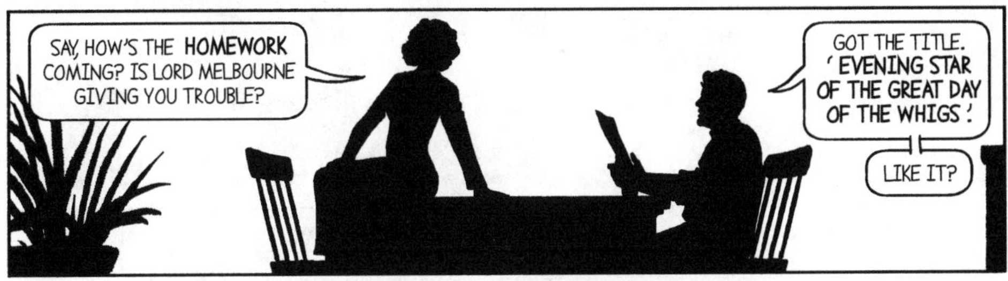
SAY, HOW'S THE HOMEWORK COMING? IS LORD MELBOURNE GIVING YOU TROUBLE?
GOT THE TITLE. 'EVENING STAR OF THE GREAT DAY OF THE WHIGS'.
LIKE IT?

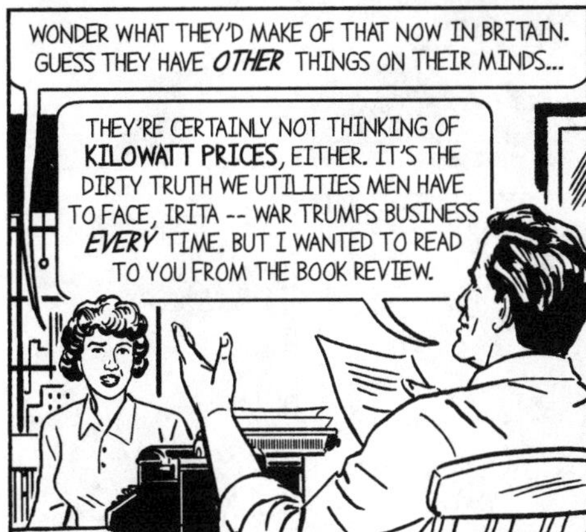
WONDER WHAT THEY'D MAKE OF THAT NOW IN BRITAIN. GUESS THEY HAVE OTHER THINGS ON THEIR MINDS...
THEY'RE CERTAINLY NOT THINKING OF KILOWATT PRICES, EITHER. IT'S THE DIRTY TRUTH WE UTILITIES MEN HAVE TO FACE, IRITA -- WAR TRUMPS BUSINESS EVERY TIME. BUT I WANTED TO READ TO YOU FROM THE BOOK REVIEW.

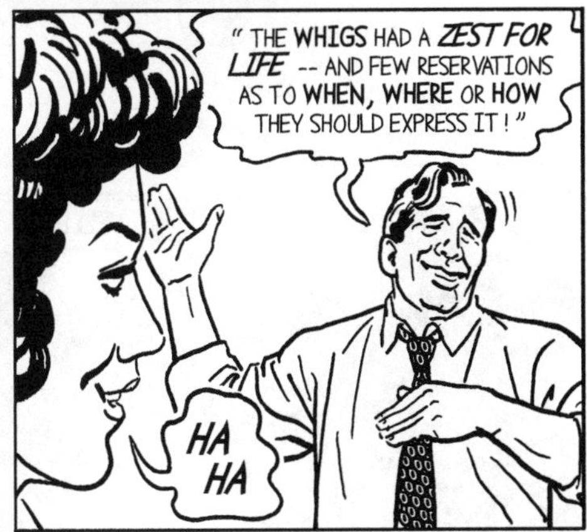
"THE WHIGS HAD A ZEST FOR LIFE -- AND FEW RESERVATIONS AS TO WHEN, WHERE OR HOW THEY SHOULD EXPRESS IT!"
HA HA

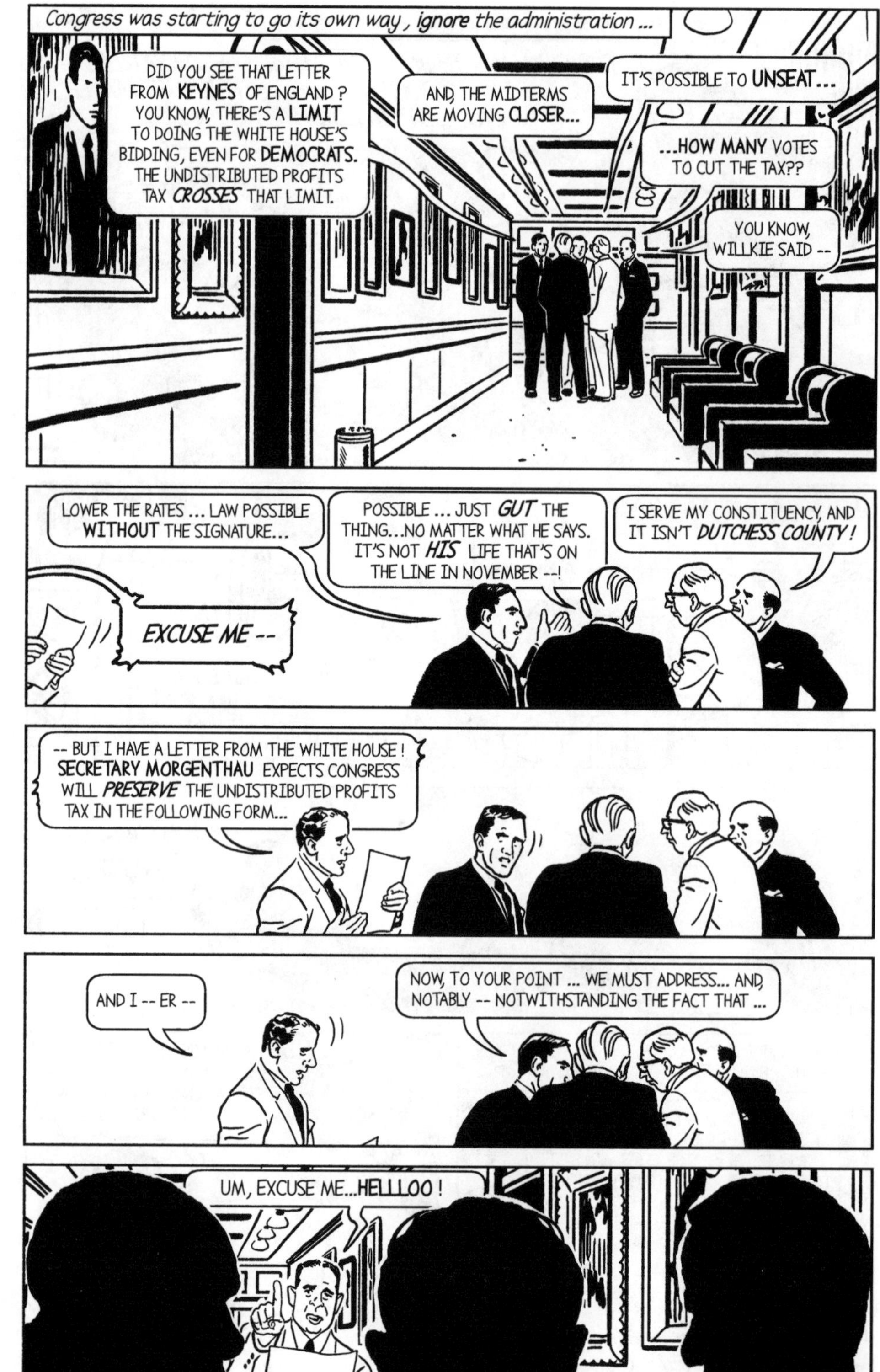

Congress was starting to go its own way, **ignore** the administration ...
DID YOU SEE THAT LETTER FROM **KEYNES** OF ENGLAND? YOU KNOW, THERE'S A **LIMIT** TO DOING THE WHITE HOUSE'S BIDDING, EVEN FOR **DEMOCRATS**. THE UNDISTRIBUTED PROFITS TAX *CROSSES* THAT LIMIT.
AND, THE MIDTERMS ARE MOVING **CLOSER...**
IT'S POSSIBLE TO **UNSEAT...**
...HOW MANY VOTES TO CUT THE TAX??
YOU KNOW, WILLKIE SAID --
LOWER THE RATES ... LAW POSSIBLE **WITHOUT** THE SIGNATURE...
POSSIBLE ... JUST ***GUT*** THE THING...NO MATTER WHAT HE SAYS. IT'S NOT ***HIS*** LIFE THAT'S ON THE LINE IN NOVEMBER --!
I SERVE MY CONSTITUENCY, AND IT ISN'T *DUTCHESS COUNTY!*
EXCUSE ME --
-- BUT I HAVE A LETTER FROM THE WHITE HOUSE! **SECRETARY MORGENTHAU** EXPECTS CONGRESS WILL *PRESERVE* THE UNDISTRIBUTED PROFITS TAX IN THE FOLLOWING FORM...
AND I -- ER --
NOW, TO YOUR POINT ... WE MUST ADDRESS... AND, NOTABLY -- NOTWITHSTANDING THE FACT THAT ...
UM, EXCUSE ME...**HELLLOO!**

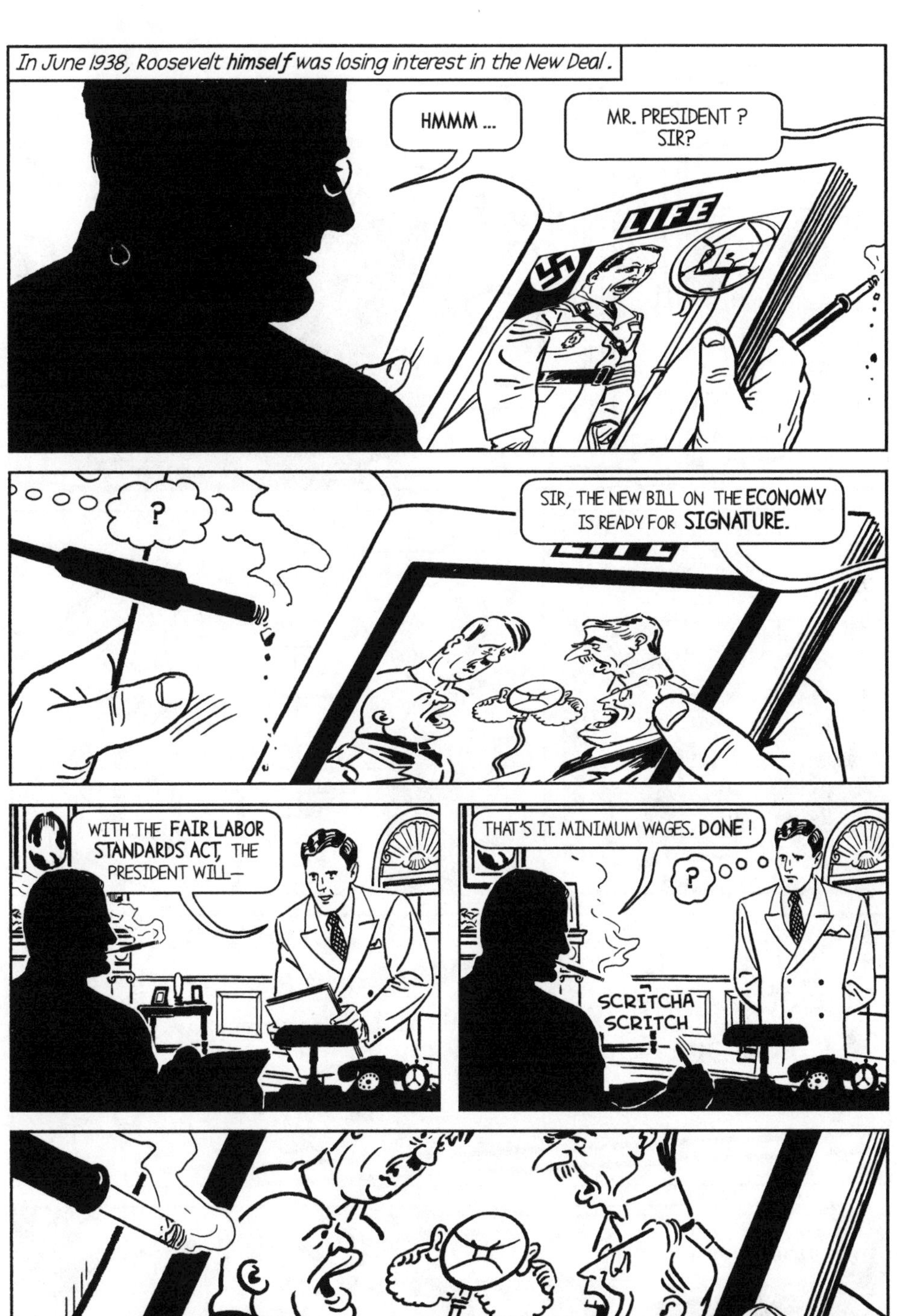
In June 1938, Roosevelt **himself** was losing interest in the New Deal.
HMMM ...
MR. PRESIDENT ? SIR?
LIFE
?
SIR, THE NEW BILL ON THE ECONOMY IS READY FOR SIGNATURE.
WITH THE FAIR LABOR STANDARDS ACT, THE PRESIDENT WILL—
THAT'S IT. MINIMUM WAGES. DONE !
?
SCRITCHA SCRITCH
HMM. OUR LITTLE DOMESTIC SQUABBLES AREN'T THE ONES THAT MATTER NOW ...

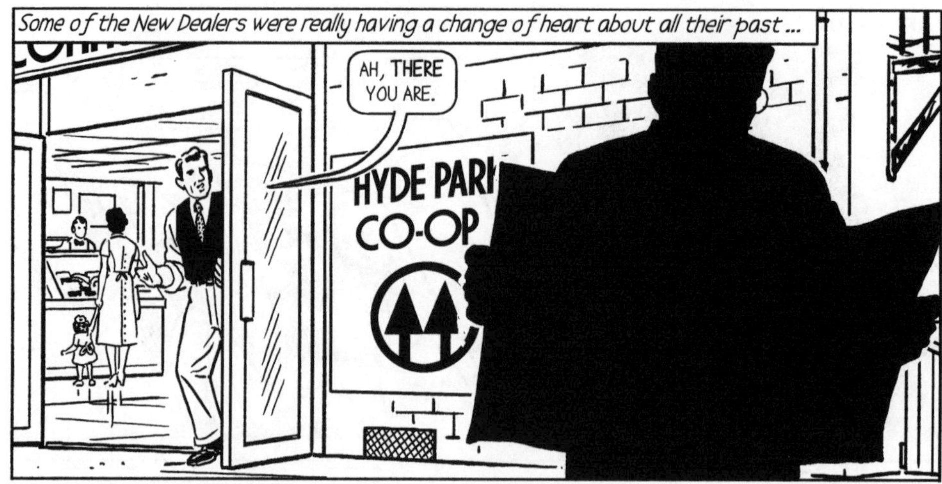

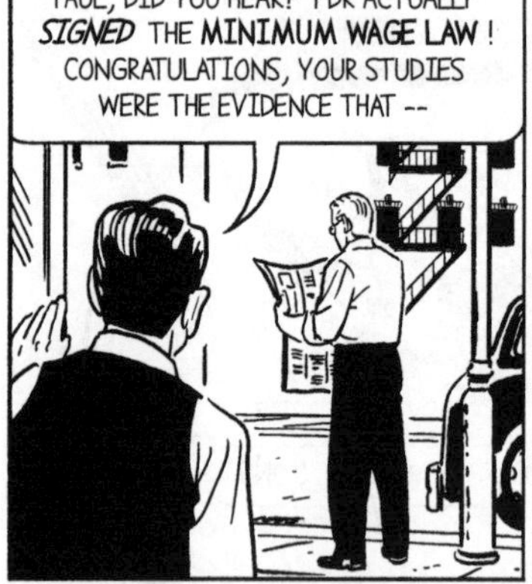

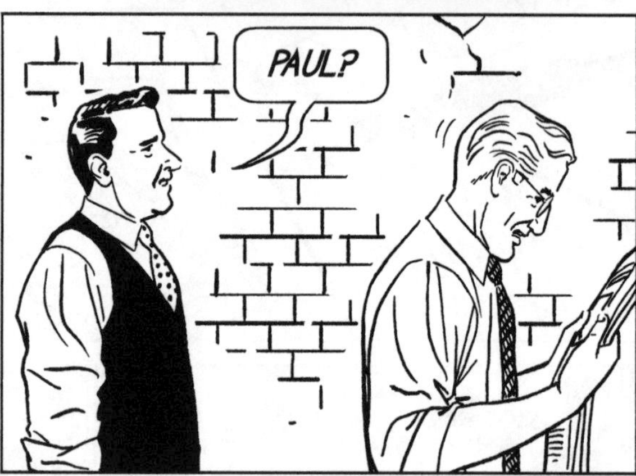

Authorities say that there is nothing to shed light on the **disappearance** a year ag of **Betty Glan,** well known to foreigners as director of Moscow's Park of Culture and Rest.

BETTY --

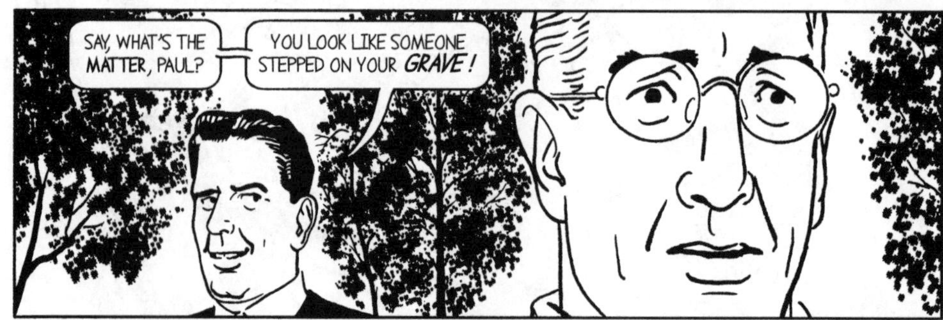

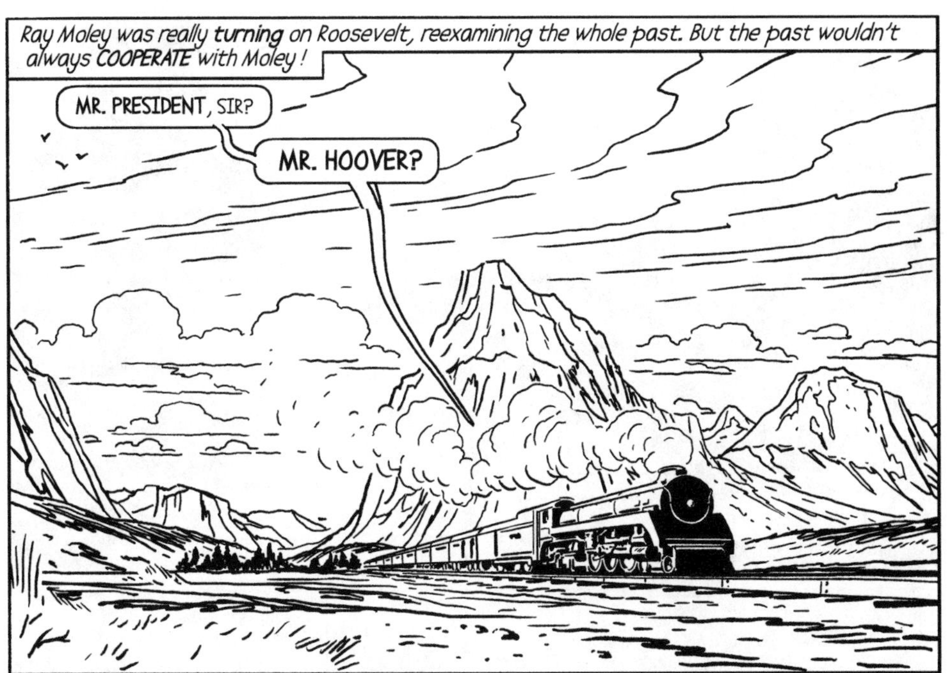
Ray Moley was really turning on Roosevelt, reexamining the whole past. But the past wouldn't always COOPERATE with Moley!
MR. PRESIDENT, SIR?
MR. HOOVER?

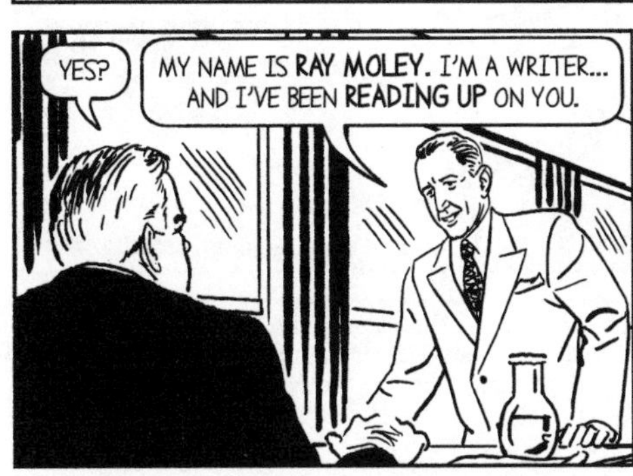
YES?
MY NAME IS RAY MOLEY. I'M A WRITER... AND I'VE BEEN READING UP ON YOU.

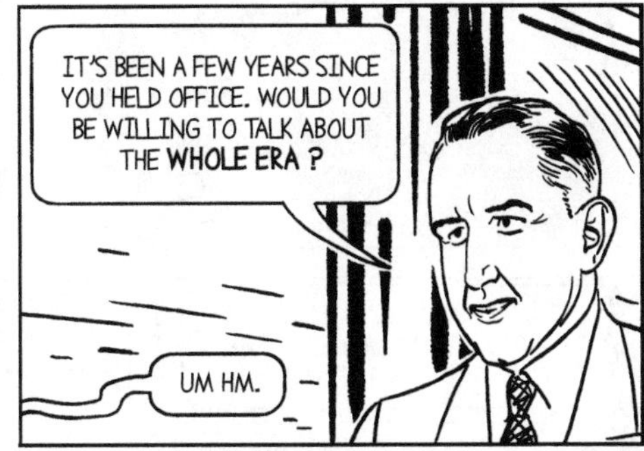
IT'S BEEN A FEW YEARS SINCE YOU HELD OFFICE. WOULD YOU BE WILLING TO TALK ABOUT THE WHOLE ERA ?
UM HM.

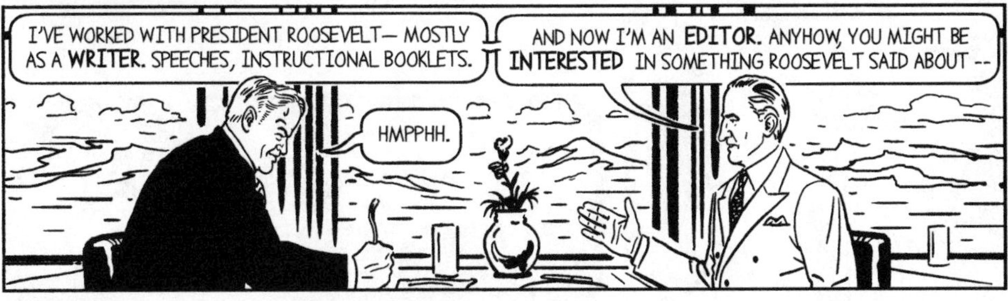
I'VE WORKED WITH PRESIDENT ROOSEVELT— MOSTLY AS A WRITER. SPEECHES, INSTRUCTIONAL BOOKLETS.
AND NOW I'M AN EDITOR. ANYHOW, YOU MIGHT BE INTERESTED IN SOMETHING ROOSEVELT SAID ABOUT --
HMPPHH.

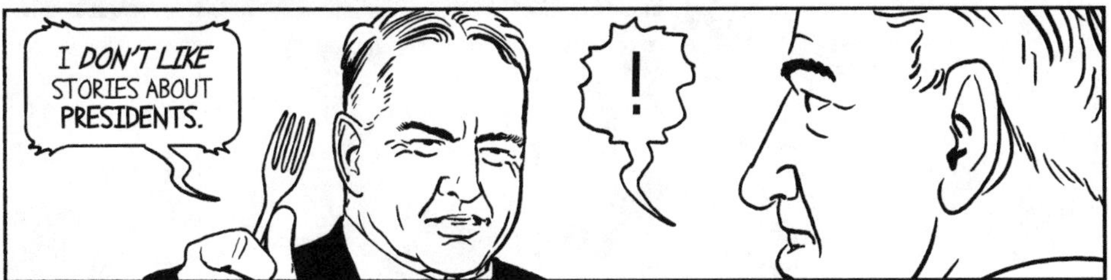
I DON'T LIKE STORIES ABOUT PRESIDENTS.
!

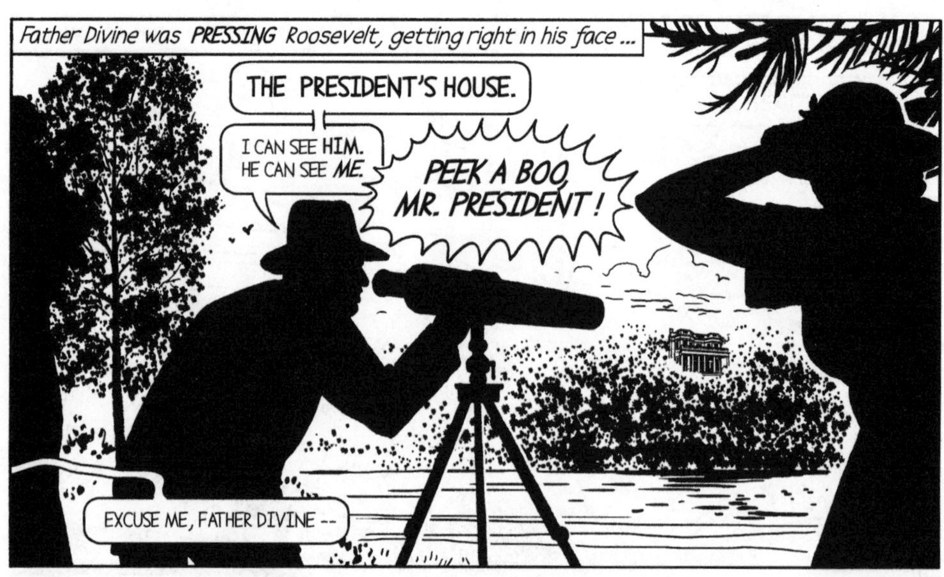

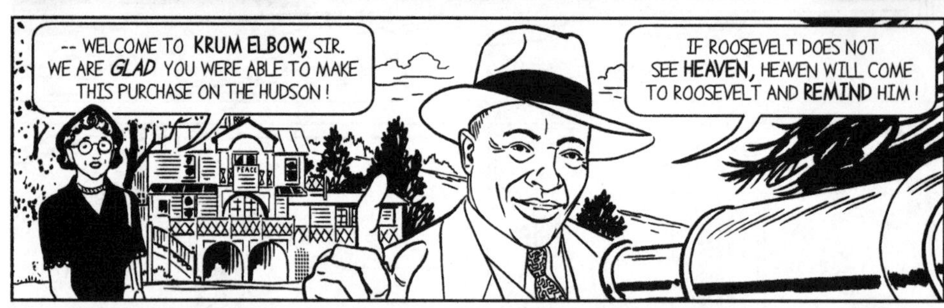

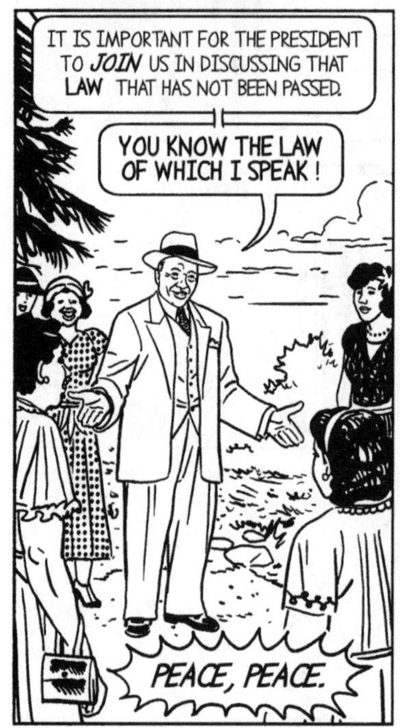

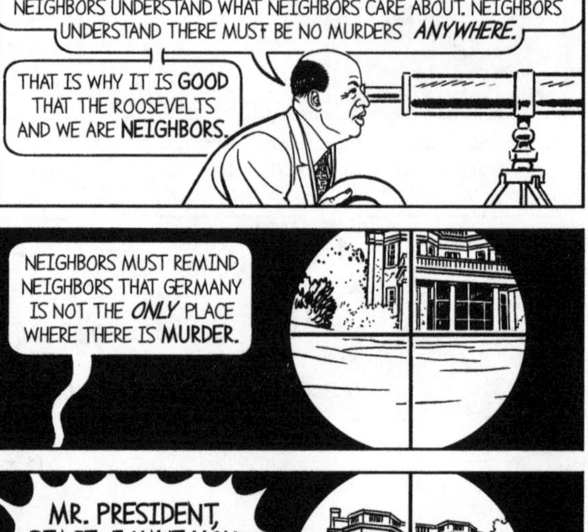

MR. PRESIDENT, PEACE. I HAVE YOU IN MY SIGHTS!

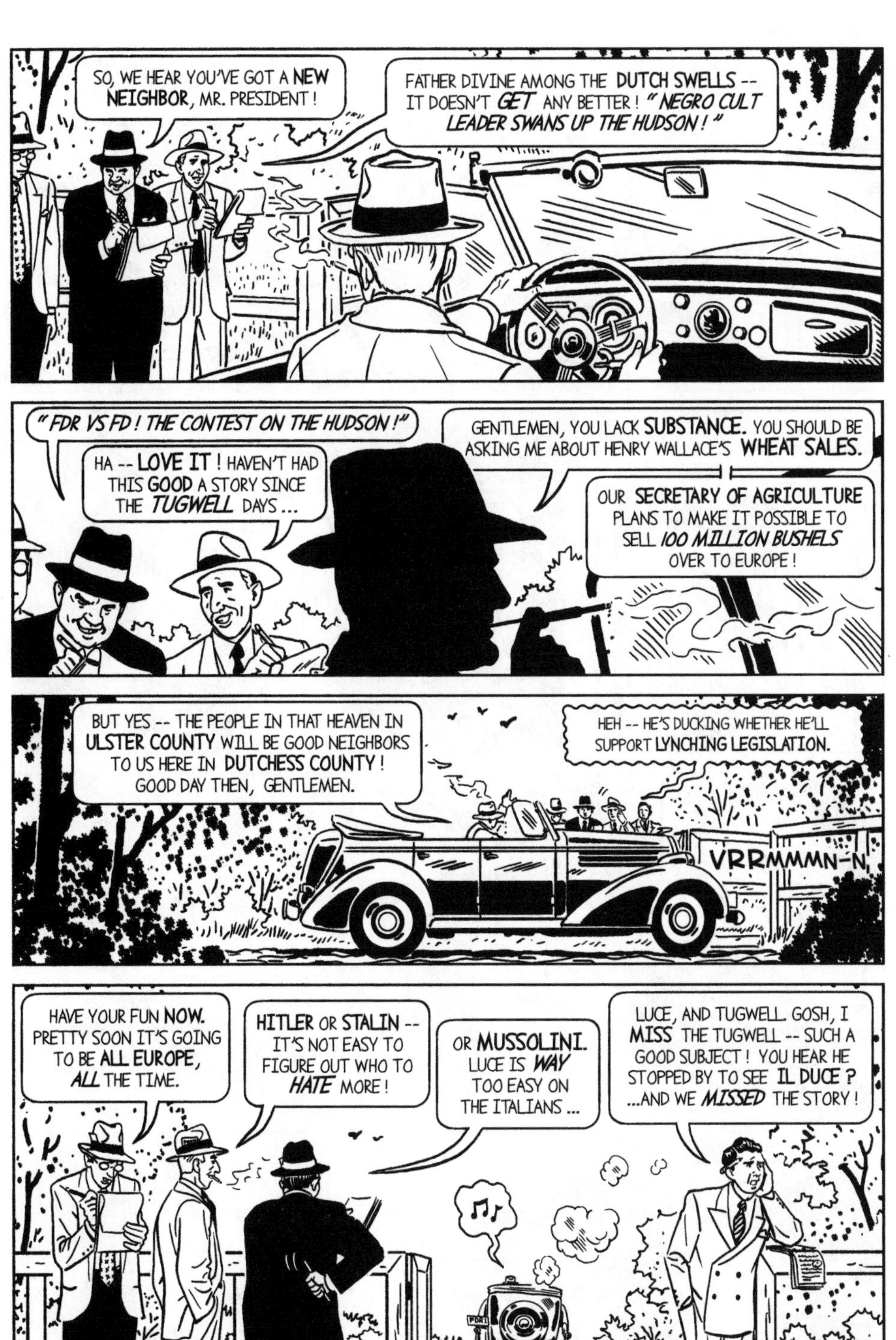
SO, WE HEAR YOU'VE GOT A NEW NEIGHBOR, MR. PRESIDENT!
FATHER DIVINE AMONG THE DUTCH SWELLS -- IT DOESN'T GET ANY BETTER! "NEGRO CULT LEADER SWANS UP THE HUDSON!"
"FDR VS FD! THE CONTEST ON THE HUDSON!"
HA -- LOVE IT! HAVEN'T HAD THIS GOOD A STORY SINCE THE TUGWELL DAYS...
GENTLEMEN, YOU LACK SUBSTANCE. YOU SHOULD BE ASKING ME ABOUT HENRY WALLACE'S WHEAT SALES.
OUR SECRETARY OF AGRICULTURE PLANS TO MAKE IT POSSIBLE TO SELL 100 MILLION BUSHELS OVER TO EUROPE!
BUT YES -- THE PEOPLE IN THAT HEAVEN IN ULSTER COUNTY WILL BE GOOD NEIGHBORS TO US HERE IN DUTCHESS COUNTY! GOOD DAY THEN, GENTLEMEN.
HEH -- HE'S DUCKING WHETHER HE'LL SUPPORT LYNCHING LEGISLATION.
VRRMMMN-N
HAVE YOUR FUN NOW. PRETTY SOON IT'S GOING TO BE ALL EUROPE, ALL THE TIME.
HITLER OR STALIN -- IT'S NOT EASY TO FIGURE OUT WHO TO HATE MORE!
OR MUSSOLINI. LUCE IS WAY TOO EASY ON THE ITALIANS...
LUCE, AND TUGWELL. GOSH, I MISS THE TUGWELL -- SUCH A GOOD SUBJECT! YOU HEAR HE STOPPED BY TO SEE IL DUCE? ...AND WE MISSED THE STORY!
FDR 1

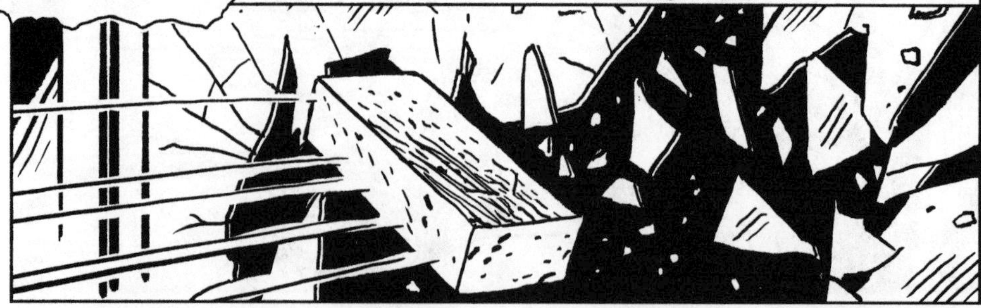
November 1938
Unemployment: 17.7 %
Dow Jones Industrial
Average (Nov. 1): 151
Roosevelt suffered his first big **setbacks** in the November midterms. But FDR's Democrats still held majorities. The midterms in any case didn't have the effect expected because of **shocking news** ...

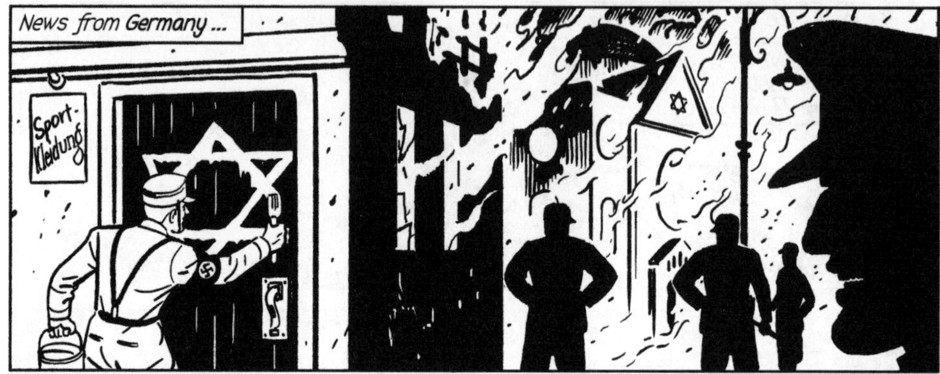
News from **Germany** ...
Sport-
Kleidung

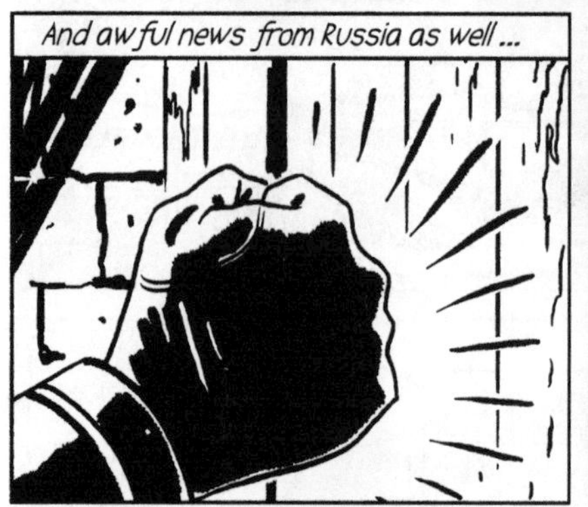
And awful news from Russia as well ...

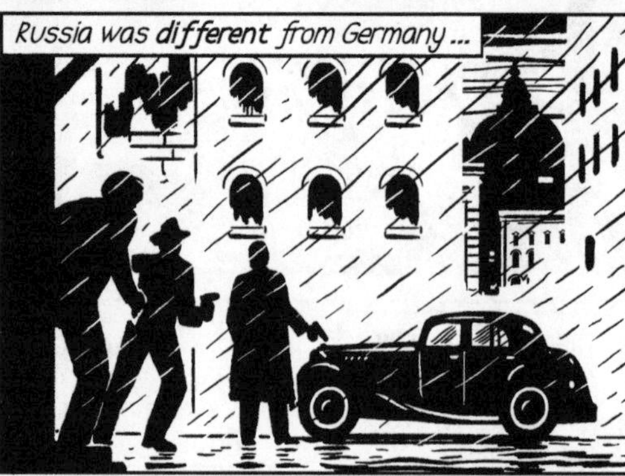
Russia was **different** from Germany ...

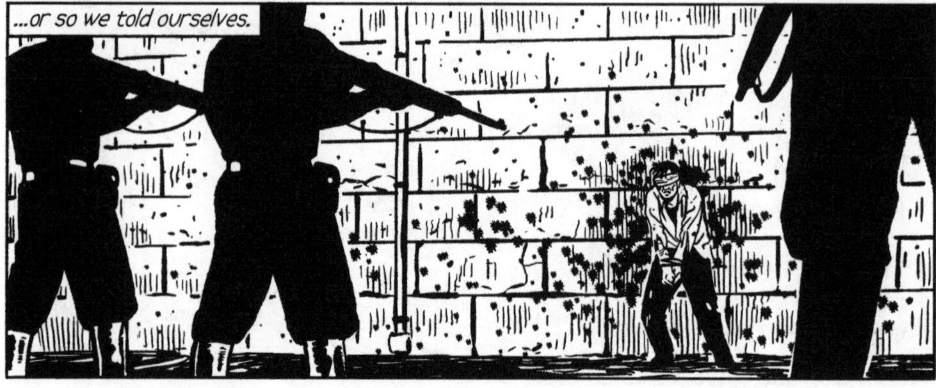
...or so we told ourselves.

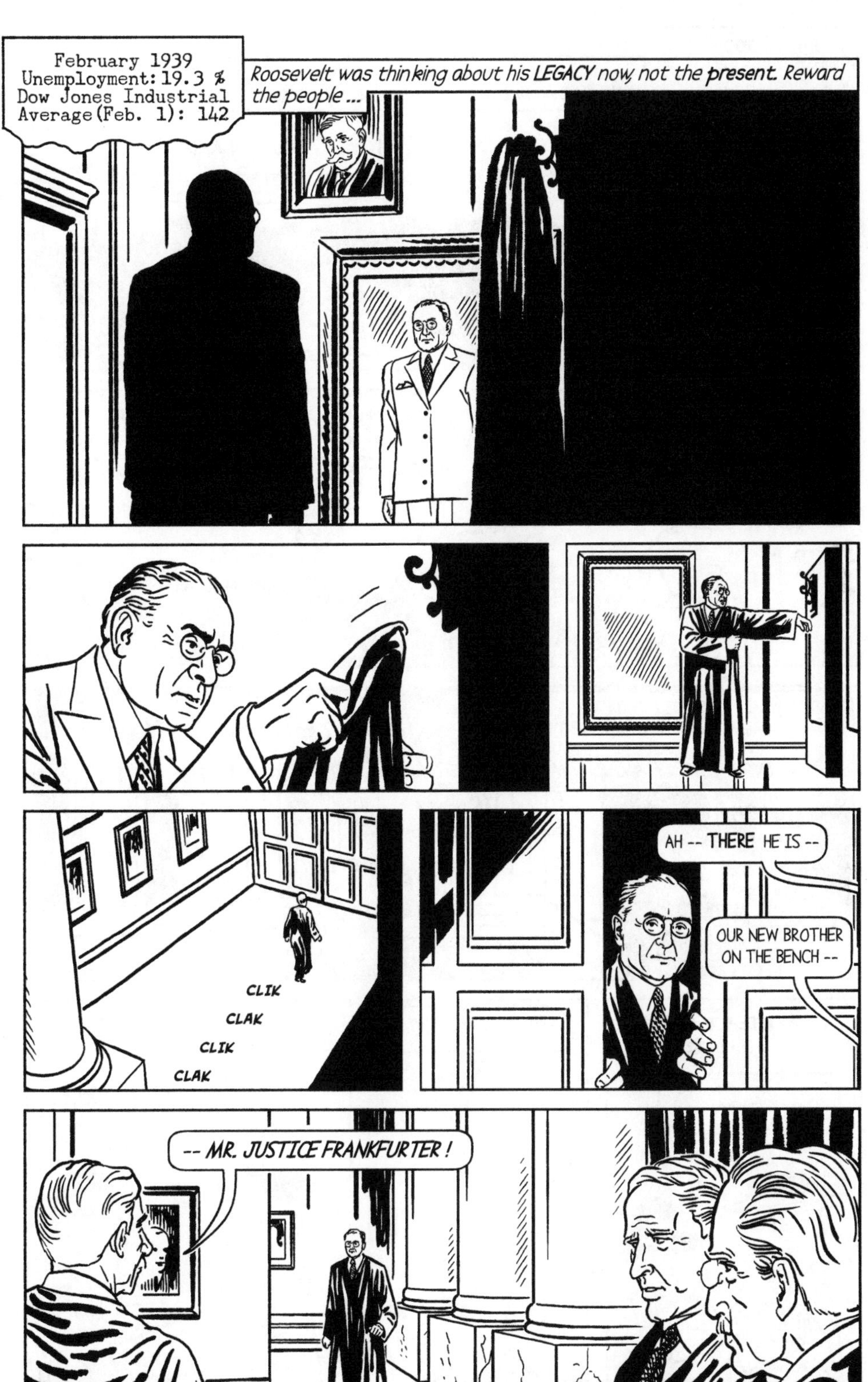
February 1939
Unemployment: 19.3 %
Dow Jones Industrial
Average (Feb. 1): 142
Roosevelt was thinking about his LEGACY now, not the present. Reward the people ...
CLIK
CLAK
CLIK
CLAK
AH -- THERE HE IS --
OUR NEW BROTHER ON THE BENCH --
-- MR. JUSTICE FRANKFURTER !

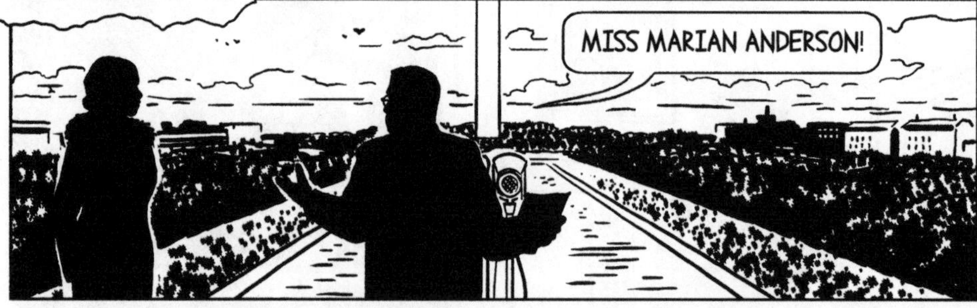
April 1939
Unemployment: 20.7 %
Dow Jones Industrial
Average (April 1): 133
I considered myself FDR's **opponent**, but I couldn't help but admire the way he and Mrs. Roosevelt supported Marian Anderson ...
MISS MARIAN ANDERSON!

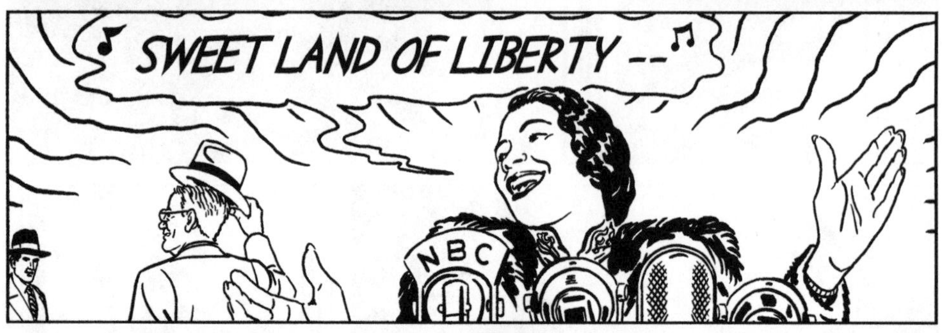
SWEET LAND OF LIBERTY --
NBC

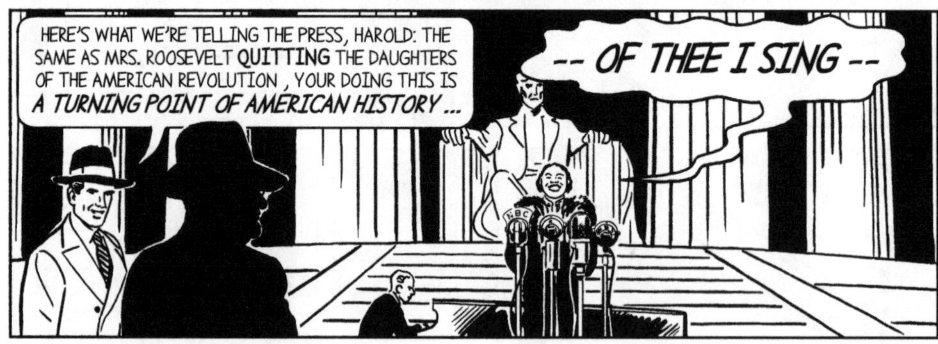
HERE'S WHAT WE'RE TELLING THE PRESS, HAROLD: THE SAME AS MRS. ROOSEVELT **QUITTING** THE DAUGHTERS OF THE AMERICAN REVOLUTION, YOUR DOING THIS IS ***A TURNING POINT OF AMERICAN HISTORY ...***
-- OF THEE I SING --

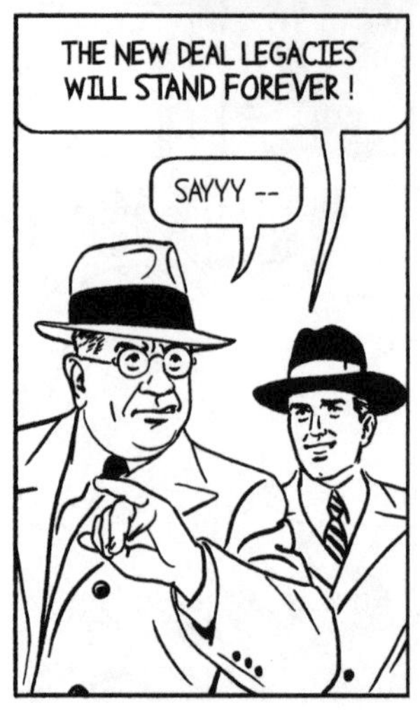
THE NEW DEAL LEGACIES WILL STAND FOREVER!
SAYYY --

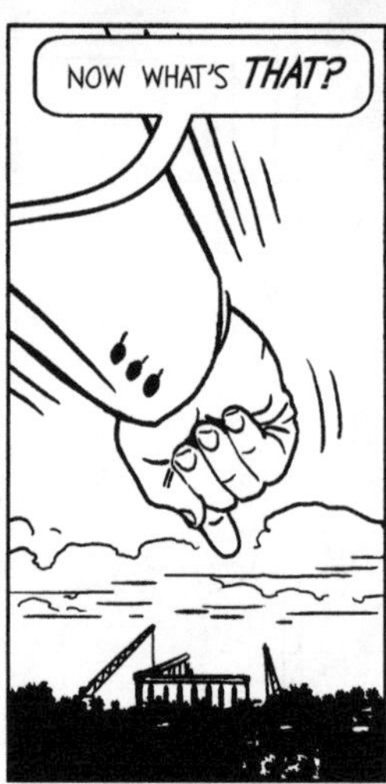
NOW WHAT'S *THAT?*

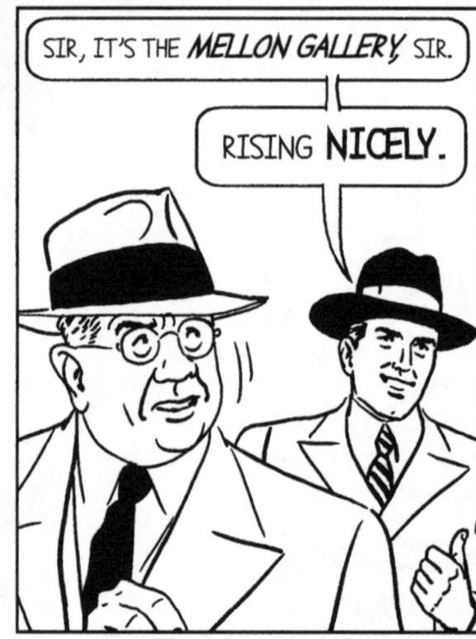
SIR, IT'S THE *MELLON GALLERY,* SIR.
RISING **NICELY.**

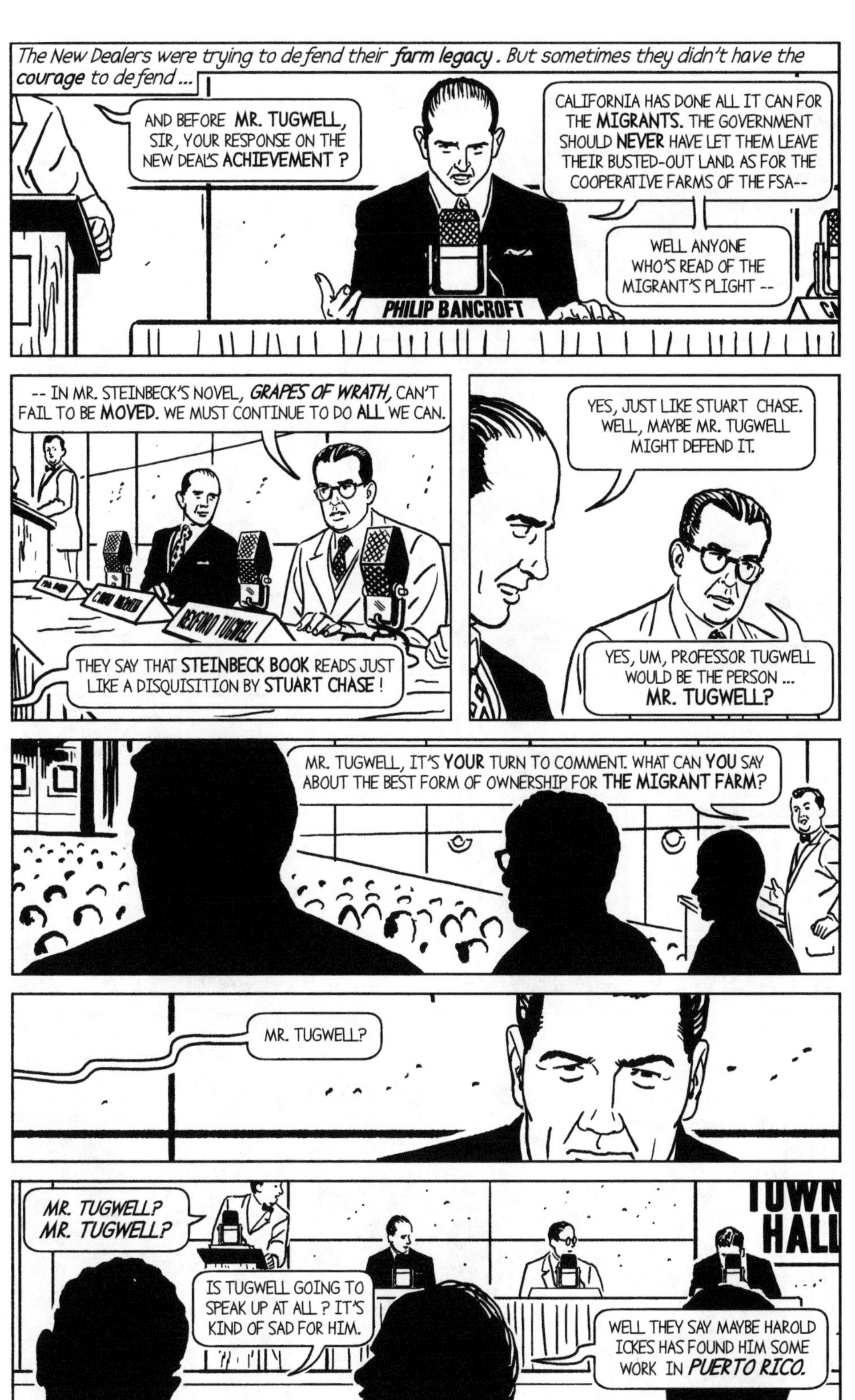
The New Dealers were trying to defend their farm legacy. But sometimes they didn't have the courage to defend ...
AND BEFORE MR. TUGWELL, SIR, YOUR RESPONSE ON THE NEW DEAL'S ACHIEVEMENT ?
CALIFORNIA HAS DONE ALL IT CAN FOR THE MIGRANTS. THE GOVERNMENT SHOULD NEVER HAVE LET THEM LEAVE THEIR BUSTED-OUT LAND. AS FOR THE COOPERATIVE FARMS OF THE FSA--
WELL ANYONE WHO'S READ OF THE MIGRANT'S PLIGHT --
PHILIP BANCROFT
-- IN MR. STEINBECK'S NOVEL, GRAPES OF WRATH, CAN'T FAIL TO BE MOVED. WE MUST CONTINUE TO DO ALL WE CAN.
THEY SAY THAT STEINBECK BOOK READS JUST LIKE A DISQUISITION BY STUART CHASE !
YES, JUST LIKE STUART CHASE. WELL, MAYBE MR. TUGWELL MIGHT DEFEND IT.
YES, UM, PROFESSOR TUGWELL WOULD BE THE PERSON ... MR. TUGWELL?
MR. TUGWELL, IT'S YOUR TURN TO COMMENT. WHAT CAN YOU SAY ABOUT THE BEST FORM OF OWNERSHIP FOR THE MIGRANT FARM?
MR. TUGWELL?
MR. TUGWELL? MR. TUGWELL?
TOWN HALL
IS TUGWELL GOING TO SPEAK UP AT ALL ? IT'S KIND OF SAD FOR HIM.
WELL THEY SAY MAYBE HAROLD ICKES HAS FOUND HIM SOME WORK IN PUERTO RICO.

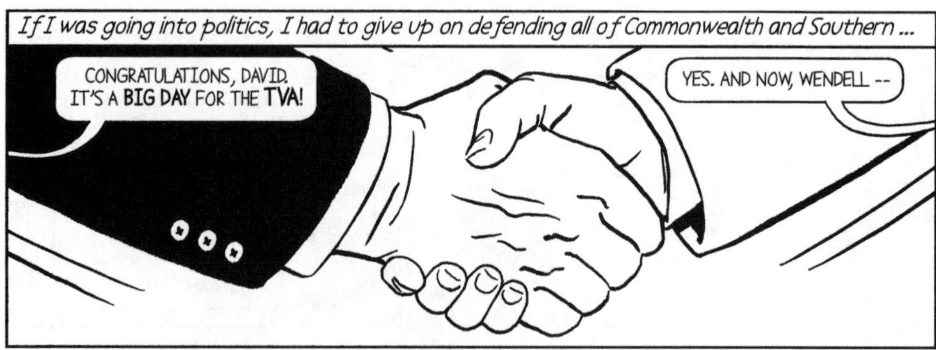
If I was going into politics, I had to give up on defending all of Commonwealth and Southern ...
CONGRATULATIONS, DAVID. IT'S A BIG DAY FOR THE TVA!
YES. AND NOW, WENDELL --

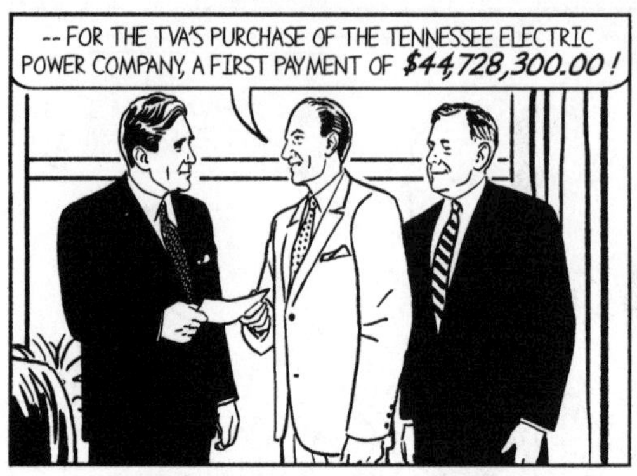
-- FOR THE TVA'S PURCHASE OF THE TENNESSEE ELECTRIC POWER COMPANY, A FIRST PAYMENT OF $44,728,300.00 !

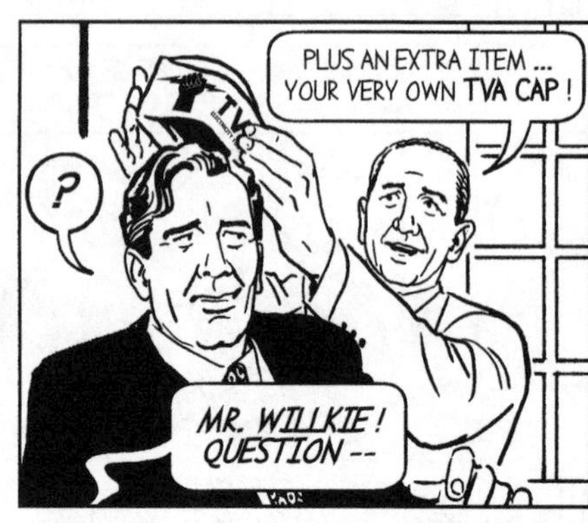
PLUS AN EXTRA ITEM ... YOUR VERY OWN TVA CAP !
?
MR. WILLKIE! QUESTION --

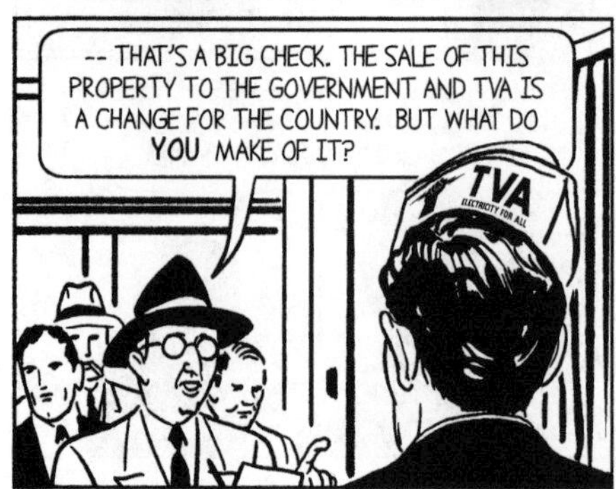
-- THAT'S A BIG CHECK. THE SALE OF THIS PROPERTY TO THE GOVERNMENT AND TVA IS A CHANGE FOR THE COUNTRY. BUT WHAT DO YOU MAKE OF IT?
TVA
ELECTRICITY FOR ALL

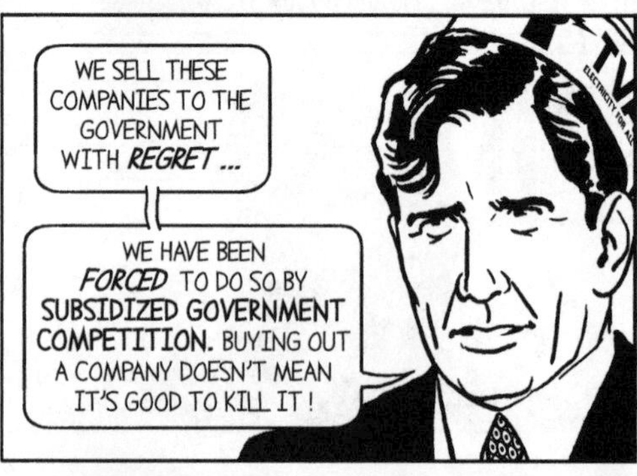
WE SELL THESE COMPANIES TO THE GOVERNMENT WITH REGRET ...
WE HAVE BEEN FORCED TO DO SO BY SUBSIDIZED GOVERNMENT COMPETITION. BUYING OUT A COMPANY DOESN'T MEAN IT'S GOOD TO KILL IT !

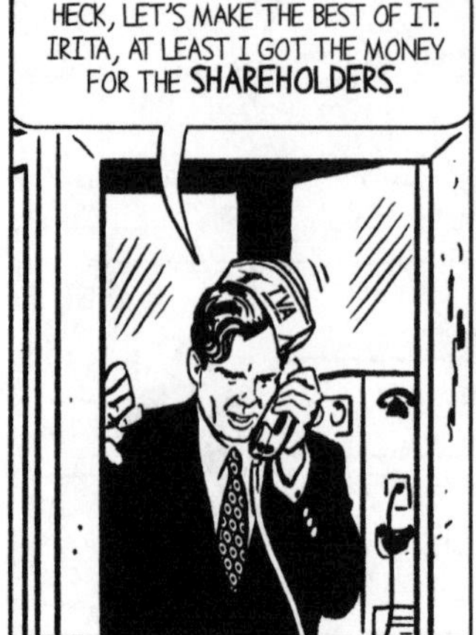
HECK, LET'S MAKE THE BEST OF IT. IRITA, AT LEAST I GOT THE MONEY FOR THE SHAREHOLDERS.

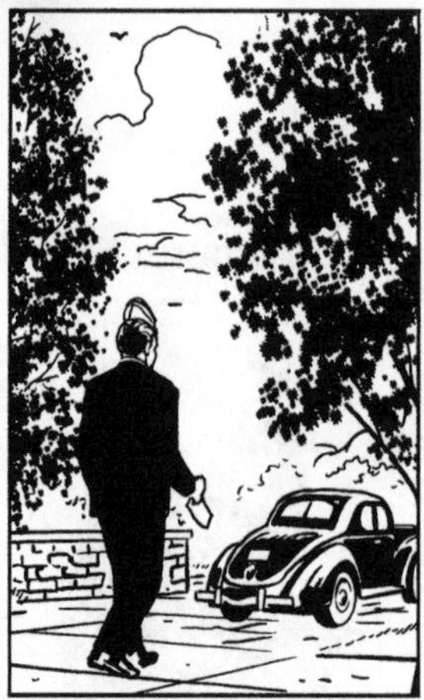

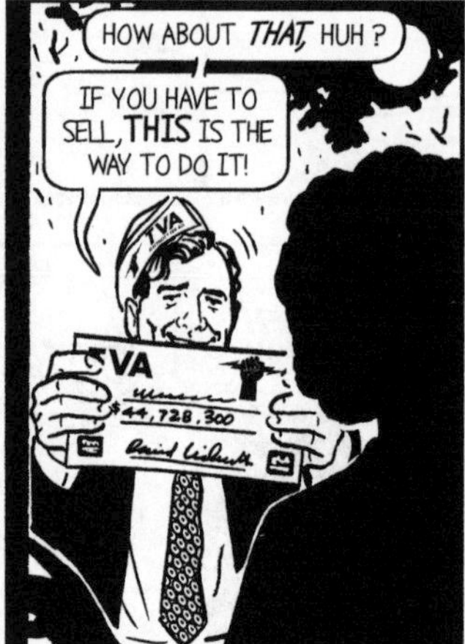
HOW ABOUT THAT, HUH ?
IF YOU HAVE TO SELL, THIS IS THE WAY TO DO IT!
TVA
$44,728,300

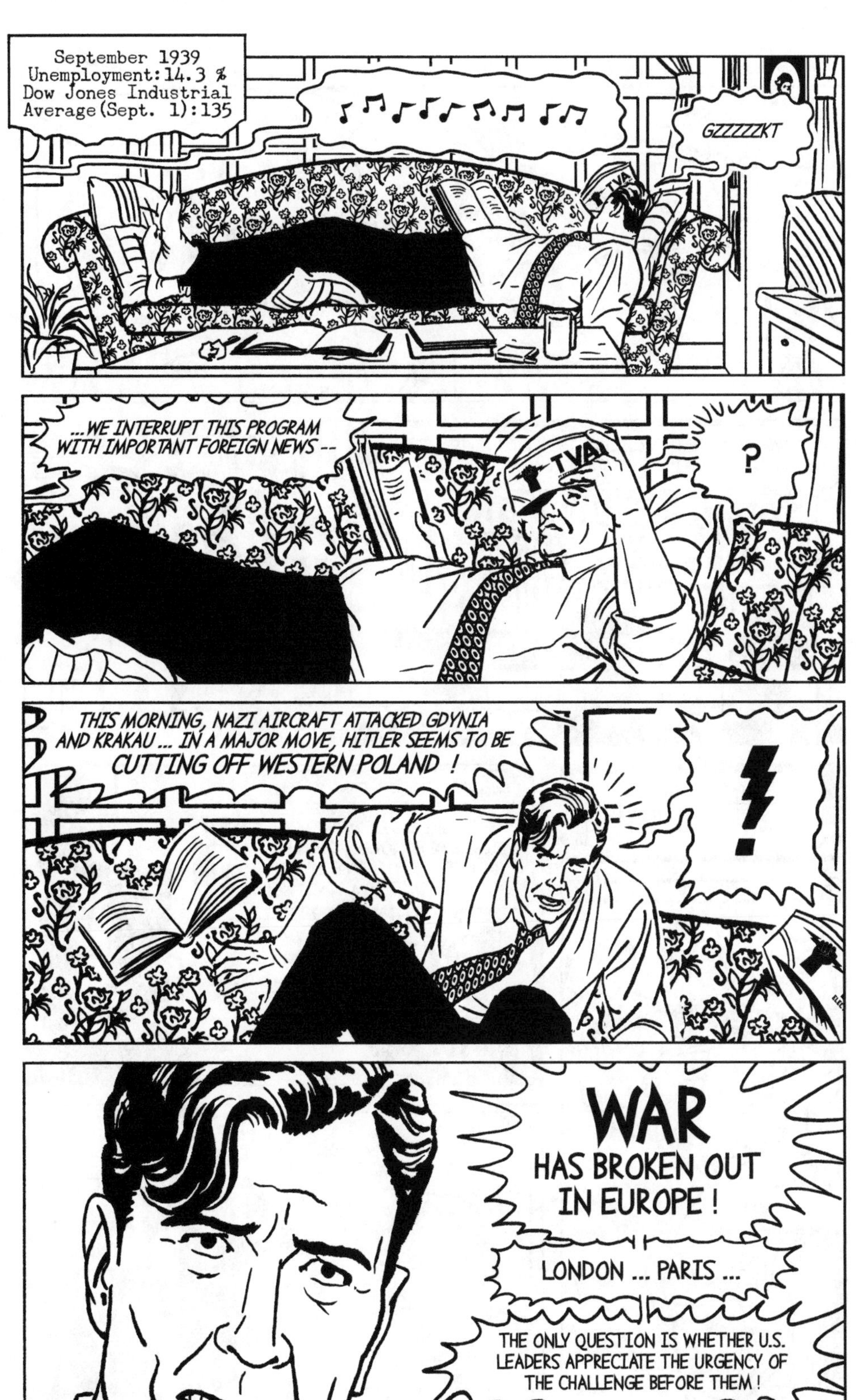
September 1939
Unemployment: 14.3 %
Dow Jones Industrial
Average (Sept. 1): 135
GZZZZZKT
TVA
...WE INTERRUPT THIS PROGRAM
WITH IMPORTANT FOREIGN NEWS --
?
THIS MORNING, NAZI AIRCRAFT ATTACKED GDYNIA
AND KRAKAU ... IN A MAJOR MOVE, HITLER SEEMS TO BE
CUTTING OFF WESTERN POLAND !
!
WAR
HAS BROKEN OUT
IN EUROPE !
LONDON ... PARIS ...
THE ONLY QUESTION IS WHETHER U.S.
LEADERS APPRECIATE THE URGENCY OF
THE CHALLENGE BEFORE THEM !

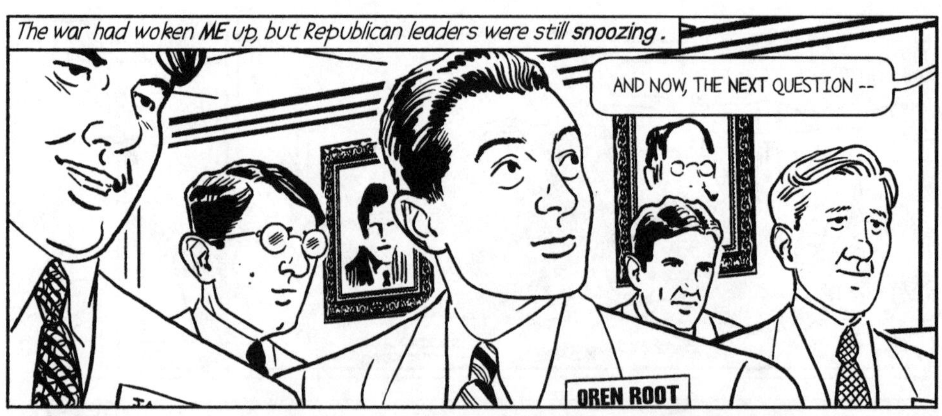
The war had woken ME up, but Republican leaders were still snoozing.
AND NOW, THE NEXT QUESTION --
OREN ROOT

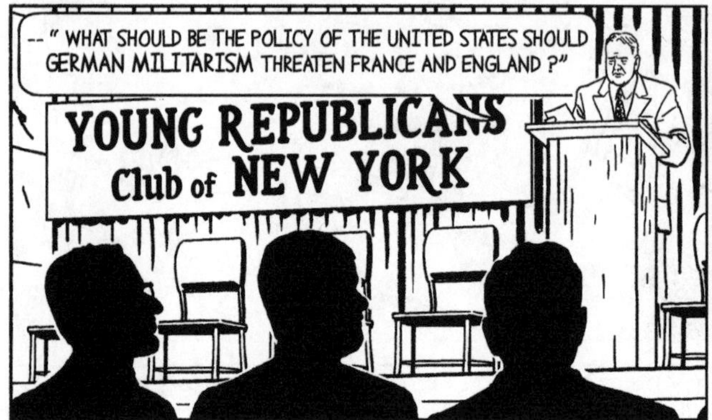
-- " WHAT SHOULD BE THE POLICY OF THE UNITED STATES SHOULD GERMAN MILITARISM THREATEN FRANCE AND ENGLAND ?"
YOUNG REPUBLICANS Club of NEW YORK

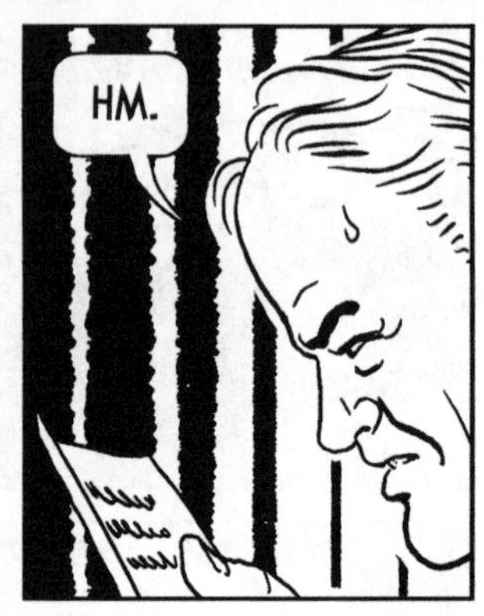
HM.

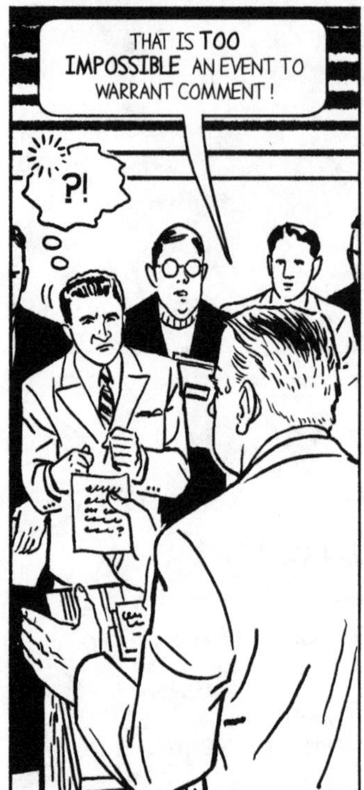
THAT IS TOO IMPOSSIBLE AN EVENT TO WARRANT COMMENT !
?!

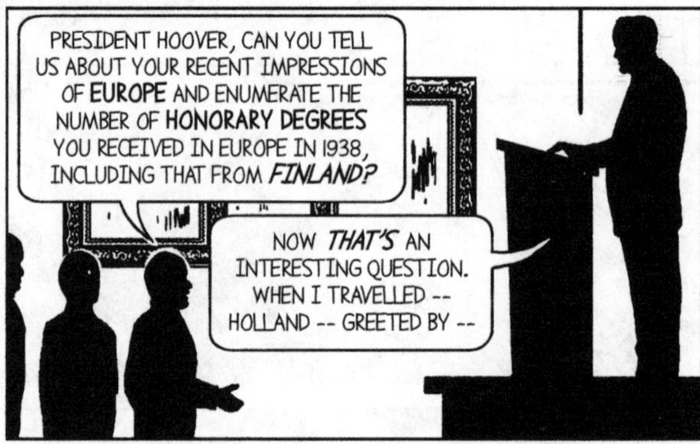
PRESIDENT HOOVER, CAN YOU TELL US ABOUT YOUR RECENT IMPRESSIONS OF EUROPE AND ENUMERATE THE NUMBER OF HONORARY DEGREES YOU RECEIVED IN EUROPE IN 1938, INCLUDING THAT FROM FINLAND?
NOW THAT'S AN INTERESTING QUESTION. WHEN I TRAVELLED -- HOLLAND -- GREETED BY --

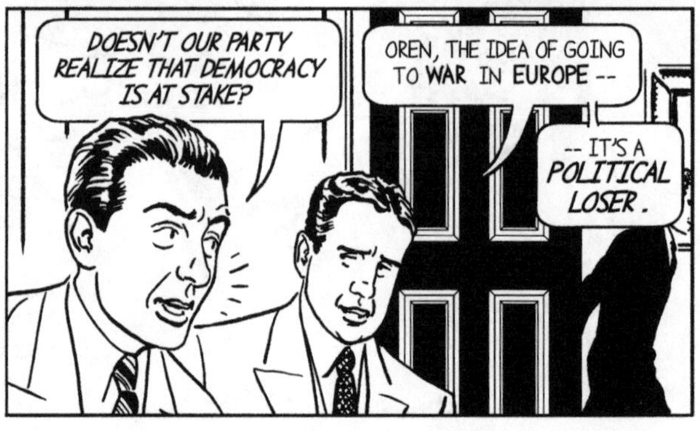
DOESN'T OUR PARTY REALIZE THAT DEMOCRACY IS AT STAKE?
OREN, THE IDEA OF GOING TO WAR IN EUROPE --
-- IT'S A POLITICAL LOSER.

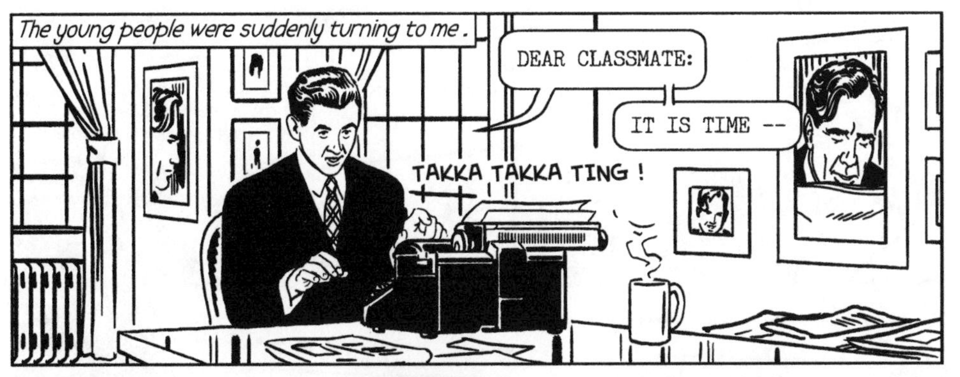
The young people were suddenly turning to me.
DEAR CLASSMATE:
IT IS TIME --
TAKKA TAKKA TING !

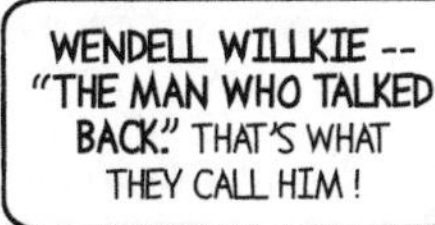
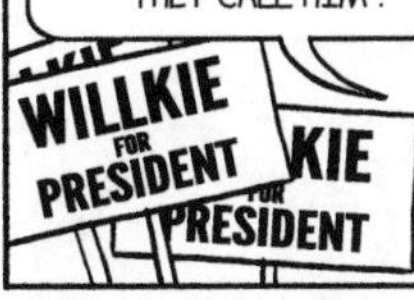
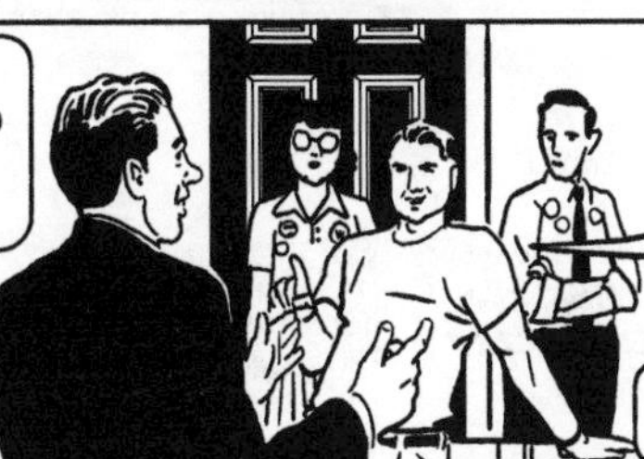
WENDELL WILLKIE -- "THE MAN WHO TALKED BACK." THAT'S WHAT THEY CALL HIM !
WILLKIE FOR PRESIDENT
WILLKIE CLUB
YUP, OREN, THAT'S THE PLAN ON THE *DOMESTIC* SIDE -- TELL THEM THE **TAXES** ARE TOO HIGH. STICK IT TO **TNEC** AND **THURMAN ARNOLD** !
-- AND ON THE FOREIGN SIDE, TELL THEM THAT WE SHOULD TAKE EUROPE **SERIOUSLY**.

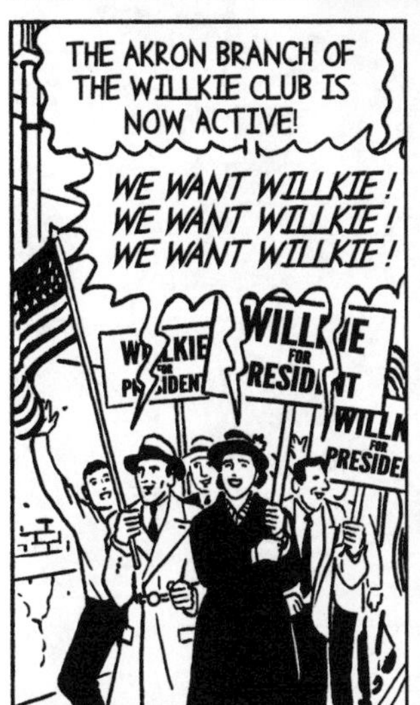
THE AKRON BRANCH OF THE WILLKIE CLUB IS NOW ACTIVE!
WE WANT WILLKIE! WE WANT WILLKIE! WE WANT WILLKIE!

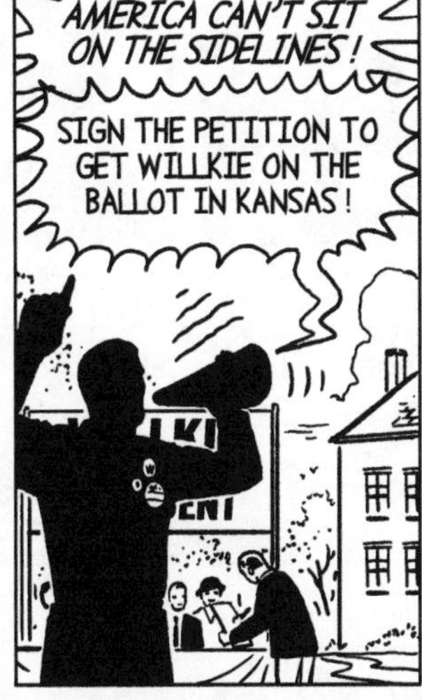
AMERICA CAN'T SIT ON THE SIDELINES!
SIGN THE PETITION TO GET WILLKIE ON THE BALLOT IN KANSAS !

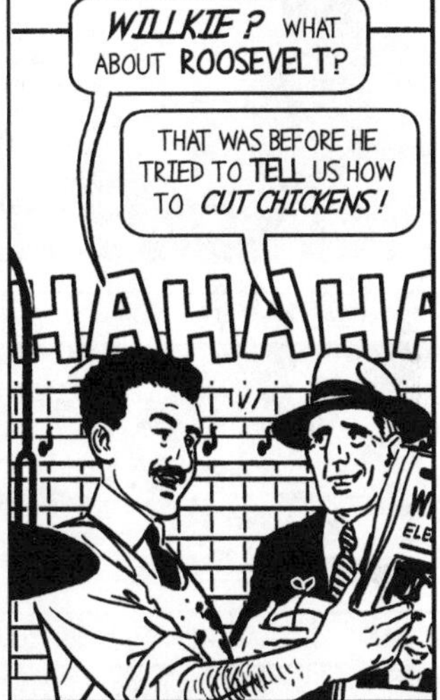
WILLKIE? WHAT ABOUT **ROOSEVELT**?
THAT WAS BEFORE HE TRIED TO **TELL** US HOW TO *CUT CHICKENS*!
HAHAHA

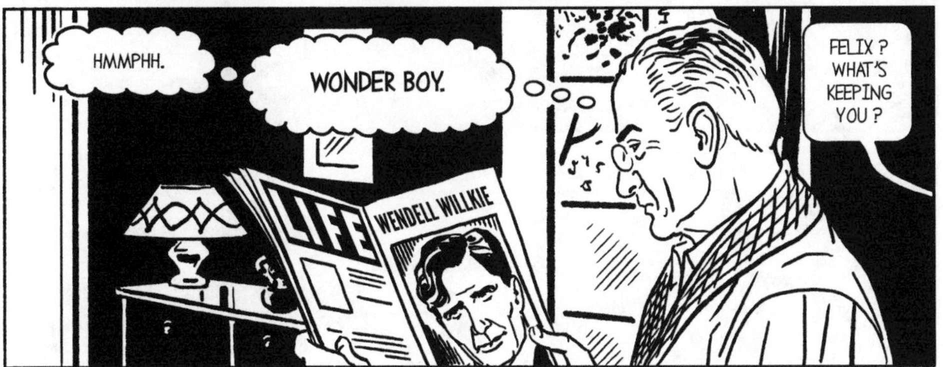
HMMPHH.
WONDER BOY.
FELIX ? WHAT'S KEEPING YOU ?
LIFE
WENDELL WILLKIE

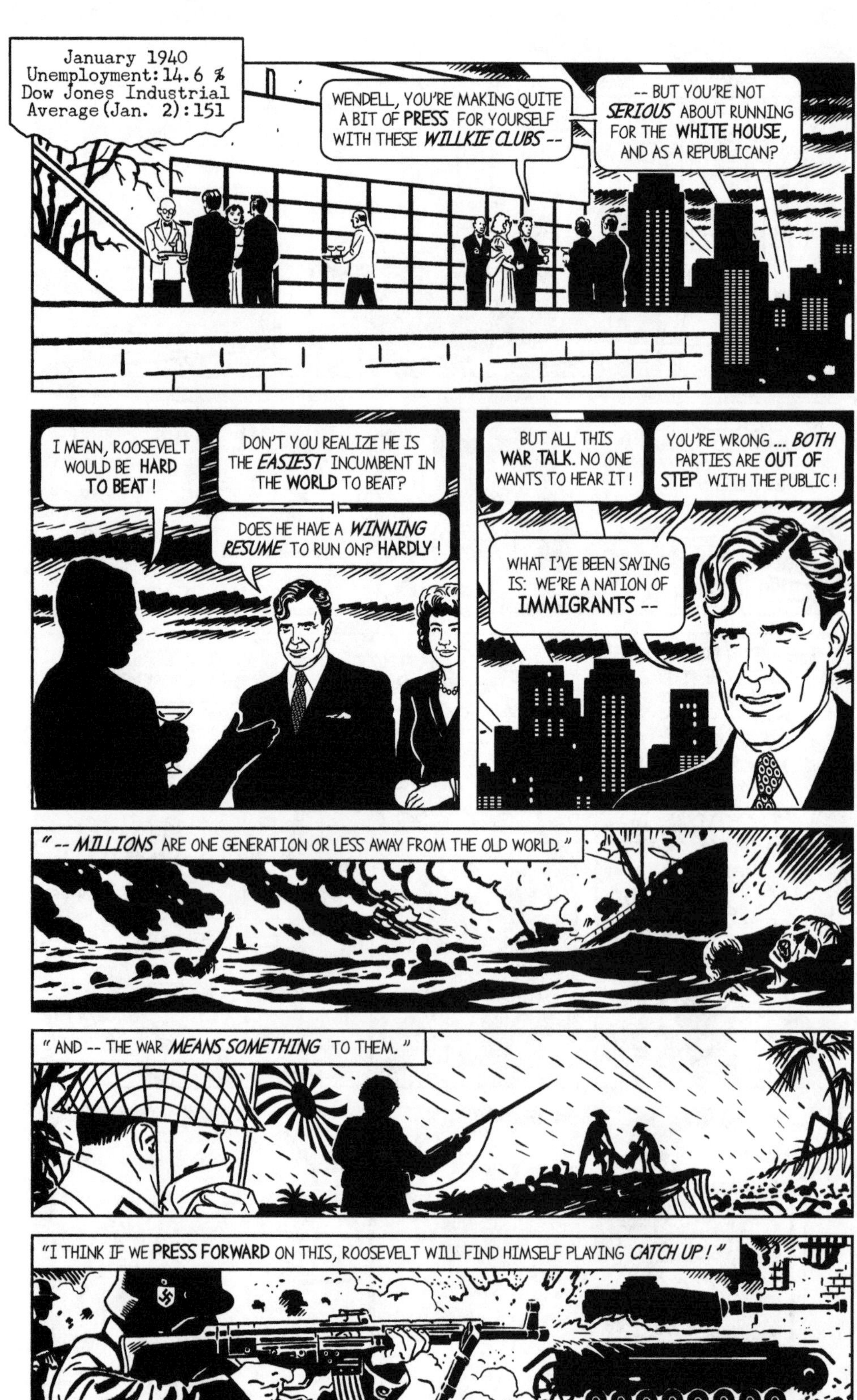
January 1940
Unemployment: 14.6 %
Dow Jones Industrial
Average (Jan. 2): 151
WENDELL, YOU'RE MAKING QUITE A BIT OF PRESS FOR YOURSELF WITH THESE WILLKIE CLUBS --
-- BUT YOU'RE NOT SERIOUS ABOUT RUNNING FOR THE WHITE HOUSE, AND AS A REPUBLICAN?
I MEAN, ROOSEVELT WOULD BE HARD TO BEAT!
DON'T YOU REALIZE HE IS THE EASIEST INCUMBENT IN THE WORLD TO BEAT?
DOES HE HAVE A WINNING RESUME TO RUN ON? HARDLY!
BUT ALL THIS WAR TALK. NO ONE WANTS TO HEAR IT!
YOU'RE WRONG ... BOTH PARTIES ARE OUT OF STEP WITH THE PUBLIC!
WHAT I'VE BEEN SAYING IS: WE'RE A NATION OF IMMIGRANTS --
" -- MILLIONS ARE ONE GENERATION OR LESS AWAY FROM THE OLD WORLD."
" AND -- THE WAR MEANS SOMETHING TO THEM."
"I THINK IF WE PRESS FORWARD ON THIS, ROOSEVELT WILL FIND HIMSELF PLAYING CATCH UP!"

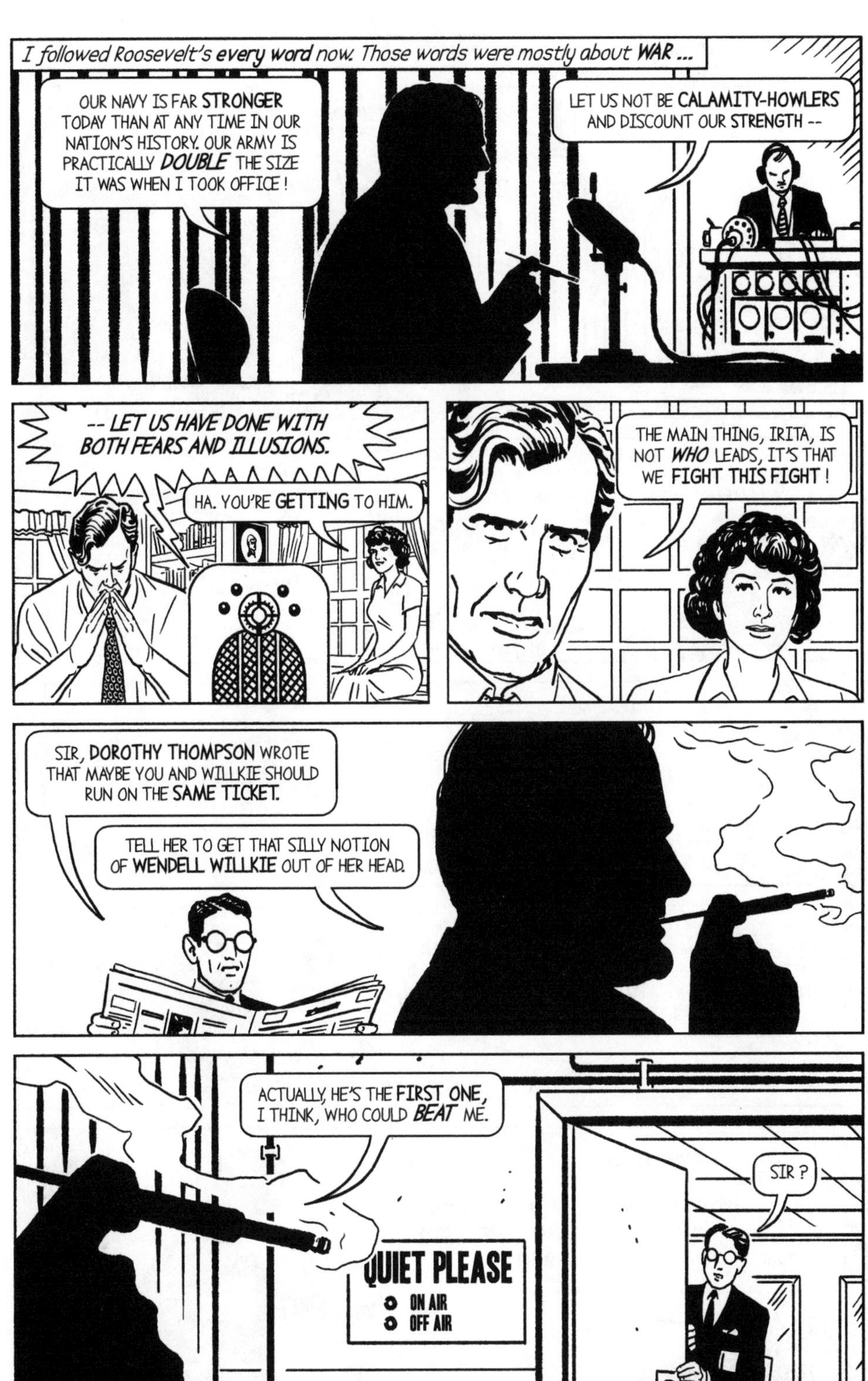
I followed Roosevelt's **every word** now. Those words were mostly about **WAR** ...
OUR NAVY IS FAR **STRONGER** TODAY THAN AT ANY TIME IN OUR NATION'S HISTORY. OUR ARMY IS PRACTICALLY ***DOUBLE*** THE SIZE IT WAS WHEN I TOOK OFFICE !
LET US NOT BE **CALAMITY-HOWLERS** AND DISCOUNT OUR **STRENGTH** --
-- LET US HAVE DONE WITH BOTH FEARS AND ILLUSIONS.
HA. YOU'RE **GETTING** TO HIM.
THE MAIN THING, IRITA, IS NOT ***WHO*** LEADS, IT'S THAT WE **FIGHT THIS FIGHT** !
SIR, **DOROTHY THOMPSON** WROTE THAT MAYBE YOU AND WILLKIE SHOULD RUN ON THE **SAME TICKET.**
TELL HER TO GET THAT SILLY NOTION OF **WENDELL WILLKIE** OUT OF HER HEAD.
ACTUALLY, HE'S THE **FIRST ONE**, I THINK, WHO COULD ***BEAT*** ME.
QUIET PLEASE
ON AIR
OFF AIR
SIR ?

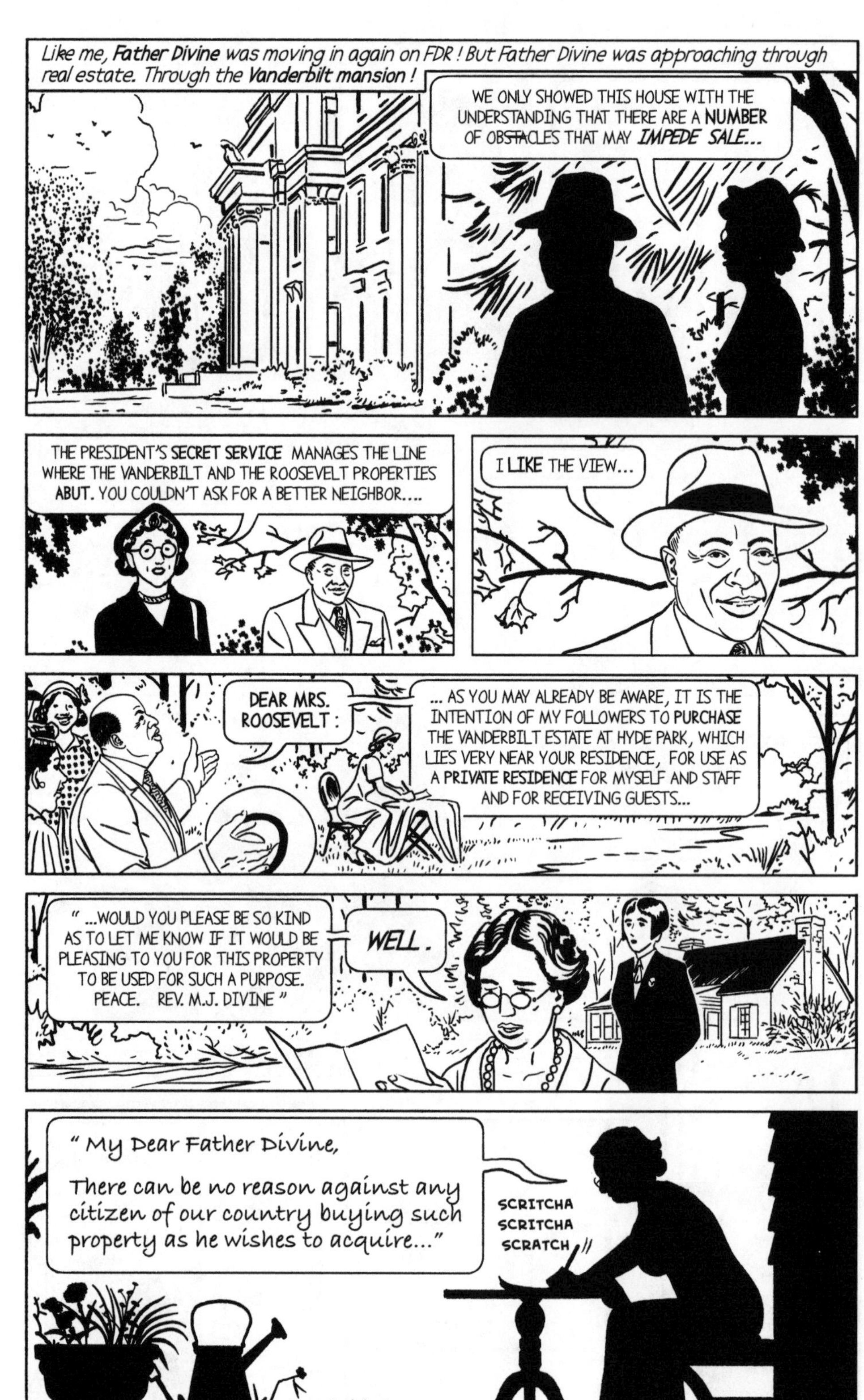
Like me, **Father Divine** was moving in again on FDR! But Father Divine was approaching through real estate. Through the **Vanderbilt mansion**!
WE ONLY SHOWED THIS HOUSE WITH THE UNDERSTANDING THAT THERE ARE A NUMBER OF OBSTACLES THAT MAY IMPEDE SALE...
THE PRESIDENT'S SECRET SERVICE MANAGES THE LINE WHERE THE VANDERBILT AND THE ROOSEVELT PROPERTIES ABUT. YOU COULDN'T ASK FOR A BETTER NEIGHBOR....
I LIKE THE VIEW...
DEAR MRS. ROOSEVELT:
... AS YOU MAY ALREADY BE AWARE, IT IS THE INTENTION OF MY FOLLOWERS TO PURCHASE THE VANDERBILT ESTATE AT HYDE PARK, WHICH LIES VERY NEAR YOUR RESIDENCE, FOR USE AS A PRIVATE RESIDENCE FOR MYSELF AND STAFF AND FOR RECEIVING GUESTS...
" ...WOULD YOU PLEASE BE SO KIND AS TO LET ME KNOW IF IT WOULD BE PLEASING TO YOU FOR THIS PROPERTY TO BE USED FOR SUCH A PURPOSE. PEACE. REV. M.J. DIVINE "
WELL.
" My Dear Father Divine,
There can be no reason against any citizen of our country buying such property as he wishes to acquire..."
SCRITCHA
SCRITCHA
SCRATCH

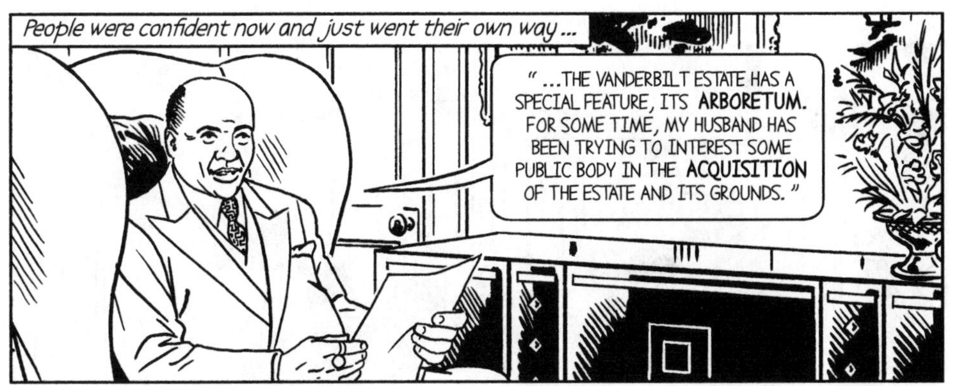
People were confident now and just went their own way...
" ...THE VANDERBILT ESTATE HAS A SPECIAL FEATURE, ITS ARBORETUM. FOR SOME TIME, MY HUSBAND HAS BEEN TRYING TO INTEREST SOME PUBLIC BODY IN THE ACQUISITION OF THE ESTATE AND ITS GROUNDS."

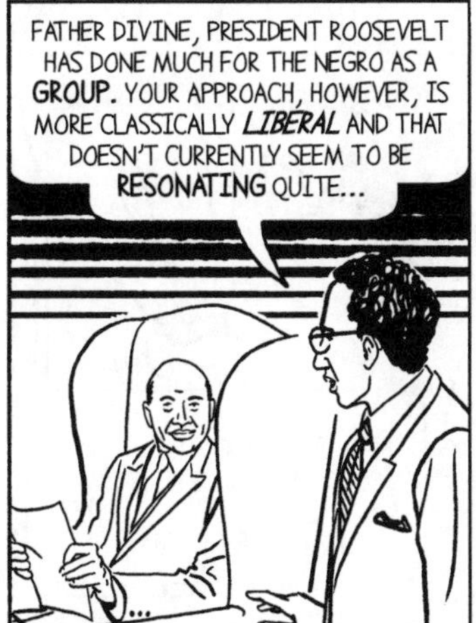
FATHER DIVINE, PRESIDENT ROOSEVELT HAS DONE MUCH FOR THE NEGRO AS A GROUP. YOUR APPROACH, HOWEVER, IS MORE CLASSICALLY LIBERAL AND THAT DOESN'T CURRENTLY SEEM TO BE RESONATING QUITE...
...

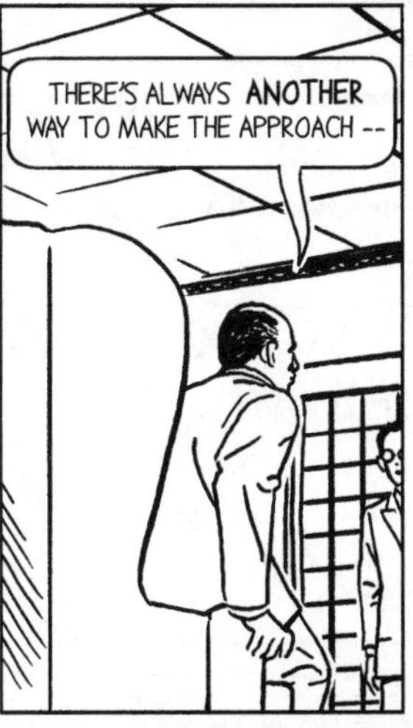
THERE'S ALWAYS ANOTHER WAY TO MAKE THE APPROACH --

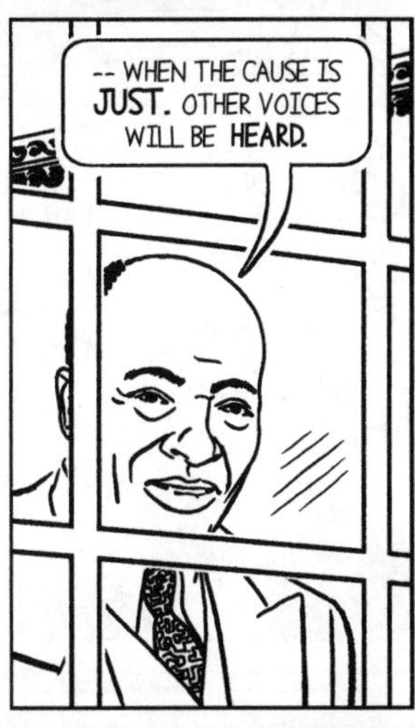
-- WHEN THE CAUSE IS JUST. OTHER VOICES WILL BE HEARD.

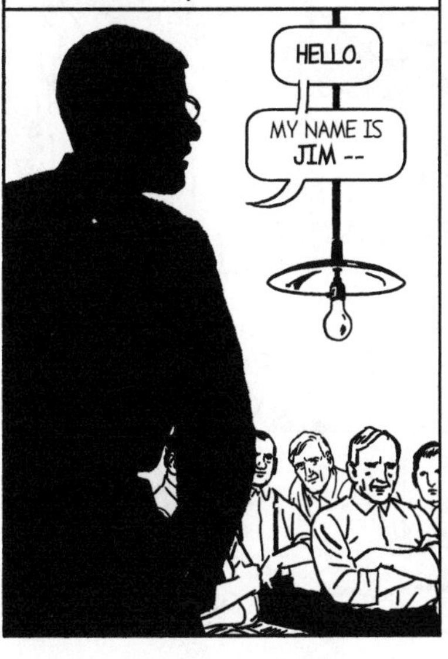
In a time of war, and in a different manner than Father Divine, Alcoholics Anonymous was helping more souls than ever find peace...
HELLO.
MY NAME IS JIM --

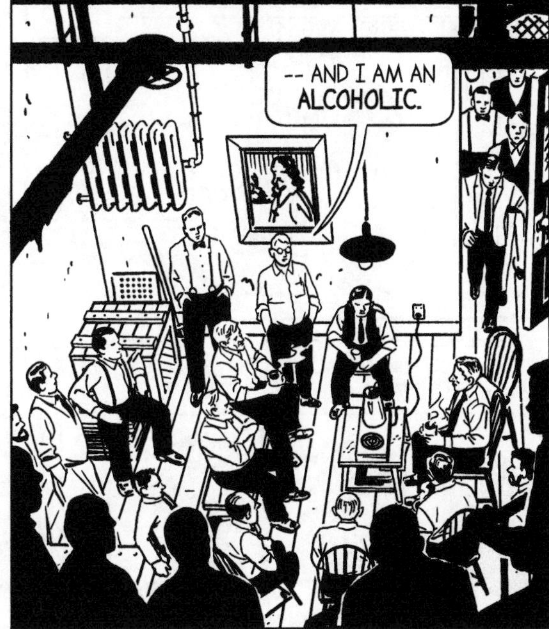
-- AND I AM AN ALCOHOLIC.

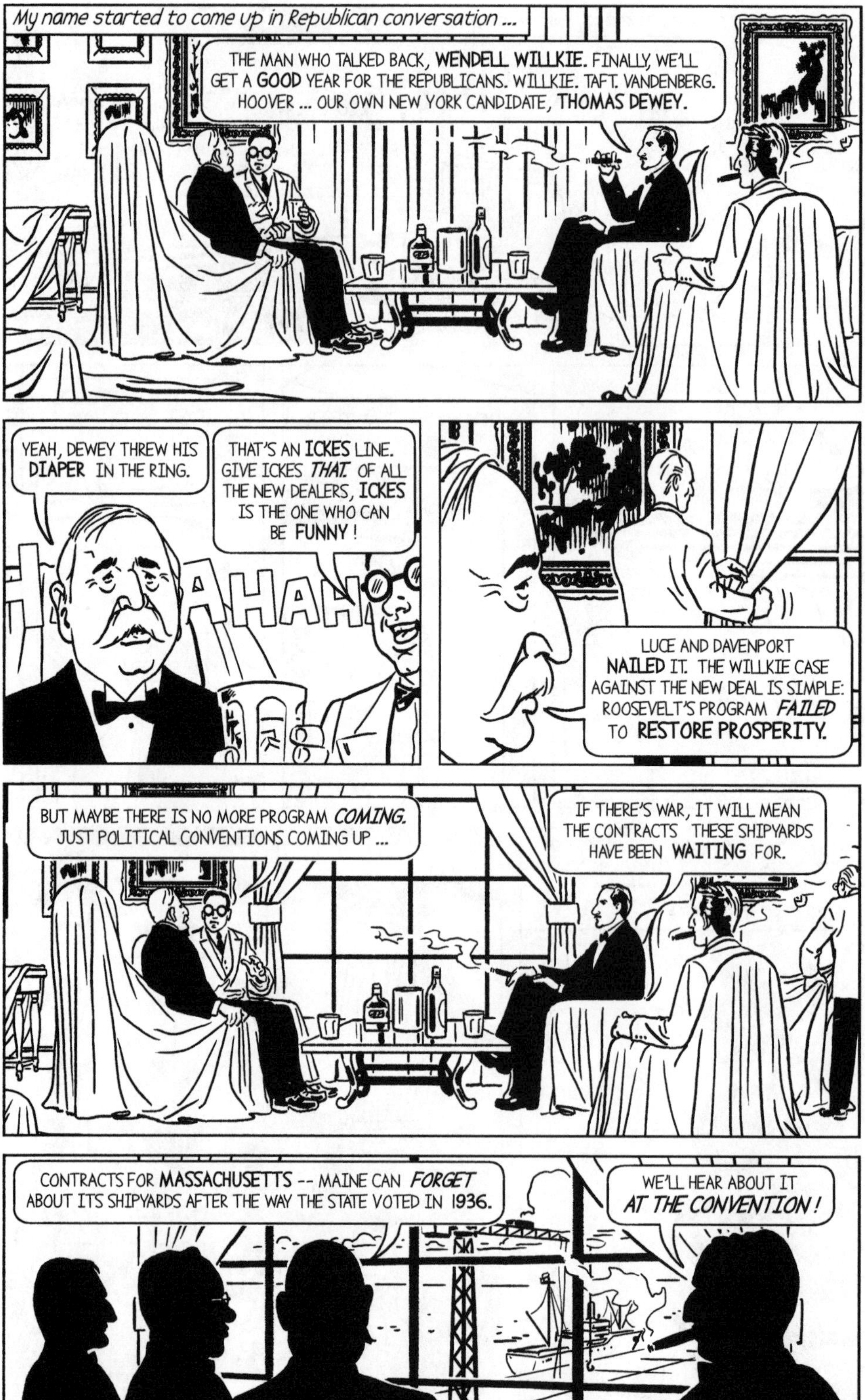

My name started to come up in Republican conversation ...

THE MAN WHO TALKED BACK, **WENDELL WILLKIE.** FINALLY, WE'LL GET A **GOOD** YEAR FOR THE REPUBLICANS. WILLKIE. TAFT. VANDENBERG. HOOVER ... OUR OWN NEW YORK CANDIDATE, **THOMAS DEWEY.**

YEAH, DEWEY THREW HIS **DIAPER** IN THE RING.

THAT'S AN **ICKES** LINE. GIVE ICKES *THAT.* OF ALL THE NEW DEALERS, **ICKES** IS THE ONE WHO CAN BE **FUNNY** !

HAHAHAH

LUCE AND DAVENPORT **NAILED** IT. THE WILLKIE CASE AGAINST THE NEW DEAL IS SIMPLE: ROOSEVELT'S PROGRAM ***FAILED*** TO **RESTORE PROSPERITY.**

BUT MAYBE THERE IS NO MORE PROGRAM *COMING.* JUST POLITICAL CONVENTIONS COMING UP ...

IF THERE'S WAR, IT WILL MEAN THE CONTRACTS THESE SHIPYARDS HAVE BEEN **WAITING** FOR.

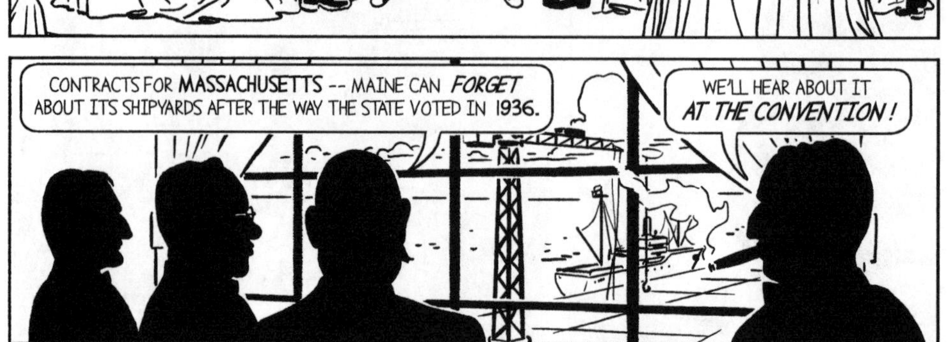

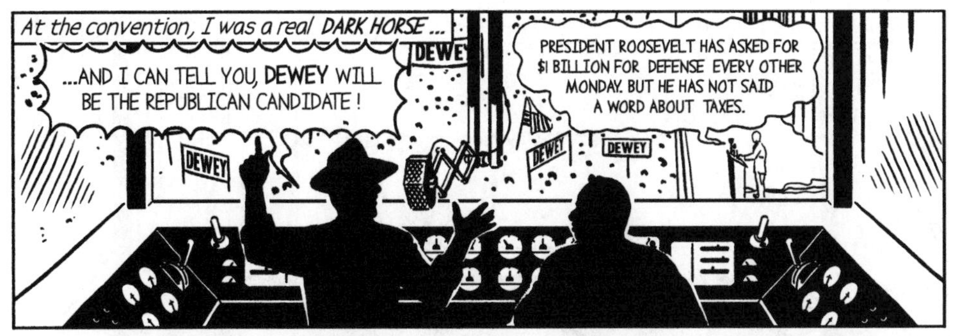
At the convention, I was a real DARK HORSE ...
...AND I CAN TELL YOU, DEWEY WILL BE THE REPUBLICAN CANDIDATE !
PRESIDENT ROOSEVELT HAS ASKED FOR $1 BILLION FOR DEFENSE EVERY OTHER MONDAY. BUT HE HAS NOT SAID A WORD ABOUT TAXES.
DEWEY
DEWEY
DEWEY
DEWEY

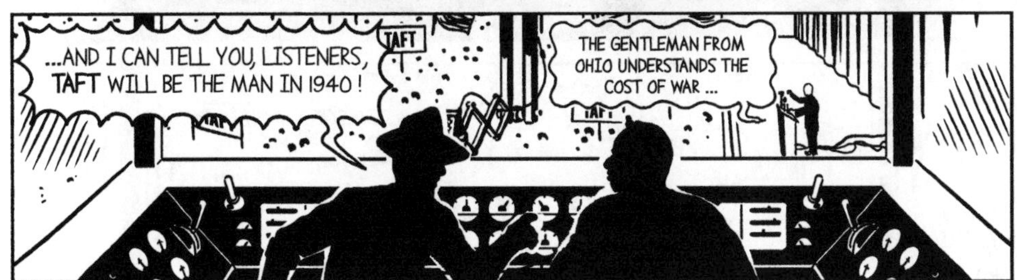
...AND I CAN TELL YOU, LISTENERS, TAFT WILL BE THE MAN IN 1940 !
THE GENTLEMAN FROM OHIO UNDERSTANDS THE COST OF WAR ...
TAFT

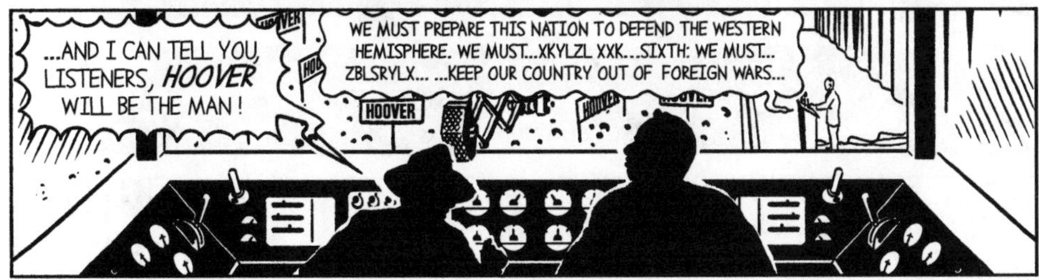
...AND I CAN TELL YOU, LISTENERS, HOOVER WILL BE THE MAN !
WE MUST PREPARE THIS NATION TO DEFEND THE WESTERN HEMISPHERE. WE MUST...XKYLZL XXK...SIXTH: WE MUST... ZBLSRYLX... ...KEEP OUR COUNTRY OUT OF FOREIGN WARS...
HOOVER

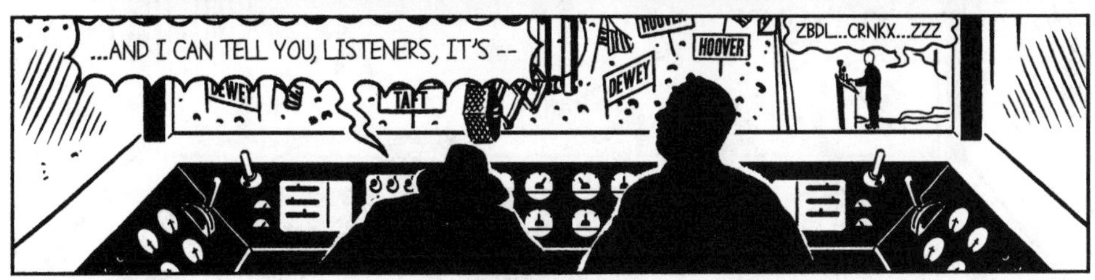
...AND I CAN TELL YOU, LISTENERS, IT'S --
ZBDL...CRNKX...ZZZ
HOOVER
DEWEY
TAFT

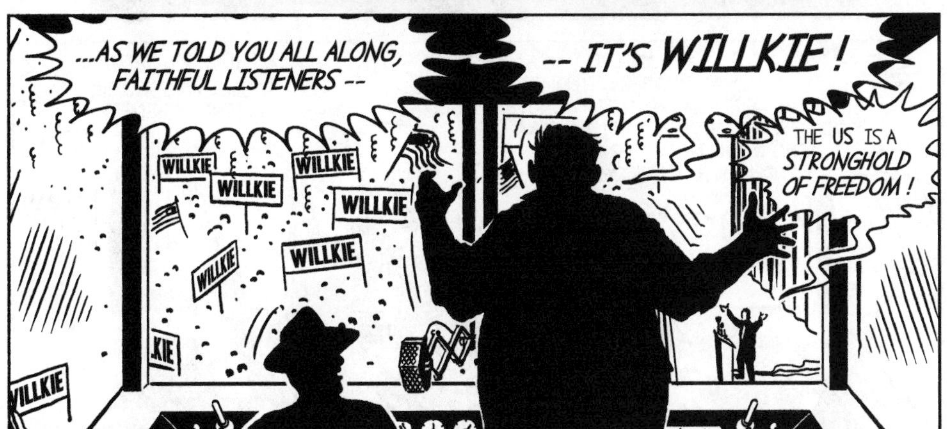
...AS WE TOLD YOU ALL ALONG, FAITHFUL LISTENERS --
-- IT'S WILLKIE !
THE US IS A STRONGHOLD OF FREEDOM !
WILLKIE
WILLKIE
WILLKIE
WILLKIE
WILLKIE
WILLKIE

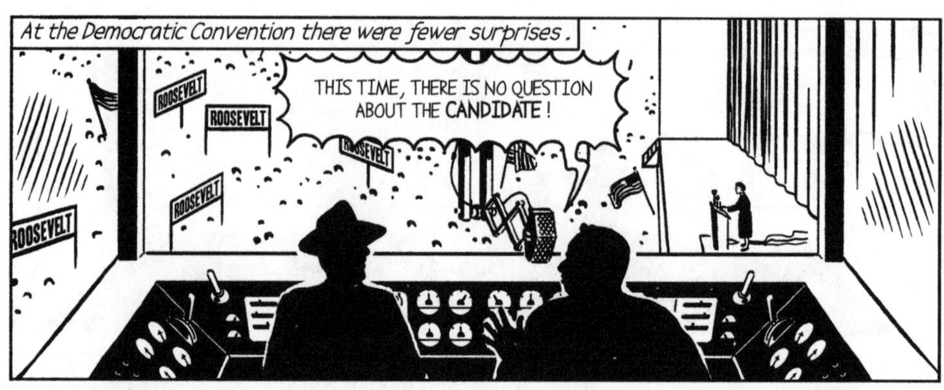
At the Democratic Convention there were fewer surprises.
ROOSEVELT
THIS TIME, THERE IS NO QUESTION ABOUT THE **CANDIDATE** !

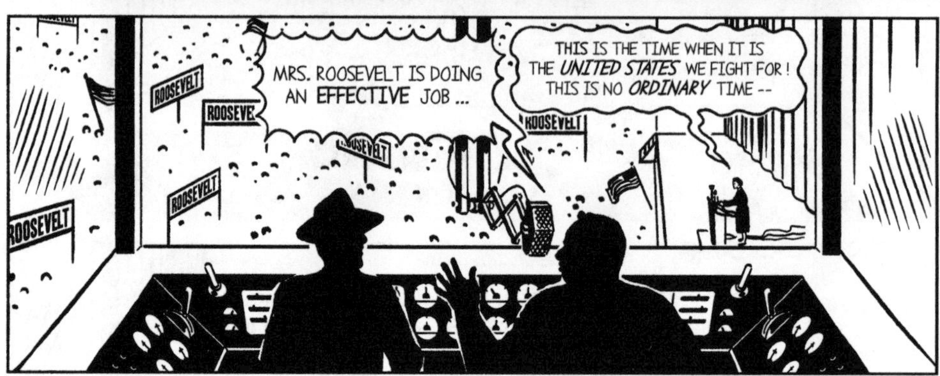
MRS. ROOSEVELT IS DOING AN **EFFECTIVE** JOB ...
THIS IS THE TIME WHEN IT IS THE *UNITED STATES* WE FIGHT FOR ! THIS IS NO *ORDINARY* TIME --
ROOSEVELT

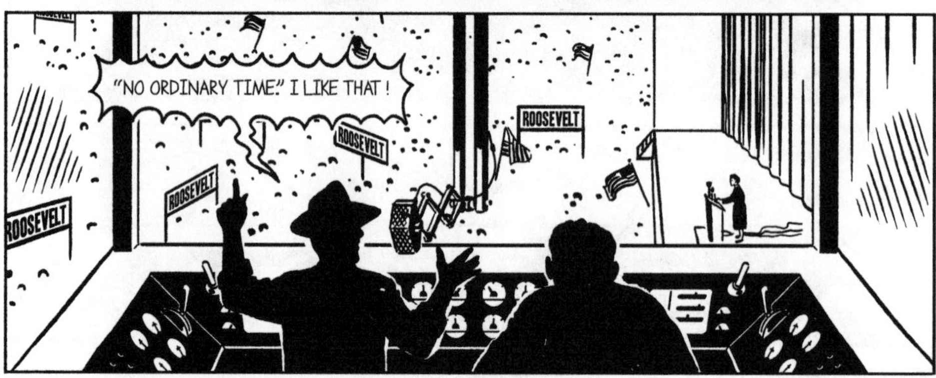
"NO ORDINARY TIME." I LIKE THAT !
ROOSEVELT

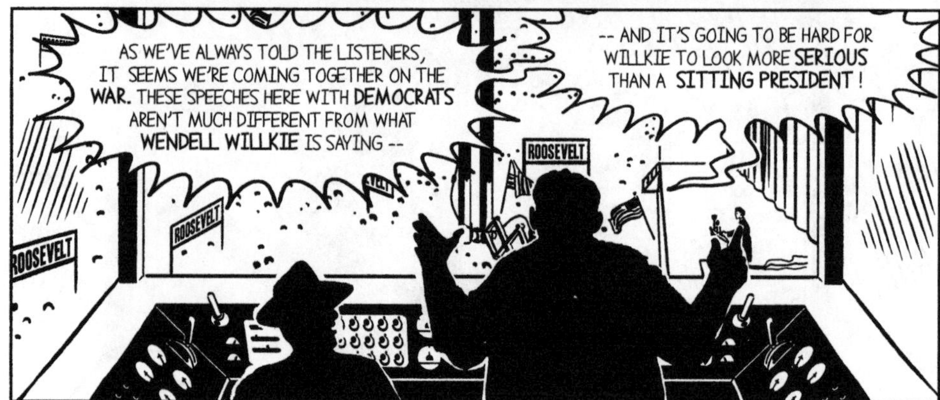
AS WE'VE ALWAYS TOLD THE LISTENERS, IT SEEMS WE'RE COMING TOGETHER ON THE **WAR.** THESE SPEECHES HERE WITH **DEMOCRATS** AREN'T MUCH DIFFERENT FROM WHAT **WENDELL WILLKIE** IS SAYING --
-- AND IT'S GOING TO BE HARD FOR WILLKIE TO LOOK MORE **SERIOUS** THAN A **SITTING PRESIDENT** !
ROOSEVELT

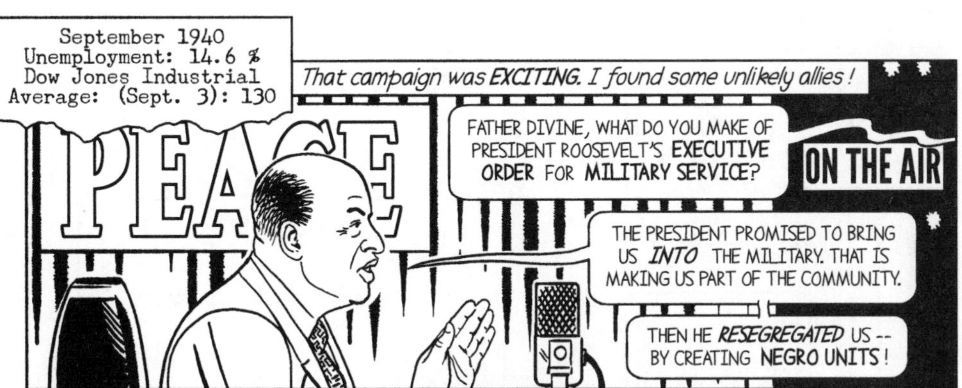
September 1940
Unemployment: 14.6 %
Dow Jones Industrial
Average: (Sept. 3): 130
That campaign was EXCITING. I found some unlikely allies!
PEACE
FATHER DIVINE, WHAT DO YOU MAKE OF PRESIDENT ROOSEVELT'S EXECUTIVE ORDER FOR MILITARY SERVICE?
ON THE AIR
THE PRESIDENT PROMISED TO BRING US INTO THE MILITARY. THAT IS MAKING US PART OF THE COMMUNITY.
THEN HE RESEGREGATED US -- BY CREATING NEGRO UNITS!

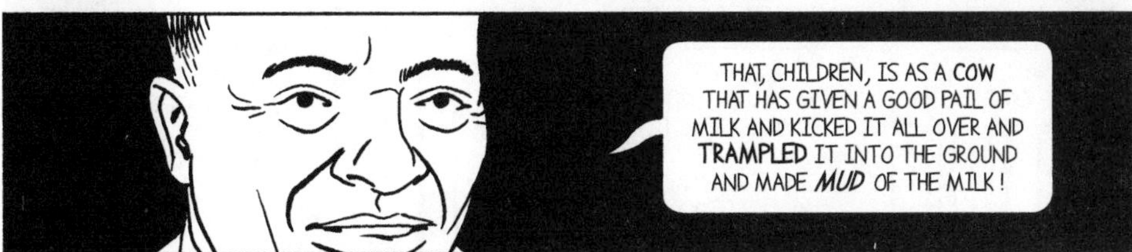
THAT, CHILDREN, IS AS A COW THAT HAS GIVEN A GOOD PAIL OF MILK AND KICKED IT ALL OVER AND TRAMPLED IT INTO THE GROUND AND MADE MUD OF THE MILK!

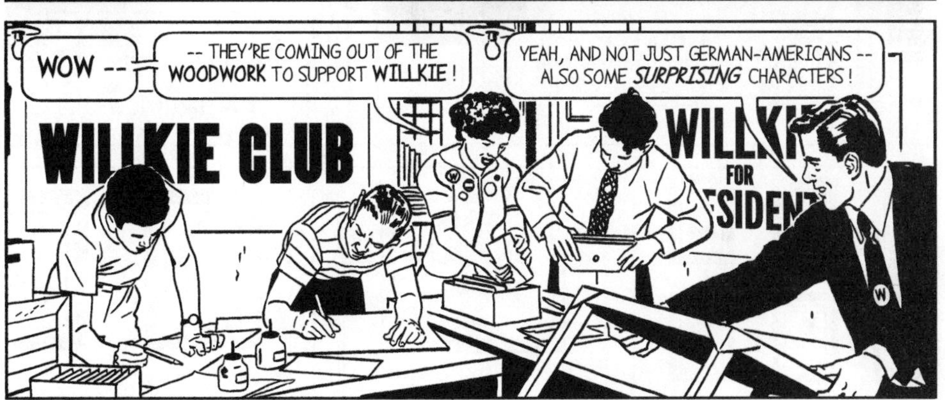
WOW --
-- THEY'RE COMING OUT OF THE WOODWORK TO SUPPORT WILLKIE!
YEAH, AND NOT JUST GERMAN-AMERICANS -- ALSO SOME SURPRISING CHARACTERS!
WILLKIE CLUB

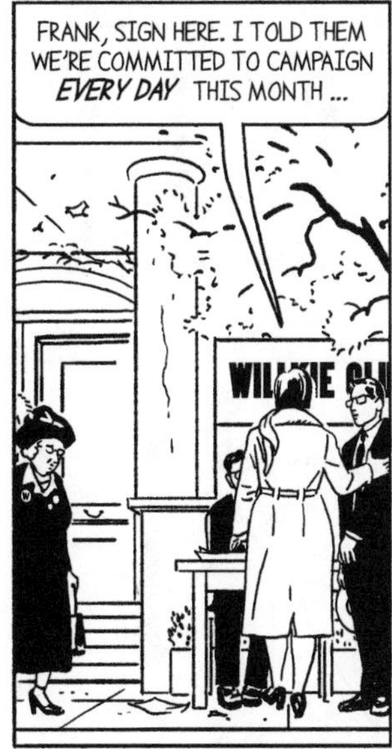
FRANK, SIGN HERE. I TOLD THEM WE'RE COMMITTED TO CAMPAIGN EVERY DAY THIS MONTH ...

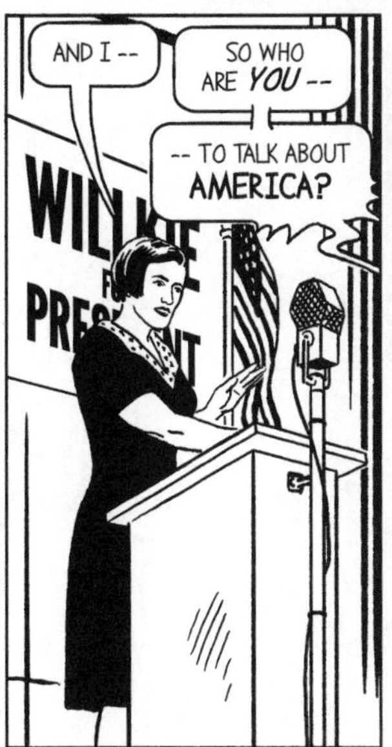
SO WHO ARE YOU --
AND I --
-- TO TALK ABOUT AMERICA?

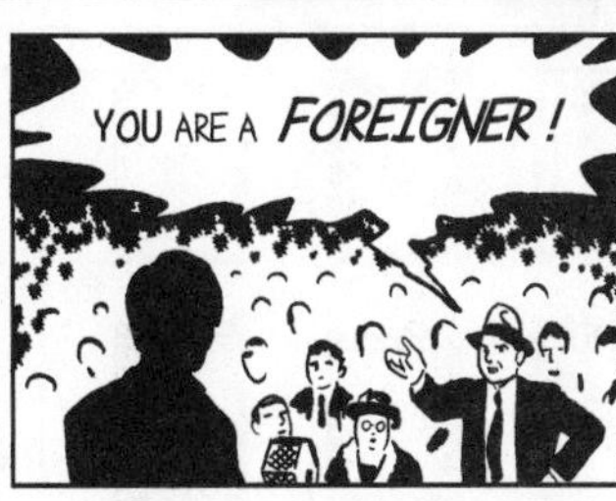
YOU ARE A FOREIGNER!

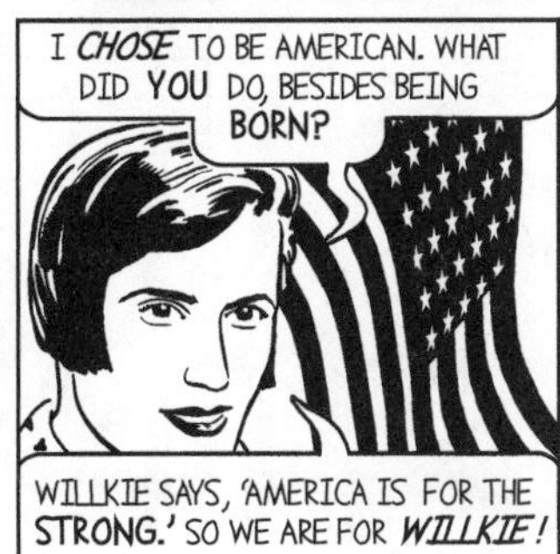
I CHOSE TO BE AMERICAN. WHAT DID YOU DO, BESIDES BEING BORN?
WILLKIE SAYS, 'AMERICA IS FOR THE STRONG.' SO WE ARE FOR WILLKIE!

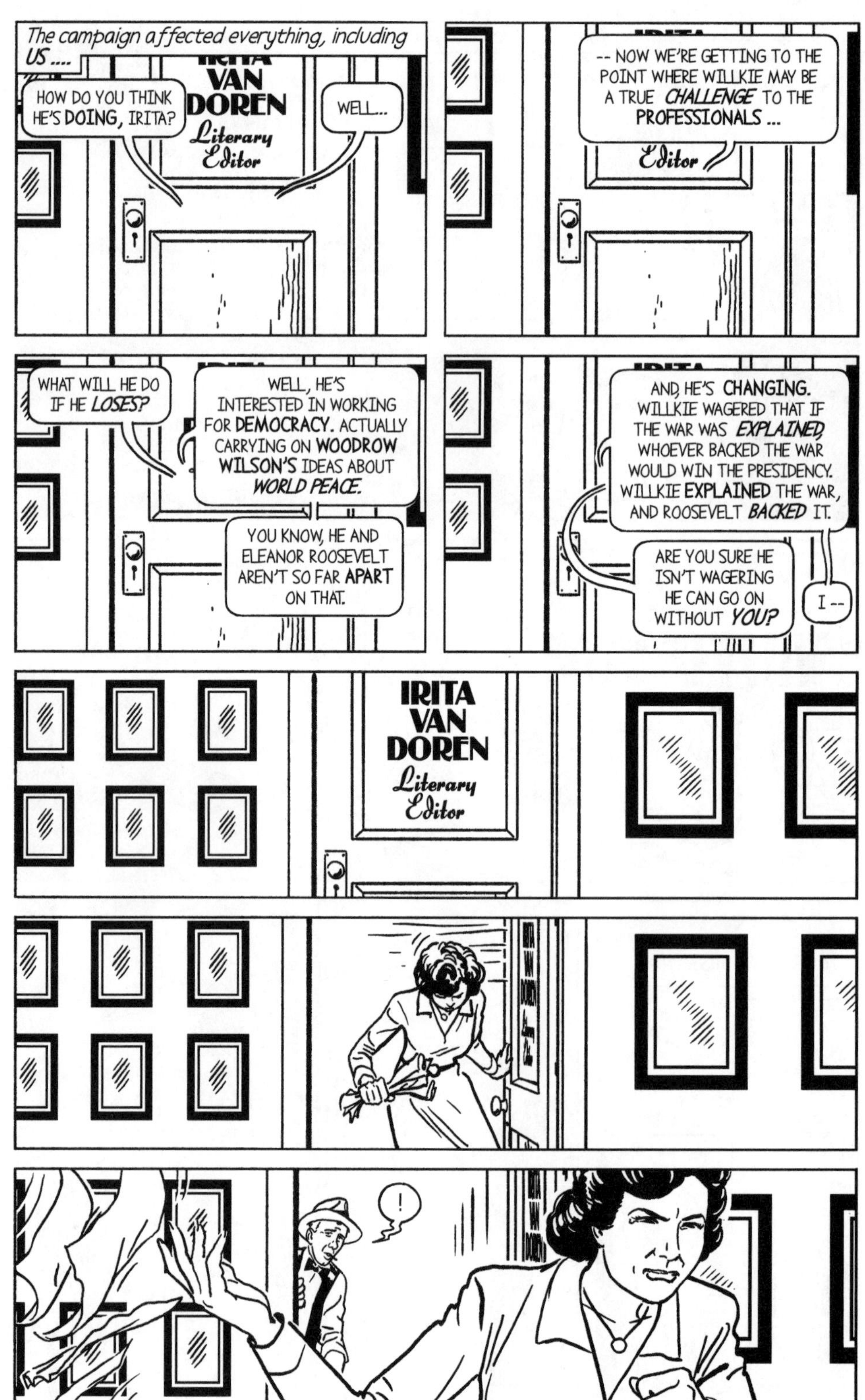
The campaign affected everything, including US ....
IRITA VAN DOREN Literary Editor
HOW DO YOU THINK HE'S DOING, IRITA?
WELL...
-- NOW WE'RE GETTING TO THE POINT WHERE WILLKIE MAY BE A TRUE CHALLENGE TO THE PROFESSIONALS ...
Editor
WHAT WILL HE DO IF HE LOSES?
WELL, HE'S INTERESTED IN WORKING FOR DEMOCRACY. ACTUALLY CARRYING ON WOODROW WILSON'S IDEAS ABOUT WORLD PEACE.
YOU KNOW, HE AND ELEANOR ROOSEVELT AREN'T SO FAR APART ON THAT.
AND, HE'S CHANGING. WILLKIE WAGERED THAT IF THE WAR WAS EXPLAINED, WHOEVER BACKED THE WAR WOULD WIN THE PRESIDENCY. WILLKIE EXPLAINED THE WAR, AND ROOSEVELT BACKED IT.
ARE YOU SURE HE ISN'T WAGERING HE CAN GO ON WITHOUT YOU?
I --
IRITA VAN DOREN Literary Editor
!

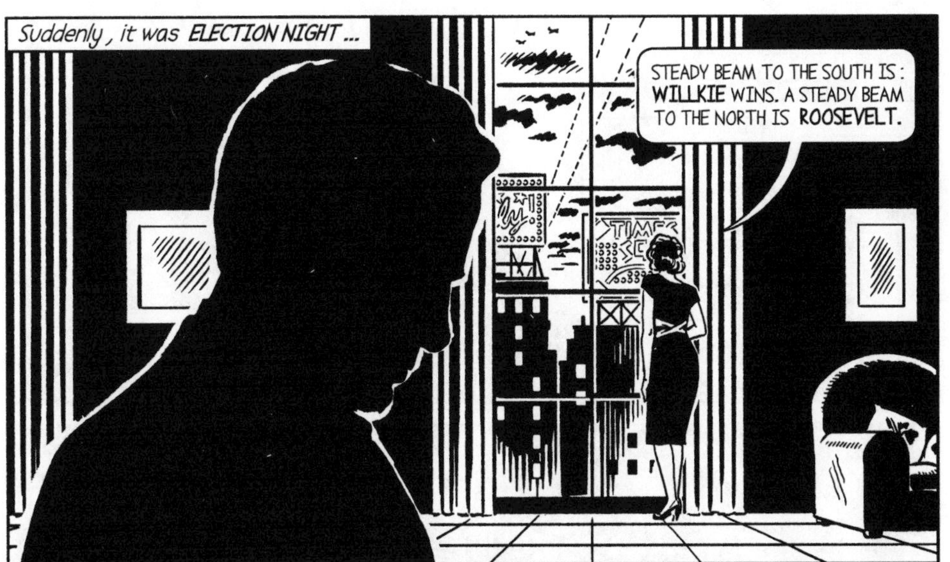
Suddenly, it was ELECTION NIGHT...
STEADY BEAM TO THE SOUTH IS: WILLKIE WINS. A STEADY BEAM TO THE NORTH IS ROOSEVELT.

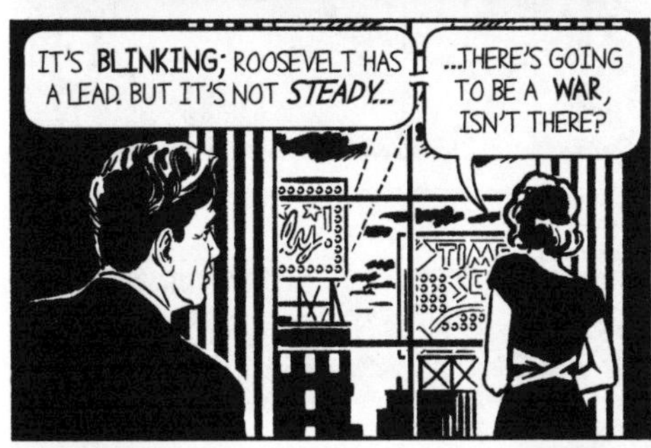
IT'S BLINKING; ROOSEVELT HAS A LEAD. BUT IT'S NOT STEADY...
...THERE'S GOING TO BE A WAR, ISN'T THERE?

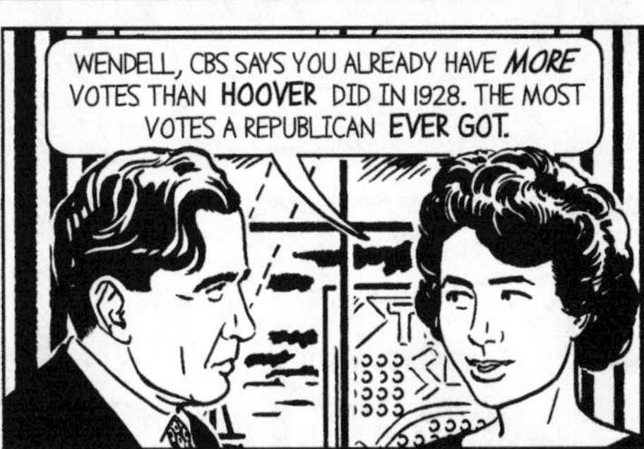
WENDELL, CBS SAYS YOU ALREADY HAVE MORE VOTES THAN HOOVER DID IN 1928. THE MOST VOTES A REPUBLICAN EVER GOT.

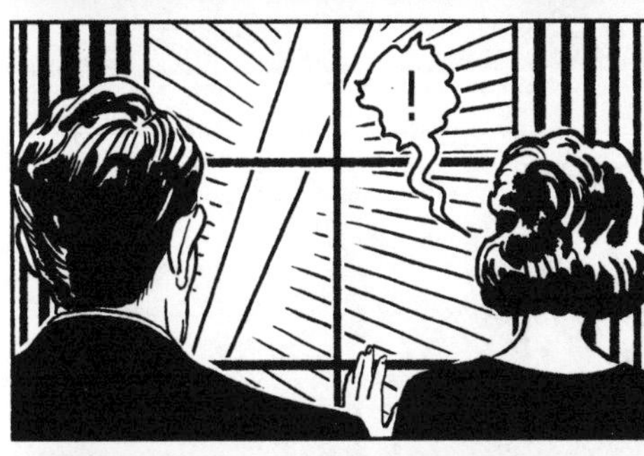
!

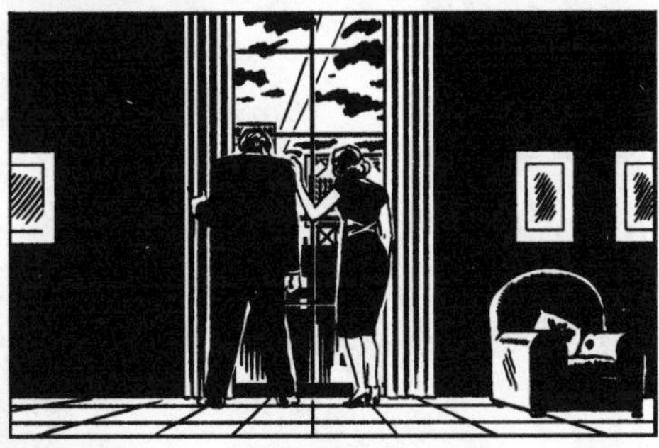

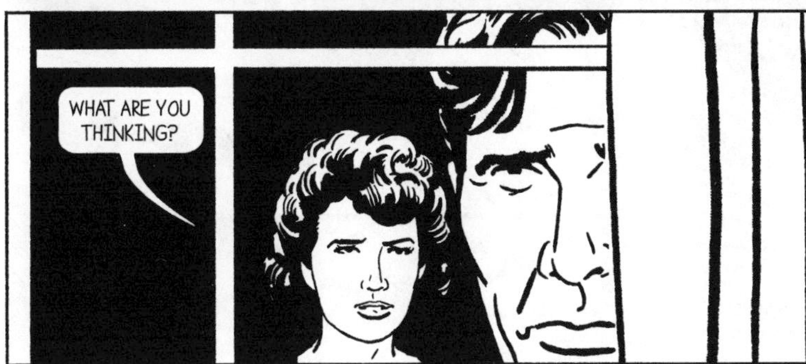
WHAT ARE YOU THINKING?

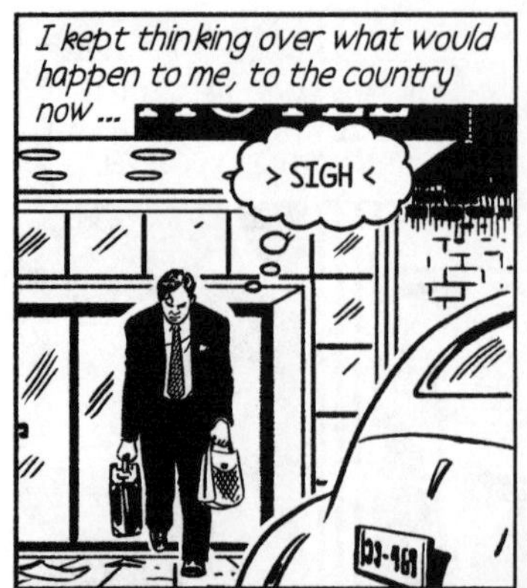
I kept thinking over what would happen to me, to the country now ...
> SIGH <

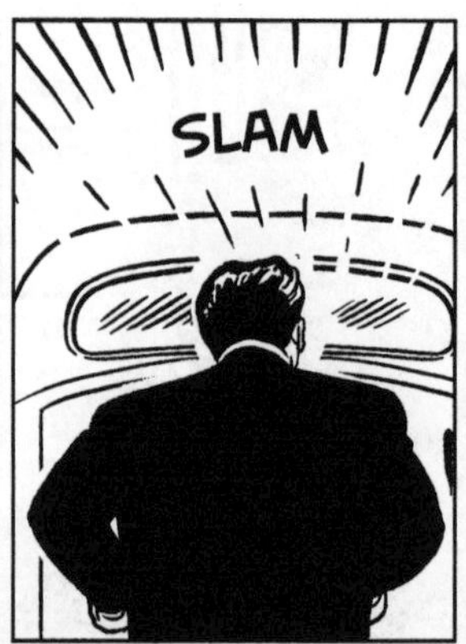
SLAM

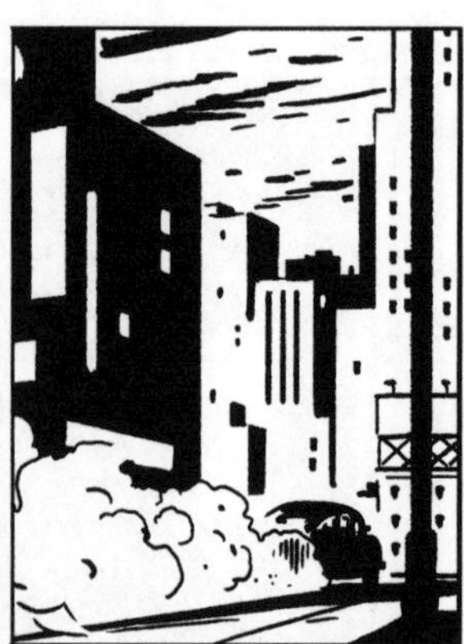

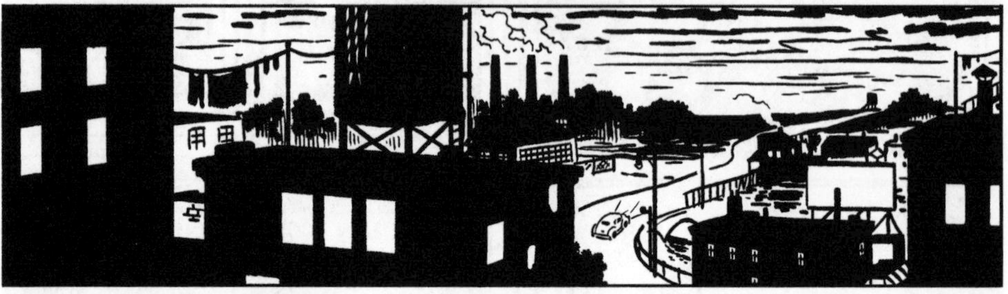

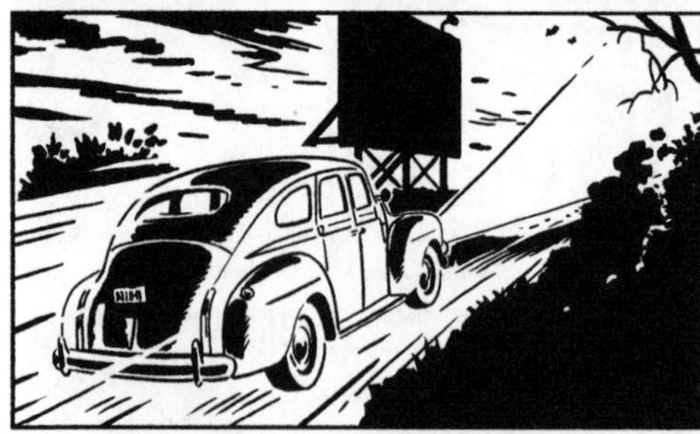

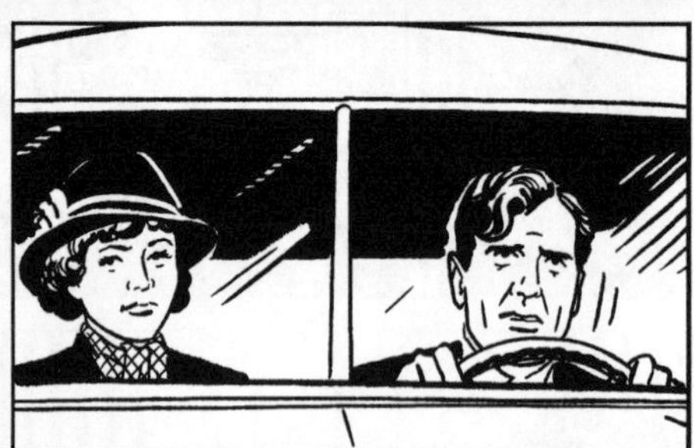

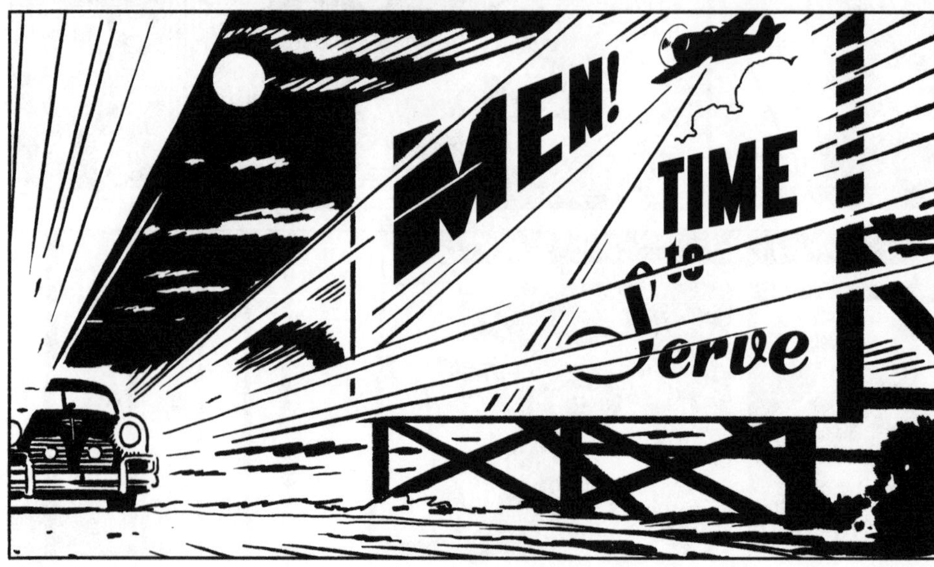
MEN!
TIME
to
Serve

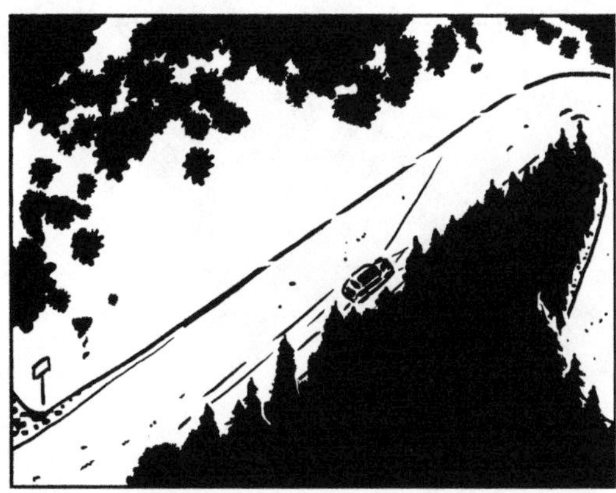

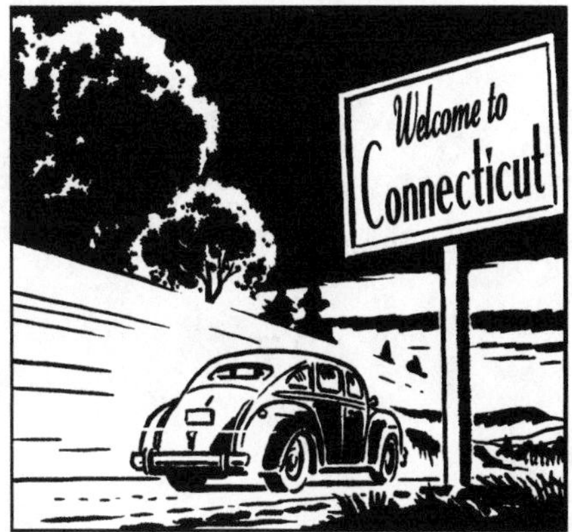
Welcome to
Connecticut

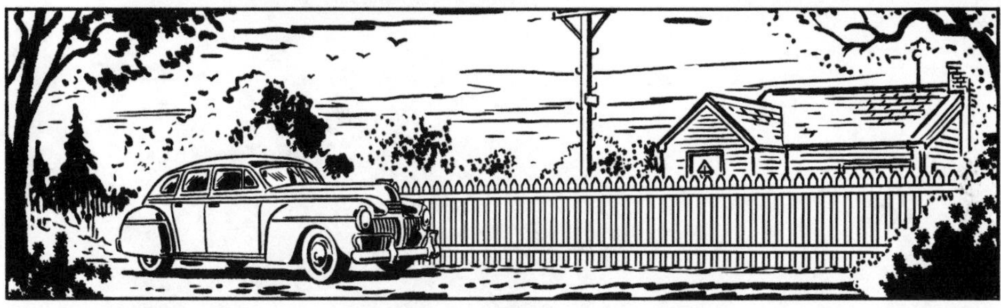

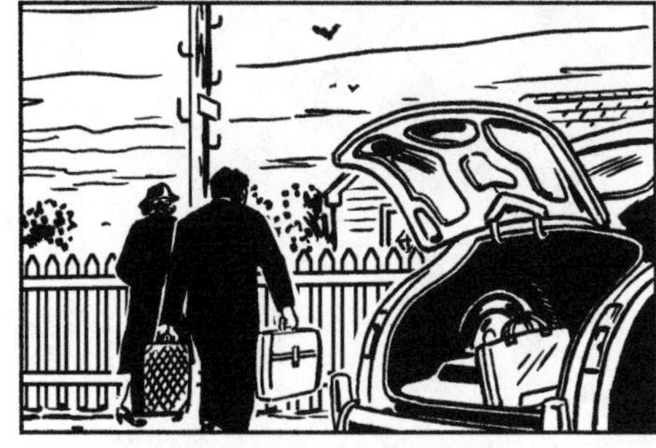

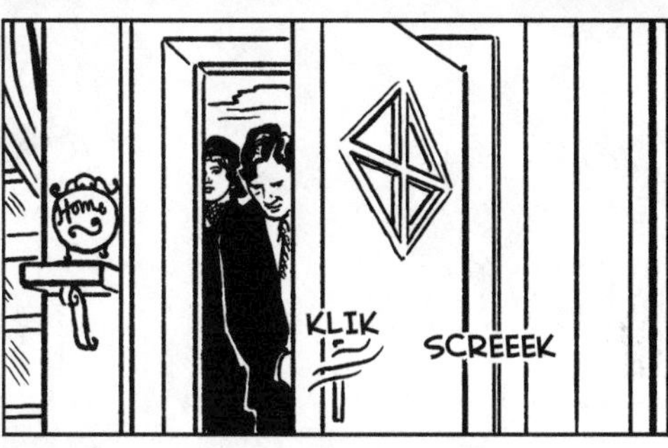
Home
KLIK
SCREEEK

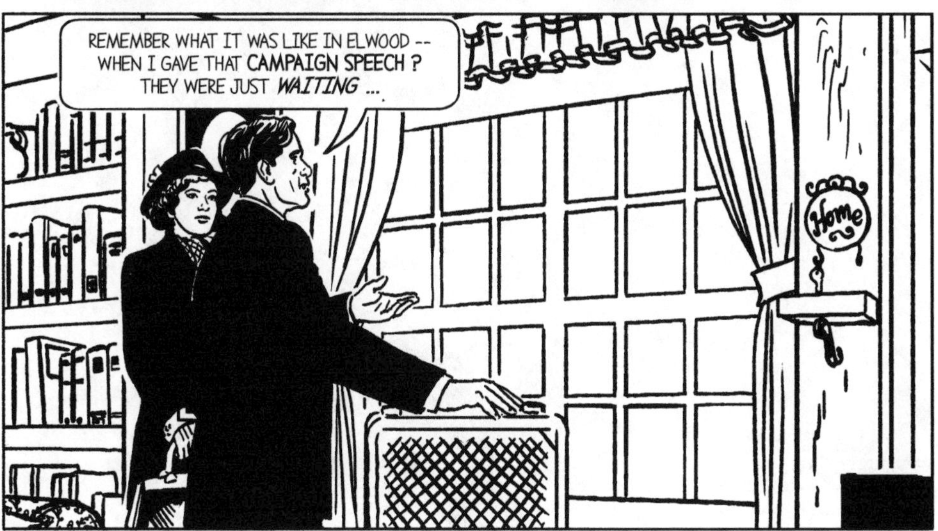
REMEMBER WHAT IT WAS LIKE IN ELWOOD -- WHEN I GAVE THAT **CAMPAIGN SPEECH** ? THEY WERE JUST ***WAITING*** ...
Home

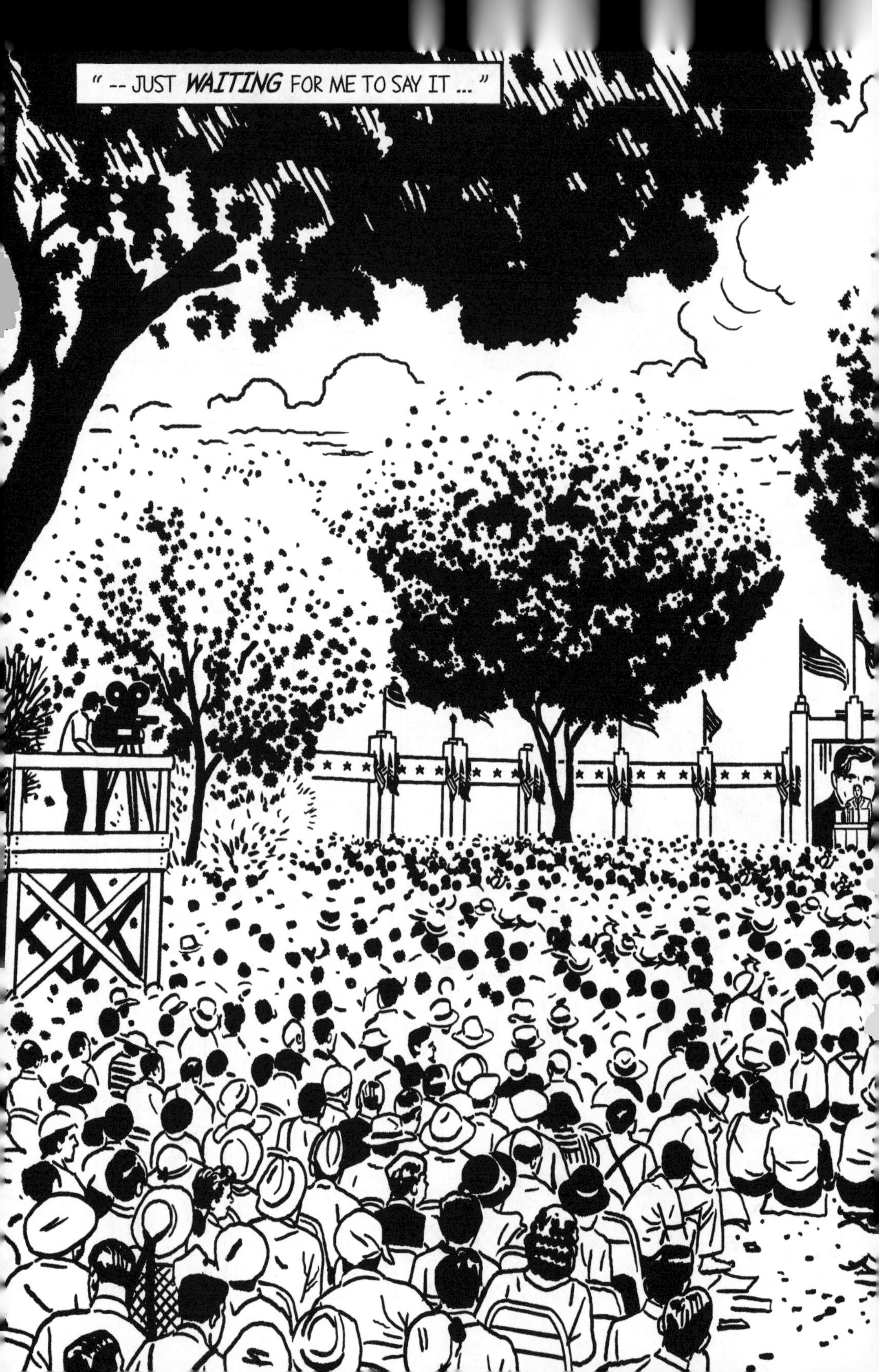
" -- JUST WAITING FOR ME TO SAY IT ... "

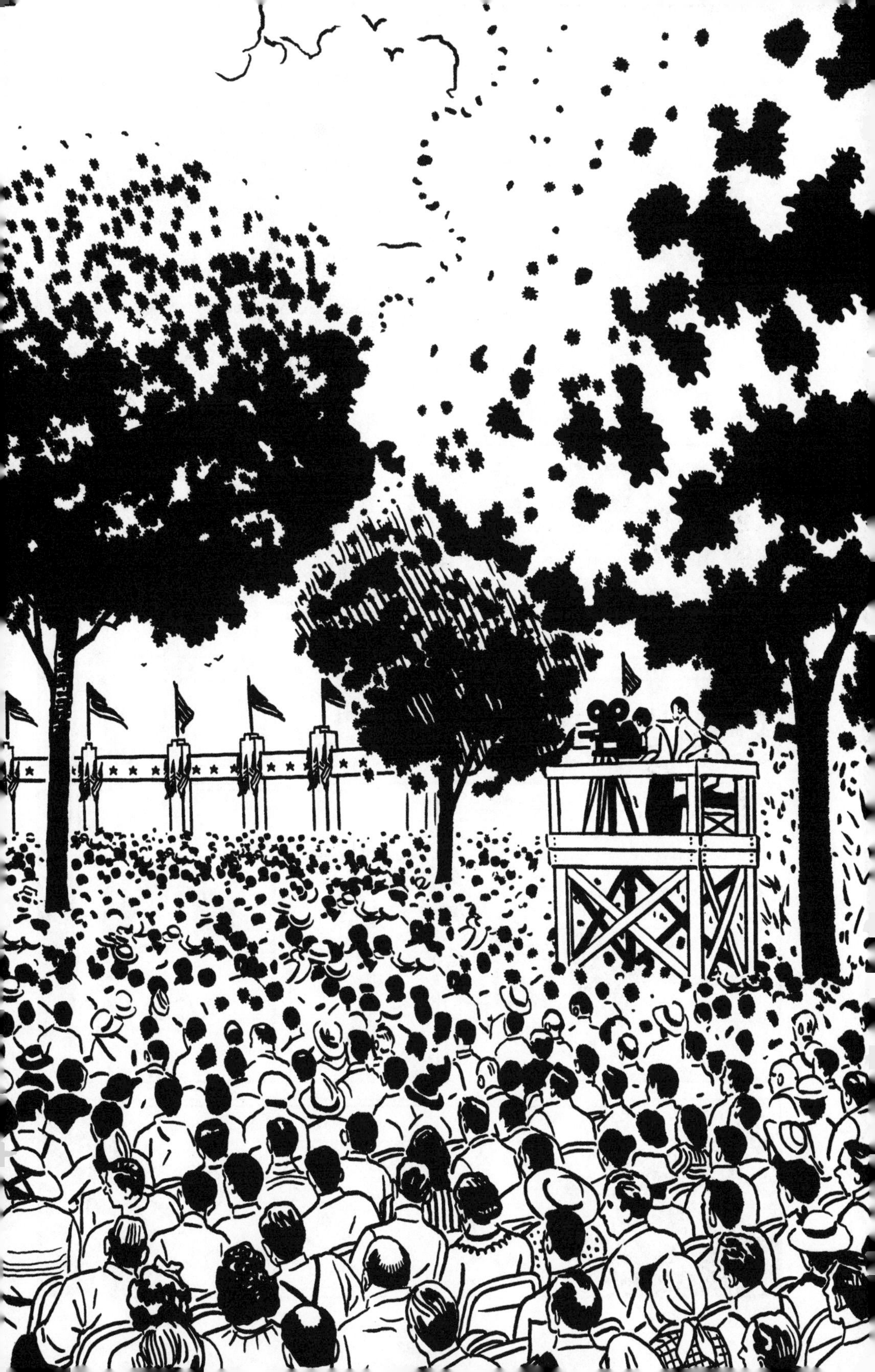

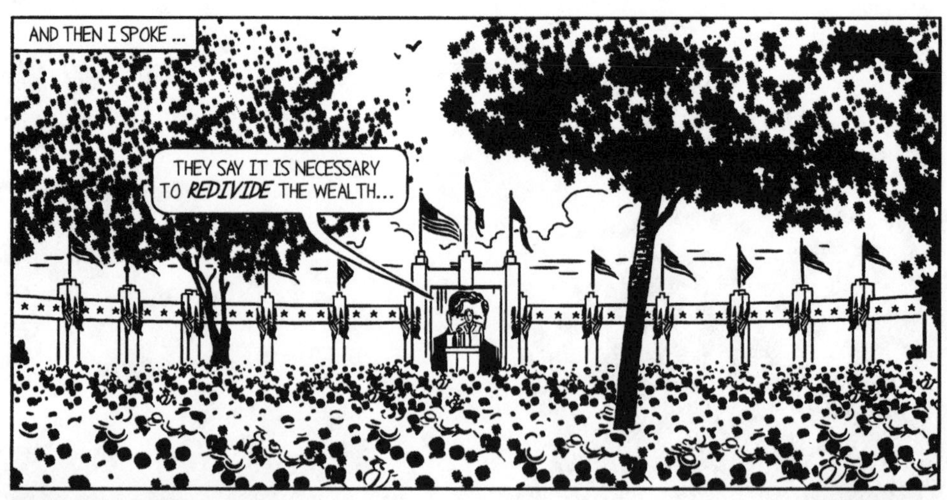
AND THEN I SPOKE ...
THEY SAY IT IS NECESSARY TO *REDIVIDE* THE WEALTH...

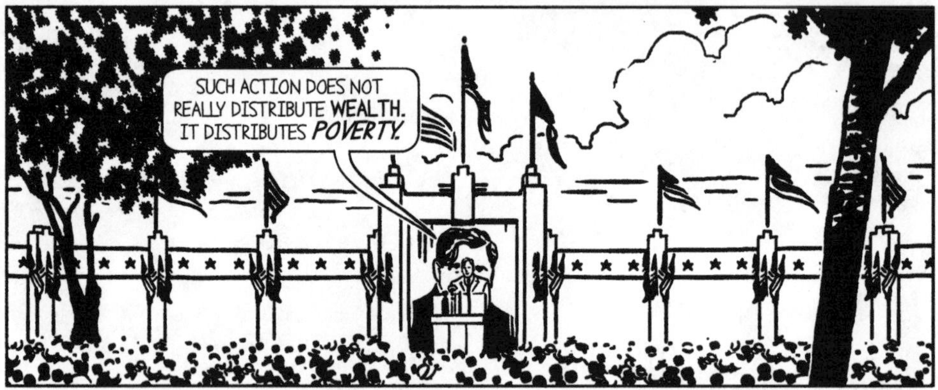
SUCH ACTION DOES NOT REALLY DISTRIBUTE **WEALTH.** IT DISTRIBUTES *POVERTY.*

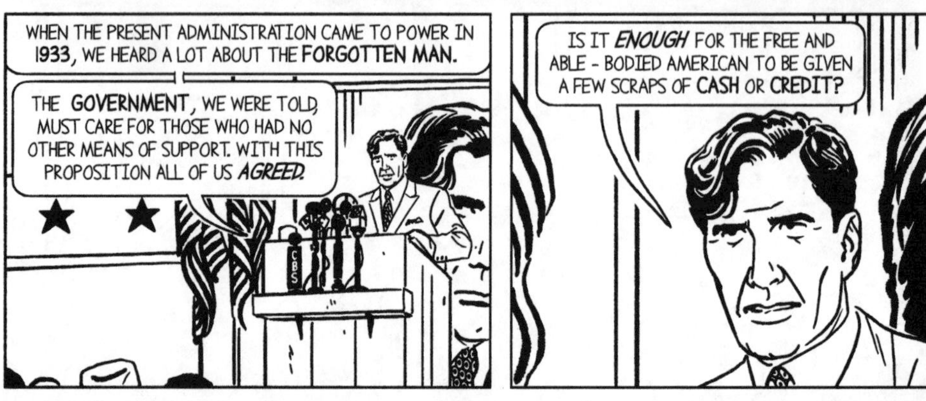
WHEN THE PRESENT ADMINISTRATION CAME TO POWER IN 1933, WE HEARD A LOT ABOUT THE **FORGOTTEN MAN.**
THE **GOVERNMENT**, WE WERE TOLD, MUST CARE FOR THOSE WHO HAD NO OTHER MEANS OF SUPPORT. WITH THIS PROPOSITION ALL OF US *AGREED.*
CBS
IS IT *ENOUGH* FOR THE FREE AND ABLE - BODIED AMERICAN TO BE GIVEN A FEW SCRAPS OF **CASH** OR **CREDIT?**

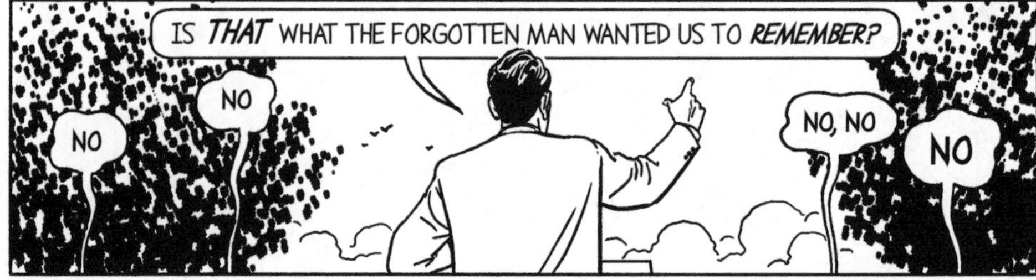
IS *THAT* WHAT THE FORGOTTEN MAN WANTED US TO *REMEMBER?*
NO
NO
NO, NO
NO

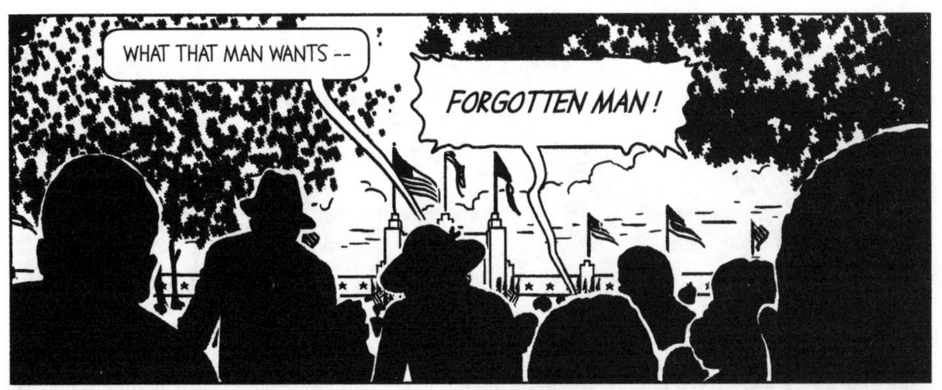
WHAT THAT MAN WANTS --
FORGOTTEN MAN!

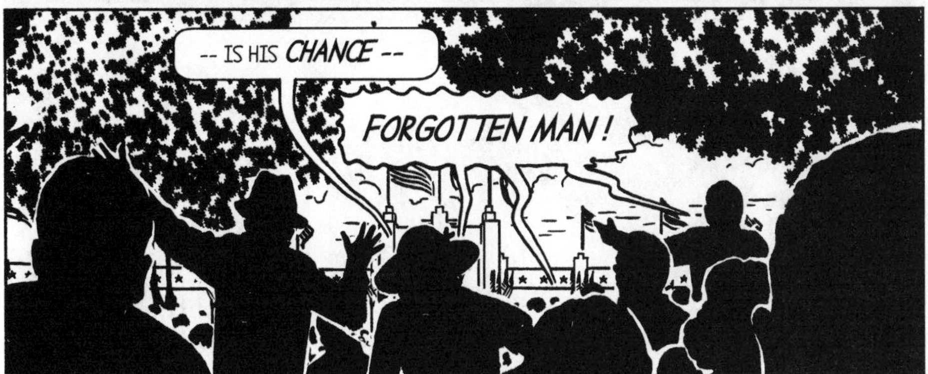
-- IS HIS CHANCE --
FORGOTTEN MAN!

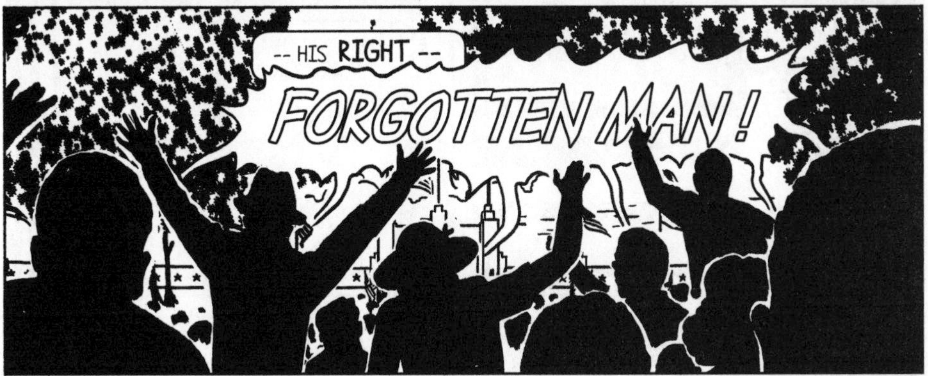
-- HIS RIGHT --
FORGOTTEN MAN!

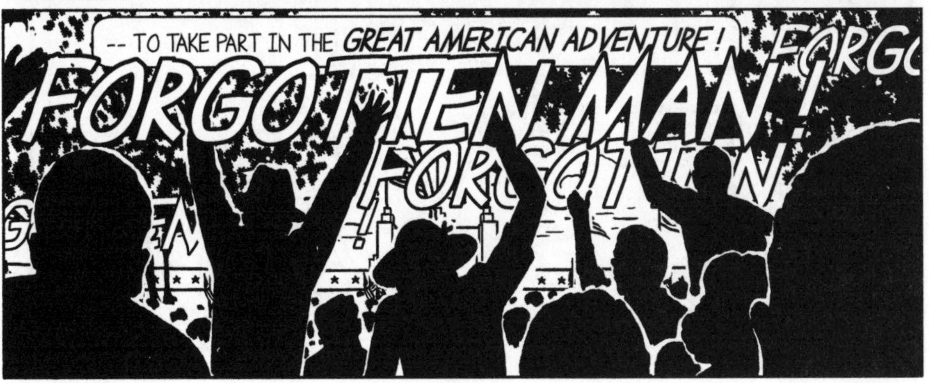
-- TO TAKE PART IN THE GREAT AMERICAN ADVENTURE!
FORGOTTEN MAN!

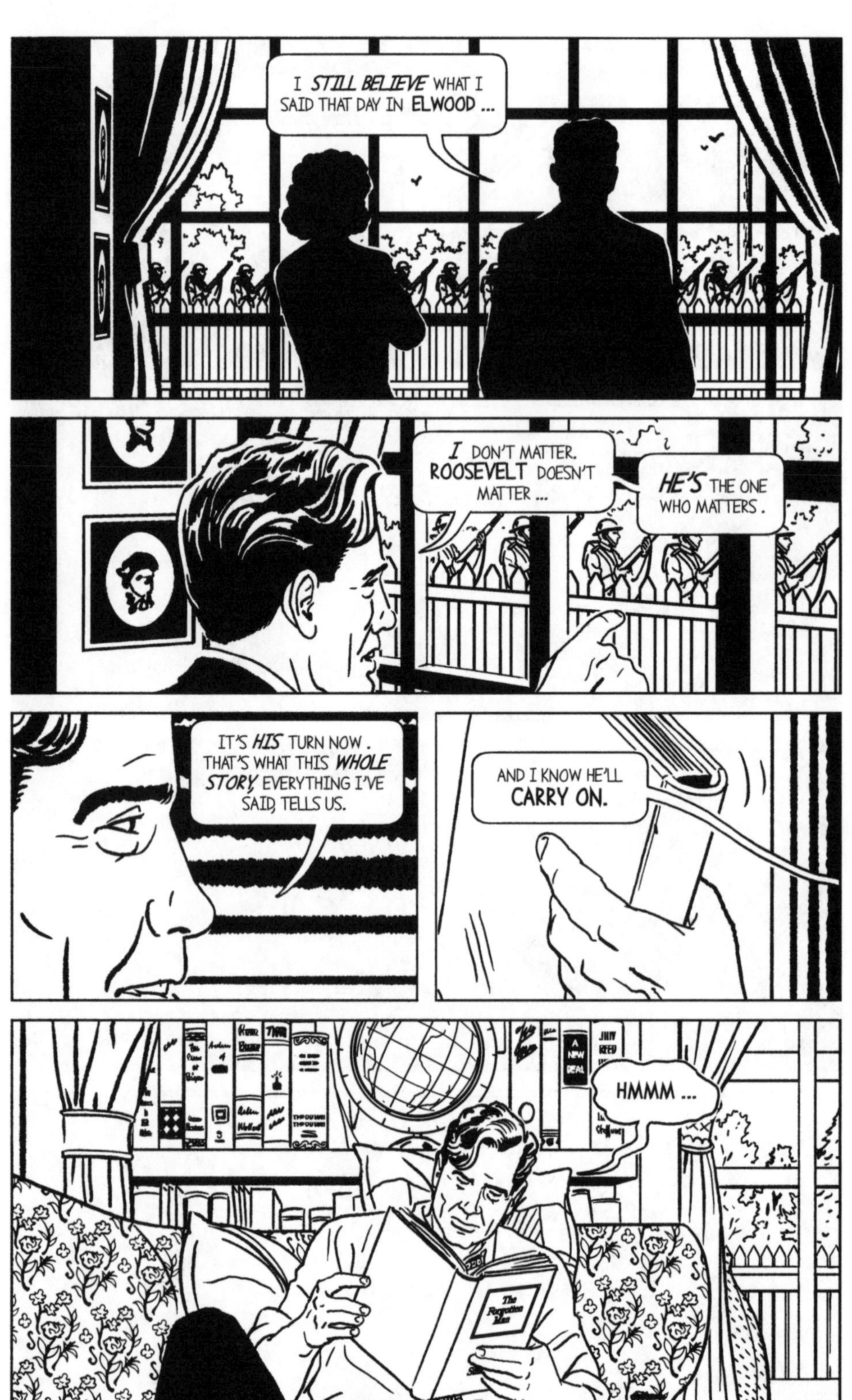
I STILL BELIEVE WHAT I SAID THAT DAY IN ELWOOD ...
I DON'T MATTER. ROOSEVELT DOESN'T MATTER ...
HE'S THE ONE WHO MATTERS.
IT'S HIS TURN NOW. THAT'S WHAT THIS WHOLE STORY, EVERYTHING I'VE SAID, TELLS US.
AND I KNOW HE'LL CARRY ON.
A NEW DEAL
HMMM ...
The Forgotten Man

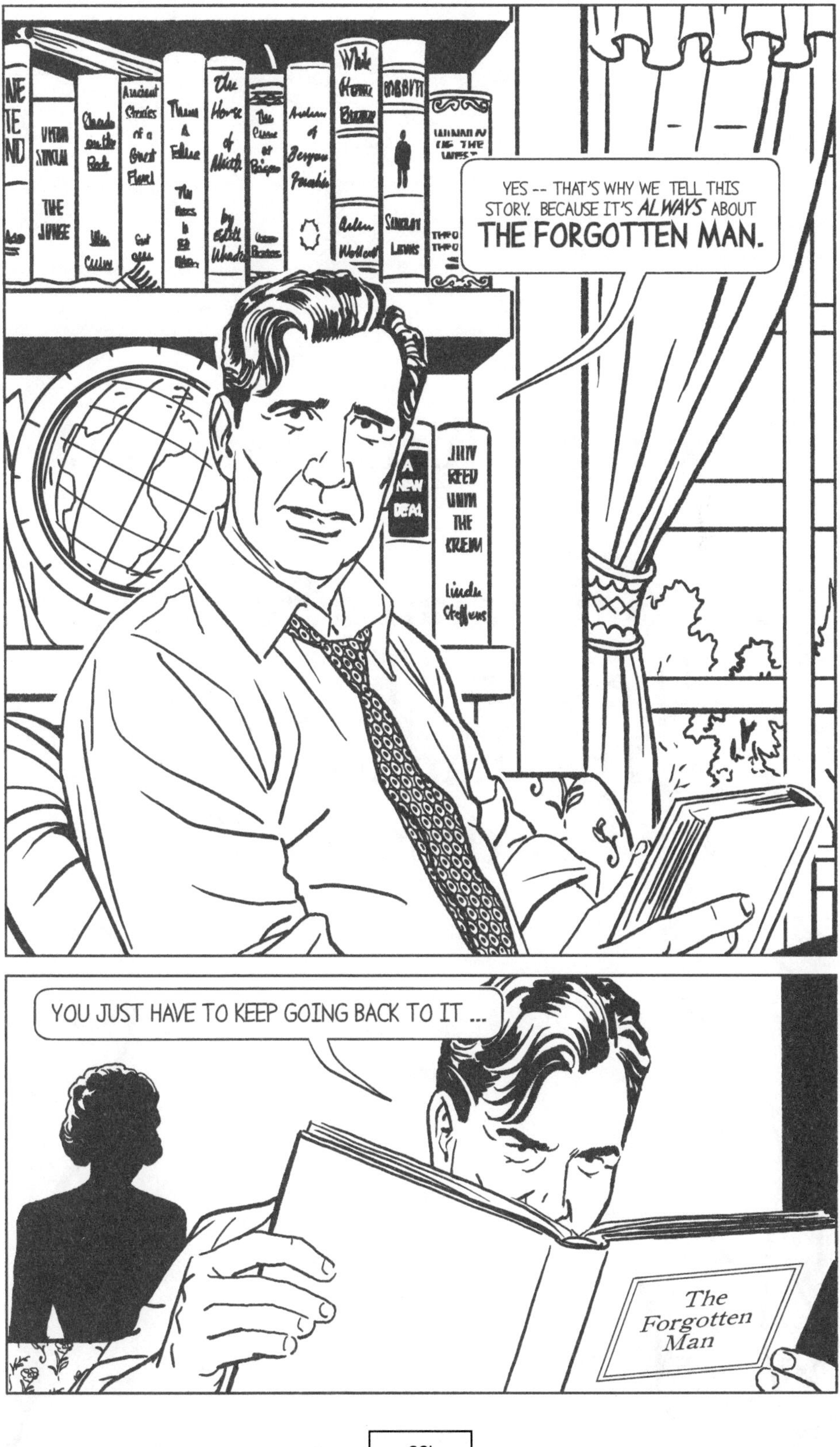

YES -- THAT'S WHY WE TELL THIS STORY. BECAUSE IT'S *ALWAYS* ABOUT **THE FORGOTTEN MAN.**

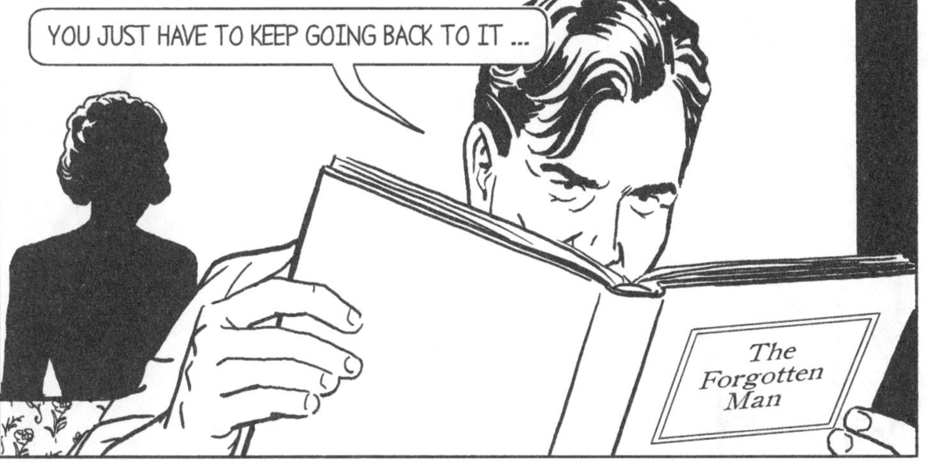

Who is the forgotten man?

He is the man who pays.
The man who prays.
The man who is
never thought of.

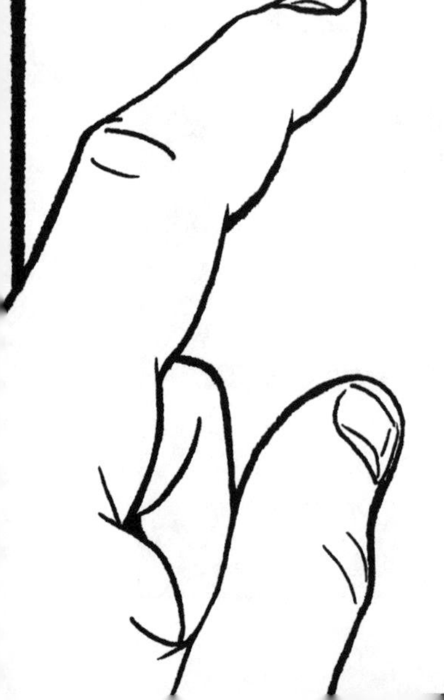

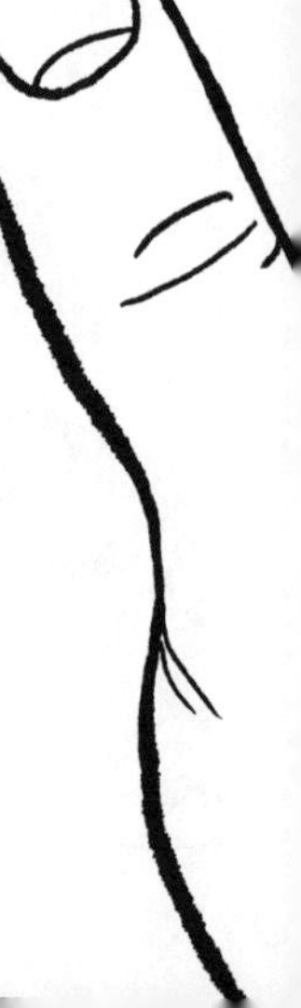

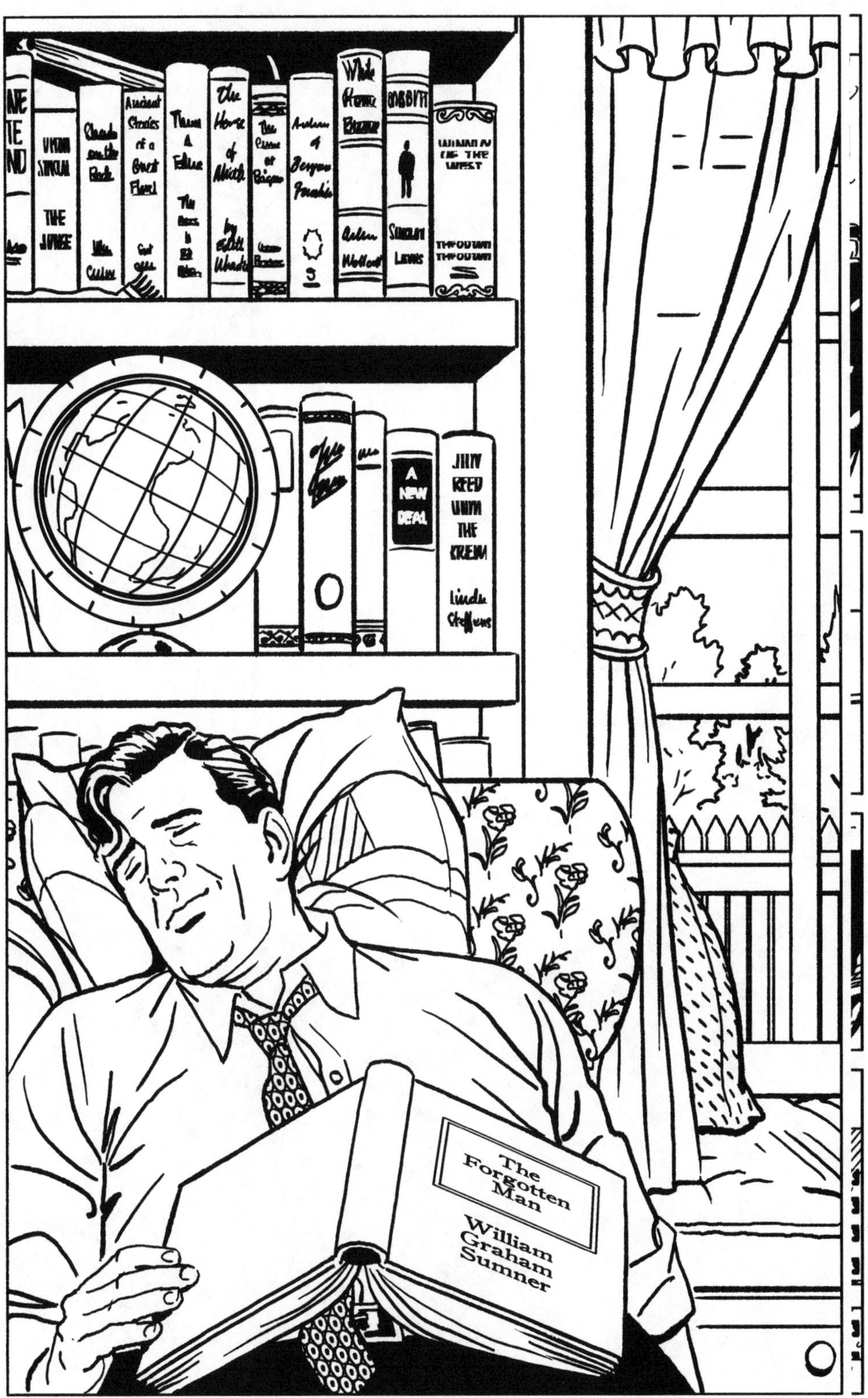
The Forgotten Man
William Graham Sumner
A NEW DEAL
The House of Mirth
Sinclair Lewis
Lincoln Steffens

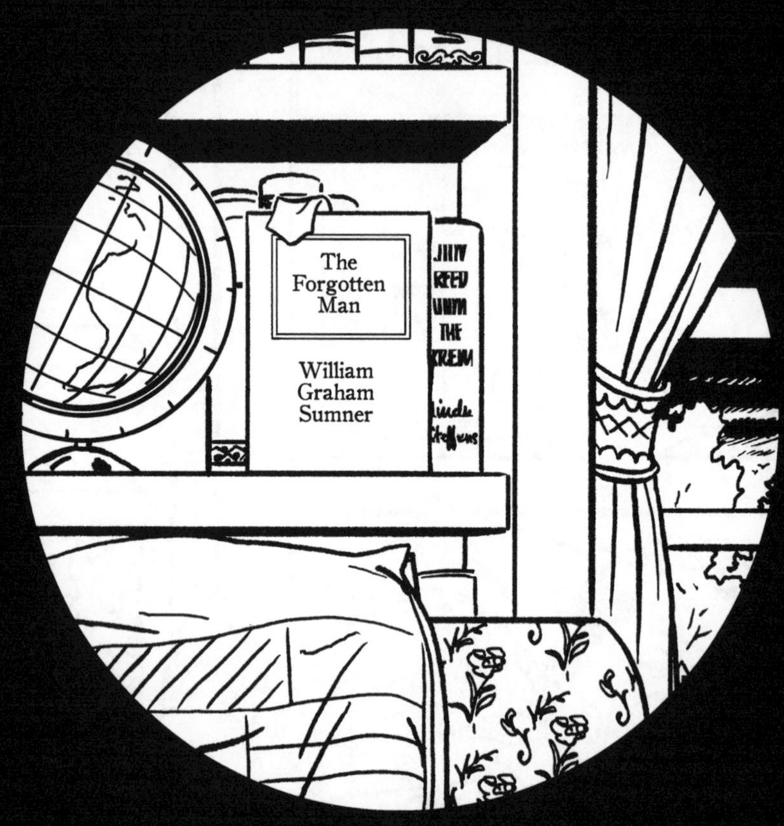
The Forgotten Man
William Graham Sumner

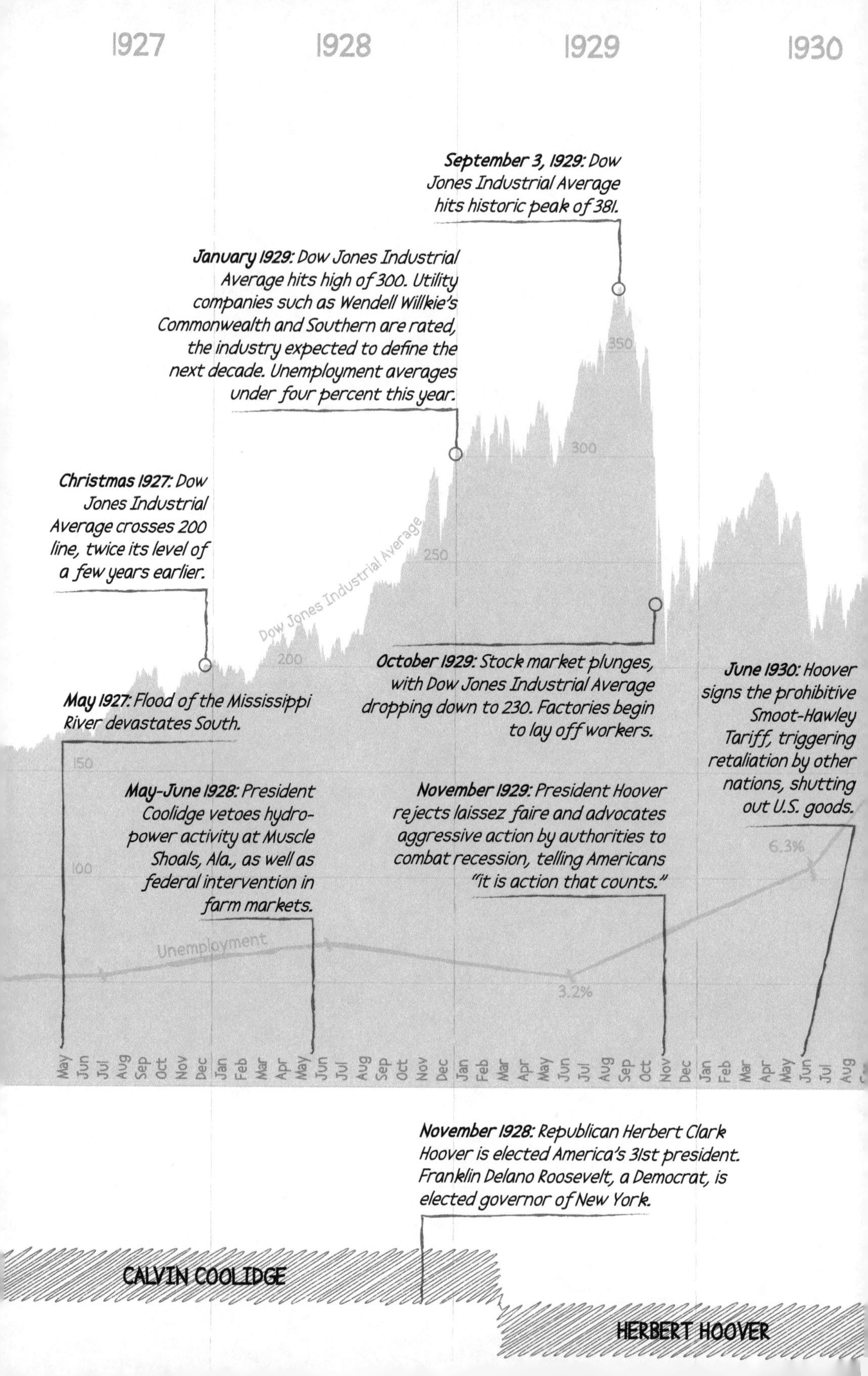

1927 1928 1929 1930

September 3, 1929: Dow Jones Industrial Average hits historic peak of 381.

January 1929: Dow Jones Industrial Average hits high of 300. Utility companies such as Wendell Willkie's Commonwealth and Southern are rated, the industry expected to define the next decade. Unemployment averages under four percent this year.

Christmas 1927: Dow Jones Industrial Average crosses 200 line, twice its level of a few years earlier.

Dow Jones Industrial Average

350 300 250 200 150 100

October 1929: Stock market plunges, with Dow Jones Industrial Average dropping down to 230. Factories begin to lay off workers.

May 1927: Flood of the Mississippi River devastates South.

June 1930: Hoover signs the prohibitive Smoot-Hawley Tariff, triggering retaliation by other nations, shutting out U.S. goods.

May-June 1928: President Coolidge vetoes hydro-power activity at Muscle Shoals, Ala., as well as federal intervention in farm markets.

November 1929: President Hoover rejects laissez faire and advocates aggressive action by authorities to combat recession, telling Americans "it is action that counts."

6.3%

Unemployment

3.2%

May Jun Jul Aug Sep Oct Nov Dec Jan Feb Mar Apr May Jun Jul Aug Sep Oct Nov Dec Jan Feb Mar Apr May Jun Jul Aug Sep Oct Nov Dec Jan Feb Mar Apr May Jun Jul Aug

November 1928: Republican Herbert Clark Hoover is elected America's 31st president. Franklin Delano Roosevelt, a Democrat, is elected governor of New York.

CALVIN COOLIDGE

HERBERT HOOVER

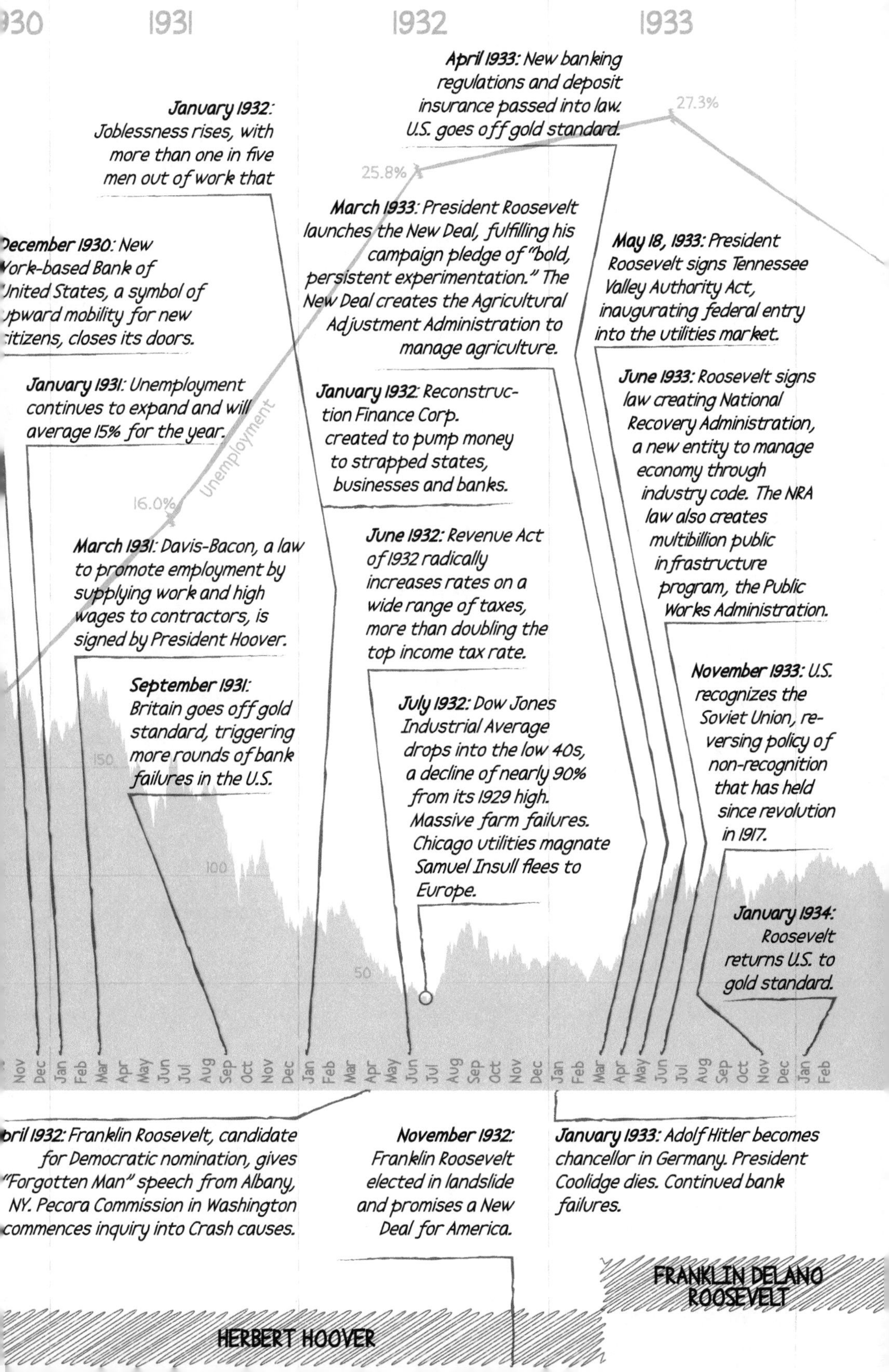

930 1931 1932 1933

April 1933: New banking regulations and deposit insurance passed into law. U.S. goes off gold standard.

27.3%

January 1932: Joblessness rises, with more than one in five men out of work that

25.8%

March 1933: President Roosevelt launches the New Deal, fulfilling his campaign pledge of "bold, persistent experimentation." The New Deal creates the Agricultural Adjustment Administration to manage agriculture.

December 1930: New York-based Bank of United States, a symbol of upward mobility for new citizens, closes its doors.

May 18, 1933: President Roosevelt signs Tennessee Valley Authority Act, inaugurating federal entry into the utilities market.

January 1931: Unemployment continues to expand and will average 15% for the year.

Unemployment

16.0%

January 1932: Reconstruction Finance Corp. created to pump money to strapped states, businesses and banks.

June 1933: Roosevelt signs law creating National Recovery Administration, a new entity to manage economy through industry code. The NRA law also creates multibillion public infrastructure program, the Public Works Administration.

March 1931: Davis-Bacon, a law to promote employment by supplying work and high wages to contractors, is signed by President Hoover.

June 1932: Revenue Act of 1932 radically increases rates on a wide range of taxes, more than doubling the top income tax rate.

September 1931: Britain goes off gold standard, triggering more rounds of bank failures in the U.S.

July 1932: Dow Jones Industrial Average drops into the low 40s, a decline of nearly 90% from its 1929 high. Massive farm failures. Chicago utilities magnate Samuel Insull flees to Europe.

November 1933: U.S. recognizes the Soviet Union, reversing policy of non-recognition that has held since revolution in 1917.

150

100

50

January 1934: Roosevelt returns U.S. to gold standard.

Nov Dec Jan Feb Mar Apr May Jun Jul Aug Sep Oct Nov Dec Jan Feb Mar Apr May Jun Jul Aug Sep Oct Nov Dec Jan Feb Mar Apr May Jun Jul Aug Sep Oct Nov Dec Jan Feb

pril 1932: Franklin Roosevelt, candidate for Democratic nomination, gives "Forgotten Man" speech from Albany, NY. Pecora Commission in Washington commences inquiry into Crash causes.

November 1932: Franklin Roosevelt elected in landslide and promises a New Deal for America.

January 1933: Adolf Hitler becomes chancellor in Germany. President Coolidge dies. Continued bank failures.

FRANKLIN DELANO ROOSEVELT

HERBERT HOOVER

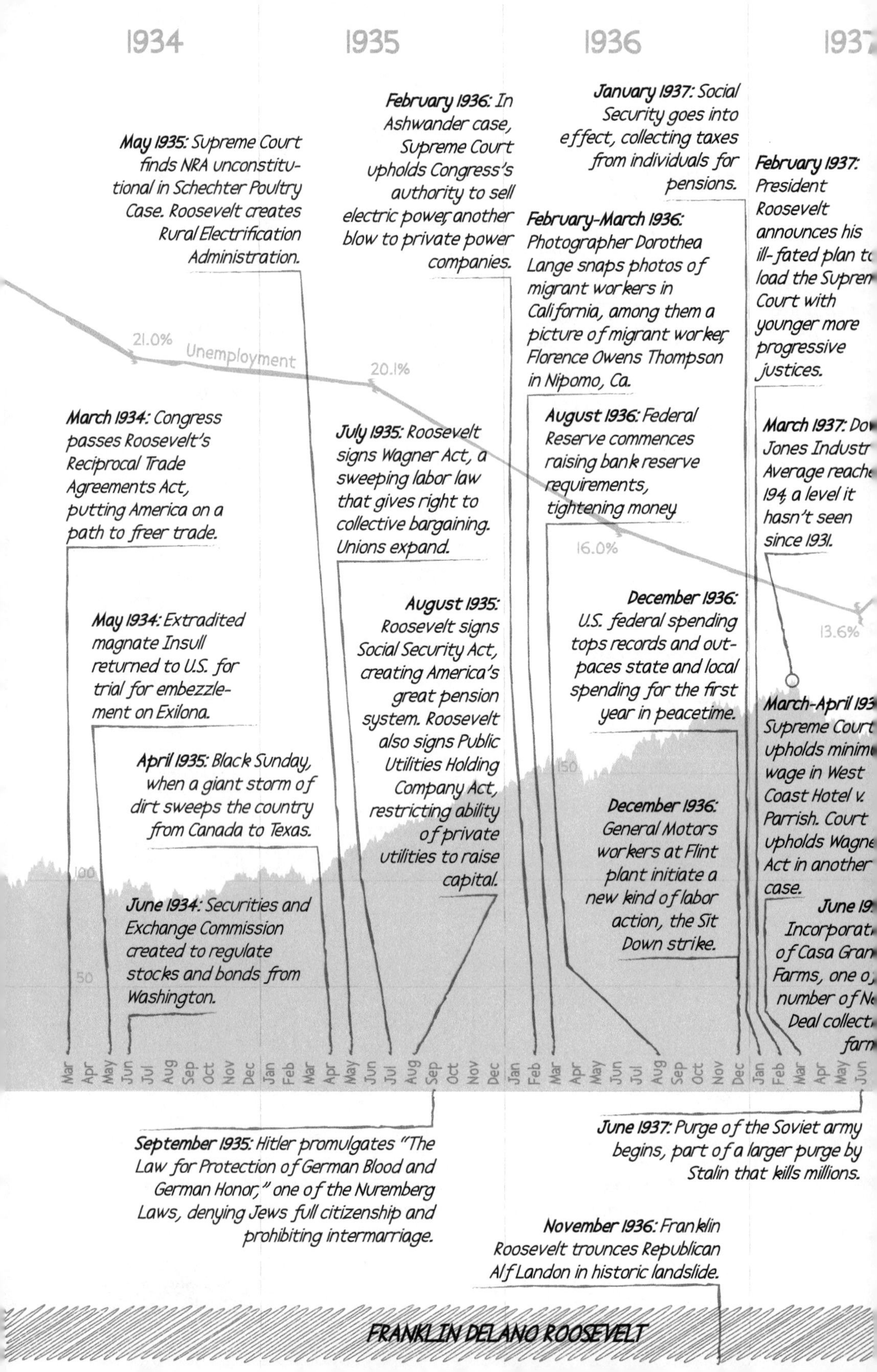

1934 1935 1936 1937

May 1935: Supreme Court finds NRA unconstitutional in Schechter Poultry Case. Roosevelt creates Rural Electrification Administration.

February 1936: In Ashwander case, Supreme Court upholds Congress's authority to sell electric power, another blow to private power companies.

January 1937: Social Security goes into effect, collecting taxes from individuals for pensions.

February 1937: President Roosevelt announces his ill-fated plan to load the Supreme Court with younger more progressive justices.

February-March 1936: Photographer Dorothea Lange snaps photos of migrant workers in California, among them a picture of migrant worker, Florence Owens Thompson in Nipomo, Ca.

21.0% Unemployment 20.1% 16.0% 13.6%

March 1934: Congress passes Roosevelt's Reciprocal Trade Agreements Act, putting America on a path to freer trade.

July 1935: Roosevelt signs Wagner Act, a sweeping labor law that gives right to collective bargaining. Unions expand.

August 1936: Federal Reserve commences raising bank reserve requirements, tightening money.

March 1937: Dow Jones Industrial Average reaches 194, a level it hasn't seen since 1931.

May 1934: Extradited magnate Insull returned to U.S. for trial for embezzlement on Exilona.

August 1935: Roosevelt signs Social Security Act, creating America's great pension system. Roosevelt also signs Public Utilities Holding Company Act, restricting ability of private utilities to raise capital.

December 1936: U.S. federal spending tops records and outpaces state and local spending for the first year in peacetime.

March-April 1937: Supreme Court upholds minimum wage in West Coast Hotel v. Parrish. Court upholds Wagner Act in another case.

April 1935: Black Sunday, when a giant storm of dirt sweeps the country from Canada to Texas.

December 1936: General Motors workers at Flint plant initiate a new kind of labor action, the Sit Down strike.

June 1934: Securities and Exchange Commission created to regulate stocks and bonds from Washington.

June 1937: Incorporation of Casa Grande Farms, one of a number of New Deal collective farms.

150 100 50

Mar Apr May Jun Jul Aug Sep Oct Nov Dec Jan Feb Mar Apr May Jun Jul Aug Sep Oct Nov Dec Jan Feb Mar Apr May Jun Jul Aug Sep Oct Nov Dec Jan Feb Mar Apr May Jun

September 1935: Hitler promulgates "The Law for Protection of German Blood and German Honor," one of the Nuremberg Laws, denying Jews full citizenship and prohibiting intermarriage.

June 1937: Purge of the Soviet army begins, part of a larger purge by Stalin that kills millions.

November 1936: Franklin Roosevelt trounces Republican Alf Landon in historic landslide.

FRANKLIN DELANO ROOSEVELT

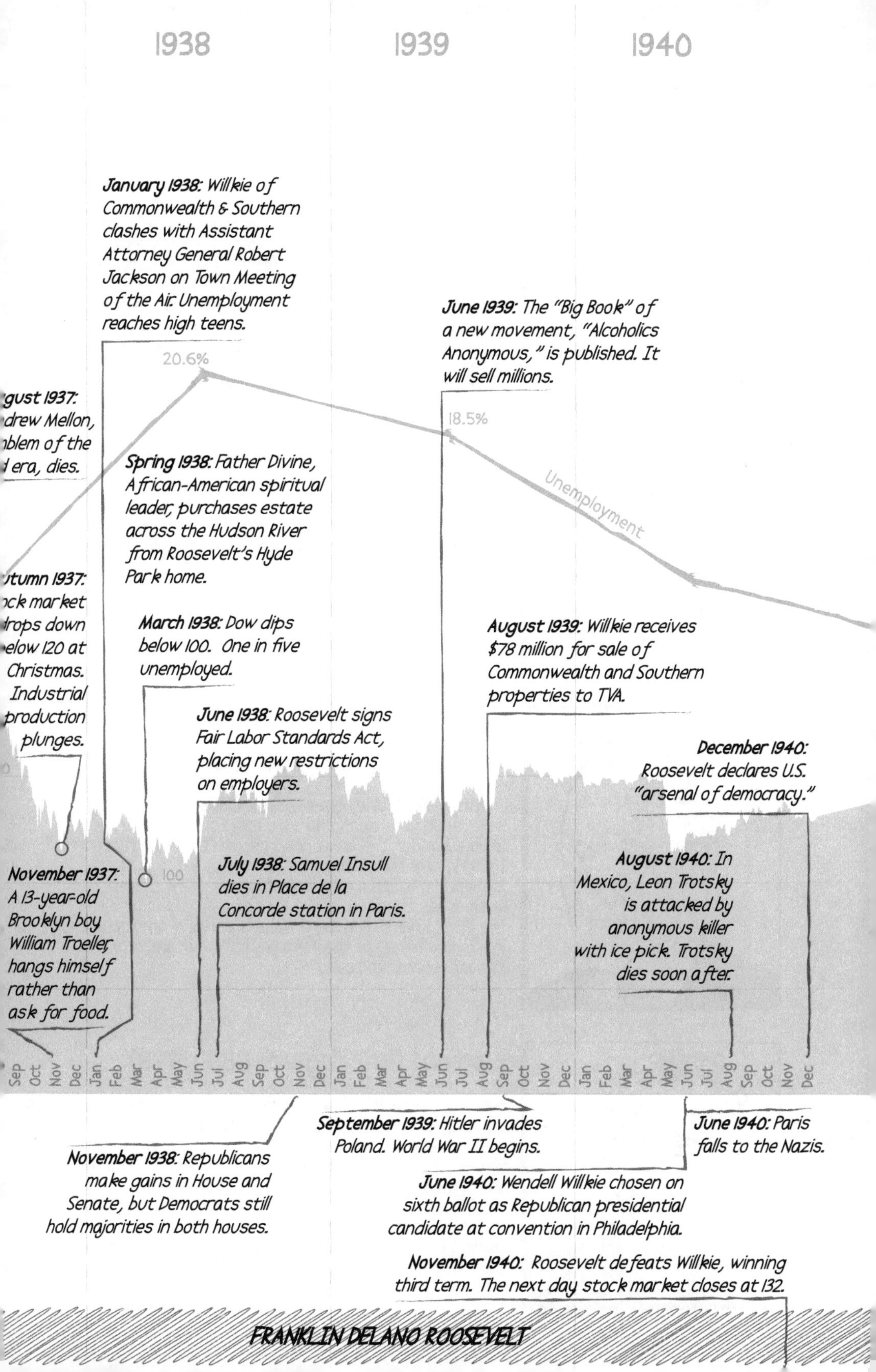

1938 1939 1940

January 1938: Willkie of Commonwealth & Southern clashes with Assistant Attorney General Robert Jackson on Town Meeting of the Air. Unemployment reaches high teens.

20.6%

June 1939: The "Big Book" of a new movement, "Alcoholics Anonymous," is published. It will sell millions.

18.5%

Unemployment

gust 1937: drew Mellon, blem of the l era, dies.

Spring 1938: Father Divine, African-American spiritual leader, purchases estate across the Hudson River from Roosevelt's Hyde Park home.

tumn 1937: ck market drops down below 120 at Christmas. Industrial production plunges.

March 1938: Dow dips below 100. One in five unemployed.

August 1939: Willkie receives $78 million for sale of Commonwealth and Southern properties to TVA.

June 1938: Roosevelt signs Fair Labor Standards Act, placing new restrictions on employers.

December 1940: Roosevelt declares U.S. "arsenal of democracy."

November 1937: A 13-year-old Brooklyn boy William Troeller, hangs himself rather than ask for food.

100

July 1938: Samuel Insull dies in Place de la Concorde station in Paris.

August 1940: In Mexico, Leon Trotsky is attacked by anonymous killer with ice pick. Trotsky dies soon after.

Sep Oct Nov Dec Jan Feb Mar Apr May Jun Jul Aug Sep Oct Nov Dec Jan Feb Mar Apr May Jun Jul Aug Sep Oct Nov Dec Jan Feb Mar Apr May Jun Jul Aug Sep Oct Nov Dec

September 1939: Hitler invades Poland. World War II begins.

June 1940: Paris falls to the Nazis.

November 1938: Republicans make gains in House and Senate, but Democrats still hold majorities in both houses.

June 1940: Wendell Willkie chosen on sixth ballot as Republican presidential candidate at convention in Philadelphia.

November 1940: Roosevelt defeats Willkie, winning third term. The next day stock market closes at 132.

CAST OF CHARACTERS

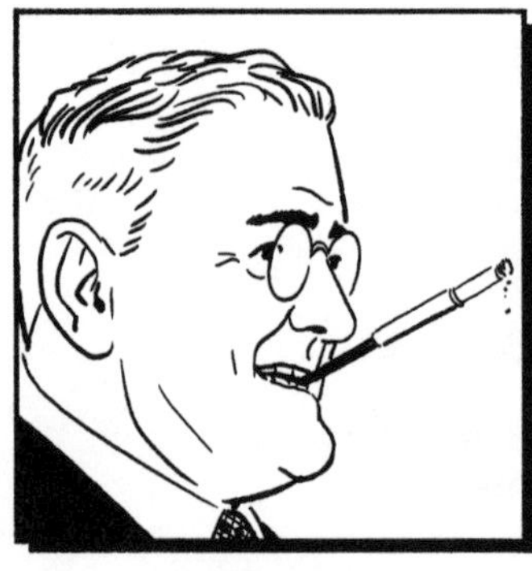

Franklin Roosevelt (1882-1945)

In 1932, at a point when one in four Americans was unemployed, this New York governor successfully campaigned as the Democratic candidate for president, promising to help "the forgotten man at the bottom of the economic pyramid." In 1933, Roosevelt launched an unprecedented government intervention in the economy, the New Deal. While popular, the New Deal failed to either return unemployment to pre-Depression levels or restore the stock market. Elected four times, Roosevelt led the country to victory in World War II.

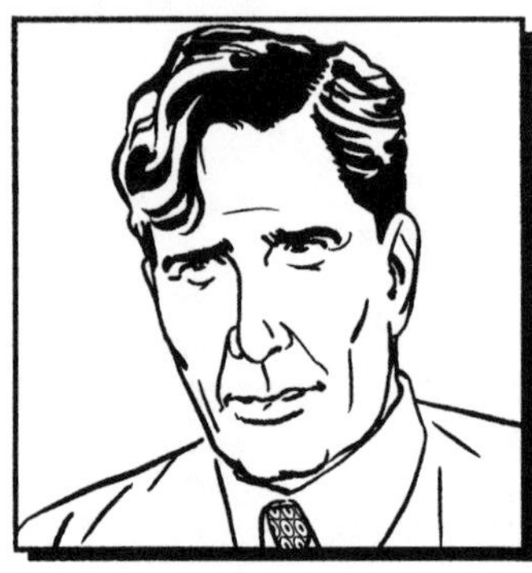

Wendell Lewis Willkie (1892-1944)

The narrator of this book, Willkie was born in Indiana. After studying law at Indiana University, Willkie married Edith "Billie" Willkie and made a career in the most exciting industry of his era, utilities. As head of the new company Commonwealth and Southern, Willkie for years tilted with David Lilienthal of the Tennessee Valley Authority. After TVA triumphed, Willkie, outraged, entered politics. Willkie ran unsuccessfully for president in 1940.

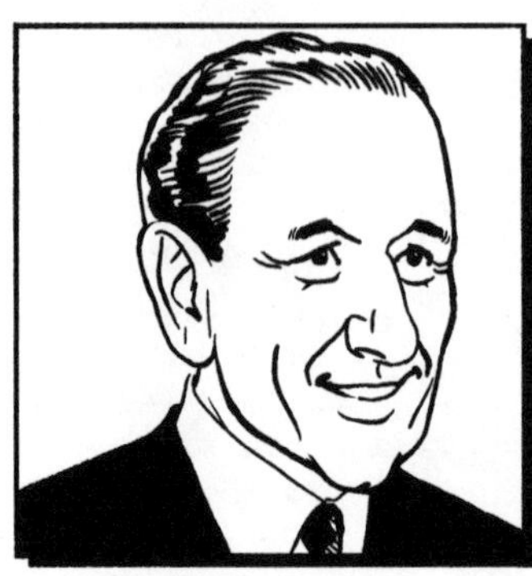

David Lilienthal (1899-1981)

Lilienthal, like Willkie, grew up in Indiana, attending DePauw University and Harvard Law School, where he studied under the great progressive Felix Frankfurter. In 1933, Lilienthal joined the Tennessee Valley Authority, which created a network of government power businesses throughout the South. Over the course of the 1930s Lilienthal became Willkie's principal antagonist in a battle between the TVA's public power and Willkie's private-sector company.

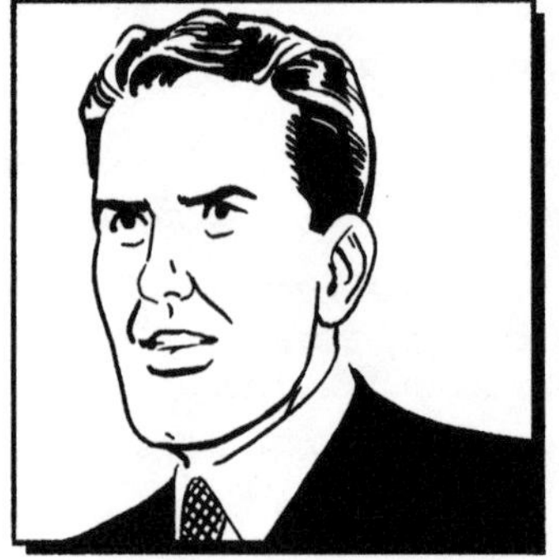

Rexford Guy Tugwell (1891-1979)

Born in rural New York and moved to action by farm poverty, Tugwell, an economist, entered the progressive movement, joining others in a study trip to Soviet Russia in 1927. After FDR's victory, the flamboyant Tugwell served in the Roosevelt Administration, including as head of the Resettlement Administration. He helped to create numerous planned communities, including Casa Grande, the Arizona collective in this book. Tugwell left the administration in 1937.

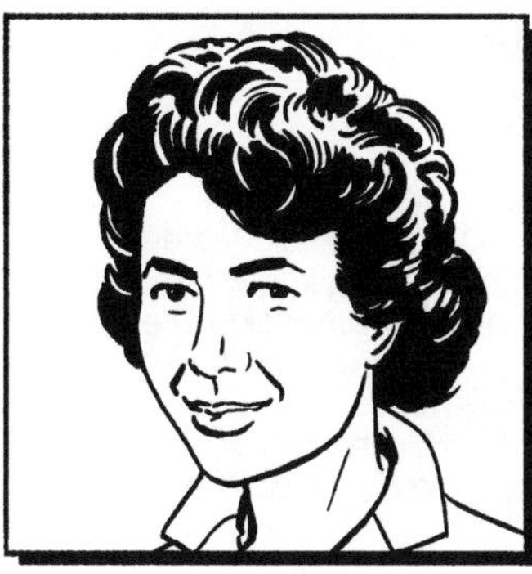

Irita Van Doren (1891-1966)

The legendary books editor at the *New York Herald Tribune* was born in Alabama. After studying at Columbia, she and her husband, Carl Van Doren, worked at the left-leaning magazine *The Nation.* Irita later moved to the *Herald Tribune* and divorced. In the late 1930s, Van Doren edited the utilities executive Wendell Willkie's articles; their friendship became romance. Many scenes in this book take place in Van Doren's West Cornwall, Ct., summer house. The pair never married.

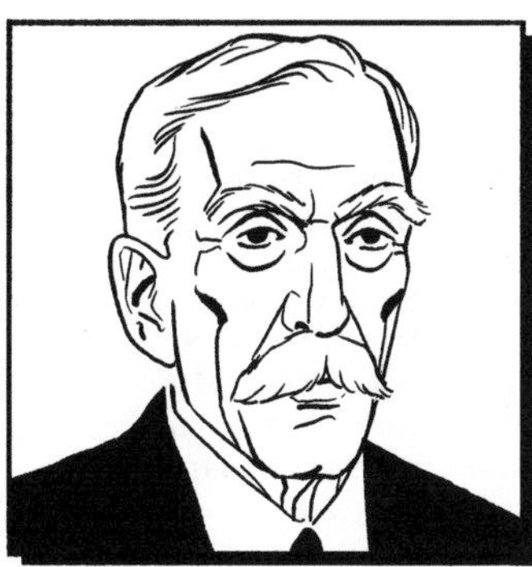

Andrew Mellon (1855-1937)

Pittsburgh-born Mellon and his family built an empire of steel, railroads and shipbuilding. Mellon developed what we today call venture capital investing: providing seed money to innovative young firms such as the one that became Aluminum Company of America. In the 1920s, Mellon served as treasury secretary to Presidents Harding, Coolidge, and Hoover, lowering the debt and cutting tax rates. In the 1930s, Roosevelt's administration turned on the former Treasury Secretary, prosecuting him for tax fraud. In the same years Mellon built the National Gallery of Art.

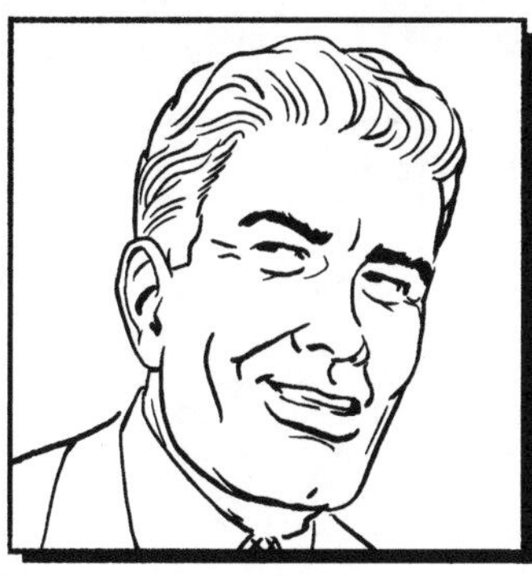

Stuart Chase (1888-1985)

A New Hampshire-born accountant and economist, Chase was one of the leaders of the technocratic movement in the 1920s. In 1927, he, Tugwell, Paul Douglas and other economists and planners visited Stalin's Soviet Union, hoping to import some Soviet ideas to the U.S. Chase authored a book titled *A New Deal*, around the time Franklin Roosevelt made the phrase the slogan of his program. Roosevelt's New Deal implemented many of the ideas that Chase favored.

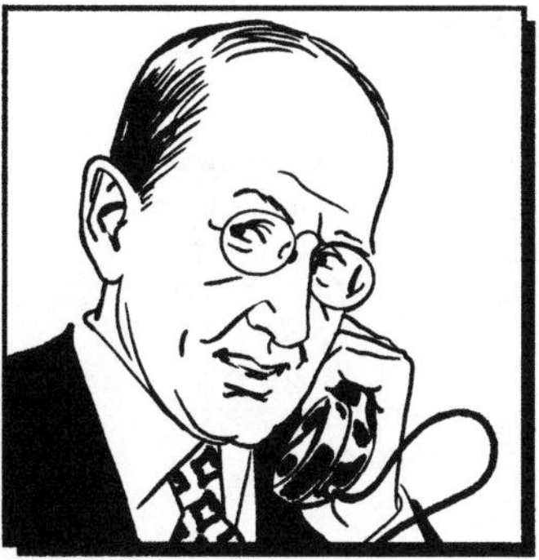

Henry Morgenthau, Jr. (1891-1967)

Born in the Hudson Valley into an eminent family, Morgenthau, along with his wife Elinor, were friends of the Roosevelts. When Roosevelt became president, he named Morgenthau to the Farm Board. When Treasury Secretary William Woodin resigned in 1934, Roosevelt promoted Morgenthau to the post. Morgenthau did not always approve of Roosevelt's policies, and often tangled with colleagues such as Marriner Eccles. Like his Treasury predecessor Mellon, Morgenthau was an avid fan of the arts.

CAST OF CHARACTERS

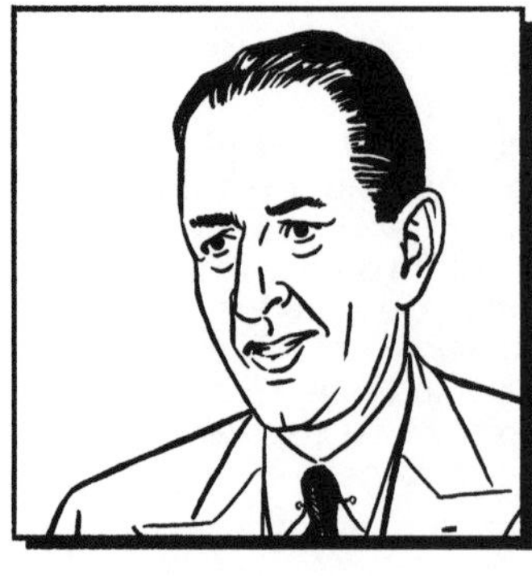

Marriner Stoddard Eccles (1890-1977)

The patriarch in a prominent Mormon family, Eccles shepherded local Utah banks through the Great Depression. Roosevelt brought Eccles to Washington, where the Utah banker helped craft a new law governing the Federal Reserve system. Eccles, a proponent of looser money and stimuli, served as Federal Reserve chairman. During the Depression within the Depression of the later 1930s, Eccles famously quarreled with Treasury Secretary Morgenthau.

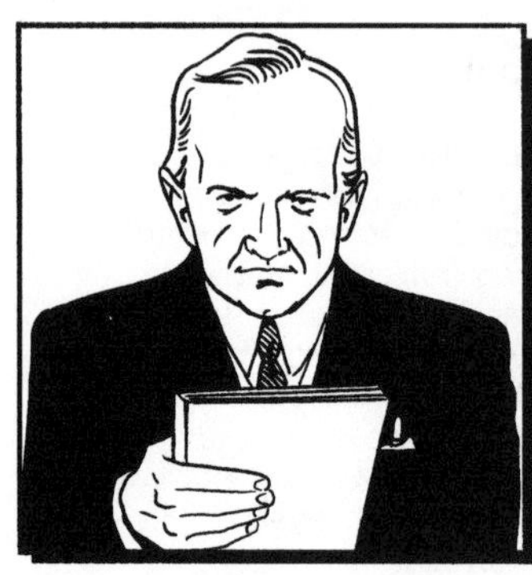

Calvin Coolidge (1872-1933)

Born in rural Vermont, Coolidge served as governor of Massachusetts, then as U.S. vice president to President Warren Harding. Harding and Coolidge advocated a policy of "normalcy," or reducing policy uncertainty. At Harding's 1923 death, "Silent Cal" became chief executive. The minimalist Coolidge, an advocate of smaller government, vetoed progressive legislation repeatedly as President, including hydropower projects and agricultural subsidy of the sort the New Deal would make reality.

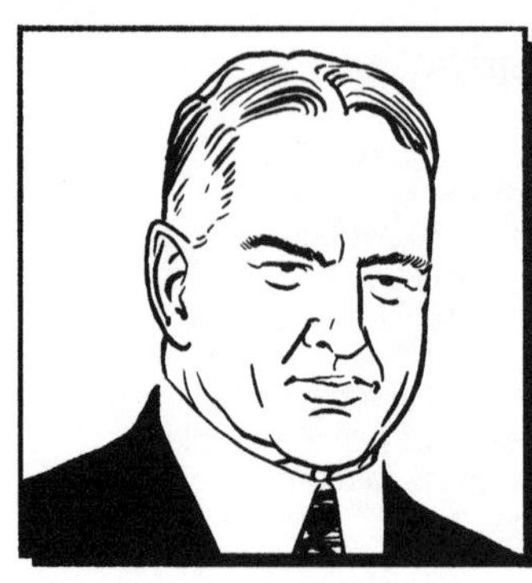

Herbert Clark Hoover (1874-1964)

The 31st president got his start as a mining engineer, training at the then-new Stanford University. After a brilliant career as a mining engineer, Hoover led the campaign to feed starving Belgians in World War I. From 1921, Hoover served as commerce secretary to Harding and Coolidge, leading the rescue effort in the South after the great 1927 flood of the Mississippi. Unlike his fellow Republican Coolidge, Hoover favored active government. Elected president in 1928, Hoover served in the early years of the Great Depression, signing the Smoot-Hawley Tariff into law.

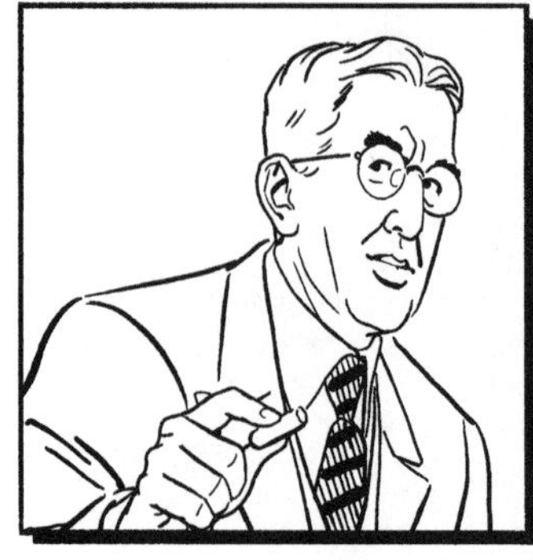

Paul Douglas (1892-1976)

A New Englander by birth, Douglas was moved by the poverty of loggers, becoming an economics professor specializing in labor. While teaching at the University of Chicago, Douglas travelled with Tugwell and Chase to Soviet Russia and drew inspiration there. One of the people Douglas chanced to meet was Betty Glan. Douglas later became disillusioned with central planning. A Roosevelt advisor, Douglas played key roles in the formation of the Wagner Act and Social Security.

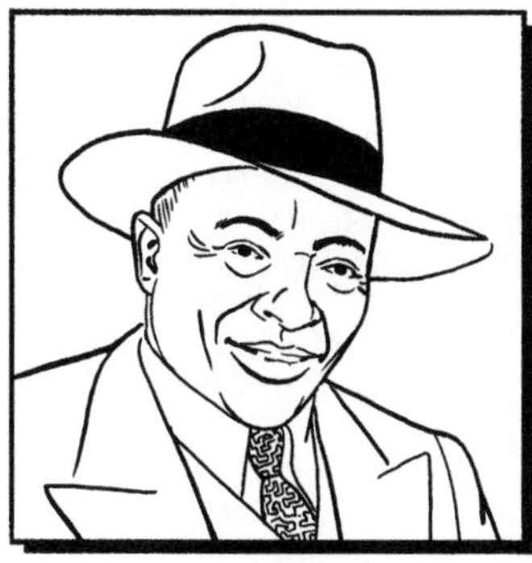

Father Divine (Ca. 1876-1965)

The African-American spiritual leader led a cult that worshipped both him and the concepts of racial equity, peace, education, individual initiative and property ownership. In the 1930s, Divine challenged Roosevelt on civil rights, hounding the president on his failure to strongly endorse anti-lynching legislation. Father Divine purchased a farm across the Hudson from Roosevelt's in order to provide a physical reminder of himself and his cause.

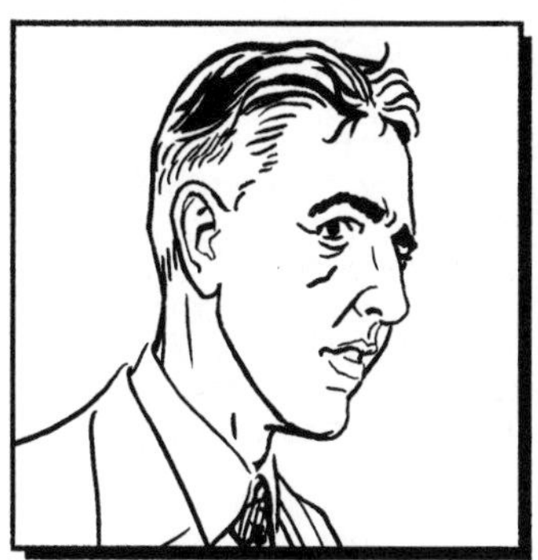

Bill Wilson (1895-1971)

Born in Vermont, Bill Wilson worked on Wall Street and fell into alcoholism. Together with "Dr. Bob," the Ohio physician Bob Smith, Wilson in 1935 founded Alcoholics Anonymous. With AA, they put forward a then-new concept: that people with troubles might help one another in group meetings. Wilson's Twelve-Step Program to Recovery gained many followers during the Depression. Wilson's book, *Alcoholics Anonymous*, has sold millions of copies.

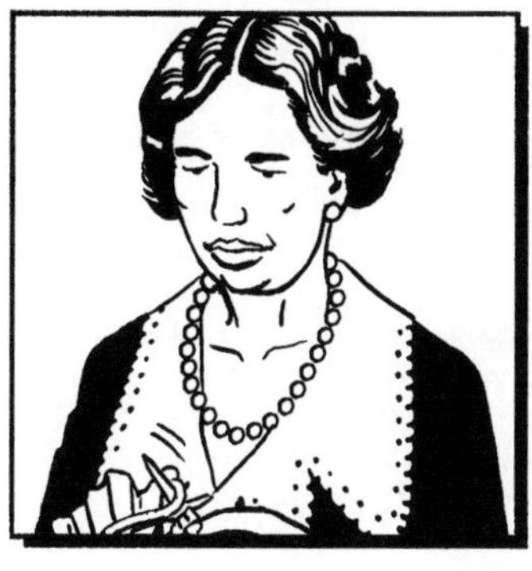

Anna Eleanor Roosevelt (1884-1962)

A niece of president Theodore Roosevelt, Eleanor Roosevelt married Franklin Roosevelt, her distant cousin, in 1905. After her husband contracted polio, she helped him find heart and herself began speaking publicly for progressive causes. As First Lady, Mrs. Roosevelt supported many social programs, especially planned communities such as Arthurdale, in West Virginia. Her column, "My Day," both supported and illuminated New Deal programs and minority rights.

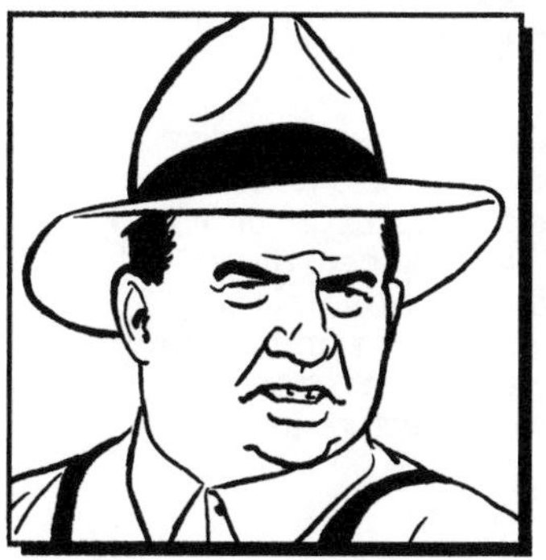

Robert Faul (1881-1963)

A farming expert, Faul was hired by the New Deal Farm Security Administration to manage the model collective farm for migrant farmers established by Tugwell's Resettlement Administration and the Farm Security Administration at Casa Grande, Arizona. Planned as a model alternative to tenant farming, Casa Grande gave farmers a share in a cooperative. Though the federal government poured cash into the farm, it failed when the workers revolted or grew disillusioned, as documented in *Government Project* by Edward C. Banfield.

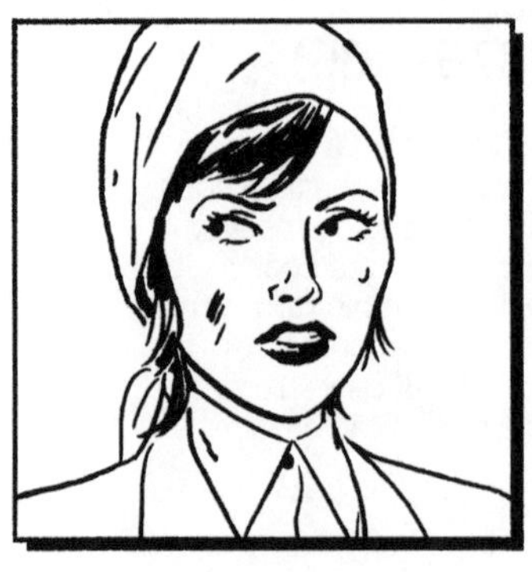

Betty Glan

An early favorite of Stalin's Soviet regime, Glan was one of the young workers introduced to the American travellers who visited Russia in 1927, catching Paul Douglas's eye at a factory meeting. Later, Glan served as director of Gorky Park in Moscow. A decade later, Douglas learned she had been purged from Stalin's regime through a chance reading of a newspaper article.

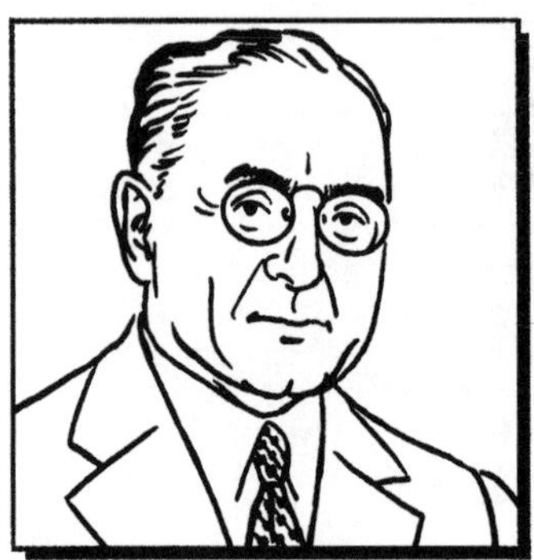

Felix Frankfurter (1882-1965)

Born in Vienna, Austria, in 1882, Frankfurter attended Harvard Law School and helped found the American Civil Liberties Union. An influential progressive instructor at the Law School, Frankfurter sent many pupils to clerk on the Supreme Court. An advisor to the Wilson Administration, Frankfurter also advised Franklin Roosevelt for many years, including on key laws such as Social Security. Roosevelt appointed Frankfurter to the Supreme Court in 1939.

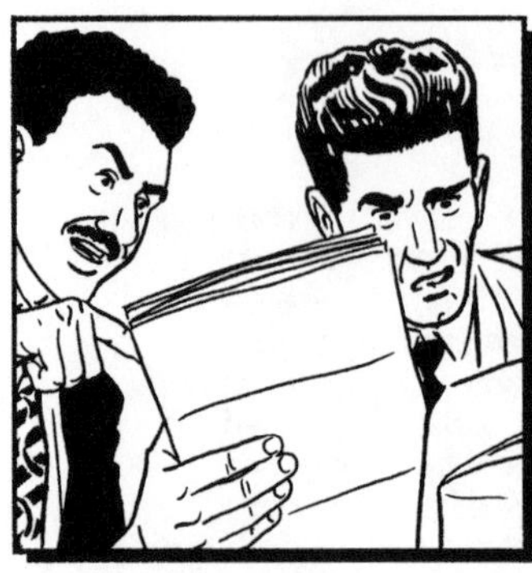

The Schechter Brothers

These Jewish immigrants built a wholesale kosher poultry business in New York City. New Deal authorities determined that Schechter Poultry labor and price policy violated the numerous rules of the New Deal's far-reaching National Recovery Administration. The Schechters were accused of paying illegally low wages and allowing customers to select their own chickens. The Supreme Court heard ALA Schechter Poultry Corp. v U.S., as an NRA test case in May 1935. Voting unanimously, justices deemed the NRA unconstitutional.

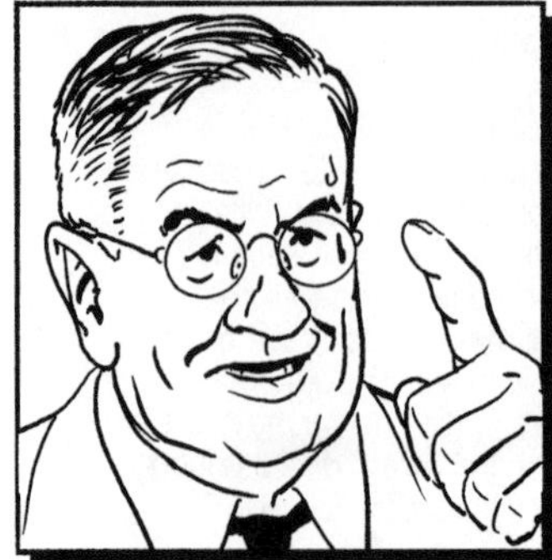

Harold L. Ickes (1874-1952)

Born in Altoona, Pa., Ickes as a young man led progressives in the Midwest in campaigns to reform industries such as utilities, making a special target of utilities magnate Samuel Insull. Switching from the progressive wing of the Republican Party to the Democrats, Ickes joined the Roosevelt Administration as both Interior Secretary and head of the Public Works Administration. Ickes's PWA infrastructure empire symbolized the New Deal.

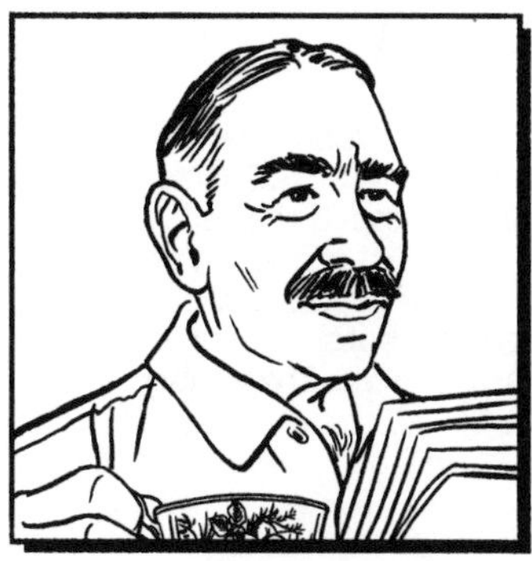

John Maynard Keynes (1883-1946)

This British economist made a worldwide name for himself with the 1919 *Economic Consequences of the Peace*, a prophetic book that warned that the harsh terms of the Versailles Treaty would destabilize a defeated Germany. Later, Keynes led a revolution in economic thinking, rating laissez faire economics retrograde and backing monetary and fiscal intervention by governments. Works such as his 1936 *General Theory*, provided justification for government spending.

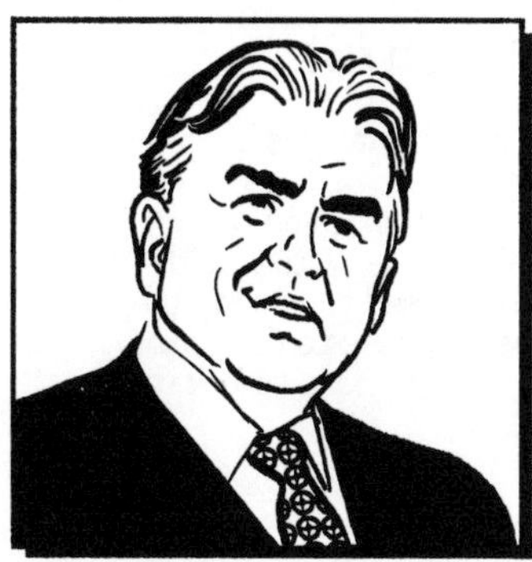

John Llewellyn Lewis (1880-1969)

Born in Iowa, Lewis, a young miner, joined the United Mine Workers and led that union in a historic 1919 coal strike. Lewis created the Committee for Industrial Organization, or CIO, which teamed up with the older, more conservative, American Federation of Labor. In 1935, Roosevelt signed America's most radical labor law, the National Labor Relations Act. The fierce Lewis seized the chance the law offered and led the giant and historic unionization of the late 1930s.

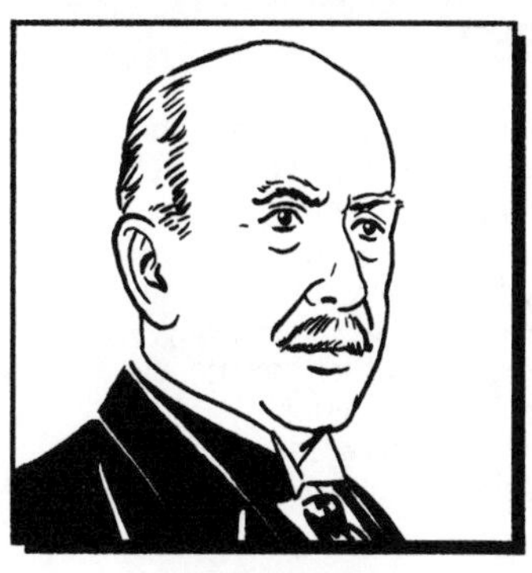

William Graham Sumner (1840-1910)

A professor at Yale University from the 1870s on, Sumner advocated classical liberalism, arguing for free trade, free markets, the gold standard and individual rights. Many scholars have vilified Sumner as a ruthless social Darwinist. Sumner's greatest influence however was his concept of the taxpaying individual as the Forgotten Man, hostage to group rights. Skeptical of the value of government relief, Sumner disapproved of what he called "jobbery." "Jobbery" was the creation of work to serve political rather than individual or economic ends.

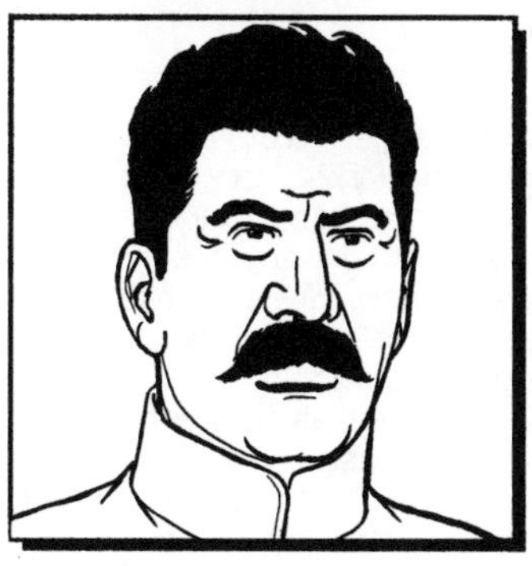

Joseph Stalin (1879-1953)

Born Joseph Vissarionivich Djugashvili in Georgia, then part of the Russian Empire, Stalin, along with Leon Trotsky, joined Vladimir Lenin in leading the 1917 Communist Revolution in Russia. The Bolsheviks expropriated businesses, seized factories, and suppressed religious freedom. After the death of Lenin in 1924, Stalin became leader. At the time the scholars in this book visited Russia, 1927, Stalin was eager that Russia make a good impression to get an alliance with Western labor unions.

CAST OF CHARACTERS

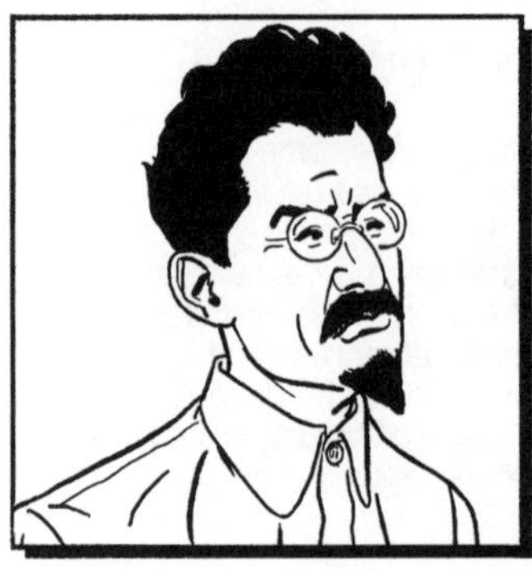

Leon Trotsky (1879-1940)

Born Lev Davidovich Bronstein, Trotsky spent years in exile from the czar, even living for a time at 1522 Vyse Avenue in New York's Bronx. Trotsky headed the Red Army at the end of World War I. Trotsky, a Stalin rival, was a favorite of foreigners. Soon after the 1927 scenes in this book, Stalin exiled him. Trotsky eventually reached Mexico and was assassinated. The weapon was an ice pick.

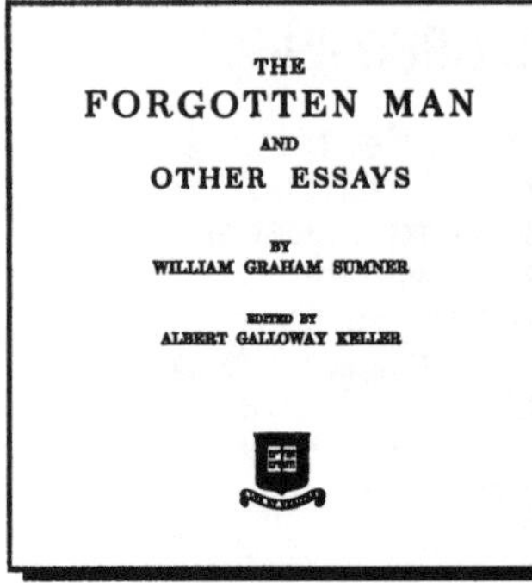

THE
FORGOTTEN MAN
AND
OTHER ESSAYS

BY
WILLIAM GRAHAM SUMNER

EDITED BY
ALBERT GALLOWAY KELLER

"The Forgotten Man" (1876)

A book in which William Sumner put forward his concept of the Forgotten Man. Sumner wrote: "As soon as A observes something which seems to him to be wrong, from which X is suffering, A talks it over with B, and A and B then propose to get a law passed to remedy the evil and help X. Their law always proposes to determine what C shall do for X ...what I want to do is to look up C... I call him the Forgotten Man..."

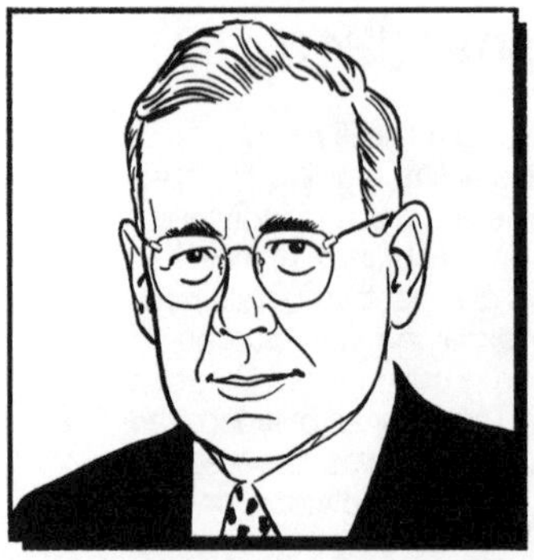

Alf Landon (1887-1987)

This Kansas governor became the Republican presidential candidate in 1936. Speaking of President Roosevelt's use of special powers to manage the economy, Landon said, "these powers were granted with the understanding that they were only temporary. But after the powers had been obtained, and after the emergency was clearly over, we were told that another emergency would be created if the power was given up." Landon's platform was moderate however: some historians have termed it "New Deal Lite." Roosevelt trounced Landon.

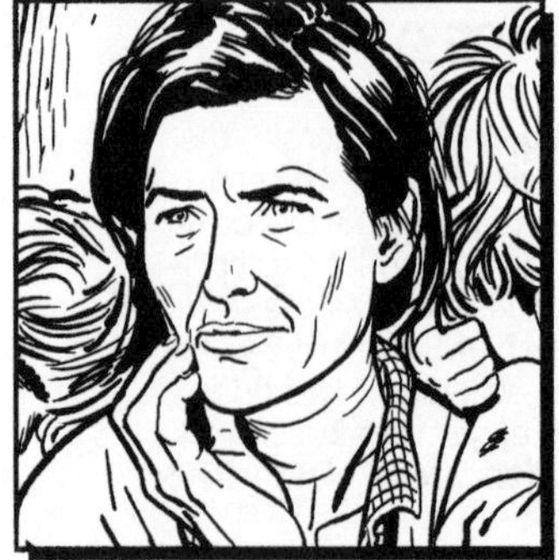

"Migrant Mother"

In the mid-1930s, New Deal photographer Dorothea Lange came across a poor migratory worker, Florence Owens Thompson, in Nipomo, California. Later Lange wrote: " I saw and approached the hungry and desperate mother, as if drawn by a magnet....She said that they had been living on frozen vegetables from the surrounding fields, and birds that the children killed." The photo of Thompson by Lange, known as "Migrant Mother, " is the icon of the Great Depression.

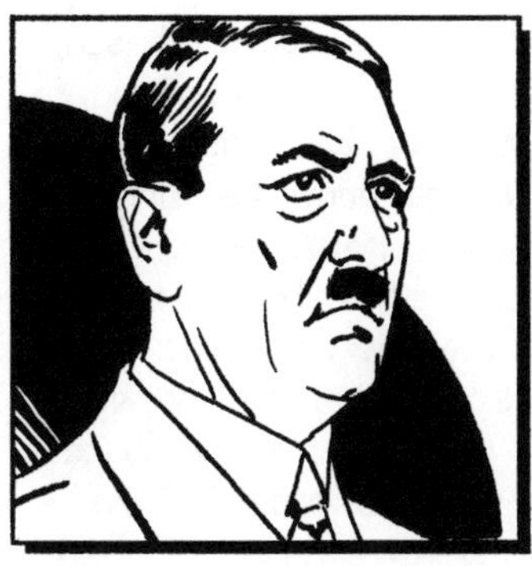

Adolf Hitler (1889-1945)

Leader of Germany's murderous National Socialist German Workers' Party in the 1920s, the World War I corporal became chancellor of Germany in 1933 and quickly seized more power, converting the democratic Weimar Republic to dictatorship. The Nazis forced dissenters into concentration camps, dissolved labor unions, rearmed Germany, and oppressed tens of thousands. In 1935 the dictator promulgated the Nuremberg Laws, the early anti-semitic measures against Jewish citizens that foreshadowed World War II and the Holocaust.

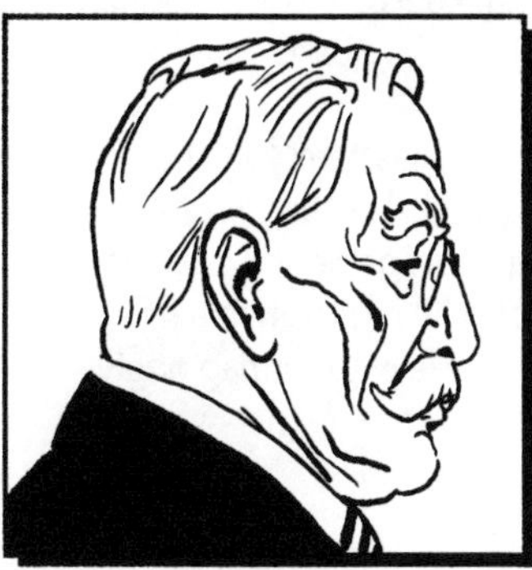

Samuel Insull (1859-1938)

The British-born Insull immigrated to the United States at the age of 21 to serve as secretary to Thomas Edison. Insull moved to Chicago and led the city's electrification, introducing or promoting such innovations as the metered system, the electric grid, and the central generating plant. At his height, Insull employed thousands. Insull's companies crashed in the Great Depression, destroying the savings of many Chicagoans.

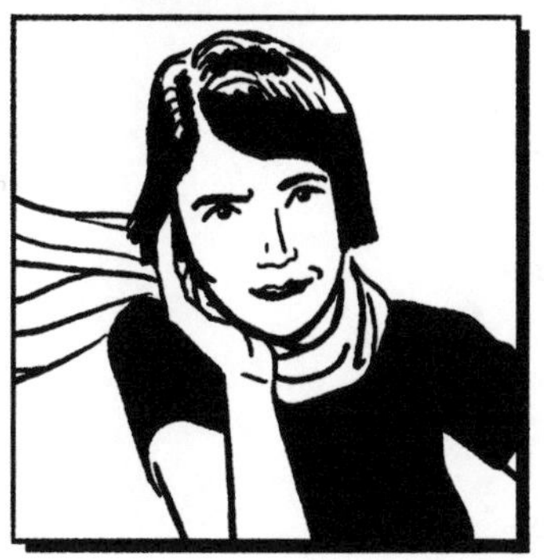

Ayn Rand (1905-1982)

Born Alisa Rosenbaum in Russia, this author saw her father's pharmacy confiscated by the Bolsheviks. Rejecting Bolshevik ideals, the young woman traveled to New York in 1926, eventually changing her name to Ayn Rand. The anti-collectivist Rand wrote *The Fountainhead,* her first hit, during the New Deal. *The Fountainhead* portrayed a hero who fought back against bureaucrats. Rand and her husband Frank O'Connor campaigned for Wendell Willkie in 1940.

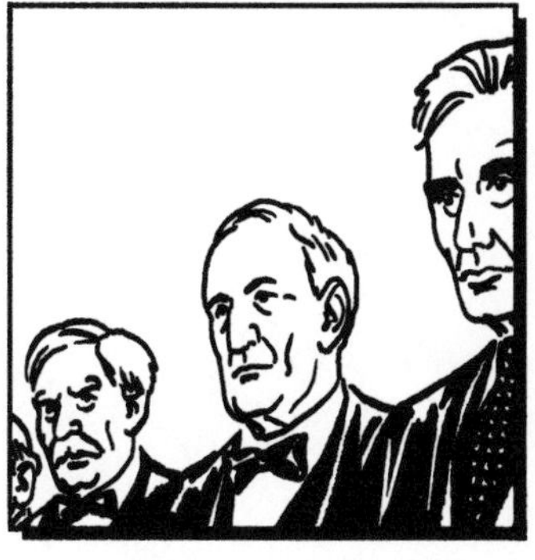

The Supreme Court

The Supreme Court in the 1930s was divided. On the one hand were conservatives and classical liberals Pierce Butler, James Clark McReynolds, George Sutherland and Willis Van Devanter. This group was known as "The Four Horsemen." Opposing the horsemen were more progressive justices such as Louis Brandeis, Benjamin Cardozo and Harlan Fiske Stone. Chief Justice Charles Evans Hughes and Justice Owen Roberts played the swing role. Though Roosevelt's court packing effort failed, the court tilted left in the later 1930s on its own.

ACKNOWLEDGMENTS

Many groups and individuals supported this quirky project. They include: David Bahnsen, T.D. Service Company, Kerry E. Reynolds, Bruce J. McDonald, Ivan Marks, Robert Loewen, David Kramer, Inland Group, Charles P. Hanlon, Albert A. Frink, Morgan Davis, Scott L. Anderson, Marilyn Palarea, Kathy Gremer, The Lincoln Club of Orange County, Paul Singer, Anne Dickerson, Amy Baker, Janine Hill, James Lindsay, Betsy Gude, and Suzanne Helm. Lawrence Kadish's support has been crucial. Nina Rosenwald cheered us all on, as did the Hudson Institute and Wendell Willkie II, as well as Kim Dennis. The Robert and Ardis James Foundation, Bob Asahina, Gaurav Tiwari, Erica Libby, the Council on Foreign Relations, and the George W. Bush Presidential Center all provided friendship or support. Thank you Cathy James for understanding this project. Andrew Wylie, Scott Moyers, Edward Orloff, Jin Auh, and others at Wylie agency were especially helpful. Nikolai Krylov, Matt Denhart, and Rebecca Sears managed tricky details. Emily Cunningham, William Ruoto, and Tim Duggan: thank you. Thank you to Chuck Dixon who contributed so much at the start.

Paul Rivoche would like to acknowledge the invaluable assistance of his family in the completion of this work, especially his mother, Stella Rivoche, and his brother, Michael Rivoche. Ken Barth and Peter Bielicki provided friendship and encouragement at a crucial moment; as did Tim Wong, who also kindly supplied a very useful 3D digital model of Irita's cottage interior. Lastly, his daughters Charlotte and Isabelle were unflaggingly supportive, encouraging, and loving throughout the lengthy time their father was away illuminating these pages.

ABOUT THE AUTHOR AND ILLUSTRATOR

Amity Shlaes writes a column for *Forbes* and serves as chairman of the Calvin Coolidge Presidential Foundation. She is the author of three *New York Times* bestsellers, *Coolidge, The Forgotten Man,* and *The Greedy Hand.* She chairs the jury for the Hayek Book Prize of the Manhattan Institute. She lives in Brooklyn, New York.

Paul Rivoche is a Toronto-based illustrator/comic book artist who cocreated the 1980s icon Mister X. His work includes making comics, writing stories for graphic novels such as *Flight 5* and Adhouse Books' *Project Superior,* illustrating comics covers for *Superman* and *Iron Man,* and creating background designs for Warner Bros. TV Animation.